Georgia Class-D Minor League Baseball Encyclopedia

A Statistical History of the
Georgia-Alabama, Georgia-Florida,
and Georgia State Leagues

by John Bell

Vabella Publishing

Vabella Publishing
P.O. Box 1052
Carrollton, Georgia 30112

A portion of the proceeds from the sale of this book will be donated to a children's recreation organization.

This book is a factual account based on sources considered to be accurate, reliable, and taken in good faith. Any information that is inaccurate or mistaken is completely unintentional. This book is sold with the understanding that the publisher and author are not responsible or liable for inaccuracies from sources considered to be reliable. The publisher and author will not be held responsible or liable for any repercussions or actions stemming from information, accurate or not, made known in this book.

Copyright © 2003 by John G. Bell

All rights reserved. No part of this book may be reproduced or utilized in any form or by any means without permission in writing from the author. All requests should be addressed to the publisher.

Manufactured in the United States of America

Library of Congress Control Number: 2003108873

10-digit ISBN 0-9712204-2-5

13-digit ISBN 978-0-9712204-2-3

For Jacob and Andrew

This book is also dedicated to all the men and women who have ever played minor league or semi-professional baseball in the state of Georgia.

Other books by John Bell:

*Shoeless Summer:
The summer of 1923 when Shoeless Joe Jackson
played baseball in Americus, Georgia*
(published 2001)

*"PICKLE IT!" – Minor League Baseball of
Carrollton, Georgia*
(published 2002)

Table of Contents

Author's Notes .... page vi

Georgia Class-D League Cities/Years .... page 1

Georgia Class-D League Yearly Reviews 1906-63 .... page 4

Georgia Class-D League All-Time Season Records .... page 204

Georgia Class-D League Player/Pitcher Register .... page 211

Georgia Class-D League Major Leaguers .... page 431

Georgia Minor League Baseball Reunion .... page 448

Index .... page 449

Bibliography .... page 503

Acknowledgements .... page 504

About the Author .... page 504

Author's Notes

The inspiration to put this book together came in August of 2001 at the first reunion of the Georgia-Florida League held in Moultrie, Georgia. While at this now historic event, I witnessed first-hand the gleam in the eyes of the former players as they took center stage and relived their days on the diamond. I realized what a special and cherished time this was to those involved and that someone must capture and preserve this piece of history.

As I researched on and off since that day, I experienced joy when new pieces of information were discovered and frustration when dead ends were hit. While the dead ends were quite daunting, the elation of unearthing new data far outweighed the missing pieces of the puzzle. I came to realize that I would probably never single-handedly get all the information I needed to complete this history. So, I decided to publish the work with a few gaps, such as the 1906 Georgia State League season missing all player statistics and the 1920 and 1921 Georgia State League having only incomplete player statistics. My hope is that those who read this book who may have data to fill in the gaps I've left and will contact me with this information. If enough improved data is surfaced through this first publication, I'll publish a revised, second edition.

I feel confident in the accuracy of the majority of the information I've put on paper here. However, I realize that there will be errors from both myself and from sources used to compile this work. I would be most appreciative to any and all readers who bring mistakes to my attention, however significant or minute the detail may seem. My goal here is to provide the most accurate information possible to those who appreciate the rich history of minor league baseball. Please write to me or e-mail me at the following addresses if you want to let me know about errors in this book or for any other reason you wish:

postal mail: e-mail:
John Bell   belljg@aol.com
Vabella Publishing
P.O. Box 1052
Carrollton, Georgia 30112

Thank you very much for taking a look at my book. I hope you experience as much joy in reading it as I had in writing it.

Georgia Class-D Minor League Baseball Encyclopedia

Georgia Class-D League Cities/Years

Georgia Class-D Minor League Baseball Cities by Year

1906 – Albany, Georgia; Americus, Georgia; Brunswick, Georgia; Columbus, Georgia; Cordele, Georgia; Valdosta, Georgia; Waycross, Georgia.

1913 – Americus, Georgia; Anniston, Alabama; Brunswick, Georgia; Cordele, Georgia; Gadsden, Alabama; LaGrange, Georgia; Newnan, Georgia; Opelika, Alabama; Talladega, Alabama; Thomasville, Georgia; Valdosta, Georgia; Waycross, Georgia.

1914 – Anniston, Alabama; Americus, Georgia; Brunswick, Georgia; Cordele, Georgia; Gadsden, Alabama; LaGrange, Georgia; Newnan, Georgia; Opelika, Alabama; Rome, Georgia; Selma, Alabama; Talladega, Alabama; Thomasville, Georgia; Valdosta, Georgia; Waycross, Georgia.

1915 – Americus, Georgia; Anniston, Alabama; Brunswick, Georgia; Dothan, Alabama; Gainesville, Florida; Griffin, Georgia; LaGrange, Georgia; Newnan, Georgia; Rome, Georgia; Talladega, Georgia; Thomasville, Georgia; Valdosta, Georgia; Waycross, Georgia.

1916 – Anniston, Alabama; Griffin, Georgia ; LaGrange, Georgia; Newnan, Georgia; Rome, Georgia; Talladega, Alabama.

1917 – Alabama City, Alabama; Anniston, Alabama; Attalla, Alabama; Gadsden, Alabama; Griffin, Georgia; LaGrange, Georgia; Rome, Georgia; Talladega, Alabama.

1920 – Carrollton, Georgia; Cedartown, Georgia; Griffin, Georgia; LaGrange, Georgia; Lindale, Georgia; Rome, Georgia.

1921 – Carrollton, Georgia; Cedartown, Georgia; Griffin, Georgia; LaGrange, Georgia; Lindale, Georgia; Rome, Georgia.

1928 – Anniston, Alabama; Carrollton, Georgia; Cedartown, Georgia; Gadsden, Alabama; Lindale, Georgia; Talladega, Alabama.

1929 – Anniston, Alabama; Carrollton, Georgia; Cedartown, Georgia; Gadsden, Alabama; Lindale, Georgia; Talladega, Alabama.

1930 – Anniston, Alabama; Carrollton, Georgia; Cedartown, Georgia; Huntsville, Alabama; Lindale, Georgia; Talladega, Alabama.

1935 – Albany, Georgia; Americus, Georgia; Moultrie, Georgia; Panama City, Florida; Tallahassee, Florida; Thomasville, Georgia.

1936 – Albany, Georgia; Americus, Georgia; Cordele, Georgia; Moultrie, Georgia; Tallahassee, Florida; Thomasville, Georgia.

1937 – Albany, Georgia; Americus, Georgia; Cordele, Georgia; Moultrie, Georgia; Tallahassee, Florida; Thomasville, Georgia.

1938 – Albany, Georgia; Americus, Georgia; Cordele, Georgia; Moultrie, Georgia; Tallahassee, Florida; Thomasville, Georgia.

1939 – Albany, Georgia; Americus, Georgia; Cordele, Georgia; Moultrie, Georgia; Tallahassee, Florida; Thomasville, Georgia; Valdosta, Georgia; Waycross, Georgia.

1940 – Albany, Georgia; Americus, Georgia; Cordele, Georgia; Moultrie, Georgia; Tallahassee, Florida; Thomasville, Georgia; Valdosta, Georgia; Waycross, Georgia.

1941 – Albany, Georgia; Americus, Georgia; Cordele, Georgia; Moultrie, Georgia; Tallahassee, Florida; Thomasville, Georgia; Valdosta, Georgia; Waycross, Georgia.

1942 – Albany, Georgia; Americus, Georgia; Cordele, Georgia; Dothan, Alabama; Moultrie, Georgia; Tallahassee, Florida; Valdosta, Georgia; Waycross, Georgia.

1946 – Albany, Georgia; Americus, Georgia; Carrollton, Georgia; Cordele, Georgia; LaGrange, Georgia; Moultrie, Georgia; Newnan, Georgia; Opelika, Alabama; Tallahassee, Florida; Tallassee, Alabama; Thomasville, Georgia; Valdosta, Georgia; Valley, Alabama; Waycross, Georgia.

1947 – Alexander City, Alabama; Albany, Georgia; Americus, Georgia; Carrollton, Georgia; Cordele, Georgia; Griffin, Georgia; LaGrange, Georgia; Moultrie, Georgia; Newnan, Georgia; Opelika, Alabama; Tallahassee, Florida; Tallassee, Alabama; Thomasville, Georgia; Valdosta, Georgia; Valley, Alabama; Waycross, Georgia.

1948 – Albany, Georgia; Alexander City, Alabama; Americus, Georgia; Baxley, Georgia; Carrollton, Georgia; Cordele, Georgia; Douglas, Georgia; Eastman, Georgia; Fitzgerald, Georgia; Griffin, Georgia; LaGrange, Georgia; Lyons, Georgia; Moultrie, Georgia; Newnan, Georgia; Opelika, Alabama; Sparta, Georgia; Vidalia, Georgia; Tallahassee, Florida; Tallassee, Alabama; Thomasville, Georgia; Valdosta, Georgia; Valley, Alabama; Waycross, Georgia.

1949 – Albany, Georgia; Alexander City, Alabama; Americus, Georgia; Baxley, Georgia; Carrollton, Georgia; Cordele,

Georgia Class-D Minor League Baseball Encyclopedia

Georgia; Douglas, Georgia; Dublin, Georgia; Eastman, Georgia; Fitzgerald, Georgia; Griffin, Georgia; Hazlehurst, Georgia; LaGrange, Georgia; Lyons, Georgia; Moultrie, Georgia; Newnan, Georgia; Opelika, Alabama; Sparta, Georgia; Tallahassee, Florida; Tallassee, Alabama; Thomasville, Georgia; Tifton, Georgia; Valdosta, Georgia; Valley, Alabama; Vidalia, Alabama; Waycross, Georgia.

1950 – Albany, Georgia; Alexander City, Alabama; Americus, Georgia; Baxley, Georgia; Carrollton, Georgia; Cordele, Georgia; Douglas, Georgia; Dublin, Georgia; Eastman, Georgia; Fitzgerald, Georgia; Griffin, Georgia; Hazlehurst, Georgia; Jesup, Georgia; LaGrange, Georgia; Lyons, Georgia; Moultrie, Georgia; Newnan, Georgia; Opelika, Alabama; Rome, Georgia; Tallahassee, Florida; Thomasville, Georgia; Tifton, Georgia; Valdosta, Georgia; Valley, Alabama, Vidalia, Georgia; Waycross, Georgia.

1951 – Albany, Georgia; Alexander City, Alabama; Americus, Georgia; Baxley, Georgia; Brunswick, Georgia; Cordele, Georgia; Douglas, Georgia; Dublin, Georgia; Eastman, Georgia; Fitzgerald, Georgia; Griffin, Georgia; Hazlehurst, Georgia; Jesup, Georgia; LaGrange, Georgia; Moultrie, Georgia; Opelika, Alabama; Rome, Georgia; Tifton, Georgia; Valdosta, Georgia; Valley, Alabama; Waycross, Georgia.

1952 – Albany, Georgia; Brunswick, Georgia; Cordele, Georgia; Douglas, Georgia; Dublin, Georgia; Eastman, Georgia; Fitzgerald, Georgia; Hazlehurst, Georgia; Jesup, Georgia; Moultrie, Georgia; Statesboro, Georgia; Thomasville, Georgia; Tifton, Georgia; Valdosta, Georgia; Vidalia, Georgia; Waycross, Georgia.

1953 – Albany, Georgia; Brunswick, Georgia; Cordele, Georgia; Douglas, Georgia; Dublin, Georgia; Eastman, Georgia; Fitzgerald, Georgia; Hazlehurst, Georgia; Jesup, Georgia; Sandersville, Georgia; Statesboro, Georgia; Thomasville, Georgia; Tifton, Georgia; Valdosta, Georgia; Vidalia, Georgia; Waycross, Georgia.

1954 – Albany, Georgia; Americus, Georgia; Baxley, Georgia; Brunswick, Georgia; Cordele, Georgia; Douglas, Georgia; Dublin, Georgia; Fitzgerald, Georgia; Hazlehurst, Georgia; Sandersville, Georgia; Statesboro, Georgia; Thomasville, Georgia; Tifton, Georgia; Valdosta, Georgia; Vidalia, Georgia; Waycross, Georgia.

1955 – Albany, Georgia; Baxley, Georgia; Brunswick, Georgia; Cordele, Georgia; Douglas, Georgia; Dublin, Georgia; Hazlehurst, Georgia; Moultrie, Georgia; Sandersville, Georgia; Statesboro, Georgia; Thomasville, Georgia; Tifton, Georgia; Valdosta, Georgia; Vidalia, Georgia; Waycross, Georgia.

1956 – Albany, Georgia; Baxley, Georgia; Brunswick, Georgia; Douglas, Georgia; Dublin, Georgia; Fitzgerald, Georgia; Hazlehurst, Georgia; Moultrie, Georgia; Sandersville, Georgia; Thomasville, Georgia; Thomson, Georgia; Tifton, Georgia; Valdosta, Georgia; Vidalia, Georgia; Waycross, Georgia.

1957 – Albany, Georgia; Brunswick, Georgia; Fitzgerald, Georgia; Moultrie, Georgia; Thomasville, Georgia; Valdosta, Georgia; Waycross, Georgia.

1958 – Albany, Georgia; Brunswick, Georgia; Dublin, Georgia; Thomasville, Georgia; Valdosta, Georgia; Waycross, Georgia.

1962 – Brunswick, Georgia; Dublin, Georgia; Moultrie, Georgia; Thomasville.

1963 – Brunswick, Georgia; Moultrie, Georgia; Thomasville, Georgia; Waycross, Georgia.

Georgia Class-D Minor League Baseball Years by City

Alabama City, Alabama – 1917

Albany, Georgia – 1906, 1935, 1936, 1937, 1938, 1939, 1940, 1941, 1942, 1946, 1947, 1948, 1949, 1950, 1951, 1952, 1953, 1954, 1955, 1956, 1957, 1958

Alexander City, Alabama – 1947, 1948, 1949, 1950, 1951

Americus, Georgia – 1906, 1913, 1914, 1915, 1935, 1936, 1937, 1938, 1939, 1940, 1941, 1942, 1946, 1947, 1948, 1949, 1950, 1951, 1954

Anniston, Alabama – 1913, 1914, 1915, 1916, 1917, 1928, 1929, 1930

Attalla, Alabama – 1917

Baxley, Georgia – 1948, 1949, 1950, 1951, 1952, 1953, 1954, 1955, 1956, 1957

Brunswick, Georgia – 1906, 1913, 1914, 1915, 1951, 1952, 1953, 1954, 1955, 1956, 1957, 1958, 1962, 1963

Carrollton, Georgia – 1920, 1921, 1928, 1929, 1930, 1946, 1947, 1948, 1949, 1950

Cedartown, Georgia – 1920, 1921, 1928, 1929, 1930

Columbus, Georgia – 1906

Cordele, Georgia – 1906, 1913, 1914, 1936, 1937, 1938, 1939, 1940, 1941, 1942, 1946, 1947, 1948, 1949, 1950, 1951, 1952, 1953, 1954, 1955

Dothan, Alabama – 1915, 1942

Douglas, Georgia – 1948, 1949, 1950, 1951, 1952, 1953, 1954, 1955, 1956

Dublin, Georgia – 1949, 1950, 1951, 1952, 1953, 1954, 1955, 1956, 1958, 1962

Eastman, Georgia – 1948, 1949, 1950, 1951, 1952, 1953

Fitzgerald, Georgia – 1948, 1949, 1950, 1951, 1952, 1953, 1954, 1956, 1957

Gadsden, Alabama – 1913, 1914, 1917, 1928, 1929

Gainesville, Florida – 1915

Griffin, Georgia – 1915, 1916, 1917, 1920, 1921, 1947, 1948, 1949, 1950, 1951

Hazlehurst, Georgia – 1949, 1950, 1951, 1952, 1953, 1954, 1955, 1956

Huntsville, Alabama – 1930

Jesup, Georgia – 1950, 1951, 1952, 1953

LaGrange, Georgia – 1913, 1914, 1915, 1916, 1917, 1920, 1921, 1946, 1947, 1948, 1949, 1950, 1951

Lanett, Alabama – see Valley, Alabama

Lindale, Georgia – 1920, 1921, 1928, 1929, 1930

Lyons, Georgia – 1948, 1949, 1950

Moultrie, Georgia – 1935, 1936, 1937, 1938, 1939, 1940, 1941, 1942, 1946, 1947, 1948, 1949, 1950, 1951, 1952, 1955, 1956, 1957, 1962, 1963

Newnan, Georgia – 1913, 1914, 1915, 1916, 1946, 1947, 1948, 1949, 1950

Opelika, Alabama – 1913, 1914, 1946, 1947, 1948, 1949, 1950, 1951

Panama City, Florida – 1935

Rome, Georgia – 1914, 1915, 1916, 1917, 1920, 1921, 1950, 1951

Sandersville, Georgia – 1953, 1954, 1955, 1956

Selma, Alabama – 1914

Sparta, Georgia – 1948, 1949

Statesboro, Georgia – 1952, 1953, 1954, 1955

Talladega, Alabama – 1913, 1914, 1915, 1916, 1917, 1928, 1929, 1930

Tallahassee, Florida – 1935, 1936, 1937, 1938, 1939, 1940, 1941, 1942, 1946, 1947, 1948, 1949, 1950

Tallassee, Alabama – 1946, 1947, 1948, 1949

Thomasville, Georgia – 1913, 1914, 1915, 1935, 1936, 1937, 1938, 1939, 1940, 1941, 1946, 1947, 1948, 1949, 1950, 1952, 1953, 1954, 1955, 1956, 1957, 1958, 1962, 1963

Thomson, Georgia – 1956

Tifton, Georgia – 1949, 1950, 1951, 1952, 1953, 1954, 1955, 1956

Valdosta, Georgia – 1906, 1913, 1914, 1915, 1939, 1940, 1941, 1942, 1946, 1947, 1948, 1949, 1950, 1951, 1952, 1953, 1954, 1955, 1956, 1957, 1958

Valley, Alabama – 1946, 1947, 1948, 1949, 1950, 1951

Vidalia, Georgia – 1948, 1949, 1950, 1952, 1953, 1954, 1955, 1956

Waycross, Georgia – 1906, 1913, 1914, 1915, 1939, 1940, 1941, 1942, 1946, 1947, 1948, 1949, 1950, 1951, 1952, 1953, 1954, 1955, 1956, 1957, 1958, 1963

Georgia Class-D Minor League Baseball Encyclopedia

Georgia Class-D League Yearly Reviews 1906-63

This section is devoted to covering each year a Class-D minor league operated under the name Georgia-Alabama League, Georgia-Florida League, or Georgia State League. Also covered are the two years that the Georgia State League went by a different name and the one year the Georgia-Florida League operated as a Class-A minor league. Each year and league listing includes information on league officials, season league standings, a map of the league cities, a short recap of each season, information on each club, seasonal league records, and all-star teams for each season. Included in the information for each club are club officials, ballparks played in, attendance, major league affiliates, and player rosters with brief statistics and other league teams played for during the season (listed in the "APF" standing for Also Played For).

1906

Georgia State League

League President: J.P. Nichols, Jr.
Umpires: E.P. Coniff, C.W. Harris, M. McGrath, Weeks.

Georgia State League Final Standings

Team	W	L	Pct	GB	Affiliate
Waycross Machinists	37	12	.755	----	Unaffiliated
Columbus River Snipes/Brunswick	29	17	.630	6.5	Unaffiliated
Cordele	24	24	.500	12.5	Unaffiliated
Valdosta Stars	22	25	.468	14.0	Unaffiliated
Albany	17	32	.347	20.0	Unaffiliated
Americus Pallbearers	13	32	.289	22.0	Unaffiliated

1906 Georgia State League Map

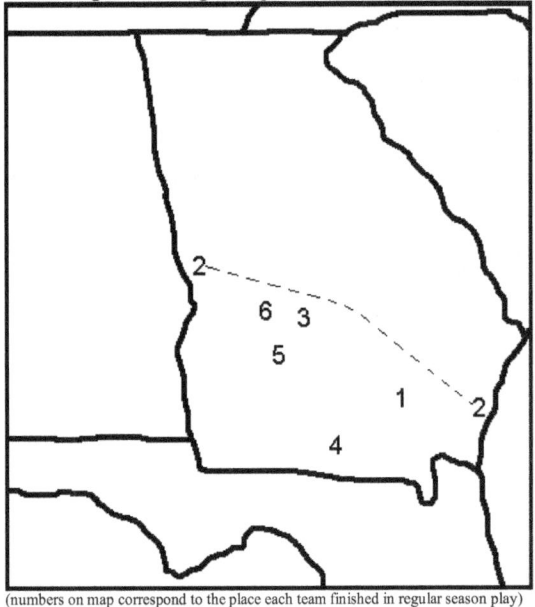

(numbers on map correspond to the place each team finished in regular season play)

The first ever class-D Georgia State League was organized in 1906 consisting of the cities of Albany, Americus, Columbus, Cordele, Valdosta, and Waycross. This six-club circuit began play on May 3 and managed to stay afloat for just over two months under the direction of president J.P. Nichols, Jr.

Financial difficulties were prevalent early on for most of the clubs and the league as a whole. On June 25, Columbus moved its operations to Brunswick hoping to get a stronger fan base to support the strapped club. Valdosta succumbed to financial problems on July 4, and Americus was close behind disbanding on July 7. Unable to keep operations going with only four teams, the entire league folded on July 9.

Although the league was defunct, a championship series was played between top finisher Waycross and second place Brunswick. The Machinists of Waycross won the best of five games series three games to one over their neighboring Brunswick.

Albany, Georgia
Manager(s): E.D. Alexander, Walter Snodgrass

Albany Team Roster

NAME	POS	APF
Alexander, E.D.	M, 1B	
Anthony, ---	P	
Boyd, Smith	P, OF, 3B	
Calder, ---	P	
Collier, ---	P	
Crosley, Umpire	P, OF	
DeCosta, ---	C, 1B	Americus
Dudley, ---	OF, 1B	Americus
Eldred, Henry	2B	
Lovelace, ---	3B	
McCormack, ---	C	
Nolley, ---	OF	
Nunley, ---	P	
Poole, ---	3B, OF	Americus
Posey, ---	P, OF	
Ramburger, ---	SS	
Siner, ---	SS	
Snodgrass, Walter	M, OF	

Georgia Class-D Minor League Baseball Encyclopedia

Americus, Georgia
Manager(s): E.P. Coniff, W.L. Harrigan, Harry Powell, James Whalen

Americus Pallbearers Team Roster

NAME	POS	APF
Averette, ---	OF	
Barnes, ---	3B	
Brenner, ---	2B	
Coniff, E.P.	M	
Crawley, ---	OF	
Crews, ---	P	
Crowley, ---	2B	
DeCosta, ---	C, 1B	Albany
Dudley, ---	OF, 1B	Albany
Everett, ---	P	
Hamilton, ---	P	
Harrigan, W.L.	M, OF	
Hawkins, ---	P	
Hines, ---	P, OF	
Hudson, ---	P	
Kiker, B.	OF	
Lamar, Nick	1B, P	
Lane, ---	3B, 2B, SS	
Marshall, ---	P	
McKnight, ---	P	
Middlebrooks, ---	OF	
Newkirk, ---	SS, 3B	
Perry, ---	OF	
Poole, ---	3B, OF	Albany
Powell, O.T. "Harry"	M	
Reynolds, ---	P, OF	
Richardson, ---	P, OF	
Rolf, ---	2B	
Sawyer, ---	P	
Smith, A.	1B	
Smith, C.	2B	
Sobor, ---	P	
Sorrells, ---	3B, 1B	
Spencer, ---	P	
Stephens, Colonel	C, 1B	
Tison, ---	OF	
Westbrook, ---	1B, C, OF	
Whalen, James	M, OF	
Yancey, ---	OF	

Columbus/Brunswick, Georgia
Manager(s): Bill Hessler, Dudly Lewis

Columbus River Snipes/ Brunswick Team Roster

NAME	POS	APF
Cranston, ---	C	
Dillard, ---	3B	
Fisher, Bob	SS	
Foster, ---	P, OF	
Goodrich, ---	OF	
Henry, ---	P, OF	
Hessler, Bill	M, 2B, C	
Lewis, Dudley D.	M, OF	
Mercer, ---	P, OF	
Weaver, ---	P	
Westervelt, ---	1B	

Cordele, Georgia
Manager(s): Trammel Scott

Cordele Team Roster

NAME	POS	APF
Cummings, ---	OF	
Davenport, ---	P, OF	
Deyo, ---	OF	
Hall, ---	P	
Harper, ---	SS	
Hart, ---	C	
Harwood, ---	C	
Lavender, ---	P	
Osment, ---	OF	
Phelan, ---	P	
Poole, ---	2B	
Ramsey, ---	P, OF	
Reagan, ---	2B	
Richards, ---	3B	
Scott, Trammel	M, 1B	
Sohni, ---	P	
Stewart, ---	OF	

Valdosta, Georgia
Manager(s): E. Bagwell, Harry Piepho, A.L. Starr, Peck Walters, Charles Willett

Valdosta Stars Team Roster

NAME	POS	APF
Bagwell, E.	M, OF	
Barber, ---	P	
Buchanan, ---	P	
Burden, ---	C, 1B	
Cassidy, ---	P	
Crowder, ---	SS	
Kipp, ---	3B	
LaMotte, ---	OF	
Mitchell, ---	2B	
O'Quinn, ---	P	
Piepho, Harry	M	
Starr, A.L.	M	
Tideman, ---	OF	
Walters, Peck	M, C	
Weakley, ---	P	
Willett, Charles R.	M	

Waycross, Georgia
Manager(s): Carl Buesse

Waycross Machinists Team Roster

NAME	POS	APF
Allen, ---	1B	
Blanton, ---	OF, 3B	
Bowen, ---	1B, C	
Buesse, Carlton "Carl"	M, P	
Buesse, F.	3B, SS	
Griffin, H.	OF	
Griffin, T.	2B	
Ham, ---	P, OF	
Tribble, ---	C, OF	
Wagnon, ---	SS, OF	
Wilson, ---	P, OF	

1913

Empire State League (Georgia State League)

League President: C.C. Vaughn / Oscar Grover

Empire State League Final Standings

Team	W	L	Pct	GB	Affiliate
Valdosta Millionaires	58	40	.592	----	Unaffiliated
Thomasville Hornets	56	40	.583	1.0	Unaffiliated
Cordele Babies	49	50	.495	9.5	Unaffiliated
Americus Muckalees	45	54	.455	13.5	Unaffiliated
Waycross Blowhards	43	52	.453	13.5	Unaffiliated
Brunswick Pilots	42	57	.424	16.5	Unaffiliated

1913 Empire State League Map

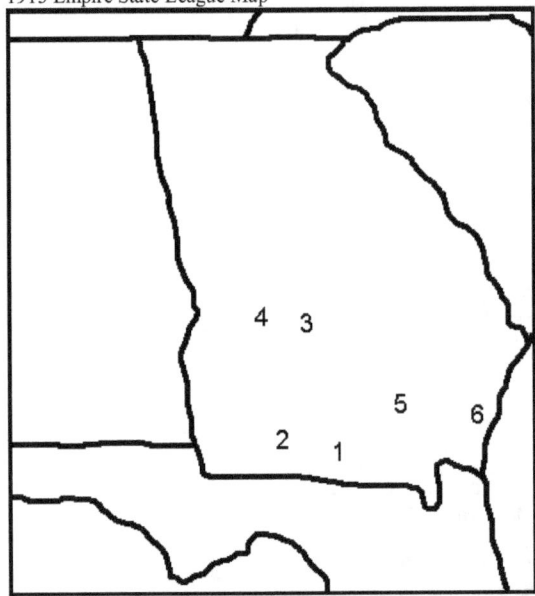

(numbers on map correspond to the place each team finished in regular season play)

After a seven-year hiatus, the Class-D Georgia State League returned to baseball action under the name Empire State League. The cities of Americus, Brunswick, Cordele, Thomasville, Valdosta, Waycross all participated in the league. Of these cities, only Thomasville did not participate in the Georgia State League in the inaugural season of 1906. Cordele dropped out of the league at the end of the first half of the season and was not replaced.

Before Cordele dropped out of the league, two of the Babies' pitchers accomplished quite an impressive feat. On July 23, Dana Fillingim and Percy Wilder both pitched no-hitters in a double header against Waycross. Fillingim won the first game 4 to 0, and Wilder won the second 5 to 0 that was shortened to seven innings.

The league played a split schedule with the winner of each half meeting at the end of the season in the league championship series. Valdosta won the first half of the season with thirty-two wins and fifteen losses. Thomasville, who placed third in the first half, came out on top in the season's second stanza earning the right to face Valdosta in the post-season championship series. In the best of seven games championship series, Thomasville emerged victorious over Valdosta, four games to two. Although the championship was lost by Valdosta, the Millionaire's overall season record was one game better than Thomasville.

Americus, Georgia
Manager(s): Hal Griffin, William Kuhlman, Harry Webber

Americus Muckalees Team Roster

NAME	G	BA	POS	W	L	PCT	APF
Bernstein, ---	27	0.278	SS				
Bowen, Grady	96	0.324	3B				
Brouthers, Walt	100	0.269	OF				Waycross
Chancey, C.M.	102	0.386	OF				
Dacey, Red	55	0.157	P, OF	9	3	0.750	
Griffin, Hal	101	0.265	M, 1B				
Kuhlman, William	73	0.289	M, 2B				
Manchester, Dick	98	0.271	C				
Pratt, ---	19	0.127	P	9	6	0.600	
Stewart, ---	16	0.191	P	4	6	0.400	
Utter, ---	27	0.132					Valdosta
Wagnon, John	81	0.263	OF				Thomasville
Webber, Harry			M				
Werner, ---	43	0.266	P	9	12	0.429	
Wolfe, ---	22	0.250	P				

Brunswick, Georgia
Manager(s): Bert Kite, Charles Moran, Whitey Morse

Brunswick Pilots Team Roster

NAME	G	BA	POS	W	L	PCT	APF
Bundy, ---	37	0.211	2B				
Cates, Eli	34	0.240	P, OF	11	11	0.500	
Franks, ---	88	0.241	OF				Valdosta
Hartner, ---	43	0.265	P, OF	15	8	0.652	
Hawkins, G.B.	60	0.332	OF				Valdosta
Kite, Bert	47	0.243	M, C				
Leininger, ---	94	0.187	3B				Valdosta
Moran, Charles			M				
Morse, Whitey	101	0.316	M, 1B				Valdosta
Mullin, ---	78	0.232	SS				
Parker, ---	85	0.257	2B				
Pierce, ---	85	0.251	C				Valdosta
Schuyler, ---	98	0.277	OF				
Seigfried, ---	93	0.238	OF				
Siefert, ---	34	0.246	C				
Stewart, ---	9		P	4	4	0.500	
Walker, ---	41	0.242	OF, P	3	10	0.231	

Cordele, Georgia
Manager(s): Kid Reagan

Cordele Babies Team Roster

NAME	G	BA	POS	W	L	PCT	APF
Bowden, ---	59	0.286	C, OF				
Brazier, ---	102	0.308	OF				
Davenport, ---	13	0.220	OF				
Day, ---	93	0.265	1B				
Eubanks, ---	91	0.282	C				
Fillingim, Dana	34	0.151	P	15	10	0.600	
Gillespie, ---	30	0.190	P	5	10	0.333	
Gray, ---	22	0.318	SS				
Hall, ---	38	0.239	P, OF	12	16	0.429	
Heidt, ---	43	0.208	SS				
Humphries, ---	44	0.203	3B				

Georgia Class-D Minor League Baseball Encyclopedia

NAME	G	BA	POS	W	L	PCT	APF
McLendon, ---	64	0.248	3B				
Reagan, Kid	102	0.237	M, 2B				
Smith, ---	36	0.248	SS				
Stone, ---	27	0.294	OF				
Wassem, ---	83	0.306	OF				
Wilder, Percy	30	0.232	P	16	10	0.615	
Wilkes, ---	50	0.213	OF				Thomasville

Thomasville, Georgia
Manager(s): Martin Dudley, George Durley

Thomasville Hornets Team Roster

NAME	G	BA	POS	W	L	PCT	APF
Barnett, ---	97	0.224	OF				
Champlain, ---	97	0.236	3B				
Cheney, ---	25	0.237	P	10	6	0.625	
Davenport, ---	60	0.279	1B				
Day, ---	24	0.283	P	16	6	0.727	
Dudley, Martin	76	0.252	M, C				
Durley, George			M				
Elrod, ---	10		P	5	5	0.500	Valdosta
Kates, ---	28	0.231	1B				
Mills, ---	14		2B				
Murch, Red	80	0.285	2B				
Murphy, ---	73	0.338	SS				
Parker, ---	23	0.321	2B				
Roth, V.	57	0.283	P, OF	18	8	0.692	
Stiles, ---	23	0.154	P	8	13	0.381	
Wagnon, John	81	0.263	OF				Americus
Wilkes, ---	50	0.213	OF				Cordele

Valdosta, Georgia
Manager(s): Dutch Jordan, Whitey Morse

Valdosta Millionaires Team Roster

NAME	G	BA	POS	W	L	PCT	APF
Elrod, ---	10		P	5	5	0.500	Thomasville
Franks, ---	88	0.241	OF				Brunswick
Hawkins, G.B.	60	0.332	OF				Brunswick
Hurley, ---	89	0.311	1B, OF				
Jordan, Dutch	96	0.344	M, 2B				
Leininger, ---	94	0.187	3B				Brunswick
Medlock, ---	79	0.251	OF				Waycross
Morse, Whitey	101	0.316	M, 1B				Brunswick
Pierce, ---	85	0.251	C				Brunswick
Schwartz, F.	71	0.205	SS				
Utter, ---	27	0.132					Americus
Van Landingham, ---	101	0.303	C, OF				
Vanderlip, ---	8		P	3	5	0.375	
Vaughn, ---	10	0.182	P	5	4	0.556	
Walker, ---	9		P				
Winges, ---	43	0.115	P, OF	17	7	0.708	
Zellers, ---	51	0.208	P, OF	15	13	0.536	

Waycross, Georgia
Manager(s): William Clark, Jack Hawkins, Charles Wahoo

Waycross Blowhards Team Roster

NAME	G	BA	POS	W	L	PCT	APF
Alperman, Whitey	14	0.250	OF				
Anderson, ---	85	0.301	SS, OF				
Bitting, Earl	35	0.262	3B				
Brouthers, Walt	100	0.269	OF				Americus
Clancey, ---	29	0.141	SS				
Clark, William	47	0.190	M, P, OF	16	9	0.640	
Coveney, Jack	29	0.169	C				
Daley, ---	17	0.197	3B				
Faircloth, ---	8		P	2	3	0.400	
Fenton, ---	98	0.259	OF				
Hawkins, Jack			M				
Herring, ---	18	0.175	P	5	8	0.385	
Holiday, ---	27	0.156	1B				
Jones, ---	42	0.260	1B				
Lloyd, ---	33	0.250	2B				
McMannus, ---	25	0.245	P	5	6	0.455	
Medlock, ---	79	0.251	OF				Valdosta
Rafferty, ---	22	0.173	OF				
Shuman, ---	82	0.238	C, OF				
Spaugh, ---	4		P				
Wahoo, Charles	25	0.250	M, C				

1913 Empire State League Records
Batting
Highest Batting Average (minimum 100 at bats)
1. C.M. Chancey – Americus .386
2. Dutch Jordan – Valdosta .344
3. --- Murphy – Thomasville .338
4. G.B. Hawkins – Vald/Brun .332
5. Grady Bowen – Americus .324

Most Hits
1. C.M. Chancey – Americus 142
2. Dutch Jordan – Valdosta 130
3. --- Van Landingham – Valdosta 128
4. --- Brazier – Cordele 121
5. Grady Bowen – Americus 118

Most Runs
1. --- Van Landingham – Valdosta 72
2. Dutch Jordan – Valdosta 69
3. C.M. Chancey – Americus 68
4. --- Wassem – Cordele 64
5. John Wagnon – Amer/Thom 60

Most Total Bases
1. C.M. Chancey – Americus 212
2. Dutch Jordan – Valdosta 174
3. --- Van Landingham – Valdosta 161
4. --- Brazier – Cordele 157
5. --- Hurley – Valdosta 148

Most Doubles
1. Dutch Jordan – Valdosta 34
2. C.M. Chancey – Americus 32
3. --- Van Landingham – Valdosta 24
4. Hal Griffin – Americus 21
5. --- Day – Cordele 20

Most Triples
1. --- Hurley – Valdosta 8
   --- Murphy – Thomasville 8
3. --- Wilkes – Thom/Cord 7
4. --- Brazier – Cordele 5
5. C.M. Chancey – Americus 4
   --- Day – Cordele 4
   --- Franks – Brun/Vald 4

Most Home Runs
1. C.M. Chancey – Americus 10
2. --- Fenton – Waycross 7
3. --- Davenport – Thomasville 5
4. *eight players tied with 4

Most Extra Base Hits
1. C.M. Chancey – Americus 46
2. Dutch Jordan – Valdosta 38

3. --- Murphy – Thomasville 30
4. --- Van Landingham – Valdosta 28
5. --- Schuyler – Brunswick 26

Fielding
Most Put-Outs
1. Hal Griffin 1B – Americus 983
2. Whitey Morse 1B – Valdosta 873
3. --- Day 1B – Cordele 768
4. --- Eubanks C – Cordele 648
5. --- Davenport 1B – Thomasville 616

Most Assists
1. E.L. Reagan 2B – Cordele 283
2. Dutch Jordan 2B – Valdosta 262
3. --- Champlain 3B – Thomasville 212
4. Grady Bowen 3B – Americus 201
5. William Kuhlman 2B – Americus 194

Most Errors
1. --- Murphy SS – Thomasville 47
2. --- Lieninger 3B – Valdosta 45
3. --- Mullin SS – Brunswick 40
4. --- Day 1B – Cordele 38
5. --- Smith SS – Cordele 35

Pitching
Most Wins
1. V. Roth – Thomasville 18
2. --- Winges – Valdosta 17
3. William Clark – Waycross 16
   --- Day – Thomasville 16
   Percy Wilder – Cordele 16

Most Losses
1. --- Hall – Cordele 16
2. --- Stiles – Thomasville 13
   --- Zellers – Valdosta 13
4. --- Werner – Americus 12
5. Eli Cates – Brunswick 11

Highest Winning Percentage (10 game minimum)
1. Red Dacey – Americus .750
2. --- Day – Thomasville .727
3. --- Winges – Valdosta .708
4. V. Roth – Thomasville .692
5. --- Hartner – Brunswick .652

1913

Georgia-Alabama League

League President: W.J. Boykin

Georgia-Alabama League Final Standings

Team	W	L	Pct	GB	Affiliate
Gadsden Steel Makers	51	38	.573	----	Unaffiliated
Newnan Cowetas	46	44	.511	5.5	Unaffiliated
Opelika Opelicans	46	45	.505	6.0	Unaffiliated
Anniston Moulders	45	45	.500	6.5	Unaffiliated
LaGrange Terrapins	42	48	.467	9.5	Unaffiliated
Talladega Indians	40	50	.444	11.5	Unaffiliated

1913 Georgia-Alabama League Map

(numbers on map correspond to the place each team finished in regular season play)

The Class-D Georgia-Alabama League was first born in 1913. Consisting of Georgia teams from LaGrange and Newnan and Alabama teams from Anniston, Gadsden, Opelika, and Talladega, the league spun off from the defunct Southeastern League. Anniston, Gadsden, and Talladega made up the core of the new circuit while Newnan, LaGrange, and Opelika took the places of Selma and Bessemer, Alabama, and Rome, Georgia from the old aggregation. Under the direction of league president W.J. Boykin of Gadsden, all six clubs stayed in operation from the start to the finish of the season.

Anniston pitcher Cecil Battson made history on August 16 when he pitched a no-hitter defeating LaGrange 8 to 0. George Rohe of Newnan set the all-time Georgia-Alabama League record for the highest single season batting average in 1913 when he hit .435.

The Gadsden Steel Makers took the pennant having the best record at the end of the season. After the unsplit, single-term season, there was no post-season play.

Georgia Class-D Minor League Baseball Encyclopedia

Anniston, Alabama
Manager(s): Chick Hannon

Anniston Moulders Team Roster

NAME	G	BA	POS	W	L	PCT	APF
Askew, ---	68	0.321	OF				
Battson, Cecil	11		P	8	3	0.727	
Donaldson, Earl	79	0.278	SS				
Glazner, Whitey	10		P	6	4	0.600	
Hannon, Chick			M				
Henry, ---	89	0.235	OF				
Hopper, ---	29	0.315	1B				
Lamar, ---	88	0.284	2B				
Lunger, ---	27	0.232	3B				
Proctor, Louis	42	0.333	OF				
Sheppard, ---	85	0.174	C				
Stephenson, ---	48	0.299	P, OF	7	7	0.500	
Young, ---	8		P	4	4	0.500	

Gadsden, Alabama
Manager(s): Elmer Randall

Gadsden Steel Makers Team Roster

NAME	G	BA	POS	W	L	PCT	APF
Clark, ---	19	0.303	2B				
Cooper, ---	59	0.266	OF				
Frentz, ---	13		P	10	3	0.769	
Jorda, ---	78	0.310	C				
King, ---	23		P	12	11	0.522	
Needles, ---	6		P	3	3	0.500	
Pezold, Larry	86	0.304	OF,				
Randall, Elmer	72	0.410	M, OF				
Reinecke, Wally	89	0.222	SS				
Roxie, ---	59	0.256	3B				
Sigmon, Jesse	43	0.182	P	14	9	0.609	
Werner, G.H.	88	0.302	OF				
Williams, ---	90	0.275	1B				

LaGrange, Georgia
Manager(s): Ducky Holmes

LaGrange Terrapins Team Roster

NAME	G	BA	POS	W	L	PCT	APF
Bannister, ---	36	0.291	P, OF	5	6	0.455	
Beasley, ---	46	0.204	P	10	14	0.417	
Billingsley, ---	80	0.284	P, C				
Brannen, ---	65	0.261	P, OF	4	4	0.500	
Clark, ---	81	0.225	3B, SS				
Donaldson, Jack	78	0.342	SS				
Guitterez, W.	55	0.234	2B				
Head, Ralph	14		P	8	6	0.571	
Holmes, Ducky			M				
Nelson, ---	80	0.265	OF, P	2	6	0.250	
Newkirk, ---	91	0.241	1B				
Robinson, ---	51	0.224	OF, P	1	2	0.333	
Vandegraff, ---	44	0.257	OF				
Waldron, William	91	0.285	3B				

Newnan, Georgia
Manager(s): E.S. Bagwell, Ed Schulze

Newnan Cowetas Team Roster

NAME	G	BA	POS	W	L	PCT	APF
Bagwell, E.S.			M				
Cole, ---	57	0.302	SS				
Craven, Jess	90	0.351	OF				
Griffin, ---	83	0.264	1B				
Hanson, Harry	17	0.250	C				
Hawkins, G.B.	19		P	7	12	0.368	
Howell, Lloyd	89	0.383	2B				
Lovett, ---	13		P	9	4	0.692	
Luttrell, ---	13		P	9	4	0.692	
Rice, ---	61	0.324	1B				
Robinson, ---	65	0.277	P, OF	4	2	0.667	
Rohe, George	42	0.435	3B				
Schulze, Ed			M				
Stark, ---	7		P	3	4	0.429	

Opelika, Alabama
Manager(s): Ed Ery

Opelika Opelicans Team Roster

NAME	G	BA	POS	W	L	PCT	APF
Allen, ---	37	0.256	C				
Blackwell, ---	90	0.311	2B				
Bone, ---	62	0.230	C				
Cantley, John	37	0.257	P	10	13	0.435	
Chambers, ---	91	0.296	3B, OF				
Ery, Ed		0.286	M, OF, P	19	5	0.792	
Hardage, ---	31	0.265	OF				
Hawkins, G.B.	36	0.277	P	10	10	0.500	
Ragsdale, Bob	87	0.236	OF				
Schwartz, Bill	88	0.256	1B				
Spitznagle, ---	88	0.218	SS				
Williams, ---	38	0.266	P	10	13	0.435	

Talladega, Alabama
Manager(s): Charles Reese

Talladega Indians Team Roster

NAME	G	BA	POS	W	L	PCT	APF
Boyd, J.S.		0.386	P	2	3	0.400	
Camp, Howie	90	0.314	OF				
Glass, ---	89	0.282	2B				
Hoch, ---	37	0.286	1B				
Kuppin, ---	4		P	2	2	0.500	
McCraney, ---	48	0.216	3B				
Powers, ---	24	0.337	SS				
Reese, Charles	73	0.376	M, OF				
Richards, J.A.	33	0.304	C				
Roberts, ---	45	0.152	P				
Whitfield, ---	39	0.185	OF				

1913 Georgia-Alabama League Records
Batting
Highest Batting Average (minimum 100 at bats)
1. George Rohe – Newnan .435
2. Elmer Randall – Gadsden .410
3. C.L. Howell – Newnan .383
4. Charles Reese – Talladega .376
5. Jess Craven – Newnan .351

Most Hits
1. Jess Craven – Newnan 121
2. Jack Donaldson – LaGrange 111
3. Elmer Randall – Gadsden 110
4. Howie Camp – Talladega 109
5. --- Blackwell – Opelika 105

Most Runs
1. Larry Pezold – Gadsden 76
2. C.L. Howell – Newnan 63
    William Waldron – LaGrange 63
4. --- Spitznagle – Opelika 62

--- Williams – Gadsden   62

Most Stolen Bases
1. --- Williams – Gadsden   40
2. --- Newkirk – LaGrange   35
   Bob Ragsdale – Opelika   35
4. --- Glass – Talladega   33
5. --- Spitznagle – Opelika   31

Fielding
Most Put-Outs

1. --- Newkirk 1B – LaGrange   862
2. --- Williams 1B – Gadsden   861
3. --- Griffin 1B – Newnan   675
4. Bill Schwartz 1B – Opelika   631
5. --- Sheppard C – Anniston   537

Most Assists
1. Wally Reinecke SS – Gadsden   257
2. --- Spitznagle SS – Opelika   252
3. C.L. Howell 2B – Newnan   232
4. Earl Donaldson SS – Anniston   214
5. --- Lamar 2B – Anniston   208

Most Errors
1. --- Lamar 2B – Anniston   45
2. Wally Reinecke SS – Gadsden   43
3. --- Clark 3B, SS – LaGrange   42
   Earl Donaldson SS – Anniston   42
   --- Spitznagle SS – Opelika   42

Pitching
Most Wins
1. Ed Ery – Opelika   19
2. Jesse Sigmon – Gadsden   14
3. --- King – Gadsden   12
4. *five players tied with   10

Most Losses
1. --- Beasley – LaGrange   14
2. John Cantley – Opelika   13
   --- Williams – Opelika   13
4. G.B. Hawkins – Newnan   12
5. --- King – Gadsden   11

Highest Winning Percentage (10 game minimum)
1. Ed Ery – Opelika   .792
2. --- Frentz – Gadsden   .769
3. Cecil Battson – Anniston   .727
4. --- Lovett – Newnan   .692
   --- Lutrell – Newnan   .692

1914

Georgia-Alabama League

League President: W.J. Boykin

Georgia-Alabama League Final Standings

Team	W	L	Pct	GB	Affiliate
Selma River Rats	60	35	.632	----	Unaffiliated
Newnan Cowetas	56	37	.602	3.0	Unaffiliated
LaGrange Terrapins	55	43	.561	6.5	Unaffiliated
Opelika Pelicans	52	45	.536	9.0	Unaffiliated
Rome Romans	46	50	.479	14.5	Unaffiliated
Anniston Moulders	41	54	.432	19.0	Unaffiliated
Talladega Indians	37	55	.402	21.0	Unaffiliated
Gadsden Steel Makers	32	60	.348	26.5	Unaffiliated

1914 Georgia-Alabama League Map

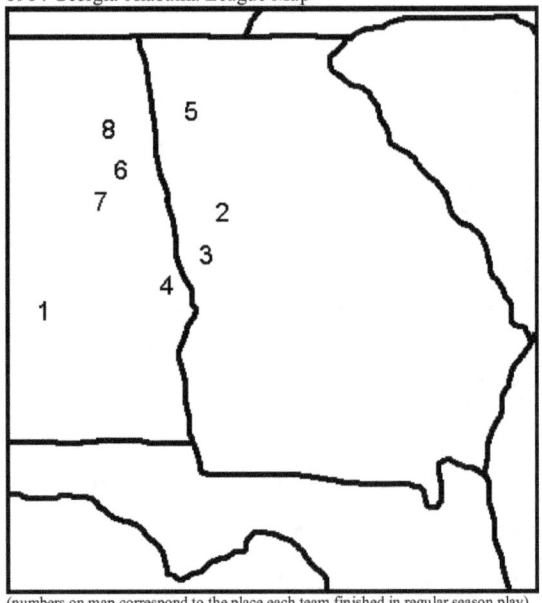

(numbers on map correspond to the place each team finished in regular season play)

The Georgia-Alabama League grew from six teams to eight during the off-season after 1913. Rome, Georgia and Selma, Alabama joined the original six clubs of the circuit after spending a season in the Appalachian and Cotton States Leagues respectively. Both teams were part of the Southeastern League in 1912, the loop that spawned the Georgia-Alabama League, but opted not to join the new organization in 1913. On August 3, Gadsden became a road-only, traveling club. The remaining games were played at the respective home fields of Gadsden's regularly scheduled opponents.

On June 5, Opelika pitcher John Cantley tossed a game against Talladega and won 19 to 1. In the game, Cantley hit three grand slams and one single driving in 15 runs. Newnan's H.P. Mackie set the single season Georgia-Alabama League record for the most runs scored in 1914 when he crossed to plate 176 times.

The River Rats of Selma were at the top of the standings when the season closed earning the league pennant. No post-season championship was played, and Selma was declared league champions.

Anniston, Alabama
Manager(s): Louis Proctor, Bob Ragsdale

Anniston Moulders Team Roster

NAME	G	BA	POS	GP	APF
Abbott, ---	86	0.209	3B		
Battson, Cecil	29	0.068	P	29	
Carter, ---	14	0.196	OF		
Donaldson, Earl	99	0.233	SS		
Glazner, Whitey	22	0.161	P	22	
Killingsworth, ---	31	0.089	P	31	
Lamar, ---	98	0.294	2B		
Proctor, Louis	54	0.167	M, OF		
Ragsdale, Bob	97	0.223	M, OF		
Sanford, Allen	33	0.200			
Stephenson, ---	47	0.290	P	47	
Tisdale, ---	75	0.279	C		

Gadsden, Alabama
Manager(s): Bruce Hayes, Louis Jordan, L. Mills

Gadsden Steel Makers Team Roster

NAME	G	BA	POS	GP	APF
Abbott, ---	31	0.128	P	31	
Askew, ---	59	0.247	1B, OF		
Baumgardner, ---	75	0.242	3B		
Brownslow, ---	23	0.220	OF		
Hayes, Bruce			M		
Jordan, Louis	68	0.287	M, C		
King, ---	27	0.175	P	27	
Mills, L.	59	0.247	M, 1B		
Selph, ---	87	0.260	3B		
Sigmon, Jesse	39	0.204	P	39	
Smith, H.T.	15	0.140	2B		
Werner, G.H.	88	0.219	OF		
Williams, ---	55	0.176	OF		
Wood, ---	48	0.177	P	48	

LaGrange, Georgia
Manager(s): Ed LaFitte

LaGrange Terrapins Team Roster

NAME	G	BA	POS	GP	APF
Allen, ---	73	0.200	OF		
Amazon, H.W.	75	0.183	1B		
Bannister, ---	78	0.270	OF		
Donaldson, Jack	50	0.305	SS		
Head, Ralph	28	0.117	P	28	
Holland, Sid	94	0.281	2B		
Jackson, Charles	10	0.250	OF		
LaFitte, Ed	95	0.278	M, C		
Waldron, William	94	0.309	3B		
Weston, E.H.	27	0.183	P	27	
Williams, ---	31	0.159	P	31	
Zellers, ---	52	0.223	P	52	

Newnan, Georgia
Manager(s): War Sanders

Newnan Cowetas Team Roster

NAME	G	BA	POS	GP	APF
Bowen, Grady	67	0.268	SS		
Craven, Jess	27	0.250	OF		
Edmondson, W.C.	74	0.228	3B		
Howell, Lloyd	82	0.332	1B		
Long, H.L.	25	0.326	P	25	
Lovett, ---	6	0.167	P	6	
Mackie, H.P.	93	0.266	2B		
Mays, ---	34	0.268	P	34	
Sanders, War	88	0.191	M, OF		
Smith, ---	92	0.247	OF		
Whitney, J.F.	23	0.175	P	23	

Opelika, Alabama
Manager(s): Kirk Newell, Jack Steele

Opelika Opelicans Team Roster

NAME	G	BA	POS	GP	APF
Blackwell, ---	88	0.287	3B		
Cantley, John	33	0.273	P	33	
Chambers, ---	93	0.267	OF		
Davis, Bud	14	0.143	P	14	
Donaldson, Jack	76	0.161	OF		
Ery, Ed	53	0.254	P	53	
Hawkins, G.B.	26	0.176	P	26	
McLin, ---	50		OF		
Newell, Kirk	91	0.258	M, 2B		
Schwartz, Bill	92	0.262	1B		
Sheppard, ---	75	0.287	C		
Spitznagle, ---	91	0.268	SS		
Steele, Jack	86	0.321	M, OF		
Williams, ---	89	0.236	C		

Rome, Georgia
Manager(s): Jack Reidy

Rome Romans Team Roster

NAME	G	BA	POS	GP	APF
Aaron, W.M.	29	0.223	P	29	
Alexander, ---	75	0.220	3B		
Barclay, Robert	16	0.184	P	16	
Boote, ---	13	0.081	P	13	
Bray, ---	75	0.244	2B		
Flowers, B.	33	0.188	P	33	
Flowers, H.	10	0.343	P	10	
Hutchins, ---	30	0.205	OF		
Kimball, ---	90	0.292	C		
Knight, ---	27	0.154	P	27	
Moorefield, ---	50	0.354	OF		
Reidy, Jack	95	0.298	M, OF		
Smith, ---	50	0.356	OF		
Stringfield, ---	71	0.258	3B		
Taylor, ---	75	0.241	C		Selma
Taylor, A.	24	0.213	SS		
Utley, ---	92	0.288	1B		

Selma, Alabama
Manager(s): W. Guitterez, Arthur Riggs

Selma River Rats Team Roster

NAME	G	BA	POS	GP	APF
Bostwick, ---	9	0.077	P	9	
Brooks, R.	27	0.397	P	27	
Burke, ---	21		OF		
Cowan, E.	69	0.284	3B		
Cowan, W. W.	67	0.316	2B		
Farmer, ---	69	0.301	SS		
Guitterez, W.	62	0.223	M, C		
Kimball, ---	18	0.169	OF		
Morrison, Harry	22	0.103	P	22	

Overton, H.A.	46	0.184	SS	
Riggs, Arthur			M	
Sharp, ---	51	0.233	SS	
Shirley, ---	6	0.421	OF	
Taylor, ---	75	0.241	C	Rome
Thomas, ---	35	0.149	OF	
Vasterling, ---	69	0.305	1B	

Talladega, Alabama
Manager(s): Howard Baker, Lovell Draper, Tige Garrett, Carl Pace

Talladega Indians Team Roster

NAME	G	BA	POS	GP	APF
Baker, Howard	78	0.271	M, C		
Black, ---	12	0.216	P	12	
Camp, Howie	57	0.283	OF		
Crow, Lee	68	0.249	2B, 3B		
Davis, Bud	38	0.207	P	38	
Decatur, Art	20	0.182	OF		
Doyle, ---	20	0.183	1B		
Draper, Lovell			M		
Garrett, Tige	39	0.214	M, 1B		
Garrison, ---	6	0.111	OF		
Graves, ---	8	0.211	3B		
Hodge, ---	15	0.275	SS		
Knox, ---	23	0.353	OF		
Moore, James	29	0.163	OF		
Pace, Carl			M		
Reinecke, Wally	54	0.162	SS		
Robinson, ---	35	0.278	OF		
Schultz, ---	12		P	12	
Shean, ---	12		P	12	
Slater, ---	24	0.205	2B		
Townsend, ---	10		OF		
Wilson, ---	72	0.222	2B		

Fielding
Most Put-Outs
1. --- Utley – Rome   923
2. C.L. Howell – Newnan   857
3. H.W. Amazon – LaGrange   683
4. --- Vasterling – Selma   664
5. Ed LaFitte – LaGrange   611

Most Assists
1. Earl Donaldson – Anniston   283
2. --- Bray – Rome   277
3. Lee Crow – Talladega   270
4. --- Spitznagle – Opelika   269
5. Kirk Newell – Opelika   261

Most Errors
1. --- Spitznagle – Opelika   61
2. Wally Reinecke – Talladega   50
3. Earl Donaldson – Anniston   47
4. --- Lamar – Anniston   46
5. --- Alexander – Rome   45

1914 Georgia-Alabama League Records
Batting
Highest Batting Average (minimum 100 at bats)
1. --- Smith – Rome   .356
2. --- Moorefield – Rome   .354
3. C.L. Howell – Newnan   .332
4. Jack Steele – Opelika   .321
5. E. Cowan – Selma   .316

Most Hits
1. Jack Reidy – Rome   117
2. C.L. Howell – Newnan   113
   --- Lamar – Anniston   113
4. William Waldron – LaGrange   106
5. --- Utley – Rome   103

Most Runs
1. H.P. Mackie – Newnan   176
2. --- Smith – Newnan   165
3. J.F. Whitney – Newnan   90
4. Jack Reidy – Rome   76
5. Earl Donaldson – Anniston   70
   --- Spitznagle – Opelika   70

Most Stolen Bases
1. --- Lamar – Anniston   43
2. Jack Reidy – Rome   31
3. Kirk Newell – Opelika   30
4. E. Cowan – Selma   27
   Earl Donaldson – Anniston   27

1914

Georgia State League

League President: I.J. Kalmon

Georgia State League Final Standings

Team	W	L	Pct	GB	Affiliate
Cordele Ramblers	57	44	.564	----	Unaffiliated
Americus Muckalees	57	47	.548	1.5	Unaffiliated
Thomasville Hornets	53	50	.515	5.0	Unaffiliated
Brunswick Pilots	53	51	.510	5.5	Unaffiliated
Waycross Grasshoppers/ Moguls	53	53	.500	6.5	Unaffiliated
Valdosta Millionaires	41	69	.410	20.5	Unaffiliated

1914 Georgia State League Map

(numbers on map correspond to the place each team finished in regular season play)

In its second year of operation under the new organization, the league went back to the old moniker of Georgia State League. The same six teams from the previous year made up the newly named circuit.

Americus pitcher Bob Geary claimed the spotlight on July 24 when he pitched a no-hitter against Valdosta winning the game 8 to 0.

A split schedule was played with the Thomasville Hornets winning the first half and the Muckalees of Americus winning the second. Americus posted an astounding turn around in the second half of the season after placing fifth in act one of the baseball year. In the post-season championship series, Americus swept Thomasville four games to none. Cordele ended the season with the best combined record between the two halves, one and a half games ahead of Americus and five full games in front of Thomasville.

Americus, Georgia
Manager(s): Dave Gaston

Americus Muckalees Team Roster

NAME	G	BA	POS	GP	APF
Baggens, ---		0.255			Valdosta
Bales, ---		0.337			
Bitting, Earl		0.307			Brunswick
Bowen, Grady		0.278			
Ellis, ---		0.317			
Gallagher, ---		0.203			Brunswick
Gaston, Dave		0.306	M		
Geary, Bob		0.308			
Hodge, ---		0.272			Brunswick
Leonard, ---		0.266			
Manchester, Dick		0.238			
Middiknight, ---		0.188			
Pierre, Bill		0.277			Brunswick
Pratt, ---		0.248			
Riley, B.		0.288			
West, ---		0.255			
Zapke, ---		0.138			

Brunswick, Georgia
Manager(s): Earl Bitting, Dutch Jordan, Bert Kite

Brunswick Pilots Team Roster

NAME	G	BA	POS	GP	APF
Bitting, Earl		0.307	M		Americus
Bowden, ---		0.317			
Dedon, ---		0.191			Valdosta
Gallagher, ---		0.203			Americus
Gordon, ---		0.190			
Gross, ---		0.309			
Hodge, ---		0.272			Americus
Jordan, Dutch		0.280	M		
Kite, Bert			M		
Leon, ---		0.212			Valdosta
Morse, Whitey		0.261			Valdosta
O'Brien, ---		0.257			Valdosta
Parker, ---		0.274			
Payne, George		0.130	P	23	
Pierre, Bill		0.277			Americus
Reynolds, Wade		0.276			
Schuman, ---		0.317			Waycross
Schuyler, ---		0.307			
Seigfried, ---		0.281			
Stewart, ---		0.125			
Telkan, ---		0.327			Thomasville
Weiler, ---		0.208			Valdosta
Wood, ---		0.132			

Cordele, Georgia
Manager(s): Kid Reagan

Cordele Ramblers Team Roster

NAME	G	BA	POS	GP	APF
Bankston, Will		0.359			
Brouthers, Walt		0.264			
Burress, ---		0.261			
Eubanks, ---		0.309			
Fillingim, Dana		0.146			
Griffin, ---		0.297			
Hall, ---		0.259			
Kuhlman, William		0.292			
Reagan, Kid		0.232	M		
Robinson, ---		0.288			
Thrasher, ---		0.412			

Vaiden, ---	0.098	
Wicker, ---	0.264	Thomasville

Thomasville, Georgia
Manager(s): Martin Dudley

Thomasville Hornets Team Roster

NAME	G	BA	POS	GP	APF
Barnett, ---		0.235			
Champlain, ---		0.306			
Cox, ---		0.253			
Davenport, ---		0.281			
Day, ---		0.231			
Dudley, Martin		0.219	M		
East, Carl		0.279			
Klump, ---		0.222			
Murch, Red		0.247			
Roth, V.		0.302			
Telkan, ---		0.327			Brunswick
Wicker, ---		0.264			Cordele
Wilkes, ---		0.226			

Valdosta, Georgia
Manager(s): Joe Herold, Frank Moffett

Valdosta Millionaires Team Roster

NAME	G	BA	POS	GP	APF
Agnew, ---		0.239			Waycross
Anderson, ---		0.139			
Baggens, ---		0.255			Americus
Davis, ---		0.118			Waycross
Dedon, ---		0.191			Brunswick
Herold, Joe		0.252	M		
Hurley, ---		0.315			
Kelley, ---		0.257			
Kipp, ---		0.214			Waycross
Leon, ---		0.212			Brunswick
Lipsey, ---		0.240			
Lowe, ---		0.315			
McMillan, Norm		0.302			
Medlock, ---		0.304			
Moffett, Frank			M		
Morse, Whitey		0.261			Brunswick
O'Brien, ---		0.257			Brunswick
Schwartz, B.		0.243			
Van Landingham, ---		0.256			
Weiler, ---		0.208			Brunswick
Winges, ---		0.227			

Waycross, Georgia
Manager(s): Langdon Clark, Jack Coveney

Waycross Grasshoppers/Moguls Team Roster

NAME	G	BA	POS	GP	APF
Agnew, ---		0.239			Valdosta
Anderson, ---		0.232			
Antley, ---		0.179			
Chapman, ---		0.155			
Clark, Langdon			M		
Coveney, Jack		0.230	M		
Davis, ---		0.118			Valdosta
Doherty, ---		0.172			
Hartner, ---		0.100			
Jones, ---		0.247			
Kipp, ---		0.214			Valdosta
McCoy, ---		0.314			
McFarland, ---		0.200			

Miller, ---	0.158	
Moore, ---	0.344	
Schuman, ---	0.317	Brunswick
Warwick, ---	0.165	
Wasem, ---	0.322	

1914 Georgia State League Records
Batting

Highest Batting Average (minimum 100 at bats)
1. --- Thrasher – Cordele .412
2. Will Bankston – Cordele .359
3. --- Wassem – Waycross .322
4. --- Schuman – Brun/Wayc .317
   --- Ellis – Americus .317

Most Hits
1. Will Bankston – Cordele 144
2. Dave Gaston – Americus 117
3. --- Medlock – Valdosta 116
4. --- Champlain – Thomasville 110
   --- Parker – Brunswick 110
   --- Seigfried – Brunswick 110

Most Runs
1. Walt Brouthers – Cordele 87
2. Will Bankston – Cordele 82
   William Kuhlman – Cordele 82
4. --- Seigfried – Brunswick 76
5. Dave Gaston – Americus 75

Most Total Bases
1. Will Bankston – Cordele 279
2. Dave Gaston – Americus 195
3. --- Ellis – Americus 186
4. --- Medlock – Valdosta 180
5. --- Seigfried – Brunswick 143

Most Doubles
1. --- Medlock – Valdosta 26
2. Dave Gaston – Americus 24
3. --- Ellis – Americus 22
4. --- Champlain – Thomasville 19
5. --- Leonard – Americus 18
   --- O'Brien – Vald/Brun 18
   --- Wicker – Cord/Thom 18

Most Triples
1. Will Bankston – Cordele 14
2. Dave Gaston – Americus 12
3. --- Medlock – Valdosta 10
4. --- Ellis – Americus 8
5. Wade Reynolds – Brunswick 7

Most Home Runs
1. Will Bankston – Cordele 31
2. --- Ellis – Americus 15
3. Bill Pierre – Brun/Amer 11
4. Dave Gaston – Americus 10
5. --- Wicker – Cord/Thom 8

Most Extra Base Hits
1. Will Bankston – Cordele 59
2. Dave Gaston – Americus 46
3. --- Ellis – Americus 45
4. --- Medlock – Valdosta 42
5. --- Wicker – Cord/Thom 32

Most Stolen Bases
1. Walt Brouthers – Cordele   41
2. Dave Gaston – Americus   38
3. --- Seigfried – Brunswick   36
4. --- Anderson – Waycross   24
5. --- Van Landingham – Valdosta   22
   --- Wilkes – Thomasville   22

1915

Florida-Alabama-Georgia "FLAG" League (Georgia State League)

League President: Richard "Dick" Jemison

FLAG League Final Standings

Team	W	L	Pct	GB	Affiliate
Dothan	45	26	.634	----	Unaffiliated
Waycross Moguls	41	30	.577	4.0	Unaffiliated
Valdosta Millionaires	35	33	.515	8.5	Unaffiliated
Brunswick Pilots	36	37	.493	10.0	Unaffiliated
Americus Muckalees/ Gainesville Sharks	29	42	.408	16.0	Unaffiliated
Thomasville Hornets	25	43	.368	18.5	Unaffiliated

1915 FLAG League Map

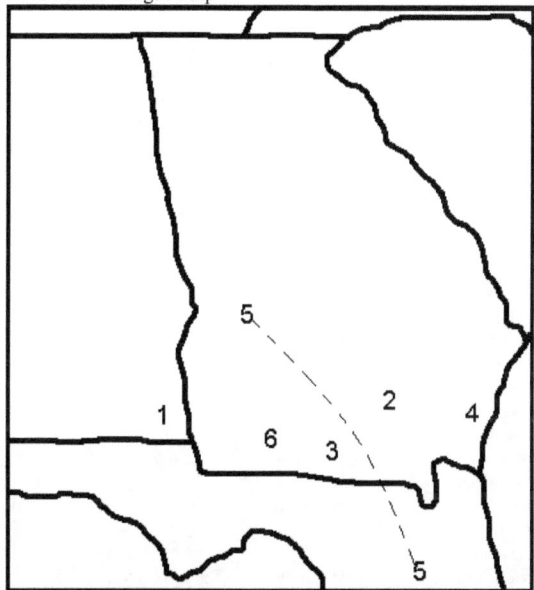

(numbers on map correspond to the place each team finished in regular season play)

In 1915, the class-D Georgia State League returned to the diamond with one modification to its lineup. Cordele had dropped out of the league during the off season, and Dothan, Alabama was picked up to fill the void.

Americus, who had been in the league since the beginning in 1913, as well as with the original Georgia State League in 1906, made some waves when the club surrendered its charter to the league on May 18. This was surprising news especially given the fact that Americus had great success winning the pennant just one season before. On May 31, the club reappeared in Gainesville, Florida expanding the league's geographic coverage to incorporate a third state. It only seemed logical for the Georgia State League to now take a new name since the circuit also covered Alabama and Florida. On June 15, league officials changed the name to the Florida-

15

Georgia Class-D Minor League Baseball Encyclopedia

Alabama-Georgia League. It would commonly go by the acronym "FLAG" League.

On June 1, Waycross pitcher John Cantley pitched a no-hitter against Valdosta but lost the game 0 to 1.

The familiar split schedule was played, and Brunswick won the first half of the season. Valdosta took the second half that was shortened when the league disbanded on July 17. Although the league was now officially defunct, Brunswick and Valdosta squared off for a championship series. Three games into the series, Valdosta was winning two games to one. Brunswick players went on strike refusing to play, and league president Richard Jemison declared Valdosta to be the winner of the series. The club that had the best overall record between the two halves was Dothan who failed to garner the top spot in either half. Dothan had four games on Waycross and eight and a half games on Valdosta in the final combined standings.

Americus, Georgia / Gainesville, Florida
Manager(s): Oscar Baker, John Wagnon

Americus Muckalees / Gainesville Sharks Team Roster

NAME	G	BA	POS	W	L	PCT	APF
Baker, Oscar	28	0.184	M, OF, P	5	3	0.625	Dothan
Bartell, ---	17	0.227					Valdosta
Betts, ---	40	0.224					
Blackwell, ---	39	0.271	2B, OF				Dothan
Blansit, ---	4	0.000	P	2	1	0.667	
Bowden, ---	5		P	2	3	0.400	
Buie, ---	<10						Thomasville
Cabera, ---	<10						
Colcolough, Tom		0.000	P	0		0.000	
Dickerson, ---	18	0.277	P	5	7	0.417	Valdosta
Dozier, ---	<10		P	0		0.000	
Dunning, Guy	74	0.316	OF				
Elrod, ---			P	0		0.000	
Fitzgerald, ---	<10						
Guess, ---	67	0.274	1B				
Hodge, ---	62	0.247	SS				
Manchester, Dick	31	0.278	C				
Middiknight, ---	19	0.254	2B, P	0		0.000	
Mills, ---	<10		P	0		0.000	
Moseley, ---	25	0.211	P	8	7	0.533	Dothan
Moseley, ---	2		P	2	0	1.000	
Peddy, ---	23	0.355	P	5	8	0.385	
Powers, ---	21	0.329	2B				
Pratt, ---	<10						
Selph, ---	71	0.242	3B, SS				
Shuman, ---	60	0.227	OF				
Spaugh, ---	27	0.179	P	5	12	0.294	
Stegal, ---	<10						
Underwood, ---	<10						Brunswick
Wagnon, John	26	0.266	M, OF				
Wilkes, ---	71	0.257	3B, OF, C				

Brunswick, Georgia
Manager(s): Wade Reynolds

Brunswick Pilots Team Roster

NAME	G	BA	POS	W	L	PCT	APF
Ansley, ---	<10						
Bope, George	74	0.279	1B, P	0		0.000	
Cooper, ---	<10		P	0		0.000	
Donaldson, Earl	<10						
Gandy, Bob	74	0.274	2B, OF, P	0		0.000	Waycross
Harvey, ---		0.000					
Hawkins, G.B.	33	0.163	OF, P	8	8	0.500	
Hill, ---		0.000					
Hutchison, ---		0.000					
Jordan, ---	69	0.298	3B, C, P	0		0.000	
Levison, ---		0.000					
L'Hommedieu, F.E.	1		P	1	0	1.000	
Livingston, F.S.	<10		P	0		0.000	
Lowther, ---	<10		P	0		0.000	
Manson, ---		0.000	P	0		0.000	
McFarlin, ---	32	0.165	OF, P	12	5	0.706	
Nance, ---	74	0.267	3B, C, P	0		0.000	
O'Brien, ---		0.000					
Rafferty, ---	70	0.214	OF				
Reilly, ---	60	0.301	2B				
Reynolds, Wade	61	0.303	M, OF, C				
Smith, ---	<10						
Stacey, ---	62	0.202	OF				Waycross
Stewart, ---	28	0.182	P	8	9	0.471	
Underwood, ---	<10						Ame-Gain
Walker, ---			P	0		0.000	
Watkins, Robert	29	0.188	P	7	8	0.467	
Weiler, ---	75	0.269	SS				
Willard, ---	46	0.310	OF				

Dothan, Alabama
Manager(s): Jack Reidy

Dothan Team Roster

NAME	G	BA	POS	W	L	PCT	APF
Alford, ---	12	0.300	C				
Askew, ---	<10						
Attride, ---	27	0.242	C				
Baker, Oscar	28	0.184	OF, P	5	3	0.625	Ame-Gain
Blackwell, ---	39	0.271	2B, OF				Ame-Gain
Burruss, ---	71	0.170	SS				
Chambers, ---	75	0.245	1B				
Hall, G.H.	27	0.267	P	14	5	0.737	
Heck, ---	74	0.250	3B				
Hodge, Shovel	23	0.282	P				
Moseley, ---	25	0.211	P	8	7	0.533	Ame-Gain
Parks, ---	62	0.326	OF				
Paschal, Ben	64	0.290	OF				
Poole, Edward	23	0.215	P	13	7	0.650	
Price, ---	31	0.287	C, P	7	3	0.700	
Reidy, Jack	75	0.279	M, OF				
Rushing, ---	<10						
Spitznagle, ---	70	0.244	2B				
Terry, Bill	<10		P	0		0.000	
Turner, ---	33	0.327	OF, C				Valdosta

Thomasville, Georgia
Manager(s): Red Murch

Thomasville Hornets Team Roster

NAME	G	BA	POS	W	L	PCT	APF
Alexander, ---		0.000					
Anderson, ---	46		SS, OF				
Baker, ---		0.000					
Barnard, ---	<10						
Brazier, ---	40	0.265	OF				
Buie, ---	<10						Ame-Gain
Conley, ---	71	0.218	2B, OF				
Corbett, ---	47	0.197	2B, OF				Valdosta
Dunham, ---		0.000					
Foss, Deeby	12	0.256	SS, P	0		0.000	
Goen, ---	2		P	1	1	0.500	
Holt, ---	2		P	1	0	1.000	
Kalena, ---	<10		P	0		0.000	
Krebs, ---		0.000					
Mays, ---	11	0.147	P	1	4	0.200	
Murch, Red	46	0.227	M, 2B				
Ostendorf, Fred	10	0.167					

Georgia Class-D Minor League Baseball Encyclopedia

Name	G	BA	POS	W	L	PCT	APF
Parker, ---	70	0.221	3B				
Pearson, ---	31	0.155	OF, P	8	11	0.421	
Perry, ---	<10						
Pittman, ---	18	0.224	OF				
Price, ---	<10						
Sells, Albert	3		P	1	1	0.500	
Sheppard, ---	54	0.178	C, P	0		0.000	
Sikes, ---	36	0.217	P	11	9	0.550	
Summerlin, ---	4	0.000	P	1	1	0.500	
Utley, ---	71	0.238	1B				
Wicker, ---	70	0.233	OF				
Winges, ---	9		P	1	6	0.143	Valdosta

Valdosta, Georgia
Manager(s): Dutch Jordan

Valdosta Millionaires Team Roster

NAME	G	BA	POS	W	L	PCT	APF
Baker, ---	9		P	4	3	0.571	
Bales, ---	30	0.237	3B				
Bartell, ---	17	0.227					Ame-Gain
Brakefield, William		0.000	P	0		0.000	
Braze, ---	<10		P	0		0.000	
Brewer, ---	10	0.343	OF				
Burns, ---	<10						
Chatham, Happy	21	0.275	SS				
Coffey, ---	18	0.250	1B				
Corbett, ---	47	0.197	2B, OF				Thomasville
Dickerson, ---	18	0.277	P	5	7	0.417	Ame-Gain
Ery, Ed	51	0.169	OF, P	13	8	0.619	
Jordan, Dutch	60	0.223	M, 1B, 2B				
Maltby, ---	12	0.234	OF				
McMillan, Norm	60	0.301	OF				
Medlock, ---	59	0.313	OF				
Mills, ---	<10		P	0		0.000	
Mulligan, ---	<10						
Parker, ---	<10		P	0		0.000	
Poland, Eugene	<10						
Sample, ---	<10						
Schwartz, B.	30	0.240	1B				
Schwartz, F.	65	0.186	2B, SS				
Skelton, ---		0.000	P	0			
Sloan, ---	29	0.223	P	12	8	0.600	
Stewart, ---	71	0.244	2B, 3B, P	0		0.000	Waycross
Taylor, ---	64	0.101	C				
Turner, ---	33	0.327	OF, C				Dothan
Vaughn, ---	<10		P	2	2	0.500	
Weston, E.H.	1	0.000	P	1	0	1.000	
Winges, ---	9		P	1	6	0.143	Thomasville
Wright, ---	22	0.229	OF				

Waycross, Georgia
Manager(s): Jesse Reynolds

Waycross Grasshoppers/Moguls Team Roster

NAME	G	BA	POS	W	L	PCT	APF
Antley, ---	38	0.190	OF, P	10	9	0.526	
Barber, ---	75	0.201	1B				
Biel, ---	12	0.147	2B				
Bowden, ---	6		P	2	2	0.500	
Burke, ---	75	0.253	OF				
Caldwell, ---	26	0.212	OF				
Chapman, ---	<10						
Clark, ---	75	0.235					
Gandy, Bob	74	0.274	2B, OF, P	0		0.000	Brunswick
Gardner, ---	20		P	12	7	0.632	
Hill, ---		0.000	P	0		0.000	
Kingery, ---	16	0.169	2B				
Reynolds, Jesse	71	0.280	M, C				
Riggins, ---	74	0.224	3B				
Stacey, ---	62	0.202	OF				Brunswick
Stewart, ---	71	0.244	2B, 3B, P	0		0.000	Valdosta
Utter, ---		0.000					
Vaiden, ---	24	0.183	P	10	8	0.556	
Wiggins, ---	30	0.256	P	7	4	0.636	

1915 FLAG League Records
Batting
Highest Batting Average (minimum 100 at bats)
1. --- Turner – Doth/Vald .327
2. --- Parks – Dothan .326
3. Guy Dunning – Amer-Gain .316
4. --- Medlock – Valdosta .313
5. --- Willard – Brunswick .310

Most Hits
1. Guy Dunning – Amer-Gain 100
2. --- Parks – Dothan 88
3. Jack Reidy – Dothan 78
4. Bob Gandy – Waycross 77
   --- Weiler – Brunswick 77

Most Runs
1. Jack Reidy – Dothan 69
2. Guy Dunning – Amer-Gain 58
3. --- Stewart – Vald/Wayc 45
4. --- Chambers – Dothan 44
5. Wade Reynolds – Brunswick 42

Most Total Bases
1. Guy Dunning – Amer-Gain 127
2. Ben Paschal – Dothan 121
3. --- Parks – Dothan 105
4. Jesse Reynolds – Waycross 104
5. Norm McMillan – Valdosta 101

Most Doubles
1. --- Chambers – Dothan 17
2. --- Utley – Thomasville 16
3. --- Guess – Amer-Gain 15
   --- Parks – Dothan 15
   Wade Reynolds – Brunswick 15

Most Triples
1. --- Medlock – Valdosta 7
2. Ben Paschal – Dothan 6
3. Guy Dunning – Amer-Gain 5
4. --- Wilkes – Amer-Gain 4
5. --- Brewer – Valdosta 3
   --- Parker – Thomasville 3

Most Home Runs
1. Ben Paschal – Dothan 7
   Jesse Reynolds – Waycross 7
3. Norm McMillan – Valdosta 5
   --- Rafferty – Brunswick 5
   --- Wilkes – Amer-Gain 5

Most Extra Base Hits
1. Ben Paschal – Dothan 26
2. Norm McMillan – Valdosta 21
   Jesse Reynolds – Waycross 21
4. Guy Dunning – Amer-Gain 20
5. *four players tied with 19

Most Stolen Bases
1. --- Stewart – Vald/Wayc 38
2. Jack Reidy – Dothan 24

	--- Wilkes – Amer-Gain	24
4.	Ben Paschal – Dothan	23
	--- Reilly – Brunswick	23

Fielding

Most Put-Outs
1. --- Barber 1B – Waycross   733
2. --- Chambers 1B – Dothan   696
3. George Bope 1B, P – Brunswick   630
4. --- Guess 1B – Amer-Gain   625
5. --- Utley 1B – Thomasville   603

Most Assists
1. --- Spitznagle 2B – Dothan   197
2. --- Buruss SS – Dothan   184
3. --- Weiler SS – Brunswick   181
4. Dutch Jordan 1B, 2B – Valdosta   139
5. --- Nance 3B, C, P – Brunswick   136

Most Errors
1. --- Weiler SS – Brunswick   40
2. --- Hodge SS – Amer-Gain   39
3. --- Parker 3B – Thomasville   31
   --- Riggins 3B – Waycross   31
5. --- Burruss SS – Dothan   30

Pitching

Most Wins
1. G.H. Hall – Dothan   14
2. Ed Ery – Valdosta   13
   Edward Poole - Dothan   13
4. --- Gardner – Waycross   12
   --- McFarlin – Brunswick   12
   --- Sloan – Valdosta   12

Most Losses
1. --- Spaugh – Amer-Gain   12
2. --- Pearson – Thomasville   11
3. --- Antley – Waycross   9
   --- Sikes – Thomasville   9
   --- Stewart – Brunswick   9

Highest Winning Percentage (10 game minimum)
1. G.H. Hall – Dothan   .737
2. --- McFarlin – Brunswick   .706
3. --- Price – Dothan   .700
4. Edward Poole – Dothan   .650
5. --- Wiggins – Waycross   .636

Most Strikeouts
1. Edward Poole – Dothan   119
2. --- Sikes – Thomasville   105
3. --- Sloan – Valdosta   101
4. --- Antley – Waycross   99
5. --- Pearson – Thomasville   98

Most Bases on Balls
1. Edward Poole – Dothan   71
2. --- Sloan – Valdosta   68
3. --- Antley – Waycross   59
4. G.B. Hawkins – Brunswick   52
5. --- Sikes – Thomasville   48

Most Hits Allowed
1. --- Spaugh – Amer-Gain   205
2. --- Sikes – Thomasville   173
3. --- Gardner – Waycross   162
4. Ed Ery – Valdosta   160
5. G.H. Hall – Dothan   146

Most Innings Pitched
1. Ed Ery – Valdosta   203
2. --- Sloan – Valdosta   190
3. Edward Poole – Dothan   185
4. --- Spaugh – Amer-Gain   179
5. G.H. Hall – Dothan   173

Georgia Class-D Minor League Baseball Encyclopedia

1915

Georgia-Alabama League

League President: C.L. Bruner

Georgia-Alabama League Final Standings

Team	W	L	Pct	GB	Affiliate
Newnan Cowetas	39	20	.661	----	Unaffiliated
Talladega Tigers	39	22	.639	1.0	Unaffiliated
Griffin Lightfoots	32	28	.533	7.5	Unaffiliated
Rome Romans	27	31	.466	11.5	Unaffiliated
Anniston Moulders	22	38	.367	17.5	Unaffiliated
LaGrange Terrapins	18	38	.327	19.5	Unaffiliated

1915 Georgia-Alabama League Map

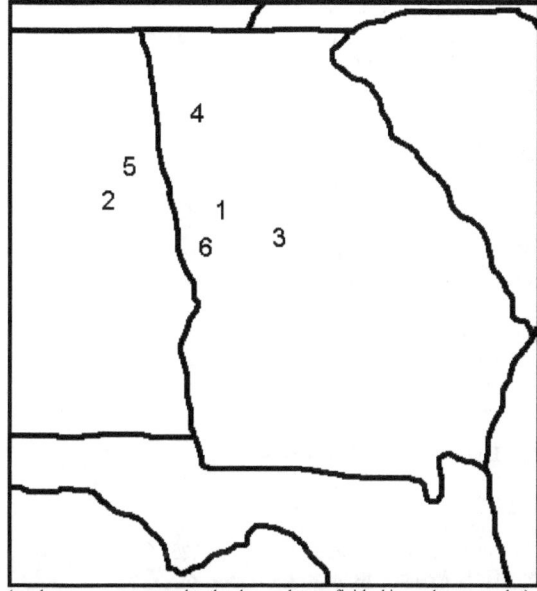

(numbers on map correspond to the place each team finished in regular season play)

As quickly as the Georgia-Alabama League grew from six to eight teams after the 1913 season, it shrunk from eight back to six after 1914. Gadsden, Opelika, and Selma, all Alabama teams, dropped out of the league, and Griffin, Georgia was picked up as a league city.

There was a pair of no-hitters pitched by Georgia-Alabama pitchers, both manning the mound for Newnan. Jack Nabors was the owner of the first one on June 15 defeating Talladega 1 to 0 in thirteen innings. Billy Terry pitched the second one when he no-hit Anniston 2 to 0 on June 30. Nabors also hurled his way to the all time single season league record for highest winning percentage between his time spent with Talladega and Newnan during the season. Winning 12 and losing only one, Nabors' boasted a .923 winning percentage.

With no post-season championship scheduled, the Newnan Cowetas were the pennant winners edging out the Talladega Tigers by one game.

Anniston, Alabama
Manager(s): Jack Steele

Anniston Moulders Team Roster

NAME	G	BA	POS	W	L	PCT	APF
Boykin, Roma	45	0.188	OF				
Brittian, ---	28	0.258	2B				
Brown, ---	22	0.197	OF				LaGrange
Chastant, ---	58	0.240	2B, OF				Newnan
Clapp, Charles	37	0.225	OF				Talladega
Donaldson, Earl	56	0.244	SS				
Ganong, ---	13	0.273					
Glazner, Whitey	25	0.127	P	8	9	0.471	
Holt, ---	40	0.195	3B				
King, ---	18	0.109	P	4	8	0.333	Rome
Leaman, ---	23	0.128	2B				Griffin
Luna, C.W.	35	0.198	C				
McDuffie, ---	10	0.138	P	3	4	0.429	
Morrison, Harry	<6		P				
Morton, ---	17	0.177	OF, P				
Shinault, Ginger	12	0.171	OF				
Sigmon, Jesse	29	0.190	P	7	13	0.350	
Steele, Jack	55	0.247	M, 1B				
Stevenson, ---	27	0.171					
Wilson, ---	13	0.190	2B				
Yon, ---	<6		P				
Young, ---	<6		P				

Griffin, Georgia
Manager(s): W.P. Martin, Kid Reagan

Griffin Lightfoots Team Roster

NAME	G	BA	POS	W	L	PCT	APF
Abercrombie, ---	<6		P				
Anderson, Victor	16	0.068	P	5	4	0.556	
Bostwick, ---	10		P	2	4	0.333	
Bowdoin, Lawrence	44	0.254	3B				
Brazier, ---	26	0.281	OF				
Brooks, R.	14	0.290	P	5	5	0.500	
Combs, ---	<6		P				
Groome, J.L.	41	0.229	3B				LaGrange
Guthrie, ---	14	0.135	P	5	6	0.455	Newnan
Hawkins, G.B.	11	0.286	P				
Hoard, ---	20	0.247	SS				
Howell, Lloyd	25	0.406	OF				
Kirke, M.M.	49	0.272	SS				
Leaman, ---	23	0.128	2B				Anniston
Manchester, Dick	28	0.186	C				
Marion, J.W.	61	0.279	SS				Talladega
Martin, W.P.	18	0.145	M, OF				
Ostendorf, Fred	<6		P				
Panella, ---	7		P	1	3	0.250	
Pope, Ashley	54	0.290	1B				
Reagan, Kid	39	0.217	M, 2B				
Rickard, ---	51	0.254	OF				
Shannon, ---	16	0.196	C				
Walker, ---	58	0.291	OF				Newnan
Watson, Henry	19	0.208	P	7	0	1.000	

LaGrange, Georgia
Manager(s): Ed LaFitte

LaGrange Terrapins Team Roster

NAME	G	BA	POS	W	L	PCT	APF
Allison, E.B.	58	0.190	2B				
Amazon, H.W.	58	0.146	1B				
Brown, ---	22	0.197	OF				Anniston
Craven, Jess	29	0.304	OF				

Georgia Class-D Minor League Baseball Encyclopedia

NAME	G	BA	POS	W	L	PCT	APF
Donaldson, Jack	58	0.250	SS				
Groome, J.L.	41	0.229	3B				Griffin
Head, Ralph	21	0.062	P	6	9	0.400	
Holland, Sid	19	0.219	2B				
LaFitte, Ed	55	0.245	M, C				
Livingston, F.S.	21	0.130	P	5	9	0.357	
Poland, Eugene	58	0.297	OF				
Raburn, Charley	21	0.138	P	2	13	0.133	
Smith, H.T.	50	0.287	3B				
Weston, E.H.	29	0.147	P	5	8	0.385	

Newnan, Georgia
Manager(s): Harry Matthews

Newnan Cowetas Team Roster

NAME	G	BA	POS	W	L	PCT	APF
Boyd, J.S.	60	0.303	OF				
Burgess, ---	27	0.260	3B				
Chastant, ---	58	0.240	2B, OF				Anniston
Donaldson, Jack	33	0.244	OF				
Edmondson, W.C.	25	0.171	3B				
Flynn, Don	58	0.358	OF				
Gentle, ---	10	0.083	P				
Golden, ---	7		P	3	2	0.600	
Griffin, Hal	60	0.206	1B				
Guthrie, ---	14	0.135	P	5	6	0.455	Griffin
Knight, ---	15	0.056	P	6	6	0.500	Rome
Mackie, H.P.	43	0.292	2B				
Matthews, Harry	58	0.266	M, C				
Methvin, ---	<6		P				
Nabors, Jack	15	0.180	P	12	1	0.923	Talladega
Newton, Cash	58	0.243	SS				
Sewell, ---	<6		P				
Terry, Bill	8		P	7	1	0.875	
Walker, ---	58	0.291	OF				Griffin
Whitney, J.F.	25	0.156	P	8	7	0.533	

Rome, Georgia
Manager(s): Art Burleson

Rome Romans Team Roster

NAME	G	BA	POS	W	L	PCT	APF
Aaron, W.M.	20	0.125	P	9	8	0.529	
Burleson, Art	10	0.120	M, P	3	2	0.600	
Cochran, John	60	0.333	OF				
Hutchins, ---	55	0.246	1B				
King, ---	18	0.109	P	4	8	0.333	Anniston
Knight, ---	15	0.056	P	6	6	0.500	Newnan
Leon, ---	47	0.228	3B				
Lowery, D.D.	<10		P				
Middiknight, ---	14	0.104	3B				
Newell, Kirk	13	0.146	3B				
Overton, H.A.	44	0.226	SS				
Richards, J.A.	51	0.244	C				
Riggs, ---	18	0.220	OF				
Smith, ---	41	0.261	OF				
Tolbert, C.	59	0.290	OF				
Werner, G.H.	58	0.332	2B				
Winchell, ---	<10		P				
Zellers, ---	10	0.292	P	3	3	0.500	

Talladega, Alabama
Manager(s): Tige Garrett

Talladega Tigers Team Roster

NAME	G	BA	POS	W	L	PCT	APF
Baker, Howard	61	0.295	C				
Bradley, Eugene	18	0.211	OF				
Camp, Howie	57	0.325	OF				
Clapp, Charles	37	0.225	OF				Anniston
Crow, Lee	61	0.220	3B				
Decatur, Art	22	0.049	P	11	8	0.579	
Garrett, Tige	53	0.259	M, 1B				
Jackson, Charles	50	0.273	OF				
Koenig, Herman	46	0.247	2B				
Marion, J.W.	61	0.279	SS				Griffin
Marshall, ---	<6		P				
Moore, James	51	0.316	OF				
Nabors, Jack	15	0.180	P	12	1	0.923	Newnan
Norman, Jesse	18	0.200	P	10	4	0.714	
Sanford, Allen	26	0.211	P	9	8	0.529	
Slater, ---	10	0.205	2B, OF				
Wiley, Joseph	<10		P	5	2	0.714	

1915 Georgia-Alabama League Records
Batting

Highest Batting Average (minimum 100 at bats)
1. Don Flynn – Newnan .358
2. John Cochran – Rome .333
3. G.H. Werner – Rome .332
4. Howie Camp – Talladega .325
5. James Moore – Talladega .316

Most Hits
1. Don Flynn – Newnan 76
2. G.H. Werner – Rome 74
3. J.S. Boyd – Newnan 72
4. John Cochran – Rome 71
5. Howie Camp – Talladega 68

Most Runs
1. John Cochran – Rome 47
2. Don Flynn – Newnan 43
3. J.S. Boyd – Newnan 40
   Lee Crow – Talladega 40
5. Eugene Poland – LaGrange 39

Most Total Bases
1. Don Flynn – Newnan 139
2. John Cochran – Rome 123
3. G.H. Werner – Rome 98
4. J.S. Boyd – Newnan 93
   Howie Camp – Newnan 93

Most Doubles
1. Ashley Pope – Griffin 20
2. G.H. Werner – Rome 18
3. Don Flynn – Newnan 16
   Charles Jackson – Talladega 16
   C. Tolbert – Rome 16

Most Triples
1. Howie Camp – Talladega 4
2. J.S. Boyd – Newnan 3
   Sid Holland – LaGrange 3
   M.M. Kirke – Griffin 3
5. *eight players tied with 2

Most Home Runs
1. Don Flynn – Newnan 15
2. John Cochran – Rome 11
3. --- Chastant – Anni/Newn 4
   Harry Matthews – Newnan 4

James Moore – Talladega   4

Most Extra Base Hits
1. Don Flynn – Newnan   32
2. John Cochran – Rome   28
3. Ashley Pope – Griffin   24
4. G.H. Werner – Rome   20
5. Howie Camp – Talladega   19
   C. Tolbert – Rome   19

Fielding
Most Put-Outs
1. Hal Griffin 1B – Newnan   663
2. H.W. Amazon 1B – LaGrange   555
3. Jack Steele 1B – Anniston   536
4. Tige Garrett 1B – Talladega   516
5. Ashley Pope 1B – Griffin   510

Most Assists
1. G.H. Werner 2B – Rome   185
2. Cash Newton SS – Newnan   177
3. Jack Donaldson SS – LaGrange   159
4. Earl Donaldson SS – Anniston   154
5. J.W. Marion SS – Grif/Tall   144

Most Errors
1. Jack Donaldson SS – LaGrange   39
2. Earl Donaldson SS – Anniston   27
   M.M. Kirke SS – Griffin   27
4. E.B. Allison 2B – LaGrange   26
   H.A. Overton SS – Rome   26

Pitching
Most Wins
1. Jack Nabors – Tall/Newn   12
2. Art Decatur – Talladega   11
3. Jesse Norman – Talladega   10
4. W.M. Aaron – Rome   9
5. Allen Sanford – Talladega   9

Most Losses
1. Charley Raburn – LaGrange   13
   Jesse Sigmon – Anniston   13
3. Whitey Glazner – Anniston   9
   Ralph Head – LaGrange   9
   F.S. Livingston – LaGrange   9

Highest Winning Percentage (10 game minimum)
1. Jack Nabors – Talladega   .923
2. Jesse Norman – Talladega   .714
3. Art Decatur – Talladega   .579
4. Victor Anderson – Griffin   .556
5. J.F. Whitney – Newnan   .533

1916

Georgia-Alabama League

League President: Richard "Dick" Jemison

Georgia-Alabama League Final Standings

Team	W	L	Pct	GB	Affiliate
Rome Romans	43	22	.662	----	Unaffiliated
Newnan Cowetas	41	26	.612	3.0	Unaffiliated
LaGrange Grangers	39	29	.574	5.5	Unaffiliated
Talladega Tigers	26	38	.406	16.5	Unaffiliated
Anniston Moulders	23	39	.371	18.5	Unaffiliated
Griffin Lightfoots	23	41	.359	19.5	Unaffiliated

1916 Georgia-Alabama League Map

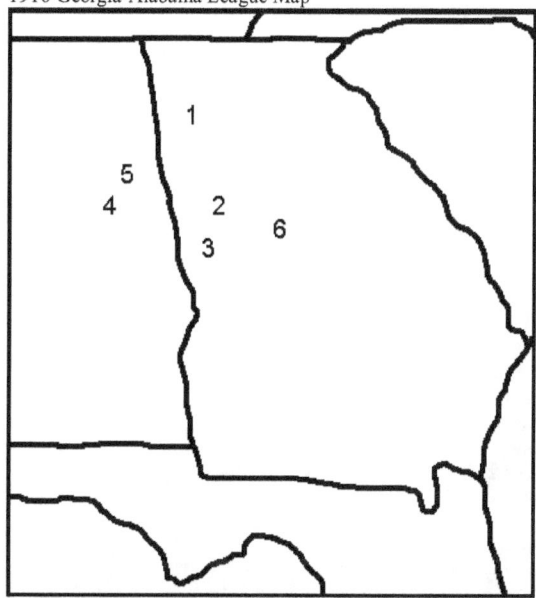

(numbers on map correspond to the place each team finished in regular season play)

The six teams that comprised the Georgia-Alabama loop in 1915 appeared to be a good mix, and all of the clubs returned to the circuit in 1916.

The Rome Romans won the pennant of the league by a three-game margin over the previous year's winner, Newnan. There was not any post-season action on the Georgia-Alabama League diamonds.

Anniston, Alabama
Manager(s): Wade Reynolds

Anniston Moulders Team Roster

NAME	G	BA	POS	APF
Bope, George	42	0.220	1B	
Bowdoin, Lawrence	66	0.160	P, 3B	Grif - New
Christenbury, Low	59	0.295	SS, OF	Newnan
Clark, ---	21	0.351	SS	
Hawkins, G.B.	25	0.141	OF, P	
Johannsen, ---	64	0.196	OF, 2B	
Lacy, Guy	49	0.226	2B	

Georgia Class-D Minor League Baseball Encyclopedia

NAME	G	BA	POS	APF
Love, B.L.	64	0.231	OF	
McDonald, ---	35	0.228	C	
Miles, R.L.	19	0.167	C	
Morrison, Harry	24	0.217	P	
Osteen, W.J.	36	0.169	OF, P	Newnan
Reynolds, Wade	65	0.329	M, OF, 1B	
Russell, ---	16	0.158	P	
Showers, ---	70	0.204	3B	Newnan
Sigmon, Jesse	24	0.164	P	
Troutman, B.K.	22	0.195	OF	Rome

Griffin, Georgia
Manager(s): Kid Reagan, Phil Wells

Griffin Lightfoots Team Roster

NAME	G	BA	POS	APF
Anderson, Victor	19	0.204	P	
Bales, ---	40	0.303	3B	
Bowdoin, Lawrence	66	0.160	P, 3B	Ann - New
Burgess, ---	70	0.261	SS, 3B	
Chalker, A.G.	61	0.190	C	LaGrange
Cheney, ---	35	0.226	P	Talladega
Hanson, Harry	70	0.246	OF, C	
Harbison, Douglas	17	0.138	OF	
Jenkins, Tom	37	0.333	OF	
Kirke, M.M.	62	0.246	OF, SS	
Methvin, ---	4	0.200		
Miller, ---	21	0.337		
Pope, Ashley	70	0.233	1B, OF, P	
Reagan, Kid	70	0.193	M, 2B	
Robertson, ---	31	0.179	P	
Watson, Henry	46	0.220	OF, P	
Wells, Phil	41	0.232	M, C	

LaGrange, Georgia
Manager(s): Grady Bowen, Ed LaFitte

LaGrange Grangers Team Roster

NAME	G	BA	POS	APF
Bowen, Grady	70	0.281	M, 3B	
Chalker, A.G.	61	0.190	C	Griffin
Ginn, Stark	60	0.232	OF	
Jones, R.E.	21	0.209	P	
LaFitte, Ed			M	
Leonard, ---	61	0.215	2B	
Livingston, F.S.	22	0.169	P	Rome
Nolly, Rufus	14	0.178	P	
Poland, Eugene	70	0.273	OF	
Poland, P.	12	0.243	OF	
Smith, H.T.	66	0.241	1B	
Thompson, ---	18	0.235	P	
Waldron, William	70	0.262	SS	
Williams, ---	26	0.169	P	
Wilson, ---	70	0.221	OF	

Newnan, Georgia
Manager(s): Harry Matthews

Newnan Cowetas Team Roster

NAME	G	BA	POS	APF
Bowdoin, Lawrence	66	0.160	P, 3B	Ann - Grif
Boyd, J.S.	70	0.242	OF	
Christenbury, Low	59	0.295	SS, OF	Anniston
Davis, Bud	52	0.301	OF, P	
Flynn, Don	68	0.365	OF	
Gondolfi, Art	70	0.252	SS	
Griffin, Hal	70	0.265	1B	
Guitterez, W.	16	0.258	OF	
Lowery, D.D.	16	0.150	P	
Mackie, H.P.	66	0.305	2B	
Matthews, Harry	67	0.224	M, C	
Osteen, W.J.	36	0.169	OF, P	Anniston
Showers, ---	70	0.204	3B	Anniston
Terry, Bill	33	0.238	P	
Watkins, Robert	27	0.200	P	

Rome, Georgia
Manager(s): Frank Manush

Rome Romans Team Roster

NAME	G	BA	POS	APF
Cates, Eli	25	0.318	P	
Donaldson, Earl	67	0.226	SS	
Hanna, ---	34	0.228	OF	
Livingston, F.S.	22	0.169	P	LaGrange
Manush, Frank	65	0.300	M, 3B	
Pierre, Bill	66	0.258	C	
Pond, ---	68	0.250	1B, OF	
Shaw, H.L.	67	0.337	OF	
Tolbert, C.	67	0.293	OF	
Troutman, B.K.	22	0.195	OF	Anniston
Watson, Jules	33	0.193	2B, P	
Webb, ---	21	0.246	1B	
Werner, G.H.	35	0.208	2B	
Weston, E.H.	27	0.209	P	
Wiley, Joseph	25	0.213	P	

Talladega, Alabama
Manager(s): Tige Garrett

Talladega Tigers Team Roster

NAME	G	BA	POS	APF
Allen, ---	18	0.220	SS	
Camp, Howie	59	0.309	OF	
Cheney, ---	35	0.226	P	Griffin
Clapp, Charles	62	0.315	OF	
Garrett, Tige	69	0.227	M, 1B	
Gooch, Johnny	70	0.177	C	
Hodge, ---	13	0.239	SS	
Knox, ---	14	0.089	OF	
Koenig, Herman	70	0.200	2B	
Krapp, Gene	13	0.324	P	
Newton, Cash	20	0.143	SS	
Raburn, Charley	22	0.180	P	
Sanford, Allen	47	0.172	OF, P	
Selph, ---	23	0.184		
Smith, H.T.	70	0.266	3B, OF	
Verratt, E.A.	24	0.123	OF, P	

1916 Georgia-Alabama League Records
Batting

Highest Batting Average (minimum 100 at bats)
1. Don Flynn – Newnan .365
2. H.L. Shaw – Rome .337
3. Tom Jenkins – Griffin .333
4. Wade Reynolds – Anniston .329
5. Charles Clapp – Talladega .315

Most Hits
1. H.L. Shaw – Rome 89
2. Don Flynn – Newnan 88
3. C. Tolbert – Rome 75
4. Wade Reynolds – Anniston 73
5. Frank Manush – Rome 72

Most Runs
1. Don Flynn – Newnan — 52
2. Frank Manush – Rome — 48
3. H.L. Shaw – Rome — 47
4. William Waldron – LaGrange — 45
   --- Wilson – LaGrange — 45

Most Stolen Bases
1. Frank Manush – Rome — 25
   H.L. Shaw – Rome — 25
3. Art Gondolfi – Newnan — 23
4. --- Wilson – LaGrange — 22
   J.S. Boyd – Newnan — 22

Pitching
Most Wins
1. Robert Watkins – Newnan — 15
   Joseph Wiley – Rome — 15
3. Rufus Nolly – LaGrange — 12

1917

Georgia-Alabama League

League President: Richard "Dick" Jemison

Georgia-Alabama League Final Standings

Team	W	L	Pct	GB	Affiliate
Anniston Moulders	13	5	.722	----	Unaffiliated
Griffin Griffs	10	7	.588	2.5	Unaffiliated
Tri-Cities Triplets	10	8	.556	3.0	Unaffiliated
Rome-Lindale Romans	9	9	.500	4.0	Unaffiliated
Talladega Tigers	6	12	.333	7.0	Unaffiliated
LaGrange Grangers	5	12	.294	7.5	Unaffiliated

1917 Georgia-Alabama League Map

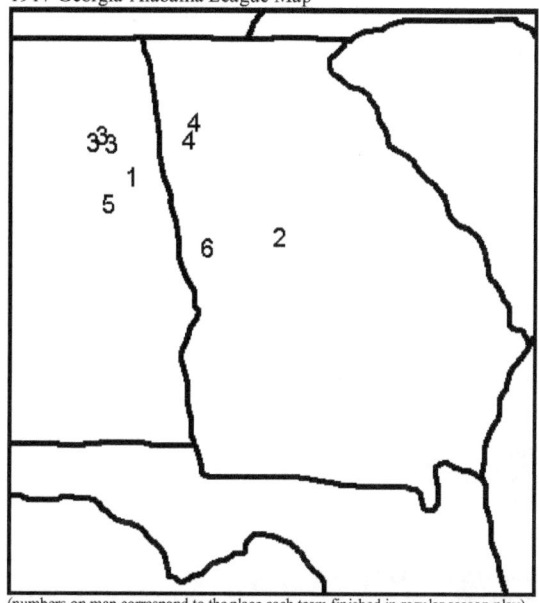

(numbers on map correspond to the place each team finished in regular season play)

Still a six-team circuit, the Georgia-Alabama League saw one change in the lineup between 1916 and 1917. Newnan, Georgia decided not to participate in the league and was replaced by Tri-Cities, Alabama. The three cities of Alabama City, Attalla, and Gadsden, Alabama collectively made up the league's new team.

With the first World War on the horizon, numerous players from every team were leaving the diamond and joining the armed forces to defend their country. With less than twenty games in the books for each club, the league directors met and decided it best to cancel the remainder of the season. The Georgia-Alabama League disbanded on May 23.

The Anniston Moulders were leading the pack with a two and a half game lead over the Griffin Griffs when the season was abruptly halted. The pennant was awarded to Anniston, and no post-season was played.

Georgia Class-D Minor League Baseball Encyclopedia

Anniston, Alabama
Manager(s): Bill Pierre

Anniston Moulders Team Roster

NAME	G	BA	POS	W	L	PCT	APF
Bope, George	5	0.154	1B, 3B				
Cashion, ---	13	0.319	1B, C				
Christenbury, Low	16	0.371	SS				
Costello, Dan	16	0.235	OF				
Holliday, ---	1	0.000	P	0	0		
Kelley, ---	15	0.234	OF				
Lacy, Guy	16	0.338	OF, 3B				
McBride, ---	2	0.167	P	2	0	1.000	
McDuff, ---	5	0.300	3B, C				
Mickle, ---	10	0.292	OF, P	2	2	0.500	
Morrison, Harry	5	0.100	P	1	1	0.500	
Nolly, Rufus	4	0.273	P	1	0	1.000	
Pickett, ---	10	0.275	3B, C				
Pierre, Bill	5	0.375	M, C				
Pratt, Frank	5	0.182	P				
Sanders, ---	3	0.000	P	0	1	0.000	
Smith, ---	7	0.214	C, 1B				
Watson, Jules	15	0.311	2B				

Griffin, Georgia
Manager(s): Matty Matthews

Griffin Griffs Team Roster

NAME	G	BA	POS	W	L	PCT	APF
Burgess, ---	10	0.290	2B, 3B, OF				
Caldwell, ---	5	0.100	P	3	1	0.750	
Flynn, Don	15	0.333	OF, P	2	0	1.000	
Gondolfi, Art	14	0.182	SS				
Griffin, Hal	16	0.230	1B				
Hanson, Harry	15	0.146	OF, C				
Jenkins, Tom	14	0.277	OF, 3B				
Matthews, Matty	16	0.233	M, C				
Miller, ---	16	0.258	OF, 3B				
Parker, ---	1	0.333	P	0	1	0.000	
Peeler, ---	2	0.333	P	0	1	0.000	
Robertson, ---	7	0.200	OF, P	1	4	0.200	
Vines, ---	3	0.143	P	2	0	1.000	
Waldron, William	16	0.381	2B, SS				

LaGrange, Georgia
Manager(s): Isom Jones

LaGrange Grangers Team Roster

NAME	G	BA	POS	W	L	PCT	APF
Banville, ---	15	0.255	OF, 1B				
Beall, ---	3	0.083	2B				
Brock, ---	12	0.302	2B, SS				
Castaing, ---	3	0.000	1B				
Fields, Conrad	8	0.294	P, 2B	2	3	0.400	
Hollingsworth, ---	7	0.118	OF, P	2	3	0.400	
Jones, Isom	3	0.091	M, OF				
Moran, ---	8	0.154	OF, P	2	1	0.667	
Nelson, ---	2	0.333	OF				
Parker, ---	8	0.222	2B				
Peterson, ---	1	0.000	OF				
Phillips, ---	5	0.267	OF				
Poland, Eugene	6	0.273	OF				
Probst, ---	16	0.288	3B				
Roberts, Red	11	0.120	OF, P	0	3	0.000	
Smith, H.T.	16	0.115	2B, SS				
Stapleton, ---	15	0.161	C				
Summerlin, Fritz	10	0.125	OF				
Wares, ---	1	0.000	2B				

Rome-Lindale (Rome & Lindale), Georgia
Manager(s): Dannie Overton

Rome-Lindale Romans Team Roster

NAME	G	BA	POS	W	L	PCT	APF
Alexander, ---	17	0.317	1B				
Benedict, ---	16	0.173	OF, C				
Crouch, ---	16	0.242	3B				
Donaldson, Earl	16	0.175	2B, SS, OF				
Hall, ---	2	0.000	P	0	2	0.000	
Overton, Dannie	9	0.357	M, OF, SS				
Peeples, ---	6	0.063	P	2	2	0.500	
Pond, ---	17	0.310	2B, C				
Ridley, ---	7	0.000	P	3	3	0.500	
Sigmon, Jesse	7	0.222	OF, P	2	2	0.500	
Taylor, ---	9	0.194	C				
Tolbert, C.	17	0.323	OF				
Weston, E.H.	17	0.262	OF, P	0	1	0.000	

Talladega, Alabama
Manager(s): Ed Goosetree

Talladega Tigers Team Roster

NAME	G	BA	POS	W	L	PCT	APF
Bailey, ---	3	0.000	3B				
Beall, ---	8	0.250	1B				
Carter, ---	2	0.200	OF				
Ellis, ---	16	0.306	OF				
Ferguson, ---	6	0.286	OF				
Flowers, ---	17	0.292	OF				
Goosetree, Ed	16	0.234	M, 3B, SS				
Hinges, ---	1	0.200	SS				
Jonnard, Bubber	16	0.231	C				
Jonnard, Claude	3	0.000	P	2	0	1.000	
Kennedy, ---	1	0.000	P				
McClellan, Harvey	16	0.323	3B				
O'Neal, ---	10	0.195	3B, SS, OF				
Raburn, Charley	6	0.231	OF, P	0	4	0.000	
Rodgers, ---	1	0.333	OF				
Stimson, Carl	5	0.182	P, 3B	0	3	0.000	
Thompson, ---	4	0.200	P	3	0	1.000	
Verratt, E.A.	9	0.250	P	3	1	0.750	
Wingfield, ---	16	0.288	1B, 3B, SS				

Tri-Cities (Alabama City, Attalla, & Gadsden), Alabama
Manager(s): Martin Dudley

Tri-Cities Triplets Team Roster

NAME	G	BA	POS	W	L	PCT	APF
Anderson, ---	16	0.266	1B				
Bennett, ---	4	0.200	P	2	1	0.667	
Bowdoin, Lawrence	16	0.242	3B				
Chastant, ---	15	0.222	OF				
Dowdy, ---	16	0.298	SS				
Dudley, Martin	15	0.212	M, C				
Gibson, ---	1	0.000	P	0	0		
Gilliland, ---	2	0.429	OF				
Livingston, F.S.	6	0.273	P	2	2	0.500	
Long, H.L.	7	0.200	P	3	2	0.600	
Matthews, Harry	11	0.211	OF				
McGlade, ---	16	0.281	2B				
Patterson, ---	16	0.125	OF				
Russell, ---	3	0.000	P	1	2	0.333	
Smith, ---	2	0.125	OF				
South, ---	2	0.000	P	0	1	0.000	

1917 Georgia-Alabama League Records

Batting

Highest Batting Average (minimum 50 at bats)
1. William Waldron – Griffin .381
2. Low Christenbury – Anniston .371
3. Guy Lacy – Anniston .338
4. Don Flynn – Griffin .333
5. Harvey McClellan – Talladega .323

Most Hits
1. William Waldron – Griffin 24
2. Low Christenbury – Anniston 23
3. Guy Lacy – Anniston 22
4. Harvey McClellan – Talladega 21
   C. Tolbert – Rome-Lindale 21

Most Runs
1. William Waldron – Griffin 19
2. Guy Lacy – Anniston 17
   C. Tolbert – Rome-Lindale 17
4. Low Christenbury – Anniston 16
5. --- Alexander – Rome-Lindale 14

Most Total Bases
1. William Waldron – Griffin 37
2. Low Christenbury – Anniston 33
   --- Flowers – Talladega 33
4. Don Flynn – Griffin 32
5. Guy Lacy – Anniston 31
   --- Ellis – Talladega 31

Most Doubles
1. William Waldron – Griffin 11
2. Don Flynn – Griffin 6
   Tom Jenkins – Griffin 6
4. *five players tied with 5

Most Triples
1. --- Flowers – Talladega 4
2. Low Christenbury – Anniston 3
3. *eight players tied with 2

Most Home Runs
1. --- McGlade – Tri-Cities 2
   --- Ellis – Talladega 2
   Don Flynn – Griffin 2
4. *five players tied with 1

Most Extra Base Hits
1. William Waldron – Griffin 12
2. Don Flynn – Griffin 8
   --- Flowers – Talladega 8
4. --- McGlade – Tri-Cities 7
   --- Ellis – Talladega 7
   Low Christenbury – Anniston 7
   Guy Lacy – Anniston 7

Most Stolen Bases
1. William Waldron – Griffin 12
2. Dan Costello – Anniston 10
3. Guy Lacy – Anniston 9
4. --- Miller – Griffin 8
5. --- Wingfield – Talladega 7

Fielding

Most Put-Outs
1. --- Alexander 1B – Rome-Lindale 189
2. Hal Griffin 1B – Griffin 158
3. --- Anderson 1B – Tri-Cities 156
4. --- Cashion 1B, C – Anniston 122
5. --- Stapleton C – LaGrange 109

Most Assists
1. William Waldron 2B, SS – Griffin 56
2. Low Christenbury SS – Anniston 55
3. Harvey McClellan 3B – Talladega 52
4. Earl Donaldson 2B, SS, OF – Rome-Lindale 51
5. Jules Watson 2B – Anniston 44
   --- Dowdy SS – Tri-Cities 44

Most Errors
1. --- Dowdy SS – Tri-Cities 11
   --- Pond 2B, C – Rome-Lindale 11
   Ed Goosetree 3B, SS – Talladega 11
   --- O'Neal 3B, SS – Talladega 11
5. Jules Watson 2B – Anniston 10
   --- McGlade 2B – Tri-Cities 10

Pitching

Most Wins
1. H.L. Long – Tri-Cities 3
   --- Ridley – Rome-Lindale 3
   E.A. Verratt – Talladega 3
   --- Caldwell – Griffin 3
   --- Thompson – Talladega 3

Most Losses
1. --- Robertson – Griffin 4
   Charley Raburn – Talladega 4
3. --- Ridley – Rome-Lindale 3
   Conrad Fields – LaGrange 3
   --- Hollingsworth – LaGrange 3
   Carl Stimson – Talladega 3
   Red Roberts – LaGrange 3

Highest Winning Percentage (4 game minimum)
1. --- Thompson – Talladega 1.000
   Don Flynn – Griffin 1.000
   Rufus Nolly – Anniston 1.000
4. E.A. Verratt – Talladega .750
   --- Caldwell – Griffin .750

Most Strikeouts
1. Conrad Fields – LaGrange 47
2. Don Flynn – Griffin 30
3. H.L. Long – Tri-Cities 27
   --- Hollingsworth – LaGrange 27
5. --- Ridley – Rome-Lindale 26

Most Bases on Balls
1. H.L. Long – Tri-Cities 15
   --- Ridley – Rome-Lindale 15
   --- Russell – Tri-Cities 15
4. --- Hollingsworth – LaGrange 14
   --- Bennett – Tri-Cities 14

Most Hits Allowed
1. --- Robertson – Griffin 43
2. H.L. Long – Tri-Cities 38
3. --- Ridley – Rome-Lindale 36
4. --- Hollingsworth – LaGrange 34
   Jesse Sigmon – Rome-Lindale 34
   --- Peeples – Rome-Lindale 34
   F.S. Livingston – Tri-Cities 34

Most Innings Pitched
1. Conrad Fields – LaGrange 52
2. --- Ridley – Rome-Lindale 51

3. H.L. Long – Tri-Cities   48
4. --- Peeples – Rome-Lindale   44
5. --- Robertson – Griffin   42
   E.A. Verratt – Talladega   42

1920

Georgia State League

Georgia State League President: J.P. Nichols, Jr.

Georgia State League Final Standings

Team	W	L	Pct	GB	Affiliate
Carrollton	53	39	.276	----	Unaffiliated
Rome	50	40	.555	2.0	Unaffiliated
Lindale Pepperels	47	43	.522	5.0	Unaffiliated
Cedartown Cedars	44	48	.478	9.0	Unaffiliated
Griffin	42	52	.447	12.0	Unaffiliated
LaGrange	39	53	.424	14.0	Unaffiliated

1920 Georgia State League Map

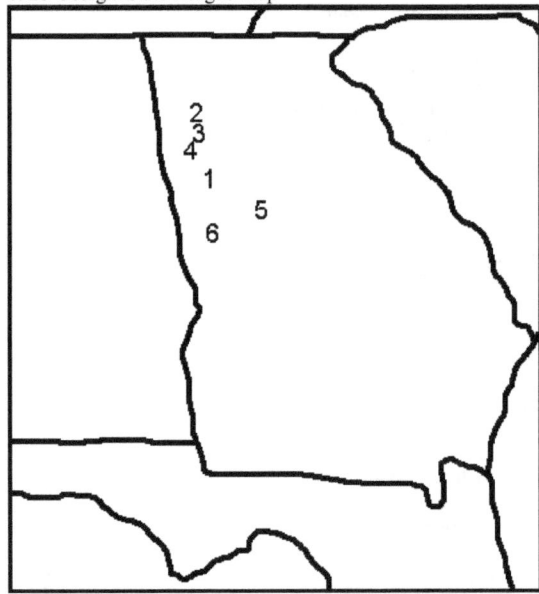

(numbers on map correspond to the place each team finished in regular season play)

A new league appeared in 1920 under the familiar name of Georgia State League. The locale of the circuit went from south Georgia to northwest Georgia with six new teams. These six clubs were Griffin, LaGrange, Lindale, and Rome, all of whom had previously played in the Georgia-Alabama League, and Carrollton and Cedartown, both of whom were making their organized baseball debuts.

Carrollton had the best record overall at the end of the season and was declared league champions. No post-season games were played.

Carrollton, Georgia
Team Operated by Carroll County Baseball Association
Team Owner: Mann Long
Team President: Jess Travis
Manager(s): Charlie Bell
Games played at South Street Baseball Field

Georgia Class-D Minor League Baseball Encyclopedia

Carrollton Team Roster

NAME	AB	BA	POS	APF
Allen, Harry	93	0.108	P, OF	
Ardis, ---	0			
Bales, ---	60	0.267		
Beck, ---	43	0.116	P, OF	
Bell, Charlie	343	0.318	M, SS, 2B, 3B, P	
Bonifay, Albert	71	0.211	P	
Brandon, Goat	284	0.306	OF	
Brinson, ---			SS	
Carter, Russ			OF	
Chaplin, Ed	281	0.310	OF, C	
Chatham, Happy	109	0.257	3B, SS, 2B	
Craven, Jess	325	0.268	OF, 1B	
Craven, Tommy	9	0.333		
Dugan, ---			P	
Fuller, Bertram	45	0.200	SS	
Henderson, Hap	40	0.200	P, OF	
Holtz, Red	13	0.308	1B	
Ingram, Jimmy	7	0.143	P	
Lassetter, Roy	8	0.250		
Long, H.L.	29	0.000	P	
McKinnon, Bill	25	0.280	P	
Pratt, Frank	205	0.293	P, OF, SS	
Pressley, Omer	112	0.313	UT	
Pulliam, J.C.	33	0.121	SS	
Reese, Red	144	0.222	C, 2B	
Register, ---	85	0.365	1B, OF, P	
Robertson, ---			P, OF	
Shaw, Pop	111	0.270	OF	
Summerlin, Fritz			OF	
Sutton, Lefty	7	0.286	P	
Swann, Ducky	26	0.000	P	
Watson, Jules	224	0.277	2B, OF	
Williams, Luke	42	0.167	SS	
Wilson, Jack	85	0.212	OF, 2B, 3B, SS	

Cedartown, Georgia
Manager(s): D. Jones

Cedartown Cedars Team Roster

NAME	AB	BA	POS	APF
Boone, Ike	274	0.412		
Carter, Russ			OF	
Craddock, ---			SS	
Durham, J.C.				
Hughes, ---			P	
Hunter, H.C.			3B	
Johnson, Earl			P	
Jones, D.	63	0.302	M, C	
Kelton, Wiley	291	0.302	1B	
Parks, James	58	0.431		
Schroeder, A.L.			P	
Sells, Albert				
Skinner, Camp	298	0.342	OF	
Suggs, Eugene			2B	
Tattler, Henry			C, OF	
Tolbert, C.	170	0.300	OF	
Vardeman, F.C.			P	

Griffin, Georgia
Manager(s): Tige Garrett

Griffin Team Roster

NAME	AB	BA	POS	APF
Bowdoin, Lawrence			2B	
Burgess, ---			2B	
Dillon, J.T.R.				
Ellington, ---			P	
Garrett, Tige			M, 1B	
Gilbert, Lewis			OF	
Hawkins, G.B.			P	
Johannsen, ---			3B	
Johnson, ---			P	
Livingston, ---			C	
Manush, Frank	166	0.301	2B	
McLaughlin, Edward			SS	
Moore, Clem			OF	
Osborne, Tiny			P, OF	
Proctor, ---			P	
Roberts, Red			OF	
Stanley, Bill			SS, 3B	
Watters, Lark				
Wheat, B.C.			C	
Wheat, Lafe			P	

LaGrange, Georgia
Manager(s): J.E. Culpepper, Red Smith

LaGrange Team Roster

NAME	AB	BA	POS	APF
Bedingfield, J.R.			P	
Bonifay, Albert			P	
Chipman, A.B.			C	
Culpepper, J.E.	41	0.341	M, P	
Foster, R.A.			P	
Gould, ---			P	
Konneman, W.H.			P	
Marbet, Otto			1B	
Martin, S.R.				
Miller, Dan			2B	
Milner, Holt	236	0.301	SS	
Moon, Eulas				
Nitram, ---			SS	
Sikes, Don			OF	
Smith, Red			M, P, OF	
Thrasher, George	258	0.302	OF, 2B	
Thrasher, Ike			3B, OF	
Williams, ---				

Lindale, Georgia
Manager(s): Hardin Herndon

Lindale Pepperells Team Roster

NAME	AB	BA	POS	APF
Brenner, Herbert			1B	
Cornelius, Rusty			P	
Donaldson, Earl			SS	
Driscoll, ---			OF	
Ennis, ---			2B	
Flohr, ---			3B	
Herndon, Hardin	171	0.304	M, OF	
Lassetter, Roy	49	0.347		
Mittewede, Walter	272	0.301	3B	
Nunn, ---			C	
Parilla, ---	39	0.308		
Rich, ---	64	0.328	OF	
Summit, ---	158	0.304		

Rome, Georgia
Manager(s): Tim Bowden

Rome Team Roster

NAME	AB	BA	POS	APF
Bachelor, Harry	46	0.152	OF	
Bowden, Tim	291	0.364	M, OF	
Gross, ---	268	0.235	OF	
Hall, ---	33	0.242		
Hawkins, Cy	248	0.302	C	
Jesmer, W.H.	267	0.228	1B	
Kane, ---	262	0.309	3B	
Lowery, D.D.	109	0.174	P, OF	
Lucus, ---	41	0.171	P	
Overton, H.A.	244	0.258	2B	
Palmantier, A.B.	296	0.304	OF	
Prince, ---			SS	
Schmidt, ---	304	0.322		
Walker, Flem	32	0.031		

1920 Georgia State League Records

Batting

Highest Batting Average (minimum 100 at bats)
1. Ike Boone – Cedartown   .412
2. Tim Bowden – Rome   .364
3. Camp Skinner – Cedartown .342
4. --- Schmidt – Rome   .322
5. Charlie Bell – Carrollton .318

Most Hits
1. Ike Boone – Cedartown   113
2. Charlie Bell – Carrollton 109
3. Tim Bowden – Rome   106
4. Camp Skinner – Cedartown 102
5. --- Schmidt – Rome   98

Most Runs
1. Ed Chaplin – Carrollton   73
2. Charlie Bell – Carrollton 68
3. Ike Boone – Cedartown   62
4. H.A. Overton – Rome   57
5. Goat Brandon – Carrollton 52
   Jess Craven – Carrollton   52

1921

Georgia State League

League President: H.P. Meikleham
League Secretary: William O. Wells

Georgia State League Final Standings

Team	W	L	Pct	GB	Affiliate
Lindale Pepperells	69	29	.704	----	Unaffiliated
Griffin	53	48	.525	17.5	Unaffiliated
LaGrange	52	49	.515	18.5	Unaffiliated
Cedartown Cedars	52	49	.525	18.5	Unaffiliated
Rome	50	49	.505	19.5	Unaffiliated
Carrollton	24	76	.240	46.0	Unaffiliated

1921 Georgia State League Map

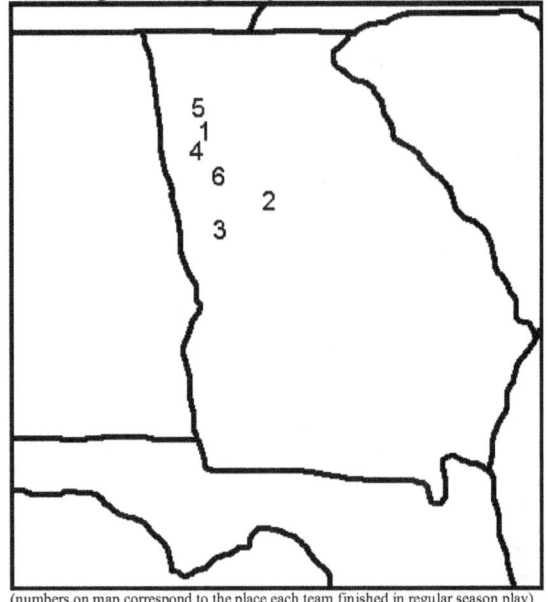

(numbers on map correspond to the place each team finished in regular season play)

The six clubs from 1920 all returned to the diamond for the 1921 season in the Georgia State League.

On June 20, LaGrange pitcher Al Williamson pitched a no-hitter against Cedartown defeating the Cedars 5 to 0. During the season, Cedartown's Ollie Tucker batted .438 setting the all-time league single season record for the highest batting average.

At the end of the first half of the split season, Lindale had the best record assuring themselves a spot in the post-season league championship series. LaGrange topped the standings in the second stanza and faced Lindale in the championship. LaGrange proved to be too much for Lindale in the scheduled seven game series winning the flag four games to one.

Financial difficulties claimed another baseball league known as the Georgia State League at the close of the season. The league would not appear again until 1948 when it popped up in the south-central part of the state.

Georgia Class-D Minor League Baseball Encyclopedia

Carrollton, Georgia
Team Operated by Carroll County Baseball Association
Team President: Jess Travis
Manager(s): Cy Hawkins, Jules Watson
Games played at South Street Baseball Field

Carrollton Team Roster

NAME	AB	BA	POS	APF
Allen, Harry	28	0.036	P	
Barber, ---	319	0.339	OF	
Barnes, ---			P	
Bruner, Bruce	104	0.135	SS	
Cannon, Shorty	195	0.303	OF, SS	
Carmichael, ---	14	0.571		
Coombs, ---			P	
Cornelius, Rusty			P	
Davenport, ---	103	0.233	2B	
Gallagher, ---			OF	
Garvey, ---			P	
Hasty, Bob			P	
Hathaway, R.H.	110	0.164	P	
Hawkins, Cy	108	0.213	M, OF	
Hicks, R.E.	56	0.250	1B, P	
Jesmer, W.H.	142	0.282	1B	
Kitts, Claude	56	0.161	P	
Lehman, Otto	20	0.100	P	
Little, ---			SS	
Long, H.L.	6	0.167	P	
Martin, S.R.	101	0.248		
Moore, Clem	95	0.400	OF	
Powers, ---			SS	
Reis, ---	52	0.173	P	
Richards, Babe	166	0.361	OF, P	
Schulte, J.	108	0.222	OF	
Sessions, Pete			3B	
Smith, J.	174	0.207	C	
Suratt, Clyde			P	
Taylor, Bill	285	0.270	3B	
Walton, Battleaxe	139	0.281	C, OF, 1B	
Watson, Jules	199	0.196	M, 2B	

Cedartown, Georgia
Manager(s): Bill Schwartz

Cedartown Cedars Team Roster

NAME	AB	BA	POS	APF
Bradley, Eugene	279	0.337	OF	
Carter, ---			C	
Chambers, ---			P	
Cook, ---			OF, P	
Culp, ---			P	
DeBosky, Edward				
Dumas, ---			SS	
Ellis, ---			2B	
Hawkins, E.J.			P	
Kelton, Wiley	285	0.302	OF, 1B	
Lehman, Otto			P	
McAuliffe, ---			2B	
Munford, ---			SS	
Sargent, ---			2B	
Schwartz, Bill			M, 1B	
Sells, Albert			P	
Shaw, Pop	127	0.323	OF	
Simon, Dewey	258	0.337	3B	
Tattler, Henry	43	0.302	C, OF	
Tucker, Ollie	246	0.439	OF	
Vardeman, F.C.			P	
Whitfield, ---			OF	
Yost, ---			SS	

Griffin, Georgia
Manager(s): Harry Matthews

Griffin Team Roster

NAME	AB	BA	POS	APF
Bates, ---			P	
Brewer, Henry				
Carlyle, Roy	48	0.458		
Davenport, ---			2B	
Dillon, J.T.R.				
Duval, ---			OF	
Fish, Hamilton	182	0.308	1B	
Gaines, R.H.			1B	
Gibson, ---			OF	
Hawkins, Cy			OF, C	
Hicks, R.E.			1B	
Hunter, Bob				
Marion, J.W.			2B	
Matthews, Harry	16	0.313	M	
McLaughlin, Edward			SS	
Mosley, C.S.			SS	
Osborne, Tiny	47	0.362	P	
Parks, James	181	0.376	OF	
Pounds, J.P.	61	0.377	OF	
Purcell, E.E.				
Sessions, Pete	9	0.333		
Stanley, Bill	285	0.302	3B	
Thrasher, Loren	253	0.368	OF	
Townsend, Arnold	144	0.347	C	
Vandergriff, H.L.	50	0.320	C	
Wheat, Lafe			P	
Wheeler, Buck				

LaGrange, Georgia
Manager(s): Fred Hager

LaGrange Team Roster

NAME	AB	BA	POS	APF
Barnhart, ---			C	
Chancey, C.M.	39	0.333		
Chestnut, H.C.			C	
Fortner, ---			SS	
Green, ---	170	0.312	SS, 2B	
Hager, Fred	166	0.313	M, C	
Konneman, W.H.			P, OF	
Krankie, ---				
McAuliffe, ---			SS, 2B	
Milner, Holt	57	0.351	3B	
Register, ---			OF	
Ricks, Lloyd	99	0.303	1B	
Sargent, ---			2B	
Schroeder, A.L.			P	
Schwartz, ---			P	
Sells, Albert			P	
Sikes, Don	66	0.348	OF	
Swann, Ducky			OF, P	
Thrasher, George	262	0.385	OF	
Williamson, Al			P	
Workman, Hoge			P	

Lindale, Georgia
Manager(s): Hardin Herndon

Lindale Pepperells Team Roster

NAME	AB	BA	POS	APF
Black, ---			P	
Bolt, ---			P	
Brenner, Herbert	166	0.319	1B	

NAME	AB	BA	POS
Cornelius, Rusty			P
Donaldson, Earl			SS
Driscoll, ---			OF
Earp, Whitfield			C
Herndon, Hardin	144	0.333	M, 1B, OF
Humphries, ---			P
Lassetter, Roy			
Mittewede, Walter	219	0.320	3B
Overton, H.A.	172	0.308	2B
Powell, ---			C
Rich, ---	116	0.371	OF
Smith, J.	250	0.376	OF
Suggs, Eugene	23	0.435	
Veazie, ---	57	0.368	OF

Rome, Georgia
Manager(s): Jim Fox

Rome Team Roster

NAME	AB	BA	POS	APF
Fortner, ---			2B	
Fox, Jim	78	0.308	M, 1B	
Gross, J.F.			P	
Hanson, C.W.	70	0.314		
Hodgin, W.H.	284	0.313	OF	
Hunter, Bob			2B	
James, R.E.			OF, P	
Kane, ---	288	0.347	3B	
Lowery, D.D.			P	
McAuliffe, ---			2B	
Morrow, ---	274	0.350	C	
Nunnally, ---			OF	
Parnell, M.R.				
Ramsey, ---			OF	
Schmidt, ---	60	0.317	SS	
Veazie, ---			OF	
Weaver, C.B.				

1921 Georgia State League Records
Batting
Highest Batting Average (minimum 100 at bats)
1. Ollie Tucker – Cedartown .438
2. George Thrasher – LaGrange .385
3. J. Smith – Lindale .376
   James Parks – Griffin .376
5. --- Rich – Lindale .371

Most Hits
1. Ollie Tucker – Cedartown 146
2. --- Barber – Carrollton 108
3. George Thrasher – LaGrange 101
4. --- Kane – Rome 100
5. --- Morrow – Rome 96

Most Runs
1. Ollie Tucker – Cedartown 76
2. --- Barber – Carrollton 62
3. Eugene Bradley – Cedartown 59
4. Dewey Simon – Cedartown 57
5. --- Kane – Rome 56

Most Home Runs
1. Ollie Tucker – Cedartown 22

1928

Georgia-Alabama League

League President: C.I. Scarborough
League Secretary: Walter M. Booz

Georgia-Alabama League Final Standings

Team	W	L	Pct	GB	Affiliate
Cedartown Sea Cows	55	34	.618	----	Unaffiliated
Carrollton Frogs	54	34	.614	0.5	Unaffiliated
Anniston Nobles	47	42	.528	8.0	Unaffiliated
Talladega Indians	45	43	.511	9.5	Unaffiliated
Gadsden Eagles	37	49	.430	16.5	Unaffiliated
Lindale Dragons	26	62	.295	28.5	Unaffiliated

1928 Georgia-Alabama League Map

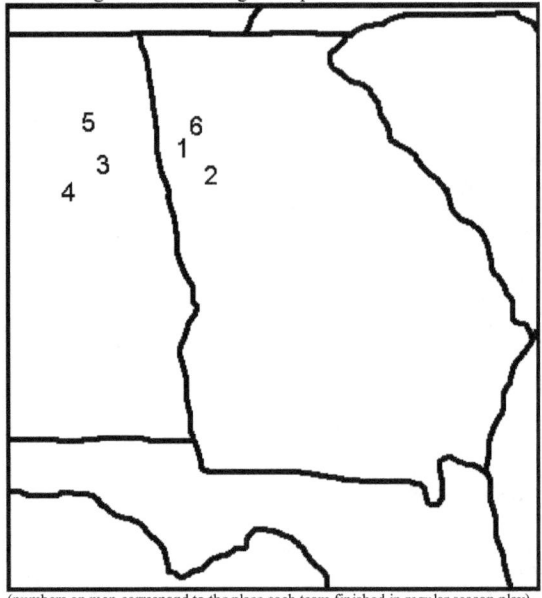

(numbers on map correspond to the place each team finished in regular season play)

After the instantaneous disbanishment of the Georgia-Alabama League in 1917, the league was revived in 1928 under the direction of league president C.I. Scarborough. Returning teams from the eleven years prior were only Anniston and Talladega. Rounding out the six-team loop were Carrollton, Cedartown, and Lindale, Georgia and Gadsden, Alabama.

On August 31, Talladega pitcher Lefty Lane pitched a no-hitter against Cedartown winning 4 to 0. Paul Fittery of Carrollton won 21 games and lost only two boasting a 1.60 earned run average. Fittery's earned run average was good enough to become the all time Georgia-Alabama League record for the lowest in a single season.

A split season was played by the circuit with the Carrollton Frogs winning the first half and the Indians of Talladega taking the second. Talladega and Anniston were tied at the end of the second half, but Talladega nobly squeezed by the Nobles in a two-game playoff to take the second half title. Carrollton then defeated Talladega four games to two in the championship series to win the league title. Although Cedartown finished second and third respectively in the first and second halves, the

Georgia Class-D Minor League Baseball Encyclopedia

Sea Cows had the best cumulative record for both halves edging Carrollton out by a half game.

Anniston, Alabama
Manager(s): Bud Ammons

Anniston Nobles Team Roster

NAME	G	BA	POS	W	L	ERA	APF
Ammons, Bud	83	0.373	M, 1B				
Atchley, Loy	61	0.319	OF, P	3	6	3.52	Car - Ced
Bailey, ---	5		P	0	0	12.00	Carrollton
Camp, Howie	91	0.303	OF				
Case, S.E.	86	0.297	C				
Craft, Molly	14	0.420	1B				Lindale
Floyd, Buck	21	0.167	P	5	9	4.90	Gadsden
Fuqua, Roger	61	0.282	SS				
Gray, ---	58	0.240	OF, P	8	2	4.86	Lindale
Hamner, R.L.	62	0.286	OF				
Harris, Joe	13	0.208	P	3	4	4.04	
Laminack, ---	77	0.251	3B				Talladega
Oldfield, Pat	21	0.240	3B				
Parks, ---	20	0.136	P	10	6	4.54	Cedartown
Sanders, ---	92	0.291	2B				
Sharpe, ---	32	0.207	P	18	6	2.56	
Stroecker, ---	21	0.247	OF				
Thompson, R.L.	68	0.319	OF				
Walker, Tom	21	0.261	P	3	4	4.50	
Washington, ---	7		P	4	3	4.76	
Williams, ---	22	0.179	P	8	8	4.15	Lindale
Wilson, ---	25	0.207	OF				

Carrollton, Georgia
Team Operated by the Carrollton Baseball Club
Team President: A.W. "Andy" Ford
Manager(s): Paul Fittery
Games played at City Athletic Field

Carrollton Frogs Team Roster

NAME	G	BA	POS	W	L	ERA	APF
Atchley, Loy	61	0.319	OF, P	3	6	3.52	Ann - Ced
Avery, ---		0.190					
Bailey, ---	5		P	0	0	12.00	Anniston
Boswell, Brant	88	0.272	2B				
Butts, ---		0.467	1B				
Carter, Homer	28	0.254	P, OF	9	8	4.00	Gadsden
Cosby, ---	15	0.293	SS				Lindale
Dumas, Otto	20	0.298	OF				
Fittery, Paul	66	0.243	M, OF, P	21	2	1.60	
Frakes, Ben	20	0.082	P	5	9	1.85	Gadsden
Garrett, Tige	30	0.194	3B				
Goggans, Cheese	87	0.309	C				
Grimes, ---	10	0.381	SS				Lindale
Howell, Red	95	0.372	OF				
Huggins, Miller	79	0.250	3B				Gadsden
James, Fob	73	0.292	1B				
Lacey, ---	6	0.133	P	4	2	3.68	
Laird, Red	32	0.238	OF, P	9	4	4.80	
Mathewson, ---		0.250					
McKinney, ---	41	0.284	C				Lindale
Moore, J.	8		P	1	2	5.85	
Rowe, Bob	68	0.316	OF				Gadsden
Taliaferro, Dick	70	0.392	SS				
White, Abe	29	0.171	P	13	10	3.36	
White, Jo-Jo	96	0.330	OF				
Wicker, K.C.		0.286	P				

Cedartown, Georgia
Manager(s): Wiley Kelton, Sherry Smith

Cedartown Sea Cows Team Roster

NAME	G	BA	POS	W	L	ERA	APF
Atchley, Loy	61	0.319	OF, P	3	6	3.52	Ann - Car
Baines, Alfred	77	0.238	SS				
Beck, ---	23	0.287	1B, OF				Talladega
Clark, R.H.	89	0.368	2B, OF, C				
Davis, W.C.	42	0.280	1B, P	11	3	2.65	
DeArman, H.P.	88	0.289	1B, P	1	1	5.25	
Glass, ---	31	0.221	P	11	9	4.73	
Hydringer, ---	21	0.149	P	7	8	4.03	
Kelton, Wiley	58	0.324	M, OF				
Knowles, Charles	86	0.332	OF, C				
Marks, Max	45	0.230	3B, P	5	8	3.51	Talladega
Mason, S.	66	0.278	OF				
Parks, ---	20	0.136	P	10	6	4.54	Anniston
Rainwater, Dewey	5		P	3	2	3.35	
Selley, ---	18	0.178	P	4	4	4.33	
Shipley, Jack	59	0.335	2B				
Smith, Sherry	17	0.353	M, P	4	1	1.57	
Thompson, William	69	0.301	2B, OF				
Treadway, Ray	90	0.362	3B, SS				

Gadsden, Alabama
Manager(s): Doc Newton, Joe Schepner

Gadsden Eagles Team Roster

NAME	G	BA	POS	W	L	ERA	APF
Abell, ---	39	0.264	1B				Lindale
Allen, Frank	38	0.259	OF, P	12	6	2.46	
Almon, ---	11	0.273	OF				
Carter, Homer	28	0.254	P, OF	9	8	4.00	Carrollton
Donahue, Matt	38	0.252	OF				
Floyd, Buck	21	0.167	P	5	9	4.90	Anniston
Frakes, Ben	20	0.082	P	5	9	1.85	Carrollton
Garner, ---	67	0.251	OF, C				
Gentry, Ed	75	0.319	2B, 3B, SS				
Greene, Ray	30	0.229	C				Lindale
Greene, Ray	68	0.302	C				
Hockette, Lefty	57	0.322	OF, P	6	10	3.95	
Howell, Lloyd	42	0.252	OF				Lindale
Huggins, Miller	79	0.250	3B				Carrollton
Hunter, ---	10	0.296	OF				
Lowry, ---	73	0.236	2B, 3B, SS				
Martz, ---	14	0.227	SS				
Moore, H.H.	64	0.292	2B, SS				
Mulkin, ---	12	0.234	OF				
Newton, Doc	16	0.211	M, P	2	3	4.83	
Rowe, Bob	68	0.316	OF				Carrollton
Schepner, Joe	40	0.286	M, 1B				
Stine, ---	24	0.264	OF				
Swift, ---	35	0.200	P	9	7	4.77	Talladega

Lindale, Georgia
Manager(s): Earl Donaldson

Lindale Dragons Team Roster

NAME	G	BA	POS	W	L	ERA	APF
Abell, ---	39	0.264	1B				Gadsden
Alexander, Bill	88	0.315	3B, SS, OF				
Burton, ---	17	0.203					
Cartwright, James	69	0.371	1B, OF				
Cash, ---	14	0.214	SS				
Cosby, ---	15	0.293	SS				Carrollton
Craft, Molly	14	0.420	1B				Anniston
Crowe, Hoyt	31	0.233	OF, P	6	11	2.49	

Name	G	BA	POS	W	L	ERA	APF
Dodson, ---	13	0.227	P	5	2	3.65	
Donaldson, Earl	67	0.252	M, 2B				
Duff, ---	12	0.186	OF				
Early, ---	79	0.300	OF, C				
Gray, ---	58	0.240	OF, P	8	2	4.86	Anniston
Greene, Ray	30	0.229	C				Gadsden
Grimes, ---	10	0.381	SS				Carrollton
Hawkins, Cy	5		P	0	3	10.29	Talladega
Holsomback, Squirt	56	0.310	3B				
Howell, Lloyd	42	0.252	OF				Gadsden
Mason, J.	10	0.107					
McCollum, ---	6		P	1	5	5.73	
McKinney, ---	41	0.284	C				Carrollton
Perryman, Parson	30	0.345	OF				
Stanfield, Ralph	64	0.259	OF, P	6	14	4.48	
Waldrip, ---	7		P	0	6	6.24	
White, E.R.	33	0.280	1B				
Wilkie, ---	30	0.195	P	5	14	5.09	
Williams, ---	22	0.179	P	8	8	4.15	Anniston

Talladega, Alabama
Manager(s): Bruce Bruner, Cy Hawkins, Lewis Walker

Talladega Indians Team Roster

NAME	G	BA	POS	W	L	ERA	APF
Beck, ---	23	0.287	1B, OF				Cedartown
Bruner, Bruce	19	0.200	M, SS				
Carroll, ---	14	0.226	OF				
Finney, Lou	70	0.307	C				
Gallagher, Charles	98	0.307	1B, OF, P	4	1	3.60	
Hawkins, Cy	5		M, P	0	3	10.29	Lindale
Laminack, ---	77	0.251	3B				Anniston
Lane, Lefty	42	0.287	OF, P	17	9	2.84	
Lewis, Bernard	94	0.363	OF				
Marks, Max	45	0.230	3B, P	5	8	3.51	Cedartown
McCarthy, ---	27	0.189	C				
McLaughlin, ---	15	0.205	P	6	5	3.45	
Roe, H.J.	14	0.242	P	3	8	5.72	
Swift, ---	35	0.200	P	9	7	4.77	Gadsden
Verner, Cliff	55	0.365	OF				
Vincent, Al	97	0.310	2B, SS				
Vincent, C.E.	69	0.269	SS				
Walker, Lewis	66	0.297	M, 3B				
Waller, ---	19	0.208	P	8	5	3.94	
Wheeler, ---	70	0.230	1B				

1928 Georgia-Alabama League Records

Batting

Highest Batting Average (minimum 100 at bats)
1. Dick Taliaferro – Carrollton .392
2. Bud Ammons – Anniston .373
3. Red Howell – Carrollton .372
4. James Cartwright – Lindale .371
5. R.H. Clark – Cedartown .368

Most Hits
1. Red Howell – Carrollton 152
2. Ray Treadway – Cedartown 135
3. Bernard Lewis – Talladega 134
4. R.H. Clark – Cedartown 129
5. Al Vincent – Talladega 126

Most Runs
1. Jo-Jo White – Carrollton 92
2. Red Howell – Carrollton 87
3. Charles Gallagher – Talladega 86
4. Al Vincent – Talladega 79
    Brant Boswell – Carrollton 79

Most Total Bases
1. Red Howell – Carrollton 256
2. Jo-Jo White – Carrollton 231
3. Bernard Lewis – Talladega 222
4. Ray Treadway – Cedartown 217
5. Charles Gallagher – Talladega 202

Most Doubles
1. Red Howell – Carrollton 34
2. Bernard Lewis – Talladega 26
3. Cheese Goggans – Carrollton 24
4. Ray Treadway – Cedartown 22
5. Charles Gallagher – Talladega 21
    R.H. Clark – Cedartown 21

Most Triples
1. Ray Treadway – Cedartown 15
2. Bernard Lewis – Talladega 13
    Cliff Verner – Talladega 13
4. Charles Gallagher – Talladega 12
    S.E. Case – Anniston 12

Most Home Runs
1. Jo-Jo White – Carrollton 27
2. Charles Knowles – Cedartown 21
3. Red Howell – Carrollton 16
4. Charles Gallagher – Talladega 14
    Cheese Goggans – Carrollton 14

Most Extra Base Hits
1. Red Howell – Carrollton 61
2. Bernard Lewis – Talladega 51
3. Jo-Jo White – Carrollton 49
4. Charles Gallagher – Talladega 47
    Ray Treadway – Cedartown 47

Most Stolen Bases
1. Bill Alexander – Lindale 24
2. Jack Shipley – Cedartown 21
3. Jo-Jo White – Carrollton 18
4. Charles Gallagher – Talladega 17
    --- Sanders – Anniston 17

Fielding

Most Put-Outs
1. H.P. DeArman 1B, P – Cedartown 785
2. Fob James 1B – Carrollton 733
3. --- Wheeler 1B – Talladega 687
4. Bud Ammons 1B – Anniston 684
5. Charles Gallagher 1B, OF – Talladega 364

Most Assists
1. --- Sanders 2B – Anniston 306
2. Brant Boswell 2B – Carrollton 269
3. Ray Treadway 3B, SS – Cedartown 252
4. Alfred Barnes SS – Cedartown 224
5. Ed Gentry 2B, 3B, SS – Gadsden 224

Most Errors
1. Al Vincent 2B, SS – Talladega 31
2. Alfred Baines SS – Cedartown 30
3. H.H. Moore 2B, SS – Gadsden 29
4. Brant Boswell 2B – Carrollton 28
    C.E. Vincent SS – Talladega 28
    --- Lowry 2B, 3B, SS – Gadsden 28

1929

Georgia-Alabama League

League President: C.I. Scarborough
League Secretary: B.A. Lancaster

Georgia-Alabama League Final Standings

Team	W	L	Pct	GB	Affiliate
Lindale Collegians	60	39	.606	----	Unaffiliated
Carrollton Champs	56	44	.560	4.5	Unaffiliated
Talladega Indians	49	49	.500	10.5	Unaffiliated
Gadsden Eagles	49	50	.495	11.0	Unaffiliated
Anniston Nobles	44	56	.440	16.5	Unaffiliated
Cedartown Sea Cows	40	60	.400	20.5	Unaffiliated

1929 Georgia-Alabama League Map

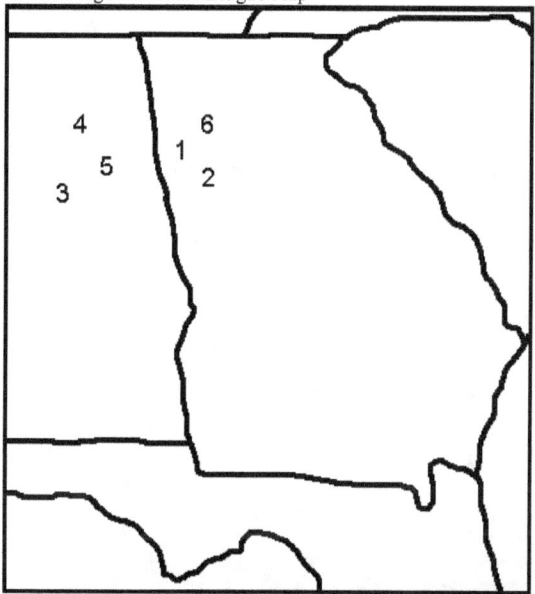

(numbers on map correspond to the place each team finished in regular season play)

The same six teams from 1928 returned to the Georgia-Alabama League lineup in 1929.

Gadsden's Earl Persons set the league's all-time single season record for the most triples when he reached third on his own bat 17 times during the year.

Another split season was played with Carrollton taking the first half and Lindale winning the second stanza. Carrollton, under the direction of returning manager/pitcher Paul Fittery, routed Lindale in the post-season championship series four games to none. Lindale boasted the best record of the two halves combined by four and a half games over league champion Carrollton.

Anniston, Alabama
Manager(s): Bud Ammons, Verdo Elmore

Pitching

Most Wins
1. Paul Fittery – Carrollton — 21
2. --- Sharpe – Anniston — 18
3. Lefty Lane – Talladega — 17
4. Abe White – Carrollton — 13
5. Frank Allen – Gadsden — 12

Most Losses
1. Ralph Stanfield – Lindale — 14
   --- Wilkie – Lindale — 14
3. Hoyt Crowe – Lindale — 11
4. Abe White – Carrollton — 10
   Lefty Hockette – Gadsden — 10

Highest Winning Percentage (10 game minimum)
1. Paul Fittery – Carrollton — .913
2. --- Gray – Lind/Anni — .800
   Charles Gallagher – Talladega — .800
4. W.C. Davis – Cedartown — .786
5. --- Sharpe – Anniston — .750

Lowest Earned Run Average (100 inning minimum)
1. Paul Fittery – Carrollton — 1.60
2. Ben Frakes – Gads/Carr — 1.85
3. Frank Allen – Gadsden — 2.46
4. Hoyt Crowe – Lindale — 2.49
5. --- Sharpe – Anniston — 2.56

Most Strikeouts
1. Abe White – Carrollton — 141
2. Paul Fittery – Carrollton — 137
3. --- Sharpe – Anniston — 90
   Lefty Lane – Talladega — 90
5. --- Glass – Cedartown — 68

Most Bases on Balls
1. --- Glass – Cedartown — 60
2. Max Marks – Tall/Ceda — 57
3. Abe White – Carrollton — 49
4. --- Hydringer – Cedartown — 48
5. --- Gray – Lind/Anni — 43

Most Hits Allowed
1. Ralph Stanfield – Lindale — 245
2. Abe White – Carrollton — 217
3. --- Swift – Tall/Gads — 215
4. --- Sharpe – Anniston — 212
5. Lefty Lane – Talladega — 198

Most Innings Pitched
1. --- Sharpe – Anniston — 225
   Paul Fittery – Carrollton — 225
3. Lefty Lane – Talladega — 212
4. Abe White – Carrollton — 206
5. Ralph Stanfield – Lindale — 193

Georgia Class-D Minor League Baseball Encyclopedia

Anniston Nobles Team Roster

NAME	G	BA	POS	W	L	PCT	APF
Ammons, Bud	37	0.307	M, 1B				
Bassett, Grady	7		P	3	2	0.600	
Burbank, ---	19	0.288	OF				
Caldwell, ---	27	0.238	OF				
Carroll, ---	30	0.292	OF				
DeArman, H.P	83	0.260	1B				
Elmore, Verdo	52	0.361	M, 1B				
Fanning, Rip	84	0.228	C				
Feeley, ---	15	0.200	OF				
Fuqua, Roger	92	0.370	SS				
Holloran, ---	37	0.342	2B				
Kelly, Harold	22	0.143	P	11	4	0.733	
Langdon, Joe	53	0.295	OF				
Long, H.L.	5		P	2	2	0.500	
Marks, Max	42	0.174	P	8	8	0.500	
Oldfield, Pat	97	0.282	3B				
Pellicier, ---	13	0.213	OF				
Posey, ---	19	0.313	OF				
Ramsey, ---	8		P	2	4	0.333	
Ray, ---	39	0.287	OF				
Reed, ---	5		P	1	1	0.500	
Smith, P.	62	0.269	OF				
Valdez, ---	8		P	2	2	0.500	
Walker, Dixie	29	0.324	OF				
Ward, ---	29	0.311	P	5	9	0.357	
Washington, ---	23	0.268	P	5	4	0.556	

Carrollton, Georgia
Team Operated by the Carrollton Baseball Club
Team President: A.W. "Andy" Ford
Manager(s): Paul Fittery
Games played at City Athletic Field

Carrollton Champs Team Roster

NAME	G	BA	POS	W	L	PCT	APF
Anderson, Marion	74	0.350	2B				
Burford, Red		0.077	OF				
Christiansen, ---		0.324					
Crowe, Hoyt	21	0.189	P	8	7	0.533	
Davis, Carl		0.105	P				
Ezzell, Bob	95	0.369	1B				
Fittery, Paul	39	0.213	M, P	16	2	0.889	
Freedman, Benny	88	0.312	OF				
Goggans, Cheese	92	0.287	C				
Harrison, ---	16	0.309	OF				
Holsomback, Squirt	98	0.269	3B				
Justiss, Red	29	0.225	P	10	12	0.455	
Lacey, ---		0.222	P				
Lopez, ---	19	0.243	OF				
Marks, Max		0.250	P				
McGhee, Bill	61	0.311	OF				
Nettles, Hoke	6	0.556	OF				
Patton, Henry	99	0.285	OF				
Reese, Eddie	37	0.278	SS				
Sappenfield, Colon	54	0.323	SS				
Stanfield, Ralph	26	0.167	P	8	8	0.500	
Tate, J.R.		0.248	2B				
White, Abe	31	0.259	P	10	11	0.476	
Winn, Breezy		0.250	OF, P				

Cedartown, Georgia
Manager(s): Sherry Smith, Ike Thrasher

Cedartown Sea Cows Team Roster

NAME	G	BA	POS	W	L	PCT	APF
Adams, Marvin	14	0.182	P	1	3	0.250	
Chitwood, Ken	24	0.333	P	9	5	0.643	
Christiansen, ---	43	0.282	OF				
Clark, R.H.	90	0.326	OF				
Davis, W.C.	29	0.254	P				
Fowler, ---	15	0.233	P	1	2	0.333	
Gault, Pat	46	0.229	P	8	10	0.444	
Gentry, Ed	87	0.273	3B				
Harris, C.	16	0.278	2B				
Huggins, Miller	21	0.310	3B				
Joyner, ---	7		P	0	4	0.000	
Kelly, George	97	0.301	1B				
Knowles, Charles	99	0.315	C				
Lessley, John	39	0.329	OF				
McDonald, ---	9		P	3	2	0.600	
Nobles, ---	6		P	1	0	1.000	
Rainwater, Dewey	39	0.159	P	7	12	0.368	
Robinson, ---	7		P	1	4	0.200	
Shipley, Jack	101	0.345	2B				
Smith, Sherry	31	0.367	M, P	7	0	1.000	
Tate, J.R.	95	0.263	SS				
Thompson, R.L.	79	0.312	OF				
Thrasher, Ike	43	0.283	M				
Truitt, D.E.	20	0.040	P	3	7	0.300	
White, Abe	8		P	0	5	0.000	

Gadsden, Alabama
Manager(s): Lewis Walker

Gadsden Eagles Team Roster

NAME	G	BA	POS	W	L	PCT	APF
Allen, Frank	6		P	0	1	0.000	
Costa, Frank	98	0.218	SS				
Costa, Tony	89	0.289	2B				
Crowder, H.F.	28	0.328	P	7	8	0.467	
Finney, Lou	81	0.333	C				
Freedman, Benny	12	0.277	OF, P	1	0	1.000	
Heidlebach, ---	28	0.194	P	10	11	0.476	
Hockette, Lefty	26	0.200	P	8	9	0.471	
King, ---	10	0.211	P	1	4	0.200	
Land, Doc	84	0.346	OF				
McDonough, ---	12	0.357	2B				
McLaughlin, ---	19	0.057	P	1	7	0.125	
Persons, Earl	101	0.374	OF				
Ray, ---	14	0.302	C				
Senn, Yancy	101	0.306	1B				
Sorrell, Jesse	95	0.246	3B				
Soward, Jim	70	0.293	P	17	6	0.739	
Stroecker, ---	26	0.259	OF				
Walker, Lewis	46	0.238	M, OF				

Lindale, Georgia
Manager(s): Jack Moulton

Lindale Collegians Team Roster

NAME	G	BA	POS	W	L	PCT	APF
Alexander, Bill	94	0.307	OF				
Baker, Jake	23	0.193	P	10	8	0.556	
Currie, Frank	82	0.317	3B				
Dobbins, Howard	57	0.318	OF				
Griffith, Ralph	33	0.214	P	11	11	0.500	
Hardwick, George	25	0.232	P	8	4	0.667	
Harris, Joe	16	0.174	P	2	6	0.250	
James, Fob	49	0.283	1B				
Lott, Edgar	59	0.355	OF				
Moulton, Jack	86	0.318	M, 1B, P	5	4	0.556	
Ogle, Hugh	13	0.167	P				
Poindexter, R.C.	80	0.316	C				
Pugh, Gordon	29	0.358	OF				
Sanford, ---	62	0.318	2B				
Smith, C.H.	94	0.281	SS				

Georgia Class-D Minor League Baseball Encyclopedia

NAME	G	BA	POS	W	L	PCT
Smith, H.T.	96	0.340	3B			
Stevens, Jim	49	0.230	C			
Stoutenborough, Y.C.	30	0.230	P	12	8	0.600
White, H.	17	0.242	SS			
Wood, Norman	18	0.156	P	5	5	0.500

Talladega, Alabama
Manager(s): Howie Camp

Talladega Indians Team Roster

NAME	G	BA	POS	W	L	PCT	APF
Beagle, H.E.	54	0.286	3B				
Boling, Edward	90	0.247	1B				
Butler, C.L.	26	0.243	2B				
Camp, Howie	85	0.327	M, OF				
Coker, E.R.	39	0.303	P	12	8	0.600	
Gray, ---	31	0.246	SS				
Greene, ---	8		P	1	3	0.250	
Harris, Jack	54	0.247	2B				
Holbrook, Sammy	81	0.276	C				
Hunnicutt, ---	28	0.176	3B				
Lacey, ---	13	0.200	P	4	6	0.400	
Laminack, ---	44	0.228	3B				
Lane, Lefty	11	0.160	P	2	6	0.250	
Lewis, Bernard	92	0.420	OF				
Lott, F.O.	38	0.266	P	16	5	0.762	
McKay, F.S.	11	0.161	P	4	7	0.364	
Query, Wray	59	0.266	P	10	7	0.588	
Verner, Cliff	79	0.339	OF				
White, E.R.	28	0.218	SS				

1929 Georgia-Alabama League Records

Batting

Highest Batting Average (minimum 100 at bats)
1. Bernard Lewis – Talladega .420
2. Earl Persons – Gadsden .374
3. Roger Fuqua – Anniston .370
4. Bob Ezzell – Carrollton .369
5. Verdo Elmore – Anniston .361

Most Hits
1. Bernard Lewis – Talladega 159
2. Earl Persons – Gadsden 157
3. Jack Shipley – Cedartown 138
4. Roger Fuqua – Anniston 137
5. H.T. Smith – Lindale 134

Most Runs
1. Charles Knowles – Cedartown 92
2. Henry Patton – Carrollton 84
3. Bob Ezzell – Carrollton 82
4. Bernard Lewis – Talladega 78
5. Bill Alexander – Lindale 72

Most Total Bases
1. Bernard Lewis – Talladega 238
2. Earl Persons – Gadsden 233
3. Bob Ezzell – Carrollton 212
4. George Kelly – Cedartown 207
5. Charles Knowles – Cedartown 206

Most Doubles
1. Bob Ezzell – Carrollton 32
2. Henry Patton – Carrollton 30
3. Bernard Lewis – Talladega 27
4. Bill Alexander – Lindale 25
   Howie Camp – Talladega 25

Most Triples
1. Earl Persons – Gadsden 17
2. Cliff Verner – Talladega 15
3. Bernard Lewis – Talladega 14
4. Bill Alexander – Lindale 11
   --- Gray – Talladega 11

Most Home Runs
1. Charles Knowles – Cedartown 25
2. George Kelly – Cedartown 16
3. Benny Freedman – Carrollton 15
4. Bob Ezzell – Carrollton 13
5. Cliff Verner – Talladega 12
   Jack Moulton – Lindale 12
   Henry Patton – Carrollton 12

Most Extra Base Hits
1. Bob Ezzell – Carrollton 50
2. Bernard Lewis – Talladega 49
3. Henry Patton – Carrollton 47
   Bill Alexander – Lindale 47
5. George Kelly – Cedartown 45

Most Stolen Bases
1. Doc Land – Gadsden 32
2. Jack Shipley – Cedartown 29
3. P. Smith – Anniston 26
4. Bernard Lewis – Talladega 23
   Earl Persons – Gadsden 23

Fielding

Most Put-Outs
1. Yancy Senn 1B – Gadsden 1,124
2. Bob Ezzell 1B – Carrollton 961
3. Edward Boling 1B – Talladega 779
4. George Kelly 1B – Cedartown 752
5. H.P. DeArman 1B – Anniston 699

Most Assists
1. Frank Costa SS – Gadsden 368
2. Jack Shipley 2B – Cedartown 348
3. C.H. Smith SS – Lindale 315
4. Tony Costa 2B – Gadsden 294
5. Roger Fuqua SS – Anniston 261

Most Errors
1. J.R. Tate SS – Cedartown 48
2. Jack Shipley 2B – Cedartown 46
   C.H. Smith SS – Lindale 46
   Roger Fuqua SS – Anniston 46
5. Frank Costa SS – Gadsden 33

Pitching

Most Wins
1. Jim Soward – Gadsden 17
2. Paul Fittery – Carrollton 16
   F.O. Lott – Talladega 16
4. Y.C. Stoutenborough – Lindale 12
   E.R. Coker – Talladega 12

Most Losses
1. Red Justiss – Carrollton 12
   Dewey Rainwater – Cedartown 12
3. Ralph Griffith – Lindale 11
   Abe White – Carrollton 11
   --- Heidlebach – Gadsden 11

Highest Winning Percentage (10 game minimum)
1. Sherry Smith – Cedartown 1.000
2. Paul Fittery – Carrollton .889

3. F.O. Lott – Talladega .762
4. Jim Soward – Gadsden .739
5. Harold Kelly – Anniston .733

Lowest Earned Run Average (100 inning minimum)
1. Paul Fittery – Carrollton 1.81

Most Strikeouts
1. Abe White – Carrollton 101
2. Jim Soward – Gadsden 100
3. F.O. Lott – Talladega 99
4. Red Justiss – Carrollton 95
5. Jake Baker – Lindale 91

Most Bases on Balls
1. Jim Soward – Gadsden 119
2. D.E. Truitt – Cedartown 64
3. Abe White – Carrollton 62
4. Pat Gault – Cedartown 60
   Wray Query – Talladega 60
   Dewey Rainwater – Cedartown 60

Most Hits Allowed
1. Dewey Rainwater – Cedartown 221
2. Abe White – Carrollton 214
3. Ralph Griffith – Lindale 212
4. Red Justiss – Carrollton 211
5. Y.C. Stoutenborough – Lindale 194

Most Innings Pitched
1. Jim Soward – Gadsden 223
2. Abe White – Carrollton 199
3. Ralph Griffith – Lindale 188
4. F.O. Lott – Talladega 185
5. Red Justiss – Carrollton 184

1930

Georgia-Alabama League

League Office: Anniston, Alabama
League President: L.H. Carre
League Secretary: L.M. Carre
Salary Limit: $1,500 per month.
Player Rule: Each club was allowed a roster of fourteen players, one of which who had played professional baseball in another league. Players who had not played more than twenty games in another league were not counted as having played elsewhere.

Georgia-Alabama League Final Standings

Team	W	L	Pct	GB	Affiliate
Lindale Pepperells	63	38	.624	----	Unaffiliated
Cedartown Braves	60	41	.594	3.0	Unaffiliated
Anniston Nobles	57	44	.564	6.0	Unaffiliated
Huntsville Springers	35	66	.347	28.0	Unaffiliated
Carrollton Champs	38	46	.452	N/A	Unaffiliated
Talladega Indians	33	51	.393	N/A	Unaffiliated

1930 Georgia-Alabama League Map

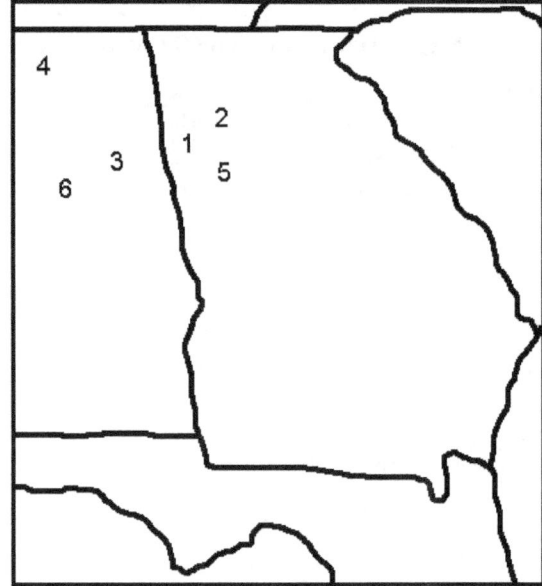

(numbers on map correspond to the place each team finished in regular season play)

The same three Georgia teams returned to the league from the year previous, but only two of the Alabama clubs came back for another season. Gadsden surrendered its franchise to the league in the off-season, and the league decided to award it to Huntsville, Alabama to complete the six-team aggregation.

During the season, Carrollton and Lindale both were forced to forfeit games they had won because of player rule violations. Both teams were found to be playing "class men" who had previously played in higher classifications of baseball. Later in the season, it was learned that Anniston, Huntsville, and Lindale, again, were each playing ineligible class men. Carrollton complained to league president L.H. Carre, but Carre refused to force any of the teams to forfeit games in which the class men had played. Carre feared that such a ruling would force the league out of business. Carrollton pulled out of the league on August 14, and Talladega, supporting Carrollton's stance, called it quits as well. The remaining four teams played out the rest of the season on an adjusted schedule.

Lindale's Bernard Lewis set the all-time league record for extra base hits in a single season with 69. Cedartown shortstop Cleveland set the league's all-time single season mark for the most errors with 74. This record was later tied by Opelika shortstop Paul Flores in 1949.

Cedartown won the first half of the split season, and Lindale won the second half. The two teams squared off in the post season that took eight games to determine a winner in the best of seven games series. One of the games was called a tie when darkness fell. The Cedartown Sea Cows emerged victorious in the series winning four games to three over the Collegians.

President Carre, working to keep the league alive, solicited Gadsden, Alabama and LaGrange, Georgia to take the places of Carrollton and Talladega for the 1931 season. When both cities turned down the offer, the league went out of business not to return until 1946.

Anniston, Alabama
Team Operated by Anniston Baseball Association
Manager(s): Paul Fittery, Dixie Walker

Anniston Nobles Team Roster

NAME	G	BA	POS	W	L	ERA	APF
Carter, Homer	20	0.093	P	6	6	5.46	
Crowder, H.F.	2		P	0	1	9.00	
DeArman, H.P	10	0.235	1B				
Dixon, ---	13	0.362	3B				
Fittery, Paul	27	0.206	M, P	11	4	3.52	
Fuqua, Roger	95	0.350	2B, SS				
Goggans, Cheese	86	0.336	C				
Hand, Dewey	14	0.429	P	4	6	5.88	
Higginbotham, ---	90	0.342	OF				
Hill, ---	2		P	1	0	5.63	
Hockette, Lefty	29	0.222	P	11	8	4.63	
Hurst, ---	13	0.318	C				
Justiss, Red	22	0.302	P	10	9	4.43	
Kelly, Harold	10	0.313	P	3	5	4.62	
Langdon, Joe	104	0.331	2B, OF				
Ledbetter, Bob	29	0.313	P	11	7	3.93	
Lott, Edgar	68	0.306	OF				
Lott, F.O.	25	0.266	P	7	14	4.91	
McGhee, Bill	96	0.328	1B				
Ray, ---	10	0.161	C				
Sappenfield, Colon	85	0.326	SS				
Stanfield, Ralph	38	0.313	OF, P	6	4	5.40	
Turner, ---	15	0.250	P	4	6	6.48	
Urquhart, ---	1		P	1	0	0.00	
Verner, Cliff	101	0.342	OF				
Walker, Dixie			M				
Watson, Jules	59	0.262	2B				
Williamson, ---	1		P	1	0	0.00	
Wright, ---	86	0.243	3B				

Carrollton, Georgia
Team Operated by Carrollton Baseball Club
Team President: A.W. "Andy" Ford
Secretary: Wiley Creel
Manager(s): Carl East, Erskine Thompson
Games played at City Athletic Field

Carrollton Champs Team Roster

NAME	G	BA	POS	W	L	ERA	APF
Alexander, Bill	85	0.343	2B, SS, OF				
Bettison, ---	<10		C				
Cain, Sugar	35	0.283	P	8	10	4.80	
Caldara, ---	1		P	0	1	18.00	
Carter, Homer		0.150	P				
Coker, E.R.		0.243	SS				
Davenport, ---		0.100					
Davis, Carl	<10		P				
East, Carl	64	0.434	M, OF				
Ezzell, Bob	84	0.312	1B				
Finney, Lou	55	0.389	OF				
Fisher, ---	19	0.284	2B				
Gallivan, Phil	7		P	1	2	4.05	
Goggans, Cheese	<10		C				
Goode, ---	19	0.184	SS				
Griffith, Ralph	19	0.229	P	5	5	7.07	
Hardwick, George	12	0.333	P	3	5	6.46	
Holcomb, Hot	2		P	1	1	7.71	
Holsomback, Squirt	84	0.302	3B				
Humphries, Roy	<10		OF				
Justiss, Red		0.288	P				
Lacey, ---	<10		P				
Manning, ---	2		P	0	1	6.75	
Martin, Amos	27	0.333	SS				
McGhee, Bill	19	0.180	SS				
Milner, Holt	<10						
Reese, Eddie		0.255	SS				
Smith, Rube	<10		C				
Soward, Jim		0.273	P				
Stanfield, Ralph		0.324	P, OF				
Taylor, Zachery	55	0.352	C				
Thompson, Erskine	28	0.272	M, C				Huntsville
Turk, ---		0.118	C				
Turner, ---	<10		P				
Wesley, ---	<10						
White, Abe		0.125	P				
White, H.	23	0.262	2B				

Cedartown, Georgia
Team Operated by Cedartown Baseball Association
Team President: J.M. Tate
Secretary: Lee Parker
Manager(s): Sherry Smith

Cedartown Braves Team Roster

NAME	G	BA	POS	W	L	ERA	APF
Adams, Marvin	6		P	0	2	12.86	
Chitwood, Ken	32	0.360	P	13	8	6.19	
Clark, R.H.	94	0.343	OF, C, P	1	1	6.75	
Cleveland, ---	96	0.288	SS				
Crowder, H.F.	34	0.305	P	9	6	6.00	
Fuller, ---	4		P	1	1	5.54	
Gault, Pat	6		P	1	1	4.34	
Gentry, Ed	84	0.337	3B				
Glass, ---	2		P	0	2	9.90	
Glazner, Whitey	14	0.091	P	4	3	5.72	
Kelly, George	96	0.358	1B				
Knowles, Charles	95	0.338	OF, C				
Lessley, John	94	0.386	OF				
Oldfield, Pat	58	0.327	2B, 3B, C				
Ozburn, ---	82	0.233	2B				
Patton, Henry	96	0.288	OF				
Pruitt, ---	25	0.227	P	9	7	7.03	
Seagraves, ---	8		P	3	4	6.16	
Shipley, Jack	101	0.384	OF				
Smith, Sherry	31	0.329	M, P	14	2	3.34	
Washington, ---	10	0.355	P	4	3	7.45	

Georgia Class-D Minor League Baseball Encyclopedia

Huntsville, Alabama
Manager(s): Dixie Carroll, Clarence Hart, Bill Pierre, Erskine Thompson, Tubby Walton

Huntsville Springers Team Roster

NAME	G	BA	POS	W	L	ERA	APF
Barnes, ---	15	0.192	3B				
Carroll, Dixie			M				
Carter, Homer	27	0.217	P	8	11	6.37	
Collier, ---	6		P	2	1	7.71	
Crosslin, ---	39	0.299	SS				
Curry, ---	20	0.167	P	4	3	5.28	
Denton, Malcolm	3		P	0	2	11.25	
Dickson, ---	5		P	1	1	7.80	
Frazee, ---	3		P	1	0	8.10	
Frey, ---	10	0.108	SS				
Gray, ---	71	0.237	1B, 2B, OF, P	2	6	6.49	
Green, Ray	30	0.288	OF, C				
Hahn, ---	15	0.158	2B				
Hammond, J.H.	103	0.355	1B, OF				
Hargis, ---	10	0.158					
Harris, C.	10	0.308	2B, P	0	2	14.00	
Hart, Clarence			M				
Hoellman, ---	6		P	0	4	10.61	
Holcomb, E.	10	0.273	P	2	4	6.85	
Lambert, ---	46	0.291	P	6	9	5.97	
McSwain, Cliff	34	0.388	OF				
Parker, ---	35	0.368	1B				
Patterson, ---	71	0.373	C				
Pierre, Bill	1		M, P	0	1	10.80	
Reese, Eddie	98	0.338	2B, 3B, SS				
Thomas, ---	7		P	1	2	6.75	
Thompson, Erskine	28	0.272	M, C				Carrollton
Walker, Lewis	58	0.339	OF				
Walton, Tubby			M				
Warren, ---	3		P	0	3	7.50	
Watson, ---	4		P	0	3	7.71	
Wesley, ---	62	0.305	OF				
Wilson, ---	28	0.336	2B, 3B				
Winn, Breezy	11	0.286	P	1	3	7.24	
Wolfe, Tom	59	0.304	3B, SS, OF				

Lindale, Georgia
Team Operated by Lindale Baseball Association
Team President: Harry P. Meikleham
Secretary: Earl Donaldson
Manager(s): Jack Moulton

Lindale Pepperells Team Roster

NAME	G	BA	POS	W	L	ERA	APF
Anderson, ---	5		P	1	0	9.00	
Baker, Jake	37	0.221	P	15	9	4.04	
Bassett, Grady	3		P	1	1	9.56	
Costa, Frank	93	0.338	SS				
Fanning, Rip	94	0.241	C				
Granger, George	51	0.325	P	14	11	5.03	
Holloran, ---	86	0.340	1B, 2B				
Land, Doc	57	0.326	1B, OF				
Lewis, Bernard	96	0.423	OF				
Moulton, Jack	59	0.303	M, 1B, OF, P	1	0	6.57	
Pugh, Gordon	94	0.416	OF				
Smith, H.T.	89	0.299	2B, 3B				
Stoutenborough, Y.C.	29	0.275	P	16	5	5.46	
Wall, ---	51	0.343	OF, P	2	1	6.84	
West, ---	85	0.377	3B				
White, Abe	29	0.152	P	11	11	4.35	
Wood, Norman	24	0.237	P	8	7	4.60	
Wright, ---	6		P	3	2	11.42	

Talladega, Alabama
Team Operated by Talladega Baseball Club, Inc.
Team President: T.S. Dick
Manager(s): Walt Barbare, Cliff Verner

Talladega Indians Team Roster

NAME	G	BA	POS	W	L	ERA	APF
Allen, Frank	12	0.250	1B				
Amadee, Joe	16	0.225	P	7	3	5.91	
Barbare, P.	19	0.339	2B, OF				
Barbare, Walt	19	0.278	M				
Boling, Edward	33	0.323	1B				
Brannon, ---	80	0.297	C				
Chadwick, ---	18	0.243	OF				
Davis, Carl			P	0	1	9.90	
Davis, W.C.	2		P	0	1	9.90	
Deal, ---	38	0.315	2B				
Giglio, Joe	1		P	0	1	45.00	
Lane, Lefty	15	0.341	P	5	6	7.20	
McDonald, ---	2		P	0	1	6.75	
McKay, F.S.	15	0.152	P	5	6	4.59	
Newsome, Skeeter	83	0.284	SS				
Picklesimer, ---	59	0.309	3B, OF				
Query, Wray	45	0.262	OF, P	0	3	7.20	
Reeves, ---	3		P	0	2	7.11	
Sidwell, ---	19	0.186	P	9	4	3.87	
Soward, Jim	42	0.285	OF, P	3	4	6.21	
Thompson, R.L.	64	0.349	OF				
Thorpe, ---	38	0.311	3B				
Tice, ---	21	0.109	P	4	9	6.69	
Verner, Cliff	3		M, P	0	2	7.20	
Warner, ---	2		P	0	1	6.75	

1930 Georgia-Alabama League Records
Batting

Highest Batting Average (minimum 100 at bats)
1. Carl East – Carrollton .434
2. Bernard Lewis – Lindale .423
3. Gordon Pugh – Lindale .416
4. Lou Finney – Carrollton .389
5. Cliff McSwain – Huntsville .388

Most Hits
1. Bernard Lewis – Lindale 175
2. John Lessley – Cedartown 161
3. Gordon Pugh – Lindale 158
4. Jack Shipley – Cedartown 155
5. George Kelly – Cedartown 152

Most Runs
1. Jack Shipley – Cedartown 131
2. Bernard Lewis – Lindale 128
3. George Kelly - Cedartown 116
4. Gordon Pugh – Lindale 105
5. --- Cleveland – Cedartown 97

Most Total Bases
1. Bernard Lewis – Lindale 303
2. George Kelly – Cedartown 263
3. J.H. Hammond – Huntsville 242
4. John Lessley – Cedartown 241
5. Gordon Pugh – Lindale 240

Most Doubles
1. Eddie Reese – Huntsville 37
2. Bernard Lewis – Lindale 35
   J.H. Hammond – Huntsville 35
4. Gordon Pugh – Lindale 34

5. Joe Langdon – Anniston 32

Most Triples
1. Cliff Verner – Anniston 13
2. Edgar Lott – Anniston 12
3. J.H. Hammond – Huntsville 10
   R.H. Clark – Cedartown 10
5. *five players tied with 9

Most Home Runs
1. George Kelly – Cedartown 26
2. Bernard Lewis – Lindale 25
3. --- Higginbotham – Anniston 23
4. --- Holloran – Lindale 21
5. Bob Ezzell – Carrollton 20

Most Extra Base Hits
1. Bernard Lewis – Lindale 69
2. J.H. Hammond – Huntsville 58
3. --- Higginbotham – Anniston 57
4. Joe Langdon – Anniston 56
   Eddie Reese – Huntsville 56

Most Stolen Bases
1. Cliff Verner – Anniston 26
2. Jack Shipley – Cedartown 21
   Edgar Lott – Anniston 21
4. Roger Fuqua – Anniston 19
5. Bernard Lewis – Lindale 18
   Bob Ezzell – Carrollton 18

Fielding
Most Put-Outs
1. George Kelly 1B – Cedartown 982
2. Bill McGhee 1B – Anniston 976
3. Bob Ezzell 1B – Carrollton 835
4. J.H. Hammond 1B, OF – Huntsville 666
5. --- Holloran 1B, 2B – Lindale 537

Most Assists
1. Frank Costa SS – Lindale 316
2. Skeeter Newsome SS – Talladega 309
3. Roger Fuqua 2B, SS – Anniston 302
4. Ed Gentry 3B – Cedartown 292
5. --- Cleveland SS – Cedartown 290

Most Errors
1. --- Cleveland SS – Cedartown 74
2. Skeeter Newsome SS – Talladega 47
3. Frank Costa SS – Lindale 46
   --- Ozburn 2B – Cedartown 46
5. Colon Sappenfield SS – Anniston 44

Pitching
Most Wins
1. Y.C. Stoutenborough – Lindale 16
2. Jake Baker – Lindale 15
3. Sherry Smith – Cedartown 14
   George Granger – Lindale 14
5. Ken Chitwood – Cedartown 13

Most Losses
1. F.O. Lott – Anniston 14
2. George Granger – Lindale 11
   Abe White – Lindale 11
   Homer Carter – Huntsville 11
5. Sugar Cain – Carrollton 10

Highest Winning Percentage (10 game minimum)
1. Sherry Smith – Cedartown .875
2. Y.C. Stoutenborough – Lindale .762
3. Paul Fittery – Anniston .733
4. Joe Amadee – Talladega .700
5. --- Sidwell – Talladega .692

Lowest Earned Run Average (100 inning minimum)
1. Sherry Smith – Cedartown 3.34
2. Paul Fittery – Anniston 3.52
3. --- Sidwell – Talladega 3.87
4. Bob Ledbetter – Anniston 3.93
5. Jake Baker – Lindale 4.04

Most Strikeouts
1. Abe White – Lindale 143
2. Sugar Cain – Carrollton 103
   Ken Chitwood – Cedartown 103
4. Jake Baker – Lindale 102
5. George Granger – Lindale 90

Most Bases on Balls
1. --- Pruitt – Cedartown 84
2. Jake Baker – Lindale 75
3. Homer Carter – Huntsville 74
4. Sugar Cain – Carrollton 58
   Ken Chitwood – Cedartown 58
   Bob Ledbetter – Anniston 58

Most Hits Allowed
1. George Granger – Lindale 264
2. Lefty Hockette – Anniston 239
3. Y.C. Stoutenborough – Lindale 230
4. Ken Chitwood – Cedartown 227
   Bob Ledbetter – Anniston 227

Most Innings Pitched
1. Bob Ledbetter – Anniston 206
2. George Granger – Lindale 204
3. Ken Chitwood – Cedartown 189
4. Jake Baker – Lindale 185
5. Abe White – Lindale 182

1930 Georgia-Alabama League All-Star Team
1B Bill McGhee – Anniston
2B Roger Fuqua – Anniston
3B Ed Gentry – Cedartown
SS Frank Costa – Lindale
OF Bernard Lewis – Lindale
OF Jack Shipley – Cedartown
OF Gordon Pugh – Lindale
C Cheese Goggans – Anniston
UT Bill Alexander – Carrollton
P Bob Ledbetter – Anniston
P Grady Bassett – Anniston
P Jake Baker – Lindale
P Ken Chitwood – Cedartown
P George Granger – Lindale

1935

Georgia-Florida League

League Office: Americus, Georgia
League President: Hollis Fort
League Vice President: W.T. Jay
Secretary: Al Block
Treasurer: A. Sullivan
Salary Limit: $1,000 per month.
Player Rule: Each club was allowed a roster of fourteen players, three of which with unlimited playing experience, not more than two with one year experience, and at least nine rookies.

Georgia-Florida League Final Standings

Team	W	L	Pct	GB	Affiliate
Albany Travelers	68	52	.567	----	Unaffiliated
Tallahassee Capitols	67	52	.563	0.5	NY-NL
Americus Cardinals	59	57	.509	7.0	Unaffiliated
Thomasville Orioles	57	61	.483	10.0	Unaffiliated
Panama City Pilots	53	64	.453	13.5	WSH-AL
Moultrie Steers	48	66	.421	17.0	CHI-AL

1935 Georgia-Florida League Map

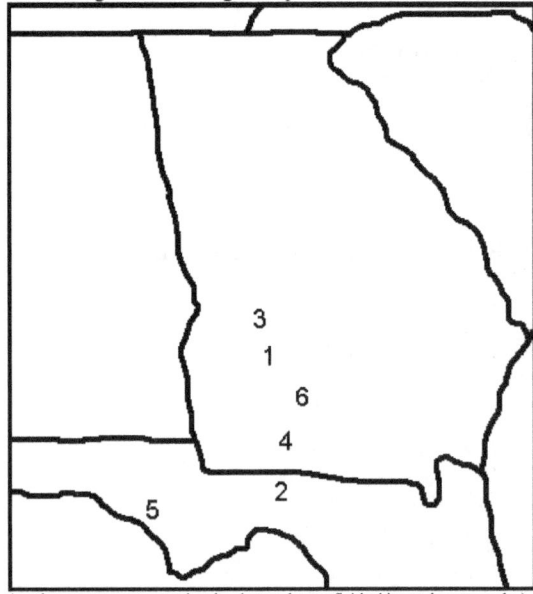

(numbers on map correspond to the place each team finished in regular season play)

On March 24, 1935, the class-D Georgia-Florida League was born in Tallahassee, Florida. The six teams participating in the inaugural season were Albany, Americus, Moultrie, and Thomasville of Georgia, and Panama City and Tallahassee of Florida. These six clubs operated under the watchful eye of the league's first president Hollis Fort of Americus.

Oza Akers of Panama City hit the new league's first home run early in the season. Panama City first baseman Ed Davis set the circuit's all-time single season record for most put outs with 1,391. On June 5, Tallahassee mayor L.A. Wesson wired Babe Ruth making a bid for him to play for the Capitols. "What we lack in salary, we can make up in fishing, golf, and other attractions," Wesson pitched. Ruth politely declined the offer.

The new league opted to play a split season with the winners of each half advancing to the league championship series at the end of the second half. Albany won the first half having the best record, and Tallahassee took the second half honors. When these two teams met in the championship series, it took all seven scheduled games for Tallahassee to finally defeat Albany four games to three.

Albany, Georgia
Team President: M.M. Wiggins
Manager(s): Bob Rice

Albany Travelers Team Roster

NAME	G	BA	POS	W	L	PCT	APF
Ammon, Walt	39	0.194	P	21	12	0.636	
Annino, Alfio	87	0.295	IF				
Barrett, Frank	19	0.089	P	8	10	0.444	
Bess, Krim	51	0.226	P	19	10	0.655	
Bourell, Roy	22	0.118	P	5	7	0.417	
Bowen, Rex	118	0.287	IF				
Cohen, Arnold	24	0.315	OF				
Elston, Dick	13	0.158	P	7	2	0.778	
Grant, Cy	13	0.333	OF				
Harrington, Hayes	103	0.325	C				
Kinsel, Bill	14	0.194	P	4	6	0.400	
Narron, Sam	93	0.349	OF				
Oehler, Vic	14	0.339	OF				
Puttman, Frank	120	0.338	IF				
Rice, Bob	86	0.296	M, IF				
Swindell, Dave	90	0.238	OF				
Unetich, Frank	13	0.120	P	4	3	0.571	
Wojcik, Frank	72	0.269	IF				

Americus, Georgia
Team President: B.B. Kent
Manager(s): Eddie Grayston, Don Sikes

Americus Cardinals Team Roster

NAME	G	BA	POS	W	L	PCT	APF
Anderson, Marion	57	0.261	IF				
Barnes, Irv	95	0.199	IF				
Berry, George	91	0.300	C				
Cannon, Harry	29	0.236	P	12	7	0.632	
Clary, Ellis	89	0.216	IF				
Cole, Sam	112	0.336	OF				
Edwards, Mac	8	0.160	P	4	3	0.571	
Grayston, Eddie	109	0.278	M, IF				
Henry, Wilbur	51	0.314	OF				
Humphries, Roy	53	0.285	OF				
Kearns, John	33	0.272	P	17	7	0.708	
Long, Hoke	21	0.309					
Mahaffey, Jim	9		P	2	4	0.333	
McQuaig, Jerry	29	0.286	OF				
Mittleman, Dick	109	0.254	OF				
Moody, Frank	114	0.267	IF				
Sikes, Don	31	0.323	M, OF				
Tomasello, Theron	19	0.244	P	3	2	0.600	
West, Dick	89	0.330	C				
Wood, W.G.	34	0.165	P	16	11	0.593	

Moultrie, Georgia
Team President: Bob Murray
Manager(s): Bob Murray
Major League Affiliate: Chicago White Sox – American League.

Georgia Class-D Minor League Baseball Encyclopedia

Moultrie Steers Team Roster

NAME	G	BA	POS	W	L	PCT	APF
Black, Wayne	90	0.260	IF				
Crisler, Joe	41	0.183	P	11	10	0.524	
DeWeese, Mal	50	0.292	C				
Dobernic, John	29	0.123	P	9	17	0.346	
Duberstein, Ed	57	0.261	IF				
Fatui, Charles	93	0.287	IF				
Givens, Bill	50	0.225	C				
Hickey, Jim	17	0.143	P	6	7	0.462	
Johnsen, Tor	52	0.296	OF				
Knox, Fred	62	0.268	OF				
Murray, Bob			M				
Pickett, Fred	93	0.254	IF				
Smith, Paul	23	0.057	P	10	7	0.588	
Strott, Art	51	0.346	OF				

Panama City, Florida
Team President: F.M. Nelson
Manager(s): Bill Snyder, Harry Snyder
Major League Affiliate: Washington Senators – American League.

Panama City Pilots Team Roster

NAME	G	BA	POS	W	L	PCT	APF
Akers, Oza	113	0.265	OF				
Bazner, Henry	58	0.212	P	9	16	0.360	
Berry, John	30	0.169	P	10	7	0.588	
Bloodworth, Jimmy	55	0.305	OF				
Chase, Ken	31	0.258	P	11	11	0.500	
Coleman, Sid	117	0.270	IF				
Davis, Ed	108	0.271	IF				
Dickson, Robin	69	0.331	C				
LaFaive, Verne	27	0.218	P	5	6	0.455	
Lanier, Joe	27	0.052	P	10	13	0.435	
Martin, Archie	17	0.203	C				
Matt, J.W.	13	0.217	C				
McKinley, Pete	13	0.194	P	5	5	0.500	
Muth, Dick	110	0.234	OF				
Owens, D.L.	105	0.229	IF				
Sewell, Guy	20	0.145	P	7	9	0.438	
Snyder, Bill			M				
Snyder, Harry	63	0.316	M, IF				

Tallahassee, Florida
Team President: Fred Lowry
Manager(s): Tex Hoffman
Major League Affiliate: New York Giants – National League.

Tallahassee Capitols Team Roster

NAME	G	BA	POS	W	L	PCT	APF
Allen, Earl	9	0.150	P	2	5	0.286	
Borom, Red	7	0.238	IF				
Castillo, Celido	57	0.243	P				
Collins, Charlie	42	0.305	OF				
Duay, Ted	55	0.266	C				
Helvey, Bob	25	0.183	P	9	9	0.500	
Hoffman, Tex	62	0.249	M, IF				
Huisking, Charles	15	0.231	P	4	4	0.500	
Martin, Charles	88	0.209	C				
Miller, Frank	47	0.247	IF				
Murray, Glenn	115	0.245	OF				
Newcomb, Tete	97	0.293	OF				
Oscher, Bob	18	0.180	P	6	10	0.375	
Ryder, Paul	110	0.235	IF				
Sauerbrun, Kip	36	0.204	P	20	7	0.741	
Scherer, Leon	14	0.244	P	9	1	0.900	
Thrasher, Lew	13	0.111	P	6	5	0.545	
Triplett, Coaker	102	0.317	OF				
Waits, Frank	116	0.295	IF				
Willoughby, John	33	0.327	C				

Thomasville, Georgia
Team President: E.O. Garner
Manager(s): Harry O'Donnell, Bob Vines

Thomasville Orioles Team Roster

NAME	G	BA	POS	W	L	PCT	APF
Anderson, Frank	9		P	2	4	0.333	
Brown, Ben	116	0.336	OF				
Coombs, Woody	109	0.227	IF				
Cox, Jim	78	0.258	IF				
Daugherty, Norm	21	0.137	P	7	8	0.467	
Fernandez, Cecil	86	0.292	C				
Ferrell, Beverly	115	0.300	OF				
Flora, Bill	23	0.053	P	13	6	0.684	
Gray, Milt	95	0.298	C				
Hand, Dewey	6		P	1	3	0.250	
Letchas, Charlie	116	0.286	IF				
McKenzie, Sherwood	71	0.289	P	9	12	0.429	
McKenzie, William	32	0.169	IF				
Neigefind, Vic	6		P	2	2	0.500	
O'Donnell, Harry			M				
Pickering, Chris	97	0.264	P	2	2	0.500	
Sansosti, Frank	17	0.176	P	6	3	0.667	
Sullivan, Joe	55	0.231	IF				
Townsend, Art	45	0.211					
Trainor, Bernard	18	0.174	P	7	6	0.538	
Vines, Bob			M				

1935 Georgia-Florida League Records
Batting
Highest Batting Average (minimum 100 at bats)
1. Sam Narron – Albany .349
2. Art Strott – Moultrie .346
3. Frank Puttman – Albany .338
4. Ben Brown – Thomasville .336
  Sam Cole – Americus .366

Most Hits
1. Sam Cole – Americus 153
2. Frank Puttman – Albany 150
3. Ben Brown – Thomasville 143
4. Glenn Murray – Tallahassee 140
5. Coaker Triplett – Tallahassee 127
  Frank Waits – Tallahassee 127

Most Runs
1. Frank Waits – Tallahassee 97
2. Rex Bowen – Albany 88
3. Sid Coleman – Panama City 84
4. Beverly Ferrell – Thomasville 83
5. Ben Brown – Thomasville 82

Most Total Bases
1. Frank Puttman – Albany 240
2. Glenn Murray – Tallahassee 223
3. Sam Narron – Albany 204
4. Beverly Ferrell – Thomasville 198
5. Ben Brown – Thomasville 195
  Sam Cole – Americus 195

Most Doubles
1. Hayes Harrington – Albany   30
2. Beverly Ferrell – Thomasville   29
   Sam Cole – Americus   29
4. Frank Puttman – Albany   28
   Dick West – Americus   28

Most Triples
1. Glenn Murray – Tallahassee   18
2. Frank Waits – Tallahassee   12
   Art Strott – Moultrie   12
4. Coaker Triplett – Tallahassee   11
5. *five players tied   7

Most Home Runs
1. Frank Puttman – Albany   18
2. Sam Narron – Albany   16
3. Oza Akers – Panama City   14
4. Beverly Ferrell – Tallahassee   11
5. Ben Brown – Thomasville   10
   Eddie Grayston – Americus   10

Most Extra Base Hits
1. Frank Puttman – Albany   50
2. Glenn Murray – Tallahassee   49
3. Beverly Ferrell – Thomasville   47
4. Sam Narron – Albany   43
5. Dick West – Americus   41

Most Stolen Bases
1. Coaker Triplett – Tallahassee   26
2. Sam Cole – Americus   24
3. D.L. Owens – Panama City   21
4. Frank Waits – Tallahassee   18
   Milt Gray – Thomasville   18

Fielding
Most Put-Outs
1. Ed Davis IF – Panama City   1,391
2. Eddie Grayston IF – Americus   1,004
3. George Berry C – Americus   665
4. Ed Duberstein IF – Moultrie   540
5. Joe Sullivan IF – Thomasville   480

Most Assists
1. Rex Bowen IF – Albany   340
2. Sid Coleman IF – Panama City   329
3. Frank Waits IF – Tallahassee   325
4. Charlie Letchas IF – Thomasville   322
5. Fred Pickett IF – Moultrie   269

Most Errors
1. Sid Coleman IF – Panama City   73
2. Ellis Clary IF – Americus   49
3. Paul Ryder IF – Tallahassee   46
4. Wayne Black IF – Moultrie   45
5. Charlie Letchas IF – Thomasville   42

Pitching
Most Wins
1. Walt Ammon – Albany   21
2. Kip Saurbrun – Tallahassee   20
3. Krim Bess – Albany   19
4. John Kearns – Americus   17
5. W.G. Wood – Americus   16

Most Losses
1. John Dobernic – Moultrie   17
2. Henry Bazner – Panama City   16
3. Joe Lanier – Panama City   13

4. Walt Ammon – Albany   12
   Sherwood McKenzie – Thomasville   12

Highest Winning Percentage (10 game minimum)
1. Leon Scherer – Tallahassee   .900
2. Dick Elston – Albany   .778
3. Kip Saurbrun – Tallahassee   .741
4. John Kearns – Americus   .708
5. Bill Flora – Thomasville   .684

Most Strikeouts
1. Ken Chase – Panama City   220
2. Henry Bazner – Panama City   180
3. John Kearns – Americus   147
4. John Dobernic – Moultrie   127
5. Kip Saurbrun – Tallahassee   126

Most Bases on Balls
1. Sherwood McKenzie – Thomasville   97
2. Ken Chase – Panama City   92
3. John Dobernic – Moultrie   86
4. Krim Bess – Albany   80
5. Kip Saurbrun – Tallahassee   76

Most Hits Allowed
1. W.G. Wood – Americus   258
2. Walt Ammon – Albany   253
3. Krim Bess – Albany   250
4. John Kearns – Americus   229
5. Kip Saurbrun – Tallahassee   198

Most Innings Pitched
1. Henry Bazner – Panama City   275
2. Walt Ammon – Albany   263
3. Krim Bess – Albany   240
4. John Dobernic – Moultrie   217
5. Kip Saurbrun – Tallahassee   209

1935 Georgia-Florida League All-Star Team
1B Ed Davis – Panama City
2B Rex Bowen – Albany
3B Frank Waits – Tallahassee
SS Sidney Coleman – Panama City
OF Beverly Ferrell – Thomasville
OF Coaker Triplett – Tallahassee
OF Glenn Murray – Tallahassee
C   George Berry – Americus
UT Sam Narron – Albany
P   Walt Ammon – Albany
P   Kip Saurbrun – Tallahassee
M   Bob Rice – Albany

Georgia Class-D Minor League Baseball Encyclopedia

1936

Georgia-Florida League

League Office: Americus, Georgia
League President: Hollis Fort
League Vice President: W.T. Jay
Secretary: Al Block
Treasurer: A. Sullivan
Salary Limit: $1,000 per month.
Player Rule: Each club was allowed a roster of fourteen players, three of which with unlimited playing experience, not more than two with Class-C experience, and at least nine rookies.
Umpires: Ike Cowart, J.M. Crowley, Basile Milazzo, John Parks, R.G. Vickers, Jesse Woolf.

Georgia-Florida League Final Standings

Team	W	L	Pct	GB	Affiliate
Tallahassee Capitols	69	50	.580	----	NY-NL
Albany Travelers	60	53	.531	6.0	STL-NL
Americus Cardinals	58	58	.500	9.5	STL-NL
Cordele Reds	56	61	.479	12.0	CIN-NL
Thomasville Orioles	51	61	.455	14.5	Unaffiliated
Moultrie Packers	51	62	.451	15.0	CHI-AL

1936 Georgia-Florida League Map

(numbers on map correspond to the place each team finished in regular season play)

After only one season in the books, the first league team dropped out of the circuit. Panama City, Florida resigned its league charter during the off-season, and Cordele, Georgia was picked up to fill the void.

The league's first ever no-hitter was pitched by Cordele moundsman Woody Davis in a 2 to 0 victory on June 25 against Thomasville. Americus utility man Lew Quinn set the all-time league mark for most assists in a single season with 677. Beverly "Red" Ferrell of Thomasville played in all 112 games of the Orioles' season.

A split season was played with the winner of each half squaring off in the post-season championship series. The Tallahassee Capitols finished the first half with the best record, and the Reds of Cordele won the second half pennant. Tallahassee handily defeated Cordele in the championship series four games to none. The Capitols went on to play the St. Augustine Saints, Florida State League champions, in the Southeast Championship. In what was also called the "Crackerland Series," St. Augustine defeated Tallahassee four games to two.

Albany, Georgia

Team Operated by Columbus, Ohio Baseball Club, Inc.
Team President: M.M. Wiggins
Business Manager: Harold G. Roettger
Manager(s): Bob Rice
Games played at Albany Baseball Park
Major League Affiliate: St. Louis Cardinals – National League.

Albany Travelers Team Roster

NAME	G	BA	POS	W	L	ERA	APF
Ammon, Walt	34	0.225	P	12	10	4.90	
Annino, Alfio	112	0.285	OF				
Barrett, Frank	11	0.172	P	5	4	4.06	
Bess, Krim	62	0.157	P	21	15	3.48	
Bleidistel, Wally			P				
Bourell, Roy			P				
Bowen, Rex	62	0.245	2B				
Burns, Bob	8	0.250	P				
Greek, Bill	22	0.305	UT				
Gremp, Buddy	60	0.208	SS				
Hader, George	10	0.227	P	2	2	3.07	
Hall, ---			P				
Johnson, Lee	113	0.275	1B				
Kratzer, Duane	113	0.303	UT				
Leistritz, Harold	32	0.194	3B				
Miller, Ken	108	0.246	OF				
Newcomb, ---			P				
Nowak, Ed	11	0.400	P	3	1	4.70	
Perry, Tom	23	0.172	P	7	5	2.70	
Pfeifer, Fred	18	0.263	SS				
Rice, Bob	93	0.324	M, 3B				
Roberts, Howard	17	0.212	OF				
Scheffing, Bob	99	0.315	C				
Schulte, Len	29	0.267	C				
Schultz, Joe		0.367	C				
Stoner, Bob	13	0.160	OF				
Tucker, Wilbur	15	0.278	OF				
Webb, ---			P				
Zajac, Henry	11	0.217	P	4	3	3.10	

Americus, Georgia

Team Operated by Americus Baseball Corporation
Team President: B.B. Kent
Secretary: J.R. Blair
Manager(s): George Berry, Joe Bonowitz, Dixie Parker
Games played at Americus Ball Park
Major League Affiliate: St. Louis Cardinals – National League.

Americus Cardinals Team Roster

NAME	G	BA	POS	W	L	ERA	APF
Berry, George	47	0.295	M, C				
Bonowitz, Joe	48	0.360	M, OF				
Burnett, L.W.	10	0.212	2B				
Clary, Ellis	21	0.188	SS				

NAME	G	BA	POS	W	L	ERA
Cole, Sam	117	0.306	OF			
Edwards, Mac	30	0.157	P	8	9	4.17
Evans, Dean	55	0.298	2B			
Feathers, Beattie	61	0.396	OF			
Grayston, Eddie	116	0.333	1B			
Guinn, Jim	118	0.323	3B			
Howton, George	8	0.083	P	2	0	4.35
Isbell, Maurice	15	0.207	P	4	2	3.27
Lindley, Jack	30	0.306	OF			
Marion, Red	66	0.336	OF			
McClure, Jim	51	0.282	P	22	9	3.92
Parker, Dixie	17	0.189	M, C			
Quick, Hal	116	0.288	SS			
Quinn, Lew	109	0.257	UT			
Silver, Charles	8	0.231	P	1	4	7.41
Sullivan, Jim	21	0.220	P	4	6	4.84
West, Dick	89	0.333	UT			
West, Stan			P	0	0	
Willoughby, John	84	0.311	C			
Wood, ---			P			
Wright, Owen	11	0.313	P	3	4	7.40

Cordele, Georgia

Team Operated by Cordele Baseball Club, Inc.
Team President: C.E. Harris
Vice President: J.H. Shipp
Secretary-Treasurer: W.D. Griffith
Manager(s): Ivy Griffin
Games played at Cordele Baseball Park
Major League Affiliate: Cincinnati Reds – National League.

Cordele Reds Team Roster

NAME	G	BA	POS	W	L	ERA	APF
Amaral, Dan	68	0.369	OF				
Averette, Dave	23	0.295	OF				
Blackstock, Hal	110	0.274	SS				
Bunch, Jake			P				
Campbell, Lem	110	0.236	2B				
Cannon, Bill	34	0.198	P	8	8	5.01	
Clonts, Ray	26	0.238	C				
Davis, Woody	27	0.058	P	17	3	1.87	
Falconi, Frank	44	0.231	OF				
Gallegos, N.F.	18	0.275	OF				
Griffin, Ivy	113	0.289	M, 1B				
Hargrove, Woody	19	0.300	P	2	2	3.19	
Hoskiewicz, ---			P	1	4	5.23	
Jumonville, George	17	0.224	SS				
Kenny, Ken	14	0.037	P	3	6	4.85	
Leamon, Jim	44	0.207	UT				
McFarlane, Alex	111	0.269	3B				
Morris, Willard	22	0.333	P	2	6	3.93	
Odom, Lilburn	115	0.268	OF				
Quackenbush, Mark	13	0.211	OF				
Rosett, Jack	41	0.261	OF				
Sewell, Guy	32	0.273	P	8	10	5.43	
Siragusa, Reano	37	0.139	P	14	10	3.45	
Spinetti, Sam			P				
Swails, Alex	22	0.100	P	4	9	5.30	
Taylor, Bill	90	0.285	C				
Tice, Paul	31	0.311	OF				
Woodington, ---			P				

Moultrie, Georgia

Team Operated by Moultrie Baseball Corporation
Team President: Alex Hall
Vice President: C.F. Jarman
Secretary-Treasurer: W.E. Young
Manager(s): Grant Gillis
Games played at Moultrie Stadium
Major League Affiliate: Chicago White Sox – American League.

Moultrie Packers Team Roster

NAME	G	BA	POS	W	L	ERA	APF
Appling, Horace	10	0.282	OF				
Coble, Dave	91	0.249	C				
Crisler, Joe	50	0.214	P	13	10	3.68	
DeWeese, Mal	106	0.276	3B				
Dobernic, John			P				
Duberstein, Ed	102	0.304	1B				
Embry, Harry	21	0.214	OF				
Feaster, ---			P	2	3	5.34	
Gillis, Grant	92	0.259	M, 2B				
Huey, O.D.	12	0.182	P				
Long, Chester	29	0.111	P	7	7	4.01	
Martin, Archie	42	0.241	C				
McQuaig, Jerry	42	0.270	OF				
Nee, Dan	19	0.235	1B				
Pelham, Bill	12	0.000					
Pensky, Stan	74	0.231	OF				
Prince, Bill	42	0.311	3B				
Smith, Paul	39	0.120	P	13	13	3.42	
Spikes, Oliver	37	0.167	P	11	17	4.20	
Thomas, Clarence	45	0.237	OF				
Tierce, Joel	107	0.276	SS				
Trainor, Bernard	30	0.167	P	8	11	5.34	
Whittaker, Charles	23	0.290	OF				

Tallahassee, Florida

Team Operated by Tallahassee Baseball Club, Inc.
Team President/Business Manager: Fred N. Lowry
Secretary: Al B. Block
Manager(s): Tex Hoffman
Games played at Centennial Field
Major League Affiliate: New York Giants – National League.

Tallahassee Capitols Team Roster

NAME	G	BA	POS	W	L	ERA	APF
Allen, Earl	48	0.207	P	19	13	3.26	
Bryant, Chic	18	0.186	P	5	8	5.06	
Dotlich, Joe	121	0.254	1B				
Ebel, Wally	122	0.294	OF				
Friar, Del	77	0.239	C				
Grimes, Glenn	25	0.264	OF				
Hofferth, Stew	102	0.334	C				
Hoffman, Tex			M				
Lippold, Greg	16	0.211	P	9	4	3.26	
Lowery, Les	41	0.176	P	15	10	4.11	
McKenzie, Bill	16	0.105	P	3	5	3.97	
Murray, Glenn	62	0.366	OF				
Newcomb, Tete	122	0.296	OF				
Pelat, Frank	121	0.273	2B				
Robinson, Wilbur	10	0.148	P	5	3	2.65	
Rospond, Walt	121	0.243	SS				
Thrasher, Lew	12	0.071	P	6	4	2.96	
Waits, Frank	113	0.031	3B				

Thomasville, Georgia

Team Operated by Thomasville Baseball Corporation
Team President: H.S. Feinberg
Secretary/Business Manager: A.D. Walker
Manager(s): Frank Sidle
Games played at City Park

Thomasville Orioles Team Roster

NAME	G	BA	POS	W	L	ERA	APF
Alleruzo, Larry			P				

Anderson, Frank	65	0.252	P	17	10	2.61
Annunzio, Joe	55	0.237	C			
Bradley, Bob	57	0.222	UT			
Brown, Ben	49	0.254	OF			
Bruce, Buster	47	0.210	P	14	17	3.37
Brunner, Sheldon			P			
Buddhu, Charles	20	0.197	SS			
Coleman, Sid	95	0.239	SS			
Corbett, Tom	65	0.315	OF			
Fernandez, Cecil	37	0.262	C			
Ferrell, Beverly	112	0.346	OF			
Flora, Bill	11	0.154	P	4	4	3.73
Hearn, Barnie	63	0.309	OF			
Kracher, Joe	45	0.260	OF			
Letchas, Charlie	89	0.284	3B			
McKenzie, Sherwood	27	0.316	1B			
McNally, Jim	29	0.227	1B			
Mitchell, Merv	19	0.243	1B, P			
Nicholas, Alvin	35	0.311	1B			
O'Higgins, Dennis	20	0.190	P	3	8	4.45
Oyler, Dick	14	0.308	P	2	2	4.98
Petrella, Joe	55	0.243	2B			
Russo, Manuel	24	0.233	3B			
Sansosti, Frank	11	0.188	P	3	4	5.69
Sidle, Frank	34	0.175	M, C			

1936 Georgia-Florida League Records

Batting

Highest Batting Average (minimum 100 at bats)
1. Beattie Feathers – Americus .396
2. Dan Amaral – Cordele .369
3. Glenn Murray – Tallahassee .366
4. Joe Bonowitz – Americus .360
5. Beverly Ferrell – Thomasville .346

Most Hits
1. Jim Guinn – Americus 161
2. Eddie Grayston – Americus 155
3. Sam Cole – Americus 153
4. Tete Newcomb – Tallahassee 141
5. Beverly Ferrell – Thomasville 139
   Wally Ebel – Tallahassee 139

Most Runs
1. Walt Rospond – Tallahassee 106
2. Duane Kratzer – Albany 101
3. Wally Ebel – Tallahassee 94
4. Jim Guinn – Americus 91
   Frank Waits – Tallahassee 91

Most Total Bases
1. Eddie Grayston – Americus 224
2. Beverly Ferrell – Thomasville 222
3. Jim Guinn – Americus 218
4. Sam Cole – Americus 207
5. Lee Johnson – Albany 205

Most Doubles
1. Eddie Grayston – Americus 33
2. Lee Johnson – Albany 27
   Walt Rospond – Tallahassee 27
   Bob Rice – Albany 27
5. Bob Scheffing – Albany 25

Most Triples
1. Walt Rospond – Tallahassee 13
2. Beverly Ferrell – Thomasville 11
3. Dan Amaral – Cordele 10
   Frank Pelat – Tallahassee 10

5. Mal DeWeese – Moultrie 9
   Glenn Murray – Tallahassee 9
   Lilburn Odom – Cordele 9

Most Home Runs
1. Lee Johnson – Albany 16
2. Beverly Ferrell – Thomasville 14
3. Lilburn Odom – Cordele 13
4. Mal DeWeese – Moultrie 12
5. Eddie Grayston – Americus 10

Most Extra Base Hits
1. Lee Johnson – Albany 48
2. Eddie Grayston – Americus 46
   Walt Rospond – Tallahassee 46
4. Beverly Ferrell – Thomasville 44
5. Bob Scheffing – Albany 40

Most Runs Batted In
1. Eddie Grayston – Americus 96
2. Lilburn Odom – Cordele 90
3. Tete Newcomb – Tallahassee 85
4. Lee Johnson – Albany 84
5. Sam Cole – Americus 81

Most Stolen Bases
1. Duane Kratzer – Albany 46
2. Barnie Hearn – Thomasville 36
3. Beverly Ferrell – Thomasville 31
4. Walt Rospond – Tallahassee 30
5. Ken Miller – Albany 28

Fielding

Most Put-Outs
1. Joe Dotlich 1B – Tallahassee 1,177
2. Eddie Grayston 1B – Americus 1,069
3. Lee Johnson 1B – Albany 1,029
4. Ivy Griffin 1B – Cordele 900
   Ed Duberstein 1B – Moultrie 900

Most Assists
1. Lew Quinn UT – Americus 677
2. Walt Rospond SS – Tallahassee 388
3. Hal Blackstock SS – Cordele 377
4. Sid Coleman SS – Thomasville 353
5. Frank Waits 3B – Tallahassee 330

Most Errors
1. Walt Rospond SS – Tallahassee 75
2. Lew Quinn UT – Americus 61
3. Hal Blackstock SS – Cordele 56
4. Sid Coleman SS – Thomasville 46
5. Frank Waits 3B – Tallahassee 42
   Alex McFarlane 3B – Cordele 42

Pitching

Most Wins
1. Jim McClure – Americus 22
2. Krim Bess – Albany 21
3. Earl Allen – Tallahassee 19
4. Frank Anderson – Thomasville 17
   Woody Davis – Cordele 17

Most Losses
1. Buster Bruce – Thomasville 17
   Oliver Spikes – Moultrie 17
3. Krim Bess – Albany 15
4. Earl Allen – Tallahassee 13
   Paul Smith – Moultrie 13

1937

Georgia-Florida League

Highest Winning Percentage (10 game minimum)
1. Woody Davis – Cordele .850
2. Ed Nowak – Albany .750
3. Jim McClure – Americus .710
4. Greg Lippold – Tallahassee .692
5. Maurice Isbell – Americus .667

Lowest Earned Run Average (100 inning minimum)
1. Woody Davis – Cordele 1.87
2. Frank Anderson – Thomasville 2.61
3. Tom Perry – Albany 2.70
4. Earl Allen – Tallahassee 3.26
   Greg Lippold – Tallahassee 3.26

Most Strikeouts
1. Jim McClure – Americus 179
2. Oliver Spikes – Moultrie 162
3. Buster Bruce – Thomasville 138
4. Frank Anderson – Thomasville 134
5. Woody Davis – Cordele 124

Most Bases on Balls
1. Buster Bruce – Thomasville 150
2. Oliver Spikes – Moultrie 129
3. Alex Swails – Cordele 105
4. Walt Ammon – Albany 99
5. Jim McClure – Americus 95

Most Innings Pitched
1. Krim Bess – Albany 290
2. Earl Allen – Tallahassee 284
3. Paul Smith – Moultrie 271
4. Jim McClure – Americus 266
5. Buster Bruce – Thomasville 259

1936 Georgia-Florida League All-Star Team
1B Eddie Grayston – Americus
2B Rex Bowen – Albany
3B Frank Waits – Tallahassee
SS Walt Rospond – Tallahassee
OF Beverly Ferrell – Thomasville
OF Red Marion – Americus
OF Dan Amaral – Cordele
C   Bob Scheffing – Albany
UT Dick West – Americus
P   Woody Davis – Cordele
P   Jim McClure – Americus

League Office: Thomasville, Georgia
League President: A.D. "Doc" Walker
League Vice President: S.E. Teague
Secretary-Treasurer: J.T. Culpepper
Salary Limit: $1,000 per month.
Player Rule: Each club was allowed a roster of fourteen players including the manager, three of which with unlimited playing experience, not more than two with Class-C experience, and nine rookies.
Umpires: Ben Brown, Tim Floyd, Ben Levin, Hugh Moore, John Parks, and Bob Vickers.

Georgia-Florida League Final Standings

Team	W	L	Pct	GB	Affiliate
Thomasville Orioles	73	49	.598	----	Unaffiliated
Cordele Reds	73	50	.593	0.5	BRK-NL
Moultrie Packers	61	61	.500	12.0	BSN-AL
Albany Travelers	59	66	.472	15.5	Unaffiliated
Tallahassee Capitols	51	70	.421	21.5	Unaffiliated
Americus Cardinals	50	71	.413	22.5	BRK-NL

1937 Georgia-Florida League Map

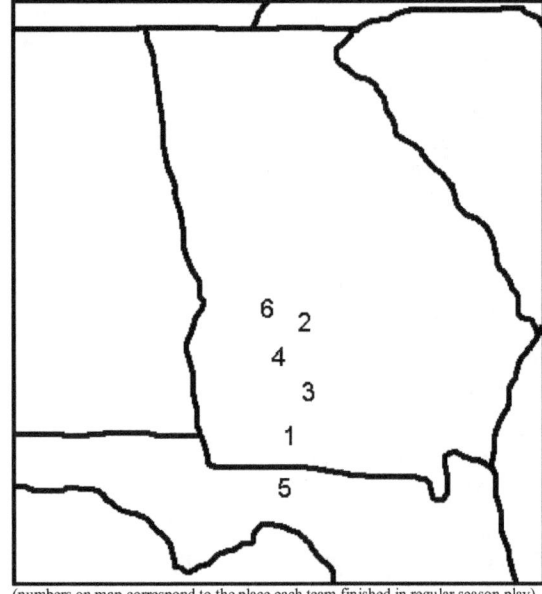

(numbers on map correspond to the place each team finished in regular season play)

The Georgia-Florida League membership remained the same from 1936 to 1937 with the same six teams.

Cordele pitcher Ace Adams set the league's all-time record for the most innings pitched in a single season with 339.

With the Shaughnessy style playoff system not yet implemented, a split season was played with the winner of each half facing each other for the title of league champions at the end of the season. Tallahassee won the first half, and Cordele garnered the second. It was Cordele who got the flag by winning the championship series over Tallahassee four games to one. As champions of the Georgia-Florida League, Cordele

Georgia Class-D Minor League Baseball Encyclopedia

earned the right to play Gainesville, the Florida State Champions, in the interleague Southeast Championship. The series went the distance, and Cordele won four games to three.

NAME	G	BA	POS	W	L	ERA
Sullivan, Jim	22	0.280	OF, P	3	2	3.88
Vaughan, Jim	101	0.294	OF			
West, Dick	103	0.326	OF			
West, Stan	29		P	12	11	2.92

Albany, Georgia
Team Operated by Columbus, Ohio Baseball Club, Inc.
Team President: M.M. Wiggins
Business Manager: Robert L. Finch, Jr.
Manager(s): Bob Rice
Games played at High School Park

Albany Travelers Team Roster

NAME	G	BA	POS	W	L	ERA	APF
Dobner, Charles		0.250	P				
Endicott, Bill	102	0.297	OF				
Esser, Bill	97	0.217	OF				
Gremp, Buddy	113	0.242	2B				
Johnson, Lee	123	0.314	1B				
Jones, Roscoe	20	0.219	OF				
Joratz, Bob	95	0.301	OF				
Kahn, Lou	67	0.252	C				
Kratzer, Duane	23	0.240	OF				
McKinley, Tom	24	0.217	C				
Melton, Rube	27	0.281	P	6	11	4.01	
Mundo, Jim	22	0.173	2B				
Nowak, Ed	26	0.215	P	5	7	6.03	
Nowak, Hank	39	0.218	P	11	13	4.19	
Orr, Dick	37	0.216	2B				
Rampola, Joe	51	0.243	P	16	11	3.31	
Reichelt, Charles	6		P	2	4	6.12	
Rice, Bob	104	0.258	M, 3B				
Schulte, Len	32	0.252	OF				
Schultz, Joe	20	0.176	C				
Thorne, Joe	7		P	1	5	5.00	
Vargo, Steve	37	0.284	P	16	10	2.18	
Wayton, Henry	127	0.303	SS				

Americus, Georgia
Team Operated by Americus Baseball Club, Inc.
Team President: W.T. Anderson
Secretary: J.R. Blair
Business Manager: James W. Smith
Manager(s): Guy Lacy, Dixie Parker, Bill Porter
Games played at Playground Ballpark
Major League Affiliate: Brooklyn Dodgers – National League.

Americus Cardinals Team Roster

NAME	G	BA	POS	W	L	ERA	APF
Annunziato, Al	59	0.231	C				
Brown, Martin	36	0.192	OF				
Center, Pete	19	0.250	P	1	8	4.38	
Cole, Sam	49	0.260	OF				
Graham, Alvin	32	0.088	P	8	9	5.14	
Grayston, Eddie	120	0.299	1B				
Guinn, Jim	125	0.299	3B				
Holland, Fred	32	0.215	C				
Hudson, Frank	26	0.262	P	8	10	4.38	
Huffaker, Wayne	34	0.101	P	7	15	4.27	
Ivey, Doug	30	0.172	P	10	11	3.34	
Keller, Bob	126	0.283	2B				
Lacy, Guy	21	0.345	M, 1B				
Looney, Russ	23	0.282	OF				
Parker, Dixie	25	0.291	M, C				
Peele, Sanford		0.318	C				
Porter, Bill			M				
Quick, Hal	121	0.224	SS				
Rowe, John	56	0.256	OF				
Smith, Jesse	19	0.220	C				

Cordele, Georgia
Team Operated by Cordele Baseball Club, Inc.
Team President: H.E. Walton
Secretary: J.W. Lenoir
Manager(s): Ivy Griffin
Games played at Cordele Baseball Park
Major League Affiliate: Brooklyn Dodgers – National League.

Cordele Reds Team Roster

NAME	G	BA	POS	W	L	ERA	APF
Adams, Ace	66	0.245	P	26	13	2.34	
Amaral, Dan	107	0.340	OF				
Bruce, Buster	34	0.241	P	12	11	2.96	
Campbell, Lem	90	0.251	SS				
Cole, Joe			P	1	0		
Cross, Don	36	0.271	SS				
Deutch, Morris	22	0.279	OF				
Griffin, Ivy	118	0.307	M, 1B				
Hahn, Earl		0.306	OF				
Hargrove, Woody	69	0.227	P	17	10	3.88	
Holloway, Jim	24	0.253	OF				
Jumonville, George	124	0.282	3B				
Peacock, T.D.	36	0.224	2B				
Rowell, Bama	101	0.241	2B				
Siragusa, Reano	10		P	1	4	5.02	
Smith, Artis		0.261	OF				
Smith, Norm	18	0.212	P	9	1	3.00	
Taylor, Bill	123	0.277	C				
Tice, Paul	120	0.287	OF				
Veale, Frank	22	0.121	P	4	7	3.39	

Moultrie, Georgia
Team Operated by Moultrie Baseball Corporation
Team President: Alex Hall
Secretary: R.B. Wright
Manager(s): Grant Gillis
Games played at Moultrie Stadium
Major League Affiliate: Boston Red Sox – American League.

Moultrie Packers Team Roster

NAME	G	BA	POS	W	L	ERA	APF
Brown, Norm	43	0.191	P	10	13	3.52	
Burtner, Lou	87	0.224	3B				
Finley, Bob	36	0.236	C				
Flair, Al	109	0.290	1B				
Foley, Walt	89	0.237	OF				
Ford, Leonard	24	0.205	P	4	9	3.86	
Freund, Norm	41	0.236	3B				
Gentile, Sam	124	0.305	OF				
Gillis, Grant	90	0.289	M, 2B				
Hughson, Tex	32	0.167	P	8	6	2.38	
Kelly, Joe	55	0.283	SS				
Lazor, Johnny	115	0.314	OF				
Maratowski, Fred	93	0.238	OF				
McNair, Ralph	76	0.279	C				
Pensky, Stan	28	0.234	2B				
Penso, John		0.250	2B				
Prezina, John			P	2	1		
Puckett, Vearel	34	0.148	P	14	7	3.97	
Quinn, Lew	36	0.248	SS				
Smith, Paul	48	0.155	P	14	12	3.04	
Steely, Stan	22	0.148	P	6	9	2.94	
Veigel, Al	10		P	3	4	5.23	

Tallahassee, Florida

Team Operated by Tallahassee Baseball Club, Inc.
Team President: Fred N. Lowry
Secretary: Al B. Block
Manager(s): Tex Hoffman
Games played at Centennial Field

Tallahassee Capitols Team Roster

NAME	G	BA	POS	W	L	ERA	APF
Barbero, Frank		0.306	1B				
Barry, Jeremiah	52	0.167	C				
Beazley, Johnny	13		P	1	7	4.50	
Clemens, Chet	34	0.232	OF				
Cox, Jim	39	0.282	SS				
Cudillo, Joe	71	0.234	1B				
Dews, Bobby	78	0.302	C				
Durheim, Harry			P	1	2		
Ebel, Wally	48	0.236	2B				
Grieger, Russ	34	0.256	OF				
Harkness, Jean	17	0.116	P	0	8	10.19	
Hearn, Barnie		0.209	OF				
Hoffman, Tex			M				
Jordan, Nance	38	0.248	1B				
Kirby, Howard	8		P	1	5	7.04	
Kyle, Leon	24	0.093	P	14	3	2.69	
Lowery, Les	41	0.141	P	6	13	4.64	
McFarlane, Alex	69	0.221	SS				
Newcomb, Tete	87	0.264	OF				
Ogle, Fred	27	0.130	P	7	5	2.14	
Pelat, Frank	115	0.254	2B				
Ridings, Jack	123	0.245	3B				
Robinson, Wilbur	47	0.225	P	17	14	3.12	
Ruddle, Ed			P	1	3		
Stack, Lawrence	28	0.302	SS				
Taylor, Ray	90	0.254	OF				
Weiss, Sid	49	0.249	OF				
Werk, Frank	16	0.308	P	3	4	3.38	

Thomasville, Georgia

Team Operated by Thomasville Baseball Corporation
Team President: H.S. Feinberg
Secretary-Business Manager: W.J. Powell
Manager(s): Cy Morgan
Games played at Municipal Park

Thomasville Orioles Team Roster

NAME	G	BA	POS	W	L	ERA	APF
Baglivi, Bill	107	0.219	SS				
Benjamin, Stan	123	0.310	3B				
Bruner, Roy	28	0.247	P	12	8	3.24	
Clark, Walt	42	0.278	P	13	9	3.57	
Corbett, Tom	124	0.349	OF				
Dezik, John	123	0.277	OF				
Isert, Fred	33	0.120	P	20	8	2.45	
Kosar, Joe	23	0.170	P	4	7	4.08	
Kracher, Joe	92	0.283	UT				
Letchas, Charlie	121	0.309	2B				
Lowman, Cal	71	0.230	C				
McKenzie, Sherwood	80	0.288	1B, P	3	3	3.42	
Morgan, Cy	109	0.320	M, OF				
Nicholas, Alvin	42	0.196	1B				
Sansosti, Frank	54	0.169	P	21	10	2.81	

1937 Georgia-Florida League Records

Batting

Highest Batting Average (minimum 100 at bats)
1. Tom Corbett – Thomasville .349
2. Dan Amaral – Cordele .340
3. Dick West – Americus .326
4. Cy Morgan – Thomasville .320
5. Lee Johnson – Albany .314
   Johnny Lazor – Moultrie .314

Most Hits
1. Tom Corbett – Thomasville 166
2. Sam Gentile – Moultrie 157
3. Charlie Letchas – Thomasville 154
4. Stan Benjamin – Thomasville 153
5. Lee Johnson – Albany 149

Most Runs
1. Charlie Letchas – Thomasville 98
2. Tom Corbett – Thomasville 97
3. Paul Tice – Cordele 90
4. Johnny Lazor – Moultrie 89
5. Sam Gentile – Moultrie 84

Most Total Bases
1. Tom Corbett – Thomasville 289
2. Charlie Letchas – Thomasville 216
3. Sam Gentile – Moultrie 204
4. Stan Benjamin – Thomasville 202
5. Henry Wayton – Albany 199
   Bob Keller – Americus 199

Most Doubles
1. Lee Johnson – Albany 29
2. Bob Joratz – Albany 27
3. Tom Corbett – Thomasville 25
   Johnny Lazor – Moultrie 25
5. Bob Keller – Americus 23

Most Triples
1. Stan Benjamin – Thomasville 13
2. Charlie Letchas – Thomasville 12
   Jim Vaughan – Americus 12
4. Dan Amaral – Cordele 11
   Ray Taylor – Tallahassee 11

Most Home Runs
1. Tom Corbett – Thomasville 26
2. Eddie Grayston – Americus 12
3. Bob Keller – Americus 9
   Bob Joratz – Albany 9
   Sanford Peele – Americus 9

Most Extra Base Hits
1. Tom Corbett – Thomasville 61
2. Bob Keller – Americus 40
3. Bob Joratz – Albany 39
4. Johnny Lazor – Moultrie 37
5. Charlie Letchas – Thomasville 36

Most Runs Batted In
1. Tom Corbett – Thomasville 113
2. Henry Wayton – Albany 93
3. John Dezik – Thomasville 81
4. Dan Amaral – Cordele 78
   Eddie Grayston – Americus 78

Most Stolen Bases
1. Jack Ridings – Tallahassee 29
2. Stan Benjamin – Thomasville 28

Georgia Class-D Minor League Baseball Encyclopedia

3. Lee Johnson – Albany   24
4. Henry Wayton – Albany   19
5. Frank Pelat – Tallahassee   17

Fielding
Most Put-Outs
1. Eddie Grayston 1B – Americus   1,076
2. Lee Johnson 1B – Albany   1,043
   Ivy Griffin 1B – Cordele   1,043
4. Al Flair 1B – Moultrie   1,015
5. Sherwood McKenzie 1B, P – Thomasville   704

Most Assists
1. Charlie Letchas 2B – Thomasville   424
2. Hal Quick SS – Americus   402
3. Henry Wayton SS – Albany   370
4. Bill Baglivi SS – Thomasville   341
5. Frank Pelat 2B – Tallahassee   336

Most Errors
1. Henry Wayton SS – Albany   58
2. Stan Benjamin 3B – Thomasville   56
3. Hal Quick SS – Americus   53
4. Bill Baglivi SS – Thomasville   50
5. George Jumonville 3B – Cordele   47

Pitching
Most Wins
1. Ace Adams – Cordele   26
2. Frank Sansosti – Thomasville   21
3. Fred Isert – Thomasville   20
4. Woody Hargrove – Cordele   17
   Wilbur Robinson – Tallahassee   17

Most Losses
1. Wayne Huffaker – Americus   15
2. Wilbur Robinson – Tallahassee   14
3. Ace Adams – Cordele   13
   Hank Nowak – Albany   13
   Norm Brown – Moultrie   13
   Les Lowery – Tallahassee   13

Highest Winning Percentage (10 game minimum)
1. Norm Smith – Cordele   .900
2. Leon Kyle – Tallahassee   .824
3. Fred Isert – Thomasville   .714
4. Frank Sansosti – Thomasville   .677
5. Ace Adams – Cordele   .667

Lowest Earned Run Average (100 inning minimum)
1. Fred Ogle – Tallahassee   2.14
2. Steve Vargo – Albany   2.18
3. Ace Adams – Cordele   2.34
4. Tex Hughson – Moultrie   2.38
5. Fred Isert – Thomasville   2.45

Most Strikeouts
1. Ace Adams – Cordele   218
2. Fred Isert – Thomasville   136
3. Hank Nowak – Albany   134
4. Wilbur Robinson – Tallahassee   133
5. Frank Sansosti – Thomasville   114

Most Bases on Balls
1. Hank Nowak – Albany   130
2. Vearel Puckett – Moultrie   119
3. Buster Bruce – Cordele   109
4. Frank Sansosti – Thomasville   105
5. Stan West – Americus   102

Most Hits Allowed
1. Ace Adams – Cordele   287
2. Wilbur Robinson – Tallahassee   272
3. Paul Smith – Moultrie   235
   Les Lowery – Tallahassee   235
5. Joe Rampola – Albany   234

Most Innings Pitched
1. Ace Adams – Cordele   339
2. Wilbur Robinson – Tallahassee   265
3. Frank Sansosti – Thomasville   263
4. Fred Isert – Thomasville   250
5. Joe Rampola – Albany   234

1937 Georgia-Florida League All-Star Team
1B Eddie Grayston – Americus
2B Charlie Letchas – Thomasville
3B Stan Benjamin – Thomasville
SS Henry Wayton – Albany
OF Johnny Lazor – Moultrie
OF Cy Morgan – Thomasville
OF Tom Corbett – Thomasville
C   Bill Taylor – Cordele
UT Dick West – Americus
P   Ace Adams – Cordele
P   Frank Sansosti – Thomasville
M Bob Rice - Albany

1938

Georgia-Florida League

League Office: Thomasville, Georgia
League President: A.D. "Doc" Walker
League Vice President: S.E. Teague
Secretary-Treasurer: Christine Walker
Salary Limit: $1,200 per month.
Player Rule: Each club was allowed a roster of fourteen players, three of which with unlimited playing experience, two with Class-C experience, two with not higher than Class-D experience, and seven rookies.
Umpires: Robert C. Austin, Leonard M. Curtis, J.E. Haslett, Curtis Hatter, Ralph Kendall, and Henry McShane.

Georgia-Florida League Final Standings

Team	W	L	Pct	GB	Affiliate
Albany Travelers	84	42	.667	----	STL-NL
Thomasville Orioles	69	54	.561	13.5	Unaffiliated
Americus Cardinals	65	61	.516	19.0	WSH-AL
Tallahassee Capitols	56	69	.448	27.5	BRK-NL
Cordele Reds	51	73	.411	32.0	Unaffiliated
Moultrie Packers	49	75	.395	34.0	Unaffiliated

1938 Georgia-Florida League Map

(numbers on map correspond to the place each team finished in regular season play)

For a third year in a row, the same six teams aggregately called themselves the Georgia-Florida League.

The all-time league record for the most hits allowed by a pitcher in a single season was set by Albany pitcher Krim Bess when he surrendered 360 hits during season.

By July 4, the Albany Travelers were running away with the season and had already won their fiftieth game. Albany kept up their winning ways and took the regular season pennant by a thirteen and a half game margin.

In its fourth year of operation, the league finally adopted the Shaughnessy playoff system for the post-season. This new system allowed four of the league's six clubs to advance to the championship tournament. Pennant winner Albany was slated to play third place Americus in round one, and second place Thomasville played the number four club Tallahassee. Albany easily went through Americus in three straight games, while Thomasville took all five scheduled games to defeat Tallahassee three games to two. Albany proved why they had won the regular season pennant when they beat Thomasville four games to two in the league championship series. Albany then advanced to the Southeast Championship against Florida State League champion Gainesville. Gainesville made easy work of Albany and won the series four games to one.

Albany, Georgia

Team Operated by Albany Baseball Club, Inc.
Team President: M.M. Wiggins
Business Manager: A.J. French
Manager(s): Johnny Keane
Games played at Municipal Stadium
Major League Affiliate: St. Louis Cardinals – National League.

Albany Travelers Team Roster

NAME	G	BA	POS	W	L	ERA	APF
Bess, Krim	35	0.165	P	18	6	3.23	
Dernback, Al	124	0.235	2B				
Endicott, Bill	108	0.354	OF				
Joratz, Bob	99	0.346	OF				
Keane, Johnny	115	0.299	M, 3B				
Lukasiuk, Lou	101	0.284	SS				
Michel, Harold	110	0.326	C				
Murphy, Ed	125	0.320	1B				
Nowak, Hank	39	0.242	P	20	11	3.78	
Rampola, Joe	47	0.191	P	13	12	3.83	
Rhawn, Bobby	81	0.246	UT				
Riley, Pat	120	0.320	OF				
Vargo, Steve	39	0.231	P	15	7	3.11	
Wilshere, Carl	33	0.250	P	17	6	4.03	

Americus, Georgia

Team Operated by Americus Baseball Club, Inc.
Team President: W.T. Anderson
Secretary: J.R. Blair
Business Manager: James W. Smith
Manager(s): Red McColl
Games played at Community Center Ballpark
Major League Affiliate: Washington Senators – American League.

Americus Cardinals Team Roster

NAME	G	BA	POS	W	L	ERA	APF
Annunziato, Al	99	0.245	C				
Baker, George	87	0.264	OF				
Davis, Homer	32	0.229	P	12	9	4.60	
Davis, Howard	13	0.267	P	6	3	3.26	
Guinn, Jim	124	0.309	3B				
Hartness, Edd	108	0.278	1B				
Kish, Alex	23	0.196	P	4	5	6.22	
Lacy, Guy	33	0.209	2B				
Layne, Hillis	112	0.315	2B				
Martin, Edwin	61	0.275	OF				
McColl, Red	37	0.123	M, P	16	3	2.04	
Newcomb, Tete	58	0.300	UT				
Price, Jake	27	0.138	P	6	16	5.41	
Quick, Hal	118	0.268	SS				
Rowe, John	126	0.316	OF				
Sigmon, Joe	29	0.184	P	15	10	3.34	
Tone, Lawrence	50	0.282	OF				

Georgia Class-D Minor League Baseball Encyclopedia

Cordele, Georgia
Team Operated by Cordele Baseball Club, Inc.
Team President: H.E. Walton
Secretary-Treasurer-Business Manager: Wiley Johnston
Manager(s): Bob Hasty
Games played at Cordele Baseball Park

Cordele Reds Team Roster

NAME	G	BA	POS	W	L	ERA	APF
Aase, Kermit	10	0.261	P	2	5	5.00	
Albanese, Joe	22	0.204	P	6	9	4.46	
Carlin, Jim	40	0.209	SS				
Carter, Mack	95	0.250	1B				
Evans, Dean	111	0.314	OF				
Hargrove, Woody	110	0.322	UT, P	5	5	3.56	
Hartley, Travis	44	0.181	P	6	9	3.24	
Hasty, Bob	28	0.097	M, P				
Ivey, Bob	63	0.236	UT				
Jumonville, George	115	0.230	3B				
Lowery, Cy	14	0.154	SS				
Marsh, Jim E.	27	0.259	P	7	7	3.37	
Melton, Ray	15	0.182	3B				
Mize, Pope	19	0.311	OF				
Parker, Dudley	82	0.295	2B				
Purcey, Walt	4		P	2	2	2.18	
Smith, Norm	12	0.276	P	2	8	3.32	
Smith, Paul	34	0.181	P	12	12	3.57	
Taylor, Bill	115	0.303	C				

Moultrie, Georgia
Team Operated by Moultrie Baseball Club, Inc.
Team President: Alex Hall
Secretary-Treasurer: R.B. Wright
Business Manager: Grant Gillis
Manager(s): Dewey Stover
Games played at Moultrie Stadium

Moultrie Packers Team Roster

NAME	G	BA	POS	W	L	ERA	APF
Brown, Norm	33	0.286	P	16	12	3.49	
Chiado, Bob	28	0.330	OF				
DeGregorio, Syl	38	0.213	2B				
Fisher, W.A.	35	0.210	OF				
Flair, Al	66	0.345	1B				
Gillis, Grant	27	0.307	3B				
Heagerty, L.E.	37	0.271	C				
Hodkey, Eli	21	0.154	P	4	4	3.31	
Hoffman, Karl	23	0.136	P	6	10	3.88	
Johnson, Jim	73	0.235	OF				
Jurkovic, Bill	45	0.225	UT				
Manning, ---	3		P	1	2	7.31	
Mazer, Al	82	0.268	2B				
Reed, Tommy	53	0.275	3B, P	1	1	1.93	
Robertson, Everett	51	0.238	C				
Sinay, Andy	30	0.250	P	6	6	4.72	
Stover, Dewey	113	0.327	M, OF				
Sullivan, Gene	56	0.315	OF				
Tierce, Joel	112	0.289	3B				
Vesek, Steve	123	0.249	SS				
Voiselle, Bill	36	0.151	P	8	15	4.52	

Tallahassee, Florida
Team Operated by Tallahassee Baseball Club, Inc.
Team President: Fred N. Lowry
Secretary: Al B. Block
Manager(s): Tim Murchison
Games played at Centennial Stadium
Major League Affiliate: Brooklyn Dodgers – National League.

Tallahassee Capitols Team Roster

NAME	G	BA	POS	W	L	ERA	APF
Bryson, Hoyle	32	0.213	P	16	10	3.52	
Charmolue, Jules	47	0.211	1B				
Collins, Bill	15	0.050	P	3	8	3.56	
Dolhrman, Paul	58	0.253	OF				
Francoline, Jim	41	0.298	3B				
Goldasich, Paul	61	0.223	UT				
Grieger, Russ	27	0.263	C				
Haden, Stan	44	0.272	2B				
Haefner, Mickey	82	0.262	P	15	10	3.27	
Heinz, Charles	9	0.278	UT				
Kimbrell, Casey	41	0.318	OF				
McAdams, Ralph	66	0.333	C				
McVay, Frosty	121	0.278	3B				
Murchison, Tim			M				
Murray, Glenn	52	0.292	OF				
Pierson, Argyle	9	0.069	P	6	3	3.43	
Potts, Cliff	25	0.200	P	8	8	3.58	
Ridings, Jack	112	0.301	2B				
Savant, Joe	112	0.298	SS				
Summ, Jack	117	0.246	OF				
Taylor, Harry			P	0	0		
Tyson, Turkey	66	0.323	1B				
Vitale, Harold	10	0.194	C				

Thomasville, Georgia
Team Operated by Thomasville Baseball Association, Inc.
Team President: H.S. Feinberg
Secretary-Treasurer: W.J. Powell
Manager(s): Cy Morgan
Games played at Municipal Stadium

Thomasville Orioles Team Roster

NAME	G	BA	POS	W	L	ERA	APF
Benjamin, Stan	97	0.343	3B				
Berry, John	4		P	1	2	5.63	
Bruner, Roy	36	0.250	P	19	8	3.87	
Clark, Walt	40	0.256	P				
Cross, Don	116	0.257	2B				
Dove, Pat	20	0.370	P	4	3	5.05	
Geary, Huck	74	0.244	SS				
Heft, Arnold			P	0	0		
Howell, Dixie	81	0.268	C				
Johnson, Marion	25	0.289	2B				
Karpel, Herb	13	0.357	P	8	1	1.54	
Kerr, Jim	33	0.213	P	13	11	3.28	
Kracher, Joe	115	0.279	UT				
Lee, Harold	95	0.301	OF				
Lee, Roy	121	0.204	1B				
McKenzie, Sherwood	119	0.307	OF, P	4	0	4.73	
Morgan, Cy	114	0.301	M, OF				
O'Kronley, Pete	10	0.214	P	5	3	3.88	
Spirida, John	30	0.280	OF				
Taylor, Ed	48	0.268	SS				
Williams, Dick	12	0.256	OF				

1938 Georgia-Florida League Records
Batting
Highest Batting Average (minimum 100 at bats)
1. Bill Endicott – Albany .354
2. Bob Joratz – Albany .346
3. Al Flair – Moultrie .345
4. Stan Benjamin – Thomasville .343
5. Ralph McAdams – Tallahassee .333

Most Hits
1. John Rowe – Americus   173
2. Ed Murphy – Albany   164
3. Jim Guinn – Americus   158
4. Bill Endicott – Albany   156
   Pat Riley – Albany   156

Most Runs
1. Pat Riley – Albany   128
2. John Rowe – Americus   115
3. Bill Endicott – Albany   96
4. Cy Morgan – Thomasville   90
5. Ed Murphy – Albany   88

Most Total Bases
1. John Rowe – Americus   237
2. Ed Murphy – Albany   232
3. Pat Riley – Albany   211
4. Hillis Layne – Americus   205
5. Stan Benjamin – Thomasville   199

Most Doubles
1. John Rowe – Americus   34
2. Ed Murphy – Albany   33
3. Stan Benjamin – Thomasville   32
4. Bill Endicott – Albany   28
5. Harold Lee – Thomasville   24

Most Triples
1. Edd Hartness – Americus   14
2. Ed Murphy – Albany   13
3. Stan Benjamin – Thomasville   12
   Hillis Layne – Americus   12
5. Joe Kracher – Thomasville   10

Most Home Runs
1. Edd Hartness – Americus   8
   Pat Riley – Albany   8
3. Hillis Layne – Americus   6
4. John Rowe – Americus   4
   Frosty McVay – Tallahassee   4
   Dean Evans – Cordele   4

Most Extra Base Hits
1. Ed Murphy – Albany   49
2. John Rowe – Americus   47
   Stan Benjamin – Thomasville   47
4. Hillis Layne – Americus   40
5. Edd Hartness – Americus   38

Most Runs Batted In
1. Ed Murphy – Albany   113
2. Sherwood McKenzie – Thomasville   89
3. Frosty McVay – Tallahassee   82
4. Woody Hargrove – Cordele   78
5. Stan Benjamin – Thomasville   77

Most Stolen Bases
1. Bill Endicott – Albany   40
   John Rowe – Americus   40
3. Dewey Stover – Moultrie   37
4. Jack Ridings – Tallahassee   31
5. Johnny Keane – Albany   29

Fielding
Most Put-Outs
1. Roy Lee 1B – Thomasville   1,161
2. Ed Murphy 1B – Albany   1,084
3. Edd Hartness 1B – Americus   1,029
4. Mack Carter 1B – Cordele   814
5. Al Flair 1B – Moultrie   642

Most Assists
1. Hal Quick SS – Americus   409
2. Steve Vesek SS – Moultrie   408
3. Joe Savant SS – Tallahassee   384
4. Hillis Layne 2B – Americus   372
5. Don Cross 2B – Thomasville   362

Most Errors
1. Al Dernback 2B – Albany   64
2. Frosty McVay 3B – Tallahassee   56
3. Steve Vesek SS – Moultrie   53
   Joe Savant SS – Tallahassee   53
5. Joel Tierce 3B – Moultrie   49

Pitching
Most Wins
1. Hank Nowak – Albany   20
2. Roy Bruner – Thomasville   19
3. Krim Bess – Albany   18
4. Carl Wilshere – Albany   17
5. Red McColl – Americus   16
   Norm Brown – Moultrie   16
   Hoyle Bryson – Tallahassee   16

Most Losses
1. Jake Price – Americus   16
2. Bill Voiselle – Moultrie   15
3. Norm Brown – Moultrie   12
   Joe Rampola – Albany   12
   Paul Smith – Cordele   12

Highest Winning Percentage (10 game minimum)
1. Red McColl – Americus   .842
2. Krim Bess – Albany   .750
3. Carl Wilshere – Albany   .739
4. Roy Bruner – Thomasville   .704
5. Steve Vargo – Albany   .682

Lowest Earned Run Average (100 inning minimum)
1. Red McColl – Americus   2.04
2. Steve Vargo – Albany   3.11
3. Krim Bess – Albany   3.23
4. Travis Hartley – Cordele   3.24
5. Mickey Haefner – Tallahassee   3.27

Most Strikeouts
1. Hank Nowak – Albany   165
2. Norm Brown – Moultrie   152
3. Jim Kerr – Thomasville   143
4. Bill Voiselle – Moultrie   135
5. Roy Bruner – Thomasville   132

Most Bases on Balls
1. Hank Nowak – Albany   137
2. Carl Wilshere – Albany   129
3. Jim Kerr – Thomasville   120
4. Bill Voiselle – Moultrie   110
5. Norm Brown – Moultrie   102

Most Hits Allowed
1. Krim Bess – Albany   360
2. Roy Bruner – Thomasville   249
3. Mickey Haefner – Tallahassee   248
4. Paul Smith – Cordele   241
5. Joe Rampola – Albany   239

Most Innings Pitched
1. Hank Nowak – Albany   243
2. Roy Bruner – Thomasville   237
3. Mickey Haefner – Tallahassee 234
4. Krim Bess – Albany   231
5. Paul Smith – Cordele   222

1938 Georgia-Florida League All-Star Team
1B Ed Murphy – Albany
2B Hillis Layne – Americus
3B Stan Benjamin – Thomasville
SS Lou Lukasiuk – Albany
OF Bill Endicott – Albany
OF Bob Joratz – Albany
OF Dean Evans – Cordele
C   Harold Michel – Albany
UT Joe Kracher – Thomasville
P   Red McColl – Americus
P   Mickey Haefner – Tallahassee
M   Cy Morgan – Thomasville

1939

Georgia-Florida League

League Office: Thomasville, Georgia
League President: A.D. "Doc" Walker
League Vice President: S.E. Teague
Secretary-Treasurer: Christine Walker
Salary Limit: $1,200 per month.
Player Rule: Each club was allowed a roster of fourteen players, three of which with unlimited playing experience, two with Class-C experience, two with not higher than Class-D experience, and seven rookies.

Georgia-Florida League Final Standings

Team	W	L	Pct	GB	Affiliate
Albany Cardinals	80	53	.607	----	STL-NL
Valdosta Trojans	71	63	.537	8.5	PIT-NL
Tallahassee Capitols	69	66	.511	12.0	CLE-AL
Waycross Bears	70	68	.507	12.5	Unaffiliated
Moultrie Packers	68	67	.504	13.0	PHI-NL
Thomasville Orioles	64	72	.491	17.5	Unaffiliated
Americus Pioneers	63	76	.471	20.0	BRK-NL
Cordele Bees	58	80	.453	24.5	Unaffiliated

1939 Georgia-Florida League Map

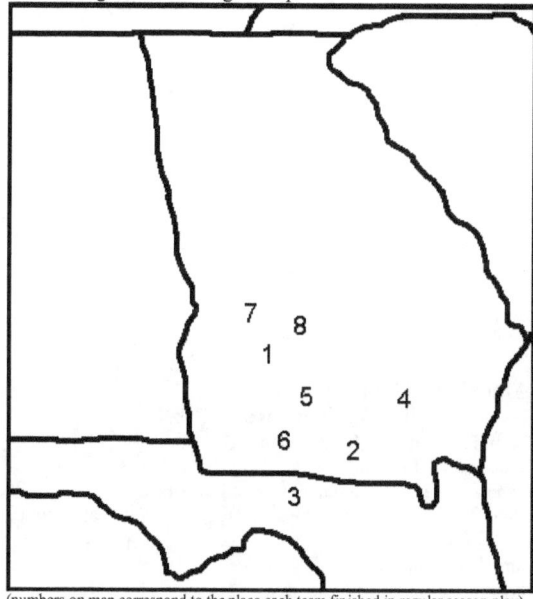

(numbers on map correspond to the place each team finished in regular season play)

Two more clubs were added to the organization making the Georgia-Florida League an eight-team circuit. Valdosta and Waycross, both Georgia cities, were added while the rest of the league remained the same.

Albany again won the regular season pennant having the best record when all the regular season games had been played. This put the club up against third place Tallahassee, the league's only Florida city, in the first round of the Shaughnessy playoffs. Second place Valdosta played fourth place Waycross on the other side of the first round bracket in the post-season. Albany defeated Tallahassee three games to one in the best of

Georgia Class-D Minor League Baseball Encyclopedia

five series, and Valdosta beat Waycross three games to two. The Albany Cardinals, easily shutout the Trojans of Valdosta four games to none in the championship series. After winning the league pennant and championship for the second year in a row, Albany went on to play Sanford, the Florida State League champions, in the Southeast Championship. Although Albany was the powerhouse team of their home league, Sanford proved to be too much winning the interleague series four games to one.

Albany, Georgia
Team Operated by Albany Baseball Club, Inc.
Team President: M.M. Wiggins
Business Manager: A.J. French
Manager(s): Johnny Keane
Games played at Municipal Stadium
Major League Affiliate: St. Louis Cardinals – National League.

Albany Cardinals Team Roster

NAME	G	BA	POS	W	L	ERA	APF
Bess, Krim			P	1	4	5.49	
Cash, Paul	10	0.421	P	3	2	4.50	
Dernback, Al	134	0.248	2B				
Dusak, Erv	134	0.309	OF				
Fingers, M.			P				
Gaddy, John			P				
Goetz, Art			P				
Horn, Vern	32	0.158	P	18	6	2.19	
Karpoe, John	27	0.262	OF				
Keane, Johnny	121	0.314	M, 3B				
Kelly, Howard	12	0.139	1B				
Lawhon, Sid			P				
Leach, Russ	116	0.285	1B				
Lukasiuk, Lou	134	0.290	SS				
McMullen, G.			P				
Michel, Harold	70	0.316	C				
Morris, Eddie	106	0.272	UT				
Polly, Henry	11	0.061	P	8	1	1.57	
Rampola, Joe			P				
Rhawn, Bobby	95	0.282	UT				
Riley, Pat	90	0.322	OF				
Schmidt, Freddy	31	0.275	P	14	5	1.81	
Weaver, Henry			P				
Whitlow, Bob	34	0.231	P	17	10	3.10	
Wilshere, Carl	38	0.221	P	8	12	3.19	
Zachritz, Charles	52	0.263	C				

Americus, Georgia
Team Operated by Americus Baseball Club, Inc.
Team President: W.T. Anderson
Manager(s): Joe Sims
Games played at Community Center Ballpark
Major League Affiliate: Brooklyn Dodgers – National League.

Americus Pioneers Team Roster

NAME	G	BA	POS	W	L	ERA	APF
Adair, Tommy	50	0.323	UT, P	8	13	3.47	
Atkinson, Don	10	0.000	P	0	4	6.89	
Baker, George	13	0.137	OF				
Beyrer, Harold	16	0.254	2B				
Blackwell, Verne	111	0.278	OF				
Brande, Ralph	118	0.277	3B, OF				
Burlick, Bill	91	0.295	3B				
Cruthers, Hal	42	0.232	2B				
Cummings, Polly	42	0.250	P	13	17	6.17	
Davis, Homer			P				
DeKoning, Bill	32	0.200	C				
Freeman, Harold	35	0.221	SS				
Freis, Clayton	37	0.160	P	10	15	3.71	
Frost, Bob	31	0.260	C				
Gusak, Tony	99	0.302	2B				
Hartness, Edd	129	0.356	OF				
Hoffman, Eddie	129	0.249	1B				
Kish, Alex			P				
Kucinski, Mickey	19	0.204	C				
Miller, Pinkie	53	0.319	OF				
Mott, Bitsy	77	0.279	SS				
Rumfield, Lyn	30	0.367	OF				
Sims, Joe	33	0.152	M, P	11	10	2.79	
Sturges, Sylvester	20	0.250	OF				
Tennant, Mal	17	0.298	C				
West, Lefty	40	0.127	P	18	11	2.91	

Cordele, Georgia
Manager(s): Harry Ris
Games played at Cordele Baseball Park

Cordele Bees Team Roster

NAME	G	BA	POS	W	L	ERA	APF
Adz, Johnny	68	0.308	UT				
Arnold, Mel	139	0.304	OF				
Ayers, W.F.			P				
Belknap, Lyle			P				
Bohonko, John	20	0.269	3B				
Boozer, Wes	28	0.098	P	4	7	4.98	
Canteley, Maxie	19	0.029	P	6	6	4.03	
Carter, Mack	95	0.251	1B				
Cearley, Wilbur	126	0.306	OF				
Harrington, Walter	23	0.290	1B				
Herndon, Roy	18	0.250	2B				
Jaeckel, Roy	72	0.259	UT				
Johnson, Marion	14	0.167	2B				
Martin, Harold	39	0.234	2B				
McPherson, Tom	16	0.222	P	5	3	4.62	
McVay, Frosty	132	0.263	SS				
Miehoff, Sol	118	0.285	OF				
Newcomb, Tete	49	0.214	UT				
Ogier, T.L.	67	0.262	3B				
Patrow, Eddie	72	0.282	SS				
Purcell, George	7		P	2	5	3.54	
Purcey, Walt	48	0.150	P	6	14	2.92	
Rice, Harry	45	0.309	UT, P	4	5	4.81	
Ris, Harry			M				
Storey, Gordon			P				
Strachan, Mearl	37	0.169	P	13	14	3.00	
Taylor, D.			P				
Thompson, Leo	27	0.282	C				
Vargo, Steve			P				
Wysocki, Stan	33	0.143	P	9	11	4.17	

Moultrie, Georgia
Team Operated by Moultrie Baseball Club, Inc.
Manager(s): Joe Halden
Games played at Moultrie Stadium
Major League Affiliate: Philadelphia Phillies – National League.

Moultrie Packers Team Roster

NAME	G	BA	POS	W	L	ERA	APF
Bearden, Gene	29	0.185	P	5	11	3.48	
Bethman, Carl	139	0.308	3B				
Christie, Jake			P				
Cielesz, Walt	113	0.287	OF				
Dulick, Pete	12	0.167	P				
Gross, Lloyd	48	0.167	P	22	10	2.76	
Halden, Joe			M				
Holden, Joe	64	0.216	C				

Georgia Class-D Minor League Baseball Encyclopedia

Name	G	BA	POS	W	L	ERA
Kunigonis, John	24	0.155	P	7	8	4.27
Lindstrom, John	37	0.069	P	9	10	3.78
Lomas, Wayne	27	0.172	P	7	11	4.97
Marnie, Hal	119	0.286	2B			
Padgett, Travis	26	0.250	OF			
Pelat, Frank	135	0.274	SS			
Podgajny, Johnny	48	0.130	P	15	10	2.92
Reeder, Clyde	139	0.287	1B			
Rist, Ray	139	0.296	OF			
Sharlinsky, L.			P			
Troy, Gordon	140	0.245	OF			
Usciak, Matt	25	0.235	SS			
Whitten, Norm	118	0.232	C			

Tallahassee, Florida
Team Operated by Tallahassee Baseball Club, Inc.
Team President: Fred N. Lowry
Manager(s): Ralph McAdams
Games played at Centennial Stadium
Major League Affiliate: Cleveland Indians – American League.

Tallahassee Capitols Team Roster

NAME	G	BA	POS	W	L	ERA	APF
Bottone, Lou	57	0.249	OF				
Bryson, Hoyle	33	0.121	P	7	15	3.76	
Burt, Tommy	13	0.209	P	5	1	3.22	
Deal, Silas			P				
Graves, Millard			P				
Headen, Ray	61	0.250	OF				
Holt, Doug	15	0.193	C				
Kimbrell, Casey	130	0.310	OF				
Lorenz, Marv	16	0.161	1B				
Lowery, Cy	134	0.266	SS				
McAdams, Ralph	49	0.278	M, C				
McClure, Oscar	132	0.276	2B				
Ogiego, Walt	39	0.202	P	17	8	3.19	
O'Neil, John	13	0.186	SS				
Patterson, Britt			P				
Pickel, Oliver	37	0.154	P	13	14	3.82	
Pierson, Argyle	39	0.233	P	18	9	2.42	
Schultz, Hal	29	0.321	SS				
Stolper, Hubert	129	0.225	C				
Summ, Jack	130	0.241	UT				
Sutter, John	54	0.239	SS				
Teague, John	69	0.207	UT, P	6	13	3.89	
Tyson, Turkey	118	0.322	1B				

Thomasville, Georgia
Manager(s): Cy Morgan
Games played at Municipal Stadium

Thomasville Orioles Team Roster

NAME	G	BA	POS	W	L	ERA	APF
Aase, Kermit			P				
Albritton, Gene	13	0.184	C				
Ballou, Don	36	0.141	P	7	12	3.31	Valdosta
Blewster, Dave			P				
Bosser, Mel	30	0.391	P	7	12	3.32	
Bowers, Stew	33	0.188	P	14	9	3.57	
Contini, Bobby	125	0.262	OF				Valdosta
Dove, Pat	115	0.266	UT, P	2	5	4.81	
Goff, Jim			P				
Hudson, Bill	23	0.212	P	3	6	3.41	
Jumonville, George	135	0.281	3B				
Maze, John			P	2	3	4.62	
McKenzie, Sherwood	136	0.303	OF, P	2	3	5.08	
Morgan, Cy	96	0.311	M, OF				
Mueninghoff, Dick	135	0.252	SS				

Name	G	BA	POS	W	L	ERA
Murray, Charlie	29	0.196	OF			
Nakunas, Steve	68	0.217	C			
Semler, Marion			P			
Swoboda, Paul	129	0.250	1B			
Taylor, Bob	14	0.256	C			
Trinkle, Ken	36	0.236	P	13	8	2.25
Ulisney, Mike	79	0.227	C			
Van Orsdol, Jack	23	0.242	P	10	8	2.36
Vandergrift, Ed	136	0.333	2B			
Williams, Lynn	12	0.273	C			
Wright, Bill	11	0.207	SS			

Valdosta, Georgia
Team Operated by Valdosta Baseball Club, Inc.
Team President: T.G. Connell
Vice President: G.H. Oliver
Secretary: Nina Connell
Treasurer: O.R. Dobbs
Manager(s): Bill Morrell
Games played at Pendleton Park
Major League Affiliate: Pittsburgh Pirates – National League.

Valdosta Trojans Team Roster

NAME	G	BA	POS	W	L	ERA	APF
Allen, L.			P				
Barnhart, Bob	26	0.217	3B				
Berry, Larry	127	0.217	C				
Bryant, Bill	18	0.243	OF				
Carmichael, Ed	15	0.314	OF				
Contini, Bobby	125	0.262	OF				Thomasville
Davis, Woody	84	0.261	UT, P	13	11	3.27	
Deal, Wally	47	0.118	P	18	11	2.95	
Harrison, Dennie	115	0.297	OF				
Hartley, Travis	39	0.185	P	9	4	3.05	
Huber, Ray	32	0.263	SS				
Leatherwood, Gil	54	0.179	1B				
Lukon, Eddie	137	0.300	OF				
Mitchell, Ed	20	0.225	OF				
Morrell, Bill	14	0.200	M, P				
Panek, Ed	32	0.274	OF				
Patterson, Joe	37	0.088	P	9	15	3.99	
Podein, George	25	0.128	UT				
Robinson, Eddie	136	0.249	1B				
Rochelli, Lou	134	0.277	2B				
Skidgel, Leon			P				
Smith, Paul	36	0.126	P	21	11	2.35	
Stewart, Russ	72	0.245	SS				
Wheeler, Waverly	131	0.272	3B				
Zimmerman, George	10	0.407	C				

Waycross, Georgia
Team Operated by Waycross Baseball Association, Inc.
Team President: Herbert Bradshaw
Vice President: W.D. Rivenbark
Secretary: O.K. Burgess
Treasurer: George Fesperman
Manager(s): Al Leitz
Games played at Ralph Newton Field

Waycross Bears Team Roster

NAME	G	BA	POS	W	L	ERA	APF
Adams, Henry	10	0.276	OF				
Atwater, Charlie	11	0.100	P	3	5	3.74	
Bennett, Frank	25	0.190	P	8	9	3.73	
Blasco, Pete	11	0.133	SS				
Bray, Buster			P				
Burchfield, Boyd			P				
Creager, Bill	79	0.259	2B				

D'Antonio, Joe	41	0.241	2B			
Evans, Dean	107	0.270	OF			
Farrar, Charles	56	0.298	OF			
Grimes, Marion			P			
Horton, Marv	12	0.300	3B			
Lawson, Elwood	23	0.326	P	8	5	4.31
Lee, George	7		P	3	2	5.20
Leitz, Al	111	0.311	M, C, 3B			
Marsh, Jim E.	23	0.188	P	7	10	3.50
Melton, Ray	23	0.067	C			
Mertz, Jim	29	0.160	P	8	7	3.00
Parker, Dudley	80	0.240	3B			
Patchin, Art	26	0.295	P	8	11	3.04
Peters, Genie	23	0.215	OF			
Petrosky, Mike	64	0.299	P, OF	15	11	2.33
Pierce, Pete	30	0.246	3B			
Smith, B.			P			
Stratton, Harry	72	0.294	OF			
Thomassie, Pete	135	0.315	OF			
Thompson, Fresco	84	0.313	1B			
Valle, Sindo	139	0.263	SS			
Vickers, Dan	62	0.229	C			
Wrobke, Joe	7	0.143	P	6	1	2.49

1939 Georgia-Florida League Records
Batting
Highest Batting Average (minimum 100 at bats)
1. Lyn Rumfield – Americus .367
2. Edd Hartness – Americus .356
3. Ed Vandergrift – Thomasville .333
4. Pat Riley – Albany .322
   Turkey Tyson – Tallahassee .322

Most Hits
1. Edd Hartness – Americus 175
   Carl Bethman – Moultrie 175
3. Pete Thomassie – Waycross 171
4. Ed Vandergrift – Thomasville 167
   Sherwood McKenzie – Thomasville 167

Most Runs
1. Frank Pelat – Moultrie 113
2. Pete Thomassie – Waycross 107
3. George Jumonville – Thomasville 95
   Casey Kimbrell – Tallahassee 95
5. Lou Rochelli – Valdosta 93

Most Total Bases
1. Carl Bethman – Moultrie 267
2. Edd Hartness – Americus 223
   Ed Vandergrift – Thomasville 223
4. Eddie Lukon – Valdosta 222
5. Sherwood McKenzie – Thomasville 218

Most Doubles
1. Carl Bethman – Moultrie 41
2. Lou Lukasiuk – Albany 34
3. Ed Vandergrift – Thomasville 32
4. Pat Riley – Thomasville 30
5. Erv Dusak – Albany 29

Most Triples
1. Eddie Lukon – Valdosta 17
2. Turkey Tyson – Talladega 14
3. Carl Bethman – Moultrie 12
   Verne Blackwell – Americus 12
5. Ray Rist – Moultrie 11
   Walt Cielesz – Moultrie 11

Most Home Runs
1. Carl Bethman – Moultrie 9
2. Bill Creager – Waycross 7
   Eddie Robinson – Waycross 7
   Eddie Hoffman – Americus 7
5. Casey Kimbrell – Tallahassee 6
   Sherwood McKenzie – Thomasville 6

Most Extra Base Hits
1. Carl Bethman – Moultrie 62
2. Eddie Lukon – Valdosta 44
3. Ed Vandergrift – Thomasville 42
   Pat Riley – Albany 42
5. Lou Lukasiuk – Albany 41

Most Runs Batted In
1. Carl Bethman – Moultrie 111
2. Eddie Lukon – Valdosta 104
3. Ray Rist – Moultrie 90
4. Eddie Robinson – Valdosta 88
5. Clyde Reeder – Moultrie 86

Most Stolen Bases
1. Dennie Harrison – Valdosta 38
2. Casey Kimbrell – Tallahassee 37
3. Jack Summ – Tallahassee 34
4. Pete Thomassie – Waycross 33
5. Eddie Lukon – Valdosta 28

Fielding
Most Put-Outs
1. Paul Swoboda 1B – Thomasville 1,300
2. Eddie Robinson 1B – Valdosta 1,227
3. Clyde Reeder 1B – Moultrie 1,223
4. Eddie Hoffman 1B – Americus 1,153
5. Turkey Tyson 1B – Tallahassee 1,064

Most Assists
1. Dick Mueninghoff SS – Thomasville 441
2. Ed Vandergrift 2B – Thomasville 433
3. Lou Lukasiuk SS – Albany 422
4. Lou Rochelli 2B – Valdosta 415
5. Al Dernback 2B – Albany 398

Most Errors
1. Lou Lukasiuk SS – Albany 63
2. Cy Lowery SS – Tallahassee 60
3. Ed Vandergrift 2B – Thomasville 59
4. Al Dernback 2B – Albany 56
5. Dick Mueninghoff SS – Thomasville 55

Pitching
Most Wins
1. Lloyd Gross – Moultrie 22
2. Paul Smith – Valdosta 21
3. Lefty West – Americus 18
   Wally Deal – Valdosta 18
   Argyle Pierson – Tallahassee 18
   Vern Horn – Albany 18

Most Losses
1. Polly Cummings – Americus 17
2. Clayton Freis – Americus 15
   Joe Patterson – Valdosta 15
   Hoyle Bryson – Tallahassee 15
5. Oliver Pickel – Tallahassee 14
   Mearl Strachan – Cordele 14
   Walt Purcey – Cordele 14

Highest Winning Percentage (10 game minimum)
1. Vern Horn – Albany .750
2. Freddy Schmidt – Albany .737
3. Travis Hartley – Valdosta .692
4. Lloyd Gross – Moultrie .688
5. Walt Ogiego – Tallahassee .680

Lowest Earned Run Average (100 inning minimum)
1. Freddy Schmidt – Albany 1.81
2. Vern Horn – Albany 2.19
3. Ken Trinkle – Thomasville 2.25
4. Mike Petrosky – Waycross 2.33
5. Paul Smith – Valdosta 2.35

Most Strikeouts
1. Lefty West – Americus 245
2. Lloyd Gross – Moultrie 168
3. Argyle Pierson – Tallahassee 149
4. Paul Smith – Valdosta 146
5. Clayton Freis – Americus 137

Most Bases on Balls
1. Oliver Pickel – Tallahassee 115
2. Lefty West – Americus 113
3. Polly Cummings – Americus 108
4. John Teague – Tallahassee 103
5. Clayton Freis – Americus 98

Most Hits Allowed
1. Lloyd Gross – Moultrie 293
2. Paul Smith – Valdosta 276
3. Wally Deal – Valdosta 263
4. Polly Cummings – Americus 250
5. Lefty West – Americus 240

Most Innings Pitched
1. Lloyd Gross – Moultrie 303
2. Lefty West – Americus 294
3. Paul Smith – Valdosta 283
4. Wally Deal – Valdosta 259
5. Argyle Pierson – Tallahassee 257

1939 Georgia-Florida League All-Star Team
1B Turkey Tyson – Tallahassee
2B Ed Vandergrift – Thomasville
3B Carl Bethman – Moultrie
SS Lou Lukasiuk – Albany
OF Edd Hartness – Americus
OF Casey Kimbrell – Tallahassee
OF Eddie Lukon – Valdosta
C Al Leitz – Waycross
UT Pat Dove – Thomasville
P Vern Horn – Albany
P Lefty West – Americus
M Cy Morgan - Thomasville

1940

Georgia-Florida League

League Office: Thomasville, Georgia
League President: A.D. "Doc" Walker
League Vice President: S.E. Teague
Secretary-Treasurer: Christine Walker
Salary Limit: $1,400 per month including manager.
Player Rule: Each club was allowed a roster of fourteen players, not more than four veterans, not more than eight limited service, and not less than two rookies.
Umpires: C.C. Forrest, Don Atkinson, Edward J. Matesic, Charles V. Varble, Otto Truhler, Pat Brady, Mason Stevenson.

Georgia-Florida League Final Standings

Team	W	L	Pct	GB	Affiliate
Waycross Bears	93	45	.674	----	Unaffiliated
Thomasville Tourists	81	58	.583	12.5	WSH-AL
Valdosta Trojans	76	61	.555	16.5	Unaffiliated
Albany Cardinals	77	63	.550	17.0	STL-NL
Americus Pioneers	67	72	.482	26.5	BRK-NL
Tallahassee Capitols	64	75	.461	29.5	Unaffiliated
Cordele Bees	49	89	.355	44.0	Unaffiliated
Moultrie Packers	47	91	.340	46.0	PHI-NL

1940 Georgia-Florida League Map

(numbers on map correspond to the place each team finished in regular season play)

All eight of the league cities from 1939 returned to the diamond for the 1940 season.

Waycross pitcher Elwood Lawson won his first 13 games of the season before he was defeated by Americus on June 14. Elmer Rummans, pitcher for Valdosta, struck out eighteen Cordele batters in one game on August 9. Moultrie pitcher John Lindstrom set the all-time league single season record for the most losses with 22.

The league's all-star team played league leader Waycross on July 14 at Albany. The Bears defeated the league's best 7 to

Georgia Class-D Minor League Baseball Encyclopedia

6 in a marathon 14-inning contest. Another long game was played on the last day of the season when Valdosta and Waycross tied up for 19 innings. Waycross scored five runs in the 19th to win the game 8 to 3.

Waycross won the regular season pennant with the best record followed in order by Thomasville, Valdosta, and Albany. These top four teams advanced to the post-season playoffs. Top seed Waycross defeated third place Valdosta three games to none, while number two Thomasville eliminated Albany three games to two in the first round. In the finals, Waycross easily defeated Thomasville four games to one to become undisputed league champions. After winning it all in their own league, the Bears of Waycross went south to play Orlando, champs of the Florida State League, in the Southeast Championship. Orlando was no match for Waycross as the Georgia-Florida champions won the series four games to two. In another interleague series also called the Southeast Championship, Waycross took on Florida East Coast League champion Ft. Lauderdale. Making the home league proud, Waycross easily won this series four games to one.

Albany, Georgia
Team Operated by St. Louis National League Baseball Club
Team President: M.M. Wiggins
Vice Presidents: Branch Rickey, William Walsingham, Jr.
Business Manager: George Sisler, Jr.
Manager(s): Joe Cusick
Games played at Municipal Stadium
Major League Affiliate: St. Louis Cardinals – National League.

Albany Cardinals Team Roster

NAME	G	BA	POS	W	L	ERA	APF
Bailey, Paul	20	0.313	2B				
Brock, Ed	10	0.360	2B				
Burns, Jim	47	0.282	2B				
Cash, Paul	73	0.276	P, IF	17	6	3.26	
Cusick, Joe	108	0.280	M, C				
Dernback, Al	73	0.240	2B				
Dixon, Stokely	14	0.040	P	4	4	3.43	
Dobbs, Gil	29	0.292	C				
Dusak, Erv	141	0.335	OF, P				
Dvorak, Ray	13	0.238	2B				
Ferens, Stan	39	0.167	P	20	11	2.34	
Filo, Ed	124	0.320	OF, C				
Goetz, Art	24	0.241	P	8	9	3.28	
Hadley, Harry	<10						
Hardin, Henry	71	0.292	OF				
Isert, Lou	36	0.187	SS				Thomasville
Leach, Russ	134	0.337	1B				
McGreal, Jimmy	<10						
Mediamolle, Frank	<10						
Moore, Hugh	98	0.241	SS				
Muhlenbein, Henry	<10		P				
Reggio, Jimmy	<10						
Sisler, George	<10		P				
Smith, Howard	<10		P				
Stickney, Floyd	135	0.300	3B				
Tefft, Charles	75	0.286	OF				
Weaver, Henry	42	0.190	P	15	13	4.41	
Wilshere, Carl	<10		P				
Yeates, Doug	24	0.071	P	8	9	3.34	

Americus, Georgia
Team Operated by Baseball Club of Americus, Inc.
Team President: W.T. Anderson
Secretary-Business Manager: E.J. Bavasi
Treasurer: John F. Collins
Manager(s): Bernie Deviveiros, Stew Hofferth
Games played at Community Center Ballpark
Major League Affiliate: Brooklyn Dodgers – National League.

Americus Pioneers Team Roster

NAME	G	BA	POS	W	L	ERA	APF
Adair, Tommy	60	0.316	P, IF	10	13	3.61	
Addison, George	19	0.343	OF				
Archipoli, Andy	84	0.259	2B				
Atkinson, Don	<10		P	4	2	7.00	
Carel, Paul	<10		P				
Cibrowski, Marion	100	0.281	OF				
Cohick, Harry	52	0.256	P, IF	12	12	2.61	
DeViveiros, Bernie	44	0.266	M, 3B				
Gusak, Tony	<10						
Hofferth, Stew	71	0.257	M, C				
Hoffman, Eddie	139	0.297	1B				
Johnson, Norm	<10						
Kienle, Fred	19	0.286	P	4	7	7.18	
Martinez, Freddie	36	0.189	2B				
Miller, Frank	79	0.310	OF, IF				
Mott, Bitsy	137	0.243	SS				
Moulder, Glen	36	0.198	P	20	9	2.65	
Pine, Ken	17	0.151	P, IF	5	5	2.78	
Rogers, Jim	39	0.267	OF				
Seymour, George	10	0.118	P				
Smith, Bob	11	0.103	P	1	8	4.80	
Smith, Norm	26	0.238	P	8	8	3.76	
Stalcup, Pete	<10		P				
Switzer, Marion	<10						
Twitchell, Beech	45	0.224	OF				
Twitchell, Dan	62	0.221	C				
Uhle, Stan	134	0.301	OF, IF, P				Thomasville
Wasiak, Stan	111	0.315	3B				

Cordele, Georgia
Team Operated by Jacksonville Baseball Exhibition Co., Inc.
Team President: Charlie Garwood
Vice-President: Joe Bridges
Secretary-Treasurer-Business Manager: Leon Hamilton
Manager(s):
Games played at Stander Stadium

Cordele Bees Team Roster

NAME	G	BA	POS	W	L	ERA	APF
Arnold, Mel	97	0.331	OF				
Avera, Jim	58	0.214	P, IF	2	11	3.45	
Barnes, Duge	14	0.156	OF				
Bobo, Bill	29	0.172	P	6	11	5.18	
Canteley, Maxie	13	0.111	P	2	5	7.02	
Ciccone, Remo	110	0.276	OF, IF, P				
Cloninger, Al	<10						
Eckenroth, Bill	<10		P				
Goldsmith, Ralph	15	0.194	2B				
Greer, Elwyn	23	0.097	P	8	8	3.42	
Heller, Harry	40	0.278	2B				
Jaeckel, Roy	118	0.292	OF, IF				Tallahassee
Killian, C.L.	90	0.243	SS				
Landis, Dick	<10		P				
Lane, Leon	15	0.200	P	4	4	4.83	Tallahassee
LaPiana, Peter	27	0.155	3B				Moultrie
Linderman, Bob	111	0.260	C				
Lokey, George	57	0.233	OF, IF				Moultrie
Long, Jim	40	0.201	SS				
McBryde, Warren	27	0.233	OF				
Ogier, T.L.	54	0.219	SS				
Pensky, Stan	44	0.252	2B				
Prince, Jim	85	0.317	3B				
Purcey, Walt	49	0.234	P, IF	15	19	3.00	
Rios, Felix	38	0.367	OF, IF				
Rutledge, Bob	74	0.247	2B				

Georgia Class-D Minor League Baseball Encyclopedia

NAME	G	BA	POS	W	L	ERA
Schmidt, Don	10	0.286	SS			
Taylor, Bill	90	0.274	M, C			
Texanne, Russ	11	0.161	P	3	6	4.94
Womack, Charles	11	0.158	OF			
Wooten, Bob	80	0.255	1B			
Wysocki, Stan	47	0.115	P	8	19	3.85

Moultrie, Georgia
Team Operated by Moultrie Baseball Club, Inc.
Team President: Charles O. Powell
Secretary: Henry S. Cohen
Manager(s): Joe Holden, George Jacobs
Games played at Moultrie Stadium
Major League Affiliate: Philadelphia Phillies – National League.

Moultrie Packers Team Roster

NAME	G	BA	POS	W	L	ERA	APF
Asinof, Eliot	15	0.296	1B				
Banta, Sterling	35	0.282	OF				
Barnett, John	23	0.171	SS				
Behrends, Al	138	0.327	OF				
Blewster, Dave	<10		P	1	6	5.91	
Bongard, Eddie	<10						
Brelich, Mike	<10						
Brickner, Walt	117	0.318	1B				
Brown, Xenophon	<10		P				
Burns, Jim	100	0.260	P, IF	5	12	7.18	
Cielesz, Walt	23	0.250	OF				
Dispenziere, Carmen	26	0.308	C				
Dixon, Percy	<10		P				
Dunlevy, Harry	16	0.217	P	1	4	5.67	
Elliott, Buck	50	0.262	SS				
Factor, Leonard	10	0.138	C				
Gardecki, Stan	<10						
Glover, Jim	<10		P				
Harris, Reese	<10						
Holden, Joe	39	0.272	M, C				
Houck, Fred	19	0.350	3B				
Jacobs, George			M				
Koval, George	<10		P				
LaPiana, Peter	27	0.155	3B				Cordele
Lindstrom, John	48	0.151	P, IF	8	22	4.69	
Lockman, Charles	<10						
Lokey, George	57	0.233	OF, IF				Cordele
Meaders, Elden	<10						
Neborak, Bill	<10						
Pelat, Frank	136	0.242	2B				
Rist, Ray	23	0.338	OF				
Roberts, Ray	23	0.262	3B				
Ryan, Bob	11	0.244	SS				
Salzman, Cy	51	0.206	SS				
Serners, Yorkey	80	0.203	C				
Singer, Hal	10	0.231	P	3	4	4.20	
Stone, Eddie	51	0.212	3B				
Swift, Fred	<10		P	0	1	4.50	
Weldon, Larry	45	0.233	P, IF	12	13	4.34	
Williams, Kerr	31	0.250	P	10	13	4.52	
Yonchuk, Walt	134	0.273	OF, IF				

Tallahassee, Florida
Team Operated by Tallahassee Baseball Club, Inc.
Team President: Fred N. Lowry
Secretary-Treasurer: Godfrey Smith
Business Manager: Franklin Powell
Manager(s): Hal Schultz
Games played at Centennial Field

Tallahassee Capitols Team Roster

NAME	G	BA	POS	W	L	ERA	APF
Burt, Tommy	40	0.135	P	9	16	4.29	Thomasville
Cappel, Lou	14	0.225	1B				
Crandall, Johnny	<10						
Hink, Bill	93	0.247	2B				Thomasville
Hisey, Ralph	56	0.178	P, IF	9	14	4.63	
Hocevar, Joe	<10		P	1	5	6.83	
Jaeckel, Roy	118	0.292	OF, IF				Cordele
Janci, Fred	45	0.244	1B				
Kimbrell, Casey	139	0.298	OF				
Kirksey, Calvin	23	0.101	P	12	8	3.03	
Lane, Leon	15	0.200	P	4	4	4.83	Cordele
Langston, Joe	12	0.182	P	5	3	2.06	
Lowe, Loui	18	0.221	3B				
Lowery, Cy	140	0.331	3B				
McVay, Frosty	106	0.248	2B				
Newcomb, Tete	127	0.288	1B, UT, P				
Radney, Joe	31	0.105	P	10	15	2.60	
Schultz, Hal	136	0.317	M, SS				
Settles, Wolf	47	0.227	P	17	14	3.72	
Smith, Del	133	0.250	OF				
Storie, Burl	117	0.252	C				

Thomasville, Georgia
Team Operated by Thomasville Baseball Association, Inc.
Team President: H.L. Key
Vice President: H.S. Feinberg
Secretary-Treasurer: W.E. Young
Business Manager: W.T. Jay
Manager(s): Moose Alexander
Games played at Municipal Stadium
Major League Affiliate: Washington Senators – American League.

Thomasville Tourists Team Roster

NAME	G	BA	POS	W	L	ERA	APF
Alexander, Moose	91	0.388	M, 1B				
Barnett, Lowell	112	0.320	P	6	7	2.89	
Bosser, Mel	49	0.246	P	23	11	3.58	
Bowers, Stew	11	0.286	P	4	6	4.71	
Burt, Tommy	40	0.135	P	9	16	4.29	Tallahassee
Cathey, Abner	38	0.194	P	20	8	3.27	
Colgan, Bill	<10						
Dove, Pat	121	0.315	P, 2B	4	4	6.11	
Ellis, Ralph	125	0.368	OF				
Gallagher, Charles	12	0.262	3B				
Gassoway, Paul	<10						
Gilstrap, John	<10						
Hink, Bill	93	0.247	2B				Tallahassee
Isert, Lou	36	0.187	SS				Albany
Ivey, Doug	<10		P				
Jordan, Kirby	52	0.318	OF				
Loveless, Deason	127	0.281	3B				
McKenzie, Sherwood	112	0.378	OF				
Pugh, Earl	<10		P				
Sauerbrun, Kip	22	0.210	P, IF	12	5	3.32	
Seat, Clayton	37	0.129	P	12	9	4.03	
Swoboda, Paul	22	0.338	1B				
Troy, Gordon	104	0.268	OF, IF				
Uhle, Stan	134	0.301	OF, IF, P				Americus
Ulisney, Mike	135	0.273	C				
Walters, Jim	12	0.148	P	2	4	7.58	
Yosipovich, Lou	10	0.100	OF				

Valdosta, Georgia
Team Operated by Valdosta Baseball Club, Inc.
Team President: T.G. Connell
Vice President: G.H. Oliver

Georgia Class-D Minor League Baseball Encyclopedia

Secretary: Nina Connell
Treasurer: O.R. Dobbs
Manager(s): Bill Morrell
Games played at Pendleton Park

Valdosta Trojans Team Roster

NAME	G	BA	POS	W	L	ERA	APF
Berry, Larry	24	0.176	C				
Brzowsky, Emil	15	0.167	P	2	4	5.94	
Contini, Bobby	16	0.311	OF				
Davis, Woody	<10		P	3	4	5.10	
Deal, Wally	52	0.200	P	18	15	3.07	
Forrest, Jim	<10		P				
Harrison, Dennie	81	0.269	3B				
Hartley, Travis	30	0.275	P	9	3	4.72	
Jackson, Gene	45	0.231	OF				
Kazak, Eddie	130	0.292	2B				
Kroll, Jim	68	0.236	OF				
Looney, Russ	24	0.288	OF, IF				
Lukon, John	116	0.226	OF				
Morrell, Bill	<10		M, P	2	2	6.35	
Patterson, Joe	54	0.274	P, IF	17	12	3.57	
Peppers, Dorsey	<10						
Podein, George	89	0.260	C, OF				
Riley, Pat	92	0.306	OF				
Robinson, Eddie	137	0.323	1B				
Rummans, Elmer	44	0.234	P	18	10	2.19	
Sierra, Andrew	15	0.161	P	4	5	3.76	
Stewart, Russ	106	0.242	SS				
Summerhill, Steve	113	0.307	OF				
Thomason, Harold	11	0.278	P	2	4	4.41	Waycross
Zimmerman, George	76	0.290	C				

Waycross, Georgia
Team Operated by Waycross Baseball Association, Inc.
Team President: Herbert Bradshaw
Vice President: W.D. Rivenbark
Secretary: O.K. Burgess
Treasurer: George Fesperman
Manager(s): Al Leitz
Games played at Ralph Newton Field

Waycross Bears Team Roster

NAME	G	BA	POS	W	L	ERA	APF
Atwater, Charlie	23	0.206	P	14	4	2.62	
Bennett, Frank	31	0.124	P	16	6	2.86	
Bevell, Pat	50	0.238	C				
Borden, Wallie	133	0.281	OF				
Brewster, Charlie	140	0.305	SS				
Clement, Ed	<10		P	2	3	1.13	
DeJohn, John	140	0.309	2B				
Embler, Jack	40	0.198	P	18	9	3.11	
Farrar, Charles	140	0.320	OF				
Hafey, Will	13	0.245	1B				
Horton, Marv	136	0.302	3B				
Hughes, Harry	127	0.338	1B				
Lawson, Elwood	43	0.174	P	26	6	3.16	
Lee, George	<10		P				
Leitz, Al	121	0.321	M, C				
Marsh, Jim E.	19	0.209	P	3	5	4.24	
Morgan, Billy	15	0.000	P	5	3	3.08	
Rados, Frank	<10						
Rucker, Bill	17	0.259	OF				
Smoll, John	<10		P				
Thomason, Harold	11	0.278	P	2	4	4.41	Valdosta
Thomassie, Pete	139	0.339	OF				
Wattigney, Ulysses	<10		P				
Wrobke, Joe	14	0.189	P	6	4	3.14	

1940 Georgia-Florida League Records
Batting

Highest Batting Average (minimum 100 at bats)
1. Moose Alexander – Thomasville .388
2. Sherwood McKenzie – Thomasville .378
3. Ralph Ellis – Thomasville .368
4. Felix Rios – Cordele .367
5. Pete Thomassie – Waycross .339

Most Hits
1. Ralph Ellis – Thomasville 203
2. Pete Thomassie – Waycross 193
3. Hal Schultz – Tallahassee 190
4. Charles Farrar – Waycross 187
5. Cy Lowery – Tallahassee 186

Most Runs
1. Russ Leach – Albany 131
2. Erv Dusak – Albany 125
3. Casey Kimbrell – Tallahassee 121
4. John DeJohn – Waycross 118
5. Ralph Ellis – Thomasville 115

Most Total Bases
1. Ralph Ellis – Thomasville 285
2. Charles Farrar – Waycross 279
3. Eddie Robinson – Valdosta 270
4. Erv Dusak – Albany 263
5. Pete Thomassie – Waycross 262

Most Doubles
1. Eddie Kazak – Valdosta 38
2. Erv Dusak – Albany 37
3. Ralph Ellis – Thomasville 35
4. Charles Farrar – Waycross 34
5. Stan Uhle – Thom/Amer 32

Most Triples
1. Casey Kimbrell – Tallahassee 22
2. Eddie Robinson – Valdosta 21
3. Ralph Ellis – Thomasville 16
4. Floyd Stickney – Albany 15
5. Charles Farrar – Waycross 14

Most Home Runs
1. Moose Alexander – Thomasville 14
2. Charlie Brewster – Waycross 12
3. Charles Farrar – Waycross 10
   Ed Filo – Albany 10
5. Eddie Robinson – Valdosta 8
   George Podein – Valdosta 8

Most Extra Base Hits
1. Charles Farrar – Waycross 58
2. Erv Dusak – Albany 56
   Ralph Ellis – Thomasville 56
4. Casey Kimbrell – Tallahassee 54
5. Moose Alexander – Thomasville 50
   Eddie Kazak – Valdosta 50

Most Runs Batted In
1. Charles Farrar – Waycross 131
2. Eddie Robinson – Valdosta 105
3. Ed Filo – Albany 103
4. Eddie Kazak – Valdosta 101
5. Erv Dusak – Albany 98
   Charlie Brewster – Waycross 98

Most Stolen Bases
1. Charlie Brewster – Waycross — 35
2. Pete Thomassie – Waycross — 34
3. Ralph Ellis – Thomasville — 25
4. Steve Summerhill – Valdosta — 23
5. Lowell Barnett – Thomasville — 22

Fielding
Most Put-Outs
1. Eddie Hoffman 1B – Americus — 1,376
2. Eddie Robinson 1B – Valdosta — 1,239
3. Harry Hughes 1B – Waycross — 1,234
4. Russ Leach 1B – Albany — 1,201
5. Walt Brickner 1B – Moultrie — 952

Most Assists
1. Charlie Brewster SS – Waycross — 475
2. Frank Pelat 2B – Moultrie — 461
3. Hal Schultz SS – Tallahassee — 441
4. Bitsy Mott SS – Americus — 409
5. John DeJohn 2B – Waycross — 390

Most Errors
1. Charlie Brewster SS – Waycross — 88
2. Bitsy Mott SS – Americus — 73
3. Marv Horton 3B – Waycross — 64
4. Hal Schultz SS – Tallahassee — 55
5. Floyd Stickney 3B – Albany — 54

Pitching
Most Wins
1. Elwood Lawson – Waycross — 26
2. Mel Bosser – Thomasville — 23
3. Glen Moulder – Americus — 20
   Abner Cathey – Thomasville — 20
   Stan Ferens – Albany — 20

Most Losses
1. John Lindstrom – Moultrie — 22
2. Walt Purcey – Cordele — 19
   Stan Wysocki – Cordele — 19
4. Tommy Burt – Thom/Tall — 16
5. Wally Deal – Valdosta — 15
   Joe Radney – Tallahassee — 15

Highest Winning Percentage (10 game minimum)
1. Elwood Lawson – Waycross — .813
2. Charlie Atwater – Waycross — .778
3. Travis Hartley – Valdosta — .750
4. Paul Cash – Albany — .739
5. Frank Bennett – Waycross — .727

Lowest Earned Run Average (100 inning minimum)
1. Elmer Rummans – Valdosta — 2.19
2. Stan Ferens – Albany — 2.34
3. Joe Radney – Tallahassee — 2.60
4. Harry Cohick – Americus — 2.61
5. Charlie Atwater – Waycross — 2.62

Most Strikeouts
1. Stan Ferens – Albany — 253
2. Elmer Rummans – Valdosta — 220
3. Abner Cathey – Thomasville — 186
4. Glen Moulder – Americus — 164
5. Joe Patterson – Valdosta — 158
   John Lindstrom – Moultrie — 158

Most Bases on Balls
1. Elwood Lawson – Waycross — 147
2. Ralph Hisey – Tallahassee — 142
3. Wolf Settles – Tallahassee — 137
4. Jim Burns – Moultrie — 125
5. Clayton Seat – Thomasville — 104

Most Hits Allowed
1. Walt Purcey – Cordele — 326
2. John Lindstrom – Moultrie — 321
3. Henry Weaver – Albany — 319
4. Mel Bosser – Thomasville — 316
5. Stan Wysocki – Cordele — 314

Most Innings Pitched
1. Wally Deal – Valdosta — 299
2. Walt Purcey – Cordele — 291
3. Stan Ferens – Albany — 289
4. Wolf Settles – Tallahassee — 281
5. Mel Bosser – Thomasville — 274

1940 Georgia-Florida League All-Star Team
1B Eddie Hoffman – Americus
2B Eddie Kazak – Valdosta
3B Cy Lowery – Tallahassee
SS Charlie Brewster – Waycross
OF Pete Thomassie – Waycross
OF Erv Dusak – Albany
OF Charles Farrar – Waycross
C Al Leitz – Waycross
UT Pat Dove – Thomasville
P Elmer Rummans – Valdosta
P Elwood Lawson – Waycross
M Moose Alexander – Thomasville

1941

Georgia-Florida League

League Office: Thomasville, Georgia
League President: A.D. "Doc" Walker
League Vice President: S.E. Teague
Secretary-Treasurer: Christine Brown
Salary Limit: $1,200 per month including manager.
Player Rule: Each club was allowed a roster of fourteen players, fifteen with bench manager, not more than four veterans, not more than six limited service, and not less than four rookies.
Umpires: C.C. Forrest, Charles V. Varble, Kenneth Day, Gus C. Hanke, J.W. Tyson, Jr. Byron Alexander, Don Atkinson, and Don Streets.

Georgia-Florida League Final Standings

Team	W	L	Pct	GB	Affiliate
Albany Cardinals	88	48	.647	----	STL-NL
Valdosta Trojans	85	51	.625	3.0	BRK-NL
Waycross Bears	84	54	.609	5.0	Unaffiliated
Thomasville Lookouts	69	67	.507	19.0	WSH-AL
Moultrie Packers	62	74	.456	26.0	PIT-NL
Americus Pioneers	56	81	.409	32.5	Unaffiliated
Cordele Reds	51	81	.386	35.0	CIN-NL
Tallahassee Capitols	47	86	.353	39.5	Unaffiliated

1941 Georgia-Florida League Map

(numbers on map correspond to the place each team finished in regular season play)

For a third straight season, the Georgia-Florida League lineup was comprised of the same eight clubs.

Albany's Eddie Kazak set the league's all-time record for the most hits in a season when he garnered 221 safe hits on the year. Ray Hamrick, Americus shortstop, set the all-time league mark for the most errors in a season when he booted 100.

After ending the season with the best record in the league, Albany faced third place Waycross in the first round of the post-season. Second place Valdosta took on Thomasville who ended up in the fourth spot of the final standings. Albany swept Waycross in three straight games, and Thomasville upset Valdosta three games to one. In the league championship series, it was Thomasville pulling another upset defeating Albany four games to three after finishing the regular season nineteen games out of first place. Thomasville went on to play in the Class D Interleague series against Florida State League champion Leesburg. That series also went the distance before it was won by Thomasville four games to three.

Albany, Georgia
Manager(s): Joe Cusick
Games played at Municipal Stadium
Major League Affiliate: St. Louis Cardinals – National League.

Albany Cardinals Team Roster

NAME	G	BA	POS	W	L	ERA	APF
Bakay, John	111	0.264	OF				
Burns, Jim	121	0.313	SS				
Cusick, Joe	123	0.310	M, C				
Dixon, Stokely	19	0.240	P	4	6		
Dudas, Al	15	0.258	OF				
Duff, Art	123	0.262	OF				
Hink, Bill	121	0.240	3B				Thomasville
Jackimchuk, Nick	34	0.296	SS				
Jefferson, Ernest	18	0.190	P	12	3	2.54	
Kazak, Eddie	135	0.378	2B				
Kleine, George	38	0.200	P	20	9	2.57	
Kopp, Clyde	19	0.193	OF				
Leach, Russ	136	0.326	1B				
LeBlanc, Rollie	116	0.318	OF				
Peterman, Irv	38	0.218	P	23	8	2.92	
Pfund, Lee	29	0.239	P	10	10	5.16	
Ragsdale, Joe	21	0.148	P	8	6	4.86	
Regan, John	8	0.133	OF				
Renko, Harry	53	0.277	P	11	6	4.44	
Sisler, George	14	0.236	2B				
Whitfield, Jim	26	0.238	OF				

Americus, Georgia
Team Operated by Americus Baseball Club, Inc.
Manager(s): Dick Luckey, Bill Rogers
Games played at Community Center Ballpark

Americus Pioneers Team Roster

NAME	G	BA	POS	W	L	ERA	APF
Armstrong, Carl	93	0.209	3B				Thomasville
Birchfield, Gilbert	40	0.149	P	12	15	4.28	
Black, Loyd	3	0.083	OF				
Brockelman, Bernard	138	0.283	1B				
Cohick, Harry	15	0.143	P	1	3	3.71	
Davis, Lisle	24	0.266	OF				
Dollard, Bob	5	0.333	P	1	1	7.04	
Duncan, Frank	24	0.135	P	2	8	4.88	
Fahan, Ed	80	0.291	2B				
Goodwin, Gil	11	0.182	2B, P	1	3	9.00	
Hamrick, Ray	138	0.272	SS				
Hoffman, Ed	30	0.268	P	3	7	5.88	
Hubbard, Herman	19	0.250	2B				
Johnson, Red	117	0.312	OF				
Kreitner, Mickey	100	0.232	C				
Kroll, Jim	134	0.260	3B				
Lampley, Bill	42	0.105	P	8	13	5.48	
Luckey, Dick	102	0.241	M, C, P	1	1	4.83	
Lukon, John	126	0.267	2B				Cordele
Manning, Tommy	35	0.169	OF				
Mehrens, Wallace	16	0.179	P	3	6	5.14	

Georgia Class-D Minor League Baseball Encyclopedia

NAME	G	BA	POS	W	L	ERA	APF
Miller, Howard	6	0.143	P	3	1	3.41	
Narieka, Joe	15	0.108	P	5	8	4.97	Moultrie
Riley, Pat	134	0.321	OF				
Rogers, Bill	8	0.071	M, P	1	2	6.50	
Smith, Norm	60	0.176	P	14	10	3.25	
Strohmeyer, Fred	13	0.077	P	3	4	5.52	
Tucker, Jim	3		P	0	2	9.00	
White, Ralph	21	0.139	2B				
Williams, Charlie	26	0.200	2B				Thomasville

Cordele, Georgia
Team Operated by Cordele Baseball Club, Inc.
Team President: W.D. Griffith
Vice President: T.E. Fletcher
Secretary-Treasurer: O.E. Scott
Manager(s): Bill Morrell
Games played at Cordele Baseball Park
Major League Affiliate: Cincinnati Reds – National League.

Cordele Reds Team Roster

NAME	G	BA	POS	W	L	ERA	APF
Berry, Larry	78	0.205	C				
Blackburn, Jim	12	0.174	P	1	3	7.16	
Brady, Ken	33	0.173	OF				
Burkholder, John	13	0.097	OF, P	1	0	4.71	
Colina, Eddie	35	0.270	2B				
Corley, Furman	22	0.267	P	1	11	4.82	
Dorin, Henry	5	0.167	P	1	3	5.52	
Fulwiler, Harold	8	0.290	OF				
High, Andy	4	0.400	2B				
Hill, Bob	40	0.133	P	18	12	7.06	
Hutcherson, Billy	14	0.255	2B				
Johnson, Eli	9	0.391	2B				
Kress, Charlie	104	0.325	1B				
Looney, Russ	64	0.263	OF				
Lukon, John	126	0.267	2B				Americus
Mackey, John	17	0.300	P	1	3	5.17	
McCorry, ---	4		P	0	3	5.29	Thomasville
Milcsik, Ray	28	0.182	SS				
Miller, Harold	57	0.179	P	13	15	4.26	
Mitchell, Joe Bob	85	0.354	OF, P	1	1	6.00	
Moore, Hugh	18	0.200	3B				
Morrell, Bill	8	0.133	M, P	2	3	8.29	
Mott, Bitsy	6	0.136	OF				
Peppers, Dorsey	7	0.200	OF				
Podein, George	114	0.238	3B				
Shannon, Jack	22	0.095	P	2	4	3.84	
Shumaker, Bob	29	0.305	3B				
Snyder, Ralph	47	0.171	C				
Stapenhorst, Jean	25	0.188	P	3	9	4.35	
Taylor, Gene	29	0.068	P	7	15	4.33	
Tysinger, Everett	122	0.242	SS				
Ward, Bill	54	0.282	OF				
Wolf, Lawrence	124	0.242	OF				

Moultrie, Georgia
Team Operated by Moultrie Baseball Club, Inc.
Team President: David Cohn
Manager(s): Buzz Arlitt, Kip Sauerbrun
Games played at Moultrie Stadium
Major League Affiliate: Pittsburgh Pirates – National League.

Moultrie Packers Team Roster

NAME	G	BA	POS	W	L	ERA	APF
Arlitt, Buzz	132	0.346	M, 1B, P	1	0	5.00	
Ball, Bob	18	0.154	C				
Brickner, Walt	132	0.337	OF				
Brooks, Warren	95	0.261	SS				
Brown, ---	3		P	1	0	5.54	

NAME	G	BA	POS	W	L	ERA	APF
Buffington, Jack	9	0.323	3B				
Burns, Jim	73	0.303	P	12	13	3.77	
Burrows, John	6		P	1	3	9.00	
Castiglione, Pete	92	0.280	3B				
Chew, Ray	4	0.167	C				
Coulling, Stan	35	0.138	P	11	11	4.04	
Demma, Sam	79	0.209	C				Waycross
Dietz, Bill	39	0.193	P	14	12	4.44	
Dispenziere, Carmen	8	0.280	OF				
Ewer, Seaborn	6	0.240	OF				
Gibson, Charlie	128	0.266	OF, P	1	1	4.71	
Grant, Charlie	46	0.219	2B				Tallahassee
Harjo, Fesser	7	0.154	P	0	2	7.64	
Lenn, Wayne	3		P	0	0	20.25	
McCloskey, Frank	7	0.185	OF				
Nafus, Virgil	28	0.143	P	9	10	2.92	
Narieka, Joe	15	0.108	P	5	8	4.97	Americus
Nelson, Bob	24	0.267					
Reeser, Eddie	28	0.267	C				
Ryan, Bob	123	0.240	2B				
Sauerbrun, Kip	20	0.178	M, P	8	5	1.40	Thomasville
Serners, Yorkey	8	0.174	C				
Shank, Doug	13	0.118	P	2	4	7.66	
Singer, Hal	4		P	0	2	15.23	
Stewart, Buford	56	0.248	C				
Strosser, Walt	110	0.284	OF				
Whalen, ---	4		P	0	1	2.57	
Willey, Joe	16	0.188	P	1	6	3.64	
Wingo, Kelly	38	0.230	3B				

Tallahassee, Florida
Team Operated by Tallahassee Baseball Club, Inc.
Team President: Fred N. Lowry
Vice President: A.E. Bagnall
Secretary-Treasurer: Godfrey Smith
Manager(s): Lance Richbourg
Games played at Centennial Field

Tallahassee Capitols Team Roster

NAME	G	BA	POS	W	L	ERA	APF
Bernat, Walt	8	0.207	SS				
Blackwell, Dan	62	0.237	OF				
Bogart, Gene	57	0.234	3B				
Bolster, Harvey	30	0.168	OF				
Brewster, Bill	20	0.264	OF				
Burton, Leonard	11	0.160	P	2	6	4.13	
Christakis, George	8	0.172	2B				
Eaton, Joe	132	0.253	1B				
Eure, Carlton	130	0.269	OF, P	0	0	4.22	
Fowler, Cecil	4	0.167	OF				
Frey, Larry	9	0.286	P	1	1	6.86	
Grant, Charlie	46	0.219	2B				Moultrie
Hinrichs, Wayne	36	0.182	P	10	14	3.82	
Jaeckel, Roy	50	0.193	OF				
Johnson, Emmitt	64	0.283	3B				
Kirksey, Calvin	88	0.245	OF, P	9	20	4.66	
Kirksey, Calvin	35	0.264	P				
Langston, Joe	36	0.169	P	5	16	4.73	
Larimer, Roger	17	0.128	P	7	7	3.06	
Lowery, Cy	81	0.311	OF				
Newlin, Bob	3		P	0	0	12.00	
Radney, Joe	44	0.200	P	12	16	3.66	
Richbourg, Lance			M				
Russo, Manuel	48	0.258	3B				
Schellhouse, Fred	26	0.198	2B				
Smith, Del	131	0.259	OF				Thomasville
Sparks, Hugh	11	0.150	P	1	5	4.25	
Storie, Burl	124	0.268	C				
Watts, Bill	44	0.223	SS				
Williams, Norm	10	0.083	SS				

Georgia Class-D Minor League Baseball Encyclopedia

Wilson, Hugh	83	0.248	2B				

Thomasville, Georgia
Team Operated by Thomasville Baseball Association, Inc.
Team President: Harry S. Feinberg
Secretary: J.H. Whiddon
Business Manager: Joseph Feinberg
Manager(s): Kip Sauerbrun
Games played at Municipal Stadium
Major League Affiliate: Washington Senators – American League.

Thomasville Lookouts Team Roster

NAME	G	BA	POS	W	L	ERA	APF
Anderson, Jack	102	0.287	1B				
Armstrong, Carl	93	0.209	3B				Americus
Atwater, Charlie	16	0.314	P	6	5	5.58	Waycross
Bevil, Lou	54	0.163	P	17	15	3.80	
Buffington, Rex	31	0.148	P	14	11	3.32	
Burt, Tommy	2		P	0	2	8.00	
Chetaitis, Stan	12	0.182	C				
Dove, Pat	64	0.337	3B				
English, Edgar	14	0.111	P	3	3	5.01	
Fortuna, Walter	9	0.167	OF				
Gaillard, Mel	54	0.285	OF				
Gaisser, Roy	5		P	0	0	13.50	
Gassoway, Paul	55	0.227	C				
Grimes, Mike	23	0.189	C				
Hargrove, Woody	46	0.322	OF, P	2	0	1.50	
Hink, Bill	121	0.240	3B				Albany
Massey, Terrance	8	0.296	OF				
McClusky, LeRoy	5	0.050	OF				
McCorry, ---	4		P	0	3	5.29	Cordele
McVay, Frosty	127	0.321	2B				
Minner, Paul	3		P	0	2	6.43	
Peterson, Jerry	21	0.242	P	1	1	8.70	
Roede, Lou	130	0.284	OF				
Rogers, Lou	16	0.222	P	3	3	3.00	
Sasse, ---	3		P	0	1	5.73	
Sauerbrun, Kip	20	0.178	M, P	8	5	1.40	Moultrie
Smith, Del	131	0.259	OF				Tallahassee
Sullivan, John	136	0.323	SS				
Ulisney, Mike	66	0.223	C				
Webb, Leroy	48	0.240	P	11	14	4.35	
Wiley, Jack	28	0.104	P	13	7	3.02	
Williams, Charlie	26	0.200	2B				Americus
Wingard, Ernie	34	0.271	1B				
Zivich, George	15	0.193	OF				

Valdosta, Georgia
Team Operated by Valdosta Baseball Club, Inc.
Team President: Charles Singleton
Vice President: Branch Rickey, Jr.
Secretary: Mickey McConnell
Business Manager: E.J. Bavasi
Manager(s): Stew Hofferth
Games played at Pendleton Park
Major League Affiliate: Brooklyn Dodgers – National League.

Valdosta Trojans Team Roster

NAME	G	BA	POS	W	L	ERA	APF
Archipoli, Andy	101	0.302	3B				
Behrman, Hank	44	0.165	P	18	10	3.11	
Brydon, Bob	78	0.330	OF				
Burpo, Howard	43	0.189	P	2	4	5.14	
Cibrowski, Marion	129	0.323	OF, P	0	1	1.13	
Danielson, Dan	88	0.286	2B				
Davis, Hargrove	8	0.200	OF				
Gordon, Melvin	27	0.048	P	16	7	1.98	
Hansen, Henry	9	0.125	P	4	3	3.49	
Hernandez, John	48	0.290	1B				
Hofferth, Stew	132	0.338	M, C				
Hoffman, Eddie	57	0.254	1B				
Keough, John	51	0.242	3B				
Koch, Art	31	0.123	P	14	10	4.04	
Lindquist, Carl	4		P	1	1	3.86	
McBride, Harold	3		P	1	0	3.21	
Nowak, Ed	2		P	0	2	54.00	
Persoskie, Metro	45	0.195	P	9	7	3.82	
Rackley, Marv	133	0.322	OF				
Rey, Emil	127	0.204	SS				
Samaklis, Charles	36	0.196	P	20	6	2.15	
Sholtzs, ---	3	0.231	1B				
Summerhill, Steve	116	0.303	3B				
Whitley, Shirley	4	0.133	OF				

Waycross, Georgia
Team Operated by Waycross Baseball Association, Inc.
Team President: M.M. Monroe
Vice President: O.K. Burgess
Secretary-Treasurer: George Fesperman
Manager(s): Al Leitz
Games played at Ralph Newton Field

Waycross Bears Team Roster

NAME	G	BA	POS	W	L	ERA	APF
Atwater, Charlie	16	0.314	P	6	5	5.58	Thomasville
Barnett, John	43	0.168	P	18	9	2.51	
Borden, Wallie	138	0.285	OF				
Brewster, Charlie	78	0.330	SS				
Colgan, Bill	72	0.249	OF				
Cronin, Frank	10	0.200	P	6	2	2.28	
Demma, Sam	79	0.209	C				Moultrie
Farrar, Charles	48	0.303	1B				
Green, ---	4		OF				
Hartz, John	27	0.185	P	17	8	3.70	
Horton, Marv	78	0.314	3B				
Johnson, Bob	29	0.255	SS				
Kelly, Jack	138	0.243	2B				
Kelly, Oliver	112	0.298	SS				
Leitz, Al	128	0.315	M, C				
McGee, Wilson	3		P	1	0	1.64	
McGowen, Mickey	32	0.158	P	14	14	2.73	
Morgan, Billy	4	0.222	P	0	2	1.64	
Morris, Teddy	27	0.210	P	11	10	3.88	
Sowell, Julian	21	0.172	P	12	6	2.22	
Spivey, Bill	13	0.154	C				
Thompson, Leon	10	0.162	1B				
Willoughby, Carl	123	0.262	1B				
Woddail, Charles	138	0.323	OF				

1941 Georgia-Florida League Records
Batting
Highest Batting Average (minimum 100 at bats)
1. Eddie Kazak – Albany .378
2. Joe Bob Mitchell – Cordele .354
3. Buzz Arlitt – Moultrie .346
4. Stew Hofferth – Valdosta .338
5. Pat Dove – Thomasville .337
   Walt Brickner – Moultrie .337

Most Hits
1. Eddie Kazak – Albany 221
2. Russ Leach – Albany 184
3. John Sullivan – Thomasville 183
   Marv Rackley – Valdosta 183

Georgia Class-D Minor League Baseball Encyclopedia

5. Charles Woddail – Waycross   174

Most Runs
1. Eddie Kazak – Albany   133
2. Russ Leach – Albany   128
3. Pat Riley – Americus   126
4. John Sullivan – Thomasville   124
5. Jim Burns – Tallahassee   121

Most Total Bases
1. Eddie Kazak – Albany   290
2. Marv Rackley – Valdosta   250
3. Buzz Arlitt – Moultrie   242
4. Russ Leach – Albany   239
5. Pat Riley – Americus   238

Most Doubles
1. Eddie Kazak – Albany   45
2. Buzz Arlitt – Moultrie   33
    Ray Hamrick – Americus   33
4. Pat Riley – Americus   32
    Stew Hofferth – Valdosta   32

Most Triples
1. Charlie Kress – Cordele   17
2. Marv Rackley – Valdosta   15
3. Lou Roede – Thomasville   14
    Oliver Kelly – Waycross   14
5. Steve Summerhill – Valdosta   13

Most Home Runs
1. Joe Bob Mitchell – Cordele   12
2. Art Duff – Albany   11
    Pat Riley – Americus   11
4. Lou Roede – Thomasville   10
5. Walt Strosser – Moultrie   9
    Red Johnson – Americus   9

Most Extra Base Hits
1. Eddie Kazak – Albany   56
2. Pat Riley – Americus   49
    Lou Roede – Thomasville   49
    Charlie Kress – Cordele   49
5. Buzz Arlitt – Moultrie   48

Most Runs Batted In
1. Russ Leach – Albany   117
2. Rollie LeBlanc – Albany   114
3. Eddie Kazak – Albany   113
4. Al Leitz – Waycross   98
5. Pat Riley – Americus   95

Most Stolen Bases
1. Charlie Brewster – Waycross   41
2. Marion Cibrowski – Valdosta   31
3. Jim Burns – Albany   29
4. Pat Riley – Americus   25
5. John Lukon – Cord/Amer   24

Fielding
Most Put-Outs
1. Bernard Brockelman 1B – Americus   1,243
2. Buzz Arlitt 1B, P – Moultrie   1,169
3. Russ Leach 1B – Albany   1,161
4. Joe Eaton 1B – Tallahassee   1,140
5. Carl Willoughby 1B – Waycross   1,081

Most Assists
1. Ray Hamrick SS – Americus   486
2. John Sullivan SS – Thomasville   471
3. Emil Rey SS – Valdosta   420
4. Eddie Kazak 2B – Albany   383
5. Jack Kelly 2B – Waycross   377

Most Errors
1. Ray Hamrick SS – Americus   100
2. John Sullivan SS – Thomasville   83
3. Everett Tysinger SS – Cordele   80
4. Jim Burns SS – Albany   75
5. Emil Rey SS – Valdosta   74

Pitching
Most Wins
1. Irv Peterman – Albany   23
2. Charles Samaklis – Valdosta   20
    George Kleine – Albany   20
4. Hank Behrman – Valdosta   18
    Bob Hill – Cordele   18
    John Barnett – Waycross   18

Most Losses
1. Calvin Kirksey – Tallahassee   20
2. Joe Radney – Tallahassee   16
    Joe Langston – Tallahassee   16
4. Lou Bevil – Thomasville   15
    Harold Miller – Cordele   15
    Gilbert Birchfield – Americus   15
    Gene Taylor – Cordele   15

Highest Winning Percentage (10 game minimum)
1. Ernest Jefferson – Albany   .800
2. Charles Samaklis – Valdosta   .769
3. Irv Peterman – Albany   .742
4. Melvin Gordon – Valdosta   .696
5. George Kleine – Albany   .690

Lowest Earned Run Average (100 inning minimum)
1. Kip Sauerbrun – Thom/Moul   1.40
2. Melvin Gordon – Valdosta   1.98
3. Charles Samaklis – Valdosta   2.15
4. Julian Sowell – Waycross   2.22
5. John Barnett – Waycross   2.51

Most Strikeouts
1. Joe Radney – Tallahassee   220
2. Lou Bevil – Thomasville   182
3. Mickey McGowan – Waycross   180
4. Bill Dietz – Moultrie   177
5. Hank Behrman – Valdosta   175

Most Bases on Balls
1. Jim Burns – Moultrie   149
2. Joe Langston – Tallahassee   148
3. Lou Bevil – Thomasville   143
4. Bill Dietz – Moultrie   127
5. Gilbert Birchfield – Americus   122

Most Hits Allowed
1. John Barnett – Waycross   287
2. Joe Radney – Tallahassee   283
    George Kleine – Albany   283
4. Calvin Kirksey – Tallahassee   263
5. Irv Peterman – Albany   261

Most Innings Pitched
1. Joe Radney – Tallahassee   273
2. Irv Peterman – Albany   262
3. George Kleine – Albany   259
4. Lou Bevil – Thomasville   256
5. Hank Behrman – Valdosta   252

1941 Georgia-Florida League All-Star Team
- 1B Russ Leach – Albany
- 2B Eddie Kazak – Albany
- 3B Pete Castiglione – Moultrie
- SS John Sullivan – Thomasville
- OF Rollie LeBlanc – Albany
- OF Lou Roede – Thomasville
- OF Marion Cibrowski – Valdosta
- C   Al Leitz – Waycross
- UT Frosty McVay – Thomasville
- P   Melvin Gordon – Valdosta
- P   Mickey McGowan – Waycross
- M   Stew Hofferth – Valdosta

1942

Georgia-Florida League

League President: W.T. Anderson

Georgia-Florida League Final Standings

Team	W	L	Pct	GB	Affiliate
Valdosta Trojans	81	45	.643	----	BRK-NL
Waycross Bears	72	54	.571	9.0	Unaffiliated
Moultrie Packers	72	54	.571	9.0	PIT-NL
Dothan Browns	64	62	.508	17.0	STL-AL
Tallahassee Capitols	62	64	.482	19.0	Unaffiliated
Albany Cardinals	56	70	.444	25.0	STL-NL
Americus Pioneers	49	77	.389	32.0	CHI-NL
Cordele Reds	48	78	.381	33.0	CIN-NL

1942 Georgia-Florida League Map

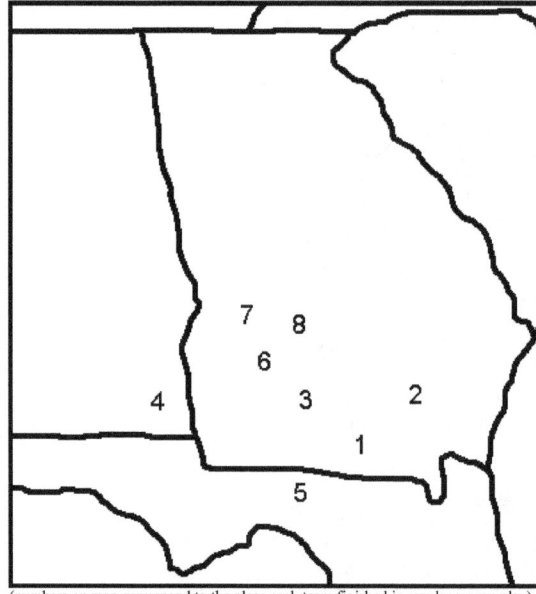

(numbers on map correspond to the place each team finished in regular season play)

For the first and only time in the history of the Georgia-Florida League, a club from Alabama was admitted. Dothan, who had always been in the Alabama-Florida League or the Alabama State League, spent their only season in another league. This new addition to the circuit came when Thomasville dropped out during the off-season.

Dave Pluss of Valdosta set the league's all-time record for the most triples in a season when he reached third 23 times from his own bat.

Valdosta topped the league at the end of the regular season. Tied for second place, Waycross and Moultrie played a one-game tie breaker. Moultrie lost this game and took on Valdosta in the first round of the post-season championship tournament, and Waycross played fourth place Dothan in round one. Valdosta defeated Moultrie three games to one, and Waycross blanked Dothan in three straight games. Waycross upset Valdosta to win the championship series four games to one.

The 1942 season was overshadowed by the beginnings of World War II. Following the baseball season, the Georgia-

Georgia Class-D Minor League Baseball Encyclopedia

Florida League, as well as many of the other minor leagues, suspended operations.

Albany, Georgia
Manager(s): Joe Cusick
Games played at Municipal Stadium
Major League Affiliate: St. Louis Cardinals – National League.

Albany Cardinals Team Roster

NAME	G	BA	POS	W	L	ERA	APF
Bakay, John	126	0.345	OF				
Barry, Gene	19	0.234	OF				
Beane, Ed	7	0.087	P	2	3	3.63	
Blevins, Jesse	2	0.333	C				
Bowen, Harold	70	0.249	OF				
Brady, ---	8		P	2	2	6.27	
Britchet, Jackson	34	0.188	P	8	10	2.51	
Cavaness, Jim	14	0.222	3B				
Cusick, Joe	96	0.312	M, C				
Diering, Chuck	126	0.305	OF				
Duda, John	18	0.217	P, OF	5	7	4.50	
Gravino, Frank	52	0.198	P	13	9	3.52	
Grish, Steve	118	0.274	3B				
Guerriero, ---	4		P	2	1	5.25	
Hanna, John	5		P	0	3	6.83	
Harms, Carl	14	0.133	P	2	5	5.31	
Haynes, Bill	3		P	0	1	4.85	
Lazar, Steve	80	0.270	2B				
Lenn, Ed	126	0.276	1B				
Linneman, Joe	11	0.105	P	3	6	6.25	
Miller, Ray	44	0.230	2B				
Moore, Hugh	1	0.200	SS				
Roe, ---	13		P	0	2	9.00	
Schoendienst, Red	68	0.269	2B, SS				
Sisler, George	11	0.381	2B				
Smith, John	42	0.214	P	14	8	3.05	
Wroblewski, Erwin	95	0.261	2B, SS				
Wulf, Gene	8	0.278	P	2	6	4.88	

Americus, Georgia
Manager(s): Jerry Tiemann
Games played at Community Center Ballpark
Major League Affiliate: Chicago Cubs – National League.

Americus Pioneers Team Roster

NAME	G	BA	POS	W	L	ERA	APF
Bartholomew, ---	7		P	0	3	2.37	
Carlson, Bob	67	0.234	2B				
Carlson, Ray	40	0.229	OF				
Collins, Bill	7	0.471	OF				
Euliss, Walt	5	0.167	P	0	4	9.00	
Fitzgerald, Lou	25	0.240	3B, SS				
Gast, Mike	8	0.083	P	6	2	2.73	
George, Johnny	6	0.091	C				
Guth, Gene	33	0.145	P	10	14	3.83	
Jameson, Don	86	0.304	C, OF				
Johnson, Red	97	0.270	OF				
Knoll, Frank	19	0.176	OF				
Koltz, Ted	9	0.087	P	3	5	3.00	
Kuwala, Ed	5	0.095	2B				
Macrinotis, Lou	126	0.276	3B				
McQuillen, Jack	73	0.217	OF				
Molinder, Walt	6	0.067	P	1	4	5.65	
Moss, Les	109	0.299	C				
Okey, Kene	7		P	3	4	4.81	
Patterson, Britt	11		P	1	4	5.95	
Phillips, Dave	23	0.073	P	6	12	4.38	
Riley, Leonard	28	0.262	SS				
Sellergren, Willard	26	0.195	2B				
Thomas, George	14	0.182	OF				
Tiemann, Jerry	121	0.316	M, 1B				
Varner, Paul	75	0.358	SS				
Vaughn, Gene	61	0.314	P, OF	10	9	2.62	
Wiggins, LeRoy	7		P	1	2	6.97	
Willis, Clarence	48	0.193	P	9	9	4.12	
Zoeller, Simon Lee	36	0.250	2B				

Cordele, Georgia
Manager(s): Frank O'Rourke
Games played at Cordele Baseball Park
Major League Affiliate: Cincinnati Reds – National League.

Cordele Reds Team Roster

NAME	G	BA	POS	W	L	ERA	APF
Blackburn, Jim	24	0.290	P	8	11	3.76	
Dittus, George	41	0.229	1B				
Evans, Robert	31	0.368	OF				
Feie, Bill	12		P	4	1	4.65	
Hoderlein, Mel	87	0.249	SS				
Hutcherson, Billy	34	0.258	OF				
Jaeckel, Roy	92	0.251	2B				
Kirby, Jim	61	0.254	OF				
Liles, Tommy	71	0.261	1B				
Malone, Frank	22	0.171	2B				
McDaniel, Ernest	38	0.160	P	11	13	4.73	
Milcsik, Ray	12	0.104	SS				
O'Rourke, Frank			M				
O'Toole, Dan	15	0.189	P	5	8	7.50	
Petty, Vern	97	0.336	3B				
Plaia, Benny	28	0.148	P	9	15	3.36	
Ramsey, Don	114	0.252	C				
Rasch, Marvin	124	0.261	OF				
Robinson, Harold	10	0.091	P	2	5	7.60	Dothan
Romello, Mike	14	0.263	SS				
Satterfield, Ben	29	0.169	P	5	9	3.96	
Satterfield, Ralph	27	0.226	SS				
Vucelich, Milan	61	0.243	P	4	10	5.47	
Wanstrath, Bill	70	0.270	OF				
Wentworth, Dick	88	0.181	C				
Werther, ---	6		P	1	4	4.50	

Dothan, Alabama
Manager(s): Holt Milner
Major League Affiliate: St. Louis Browns – American League.

Dothan Browns Team Roster

NAME	G	BA	POS	W	L	ERA	APF
Appleby, Ellis	33	0.189	3B				
Ashworth, Johnny	6	0.231	P	1	2	7.31	
Austin, Bob	8		P	3	5	5.57	
Austin, Forrest	56	0.292	OF				
Brannon, Shaw	23	0.154	C				
Ciccimarro, John	33	0.164	SS				
Click, Jim	39	0.313	OF				
Fair, Paul	53	0.369	2B				
Fraker, Dick	34	0.180	OF				
Graham, Tom	15	0.143	P	7	8	2.52	
Grant, Charlie	70	0.288	2B				
Hair, Bill	40	0.162	P	12	11	3.36	
Howell, Dixie	32	0.345	SS				
Johnson, Marion	32	0.285	3B				
Kimbrell, Wilbur	11	0.238	SS				
Knapp, Roy	82	0.241	C				
Maxwell, Bob	72	0.214	P	18	12	2.89	
Milner, Holt	110	0.294	M, 1B				
Milner, Jim	108	0.316	OF				
Moore, Ed	7	0.217	OF				
Pride, Jude	53	0.218	SS				

Georgia Class-D Minor League Baseball Encyclopedia

Name	G	BA	POS	W	L	ERA	APF
Robinson, Harold	10	0.091	P	2	5	7.60	Cordele
Snider, Floyd	20	0.250	OF				
Stevens, ---	2		P	1	1	0.00	
Stokes, Don	51	0.256	3B				
Taylor, Q.P.	112	0.262	C				
West, Tom	29	0.253	P	7	11	4.76	
Wiggins, LeRoy	13	0.080	P	4	1	4.18	
Williams, Wallace	17	0.250	P	8	3	3.98	
Young, Bill	26	0.265	OF				

Moultrie, Georgia
Manager(s): Frosty McVay
Games played at Moultrie Stadium
Major League Affiliate: Pittsburgh Pirates – National League.

Moultrie Packers Team Roster

NAME	G	BA	POS	W	L	ERA	APF
Benson, Gene	21	0.250	OF				
Brooks, Warren	104	0.285	SS				
Burns, Jim	73	0.241	P	15	15	3.46	
Butkus, Carl	15	0.250	C				
Carter, Larry	125	0.298	1B				
Coccetti, Al	125	0.274	OF				
Coulling, Stan	26	0.153	P	10	9	2.75	
Dukovich, ---	11		P	1	5	6.64	
Ganss, Bob	83	0.240	C				
Gibson, Charlie	122	0.279	OF, P	2	2	4.50	
Johnson, ---	4		P	0	3	6.38	
McGee, Wilson	26	0.210	P	9	8	4.34	
McVay, Frosty	120	0.294	M, 2B				
Myers, Jim	126	0.235	OF				
Petroziello, Carl	125	0.250	3B				
Sauerbrun, Kip	23	0.203	P	13	5	1.83	
Skaggs, Earl	13	0.179	C				
Wright, Paul	41	0.180	P	20	8	2.57	

Tallahassee, Florida
Manager(s): Will Good
Games played at Centennial Stadium

Tallahassee Capitols Team Roster

NAME	G	BA	POS	W	L	ERA	APF
Ballentine, Curtis	103	0.234	1B, OF				
Davids, Roland	42	0.140	P	7	13	5.16	
Dixon, Stokely	29	0.147	P	10	8	3.69	
Dulancy, C.A.	13	0.122	OF				
Eckenroth, Leroy	21	0.203	3B				
Good, Will			M				
Groat, Clarence	104	0.300	OF				
Herrell, Don	68	0.235	1B				
Jackson, Earl	99	0.275	3B				
Kirkland, Dan	43	0.254	OF				
Kirksey, Bill	50	0.186	C				
Kirksey, Calvin	45	0.198	P	20	18	2.82	
Krinsky, Robert	60	0.197	C				
Latsko, George	122	0.307	OF				
Nemier, ---	4	0.308	C				
Radney, Joe	41	0.192	P	18	14	3.54	
Reid, Warren	16	0.087	P	3	6	5.85	
Salter, Desmond	64	0.275	3B				
Seiler, Dan	113	0.226	2B				
Smith, Ed	11	0.048	P	3	1	4.15	
Tarzi, ---	7	0.115	2B				
Trammell, Wes	122	0.274	SS				

Valdosta, Georgia
Manager(s): Stew Hofferth, Clancy Odell
Games played at Pendleton Park
Major League Affiliate: Brooklyn Dodgers – National League.

Valdosta Trojans Team Roster

NAME	G	BA	POS	W	L	ERA	APF
Basgall, Monty	126	0.253	2B				
Beringhele, Basil	53	0.252	1B				
Bodan, Joe	86	0.258	OF				
Bowland, Art	126	0.302	OF				
Clancy, Bud	48	0.287	1B				
Demchuk, Bill	4		P	1	0	3.18	
Dunn, Ed	7		P	2	4	2.80	
Henderson, Chuck	81	0.329	3B				
Hofferth, Stew	62	0.365	M, C				
Koch, Art	22	0.100	P	14	7	2.61	
Lown, Turk	29	0.247	P	18	8	1.94	
McBride, Harold	16	0.171	P	7	5	2.94	
McCann, Cliff	20	0.102	P	6	8	3.63	
McCorkle, Bob	14	0.260	C				
Morgan, Fred	43	0.263	P	16	6	2.80	
Odell, Clancy			M				
Pluss, Dave	118	0.305	OF				
Rey, Emil	115	0.251	SS				
Ruminski, Frank	8	0.300	P	6	0	1.42	
Silky, Harold	14	0.152	P	6	1	2.82	
Summerhill, Steve	114	0.350	OF				
Taylor, Furman	13	0.341	P	5	6	4.22	
Thomas, Jim	10	0.378	OF				
Urban, Hubert	3		P	1	0	4.15	
Welp, Bill	59	0.340	C				

Waycross, Georgia
Manager(s): Al Leitz
Games played at Ralph Newton Field

Waycross Bears Team Roster

NAME	G	BA	POS	W	L	ERA	APF
Bryant, Jim	13	0.351	P	7	2	2.60	
Chambers, Inman	34	0.256	P	13	13	3.08	
Cronin, Frank	18	0.200	P	9	5	4.29	
Curley, Jim	17	0.188	SS				
Curtis, Turk	3	0.273	P	3	0	0.33	
Douglas, David	26	0.233	OF				
Flair, Elmer	44	0.250	OF				
Gautreaux, Joe	22	0.103	P	7	12	3.27	
Hill, Bob	27	0.322	P	19	4	2.03	
Howell, Bryan	127	0.314	OF				
Kelly, Jack	123	0.245	2B				
Leitz, Al	107	0.315	M, C				
Mathis, Willie	103	0.037	3B				
Mediamolle, Frank	126	0.247	1B				
Pinner, Ted	69	0.242	SS				
Ramsey, Bill	31	0.201	OF				
Robinson, Tom	117	0.299	OF				
Tracy, Bill	59	0.234	C				
Vitari, Joe	21	0.253	SS				
Walker, Bill	31	0.219	P	9	11	2.52	
Zernial, Gus	95	0.286	OF				

1942 Georgia-Florida League Records
Batting
Highest Batting Average (minimum 100 at bats)
1. Robert Evans – Cordele   .368
2. Stew Hofferth – Valdosta   .365
3. Paul Varner – Americus   .358
4. Steve Summerhill – Valdosta   .350

Georgia Class-D Minor League Baseball Encyclopedia

5. Dixie Howell – Dothan .345

Most Hits
1. Steve Summerhill – Valdosta 165
2. John Bakay – Albany 163
3. Bryan Howell – Waycross 160
4. Art Bowland – Valdosta 149
5. Jim Milner – Dothan 147

Most Runs
1. Chuck Diering – Albany 102
2. Art Bowland – Valdosta 100
3. Dave Pluss – Valdosta 94
4. George Latsko – Tallahassee 90
5. Clarence Groat – Tallahassee 89

Most Total Bases
1. Steve Summerhill – Valdosta 232
2. Dave Pluss – Valdosta 228
3. John Bakay – Albany 211
4. Bryan Howell – Waycross 210
5. Chuck Diering – Albany 190
   Jim Milner – Dothan 190

Most Doubles
1. Vern Petty – Cordele 38
2. Steve Summerhill – Valdosta 33
3. Frosty McVay – Moultrie 30
4. Jim Milner – Dothan 27
5. *five players tied with 26

Most Triples
1. Dave Pluss – Valdosta 23
2. Steve Summerhill – Valdosta 14
3. Steve Grish – Albany 13
4. Carl Petroziello – Moultrie 12
   Stew Hofferth – Valdosta 12

Most Home Runs
1. Dave Pluss – Valdosta 9
   Red Johnson – Americus 9
3. Marvin Rasch – Cordele 7
4. Al Coccetti – Moultrie 4
5. *nine players tied with 3

Most Extra Base Hits
1. Steve Summerhill – Valdosta 49
2. Dave Pluss – Valdosta 48
3. Vern Petty – Cordele 43
4. Red Johnson – Americus 38
   Charlie Gibson – Moultrie 38

Most Runs Batted In
1. Dave Pluss – Valdosta 105
2. Steve Summerhill – Valdosta 95
3. John Bakay – Albany 94
4. Charlie Gibson – Moultrie 88
5. Ed Lenn – Albany 86

Most Stolen Bases
1. Art Bowland – Valdosta 26
2. Willie Mathis – Waycross 25
3. Roy Knapp – Dothan 24
4. Steve Summerhill – Valdosta 21
5. Jim Milner – Dothan 19
   Erwin Wroblewski – Albany 19
   Chuck Henderson – Valdosta 19

Fielding
Most Put-Outs
1. Frank Mediamolle 1B – Waycross 1,186
2. Larry Carter 1B – Moultrie 1,107
3. Jerry Tiemann 1B – Americus 1,080
4. Ed Lenn 1B – Albany 1,069
5. Holt Milner 1B – Dothan 1,022

Most Assists
1. Monty Basgall 2B – Valdosta 502
2. Emil Rey SS – Valdosta 402
3. Frosty McVay 2B – Moultrie 360
4. Jack Kelly 2B – Waycross 357
5. Erwin Wroblewski 2B, SS – Albany 315

Most Errors
1. Mel Hoderlein SS – Cordele 64
2. Warren Brooks SS – Moultrie 59
3. Erwin Wroblewski 2B, SS – Albany 52
4. Wes Trammell SS – Tallahassee 51
5. Steve Grish 3B – Albany 47

Pitching
Most Wins
1. Calvin Kirksey – Tallahassee 20
   Paul Wright – Moultrie 20
3. Bob Hill – Waycross 19
4. Joe Radney – Tallahassee 18
   Turk Lown – Valdosta 18
   Bob Maxwell – Dothan 18

Most Losses
1. Calvin Kirksey – Tallahassee 18
2. Jim Burns – Moultrie 15
   Benny Plaia – Cordele 15
4. Joe Radney – Tallahassee 14
   Gene Guth – Americus 14

Highest Winning Percentage (10 game minimum)
1. Harold Silky – Valdosta .857
2. Bob Hill – Waycross .826
3. LeRoy Wiggins – Dothan .800
   Bill Feie – Cordele .800
5. Jim Bryant – Waycross .778

Lowest Earned Run Average (100 inning minimum)
1. Kip Sauerbrun – Moultrie 1.83
2. Turk Lown – Valdosta 1.94
3. Bob Hill – Waycross 2.03
4. Jackson Britchet – Albany 2.51
5. Tom Graham – Dothan 2.52

Most Strikeouts
1. Jim Burns – Moultrie 246
2. Joe Radney – Tallahassee 210
3. Turk Lown – Valdosta 204
4. Calvin Kirksey – Tallahassee 183
5. Bob Hill – Waycross 154

Most Bases on Balls
1. Jim Burns – Moultrie 174
2. Joe Radney – Tallahassee 146
3. Frank Gravino – Albany 139
4. Bill Hair – Dothan 115
5. Turk Lown – Valdosta 113

Most Hits Allowed
1. Bob Maxwell – Dothan 280
2. Joe Radney – Tallahassee 273
3. Ernest McDaniel – Cordele 269

4. Calvin Kirksey – Tallahassee   266
5. Paul Wright – Moultrie   232

Most Innings Pitched
1. Calvin Kirksey – Tallahassee   310
2. Joe Radney – Tallahassee   285
3. Bob Maxwell – Dothan   277
4. Jim Burns – Moultrie   255
5. Paul Wright – Moultrie   235

1946

Georgia-Alabama League

League Office: Carrollton, Georgia
League President: Carl W. East
League Vice President: A.W. Ford
Salary Limit: $1,800 per month.
Player Rule: Each club was allowed a roster of fifteen players, not more than three class men, not more than seven limited service, and not less than five rookies.
Umpires: Merritt Cain, Wilkins T. Smith, William E. Owens, E.M. Elliott, Clayton D. Vick, W.S. Gaston, and Hop Mills.

Georgia-Alabama League Final Standings

Team	W	L	Pct	GB	Affiliate
Carrollton Hornets	75	55	.577	----	Unaffiliated
Valley Rebels	72	58	.554	3.0	Unaffiliated
Tallassee Indians	71	59	.546	4.0	PIT-NL
Newnan Brownies	68	62	.523	7.0	Unaffiliated
LaGrange Troupers	59	71	.454	16.0	Unaffiliated
Opelika Owls	45	85	.346	30.0	Unaffiliated

1946 Georgia-Alabama League Map

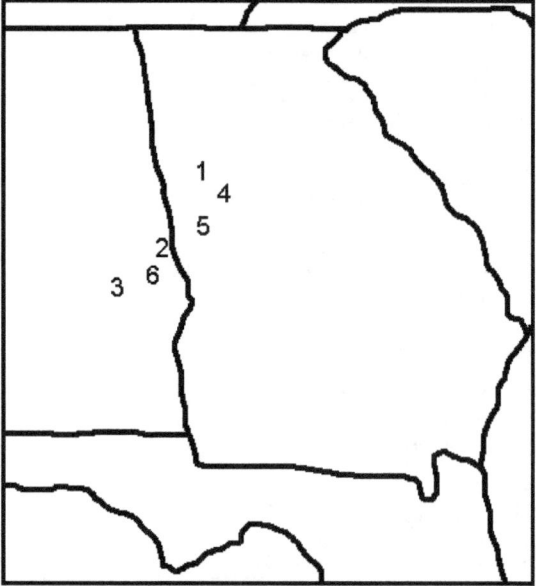

(numbers on map correspond to the place each team finished in regular season play)

In 1946, the Georgia-Alabama league reappeared during the resurgence of local baseball following World War II. Carl W. East, an alumnus of the league from 1930, was named president of the circuit. Carrollton was the only club from the 1930 loop to play in the new league with the familiar name. LaGrange and Newnan joined Carrollton as the Georgia cities, while Opelika, Tallassee, and Valley made up the Alabama portion of the six-team diamond loop. Valley represented the cities of Lanett, Alabama and West Point, Georgia.

On August 21, Newnan pitcher John Johnson became an "Iron Man" when he pitched and won both games of a double header against Valley. Johnson shutout Valley in both contests, 1 to 0 and 7 to 0, and gave up 10 and 6 hits respectively.

Georgia Class-D Minor League Baseball Encyclopedia

The post-season was played using the Shaughnessy style playoff system, which was new to the Georgia-Alabama League. With the top four teams of the league advancing to the two-tiered post-season tournament, more teams had a chance of being crowned league champions. Carrollton, who had the best record at the end of the regular season, played third place Tallassee in the first round of the playoffs, and second place Valley squared off against fourth place Newnan on the other side of the bracket. Tallassee defeated Carrollton three games to two, and Valley did the same to Newnan with the same final score. The Indians of Tallassee then beat the Valley Rebels by the familiar three games to two in the five-game series. Tallassee went on to play in an interleague championship series against Geneva, Alabama, the champions of the Alabama State League, in the Class D Series. Tallassee won the series four games to none.

Carrollton, Georgia
Team Operated by Carrollton Baseball Club, Inc.
Team President: A.W. Ford
Secretary: Earl Stoples
Treasurers: Harvey Copeland and Earl Stoples
Manager(s): Luther Gunnells
Games played at City Athletic Field

Carrollton Hornets Team Roster

NAME	G	BA	POS	W	L	ERA	APF
Anderson, ---	<10						
Barkley, ---	4		P	2	1	0.00	
Beasley, ---	<10						
Bieser, Fred	24	0.111	OF				
Borders, Aubrey	29	0.267	P	7	6	3.82	Newnan
Bosser, Mel	4		P	1	2	0.00	
Brock, Paul	12	0.333	P	10	2	3.46	
Cain, George	7		P	1	1	0.00	
Childs, Frank	39	0.178	OF, P	0	3	0.00	Newnan
Colter, ---	1		P	0	0	0.00	
Condit, ---	18	0.167	P	8	7	3.02	Opelika
Crowson, Marv	6		P	3	1	0.00	
Dean, Harry	2		P	1	0	0.00	
Farr, Red	<10						
Fincher, Bob	10	0.242					
Flowers, Burnice	<10						
Foster, ---	<10						
Fraker, Dick	38	0.263	OF				
Garner, Bob	67	0.281	OF, P	3	4	6.10	
Gulliver, Clark	90	0.201	OF, P	0	0		
Gunnells, Luther	117	0.381	M, SS, P	0	1	0.00	
Gurdy, ---	1		P	0	0	0.00	
Guyton, ---	24	0.174	3B				
Hill, Jim	121	0.257	C				
Hurley, ---	1		P	0	0	0.00	
Israel, Bill	30	0.242	P	12	8	3.96	
Kirschner, George	1		P	0	0	0.00	
Langley, Jim	19	0.250	1B				
Little, Walt	2		P	1	1	0.00	
Marshall, Shorty	128	0.273	2B				
Matthews, Bob	35	0.107	P	16	13	6.88	
Milo, ---	<10						
Oglesby, Hugh	26	0.149	OF				
Patterson, Bill	<10						
Pittman, Al	12	0.120	P	4	4	4.43	
Reed, Jim	8		P	0	5	0.00	LaGrange
Roberts, Red	67	0.308	3B, SS				
Robison, Roy	<10						
Seigler, Bill	26	0.220	P	4	4	5.34	
Shivers, ---	<10						
Snider, Floyd	38	0.221	OF				Newnan
Souter, George	58	0.321	3B, OF, P	1	2	0.00	
Spencer, Bill	1		P	0	0	0.00	
Sprayberry, Jim	2		P	0	0	0.00	Valley
Steel, ---	1		P	0	0	0.00	
Stoyle, Jim	90	0.351	1B				
Terry, Horace	<10						
Thomas, Dallas	16	0.254	OF				
Westbrook, John	16	0.057	P	6	7	2.51	Tallassee
Williams, Paul	39	0.261	3B				
Yearty, Sam	6		P	1	0	0.00	
York, Lew	121	0.302	1B, OF, P	0	0	0.00	

LaGrange, Georgia
Team Operated by LaGrange Baseball Club, Inc.
Team President: G.L. Cahall
Vice President: R.C. Davis
Secretary-Treasurer-Business Manager: Oliver Hunnicutt
Manager(s): Jake Daniel, Newton Parker
Games played at Callaway Stadium

LaGrange Troupers Team Roster

NAME	G	BA	POS	W	L	ERA	APF
Allen, Johnny	129	0.257	2B, 3B, OF, P	0	0	0.00	
Bennett, Charles	3		P	1	0	0.00	
Bridges, Harold	16	0.063	P	3	5	6.52	Valley
Camp, Loy	39	0.163	P	10	14	4.16	
Carter, Emil	<10						
Connor, ---	<10						
Copeland, Elmer	36	0.123	P	14	10	4.50	
Cox, Max	7		P	0	3	0.00	
Daniel, Jake	129	0.357	M, 1B, P	0	0	0.00	Valley
Davis, ---	1		P	0	1	0.00	
Deal, Nip	<10						
Dean, Charles	59	0.249	3B, OF, P	0	0	0.00	
Dickerson, ---	2		P	0	0	0.00	
Duncan, Troy	<10						
Edmondson, Lee	<10						
Gilson, John	12	0.316	P	0	4	5.14	
Green, ---	1		P	0	0	0.00	
Griggs, Bill	1		P	0	1	0.00	
Harper, Bill	14	0.186	3B				
Hoflac, Joe	26	0.250	OF				
Holmes, Jim	2		P	1	0	0.00	
Hubbard, Carl	1		P	0	0	0.00	
Humberson, Roxie	<10						
Jeter, Cleo	45	0.286	P, OF	14	11	3.86	Opelika
Johnson, Joe	100	0.228	OF, P	0	0	0.00	Valley
Kilgore, Bill	<10						
Kirksey, Calvin	21	0.208	P	8	9	4.16	Valley
Lowe, ---	<10						
Lyons, Ray	<10						
Malcolm, Lew	12	0.143					
Mashburn, Ernest	19	0.185	OF, P	0	2	0.00	
McRae, Bill	38	0.138	3B				Newnan
Melton, Ray	<10						
Minor, Howard	<10						
Murray, Ralph	27	0.151	3B				
Murray, Tom	24	0.250	P	6	3	5.04	
Padgett, Charles	48	0.194	SS				Newnan
Parker, Newton	27	0.278	M, 1B, P	0	0	0.00	
Pratt, Tom	45	0.291	OF				
Pritchett, Doug	12	0.179	SS				
Putnam, Basil	13	0.157	OF				
Reed, Jim	8		P	0	5	0.00	Carrollton
Reese, Eddie	93	0.222	2B				
Rucker, ---	<10						
Satterfield, Cicero	35	0.184	C				Valley
Scobbins, ---	<10						
Smith, Reuben	25	0.172	P	8	6	3.08	
Spitzer, Lloyd	14	0.200	OF				Tallassee
Standard, ---	1		P	0	1	0.00	
Stephens, T.W.	<10						

Georgia Class-D Minor League Baseball Encyclopedia

NAME	G	BA	POS	W	L	ERA	APF
Stowe, John	77	0.343	OF, P	0	2	0.00	
Sweatt, Bill	3		P	0	0	0.00	
Towns, Jim	99	0.305	SS				
Walls, Howard	117	0.234	C, P	0	0	#REF!	
Ward, ---	<10						
Ware, Dan	<10						
Webb, ---	<10						
White, Bill	24	0.229	3B				
Whitley, Tom	17	0.160					
Woodruff, Ridley	<10						

Newnan, Georgia
Team Operated by Newnan Baseball Club
Team President: J.R. Brown
Manager(s): Gimpy Brown, George Nix
Games played at Pickett Field

Newnan Brownies Team Roster

NAME	G	BA	POS	W	L	ERA	APF
Astin, Bob	3		P	1	0	0.00	
Ball, John	67	0.325	2B, P	0	1	0.00	
Borders, Aubrey	29	0.267	P	7	6	3.82	Carrollton
Bottoms, Woodrow	80	0.421	3B, SS				
Brown, Gimpy	38	0.214	M, P	9	8	2.17	
Brown, Hubert	10	0.136	OF, P	3	5	4.36	
Browning, Ted	123	0.301	OF, P	0	0	0.00	
Bucek, John	98	0.300	3B, OF, P	0	0	0.00	
Carpenter, John	2		P	1	0	0.00	
Childs, Frank	39	0.178	OF, P	0	3	0.00	Carrollton
Collum, Ambrose	1		P	0	0	0.00	
Daugherty, Mike	13	0.245	OF				
Denny, Horace	<10						
Dickinson, John	5		P	2	2	0.00	
Dye, Hoyle	<10						
Evans, Millard	32	0.206	P	5	13	3.99	
Faucette, Lew	<10						
Gallart, Armando	76	0.290	3B, SS, P	0	0		
George, Milt	<10						
Grimes, Dave	<10						
Harris, ---	1		P	0	0		
Hitt, Jack	2		P	0	0	0.00	
Hunt, Ray	34	0.235	C				
Johnson, John	32	0.183	P	20	8	2.92	
Jones, Bill	21	0.302	P	7	6	2.57	
Jones, Jim	3		P	1	0	0.00	
Jones, Ward	52	0.247	2B				
Lutes, Jim	<10						
McCravy, Charles	2		P	0	1	0.00	
McGee, Wilson	29	0.157	P	13	10	4.06	
McRae, Bill	38	0.138	3B				LaGrange
Melvin, ---	<10						
Najour, George	24	0.212	3B				
Nix, George	<10		M				
O'Connell, Tom	<10						
Padgett, Charles	48	0.194	SS				LaGrange
Satterfield, Ralph	101	0.294	1B				
Shoemake, Claude	124	0.316	1B, OF, P	4	2	2.39	
Sinnott, John	<10						
Snider, Floyd	38	0.221	OF				Carrollton
Stanley, Bob	103	0.275	C, P	0	1	0.00	
Webb, Lawrence	<10						
Whiteside, Bright	<10						
Willingham, Coney	<10						

Opelika, Alabama
Team Operated by Opelika Baseball Club
Team President: L.H. Rice
Vice President: Eason Cook
Secretary-Treasurer: Douglas Hearn
Manager(s): Jim Hitchcock, Zach Schuessler
Games played at Pepperell Park

Opelika Owls Team Roster

NAME	G	BA	POS	W	L	ERA	APF
Bailey, Don	94	0.324	1B, OF, P	0	1	0.00	
Boyer, Milt	5		P	0	1	0.00	
Brogden, Otis	52	0.223	2B				
Bryson, Joe	8		P	2	2	0.00	
Burnett, Ed	58	0.280	1B, 3B, P	4	6	5.14	
Condit, ---	18	0.167	P	8	7	3.02	Carrollton
Davis, Jim	4		P	0	1	0.00	
Day, ---	5		P	0	2	0.00	
Dennis, C.T.	1		P	0	0	0.00	
Finney, Lou	45	0.299	1B, OF				Valley
Frederick, Bill	3		P	2	1	0.00	
Gill, Audis	52	0.265	3B, OF				
Godwin, Bill	40	0.275	3B				
Harrell, Ben	42	0.200	P	5	12	4.14	
Hayes, Frank	5		P	0	1	0.00	
Hitchcock, Jim	66	0.242	M, 2B, SS, P	0	0	0.00	
Hitson, John	44	0.238	SS				
Humbracht, Hal	12	0.100	1B, P	0	0	0.00	
Jackson, Claude	1		P	0	0	0.00	
Jeter, Cleo	45	0.286	P, OF	14	11	3.86	LaGrange
Jones, Murray	<10						
Kenmore, ---	<10						
Kent, Otis	26	0.177	P	9	5	3.77	Valley
Kreamcheck, Ed	113	0.258	1B, OF, P	0	0	0.00	
Kritsky, Walt	9		P	1	4	6.40	
McConnell, Ed	<10						
McGarity, Les	49	0.297	C, P	1	0	0.00	Tallassee
Medlock, Frank	<10						
Moore, Jewell	11	0.282					
Morris, Ray	5		P	0	1	0.00	
Nelson, Jim	37	0.280	C				
Newhall, Bob	84	0.228	2B, C, P	0	0	0.00	
Noto, Phil	40	0.181	SS				
O'Kelley, Clyde	22	0.159	C				
Peacock, Cecil	15	0.103	P	3	9	6.55	
Peake, ---	4		P	1	3	0.00	
Plyn, Percy	23	0.198	SS				
Pope, C.	9		P	2	4	0.00	
Quick, John	105	0.291	OF				
Rhodes, Herb	<10						
Rollo, Charles	13	0.241	2B				
Schuessler, Zach	8		M, P	0	5	0.00	
Scott, Jim	34	0.358	P	6	8	5.72	
Smeltzer, Charles	31	0.265	C				
Tarvin, Art	2		P	0	1	0.00	
Thompson, Jack	127	0.290	OF, P	0	0	0.00	
Tolbert, ---	1		P	0	0	0.00	
Vickers, Jim	35	0.177	P	9	15	3.84	
Wallin, Carl	12	0.091	P	1	2	0.00	Tallassee
Wallis, Arnold	<10						

Tallassee, Alabama
Team Operated by Tallassee Baseball Club, Inc.
Team President: A.T. Holloway
Vice President-Secretary: Clyde Pruitt
Treasurer: W.F. Gulledge
Manager(s): Johnnie Heving
Games played at Tallassee Ballpark
Major League Affiliate: Pittsburgh Pirates – National League.

Tallassee Indians Team Roster

NAME	G	BA	POS	W	L	ERA	APF
Buck, Joe	<10						
Bundrick, Clinton	14	0.224	SS				
Bush, Carl	<10						

Georgia Class-D Minor League Baseball Encyclopedia

NAME	G	BA	POS	W	L	ERA	APF
Chandler, Jack	105	0.241	OF				
Dabbs, Chester	20	0.175	3B				
Davis, Clarence	<10						
Downs, Wilburn	22	0.129	2B				
Duncan, John	11	0.190	P	2	5	6.47	
Hall, Carl	23	0.130	P	4	8	3.68	
Hammock, Bill	34	0.175	C				
Hathcock, Marlin	117	0.275	2B, SS				
Heving, Johnnie	11	0.364	M				
Higginbotham, Morris	<10						
Hill, John	97	0.341	3B				
Hornsby, Leonard	1		P	0	1	0.00	
Jones, Bill	124	0.272	1B				
Knowles, Earl	116	0.262	OF, P	0	0	0.00	
Lamb, ---	1		P	0	1	0.00	
Land, Dick	11	0.176	P	1	2	0.00	
Lantrip, Bill	27	0.281	P	11	9	4.59	
Latta, John	11	0.133					
Leitz, Al	<10						
Lohr, Larry	34	0.101	P	15	10	3.56	
Lowell, ---	1		P	0	0	0.00	
Mahoney, ---	1		P	0	0	0.00	
Manheim, Francis	16	0.136	P	6	7	4.38	
McGarity, Les	49	0.297	C, P	1	0	0.00	Opelika
Mihalik, Mickey	13	0.050	P	2	4	3.88	
Muti, Nick	<10						
Nelson, Burel	7		P	1	2	0.00	
Parks, Jack	87	0.249	C				
Parks, Woodford	7		P	6	1	2.75	
Poole, Ralph	31	0.175	P	19	6	2.80	
Porterfield, Lee	1		P	1	0	0.00	
Posey, Walt	74	0.262	OF				
Schivone, Ralph	<10						
Smeraglia, Anthony	<10						
Smithley, ---	<10						
Spitzer, Lloyd	14	0.200	OF				LaGrange
Wallin, Carl	12	0.091	P	1	2	0.00	Opelika
Wellman, Bob	65	0.332	OF				
Westbrook, John	16	0.057	P	6	7	2.51	Carrollton
Wilson, Nesby	31	0.320	OF				
Wright, Maurice	93	0.265	SS				
Folson, ---	<10						
Frazier, Lance	29	0.220	1B, C				
Frazier, Ralph	102	0.261	OF				
Gilbert, Art	38	0.200	P	15	12	4.52	
Green, ---	<10						
Groves, ---	<10						
Hall, Floyd	44	0.197	OF				
Herring, Bill	<10						
Hornsberg, Art	10	0.167	P	1	1	0.00	
Johnson, Joe	100	0.228	OF, P	0	0	0.00	LaGrange
Kent, Otis	26	0.177	P	9	5	3.77	Opelika
Kirksey, Calvin	21	0.208	P	8	9	4.16	LaGrange
Lewis, Jim	93	0.328	1B				
Marshall, ---	1		P	1	0	0.00	
Milner, Walt	19	0.222	M, P	7	7	3.67	
Montalvo, Jose	67	0.288	OF, C, P	0	0	0.00	
Morgan, Malvern	96	0.299	3B, OF, P	2	0	0.00	
Morrison, Dean	19	0.174	P	4	5	4.69	
Newsome, Art	12	0.400	P	1	3	0.00	
Peters, Charles	1		P	0	0	0.00	
Place, Paul	24	0.299	C				
Ray, Stan	<10						
Robinson, Tom	84	0.279	OF				
Rowe, ---	<10						
Satterfield, Cicero	35	0.184	C				LaGrange
Sharp, Bill	17	0.255	OF				
Shaw, Floyd	16	0.167	P	8	5	2.08	
Siegfield, ---	1		P	0	0	0.00	
Smith, Luther	26	0.155	P	6	5	4.04	
Sprayberry, Jim	2		P	0	0	0.00	Carrollton
Tillery, Tom	<10						
Tomlin, Ed	<10						
Whitten, Norm	<10						
Wiggins, LeRoy	25	0.083	P	11	5	3.77	
Williams, Ed	18	0.172	P	7	5	3.47	

Valley (Lanett, Alabama & West Point, Georgia), Alabama

Team Operated by Valley Baseball Club, Inc.
Team President: G.E. Goggans
Vice President: Fob James
Secretary-Business Manager: J. Hoyd Gay
Treasurer: Donald G. Lord
Manager(s): Walt Milner
Games played at Lanett Ballpark

Valley Rebels Team Roster

NAME	G	BA	POS	W	L	ERA	APF
Bartula, Matthew	2		P	0	0	0.00	
Benezue, ---	1		P	0	0	0.00	
Blackstock, Hal	47	0.273	3B				
Blaze, Frank	<10						
Bosarge, Vince	120	0.220	SS				
Bridges, Harold	16	0.063	P	3	5	6.52	LaGrange
Casey, Charles	25	0.172	C				
Chambers, Joe	128	0.291	2B				
Colley, Owen	11	0.081	3B				
Crow, Paul	80	0.268	OF				
Crowder, ---	<10						
Daniel, Jake	129	0.357	1B, P	0	0	0.00	LaGrange
Ellington, Paul	<10						
Ferguson, ---	<10						
Finney, Bob	23	0.162	C				
Finney, Lou	45	0.299	1B, OF				Opelika

1946 Georgia-Alabama League Records

Batting

Highest Batting Average (minimum 100 at bats)
1. Woodrow Bottoms – Newnan .421
2. Luther Gunnells – Carrollton .381
3. Jake Daniel – LaGr/Vall .357
4. Jim Stoyle – Carrollton .351
5. John Stowe – LaGrange .343

Most Hits
1. Jake Daniel – LaGr/Vall 159
2. Ted Browning – Newnan 154
3. Luther Gunnells – Carrollton 153
4. Claude Shoemake – Newnan 152
5. Shorty Marshall – Carrollton 143

Most Runs
1. Jake Daniel – LaGr/Vall 118
2. Joe Chambers – Valley 95
3. Ted Browning – Newnan 90
4. Luther Gunnells – Carrollton 89
5. Shorty Marshall – Carrollton 88

Most Total Bases
1. Jake Daniel – LaGr/Vall 285
2. Luther Gunnells – Carrollton 256
3. Claude Shoemake – Newnan 224
4. Lew York – Carrollton 205
5. Marlin Hathcock – Tallassee 204

Most Doubles
1. Jake Daniel – LaGr/Vall 30
2. Shorty Marshall – Carrollton 28

3. Luther Gunnells – Carrollton   27
4. Claude Shoemake – Newnan   26
5. Malvern Morgan – Valley   25

Most Triples
1. Joe Chambers – Valley   15
2. Marlin Hathcock – Tallassee   14
3. Ted Browning – Newnan   9
   Jack Thompson – Opelika   9
5. Ralph Satterfield – Newnan   8

Most Home Runs
1. Jake Daniel – LaGr/Vall   30
2. Luther Gunnells – Carrollton   24
3. Lew York – Carrollton   19
4. Claude Shoemake – Newnan   14
5. John Stowe – LaGrange   13

Most Extra Base Hits
1. Jake Daniel – LaGr/Vall   63
2. Luther Gunnells – Carrollton   53
3. Claude Shoemake – Newnan   42
4. Shorty Marshall – Carrollton   39
   Marlin Hathcock – Tallassee   39

Most Runs Batted In
1. Jake Daniel – LaGr/Vall   122
2. Claude Shoemake – Newnan   107
3. Luther Gunnells – Carrollton   96
4. Lew York – Carrollton   84
5. Jim Stoyle – Carrollton   83

Most Stolen Bases
1. Luther Gunnells – Carrollton   31
2. Vince Bosarge – Valley   24
   Jim Towns – LaGrange   24
4. Joe Chambers – Valley   21
5. Shorty Marshall – Carrollton   20

Fielding
Most Put-Outs
1. Jake Daniel 1B, P – LaGr/Vall   1,108
2. Bill Jones 1B – Tallassee   1,066
3. Jim Stoyle 1B – Carrollton   947
4. Ralph Satterfield 1B – Newnan   900
5. Jim Lewis 1B – Valley   813

Most Assists
1. Joe Chambers 2B – Valley   370
2. Luther Gunnells SS, P – Carrollton   326
   Vince Bosarge SS – Valley   326
4. Shorty Marshall 2B – Carrollton   316
5. Marlin Hathcock 2B, SS – Tallassee   310

Most Errors
1. Vince Bosarge SS – Valley   57
2. Jim Towns SS – LaGrange   46
3. Luther Gunnells SS, P – Carrollton   40
   Marlin Hathcock 2B, SS – Tallahassee   40
5. John Hitson SS – Opelika   36

Pitching
Most Wins
1. John Johnson – Newnan   20
2. Ralph Poole – Tallassee   19
3. Bob Matthews – Carrollton   16
4. Larry Lohr – Tallassee   15
   Art Gilbert – Valley   15

Most Losses
1. Jim Vickers – Opelika   15
2. Loy Camp – LaGrange   14
3. Bob Matthews – Carrollton   13
   Millard Evans – Newnan   13
5. Art Gilbert – Valley   12
   Ben Harrell – Opelika   12

Highest Winning Percentage (10 game minimum)
1. Paul Brock – Carrollton   .833
2. Ralph Poole – Tallassee   .760
3. John Johnson – Newnan   .714
4. LeRoy Wiggins – Valley   .688
5. *four players tied with   .667

Lowest Earned Run Average (100 inning minimum)
1. Floyd Shaw – Valley   2.08
2. Gimpy Brown – Newnan   2.17
3. John Westbrook – Carr/Tall   2.51
4. Bill Jones – Newnan   2.57
5. Ralph Poole – Tallassee   2.80

Most Strikeouts
1. John Johnson – Newnan   138
2. Art Gilbert – Valley   123
3. Wilson McGee – Newnan   117
4. Millard Evans – Newnan   115
5. Larry Lohr – Tallahassee   114

Most Bases on Balls
1. Jim Vickers – Opelika   84
2. Millard Evans – Newnan   81
3. Art Gilbert – Valley   80
   Larry Lohr – Tallassee   80
5. Bill Lantrip – Tallassee   76

Most Hits Allowed
1. John Johnson – Newnan   228
2. Bob Matthews – Carrollton   227
3. Art Gilbert – Valley   226
4. Jim Vickers – Opelika   201
5. Wilson McGee – Newnan   196

Most Innings Pitched
1. Art Gilbert – Valley   233
2. John Johnson – Newnan   231
3. Ralph Poole – Tallassee   215
4. Jim Vickers – Opelika   204
5. Larry Lohr – Tallassee   197

1946 Georgia-Alabama League All-Star Team
1B Jake Daniel – LaGrange
2B Joe Chambers – Valley
3B John Hill – Tallassee
SS Luther Gunnells – Carrollton
OF Bob Wellman – Tallassee
OF Ted Browning – Newnan
OF Jack Thompson – Opelika
C   Jim Hill – Carrollton
P   Ralph Poole – Tallassee
P   Hubert Brown – Newnan
UT Woodrow Bottoms – Newnan
M   John Hill – Tallassee

1946

Georgia-Florida League

League Office: Leslie, Georgia
League President: W.T. Anderson
League Vice President: Guy Connell
Secretary: J.R. Blair
Salary Limit: $1,800 per month.
Player Rule: Each club was allowed a roster of fifteen players, not more than four veterans, not more than six limited service, and not less than five rookies.
Umpires: Robert W. Vocial, David C. Kirkwood, Edward P. Czjka, Vito C. Baolto, Nicholas McKay, E.M. Spurlock, Rocco Thomas Flammia, and Robert L. Fisher.

Georgia-Florida League Final Standings

Team	W	L	Pct	GB	Affiliate
Americus Phillies	87	37	.702	----	PHI-NL
Moultrie Packers	76	47	.618	10.5	Unaffiliated
Waycross Bears	75	50	.600	12.5	Unaffiliated
Valdosta Dodgers	64	61	.512	23.5	BRK-NL
Tallahassee Pirates	63	62	.504	24.5	PIT-NL
Albany Cardinals	54	71	.432	33.5	STL-NL
Thomasville Tigers	45	80	.360	42.5	Unaffiliated
Cordele White Sox	35	91	.278	53.0	CHI-AL

1946 Georgia-Florida League Map

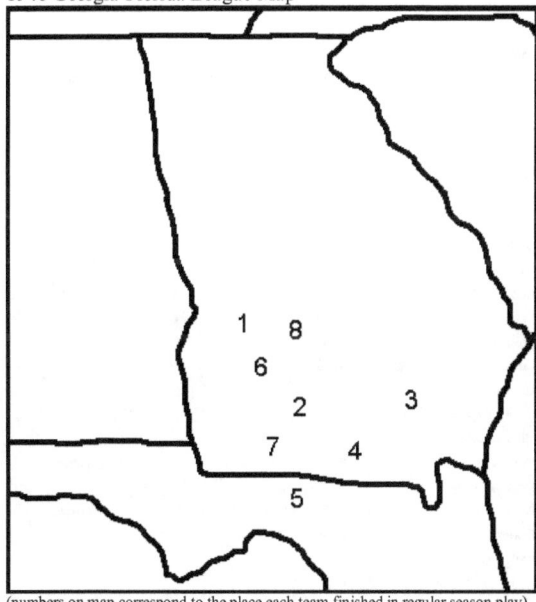

(numbers on map correspond to the place each team finished in regular season play)

With World War II now over, the minor league baseball world experienced resurgence all over America. The Georgia-Florida League returned to the diamond with only one change in the lineup from the 1942 season. Dothan, Alabama, who had taken the place of Thomasville in 1942, returned to the Alabama-Florida League, and Thomasville came back to play in the Georgia-Florida circuit.

On May 3, Moultrie first baseman Ken Rhyne hit four home runs in one game against Thomasville. Rhyne also drove in 9 runs in the 12 to 2 Packers victory. Another diamond feat was accomplished on this date when Cordele rookie pitcher Greg "Lefty" Parente struck out 23 Tallahassee batters winning the game for the White Sox 16 to 2. Gaylord Lemish, Moultrie moundsman, pitched the league's first no-hitter of the year when he blanked Albany 10 to 0 on May 14. The second and last no-hitter of the season also came against Albany when Thomasville's Al Comotti went untouched in a 6 to 0 victory on August 16.

Americus won the league pennant in regular season play with a .702 winning percentage, the highest in league history. Facing third place Waycross in the first round of the post-season, Americus won the series three games to two. On the other side of the bracket, second place Moultrie defeated fourth slotted Valdosta three games to one. In the league championship series, Moultrie edged out Americus four games to three. As champions of the Georgia-Florida League, the Packers went on to play the winners of the Florida State League, Orlando, in the Southeastern Championship. Orlando made easy work of Moultrie sweeping the interleague series in four straight games.

Albany, Georgia

Team Operated by Albany Baseball Club, Inc.
Team President: Morton M. Wiggins
Vice President: S. Breadon
Secretary-Treasurer: Edward W. Roth
Business Manager: Thomas P. Johnson, Jr.
Manager(s): Herb Moore
Games played at Tift Stadium
Major League Affiliate: St. Louis Cardinals – National League.

Albany Cardinals Team Roster

NAME	G	BA	POS	W	L	ERA	APF
Balen, John	<10						
Bell, Jefferson	127	0.267	2B, 3B				
Bishop, Charlie	33	0.228	OF, P	8	4	2.93	
Brand, Clarence	35	0.145	3B, OF				
Carlson, Les	4		P	0	3	0.00	
Dance, John	77	0.235	OF				
Denny, Fred	4		P	0	2	0.00	
Desmuke, Harry	7		P	1	2	0.00	
DiMartino, Joe	91	0.271	C				
Duda, John	13	0.286	P	1	1	0.00	
Garrison, Lyle	38	0.208	P	6	12	4.08	Cordele
German, Preston	103	0.287	2B				
Gilmore, Don	35	0.196	P	5	11	4.58	
Glass, Dick	<10						
Hardegree, Bill	<10						
Hartman, Earl	112	0.269	1B				
Hodge, Clarence	32	0.156	OF				
Hoffman, Bob	46	0.231	P	15	14	3.06	
Jones, Charles	10	0.083					
Katkaveck, Mickey	57	0.234	C				
Lee, Jim	20	0.241	P	2	8	4.87	
Liming, Jim	12	0.095	P	3	3	2.91	
Luckman, Jack	16	0.182	SS				
Michaels, Bill	3		P	0	0	0.00	
Moore, Herb	116	0.323	M, 1B, OF, P	15	3	1.44	
Nix, Henry	44	0.229	2B, OF				Cordele
Olmstead, Ted	8		P	1	4	0.00	
Pavone, Nick	14	0.235	OF				
Pfeiffer, Harry	21	0.128	OF				
Puent, Larry	15	0.188	P	0	7	6.24	
Reilly, Ed	<10						
Roberts, Jim	<10						
Sanders, Lou	83	0.215	OF				
Schmidhausler, Vern	13	0.120					
Schoendienst, Elmer	99	0.205	SS				

Georgia Class-D Minor League Baseball Encyclopedia

Name	G	BA	POS	W	L	ERA	APF
Swygert, Alan	28	0.310	OF				
Thompson, Emery	29	0.214	OF, C				
Thorn, George	2		P	0	1	0.00	
Walker, Bill	28	0.050	P	6	3	3.36	Tal - Way

Americus, Georgia
Team Operated by Philadelphia National League Baseball Club
Team President: H. Phil Jones
Vice President: Raymond Holt
Secretary: J.R. Blair
Treasurer: George A. Fletcher
Business Manager: Rodney H. Blaylock
Manager(s): Jack Sanford
Games played at Community Center Ballpark
Major League Affiliate: Philadelphia Phillies – National League.

Americus Phillies Team Roster

NAME	G	BA	POS	W	L	ERA	APF
Adair, Tommy	29	0.241	P	12	8	2.72	
Asmer, John	46	0.230	P	24	6	2.81	
Clair, Tom	1		P	0	0	0.00	
Corley, Ken	116	0.317	OF				
Cusick, Jack	93	0.272	3B				
Dommer, Chuck	38	0.151	P	17	5	2.15	
Dykes, Charlie	123	0.263	2B				
Edwards, Elmer	120	0.237	3B, OF				Cordele
Glynn, Bill	114	0.328	1B				
Hoflack, Dan	11	0.257	OF				
Howard, Crawford	82	0.232	OF				
Kerr, Tom	5		P	1	2	0.00	
Leili, Joe	65	0.253	C				
McCarthy, Dick	1		P	0	0	0.00	
Murray, Bill	33	0.141	P	21	6	3.22	
Nobles, Julian	29	0.250	P	6	11	4.60	Thomasville
Palantino, Bob	19	0.105	P	4	3	3.57	
Romello, Mike	114	0.274	SS				
Sanford, Jack	38	0.253	M, 1B, P	0	1	0.00	
Turner, Jim	106	0.278	OF, C				
Utke, John	84	0.225	3B, OF				
West, Lewis	16	0.176	P	5	4	3.17	
Whalen, Frank	119	0.268	OF				
Wilson, George	7		P	3	2	4.70	

Cordele, Georgia
Team Operated by Cordele Athletic Association, Inc.
Team President: C.L. Thompson
Vice President: J.W. Bridges
Secretary-Treasurer: W.D. Griffith
Business Manager: William G. Purnhage
Manager(s): Joe Holden
Games played at City Park
Major League Affiliate: Chicago White Sox – American League.

Cordele White Sox Team Roster

NAME	G	BA	POS	W	L	ERA	APF
Bakunas, Al	<10						
Burkwitt, Irwin	105	0.246	OF				Moultrie
Chernetsky, Anthony	90	0.271	OF, C				
Chulick, Bill	<10						
Ciccone, Nick	<10						
Dorough, John	<10						
Dove, Pat	111	0.292	1B, 2B, 3B				Thomasville
Edwards, Elmer	120	0.237	3B, OF				Americus
Elenchin, John	97	0.255	OF, P	1	1	5.60	
Garrison, Lyle	38	0.208	P	6	12	4.08	Albany
Graffeo, John	12	0.239	OF				
Hamm, Francis	19	0.098	P	1	9	3.86	
Haschak, Bill	<10						
Heffline, Bob	65	0.284	OF				
Holden, Joe	<10		M				
Hurd, Tom	122	0.227	SS				
Jobe, Lew	30	0.286	P	5	12	3.75	
Leary, Bill	17	0.238	P	2	10	6.64	Waycross
Luby, Jim	12	0.205	OF				
Maelwig, ---	<10						
Mashburn, Ernest	<10						
Mazzone, ---	41	0.174	3B				Moultrie
McMahon, Jim	42	0.127	P	5	15	4.01	
Nicolai, Mel	39	0.127	P	10	19	3.53	
Nix, Henry	44	0.229	2B, OF				Albany
O'Brien, Jim	9		P	0	2	0.00	
Paison, Bob	<10						
Parente, Greg	49	0.323	P	6	11	4.29	
Plante, ---	<10						
Rautzhan, Bill	118	0.277	1B				
Sarros, Jim	77	0.202	2B, 3B				
Simon, Jerry	5		P	0	0	0.00	
Smith, Andy	67	0.232	C				
Stouch, John	50	0.194	2B, 3B				
Strauss, Harold	11	0.250	2B				
Szolwinski, Sylvester	10	0.000	P	0	6	0.00	

Moultrie, Georgia
Team Operated by Moultrie Baseball Association, Inc.
Team President: F.R. Pidcock, Jr.
Vice President: W.C. Vereen, Jr.
Secretary-Treasurer-Business Manager: C.W. Vandiver
Manager(s): Dixie Parsons, Jim Poole
Games played at League Park

Moultrie Packers Team Roster

NAME	G	BA	POS	W	L	ERA	APF
Barnes, Bill	21	0.305	3B				
Batchko, Joe	26	0.167	OF, P	0	0	0.00	Thomasville
Blackwell, Tom	99	0.243	3B				
Brooks, Floyd	103	0.314	2B				
Brooks, Warren	15	0.435	2B				
Burkwitt, Irwin	105	0.246	OF				Cordele
Coats, Glenn	<10						
Davis, Art	1		P	0	0	0.00	
Del Papa, Frank	104	0.274	OF				
Hall, Jesse	<10						
Holloman, Bobo	44	0.212	P	20	5	2.33	
Kinnas, Christ	12	0.200	P	2	4	5.17	
Kivett, Bill	77	0.264	C				
LaFrance, Bill	72	0.318	OF				
Laumann, Andrew	103	0.219	SS				
Lemish, Gaylord	38	0.189	P	14	13	3.33	
Masterson, Bill	<10						
Mazzone, ---	41	0.174	3B				Cordele
McMillan, Frank	60	0.279	OF				
Parsons, Dixie	87	0.359	M, OF, C				Waycross
Paulick, Frank	71	0.268	OF, C				
Poole, Jim	49	0.271	2B, SS				
Poole, Jim	22	0.286	M, 1B				
Rhyne, Ken	123	0.304	1B, OF, P	1	0	0.00	
Steedly, Alvin	3		P	1	1	0.00	
Stewart, Buford	15	0.200	OF				
Swain, Harold	<10						
Taylor, Furman	66	0.271	OF, P	13	6	2.66	
Vukas, Steve	45	0.243	P	14	8	2.98	
Whitmore, Don	34	0.217	P	11	10	4.18	

Georgia Class-D Minor League Baseball Encyclopedia

Tallahassee, Florida
Team Operated by Tallahassee Pirates, Inc.
Team President: Fred N. Lowry
Vice Presidents: W.E. Benswanger, S.E. Watters
Secretary: Robert T. Rice
Business Manager: John Y. Humphress
Manager(s): Art Doll
Games played at Centennial Field
Major League Affiliates: Pittsburgh Pirates – National League.

Tallahassee Team Roster

NAME	G	BA	POS	W	L	ERA	APF
Angeli, Joe	125	0.256	OF				
Anjeski, Elmer	63	0.325	OF				
August, Joe	13	0.216	OF				
Bailey, ---	<10						
Bennett, Craig	26	0.156	P	5	6	5.05	
Brannan, Charles	112	0.292	1B, OF				
Cagle, Lamar	<10						
Castelgrande, Vito	113	0.251	OF				
Clawson, Charles	5		P	1	3	0.00	
Cook, Ron	5		P	0	2	0.00	
Doll, Art	63	0.290	M, C, P	6	6	2.75	
Dravecky, Andrew	83	0.224	C				
Fain, Stan	10	0.105	P	3	5	3.84	
Fink, Jim	90	0.244	3B, SS				
Goodwin, Gervin	14	0.250					
Green, Bob	30	0.153	P	14	8	2.75	
Haddican, Harold	85	0.274	OF, C				
Heck, ---	78	0.267	2B, SS				
Jeffcoat, William	1		P	0	0	0.00	
Johnson, Doug	124	0.302	3B, SS, P	0	0	0.00	
Muskulin, John	4		P	0	1	0.00	
Oliver, Ben	27	0.146	P	7	7	4.94	
Paisley, Bill	<10						
Palumbo, ---	1		P	0	0	0.00	
Pegram, George	<10						
Petty, Jim	21	0.298	1B				
Quinlan, Bud	4		P	0	3	0.00	
Shapiro, Al	9		P	2	4	4.15	
Stasko, Julius	115	0.276	2B				
Telford, Dave	28	0.143	P	12	7	3.42	
Walker, Bill	28	0.050	P	6	3	3.36	Alb - Way
Williams, ---	<10						
Yancek, Frank	30	0.128	P	8	9	4.74	

Thomasville, Georgia
Team Operated by Thomasville Amusements, Inc.
Team President: Heeth Varnedoe
Vice President: O.B. Anderson
Secretary-Treasurer: Lee Singletary
Manager(s): Vincent Mullen
Games played at Municipal Stadium

Thomasville Tigers Team Roster

NAME	G	BA	POS	W	L	ERA	APF
Alexander, Ted	<10						
Atchison, John	3		P	1	2	0.00	
Batchko, Joe	26	0.167	OF, P	0	0	0.00	Moultrie
Belcher, Neil	2		P	0	0	0.00	
Booth, Wayne	1		P	0	0	0.00	
Bozeman, Jim	1		P	0	0	0.00	
Brown, ---	1		P	0	0	0.00	
Campbell, Cliff	6		P	2	2	0.00	
Catchpole, Jim	5		P	0	2	0.00	
Colgan, Bill	113	0.236	3B, OF				
Comotti, Elmo	25	0.157	P	14	8	2.02	
Dove, Pat	111	0.292	1B, 2B, 3B				Cordele
Dull, Bob	<10						
Edge, Roy	<10						
Fairley, Florian	15	0.250	P	1	2	0.00	
Ferra, Joe	16	0.128	1B				
Izzo, John	3		P	0	1	0.00	
Kinney, Bill	11	0.045	P	3	4	5.10	
Knappe, John	3		P	0	1	0.00	
Lillie, Jim	1		P	0	0	0.00	
Macli, Al	77	0.197	C				
Mann, Tom	27	0.206	OF				
Markham, Ken	33	0.203	P	5	11	5.39	
McBryde, Warren	88	0.336	OF				
McRae, Jim	31	0.202	OF				
Mendillo, Anthony	<10						
Moore, Earl	4		P	0	1	0.00	
Mullen, Vincent	90	0.325	M, 2B, 3B				
Nobles, Julian	29	0.250	P	6	11	4.60	Americus
Peterson, Wright	8		P	1	5	0.00	
Phillips, Ray	52	0.286	OF				
Reese, Joe	82	0.344	2B				
Riolo, Joe	17	0.271	3B				
Schaeffer, Bernard	27	0.235	P	1	9	6.03	
Simonec, Reuben	11	0.000	P	2	4	0.00	
Smith, Tom	31	0.140	P	5	10	4.40	
Spaziano, Al	108	0.303	1B, OF, C				
Sullivan, Woodward	3		P	0	0	0.00	
Tanner, J.D.	10	0.313	P	0	0	0.00	
Ward, Warren	5		P	0	2	0.00	
Willett, Ray	126	0.248	SS				
Williams, Charlie	17	0.169	2B				
Williams, Wiley	46	0.197	1B				
Willingham, Ralph	15	0.233	P	4	5	3.97	
Willis, Joel	<10						
Witkowski, John	<10						
Woleen, Raymond	120	0.210	OF				

Valdosta, Georgia
Team Operated by Valdosta Dodgers Baseball Club, Inc.
Team President: C.W. Singleton
Vice Presidents: Branch Rickey, Jr., Harold G. Roettger
Secretary: Fresco Thompson
Treasurer: D.E. Beach
Business Manager: Victor A. Zodda
Manager(s): Bill Welp
Games played at Pendleton Park
Major League Affiliate: Brooklyn Dodgers – National League.

Valdosta Dodgers Team Roster

NAME	G	BA	POS	W	L	ERA	APF
Amoroso, Dante	3		P	0	1	0.00	
Barlam, Barnett	24	0.116	P	4	6	4.69	
Bauer, Ed	24	0.221	OF				
Berman, Buddy	<10						
Brancato, Jim	28	0.148	OF				
Braun, Ken	64	0.257	OF, P	10	6	2.28	
Brightwell, Bill	24	0.135	P	4	6	2.57	
Cahill, Norm	12	0.242	OF				
Coapland, Bernis	3		P	0	2	0.00	
Crumly, Ivan	125	0.276	1B				
Fields, Walt	20	0.209	OF				
Howig, Donald	<10						
Kane, Murray	7		P	2	2	0.00	
Koch, Art	25	0.059	P	7	9	3.82	
Lane, Eli	<10						
Larivee, Armand	20	0.280					
Leveille, Roland	<10						
Loschke, Leo	31	0.149	P	10	7	4.89	
Lynn, Fred	25	0.122	P	7	6	4.67	
Maloney, Pat	3		P	0	0	0.00	
Mize, Mike	<10						
Myers, Don	25	0.303	OF				
Ouchterloney, Don	12	0.191					

Georgia Class-D Minor League Baseball Encyclopedia

NAME	G	BA	POS	W	L	ERA	APF
Pepitone, John	<10						
Purdy, John	<10						
Reichert, Arnold	2		P	0	1	0.00	
Reichert, Paul	37	0.183	OF				
Rey, Emil	123	0.180	SS				
Robinson, Orem	19	0.194	P	8	6	4.36	
Rogers, Walt	123	0.314	3B				
Rose, Russ	111	0.252	2B				
Samson, Charles	41	0.303	OF				
Smith, Jim	34	0.260	OF				
Staley, Don	1		P	0	0	0.00	
Swindle, Jim	36	0.203	OF				
Valencik, Ed	11	0.214	OF				
Villa, Antonio	46	0.230	OF				
Weisenberg, Aaron	32	0.098	P	12	9	2.94	
Welp, Bill	111	0.310	M, C, P	0	0	0.00	
Zodda, Vic	76	0.249	OF, C				

Waycross, Georgia

Team Operated by Waycross Baseball Association, Inc.
Team President: Herbert Bradshaw
Vice President: William D. Rivenbark
Treasurer: Charles H. Andrews
Manager(s): LeGrant Scott
Games played at Newton Field

Waycross Bears Team Roster

NAME	G	BA	POS	W	L	ERA	APF
Blackmon, Grover	<10						
Chambers, Inman	25	0.143	P	7	5	3.05	
Cherry, Dick	2		P	0	0	0.00	
Coates, Dick	13	0.229	1B				
Coppola, Herb	10	0.053	P	4	2	5.00	
Cronic, Guin	31	0.284	P	12	9	3.27	
Doane, Carl	13	0.207	P	6	2	3.89	
Dwyer, Bill	124	0.274	2B				
Eskridge, Jim	24	0.188	SS				
Euliss, Walt	2		P	0	0	0.00	
Farrar, Charles	31	0.313	OF				
Garrett, ---	<10						
Gautreaux, Joe	20	0.077	P	8	7	3.46	
Grupposo, Vince	20	0.177	3B				
Hill, Bob	7		P	3	1	0.00	
Johnson, George	<10						
Lauria, Cosmo	46	0.193	3B				
Leary, Bill	17	0.238	P	2	10	6.64	Cordele
Leeper, Mason	12	0.400	P	2	4	0.00	
Long, Howard	2		P	0	0	0.00	
McCarnes, Jim	125	0.336	OF				
Mock, George	106	0.254	3B, SS				
Moody, Joe	122	0.313	OF				
Murray, Francis	14	0.167	P	8	3	3.96	
Njirich, Gildo	40	0.237	OF, C				
Osborne, Pete	63	0.277	OF, P	18	8	3.95	
Parsons, Dixie	87	0.359	OF, C				Moultrie
Raulerson, Harry	6		P	1	2	0.00	
Savage, John	25	0.222	P	4	7		
Scott, LeGrant	88	0.368	M, OF, P	1	0	0.00	
Sofia, Mike	54	0.184	SS				
Teal, Harry	65	0.247	1B				
Walker, Bill	28	0.050	P	6	3	3.36	Alb - Tal
Watts, George	<10						
Willingham, Jack	<10						
Wilson, Martin	47	0.229	1B				
Wilson, Norm	106	0.288	C				

1946 Georgia-Florida League Records

Batting

Highest Batting Average (minimum 100 at bats)
1. LeGrant Scott – Waycross .368
2. Dixie Parsons – Wayc/Moul .359
3. Joe Reese – Thomasville .344
4. Warren McBryde – Thomasville .336
   Jim McCarnes – Waycross .336

Most Hits
1. Jim McCarnes – Waycross 169
2. Bill Glynn – Americus 154
   Walt Rogers – Valdosta 154
4. Ken Corley – Americus 150
5. Joe Moody – Waycross 147

Most Runs
1. Jim McCarnes – Waycross 111
2. Frank Whalen – Americus 109
3. Floyd Brooks – Moultrie 104
4. Joe Moody – Waycross 102
5. Ken Rhyne – Moultrie 101

Most Total Bases
1. Bill Glynn – Americus 269
2. Ken Rhyne – Moultrie 242
3. Jim McCarnes – Waycross 218
4. Walt Rogers – Valdosta 216
5. Joe Moody – Waycross 203

Most Doubles
1. Bill Glynn – Americus 34
   Jim McCarnes – Waycross 34
3. Ken Rhyne – Moultrie 28
4. Joe Moody – Waycross 27
5. Herb Moore – Albany 25

Most Triples
1. Bill Glynn – Americus 18
   Doug Johnson – Tallahassee 18
3. Ivan Crumly – Valdosta 14
4. Walt Rogers – Valdosta 13
5. Irwin Burkwitt – Moul/Cord 12

Most Home Runs
1. Ken Rhyne – Moultrie 22
2. Bill Glynn – Americus 15
3. Frank Del Papa – Moultrie 10
4. LeGrant Scott – Waycross 8
5. Dixie Parsons – Wayc/Moul 7

Most Extra Base Hits
1. Bill Glynn – Americus 63
2. Ken Rhyne – Moultrie 53
3. Jim McCarnes – Waycross 41
4. Walt Rogers – Valdosta 39
   Joe Moody – Waycross 39

Most Runs Batted In
1. Ken Rhyne – Moultrie 129
2. Bill Glynn – Americus 101
3. Joe Moody – Waycross 98
4. Ivan Crumly – Valdosta 89
5. Doug Johnson – Tallahassee 83

Most Stolen Bases
1. Harold Haddican – Tallahassee 34
2. Floyd Brooks – Moultrie 31
3. Frank Whalen – Americus 28
4. Bill Dwyer – Waycross 24

5. Charlie Dykes – Americus 23
   Lou Sanders – Albany 23

Fielding
Most Put-Outs
1. Bill Glynn 1B – Americus 1,037
2. Ivan Crumly 1B – Valdosta 988
3. Bill Rautzhan 1B – Cordele 961
4. Ken Rhyne 1B, OF, P – Moultrie 943
5. Earl Hartman 1B – Albany 927

Most Assists
1. Ray Willett SS – Thomasville 432
2. Tom Hurd SS – Cordele 382
3. Emil Rey SS – Valdosta 367
4. Bill Dwyer 2B – Waycross 338
5. Charlie Dykes 2B – Americus 308

Most Errors
1. Tom Hurd SS – Cordele 88
2. Ray Willett SS – Thomasville 75
3. Doug Johnson 3B, SS, P – Tallahassee 74
4. Charlie Dykes 2B – Americus 70
5. Emil Rey SS – Valdosta 63

Pitching
Most Wins
1. John Asmer – Americus 24
2. Bill Murray – Americus 21
3. Bobo Holloman – Moultrie 20
4. Pete Osborne – Waycross 18
5. Chuck Dommer – Americus 17

Most Losses
1. Mel Nicolai – Cordele 19
2. Jim McMahon – Cordele 15
3. Bob Hoffman – Albany 14
4. Gaylord Lemish – Moultrie 13
5. Lyle Garrison – Cord/Alba 12
   Lew Jobe – Cordele 12

Highest Winning Percentage (10 game minimum)
1. Herb Moore – Albany .833
2. John Asmer – Americus .800
   Bobo Holloman – Moultrie .800
4. Bill Murray – Americus .778
5. Chuck Dommer – Americus .773

Lowest Earned Run Average (100 inning minimum)
1. Herb Moore – Albany 1.44
2. Elmo Comotti – Thomasville 2.02
3. Chuck Dommer – Americus 2.15
4. Ken Braun – Valdosta 2.28
5. Bobo Holloman – Moultrie 2.33

Most Strikeouts
1. Gaylord Lemish – Moultrie 278
2. Herb Moore – Albany 214
3. Bobo Holloman – Moultrie 184
4. Chuck Dommer – Americus 182
5. Mel Nicolai – Cordele 157

Most Bases on Balls
1. Gaylord Lemish – Moultrie 140
2. Lyle Garrison – Cord/Alba 130
3. Greg Parente – Cordele 119
4. Bobo Holloman – Moultrie 114
5. Don Gilmore – Albany 108

Most Hits Allowed
1. Bill Murray – Americus 249
2. Jim McMahon – Cordele 221
3. Mel Nicolai – Cordele 219
4. Pete Osborne – Waycross 217
5. John Asmer – Americus 209

Most Innings Pitched
1. Bob Hoffman – Albany 244
2. John Asmer – Americus 240
3. Gaylord Lemish – Moultrie 238
4. Bill Murray – Americus 232
5. Chuck Dommer – Americus 222

1946 Georgia-Florida League All-Star Team
1B Bill Glynn – Americus
2B Warren Brooks – Moultrie
3B Walt Rogers – Valdosta
SS Mike Romello – Americus
OF Joe Angeli – Tallahassee
OF Joe Moody – Waycross
OF Jim McCarnes – Waycross
C Norm Wilson – Waycross
UT Harold Haddican – Tallahassee
P Bobo Holloman – Moultrie
P Guin Cronic – Waycross
M Jack Sanford – Americus

1947

Georgia-Alabama League

League Office: Talladega, Alabama
League President: Arthur R. Decatur
League Vice President: George Cahall
Salary Limit: $2,250 per month.
Player Rule: Each club was allowed a roster of fifteen players, not more than three veterans, not more than six limited service, and not less than six rookies.
Umpires: Paul W. Bernebrok, Arthur J. Cornacchia, Earl R. Keller, William Kokinchak, William G. Malesky, Lester R. Sanoers, Herald Taylor, and Everett C. Terry.

Georgia-Alabama League Final Standings

Team	W	L	Pct	GB	Affiliate
Carrollton Hornets	75	49	.605	----	Unaffiliated
Opelika Owls	76	50	.603	----	Unaffiliated
Valley Rebels	75	51	.595	1.0	Unaffiliated
Newnan Brownies	72	53	.576	3.5	Unaffiliated
Tallassee Indians	62	63	.496	13.5	Unaffiliated
Griffin Pimientos	53	68	.438	20.5	Unaffiliated
LaGrange Troupers	46	78	.371	29.0	Unaffiliated
Alexander City Millers	39	86	.312	36.5	Unaffiliated

1947 Georgia-Alabama League Map

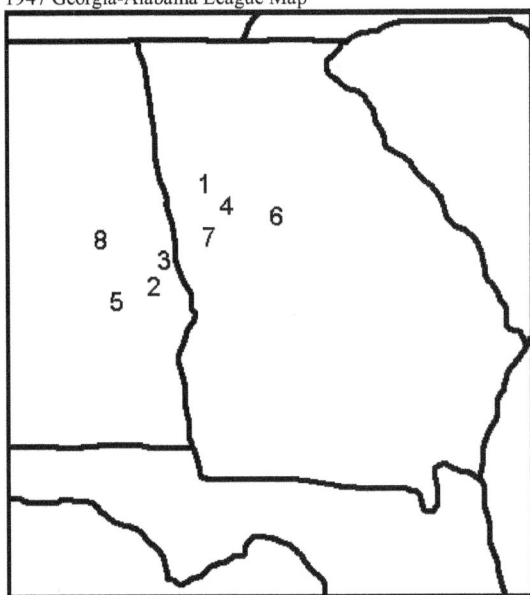

(numbers on map correspond to the place each team finished in regular season play)

After a successful first season back on the diamond in 1946, the Georgia-Alabama League returned in 1947 with two new members. Alexander City, Alabama, and Griffin, Georgia joined the six teams from the previous year to make the league an expanded, eight-club loop.

On May 3, Valley pitcher Ed Wiilliams pitched a no-hitter routing Carrollton 12 to 0. LaGrange pitcher Bill Regan pitched the season's second no-hitter on August 18 against Alexander City. Regan won by a final of 5 to 0 in the shortened, seven-inning contest. Malvern Morgan of Valley had 184 hits during the year setting the all-time single season most hits record for the Georgia-Alabama League. Newnan pitcher Paul Brock set the league's all-time single season mark for the most wins with 23. This record was later tied in 1948 by Opelika's Bill Kallaher and Carrollton's Gene Doerflinger. Brock also set the all-time single season league records for most hits allowed with 282 and most innings pitched with 313. Pitcher Jesse Danna of Valley lost 18 games setting the all-time record for the most losses in a season for the Georgia-Alabama League.

Carrollton won the regular season pennant with the best record edging out Opelika by .002 points. Carrollton played third place Valley in the first round of the playoffs to see who would advance to the league championship series, and Opelika and Newnan, second and fourth places respectively, squared off for the other championship series berth. Valley defeated Carrollton three games to one, and Opelika eliminated Newnan by the exact same score. Valley won the seven-game championship series over Opelika four games to two to become league champions.

Alexander City, Alabama

Team Operated by Douglas Taitt and James Outlaw
Team President: James Callahan
Vice President: George Hulme
Manager(s): Doug Taitt
Games played at Benjamin C. Russell Field

Alexander City Millers Team Roster

NAME	G	BA	POS	W	L	ERA	APF
Adkinson, Bill	14	0.083	C				
Alexander, Bill	46	0.289	1B				
Boatman, Jim	37	0.212	SS, OF				
Boos, Wendell	35	0.145	P	11	14	4.38	
Carmichael, Ed	124	0.324	OF				Tallassee
Carter, Steve	26	0.232	3B, OF				Tallassee
Chappell, Marv	61	0.227	OF, P	7	13	3.42	
Chitwood, Ed	27	0.091	P	5	15	6.10	
Collins, Lee	47	0.201	OF				Ca - Ne - Ta
Culpepper, Bill	65	0.329	3B, OF				
Davis, Fred	12	0.133	P	0	4	5.09	
Davis, Max	120	0.294	1B, OF				
Davis, Ralph	30	0.248	2B, 3B				
Doerflinger, Gene	25	0.222	P	8	7	3.47	
Driskell, Roy	36	0.185	OF				
Ellison, Lee	19	0.212	P	2	10	5.57	
Harrell, Joe	56	0.212	SS				
Hebert, Walter	15	0.135	3B				
Huesman, Jack	62	0.271	2B				
Huffman, Bob	59	0.146	C				
Mann, Elbert	10	0.321					
McKinney, Bill	34	0.135	C				
Mitchell, Joe Bob	17	0.273					
Nichols, Fred	62	0.252	OF				
Osteen, Bill	10	0.300					
Osteen, Frank	17	0.132	OF				
Patterson, Derward	19	0.220					
Persons, Jim	32	0.210	3B, C				
Reed, Bob	16	0.222	OF				Opelika
Rizzetta, Anthony	10	0.186	OF				Tallassee
Spencer, Dave	18	0.306	2B				
Stephens, Frank	14	0.273	P				
Taitt, Doug	52	0.213	M, 1B				
Teyema, Dave	113	0.302	SS, OF				
Wenclewicz, Walt	19	0.118	P	3	5	3.26	
Williams, Bill	12	0.192					
Yawn, Sid	23	0.258	C				

Georgia Class-D Minor League Baseball Encyclopedia

Carrollton, Georgia
Team Operated by Carrollton Baseball Club, Inc.
Team President: Andy W. Ford
Vice President-Secretary-Treasurer: R. E. Muse
Manager(s): Red Roberts
Games played at City Athletic Field

Carrollton Hornets Team Roster

NAME	G	BA	POS	W	L	ERA	APF
Alexander, Bill	16	0.125	P	3	4	5.42	Griffin
Allen, Johnny	83	0.242	2B, OF				LaGrange
Bozzuto, Bert	26	0.113	P	10	6	3.09	
Collins, Lee	47	0.201	OF				AC - Ne - Ta
Crain, Paul	41	0.205	P	19	14	2.93	Valley
Dendinger, Dick	23	0.260	C				
DiMasi, Joe	17	0.246	OF				
Ello, Jim	89	0.224	C				Griffin
Goicoechea, Leo	12	0.160	P	5	2	3.46	
Hill, Jim	90	0.295	C				
Jones, Bill	70	0.276	OF, P	14	11	3.41	Newnan
Kelly, Dick	122	0.303	3B				
Langley, Jim	89	0.277	1B				
Little, Walt	10	0.129	P	7	3	3.60	
Marshall, Shorty	121	0.330	2B, SS				
Matthews, Bob	40	0.182	P	18	16	2.54	Newnan
Monarchi, Pete	70	0.270	2B, OF				
Murphee, Bill	39	0.304	1B				
Padgett, Charles	17	0.162	SS				
Patterson, Bill	81	0.249	OF, C				
Roberts, Red	97	0.385	M, SS				
Singley, Hulen	17	0.091	P	9	4	4.45	
Smith, ---	5		P	3	2		
Snider, Floyd	124	0.307	OF				
Thomas, Dallas	107	0.284	OF				
Tilley, Travis	28	0.244	OF				LaGrange
Webb, Bill	31	0.406	P	22	5	2.40	

Griffin, Georgia
Team Operated by Griffin Baseball Club, Inc.
Team President: Louis George
Vice President: Joseph George
Secretary-Treasurer-Business Manager: T.D. Westmoreland
Manager(s): Abe White
Games played at Pimiento Park

Griffin Pimientos Team Roster

NAME	G	BA	POS	W	L	ERA	APF
Alexander, Bill	16	0.125	P	3	4	5.42	Carrollton
Anderson, Dick	30	0.128	C				
Ayers, Lonzo	47	0.209	P	5	4	3.20	Newnan
Blackstock, Hal	114	0.316	3B, SS				Valley
Blackwell, Tom	118	0.246	3B				
Brodzinski, Jim	31	0.172	P	9	9	4.44	Tallassee
Brooks, Warren	75	0.330	2B				
Childs, Frank	61	0.231	OF, P	11	11	4.83	
Ello, Jim	89	0.224	C				Carrollton
Forrester, Frank	115	0.235	OF				
Guettler, Ken	109	0.334	OF				
Harrelson, John	34	0.207	P	12	12	4.15	
Hartman, Earl	117	0.295	1B				
Jones, Roser	31	0.281	OF				LaGrange
King, Claude	11	0.222	P	2	4	6.45	
Kirkland, Bill	10	0.222					
Lohr, Larry	22	0.132	P	6	8	4.67	New - Tal
McWhorter, Marcus	22	0.114	P	8	7	4.15	
Murphy, Jim	112	0.276	OF				
Swanson, Dale	16	0.208	2B				Newnan
Swanson, Ralph	19	0.380	SS				Newnan
White, Abe	39	0.225	M, P	10	13	3.44	
Wiggins, LeRoy	27	0.141	P	8	7	3.74	Valley

| Witzke, Howard | 25 | 0.242 | 2B | | | | |

LaGrange, Georgia
Team Operated by LaGrange Baseball Club, Inc.
Team President: G.L. Cahall
Secretary-Treasurer-Business Manager: Oliver Hunnicutt
Manager(s): Carl East, Howard Ermisch
Games played at Callaway Stadium

LaGrange Troupers Team Roster

NAME	G	BA	POS	W	L	ERA	APF
Adams, Bob	14	0.286	SS				
Allen, Johnny	83	0.242	2B, OF				Carrollton
Balais, Alex	11	0.214					
Briggs, Harold	13	0.158	P	1	5	6.71	
Camp, Loy	11	0.217	P	3	3	2.70	
Chandler, Dave	20	0.185	P	3	4	5.45	
Copeland, Elmer	41	0.149	P	13	15	3.95	
Daniel, Jake	95	0.313	1B				Newnan
Danish, Chris	73	0.298	C				
East, Carl			M				
Ermisch, Howard	62	0.274	M, 3B, SS				
Ford, Don	37	0.204	C				Tallassee
Glaze, Hugh	66	0.279	SS				
Griffin, Ed	89	0.197	3B, OF, C				
Hall, Bob	64	0.253	1B, OF				
Hammack, Shurley	78	0.188	2B				
Hamrick, Charles	41	0.245	OF				Newnan
Hamrick, Roy	21	0.286	1B				
Hoflack, Dan	40	0.243	OF				
Jones, Roser	31	0.281	OF				Griffin
Lomberger, John	68	0.261	OF				
Melton, Ray	48	0.235	3B				
Murray, Tom	27	0.265	P	5	5	4.45	
Murray, Walt	10	0.083					
Regan, Bill	11	0.182	P	3	3	3.32	
Sloan, George	29	0.293	2B				
Tilley, Travis	28	0.244	OF				Carrollton
Travers, Tom	12	0.095	P	1	7	4.78	
Walls, Boyd	13	0.159	C				
Ware, Bruce	98	0.293	OF				
Watson, Ed	11	0.150	P	2	5	4.96	
Williams, Curtis	14	0.176	P	3	4	9.60	
Wilson, Walt	17	0.227	P	7	9	4.23	

Newnan, Georgia
Team Operated by Newnan Baseball Association, Inc.
Team President: A.L. Fuller
Vice President: Hamilton C. Arnall
Secretary-Treasurer-Business Manager: A.L. Potts
Manager(s): Joe Abreu, Ed Westbrook
Games played at Pickett Field

Newnan Brownies Team Roster

NAME	G	BA	POS	W	L	ERA	APF
Abreu, Joe	104	0.290	M, 2B				
Astin, Bob	32	0.289	OF				
Ayers, Lonzo	47	0.209	P	5	4	3.20	Griffin
Bottoms, Woodrow	48	0.337	3B, SS				
Brock, Paul	67	0.225	OF, P	23	11	2.33	
Browning, Ted	123	0.311	OF				
Collins, Lee	47	0.201	OF				AC - Ca - Ta
Daniel, Jake	95	0.313	1B				LaGrange
DePillo, George	22	0.301	2B				
Eidson, Lewis	18	0.114	P	10	4	2.92	
Hamrick, Charles	41	0.245	OF				LaGrange
Harrell, Ben	12	0.053					
Hill, John	125	0.288	3B				Tallassee
Jones, Bill	70	0.276	OF, P	14	11	3.41	Carrollton

Georgia Class-D Minor League Baseball Encyclopedia

NAME	G	BA	POS	W	L	ERA	APF
Krohn, Duane	20	0.156	P	4	3	3.68	
Lohr, Larry	22	0.132	P	6	8	4.67	Grif - Tal
Mason, George	52	0.242	OF				Tallassee
Matthews, Bob	40	0.182	P	18	16	2.54	Carrollton
McCravy, Charles	16	0.121	P	3	8	6.00	Valley
McFarland, Bill	20	0.268	1B				
Morris, Dave	18	0.182	OF				
Powers, Tom	15	0.137	SS				Tallassee
Shoemake, Claude	123	0.341	OF				
Skalski, Chester	99	0.294	SS				
Stanley, Bob	115	0.252	C				
Stoyle, Jim	80	0.358	1B				
Swanson, Dale	16	0.208	2B				Griffin
Swanson, Ralph	19	0.380	SS				Griffin
Swygert, Alan	15	0.268	OF				
Westbrook, Ed	29	0.197	M, P	9	5	3.14	Tallassee
Whitney, Jim	29	0.175	C				

Opelika, Alabama
Team Operated by Opelika Baseball Club, Inc.
Team President: I.J. Scott
Vice President: Eason Cook
Secretary: Webb Kennedy
Treasurer: Phil Hudson
Business Manager-Travel Secretary: Zack Schuessler
Manager(s): Luther Gunnells
Games played at Pepperell Park

Opelika Owls Team Roster

NAME	G	BA	POS	W	L	ERA	APF
Bailey, Don	126	0.318	OF				
Ball, Jim	122	0.305	OF				
Burnette, Etheridge	64	0.276	3B, P	5	3	3.21	
Cole, Ken	28	0.165	C				
Dennany, Bob	29	0.090	P	8	5	3.70	
Flemming, Wheeler	125	0.239	1B				
Glaze, Claude	20	0.229	P	5	5	4.19	
Godwin, Bill	91	0.303	3B				
Gunnells, Luther	123	0.314	M, SS				
Hicks, Elroy	15	0.130	P				
Jeter, Cleo	13	0.250					
Jones, Tom	32	0.224	P	12	11	4.04	
Kallaher, Bill	38	0.268	P	16	10	3.09	
Nelson, Jim	88	0.251	C				
Noto, Phil	24	0.207	2B				Tallassee
Reed, Bob	16	0.222	OF				Alex City
Riddle, Jim	126	0.287	OF				
Schuessler, Zach	11	0.280	P	7	3	4.05	
Sinquefield, Roy	32	0.154	P	15	7	2.94	
Vinson, Earl	125	0.299	2B				

Tallassee, Alabama
Team Operated by Tallassee Baseball Club, Inc.
Team President: A.T. Holloway
Vice President: O.F. Kelly
Secretary: Clyde Pruitt
Treasurer: W.F. Gulledge
Manager(s): John Hill
Games played at Stumberg Field

Tallassee Indians Team Roster

NAME	G	BA	POS	W	L	ERA	APF
Aurelio, Ed	48	0.248	1B				
Beavers, Jim	26	0.125	P	10	9	4.75	
Brawner, Ralph	36	0.270	OF				
Brodzinski, Jim	31	0.172	P	9	9	4.44	Griffin
Campo, Ray	41	0.256	C				
Carmichael, Ed	124	0.324	OF				Alex City
Carter, Steve	26	0.232	3B, OF				Alex City
Collins, Lee	47	0.201	OF				AC - Ca - Ne
Corley, Art	10	0.087	P	7	2	2.25	
Edwards, Ray	125	0.273	3B, OF				
Ford, Don	37	0.204	C				LaGrange
Hill, John	125	0.288	M, 3B				Newnan
Knowles, Earl	69	0.311	OF				
Lohr, Larry	22	0.132	P	6	8	4.67	Grif - New
Mason, George	52	0.242	OF				Newnan
Medlock, Frank	64	0.180	C				
Nelson, Burel	37	0.160	P	13	14	3.26	
Noto, Phil	24	0.207	2B				Opelika
Powers, Tom	15	0.137	SS				Newnan
Rhyne, Marvel	13	0.200	1B				
Rizzetta, Anthony	10	0.186	OF				Alex City
Robertson, Preston	12	0.121	P	6	6	3.60	
Ryan, Jim	20	0.239					
Schwab, Bob	11	0.200	OF				
Smith, Joe	45	0.331	OF				
Urso, Joe	116	0.281	2B				
Ward, Milt	77	0.265	1B, OF				
Westbrook, Ed	29	0.197	P	9	5	3.14	Newnan
Wollitz, Herman	14	0.257	P	5	3	2.97	
Wright, Maurice	125	0.255	SS				

Valley (Lanett), Alabama
Team Operated by Valley Baseball Club, Inc.
Team President: G.E. "Cheese" Goggans
Vice President: Fob James
Secretary-Business Manager: J.Hoyt Gay
Treasurer: Donald G. Lord
Manager(s): Art Luce
Games played at Jennings Field

Valley Rebels Team Roster

NAME	G	BA	POS	W	L	ERA	APF
Anderson, Martin	22	0.306	P	8	6	3.71	
Blackburn, Tom	100	0.286	3B, OF				
Blackstock, Hal	114	0.316	3B, SS				Griffin
Bosarge, Vince	48	0.243	SS				
Chambers, Joe	126	0.317	2B				
Crain, Paul	41	0.205	P	19	14	2.93	Carrollton
Danna, Charles	110	0.318	C				
Danna, Jesse	51	0.171	OF, P	17	18	2.15	
Edwards, Bob	116	0.305	OF, P				
Frazier, Lance	14	0.390	C				
Frazier, Ralph	12	0.244	1B				
Giglio, Joe	10	0.059	P	3	2	3.63	
Hartlein, Bill	97	0.297	OF				
Jones, Barry	57	0.240	SS				
Lewis, Jim	90	0.320	1B				
Luce, Art	18	0.200	M, OF				
McCravy, Charles	16	0.121	P	3	8	6.00	Newnan
Milner, Bruce	23	0.220	OF				
Minarck, Bill	14	0.104	SS				
Morgan, Malvern	126	0.364	1B, 3B				
White, John	28	0.223	P				
Wiggins, Bob	16	0.125	P	2	4	5.17	
Wiggins, LeRoy	27	0.141	P	8	7	3.74	Griffin
Williams, Ed	9		P	4	3	3.33	

1947 Georgia-Alabama League Records
Batting
Highest Batting Average (minimum 100 at bats)
1. Red Roberts – Carrollton .385
2. Malvern Morgan – Valley .364
3. Jim Stoyle – Newnan .358
4. Claude Shoemake – Newnan .341
5. Woodrow Bottoms – Newnan .337

Georgia Class-D Minor League Baseball Encyclopedia

Most Hits
1. Malvern Morgan – Valley   184
2. Shorty Marshall – Carrollton   171
3. Claude Shoemake – Newnan   170
4. Ted Browning – Newnan   162
5. Don Bailey – Opelika   160

Most Runs
1. Ted Browning – Newnan   122
2. Joe Chambers – Valley   102
3. Bob Edwards – Valley   101
4. Shorty Marshall – Carrollton   99
5. Malvern Morgan – Valley   96

Most Total Bases
1. Malvern Morgan – Valley   259
2. Claude Shoemake – Newnan   249
3. Floyd Snider – Carrollton   245
4. Luther Gunnells – Opelika   241
5. Ken Guettler – Griffin   240

Most Doubles
1. Malvern Morgan – Valley   34
   Claude Shoemake – Newnan   34
   Hal Blackstock – Grif/Newn   34
4. Luther Gunnells – Opelika   30
5. Shorty Marshall – Carrollton   29

Most Triples
1. Joe Chambers – Valley   13
2. Max Davis - Alexander City   12
3. Earl Hartman – Griffin   11
   Jim Ball – Opelika   11
5. Bob Edwards – Valley   10

Most Home Runs
1. Ken Guettler – Griffin   25
2. Floyd Snider – Carrollton   21
   Luther Gunnells – Opelika   21
4. Jim Langley – Carrollton   18
5. Earl Hartman – Griffin   15

Most Extra Base Hits
1. Luther Gunnells – Opelika   53
2. Floyd Snider – Carrollton   52
   Earl Hartman – Griffin   52
4. Claude Shoemake – Newnan   51
5. Malvern Morgan – Valley   50

Most Runs Batted In
1. Ken Guettler – Griffin   103
2. Floyd Snider – Carrollton   102
3. Claude Shoemake – Newnan   101
   John Hill – Newn/Tall   101
5. Joe Chambers – Valley   96

Most Stolen Bases
1. Ted Browning – Newnan   42
2. Jim Ball – Opelika   39
3. Bob Edwards – Valley   35
4. Jim Murphy – Griffin   30
5. Luther Gunnells – Opelika   27
   Joe Urso – Tallassee   27

Fielding
Most Put-Outs
1. Wheeler Flemming 1B – Opelika   1,088
2. Earl Hartman 1B – Griffin   949
3. Jake Daniel 1B – LaGrange   788
4. Jim Langley 1B – Carrollton   771
5. Jim Lewis 1B – Valley   747

Most Assists
1. Maurice Wright SS – Tallassee   389
2. Luther Gunnells SS – Opelika   362
3. Joe Chambers 2B – Valley   345
4. Joe Abreu 2B – Newnan   333
5. Hal Blackstock 3B, SS – Grif/Vall 328

Most Errors
1. Maurice Wright SS – Tallassee   58
2. Luther Gunnells SS – Opelika   57
3. Dick Kelly 3B – Carrollton   53
4. Hal Blackstock 3B, SS – Grif/Vall 47
5. Joe Urso 3B – Tallassee   45
   Dave Teyema SS, OF - Alexander City 45

Pitching
Most Wins
1. Paul Brock – Newnan   23
2. Bill Webb – Carrollton   22
3. Paul Crain – Carr/Vall   19
4. Bob Matthews – Carr/Newn   18
5. Jesse Danna – Valley   17

Most Losses
1. Jesse Danna – Valley   18
2. Bob Matthews – Carr/Newn   16
3. Elmer Copeland – LaGrange   15
   Ed Chitwood - Alexander City   15
5. Paul Crain – Carr/Vall   14
   Burel Nelson – Tallassee   14
   Wendell Boos - Alexander City   14

Highest Winning Percentage (10 game minimum)
1. Bill Webb – Carrollton   .815
2. Art Corley – Tallassee   .778
3. Lewis Eidson – Newnan   .714
   Leo Goicoechea – Carrollton   .714
5. Zach Schuessler – Opelika   .700
   Walt Little – Carrollton   .700

Lowest Earned Run Average (100 inning minimum)
1. Jesse Danna – Valley   2.15
2. Paul Brock – Newnan   2.33
3. Bill Webb – Carrollton   2.40
4. Bob Matthews – Carr/Newn   2.54
5. Lewis Eidson – Newnan   2.92

Most Strikeouts
1. Paul Brock – Newnan   220
2. Burel Nelson – Tallassee   161
3. Roy Sinquefield – Opelika   155
4. Paul Crain – Carr/Vall   152
5. Bill Kallaher – Opelika   143

Most Bases on Balls
1. Jim Beavers – Tallassee   108
   Jim Brodzinski – Grif/Tall   108
3. Frank Childs – Griffin   92
4. Ed Chitwood - Alexander City   87
5. Burel Nelson – Tallassee   85

Most Hits Allowed
1. Paul Brock – Newnan   282
2. Elmer Copeland – LaGrange   268
3. Paul Crain – Carr/Vall   255
4. Abe White – Griffin   244
5. Bob Matthews – Carr/Newn   229

Most Innings Pitched
1. Paul Brock – Newnan   313
2. Paul Crain – Carr/Vall   261
3. Bob Matthews – Carr/Newn   248
4. Elmer Copeland – LaGrange   244
5. Burel Nelson – Tallassee   232
   Bill Jones – Newn/Carr   232

1947 Georgia-Alabama League All-Star Team
1B Jim Stoyle – Newnan
2B Joe Chambers – Valley
3B Hal Blackstock – Griffin
SS Red Roberts – Carrollton
OF Bob Edwards – Valley
OF Ted Browning – Newnan
OF Ken Guettler – Griffin
C   Charles Danna – Valley
C   Jim Hill – Carrollton
UT Shorty Marshall – Carrollton
UT Claude Shoemake – Newnan
P   Bill Webb – Carrollton
P   Jesse Danna – Valley

1947

Georgia-Florida League

League Office: Leslie, Georgia
League President: W.T. Anderson
League Vice President: Guy Connell
Salary Limit: $2,200 per month.
Player Rule: Each club was allowed a roster of fifteen players, not more than four veterans, not more than six limited service, and not less than five rookies.
Umpires: Robert W. Vocial, Lewis E. Anderson, M.E. Combs, Harry P. Holmes, Gerald W. LaCount, Michael J. Marino, Charles W. Smeltzer, Francis J. Stiles, and H.W. Stover.

Georgia-Florida League Final Standings

Team	W	L	Pct	GB	Affiliate
Moultrie Packers	85	53	.616	----	Unaffiliated
Waycross Bears	79	59	.572	6.0	Unaffiliated
Tallahassee Pirates	80	60	.571	6.0	PIT-NL
Albany Cardinals	78	62	.557	8.0	STL-NL
Thomasville Tigers	68	69	.498	16.5	DET-AL
Americus Phillies	65	74	.468	20.5	PHI-NL
Valdosta Dodgers	54	84	.391	31.0	BRK-NL
Cordele Indians	45	93	.326	40.0	CLE-AL

1947 Georgia-Florida League Map

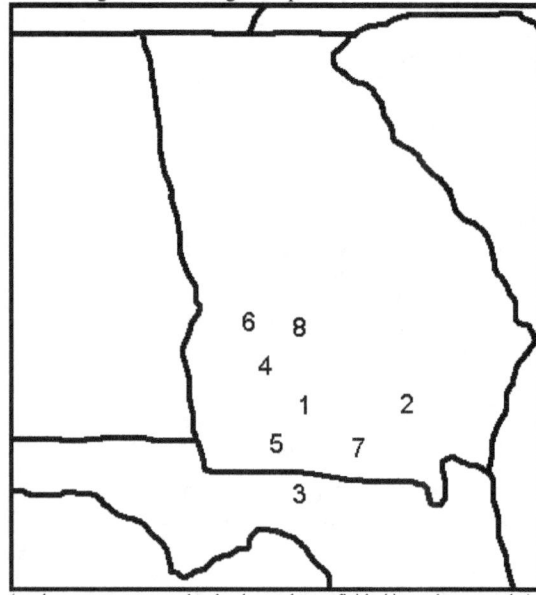

(numbers on map correspond to the place each team finished in regular season play)

The composition of the Georgia-Florida League stayed the same from 1946 in the 1947 baseball season.
Valdosta pitcher Don Otten pitched the year's first no-hitter when he defeated Albany 2 to 0 on May 18. In a 15 to 0 routing of Valdosta, Waycross hurler Bob Galey threw the second no-hitter of the season on July 22. Davey Williams of Waycross set the league's all-time record for scoring the most runs in a single season when he crossed the plate 147 times during the year.

Georgia Class-D Minor League Baseball Encyclopedia

Moultrie won the regular season pennant for the league, and Waycross, Tallahassee, and Albany finished behind the Packers in order. Waycross and Tallahassee were both six games behind Moultrie, but Waycross' winning percentage was .001 points higher than Moultrie's. The league switched the places that played each other in the first round of the Shaughnessy playoffs. Previously, first and third places faced off as did second and fourth. This year, first place, Moultrie, played fourth place, Albany, and second, Waycross, played against third, Tallahassee. Moultrie swept Albany in three straight games, and Tallahassee took all five games to beat Waycross three to two. When Moultrie and Tallahassee squared off in the championship series, the Packers defeated the sole Florida team four games to two. Following the series, Moultrie advanced to the Southern Championship interleague series against Gainesville, champions of the Florida State League. Moultrie also won this series four games to three.

Albany, Georgia
Team Operated by Albany Baseball Club, Inc.
Team President: Morton M. Wiggins
Vice President: S. Breadon
Secretary-Treasurer: Edward W. Roth
Business Manager: L.W. Bergesch
Manager(s): Mickey Katkaveck
Games played at Tift Stadium
Major League Affiliate: St. Louis Cardinals – National League.

Albany Cardinals Team Roster

NAME	G	BA	POS	W	L	ERA	APF
Bell, Jefferson	32	0.180	2B				
Bricker, Cy	9		P	0	3	2.54	
Cyrus, Dave	70	0.321	OF, P	13	13	3.31	
Dance, John	13	0.162	OF				
Ewaniak, John	140	0.322	OF				
Frisinger, Jack	34	0.207	P	20	7	2.18	
Golembiewski, Marion	107	0.277	1B, OF, P	8	3	4.50	
Herbison, Jim	140	0.255	2B, SS				
Jacquot, Jim	12	0.147	OF				
Jones, Vern	12	0.250	P	1	4	6.51	
Katkaveck, Mickey	102	0.224	M, C				
McCulley, Melvin	48	0.259	OF				
McGovern, Russ	128	0.248	OF				
Porreca, Frank	134	0.271	1B				
Scheidts, Ed	24	0.216	P	5	8	3.60	
Schoendienst, Elmer	133	0.254	3B, SS				
Selbee, Bill	12	0.135	OF				
Simpson, Cliff	108	0.274	SS				
Stephens, Don	37	0.211	P	12	12	3.44	
Thompson, Bob	62	0.186	C				
Vogeltanz, Bob	48	0.250	P	15	6	3.17	

Americus, Georgia
Team Operated by Philadelphia National League Baseball Club
Team President: H. Phil Jones
Vice President: Raymond Holt
Secretary: J.R. Blair
Treasurer: George A. Fletcher
Business Manager: Grady L. "Pete" Rockett
Manager(s): Lew Krausse, Jack Sanford
Games played at Community Center Ballpark
Major League Affiliate: Philadelphia Phillies – National League.

Americus Phillies Team Roster

NAME	G	BA	POS	W	L	ERA	APF
Asmer, John	39	0.169	OF, P	7	11	6.02	
Bacha, Bill	98	0.245	3B				
Barrow, Ray	16	0.160	P	1	4	7.42	
Burnett, Ray	64	0.185	P	21	10	3.81	
Crucitti, Tony	11	0.114	SS				
Eilstrop, ---	30		OF				
Epps, George	17	0.270	OF				
Gilstrap, John	34	0.241					
Healy, Francis	35	0.139	P	12	15	3.57	
Hill, Bob	103	0.283	1B				
Howard, Crawford	139	0.303	OF				
Kelly, Art	123	0.281	3B, OF				
Kerr, Tom	9		P	4	4	4.13	
Krausse, Lew			M				
Kremer, George	65	0.171	SS				
McCullough, John	139	0.290	2B				
Moore, Vern	38	0.238	OF				
Pliszka, Matt	112	0.235	1B, OF, C				
Restic, Joe	20	0.088	P	2	8	6.70	
Riley, Bob	60	0.318	SS				
Sabine, Frank	41	0.107	P	9	9	3.66	
Sanford, Jack	14	0.404	M				
Smith, Harold	14	0.125	P				
Tanner, Bill	33	0.279	OF				
Volan, Ed	21	0.292	OF				
Walters, Ray	103	0.343	OF, C				
Witz, Tom	12	0.071	P	1	2	6.80	
Zwierzynski, Adam	20	0.182	OF				

Cordele, Georgia
Team Operated by Cordele Indians Baseball Club, Inc.
Team President: J.W. Bridges
Vice President: H.B. "Buzz" Wetzel
Secretary-Treasurer: Rudie Chaffer
Business Manager: Bob Reynolds
Manager(s): Mercer Harris
Games played at City Park
Major League Affiliate: Cleveland Indians – American League.

Cordele Indians Team Roster

NAME	G	BA	POS	W	L	ERA	APF
Brown, Arles	14	0.114	P	3	4	2.70	
Callaway, Bill	12	0.409					
Chredar, Steve	26	0.182	P	3	3	5.23	Tallahassee
Coker, Jim	21	0.218	C				
Cooper, Stewart	20	0.322	OF				
Crouch, Les	10	0.300	SS				
Davis, Spencer	12	0.214	P	1	4	4.79	
Fouts, Paul	71	0.290	2B				
Freeland, John	75	0.248	C				
Gregg, Fred	105	0.326	3B, SS				
Gross, Don	101	0.221	2B, 3B, C				
Harris, Mercer	55	0.299	M, 1B, 3B				
Howell, Jim	16	0.176	3B				
Jobe, Lew	28	0.216	P	2	8	4.70	
Lee, Frank	14	0.304	OF				
Lee, Hal	35	0.254	3B				
Lefler, Henry	113	0.271	1B, 3B, SS				
Mashburn, Ernest	33	0.176	OF				
McCormick, Dick	21	0.151	2B				
McDonald, Bob	33	0.321	2B				
Milam, Lawrence	10	0.133					
Park, Maynard	21	0.163	P	10	8	3.63	
Pettis, Tom	12	0.150	1B				
Pompelia, Gene	98	0.264	OF				
Rawlings, Vern	13	0.152	OF				
Scott, Bill	21	0.182	OF				
Sharpless, Seaborne	109	0.254	OF				
Sheffield, Frank	30	0.140	P	6	9	5.76	
Simpson, Charles	32	0.160	P, C	1	13	4.35	
Stewart, Ray	14	0.308	3B				

Georgia Class-D Minor League Baseball Encyclopedia

NAME	G	BA	POS	W	L	ERA
Strickland, Norris	89	0.300	1B, OF			
Vitter, Jim	44	0.236	P	11	16	4.24
Young, Tex	19	0.139	P	0	8	3.80

Moultrie, Georgia
Team Operated by J.R. Poole, Eva B. Poole, and Phil S. Poole
Team President: F.R. Pidcock, Jr.
General Manager: J.R. Poole
Secretary: Eva B. Poole
Treasurer: Phil S. Poole
Business Manager: C.W. Vandiver
Manager(s): Buster Kinard, Jim Poole
Games played at Municipal Park

Moultrie Packers Team Roster

NAME	G	BA	POS	W	L	ERA	APF
Bargas, John	34	0.205	C				
Barnes, Bill	89	0.294	3B				
Brewer, Orbie	72	0.262	OF				
Brooks, Warren	24	0.361	2B				
Bryant, Harold	65	0.219	3B, OF				
Burkhardt, John	12	0.304					
Colombatto, Pete	104	0.262	2B				
Gowan, Reid	14	0.298	P	4	2	3.50	
Herbik, John	46	0.168	P	15	3	3.58	
Icenhour, Phil	43	0.250	OF				
Kinard, Buster	33	0.289	M, OF				
LaFrance, Bill	138	0.304	OF, P	6	3	3.46	
Langemeier, Paul	29	0.135	P	9	5	5.06	
Laumann, Andrew	137	0.275	SS				
Lemish, Gaylord	20	0.188	P	8	6	3.82	
Lentz, Walt	33	0.215	P	12	7	2.95	
Miller, Gibbs	14	0.242					
Poole, Jim			M				
Rhyne, Ken	138	0.304	1B				
Sowins, Ray	103	0.280	OF				
Steedly, Alvin	42	0.210	P	14	10	3.97	
Vukas, Steve	27	0.138	P	8	6	3.10	
Whitmore, Don	13	0.103	P	3	4	3.88	
Wilson, Clyde	24	0.132	C				
Wrenn, Milt	100	0.290	C				

Tallahassee, Florida
Team Operated by Pittsburgh National League Baseball Club
Team President: Fred N. Lowry
Vice President: H. Roy Hamey
Secretary: Ray Kennedy
Business Manager: Bob Bonifay
Manager(s): Phil Seghi
Games played at Centennial Field
Major League Affiliate: Pittsburgh Pirates – National League.

Tallahassee Pirates Team Roster

NAME	G	BA	POS	W	L	ERA	APF
Anjeski, Elmer	141	0.317	OF				
Bandoch, Ed	73	0.225	3B, C				
Bartolozzi, Ralph	133	0.236	1B				
Brannan, Charles	10	0.269					
Campbell, Earl	12	0.268					
Chredar, Steve	26	0.182	P	3	3	5.23	Cordele
Dravecky, Andrew	100	0.257	C				
Fink, Jim	12	0.240	3B				
Fisher, Harry	39	0.318	P	16	9	3.15	
Holder, Charles	129	0.268	SS				
Judy, George	24	0.245	P	7	8	2.50	
Lutes, Bill	126	0.281	OF				
Maxwell, Elmo	<10						
Munch, Bill	12	0.533	P				

NAME	G	BA	POS	W	L	ERA
Page, Glen	57	0.239	P	15	6	2.63
Pierro, Bill	14	0.000	P			
Rixey, Ben	38	0.234	OF			
Seghi, Phil	83	0.276	M, 3B			
Sezna, Tom	130	0.252	OF			
Smart, Charles	36	0.308	3B, SS			
Stasko, Julius	141	0.266	2B			
Tafaro, Dan	16	0.261	P	0	4	5.26
Walker, Jack	40	0.219	P	15	14	4.73
Yebernetsky, George	36	0.313	P	13	9	3.69

Thomasville, Georgia
Team Operated by Thomasville Baseball Company
Team President: Heeth Varnedoe
Vice Presidents: G.E. Gilliland, Richard Wagner
Secretary-Treasurer: O.B. Anderson
Assistant Secretary: H.M. Sisson
Manager(s): Vincent Mullen
Games played at Municipal Stadium
Major League Affiliate: Detroit Tigers – American League.

Thomasville Tigers Team Roster

NAME	G	BA	POS	W	L	ERA	APF
Bowden, Ray	88	0.277	2B				
Cronin, Jim	130	0.292	OF				
Dimitriadis, Jim	28	0.226	P	6	10	4.06	
Frew, Bill	32	0.161	P	6	12	3.88	
Grice, John	137	0.340	OF				
Hassler, Percy	50	0.223	3B, SS				
Henkel, Howard	40	0.328	2B				
Markham, Ken	41	0.224	P	13	12	4.00	
Mason, George	11	0.171	OF				
Mullen, Vincent	54	0.277	M, 2B, 3B, SS				
Nedelco, Alex	17	0.139	P	6	3	3.49	
Pelot, Harold	13	0.188	P				
Phillips, Ray	119	0.301	OF				
Snyder, Paul	34	0.145	P	12	10	4.34	
Snyder, Ron	108	0.271	C				
Stamos, Pete	17	0.160	P	8	2	1.83	
Verbish, George	20	0.231	C				
Warren, Bob	47	0.261	3B				
Waugh, Art	47	0.273	C				
Weeks, Ralph	138	0.321	1B				
Willett, Ray	42	0.250	SS				
Yohn, Charles	39	0.188	P	15	7	2.44	
Zabek, Ed	118	0.233	3B, SS				

Valdosta, Georgia
Team Operated by Brooklyn National League Baseball Club
Team President: C.W. Singleton
Vice President: Harold G. Roettger
Secretary: Fresco Thompson
Treasurer: D.E. Beach
Public Relations-Travel Secretary-Business Manager:
    Victor A. Zodda
Manager(s): Hugh Holliday
Games played at Pendleton Park
Major League Affiliate: Brooklyn Dodgers – National League.

Valdosta Dodgers Team Roster

NAME	G	BA	POS	W	L	ERA	APF
Baskin, Al	37	0.070	P	6	11	3.83	
Blackman, Don	27	0.186	2B				
Bradshaw, George	18	0.268	C				
Brophy, Jim	13	0.196	OF				
DeArmond, Hollis	43	0.314	C				
Gillet, Al	21	0.141	C				
Hoak, Don	134	0.295	3B				

Georgia Class-D Minor League Baseball Encyclopedia

NAME	G	BA	POS	W	L	ERA
Holliday, Hugh	26	0.257	M			
Kane, Murray	16	0.222	P	4	3	2.57
Koch, Art	35	0.044	P	9	9	3.65
Koenig, Leon	120	0.252	OF			
Lehman, Ken	25	0.218	P	5	11	2.49
Lynn, Fred	22	0.065	P	6	5	5.13
Mack, Jerome	23	0.238	OF			
McNulty, Jim	125	0.243	2B, SS			
Mills, Gil	84	0.256	OF, P	5	11	4.36
Noah, Harold	47	0.241	OF			
Otten, Don	22	0.178	P	6	10	4.33
Pinkston, Ewell	21	0.246				
Pulcini, John	96	0.199	1B			
Rey, Emil	112	0.217	SS			
Robinson, Orem	29	0.250	P	10	10	2.66
Smith, Gil	101	0.243	OF, C			
Steger, Dave	85	0.292	1B, OF			
Taylor, Don	31	0.229	OF			
Tomkinson, Phil	78	0.345	C			
Watts, Bill	11	0.227	P	2	6	4.42

Waycross, Georgia
Team Operated by Waycross Baseball Association, Inc.
Team President: Herbert Bradshaw
Vice President: William D. Rivenbark
Treasurer: Charles H. Andrews
Manager(s): LeGrant Scott
Games played at Newton Field

Waycross Bears Team Roster

NAME	G	BA	POS	W	L	ERA	APF
Anderson, Harrison	11	0.255	1B				
Bremer, Walt	133	0.285	3B				
Cherry, Dick	12	0.143	P	4	3	4.37	
Coker, Jack	33	0.250	P	12	10	3.95	
Colgan, Bill	18	0.241	OF				
Cronic, Guin	14	0.250	P	4	4	5.34	
Doane, Carl	13	0.300	P				
Dwyer, Bill	119	0.279	1B, 2B, SS, OF				
Galey, Bob	41	0.277	P	18	8	4.11	
Harwood, Don	32	0.222	P	13	10	3.67	
Jones, Rudy	108	0.333	1B, OF				
Kreider, Jesse	26	0.344	OF				
Leatherwood, Gil	39	0.192	1B				
Leeper, Mason	7		P	3	1	4.50	
McNulty, John	114	0.277	SS				
McWhorter, Pierce	96	0.250	C				
Njirich, Gildo	82	0.246	OF, C				
Paulick, Frank	53	0.274	OF				
Scott, LeGrant	76	0.359	M, OF				
Seidel, Ray	48	0.234	P	13	9	3.42	
Underwood, Glenn	43	0.075	P	5	6	5.94	
Voitier, Bob	104	0.339	OF				
Weathers, Charlie	43	0.184	OF				
Williams, Davey	132	0.282	2B				

1947 Georgia-Florida League Records
Batting
Highest Batting Average (minimum 100 at bats)
1. LeGrant Scott – Waycross .359
2. Phil Tomkinson – Valdosta .345
3. Ray Walters – Americus .343
4. John Grice – Thomasville .340
5. Bob Voitier – Waycross .339

Most Hits
1. John Grice – Thomasville 182
2. Elmer Anjeski – Tallahassee 177
3. Ralph Weeks – Thomasville 170
4. Crawford Howard – Americus 169
5. John Ewaniak – Albany 167

Most Runs
1. Davey Williams – Waycross 147
2. John McCullough – Americus 130
3. Andrew Laumann – Moultrie 128
4. Elmer Anjeski – Tallahassee 116
5. Julius Stasko – Tallahassee 115

Most Total Bases
1. Ken Rhyne – Moultrie 273
2. Bill LaFrance – Moultrie 254
3. John Ewaniak – Albany 248
4. John Grice – Thomasville 242
5. Elmer Anjeski – Tallahassee 238

Most Doubles
1. Davey Williams – Waycross 34
2. Bill LaFrance – Moultrie 33
3. John Ewaniak – Albany 32
   Art Kelly – Americus 32
5. Crawford Howard – Americus 31
   John McCullough – Americus 31

Most Triples
1. Fred Gregg – Cordele 13
2. Elmer Anjeski – Tallahassee 12
   Don Hoak – Valdosta 12
   Tom Sezna – Tallahassee 12
5. John Grice – Thomasville 11
   Bill Lutes – Tallahassee 11

Most Home Runs
1. Ken Rhyne – Moultrie 24
2. Bill LaFrance – Moultrie 18
3. Ray Sowins – Moultrie 16
4. John Ewaniak – Albany 11
5. Bob Voitier – Waycross 10
   Walt Bremer – Waycross 10

Most Extra Base Hits
1. Bill LaFrance – Moultrie 58
2. Ken Rhyne – Moultrie 57
3. Davey Williams – Waycross 52
4. John Ewaniak – Albany 51
5. Bob Voitier – Waycross 44
   Walt Bremer – Waycross 44

Most Runs Batted In
1. Ken Rhyne – Moultrie 141
2. Walt Bremer – Waycross 115
3. Crawford Howard – Americus 113
4. Bill LaFrance – Moultrie 111
5. John Ewaniak – Albany 99
   John Grice – Thomasville 99

Most Stolen Bases
1. John McCullough – Americus 42
2. Tom Sezna – Tallahassee 30
   Bill Dwyer – Waycross 30
4. Crawford Howard – Americus 28
   Davey Williams – Waycross 28

Fielding
Most Put-Outs
1. Ralph Weeks 1B – Thomasville 1,260
2. Ken Rhyne 1B – Moultrie 1,134

3. Ralph Bartolozzi 1B – Tallahassee 1,097
4. Frank Porreca 1B – Albany 1,089
5. Bob Hill 1B – Americus 807

Most Assists
1. Andrew Laumann SS – Moultrie 460
2. Jim McNulty 2B, SS – Valdosta 441
3. Julius Stasko 2B – Tallahassee 405
4. Charles Holder SS – Tallahassee 399
5. Jim Herbison 2B, SS – Albany 377

Most Errors
1. Cliff Simpson SS – Albany 75
2. Fred Gregg 3B, SS – Cordele 66
3. Andrew Laumann SS – Moultrie 57
   Charles Holder SS – Tallahassee 57
5. John McNulty SS – Waycross 53

Pitching
Most Wins
1. Ray Burnett – Americus 21
2. Jack Frisinger – Albany 20
3. Bob Galey – Waycross 18
4. Harry Fisher – Tallahassee 16
5. *five players tied with 15

Most Losses
1. Jim Vitter – Cordele 16
2. Francis Healy – Americus 15
3. Jack Walker – Tallahassee 14
4. Dave Cyrus – Albany 13
   Charles Simpson – Cordele 13

Highest Winning Percentage (10 game minimum)
1. John Herbik – Moultrie .833
2. Pete Stamos – Thomasville .800
3. Jack Frisinger – Albany .741
4. Marion Golembiewski – Albany .727
5. Glen Page – Tallahassee .714

Lowest Earned Run Average (100 inning minimum)
1. Jack Frisinger – Albany 2.18
2. Charles Yohn – Thomasville 2.44
3. Ken Lehman – Valdosta 2.49
4. George Judy – Tallahassee 2.50
5. Glen Page – Tallahassee 2.63

Most Strikeouts
1. Jack Frisinger – Albany 274
2. Ray Burnett – Americus 262
3. Bob Galey – Waycross 223
4. Harry Fisher – Tallahassee 209
5. Jack Coker – Waycross 198

Most Bases on Balls
1. Ray Burnett – Americus 179
2. Jack Coker – Waycross 159
3. Paul Snyder – Thomasville 142
4. Jack Frisinger – Albany 137
5. Art Koch – Valdosta 136

Most Hits Allowed
1. Dave Cyrus – Albany 242
2. Jim Vitter – Cordele 237
3. Jack Walker – Tallahassee 228
4. Ray Burnett – Americus 225
5. Francis Healy – Americus 222

Most Innings Pitched
1. Ray Burnett – Americus 253
2. Dave Cyrus – Albany 226
3. Bob Galey – Waycross 219
   Jack Frisinger – Albany 219
5. Ken Markham – Thomasville 218

1947 Georgia-Florida League All-Star Team
1B Ralph Weeks – Thomasville
2B Davey Williams – Waycross
3B Elmer Schoendienst – Albany
SS Emil Rey – Valdosta
OF John Ewaniak – Albany
OF Elmer Anjeski – Tallahassee
OF Crawford Howard – Americus
C Phil Tomkinson – Valdosta
UT Bill Dwyer – Waycross
UT Bill LaFrance – Moultrie
P Bob Galey – Waycross
P Jack Frisinger – Albany
M LeGrant Scott – Waycross

1948

Georgia-Alabama League

League Office: Talladega, Alabama
League President: Arthur R. Decatur
League Vice President: George Cahall
Salary Limit: $2,600 per month
Player Rule: Each club was allowed a roster of sixteen players, not more than one veteran, not more than six limited service, and not less than nine rookies.
Umpires: Paul W. Berenbrok, Everett C. Terry, William E. Owens, Arthur Nossokoff, Frank S. Sirocki, Leslie V. Zabel, Lakey Sullivan, and Ellis K. Taylor.

Georgia-Alabama League Final Standings

Team	W	L	Pct	GB	Affiliate
Valley Rebels	75	51	.595	----	BSN-AL
Carrollton Hornets	73	53	.579	2.0	Unaffiliated
Newnan Brownies	68	58	.540	7.0	Unaffiliated
Alexander City Millers	63	63	.500	12.0	Unaffiliated
Opelika Owls	62	64	.492	13.0	Unaffiliated
Griffin Pimientos	55	71	.437	20.0	STL-AL
LaGrange Troupers	54	72	.429	21.0	NY-AL
Tallassee Indians	54	72	.429	21.0	STL-NL

1948 Georgia-Alabama League Map

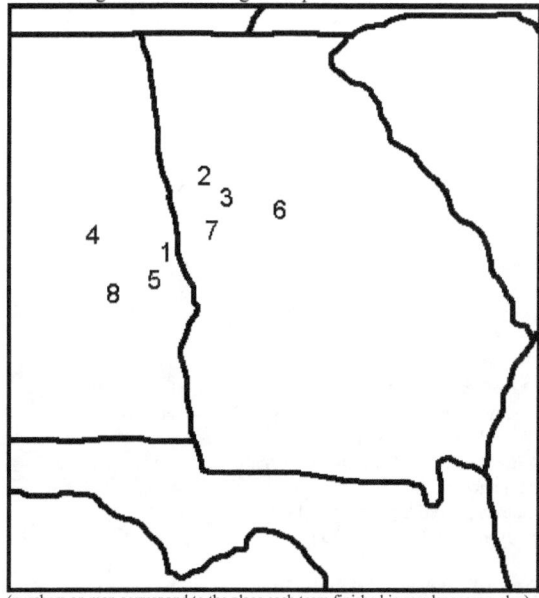

(numbers on map correspond to the place each team finished in regular season play)

In 1948, the eight-club Georgia-Alabama League remained in tact as the same eight-city aggregation from the 1947 season.

On April 29, 1948, Griffin outfielder Bill Savage stole home twice in the 9-run eighth inning of a game against Alexander City. Griffin won the game 16 to 4. Tallassee pitcher Johnny Taylor hurled a 1 to 0 no-hitter against Alexander City on June 23. Bill Revels of Carrollton pitched the season's second no-hitter on August 16 but lost the game to Valley 0 to 1 in seven innings. Tallassee first baseman Henry Zich set the league's all-time single season record for the most put outs with 1,143. Bill Kallaher and Gene Doerflinger, pitching for Opelika and Carrollton respectively, each tied the all-time league single season record for most wins when they each won 23 games. The original record was set by Paul Brock of Newnan in 1947. Doerflinger also set the all-time league mark for the most strikeouts in a season when he fanned 233 batters. Newnan pitcher Mickey Mihalik set the all-time single season record in the league for the most bases on balls when he walked 149 over the course of the season.

After Valley won the regular season pennant by a two game margin over Carrollton, the two teams along with third place Newnan and fourth place Alexander City advanced to the post-season championship tournament. Valley defeated Newnan three games to one in the first round, and Carrollton eliminated Alexander City three games to two. In the championship series, it was all the Valley Rebels upsetting the Hornets of Carrollton in four straight games to take the league title.

Alexander City, Alabama
Team Operated by Alexander City Millers, Inc.
Team President: D.W. Hodo
Vice President: James Callahan
Secretary-Treasurer: L.C. Howell
Business Manager: Zack Schuessler
Manager(s): Ben Catchings, Marv Chappell, Luther Gunnells
Games played at Benjamin C. Russell Field
Season attendance: 44,053

Alexander City Millers Team Roster

NAME	G	BA	POS	W	L	ERA	APF
Booker, John	25	0.159	SS				
Brodzinski, Jim	11	0.083	P				
Brown, Bill	126	0.244	1B				
Catchings, Ben	93	0.208	M, 3B, SS				
Chappell, Marv	75	0.216	M, OF, P	9	12	4.38	
Coker, Jim	50	0.152	C				
Culpepper, Bill	116	0.263	OF				
Davis, Fred	22	0.143	P	7	6	4.21	
Davis, Max	59	0.301	OF				
Dorsky, Mike	80	0.206	OF				Opelika
Ello, Jim	103	0.294	C				Griffin
Farrar, Bill	16	0.100	OF				
Glaze, Claude	22	0.304	P	2	8	4.30	Opelika
Glover, Omer	49	0.172	C				Carrollton
Gunnells, Luther	117	0.323	M, SS				Opelika
Haynes, Willard	13	0.105	P	1	5	5.74	
Huesman, Jack	123	0.262	2B				
Johnson, George	71	0.242	3B				
Keller, George	15	0.100					Opelika
Lindsey, John	48	0.093	P	19	12	2.00	
McCraney, Wayne	37	0.224	P	9	11	3.85	
McTaggert, Charles	22	0.156	P	8	3	3.86	
Miller, Charles	15	0.214	C				
Powell, John	49	0.268	SS, P				
Reach, Cliff	31	0.163	3B, OF				
Ross, Jerome	24	0.247	3B				
Wooley, Jim	102	0.267	OF				

Carrollton, Georgia
Team Operated by Carrollton Baseball Club, Inc.
Team President: Harvey J. Copeland
Secretary-Treasurer: William O. Cobb
Manager(s): John Hill, Red Roberts
Games played at City Athletic Field
Season attendance: 53,000

Georgia Class-D Minor League Baseball Encyclopedia

Carrollton Hornets Team Roster

NAME	G	BA	POS	W	L	ERA	APF
Arroyo, Blas	65	0.210	3B, OF, P	2	2	3.00	
Bertha, Elmer	37	0.183	1B				
Bozzuto, Bert	14	0.100	P	5	5	3.84	
Burke, Joe	15	0.257	P	3	3	2.39	
Cain, George	25	0.154	P	8	6	4.29	
Cichon, Frank	108	0.266	OF				
Dendinger, Dick	16	0.283	OF				
Doerflinger, Gene	41	0.182	P	23	11	2.13	
Edwards, Hoyt	28	0.091	P	8	6	4.34	Newnan
Giombetti, Eddie	1		P	0	0		
Glover, Omer	49	0.172	C				Alex City
Hill, Jim	95	0.239	C				
Hill, John	12	0.170	M, 3B				
Jefts, Virgil	12	0.344	C				
Little, Walt	27	0.177	P	13	7	3.92	
Lovelady, Willard	15	0.188	P	2	1	3.56	
Marshall, Shorty	121	0.307	2B				
Monarchi, Gene	111	0.236	SS				
Monarchi, Pete	<10		2B				
Nagle, Bob	32	0.190	3B				
Nasworthy, Luther	10	0.120					
Przeworski, Ted	123	0.246	3B, OF				LaGrange
Revels, Bill	12	0.192	P	4	5	2.81	
Roberts, Red	86	0.337	M, 3B, SS				
Roedel, Bob	12	0.095	C				
Roman, Carl	23	0.218	OF				
Russell, Bing	78	0.255	OF				
Silverman, Jerome	77	0.315	1B				
Snider, Floyd	48	0.277	1B, OF				
Varner, Buck	66	0.292	OF				
Williams, Bob	11	0.167					

Griffin, Georgia

Team Operated by Griffin Baseball Club, Inc.
Team President: Louis George
Vice President: Joseph George
Secretary-Treasurer-Business Manager: H.T. Green
Manager(s): Paul Campbell, Abe White
Games played at Griffin Ballpark
Season attendance: 63,672
Major League Affiliate: St. Louis Browns – American League.

Griffin Pimientos Team Roster

NAME	G	BA	POS	W	L	ERA	APF
Allen, Johnny	23	0.258	3B				
Blackwell, Tom	50	0.281	2B, 3B				
Brinkman, Frank	77	0.262	OF				
Campbell, Fred	123	0.357	SS, C				
Campbell, Paul			M				
Carroll, Bill	13	0.171	1B				
Creamer, Brice	14	0.257	P	3	7	5.85	
Ellis, Gerhart	13	0.095	P	2	5	3.09	
Ello, Jim	103	0.294	C				Alex City
Evins, John	22	0.235	OF				
Hale, Don	22	0.147	P	2	7	5.29	
Hammett, Miles	18	0.088	P	1	6	3.03	
Kane, Henry	126	0.335	OF				
Knoke, John	14	0.143	P	2	6	4.85	
Knopp, Mel	45	0.212	2B				
Kulig, Al	31	0.244	P	18	9	3.28	
Lovett, Bill	37	0.194	2B, OF				
Mlynarek, Anthony	70	0.267	C				
Noga, George	98	0.281	3B				
O'Donnell, John	68	0.311	OF, P	15	12	3.23	
Porco, Frank	14	0.150					
Rettie, Joe	<10						
Rolfs, Frank	106	0.294	1B				
Sanders, Lou	16	0.375	OF				
Savage, Bill	112	0.279	OF				
Stock, Lloyd	42	0.218	2B, SS				
Votaw, Jim	10	0.091	P				
White, Abe			M				

LaGrange, Georgia

Team Operated by LaGrange Baseball Club, Inc.
Team President: Oliver Hunnicutt
Secretary: Alvin Davis
Manager(s): Jim Acton
Games played at Callaway Stadium
Season attendance: 53,589
Major League Affiliate: New York Yankees – American League.

LaGrange Troupers Team Roster

NAME	G	BA	POS	W	L	ERA	APF
Acton, Jim	97	0.331	M, 1B, OF, C				
Adams, Bob	122	0.231	2B, SS				
Bobowski, Ed	22	0.147	P	2	4	4.64	
Cohen, Hy	28	0.171	P	7	5	5.50	
Dan, Virgil	10		1B				
Dyser, Bill	8		P	4	0	4.50	
Federow, Emil	25	0.237	P	4	5	5.49	
Garone, Mike	10	0.094	OF				
Griffin, Ed	12	0.222					
Guido, Ed	35	0.176	3B, OF				
Hall, Bob	36	0.272	1B				
Heisig, Bill	44	0.127	P	7	16	5.20	
Kramer, Bob	108	0.234	3B, OF, C				
Liddy, George	108	0.332	OF				
Magnatta, Jim	37	0.092	P	9	15	4.16	
McLeod, Jim	23	0.163	P	6	6	4.19	
Muse, Don	79	0.288	3B, C				
Nazzaro, Carman	11	0.262	OF				
Pheister, Paul	67	0.271	1B, 3B, OF				
Poulas, Nick	14	0.207					
Przeworski, Ted	123	0.246	3B, OF				Carrollton
Raehse, Bill	43	0.250	1B				
Roth, Jac	43	0.274	2B				
Striffler, Charles	37	0.259	OF				
Travers, Tom	16	0.135	P	3	3	5.94	
Trotter, Bill	59	0.243	2B, 3B				
Virgil, Dan	10	0.162					
Watson, Ed	39	0.197	P	9	10	3.81	
Webb, Marion	65	0.284	3B, SS				
Zazzera, Ben	13	0.205	OF				

Newnan, Georgia

Team Operated by Newnan Baseball Association
Team President: A.L. Potts
Vice President: Hamilton C. Arnall
Manager(s): Norm Veazey
Games played at Pickett Field
Season attendance: 65,257

Newnan Brownies Team Roster

NAME	G	BA	POS	W	L	ERA	APF
Barger, John	47	0.269	P	20	9	2.17	
Campbell, Ben	69	0.215	OF, C, P	8	5	3.69	
Chaptman, Devon	16	0.121	P	6	5	3.03	
Devaney, Bob	23	0.128	P	10	1	2.63	
Dunn, Ed	8		P	2	4	3.96	
Edwards, Hoyt	28	0.091	P	8	6	4.34	Carrollton
Franson, Carl	123	0.238	3B				
Joyce, Arnold	32	0.270	OF, P	3	5	8.63	
Lassiter, Bob	11	0.350	P	3	4	3.26	
Lewis, Bill	104	0.326	C				

Georgia Class-D Minor League Baseball Encyclopedia

NAME	G	BA	POS	W	L	ERA	APF
McAfee, Alton	124	0.293	1B				
McBride, Tom	29	0.209	P				
McLeod, Pete	30	0.264	OF				
Mihalik, Mickey	37	0.122	P	15	14	3.47	
Millard, John	126	0.263	SS				
Ortiz, Otoniel	109	0.300	2B				
Reid, Russ	13	0.286	3B				
Turner, McDonald	125	0.295	OF				
Veazey, Norm	110	0.306	M, OF				
Wiacek, Ray	92	0.290	OF				

Opelika, Alabama

Team Operated by Opelika Baseball Club, Inc.
Team President: W.L. Powell
Vice President: Dan Rancher
Secretary: T.K. Davis
Treasurer: Thomas Spain
Manager(s): Jim Ball, Luther Gunnells
Games played at Pepperell Park
Season attendance: 59,000

Opelika Owls Team Roster

NAME	G	BA	POS	W	L	ERA	APF
Bailey, George	125	0.357	OF				
Ball, Jim	117	0.333	M, OF				
Beavers, Jim	23	0.267	P	5	12	3.44	
Collins, Charlie	15	0.107	P	3	5	6.65	
Conovan, Mike	34	0.125	P	3	14	6.15	Tallassee
Dennany, Bob	25	0.207	P	9	9	3.73	
Diffly, Peter	42	0.223	SS				
Dorsky, Mike	80	0.206	OF				Alex City
Flemming, Wheeler	104	0.278	1B				
Gilmore, John	115	0.180	2B				
Glaze, Claude	22	0.304	P	2	8	4.30	Alex City
Gunnells, Luther	117	0.323	M, SS				Alex City
Hudson, Bill	90	0.298	OF				
Irvin, Jim	33	0.221	C				
Jackson, Claude	51	0.149	P	13	15	4.28	
Jarvis, Bob	123	0.276	3B				
Kallaher, Bill	82	0.251	1B, P	23	5	2.08	
Keller, George	15	0.100					Alex City
Kilgore, Bill	12	0.269	P	5	2	3.75	
Olayko, Alex	99	0.209	C				
Philpott, Carey	18	0.149	C				
Yancey, Carl	20	0.190	SS				

Tallassee, Alabama

Team Operated by Tallassee Baseball Club, Inc.
Team President: C.A. Pruitt
Vice Presidents: R.L. Cottle, O.F. Kelly
Secretary: P.S. Land
Treasurer: C.G. Mann
Business Manager: J.C. Bowen
Manager(s): Bob Comiskey, Hugh East
Games played at Stumberg Field
Season attendance: 34,696
Major League Affiliate: St. Louis Cardinals – National League

Tallassee Indians Team Roster

NAME	G	BA	POS	W	L	ERA	APF
Adams, Bob	101	0.299	2B, 3B, SS, OF				
Berg, Ed	80	0.182	2B				
Betz, Bob	30	0.232	OF				
Boyer, Milt	52	0.268	OF, P	8	10	4.66	
Brunson, Marion	11	0.091	P	1	7	4.17	
Childs, Delton	126	0.348	OF				
Comiskey, Bob	64	0.325	M, C				
Conovan, Mike	34	0.125	P	3	14	6.15	Opelika
Coss, Royden	31	0.173	P	7	8	5.16	
Deibler, Mason	24	0.111	P	7	5	2.68	
Duke, Willie	10	0.192					
Duncan, Charles	23	0.143	P	4	12	4.03	
East, Hugh			M				
Edwards, Ray	78	0.255	3B				
Fisher, Ron	62	0.270	C				
Galloway, Oliver	27	0.278	C				
Gregory, Bob	7		P	4	1	2.68	
Hathcock, Marlin	11	0.212	2B				
Martini, Fernando	85	0.276	OF				Valley
Mellinger, Jim	48	0.293	P	9	8	3.70	
Monaco, Frank	92	0.223	SS				
Popovich, Charles	<10						
Pruett, John	23	0.257	SS				
Rikard, Denver	90	0.312	OF				
Sutton, Jim	18	0.283	OF				
Taylor, John	19	0.038	P	4	5	5.09	
Tefft, Al	14	0.234	3B				
Tiefenauer, Bobby			P	3	2	4.40	
Zich, Henry	126	0.292	1B				

Valley (Lanett), Alabama

Team Operated by Valley Baseball Club, Inc.
Team President: Fob James
Vice President: G.E. "Cheese" Goggans
Secretary-Business Manager: J.H. Gay
Treasurer: Donald G. Lord
Assistant Business Manager: Kenneth J. Rees
Manager(s): Jesse Danna
Games played at Jennings Field
Season attendance: 60,163

Valley Rebels Team Roster

NAME	G	BA	POS	W	L	ERA	APF
Chambers, Joe	125	0.327	2B				
Clark, Ray	112	0.235	SS				
Danna, Charles	115	0.288	C				
Danna, Jesse	61	0.276	M, OF, P	22	6	2.06	
Edge, Harvey	22	0.214	P	2	5	4.68	
Edmondson, Lee	19	0.189	C				
Edwards, Bob	125	0.319	OF				
Embry, Joel	27	0.226	P	8	6	3.24	
Eustice, Willis	44	0.283	P	10	8	3.76	
Frazier, John	35	0.196	OF				
Gustavson, Carl	34	0.165	P	15	8	2.88	
Hall, Jesse	42	0.273	OF				
Hammons, Herb	14	0.189					
Lee, Frank	32	0.200	OF				
Lewis, Jim	121	0.313	1B				
Martini, Fernando	85	0.276	OF				Tallassee
McWhorter, Marcus	35	0.176	P	14	13	3.01	
Ray, Tom	10	0.194	SS, OF				
Spruill, Jack	124	0.245	3B				
Still, Jim	58	0.263	OF				
Swigler, Norm	27	0.198	OF				

1948 Georgia-Alabama League Records

Batting

Highest Batting Average (minimum 100 at bats)
1. Fred Campbell – Griffin   .357
   George Bailey – Opelika   .357
3. Delton Childs – Tallassee   .348
4. Red Roberts – Carrollton   .337
5. Henry Kane – Griffin   .335

Georgia Class-D Minor League Baseball Encyclopedia

Most Hits
1. George Bailey – Opelika   174
2. Fred Campbell – Griffin   168
3. Delton Childs – Tallassee   166
4. Henry Kane – Griffin   159
5. Bob Edwards – Valley   156

Most Runs
1. Bob Edwards – Valley   114
2. McDonald Turner – Newnan   103
3. Delton Childs – Tallassee   100
4. Shorty Marshall – Carrollton   99
5. Fred Campbell – Griffin   98

Most Total Bases
1. Bob Edwards – Valley   234
2. Shorty Marshall – Carrollton   229
3. Fred Campbell – Griffin   223
4. Henry Kane – Griffin   218
5. Delton Childs – Tallassee   216

Most Doubles
1. Fred Campbell – Griffin   34
2. Shorty Marshall – Carrollton   32
3. Bob Edwards – Valley   31
4. Henry Zich – Tallassee   29
    Alton McAfee – Newnan   29

Most Triples
1. Bob Edwards – Valley   16
2. John Millard – Newnan   15
3. Frank Rolfs – Griffin   13
4. Henry Zich – Tallassee   12
    Joe Chambers – Valley   12
    Delton Childs – Tallassee   12

Most Home Runs
1. Jim Acton – LaGrange   14
2. Carl Franson – Newnan   13
    Shorty Marshall – Carrollton   13
    Luther Gunnells – Opel/Alex   13
5. Frank Cichon – Carrollton   12

Most Extra Base Hits
1. Bob Edwards – Valley   52
2. Shorty Marshall – Carrollton   48
3. Fred Campbell – Griffin   43
4. Alton McAfee – Newnan   41
    Henry Zich – Tallassee   41

Most Runs Batted In
1. Fred Campbell – Griffin   105
2. Jim Lewis – Valley   102
3. Joe Chambers – Valley   99
4. Alton McAfee – Newnan   94
5. Luther Gunnells – Opel/Alex   91

Most Stolen Bases
1. Bob Edwards – Valley   67
2. Delton Childs – Tallassee   50
3. George Liddy – LaGrange   44
4. Jack Huesman – Alexander City   41
5. Jim Ball – Opelika   37

Fielding
Most Put-Outs
1. Henry Zich 1B – Tallassee   1,143
2. Bill Brown 1B – Alexander City   1,102
3. Jim Lewis 1B – Valley   1,058
4. Alton McAfee 1B – Newnan   1,057
5. Wheeler Flemming 1B – Opelika   933

Most Assists
1. John Millard SS – Newnan   395
2. Joe Chambers 2B – Valley   364
3. Ray Clark SS – Valley   362
4. Bob Adams 2B, SS – LaGrange   342
5. Jack Huesman 2B - Alexander City   339

Most Errors
1. Luther Gunnells SS – Opel/Alex   53
    Fred Campbell SS, C – Griffin   53
3. Ray Clark SS – Valley   51
4. John Millard SS – Newnan   47
5. Frank Monaco SS – Tallassee   45

Pitching
Most Wins
1. Bill Kallaher – Opelika   23
    Gene Doerflinger – Carrollton   23
3. Jesse Danna – Valley   22
4. John Barger – Newnan   20
5. John Lindsey - Alexander City   19

Most Losses
1. Bill Heisig – LaGrange   16
2. Claude Jackson – Opelika   15
    Jim Magnatta – LaGrange   15
4. Mickey Mihalik – Newnan   14
    Mike Conovan – Tall/Opel   14

Highest Winning Percentage (10 game minimum)
1. Bob Devaney – Newnan   .909
2. Bill Kallaher – Opelika   .821
3. Jesse Danna – Valley   .786
4. Charles McTaggert – Alexander City   .727
5. Bill Kilgore – Opelika   .714

Lowest Earned Run Average (100 inning minimum)
1. John Lindsey - Alexander City   2.00
2. Jesse Danna – Valley   2.06
3. Bill Kallaher – Opelika   2.08
4. Gene Doerflinger – Carrollton   2.13
5. John Barger – Newnan   2.17

Most Strikeouts
1. Gene Doerflinger – Carrollton   233
2. Mickey Mihalik – Newnan   214
3. John O'Donnell – Griffin   191
4. Bill Kallaher – Opelika   181
5. John Lindsey - Alexander City   156

Most Bases on Balls
1. Mickey Mihalik – Newnan   149
2. John O'Donnell – Griffin   143
3. Claude Jackson – Opelika   132
4. Gene Doerflinger – Carrollton   123
    Wayne McCraney - Alexander City   123

Most Hits Allowed
1. Marcus McWhorter – Valley   242
2. Jim Magnatta – LaGrange   230
3. John Barger – Newnan   228
4. Claude Jackson – Opelika   224
5. Bill Heisig – LaGrange   222

Most Innings Pitched
1. John Lindsey - Alexander City   275
2. Gene Doerflinger – Carrollton   253
3. Bill Kallaher – Opelika   251

4. John Barger – Newnan   249
5. Jesse Danna – Valley   236

1948 Georgia-Alabama League All-Star Team
Georgia Team:
1B Alton McAfee – Newnan
2B Shorty Marshall - Carrollton
3B Red Roberts – Carrollton
SS Fred Campbell - Griffin
OF Frank Cichon - Carrollton
OF George Liddy - LaGrange
OF Henry Kane – Griffin
C   Jim Acton – LaGrange
C   Bill Lewis – Newnan
UT John Millard – Newnan
UT Ted Przeworski – LaGrange
P   John Barger – Newnan
P   Devon Chaptman – Newnan
P   Bill Dyser – LaGrange
P   Mickey Mihalik – Newnan
P   Gene Doerflinger – Carrollton
P   Al Kulig – Griffin

Alabama Team:
1B Jim Lewis – Valley
2B Joe Chambers – Valley
3B Ray Edwards – Tallassee
SS Luther Gunnells – Opelika
OF Delton Childs – Tallassee
OF Bob Edwards – Valley
OF George Bailey – Opelika
C   Charles Danna – Valley
C   Ron Fisher – Tallassee
UT Ben Catchings - Alexander City
UT Jim Ball – Opelika
P   Bill Kallaher – Opelika
P   Jesse Danna – Valley
P   John Lindsey - Alexander City
P   Bob Dennany – Opelika
P   Willis Eustice – Valley
P   Royden Coss – Tallassee

1948

Georgia-Florida League

League Office: Leslie, Georgia
League President: W.T. Anderson
League Vice President: C.L. Thompson
Salary Limit: $2,600 per month.
Player Rule: Each club was allowed a roster of seventeen players, not more than three veterans, not more than seven limited service, and not less than seven rookies.
Umpires: Lewis E. Anderson, Harry P. Holmes, Junius F. Beck, Gerald M. Anderson, Donald J. Atkinson, Charles T. Muller, Spike Davis, Archie Martin, and R.G. Vickers.

Georgia-Florida League Final Standings

Team	W	L	Pct	GB	Affiliate
Waycross Bears	85	55	.607	----	Unaffiliated
Valdosta Dodgers	81	58	.583	3.5	BRK-NL
Albany Cardinals	71	69	.507	14.0	STL-NL
Tallahassee Pirates	70	69	.504	14.5	PIT-NL
Moultrie Athletics	69	71	.493	16.0	PHI-AL
Thomasville Tigers	68	71	.489	16.5	DET-AL
Cordele Indians	64	76	.457	21.0	CLE-AL
Americus Phillies	50	89	.360	34.5	PHI-NL

1948 Georgia-Florida League Map

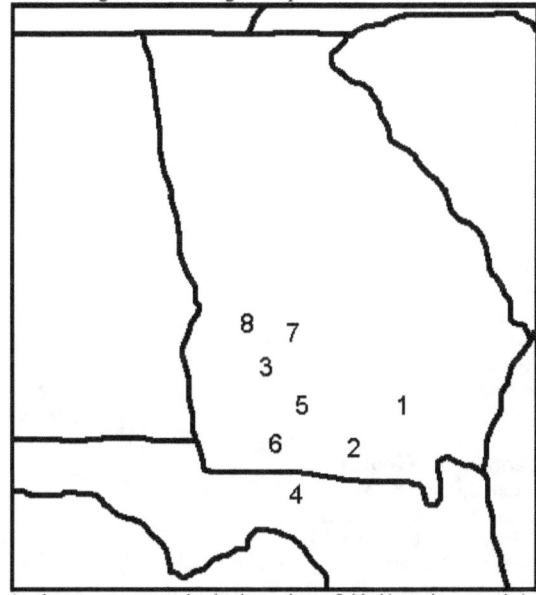

(numbers on map correspond to the place each team finished in regular season play)

All eight cities from the previous season returned to the league for action in 1948 keeping the makeup of the circuit unchanged.

Donald Stephens, pitcher for Albany, threw a no-hitter on April 15 against Moultrie winning 10 to 0. Thomasville moundsman Bob Cruze also tossed a no-hitter during the season on September 1 defeating Tallahassee 4 to 0 in a seven inning contest. Marv Leib of Valdosta set the all-time league record for the most doubles in a season by reaching second 47 times during the year.

Georgia Class-D Minor League Baseball Encyclopedia

Waycross won the regular season pennant and the top seed in the post-season playoffs against fourth place Tallahassee. Valdosta and Albany, second and third places respectively, also squared off in the first round of the post-season. Tallahassee succumbed to Waycross three games to one, and Albany upset Valdosta by the same score. Waycross easily defeated Albany in four straight games to win the league championship series. The Bears then advanced to the Southeastern Championship interleague series where they faced Daytona Beach, champions of the Florida State League. Waycross swept this series as well four games to none.

Albany, Georgia
Team Operated by Albany Baseball Club, Inc.
Team President: Morton M. Wiggins
Vice Presidents: Robert E. Hannegan, William Walsingham, Jr.
Secretary-Treasurer: Fred M. Saigh, Jr.
Business Manager: L.W. Bergesch
Manager(s): Bob Stanton
Games played at Albany Stadium
Season attendance: 61,971
Major League Affiliate: St. Louis Cardinals – National League.

Albany Cardinals Team Roster

NAME	G	BA	POS	W	L	ERA	APF
Adamcewicz, Erwin	140	0.279	OF				
Attaway, Bob	133	0.287	C				
Beck, Ted	43	0.345	2B, P	8	8	3.80	
Corley, Harold	35	0.172	SS				
Cyrus, Dave	55	0.261	P	15	12	3.74	
Deibler, Mason	11	0.000	P				
Frank, Morris	11	0.043	P	4	4	2.45	
Franz, Bill	15	0.400	P				
Galasso, Lou	26	0.245	3B				
Hinkle, Jack	<10						
Kerce, Bob	22	0.191	P	9	7	3.26	
Knoblauch, Ray	27	0.219	P	4	5	5.04	
Loeser, Dick	114	0.282	3B				
Long, Bill	135	0.305	OF				
Louis, Bob	102	0.300	SS				
Marlow, Walt	11	0.000	P	2	3	6.13	
Marolewski, Fred	140	0.271	1B				
McKenney, Bill	36	0.185	OF				Moultrie
McLean, Charles	103	0.262	OF				
Popovich, Charles	16	0.270	OF				
Reiter, Jim	25	0.197	C				
Smith, Walt	17	0.083	P	2	5	5.50	
Stanton, Bob	119	0.259	M, 2B				
Stephens, Don	42	0.273	P	17	14	2.27	
Taylor, John	10	0.300					

Americus, Georgia
Team Operated by Americus Phillies, Inc.
Team President: H. Phil Jones
Vice President: Joseph F. Reardon
Secretary-Treasurer: George A. Fletcher
Business Manager: Grady L. "Pete" Rockett
Manager(s): Ed Murphy
Games played at Americus Baseball Park
Season attendance: 34,333
Major League Affiliate: Philadelphia Phillies – National League.

Americus Phillies Team Roster

NAME	G	BA	POS	W	L	ERA	APF
Adair, Tommy	17	0.245	P	7	6	4.19	
Bucha, Anthony	51	0.221	C				
Burkey, Melvin	27	0.105	P	5	9	6.49	
Comolli, Vic	92	0.255	1B, C				
Dabbs, Chester	31	0.188	OF				
Fetter, Ken	24	0.169	C				
Fogg, Bill	30	0.185	P	11	14	4.70	
Francis, Ed	24	0.192	OF				
Geehring, Don	46	0.234	2B, 3B				
Goode, Noah	54	0.252	3B				
Guinty, Charles	15	0.188	P	3	6	5.85	
Hay, Derl	10	0.111	P				
Howard, Crawford	140	0.318	OF				
Koellmer, Bill	18	0.169	OF				
Kranitzky, Chuck	11	0.100	C				
Massey, Horace	38	0.277	OF				
Mikesell, Maurice	12	0.167	SS				
Murphy, Ed	14	0.129	M				
Pasch, Allan	39	0.258	3B				
Pizzo, Joe	28	0.305	3B				
Potocnik, Elmer	16	0.129	P	3	5	6.60	
Raisch, Harry	30	0.196	P	1	5	9.18	
Scott, LeGrant	50	0.327	M, OF				
Stamey, Harold	132	0.325	OF				
Stefano, Nick	40	0.265	2B				
Sullivan, Joe	13	0.048	P	2	4	5.08	
Tracy, Jim	30	0.213	P	6	11	5.64	
Tripp, Bob	101	0.299	1B				
Trojanowski, Ed	96	0.264	SS				
Willard, Stan	126	0.302	2B, SS				
Wingo, Jim	31	0.203	P	11	11	5.02	

Cordele, Georgia
Team Operated by Cordele Indians Baseball Club, Inc.
Team President: J.W. Bridges
Vice President: H.B. "Buzz" Wetzel
Secretary-Treasurer: Rudie Schaffer
Business Manager: Harry J. O'Brien
Manager(s): Hal Lee
Games played at City Park
Season attendance: 40,946
Major League Affiliate: Cleveland Indians – American League.

Cordele Indians Team Roster

NAME	G	BA	POS	W	L	ERA	APF
Bishop, Pat	13	0.000	P				
Callaway, Bill	12	0.214	P	5	4	6.16	
Cobb, Neal	<10						
Conner, John	136	0.291	2B, 3B, SS, OF				
Cooper, Bill	33	0.202	P	16	9	3.25	
Crouch, Les	135	0.233	2B, SS				
Dalton, Elroy	53	0.267	1B				
Geis, Harry	85	0.267	1B, OF				
Graddick, John	24	0.143	P	3	6	5.20	
Gregg, Fred	121	0.312	3B				
Hagle, Don	14	0.135					
Lee, Hal	107	0.311	M, 1B, 2B				
Lisinski, Don	12	0.063	P	3	3	4.70	
Lynch, Wayne	27	0.207	P	10	12	3.13	
Mitskavich, Nestor	32	0.133	P	10	12	3.50	
Reeves, Harold	81	0.230	C				
Reid, Jim	40	0.201	SS				
Rentz, Irv	86	0.259	C				
Sheffield, Frank	10	0.143	P				
Smith, Tom	67	0.289	OF				
Spain, Hank	121	0.309	OF				
Strickland, Norris	133	0.354	OF				
Wilder, Ralph	38	0.247	P	13	13	3.46	
Wolfe, Earl	19	0.200	2B				

Georgia Class-D Minor League Baseball Encyclopedia

Moultrie, Georgia
Team Operated by Moultrie Athletics, Inc.
Team President: Connie Mack
Vice President: A.H. Ehlers
Business Manager: C.W. Vandiver
Manager(s): Joe Antolick
Games played at Municipal Park
Season attendance: 48,962
Major League Affiliate: Philadelphia Athletics – American League.

Moultrie Athletics Team Roster

NAME	G	BA	POS	W	L	ERA	APF
Addison, John	12	0.132	OF				
Antolick, Joe	98	0.256	M, C				
Atzert, George	13	0.125	P				
Baker, Royal	29	0.188	OF				
Barnes, Bill	40	0.252	3B				
Bryant, Harold	65	0.195	2B, 3B				
Busa, Al	41	0.140	P	9	4	3.88	
Cantler, Don	21	0.282	OF				
Carey, Elwood	52	0.228	P	13	13	3.40	
Dorwin, Rod	132	0.254	OF, P	7	9	4.36	
Garner, Bill	27	0.148	P	5	6	5.14	
Gavaghan, Tom	11	0.167	P				
Godbold, Gus	135	0.280	2B, SS, OF				
Gohl, Vince	15	0.150	P	3	2	3.98	
Gruber, Bob	44	0.266	3B				
Herbik, John	11	0.154					
Ippolito, Rocco	124	0.370	OF, P	8	6	2.81	
Langemeier, Paul	17	0.120	P	7	5	4.68	
Laumann, Andrew	96	0.263	SS				
Lewetag, Al	18	0.193	3B				
McCrary, Jim	31	0.188	3B				
McKenney, Bill	36	0.185	OF				Albany
Menig, Sam	98	0.252	C				
Nojunas, Al	10	0.222					
Pancoe, Joe	19	0.362	OF				
Plyn, Percy	58	0.218	SS, OF				
Rhyne, Ken	140	0.291	1B				
Singleton, Joe	70	0.238	OF				
Storch, Charles	22	0.192	P	1	5	3.63	
Wall, Curtis	11	0.214					
Warren, Jeff	24	0.188	P	7	6	4.41	

Tallahassee, Florida
Team Operated by Tallahassee Pirates, Inc.
Team President: Fred N. Lowry
Vice President: H. Roy Hamey
Secretary: Ray Kennedy
Business Manager: Bush Perry
Manager(s): Jack Rothrock
Games played at Centennial Field
Season attendance: 63,625
Major League Affiliate: Pittsburgh Pirates – National League.

Tallahassee Pirates Team Roster

NAME	G	BA	POS	W	L	ERA	APF
Bandoch, Ed	22	0.250	C				
Beverly, Jack	<10		P	0	0		
Craig, Steve	40	0.186	C				
Cromartie, Bill	39	0.265	P	10	7	4.95	
Del Isola, Sal	13	0.219	P	4	5	3.88	
Dravecky, Andrew	117	0.274	C				
Gormish, Mike	25	0.167	P	6	8	4.43	
Hersimaki, Fred	58	0.313	OF				
Judy, George	28	0.192	P	14	10	4.11	
Kraus, Jim	26	0.214	P	10	12	5.52	
Manning, Bill	65	0.265	1B				
McCallum, Dick	11	0.063	P	0	6	7.09	
McCord, Norm	30	0.152	1B				
O'Brien, Bill	24	0.253	OF				
Overland, John	37	0.319	1B				Valdosta
Petchulat, George	12	0.158	P	1	3	4.67	
Rhodes, Herb	30	0.294	OF				
Rothrock, Jack			M				
Sezna, Tom	128	0.300	OF				
Stasko, Julius	136	0.296	2B				
Swanson, Les	19	0.083					
Thomas, Frank	138	0.295	OF				
Turner, Dick	20	0.256	OF				
Woolford, Ralph	7		P	7	0	1.64	
Wopinek, George	136	0.313	SS				
Yebernetsky, George	34	0.275	P	16	13	3.74	
Zeccola, Pete	13	0.231					
Zeiser, Harry	139	0.219	3B				

Thomasville, Georgia
Team Operated by Thomasville Baseball Company
Team President: Heeth Varnedoe
Vice Presidents: Robert Rolfe, Cedric Tallis
Secretary-Treasurer: O.B. Anderson
Assistant Secretary: H.M. Sisson
General Manager: Cedric Tallis
Manager(s): Bob Engle
Games played at Municipal Stadium
Season attendance: 54,894
Major League Affiliate: Detroit Tigers – American League.

Thomasville Tigers Team Roster

NAME	G	BA	POS	W	L	ERA	APF
Andres, Bob	15	0.200	P	3	5	4.21	
Arduini, Sal	137	0.263	3B				
Cann, Bill	27	0.139	P	4	6	5.05	
Cruze, Bob	39	0.219	P	10	11	4.34	
Curtis, Ira	13	0.129	P	7	3	2.89	
Engle, Bob	59	0.248	M, OF				
Funk, Ernie	43	0.207	P	19	13	2.43	
Hassler, Percy	136	0.261	SS				
Henderson, Bob	39	0.188	P	12	11	3.47	
Henkel, Howard	138	0.337	2B				
Knabe, Dick	32	0.119	P	2	9	5.41	
Komisarek, Ed	136	0.266	OF, C				
Law, Gordon	27	0.135	OF				
Little, Keith	131	0.266	1B				
Markham, Dick	23	0.224	OF				
Nelson, Jim	101	0.296	C				
Shaw, Bennie	132	0.279	OF				
Stamos, Pete	19	0.370	P	2	1	4.02	
Tessier, Lawrence	35	0.143	P	7	8	4.46	
Turtzo, Paul	131	0.273	OF				

Valdosta, Georgia
Team Operated by Valdosta Dodgers Baseball Club, Inc.
Team President: C.W. Singleton
Vice President: Harold G. Roettger
Secretary: Fresco Thompson
Treasurer: D.E. Beach
Business Manager: Victor A. Zodda
Manager(s): Lou Rochelli
Games played at Pendleton Park
Season attendance: 71,507
Major League Affiliate: Brooklyn Dodgers – National League.

Valdosta Dodgers Team Roster

NAME	G	BA	POS	W	L	ERA	APF
Adams, Phil	<10						
Adams, Tom	11	0.231					
Barbella, Vic	12	0.278	P				
Byrne, John	38	0.174	P	15	10	3.21	
Cater, Jim	33	0.146	P	10	8	4.02	
Darden, Bill	36	0.100	P	12	7	3.47	
DeLucia, Pasquale	14	0.218	OF				
Fernandez, Rafael	<10						
Fricano, Marion	39	0.200	P	13	7	3.13	
Jenkins, Lee	126	0.345	OF				
Jones, Dick	27	0.211	OF				
Kirk, Walt	21	0.333	2B				
Kwiatkowski, Joe	118	0.371	OF				
Leib, Marv	138	0.328	1B				
Luberto, Santo	124	0.313	3B				
Overland, John	37	0.319	1B				Tallahassee
Palumbo, Bill	131	0.294	2B, 3B				
Rochelli, Lou	131	0.296	M, SS				
Schroeder, Al	23	0.225	OF				
Smith, Gil	24	0.267	OF				
Stamey, John	37	0.227	P	10	3	2.41	
Stammen, Pete	132	0.323	C				
Stocker, Stan	41	0.143	P	12	12	3.05	
Umstead, Ed	12	0.432	OF				
Walker, John	22	0.364	OF				
Whitaker, Jim	43	0.204	OF				
Willis, Clarence	14	0.308	P	3	5	3.63	
Woodring, Dick	22	0.295	OF				

Waycross, Georgia

Team Operated by Waycross Baseball Association, Inc.
Team President: Herbert Bradshaw
Vice President: William D. Rivenbark
Treasurer: Charles H. Andrews
Manager(s): Mickey Katkaveck
Games played at Newton Field
Season attendance: 65,397

Waycross Bears Team Roster

NAME	G	BA	POS	W	L	ERA	APF
Austin, Alvin	94	0.273	OF				
Bell, Jefferson	135	0.267	3B				
Bremer, Walt	53	0.306	OF				
Brewster, Charlie	92	0.295	SS				
Cook, Bob	21	0.074	P	3	4	4.30	
Fisher, George	133	0.307	2B, OF				
Fultz, George	11	0.190	P	6	3	2.32	
Galinkin, Norm	93	0.297	1B				
Gottesman, Bert	11	0.000	P				
Gross, Don	107	0.256	1B, OF, C				
Hardegree, Bill	48	0.230	OF				
Harwood, Don	19	0.289	P	6	6	5.13	
Horton, Roger	22	0.113					
Ingalls, Jack	35	0.216	P	12	9	5.23	
Katkaveck, Mickey	109	0.239	M, C				
Lyons, Bob	119	0.304	2B, SS				
Raulerson, Harry	38	0.274	P	13	11	4.74	
Seidel, Ray	55	0.250	P	23	7	3.54	
Weathers, Charlie	138	0.287	OF				
Young, Herb	47	0.311	P	13	8	4.39	

1948 Georgia-Florida League Records
Batting
Highest Batting Average (minimum 100 at bats)
1. Joe Kwiatkowski – Valdosta .371
2. Rocco Ippolito – Moultrie .370
3. Norris Strickland – Cordele .354
4. Lee Jenkins – Valdosta .345
   Ted Beck – Albany .345

Most Hits
1. Howard Henkel – Thomasville 189
2. Norris Strickland – Cordele 185
3. Rocco Ippolito – Moultrie 183
4. Lee Jenkins – Valdosta 178
5. Joe Kwiatkowski – Valdosta 176
   Frank Thomas – Tallahassee 176

Most Runs
1. Charlie Weathers – Waycross 129
2. George Fisher – Waycross 123
3. Crawford Howard – Americus 122
   Gus Godbold – Moultrie 122
   Bill Palumbo – Valdosta 122

Most Total Bases
1. Rocco Ippolito – Moultrie 290
2. Frank Thomas – Tallahassee 273
3. Norris Strickland – Cordele 264
4. Ken Rhyne – Moultrie 261
   Marv Leib – Valdosta 261

Most Doubles
1. Marv Leib – Valdosta 47
2. Fred Marolewski – Albany 43
3. Norris Strickland – Cordele 41
4. Frank Thomas – Tallahassee 39
5. Crawford Howard – Americus 34

Most Triples
1. Lee Jenkins – Valdosta 20
2. Charlie Weathers – Waycross 18
3. Fred Gregg – Cordele 17
4. Norris Strickland – Cordele 13
   Bob Tripp – Americus 13
   Charles McLean – Albany 13

Most Home Runs
1. Ken Rhyne – Moultrie 27
2. Rocco Ippolito – Moultrie 21
3. Frank Thomas – Tallahassee 14
4. Charlie Weathers – Waycross 13
5. Charlie Brewster – Waycross 10

Most Extra Base Hits
1. Marv Leib – Valdosta 64
2. Frank Thomas – Tallahassee 61
3. Norris Strickland – Cordele 58
4. Rocco Ippolito – Moultrie 57
   Fred Marolewski – Albany 57

Most Runs Batted In
1. Frank Thomas – Tallahassee 132
2. Charlie Weathers – Waycross 117
3. Ken Rhyne – Moultrie 115
4. Crawford Howard – Americus 111
5. Lou Rochelli – Valdosta 105

Most Stolen Bases
1. George Fisher – Waycross 60
2. Rocco Ippolito – Moultrie 30
3. Tom Sezna – Tallahassee 29
4. Fred Gregg – Cordele 28
5. Lee Jenkins – Valdosta 27

Fielding

Most Put-Outs
1. Marv Leib 1B – Valdosta — 1,165
2. Ken Rhyne 1B – Moultrie — 1,118
3. Fred Marolewski 1B – Albany — 1,084
4. Keith Little 1B – Thomasville — 1,063
5. Bob Tripp 1B – Americus — 907

Most Assists
1. George Wopinek SS – Tallahassee — 463
2. Percy Hassler SS – Thomasville — 419
3. Julius Stasko 2B – Tallahassee — 414
4. Lou Rochelli SS – Valdosta — 399
5. Howard Henkel 2B – Thomasville — 389

Most Errors
1. Percy Hassler SS – Thomasville — 96
2. George Wopinek SS – Tallahassee — 82
3. Stan Willard 2B, SS – Americus — 74
4. Les Crouch 2B, SS – Cordele — 62
5. Gus Godbold 2B, SS, OF – Moultrie — 59

Pitching

Most Wins
1. Ray Seidel – Waycross — 23
2. Ernie Funk – Thomasville — 19
3. Don Stephens – Albany — 17
4. Bill Cooper – Cordele — 16
   George Yebernetsky – Tallahassee — 16

Most Losses
1. Don Stephens – Albany — 14
   Bill Fogg – Americus — 14
3. Ernie Funk – Thomasville — 13
   George Yebernetsky – Tallahassee — 13
   Ralph Wilder – Cordele — 13
   Elwood Carey – Moultrie — 13

Highest Winning Percentage (10 game minimum)
1. John Stamey – Valdosta — .769
2. Ray Seidel – Waycross — .767
3. Ira Curtis – Thomasville — .700
4. Al Busa – Moultrie — .692
5. George Fultz – Waycross — .667

Lowest Earned Run Average (100 inning minimum)
1. Don Stephens – Albany — 2.27
2. John Stamey – Valdosta — 2.41
3. Ernie Funk – Thomasville — 2.43
4. Stan Stocker – Valdosta — 3.05
5. Wayne Lynch – Cordele — 3.13
   Marion Fricano – Valdosta — 3.13

Most Strikeouts
1. Don Stephens – Albany — 221
2. Bob Cruze – Thomasville — 213
3. Jack Ingalls – Waycross — 197
4. Bill Fogg – Americus — 168
5. Ray Seidel – Waycross — 164

Most Bases on Balls
1. John Byrne – Valdosta — 185
2. Jack Ingalls – Waycross — 148
3. Jim Wingo – Americus — 137
4. Bob Cruze – Thomasville — 135
5. Bill Fogg – Americus — 132

Most Hits Allowed
1. Ray Seidel – Waycross — 303
2. George Yebernetsky – Tallahassee — 281
3. Dave Cyrus – Albany — 252
4. Harry Raulerson – Waycross — 234
5. Bill Cooper – Cordele — 232

Most Innings Pitched
1. Ray Seidel – Waycross — 282
2. Don Stephens – Albany — 254
3. George Yebernetsky – Tallahassee — 236
4. Ernie Funk – Thomasville — 230
5. Bob Henderson – Thomasville — 223

1948 Georgia-Florida League All-Star Team

1B Bob Tripp – Americus
2B Howard Henkel – Thomasville
3B Santo Luberto – Valdosta
SS Charlie Brewster – Waycross
OF Rocco Ippolito – Moultrie
OF Frank Thomas – Tallahassee
OF Joe Kwiatkowski – Valdosta
OF Norris Strickland – Cordele
C Bob Attaway – Albany
C Pete Stammen – Valdosta
UT Don Gross – Waycross
P Ernie Funk – Thomasville
P Don Stephens – Albany
P Ray Seidel – Waycross
P George Yebernetsky – Tallahassee
M Mickey Katkaveck – Waycross

1948

Georgia State League

League Office: Cochran, Georgia
League President: Joseph W. Matt Jr.
League Vice President: Fred Gilbert
Salary Limit: $2,600 per month.
Player Rule: Each club was allowed a roster of fifteen players, not more than one class man, not more than ten limited service, and not less than four rookies.
Umpires: Francis Dye, Donald G. Billingsley, Paul Masluk, Eugene Palazzo, Gabriel Koury, and Walter Doyle, Jr.

Georgia State League Final Standings

Team	W	L	Pct	GB	Affiliate
Sparta Saints	81	37	.686	----	Unaffiliated
Baxley Red Sox	66	54	.550	16.0	Unaffiliated
Fitzgerald Pioneers	65	55	.542	17.0	Unaffiliated
Eastman Dodgers	58	61	.487	23.5	Unaffiliated
Vidalia-Lyons Twins	54	66	.446	28.0	Unaffiliated
Douglas Rebels	34	85	.292	47.5	Unaffiliated

1948 Georgia State League Map

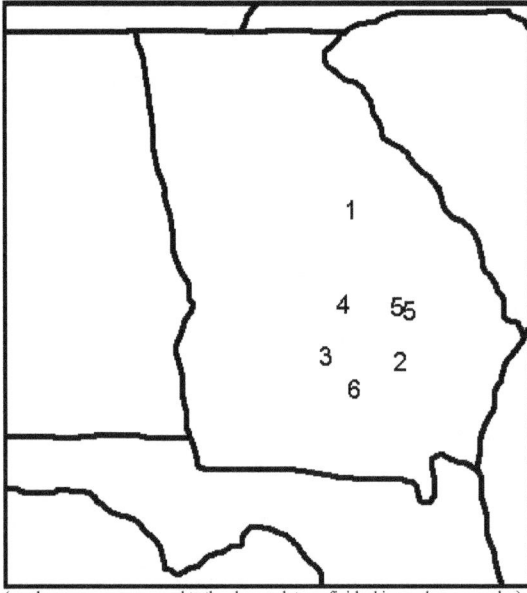

(numbers on map correspond to the place each team finished in regular season play)

The Georgia State League returned in 1948 this time located in south-central Georgia. Having officially organized on March 10, the league became the 58th league to operate that year under the National Association. The new six-club organization consisted of teams from Douglas, Baxley, Fitzgerald, Eastman, Sparta, and a Vidalia-Lyons combined team.

During this first season for the new organization, Fitzgerald's Charlie Ridgeway set the all-time league record for the most stolen bases in a single season with 80 safe swipes. Eastman pitcher Jim Harden also set an all-time league single season mark for the highest winning percentage with .929 on a record of 13 wins and 1 loss. Harden's season earned run average of 1.36 was also an all time single season record for the league. Sparta pitcher Paul Brock fanned 270 batters during the year to set the league's all-time single season record for the most strikeouts.

Sparta finished the regular season in first place by a sixteen game margin over second place Baxley. Fitzgerald and Eastman finished third and fourth respectively. In the Shaughnessy playoffs, Sparta defeated Eastman three games to two, and Fitzgerald upset Baxley three games to one. Fitzgerald went the distance and pulled an upset over Sparta in the championship series winning by a final of four games to three.

Baxley, Georgia

Team Operated by Baxley Baseball, Inc.
Team President: C.A. Whitaker
Vice President: W.M. Barron
Business Manager-Travel Secretary: Steve Maglio
Manager(s): Bud Metheny
Games played at Baxley Baseball Park
Season attendance: 24,901

Baxley Red Sox Team Roster

NAME	G	BA	POS	W	L	ERA	APF
Arcoleo, Frank	118	0.250	SS				
Carmichael, Bryce	121	0.248	2B				
Dobbins, Ralph	48	0.229	OF				
Ecklund, Bill	10	0.100	P	4	4	2.91	
Finley, Doug	121	0.226	OF				
Gilbert, Jack	28	0.208	P	16	8	2.64	
Harris, Bill	84	0.246	C				
Hutchinson, Jim	104	0.163	1B, OF				
Kanavage, Chet	84	0.238	1B, C				
Metheny, Bud	85	0.313	M, 1B				
Miskulin, John	30	0.104	P	12	12	2.49	
Oldershaw, Howard	16	0.156	P	5	6	3.78	
Parri, Carlo	16	0.000	P				
Pollack, Leonard	30	0.153	P	10	5	3.79	
Rauseo, Mike	109	0.199	3B				
Rodd, Don	27	0.152	P	17	6	3.30	
Westfall, Elmer	115	0.215	3B, OF				
Zera, Angelo	15	0.109	OF				

Douglas, Georgia

Team Operated by Douglas Baseball Corporation
Team President: F.L. Greer
Vice Presidents: Gerald Lott, Edward Dowling
Secretary-Treasurer: William Griffin
Business Manager: W.P. Ward, Jr.
Manager(s): Bill Barnes, Johnny Humphries, Emil Rey
Games played at Municipal Park
Season attendance: 34,709

Douglas Rebels Team Roster

NAME	G	BA	POS	W	L	ERA	APF
Aurelio, Ed	13	0.186	OF				
Barnes, Bill	39	0.273	M, 3B				
Barnes, Luther	39	0.192	3B, OF				
Belakovy, Rudy	41	0.169	P	9	15	3.73	
Bess, Bob	24	0.031	P	2	6	5.00	Vid-Lyo
Bryant, Harold	49	0.212	3B				
Hammel, Wayne	76	0.249	OF, C				
Hausfeld, Walt	15	0.146	OF				
Humphries, Johnny	11	0.185	M, P	3	2	3.16	
Koellmer, Bill	78	0.214	OF				
Littell, Don	20	0.180	P	3	6	5.04	
Long, Jim	29	0.217	2B				
Lovell, Hugh	12	0.167					

Georgia Class-D Minor League Baseball Encyclopedia

NAME	G	BA	POS	W	L	ERA	APF
Loveys, Bill	27	0.085	P	3	12	4.99	
Martin, Jim	95	0.244	OF				
Mazak, Leo	27	0.164	P, OF	6	9	4.54	
McDonald, Bob	46	0.234	2B, P	5	8	4.10	
McGhee, Bill	54	0.284	3B, OF				
Mink, Joe	10	0.185	OF				Fitzgerald
Nickerson, Frank	15	0.143	P	1	6	5.95	Vid-Lyo
Overstreet, Charles	20	0.118	P	3	6	3.58	
Prince, Howard	109	0.251	1B				
Rey, Emil	118	0.240	M, SS				
Rohrbaugh, Glenn	35	0.250	OF, C				
Smith, Gil	71	0.211	C				
Stenger, Dick	16	0.000	P	1	7	5.77	
Tomek, Joe	76	0.204	2B, C				

Eastman, Georgia
Team Operated by Eastman Baseball Club
Team President: J.Z. Hargrove
Vice President: O.B. Peacock
Secretary-Treasurer: O.C. Pound
Business Manager: W.W. Taylor
Manager(s): Charles Farrar, John Pare
Games played at Legion Park
Season attendance: 43,891

Eastman Dodgers Team Roster

NAME	G	BA	POS	W	L	ERA	APF
Bruno, Bob	29	0.193	OF				Sparta
Burns, Bill	10	0.172	P	3	5	3.63	
Caldwell, Wilbur	99	0.244	3B, SS, OF				
Cook, Bill	28	0.178	P	8	11	3.55	
Farrar, Charles	112	0.283	M, OF				Fitzgerald
Gagnon, Russ	78	0.212	2B				
Hardegree, Bill	74	0.208	OF				
Harden, Jim	16	0.190	P	13	1	1.36	
Horton, Roger	10	0.205	SS				
Karpinec, Everett	96	0.273	SS				
Lapovicy, Frank	44	0.200	1B, OF				
Long, Jim	13	0.128					
Mauldin, Mason	76	0.239	OF				
Nelson, Dick	23	0.151	P	4	13	4.40	
North, Lamar	105	0.271	OF				
Pare, John	97	0.249	M, C				
Perello, Dave	63	0.247	3B, OF				
Prados, Bob	25	0.022	3B				
Pruett, Milton	100	0.241	1B				
Reese, Joe	19	0.408	2B				
Rose, Bob	31	0.123	P	16	8	3.55	
Underwood, Glenn	20	0.176	P	3	9	4.34	
Wright, Dixie	55	0.257	C				

Fitzgerald, Georgia
Team Operated by Fitzgerald Baseball Club, Inc.
Team President: A.A. Boggus
Vice President: N.E. Knighton
Secretary: W.E. Hoyle, Sr.
Treasurer-Business Manager: W.E. Hoyle, Jr.
Manager(s): Bill Good
Games played at Fitzgerald Ballpark
Season attendance: 44,877

Fitzgerald Pioneers Team Roster

NAME	G	BA	POS	W	L	ERA	APF
Crago, Bill	105	0.223	OF				
Davis, Bill	13	0.250	P				
Dougan, John	83	0.232	OF				Sparta
Dougan, Stan	14	0.042	P	4	3	3.82	Sparta
Farrar, Charles	112	0.283	OF				Eastman
Friedman, Stan	60	0.243	C				
Futcher, John	12	0.250	SS				
Galoffin, Jose	11	0.000	P	2	3	4.78	Vid-Lyo
Good, Bill	114	0.316	M, 3B, SS, OF, P	5	2	3.91	
Henrickson, Ed	119	0.254	OF				Vid-Lyo
Kash, Les	28	0.132	P	13	8	2.77	
Meadows, Herman	9		P	5	1	3.24	
Mink, Joe	10	0.185	OF				Douglas
Pearson, Tom	78	0.246	1B				
Puffer, Gerald	58	0.210	OF, P	14	11	2.66	
Ridgeway, Charlie	120	0.296	2B				
Roberts, Marv	10	0.200	SS				
Schmidt, Kermit	34	0.169	P	11	7	1.78	
Screen, Jim	16	0.138	P	4	6	4.40	Spa - Vid-Lyo
Shaw, Jim	14	0.133	SS				
Simmons, Paul	113	0.282	1B, C				
Smart, Charles	98	0.275	3B				
Teichert, Bob	28	0.053	P	6	11	3.75	
Wishba, Joe	16	0.059	OF				

Sparta, Georgia
Team Operated by Sparta Baseball Association
Team President: Marvin E. Moate
Vice Presidents: M.A. Cohen, B.A. Beall
Secretary: Dr. Ray Cole
Manager(s): Woodrow Bottoms
Games played at Sparta Baseball Park
Season attendance: 27,191

Sparta Saints Team Roster

NAME	G	BA	POS	W	L	ERA	APF
Bottoms, Woodrow	99	0.375	M, SS				
Brock, Paul	46	0.325	P	21	10	1.38	
Bruno, Bob	29	0.193	OF				Eastman
Collins, Jack	119	0.279	3B				
Cook, George	24	0.071	P	12	7	2.56	
Dougan, John	83	0.232	OF				Fitzgerald
Dougan, Stan	14	0.042	P	4	3	3.82	Fitzgerald
Evans, Willard	9		P	9	0	1.50	
Goggans, Bryant	44	0.175	OF, P	5	8	5.01	
Gula, Pete	108	0.311	OF				
Hartley, Don	35	0.213	OF				
Hartman, Earl	60	0.295	1B				
Leon, Sid	29	0.237	P	20	4	1.48	
McCormick, John	19	0.200	P	10	6	2.11	
Patterson, Ted	101	0.306	2B				
Ruark, Jim	119	0.294	C				
Screen, Jim	16	0.138	P	4	6	4.40	Fit - Vid-Lyo
Sinnott, John	59	0.269	OF				
Stevens, Paul	83	0.225	2B, SS, OF				
Swygert, Alan	108	0.339	1B, OF				

Vidalia-Lyons, Georgia
Team Operated by Vidalia-Lyons Baseball Club
Team President: L.L. Waller
Vice President: E.J. Harter
Secretary-Treasurer: William T. Darby
Business Manager: Carl W. East
Manager(s): Sugar Cain, Truman Connell
Games played at Twin Cities Stadium
Season attendance: 31,580

Vidalia-Lyons Team Roster

NAME	G	BA	POS	W	L	ERA	APF
Bess, Bob	24	0.031	P	2	6	5.00	Douglas
Cain, Sugar			M				
Ceravolo, Joe	23	0.169	2B				
Connell, Truman	118	0.358	M, OF				

Name	G	AVG	POS			ERA	Team
Davenport, Nevil	34	0.227	3B				
Galoffin, Jose	11	0.000	P	2	3	4.78	Fitzgerald
Hamrick, Ray	40	0.273	1B, C				
Henrickson, Ed	119	0.254	OF				Fitzgerald
Hill, Marion	26	0.258	P	5	9	4.89	
Johnson, Harold	35	0.160	P	17	13	3.35	
McGarity, Les	68	0.257	C				
Monarchi, Pete	72	0.181	1B				
Morgan, Julian	15	0.220	P	7	4	2.23	
Murray, Milt	36	0.224	SS				
Nickerson, Frank	15	0.143	P	1	6	5.95	Douglas
Patterson, Bill	39	0.248	C				
Ricketson, Don	14	0.213					
Screen, Jim	16	0.138	P	4	6	4.40	Fit - Spa
Silverman, Jerome	34	0.293	1B				
Sims, Dewey	69	0.222	OF				
Smith, Jim	118	0.206	3B, SS				
Snider, Floyd	83	0.220	1B, OF				
Solt, Gene	121	0.285	3B, OF				
Sullivan, Dan	59	0.190	2B				
Vidal, George	41	0.227	1B, P	1	7	6.39	
Young, Tex	33	0.226	P	14	11	2.82	

1948 Georgia State League Records

Batting

Highest Batting Average (minimum 100 at bats)
1. Woodrow Bottoms – Sparta .375
2. Truman Connell – Vidalia-Lyons .358
3. Alan Swygert – Sparta .339
4. Paul Brock – Sparta .325
5. Bill Good – Fitzgerald .316

Most Hits
1. Truman Connell – Vidalia-Lyons 146
2. Alan Swygert – Sparta 145
   Jack Collins – Sparta 145
4. Gene Solt – Vidalia-Lyons 143
5. Charlie Ridgeway – Fitzgerald 141

Most Runs
1. Charlie Ridgeway – Fitzgerald 106
2. Jack Collins – Sparta 83
3. Truman Connell – Vidalia-Lyons 82
4. Woodrow Bottoms – Sparta 78
5. Gene Solt – Vidalia-Lyons 77

Most Total Bases
1. Truman Connell – Vidalia-Lyons 217
2. Gene Solt – Vidalia-Lyons 209
3. Alan Swygert – Sparta 188
4. Pete Gula – Sparta 174
5. Ed Henrickson – Vid-Lyo/Fitz 173

Most Doubles
1. Alan Swygert – Sparta 29
2. Jim Ruark – Sparta 27
3. Gene Solt – Vidalia-Lyons 26
4. Truman Connell – Vidalia-Lyons 24
5. Ed Henrickson – Vid-Lyo/Fitz 21

Most Triples
1. Ed Henrickson – Vid-Lyo/Fitz 12
2. Gene Solt – Vidalia-Lyons 11
3. Ted Patterson – Sparta 10
4. Pete Gula – Sparta 9
   Bill Crago – Fitzgerald 9

Most Home Runs
1. Truman Connell – Vidalia-Lyons 11
2. Bryce Carmichael – Baxley 10
3. Bud Metheny – Baxley 7
4. Gene Solt – Vidalia-Lyons 6
   Earl Hartman – Sparta 6
   Elmer Westfall – Baxley 6

Most Extra Base Hits
1. Gene Solt – Vidalia-Lyons 43
2. Truman Connell – Vidalia-Lyons 42
3. Jim Ruark – Sparta 37
4. Ed Henrickson – Vid-Lyo/Fitz 35
   Alan Swygert – Sparta 35

Most Runs Batted In
1. Alan Swygert – Sparta 88
2. Truman Connell – Vidalia-Lyons 82
3. Jim Ruark – Sparta 66
4. Bill Good – Fitzgerald 65
5. Pete Gula – Sparta 64

Most Stolen Bases
1. Charlie Ridgeway – Fitzgerald 80
2. Ted Patterson – Sparta 35
3. Dave Perello – Eastman 27
4. Charles Smart – Fitzgerald 22
5. Frank Arcoleo – Baxley 20

Fielding

Most Put-Outs
1. Howard Prince 1B – Douglas 1,006
2. Jim Ruark C – Sparta 806
3. Paul Simmons 1B, C – Fitzgerald 703
4. Milton Pruett 1B – Eastman 676
5. Tom Pearson 1B – Fitzgerald 660

Most Assists
1. Emil Rey SS – Douglas 378
2. Charlie Ridgeway 2B – Fitzgerald 313
3. Everett Karpinec SS – Eastman 302
4. Woodrow Bottoms SS – Sparta 287
5. Jim Smith 3B, SS – Vidalia-Lyons 286

Most Errors
1. Jim Smith 3B, SS – Vidalia-Lyons 61
2. Frank Arcoleo SS – Baxley 54
3. Everett Karpinec SS – Eastman 43
4. Bryce Carmichael 2B – Baxley 42
5. Emil Rey SS – Douglas 38
   Bill Good 3B, SS, OF - Fitzgerald 38
   Mike Rauseo 3B – Baxley 38

Pitching

Most Wins
1. Paul Brock – Sparta 21
2. Sid Leon – Sparta 20
3. Harold Johnson – Vidalia-Lyons 17
   Don Rodd – Baxley 17
5. Bob Rose – Eastman 16
   Jack Gilbert – Baxley 16

Most Losses
1. Rudy Belakovy – Douglas 15
2. Harold Johnson – Vidalia-Lyons 13
   Dick Nelson – Eastman 13
4. John Miskulin – Baxley 12
   Bill Loveys – Douglas 12

Highest Winning Percentage (10 game minimum)
1. Jim Harden – Eastman .929
2. Sid Leon – Sparta .833

3. Don Rodd – Baxley .739
4. Bill Good – Fitzgerald .714
5. Paul Brock – Sparta .677

Lowest Earned Run Average (100 inning minimum)
1. Jim Harden – Eastman 1.36
2. Paul Brock – Sparta 1.38
3. Sid Leon – Sparta 1.48
4. Kermit Schmidt – Fitzgerald 1.78
5. John McCormick – Sparta 2.11

Most Strikeouts
1. Paul Brock – Sparta 270
2. John Miskulin – Baxley 187
3. Sid Leon – Sparta 173
4. Les Kash – Fitzgerald 166
5. Harold Johnson – Vidalia-Lyons 150

Most Bases on Balls
1. Harold Johnson – Vidalia-Lyons 97
2. John Miskulin – Baxley 89
   Marion Hill – Vidalia-Lyons 89
4. Bob Teichert – Fitzgerald 86
5. Bill Cook – Eastman 85

Most Hits Allowed
1. Harold Johnson – Vidalia-Lyons 210
2. Rudy Belakovy – Douglas 196
3. Sid Leon – Sparta 186
4. Don Rodd – Baxley 182
5. Tex Young – Vidalia-Lyons 181

Most Innings Pitched
1. Paul Brock – Sparta 260
2. Sid Leon – Sparta 244
3. Harold Johnson – Vidalia-Lyons 226
4. John Miskulin – Baxley 217
5. Jack Gilbert – Baxley 208

1949

Georgia-Alabama League

League Office: Talladega, Alabama
League President: Arthur R. Decatur
League Vice President: George Cahall
Salary Limit: $2,600 per month.
Player Rule: Each club was allowed a roster of sixteen players, not more than one veteran, not more than nine limited service, and not less than six rookies.
Umpires: Leslie V. Zabel, L.H. Darden, Eldridge Mote, Merritt "Sugar" Cain, Charles Roberts, Ed Owens.

Georgia-Alabama League Final Standings

Team	W	L	Pct	GB	Affiliate
Newnan Brownies	74	52	.587	----	Unaffiliated
Alexander City Millers	69	57	.548	5.0	Unaffiliated
Tallassee Cardinals	66	60	.527	8.0	STL-NL
LaGrange Troupers	65	61	.516	9.0	NY-AL
Valley Rebels	62	64	.492	12.0	BSN-AL
Opelika Owls	62	64	.492	12.0	Unaffiliated
Carrollton Hornets	56	70	.444	18.0	Unaffiliated
Griffin Pimientos	50	76	.397	24.0	Unaffiliated

1949 Georgia-Alabama League Map

(numbers on map correspond to the place each team finished in regular season play)

For the third consecutive year, the face of the Georgia-Alabama League remained the same with all eight teams returning to the diamond.

LaGrange pitcher Alex Gounaris wrote his name in the record book on July 5 when he pitched a no-hitter against Griffin winning 5 to 0 in seven innings. On August 9, Valley pitcher Eddie Beach pitched the league's second no-hitter of the season blanking Carrollton 4 to 0 in a seven-inning contest. The league's all time record for the most stolen bases in a season was set at 80 by Jack Huesman of Alexander City. Tallassee shortstop Bob Adams set the all time league mark for the most assists in a season at 401, and Opelika shortstop Paul Flores tied the league's all time single season record for the most errors when he booted 74. The original record was set by Cedartown shortstop Cleveland in 1930.

At the end of the season, the Newnan Brownies were at the top of the standings by five games. Second, third, and fourth places went to Alexander City, Tallassee, and LaGrange. In the post-season playoffs, Newnan defeated Tallassee three games to two. On the other side of the bracket, Alexander City beat LaGrange three games to one. Alexander City upset Newnan in the league championship series four games to two.

Alexander City went on to face Waycross, champions of the Georgia-Florida League, in the Class D Series. Waycross won four games to one.

Alexander City, Alabama
Team Operated by Alexander City Miller, Inc.
Team President: D.W. Hodo
Vice President: James Callahan
Secretary: L.C. Howell
Treasurer-Business Manager: William W. Cowart
Manager(s): Red Roberts
Games played at Benjamin C. Russell Field
Season attendance: 37,373

Alexander City Millers Team Roster

NAME	G	BA	POS	W	L	ERA	APF
Alonso, John	72	0.253	OF				
Bozzuto, Bert	26	0.186	P	5	14	5.12	Carrollton
Brown, Bill	112	0.297	1B				
Chappell, Marv	89	0.315	OF, P	20	7	2.34	
Coker, Jim	10	0.243	1B				
Deibler, Mason	13	0.000	P	3	4	4.50	Tallassee
Edwards, Ray	117	0.210	3B				
Ello, Jim	115	0.229	C				
Hartman, Dick	39	0.161	C				
Hovell, Bob	123	0.251	OF				
Huesman, Jack	126	0.265	2B, SS				
Kittrell, Ed	15	0.154	P	3	5	5.03	Opelika
Little, Walt	12	0.083	P	4	6	5.12	Carrollton
McBride, Delton	12	0.160					
McCraney, Wayne	25	0.230	P	7	10	4.57	
McTaggert, Charles	28	0.136	P	9	7	3.16	
Mink, Joe	15	0.326	OF				Newnan
Reach, Cliff	82	0.206	2B, OF				
Rinaldi, Charles	22	0.150	P	7	7	4.00	
Roberts, Red	107	0.317	M, SS				
Sprayberry, Jim	11	0.267	P	2	4	4.30	
Thompson, Dick	46	0.200	P	14	6	2.72	
Wooley, Jim	106	0.287	OF				

Carrollton, Georgia
Team Operated by Carrollton Baseball Club, Inc.
Team President: William O. Cobb, P.L. Shaefer
Secretary: Eugene R. McGee
Treasurer: Harvey J. Copeland
Manager(s): Bill Rucker, Bill Seal
Games played at City Athletic Field
Season attendance: 36,029

Carrollton Hornets Team Roster

NAME	G	BA	POS	W	L	ERA	APF
Bartholomew, Jack	25	0.219	2B				
Berman, Buddy	112	0.227	2B				
Bobowski, Ed	33	0.239	P	10	13	3.51	LaGrange
Bozzuto, Bert	26	0.186	P	5	14	5.12	Alex City
Burnstein, Leonard	17	0.244	OF				
Calkins, Dick	1		OF				
Callen, Jim	4		OF				
Cichon, Frank	55	0.276	OF				
Conhenney, Jim	94	0.218	3B				
Fullington, ---	4	0.500					
Hudson, Bill	24	0.323	1B				
Hutchins, Bob	7		P	4	3	2.33	
Jefts, Virgil	114	0.241	C				
Jones, Casey	22	0.136	P	4	3	2.57	
Kuras, Walt	27	0.266	P	12	8	2.77	
Langemeier, Paul	14	0.059	P	4	4	3.13	
Laubach, Carl	<10		1B				
Little, Walt	12	0.083	P	4	6	5.12	Alex City
Maloof, Joe	11	0.188	P				
Matthews, Luther	8		P	3	3	2.52	
Morelli, Jim	107	0.259	OF				
Nasworthy, Luther	93	0.244	SS, OF				
Nelson, Burel	22		P	5	8		
Nelson, Dick	26	0.212	P	5	5	4.60	
Poole, Buddy	12	0.200	P	1	3	4.78	
Ridenour, Roy	14	0.132	SS				
Rucker, Bill	120	0.279	M, 1B, OF				
Russell, Bing	11	0.182	OF				
Seal, Bill	85	0.341	M, 3B, SS				
Shirley, Jim	85	0.215	1B				
Thompson, Jim	19	0.219	OF				
Tidwell, John	39	0.316	OF				
Umscheid, Don	11	0.000	P				Griffin
Wadewitz, Oswin	11	0.087	P	2	7	1.88	
Whited, Gerald	12	0.200	1B				
Yarborough, Mack	4		SS				

Griffin, Georgia
Team Operated by Griffin Baseball Club, Inc.
Team President: Louis George
Vice President: Joseph George
Secretary-Treasurer-Business Manager: H.T. Green
Manager(s): Buck Etchison, Sam Gibson, Lou Sanders, Rudy York
Games played at Pimiento Park
Season attendance: 47,825

Griffin Pimientos Team Roster

NAME	G	BA	POS	W	L	ERA	APF
Adcock, Bob	92	0.346	OF				
Battistelli, Angelo	18	0.186	SS				
Bianchi, Frank	17	0.200	P	2	4	7.53	
Chafin, Bobbie	17	0.094	P	1	4	5.57	
Chechile, Bill	121	0.275	OF				Newnan
DeFeo, Bob	43	0.303	3B				Tallassee
Ebetino, John	37	0.128	P	5	11	4.47	
Etchison, Buck	44	0.272	M, 1B				
Fleisch, Don	14	0.114	SS				
Forrester, Frank	43	0.229	OF				
Gibson, Sam	<10		M, P	0	2		
Green, Paul	12	0.167	SS				
Hardegree, Bill	16	0.156	P				
Hargis, Jim	17	0.264	OF				Newnan
Hart, Norm	10	0.125	P				
Jackson, Frank	12	0.115	OF				
Kemmerer, Nathaniel	31	0.211	P	11	11	4.69	
Laney, Floyd	51	0.231	3B, C				
Lopez, Carlos	43	0.205	P	12	15	4.04	
McAndrew, Bob	111	0.254	2B				
Noga, George	122	0.264	3B, SS				
Pollard, Gene	73	0.250	1B, OF				
Rinker, Bob	112	0.285	C				
Sanders, Lou	110	0.259	M, SS, OF				
Sewell, Bill	26	0.386	OF				
Tomasic, George	32	0.200	P	11	12	3.74	
Umscheid, Don	11	0.000	P				Carrollton

Georgia Class-D Minor League Baseball Encyclopedia

NAME	G	BA	POS	W	L	ERA	APF
Wassel, Bill	20	0.167	OF				Newnan
York, Rudy	33	0.188	M, 1B				

LaGrange, Georgia
Team Operated by LaGrange Baseball Club, Inc.
Team President: Oliver Hunnicutt
Vice President: C.L. Cahall
Secretary: Alvin Davis
Manager(s): Carl Cooper
Games played at Callaway Stadium
Season attendance: 59,952
Major League Affiliate: New York Yankees – American League.

LaGrange Troupers Team Roster

NAME	G	BA	POS	W	L	ERA	APF
Beaird, Dick	<10						
Bobowski, Ed	33	0.239	P	10	13	3.51	Carrollton
Braganca, Joe	47	0.209	C				
Burk, Ron	48	0.229	2B				
Charles, Jim	24	0.229	P	13	5	4.10	
Cohen, Hy	40	0.218	P	11	15	3.33	
Cooper, Carl	112	0.306	M, 1B, OF				
Dembinski, Dan	17	0.170	C				
Feinstien, Joe	22	0.276	P	6	1	5.51	
Ferra, Joe	32	0.327	OF				
Flaherty, Chris	98	0.266	1B, 3B				
Goff, Jim	84	0.241	OF				
Gounaris, Alex	33	0.158	P	5	8	4.15	
Hammack, Shurley	99	0.259	2B, SS				
Hayden, John	16	0.111	P	2	4	4.50	
Katalinic, John	22	0.152	P	6	5	4.55	
Krings, Dave	48	0.220	SS				
Krochina, John	107	0.276	OF				
Lawson, Leroy	30	0.250	1B, OF				
Lyons, Pat	19	0.200	OF				
Mancini, Herb	53	0.227	3B				
Morrongiello, Mike	35	0.344	2B				
Muse, Don	112	0.288	SS, C				
Stevenson, Fred	13	0.115	OF				
Thrift, Syd	52	0.306	1B, P	4	2	3.67	
Wallace, Jim	10	0.111	P				
Wallis, Gerald	33	0.123	P	16	8	2.64	
Woodruff, Ernest	17	0.241	OF				

Newnan, Georgia
Team Operated by Newnan Baseball Association, Inc.
Team President: A.L. Potts
Vice President-Secretary-Treasurer: J.R. Brown
Manager(s): Joe Schmidt
Games played at Pickett Field
Season attendance: 56,976

Newnan Brownies Team Roster

NAME	G	BA	POS	W	L	ERA	APF
Chechile, Bill	121	0.275	OF				Griffin
Dickson, Ed	63	0.233	OF				
Franson, Carl	124	0.269	3B				
Fulton, Bob	113	0.282	OF, C				
Garner, Homer	20	0.188	P	7	9	4.50	
Hargis, Jim	17	0.264	OF				Griffin
Konek, Pete	10	0.276					
Lazzari, Jim	36	0.200	OF				
McAfee, Alton	121	0.258	1B				
McCulloch, Bob	54	0.212	C				
McFadden, John	37	0.184	P	21	9	2.55	
Millard, John	124	0.292	SS				
Mink, Joe	15	0.326	OF				Alex City
Nierpoetter, Billy	34	0.159	P	15	12	4.26	
Powers, Fred	12	0.209					Opelika
Rees, Ernest	12	0.167	OF				
Schmidt, Joe	123	0.308	M, 2B				
Shoemake, Benton	114	0.268	1B, OF				Valley
Taylor, Spafford	89	0.222	OF				
Tenney, Jim	18	0.148	P	4	5	3.64	
Thomas, Parks	26	0.271	P	12	8	2.59	
Wagner, Dick	13	0.200	P	5	3	3.60	
Wallace, Elmer	42	0.060	P	9	2	2.02	
Wassel, Bill	20	0.167	OF				Griffin

Opelika, Alabama
Team Operated by Opelika Baseball Club, Inc.
Team President: D.M. Bailey
Vice Presidents: Phil Hudson, Jack Finney
Secretary-Treasurer: Herman Turner
Manager(s): Jim Ball
Games played at Pepperell Park
Season attendance: 44,885

Opelika Owls Team Roster

NAME	G	BA	POS	W	L	ERA	APF
Ball, Jim	115	0.341	M, OF				
Bottorff, Tom	21	0.255	1B				
Flemming, Wheeler	111	0.257	1B				
Flores, Paul	119	0.306	SS				
Howton, Frank	24	0.100	P	11	6	2.94	
Hudson, Bill	113	0.324	OF				
Jackson, Claude	48	0.250	P	16	17	3.35	
Jarvis, Bob	113	0.266	3B				
Julian, Al	119	0.287	OF				
Julian, Bob	113	0.237	2B				
Kilgore, Bill	38	0.229	P	17	8	3.00	
Kittrell, Ed	15	0.154	P	3	5	5.03	Alex City
Martin, Billie	30	0.169	P	6	7	4.54	
Noto, Phil	100	0.288	C				
Perdue, Glenn	17	0.171	P	3	4	3.80	
Powers, Fred	12	0.209					Newnan
Steadman, Bob	10	0.235					
Vanatistein, Herb	15	0.190	C				

Tallassee, Alabama
Team Operated by Tallassee Baseball Club, Inc.
Team President: C. Ray Loving
Vice President: B.G. Stumberg
Secretary: Ed Ingram
Business Manager: Charlie Bowen
Manager(s): Bill Blackwell, Bob Comiskey
Games played at Stumberg Field
Season attendance: 43,364
Major League Affiliate: St. Louis Cardinals – National League.

Tallassee Cardinals Team Roster

NAME	G	BA	POS	W	L	ERA	APF
Adams, Bob	121	0.251	SS				
Berg, Ed	117	0.234	2B				
Blackwell, Bill	115	0.289	M, OF				
Ciani, Nick	117	0.232	OF				
Clements, Ralph	36	0.301	P	14	7	2.21	
Comiskey, Bob	80	0.249	M, C				
Courtney, James	11	0.192					
Davis, Jim	17	0.333	P				
DeFeo, Bob	43	0.303	3B				Griffin
Deibler, Mason	13	0.000	P	3	4	4.50	Alex City
Dickerman, Ed	34	0.261	3B				
Herdt, Don	94	0.219	3B, C				
Hinkle, Leon	23	0.115	P	3	4	4.66	

Name	G	BA	POS	W	L	ERA
Jacobs, Ottis	12	0.077	P			
Joyner, Julian	31	0.125	P	7	10	3.77
Mathey, Bud	20	0.351				
Owen, Maurice	22	0.089	P	9	9	2.20
Pinson, Harold	115	0.256	1B			
Reinagle, Ed	17	0.067	P	3	8	4.73
Rikard, Denver	121	0.290	OF			
Teater, Rollie	54	0.187	C			
Tiefenauer, Bobby	38	0.200	P	17	6	2.27

Valley (Lanett), Alabama

Team Operated by Valley Baseball Club, Inc.
Team President: Fob James
Vice President: G.E. "Cheese" Goggans
Secretary: J.H. Gay
Treasurer: Mrs. Luther S. Turner
Manager(s): Woodrow Bottoms, Jesse Danna, Malvern Morgan
Games played at Jennings Field
Season attendance: 52,859
Major League Affiliate: Boston Red Sox – American League.

Valley Rebels Team Roster

NAME	G	BA	POS	W	L	ERA	APF
Beach, Ed	32	0.155	P	13	9	2.29	
Blackburn, Tom	119	0.260	OF				
Bottoms, Woodrow	20	0.308	M, 3B				
Casey, Charles	15	0.167	C				
Chapman, Herb	83	0.351	1B, OF				
Clark, Ray	44	0.247	SS				
Colson, Rod	38	0.230	OF				
Danna, Jesse	10	0.267	M				
Davenport, Nevil	22	0.200	2B				
Edge, Harvey	37	0.118	P	6	10	3.87	
Frazier, Lance	10	0.243	C				
Galloway, Oliver	63	0.288	C				
Griggs, Bill	16	0.000	P	2	4	3.70	
Harrison, Bill	13	0.176	2B				
Haynes, Hoover	32	0.178	P	12	6	3.11	
Henegar, Russ	28	0.350	P	6	5	4.07	
Johnson, George	14	0.200	2B				
Langdon, Joe	35	0.158	P	8	9	4.80	
Mason, John	57	0.241	OF, C				
Morgan, Malvern	77	0.375	M, 1B, 2B				
Nance, Hoover	15	0.106	OF				
Pappas, Nick	21	0.196	P	8	4	4.58	
Powers, John	62	0.319	OF				
Ray, Tom	85	0.238	SS				
Shoemake, Benton	114	0.268	1B, OF				Newnan
Spruill, Jack	126	0.321	2B, 3B				
Steckel, Bob	56	0.254	2B				
Stuckey, Rex	19	0.264	C				

1949 Georgia-Alabama League Records

Batting
Highest Batting Average (minimum 100 at bats)
1. Bill Sewell – Griffin .386
2. Malvern Morgan – Valley .375
3. Herb Chapman – Valley .351
4. Bob Adcock – Griffin .346
5. Mike Morrongiello – LaGrange .344

Most Hits
1. Jack Spruill – Valley 153
2. Jim Ball – Opelika 143
3. Al Julian – Opelika 141
4. Joe Schmidt – Newnan 140
5. John Millard – Newnan 135

Most Runs
1. Jack Huesman - Alexander City 108
2. Carl Franson – Newnan 106
3. Joe Schmidt – Newnan 102
4. Jack Spruill – Valley 95
5. Lou Sanders – Griffin 91

Most Total Bases
1. Carl Franson – Newnan 264
2. Joe Schmidt – Newnan 220
3. Denver Rikard – Tallassee 216
4. Jack Spruill – Valley 210
5. Bill Hudson – Opelika 208

Most Doubles
1. Carl Franson – Newnan 34
2. Jack Spruill – Valley 29
   Bob Adams – Tallassee 29
4. Malvern Morgan – Valley 27
5. Bob Rinker – Griffin 23

Most Triples
1. John Krochina – LaGrange 16
2. Bill Hudson – Opelika 15
3. Bob Adcock – Griffin 13
   Bill Chechile – Newn/Grif 13
5. Bob Adams – Tallassee 9
   Paul Flores – Opelika 9

Most Home Runs
1. Carl Franson – Newnan 28
2. Bill Seal – Carrollton 23
3. Carl Cooper – LaGrange 20
4. Denver Rikard – Tallassee 17
   Joe Schmidt – Newnan 17

Most Extra Base Hits
1. Carl Franson – Newnan 68
2. Bill Seal – Carrollton 47
3. Denver Rikard – Tallassee 45
4. Bill Hudson – Opelika 44
5. Joe Schmidt – Newnan 42
   Bob Adams – Tallassee 42

Most Runs Batted In
1. Joe Schmidt – Newnan 108
2. Bill Hudson – Opelika 107
3. Carl Franson – Newnan 104
4. Bill Seal – Carrollton 97
5. Carl Cooper – LaGrange 94

Most Stolen Bases
1. Jack Huesman - Alexander City 80
2. Bill Rucker – Carrollton 75
3. Al Julian – Opelika 47
4. Jim Wooley - Alexander City 29
5. Bob Julian – Opelika 25

Fielding
Most Put-Outs
1. Harold Pinson 1B – Tallassee 1,025
2. Alton McAfee 1B – Newnan 991
3. Wheeler Flemming 1B – Opelika 913
4. Bill Brown 1B - Alexander City 872
5. Jim Shirley 1B – Carrollton 645

Most Assists
1. Bob Adams SS – Tallassee 401
2. Jack Huesman 2B, SS - Alexander City 362

3. John Millard SS – Newnan 326
4. Ed Berg 2B – Tallassee 321
5. Paul Flores SS – Opelika 314

Most Errors
1. Paul Flores SS – Opelika 74
2. John Millard SS – Newnan 61
3. Bob McAndrew 2B – Griffin 53
4. Tom Ray SS – Valley 50
5. Jack Spruill 2B, 3B – Valley 40
   Don Herdt 3B, C – Tallassee 40

Pitching
Most Wins
1. John McFadden – Newnan 21
2. Marv Chappell - Alexander City 20
3. Bobby Tiefenauer – Tallassee 17
   Bill Kilgore – Opelika 17
5. Gerald Wallis – LaGrange 16
   Claude Jackson – Opelika 16

Most Losses
1. Claude Jackson – Opelika 17
2. Carlos Lopez – Griffin 15
   Hy Cohen – LaGrange 15
4. Bert Bozzuto – Carr/Alex 14
5. Ed Bobowski – LaGr/Carr 13

Highest Winning Percentage (10 game minimum)
1. Joe Feinstein – LaGrange .857
2. Elmer Wallace – Newnan .818
3. Marv Chappell - Alexander City .741
4. Bobby Tiefenauer – Tallassee .739
5. Jim Charles – LaGrange .722

Lowest Earned Run Average (100 inning minimum)
1. Elmer Wallace – Newnan 2.02
2. Maurice Owen – Tallassee 2.20
3. Ralph Clements – Tallassee 2.21
4. Bobby Tiefenauer – Tallassee 2.27
5. Ed Beach – Valley 2.29

Most Strikeouts
1. John McFadden – Newnan 180
2. Marv Chappell - Alexander City 162
3. Hy Cohen – LaGrange 148
4. Gerald Wallis – LaGrange 144
5. Billy Nierpoetter – Newnan 142

Most Bases on Balls
1. Bill Kilgore – Opelika 140
2. Carlos Lopez – Griffin 135
3. Marv Chappell - Alexander City 129
4. Claude Jackson – Opelika 118
5. Billy Nierpoetter – Newnan 116

Most Hits Allowed
1. Claude Jackson – Opelika 226
2. Carlos Lopez – Griffin 213
3. John McFadden – Newnan 196
4. Billy Nierpoetter – Newnan 189
5. Ed Bobowski – LaGr/Carr 187
   Nathaniel Kemmerer – Griffin 187

Most Innings Pitched
1. John McFadden – Newnan 244
2. Marv Chappell - Alexander City 235
3. Claude Jackson – Opelika 234
4. Carlos Lopez – Griffin 223
5. Bill Kilgore – Opelika 219

1949 Georgia-Alabama League All-Star Team
Georgia Team:
1B Alton McAfee – Newnan
2B Joe Schmidt – Newnan
3B Bill Seal – Carrollton
SS John Millard – Newnan
OF Carl Cooper – LaGrange
OF Bob Adcock – Griffin
OF Frank Cichon – Carrollton
C Bob Fulton – Newnan
C Don Muse – LaGrange
UT Herb Mancini – LaGrange
UT George Noga – Griffin
UT Jim Morelli – Carrollton
P Jim Charles – LaGrange
P John McFadden – Newnan
P Walt Kuras – Carrollton
P Parks Thomas – Newnan
P Carlos Lopez – Griffin
P Gerald Wallis – LaGrange

Alabama Team:
1B Bill Brown – Alexander City
2B Jack Huesman – Alexander City
3B Jack Spruill – Valley
SS Paul Flores – Opelika
OF Bill Hudson – Opelika
OF Jim Ball – Opelika
OF John Powers – Valley
C Bob Comiskey – Tallassee
C Jim Ello - Alexander City
UT Bob Adams – Tallassee
UT Malvern Morgan – Valley
UT Denver Rikard – Tallassee
P Bobby Tiefenauer – Tallassee
P Ralph Clements – Tallassee
P Joe Langdon – Valley
P Frank Howton – Opelika
P Bill Kilgore – Opelika
P Marv Chappell – Alexander City

Georgia Class-D Minor League Baseball Encyclopedia

1949

Georgia-Florida League

League Office: Leslie, Georgia
League President: W.T. Anderson
League Vice President: C.L. Thompson
Secretary: James R. Blair
Salary Limit: $2,600 per month.
Player Rule: Each club was allowed a roster of seventeen players, not more than three veterans, not more than seven limited service, and not less than seven rookies.

Georgia-Florida League Final Standings

Team	W	L	Pct	GB	Affiliate
Albany Cardinals	96	42	.696	----	STL-NL
Valdosta Dodgers	86	54	.614	11.0	BRK-NL
Waycross Bears	83	56	.597	13.5	Unaffiliated
Americus Phillies	71	67	.514	25.0	PHI-NL
Thomasville Tigers	60	80	.429	37.0	DET-AL
Moultrie Athletics	56	82	.406	40.0	PHI-AL
Cordele Indians	54	85	.388	42.5	CLE-AL
Tallahassee Pirates	49	89	.355	47.0	PIT-NL

1949 Georgia-Florida League Map

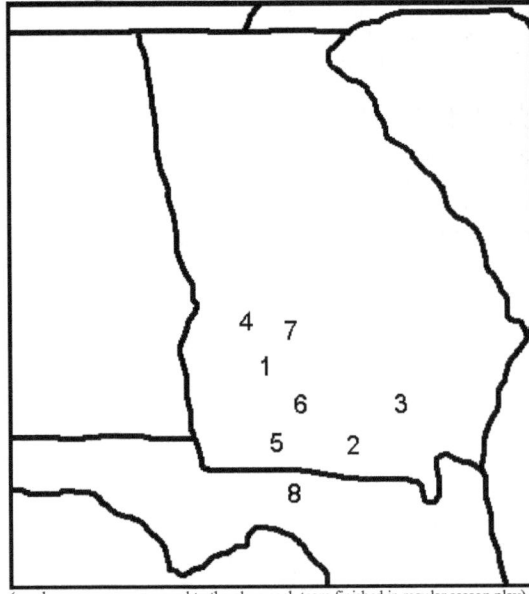

(numbers on map correspond to the place each team finished in regular season play)

For the fourth year in a row, the same eight teams made up the Georgia-Florida League.

On August 27, Moultrie pitcher Henry Penton pitched a no-hitter against Waycross pounding the Bears 18 to 0. Art Ceccarelli, pitching for Valdosta, set the all-time league mark for the most strikeouts by fanning 294 batters during the season.

The regular season pennant was copped by Albany followed in order in the standings by Valdosta, Waycross, and Americus. Albany defeated Americus in the first round of the playoffs three games to one, and Waycross eliminated Valdosta three games to none. It was Waycross pulling the upset over Albany in the league championship series winning four games to one. After winning the league championship for the second year in a row, Waycross went on to play Alexander City, Alabama, champion of the Georgia-Alabama League, in the Class D Series. Waycross won the interleague series four games to one.

Albany, Georgia
Team Operated by Albany Baseball Club, Inc.
Team President: Morton M. Wiggins
Vice Presidents: Fred M. Saigh, Jr., William Walsingham, Jr.
Secretary: Edward W. Roth
Treasurer: Fred M. Saigh, Jr.
Business Manager: L.E. "Chick" Walmsley
Manager(s): Chief Bender
Games played at Cardinal Field
Season attendance: 93,096
Major League Affiliate: St. Louis Cardinals – National League.

Albany Cardinals Team Roster

NAME	G	BA	POS	W	L	ERA	APF
Adamcewicz, Erwin	27	0.271	OF				
Bender, Chief	41	0.221	M, P	11	3	2.42	
Bodnar, Elmer	132	0.232	2B				
Boggan, George	28	0.152	P	15	5	3.52	
Childs, Delton	113	0.343	OF				
Cyrus, Dave	47	0.242	P	18	7	3.42	Americus
Foreman, Don	25	0.215	OF				
Frank, Morris	39	0.148	P	22	9	1.94	
Frantell, Don	32	0.128	2B				Valdosta
Hawley, Rondell	15	0.250	P	1	4	5.10	
Henley, Howard	33	0.246	P	13	7	2.51	
Hertweck, Neal	139	0.254	1B				
Hinkle, Jack	33	0.227	SS				
Klobe, Ray	23	0.282	P	7	1	5.61	
Koppenhaver, Bob	93	0.291	SS				
Lamey, Walt	11	0.192					
Mizell, Vinegar Bend	23	0.102	P	12	3	1.98	
Osteen, Bill	81	0.325	C				
Rac, Russell	136	0.316	OF				
Reale, John	137	0.250	3B				
Smith, Hal	99	0.224	C				
Sowins, Ray	110	0.283	OF				
Watts, Don	33	0.286	P	13	7	2.71	

Americus, Georgia
Team Operated by Americus Phillies, Inc.
Team President: H. Phil Jones
Vice President: Joseph F. Reardon
Secretary-Treasurer: George A. Fletcher
Business Manager: Orion Mitchell
Manager(s): Ed Murphy
Games played at Americus Baseball Park
Season attendance: 46,906
Major League Affiliate: Philadelphia Phillies – National League.

Americus Phillies Team Roster

NAME	G	BA	POS	W	L	ERA	APF
Bonds, Ken	42	0.176	C				
Brown, Gene	76	0.214	3B, OF				
Bucco, Dick	27	0.255	OF				
Colflesh, Jack	22	0.202	OF				
Comolli, Vic	100	0.307	C				
Cyrus, Dave	47	0.242	P	18	7	3.42	Albany
Dubbs, Clayton	16	0.204	3B				
Evans, Frank	38	0.241	3B				
Gould, Pete	102	0.276	3B, SS, C				Waycross

Georgia Class-D Minor League Baseball Encyclopedia

NAME	G	BA	POS	W	L	ERA	APF
Hubbard, Charles	10	0.000					
McArthur, Don	98	0.266	3B, OF				
McCain, Sam	126	0.275	1B, OF				
McKay, Dick	39	0.118	P	7	8	5.59	
Murphy, Ed	49	0.344	M, 1B				
Roop, Harvey	137	0.271	OF, P	11	6	4.11	
Sanford, Jack	35	0.310	P	15	9	4.39	
Stamey, Harold	134	0.311	OF				
Tracy, Jim	36	0.157	P	16	11	2.91	
Trojanowski, Ed	137	0.264	2B				
Wenitski, Bernie	136	0.214	SS				
Wingo, Jim	16	0.174	P	3	7	6.31	
Zirafi, Antonio	13	0.136	P	2	8	4.13	

Cordele, Georgia
Team Operated by Cordele Indians Baseball Club, Inc.
Team President: J.W. Bridges
Vice President: H.B. "Buzz" Wetzel
Secretary-Treasurer: Rudie Schaffer
Business Manager: Bill Brown
Manager(s): Hal Lee
Games played at City Park
Season attendance: 40,198
Major League Affiliate: Cleveland Indians – American League.

Cordele Indians Team Roster

NAME	G	BA	POS	W	L	ERA	APF
Broukal, Bill	137	0.263	SS				
Brown, Al	36	0.130	P	5	9	4.57	
Cluley, Mike	31	0.087	P	4	5	5.63	
Cromartie, Henry	31	0.200	1B				
Cutcliff, Tom	134	0.199	2B				
Froug, Mel	53	0.293	1B				
Gall, Bill	30	0.232	P	7	11	4.47	
Geis, Harry	118	0.322	1B, OF				
Howell, Pete	31	0.178	OF				
Johnson, Oscar	38	0.213	P	8	14	4.22	
Kaye, Charles	25	0.156	OF				
Koby, Dick	103	0.253	3B				
Kozimer, Harry	13	0.157	3B				
Lee, Hal	71	0.315	M, 1B, 3B				
Lynch, Wayne	33	0.145	P	11	15	3.45	
Rentz, Irv	110	0.275	C				
Roberts, Ray	55	0.254	OF				
Smith, Tom	136	0.319	OF				
Soumma, Gene	50	0.211	P	17	17	3.59	
Spain, Hank	76	0.269	OF				
Steffensen, Dick	22	0.111	P	2	3	3.86	
Strickland, Norris	29	0.311	OF				
Stroeker, Arnold	43	0.194	C				
Stryker, Ernest	10	0.200					
Whiddon, John	11	0.000	P				

Moultrie, Georgia
Team Operated by Moultrie Athletics, Inc.
Team President: Connie Mack
Vice President: Arthur Ehler
Secretary: Connie Mack, Jr.
Treasurer: Roy Mack
Business Manager: C.W. Vandiver
Manager(s): Bill Peterman
Games played at Municipal Park
Season attendance: 28,911
Major League Affiliate: Philadelphia Athletics – American League.

Moultrie Athletics Team Roster

NAME	G	BA	POS	W	L	ERA	APF
Asmer, John	25	0.224	P	11	4	4.14	
Atzert, George	25	0.204	P	9	6	3.00	
Boatwright, John	24	0.245	OF				
Brennan, Wilbert	18	0.136	OF				
Brill, Stan	137	0.262	2B				
Busa, Al	19	0.105	P	2	6	3.76	
Carr, Bill	53	0.201	SS, OF				
Cathey, Bob	70	0.235	1B				
DeFeo, Bob	17	0.191	3B				
Deitch, Mike	27	0.143	P	5	8	4.96	
Demont, Paul	103	0.249	3B, SS				
Deporto, Jesse	10	0.091					
Dotson, Gene	122	0.212	C				
Garner, Bill	35	0.088	P	10	12	3.10	
Kell, Skeeter	82	0.288	SS				
Lewison, Bill	33	0.180	3B				
McClatchey, Bob	99	0.237	OF				
Nichols, Jim	11	0.125					
Niedowicz, Frank	111	0.315	1B, OF				
Penton, Henry	50	0.200	P	9	9	5.30	
Peterman, Bill	31	0.224	M, C				
Rhyne, Ken	55	0.298	1B				
Singleton, Joe	138	0.293	OF				
Storch, Charles	11	0.111	P				
Swingle, Russ	29	0.222	P	7	12	3.60	
Taylor, Bob	14	0.048	P	1	10	5.29	
Wherry, Kendall	22	0.219	OF				
Wrenn, Milt	16	0.152	C				

Tallahassee, Florida
Team Operated by Tallahassee Pirates, Inc.
Team President: Fred N. Lowry
Vice President: H. Roy Hamey
Secretary: Fred Hering
Business Manager: Lou London
Manager(s): Gerald Cabaniss, Johnnie Heving, Bob Shawkey, Norm Veazey
Games played at Centennial Field
Season attendance: 48,079
Major League Affiliate: Pittsburgh Pirates – National League.

Tallahassee Pirates Team Roster

NAME	G	BA	POS	W	L	ERA	APF
Bandoch, Ed	26	0.175	C				
Bollman, Bill	130	0.235	1B, 2B, 3B, SS				
Bradshaw, Hugh	25	0.224	C				
Cabaniss, Gerald	71	0.284	M, 2B				
Clarich, Jim	12	0.353	P	1	4	3.83	
Costello, Dan	46	0.170	1B, P	6	11	3.20	
Crowley, Walt	75	0.196	P	14	14	3.54	
Delo, Lawrence	27	0.125	P	3	8	5.91	
Fiori, Ben	16	0.071					
Fitzgerald, John	32	0.262	P	5	15	5.90	
Forbes, John	10	0.265					
Handel, Henry	19	0.143	P	4	7	4.39	
Hegedorn, Gary	25	0.179	1B				
Heving, Johnnie			M				
Kinnamon, Bill	34	0.224	C				
Knutson, Ron	10	0.214					
Koart, Bill	34	0.193	C				
Martinich, Tony	87	0.283	OF				
O'Brien, Bill	90	0.282	OF				
Petraglia, Joe	52	0.222	2B, 3B				
Regan, Jim	91	0.244	1B				
Rhodes, Herb	29	0.239	OF				
Riley, ---	55		3B				
Secoli, Frank	10	0.091	P				
Shawkey, Bob			M				

Georgia Class-D Minor League Baseball Encyclopedia

NAME	G	BA	POS	W	L	ERA
Stark, Don	46	0.239	OF			
Stingley, Dick	66	0.233	C			
Stoops, Bill	48	0.210	3B, OF			
Sutter, Dick	19	0.125	P	3	13	5.32
Tarolli, Lou	10	0.111	P			
Thomas, Frank	74	0.326	OF			
Tond, Lou	10	0.250	P	5	3	3.44
Turturro, Mike	115	0.213	2B, SS			
Veazey, Norm	35	0.196	M, OF			
Williams, Cliff	12	0.200	P	1	1	7.71

Thomasville, Georgia
Team Operated by Thomasville Baseball Company
Team President: Heeth Varnedoe
Vice Presidents: Ray L. Kennedy, Robert L. Bergen
Secretary: H.M. Sisson
General Manager: Robert L. Bergen
Manager(s): Ralph DiLullo
Games played at Municipal Stadium
Season attendance: 44,072
Major League Affiliate: Detroit Tigers – American League.

Thomasville Tigers Team Roster

NAME	G	BA	POS	W	L	ERA	APF
Adcock, Bob	25	0.281	OF				
Andres, Bob	12	0.250	P	2	3	2.60	
Bales, Jack	69	0.240	C				
Collins, Bob	13	0.138	P	2	9	3.52	
Didier, Mel	32	0.200	P	7	11	6.35	
DiLullo, Ralph			M				
Eaton, Dick	108	0.257	1B				
Foytack, Paul	35	0.118	P	14	10	3.29	
Frazier, Andy	130	0.251	2B				
Garrecht, Bob	35	0.196	P	7	12	3.91	
Greenamoyer, Bill	13	0.273	P	4	3	7.44	
Hare, Bernard	52	0.270	OF				
Herbert, Don	41	0.192	C				
Hoffman, Myron	41	0.206	P	9	8	3.10	
Johnson, Charles	137	0.211	3B				
Jones, ---	8		P	2	5	4.88	
Klimash, Walt	12	0.308	P				
Knabe, Dick	34	0.172	P	11	11	3.23	
Lagorio, George	13	0.250					
Mlynarek, Lawrence	46	0.247	OF				
Navarro, Henry	141	0.243	SS				
Newell, Bob	33	0.160	1B				
Petrolongo, Joe	45	0.221	C				
Phillips, Bubba	138	0.329	OF				
Restaino, Emil	80	0.388	OF				
Sowell, Bill	50	0.234	OF				
Stamos, Pete	55	0.255	2B, OF				
Stanley, Ken	36	0.275	OF				

Valdosta, Georgia
Team Operated by Valdosta Dodgers Baseball Club, Inc.
Team President: D.S. Wainer
Vice President: Branch Rickey, Jr.
Secretary: Fresco Thompson
Treasurer: D.E. Beach
General Manager: Victor A. Zodda
Manager(s): Andy Alexson
Games played at Pendleton Park
Season attendance: 51,105
Major League Affiliate: Brooklyn Dodgers – National League.

Valdosta Dodgers Team Roster

NAME	G	BA	POS	W	L	ERA	APF
Alexson, Andy	131	0.309	M, 1B				
Bledsoe, Billy	30	0.147	P	8	2	3.00	
Cater, Jim	31	0.152	P	9	4	2.85	
Ceccarelli, Art	34	0.125	P	17	8	3.21	
Dean, Ted	89	0.226	2B, 3B, SS				
Deppersschmidt, Gene	128	0.338	OF				
Frantell, Don	32	0.128	2B				Albany
Gill, Bill	129	0.266	C				
Grote, Harold	125	0.276	3B, OF				
Jenkins, Lee	81	0.332	OF				
Jones, Dick	123	0.327	3B, OF				
Kirk, Walt	18	0.262	2B				
Korcheck, Mike	89	0.253	SS				
Mintz, Dwain	43	0.236	SS				
Moeller, George	115	0.287	OF, P	5	2	2.53	
Moore, Ed	32	0.152	P	8	6	4.11	
Negray, Ron	36	0.173	P	21	6	2.17	
Smith, Marion	13		P	5	6	5.08	
Spears, Jasper	28	0.266	2B				
Troy, Don	19	0.320	2B				
Williams, Marv	36	0.160	P	15	11	2.41	
Willis, Charles	29	0.191	P	3	13	4.35	
Wiren, John	72	0.222	OF, C				

Waycross, Georgia
Team Operated by Waycross Baseball Association, Inc.
Team President: Herbert Bradshaw
Vice President: William D. Rivenbark
Secretary-Treasurer: Fred W. Voight
Business Manager: Gilbert F. Bell
Manager(s): Mickey Katkaveck
Games played at Newton Field
Season attendance: 54,508

Waycross Bears Team Roster

NAME	G	BA	POS	W	L	ERA	APF
Abadie, Ben	76	0.291	OF				
Austin, Alvin	122	0.256	OF				
Beverly, Charles	12	0.220	2B				
Bloodworth, Charles	95	0.258	OF				
Bremer, Walt	102	0.235	3B				
Childs, Dick	20	0.102	P	9	6	2.91	
Dorwin, Rod	77	0.243	OF, P	2	6	7.60	
Fisher, George	61	0.335	1B				
Futcher, John	13	0.283					
Galey, Bob	21	0.240	P	5	3	3.87	
Gould, Pete	102	0.276	3B, SS, C				Americus
Gross, Don	20	0.288					
Ingalls, Jack	15	0.097	P	4	5	7.89	
Jay, Paul	60	0.215	OF, P	21	8	3.30	
Johnson, Howie	27	0.159	C				
Katkaveck, Mickey	95	0.237	M, C				
Lyons, Bob	116	0.289	2B				
Morrison, Jim	10	0.275	SS				
O'Coine, Marshall	22	0.308	P	8	4	3.86	
Olmstead, Paul	28	0.220	P	6	5	5.21	
Raulerson, Harry	43	0.355	P	18	3	3.32	
Shiles, Harold	127	0.262	3B, SS				
Smith, Morton	131	0.324	1B, OF				
Thomassie, Pete	23	0.216	OF				
Young, Herb	21	0.357	P	2	7	7.36	

Georgia Class-D Minor League Baseball Encyclopedia

1949 Georgia-Florida League Records

Batting

Highest Batting Average (minimum 100 at bats)
1. Emil Restaino – Thomasville .388
2. Ed Murphy – Americus .344
3. Delton Childs – Albany .343
4. Gene Depperschmidt – Valdosta .338
5. George Fisher – Waycross .335

Most Hits
1. Bubba Phillips – Thomasville 192
2. Morton Smith – Waycross 178
   Tom Smith – Cordele 178
4. Russell Rac – Albany 164
5. Dick Jones – Valdosta 163

Most Runs
1. Ed Trojanowski – Americus 141
2. Bob Lyons – Waycross 135
3. Harold Shiles – Waycross 134
4. Bubba Phillips – Thomasville 114
5. Delton Childs – Albany 109

Most Total Bases
1. Bubba Phillips – Thomasville 267
   Russell Rac – Albany 267
3. Tom Smith – Cordele 249
4. Harold Stamey – Americus 247
5. Harry Geis – Cordele 242
   Harvey Roop – Americus 242

Most Doubles
1. Harold Stamey – Americus 39
2. Dick Jones – Valdosta 33
3. Russell Rac – Albany 31
4. Gene Depperschmidt – Valdosta 29
   Henry Navarro – Thomasville 29

Most Triples
1. Harry Geis – Cordele 18
2. Bill Broukal – Cordele 14
3. Harold Stamey – Americus 12
   Russell Rac – Albany 12
   Emil Restaino – Thomasville 12
   Lee Jenkins – Valdosta 12

Most Home Runs
1. Harold Shiles – Waycross 21
2. Harvey Roop – Americus 17
3. Russell Rac – Albany 16
4. Ray Sowins – Albany 15
5. Bubba Phillips – Thomasville 12
   Neal Hertweck – Albany 12

Most Extra Base Hits
1. Harold Stamey – Americus 62
2. Russell Rac – Albany 59
3. Harold Shiles – Waycross 54
4. Harvey Roop – Americus 50
   Harry Geis – Cordele 50

Most Runs Batted In
1. Russell Rac – Albany 134
2. Morton Smith – Waycross 114
3. Neal Hertweck – Albany 109
4. Harvey Roop – Americus 107
5. Tom Smith – Cordele 102

Most Stolen Bases
1. Ed Trojanowski – Americus 69
2. Bubba Phillips – Thomasville 60
3. Gene Depperschmidt – Valdosta 54
4. Harold Shiles – Waycross 47
5. Dick Jones – Valdosta 37

Fielding

Most Put-Outs
1. Neal Hertweck 1B – Albany 1,273
2. Bill Gill C – Valdosta 1,169
3. Andy Alexson 1B – Valdosta 956
4. Dick Eaton 1B – Thomasville 867
5. Jim Regan 1B – Tallahassee 770

Most Assists
1. Henry Navarro SS – Thomasville 468
2. Bernie Wenitski SS – Americus 427
3. Bill Broukal SS – Cordele 425
4. Ed Trojanowski 2B – Americus 422
5. Stan Brill 2B – Moultrie 421

Most Errors
1. Bill Broukal SS – Cordele 86
2. Bernie Wenitski SS – Americus 81
3. Henry Navarro SS – Thomasville 76
4. Bill Bollman UT – Tallahassee 65
5. Charles Johnson 3B – Thomasville 60

Pitching

Most Wins
1. Morris Frank – Albany 22
2. Ron Negray – Valdosta 21
   Paul Jay – Waycross 21
4. Dave Cyrus – Amer/Alba 18
   Harry Raulerson – Waycross 18

Most Losses
1. Gene Soumma – Cordele 17
2. Wayne Lynch – Cordele 15
   John Fitzgerald – Tallahassee 15
4. Walt Crowley – Tallahassee 14
   Oscar Johnson – Cordele 14

Highest Winning Percentage (10 game minimum)
1. Ray Klobe – Albany .875
2. Harry Raulerson – Waycross .857
3. Vinegar Bend Mizell – Albany .800
   Billy Bledsoe – Valdosta .800
5. Chief Bender – Albany .786

Lowest Earned Run Average (100 inning minimum)
1. Morris Frank – Albany 1.94
2. Vinegar Bend Mizell – Albany 1.98
3. Ron Negray – Valdosta 2.17
4. Marv Williams – Valdosta 2.41
5. Chief Bender – Albany 2.42

Most Strikeouts
1. Art Ceccarelli – Valdosta 294
2. Morris Frank – Albany 254
3. Ron Negray – Valdosta 242
4. Marv Williams – Valdosta 226
5. Paul Foytack – Thomasville 207

Most Bases on Balls
1. Art Ceccarelli – Valdosta 149
2. Jack Sanford – Americus 135
3. Walt Crowley – Tallahassee 134
4. Paul Foytack – Thomasville 133
5. Dick McKay – Americus 127

Most Hits Allowed
1. Gene Soumma – Cordele 262
2. Wayne Lynch – Cordele 251
3. Dave Cyrus – Amer/Alba 241
4. Jim Tracy – Americus 237
5. Paul Jay – Waycross 232

Most Innings Pitched
1. Gene Soumma – Cordele 248
2. Walt Crowley – Tallahassee 244
3. Jim Tracy – Americus 238
4. Paul Jay – Waycross 237
5. Morris Frank – Albany 236

1949 Georgia-Florida League All-Star Team
1B Neal Hertweck – Albany
2B Ed Trojanowski – Americus
3B Harold Grote – Valdosta
SS Bob Koppenhaver – Albany
OF Gene Depperschmidt – Valdosta
OF Dick Jones – Valdosta
OF Russell Rac – Albany
C Vic Comolli – Americus
P Morris Frank – Albany
P Art Ceccarelli – Valdosta

1949

Georgia State League

League Office: Cochran, Georgia
League President: Joseph W. Matt Jr.
League Vice President: Fred Gilbert
Salary Limit: $2,600 per month.
Player Rule: Each club was allowed a roster of seventeen players, not more than three class man, not more than ten limited service, and not less than four rookies.
Umpires: Carlton Goffney, William Koval, Dudley Radak, William H. Walsh, Walter Kovak, Ray Bridenbaker, Joseph Fenz, and Steve Summerhill.

Georgia State League Final Standings

Team	W	L	Pct	GB	Affiliate
Eastman Dodgers	86	51	.628	----	Unaffiliated
Douglas Trojans	77	62	.554	10.0	Unaffiliated
Tifton Blue Sox	74	63	.540	12.0	Unaffiliated
Vidalia-Lyons Twins	72	65	.526	14.0	Unaffiliated
Sparta Saints	69	68	.504	17.0	Unaffiliated
Dublin Green Sox	63	75	.457	23.5	Unaffiliated
Hazlehurst-Baxley Red Socks	57	81	.413	29.5	Unaffiliated
Fitzgerald Pioneers	52	85	.386	34.0	Unaffiliated

1949 Georgia State League Map

(numbers on map correspond to the place each team finished in regular season play)

After good success in the Georgia State League in 1948, the circuit expanded from six to eight clubs. Dublin and Tifton were both added to the mix, and Baxley became a combined team also representing the city of Hazlehurst.

On July 16, Vidalia-Lyons pitcher Mike Rossi tossed a no-hitter blanking Tifton 2 to 0 in seven innings. Rossi also set the all-time single season league mark for the most innings pitched working 325 on the year. The all-time league record for the most triples in a season was set at 24 by Sparta's Ted Patterson.

Pitcher Ralph Hisey set the all-time league single season record for the most bases on balls when he walked 187 batters while playing for Dublin and Eastman during the season.

At the end of the regular season, Eastman stood at the top of the heap followed in order by Douglas, Tifton, and Vidalia-Lyons. In the first round of playoff action, Vidalia-Lyons upset Eastman three games to two in the best of five series. On the other side of the bracket, Tifton also pulled an upset defeating Douglas by the same score. Tifton bested Vidalia-Lyons in the final series four games to two to become Georgia State League champs.

Douglas, Georgia
Team Operated by Douglas Baseball Corporation
Team President: John L. "Si" Slocumb, Jr.
Vice President: Dr. T.H. Clark
Secretary-Treasurer: Floyd W. Tingley
General Manager: Dave Coble
Manager(s): Dave Coble
Games played at City Park
Season attendance: 45,403

Douglas Trojans Team Roster

NAME	G	BA	POS	W	L	ERA	APF
Baker, Roy	75	0.258	3B				
Coble, Dave			M				
Dodgin, Jim	135	0.261	OF				
Grasso, Joe	32	0.150	P	13	17	3.65	
Greco, Al	12	0.091	P	2	6	6.67	
Hominsky, Ivan	25	0.130	3B				
Koellmer, Bill	49	0.262	OF, 1B				Fitzgerald
Krauss, Bernard	29	0.185	P	14	10	2.98	
Loveys, Bill	33	0.114	P	15	7	3.90	
Marcello, Anthony	13	0.083	P	5	2	6.13	Tifton
Martin, Jim	130	0.272	3B, OF				
Mazak, Leo	32	0.175	P	12	11	5.66	
McGhee, Dick	103	0.266	OF				
Mincy, Red	146	0.293	OF				
Perada, Orestes	132	0.298	2B				
Rey, Emil	142	0.237	SS				
Robertson, Sam	136	0.269	1B				
Royal, Julian	13	0.000	P				
Salter, Desmond	28	0.299	OF				Eastman
Shanle, Del	21	0.074	C				
Tschudin, Fred	135	0.350	C				
Zolliecoffer, Bob	25	0.121	P	13	9	4.29	

Dublin, Georgia
Team Operated by Dublin Baseball Club
Team President: W.H. Lovett
Vice President: W.E. Lovett
Secretary: Frank Johnson
Manager(s): Joe Chambers, Wendell Davis, Bill Phebus
Games played at Lovett Park
Season attendance: 62,019

Dublin Green Sox Team Roster

NAME	G	BA	POS	W	L	ERA	APF
Bearden, Jack	43	0.310	OF				
Bottorff, Tom	<10						
Burgamy, Ralph	131	0.317	3B				Eastman
Chambers, Joe	100	0.263	M, 2B				
Clark, Roy	79	0.209	SS				
Davenport, Nevil	35	0.200	OF				Eastman
Davis, Wendell	13	0.231	M, P	3	1	4.00	
Gardner, Joel	75	0.263	OF				
George, Johnny	24	0.212	C				
Grigg, Bill	12	0.063					
Haber, Nate	20	0.258	OF				
Halsall, Walt	40	0.324	SS				
Hardegree, Bill	38	0.252	OF				Eas - Fit
Hisey, Ralph	42	0.203	P, IF	17	8	3.78	Eastman
Howell, Jim	87	0.264	OF				
Ivey, Bob	45	0.208	P, C	12	12	4.05	
Kuhn, George	14	0.197	3B				
Liedtke, Clyde	20	0.138	P	4	5	6.68	Tifton
Lowe, John	19	0.217	OF				
Marshall, Reavis	10	0.140	OF				
Mendoza, Ray	105	0.255	1B				
Moore, Jack	12	0.238	2B				
Mottler, Ernest	34	0.191	C				Vid-Lyo
Osthoff, Wilbur	114	0.265	SS, P	9	1	2.48	
Pendergraft, Jim	19	0.229	P	6	6	4.89	
Phebus, Bill			M				
Pollard, Gene	48	0.244	1B				
Raines, Bill	10	0.417					
Ray, Stan	22	0.191	OF				
Roig, Tony	14	0.256	OF				
Shaddix, Willard	11	0.294	P	1	3	6.35	
Simmons, Paul	99	0.324	C				
Simon, Jerry	37	0.181	P	17	12	3.43	Tifton
Starnes, Kendell	11	0.121	P	8	1	1.47	
Stinson, Bob	61	0.310	C				Eastman
Weldon, Bill	10	0.182	P	2	9	6.14	
Whaley, Walker	11	0.265	P	3	6	7.00	
Woodruff, Ernest	12	0.213	OF				
Young, Tex	23	0.238	P	7	10	6.02	Vid-Lyo

Eastman, Georgia
Team Operated by Eastman Dodgers, Inc.
Team President: H.R. Ragan
Vice President: M.M. Smith
Secretary: O.C. Pound
Business Manager: W.W. Taylor
Manager(s): Edd Hartness
Games played at Legion Park
Season attendance: 43,691

Eastman Dodgers Team Roster

NAME	G	BA	POS	W	L	ERA	APF
Beaty, Frank	26	0.246	P	7	7	5.02	
Biggerstaff, Jack	22	0.219	OF				
Burgamy, Ralph	131	0.317	3B				Dublin
Caldwell, Wilbur	116	0.259	3B				
Chafin, Cotton	135	0.332	OF				
Chilton, Warren	51	0.206	SS				
Davenport, Nevil	35	0.200	OF				Dublin
Foster, Ralph	13	0.067	P	2	1	5.48	
Gagnon, Russ	121	0.257	SS				
Gillespie, Frank	14	0.231	P	5	6	6.25	
Gregg, Jim	18	0.279	OF				
Hardegree, Bill	38	0.252	OF				Dub - Fit
Harden, Jim	27	0.247	P	20	5	2.62	
Harp, Jim	35	0.193	P	20	11	3.07	
Hartness, Edd	139	0.364	M, 1B				
Hisey, Ralph	42	0.203	P, IF	17	8	3.78	Dublin
Hood, Milt	43	0.163	C				Fitzgerald
Jakubov, John	27	0.094	P	15	9	3.84	
Lovett, Bill	11	0.182	SS				
Mauldin, Mason	110	0.244	OF				Sparta
North, Lamar	117	0.322	C				
Parker, Charles	125	0.273	2B				
Salter, Desmond	28	0.299	OF				Douglas
Stinson, Bob	61	0.310	C				Dublin
Svenke, ---	22		OF				
Wiebel, Mel	116	0.267	OF				
Woods, Julian	53	0.286	OF				
Worsham, Ben	18	0.194	P	4	7	7.60	

Wright, Dixie	46	0.228	C

Fitzgerald, Georgia
Team Operated by Fitzgerald Baseball Club, Inc.
Team President: John W. Garrison
Vice President: Eugene W. Strickland
Secretary: W.E. Hoyle, Sr.
Treasurer-Business Manager: Arthur Surprise
Manager(s): Charles DiCola, Bill Good, John Pawlick
Games played at Blue-Gray Park
Season attendance: 38,736

Fitzgerald Pioneers Team Roster

NAME	G	BA	POS	W	L	ERA	APF
Alvares, Ramon	38	0.238	1B				
Anderson, Walt	13	0.103	P	0	4	5.00	
Connell, Truman	35	0.223	OF				
Crago, Bill	137	0.277	OF				
DiCola, Charles			M				
DiFranco, Sam	84	0.256	SS				
Friedman, Stan	18		C				
Good, Bill	64	0.252	M, SS				
Goodwin, Troy	11	0.250	3B				
Hardegree, Bill	38	0.252	OF				Dub - Eas
Henrickson, Ed	18		OF				
Hood, Milt	43	0.163	C				Eastman
Koellmer, Bill	49	0.262	OF, 1B				Douglas
Lawson, Leroy	36	0.269	1B				
Markham, Dick	34	0.159	OF				
McNease, Harry	12	0.163	2B				
Meadows, Herman	33	0.211	P	10	14	5.45	Sparta
Oliveri, Fred	14		1B				
Oquendo, Noel	54	0.225	P, OF	17	19	4.06	
Orlandi, Ron	78	0.204	C, P	5	9	6.05	
Paulick, Frank	20	0.164	C				
Pawlick, John	93	0.245	M, OF				
Perello, Dave	82	0.245	3B				
Price, Lou	40	0.116	2B				
Ridgeway, Charlie	48	0.264	SS				
Scalisi, Bob	31	0.192	P	7	12	5.13	
Schmidt, Kermit	58	0.295	P, IF	13	9	4.17	
Teichert, Bob	16	0.265	P	0	8	6.65	
Wadsworth, Hal	53	0.145	2B				Vid-Lyo
Wahl, Bill	37	0.212	SS				

Hazlehurst-Baxley (Hazlehurst & Baxley), Georgia
Team Operated by Hazleurst-Baxley Baseball, Inc.
Team President: C.A. Whitaker
Vice President: W.M. Barron
Business Manager: Steve Maglio
Manager(s): Ray Baker, Mike Milosevich
Games played at Baxley Baseball Park
Season attendance: 29,257

Hazlehurst-Baxley Red Socks Team Roster

NAME	G	BA	POS	W	L	ERA	APF
Baker, Ray			M				
Banas, George	68	0.242	OF				
Bandini, Phil	11	0.391	OF				
Bassignani, Al	88	0.216	1B				
Carmichael, Bryce	137	0.313	2B				
Cromartie, Henry	41	0.201	1B				
Dardes, Nick	59	0.166	SS				
Dempsey, Frank	32	0.236	OF				
Dendy, Bob	23	0.195	2B				
Fasano, Benny	104	0.237	OF, P	7	10	4.65	
Gilbert, Clarence	17	0.175	OF				
Ivester, Neal	85	0.246	C				
Kanavage, Chet	127	0.363	C				
Kops, Willard	26	0.258	P	6	10	5.24	
Lazaro, Joe	10	0.289	OF				
Lucarella, Rinaldo	56	0.223	OF				
McNamara, Charles	19	0.167	OF				
Milosevich, Mike	75	0.289	M, 3B				
Montgomery, Bob	11	0.308					
Naphole, John	26	0.233	P	8	9	5.00	
Oldershaw, Howard	52	0.212	P, OF	10	13	6.09	
Ryan, Dick	34	0.228	P	20	11	3.32	
Sammons, ---	9		P	3	3	6.43	
Shirley, Ralph	30	0.071	P	2	10	6.44	
Smith, J.W.	13	0.028	OF				
Thompson, J.B.	10	0.083	P	1	4	3.75	Sparta
Vargo, Steve	10	0.111	SS				
Wilson, Jim	116	0.187	SS				

Sparta, Georgia
Team Operated by Sparta Baseball Association
Team President: Robert L. Harrison
Vice Presidents: M.A. Cohen, B.A. Beall
Secretary: Dr. Ray Cole
Manager(s): Woodrow Bottoms, Jim Ruark
Games played at Sparta Baseball Park
Season attendance: 33,436

Sparta Saints Team Roster

NAME	G	BA	POS	W	L	ERA	APF
Acree, John	15	0.326	OF				
Alrick, Ed	13	0.333	P	2	6	9.55	Vid-Lyo
Booth, Jim	20	0.246	C				
Bottoms, Woodrow	50	0.253	M, SS				
Brock, Paul	15	0.277	P	9	4	2.29	
Burns, Bill	19	0.200	P	5	8	5.79	
Collins, Jack	137	0.276	3B				
Cook, George	34	0.194	P	21	12	3.07	
Evans, Willard	28	0.262	P	14	10	3.45	
Gula, Pete	107	0.349	OF				
Hartley, Don	117	0.244	OF				
Kovaluk, Ted	11	0.095	OF				
Mauldin, Mason	110	0.244	OF				Eastman
Meadows, Herman	33	0.211	P	10	14	5.45	Fitzgerald
O'Barr, Tom	12	0.133	P	2	3	5.71	
Patterson, Ted	135	0.307	2B				
Ruark, Jim	118	0.302	M, C				
Ruark, Parnell	125	0.339	SS				
Stoyle, Jim	121	0.400	1B				
Taylor, John	<10		P				
Thompson, J.B.	10	0.083	P	1	4	3.75	Haz-Bax
Warren, Jim	22	0.276	P	7	2	3.00	

Tifton, Georgia
Team Operated by Tifton Baseball Club
Team President: R.B. Hall
Vice President: Herman L. Dusmuke
Secretary-Treasurer-Business Manager: Eugene Slack
Manager(s): Charles Farrar
Games played at Eve Park
Season attendance: 53,846

Tifton Blue Sox Team Roster

NAME	G	BA	POS	W	L	ERA	APF
Anderson, Bill	11	0.154	P	4	1	4.19	
Barnes, Bill	147	0.289	2B				
Baskin, Al	15	0.080	P	5	5	5.48	
Christie, Frank	28	0.258	P	12	7	5.74	
Cottengim, Charles	22	0.266	C				

NAME	G	BA	POS	W	L	ERA	APF
Daley, Gil	167	0.300	OF				
Dobbins, Ralph	139	0.219	OF				Vid-Lyo
Dorwin, Rod	66	0.286	OF				
Farrar, Charles	136	0.307	M, OF				
Fernandez, Luis	36	0.134	P	21	11	3.12	
Finley, Doug	134	0.286	OF				
Fowler, Lincoln	17	0.188	P	3	6	6.91	
Hartman, Earl	146	0.300	1B				
Kennedy, Joe	22	0.226	SS				
LaCarter, Ray	22	0.089	P	5	4	4.76	
Liedtke, Clyde	20	0.138	P	4	5	6.68	Dublin
Marcello, Anthony	13	0.083	P	5	2	6.13	Douglas
Morrison, Jim	89	0.286	SS				
Pollack, Leonard	30	0.216	P	9	13	5.01	
Rauseo, Mike	146	0.257	3B				
Richardson, Hugh	13	0.326	SS				
Simon, Jerry	37	0.181	P	17	12	3.43	Dublin
Stratton, George	50	0.251	SS				
Swain, Kurtis	118	0.239	C				
Terrell, Thurman	14	0.242	P	8	6	4.64	

Vidalia-Lyons (Vidalia & Lyons), Georgia

Team Operated by Vidalia-Lyons Baseball Club
Team President: Bill Estroff
Vice President: L.L. Waller
Business Manager: Jack Mosley
Manager(s): Julian Morgan, Mike Rossi, Joe Santomauro
Games played at Twin Cities Stadium
Season attendance: 45,463

Vidalia-Lyons Twins Team Roster

NAME	G	BA	POS	W	L	ERA	APF
Alrick, Ed	13	0.333	P	2	6	9.55	Sparta
Beauchamp, Walt	75	0.266	2B				
Coleman, Malcolm	13	0.213	SS				
Culpepper, Bill	24	0.301	OF				
Dabbs, Chester	15	0.175	OF				
Dobbins, Ralph	139	0.219	OF				Tifton
Fall, Ralph	76	0.245	SS				
Fernandez, Marcelo	29	0.284	P, IF	14	9	3.26	
Hamrick, Roy	124	0.269	C				
Mathieson, Bob	11	0.053	P	4	4	5.68	
Morgan, Julian			M				
Mottler, Ernest	34	0.191	C				Dublin
Murray, Milt	42	0.292	SS				
Ricketson, Don	146	0.284	OF				
Rossi, Mike	54	0.280	M, P, OF	25	13	2.80	
Santomauro, Joe	6		M, P	2	3	2.59	
Silverman, Jerome	144	0.298	1B				
Smith, Jim	146	0.310	3B				
Snider, Floyd	142	0.243	OF				
Stern, Jerome	16	0.224	2B				
Stroud, Earl	10	0.217	C				
Swain, Lloyd	33	0.296	P	5	6	5.86	
Wadsworth, Hal	53	0.145	2B				Fitzgerald
Wells, Les	25	0.125	P	13	9	4.30	
Young, Tex	23	0.238	P	7	10	6.02	Dublin

1949 Georgia State League Records

Highest Batting Average (minimum 100 at bats)
1. Jim Stoyle – Sparta .400
2. Edd Hartness – Eastman .364
3. Chet Kanavage - Hazlehurst-Baxley .363
4. Fred Tschudin – Douglas .350
5. Pete Gula – Sparta .349

Most Hits
1. Jim Stoyle – Sparta 191
2. Ted Patterson – Sparta 189
3. Fred Tschudin – Douglas 182
   Cotton Chafin – Eastman 182
   Jim Smith – Vidalia-Lyons 182

Most Runs
1. Jim Martin – Douglas 130
2. Cotton Chafin – Eastman 128
3. Bill Crago – Fitzgerald 125
4. Jim Smith – Vidalia-Lyons 123
5. Edd Hartness – Eastman 119

Most Total Bases
1. Jim Stoyle – Sparta 319
2. Ralph Burgamy – East/Dubl 286
3. Edd Hartness – Eastman 281
   Ted Patterson – Sparta 281
5. Chet Kanavage - Hazlehurst-Baxley 277

Most Doubles
1. Chet Kanavage - Hazlehurst-Baxley 43
2. Bill Barnes – Tifton 42
3. Edd Hartness – Eastman 41
4. Earl Hartman – Tifton 40
5. Jim Stoyle – Sparta 38
   Ted Patterson – Sparta 38
   Parnell Ruark – Sparta 38

Most Triples
1. Ted Patterson – Sparta 24
2. Jim Stoyle – Sparta 18
3. Parnell Ruark – Sparta 17
4. Cotton Chafin – Eastman 15
5. Edd Hartness – Eastman 12

Most Home Runs
1. Ralph Burgamy – East/Dubl 28
2. Don Ricketson – Vidalia-Lyons 26
3. Earl Hartman – Tifton 23
4. Jim Stoyle – Sparta 18
5. Chet Kanavage - Hazlehurst-Baxley 17
   Charles Farrar – Tifton 17

Most Extra Base Hits
1. Jim Stoyle – Sparta 74
2. Earl Hartman – Tifton 67
3. Ralph Burgamy – East/Dubl 66
   Edd Hartness – Eastman 66
5. Parnell Ruark – Sparta 65

Most Runs Batted In
1. Edd Hartness – Eastman 136
2. Earl Hartman – Tifton 134
3. Don Ricketson – Vidalia--Lyons 133
4. Ralph Burgamy – East/Dubl 123
5. Jim Stoyle – Sparta 116

Most Stolen Bases
1. Jim Martin – Douglas 54
2. Cotton Chafin – Eastman 51
3. Charlie Ridgeway – Fitzgerald 36
4. Ted Patterson – Sparta 35
5. Red Mincy – Douglas 30

Fielding
Most Put-Outs
1. Sam Robertson 1B – Douglas 1,271
2. Earl Hartman 1B – Tifton 1,255

3. Jerome Silverman 1B – Vidalia-Lyons 1,224
4. Edd Hartness 1B – Eastman   1,212
5. Jim Stoyle 1B – Sparta   1,004

Most Assists
1. Emil Rey SS – Douglas   446
2. Bill Barnes 2B – Tifton   415
3. Orestes Perada 2B – Douglas   410
4. Ted Patterson 2B – Sparta   367
5. Charles Parker 2B – Eastman   358

Most Errors
1. Bryce Carmichael 2B - Hazlehurst-Baxley 62
2. Russ Gagnon SS – Eastman   55
3. Jim Smith 3B – Vidalia-Lyons   53
   Jim Wilson SS – Hazlehurst-Baxley   53
5. Ted Patterson 2B – Sparta   48

Pitching
Most Wins
1. Mike Rossi – Vidalia-Lyons   25
2. Luis Fernandez – Tifton   21
   George Cook – Sparta   21
4. Jim Harp – Eastman   20
   Jim Harden – Eastman   20
   Dick Ryan - Hazlehurst-Baxley   20

Most Losses
1. Noel Oquendo – Fitzgerald   19
2. Joe Grasso – Douglas   17
3. Herman Meadows – Spar/Fitz   14
4. Mike Rossi – Vidalia-Lyons   13
   Howard Oldershaw - Hazlehurst-Baxley 13
   Leonard Pollack – Tifton   13

Highest Winning Percentage (10 game minimum)
1. Wilbur Osthoff – Dublin   .900
2. Kendall Starnes – Dublin   .889
3. Jim Harden – Eastman   .800
   Bill Anderson – Tifton   .800
5. Jim Warren – Sparta   .778

Lowest Earned Run Average (100 inning minimum)
1. Paul Brock – Sparta   2.29
2. Jim Harden – Eastman   2.62
3. Mike Rossi – Vidalia-Lyons   2.80
4. Bernard Krauss – Douglas   2.98
5. George Cook – Sparta   3.07
   Jim Harp – Eastman   3.07

Most Strikeouts
1. Noel Oquendo – Fitzgerald   224
2. Ralph Hisey – East/Dubl   203
3. George Cook – Sparta   184
4. Jerry Simon – Tift/Dubl   162
5. Dick Ryan - Hazlehurst-Baxley   157

Most Bases on Balls
1. Ralph Hisey – East/Dubl   187
2. Noel Oquendo – Fitzgerald   171
3. Joe Grasso – Douglas   150
4. Jerry Simon – Tift/Dubl   138
5. Bill Loveys – Douglas   135

Most Hits Allowed
1. Noel Oquendo – Fitzgerald   175
2. Howard Oldershaw - Hazlehurst-Baxley 157
3. Mike Rossi – Vidalia-Lyons   140
4. George Cook – Sparta   137
   Kermit Schmidt – Fitzgerald   137

Most Innings Pitched
1. Mike Rossi – Vidalia-Lyons   325
2. Noel Oquendo – Fitzgerald   297
3. George Cook – Sparta   276
4. Luis Fernandez – Tifton   271
5. Jerry Simon – Tift/Dubl   268

1949 Georgia State League All-Star Team
1B Edd Hartness – Eastman
2B Orestes Pereda – Douglas
3B Jack Collins – Sparta
SS Emil Rey – Douglas
OF Red Mincy – Douglas
OF Pete Gula – Sparta
OF Don Ricketson – Vidalia-Lyons
C   Fred Tschudin - Douglas
P   Jim Harden – Eastman
P   George Cook – Sparta

1950

Georgia-Alabama League

League Office: Talladega, Alabama
League President: Arthur R. Decatur
League Vice President: George Cahall
Salary Limit: $2,600 per month.
Player Rule: Each club was allowed a roster of sixteen players, not more than two veterans, not more than nine limited service, and not less than five rookies.
Umpires: Harry E. Allen, Howard O'Brentz, Henry Krane, Jerome A. Neudecker, and Silvio J. Fappiano.

Georgia-Alabama League Final Standings

Team	W	L	Pct	GB	Affiliate
LaGrange Troupers	73	48	.603	----	NY-AL
Alexander City Millers	73	53	.579	2.5	Unaffiliated
Carrollton Hornets	66	57	.537	8.0	Unaffiliated
Newnan Brownies	62	60	.508	11.5	Unaffiliated
Valley Rebels	58	65	.472	16.0	Unaffiliated
Griffin Tigers	57	64	.471	16.0	Unaffiliated
Opelika Owls	52	72	.419	22.5	Unaffiliated
Rome Red Sox	49	71	.408	23.5	WSH-AL

1950 Georgia-Alabama League Map

(numbers on map correspond to the place each team finished in regular season play)

Tallassee, Alabama dropped out of the league during the off-season after finishing third in 1949. To maintain an even number of teams, the league picked up Rome, Georgia rounding out the eight-club loop. Rome was no stranger to the circuit having been a mainstay from 1914-1917.

Newnan pitcher Bill Sweatt pitched a no-hitter against Alexander City winning 6 to 0 on July 13. On his 59th birthday, former semi-pro baseball pitcher Charlie Milner made his organized baseball debut taking the mound for Valley. He pitched four innings and gave up four singles and one run. In a playoff game against Carrollton on September 4, LaGrange pitcher Don Bessent hurled a no-hitter routing the Hornets 14 to 0. Carrollton slugger Gene Solt set the all-time league record for the most home runs in a single season with 38. Solt also set the all-time league marks for most total bases with 311 and most runs batted in with 151. Carrollton moundsman Ed Bobowski had a pair of Iron Man performances winning both games of double headers just over a week apart. The first one occurred on July 24 as he defeated Newnan 7 to 5 and 9 to 1. He even hit a home run in the second game on that date. Bobowski completed his second Iron Man stunt on August 2 against the Valley Rebels with the game scores being 5 to 0 and 14 to 4 respectively.

When regular season play was finished, LaGrange held the best record with Alexander City, Carrollton, and Newnan following in order. These four teams played in the post-season, Shaughnessy style championship tournament with LaGrange playing Carrollton and Alexander City facing Newnan in the first round. LaGrange easily handled Carrollton winning two games to none, and Alexander City carbon copied the task against Newnan. LaGrange then defeated Alexander City three games to two in the final championship series.

Alexander City, Alabama

Team Operated by Alexander City Baseball, Inc.
Team President: James Callahan
Vice President: Robert Russell
Secretary: Mrs. B.C. Russell
Business Manager: Percy Yeargan
Manager(s): Red Roberts
Games played at Benjamin C. Russell Field
Season attendance: 36,546

Alexander City Millers Team Roster

NAME	G	BA	POS	W	L	ERA	APF
Adams, Bob	126	0.280	2B, 3B, SS				
Barker, Norb	24	0.323	2B				
Bastion, Marv	30	0.163	P	3	6	4.59	
Berman, Buddy	18	0.323	2B				Carrollton
Brown, Bill	126	0.327	1B				
Chappell, Marv	74	0.189	OF, P	17	10	3.49	LaGrange
Collins, Charlie	63	0.241	OF, P	16	6	3.52	
Falcigno, Harry	117	0.257	OF				
Hanson, J.W.	36	0.193	3B, SS				Valley
Harrelson, Cleveland	22	0.129	2B				
Hartman, Dick	16	0.264	C				
Herring, Earl	44	0.142	C				
Hovell, Bob	106	0.268	OF				
Krohn, Layton	35	0.202	P	15	11	3.06	
Langley, Jim	10	0.351					
Lindsley, John	35	0.110	P	18	8	2.43	
Lopez, Carlos	65	0.307	OF, P	8	8	6.60	Griffin
Moss, Joe	19	0.305	OF				Opelika
Nierpoetter, Billy	17	0.143	P	2	8	6.18	Valley
Patterson, Bill	109	0.233	C				Ca - Gr - Va
Roberts, Red	43	0.291	M, SS				
Rucker, Bill	105	0.267	3B, OF				
Savarese, Al	68	0.161	SS				Rom - Val
Steave, John	68	0.191	C				
Venditto, Al	30	0.327	3B				
Wooley, Jim	107	0.294	OF				

Carrollton, Georgia

Team Operated by Carrollton Baseball Club, Inc.
Team President: P.L. Shaeffer
Vice Presidents: E.V. Folds, M.C. Roop
Secretary: William O. Cobb
Treasurer: Walter New
General Manager: Harvey J. Copeland

Georgia Class-D Minor League Baseball Encyclopedia

Manager(s): Shorty Marshall
Games played at City Athletic Field
Season attendance: 26,365

Carrollton Hornets Team Roster

NAME	G	BA	POS	W	L	ERA	APF
Arroyo, Blas	33	0.282	P	9	7	5.37	
Beasley, John	39	0.200	SS				Rome
Beauchamp, Walt	27	0.303	2B				
Berman, Buddy	18	0.323	2B				Alex City
Bobowski, Ed	32	0.169	P	17	7	4.96	
Clark, Ray	119	0.338	SS				
Cobiella, Ricardo	21	0.212	2B				
Corrales, Reggie	32	0.284	C				
Coulling, Stan	14	0.182	P	3	3	4.59	
Dennis, Jack	10	0.333					
DeSouza, Freddie	122	0.299	3B				
Fernandez, Mike	4		P	1	3		
Fetner, Charles	16	0.271	1B				
Gonzalez, Cotayo	8		P	4	2	4.19	
Hutchins, Bob	24	0.225	P	9	3	5.21	Rome
Jones, Casey	34	0.137	C, P	11	7	5.12	Newnan
Kelly, Mason	1	0.000	P	0	0		
Lee, Fred	108	0.260	OF				
Marshall, Shorty	80	0.354	M, 2B				
Mazak, Leo	26	0.208	P	4	9	6.24	
Morelli, Jim	113	0.291	OF				
Patterson, Bill	109	0.233	C				AC - Gr - Va
Reach, Cliff	97	0.202	2B, OF				Opelika
Shirley, Jim	105	0.236	1B				
Shoemake, Claude	62	0.342	OF				
Solt, Gene	119	0.365	OF, C				
Victor, Ernie	1		P				
Weldon, Bill	27	0.098	P	8	9	5.33	
White, Curtis	16	0.214	P	4	5	5.55	

Griffin, Georgia

Team Operated by Griffin Baseball Club, Inc.
Team President: Louis George
Vice President: Joseph George
Secretary-Treasurer-Business Manager: H.T. Green
Manager(s): Jack Bearden, Abe White
Games played at Tiger Park
Season attendance: 37,167

Griffin Tigers Team Roster

NAME	G	BA	POS	W	L	ERA	APF
Battistelli, Angelo	14	0.111	3B				
Bearden, Jack	121	0.354	M, OF				
Busch, George	34	0.133	P	11	11	4.56	Rome
Byrd, Walt	16	0.186	OF				
Collins, Bob	15	0.000	P	2	5	6.24	
Columbano, Aldo	15	0.132	3B				Rome
Corley, Earl	17	0.246	C				
Ebetino, John	40	0.263	P	9	4	3.93	
Hudson, Bill	105	0.262	OF				
Jarvis, Bob	83	0.238	3B, SS				Valley
Jones, Lou	86	0.263	3B, OF				Valley
Kelecava, Clem	46	0.183	P	10	10	5.35	
Kemmerer, Nathaniel	20	0.122	P	5	9	5.45	Valley
Kulesa, John	23	0.209	P	3	3	6.62	
Lopez, Carlos	65	0.307	OF, P	8	8	6.60	Alex City
McAndrew, Bob	118	0.239	2B				
Noga, George	120	0.298	SS				
Padgett, Bill	29	0.059	P	2	9	5.81	Rome
Patterson, Bill	109	0.233	C				AC - Ca - Va
Schmitt, Fred	119	0.308	OF				
Sowell, Bill	34	0.345	3B				
Stoyle, Jim	117	0.362	1B				
Upshaw, Charles	25	0.300	P	5	7	4.56	
Utley, Ewell	26	0.205	P	7	5	4.93	
White, Abe			M				
Winters, Bill	16	0.190	P				

LaGrange, Georgia

Team Operated by LaGrange Baseball Club, Inc.
Team President: Oliver Hunnicutt
Vice President: G.L. Cahall
Secretary-Treasurer: Alvin Davis
Manager(s): Carl Cooper
Games played at Callaway Stadium
Season attendance: 53,781
Major League Affiliate: New York Yankees – American League.

LaGrange Troupers Team Roster

NAME	G	BA	POS	W	L	ERA	APF
Bessent, Don	43	0.275	P	22	7	2.23	
Braganca, Joe	67	0.198	C				
Cacciola, Jim	11	0.286	OF				
Carter, Leon	122	0.326	3B				
Chappell, Marv	74	0.189	OF, P	17	10	3.49	Alex City
Cooper, Carl	108	0.332	M, OF				
Dawkins, Bob	15	0.150	P	1	3	6.89	
DeGourscey, Joe	26	0.059	P	3	6	3.77	
Durkin, Jim	53	0.260	C				
Gaillard, Ted	13	0.121	P	5	4	4.50	
Goff, Jim	113	0.276	1B, OF				
Jeakle, Ed	89	0.274	OF				
Johengen, George	33	0.246	1B, P	9	3	2.66	
Krings, Dave	116	0.319	OF				
Marshall, Dick	30	0.185	P	9	8	4.78	
Pescitelli, Pasquale	22	0.268	2B				
Russell, Dick	21	0.214	OF				
Taussig, Don	<10						
Troy, Jim	12	0.200					
Umbach, Ken	34	0.230	1B				
Wallis, Gerald	30	0.286	C, P	17	4	3.04	
Walls, Boyd	24	0.319					
Webster, Ed	11	0.250	P				
Wingard, Ernie	103	0.306	2B				
Winkelspecht, Bob	132	0.240	SS				

Newnan, Georgia

Team Operated by Newnan Baseball Association, Inc.
Team President: A.L. Potts
Vice President: J.R. Brown
General Manager-Business Manager: James R. Poole, Sr.
Manager(s): Joe Schmidt
Games played at Pickett Field
Season attendance: 37,215

Newnan Brownies Team Roster

NAME	G	BA	POS	W	L	ERA	APF
Bradshaw, Hugh	45	0.294	C				
Bustle, Bill	79	0.286	1B, OF, P	21	10	3.49	
Chechile, Bill	122	0.270	OF				
Cudemo, Mike	60	0.205	C				
Diehl, Leonard	67	0.188	SS				
Franson, Carl	121	0.245	3B				
Heath, Norm	63	0.238	SS				
Hobbs, ---	7		P	3	2	4.76	
Hooks, Dave	44	0.340	OF				
Jones, Casey	34	0.137	C, P	11	7	5.12	Carrollton
Kozubal, Alex	115	0.268	OF				
Laney, Lee	101	0.277	1B				
McAfee, Alton	10	0.258	1B				
Punyko, Art	51	0.302	OF				

Georgia Class-D Minor League Baseball Encyclopedia

Name	G	BA	POS	W	L	ERA
Saffer, Les	20	0.146	P	6	5	5.69
Schmidt, Joe	113	0.318	M, 2B			
Seaman, Al	25	0.185	P	2	5	6.93
Simmons, Jack	47	0.235	2B, C			
Spamer, Bill	16	0.265				
Subbiondo, Joe	10	0.212				
Sweatt, Bill	20	0.304	P	7	10	3.88
Tenney, Jim	27	0.133	P	5	10	6.05
Terrell, Thurman	20	0.163	P	6	5	6.31
Thomas, Parks	10	0.103	P	5	4	3.51

Opelika, Alabama

Team Operated by Opelika Baseball Club, Inc.
Team President: D.M. Rencher
Vice President: Al Rigell
Secretary: Phil Hudson
Treasurer: Joe Sanderson
Manager(s): Don Bailey, Woodrow Bottoms, Wheeler Flemming
Games played at Pepperell Park
Season attendance: 36,912

Opelika Owls Team Roster

NAME	G	BA	POS	W	L	ERA	APF
Anthony, Stan	23	0.104	2B				
Azzarello, Frank	23	0.180	1B				
Bailey, Don			M				
Baker, Allen	52	0.219	C				
Booker, John	24	0.148	SS				
Bottoms, Woodrow	18	0.275	M				
Bryant, Irwin	10	0.167	OF				
Chandler, Ray	15	0.139					
Creel, Jim	47	0.276	OF, P	8	8	4.07	
Creel, Scobie	67	0.258	2B, OF, P	2	6	5.46	
DeFeo, Bob	11	0.171	3B				
Dorsky, Mike	38	0.236	OF				
Ellis, George	11	0.154	P				
Flemming, Wheeler	91	0.225	M, 1B				
Hamilton, George	39	0.271	2B				
Harris, Bob	10	0.053					
Irons, Ed	55	0.360	3B, C				
Jackson, Claude	23	0.179	P	13	3	2.46	
Jones, Tom	16	0.174	P	3	7	5.18	
Julian, Al	14	0.204	OF				
Julian, Bob	126	0.236	3B, SS				
Letlow, Lou	29	0.186	OF				
Liedtke, Clyde	12	0.063	P	5	4	5.08	
Maddox, Delma	40	0.143	P	10	12	4.36	
Martin, Billie	38	0.185	P	3	10	4.80	
Meads, Charles	24	0.179	2B				
Michael, J.E.	16	0.238	OF				
Moss, Joe	19	0.305	OF				Alex City
Reach, Cliff	97	0.202	2B, OF				Carrollton
Riddle, Jim	82	0.292	OF				
Rigdon, Bill	59	0.338	SS				
Schultz, Otto	18	0.194	OF				
Sims, Dewey	44	0.227	OF				
Smith, Ken	23	0.127	1B				Valley
Stevens, Bill	16	0.145					
Tisdale, Bill	14	0.106	OF				
Zaden, Lou	41	0.378	OF, C				

Rome, Georgia

Team Operated by Rome Baseball Club
Team President: F.G. "Jack" Cole
Secretary-Treasurer: Mrs. F.G. Cole
Business Manager-General Manager: Norman Veazey
Manager(s): Myril Hoag, John Stowe, Norm Veazey
Games played at Cole Stadium
Season attendance: 30,482
Major League Affiliate: Washington Senators – American League.

Rome Red Sox Team Roster

NAME	G	BA	POS	W	L	ERA	APF
Beasley, John	39	0.200	SS				Carrollton
Brown, Al	37	0.244	OF, P	3	8	6.64	
Bryant, Jim	57	0.219	C				
Busch, George	34	0.133	P	11	11	4.56	Griffin
Caruso, Enrico	18	0.407	P	3	2	6.53	
Clements, Mason	31	0.235	3B				
Cole, Harold	103	0.301	OF				
Columbano, Aldo	15	0.132	3B				Griffin
Crawford, Wayne	102	0.244	OF, C				
Crowl, Ernest	19	0.214	P	4	4	4.68	
DeMatteis, John	16	0.234	OF				
DeMatteis, Sal	106	0.263	OF				
Frady, Herb	69	0.265	3B				
Hoag, Myril	56	0.290	M, P	15	11	2.60	Valley
Hutchins, Bob	24	0.225	P	9	3	5.21	Carrollton
Joyce, Arnold	16	0.167	P	3	5	3.90	
Knowles, Lowe	99	0.353	1B				
Padgett, Bill	29	0.059	P	2	9	5.81	Griffin
Padgett, Charles	15	0.245	SS				
Patterson, Derward	12	0.185					Valley
Pinson, John	81	0.311	2B				
Reeves, Herb	11	0.190	P	2	4	5.33	
Roig, Tony	119	0.327	2B, 3B, SS, OF				
Savarese, Al	68	0.161	SS				AC - Val
Sommer, Bill	23	0.268	3B				Valley
Sparks, Jimmy	32	0.182	P	10	16	2.83	
Stowe, John	111	0.332	M, 1B, 3B, OF, P	4	0	5.44	
Talley, Sam	38	0.216	2B				
Veazey, Norm	16	0.366	M, OF				

Valley (Lanett), Alabama

Team Operated by Valley Baseball Club, Inc.
Team President: Albert Johnson
Vice Presidents: G.E. "Cheese" Goggans, Fob James, J.C. Magee.
General Manager: J.H. Gay
Secretary-Treasurer: Ralph Hodnett
Business Manager: J.L. Brock
Manager(s): Myril Hoag
Games played at Jennings Field
Season attendance: 31,619

Valley Rebels Team Roster

NAME	G	BA	POS	W	L	ERA	APF
Albritton, Ervin	10	0.250					
Ard, Tom	10	0.200	P				
Cook, Hugh	106	0.277	1B, 3B, OF, P	0	3	6.75	
Daniel, Jake	36	0.346	1B				
Dragotto, Ralph	86	0.277	OF				
Hanson, J.W.	36	0.193	3B, SS				Alex City
Haynes, Willard	24	0.119	P	11	5	5.44	
Hoag, Myril	56	0.290	M, P	15	11	2.60	Rome
Hughes, George	100	0.332	OF				
Jarvis, Bob	83	0.238	3B, SS				Griffin
Jones, Lou	86	0.263	3B, OF				Griffin
Kemmerer, Nathaniel	20	0.122	P	5	9	5.45	Griffin
Lazicky, Dick	31	0.069	P	4	5	6.55	
Maricich, Eli	84	0.307	2B, SS				
Milner, Charlie	1		P	0	0	2.25	
Nierpoetter, Billy	17	0.143	P	2	8	6.18	Alex City
Patterson, Bill	109	0.233	C				AC - Ca - Gr
Patterson, Derward	12	0.185					Rome

Perry, Bob	62	0.246	3B				
Philpott, Carey	87	0.198	C				
Puffer, Gerald	45	0.231	P	11	8	3.81	
Rogers, Marion	35	0.188	P	7	10	5.71	
Roth, Jac	95	0.288	2B				
Savarese, Al	68	0.161	SS				AC - Rom
Smith, Ken	23	0.127	1B				Opelika
Socha, George	15	0.250	P	5	4	4.00	
Sommer, Bill	23	0.268	3B				Rome
Thompson, Jim	104	0.285	OF				
Wachtman, Dave	11	0.067	P	4	4	5.25	
Walker, Milt	80	0.264	1B, 2B, OF				

1950 Georgia-Alabama League Records

Batting

Highest Batting Average (minimum 100 at bats)
1. Lou Zaden – Opelika .378
2. Gene Solt – Carrollton .365
3. Jim Stoyle – Griffin .362
4. Ed Irons – Opelika .360
5. Shorty Marshall – Carrollton .354
   Jack Bearden – Griffin .354

Most Hits
1. Gene Solt – Carrollton 168
2. Leon Carter – LaGrange 162
3. Jim Stoyle – Griffin 159
4. Tony Roig – Rome 158
5. Ray Clark – Carrollton 155

Most Runs
1. Freddie DeSouza – Carrollton 149
2. Leon Carter – LaGrange 113
3. Jim Morelli – Carrollton 112
4. Carl Franson – Newnan 111
5. Jack Bearden – Griffin 108
   Dave Krings – LaGrange 108

Most Total Bases
1. Gene Solt – Carrollton 311
2. Jack Bearden – Griffin 254
3. Leon Carter – LaGrange 252
4. Tony Roig – Rome 245
5. Freddie DeSouza – Carrollton 243

Most Doubles
1. Ray Clark – Carrollton 38
2. Tony Roig – Rome 34
3. Freddie DeSouza – Carrollton 33
4. Jack Bearden – Griffin 31
   Joe Schmidt – Newnan 31

Most Triples
1. Jim Wooley - Alexander City 11
2. Fred Schmitt – Griffin 10
3. Dave Krings – LaGrange 9
   Ernie Wingard – LaGrange 9
   John Pinson – Rome 9

Most Home Runs
1. Gene Solt – Carrollton 38
2. Carl Franson – Newnan 31
3. Freddie DeSouza – Carrollton 24
4. Lowe Knowles – Rome 23
5. Carl Cooper – LaGrange 22

Most Extra Base Hits
1. Gene Solt – Carrollton 66
2. Freddie DeSouza – Carrollton 63
3. Jack Bearden – Griffin 56
4. Tony Roig – Rome 53
5. Lowe Knowles – Rome 52
   Ray Clark – Carrollton 52

Most Runs Batted In
1. Gene Solt – Carrollton 151
2. Jim Stoyle – Griffin 121
3. Bill Brown - Alexander City 106
4. Leon Carter – LaGrange 105
5. Tony Roig – Rome 104

Most Stolen Bases
1. Bob Julian – Opelika 38
2. Jac Roth – Valley 34
3. Dave Krings – LaGrange 30
4. Bill Chechile – Newnan 29
   Bob Hovell - Alexander City 29
   Jim Wooley - Alexander City 29

Fielding

Most Put-Outs
1. Bill Brown 1B – Alexander City 969
2. Jim Stoyle 1B – Griffin 888
3. Lowe Knowles 1B – Rome 749
4. Wheeler Flemming 1B – Opelika 735
5. Jake Daniel 1B – Valley 724

Most Assists
1. George Noga SS – Griffin 371
2. Bob Winkelspecht SS – LaGrange 358
3. Bob McAndrew 2B – Griffin 314
4. Bob Adams 2B, 3B, SS - Alexander City 312
5. Bob Julian 3B, SS – Opelika 303

Most Errors
1. Eli Maricich 2B, SS – Valley 48
2. Tony Roig 2B, 3B, SS, OF – Rome 47
3. George Noga SS – Griffin 44
4. Bob Winkelspecht SS – LaGrange 38
   Ray Clark SS – Carrollton 38

Pitching

Most Wins
1. Don Bessent – LaGrange 22
2. Bill Bustle – Newnan 21
3. John Lindsley - Alexander City 18
4. Marv Chappell – LaGr/Alex 17
   Ed Bobowski – Carrollton 17
   Gerald Wallis – LaGrange 17

Most Losses
1. Jimmy Sparks – Rome 16
2. Delma Maddox – Opelika 12
3. Layton Krohn - Alexander City 11
   Myril Hoag – Vall/Rome 11
   George Busch – Rome/Grif 11

Highest Winning Percentage (10 game minimum)
1. John Stowe – Rome 1.000
2. Claude Jackson – Opelika .813
3. Gerald Wallis – LaGrange .810
4. Don Bessent – LaGrange .759
5. George Johengen – LaGrange .750
   Bob Hutchins – Rome/Carr .750

Lowest Earned Run Average (100 inning minimum)
1. Don Bessent – LaGrange 2.23
2. John Lindsley - Alexander City 2.43
3. Claude Jackson – Opelika 2.46

4. Myril Hoag – Vall/Rome — 2.60
5. George Johengen – LaGrange — 2.66

Most Strikeouts
1. Don Bessent – LaGrange — 229
2. Bill Bustle – Newnan — 228
3. John Lindsley - Alexander City — 168
4. Layton Krohn - Alexander City — 155
5. Bill Sweatt – Newnan — 147

Most Bases on Balls
1. Marv Chappell – LaGr/Alex — 135
2. Jimmy Sparks – Rome — 120
3. Ed Bobowski – Carrollton — 118
4. Dick Marshall – LaGrange — 116
5. Charlie Collins - Alexander City — 114

Most Hits Allowed
1. John Lindsley - Alexander City — 233
2. Bill Bustle – Newnan — 228
3. Marv Chappell – LaGr/Alex — 215
4. Layton Krohn - Alexander City — 203
5. Delma Maddox – Opelika — 197

Most Innings Pitched
1. Don Bessent – LaGrange — 242
2. John Lindsley - Alexander City — 241
3. Bill Bustle – Newnan — 237
4. Marv Chappell – LaGr/Alex — 222
5. Layton Krohn - Alexander City — 218

1950 Georgia-Alabama League All-Star Team
1B Jim Stoyle – Griffin
2B Joe Schmidt – Newnan
3B Leon Carter – LaGrange
SS George Noga – Griffin
OF Jack Bearden – Griffin
OF George Hughes – Valley
OF Carl Cooper – LaGrange
C Gene Solt – Carrollton
C Jim Durkin – LaGrange
UT Bill Rigdon – Opelika
UT Dave Krings – LaGrange
P Don Bessent – LaGrange
P John Lindsley - Alexander City
P Bill Bustle – Newnan
P Ed Bobowski – Carrollton

1950

Georgia-Florida League

League Office: Leslie, Georgia
League President: W.T. Anderson
League Vice President: C.L. Thompson
Secretary: James R. Blair
Salary Limit: $2,600 per month.
Player Rule: Each club was allowed a roster of seventeen players, not more than three veterans, not more than seven limited service, and not less than seven rookies.
Umpires: Charles R. Albury, William A. Austin, Pat Fiore, Gerald J. Morrisey, Harvey D. Odom, Charles N. Rector, Harless W. Stover, Frank Augugliaro, and Hilliery E. Bothell.

Georgia-Florida League Final Standings

Team	W	L	Pct	GB	Affiliate
Albany Cardinals	83	57	.592	----	STL-NL
Valdosta Dodgers	81	56	.591	0.5	BRK-NL
Tallahassee Pirates	77	58	.570	3.5	PIT-NL
Americus Phillies	70	67	.510	11.5	PHI-NL
Moultrie Cubs	71	69	.507	12.0	CHI-NL
Waycross Bears	57	81	.413	25.0	Unaffiliated
Cordele A's	55	80	.407	25.5	PHI-AL
Thomasville Tigers	55	81	.404	26.0	DET-AL

1950 Georgia-Florida League Map

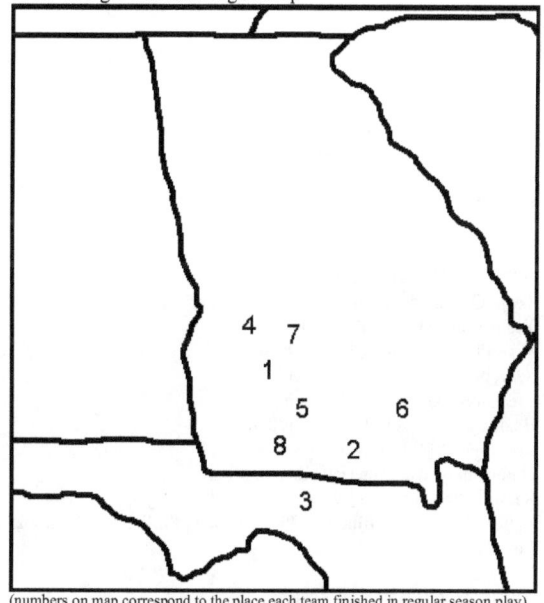

(numbers on map correspond to the place each team finished in regular season play)

The 1950 season made it five consecutive years together for the eight teams that comprised the Georgia-Florida League.

The season's only no-hitter in the league was tossed on July 22, by Thomasville's Wes Breschini in a 2 to 1 defeat of Albany.

Albany finished the regular season in first place for the second straight year. Valdosta, Tallahassee, and Americus finished second, third, and fourth respectively. Americus pulled out the upset over Albany in the first round of playoff

Georgia Class-D Minor League Baseball Encyclopedia

action by defeating the Cardinals four games to one. Tallahassee and Valdosta went the distance on the other side of the bracket before Valdosta won the series four games to three. Tallahassee was crowned league champions when they defeated Americus four games to one in the final championship series.

Albany, Georgia
Team Operated by Albany Baseball Club, Inc.
Team President: Morton M. Wiggins
Vice Presidents: Fred M. Saigh, Jr., William Walsingham, Jr.
Secretary: Edward R. Roth
Treasurer: Fred M. Saigh, Jr.
Business Manager: L.E. "Chick" Walmsley
Manager(s): Chief Bender
Games played at Cardinal Field
Season attendance: 62,950
Major League Affiliate: St. Louis Cardinals – National League.

Albany Cardinals Team Roster

NAME	G	BA	POS	W	L	ERA	APF
Bass, Danny	17	0.226	OF				
Behrens, Ed	141	0.274	1B				
Bender, Chief	39	0.250	M, P	12	5	2.78	
Benedict, Hoyt	30	0.089	P	10	8	3.45	
Drake, Jay	111	0.248	OF, C				
Eames, Paul	97	0.254	OF, C				
Ferguson, Art	64	0.228	2B, 3B, OF				
Ford, Lonnie	12	0.261	P	4	4	4.22	
Joyner, Julian	40	0.195	P	16	6	3.21	
Lageman, Ralph	142	0.312	OF				
Leftridge, Lee	123	0.304	OF				
Montgomery, Walt	30	0.160	P	7	9	4.73	
O'Barr, Tom	12	0.000	P				
Penczak, Joe	35	0.243	3B				
Pounds, Roy	41	0.158	P	15	5	2.58	
Puro, Ray	94	0.220	2B, 3B				
Rowe, Edgar	19	0.186	3B				
Ryan, Fred	138	0.251	SS				
Seymour, Tex	115	0.272	OF				
Simms, Charles	88	0.237	2B, 3B				
Smith, George	15	0.273	OF				
Wood, Don	10	0.100					
Wooldridge, Floyd	54	0.234	P	14	12	3.36	

Americus, Georgia
Team Operated by Americus Phillies, Inc.
Team President: H. Phil Jones
Vice President: Joseph F. Reardon
Secretary: George A. Fletcher
Treasurer: George F. Harrison
Business Manager: Orion Mitchell
Manager(s): Ed Murphy
Games played at Americus Baseball Park
Season attendance: 38,939
Major League Affiliate: Philadelphia Phillies – National League.

Americus Phillies Team Roster

NAME	G	BA	POS	W	L	ERA	APF
Cercek, Ed	60	0.241	OF				
Fredericks, Harry	25	0.278	OF				
Genevrino, Mike	70	0.284	1B				
Grogel, Don	61	0.222	OF				
Harper, Charles	13	0.222	P	4	6	3.70	
Hoyle, Alex	33	0.194	P	12	13	2.68	
Hushebeck, John	35	0.218	P	22	8	3.22	
Jakowczyk, Wally	109	0.280	OF				
Kret, Anthony	139	0.253	3B				
LiPetri, Angelo	18	0.241	SS				
Moore, Gene	21	0.215	OF				
Murphy, Ed	42	0.306	M, 1B				
Neely, Jess	31	0.156	2B				
Piet, Ernie	36	0.217	P	11	9	4.14	
Satkowiak, Phil	62	0.269	1B				
Savage, Cliff	37	0.213	P	9	11	2.97	
Saverine, Chuck	122	0.257	C				
Schindler, Al	125	0.202	2B				
Smith, Bob	20	0.178	OF				
Thompson, Leroy	17	0.147	P	6	6	5.65	
Wenitski, Bernie	114	0.258	SS				
Wigle, Bob	139	0.274	OF				

Cordele, Georgia
Team Operated by Cordele Athletics, Inc.
Team President: Connie Mack
Vice Presidents: Arthur Ehlers, Earle mack
Secretary: Connie Mack, Jr.
Treasurer: Roy mack
Business Manager; Carl M. Martin
Manager(s): Bill Peterman
Games played at City Park
Season attendance: 32,655
Major League Affiliate: Philadelphia Athletics – American League.

Cordele A's Team Roster

NAME	G	BA	POS	W	L	ERA	APF
Bonnett, Luther	13	0.205	OF				
Daly, Hugh	76	0.196	OF, C				
Deitch, Elliott	26	0.129	P	3	9	6.25	
DeMont, Paul	138	0.259	2B, 3B				
Dingler, George	84	0.218	C				
Donaldson, George	10	0.415	1B				
Dotson, Gene	15	0.196	C				
Dugger, Charles	27	0.172	2B				
Kell, Skeeter	122	0.353	2B				
Marino, Emil	16	0.179	OF				
Mills, Dick	48	0.123	P	10	12	3.48	
Moorehead, Dick	83	0.273	OF				
Peterman, Bill			M				
Phillips, Randolph	44	0.170	P	17	11	2.92	
Schiavo, Bill	23	0.171	P	6	6	3.60	
Sides, Bill	103	0.236	OF				
Spain, Hank	138	0.240	OF				
Spruill, Jack	121	0.354	1B				
Stempel, Courtney	44	0.205	P	11	15	4.25	
Wallace, Bill	38	0.146	P	6	7	4.21	
Welch, George	18	0.175	OF				
Yarborough, Mack	138	0.174	SS				
Zelinsky, Matt	48	0.290	3B, OF				

Moultrie, Georgia
Team Operated by Moultrie Baseball Company, Inc.
Team President: F.R. Pidcock, Jr.
Vice President: W.C. Vereen
Secretary-Treasurer-Business Manager: C.W. Vandiver
Manager(s): Steve Collins, Jim Trew
Games played at Municipal Park
Season attendance: 48,458
Major League Affiliate: Chicago Cubs – National League.

Moultrie Cubs Team Roster

NAME	G	BA	POS	W	L	ERA	APF
Brosnan, Pat	16	0.179	P	4	5	5.10	
Collins, Steve	28	0.255	M, 3B				
Courtney, Bill	139	0.253	SS				

Georgia Class-D Minor League Baseball Encyclopedia

NAME	G	BA	POS	W	L	ERA
Davis, Wendell	71	0.305	1B, 3B			
Day, Dwight	12	0.053	P	2	6	6.10
Del Piano, Mike	60	0.098	P	9	6	4.24
Earl, Les	23	0.243	C			
Garner, Bill	13	0.257	P	5	6	3.75
Golembiewski, Marion	101	0.275	1B, OF, P	4	3	4.89
Hatcher, Marv	17	0.154	P	8	5	4.46
Hightower, Gene	11	0.056	P			
Hulet, Fred	12	0.105	P	1	4	9.00
Ivy, Harold	118	0.318	OF			
Kelly, Jesse	75	0.206	2B, 3B			
Kossuth, Otto	12	0.222	P	5	4	4.71
Markland, John	34	0.324	C			
Munday, Charles	46	0.229	C			
Myers, Bob	21	0.097	P	5	4	4.89
Nelson, Gene	17	0.182	P	4	3	5.61
Perchak, Charles	139	0.289	OF			
Rendlesham, Jerry	95	0.244	1B			
Riles, Stewart	58	0.187	C			
Rose, Hubert	124	0.339	2B			
Smith, Bob	17	0.125	P	2	2	5.81
Stroud, Earl	17	0.118	C			
Tessin, Elmer	35	0.226	P	16	8	3.97
Trew, Jim	111	0.336	M, 3B, OF			
Wendell, Herb	22	0.224	OF			

Tallahassee, Florida
Team Operated by Tallahassee Pirates, Inc.
Team President: Fred N. Lowry
Vice President: H. Roy Hamey
Secretary: Fred Hering
Treasurer: Albert H. Schlensker
Business Manager: Lou London
Manager(s): Walt Tauscher
Games played at Centennial Field
Season attendance: 55,475
Major League Affiliate: Pittsburgh Pirates – National League.

Tallahassee Pirates Team Roster

NAME	G	BA	POS	W	L	ERA	APF
Costello, Dan	21	0.156	P	3	3	6.04	
Gladich, Frank	49	0.234	1B				
Handel, Henry	19	0.139	P	9	6	4.05	
Jones, Lawrence	10	0.105	P	1	4	3.46	
Kimber, Ray	32	0.146	P	10	8	4.76	
Lefevre, Leroy	138	0.316	2B				
Lewis, Ralph	33	0.207	3B				
Lichti, Russell	10	0.033					
Lindermuth, Dick	132	0.324	OF, C				
Lindermuth, Glen	135	0.281	1B, OF				
Maiden, John	102	0.251	1B				
McCallum, Dick	12	0.261	P	3	2	2.77	
McGhee, Tom	21	0.255	OF				
McGrath, John	32	0.192	P	9	4	4.80	
McNally, Don	138	0.248	SS				
Moeller, Rolf	37	0.170	P	9	8	4.53	
Oglesby, Alex	16	0.130	C				
Peterson, Hardy	45	0.275	C				
Pomykala, Jim	17	0.189	P	4	8	3.80	
Quattrone, Joe	32	0.265	OF				
Quilici, Gabe	15	0.050	P	6	1	4.22	
Smith, Dick	100	0.339	3B				
Smith, Paul	139	0.319	OF				
Stoops, Bill	11	0.241					
Talas, Eftimeo	33	0.141	P	20	5	2.73	
Tauscher, Walt			M				

Thomasville, Georgia
Team Operated by Thomasville Baseball Company
Team President: Heeth Varnedoe
Vice Presidents: Ray L. Kennedy, James A. Campbell
Secretary: H.M. Sisson
Business Manager: James A. Campbell
Manager(s): Bob Benish
Games played at Municipal Stadium
Season attendance: 27,760
Major League Affiliate: Detroit Tigers – American League.

Thomasville Tigers Team Roster

NAME	G	BA	POS	W	L	ERA	APF
Adams, Carl	21	0.220	P	12	6	3.66	
Bagwell, Jim	50	0.227	OF				
Benish, Bob	83	0.265	M, 1B, OF, P	4	5	4.80	
Breaux, Cliff	56	0.246	OF				
Breschini, Wes	31	0.219	P	14	14	3.64	
Burt, Dick	34	0.141	C				
Collins, Bob	14	0.200	P	1	3	5.63	
Craig, Myron	14	0.207	2B				
DeRieux, Bob	129	0.200	3B				
Fulton, Bob	129	0.289	C				
Hoffman, Myron	14	0.429	P				
Hurst, John	104	0.235	2B				
Keller, Ken	14	0.269					
Lary, Frank			P	4	0	3.00	
Lehrman, Charles	34	0.120	P	4	14	4.26	
Long, Wallace	79	0.285	OF				
Lyons, Tom	11	0.227					
Moore, Charles	33	0.216	2B				
Newell, Bob	125	0.251	1B				
Perry, Bob	21	0.242	OF				
Sowell, Bill	55	0.211	OF				
Stanley, Ken	73	0.315	OF				
Strickland, Don	81	0.296	OF				
Utley, Ewell	19	0.344	P	4	5	6.85	
Utter, Dick	35	0.140	P	3	8	5.46	
Waldrop, Berman	34	0.169	P	10	16	5.13	
Wetherton, Carl	35	0.236	SS				

Valdosta, Georgia
Team Operated by Valdosta Dodgers Baseball Club, Inc.
Team President: D.S. Wainer
Vice President: Branch Rickey, Jr.
Secretary: Fresco Thompson
Treasurer: D.E. Beach
General Manager: Victor A. Zodda
Manager(s): Stan Wasiak
Games played at Pendleton Park
Season attendance: 56,089
Major League Affiliate: Brooklyn Dodgers – National League.

Valdosta Dodgers Team Roster

NAME	G	BA	POS	W	L	ERA	APF
Adelhelm, Bill	122	0.279	1B				
Barker, George	27	0.214	P	10	7	4.07	
Bledsoe, Billy	40	0.198	P	16	13	3.54	
Brown, Roger	10	0.148	SS				
Coles, Chuck	111	0.355	OF				
Craig, Roger	25	0.121	P	14	7	3.13	
Cuoco, Al	88	0.274	3B				
Delich, Bill	20	0.263	SS				
Dendy, Bob	45	0.238	3B				
Giaquinto, Frank	13	0.143	P	7	2	3.14	
Hamric, Bert	138	0.312	OF				
Hatcher, Jerry	21	0.171	P	7	3	4.72	
Jenkins, Bob	35	0.210	C				
Korcheck, Mike	88	0.260	SS				

Georgia Class-D Minor League Baseball Encyclopedia

Name	G	BA	POS	W	L	ERA
Meeres, Gordon	25	0.212				
Michelson, Warren	13	0.182	P			
Pignatano, Joe	127	0.285	OF, C			
Rees, Ernest	121	0.232	2B, SS				Waycross
Sbashnig, Pete	12	0.174				
Singer, George	31	0.209	C			
Stephenson, Sonny	129	0.279	1B, OF			
Stocker, Stan	19	0.087	P	5	4	5.14
Strickland, Walt	24	0.148	P	9	4	2.71
Wasiak, Stan	138	0.312	M, 2B			
Watts, Lee	29	0.250	OF			
Zeski, Don	26	0.132	P	10	8	4.33

Waycross, Georgia
Team Operated by Waycross Baseball Association, Inc.
Team President: Erin O. Johnson
Vice President: O.E. Edenfield
Treasurer: Fred W. Voight
Business Manager: Charlie Andrews
Manager(s): Don Manno, Charles Webb
Games played at Memorial Stadium
Season attendance: 43,638

Waycross Bears Team Roster

NAME	G	BA	POS	W	L	ERA	APF
Allen, Bill	38	0.102	P	6	14	5.08	
Austin, Alvin	128	0.273	3B, OF				
Bloodworth, Charles	18	0.280	OF				
Bremer, Walt	62	0.384	3B, OF				
Childs, Dick	33	0.150	P	7	18	5.78	
Currie, Bill	46	0.242	P	15	11	3.77	
Dodson, Dick	14	0.174	P	3	3	7.09	
Foltmer, Harold	80	0.202	3B, C				
Ford, Don	84	0.256	C				
Herring, Earl	18	0.200	C				
Hilliard, Grady	92	0.279	1B, P	16	10	4.55	
Johnston, Bob	42	0.235	3B				
Luchetta, Frank	72	0.239	OF				
Manno, Don	77	0.286	M, 1B, 3B, SS, OF				
Martini, Paul	140	0.255	2B, SS				
Musial, Ed	47	0.275	OF				
Niklas, Roger	11	0.265	OF				
O'Callaghan, Tom	32	0.228	P	4	6	4.70	
Palmer, Max	25	0.151	OF				
Petty, Gene	14	0.227	OF				
Powell, Jack	66	0.289	1B				
Raulerson, Harry	7		P	2	5	5.94	
Rees, Ernest	121	0.232	2B, SS				Valdosta
Sparacino, Frank	33	0.241	SS				
Walker, Milt	31	0.198	OF				
Webb, Charles	47	0.309	M, 3B				
Young, Herb	29	0.247	OF				

1950 Georgia-Florida League Records

Batting

Highest Batting Average (minimum 100 at bats)
1. Walt Bremer – Waycross .384
2. Chuck Coles – Valdosta .355
3. Jack Spruill – Cordele .354
4. Skeeter Kell – Cordele .353
5. Dick Smith – Tallahassee .339
   Hubert Rose – Moultrie .339

Most Hits
1. Paul Smith – Tallahassee 196
2. Bert Hamric – Valdosta 174
3. Jack Spruill – Cordele 163
   Stan Wasiak – Valdosta 163
5. Chuck Coles – Valdosta 161

Most Runs
1. Hubert Rose – Moultrie 145
2. Charles Perchak – Moultrie 130
3. Bob Wigle – Americus 128
4. Paul Smith – Tallahassee 127
5. Leroy Lefevre – Tallahassee 126

Most Total Bases
1. Bert Hamric – Valdosta 265
2. Paul Smith – Tallahassee 257
3. Chuck Coles – Valdosta 250
4. Dick Lindermuth – Tallahassee 228
5. Ralph Lageman – Albany 222

Most Doubles
1. Jack Spruill – Cordele 33
2. Skeeter Kell – Cordele 30
3. Ralph Lageman – Albany 29
   Charles Perchak – Moultrie 29
   Fred Ryan – Albany 29

Most Triples
1. Bert Hamric – Valdosta 18
2. Bob Wigle – Americus 17
   Joe Pignatano – Valdosta 17
4. Dick Lindermuth – Tallahassee 16
5. Chuck Coles – Valdosta 14

Most Home Runs
1. Bob Fulton – Thomasville 15
2. Chuck Coles – Valdosta 14
3. Harold Ivy – Moultrie 13
4. Charles Perchak – Moultrie 11
   Joe Quattrone – Tallahassee 11

Most Extra Base Hits
1. Bert Harmic – Valdosta 53
2. Dick Lindermuth – Tallahassee 49
3. Chuck Coles – Valdosta 47
4. Fred Ryan – Albany 45
   Bob Wigle – Americus 45

Most Runs Batted In
1. Harold Ivy – Moultrie 131
2. Charles Perchak – Moultrie 116
3. Dick Lindermuth – Tallahassee 105
4. Glen Lindermuth – Tallahassee 97
5. Bert Hamric – Valdosta 96
   Bob Fulton – Thomasville 96

Most Stolen Bases
1. Ralph Lageman – Albany 46
2. Paul Smith – Tallahassee 43
3. Chuck Coles – Valdosta 32
4. Leroy Lefevre – Tallahassee 28
5. Paul DeMont – Cordele 27

Fielding

Most Put-Outs
1. Bob Newell 1B – Thomasville 992
2. Jack Spruill 1B – Cordele 916
3. Bill Adelhelm 1B – Valdosta 851
4. Ed Behrens 1B – Albany 842
5. Bob Fulton C – Thomasville 827

Most Assists
1. Paul Martini 2B, SS – Waycross 433
2. Stan Wasiak 2B – Valdosta 429

Georgia Class-D Minor League Baseball Encyclopedia

3. Leroy Lefevre 2B – Tallahassee — 428
4. Bill Courtney SS – Moultrie — 419
5. Fred Ryan SS – Albany — 398

Most Errors
1. Don McNally SS – Tallahassee — 77
2. Bill Courtney SS – Moultrie — 75
3. Mack Yarborough SS – Cordele — 74
4. Carl Wetherton SS – Thomasville — 71
5. Bob DeRieux 3B – Thomasville — 62

Pitching
Most Wins
1. John Hushebeck – Americus — 22
2. Eftimeo Talas – Tallahassee — 20
3. Randolph Phillips – Cordele — 17
4. Grady Hilliard – Waycross — 16
   Billy Bledsoe – Valdosta — 16
   Elmer Tessin – Moultrie — 16
   Julian Joyner – Albany — 16

Most Losses
1. Dick Childs – Waycross — 18
2. Berman Waldrop – Thomasville — 16
3. Courtney Stempel – Cordele — 15
4. Wes Breschini – Thomasville — 14
   Bill Allen – Waycross — 14
   Charles Lehrman – Thomasville — 14

Highest Winning Percentage (10 game minimum)
1. Gabe Quilici – Tallahassee — .800
2. Eftimeo Talas – Tallahassee — .778
3. Frank Giaquinto – Valdosta — .750
4. Roy Pounds – Albany — .733
5. John Hushebeck – Americus — .727

Lowest Earned Run Average (100 inning minimum)
1. Roy Pounds – Albany — 2.58
2. Alex Hoyle – Americus — 2.68
3. Walt Strickland – Valdosta — 2.71
4. Eftimeo Talas – Tallahassee — 2.73
5. Chief Bender – Albany — 2.78

Most Strikeouts
1. Bill Currie – Waycross — 240
2. Eftimeo Talas – Tallahassee — 222
3. Wes Breschini – Thomasville — 209
4. Don Zeski – Valdosta — 203
5. Cliff Savage – Americus — 195

Most Bases on Balls
1. Wes Breschini – Thomasville — 166
   Courtney Stempel – Cordele — 166
3. Rolf Moeller – Tallahassee — 162
4. Don Zeski – Valdosta — 157
5. Roger Craig – Valdosta — 150

Most Hits Allowed
1. Bill Currie – Waycross — 245
2. Berman Waldrop – Thomasville — 240
3. Julian Joyner – Albany — 216
4. Elmer Tessin – Moultrie — 215
5. Billy Bledsoe – Valdosta — 212

Most Innings Pitched
1. Bill Currie – Waycross — 272
2. Eftimeo Talas – Tallahassee — 247
3. Elmer Tessin – Moultrie — 231
4. Billy Bledsoe – Valdosta — 229
5. Cliff Savage – Americus — 227

1950 Georgia-Florida League All-Star Team
1B Jack Spruill – Cordele
2B Skeeter Kell – Cordele
3B Dick Smith – Tallahassee
SS Mike Korcheck – Valdosta
SS Fred Ryan – Albany
OF Chuck Coles – Valdosta
OF Paul Smith – Tallahassee
OF Ralph Lageman – Albany
C Dick Lindermuth – Tallahassee
P Eftimeo Talas – Tallahassee
P Julian Joyner – Albany
P Roy Pounds – Albany
P Wes Breschini – Thomasville

1950

Georgia State League

League Office: Columbia, South Carolina
League President: Earl Blue
League Vice President: W.H. Lovett
Salary Limit: $2,600 per month.
Player Rule: Each club was allowed a roster of sixteen players, not more than two veterans, not more than seven limited service, and not less than seven rookies.
Umpires: Joseph T. Braica, Michael R. Ganakas, Richard F. Leonard, Nicholas J. Mangieri, David J. McVey, Anthony Venzon, James M. Wells, and Marvin E. Whitley.

Georgia State League Final Standings

Team	W	L	Pct	GB	Affiliate
Dublin Green Sox	84	56	.600	----	Unaffiliated
Douglas Trojans	78	60	.565	5.0	Unaffiliated
Eastman Dodgers	79	61	.564	5.0	Unaffiliated
Fitzgerald Pioneers	73	66	.525	10.5	Unaffiliated
Jesup Bees	69	69	.500	14.0	Unaffiliated
Tifton Blue Sox	69	70	.496	14.5	Unaffiliated
Vidalia-Lyons Twins	56	83	.403	29.5	Unaffiliated
Hazlehurst-Baxley Red Sox	48	91	.345	35.5	Unaffiliated

1950 Georgia State League Map

(numbers on map correspond to the place each team finished in regular season play)

After the 1949 season, Sparta dropped out of the league and was replaced by the new ball club from Jesup.
On June 30, Eastman pitcher Clarence Richardson pitched a no-hitter against Douglas winning the game 5 to 0. Another no-hitter was pitched in the form of a perfect game on August 25 by Douglas pitcher Higgins Duncan against Fitzgerald. Higgins won the game 4 to 0. Douglas shortstop Emil Rey set the league's all-time mark for the most assists in a single season when he helped out on 449 putouts during the year.

In Eastman, it was the Edd Hartness show that entertained baseball fans. Hartness set four all-time single season league records during the season for the most total bases with 331, the most doubles with 48, the most extra base hits with 79, and from his defensive post at first base, the most put outs with 1,307.
Dublin finished the season in first place and was followed by Douglas, Eastman, and Fitzgerald in order. Douglas and Eastman, both five games behind the leader Dublin, were separated by only .001 points. In the first round of playoffs, Dublin defeated Fitzgerald three games to two, and Eastman ousted Douglas three games to one advancing each winner to the league championship series. In the final series that went the seven-game distance, Eastman pulled the upset over Dublin four games to three.

Douglas, Georgia

Team Operated by Douglas Baseball Club, Inc.
Team President: John I. "Si" Slocumb, Jr.
Vice President-General Manager: Dave Coble
Business Manager: H.P. Ward
Manager(s): Dave Coble, Fred Tschudin
Games played at Municipal Stadium
Season attendance: 32,590

Douglas Trojans Team Roster

NAME	G	BA	POS	W	L	ERA	APF
Allen, Joel	66	0.220	OF				
Alonso, John	29	0.269	OF				
Baker, Roy	134	0.244	2B				
Baldwin, Lamar	75	0.208	OF, C				
Brewer, George	26	0.267	P	9	7	5.13	
Catalano, Pete	33	0.346	OF				
Coble, Dave			M				Tifton
Davis, Van	138	0.295	1B				
Duncan, Higgins	42	0.125	P	19	12	3.13	
Garcia, Jose	15	0.170	OF				
Hominsky, Ivan	135	0.202	3B				
Jiminez, Dario	70	0.142	P	21	10	2.93	
Martin, Jim	135	0.251	OF				
McGhee, Bill	96	0.298	1B, OF				Fitzgerald
Parnell, Gene	27	0.125	P	4	4	5.38	Tifton
Randolph, Harry	50	0.372	OF				
Rey, Emil	131	0.243	SS				
Sala, Fred	20	0.129	OF				Jesup
Thomas, Wilbert	27	0.159	P	9	8	3.81	
Tschudin, Fred	137	0.285	M, C				
Wright, George	12	0.286	P	3	4	4.21	
Yablon, Nathan	44	0.160	P	9	12	3.79	Tifton
Yow, Forrest	95	0.281	OF				Tifton

Dublin, Georgia

Team Operated by Dublin Baseball Club, Inc.
Team President: W.H. Lovett
Vice Presidents: W.E. Lovett, W.W. Brinson
Secretary: Frank Johnson
Business Manager: Eddie Williams, Jr.
Manager(s): Parnell Ruark, Bill Seal, Ed Wissman
Games played at Lovett Park
Season attendance: 50,160

Dublin Green Sox Team Roster

NAME	G	BA	POS	W	L	ERA	APF
Blanton, Hugh	89	0.273	1B, OF, P	12	7	5.05	
Boddy, Bob	37	0.319	2B, SS				Eastman
Clifton, Henry	102	0.267	1B, P	13	7	3.83	
Collins, Jack	138	0.284	3B				
Cudemo, Mike	29	0.257	OF, C				

Georgia Class-D Minor League Baseball Encyclopedia

NAME	G	BA	POS	W	L	ERA	APF
Davis, Howard	78	0.212	SS, OF				Fitzgerald
Galloway, Oliver	89	0.275	C				
Gilbert, Jack	10	0.214					Jesup
Hudson, Bill	22	0.232	OF				
Johnson, Rudolph	103	0.264	OF				
Johnston, Jim	85	0.252	2B				
Jones, Stan	23	0.067	P	4	7	4.50	
Lovett, Bill	117	0.197	3B				Fitzgerald
Marrero, Leonilo	17	0.183	C				
Reeves, Herb	17	0.182	P	4	4	6.62	
Ruark, Parnell	113	0.327	M, OF				
Seal, Bill	38	0.359	M, 2B				
Smalley, Charles	38	0.202	P	23	7	2.46	
Starnes, Kendell	24	0.145	P	10	6	3.94	Eastman
Swain, Lloyd	25	0.306	P	9	5	5.30	Vid-Lyo
Thomas, Parks	18	0.146	P	8	5	3.53	
Tidwell, John	136	0.307	OF				
Tyler, Jim	19	0.250	P	7	7	4.04	Eastman
Warren, Jim	98	0.328	OF, P	11	5	4.65	Jesup
Wissman, Ed	62	0.229	M, 1B, P	9	4	3.23	
Wright, Jim	117	0.296	SS				

Eastman, Georgia
Team Operated by Eastman Dodgers, Inc.
Team President: H.R. Ragan
Secretary: O.C. Pound
General Manager-Business Manager: W.W. Taylor
Manager(s): Edd Hartness
Games played at Legion Park
Season attendance: 35,000

Eastman Dodgers Team Roster

NAME	G	BA	POS	W	L	ERA	APF
Albertson, Jerry	55	0.167	C				
Anderson, T.P.	97	0.285	OF				
Beaird, Dick	<10						
Bird, Jim	20	0.197	2B				
Black, Ralph	11	0.100	P	3	4	7.17	
Boddy, Bob	37	0.319	2B, SS				Dublin
Burgamy, Ralph	141	0.305	3B, OF				
Caldwell, Wilbur	138	0.278	3B, SS, P	2	6	4.62	
Dobbins, Mayes	120	0.258	2B, SS				
Griggs, Bill	27	0.160	P	11	6	2.83	
Harden, Jim	31	0.198	P	14	14	2.96	
Harp, Jim	30	0.083	P	13	6	3.53	
Hartness, Edd	142	0.400	M, 1B				
Hoard, Dan	39	0.265	OF				
Loudermilk, Joe	73	0.172	SS				
Pender, Marcus	18	0.115	P	3	6	7.39	
Pinson, John	26	0.312	SS				
Richardson, Clarence	34	0.212	P	13	6	3.13	
Roberts, Glenn	12	0.289					
Starnes, Kendell	24	0.145	P	10	6	3.94	Dublin
Stinson, Bob	114	0.302	C				
Thompson, Herman	11	0.179					
Tyler, Jim	19	0.250	P	7	7	4.04	Dublin
Vitali, Joe	36	0.230	OF				
Woods, Julian	137	0.274	OF				

Fitzgerald, Georgia
Team Operated by Pioneer Baseball Club, Inc.
Team President: Martin Gottlieb
Vice President: John F. McCowan
Secretary-Treasurer: E.W. Mann, Jr.
Manager(s): Ray Harrell
Games played at Blue-Gray Park
Season attendance: 42,227

Fitzgerald Pioneers Team Roster

NAME	G	BA	POS	W	L	ERA	APF
Burgess, Jay	13	0.244	1B				
Calabrese, Joe	114	0.266	OF				
Crago, Bill	140	0.324	OF				
Davis, Howard	78	0.212	SS, OF				Dublin
DiFranco, Sam	25	0.283	3B				
Harrell, Ray	28	0.239	M, P	15	10	4.17	
Henderson, Bill	82	0.370	OF				
Howard, Bobby	136	0.287	SS				
Koellmer, Bill	50	0.177	1B, OF				
Koss, Ed	51	0.221	1B				
Leslie, Paul	32	0.073	P	9	10	4.65	
Lovett, Bill	117	0.197	3B				Dublin
McGhee, Bill	96	0.298	1B, OF				Douglas
Oquendo, Noel	40	0.208	P	9	15	5.29	
Orlandi, Ron	128	0.283	C				
O'Toole, Jim	27	0.259	C				
Ridgeway, Charlie	140	0.322	2B				
Rivera, Luis	34	0.103	P	3	6	5.63	
Scalisi, Bob	35	0.184	P	19	14	3.74	
Schmidt, Kermit	43	0.216	P	18	8	3.43	
Sules, John	21	0.212	1B				

Hazlehurst-Baxley (Hazlehurst & Baxley), Georgia
Team Operated by Hazlehurst-Baxley Baseball, Inc.
Team President: Earl B. Baker
Vice President: Claude P. Cook
Secretary-Treasurer: Marion W. Barron
General Manager: Steve Maglio
Manager(s): Bill Enos
Games played at Baxley Baseball Park
Season attendance: 25,000

Hazlehurst-Baxley Red Sox Team Roster

NAME	G	BA	POS	W	L	ERA	APF
Ashcraft, Bill			P	0	0		
Barone, Anthony	108	0.234	SS				
Bolch, Bill	27	0.205	OF				
Bryant, Harold	55	0.214	3B, SS				
Cannon, Bob	17	0.118	P	4	6	4.10	
Christopher, Leo	38	0.216	3B, OF				
Conner, Jim	10	0.136	P	3	5	4.17	
Cunningham, Larry	100	0.249	OF				Vid-Lyo
Daniel, Doug	23	0.282	OF				
Enos, Bill	134	0.289	M, 1B				
Gehringer, Paul	61	0.208	P	13	12	3.84	
Granger, Gerald	19	0.143	P				
Harris, Bill	98	0.273	OF, C				
Hopkins, Bill	44	0.141	P	4	15	6.11	
Kushta, Bill	114	0.279	C				
Lewis, Don	127	0.322	OF				
McCalman, Jack			P	0	0		
Milster, Jack	11	0.242	SS				
Oertel, Chuck	92	0.352	3B, SS				
O'Malley, Dan	17	0.304	OF				
Rodriguez, Charles	58	0.242	2B				
Sengstock, Wayne	74	0.223	OF, P	13	11	4.78	
Sowers, Walt	75	0.386	OF				
Stackpole, Cecil	10	0.143	OF				
Tripod, Jerry	19	0.175	C				
Wargo, Clarence	33	0.111	P	5	10	4.40	
Wick, Gil	11	0.250	P	3	7	5.63	
Wills, Bill	16	0.143	OF				
Zwirko, Bill	79	0.187	2B				

Georgia Class-D Minor League Baseball Encyclopedia

Jesup, Georgia

Team Operated by Jesup Baseball Club
Team President: Robert L. Harrison
Vice President: Dr. T.G. Ritch
Secretary-Treasurer: R.M. Sanderson
Business Manager-General Manager: Lanier Harrell
Manager(s): Herb Stein
Games played at Milikin Park
Season attendance: 23,893

Jesup Bees Team Roster

NAME	G	BA	POS	W	L	ERA	APF
Boxer, Seymour	37	0.157	P	13	12	3.54	
Butts, Gene	11	0.083					
Craven, Bob	17	0.063	P	3	3	2.47	
Cumpson, Bill	34	0.236	OF				Vid-Lyo
Daniel, Stewart	83	0.215	OF				
Dillard, Rudy	34	0.157	P	10	11	4.87	
Dodson, Dick	24	0.086	P	5	3	5.32	
Dunn, Ed	25	0.150	P	5	10	5.81	
Gaines, Sam	15	0.258	P	3	5	6.87	
Gilbert, Jack	10	0.214					Dublin
Haber, Nate	111	0.234	OF				
Hallford, Lew	133	0.317	SS				
Hay, Bob	110	0.261	2B				
Heavner, Jim	24	0.205	1B				
Herringdine, Cecil	24	0.279	OF				
Holt, Bill	18	0.225	OF				
Kerr, Bill	24	0.187	2B				
Maggi, Ernest	30	0.233	OF				
Marotta, Dan	28	0.134					
Padgett, Charles	99	0.272	3B				
Reeves, Harold	140	0.264	C				
Rudolph Don	44	0.202	P	13	10	3.13	
Sala, Fred	20	0.129	OF				Douglas
Sanders, Al	11	0.182					
Shaddix, Willard	13	0.172	P	4	3	4.09	
Stein, Herb	127	0.304	M, 1B, 2B				
Vetter, Bob	13	0.098	3B				
Warren, Jim	98	0.328	OF, P	11	5	4.65	Dublin
Wilson, Ed	82	0.359	OF				

Tifton, Georgia

Team Operated by Tifton Baseball Club
Team President: R.B. Hall
Vice President: H.V. Hall
Secretary-Treasurer-Business Manager: Eugene Slack
Manager(s): Bill Barnes, Dave Coble
Games played at Eve Park
Season attendance: 54,784

Tifton Blue Sox Team Roster

NAME	G	BA	POS	W	L	ERA	APF
Barnes, Bill	92	0.269	M, 2B				
Barnes, Bob	47	0.204	P	11	9	4.92	
Baskin, Al	20	0.094	P	2	5	5.46	
Batty, Tom	15	0.160	OF				
Betancourt, Roberto	31	0.238	3B, P	3	4	4.80	
Bowen, Howard	10	0.000	P				
Christie, Frank	25	0.188	P	12	7	3.76	
Coble, Dave			M				Douglas
Cooper, Frank	11	0.263					
Daley, Gil	125	0.316	OF				
Dickerman, Ed	40	0.304	2B				
Druga, Tom	133	0.236	1B				
Fernandez, Luis	28	0.188	P	9	9	4.61	
Hobbs, Tigner	56	0.236	3B				
Manno, Don	50	0.288	2B, OF				
McDougald, Julius	33	0.222	3B				
McKenna, Bob	27	0.216	3B				
McKinney, Clarence	106	0.264	OF				
Miller, Bob	21	0.270	OF				
Morrison, Jim	130	0.292	SS				
Myers, Dick	11	0.174	P	3	4	5.37	
Noah, Harold	25	0.261	OF				
Parnell, Gene	27	0.125	P	4	4	5.38	Douglas
Riles, Stewart	25	0.176	C				
Simon, Jerry	36	0.131	P	13	13	3.94	
Stockton, Ray	13	0.188	OF				
Swain, Kurtis	123	0.255	C				
Whitehead, Don	14	0.167	P	3	4	4.34	
Wolf, Hugh	23	0.149	C				
Yablon, Nathan	44	0.160	P	9	12	3.79	Douglas
Yow, Forrest	95	0.281	OF				Douglas

Vidalia-Lyons (Vidalia & Lyons), Georgia

Team Operated by Vidalia-Lyons Baseball Club
Team President: William Estroff
Vice President: L.L. Waller
Secretary-Treasurer-Business Manager: Jack Mosley
Manager(s): Mike Kreshka, Jim Smith
Games played at Twin Cities Stadium
Season attendance: 30,350

Vidalia-Lyons Twins Team Roster

NAME	G	BA	POS	W	L	ERA	APF
Beauchamp, Walt	92	0.263	2B				
Bubeck, Bob	32	0.282	OF				
Claypool, Jim	89	0.303	OF, C				
Coleman, Malcolm	16	0.185					
Cumpson, Bill	34	0.236	OF				Jesup
Cunningham, Larry	100	0.249	OF				Haz-Bax
Deitch, Elliott	10	0.158	P	1	8	6.33	
Dobbins, Ralph	136	0.213	OF				
Esposito, Anthony	136	0.259	1B, OF				
Fall, Ralph	96	0.230	SS				
Fernandez, Marcelo	36	0.247	P	14	10	3.47	
Harvey, Gene	79	0.197	2B, SS				
Itkin, Al	37	0.132	P	11	14	5.10	
Kreshka, Mike	82	0.288	M, OF				
Matican, Marv	14	0.235					
Merget, John	36	0.156	P	7	18	4.85	
Orner, Charles	82	0.275	C				
Sherman, Ed	31	0.160	P	11	15	4.72	
Silverman, Jerome	23	0.329	1B				
Sisco, Ed	16	0.029	P	5	9	5.52	
Smith, Jim	128	0.316	M, 3B				
Stroud, Earl	16	0.189	C				
Swain, Lloyd	25	0.306	P	9	5	5.30	Dublin
Young, Claude	60	0.318	2B, OF				

1950 Georgia State League Records

Batting

Highest Batting Average (minimum 100 at bats)
1. Edd Hartness – Eastman .400
2. Walt Sowers – Hazlehurst-Baxley .386
3. Harry Randolph – Douglas .372
4. Bill Henderson – Fitzgerald .370
5. Ed Wilson – Jesup .359
   Bill Seal – Dublin .359

Most Hits
1. Edd Hartness – Eastman 201
2. Charlie Ridgeway – Fitzgerald 183
3. John Tidwell – Dublin 178
4. Don Lewis – Hazlehurst-Baxley 174
5. Jack Collins – Dublin 173

Georgia Class-D Minor League Baseball Encyclopedia

Most Runs
1. Edd Hartness – Eastman — 137
2. Charlie Ridgeway – Fitzgerald — 129
3. Ralph Burgamy – Eastman — 127
4. Jim Morrison – Tifton — 123
5. John Tidwell – Dublin — 122

Most Total Bases
1. Edd Hartness – Eastman — 331
2. John Tidwell – Dublin — 292
   Parnell Ruark – Dublin — 292
4. Don Lewis - Hazlehurst-Baxley — 263
5. Van Davis – Douglas — 261
   Jack Collins – Dublin — 261

Most Doubles
1. Edd Hartness – Eastman — 48
2. Bill Crago – Fitzgerald — 41
3. John Tidwell – Dublin — 39
4. Lew Hallford – Jesup — 35
5. Charlie Ridgeway – Fitzgerald — 34
   Wilbur Caldwell – Eastman — 34

Most Triples
1. Chuck Oertel - Hazlehurst-Baxley — 19
2. Don Lewis - Hazlehurst-Baxley — 12
3. Edd Hartness – Eastman — 11
4. Lew Hallford – Jesup — 10
   Ed Wilson – Jesup — 10

Most Home Runs
1. Parnell Ruark – Dublin — 39
2. Van Davis – Douglas — 30
3. John Tidwell – Dublin — 21
   Jim Warren – Jesu/Dubl — 21
5. Edd Hartness – Eastman — 20

Most Extra Base Hits
1. Edd Hartness – Eastman — 79
2. Parnell Ruark – Dublin — 67
3. John Tidwell – Dublin — 66
4. Van Davis – Douglas — 59
5. Bill Crago – Fitzgerald — 56

Most Runs Batted In
1. Edd Hartness – Eastman — 134
2. Parnell Ruark – Dublin — 127
3. Wilbur Caldwell – Eastman — 120
4. John Tidwell – Dublin — 114
5. Ralph Burgamy – Eastman — 106

Most Stolen Bases
1. Charlie Ridgeway – Fitzgerald — 63
   Jim Martin – Douglas — 63
3. Bill Henderson – Fitzgerald — 52
4. Gil Daley – Tifton — 35
5. Bobby Howard – Fitzgerald — 30

Fielding
Most Put-Outs
1. Edd Hartness 1B – Eastman — 1,307
2. Van Davis 1B – Douglas — 1,274
3. Tom Druga 1B – Tifton — 1,138
4. Bill Enos 1B - Hazlehurst-Baxley — 1,128
5. Anthony Esposito 1B, OF – Vidalia-Lyons — 1,100

Most Assists
1. Emil Rey SS – Douglas — 449
2. Lew Hallford SS – Jesup — 442
3. Jim Morrison SS – Tifton — 434
4. Roy Baker 2B – Douglas — 423
5. Charlie Ridgeway 2B – Fitzgerald — 372

Most Errors
1. Bobby Howard SS – Fitzgerald — 65
2. Lew Hallford SS – Jesup — 61
3. Ralph Fall SS – Vidalia-Lyons — 60
4. Jack Collins 3B – Dublin — 57
5. Jim Wright SS – Dublin — 53

Pitching
Most Wins
1. Charles Smalley – Dublin — 23
2. Dario Jiminez – Douglas — 21
3. Higgins Duncan – Douglas — 19
   Bob Scalisi – Fitzgerald — 19
5. Kermit Schmidt – Fitzgerald — 18

Most Losses
1. John Merget – Vidalia-Lyons — 18
2. Ed Sherman – Vidalia-Lyons — 15
   Noel Oquendo – Fitzgerald — 15
   Bill Hopkins - Hazlehurst-Baxley — 15
5. Bob Scalisi – Fitzgerald — 14
   Jim Harden – Eastman — 14
   Al Itkin – Vidalia-Lyons — 14

Highest Winning Percentage (10 game minimum)
1. Charles Smalley – Dublin — .767
2. Kermit Schmidt – Fitzgerald — .692
   Ed Wissman – Dublin — .692
4. Jim Warren – Jesu/Dubl — .688
5. Clarence Richardson – Eastman — .684
   Jim Harp – Eastman — .684

Lowest Earned Run Average (100 inning minimum)
1. Charles Smalley – Dublin — 2.46
2. Bill Griggs – Eastman — 2.83
3. Dario Jiminez – Douglas — 2.93
4. Jim Harden – Eastman — 2.96
5. Don Rudolph – Jesup — 3.13
   Clarence Richardson – Eastman — 3.13
   Higgins Duncan – Douglas — 3.13

Most Strikeouts
1. Charles Smalley – Dublin — 237
2. Bob Scalisi – Fitzgerald — 236
3. Kermit Schmidt – Fitzgerald — 197
4. Marcelo Fernandez – Vidalia-Lyons — 168
5. Higgins Duncan – Douglas — 133

Most Bases on Balls
1. Marcelo Fernandez – Vidalia-Lyons — 170
2. Noel Oquendo – Fitzgerald — 148
3. Ed Sherman – Vidalia-Lyons — 141
4. Bill Hopkins - Hazlehurst-Baxley — 137
5. Kermit Schmidt – Fitzgerald — 135

Most Hits Allowed
1. Bob Scalisi – Fitzgerald — 273
2. Paul Gehringer - Hazlehurst-Baxley — 258
3. Dario Jiminez – Douglas — 252
4. Ed Sherman – Vidalia-Lyons — 248
5. John Merget – Vidalia-Lyons — 236

Most Innings Pitched
1. Bob Scalisi – Fitzgerald — 274
2. Higgins Duncan – Douglas — 267

3. Charles Smalley – Dublin   256
4. Paul Gehringer – Hazlehurst-Baxley 253
5. Dario Jiminez – Douglas   240

1950 Georgia State League All-Star Team
1B Edd Hartness – Eastman
2B Charlie Ridgeway – Fitzgerald
3B Jim Smith – Vidalia-Lyons
SS Lew Hallford – Jesup
OF Parnell Ruark – Dublin
OF Bill Crago – Fitzgerald
OF John Tidwell – Dublin
C   Fred Tschudin – Douglas
UT Wilbur Caldwell – Eastman
UT Don Lewis - Hazlehurst-Baxley
P   Clarence Richardson – Eastman
P   Charles Smalley – Dublin
M   Ray Harrell – Fitzgerald

1951

Georgia-Alabama League

League Office: Talladega, Alabama
League President: Arthur R. Decatur
League Vice President: George Cahall
Secretary: J. Hoyt Gay
Salary Limit: $2,600 per month excluding manager.
Player Rule: Each club was allowed a roster of sixteen players, not more than four veterans, not more than seven limited service, and not less than five rookies.
Umpires: Harry E. Allen, Luther B. Gunnells, Ray Davis, J.R. Poole, H.L. Ayers, Macon Ray, Peter Doherty, and Gerald Pierotti.

Georgia-Alabama League Final Standings

Team	W	L	Pct	GB	Affiliate
LaGrange Troupers	67	47	.588	----	NY-AL
Valley Rebels	64	52	.552	4.0	Unaffiliated
Rome Red Sox	58	57	.504	9.5	Unaffiliated
Griffin Pimientos	58	58	.500	10.0	Unaffiliated
Alexander City Millers	33	45	.423	N/A	Unaffiliated
Opelika Owls	23	44	.343	N/A	Unaffiliated

1951 Georgia-Alabama League Map

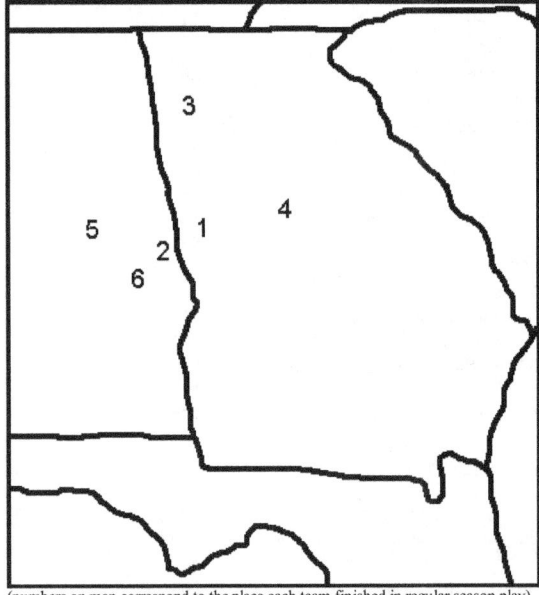

(numbers on map correspond to the place each team finished in regular season play)

After four consecutive years as an eight-team league, the Georgia-Alabama League dropped back to a six-team loop. Carrollton and Newnan both dropped out of the league following the 1950 season. The size of the league continued to decline when the Opelika club disbanded on July 1. Alexander City followed closely by calling it quits on July 15. The remaining four teams adjusted their schedules and continued on with the remainder of the season.

On June 20, Valley pitcher Gene Black pitched a no-hitter against LaGrange winning 4 to 0. Slugger John Stowe of Rome

Georgia Class-D Minor League Baseball Encyclopedia

set the league's all-time single season record for the most doubles when he reached second 39 times during the year.

With the slimmed down league roster, there was no post-season activities. The Georgia-Alabama League went out of business after the 1951 season never to return to organized baseball.

Alexander City, Alabama
Team Operated by Alexander City Baseball, Inc.
Team President: James Callahan
Vice President: Robert Russell
Secretary: Mrs. B.C. Russell
Business Manager: Murray S. Hammond
Manager(s): Bill Brown, Sam Demma
Games played at Benjamin C. Russell Field
Season attendance: 19,737

Alexander City Millers Team Roster

NAME	G	BA	POS	W	L	ERA	APF
Allen, Johnny	62	0.286	2B, 3B, OF				Valley
Alvarez, Luis	32	0.136	P	8	10	4.95	
Brown, Bill	78	0.294	M, 1B				
Cataldo, Tom	37	0.299	3B				
Culpepper, Bill	21	0.320					
Demma, Sam	45	0.231	M, C				
Falcigno, Harry	78	0.278	OF				
Haber, Nate	37	0.270	OF				
Johnson, Roy	23	0.188	C				
Krohn, Layton	21	0.250	P	9	7	3.78	
Murphy, Lamar	69	0.328	OF				
Rodriguez, Charles	67	0.273	2B				
Sanchez, Armando	29	0.260	C				Valley
Villamea, Raul	41	0.219	P	12	12	5.66	
Vitti, Ralph	11	0.571	SS				
Welch, Eacie	77	0.205	3B, SS				
White, Curtis	11	0.250	P	1	6	7.83	Valley
Winters, Charles	10	0.154					
Wooley, Jim	23	0.244	OF				

Griffin, Georgia
Team Operated by Griffin Baseball Club, Inc.
Team President: Louis George
Vice President: Joseph George
Secretary-Treasurer: T.D. Westmoreland
General Manager: Michael V. Conte
Manager(s): Jack Bearden, Fred Campbell, Michael Conte
Games played at Pimiento Park
Season attendance: 24,804

Griffin Pimientos Team Roster

NAME	G	BA	POS	W	L	ERA	APF
Bearden, Jack	115	0.320	M, OF				
Bell, John	13	0.118	P	1	4	9.39	
Campbell, Fred	102	0.326	M, SS				
Campbell, Joe	77	0.379	2B				
Catterton, Frank	59	0.248	P	12	11	5.07	
Chambers, Joe	34	0.241	2B				
Conte, Michael			M				
Drews, Roy	107	0.317	OF, C				
Griffy, Jim	29	0.283	3B, P				
Kelecava, Clem	34	0.200	P	12	12	4.62	
Maruschak, Nick	113	0.270	1B				
Oglesby, Alex	40	0.162	C				
Padgett, Bill	34	0.134	P	13	9	3.75	
Salerno, Lou	103	0.264	OF				
Sanders, Lou	60	0.275	OF				
Schultz, Herb	99	0.255	3B, OF				
Sirrine, Ernest	42	0.297	3B, C				

| Stolte, Bill | 53 | 0.174 | P | 14 | 11 | 4.30 | |

LaGrange, Georgia
Team Operated by LaGrange Baseball Club, Inc.
Team President: Oliver Hunnicutt
Vice President: G.L. Cahall
Secretary-Treasurer: Cliff Kerby
Manager(s): Bill Cooper
Games played at Callaway Stadium
Season attendance: 33,734
Major League Affiliate: New York Yankees – American League.

LaGrange Troupers Team Roster

NAME	G	BA	POS	W	L	ERA	APF
Adams, Bob	111	0.333	2B, 3B, SS				
Archer, Jim	9		P	2	3	7.24	
Beck, Dale	37	0.305	OF				
Chappell, Marv	62	0.228	P	21	8	2.55	
Cooper, Bill	39	0.212	M, 1B				
Cooper, Carl	92	0.369	OF				
DiBello, Don	99	0.261	OF				
Feldman, Nathan	11	0.167	P	2	2	4.04	
Foell, George	37	0.227	3B, SS				
Foster, Dick	47	0.305	SS				
Fucci, Dom	23	0.296	OF				
Grilliot, Bill	45	0.239	3B, C				
Harrison, Charles	28	0.215	P	19	3	3.73	
Knight, Harold	19	0.214	P	7	5	5.93	
Lourik, Alex	10	0.105					
Maurer, Ray	16	0.230	3B				
Maurer, Walt	20	0.143	OF				
McDevitt, Danny	12	0.250	P				
Murphy, Dan	110	0.322	1B				
Prappas, Jim	85	0.319	OF				
Troy, Jim	99	0.279	2B, 3B, OF				
Turner, Jim	27	0.159	P	9	4	4.67	
Vitale, Pete	24	0.245	2B				
Walls, Boyd	92	0.246	C				

Opelika, Alabama
Team Operated by Opelika Baseball Club, Inc.
Team President: Don Bailey
Vice President: Al Rigell
Secretary: Phil Hudson
Treasurer: Marion Hyatt
Manager(s): Don Bailey, Wheeler Flemming
Games played at Pepperell Park
Season attendance: 18,000

Opelika Owls Team Roster

NAME	G	BA	POS	W	L	ERA	APF
Bailey, Don			M				
Creel, Jim	29	0.286	P	8	6	4.38	
Dobbins, Mayes	37	0.250	2B				Valley
Flemming, Wheeler	55	0.230	M, 1B				
Godwin, Bill	66	0.303	3B, OF, C				
Goodwin, Fred	51	0.272					
Grinnells, Harold	13	0.357	P	1	6	6.35	
Grizzell, Bob	14	0.231	OF				
Hill, George	12	0.053	P				
Hughes, Jim	13	0.219	P	4	1	5.61	
Jackson, Claude	19	0.190	P	1	9	6.55	
Johns, Jim	29	0.237	2B				
Julian, Al	52	0.272	OF				
Julian, Bob	61	0.238	SS				
Lehner, Collis	25	0.206	P	4	9	6.03	Valley
Moss, Joe	41	0.241	OF				

Name	G	BA	POS	W	L	ERA	APF
Murphy, Bob	41	0.331	OF				
Nelson, Jim	38	0.225	C				
Rigdon, Bill	14	0.306					
Robison, Vince	12	0.231	OF				
Satterfield, Arnold	27	0.238	C				
Steadman, Bob	17	0.222	P	3	3	3.75	
Zaden, Lou	13	0.220	OF				

Rome, Georgia
Team Operated by Rome Baseball Club
Team President: F.G. "Jack" Cole
Secretary-Treasurer: Mrs. F.G. Cole
Manager(s): Leon Culberson
Games played at Cole Stadium
Season attendance: 41,000

Rome Red Sox Team Roster

NAME	G	BA	POS	W	L	ERA	APF
Cash, Jack	111	0.306	2B				
Cole, Jack	99	0.307	OF				
Cudemo, Mike	105	0.277	C				
Culberson, Leon	103	0.319	M, 3B, SS, OF				
Dacus, Joe	87	0.248	SS, OF, P	5	3	3.63	
Goeken, Don	68	0.284	OF, C				
Heyer, Dick	12	0.200	P				Valley
Hutchins, Bob	10	0.125	P				
Langston, Jim	16	0.324	P	4	6	6.51	
LaPadula, Nick	35	0.347	OF				
McManus, Joe	41	0.286	P	16	5	5.77	
Meadows, John	21	0.235	P	8	4	4.42	
O'Barr, Tom	48	0.187	P	13	15	3.89	
Rucker, Bob	114	0.331	3B, OF				
Schubele, Bruce	46	0.228	SS				
Shoemake, Claude	110	0.373	1B, OF				
Stowe, John	104	0.369	1B				
Wood, Gordon	48	0.158	P	6	14	4.87	

Valley (Lanett), Alabama
Team Operated by Valley Baseball Club, Inc.
Team President: Robert L. Rearden
Vice Presidents: G.E. "Cheese" Goggans, Fob James
Secretary-Treasurer: Joseph Nickols
General Manager: Ernest L. Jenkins
Manager(s): Gabby Grant
Games played at Jennings Field
Season attendance: 37,515

Valley Rebels Team Roster

NAME	G	BA	POS	W	L	ERA	APF
Allen, Johnny	62	0.286	2B, 3B, OF				Alex City
Barath, Dave	47	0.308	OF				
Black, Gene	38	0.167	P	10	11	4.64	
DiGirolomo, Rocco	17	0.294	C				
Dobbins, Mayes	37	0.250	2B				Opelika
Fappiano, Gene	106	0.286	2B				
Frazier, Dan	21	0.273	OF				
Goodwin, Hoyt	63	0.264	OF				
Grant, Gabby	108	0.318	M, C				
Heyer, Dick	12	0.200	P				Rome
Howe, Bob	16	0.179	P	7	3	3.28	
Hughes, George	115	0.359	OF				
Lazicky, Dick	31	0.225	P	10	5	3.46	
Lehner, Collis	25	0.206	P	4	9	6.03	Opelika
Maricich, Eli	111	0.284	SS				
Morgan, Malvern	116	0.319	1B, 3B				
Pennington, Joe	37	0.203	P	13	9	2.45	
Puffer, Gerald	88	0.275	3B, P	3	5	4.50	
Rogers, Ernest	36	0.143	P	11	7	4.30	
Roth, Jac	16	0.304	2B				
Sanchez, Armando	29	0.260	C				Alex City
Scott, Vic	13	0.303	P	5	2	5.30	
Thompson, Jim	115	0.271	OF				
White, Curtis	11	0.250	P	1	6	7.83	Alex City

1951 Georgia-Alabama League Records
Batting

<u>Highest Batting Average (minimum 100 at bats)</u>
1. Joe Campbell – Griffin .379
2. Claude Shoemake – Rome .373
3. Carl Cooper – LaGrange .369
   John Stowe – Rome .369
5. George Hughes – Valley .359

<u>Most Hits</u>
1. Claude Shoemake – Rome 171
2. George Hughes – Valley 168
3. John Stowe – Rome 166
4. Bob Adams – LaGrange 158
5. Bob Rucker – Rome 156

<u>Most Runs</u>
1. Fred Campbell – Griffin 111
2. George Hughes – Valley 110
3. Dan Murphy – LaGrange 105
4. Lou Salerno – Griffin 104
5. Jack Cash – Rome 103
   Eli Maricich – Valley 103

<u>Most Total Bases</u>
1. Claude Shoemake – Rome 290
2. Jack Bearden – Griffin 233
3. John Stowe – Rome 231
4. Bob Rucker – Rome 229
5. George Hughes – Valley 223

<u>Most Doubles</u>
1. John Stowe – Rome 39
2. Claude Shoemake – Rome 37
3. Malvern Morgan – Valley 32
4. Gabby Grant – Valley 30
5. Bob Rucker – Rome 28
   Bob Adams – LaGrange 28

<u>Most Triples</u>
1. George Hughes – Valley 14
2. Fred Campbell – Griffin 10
   Lou Salerno – Griffin 10
4. Bob Adams – LaGrange 7
5. *five players tied with 6

<u>Most Home Runs</u>
1. Claude Shoemake – Rome 26
2. Jack Bearden – Griffin 19
3. Carl Cooper – LaGrange 17
4. Jim Prappas – LaGrange 16
5. Eli Maricich – Valley 14
   Leon Culberson – Rome 14

<u>Most Extra Base Hits</u>
1. Claude Shoemake – Rome 65
2. Jack Bearden – Griffin 51
3. John Stowe – Rome 49
4. Eli Maricich – Valley 45
5. Bob Rucker – Rome 44

<u>Most Runs Batted In</u>
1. Claude Shoemake – Rome 135
2. Jack Bearden – Griffin 127

3. Bob Adams – LaGrange 106
4. Malvern Morgan – Valley 105
5. Bob Rucker – Rome 100

Most Stolen Bases
1. Eli Maricich – Valley 41
2. Fred Campbell – Griffin 28
3. Bob Adams – LaGrange 25
4. Lou Sanders – Griffin 19
5. Bob Julian – Opelika 18

Fielding
Most Put-Outs
1. Nick Maruschak 1B – Griffin 988
2. Dan Murphy 1B – LaGrange 950
3. John Stowe 1B – Rome 846
4. Bill Brown 1B - Alexander City 723
5. Malvern Morgan 1B, 3B – Valley 647

Most Assists
1. Eli Maricich SS – Valley 337
2. Fred Campbell SS – Griffin 321
3. Bob Adams 2B, 3B, SS – LaGrange 315
4. Jack Cash 2B – Rome 274
5. Gene Fappiano 2B – Valley 272

Most Errors
1. Eli Maricich SS – Valley 47
   Bob Adams 2B, 3B, SS – LaGrange 47
3. Joe Dacus 2B – Rome 44
4. Gene Fappiano 2B – Valley 42
5. Fred Campbell SS – Griffin 40

Pitching
Most Wins
1. Marv Chappell – LaGrange 21
2. Charles Harrison – LaGrange 19
3. Joe McManus – Rome 16
4. Bill Stolte – Griffin 14
5. Tom O'Barr – Rome 13
   Joe Pennington – Valley 13
   Bill Padgett – Griffin 13

Most Losses
1. Tom O'Barr – Rome 15
2. Gordon Wood – Rome 14
3. Raul Villamea - Alexander City 12
   Clem Kelecava – Griffin 12
5. Bill Stolte – Griffin 11
   Frank Catterton – Griffin 11
   Gene Black – Valley 11

Highest Winning Percentage (10 game minimum)
1. Charles Harrison – LaGrange .864
2. Jim Hughes – Opelika .800
3. Joe McManus – Rome .762
4. Marv Chappell – LaGrange .724
5. Vic Scott – Valley .714

Lowest Earned Run Average (100 inning minimum)
1. Joe Pennington – Valley 2.45
2. Marv Chappell – LaGrange 2.55
3. Bob Howe – Valley 3.28
4. Dick Lazicky – Valley 3.46
5. Charles Harrison – LaGrange 3.73

Most Strikeouts
1. Marv Chappell – LaGrange 120
2. Bill Stolte – Griffin 115
3. Charles Harrison – LaGrange 114

4. Tom O'Barr – Rome 107
   Clem Kelecava – Griffin 107

Most Bases on Balls
1. Tom O'Barr – Rome 132
2. Marv Chappell – LaGrange 128
   Clem Kelecava – Griffin 128
4. Bill Padgett – Griffin 110
5. Charles Harrison – LaGrange 101

Most Hits Allowed
1. Bill Stolte – Griffin 273
2. Tom O'Barr – Rome 232
3. Marv Chappell – LaGrange 225
4. Gene Black – Valley 224
5. Bill Padgett – Griffin 222
   Raul Villamea - Alexander City 222

Most Innings Pitched
1. Marv Chappell – LaGrange 251
2. Bill Stolte – Griffin 226
3. Tom O'Barr – Rome 208
4. Bill Padgett – Griffin 199
5. Gene Black – Valley 194

1951 Georgia-Alabama League All-Star Team
1B John Stowe – Rome
2B Joe Campbell – Griffin
3B Bill Godwin – Opelika
SS Fred Campbell – Griffin
OF Claude Shoemake – Rome
OF George Hughes – Valley
OF Jack Bearden – Griffin
C Roy Drews – Griffin
P Charles Harrison – LaGrange
P Marv Chappell – LaGrange
P Joe McManus – Rome
P Dick Lazicky – Valley

1951

Georgia-Florida League

League Office: Leslie, Georgia
League President: W.T. Anderson
League Vice President: C.L. Thompson
Secretary: James R. Blair
Salary Limit: $2,600 per month.
Player Rule: Each club was allowed a roster of seventeen players, not more than four veterans, not more than eight limited service, and not less than five rookies.
Umpires: Pat Fiore, Gerald J. Morissey, Harvey D. Odom, Frank Augugliaro, Louis Chivari, John Telford, Earl V. Upton, Earl Wheeler, and Michael R. Ganakas.

Georgia-Florida League Final Standings

Team	W	L	Pct	GB	Affiliate
Valdosta Dodgers	81	45	.643	----	BRK-NL
Albany Cardinals	76	50	.603	5.0	STL-NL
Waycross Bears	70	55	.560	10.5	Unaffiliated
Tifton Blue Sox	62	63	.496	18.5	Unaffiliated
Brunswick Pirates	60	66	.476	21.0	PIT-NL
Americus Rebels	55	70	.440	25.5	Unaffiliated
Moultrie To-baks	52	74	.413	29.0	Unaffiliated
Cordele A's	46	79	.368	34.5	PHI-AL

1951 Georgia-Florida League Map

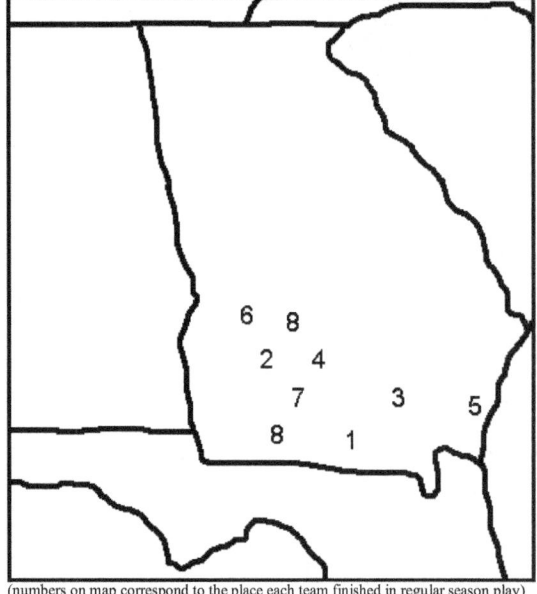

(numbers on map correspond to the place each team finished in regular season play)

After five years and no changes in league cities, the Georgia-Florida league not only had two changes in the lineup but also lost the only Florida city in the loop. Tallahassee and Thomasville dropped out of the league during the off-season, and Brunswick and Tifton were added to fill the empty spots. Hence forth, the Georgia-Florida League did not have any Florida teams playing baseball.

This was the season for no-hitters in the league, as three were pitched two being against Americus. The first came from the arm of Tifton's Roberto Betancourt on May 26 when he defeated Americus 4 to 1. Taylor Phillips of Waycross hurled the season's second no-hitter routing Moultrie 11 to 0 on May 26. And the third no-hitter of the year occurred on August 12 when Valdosta pitcher Don Shaffer shutout Americus 1 to 0 in a shortened, six-inning game.

The Dodgers of Valdosta won the regular season pennant with the best record. Albany came in second, Waycross third, and Tifton finished the season in fourth place rounding out the clubs advancing to the playoffs. Tifton, who finished 18 and a half games behind Valdosta, upset the Dodgers in the first round of playoff action four games to one. Waycross also pulled an upset in round one defeating Albany in four straight games. Waycross earned the league title by defeating Tifton four games to one in the circuit championship series.

Albany, Georgia

Team Operated by Albany Baseball Club, Inc.
Team President: Morton M. Wiggins
Vice Presidents: Fred M. Saigh, Jr., William Walsingham, Jr.
Secretary: Edward W. Roth
Treasurer: Fred M. Saigh, Jr.
Business Manager: Richard A. Roth
Manager(s): Chief Bender
Games played at Cardinal Field
Season attendance: 45,694
Major League Affiliate: New York Yankees – American League.

Albany Cardinals Team Roster

NAME	G	BA	POS	W	L	ERA	APF
Ban, Dick	34	0.213	P	12	3	3.17	
Bender, Chief	27	0.227	M, P	10	4	2.51	
Bridges, Frank	70	0.255	OF				Brunswick
Brown, Don	101	0.223	3B				
Clark, Phil	38	0.181	P	18	7	2.96	
Daley, Gil	110	0.323	OF				
DeFore, Ed	34	0.221	OF				
Eames, Paul	37	0.231	C				
Giavedoni, Nilo	14	0.200					
Heins, Bob	17	0.152	P	4	5	3.97	
Janelle, Ray	15	0.065	P	6	6	4.55	
Loehr, Dave	51	0.287	C				
Moore, Lloyd	27	0.235	P	9	5	3.92	
Murphy, Bill	126	0.301	1B				
Rikard, Denver	125	0.327	OF				
Smith, George	125	0.256	3B, OF				
Troxell, Clair	85	0.233	C				
Tschannen, Ron	124	0.248	SS				
Watts, Don	13	0.167	P				
Weed, Clarence	32	0.277	P	11	6	3.75	
Yance, Jim	14	0.188	P	3	0	5.55	
Zangari, Frank	124	0.189	2B				

Americus, Georgia

Team Operated by Americus Professional Baseball Club
General Manager: James J. Francoline
Business Manager: Stephan G. Gross
Manager(s): Mike Milosevich
Games played at Community Center Ballpark
Season attendance: 38,047

Americus Rebels Team Roster

NAME	G	BA	POS	W	L	ERA	APF
Ash, George	26	0.192	P	0	8	4.98	
Baktis, Simon	69	0.265	C				
Bernier, Bill	26	0.085	P	9	10	2.76	
Braganca, Joe	52	0.179					

Georgia Class-D Minor League Baseball Encyclopedia

NAME	G	BA	POS	W	L	ERA	APF
Darr, Don	27	0.213	P	11	5	3.49	
Dye, Ben	107	0.238	SS, OF, C				
Fasano, Benny	60	0.214	OF, P	13	4	3.83	
Francoline, Jim	108	0.255					
Genevrino, Mike	95	0.268	1B				Tifton
George, Greek	37	0.267	1B				Tifton
Gerace, John	31	0.141	P	11	7	3.23	
Heflin, Phil	122	0.224	1B				Tifton
Hession, Bill	20	0.257	OF				
Kloss, Walt	37	0.223	3B, SS				
Lagan, John	13	0.156	P	3	4	3.69	
Liptak, Bill	71	0.269					
Markle, Lou	22	0.258	OF				
Milosevich, Mike	105	0.227	M, 2B, SS				
Musumeci, John	76	0.305	3B				
Mytrysak, John	8		P	1	7	5.33	
Passarella, Bob	120	0.221	3B, SS				Cordele
Quartuci, Ray	34	0.114	2B				
Sellars, A.D.	26	0.056	P	2	11	5.93	
Stevens, Walt	20	0.152	P	2	5	5.80	
Wilcox, Stan	35	0.238	OF				
Yudin, Bob	14	0.045	OF				
Zimmerman, Glenn	76	0.299	2B				

Brunswick, Georgia
Team Operated by Brunswick Pirates, Inc.
Team President: Edo Miller
Vice Presidents: Branch Rickey, Jr., Harold G. Roettger
Secretary: Walter Bunt
Treasurer: Jim Herron
Business Manager: Harold Hays
Manager(s): Mickey O'Neil
Games played at Lanier Field
Season attendance: 46,522
Major League Affiliate: Pittsburgh Pirates – National League.

Brunswick Pirates Team Roster

NAME	G	BA	POS	W	L	ERA	APF
Beran, Lee	46	0.159	P	9	5	5.27	
Bolam, Bob	76	0.270	2B, OF				
Bonaparte, Bob	126	0.302	1B, OF				
Bridges, Frank	70	0.255	OF				Albany
Butchko, Steve	10	0.214					
Carlson, Bob	35	0.207	SS				
Ceran, ---	32		P				
Chergey, Paul	20	0.133	P	4	8	4.55	
Clark, Lou	24	0.148	P	3	1	4.08	
Cline, Leonard	50	0.211	SS				
Cochran, Bill	11	0.190	P	2	5	3.99	
Corso, Gene	23	0.238	OF				
Cunningham, Ed	18	0.137	OF				
Dillon, Charles	12	0.409					
Felaz, John	14	0.069					
Hayes, Ed	51	0.230	C				
Herald, Ray	25	0.275	OF				
Jacob, Vince	57	0.228	C				
Jacobs, Will	20	0.118	P	9	8	2.57	
Jacobsen, Ed	110	0.261	OF				
Lande, Gil	27	0.212	OF				
Lasry, Jack	15	0.188	C				
Lipstas, Bob	24	0.111	OF				
Martin, Fred	60	0.293	P	13	5	3.07	
McNally, Don	95	0.267	2B, SS				
O'Neil, Mickey			M				
Perez, Tom	39	0.209	1B				
Sallis, Ed	51	0.191	C				
Slivocka, Ray	20	0.111	P	4	3	5.07	
Squillace, John	47	0.191	2B				
Warren, Jeff	20	0.074	P	4	7	5.02	
Waugh, Jim	18	0.100	P	10	8	3.40	
Wilcox, Ralph	126	0.250	3B				
Winters, Charles	11	0.125	P	0	7	7.31	

Cordele, Georgia
Team Operated by Cordele Amusement Company, Inc.
Team President: Connie Mack
Vice Presidents: Arthur Ehlers, Roy Mack, Earle Mack
Secretary: Earle Mack
Business Manager: Carl M. Martin
Manager(s): Jimmie DeShong, Ducky Detweiler
Games played at City Park
Season attendance: 25,857
Major League Affiliate: Philadelphia Athletics – American League.

Cordele A's Team Roster

NAME	G	BA	POS	W	L	ERA	APF
Arterburn, Harry	109	0.256	1B				
Betcher, George	59	0.322	3B				
Bettleyon, Bob	108	0.218	1B, 2B, 3B				
Comegys, Clarence	25	0.128	P	4	3	4.68	
Costello, Tom	28	0.132					
Daly, Hugh	42	0.190	C				
Day, Don	120	0.297	OF				
DeShong, Jimmie			M				
Detweiler, Ducky	38	0.381	M, 2B				
DiNecci, Al	42	0.215	2B				
Evernham, George	19	0.091	C				
Hamlin, Bill	18	0.100	P	2	6	5.12	
Itkin, Al	14	0.194	P	6	6	3.75	
Kallas, Harry	35	0.189	SS				
Merget, John	24	0.217	P	6	9	4.01	
Molokie, Leon	87	0.314	2B, OF				
Passarella, Bob	120	0.221	3B, SS				Americus
Ramsey, Paul	11	0.185	C				
Scotese, Bob	56	0.174	OF				
Shimko, Bob	37	0.180	P	2	11	5.10	
Sides, Bill	125	0.298	OF				
Steave, John	95	0.236	C				
Vereault, George	37	0.197	P	7	14	3.92	
Wallace, Bill	34	0.127	P	16	14	4.44	
Wiegand, Don	29	0.186	2B				

Moultrie, Georgia
Team Operated by Moultrie Baseball Club
Owner: Dr. A.G. Funderburk
Director: Thomas V. Lassiter
Business Manager: C.W. Vandiver
Manager(s): Jim Poole
Games played at Municipal Park
Season attendance: 40,910

Moultrie To-baks Team Roster

NAME	G	BA	POS	W	L	ERA	APF
Campbell, Cliff	15	0.107	P	4	4	5.09	
Cavallaro, Fred	18	0.260	OF				
Cowan, Jim	58	0.187	C				
Davis, Wayne	31	0.214	OF				Waycross
Davis, Wendell	119	0.343	1B, OF				
Del Piano, Mike	29	0.226	P	6	6	4.34	
Dove, Pat	34	0.296	C				
Eury, Glenn	111	2.810	OF				
Franson, Carl	88	0.294	3B				
Frazier, Bill	49	0.222	OF, P	11	9	3.86	
Gendreau, Ron	123	0.244	SS				
Green, Claude	12	0.306	1B				
Hatcher, Marv	60	0.180	P	14	9	2.71	
Helbig, Anthony	104	0.282	2B				

Georgia Class-D Minor League Baseball Encyclopedia

NAME	G	BA	POS	W	L	ERA	APF
Herbik, John	34	0.151	P	8	11	4.32	
Howe, F.E.	17	0.160	3B				
Jones, Bill	42	0.291	OF, P	2	11	6.23	
Jones, Bill	22	0.053	3B				
Keen, Elmer	12	0.100	P				
Poole, Jim			M				
Reichert, Stan	24	0.203	2B				
Rhyne, Ken	48	0.249	1B				
Smith, Frank	29	0.180	P	3	12	4.08	
Starrette, George	11	0.083	P				
Still, Jim	28	0.252	OF				
Weaver, Fred	13	0.154					
Wood, Bill	49	0.333	OF				
Wrenn, Milt	104	0.223	OF, C				Tifton

Tifton, Georgia
Team Operated by Tifton Baseball Club, Inc.
Team President: R.B. Hall
Vice President: H.V. Hall
Secretary-Treasurer: Eugene Slack
Manager(s): Fred Tschudin
Games played at Eve Park
Season attendance: 48,472

Tifton Blue Sox Team Roster

NAME	G	BA	POS	W	L	ERA	APF
Baldwin, Lamar	64	0.276	OF, C				
Betancourt, Roberto	74	0.211	3B, P	18	14	2.87	
Carter, Emil	123	0.231	2B				
Christie, Frank	9		P	3	5	3.40	
Dickerman, Ed	108	0.302	3B, SS				
Dodgin, Jim	108	0.328	OF				
Freeman, Jim	11	0.167	P				
Genevrino, Mike	95	0.268	1B				Americus
George, Greek	37	0.267	1B				Americus
Glover, Charles	32	0.264	OF				
Heflin, Phil	122	0.224	1B				Americus
Jacobs, Ottis	47	0.136	P	20	12	3.12	
Jiminez, Dan	13	0.050					
Johnson, Lee	22	0.200					
Lastres, Danilo	47	0.233	SS				
Mayorquinn, Ernesto	16	0.143	P	6	5	6.04	
Quattrini, Rino	28		P	8	13	4.35	
Rotondi, Lou	93	0.293	3B, SS, OF				
Ryan, Fred	36	0.252	SS				
Tidwell, John	98	0.321	OF				
Tschudin, Fred	122	0.300	M, C, P	4	1	2.65	
Vastano, Pat	20	0.243	SS				
Wrenn, Milt	104	0.223	OF, C				Moultrie

Valdosta, Georgia
Team Operated by Valdosta Dodgers Baseball Club, Inc.
Team President: D.S. Wainer
Vice President: Fresco Thompson
Secretary: Matthew Burns
Treasurer: William Gibson
Business Manager: Warren S. Keyes
Manager(s): Stan Wasiak
Games played at Pendleton Park
Season attendance: 51,546
Major League Affiliate: Brooklyn Dodgers – National League.

Valdosta Dodgers Team Roster

NAME	G	BA	POS	W	L	ERA	APF
Alberts, Henry	80	0.231	C				
Barbieri, Fernando	23	0.242	2B				
Cook, Don	17	0.206	P	6	2	3.70	
Crumley, John	119	0.270					
Dziedzic, Walt	12	0.172					
Gates, ---	8		P	4	2	2.52	
Geary, Henry	124	0.268	OF				
Gergely, Bill	125	0.292	3B, OF				
Giordano, Al	50	0.245	C				
Gray, Dick	110	0.302	3B				
Greener, Andrew	14	0.061	OF				
Harris, Bill	40	0.284	P	18	9	2.19	
Hoffman, Bob	25	0.160	P	17	4	2.38	
Kendall, George	120	0.325	1B, OF				
Klingert, John	20	0.267	1B				
Large, George	13	0.222	SS				
Manfredi, Ralph	113	0.279					
Sanchez, Armando	10	0.100					
Shaffer, Don	31	0.279	P	12	6	2.77	
Siemasz, Nick	13	0.368	OF				
Strom, Ken	13	0.200	P	7	2	2.87	
Wasiak, Stan	107	0.320	M, 2B				
White, Ed	33	0.020	P	10	8	3.99	

Waycross, Georgia
Team Operated by Waycross Baseball Association, Inc.
Team President: Erin W. Johnson
Vice Presidents: William Rivenbark, O.E. Edenfield
Secretary-Treasurer: B.M. "Buck" Walker
Director: Herbert Bradshaw
General Manager: Harry Lee, Jr.
Manager(s): Papa Williams
Games played at Memorial Stadium
Season attendance: 54,448

Waycross Bears Team Roster

NAME	G	BA	POS	W	L	ERA	APF
Beaird, Dick	21	0.183	OF				
Bethea, George	19	0.111	P	5	5	4.03	
Bledsoe, Charles	125	0.261	C				
Bremer, Walt	44	0.313	3B				
Brinson, Luther	114	0.265	3B, SS, OF				
Caro, Jack	115	0.298	SS				
Cloude, Bill	30	0.295	OF				
Davis, Wayne	31	0.214	OF				Moultrie
Dembek, Joe	66	0.236	OF				
DiGirolomo, Al	22	0.269	3B				
Ellis, Roy	14	0.000	P	1	6	4.98	
Hall, Bob	40	0.224	OF				
Herrington, George	11	0.130	OF				
Meador, Bob	68	0.279	OF				
Miller, Dick	16	0.136	P	2	3	4.98	
Munroe, Ken	25	0.233	P	6	4	2.69	
Pacanowski, Art	12	0.250					
Parker, Ray	31	0.269	OF				
Phillips, Taylor	32	0.094	P	10	8	4.26	
Pizzitola, Vince	34	0.239	OF				
Raulerson, Harry	56	0.329	P	22	10	1.99	
Reeves, Herb	28	0.145	P	13	7	3.79	
Rogers, Francis	23	0.218	P				
Sappenfield, Roger	16	0.147	P	7	6	2.21	
Simmons, Roy	28	0.168	3B				
Webb, Charles	123	0.283	2B				
Williams, Papa	120	0.295	M, 1B				

1951 Georgia-Florida League Records
Batting

Highest Batting Average (minimum 100 at bats)
1. Ducky Detweiler – Cordele .381
2. Wendell Davis – Moultrie .343
3. Bill Wood – Moultrie .333
4. Harry Raulerson – Waycross .329

Georgia Class-D Minor League Baseball Encyclopedia

5. Jim Dodgin – Tifton .328

Most Hits
1. Wendell Davis – Moultrie 160
2. Denver Rikard – Albany 150
   George Kendall – Valdosta 150
   Bob Bonaparte – Brunswick 150
5. Gil Daley – Albany 141
   Bill Murphy – Albany 141

Most Runs
1. Dick Gray – Valdosta 118
2. Henry Geary – Valdosta 103
3. Gil Daley – Albany 100
4. Denver Rikard – Albany 98
5. Bill Murphy – Albany 95

Most Total Bases
1. Wendell Davis – Moultrie 268
2. Denver Rikard – Albany 238
3. Bob Bonaparte – Brunswick 237
4. Glenn Eury – Moultrie 225
5. George Kendall – Valdosta 218

Most Doubles
1. John Tidwell – Tifton 34
2. Wendell Davis – Moultrie 30
3. Denver Rikard – Albany 29
4. Ed Dickerman – Tifton 28
   Fred Tschudin – Tifton 28

Most Triples
1. George Kendall – Valdosta 14
2. Dick Gray – Valdosta 12
3. Denver Rikard – Albany 10
4. *five players tied with 9

Most Home Runs
1. Glenn Eury – Moultrie 29
2. Wendell Davis – Moultrie 22
3. Bob Bonaparte – Brunswick 16
4. Carl Franson – Moultrie 15
5. Denver Rikard – Albany 13

Most Extra Base Hits
1. Wendell Davis – Moultrie 58
2. Denver Rikard – Albany 52
3. Glenn Eury – Moultrie 49
4. Bob Bonaparte – Brunswick 48
5. Gil Daley – Albany 44
   John Tidwell – Tifton 44
   George Kendall – Valdosta 44

Most Runs Batted In
1. Bill Murphy – Albany 100
2. Wendell Davis – Moultrie 96
   Denver Rikard – Albany 96
4. John Tidwell – Tifton 92
5. Jim Francoline – Americus 90

Most Stolen Bases
1. Bob Meador – Waycross 39
2. Gil Daley – Albany 32
3. Dick Gray – Valdosta 31
4. Bob Bonaparte – Brunswick 27
   Glenn Zimmerman – Americus 27

Fielding
Most Put-Outs
1. Bill Murphy 1B – Albany 1,138
2. Phil Heflin 1B – Tift/Amer 1,122
3. Papa Williams 1B – Waycross 1,072
4. Mike Genevrino 1B – Tift/Amer 883
5. George Kendall 1B, OF – Valdosta 875

Most Assists
1. Ron Gendreau SS – Moultrie 434
2. Ron Tschannen SS – Albany 432
3. Frank Zangari 2B – Albany 376
4. Jack Caro SS – Waycross 361
5. Mike Milosevich 2B, SS – Americus 345

Most Errors
1. Ron Gendreau SS – Moultrie 71
2. Ron Tschannen SS – Albany 59
   Bob Passarella 3B, SS – Cord/Amer 59
4. Jack Caro SS – Waycross 55
5. Don Brown 3B – Albany 52

Pitching
Most Wins
1. Harry Raulerson – Waycross 22
2. Ottis Jacobs – Tifton 20
3. Roberto Betancourt – Tifton 18
   Phil Clark – Albany 18
   Bill Harris – Valdosta 18

Most Losses
1. Roberto Betancourt – Tifton 14
   Bill Wallace – Cordele 14
   George Vereault – Cordele 14
4. Rino Quattrini – Tifton 13
5. Ottis Jacobs – Tifton 12
   Frank Smith – Moultrie 12

Highest Winning Percentage (10 game minimum)
1. Bob Hoffman – Valdosta .810
2. Dick Ban – Albany .800
3. Ken Strom – Valdosta .778
4. Benny Fasano – Americus .765
5. Don Cook – Valdosta .750

Lowest Earned Run Average (100 inning minimum)
1. Harry Raulerson – Waycross 1.99
2. Bill Harris – Valdosta 2.19
3. Roger Sappenfield – Waycross 2.21
4. Bob Hoffman – Valdosta 2.38
5. Chief Bender – Albany 2.51

Most Strikeouts
1. Roberto Betancourt – Tifton 201
2. Ottis Jacobs – Tifton 190
3. Bill Harris – Valdosta 189
4. Harry Raulerson – Waycross 165
5. Roger Sappenfield – Waycross 143

Most Bases on Balls
1. Roberto Betancourt – Tifton 162
   Taylor Phillips – Waycross 162
3. Ed White – Valdosta 134
4. Ottis Jacobs – Tifton 128
5. Lee Beran – Brunswick 126

Most Hits Allowed
1. Bill Wallace – Cordele 258
2. George Vereault – Cordele 249
3. Harry Raulerson – Waycross 243

4. Marv Hatcher – Moultrie — 235
5. Ottis Jacobs – Tifton — 217

Most Innings Pitched
1. Harry Raulerson – Waycross — 290
2. Roberto Betancourt – Tifton — 279
3. Marv Hatcher – Moultrie — 256
4. Ottis Jacobs – Tifton — 251
5. Bill Wallace – Cordele — 223

1951 Georgia-Florida League All-Star Team
1B George Kendall – Valdosta
2B Charles Webb – Waycross
3B Dick Gray – Valdosta
SS Jack Caro – Waycross
OF John Tidwell – Tifton
OF Gil Daley – Albany
OF Denver Rikard – Albany
OF Glenn Eury – Moultrie
C Charles Bledsoe – Waycross
C Al Giordano – Valdosta
P Roberto Betancourt – Tifton
P Harry Raulerson – Waycross
P Phil Clark – Albany
P Ottis Jacobs – Tifton
P Bill Harris – Valdosta
P Bob Hoffman – Valdosta
M Stan Wasiak – Valdosta

1951

Georgia State League

League Office: Cochran, Georgia
League President: J.T. Morris
League Vice President: J.Z. Hargrove
Salary Limit: $2,600 per month.
Player Rule: Each club was allowed a roster of seventeen players, not more than four veterans, not more than nine limited service, and not less than four rookies. Player limit effective twenty days after the opening of the season and twenty days before the close of the season.
Umpires: Joseph T. Braica, Richard F. Leonard, Nicholas J. Mangieri, James M. Wells, Marvin E. Whitley, and Stephen Summerhill.

Georgia State League Final Standings

Team	W	L	Pct	GB	Affiliate
Jesup Bees	86	43	.667	----	Unaffiliated
Dublin Green Sox	78	50	.609	7.5	Unaffiliated
Eastman Dodgers	76	54	.585	10.5	Unaffiliated
Douglas Trojans	62	68	.477	24.5	Unaffiliated
Hazlehurst-Baxley Red Sox	52	77	.403	34.0	Unaffiliated
Fitzgerald Pioneers	34	96	.262	52.5	Unaffiliated

1951 Georgia State League Map

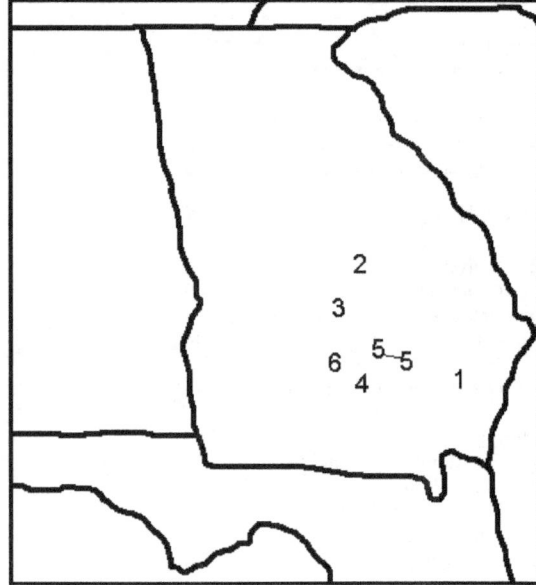

(numbers on map correspond to the place each team finished in regular season play)

No new clubs were added to the Georgia State League, but two of the existing clubs decided to call it quits. Tifton dropped out as did the combined team from Vidalia and Lyons turning the league into a six-team circuit.

Jesup, in only its second year of operation in the league, had two players to set all-time single season league records during the season. Alvin Jenkins set the record for the most hits with 207, and pitcher Don Rudolph set the mark for the most wins with 28.

Georgia Class-D Minor League Baseball Encyclopedia

Jesup also finished the season at the top of the standings garnering the regular season pennant. Dublin, Eastman, and Douglas rounded out the top four teams who would advance to the post-season playoffs. The first round series', which had previously been best of five games series, were now best of seven games series'. Both first round sets were upsets as Eastman defeated Dublin four games to two, and Douglas beat Jesup in four straight. In a hard fought championship series that needed all seven games to decide a winner, Douglas out lasted Eastman four games to three.

Douglas, Georgia
Team Operated by Douglas Trojans, Inc.
Team President: H.B. Chitty
Vice Presidents: Charles Anderson, John I. "Si" Slocumb, Jr.
Secretary-Treasurer: Robert S. Pattillo
General Manager: Witt O. "Lefty" Guise
Manager(s): Lefty Guise
Games played at Municipal Park
Season attendance: 21,839

Douglas Trojans Team Roster

NAME	G	BA	POS	W	L	ERA	APF
Baldwin, Lamar	10	0.333					
Bastion, Marv	26	0.200	P	6	9	3.51	
Beauchamp, Walt	37	0.257	2B				
Cain, Charles	19	0.132	P	4	8	6.17	
Catalano, Pete	125	0.273	OF				
Cathey, John	19	0.163	P	7	4	5.57	
Coleman, Malcolm	54	0.220	2B, 3B				Fitzgerald
Davis, Thurman	111	0.235	3B, SS				Dub - Fit
Davis, Van	129	0.333	1B				
Easterling, Gene	34	0.169	P	5	13	4.75	
Graham, Tom	13	0.000	P				
Guise, Lefty	23	0.270	M, P	14	6	2.16	
Johnson, Lee	11	0.175	SS				Dublin
Jones, Casey	28	0.134	P	10	12	4.96	
Lee, Fred	44	0.270	OF				Eastman
Monroe, Ray	120	0.207	3B				
Morelli, Jim	90	0.356	OF				
Nelson, Charles	17	0.077	P	3	7	2.56	
Perada, Orestes	80	0.220	2B				
Rey, Emil	86	0.228	SS				
Sanchez, Armando	27	0.282	OF, C				
Sassano, Bob	14	0.178	OF				
Schmidt, Kermit	63	0.253	3B, OF, P	10	6	3.36	
Swain, Kurtis	125	0.279	C				
Sweat, LeRoy	16	0.300					Haz-Bax
Yow, Forrest	124	0.292	OF				

Dublin, Georgia
Team Operated by Dublin Baseball Club, Inc.
Team President: W.H. Lovett
Vice Presidents: W.E. Lovett, W.W. Brinson
Secretary: Frank Johnson
Manager(s): Bill Kushta, Parnell Ruark
Games played at Lovett Park
Season attendance: 40,166

Dublin Green Sox Team Roster

NAME	G	BA	POS	W	L	ERA	APF
Blanton, Hugh	67	0.216	1B, OF, P	12	10	4.20	
Brennan, Don	83	0.420	2B				
Collins, Jack	28	0.342	3B				
Cook, George	20	0.105	P	10	3	5.24	
Cordero, Manuel	77	0.300	1B				
Crum, McPherson	16	0.171	P	8	5	5.47	
Davis, Thurman	111	0.235	3B, SS				Dou - Fit
Falcigno, Harry	45	0.250	OF				Fitzgerald
Fall, Ralph	127	0.234	SS				Jesup
Galloway, Oliver	125	0.285	C				
Herringdine, Cecil	113	0.267	OF				
Johnson, Lee	11	0.175	SS				Douglas
Johnson, Rudolph	128	0.279	2B, OF				Fitzgerald
Kushta, Bill	118	0.297	M, 2B, 3B, SS, OF, C, P	0	2	6.51	Haz-Bax
Lonzano, Manuel	21	0.233	3B				Fitzgerald
Moore, Jim	128	0.318	1B, OF				Fitzgerald
Oquendo, Noel	44	0.309	P	13	9	3.56	
Ridgeway, Charlie	93	0.315	2B, 3B				Fitzgerald
Rivera, Florencio	26	0.114	P	7	7	4.81	
Ruark, Parnell	126	0.329	M, OF				
Sarmiento, Antonio	30	0.130	P	10	6	4.08	
Sherman, Ed	10	0.182	P	1	7	7.66	Fit - Jes
Tenney, Jim	25	0.091	P	6	9	4.50	Fitzgerald
Tidwell, John	27	0.304	OF				
Villamea, Raul	15	0.227	P	8	2	1.95	
Young, Claude	72	0.382	3B				

Eastman, Georgia
Team Operated by Eastman Dodgers, Inc.
Team President: W.S. Stuckey
Secretary-Treasurer: E.L. Jones
General Manager: W.W. Taylor
Manager(s): Pep Rambert
Games played at Legion Park
Season attendance: 22,736

Eastman Dodgers Team Roster

NAME	G	BA	POS	W	L	ERA	APF
Adcock, Bob	40	0.366	OF				
Beecher, Bob	35	0.220	OF				Haz-Bax
Caldwell, Wilbur	126	0.283	1B, 3B, SS, OF, P	5	3	3.52	
Griggs, Bill	33	0.169	P	13	10	3.44	
Hamilton, Bill	31	0.165	1B				
Harden, Jim	28	0.169	P	15	7	3.02	
Harp, Jim	45	0.268	P	23	12	2.30	
Hoard, Dan	123	0.333	OF				
Johnston, Jim	129	0.258	2B				
Lee, Fred	44	0.270	OF				Douglas
Loudermilk, Joe	94	0.279	SS				
O'Bryant, Oscar	17	0.043	P	1	3	4.73	
Rambert, Pep	103	0.344	M, 1B, OF, P				
Rhodes, Hilman	111	0.247	OF, C				
Ricketson, Don	18	0.188	OF				
Simonian, Joe	65	0.249	OF				
Smith, Jim	115	0.260	3B				
Stinson, Bob	42	0.302	C				
Sullivan, John	30	0.043	P	6	13	6.35	Fitzgerald
Tyler, Jim	22	0.138	P	9	9	3.48	
Wilson, Ed	18	0.360	OF				
Worsham, Ben	8		P	2	3	4.17	
Wright, Dixie	16	0.267	C				

Fitzgerald, Georgia
Team Operated by Pioneer Baseball Club, Inc.
Team President: Homer Waters
Manager(s): John Duncan, Bill McGhee, Charlie Ridgeway, Jim Ruark
Games played at Blue-Gray Park
Season attendance: 26,247

Fitzgerald Pioneers Team Roster

NAME	G	BA	POS	W	L	ERA	APF
Caldwell, Calvin	20	0.265	OF				
Celiberti, Frank	15	0.174	OF				
Claypool, Jim	124	0.318	OF, C				

NAME	G	BA	POS	W	L	ERA	APF
Coleman, Malcolm	54	0.220	2B, 3B				Douglas
Cozens, John	28	0.240	OF				
Cronic, George	21	0.220	P	4	10	6.09	
Davis, Thurman	111	0.235	3B, SS				Dou - Dub
Duncan, John			M				
Falcigno, Harry	45	0.250	OF				Dublin
Hamlin, Nat	20	0.196	P	6	10	4.65	
Jamison, Tom	18	0.129	P	2	4	6.25	
Jiminez, Dan	45	0.149	3B, OF				
Johnson, Rudolph	128	0.279	2B, OF				Dublin
Kinnas, Christ	18	0.167	P	4	5	3.82	
Lonzano, Manuel	21	0.233	3B				Dublin
McGhee, Bill	127	0.322	1B, OF				Haz-Bax
McGhee, Bill			M				
McMahon, Mike	11	0.167	P				
Moore, Jim	128	0.318	1B, OF				Dublin
Mote, John	31	0.102	P	5	12	5.43	
Nichting, Ray	74	0.275	OF				
Procopio, Andrew	13	0.205	SS				
Reichert, Stan	22	0.224	2B				
Ridgeway, Charlie	93	0.315	M, 2B, 3B				Dublin
Ruark, Jim	94	0.301	M, OF, C				Jesup
Ryder, John	34	0.245	OF				
Sbashnig, Pete	88	0.245	1B, P	1	5	9.16	
Sherman, Ed	10	0.182	P	1	7	7.66	Dub - Jes
Sullivan, John	30	0.043	P	6	13	6.35	Eastman
Tenney, Jim	25	0.091	P	6	9	4.50	Dublin
Upton, Lawrence	31	0.245	2B				
Vastano, Pat	<10						
Wade, Loren	17	0.138					
Weaver, Fred	98	0.202	2B, SS				
Williams, Ben	16	0.227	3B				

Hazlehurst-Baxley (Hazlehurst & Baxley), Georgia

Team Operated by Hazlehurst-Baxley Baseball Club, Inc.
Team President: Mack Aaron
Vice President: Dr. C.R. Youmans
Secretary-Treasurer: Kenneth Martin
General Manager: Al Faehr
Manager(s): Al Faehr, Bill Kushta
Games played at Jeff Davis Stadium
Season attendance: 24,120

Hazlehurst-Baxley Red Sox Team Roster

NAME	G	BA	POS	W	L	ERA	APF
Beecher, Bob	35	0.220	OF				Eastman
Berry, Sam	50	0.244	OF				
Brown, ---	9		P	1	2	5.12	
Cannon, Bob	35	0.183	P	13	12	3.95	
Collins, Bill	48	0.242	OF				
DeFore, Ed	27	0.194	OF				
Easterling, Paul	32	0.282	OF				
Faehr, Al			M				
Ferko, Bob	10	0.214					
Fountain, Harvey	17	0.143	P	1	8	7.50	
Fowler, Wheeler	87	0.237	3B				
Gallucci, Frank	65	0.289	SS, OF				
Gilbert, Phil	19	0.222	P	2	6	5.92	
Harper, Luther	15	0.149	2B				
Harris, Bill	126	0.304	OF, C				
Kanavage, Chet	103	0.339	2B				
Kushta, Bill	118	0.297	M, 2B, 3B, SS, OF, C, P	0	2	6.51	Dublin
Love, ---	8		P	0	4	5.43	
Mapes, Carl	58	0.220	OF, P	14	4	2.88	
McGhee, Bill	127	0.322	1B, OF				Fitzgerald
Pappas, Nick	35	0.177	P	12	11	4.58	
Ploszaj, Chester	35	0.191	SS				
Pollard, Gene	55	0.343	1B				

NAME	G	BA	POS	W	L	ERA	APF
Sengstock, Wayne	68	0.282	SS, OF, P				
Sodupe, Francisco	14	0.256					
Sweat, LeRoy	16	0.300					Douglas
Timberlake, Ray	107	0.251	OF				
Vastano, Pat	32	0.235	SS				
Wargo, Clarence	20	0.167	P	0	5	6.40	
Whaley, Walker	18	0.283	P	4	6	5.18	

Jesup, Georgia

Team Operated by Jesup Baseball Club
Team President: Robert L. Harrison
Secretary-Treasurer: R.M. Sanderson
Business Manager: Ben E. Park
Manager(s): Jim Stoyle
Games played at Milikin Park
Season attendance: 23,931

Jesup Bees Team Roster

NAME	G	BA	POS	W	L	ERA	APF
Clements, Mason	111	0.285	3B				
Craven, Bob	41	0.215	P	14	6	2.82	
Daniel, Doug	11	0.216	OF				
Fall, Ralph	127	0.234	SS				Dublin
Hallford, Lew	107	0.268	SS				
Hartley, Jim	34	0.197	P	13	5	2.95	
Hay, Bob	123	0.224	2B				
Jefts, Virgil	120	0.271	C				
Jenkins, L. Alvin	125	0.376	OF				
Nix, Henry	105	0.242	1B, OF				
Parrish, Ron	57	0.136	OF, P	15	11	3.48	
Patterson, Ted	22	0.343	OF				
Rossi, Mike	63	0.258	OF, P	12	9	3.81	
Ruark, Jim	94	0.301	OF, C				Fitzgerald
Rudolph, Don	57	0.196	P	28	8	2.91	
Sherman, Ed	10	0.182	P	1	7	7.66	Dub - Fit
Sosebee, Jim	110	0.347	OF				
Stoyle, Jim	107	0.303	M, 1B				

1951 Georgia State League Records

Batting

Highest Batting Average (minimum 100 at bats)
1. Don Brennan – Dublin .420
2. Claude Young – Dublin .382
3. Alvin Jenkins – Jesup .376
4. Bob Adcock – Eastman .366
5. Jim Morelli – Douglas .356

Most Hits
1. Alvin Jenkins – Jesup 207
2. Dan Hoard – Eastman 170
3. Jim Moore – Fitz/Dubl 163
4. Parnell Ruark – Dublin 161
5. Bill McGhee – Haz-Bax/Fitz 158

Most Runs
1. Alvin Jenkins – Jesup 135
2. Parnell Ruark – Dublin 130
3. Wilbur Caldwell – Eastman 104
4. Van Davis – Douglas 101
5. Rudolph Johnson – Fitz/Dubl 100
   Lew Hallford – Jesup 100

Most Total Bases
1. Parnell Ruark – Dublin 292
2. Alvin Jenkins – Jesup 273
3. Van Davis – Douglas 271
4. Jim Moore – Fitz/Dubl 262
5. Bill McGhee – Haz-Bax/Fitz 245

Georgia Class-D Minor League Baseball Encyclopedia

Most Doubles
1. Jim Claypool – Fitzgerald 37
2. Alvin Jenkins – Jesup 35
3. Dan Hoard – Eastman 34
4. Van Davis – Douglas 30
5. *four players tied with 29

Most Triples
1. Alvin Jenkins – Jesup 11
   Jim Moore – Fitz/Dubl 11
3. Jim Morelli – Douglas 9
4. Jim Claypool – Fitzgerald 8
   Wilbur Caldwell – Eastman 8

Most Home Runs
1. Parnell Ruark – Dublin 32
2. Van Davis – Douglas 29
3. Bill McGhee – Haz-Bax/Fitz 18
4. Jim Moore – Fitz/Dubl 16
5. Claude Young – Dublin 15
   Hilman Rhodes – Eastman 15

Most Extra Base Hits
1. Parnell Ruark – Dublin 64
2. Van Davis – Douglas 61
3. Jim Moore – Fitz/Dubl 56
4. Alvin Jenkins – Jesup 49
5. Bill McGhee – Haz-Bax/Fitz 48
   Jim Claypool – Fitzgerald 48

Most Runs Batted In
1. Parnell Ruark – Dublin 140
2. Van Davis – Douglas 139
3. Jim Stoyle – Jesup 112
4. Jim Moore – Fitz/Dubl 104
5. Jim Sosebee – Jesup 95

Most Stolen Bases
1. Alvin Jenkins – Jesup 41
2. Wilbur Caldwell – Eastman 35
3. Lew Hallford – Jesup 28
4. Charlie Ridgeway – Fitz/Dubl 26
5. Jim Morelli – Douglas 23

Fielding
Most Put-Outs
1. Van Davis 1B – Douglas 1,228
2. Jim Stoyle 1B – Jesup 929
3. Jim Moore 1B, OF, P – Fitz/Dubl 869
4. Pep Rambert 1B, OF, P – Eastman 810
5. Bill McGhee 1B, OF – Haz-Bax/Fitz 736

Most Assists
1. Ralph Fall SS – Jesu/Dubl 392
2. Lew Hallford SS – Jesup 343
3. Bob Hay 2B – Jesup 328
4. Emil Rey SS – Douglas 312
5. Jim Johnston 2B – Eastman 310

Most Errors
1. Thurman Davis 3B, SS – Fitz/Doug/Dubl 54
2. Ralph Fall SS – Jesu/Dubl 53
   Mason Clements 3B – Jesup 53
4. Jim Smith 3B – Eastman 39
5. Ray Monroe 3B – Douglas 37

Pitching
Most Wins
1. Don Rudolph – Jesup 28
2. Jim Harp – Eastman 23
3. Ron Parrish – Jesup 15
   Jim Harden – Eastman 15
5. Carl Mapes - Hazlehurst-Baxley 14
   Bob Craven – Jesup 14
   Lefty Guise – Douglas 14

Most Losses
1. John Sullivan – Fitz/East 13
   Gene Easterling – Douglas 13
3. Jim Harp – Eastman 12
   Bob Cannon - Hazlehurst-Baxley 12
   Casey Jones – Douglas 12
   John Mote – Fitzgerald 12

Highest Winning Percentage (10 game minimum)
1. Raul Villamea – Dublin .800
2. Don Rudolph – Jesup .778
   Carl Mapes - Hazlehurst-Baxley .778
4. George Cook – Dublin .769
5. Jim Hartley – Jesup .722

Lowest Earned Run Average (100 inning minimum)
1. Lefty Guise – Douglas 2.16
2. Jim Harp – Eastman 2.30
3. Bob Craven – Jesup 2.82
4. Carl Mapes - Hazlehurst-Baxley 2.88
5. Don Rudolph – Jesup 2.91

Most Strikeouts
1. Don Rudolph – Jesup 148
2. Bob Craven – Jesup 129
3. Lefty Guise – Douglas 127
4. Gene Easterling – Douglas 116
5. Jim Harp – Eastman 115

Most Bases on Balls
1. John Sullivan – Fitz/East 153
2. Don Rudolph – Jesup 139
   John Mote – Fitzgerald 139
4. Ron Parrish – Jesup 138
5. Gene Easterling – Douglas 123

Most Hits Allowed
1. Jim Harp – Eastman 250
2. Don Rudolph – Jesup 245
3. Carl Mapes - Hazlehurst-Baxley 214
4. Jim Harden – Eastman 203
5. Ron Parrish – Jesup 198

Most Innings Pitched
1. Don Rudolph – Jesup 285
2. Jim Harp – Eastman 254
3. Ron Parrish – Jesup 217
4. Carl Mapes - Hazlehurst-Baxley 206
5. Bob Cannon - Hazlehurst-Baxley 198

1952

Georgia-Florida League

League Office: Leslie, Georgia
League President: W.T. Anderson
League Vice President: C.L. Thompson
Secretary: James R. Blair
Salary Limit: $2,600 per month.
Player Rule: Each club was allowed a roster of sixteen players, not more than four veterans, not more than seven limited service, and not less than five rookies.
Umpires: Earl Wheeler, Michael R. Ganakas, Samuel J. Brackens, Alfred Celli, Bernard D. Deary, Ralph DeLeonardis, Powell D. Gibbs, Joseph T. Hanley, and William Van Gilder.

Georgia-Florida League Final Standings

Team	W	L	Pct	GB	Affiliate
Valdosta Dodgers	81	58	.583	----	BRK-NL
Albany Cardinals	81	59	.579	0.5	STL-NL
Waycross Bears	80	59	.576	1.0	Unaffiliated
Tifton Blue Sox	78	61	.561	3.0	Unaffiliated
Cordele A's	66	73	.475	15.0	PHI-AL
Thomasville Tomcats	66	74	.471	15.5	Unaffiliated
Brunswick Pirates	62	78	.443	19.5	PIT-NL
Moultrie Giants	44	96	.314	37.5	NY-NL

1952 Georgia-Florida League Map

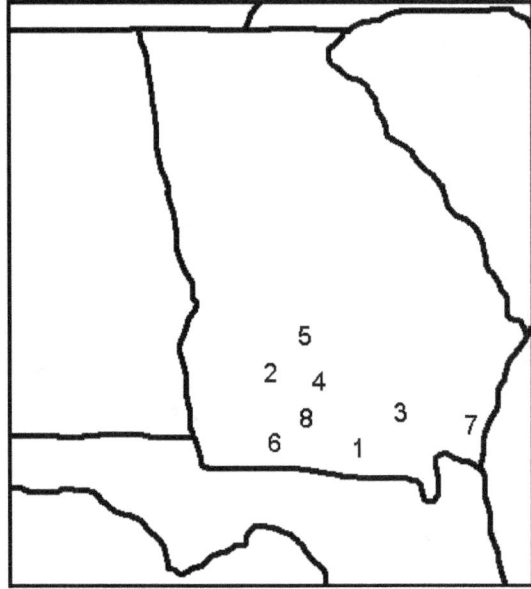

(numbers on map correspond to the place each team finished in regular season play)

One change was made in the league's lineup when Americus dropped out, and Thomasville came back after a one-year absence.

The only no-hitter of the season came on June 17 when Valdosta's Don Terwedow hurled a 7 to 0 defeat of Moultrie. Cordele went the whole season with only one home run hit by the entire team. Froggie Betcher hit the club's only dinger on July 3, the 73rd of the 139 games played by the A's. Tifton pitcher Antonio Sarmiento set the league's all-time record for the lowest earned run average in a season with 1.26. Fred Green, pitcher for Brunswick, set the all-time league single season mark for the most bases on balls when he walked 190 batters over the course of the year.

Valdosta and Waycross were tied for first at the end of the regular season, and the two clubs played a one-game tie breaker. When Valdosta won the game, the loss pushed Waycross into third place, one-half game behind Albany, who was only a half game out of first at the end of the season. Valdosta faced fourth place Tifton in round one of the playoffs, and second place Albany played third slotted Waycross. Tifton repeated their playoff upset of Valdosta from the previous year by ousting the Dodgers four games to none. Albany advanced to the championship series by defeating Waycross four games to two. The Cardinals of Albany emerged victorious over the Tifton Blue Sox in the league championship series by a four games to two final.

Albany, Georgia

Team Operated by Albany Baseball Club, Inc.
Team President: Morton M. Wiggins
Vice Presidents: Fred M. Saigh, Jr., William Walsingham, Jr.
Secretary: Edward W. Roth
Treasurer: Fred M. Saigh, Jr.
Business Manager: Richard A. Roth
Manager(s): Gene Corbett
Games played at Cardinal Park
Season attendance: 63,244
Major League Affiliate: St. Louis Cardinals – National League

Albany Cardinals Team Roster

NAME	G	BA	POS	W	L	ERA	APF
Ban, Dick	42	0.133	P	12	9	3.10	
Chaplin, Mel	34	0.184	P	15	6	2.18	
Cheney, Tom			P	0	1	27.00	
Corbett, Gene	12	0.143	M, 1B				
Cox, Frank	28	0.222	P	10	4	2.23	
Earley, Jerry	11	0.205	1B				
Goody, Sam	141	0.280	2B				
Heins, Bob	41	0.117	P	11	10	2.47	
Hollingsworth, Charles	18	0.222	P	7	4	2.88	
Ingram, Clarence	37	0.133	P	4	9	3.60	
Joyner, Julian	41	0.128	P	19	9	2.15	
Lassetter, Don	13	0.220	OF				
Looney, Bill	37	0.271	OF				
Merandi, Gene	139	0.228	SS				
Murphy, Bob	95	0.274	OF				
Plaza, Ron	135	0.211	3B				
Rice, Rollie	134	0.225	OF				
Rikard, Denver	138	0.304	OF				
Shannon, Wally	124	0.310	1B				
Skelton, Bob	47	0.167	C				
Troxell, Clair	105	0.210	C				

Brunswick, Georgia

Team Operated by Brunswick Pirates, Inc.
Team President: Edo Miller
Vice Presidents: Branch Rickey, Jr., Harold G. Roettger
Secretary: Walter Bunt
Treasurer: Jim Herron
General Manager: Harold Hays
Manager(s): George Kinnamon, Mickey O'Neil, George Pratt
Games played at Lanier Field
Season attendance: 50,605
Major League Affiliate: Pittsburgh Pirates – National League.

Georgia Class-D Minor League Baseball Encyclopedia

Brunswick Pirates Team Roster

NAME	G	BA	POS	W	L	ERA	APF
Bartley, Don	10	0.429	P				
Boyce, George	96	0.213	C				
Bussan, Don	58	0.243	OF				
Chambers, Bob	32	0.180	3B				
Cuomo, Mario	81	0.244	OF				
Davis, Sterling	30	0.162	3B, OF				
Deal, Marv	26	0.227	P	8	12	4.27	
Duncan, Dick	24	0.196	OF				
Fackler, Earl	110	0.247	1B, OF				
Glamp, Francis	39	0.234	3B				
Green, Fred	40	0.149	P	20	12	2.54	
Hicks, Robah	11	0.256	OF				
Huelfer, Dennis	48	0.218	OF, P	0	4	5.82	
Jorgenson, Merlin	34	0.083	P	3	10	3.88	
Kinnamon, George	28	0.236	M, C				
Konek, Pete	15	0.107	P	4	4	2.51	
Kovaleski, John	127	0.296	2B				
Liszewski, Joe	33	0.183	P	13	13	5.04	
Marsilisi, Mike	10	0.207					
McCrone, Tom	109	0.233	3B, OF, C				
Monahan, Jim	43	0.329	3B, OF				
O'Neil, Mickey			M				
Pratt, George			M				
Rada, Roger	115	0.286	1B				
Raphael, Mark	40	0.219	SS, OF				
Sawyer, Roger	14	0.094	P	5	6	2.43	
Sisolak, Fred	128	0.219	2B, SS				
Southard, Ken	12	0.346	P	2	3	4.70	
Super, Joe	29	0.211	P	3	5	5.44	
Swanson, Don	65	0.295	OF				
Whitecavage, Tony	19	0.131	3B				

Cordele, Georgia

Team Operated by Cordel Amusement Company, Inc.
Team President: Connie Mack
Vice President: Aruthur Ehlers
Secretary: Earle Mack
Treasurer: Roy Mack
Business Manager: Carl M. Martin
Manager(s): Norm Wilson
Games played at City Park
Season attendance: 32,549
Major League Affiliate: Philadelphia Athletics – American League.

Cordele A's Team Roster

NAME	G	BA	POS	W	L	ERA	APF
Barbier, John	41	0.096	P	16	14	2.64	
Betcher, Ralph	121	0.306	3B				
Brisson, Virgil	20	0.114	P	5	8	3.50	
Colflesh, Jack	39	0.208	SS, OF				
Davidson, Bob	112	0.303	2B, OF				
Day, Don	133	0.300	OF				
DeMont, Paul	128	0.301	2B				
Gronsky, Steve	38	0.125	P	9	4	3.16	
Hahn, Lou	18	0.303	OF				
Hardish, Dick	21	0.048	P	1	5	4.94	
Hogarth, Art	124	0.248	1B				
Kinard, Jim	31	0.253	3B, OF				
Lechtansky, Ed	52	0.218	C				
Mills, Dick	28	0.123	P	7	10	2.82	
Sanders, Bob	35	0.184	P	13	11	3.63	
Schulte, Bob	20	0.156	C				
Schypinski, Jerry	125	0.297	SS				
Sermania, Vince	10	0.000	P	1	7	6.07	
Stamper, Ken	61	0.220	1B, 3B				Thomasville
Walters, Milt	124	0.217	OF				
Watson, Carl	55	0.260	P	13	12	2.90	
Wilson, Norm	121	0.231	M, C				

Moultrie, Georgia

Team Operated by Moultrie Baseball Association
Team President: Dr. A.G. Funderburk
Business Manager: Thomas V. Lassiter
Manager(s): Dick Klaus
Games played at Municipal Park
Season attendance: 33,083
Major League Affiliate: New York Giants – National League.

Moultrie Giants Team Roster

NAME	G	BA	POS	W	L	ERA	APF
Asbill, Joe	12	0.150					
Balla, John	66	0.200	OF				
Bennett, Charles	14	0.211					
Bogardus, Earl	20	0.115	C				
Commisso, Dom	52	0.249	2B, 3B, SS				
Corder, Bob	80	0.178	SS				
Dodgin, Jim	65	0.270	OF				Tifton
Flanagan, Bill	29	0.182	P	3	9	5.82	
Galen, Joe	42	0.261	3B, SS				
Grimsley, Weldon	17	0.159	OF				
Gross, Jerrold	15	0.083	P	2	5	2.57	
Hall, Jack	16	0.225	C				
Joergen, Jim	<10						
Johnson, Jim	16	0.182	OF				
Klaus, Dick	130	0.288	M, 2B, SS, OF, P				
Klemme, Stan	118	0.225	OF				
Kott, Charles	39	0.123	P	9	18	2.82	
Lankford, Jerry	22	0.083	P	2	2	4.56	
Lloyd, Bob	17	0.262	P	4	7	3.77	
Lovell, Charles	30	0.205	P	0	9	6.04	
Reime, Bob	16	0.133	P				
Scala, Bob	32	0.225	3B				
Scheidt, Ray	47	0.128	P	11	21	3.21	
Schuck, Charles	71	0.199	C				
Scollard, John	65	0.211	1B, OF				
Shapiro, Bob	33	0.184	2B				Valdosta
Standering, Dennis	39	0.189	1B				
Suspenski, Vic	63	0.166	C				
Thorpe, Jack	29	0.273	2B				
Upper, Wray	39	0.234	3B				
Volk, Fred	48	0.131	1B, P	10	9	2.28	
Walsh, Chris	93	0.220	1B, OF				
Wrenn, Milt	33	0.238	C				
Young, Bill	141	0.244	3B, OF				

Thomasville, Georgia

Team Operated by Thomasville Baseball Club
Team President: Heeth Varnedoe
General Manager: Gardner Landon
Manager(s): Frank Lucchesi
Games played at Municipal Stadium
Season attendance: 45,651

Thomasville Tomcats Team Roster

NAME	G	BA	POS	W	L	ERA	APF
Buckles, Jim	38	0.087	P	7	3	3.07	
Burcham, Tom	90	0.288	3B				
Carolan, Joe	134	0.248	OF				
Chandler, Billy	35	0.293	P	13	12	3.71	
Cholakian, Ed	45	0.282	2B				
Clifford, Ernest	37	0.067	P	9	15	3.57	
Eames, Paul	133	0.317	C				
Heathcock, Ennis	17	0.240	P	2	5	6.00	
Heistand, Charles	11	0.333	P				
Henne, Bob	<10						

Georgia Class-D Minor League Baseball Encyclopedia

Name	G	BA	POS	W	L	ERA	APF
Hollenkamp, Dick	71	0.147	OF, 1B				
Lineberger, Don	69	0.245	OF				
Lucchesi, Frank	138	0.307	M, OF				
McLemore, Roy	46	0.198	P	20	11	2.14	
Molck, Larry	20	0.213	OF				
Moriarity, Dean	22	0.195	2B				
Peacock, Arlen	10	0.000	P	2	4	3.36	
Roberts, Tom	31	0.029	P	6	6	3.38	
Robinett, Ken	138	0.352	1B				
Schaive, Johnny	22	0.190	2B				
Schnell, Fred	17	0.103	P	4	8	3.31	
Simmons, Dick	13	0.100	OF				
Stamper, Ken	61	0.220	1B, 3B				Cordele
Turtzo, Paul	33	0.262	OF				
Willett, Ray	132	0.242	SS				
Zangari, Frank	53	0.200	2B				

Tifton, Georgia
Team Operated by Tifton Baseball Club, Inc.
Team President: H.C. Woodall
Vice President: T.L. Patrick
Secretary-Treasurer: M.H. Barlow
Business Manager: A.F. "Yank" Lamb, Jr.
Manager(s): Ed Dickerman, Greek George, Parnell Ruark
Games played at Eve Park
Season attendance: 37,805

Tifton Blue Sox Team Roster

NAME	G	BA	POS	W	L	ERA	APF
Carlesi, Vince	116	0.183	1B				
Carter, Emil	133	0.220	2B				
Cater, Jim	16	0.279	P	6	9	3.60	
Celardo, Ed	118	0.238	C				
Clapham, Brad	48	0.148	P	18	12	2.33	
Cooper, Frank	133	0.228	OF				
Deleso, Vinny	15	0.167	OF				
Dickerman, Ed	137	0.280	M, 3B				
Dodgin, Jim	65	0.270	OF				Moultrie
George, Greek	31	0.331	M, 1B, C				
Gibbons, Bill	11	0.077	P				
Griffith, Dick	26	0.245	P	5	5	2.52	
Harper, Dean	22	0.149	OF				
Johnson, Harry	40	0.183	P	19	12	2.54	
Jones, Bill	137	0.264	3B, SS, OF				
Pfeifer, Tony	24	0.086	P	7	6	3.17	
Powell, Joe	11	0.147					
Rauseo, Mike	89	0.253	SS				
Robinson, Don	57	0.259	OF, P	5	9	4.33	
Ruark, Parnell	95	0.287	M, OF				
Sarmiento, Antonio	28	0.143	P	16	3	1.26	

Valdosta, Georgia
Team Operated by Valdosta Dodgers Baseball Club, Inc.
Team President: D.S. Wainer
Vice President: Fresco Thompson
Secretary: Matthew Burns
Treasurer: William Gibson
Business Manager: Robert B. Eastman
Manager(s): John Angelone
Games played at Pendleton Park
Season attendance: 47,127
Major League Affiliate: Brooklyn Dodgers – National League.

Valdosta Dodgers Team Roster

NAME	G	BA	POS	W	L	ERA	APF
Alberts, Henry	90	0.210	C				
Angelone, John	127	0.257	M, SS				
Denison, Jack	75	0.318	OF				
Edelstein, Jacob	140	0.265	1B				
Falter, Tom	101	0.266	2B, 3B				
Fountain, Ron	129	0.252	OF				
Gergely, Bill	11	0.250	OF				
Giordano, Al	53	0.234	C				
Green, Ray	88	0.253	3B, SS				
Gurri, Anibal	48	0.209	3B, OF				
Hearn, Joshua	28	0.135	P	7	5	2.88	
Hines, ---	10		C				
Hughes, Jim	22	0.141	OF				
Lines, Don	18	0.295					
Mink, Deane	15	0.160	P	5	4	3.38	
Nelson, Charles	12	0.135	OF				
Ramsey, Silas	31	0.092	P	9	14	2.87	
Rellihan, Jerry	34	0.098	P	10	7	3.81	
Ressel, Paul	10	0.095					
Salerno, Pasquale	99	0.201	OF				
Shaffer, Don	43	0.245	P				
Shapiro, Bob	33	0.184	2B				Moultrie
Shifflett, Harry	97	0.262	2B, OF				
Terwedow, Don	39	0.259	P	14	12	2.89	
Walker, Milt	28	0.305	OF				
Wasconis, George	10	0.222	P				
White, Ed	19	0.154	P	8	4	3.92	

Waycross, Georgia
Team Operated by Waycross Baseball Association, Inc.
Team President: Erin W. Johnson
Vice Presidents: H.H. McGregor, M.M. Monroe
Secretary-Treasurer: B.M. "Buck" Walker
General Manager: W. Carlton Sweat
Manager(s): Papa Williams
Games played at Memorial Stadium
Season attendance: 53,428

Waycross Bears Team Roster

NAME	G	BA	POS	W	L	ERA	APF
Baker, Winford	19	0.145					
Bearden, Billy	17	0.033	OF				
Bledsoe, Charles	140	0.239	C				
Bremer, Walt	137	0.309	3B				
Brinson, Luther	105	0.289	2B, SS, OF				
Brown, Lamar	115	0.283	OF				
Cash, Al	45	0.276	2B				
Chandler, Norm	30	0.145	P	13	8	1.99	
Chumbris, Nick	36	0.297	OF				
Ellis, Roy	15	0.000	P	3	4	6.26	
Ensley, Jim	75	0.286	P	18	9	2.36	
Faberlle, Hector	58	0.270	P				
Fragela, Alberto	12	0.171	SS				
Hall, Bob	30	0.284	2B, OF				
Harrod, Jerrel	84	0.247	OF				
Herbert, Bentley	13	0.179	P	5	5	2.37	
Howell, Bryan	17	0.262	OF				
McGravy, Hoyt	94	0.275	OF				
Phillips, Taylor	47	0.124	P	21	10	1.39	
Reeves, Herb	42	0.190	P	15	12	2.45	
Rivers, Joe	44	0.156	SS				
Rowzee, Bob	10	0.000					
Tang, Antonio	18	0.132	SS				
Webb, Charles	65	0.217	2B				
Wilcox, Ron	21	0.118	1B				
Williams, Papa	113	0.246	M, 1B				

Georgia Class-D Minor League Baseball Encyclopedia

1952 Georgia-Florida League Records

Batting

Highest Batting Average (minimum 100 at bats)
1. Ken Robinett – Thomasville .352
2. Greek George – Tifton .331
3. Jim Monahan – Brunswick .329
4. Jack Denison – Valdosta .318
5. Paul Eames – Thomasville .317

Most Hits
1. Ken Robinett – Thomasville 176
2. Sam Goody – Albany 167
3. Frank Lucchesi – Thomasville 161
4. Denver Rikard – Albany 160
5. Paul DeMont – Cordele 156

Most Runs
1. Sam Goody – Albany 95
2. Ken Robinett – Thomasville 94
3. Rollie Rice – Albany 88
4. Frank Lucchesi – Thomasville 87
    Denver Rikard – Albany 87
    Bill Jones – Tifton 87

Most Total Bases
1. Denver Rikard – Albany 231
2. Paul Eames – Thomasville 220
3. Ken Robinett – Thomasville 211
4. Sam Goody – Albany 208
5. Frank Lucchesi – Thomasville 199

Most Doubles
1. Denver Rikard – Albany 30
2. Ken Robinett – Thomasville 29
    Frank Lucchesi – Thomasville 29
4. Dick Klaus – Moultrie 27
    Gene Merandi – Albany 27
    Earl Fackler – Brunswick 27

Most Triples
1. Denver Rikard – Albany 10
    Paul DeMont – Cordele 10
    Don Day – Cordele 10
4. Art Hogarth – Cordele 8
    Rollie Rice – Albany 8
    Fred Sisolak – Brunswick 8

Most Home Runs
1. Parnell Ruark – Tifton 19
2. Joe Carolan – Thomasville 15
3. Paul Eames – Thomasville 12
4. Ron Plaza – Albany 9
    Paul Turtzo – Thomasville 9

Most Extra Base Hits
1. Denver Rikard – Albany 47
2. Paul Eames – Thomasville 41
3. Parnell Ruark – Tifton 40
4. Joe Carolan – Thomasville 36
    Ed Dickerman – Tifton 36
    Gene Merandi – Albany 36

Most Runs Batted In
1. Denver Rikard – Albany 111
2. Walt Bremer – Waycross 95
3. Joe Carolan – Thomasville 93
4. Pasquale Salerno – Valdosta 86
5. Paul Eames – Thomasville 83

Most Stolen Bases
1. Hector Faberlle – Waycross 37
2. Frank Lucchesi – Thomasville 31
3. Bill Young – Moultrie 30
4. Fred Sisolak – Brunswick 26
5. Rollie Rice – Albany 24

Fielding

Most Put-Outs
1. Ken Robinett 1B – Thomasville 1,262
2. Jacob Edelstein 1B – Valdosta 1,210
3. Wally Shannon 1B – Albany 1,117
4. Art Hogarth 1B – Cordele 1,050
5. Papa Williams 1B – Waycross 974

Most Assists
1. Gene Merandi SS – Albany 460
2. Sam Goody 2B – Albany 455
3. John Angelone SS – Valdosta 407
4. Ray Willett SS – Thomasville 399
5. Emil Carter 2B – Tifton 386

Most Errors
1. Gene Merandi SS – Albany 61
2. Fred Sisolak 2B, SS – Brunswick 49
    Mike Rauseo SS – Tifton 49
4. Jerry Schypinski SS – Cordele 45
5. Bill Jones 3B, SS, OF – Tifton 44

Pitching

Most Wins
1. Taylor Phillips – Waycross 21
2. Roy McLemore – Thomasville 20
    Fred Green – Brunswick 20
4. Harry Johnson – Tifton 19
    Julian Joyner – Albany 19

Most Losses
1. Ray Scheidt – Moultrie 21
2. Charles Kott – Moultrie 18
3. Ernest Clifford – Thomasville 15
4. John Barbier – Cordele 14
    Silas Ramsey – Valdosta 14

Highest Winning Percentage (10 game minimum)
1. Antonio Sarmiento – Tifton .842
2. Mel Chaplin – Albany .714
    Frank Cox – Albany .714
4. Jim Buckles – Thomasville .700
5. Steve Gronsky – Cordele .692

Lowest Earned Run Average (100 inning minimum)
1. Antonio Sarmiento – Tifton 1.26
2. Taylor Phillips – Waycross 1.39
3. Norm Chandler – Waycross 1.99
4. Roy McLemore – Thomasville 2.14
5. Julian Joyner – Albany 2.15

Most Strikeouts
1. Taylor Phillips – Waycross 265
    Fred Green – Brunswick 265
3. Norm Chandler – Waycross 146
4. Ray Scheidt – Moultrie 140
5. Julian Joyner – Albany 137
    Herb Reeves – Waycross 137

Most Bases on Balls
1. Fred Green – Brunswick 190
2. Taylor Phillips – Waycross 182
3. Charles Kott – Moultrie 151

4. Don Terwedow – Valdosta   142
5. Billy Chandler – Thomasville   139

Most Hits Allowed
1. Roy McLemore – Thomasville   271
2. Roger Sawyer – Brunswick   242
3. Brad Clapham – Tifton   240
   Harry Johnson – Tifton   240
5. John Barbier – Cordele   233

Most Innings Pitched
1. Taylor Phillips – Waycross   297
2. Roy McLemore – Thomasville   273
3. Fred Green – Brunswick   269
4. Harry Johnson – Tifton   262
5. Roger Sawyer – Brunswick   259
   Jim Ensley – Waycross   259

1952 Georgia-Florida League All-Star Team
1B Wally Shannon – Albany
2B Paul DeMont – Cordele
3B Walt Bremer – Waycross
SS Jerry Schypinski – Cordele
OF Denver Rikard – Albany
OF Jack Denison – Valdosta
OF Don Day – Cordele
OF Bob Murphy – Albany
C Paul Eames – Thomasville
C Clair Troxell – Albany
P Fred Green – Brunswick
P Taylor Phillips – Waycross
P Don Shaffer – Valdosta
P Julian Joyner – Albany
P Antonio Sarmiento – Tifton
M Papa Williams – Waycross

1952

Georgia State League

League Office: Soperton, Georgia
League President: Bill Estroff
League Vice President: Claude Cook
Secretary: Frank Johnson
Salary Limit: $2,600 per month.
Player Rule: Each club was allowed a roster of sixteen players, not more than three veterans, not more than five limited service, and not less than eight rookies. Player limit effective twenty days after the opening of the season and twenty days before the close of the season.
Umpires: James R. Lathrop, Raymond F. Brackett, Calvin T. Drummond, Francis M. Terres, Robert J. Kerrigan, William S. Haines, Jr. Nick F. Reff, and Ed Kubrick.

Georgia State League Final Standings
Team	W	L	Pct	GB	Affiliate
Eastman Dodgers	75	49	.605	----	Unaffiliated
Hazlehurst-Baxley Cardinals	72	52	.581	3.0	STL-NL
Vidalia Indians	66	58	.532	9.0	Unaffiliated
Douglas Trojans	64	61	.512	11.5	Unaffiliated
Statesboro Pilots	59	65	.476	16.0	Unaffiliated
Fitzgerald Pioneers	56	70	.444	20.0	Unaffiliated
Dublin Green Sox	55	71	.437	21.0	CIN-NL
Jesup Bees	52	73	.416	23.5	Unaffiliated

1952 Georgia State League Map

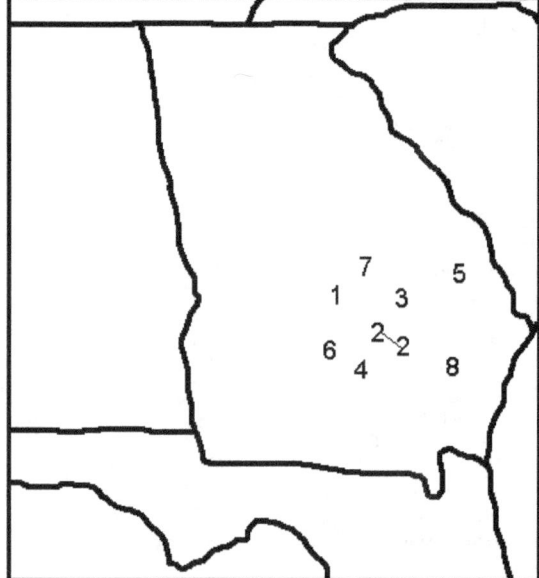

(numbers on map correspond to the place each team finished in regular season play)

Just as quickly as the Georgia State League went from eight clubs to six, the loop was back to eight again. Statesboro and Vidalia were each granted admission into the league for the 1952 season.

On May 12, Eastman pitcher Phil "Chicken" Gilbert pitched a no-hitter blanking Fitzgerald 3 to 0. A second no-hitter came on June 28 when Vidalia pitchers Doug McDermid and Fred Plushanski combined to pitch a no-hitter against Eastman winning the game 4 to 2. The third and final no-hitter of the season was hurled by Hazlehurst-Baxley pitcher Walter Bauman on Independence Day in a 14 to 0 crushing of Fitzgerald. A pair of all-time league single season league records were set by Dublin pitcher Raul Villamea, but they were not really the kind of records most pitchers are proud of. Villamea set the record for the most losses in a season with 20 and the most hits allowed at 288.

Baseball history was made on July 19 in a game between Fitzgerald and Statesboro when Joe Louis Reliford, the Fitzgerald batboy, became the first African-American to play in the league. In the same instance, Reliford also became the youngest player to ever play professional baseball. In the game at Statesboro, the home team was pounding Fitzgerald 13 to 0. The local fans were having a great time jeering the visitors and began to chant "put in the batboy." In the top of the eighth inning, Fitzgerald manager Charlie Ridgeway took the offer and sent 12-year old batboy Joe Reliford in to pinch-hit with permission from umpire Ed Kubrick. Reliford grounded one sharply to third off pitcher Curtis White in his only at bat and was thrown out by a split second. Ridgeway, not ready to pull Reliford from the game, sent him out to play right field where the youngster made history again. Statesboro's Harold Shuster, who had a 21-game hitting streak going and needed a hit to keep the streak alive, drove a ball toward Reliford. On the run, Reliford made a diving catch for the out and ended Shuster's hitting streak. As a result of allowing Reliford to play, manager Ridgeway was fined and suspended for five games, and umpire Kubrick was terminated.

Eastman finished the regular season at the top of the heap with Hazlehurst-Baxley, Vidalia, and Douglas coming in second, third, and fourth respectively. Douglas upset Eastman in the first round of the playoffs four games to two, and Vidalia pulled an upset over Hazlehurst-Baxley by the same score. In the championship series, Vidalia emerged victorious over Douglas four games to two.

Douglas, Georgia
Team Operated by Douglas Trojans, Inc.
Team President: H.B. Chitty
Vice President: G.W. Giles
Secretary-Treasurer-General Manager: Johnny Griffith
Manager(s): Van Davis
Games played at City Park
Season attendance: 27,532

Douglas Trojans Team Roster

NAME	G	BA	POS	W	L	ERA	APF
Barone, Frank	13	0.273	3B				
Cash, Jack	28	0.290	2B				
Catalano, Pete	91	0.262	OF				Fitzgerald
Cato, Roy	101	0.235	C				
Davis, Joe	83	0.304	1B, OF				
Davis, Van	100	0.326	M, 1B				
Faberlle, Hector	55	0.310	OF				
Foster, Duell	26	0.241	P	5	7	3.83	
Garcia, Jesus	37	0.301	2B				
Gore, Jack	94	0.207	3B				
Johnston, Jim	36	0.172	2B				
Jones, Jerry	46	0.324	P	12	2	3.64	
Jones, Ray	16	0.097	P	5	5	4.92	Vidalia
Kostner, Dick	63	0.222	2B, 3B, P	9	5	3.42	
Nelson, Charles	17	0.234	P	3	3	4.58	
O'Barr, Tom	43	0.333	OF, P	9	7	2.89	
Portomene, Angelo	50	0.185	SS				Dub - Sta
Rey, Emil	124	0.248	SS				
Rogers, Ernest	24	0.128	P	10	6	3.20	
Schuck, Charles	36	0.259	C				
Suarez, Oscar	15	0.261	P	2	7	4.43	
Timberlake, Ray	74	0.269	OF				
Vinson, Gene	14	0.000	P				
Wilcox, Ron	17	0.195	P	6	4	3.89	
Yow, Forrest	77	0.262	OF				

Dublin, Georgia
Team Operated by Dublin Baseball Club, Inc.
Team President: W.H. Lovett
Vice Presidents: W.E. Lovett, W.W. Brinson
Secretary: Frank Johnson
Manager(s): Jack Bearden, George Hearn, Cy Pfeifer
Games played at Lovett Park
Season attendance: 34,334
Major League Affiliate: Cincinnati Reds – National League.

Dublin Green Sox Team Roster

NAME	G	BA	POS	W	L	ERA	APF
Androvich, Joe	14	0.154					
Bahnson, Dick	47	0.181	3B				
Bearden, Jack	126	0.296	M, OF				Jesup
Boehme, Ken	48	0.252	C				
Clarke, Bill	16	0.156	OF				
Clifton, Henry	18	0.226	P	2	4	6.95	
Creighton, Joe	60	0.216	SS				
Gupton, Harry	41	0.293	SS				
Hallman, George	16	0.204	OF				
Hearn, George	100	0.278	M, 1B, C				
Heughens, Ron	11	0.125	C				
Johnson, Bill	11	0.077	P				
MacDonald, Don	23	0.271	1B				
Mays, Everett	125	0.288	OF				
McLaughlin, Pat	49	0.251	OF				
Mikulski, Stan	20	0.203	3B				
Oquendo, Noel	86	0.273	OF, P	20	10	3.68	
Pfeifer, Cy	84	0.329	M, 1B				
Portomene, Angelo	50	0.185	SS				Dou - Sta
Reid, Harold	15	0.288	SS				
Sarmiento, Antonio	17	0.214	P	5	6	7.00	
Scala, Bob	22	0.176	3B				Vidalia
Stamper, Ken	43	0.264	3B				
Vaughn, Don	44	0.213	P	8	12	4.98	
Villamea, Raul	73	0.202	OF, P	11	20	4.05	
Wagner, Allen	116	0.238	2B				
Wilkinson, Dave	17	0.190	P	1	3	6.88	
Zimmer, Harold	118	0.276	OF, P	3	2	6.67	

Eastman, Georgia
Team Operated by Eastman Dodgers, Inc.
Team President: W.S. Stuckey
Vice President: H.H. Burch
Treasurer: E.L. Jones
General Manager: W.W. Taylor
Manager(s): Bob Reid
Games played at Legion Park
Season attendance: 32,600

Eastman Dodgers Team Roster

NAME	G	BA	POS	W	L	ERA	APF
Balogh, Steve	37	0.203	2B				
Brennan, Don	30	0.270	2B				
Burgamy, Ralph	18	0.219	OF				
Buttice, Lou	42	0.198	3B, OF				
Caldwell, Wilbur	121	0.300	3B, P	9	7	3.67	
Caudle, Jim	69	0.306	OF				
Chadwick, Reed	55	0.307	C				Fitzgerald
Clements, Frank	20	0.164	P	13	3	3.25	

Georgia Class-D Minor League Baseball Encyclopedia

NAME	G	BA	POS	W	L	ERA
Copeland, Jim	17	0.189	P	3	9	5.73
Gilbert, Phil	28	0.235	P	17	6	2.97
Hamlin, Nat	15	0.213	P	8	5	4.77
Harp, Jim	48	0.224	1B, P	15	10	2.40
Herringdine, Cecil	89	0.294	OF			
Hoard, Dan	119	0.347	OF, C			
Kloss, Walt	79	0.215	2B, 3B, SS			
McPherson, Ron	20	0.260	OF			
Pratt, Art	53	0.223	OF			
Reid, Bob	120	0.288	M, 1B			
Spilman, Harry	69	0.239	C			
Tyler, Jim	13	0.100	P	6	3	4.77
Wright, Dixie	42	0.222	C			
Yanchura, John	108	0.247	SS			

Fitzgerald, Georgia
Team Operated by Fitzgerald Baseball Club, Inc.
Team President: Ace T. Adams
Secretary-Treasurer: Ellie Adams
General Manager: Ben Langella
Manager(s): Ace Adams, Charlie Ridgeway
Games played at Blue-Gray Park
Season attendance: 33,172

Fitzgerald Pioneers Team Roster

NAME	G	BA	POS	W	L	ERA	APF
Adams, Ace	10	0.571	M				
Adams, Ken	42	0.280	OF, P	5	9	3.73	
Avinger, Frank	62	0.307	1B, OF				
Catalano, Pete	91	0.262	OF				Douglas
Chadwick, Reed	55	0.307	C				Eastman
Christie, Frank	14	0.381	P	2	4	5.60	
Daniels, Dick	99	0.272	1B, OF				
Davis, Thurman	121	0.266	3B				
Drew, Dick	14	0.000	P				
Fantasia, Sal	26	0.205	OF				
Holmes, Jeptha	74	0.256	C				
McCarthy, John	15	0.250	P	2	3	5.83	Vidalia
Nichting, Ray	126	0.309	OF				
Pate, Bob	63	0.184	2B, OF				
Pippin, Fred	57	0.242	P	16	15	4.29	
Reliford, Joe	1	0.000	OF				
Ridgeway, Charlie	120	0.361	M, 2B				
Sermania, Vince	14	0.053	P	3	4	7.10	
Sinquefield, Ben	48	0.273	OF, P				
Smith, Mike	11	0.250	P	3	2	4.59	
Stoyle, Jim	98	0.324	1B				Jesup
Sullivan, John	34	0.140	P	7	9	3.54	
Super, Joe	17	0.135	P	6	5	3.13	
Tucker, Roy	18	0.197	OF				
Weaver, Fred	120	0.276	SS				
White, Randolph	23	0.171	OF				

Hazlehurst-Baxley (Hazlehurst & Baxley), Georgia
Team Operated by Hazlehurst-Baxley Baseball Club, Inc.
Team President: Mack Aaron
Vice President: Dr. C.R. Youmans
Secretary: Kenneth Martin
Treasurer: Walter W. Thompson
General Manager: Charles A. Odom
Manager(s): Arnold Riesgo
Games played at Roland Cook Stadium
Season attendance: 27,586
Major League Affiliate: St. Louis Cardinals – National League.

Hazlehurst-Baxley Cardinals Team Roster

NAME	G	BA	POS	W	L	ERA	APF
Bauman, Walt	31	0.232	P	20	5	2.75	
Beavers, Jim	122	0.363	1B				
Burnett, Gerald	16	0.238	OF				
Burton, Jim	89	0.209	C				
Dundee, Pat	23	0.197	3B				
Hemings, Fay	10	0.156					
Huthmaker, Fred	21	0.200	P	7	4	3.69	
Mapes, Carl	12	0.091	P	2	4	4.06	
McGhee, Bill	115	0.337	OF				
Pinion, Willis	17	0.147	P	4	4	4.80	
Ploszaj, Chester	120	0.236	2B				
Quinn, Don	38	0.140	P	12	9	4.65	
Rapert, Howard	25	0.196	P	8	8	5.31	
Riesgo, Arnold	86	0.298	M, OF, C				
Royer, Charles	32	0.241	P	14	7	3.78	
Shawver, Bob	122	0.309	SS				
Wilson, Bill	100	0.302	3B				
Wyatt, Gene	103	0.281	OF				
Zuccarini, Bob	124	0.256	OF				

Jesup, Georgia
Team Operated by Jesup Baseball Club
Team President: G.H. Zorn
Vice President: O.L. Harper
Secretary-Treasurer-Business Manager: W.A. Zorn
Manager(s): Jim Stoyle, Jim Warren
Games played at Milikin Park
Season attendance: 16,657

Jesup Bees Team Roster

NAME	G	BA	POS	W	L	ERA	APF
Altomare, John	42	0.136	P	11	8	4.72	
Bearden, Jack	126	0.296	OF				Dublin
Box, ---	11		P				
Bridges, Floyd	18	0.167	P	6	4	4.46	
Castillo, Sergio	15	0.190	2B				
Cook, ---	6		P	3	3	3.31	
Cotney, Vern	67	0.242	2B, OF				
Crawford, Jim	112	0.251	3B				
Daniel, Doug	24	0.255	P				
Glover, Omer	10	0.205	C				
Gordey, Alex	16	0.065	P	3	6	6.08	
Hagan, ---	7		P	1	6	3.05	
Hay, Bob	51	0.281	SS				
Layton, Fred	46	0.203	OF				
Marshall, Shorty	66	0.282	SS				
North, Bob	22	0.227	2B				
Oglesby, Alex	67	0.213	C				
Patterson, Ted	50	0.332	2B				
Ready, Charlie	53	0.133	OF, P	4	7	5.56	
Rommel, John	45	0.178	OF, P	9	5	4.60	
Ruark, Jim	36	0.238	C				
Siff, Alan	11	0.133	P				
Sosebee, Jim	125	0.323	1B, OF				
Stoyle, Jim	98	0.324	M, 1B				Fitzgerald
Swidorski, Don	11	0.034	P	1	5	3.57	
Warren, Jim	126	0.314	M, OF, P	6	11	5.26	
Youngblood, Jack	11	0.120					

Statesboro, Georgia
Team Operated by Statesboro Athletics Association, Inc.
Team President: C.B. McAllister
Vice President: Alfred Dorman
Secretary: Herbert E. Kingery
Treasurer: Herman E. Bray
Business Manager: R.F. Donaldson, Jr.

Georgia Class-D Minor League Baseball Encyclopedia

Manager(s): Chuck Quimby
Games played at Pilots Field
Season attendance: 32,146

Statesboro Pilots Team Roster

NAME	G	BA	POS	W	L	ERA	APF
Berzonski, John	16	0.147	P	5	6	5.89	
Calobrisi, Frank	12	0.255	SS				
Carn, Irv	124	0.284	OF				
Cibulski, Floyd	43	0.163	OF, P	14	11	4.10	
Genevrino, Mike	63	0.292	1B				
Gordon, Bob	49	0.274	2B, OF				
Gurri, Anibal	44	0.276	3B				
Jimenez, Felipe	66	0.242	3B, OF, C, P	1	1	3.45	
Menapace, Ed	47	0.315	C				
Murphy, Dan	36	0.290	SS				
Parsons, Harold	24	0.114	P	3	5	3.87	
Peters, Gerald	71	0.293	OF				
Pompelia, Augie	77	0.278	2B, SS				
Portomene, Angelo	50	0.185	SS				Dou - Dub
Quimby, Chuck	122	0.333	M, 1B, 2B, 3B, OF				
Rodriguez, Charles	13	0.235	2B				
Serbin, Cliff	10	0.091	P				
Shuster, Harold	121	0.339	OF				
Snider, Walt	39	0.244	1B, P	5	4	3.36	
Thrasher, Cliff	53	0.255	C				
Tuggle, Bill	39	0.239	3B				
Whaley, Charles	9		P	6	2	3.10	
Whaley, Walker	16	0.250	P	2	5	5.14	
White, Curtis	53	0.239	P	16	11	2.63	

Vidalia, Georgia

Team Operated by Vidalia Baseball Association, Inc.
Team President: G.H. Threlkeld
Vice President: W. Coite Somers
Secretary-Treasurer: G.H. Gibson
Manager(s): Bull Hamons
Games played at Vidalia Municipal Stadium
Season attendance: 37,485

Vidalia Indians Team Roster

NAME	G	BA	POS	W	L	ERA	APF
Anderson, Carl	95	0.257	C				
Barnett, Byron	11	0.250	P				
Bennett, Charles	12	0.231	P	0	6	8.17	
Bettineschi, Frank	78	0.291	3B				
Boyer, Ken	87	0.223	3B, OF, C				
Burns, Jim	125	0.334	OF				
Collins, Bill	112	0.288	OF				
Daniel, Jake	44	0.238	1B				
Dobbins, Mayes	122	0.257	2B				
Hamons, Bull			M				
Heaton, Ralph	34	0.194	P	16	5	4.03	
Howard, Alton	120	0.203	OF				
Hughes, Jim	13	0.185					
Jones, Ray	16	0.097	P	5	5	4.92	Douglas
Lehmann, Chauncey	16	0.139					
McCarthy, John	15	0.250	P	2	3	5.83	Fitzgerald
McDermid, Doug	19	0.065	P	5	7	6.16	
McPherson, Roger	81	0.228	1B				
Miller, Frank	13	0.235	P				
Plushanski, Fred	15	0.167	P	5	5	4.35	
Price, Charles	31	0.188	P	12	7	3.69	
Scala, Bob	22	0.176	3B				Dublin
Tepedino, Frank	116	0.303	SS				
Tingle, Tom	17	0.224	SS				
Ward, Bob	30	0.136	P	13	7	3.62	
Yeider, Marshall	19	0.190	P	6	8	5.61	

1952 Georgia State League Records
Batting

Highest Batting Average (minimum 100 at bats)
1. Jim Beavers - Hazlehurst-Baxley .363
2. Charlie Ridgeway – Fitzgerald .361
3. Dan Hoard – Eastman .347
4. Harold Shuster – Statesboro .339
5. Bill McGhee - Hazlehurst-Baxley .337

Most Hits
1. Jim Beavers - Hazlehurst-Baxley 191
2. Charlie Ridgeway – Fitzgerald 173
   Jim Sosebee – Jesup 173
4. Dan Hoard – Eastman 165
   Jim Warren – Jesup 165

Most Runs
1. Jim Beavers - Hazlehurst-Baxley 119
2. Wilbur Caldwell – Eastman 118
3. Chuck Quimby – Statesboro 116
4. Bill McGhee - Hazlehurst-Baxley 112
5. Bill Collins – Vidalia 111

Most Total Bases
1. Jim Beavers - Hazlehurst-Baxley 310
2. Jim Burns – Vidalia 284
3. Bill McGhee - Hazlehurst-Baxley 278
4. Jim Sosebee – Jesup 269
5. Jim Warren – Jesup 268

Most Doubles
1. Jim Burns – Vidalia 47
2. Jim Beavers - Hazlehurst-Baxley 46
3. Dan Hoard – Eastman 43
4. Jim Sosebee – Jesup 40
5. Bill McGhee - Hazlehurst-Baxley 37

Most Triples
1. Bob Shawver - Hazlehurst-Baxley 11
2. Ray Nichting – Fitzgerald 10
3. Everett Mays – Dublin 9
4. Jim Sosebee – Jesup 7
5. *four players tied with 5

Most Home Runs
1. Chuck Quimby – Statesboro 31
2. Bill McGhee - Hazlehurst-Baxley 25
   Jim Burns – Vidalia 25
4. Jim Warren – Jesup 23
5. Van Davis – Douglas 22

Most Extra Base Hits
1. Jim Burns – Vidalia 72
   Jim Beavers - Hazlehurst-Baxley 72
3. Bill McGhee - Hazlehurst-Baxley 67
4. Jim Sosebee – Jesup 61
5. Chuck Quimby – Statesboro 57

Most Runs Batted In
1. Jim Burns – Vidalia 155
2. Chuck Quimby – Statesboro 126
3. Bill McGhee - Hazlehurst-Baxley 118
4. Jim Warren – Jesup 117
5. Dan Hoard – Eastman 111

Most Stolen Bases
1. Wilbur Caldwell – Eastman 58
2. Charlie Ridgeway – Fitzgerald 52
3. Hector Faberlle – Douglas 49
4. Allen Wagner – Dublin 45

5. Gerald Peters – Statesboro 32

Fielding
Most Put-Outs
1. Bob Reid 1B – Eastman 1,198
2. Jim Beavers 1B - Hazlehurst-Baxley 975
3. Van Davis 1B – Douglas 811
4. Jim Stoyle 1B – Jesup 768
5. Roger McPherson 1B – Vidalia 654

Most Assists
1. Emil Rey SS – Douglas 386
2. Frank Tepedino SS – Vidalia 369
3. Bob Shawver SS - Hazlehurst-Baxley 362
4. Charlie Ridgeway – Fitzgerald 348
5. John Yanchura SS – Eastman 338

Most Errors
1. Bob Shawver SS - Hazlehurst-Baxley 68
2. Fred Weaver SS – Fitzgerald 59
3. John Yanchura SS – Eastman 57
4. Jim Crawford 3B – Jesup 45
5. Chester Ploszaj 2B - Hazlehurst-Baxley 38

Pitching
Most Wins
1. Noel Oquendo – Dublin 20
   Walt Bauman - Hazlehurst-Baxley 20
3. Phil Gilbert – Eastman 17
4. Ralph Heaton – Vidalia 16
   Curtis White – Statesboro 16
   Fred Pippin – Fitzgerald 16

Most Losses
1. Raul Villamea – Dublin 20
2. Fred Pippin – Fitzgerald 15
3. Don Vaughn – Dublin 12
4. Curtis White – Statesboro 11
   Floyd Cibulski – Statesboro 11
   Jim Warren – Jesup 11

Highest Winning Percentage (10 game minimum)
1. Jerry Jones – Douglas .857
2. Frank Clements – Eastman .813
3. Walt Bauman - Hazlehurst-Baxley .800
4. Ralph Heaton – Vidalia .762
5. Phil Gilbert – Eastman .739

Lowest Earned Run Average (100 inning minimum)
1. Jim Harp – Eastman 2.40
2. Curtis White – Statesboro 2.63
3. Walt Bauman - Hazlehurst-Baxley 2.75
4. Tom O'Barr – Douglas 2.89
5. Phil Gilbert – Eastman 2.97

Most Strikeouts
1. Noel Oquendo – Dublin 245
2. Curtis White – Statesboro 154
3. Don Vaughn – Dublin 153
4. Phil Gilbert – Eastman 150
5. Raul Villamea – Dublin 149

Most Bases on Balls
1. Fred Pippin – Fitzgerald 183
2. Don Vaughn – Dublin 173
3. Noel Oquendo – Dublin 147
4. Curtis White – Statesboro 146
5. Bob Ward – Vidalia 126

Most Hits Allowed
1. Raul Villamea – Dublin 288
2. Fred Pippin – Fitzgerald 269
3. Ralph Heaton – Vidalia 229
4. Noel Oquendo – Dublin 223
5. Floyd Cibulski – Statesboro 217

Most Innings Pitched
1. Noel Oquendo – Dublin 269
2. Raul Villamea – Dublin 258
   Fred Pippin – Fitzgerald 258
4. Jim Harp – Eastman 229
   Curtis White – Statesboro 229

1952 Georgia State League All-Star Team
1B Jim Beavers – Hazlehurst-Baxley
2B Charlie Ridgeway – Fitzgerald
3B Chuck Quimby – Statesboro
SS Frank Tepedino – Vidalia
OF Bill McGhee – Hazlehurst-Baxley
OF Ray Nichting – Fitzgerald
OF Jim Burns – Vidalia
C Arnold Riesgo – Hazlehurst-Baxley
P Noel Oquendo – Dublin
P Phil Gilbert – Eastman
P Walt Bauman – Hazlehurst-Baxley
P Jerry Jones – Douglas

Georgia Class-D Minor League Baseball Encyclopedia

1953

Georgia-Florida League

League Office: Leslie, Georgia
League President: W.T. Anderson
League Vice President: C.L. Thompson
Salary Limit: $2,600 per month.
Player Rule: Each club was allowed a roster of sixteen players, not more than four veterans, not more than seven limited service, and not less than five rookies.
Umpires: Samuel J. Brackens, Alfred Celli, Bernard D. Deary, Ralph DeLeonardis, Joseph T. Hanley, Raymond F. Brackett, John H. Lockamy, Ted Lopat, and Philip Reeves.

Georgia-Florida League Final Standings

Team	W	L	Pct	GB	Affiliate
Thomasville Dodgers	90	47	.657	----	BRK-NL
Brunswick Pirates	85	54	.612	6.0	PIT-NL
Tifton Blue Sox	84	55	.604	7.0	Unaffiliated
Albany Cardinals	82	56	.594	8.5	STL-NL
Fitzgerald Pioneers	62	77	.446	29.0	CIN-NL
Waycross Bears	59	78	.431	31.0	Unaffiliated
Valdosta Browns	55	81	.404	34.5	STL-AL
Cordele A's	35	104	.252	56.0	PHI-AL

1953 Georgia-Florida League Map

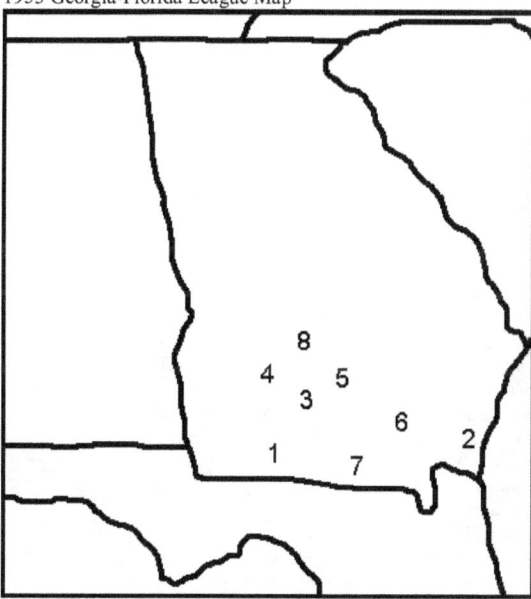

(numbers on map correspond to the place each team finished in regular season play)

Moultrie, who had been in the league since its inception, decided not to participate in the 1953 season. Filling the void was Fitzgerald, formerly of the Georgia State League.
On July 20, Thomasville pitcher George Wasconis pitched a no-hitter against Valdosta winning 1 to 0 in seven innings. Valdosta pitcher Ted Koenigsmark hurled a no-hitter on August 21 pounding Cordele 10 to 0.
Thomasville was atop the standings at the end of the regular season, and Brunswick, Tifton, and Albany followed in order. Thomasville defeated Albany four games to two in the first round of playoff action. Brunswick won the other spot in the league championship series by eliminating Tifton in four straight games. Brunswick and Thomasville fought it out in the championship series until the Pirates from the coast finally emerged victorious four games to three.

Albany, Georgia
Team Operated by Albany Baseball Club, Inc.
Team President: Morton M. Wiggins
Vice Presidents: August Busch, Jr., William Walsingham, Jr.
Business Manager: Richard A. Roth
Manager(s): Russ McGovern
Games played at Cardinal Park
Season attendance: 51,870
Major League Affiliate: St. Louis Cardinals – National League.

Albany Cardinals Team Roster

NAME	G	BA	POS	W	L	ERA	APF
Bisesi, John	132	0.226	SS				
Bourgeois, Joe	49	0.210	P	16	7	3.16	
Cheney, Tom	36	0.200	P	9	12	3.61	
Clark, Phil	8	0.083	P	1	3		
Davis, Gene	131	0.278	3B				
Duby, Bob	4	0.000	P	0	0		
Elliott, Art	4	1.000	P	0	0		
Flanigan, Cheri Jim	10	0.188	P	3	4		
Fleisch, Don	49	0.213	OF				
Fryman, Howard	5	0.125	P	3	0		
Garcia, David	2	0.286					
Gary, Lou	4	0.056					
Grabert, Herman	131	0.298	1B				
Hilyer, Ken	136	0.334	2B				
Ivey, Bill	19	0.190	OF				
Joyner, Julian	23	0.205	P	7	10	2.20	
Keggereis, Bill	21	0.120	P	4	1	5.48	
Lee, Dick	8	0.000	P	1	1		
McGovern, Russ	132	0.273	M, OF				
McKinney, Heaford	137	0.317	OF				
Ostopchuck, Joe	27	0.184	P	11	3	3.09	
Rand, Bob	122	0.267	C				
Robinson, Ben	7	0.200					
Rohs, Norm	103	0.249	OF, C				
Sarmiento, Antonio	28	0.233	P	12	7	2.63	Tifton
Shiver, Floyd	26	0.161	P	11	7	4.25	
Skelton, Bob	37	0.254	3B, C				
Slike, Max B.	18	0.204	P	7	4	4.02	
Steele, Ron	38	0.316	OF, P	2	1		
Upchurch, Bill	2	0.200					
Wilhelm, Bill	1	0.000					

Brunswick, Georgia
Team Operated by Brunswick Pirates, Inc.
Team President: Blanton Miller
Vice President: Branch Rickey, Jr., Harold G. Roettger
Secretary: Walter Bunt
Treasurer: James A. Herron
General Manager: Harold L. Hays
Manager(s): Jack Paepke
Games played at Edo Miller Park
Season attendance: 47,077
Major League Affiliate: Pittsburgh Pirates – National League.

Brunswick Pirates Team Roster

NAME	G	BA	POS	W	L	ERA	APF
Anile, Joe	9	0.263					
Bach, Phil	10	0.200	P	4	2	4.09	
Bolin, Pete	84	0.317	OF				
Brumbaugh, John	41	0.215	SS				

Georgia Class-D Minor League Baseball Encyclopedia

NAME	G	BA	POS	W	L	ERA
Capone, Bob	128	0.261	3B			
Cook, John	25	0.260	OF			
Deal, Marv	22	0.277	P	9	5	4.34
Farless, Sam	53	0.275	OF			
Faust, Floyd	126	0.280	OF			
Fleming, Doug	38	0.199	2B			
Freese, Gene	117	0.309	2B, SS, P	0	0	
Garton, Ed	17	0.280	P	4	4	4.58
Gilbert, Harry	3	0.000	P	0	0	
Gladich, Frank	36	0.228	P	14	13	3.13
Huelfer, Dennis	49	0.214	OF, P	10	8	2.91
Kelly, Ken	25	0.225	SS			
Kildoo, Don	17	0.143	P	9	5	2.25
Kirby, Jim	68	0.208	OF, C, P	0	0	
Kriczky, Mike	11	0.217	P	5	3	1.80
McGuire, Ed	5	0.000	P	0	0	
McNally, Don	30	0.179	SS, P	1	0	
Miller, Dean	35	0.265	2B, P	0	0	
Minjock, John	11	0.000	P	2	0	
Morris, Ted	10	0.429	P	1	4	
Navarro, Ignatius	3	0.500	P	0	1	
Nisewonger, Jim	48	0.223	P	18	6	1.99
Paepke, Jack	115	0.318	M, C, P	4	1	
Pillar, Bill	6	0.167	P	2	0	
Quinn, Paul	5	1.000	P	0	0	
Scarth, Jim	13	0.178				
Sinquefield, Ben	128	0.264	OF, P	0	0	
Smith, Earl	6	0.000	P	1	0	
Van Burkleo, Dutch	132	0.269	1B			
Vanasse, Bob	6	0.182	P	1	2	

Cordele, Georgia

Team Operated by Cordel Baseball and Amusement Co, Inc.
Team President: J.W. Bridges
Vice President-Secretary-Treasurer: Jim Hayward
Business Manager-Travel Secretary: Chet Morrisey
Manager(s): Lew Richardson, Joe Rullo
Games played at City Park
Season attendance: 17,705
Major League Affiliate: Philadelphia Athletics – American League.

Cordele A's Team Roster

NAME	G	BA	POS	W	L	ERA	APF
Abrams, Norm	137	0.239	2B, 3B, SS				
Alves, Joe	57	0.182	2B				
Baker, Jerry	19	0.175	C				
Barberra, Clem	20	0.237	OF				
Bartholomew, Jack	7	0.208					
Bateman, Ed	14	0.256	OF				
Blackwell, Ken	28	0.067	P	5	6	4.88	
Comegys, Howard	13	0.231	P	1	5	6.66	
Daly, Hugh	66	0.178	OF, C				
DeSpirito, Joe	4	0.000	P	0	0		
Dobias, John	67	0.294	OF, P	0	0		
Donnelly, Bob	22	0.196	P	2	5	5.26	
Donofry, Don	126	0.235	OF, P	0	0		
Dudley, John	97	0.206	3B, SS				
Fabrizio, Anthony	45	0.192	P	6	18	6.55	
Gaidzis, John	15	0.105					
Griffin, Alva	33	0.143	C				
Horine, Lawrence	70	0.265	OF				
Josephs, Al	15	0.231	P	3	4	5.61	
Kemp, Roy	36	0.115	P	4	14	5.25	
Langley, Buddy	34	0.075	1B				Waycross
Matesich, Joe	26	0.213	OF				
McCrary, Jim	48	0.240	SS				
McDonald, John	3	0.091					
Meagher, Bob	32	0.109	P	3	15	9.69	
Osburn, Herman	21	0.086	P	2	8	3.55	

NAME	G	BA	POS	W	L	ERA
Perna, Frank	3	0.000	P	0	2	
Phillips, Sam	4	0.000	P	0	1	
Richardson, Lew	77	0.258	M, C, P	0	0	
Rullo, Joe	40	0.299	M, C, P	0	0	
Sardoff, Marty	16	0.095	P	1	2	
Sayle, Bob	33	0.191	P	4	14	6.72
Shea, Dave	129	0.298	1B, OF, P	0	0	
Shiffner, Ray	39	0.221	OF			
Stern, Austin	26	0.238	3B, OF			
Stroud, Earl	5	0.000	P	1	1	
Warner, Henry	49	0.209	2B			
Watson, Carl	37	0.149	1B, P	3	9	3.87

Fitzgerald, Georgia

Team Operated by Fitzgerald Pioneers, Inc.
Team President: R.C. "Bob" Aldridge
Vice President: Philip Halperin, Raymond Harris
Secretary-Treasurer: Curtis E. Green
Business Manager: Theodore R. "Ted" Doty
Manager(s): Bob Carlson, Bull Hamons, Charlie Ridgeway
Games played at Blue-Gray Park
Season attendance: 39,264
Major League Affiliate: Cincinnati Reds – National League.

Fitzgerald Pioneers Team Roster

NAME	G	BA	POS	W	L	ERA	APF
Adams, Ken	28	0.186	P	3	3	4.65	
Barnett, Byron	1	0.000	P	0	0		
Bearden, Jack	15	0.294	OF				
Brock, Paul	17	0.040	P	2	6	6.20	
Bumstead, Dan	2	0.000	P	0	0		
Calloway, Don	3	0.000					
Carlson, Bob	44	0.288	M, SS				
Cavallaro, Fred	47	0.246	OF				
Claset, John	32	0.146	P	13	15	3.75	
Colvin, Jack	6	0.500					
Cooper, Bill	1	0.000	P	0	0		
Davis, Howard	135	0.247	3B				
Fabbio, Anthony	134	0.230	C				
Falcone, Nick	7	0.222					
Hamons, Bull			M				
Hill, Van	70	0.263	OF, P	0	0		
Hondzinski, Fred	17	0.200	OF				
Husich, John	38	0.203	P	13	8	2.90	
Jack, Dick	11	0.000	P	2	4		
Jones, Billy Joe	4	0.000	P	0	0		
Knodel, Len	18	0.000	P	1	6	4.67	
Lugo, Lou	1	0.000	P	0	0		
McDaniel, Dan	6	0.150	P	0	1		
McLeod, George	14	0.296	P	1	7	6.45	
Miarka, Stan	27	0.190	3B				Tifton
Newmarch, Ron	8	0.000	P	2	1		
Park, Loyal	88	0.291	OF				
Pierce, Jerome	95	0.197	SS				
Podolski, Dick	34	0.170	P	7	7	4.20	
Popwell, Julius	8	0.348					
Ridgeway, Charlie	136	0.276	M, 2B, P	0	0		
Roberts, Bob	4	0.000	P	1	0		
Robinette, Jimmie	28	0.212	OF				
Schneider, Ed	24	0.349	P	6	6	2.96	
Sheldon, Bill	4	0.444					
Smith, Max	45	0.258	OF				
Stoyle, Jim	127	0.331	1B, P	0	1		
Stutts, Bob	114	0.285	OF, C				
Thompson, Bill	55	0.278	1B, OF, P	0	2		
Vaughn, Don	32	0.132	P	11	9	3.73	

Georgia Class-D Minor League Baseball Encyclopedia

Thomasville, Georgia
Team Operated by Thomasville Dodgers, Inc.
Team President: Heeth Varnedoe
Vice President: Fresco Thompson
Secretary: Matthew A. Burns
Treasurer: William Gibson
Business Manager: Robert B. Eastman
Manager(s): John Angelone
Games played at Municipal Stadium
Season attendance: 41,223
Major League Affiliate: Brooklyn Dodgers – National League.

Thomasville Dodgers Team Roster

NAME	G	BA	POS	W	L	ERA	APF
Alvarez, Ultus	139	0.300	SS, OF				
Ammons, Dewey	2	0.500					
Angelone, John	131	0.305	M, SS, P	0	0		
Anthony, George	2	0.000	P	0	0		
Bledsoe, Billy	12	0.211	P	3	2		
Boykin, Gayle	19	0.059	P	0	2	5.40	
Carter, Bob	59	0.283	OF, C				
Chandler, Billy	15	0.143	P	7	4	4.16	
Dixon, Bill	136	0.231	C				
Elkins, Bobby	82	0.252	3B				
Gonet, Bill	39	0.217	OF				
Gravino, Joe	2	0.143					
Gulvas, Joe	56	0.267	3B, OF				
Hampshire, Larry	139	0.288	OF				
Hearn, Joshua	5	0.167	P	1	1		
Hughes, Jim	22	0.333	2B				
Jezek, Ed	26	0.208	P	11	5	2.61	
Koczwara, Bob	47	0.143	P	15	2	2.28	
Koranda, Jim	65	0.267	OF				
Marrochi, Hugo	14	0.229	1B				
McCombie, Charles	18	0.087	P	9	6	2.82	
McLean, John	23	0.073	P	9	6	4.11	
Mink, Deane	18	0.138	P	8	3	3.00	
Mixon, Clark	11	0.385	P	2	1		
Naylor, Dick	15	0.250	P	2	1		
Norris, Jim	4	0.286					
Ramsey, Silas	20	0.245	P	7	8	3.44	
Randle, Fred	21	0.160	P	6	1	4.17	Waycross
Riepple, Jim	24	0.182	3B				
Rogers, Lynn	9	0.143	P	2	1		
Salas, Bienvenido	35	0.233	2B, SS				
Stephenson, Sonny	140	0.333	1B, OF				
Wasconis, George	24	0.184	P	14	2	3.46	
Wright, Jerry	13	0.059	P	2	1	3.72	
Yoder, Bob	90	0.301	2B				

Tifton, Georgia
Team Operated by Tifton Baseball Club, Inc.
Team President: H.C. Woodall
Vice President: T.L. Patrick
Secretary-Treasurer: M.H. Barlow
Business Manager: Edd Hartness
Manager(s): Edd Hartness
Games played at Eve Park
Season attendance: 31,260

Tifton Blue Sox Team Roster

NAME	G	BA	POS	W	L	ERA	APF
Adams, Jerome	22	0.098	C				
Ashton, Andrew	2	0.000	P	0	0		
Badour, Bob	7	0.000	P	0	0		
Boyce, Ken	3	0.000					
Braun, Leon	3	0.000	P	0	1		
Bush, Ray	4	0.000	P	0	0		
Calobrisi, Frank	128	0.257	2B, 3B, SS, OF				
Carn, Irv	2	0.125					
Cater, Jim	36	0.190	P	21	10	2.66	
Celardo, Ed	127	0.241	C				
Chafin, Cotton	133	0.312	2B, 3B, OF				
Clapham, Brad	59	0.256	P	15	11	3.78	
Cooper, Frank	136	0.283	OF				
Davis, Alton	24	0.184	P	6	5	3.12	
DeFore, Ed	17	0.186	OF				
DiRoberto, John	20	0.250	3B				
Ford, Bob	46	0.240	SS				
Harrison, L.H.	50	0.205	SS				
Hartness, Edd	135	0.322	M, 1B				
Hughes, Norm	1	0.000	P	0	0		
Johnson, Harry	38	0.243	P	16	10	3.24	
Johnson, Ivy	27	0.175	3B				
Johnston, Bob	40	0.205	2B				
Little, Jim	39	0.178	3B, C				
Lopez, Carlos	8	0.133	P	0	3		
McPartland, Doug	7	0.286	P	0	1		
Menapace, Ed	3	0.333					
Miarka, Stan	27	0.190	3B				Fitzgerald
Musser, Dick	7	0.150					
Roberts, Tom	36	0.113	P	15	10	3.32	Valdosta
Robinson, Don	93	0.255	OF, P	3	0		
Sarmiento, Antonio	28	0.233	P	12	7	2.63	Albany
Turtzo, Paul	135	0.288	OF, P	0	0		
Upchurch, Bill	6	0.190					
Volpe, Joe	15	0.000	P	3	1	6.32	
Ware, Charles	28	0.282	3B				

Valdosta, Georgia
Team Operated by Valdosta Baseball Club, Inc.
Team President: Henry J. Hicks
Vice President: John W. Lastinger
Secretary-Treasurer: Francis Wilcox
Director: T. Guy Connell
General Manager: R.B. "Bob" Bonifay
Manager(s): Rollie Stuckmeyer, Gil Torres
Games played at Pendleton Park
Season attendance: 42,353
Major League Affiliate: St. Louis Browns – American League.

Valdosta Browns Team Roster

NAME	G	BA	POS	W	L	ERA	APF
Archaumbault, Charles	15	0.240	OF				
Bonet, Hector	31	0.300	OF				
Burcham, Tom	93	0.318	3B				
Burford, Lamar	122	0.302	OF				
Campbell, Doug	122	0.241	3B, SS				
Childers, Jimmy	1	0.000					
Deneau, Belmont	17	0.160	P	3	6	5.55	
England, Jim	40	0.226	2B, P	0	0		
Evans, Jim	132	0.252	2B, 3B				
Fenster, Aaron	75	0.234	C				
Fisher, Vern	38	0.188	P	15	13	3.67	
Gaisford, Jerry	16	0.157	OF				
Gilmore, Russ	6	0.125					
Hammen, Floyd	130	0.235	SS, OF				
Hollenkamp, Dick	24	0.185	C				
Horne, Tom	19	0.105	P	4	5	5.14	
Keller, Ed	9	0.429	P	0	4		
Koenigsmark, Ted	19	0.130	P	8	8	3.51	
Lee, Rick	37	0.177	P	5	10	5.37	
Lemons, Carol	37	0.228	OF, P	0	0		
McLemore, Roy	21	0.143	P	3	10	4.43	
Norton, Harold	118	0.283	OF				
Roberts, Tom	36	0.113	P	15	10	3.32	Tifton
Scheel, Rolf	33	0.163	P	5	8	5.47	
Schultz, Dick	17	0.270	P	4	3	5.60	
Smathers, Fred	28	0.173	C				

Name	G	BA	POS	W	L	ERA	APF
Strawser, Croyden	69	0.221	1B, OF, C				
Stuckmeyer, Rollie	79	0.294	M, 1B				
Taylor, Jim	14	0.163	OF				
Thode, Neil	18	0.161	P	3	7	4.55	
Torres, Gil	46	0.296	M, P, 1B, 2B	4	5	3.15	

Waycross, Georgia
Team Operated by Waycross Baseball Association, Inc.
Team President: O.E. Edenfield
Vice President: B.M. "Buck" Walker
Secretary-Treasurer: J.B. O'Neal
Business Manager: Joseph Paul
Manager(s): Al Aucoin, Morton Smith
Games played at Memorial Stadium
Season attendance: 27,994

Waycross Bears Team Roster

NAME	G	BA	POS	W	L	ERA	APF
Adair, Hubert	21	0.143	OF				
Adams, John	30	0.217	P	8	10	3.57	
Allen, Bill	59	0.172	OF, P	9	17	3.28	
Aucoin, Al	82	0.318	M, OF, C, P	3	1	5.75	
Bachars, Medar	50	0.215	OF				
Bearden, Billy	31	0.208	OF				
Bosch, Ortelio	74	0.265	SS				
Cash, Al	112	0.254	2B, SS				
Cato, Roy	127	0.255	3B, C				
Clifton, John	82	0.268	OF				
Cobb, Jim	5	0.333	P	0	2		
Dacus, Joe	79	0.288	3B, OF, P	0	0		
Foster, Duell	35	0.215	P	13	12	2.79	
Gilliam, Earl	38	0.179	2B, SS				
Hopkins, Bob	13	0.111	P	2	7	5.67	
Jones, Jerry	2	0.000	P	1	0		
Kostner, Dick	4	0.200	P	0	0		
Langley, Buddy	34	0.075	1B				Cordele
McGravy, Hoyt	79	0.249	OF				
Pope, Jim	23	0.200	C				
Powell, Cliff	37	0.258	OF				
Randle, Fred	21	0.160	P	6	1	4.17	Thomasville
Reese, Aaron	6	0.000	P	0	1		
Smith, Bill	58	0.189	OF				
Smith, Frank	79	0.216	1B				
Smith, Morton	52	0.246	M, 1B, P	0	3		
Spence, Steve	1	0.000	P	0	1		
Timberlake, Ray	8	0.083					
Umbricht, Jim	54	0.246	SS, P	4	3	2.87	
Utley, George	39	0.152	P	11	15	3.78	
Vinson, Gene	11	0.316	P	0	4		
Walters, Billy	77	0.253	2B, 3B				

1953 Georgia-Florida League Records
Batting
Highest Batting Average (minimum 100 at bats)
1. Ken Hilyer – Albany .334
2. Sonny Stephenson – Thomasville .333
3. Jim Stoyle – Fitzgerald .331
4. Edd Hartness – Tifton .322
5. Tom Burcham – Valdosta .318
   Jack Paepke – Brunswick .318
   Al Aucoin – Waycross .318

Most Hits
1. Ken Hilyer – Albany 171
2. Cotton Chafin – Tifton 166
3. Ultus Alvarez – Thomasville 164
4. Sonny Stephenson – Thomasville 161
5. Jim Stoyle – Fitzgerald 158

   Edd Hartness – Tifton 158

Most Runs
1. Russ McGovern – Albany 133
2. Floyd Faust – Brunswick 123
3. Ken Hilyer – Albany 118
4. Ultus Alvarez – Thomasville 113
5. Larry Hampshire – Thomasville 112

Most Total Bases
1. Ultus Alvarez – Thomasville 268
2. Ken Hilyer – Albany 256
3. Jim Stoyle – Fitzgerald 229
4. Gene Davis – Albany 221
5. Heaford McKinney – Albany 216
   Jack Paepke – Brunswick 216

Most Doubles
1. Jim Stoyle – Fitzgerald 46
2. Jack Paepke – Brunswick 32
3. Ken Hilyer – Albany 30
   Gene Davis – Albany 30
   Dave Shea – Cordele 30
   Frank Cooper – Tifton 30

Most Triples
1. Ultus Alvarez – Thomasville 21
2. Gene Davis – Albany 14
3. Cotton Chafin – Tifton 13
4. Heaford McKinney – Albany 12
5. John Dobias – Cordele 10

Most Home Runs
1. Jack Paepke – Brunswick 21
2. Dutch Van Burkleo – Brunswick 16
3. Ken Hilyer – Albany 15
4. Bill Thompson – Fitzgerald 13
5. Ultus Alvarez – Thomasville 12

Most Extra Base Hits
1. Ultus Alvarez – Thomasville 59
2. Jim Stoyle – Fitzgerald 55
3. Jack Paepke – Brunswick 54
4. Ken Hilyer – Albany 50
5. Gene Davis – Albany 49

Most Runs Batted In
1. Ultus Alvarez – Thomasville 123
2. Ken Hilyer – Albany 116
3. Jack Paepke – Brunswick 109
   Dutch Van Burkleo – Brunswick 109
5. Jim Stoyle – Fitzgerald 99

Most Stolen Bases
1. Floyd Faust – Brunswick 54
2. Charlie Ridgeway – Fitzgerald 39
3. Cotton Chafin – Tifton 38
4. Ken Hilyer – Albany 24
5. Russ McGovern – Albany 23

Fielding
Most Put-Outs
1. Edd Hartness – 1B – Tifton 1,074
2. Dutch Van Burkleo 1B – Brunswick 1,031
3. Sonny Stephenson 1B, OF – Thomasville 1,024
4. Herman Grabert 1B – Albany 1,015
5. Jim Stoyle 1B, P – Fitzgerald 875

Most Assists
1. Ken Hilyer 2B – Albany   350
2. John Angelone SS, P – Thomasville 343
3. Jim Evans 2B, 3B – Valdosta   320
   John Bisesi SS – Albany   320
5. Charlie Ridgeway 2B, P – Fitzgerald 318

Most Errors
1. Norm Abrams 2B, 3B, SS – Cordele 70
2. John Bisesi SS – Albany   66
3. Jerome Pierce SS – Fitzgerald   52
4. Doug Campbell 3B, SS – Valdosta 48
5. Frank Calobrisi UT – Tifton   43
   Bob Capone 3B – Brunswick   43

Pitching
Most Wins
1. Jim Cater – Tifton   21
2. Jim Nisewonger – Brunswick   18
3. Joe Bourgeois – Albany   16
   Harry Johnson – Tifton   16
5. *four players tied with   15

Most Losses
1. Anthony Fabrizio – Cordele   18
2. Bill Allen – Waycross   17
3. John Claset – Fitzgerald   15
   George Utley – Waycross   15
   Bob Meagher – Cordele   15

Highest Winning Percentage (10 game minimum)
1. Bob Koczwara – Thomasville   .882
2. George Wasconis – Thomasville   .875
3. Fred Randle – Wayc/Thom   .857
4. Bill Keggereis – Albany   .800
5. Joe Ostopchuck – Albany   .786

Lowest Earned Run Average (100 inning minimum)
1. Jim Nisewonger – Brunswick   1.99
2. Julian Joyner – Albany   2.20
3. Don Kildoo – Brunswick   2.25
4. Bob Koczwara – Thomasville   2.28
5. Ed Jezek – Thomasville   2.61

Most Strikeouts
1. Jim Cater – Tifton   251
2. John Claset – Fitzgerald   186
3. Brad Clapham – Tifton   179
4. Bill Allen – Waycross   161
5. Joe Bourgeois – Albany   131

Most Bases on Balls
1. Jim Cater – Tifton   155
   John Claset – Fitzgerald   155
3. Bob Meagher – Cordele   147
4. Roy Kemp – Cordele   133
5. Bill Allen – Waycross   128

Most Hits Allowed
1. Vern Fisher – Valdosta   242
2. Brad Clapham – Tifton   230
3. Harry Johnson – Tifton   225
4. John Claset – Fitzgerald   222
5. George Utley – Waycross   219

Most Innings Pitched
1. Jim Cater – Tifton   254
2. Brad Clapham – Tifton   231
3. John Claset – Fitzgerald   228
4. Bill Allen – Waycross   225

5. Vern Fisher – Valdosta   223

1953 Georgia-Florida League All-Star Team
1B Dutch Van Burkleo – Brunswick
2B Ken Hilyer – Albany
3B Tom Burcham – Valdosta
SS Gene Freese – Brunswick
OF Ultus Alvarez – Thomasville
OF Heaford McKinney – Albany
OF Larry Hampshire – Thomasville
OF Lamar Burford – Valdosta
OF Ben Sinquefield – Brunswick
C   Bob Rand – Albany
C   Bill Dixon – Thomasville
P   Jim Cater – Tifton
P   Jim Nisewonger – Brunswick
P   Bob Koczwara – Thomasville
P   Don Kildoo – Brunswick
P   George Wasconis – Thomasville
M   John Angelone – Thomasville

1953

Georgia State League

League Office: Sylvania, Georgia
League President: Bill Estroff
League Vice President: C.B. McAllister
Secretary: Charlie Odom
Salary Limit: $2,600 per month.
Player Rule: Each club was allowed a roster of sixteen players, not more than three veterans, not more than five limited service, and not less than eight rookies.
Umpires: Calvin T. Drummond, Francis M. Terres, Michael Angelo Genevrino, B.W. King, Jr., Nickey Mann, Theodore Max Howe, Raymond T. Young, George P. Kelly, and Jospeh T. Vanak.

Georgia State League Final Standings

Team	W	L	Pct	GB	Affiliate
Hazlehurst-Baxley Cardinals	84	41	.672	----	STL-NL
Jesup Bees	78	46	.629	5.5	Unaffiliated
Eastman Dodgers	77	49	.611	7.5	Unaffiliated
Douglas Trojans	76	50	.603	8.5	Unaffiliated
Statesboro Pilots	49	77	.389	35.5	Unaffiliated
Sandersville Wacos	48	77	.384	36.0	MIL-NL
Dublin Irish	47	78	.376	37.0	PIT-NL
Vidalia Indians	41	82	.333	42.0	Unaffiliated

1953 Georgia State League Map

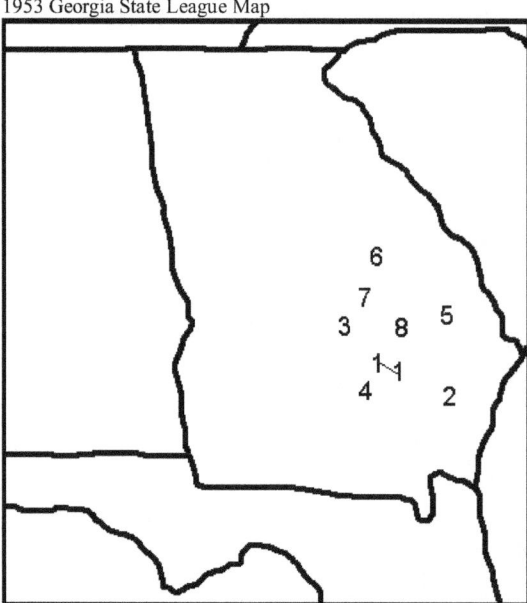

(numbers on map correspond to the place each team finished in regular season play)

During the off season between the 1952 and 1953 seasons, Fitzgerald dropped out of the Georgia State League, and Sandersville was added to fill the gap.

June 9 saw Douglas pitcher Don Quinn pitch a no-hitter against Jesup winning the game 4 to 1 for the league's only no-hitter of the season. Douglas slugger Van Davis set the all-time single season record for the most home runs in the league with 44 long balls. Davis also set the league's all time single season record for the most runs batted in with 159.

Hazlehurst-Baxley came in first place in regular season play with the best record of all the clubs. Jesup took second, Eastman third, and Douglas got fourth place in the end. Both first round playoff series' were routings as Hazlehurst-Baxley defeated Douglas four games to one, and Eastman blew out Jesup in four straight contests. The championship series, however, was a different story as it went the full, seven-game distance. In the end, it was Hazlehurst-Baxley coming out on top four games to three over Eastman.

Douglas, Georgia

Team Operated by Douglas Trojans, Inc.
Team President: H.B. Chitty
Vice President-Secretary-Treasurer-General Manager: W.P. Ward
Business Manager: Harry Roberts
Manager(s): Charles Bledsoe
Games played at City Municipal Park
Season attendance: 26,613

Douglas Trojans Team Roster

NAME	G	BA	POS	W	L	ERA	APF
Bledsoe, Charles	123	0.322	M, C, P	0	0		
Blume, Jim	17	0.250	P	0	1		Jesup
Brown, Lamar	90	0.310	OF				
Carpenter, Max	29	0.167	P	11	6	5.13	
Cash, Sewell	7	0.063	P	1	2		
Cathey, John	14	0.200	P	5	6	4.88	
Cavallaro, Fred	20	0.253	3B				
Chergey, Paul	16	0.115	P	5	5	4.14	
Clifton, John	1	0.000					
Collins, Jim	2	0.000					
Conn, Bob	122	0.304	2B				
Crouch, Les	80	0.295	SS				Statesboro
Dacus, Joe	21	0.289	OF				
Davis, Van	126	0.340	1B, P	0	1		
DeStafano, Lou	17	0.186	C				
Hutchins, Barry	8	0.286	P	1	2		
Johnson, Clyde	2	0.000	P	0	1		
Kemp, Roy	3	0.000	P	0	0		
Knodel, Len	13	0.233	P	6	4	4.12	
Kostner, Dick	87	0.296	SS, P	16	6	3.07	
McDaniels, Don	22	0.192	3B				
McGravy, Hoyt	38	0.333	OF				
McKay, Roy	33	0.157	P	11	6	6.08	
Morrison, Ron	1	0.000					
Mosley, Bob	1	0.000	P	0	1		
Murray, Don	123	0.287	OF				
O'Barr, Tom	1	0.000	P	0	1		
Padgett, Tom	2	0.000	P	0	1		
Petty, Virgil	31	0.240	OF				Jesup
Quinn, Don	27	0.000	P	11	1	4.81	
Rogers, Ernest	5	0.000	P	2	2		
Sarno, Anthony	35	0.256	3B				
Smith, Earl	10	0.200	P	2	1		
Sullivan, John	1	0.000	P	0	0		
Taylor, Ford	68	0.275	3B, SS				
Thomas, Wilbert	2	0.000	P	0	0		
Timberlake, Ray	99	0.302	OF				
Vest, Charles	1	0.000	P	0	0		
Weaver, Fred	4	0.231					
White, Bill	2	0.500					
Wieber, Joe	2	0.000	P	0	0		
Willis, Bob	2	0.333	P	0	1		
Wilson, Ward	12	0.150	P	3	3	3.88	
Yates, Bill	31	0.225	3B				

Georgia Class-D Minor League Baseball Encyclopedia

Dublin, Georgia
Team Operated by Dublin Baseball, Inc.
Team President: A.O. Hadden
Vice President: John D. George
Secretary-Treasurer-General Manager: F.M. Howell
Business Manager: C.T. Woodall
Manager(s): Johnny George, Frank Oceak, Parnell Ruark
Games played at Lovett Park
Season attendance: 25,394
Major League Affiliate: Pittsburgh Pirates – National League.

Dublin Irish Team Roster

NAME	G	BA	POS	W	L	ERA	APF
Ambrose, Dick	24	0.080	P	2	4	6.23	
Archer, Dick	4	0.000	P	0	0		
Bettin, Bob	54	0.305	OF, C				
Brumbaugh, John	56	0.195	SS				
Buheller, Clarence	50	0.258	2B, OF				
Carter, Arlen	20	0.115	P	3	10	7.54	
Chaillot, Emil	54	0.284	1B, P	5	4	5.48	
Clifton, Henry	94	0.291	1B, OF, P	14	8	5.07	
Combs, Ralph	79	0.297	3B, OF				
Crutchfield, Gene	7	0.125	P	0	1		
Dittmer, Charles	106	0.261	OF, C				
Falcione, Andrew	20	0.119					Jesup
Fleischer, Herb	8	0.000	P	2	3		
George, Johnny	44	0.233	M, C, P	1	2	9.40	
Gordon, Jerry	24	0.253	OF				
Harris, Oliver	44	0.188	1B				
Henkel, Ernest	14	0.208	P 2B, 3B, OF, C,	2	5	6.04	
Howell, Francis	124	0.269	P	0	0		Eastman
Long, Jim	39	0.192	P	11	6	4.88	Eas - San
Lugo, Lou	2	0.000	P	0	0		
Luker, John	8	0.000	P	2	0		
Marhoover, Gary	6	0.000	P	0	3		
Meier, John	13	0.189	1B				
Mena, Ignacio	64	0.289	3B, OF				Sandersville
Oceak, Frank			M				
O'Connell, Joe	8	0.250					
O'Rourke, Tom	16	0.317					
Owen, Bill	20	0.225	P	1	6	8.39	Jesup
Patten, Roger	8	0.222	P	1	2		
Petrick, John	56	0.322	OF				
Powell, Quincie	15	0.200	P	2	3	5.88	
Reagin, Bill	58	0.226	3B, P	3	2		Sandersville
Rich, Benny	19	0.152	P	1	6	6.52	
Ruark, Jim	41	0.244	C				
Ruark, Parnell	95	0.372	M, OF, P	0	1		Sandersville
Schrom, Sam	2	0.000					
Siff, Alan	13	0.160	P	2	4	6.17	
Stanziani, Nick	56	0.300	SS				
Swanson, Don	38	0.246	OF				
Titus, Lee	12	0.000	P	2	3		
Uzelatz, Max	2	0.000					
Vanasse, Bob	37	0.238	OF, P	2	8	4.67	
Vanowski, ---	1	0.000					
Walsh, Mike	53	0.265	2B				
Whaley, Walker	36	0.179	OF, P	4	6	7.08	

Eastman, Georgia
Team Operated by Eastman Dodgers, Inc.
Team President: E.L. Jones
Secretary-Treasurer: Thomas J. Sappington
General Manager: W.W. Taylor
Manager(s): Bob Reid
Games played at Legion Park
Season attendance: 29,232

Eastman Dodgers Team Roster

NAME	G	BA	POS	W	L	ERA	APF
Barnett, Byron	13	0.167	P	3	2	6.86	
Buttice, Lou	11	0.222					
Caldwell, Maurice	1	0.000					
Caldwell, Wilbur	122	0.297	3B, OF, P	13	6	4.43	
Caudle, Jim	125	0.331	1B, OF, P	0	0		
Clements, Frank	17	0.122	P	8	3	4.22	
Collins, Bill	39	0.270	OF				
Danowski, Bill	39	0.284	P	4	6	5.28	
DeFore, Ed	6	0.120					
DiRoberto, John	93	0.294	SS, OF				
Goins, Preston	15	0.087	P	0	0		
Hamlin, Nat	25	0.167	P	13	8	4.52	
Harp, Jim	51	0.219	P	19	11	3.33	
Heaton, Ralph	11	0.333	P	3	7	7.35	Sta - Vid
Howard, Alton	115	0.272	OF 2B, 3B, OF, C,				Vidalia
Howell, Francis	124	0.269	P	0	0		Dublin
Hughes, Norm	31	0.167	P	12	5	4.70	
Hunnicutt, Warner	4	0.000	P	0	2		
Kloss, Walt	123	0.242	2B				
Layton, Fred	4	0.273					Sandersville
Long, Jim	39	0.192	P	11	6	4.88	Dub - San
Maricich, Eli	124	0.323	3B, SS				
McLean, Harvey	4	0.000					
Patterson, Ted	49	0.365	1B				Sandersville
Reid, Bob	113	0.297	M, 1B				
Seaone, Manuel	9	0.345					
Veal, Bill	7	0.150					
Warzyniak, Ray	120	0.367	C				
Weaver, Bill	1	0.000	P	0	0		
Yanchura, John	29	0.265	SS				

Hazlehurst-Baxley (Hazlehurst & Baxley), Georgia
Team Operated by Hazlehurst-Baxley Baseball Club, Inc.
Team President: Mack Aaron
Vice President: Dr. C.R. Youmans
Secretary: Kenneth S. Martin
General Manager: Charles A. Odom
Manager(s): Arnold Riesgo
Games played at Roland Cook Stadium
Season attendance: 19,010
Major League Affiliate: St. Louis Cardinals – National League.

Hazlehurst-Baxley Cardinals Team Roster

NAME	G	BA	POS	W	L	ERA	APF
Allen, Jim	8	0.167	P	1	1		
Ball, John	33	0.169	P	15	8	3.34	
Barone, Anthony	4	0.200					
Barrett, Garland	2	0.000	P	0	1		
Cop, Milan	36	0.033	P	16	4	4.58	
Dal Porto, Angelo	124	0.272	SS				
Gehringer, Paul	18	0.100	P	4	4	2.82	
Ghelfi, Dick	22	0.208	P	11	4	3.23	
Guenst, Charles	13	0.298	OF				
Herrera, Ray	122	0.263	3B				
Horne, Armine	3	0.167	P	1	0		
Huthmaker, Fred	41	0.176	P	19	9	4.02	
Johnson, Earl	82	0.294	C				
Kamenski, Bernard	125	0.309	1B				
McClinton, Gene	25	0.216	P	8	3	4.50	
McLennan, Don	97	0.346	OF, P	5	5	4.82	
Newmarch, Ron	26	0.093	P	8	10	4.28	Sandersville
Petty, Fred	27	0.264	OF				
Ponce, Catarino	14	0.118	P	2	0		
Poppell, Jack	112	0.265	2B				
Recipko, Bill	13	0.190	P	1	0		
Riesgo, Arnold	90	0.306	M, 2B, C				

Georgia Class-D Minor League Baseball Encyclopedia

NAME	G	BA	POS	W	L	ERA	APF
Robinson, Ben	40	0.264	OF				
Sheeks, Bill	1	0.000	P	0	1		
Vasquez, Regino	4	0.000	P	0	1		
Westbrook, Price	1	0.333					
Wyatt, Gene	98	0.263	OF				
Zuccarini, Bob	119	0.350	OF				

Jesup, Georgia

Team Operated by Jesup Baseball Club
Team President: Dr. Alvin Leaphart
Vice President-Treasurer: L.T. Lloyd
Secretary: Bob White
Business Manager: Bill Steinecke
Manager(s): Bill Steinecke
Games played at Milikin Park
Season attendance: 20,629

Jesup Bees Team Roster

NAME	G	BA	POS	W	L	ERA	APF
Bartholomew, Jack	4	0.313					
Blume, Jim	17	0.250	P	0	1		Douglas
Boxer, Seymour	37	0.229	P	18	11	3.82	
Charette, Don	21	0.107	P	3	2	5.69	
Childers, Jimmy	4	0.167					
Cornett, Homer	2	0.000	P	0	0		
Daniel, Doug	4	0.750					
Enquist, Ernest	44	0.267	3B, SS				
Falcione, Andrew	20	0.119					Dublin
Geary, Henry	29	0.314	3B				
Harvey, Joe	5	0.167	P	1	1		
Hutson, Cecil	75	0.176	P	17	12	3.46	
Jackson, Harold	34	0.148	3B, P	2	4	3.81	
Keller, Ed	1	0.500	P	0	0		
Kovaleski, John	67	0.306	2B				
Landers, Ken	2	0.286					
Licata, Vince	24	0.227	3B				
Livingston, Doug	3	0.500					
Lyons, John	2	0.000	P	0	1		
Mallard, John	122	0.287	2B, SS				
Mansfield, Cliff	124	0.303	1B				
Medley, Carl	124	0.301	OF, C				
Miller, Stan	27	0.260	P	11	3	4.17	
Mirande, Anthony	9	0.185					
Osborne, Wilson	8	0.400					
Owen, Bill	20	0.225	P	1	6	8.39	Dublin
Parrish, Ron	2	0.500	P	1	0		
Pawlick, John	109		C				
Petty, Virgil	31	0.240	OF				Douglas
Ready, Charlie	36	0.218	P	17	7	4.26	
Sherba, Elmer	5	0.190					
Soja, Tom	7	0.273					
Sosebee, Jim	123	0.369	OF				
Steinecke, Bill			M				
Stone, Art	19	0.128					
Sutfin, Harry	4	0.333	P	0	0		
Virgona, Al	52	0.216	OF				
Warren, Jim	94	0.301	OF, P	6	1	2.02	
Williams, John	6	0.000	P	0	3		
Young, Harmon	54	0.290	3B				

Sandersville, Georgia

Team Operated by Washington County Baseball Corporation
Team President: Marvin E. Moate
Vice President-Secretary: H.C. Blackburn
Business Manager-Travel Secretary: Mike Merola
Manager(s): Gabby Grant, Julian Morgan, Lucius Morgan, Parnell Ruark
Games played at Sandersville Baseball Park
Season attendance: 33,895
Major League Affiliate: Milwaukee Braves – National League.

Sandersville Wacos Team Roster

NAME	G	BA	POS	W	L	ERA	APF
Allen, Bill	10	0.125	P	0	2		
Altomer, Lou	8	0.308	P	2	2		
Babcock, Harry	27	0.279	OF				
Baker, Jerry	2	0.000					
Boggs, Pat	13	0.103					
Boswell, John	1	0.000	P	1	0		
Braun, Leon	2	0.000	P	0	1		Statesboro
Breidt, Bob	65	0.217	C				
Castalado, Jerry	6	0.000	P	1	0		
Celozzi, Joe	8	0.077	P	0	2		
Colvin, Jack	7	0.364					
Cooper, Bob	4	0.250	P	0	1		
Davis, Carl	4	0.222	P	0	4		
Dobek, John	63	0.267	1B				
Doehler, Charles	31	0.235	OF				
Dolan, Lonnie	3	0.000					
Dunlap, Bob	3	0.500	P	2	1		
Faulk, Leon	5	0.286					
Fernandez, Jose	6	0.364	P	1	1		
Finch, ---	4	0.000	P	0	0		
Ford, Bob	87	0.264	SS				
Freeman, Jim	42	0.267	P	3	5	7.74	
Garcia, Jesus	60	0.259	2B				
Garmon, Ray	19	0.333	P	3	4	4.35	
Grant, Gabby	53	0.291	M, C, P	0	2		
Harrow, Herb	36	0.229	2B				
Herringdine, Cecil	122	0.288	OF, C				
Hoyal, Craig	48	0.144	OF, P	2	4	6.30	
Johnson, Sid	27	0.317	SS				
Jones, Harry	8	0.308					
Keleher, Oscar	6	0.095					
Kenny, Sherman	36	0.266	OF				
Kirby, Bob	5	0.083	P	1	1		
Layton, Fred	4	0.273					Eastman
Long, Jim	39	0.192	P	11	6	4.88	Dub - Eas
Luddy, Harold	3	0.200					
Manes, Jerry	3	0.000					
Maxwell, John	4	0.333	P	0	2		
McPartland, Doug	3	0.000	P	0	1		Statesboro
Mena, Ignacio	64	0.289	3B, OF				Dublin
Mock, ---	1	0.500					
Moore, Willard	19	0.154	P	3	7	7.20	
Morgan, Julian			M				
Morgan, Lucius	105	0.330	M, 2B, 3B, SS, P	0	0		
Newmarch, Ron	26	0.093	P	8	10	4.28	Haz-Bax
Parrott, Willie	26	0.236	P	5	8	5.76	
Patterson, Ted	49	0.365	1B				Eastman
Reagin, Bill	58	0.226	3B, P	3	2		Dublin
Reckelhoff, Bob	8	0.071					
Ruark, Parnell	95	0.372	M, OF, P	0	1		Dublin
Sanders, Henry	33	0.245	3B				
Saporito, John	5	0.000	P	0	1		Vidalia
Seaman, Bob	5	0.059					
Shuryn, Bill	8	0.250	P	2	3		
Smith, Max	20	0.215	1B				
Stewart, Rudy	8	0.367					
Tyler, Jim	4	0.375	P	2	1		
Ware, Charles	3	0.357					
Yearty, Sam	25	0.160	P	6	6	4.70	
Youngblood, Jack	3	0.000	P	0	1		

Statesboro, Georgia

Team Operated by Statesboro Athletic Association, Inc.
Team President: C.B. McAllister
Vice President: Alfred Dorman

Georgia Class-D Minor League Baseball Encyclopedia

Secretary: R. Herbert Kingery
Treasurer: Herman E. Bray
Business Manager: R.F. Donaldson, Jr.
Manager(s): Jack Hines, Cliff Thrasher
Games played at Pilots Field
Season attendance: 38,431

Statesboro Pilots Team Roster

NAME	G	BA	POS	W	L	ERA	APF
Bachars, Medar	20	0.210	OF				
Berzonski, John	12	0.214	P	0	4	5.44	
Braun, Leon	2	0.000	P	0	1		Sandersville
Browning, Doug	2	1.000	P	1	0		
Carn, Irv	13	0.245	OF				
Crouch, Les	80	0.295	SS				Douglas
DiMare, Dom	9	0.037					
Dyer, Vaughn	100	0.354	1B				
Elliott, Art	38	0.158	P	6	12	5.49	
Ford, Bob	89	0.261	3B, OF				
Frady, Bill	8	0.080	P	5	3	4.50	
Gunter, Ray	7	0.000	P	0	2		
Gurri, Anibal	93	0.272	OF, P	2	4		
Hay, Howard	4	0.250	P	0	1		
Heaton, Ralph	11	0.333	P	3	7	7.35	Eas - Vid
Hernandez, Sam	125	0.296	2B				
Heughens, Ron	3	0.250					
Hines, Jack			M				
Jiminez, Dan	85	0.284	3B, OF, P	4	3	5.16	
King, Ken	17	0.265	3B				
Lane, Clyde	31	0.140	P	9	12	5.32	
Lane, Dave	4	0.300					
Lee, Norm	7	0.313					
Lopez, Carlos	36	0.250	OF, P	10	4	2.37	
Lowery, Jason	38	0.289	OF				
Martin, John	19	0.267	P	2	6	6.08	
Masatto, Frank	1	0.250					
McCormack, Tom	3	0.667					
McPartland, Doug	3	0.000	P	0	1		Sandersville
Menapace, Ed	72	0.256	3B, C				Vidalia
Moore, John	19	0.100	P	2	6	6.32	
Peters, Gerald	126	0.251	1B, OF				
Romeo, John	10	0.063	P	0	0		Vidalia
Rovai, Rudy	25	0.179	P	6	6	4.88	
Sanchez, Jerry	1	0.000					
Smith, Gene	4	0.000	P	0	1		
Tepedino, Frank	119	0.283	3B, SS				Vidalia
Thrasher, Cliff	122	0.260	M, C, P	2	3		
Tipton, Bill	2	0.000					
Walston, Bob	51	0.276	OF				
Warshaw, Art	2	0.000	P	0	1		
White, Curtis	5	0.250					
White, Jack	6	0.667	P	0	4		

Vidalia, Georgia
Team Operated by Vidalia Baseball Association, Inc.
Team President: H.S. Vandiver
Secretary-Treasurer: G.H. Gibson
Manager(s): Don Cross, Jake Daniel, Bull Hamons
Games played at Vidalia Municipal Stadium
Season attendance: 28,665

Vidalia Indians Team Roster

NAME	G	BA	POS	W	L	ERA	APF
Badour, Bob	10	0.278	P	1	3	6.85	
Bauer, Ed	38	0.312	OF				
Beal, Bill	7	0.167	P	0	4		
Benson, John	2	0.125					
Bettineschi, Frank	29	0.273	3B				
Boyce, Ken	8	0.105					
Briscoe, Bertram	34	0.286	3B, OF				
Brown, John	5	0.050					
Burns, Jim	120	0.347	OF				
Callahan, Mike	24	0.163	P	7	10	4.36	
Colangelo, Stan	3	0.000	P	0	0		
Corder, Bob	51	0.255	SS				
Cross, Don	28	0.295	M, SS, P	0	0		
Daniel, Jake	37	0.284	M, 1B				
Dawson, Ron	2	0.000	P	0	0		
Dobbins, Mayes	105	0.259	2B				
Driggers, Bobby	82	0.311	OF, C				
Feola, Charles	3	0.000	P	0	0		
Hamons, Bull			M				
Haney, Clay	29	0.255	P	3	6	7.64	
Hanna, Perry	10	0.375	P	0	4		
Heaton, Ralph	11	0.333	P	3	7	7.35	Eas - Sta
Heisler, Allen	7	0.167	P	1	0		
Hollis, Grady	60	0.246	OF				
Howard, Alton	115	0.272	OF				Eastman
Jones, Jack	7	0.250	P	2	2		
Kopacz, Ed	35	0.211	1B, OF				
Kruppa, Paul	4	0.000	P	0	0		
McCluskey, Austin	14	0.250	P	0	5		
McGowan, Frank	7	0.154					
Menapace, Ed	72	0.256	3B, C				Statesboro
Musser, Dick	18	0.233	OF				
Myers, Bill	17	0.273	OF				
O'Neal, Tom	10	0.222	P	2	2		
Patriss, Bill	64	0.224	3B, SS				
Plushanski, Fred	46	0.186	P	6	16	4.23	
Price, Charles	16	0.150	P	7	7	4.78	
Raeburn, John	3	0.000					
Reeves, Harold	4	0.100					
Richter, Phil	2	0.333	P	1	1		
Ricketson, Don	25	0.281	C				
Romeo, John	10	0.063	P	0	0		Statesboro
Russell, Ed	68	0.292	1B, OF				
Saporito, John	5	0.000	P	0	1		Sandersville
Schultz, Glen	31	0.091	P	3	5	5.14	
Schultz, Jack	1	0.667	P	0	0		
Scriptjack, Ray	5	0.167	P	0	0		
Shipley, Joe	15	0.111	P	1	6	6.04	
Sterrette, Bob	8	0.212					
Sweet, Harold	23	0.235	C				
Tepedino, Frank	119	0.283	3B, SS				Statesboro
Trapasso, Lawrence	5	0.250	P	0	1		
VanDerBeek, Jim	23	0.121	P	4	5	4.19	
Watkins, Lou	3	0.444					
Wright, Ken	27	0.220	2B, SS				
Young, Bill	5	0.000					

1953 Georgia State League Records
Batting
Highest Batting Average (minimum 100 at bats)
1. Parnell Ruark – Sand/Dubl   .372
2. Jim Sosebee – Jesup   .369
3. Ray Warzyniak – Eastman   .367
4. Ted Patterson – Sand/East   .365
5. Vaughn Dyer – Statesboro   .354

Most Hits
1. Jim Sosebee – Jesup   186
2. Ray Warzyniak – Eastman   183
3. Jim Caudle – Eastman   167
4. Eli Maricich – Eastman   163
5. Charles Bledsoe – Douglas   162

Most Runs
1. Eli Maricich – Eastman   139
2. Bob Zuccarini - Hazlehurst-Baxley 131
3. Van Davis – Douglas   130

Georgia Class-D Minor League Baseball Encyclopedia

4. Jim Sosebee – Jesup 118
5. Bernard Kamenski - Hazlehurst-Baxley 112

Most Total Bases
1. Van Davis – Douglas 308
2. Ray Warzyniak – Eastman 291
3. Jim Caudle – Eastman 290
4. Eli Marcich – Eastman 289
5. Jim Sosebee – Jesup 282

Most Doubles
1. Jim Sosebee – Jesup 42
2. Ray Warzyniak – Eastman 41
3. Wilbur Caldwell – Eastman 36
4. Parnell Ruark – Sand/Dubl 31
5. Carl Medley – Jesup 29
   Jim Burns – Vidalia 29
   Sam Hernandez – Statesboro 29

Most Triples
1. Ted Patterson – Sand/East 19
2. Ray Warzyniak – Eastman 11
3. Jim Sosebee – Jesup 9
   Bernard Kamenski - Hazlehurst-Baxley 9
   Frank Tepedino – Vidalia 9

Most Home Runs
1. Van Davis – Douglas 44
2. Eli Maricich – Eastman 29
3. Jim Caudle – Eastman 27
4. Carl Medley – Jesup 23
5. Jim Burns – Vidalia 21
   Cecil Herringdine – Sandersville 21

Most Extra Base Hits
1. Van Davis – Douglas 69
2. Ray Warzyniak – Eastman 67
3. Jim Sosebee – Jesup 63
4. Eli Maricich – Eastman 62
5. Jim Caudle – Eastman 61

Most Runs Batted In
1. Van Davis – Douglas 159
2. Ray Warzyniak – Eastman 140
3. Jim Caudle – Eastman 134
4. Carl Medley – Jesup 129
5. Jim Sosebee – Jesup 118

Most Stolen Bases
1. Eli Maricich – Eastman 47
2. Gerald Peters – Statesboro 44
3. Wilbur Caldwell – Eastman 38
4. Sam Hernandez – Statesboro 36
5. Cliff Mansfield – Jesup 35

Fielding
Most Put-Outs
1. Cliff Mansfield 1B – Jesup 1,118
2. Bob Reid 1B – Eastman 986
3. Van Davis 1B, P – Douglas 973
4. Bernard Kamenski 1B - Hazlehurst-Baxley 941
5. Vaughn Dyer 1B – Statesboro 874

Most Assists
1. John Mallard 2B, SS – Jesup 381
2. Sam Hernandez 2B – Statesboro 376
3. Frank Tepedino 3B, SS – Vidalia 359
4. Walt Kloss 2B – Eastman 343
5. Eli Maricich 3B, SS – Eastman 335

Most Errors
1. Angelo Dal Porto SS - Hazlehurst-Baxley 58
2. Eli Maricich 3B, SS – Eastman 44
3. John Mallard 2B, SS – Jesup 43
4. Bob Ford SS – Sandersville 39
5. Lucius Morgan 2B, 3B, SS, P – Sandersville 36
   Bill Patriss 3B, SS – Vidalia 36

Pitching
Most Wins
1. Jim Harp – Eastman 19
   Fred Huthmaker - Hazlehurst-Baxley 19
3. Seymour Boxer – Jesup 18
4. Charlie Ready – Jesup 17
   Cecil Hutson – Jesup 17

Most Losses
1. Fred Plushanski – Vidalia 16
2. Cecil Hutson – Jesup 12
   Clyde Lane – Statesboro 12
   Art Elliott – Statesboro 12
5. Jim Harp – Eastman 11
   Seymour Boxer – Jesup 11

Highest Winning Percentage (10 game minimum)
1. Don Quinn – Douglas .917
2. Milan Cop - Hazlehurst-Baxley .800
3. Stan Miller – Jesup .786
4. Dick Ghelfi - Hazlehurst-Baxley .733
5. Dick Kostner – Douglas .727
   Frank Clements – Eastman .727

Lowest Earned Run Average (100 inning minimum)
1. Carlos Lopez – Statesboro 2.37
2. Dick Kostner – Douglas 3.07
3. Dick Ghelfi - Hazlehurst-Baxley 3.23
4. Jim Harp – Eastman 3.33
5. John Ball - Hazlehurst-Baxley 3.34

Most Strikeouts
1. Charlie Ready – Jesup 161
2. Cecil Hutson – Jesup 156
3. Roy McKay – Douglas 140
4. Milan Cop - Hazlehurst-Baxley 130
5. John Ball - Hazlehurst-Baxley 124

Most Bases on Balls
1. Roy McKay – Douglas 140
2. Henry Clifton – Dublin 131
3. Milan Cop - Hazlehurst-Baxley 129
4. Seymour Boxer – Jesup 128
5. Charlie Ready – Jesup 126

Most Hits Allowed
1. Fred Plushanski – Vidalia 247
2. Cecil Hutson – Jesup 246
3. Jim Harp – Eastman 228
4. Fred Huthmaker - Hazlehurst-Baxley 216
5. Charlie Ready – Jesup 208

Most Innings Pitched
1. Cecil Huston – Jesup 265
2. Jim Harp – Eastman 227
3. Charlie Ready – Jesup 224
4. Fred Plushanski – Vidalia 217
   Fred Huthmaker - Hazlehurst-Baxley 217
   Seymour Boxer – Jesup 217

1953 Georgia State League All-Star Team
1B Vaughn Dyer – Statesboro
2B Sam Hernandez – Statesboro
3B Ray Herrera - Hazlehurst-Baxley
SS Eli Maricich – Eastman
OF Jim Sosebee – Jesup
OF Bob Zuccarini - Hazlehurst-Baxley
OF Jim Caudle – Eastman
C Ray Warzyniak – Eastman
P Fred Huthmaker - Hazlehurst-Baxley
P Jim Harp – Eastman
P Milan Cop - Hazlehurst-Baxley
P Don Quinn – Douglas

1954

Georgia-Florida League

League Office: Leslie, Georgia
League President: W.T. Anderson
League Vice President: Guy Connell
Salary Limit: $2,600 per month plus $600.
Player Rule: Each club was allowed a roster of sixteen players, not more than three veterans, not more than eight limited service, and not less than five rookies.

Georgia-Florida League Final Standings

Team	W	L	Pct	GB	Affiliate
Brunswick Pirates	88	52	.629	----	PIT-NL
Fitzgerald Redlegs	80	59	.576	7.5	CIN-NL
Albany Cardinals	73	65	.529	14.0	STL-NL
Waycross Bears	68	67	.504	17.5	Unaffiliated
Valdosta Tigers	68	70	.493	19.0	DET-AL
Thomasville Dodgers	64	71	.474	21.5	BRK-NL
Tifton Indians	60	80	.429	28.0	CLE-AL
Americus-Cordele Orioles	51	88	.367	36.5	BAL-AL

1954 Georgia-Florida League Map

(numbers on map correspond to the place each team finished in regular season play)

The composition of the league remained the same as it was in the prior season, but Cordele became a combined team representing Americus as well.

Four no-hitters were pitched during the 1954 season, two of which were dealt to Americus-Cordele. The first no-hitter was on April 22 pitched by Waycross' John Scroggs to shutout Thomasville 3 to 0. Tom McMullen of Thomasville hurled the second no-hitter on June 9 when he defeated Americus-Cordele 8 to 1. Tifton pitcher Tony Sarmiento handed Americus-Cordele their second blank slate of the year on June 23 shutting the Orioles down 10 to 0 in seven innings. And the season's final no-hitter came from the arm of Waycross moundsman

John O'Neill on August 19 to shutout Tifton 4 to 0. Brunswick's Floyd "Dynamite" Faust set the all-time league single season record for the most stolen bases with 76 safe swipes. Charles "Whammy" Douglas, also of Brunswick, set the league's all-time mark for the most wins by a pitcher in a single season when he won 27 games.

Brunswick won the regular season pennant by having the best record of all the league's clubs. Fitzgerald finished second, Albany third, and Waycross came in fourth place finishing out the list of clubs advancing to the post-season. Brunswick easily defeated Waycross in the first round four games to one, and Fitzgerald beat Albany by the same score in the other first round series. Fitzgerald won three games in the league championship series, and Brunswick won two. The series was never finished due to numerous rainouts, and no league champion was declared.

Albany, Georgia
Team Operated by Albany Baseball Club, Inc.
Team President: Morton M. Wiggins
Vice Presidents: August Busch, Jr., William Walsingham, Jr.
Secretary: Nadine Cravey
General Manager: Sheldon A. "Chief" Bender
Manager(s): Russ McGovern
Games played at Cardinal Park
Season attendance: 47,092
Major League Affiliate: St. Louis Cardinals – National League.

Albany Cardinals Team Roster

NAME	G	BA	POS	W	L	ERA	APF
Allman, Frank	23	0.214					
Barton, Cecil	6	0.000	P	1	1		
Batty, Bill	112	0.263	2B, 3B, SS				
Benedict, Cletus	52	0.169	1B				
Carolan, Joe	15	0.218	OF				
Cassell, Carl	43	0.167	C				
Craig, Royal	1	0.000	P	0	0		
Curl, Kedy	1	0.000	P	0	0		
Doke, Ted	2	0.000	P	0	0		
Dutton, Charles	8	0.000					
Edwards, Don	45	0.188	OF				
Elliott, Art	5	0.000	P	0	3		
Fleisch, Don	26	0.260	OF				
Fraley, Carroll	7	0.000	P	0	1		
Hanna, Vic	8	0.333	P	0	0		
Henderson, Bill	13	0.063	P	2	2	4.89	Brunswick
Johnson, Earl	131	0.277	OF, C				
Joyner, Julian	40	0.119	P	10	9	2.64	
Keggereis, Bill	7	0.000	P	1	2		
Keister, Harry	111	0.286	OF				
Knox, Bill	43	0.200	P	20	9	1.80	
Kusmierski, Dick	4	0.000	P	0	0		
Luciano, Mike	12	0.208	OF				
Martin, Lane	33	0.154	P	10	12	4.76	
McGovern, Russ	134	0.257	M, OF				
Miller, Gerald	57	0.198	3B, SS				Waycross
Payne, John	32	0.156	P	10	8	3.85	
Peterson, Tom	13	0.262	SS				
Podowski, Phil	2	0.000	P	0	0		
Poppell, Jack	103	0.243	2B				
Proctor, Tom	18	0.308	P	3	3	2.76	
Rosa, Charles	1	0.000					
Salazar, Enrique	107	0.221	SS				Thomasville
Sanders, Al	15	0.077	P	7	4	3.79	
Schaffer, Bob	42	0.225	P	9	12	3.10	
Solberg, Herb	4	0.000	P	2	0		
Thomas, George	52	0.285	OF				
Vingers, Leonard	65	0.252	1B				
Way, Walt	134	0.272	1B, 3B, OF, P	0	0		
Woolford, Ed	26	0.214	2B				
Wright, Dick	1	0.000	P	0	0		

Americus-Cordele (Americus & Cordele), Georgia
Team Operated by Americus-Cordele Baseball Club
Team President: J.W. Bridges
Vice President: H.W. Moon
Secretary: James R. Blair
Treasurer: George Cochran
General Manager: J.L. Robertson, Jr.
Manager(s): Jack Landis, Cliff Melton
Games played at Community Center Ball park (half home games in Americus) and City Park (half home games in Cordele)
Season attendance: 26,136
Major League Affiliate: Baltimore Orioles – American League.

Americus-Cordele Orioles Team Roster

NAME	G	BA	POS	W	L	ERA	APF
Banks, Gerald	21	0.167	P	2	5	5.76	Fitzgerald
Bohn, Lloyd	15	0.188	P	2	3		
Brandenburg, Charles	47	0.257	OF, C				
Bunce, Jack	46	0.261	P	9	15	3.96	
Burford, Larry	138	0.249	OF				
Cartwright, Don	6	0.000	P	0	3		
Castaneda, Jim	79	0.247	1B				
Coho, Russ	72	0.221	C				
Cotter, Jim	19	0.224	OF				
Cottier, Chuck	138	0.250	2B				
DeSousa, John	10	0.214					
Eilbacher, Leo	92	0.270	OF				
Ferguson, Jim	95	0.245	3B, OF, C				
Gonzales, Oscar	25	0.107					
Hammen, Floyd	95	0.238	3B, SS				
Harrison, Randy	10	0.265					
Horne, Tom	22	0.107	P	5	6	3.48	
Kallas, Harry	59	0.257	SS				
Landis, Jack	74	0.215	M, 1B, 3B				
Lucabaugh, Charles	118	0.229	OF, P	5	6	2.25	
Lutz, Dave	14	0.250	P	2	3	5.09	
Lyons, Don	9	0.200					
Manahan, Gerald	2	0.000					
McCormack, Tom	51	0.210	1B				
McDonald, Russ	6	0.000	P	0	4		
Melton, Cliff	17	0.375	M				
Moore, Bill	20	0.143	P	4	7	4.74	
Myatt, Charles	17	0.288	3B				
Schall, Gene	23	0.128	P	4	7	4.27	
Schultz, Dick	20	0.259	P	8	7	3.41	
Silva, Gil	6	0.143	P	3	3	1.36	
Thomas, Bob	22	0.156	3B				
Tomter, Harvey	36	0.179	P	6	17	5.00	
Williams, John	60	0.207	OF				Thomasville
Wilson, Ed	5	0.000					

Brunswick, Georgia
Team Operated by Brunswick Pirates, Inc.
Team President: Blanton Miller
Vice Presidents: Branch Rickey, Jr., Harold G. Roettger
Secretary: Walter Bunt
Treasurer: James A. Herron
General Manager: Jack Berger
Manager(s): Frank Oceak
Games played at Edo Miller Park
Season attendance: 54,475
Major League Affiliate: Pittsburgh Pirates – National League.

Georgia Class-D Minor League Baseball Encyclopedia

Brunswick Pirates Team Roster

NAME	G	BA	POS	W	L	ERA	APF
Arent, George	24	0.244	1B				
Brockell, Charlie	134	0.269	3B, SS, P	0	1		
Brumbaugh, John	9	0.208					
Buheller, Clarence	141	0.325	1B, OF				
Canuso, Joe	131	0.226	C				
Capone, Bob	118	0.256	3B, OF				
Chadner, Dick	7	0.500	P	0	0		
Chlebek, Stan	6	0.000	P	1	1		
Deveney, Jim	6	0.222					
Douglas, Whammy	39	0.176	P	27	6	2.06	
Farless, Sam	127	0.285	OF				
Faust, Floyd	141	0.273	OF				
Gay, Bill	24	0.161	C				
Graham, Bernard	16	0.154	P	2	3	6.28	
Gray, Ron	34	0.125	P	19	4	2.71	
Hayden, Jim	26	0.120	P	1	3	7.50	
Hayes, Tom	5	0.250	P	1	0		
Henderson, Bill	13	0.063	P	2	2	4.89	Albany
Hensley, Paul	4	0.000	P	1	1		
Honkus, Stan	26	0.261	P	9	6	3.36	
Mathes, Ed	13	0.148					
McClenaghan, Russ	5	0.200					
McNally, Don	82	0.217	2B, SS, P	1	1		
Moriskiewicz, John	117	0.254	OF				
Oceak, Frank			M				
Patchell, Stan	17	0.156	P	3	9	3.64	
Payne, Dick	44	0.130	P	14	8	3.48	
Rechichar, Adrian	126	0.273	2B				
Smith, Tom	7	0.000	P	1	0		
Tyndall, Dick	17	0.280	P	0	0		
Vest, Milt	17	0.115	P	4	6	5.67	
Wolfman, Cedric	8	0.182	P	2	2		
Zaski, Regis	14	0.314					

Fitzgerald, Georgia
Team Operated by Fitzgerald Pioneers, Inc.
Team President: Al H. Evans
Vice Presidents: Philip Halperin, Raymond Harris
Secretary-Treasurer: Curtis E. Green
Business Manager: Michael R. Harrison
Manager(s): Red Treadway
Games played at Blue-Gray Park
Season attendance: 38,652
Major League Affiliate: Cincinnati Reds – National League.

Fitzgerald Redlegs Team Roster

NAME	G	BA	POS	W	L	ERA	APF
Banks, Gerald	21	0.167	P	2	5	5.76	Ame-Cor
Bradberry, Buck	12	0.250	P	1	6	5.64	
Claset, John	42	0.177	P	19	11	2.90	
Davis, Thurman	130	0.252	3B				
DeStefano, Lou	13	0.160	C				
Dinkelacker, Tim	36	0.228	P	16	8	3.16	
Dotterer, Tom	97	0.210	3B, SS				
Drostie, Carroll	13	0.174	P	4	6	5.16	
Fregin, Arnold	54	0.216	OF				
Gearhart, Earl	48	0.246	P	20	9	3.07	
Grobar, Jim	72	0.268	OF				
Higgenbottom, Dizzy	12	0.077	P	1	2		
Hill, Van	133	0.265	OF				
Husich, John	50	0.256	P	9	10	4.23	
Maricich, Eli	31	0.280	SS, OF				
Pierce, Jerome	32	0.203	2B				
Pollock, Stan	1	0.000					
Sangalli, Frank	95	0.231	2B				
Shartzer, Phil	59	0.239	SS				
Stone, Allan	30	0.245	P	10	7	3.95	
Stutts, Bob	65	0.264	OF, C				
Thompson, Bill	139	0.296	1B				
Tilley, Terry	9	0.174					
Treadway, Red	117	0.363	M, OF, P	0	0		
Wehman, Dick	121	0.285	C				
Yarbrough, Jim	9	0.150					

Thomasville, Georgia
Team Operated by Thomasville Dodgers, Inc.
Team President: Heeth Varnedoe
Vice President: Fresco Thompson
Secretary: Matthew A. Burns
Treasurer: William Gibson
General Manager: George E. Pfister
Manager(s): John Angelone, Boyd Bartley
Games played at Municipal Stadium
Season attendance: 36,079

Thomasville Dodgers Team Roster

NAME	G	BA	POS	W	L	ERA	APF
Angelone, John	13	0.233	M, 3B, P	0	0		
Barbier, John	28	0.234	P	9	9	3.14	
Bartley, Boyd			M				
Battle, Don	11	0.208					
Beiler, Carl	33	0.265	OF				
Brandt, Fred	8	0.000	P	1	0		
Brown, Bobby	102	0.230	OF				
Caldwell, Jim	22	0.211	SS				
Callaway, Charles	5	0.231					
Castelli, Anthony	6	0.059					
Corthell, Dick	15	0.265	3B				
Cozart, Paul	111	0.272	3B, SS, OF				
Crisp, Ransom	24	0.234	C				
Deal, Bill	22	0.175	OF				
DiMott, Don	75	0.280	1B, OF				
Draper, Dick	9	0.000	P	0	1		
Elder, Gene	116	0.262	2B, OF				
Ford, Bob	2	0.000					
Gisclair, Clyde	35	0.279	OF				
Hall, Morris	8	0.190					
Heinz, Martin	11	0.167	P	1	2		
Holderfield, Harold	78	0.277	OF				
Lauderdale, Tom	2	0.000					
Lightfoot, Frank	9	0.179					
McCall, Gordon	10	0.143	P	2	3		
McCasland, Stan	7	0.429	P	2	0		
McLean, John	6	0.000	P	0	3		
McMullen, Tom	21	0.196	P	8	8	2.18	
Mixon, Clark	9	0.333	P	0	2		
Ohr, Cliff	4	0.000	P				
Pavuk, Tom	14	0.318					
Pawlak, Walt	52	0.239	2B				
Pender, Wilbert	26	0.226	P	9	11	4.35	
Perkins, Dave	4	0.250	P	0	1		
Petrovich, Ron	8	0.000	P	1	4		
Pillow, Clarence	114	0.277	1B, 3B				
Pohutsky, Chester	19	0.227	1B				
Poole, Benny	10	0.111	P	0	2		
Royce, Gordon	12	0.125	P	4	1	3.29	
Russell, Dave	81	0.278	OF				
Salazar, Enrique	107	0.221	SS				Albany
Tracewski, Dick	72	0.277	SS				
Turek, Don	4	0.000	P	0	1		
Turner, Bob	12	0.125					
Virkstis, Bob	50	0.243	P	11	8	2.70	
Wells, Bill	6	0.333	P	2	1		
Wells, Ronald	34	0.143	P	14	11	3.04	
Williams, Don	123	0.311	C, P	0	0		
Williams, John	60	0.207	OF				Ame-Cor
Zimmerman, Dick	3	0.000	P	0	2		

Georgia Class-D Minor League Baseball Encyclopedia

Tifton, Georgia
Team Operated by Tiftarea Baseball Club, Inc.
Team President: Dr. L.O. Shaw
Vice President: R.L. Hargrett
Secretary-Treasurer: E.D. Hamilton
Business Manager: Edd Hartness
Manager(s): Edd Hartness
Games played at Eve Park
Season attendance: 30,143
Major League Affiliate: Cleveland Indians – American League.

Tifton Indians Team Roster

NAME	G	BA	POS	W	L	ERA	APF
Badia, Armenio	99	0.249	OF, P	0	0		
Brosnan, Pat	9	0.286	P	1	2		
Casanega, Dave	26	0.220	SS				
Chafin, Cotton	59	0.285	2B				
Cobb, Joe	6	0.000	P	0	1		
Company, Ron	90	0.260	OF				
Conti, Lou	3	0.091					
Cornwell, John	25	0.221	2B				
Davis, Hazen	6	0.222	P	1	4		
Deering, Verne	15	0.095	P	2	7	5.29	
DeStefano, Mike	18	0.146	OF				
Farmer, Dennis	56	0.240	2B, SS				
Fowler, Ted	21	0.050	P	2	5	4.77	
Gentry, Dick	44	0.189	SS				
Haney, Joe	34	0.208	P	3	4	3.81	
Hartness, Edd	113	0.364	M, 1B, OF				
Hemmerle, Dick	30	0.145	P	13	10	3.45	
Johnson, Tom	12	0.162	2B				
Johnson, Wilbur	27	0.226	P	7	10	4.20	
Jones, Jack	26	0.203	SS				
Jones, Ron	27	0.172					
Koszenski, Stan	13	0.158	P	2	3	4.58	
Langston, Howard	3	0.222					
Larned, Harold	18	0.031	P	6	5	2.57	
Lawman, Gerald	13	0.175	SS				
Lewis, Bob	28	0.169	OF				
Monasterio, Eduardo	42	0.245	3B				
Pare, Al	31	0.150	OF				
Price, Ron	2	0.000	P	0	0		
Retzer, Ken	130	0.307	C				
Roberts, Kelvin	140	0.331	1B, OF				
Robinson, Don	15	0.267	P	0	0		
Sarmiento, Antonio	38	0.159	P	15	13	3.66	
Senkowitz, John	3	0.000					
Smiley, Charles	42	0.273	1B				
Spinner, Larry	136	0.286	3B, OF, C				
Sroda, Ted	6	0.000					
Stigman, Dick	12	0.000	P	0	6	6.71	
Swanson, Phill	11	0.133	P	3	5	7.28	
Torres, Ed	23	0.234	SS				
Trossen, Tom	21	0.000	P	5	4	4.67	
Vejsicky, Gene	4	0.091					

Valdosta, Georgia
Team Operated by Valdosta Baseball Company, Inc.
Team President: Walter O. Briggs, Jr.
Vice President: John J. McHale
Secretary-Treasurer: H.M. Sisson
Director: T. Guy Connell
General Manager: R.B. "Bob" Bonifay
Manager(s): Marv Owen, Stan Wasiak
Games played at Pendleton Park
Season attendance: 52,911
Major League Affiliate: Detroit Tigers – American League.

Valdosta Tigers Team Roster

NAME	G	BA	POS	W	L	ERA	APF
Barna, Mike	22	0.184	2B				
Brick, Jerome	25	0.185	OF				
Cartier, Dale	11	0.000	P	0	1		
Ciatto, Rosario	9	0.226					
Douglas, Leroy	23	0.211	OF				
Estep, Virgil	54	0.284	C				
Franks, Paul	1	0.000	P	0	1		
Green, Jim	13	0.121	OF				
Greenan, Bill	3	0.077					
Greene, Joe	21	0.244	P	11	4	1.70	
Halter, Dick	1	0.000	P	0	0		
Heller, Ron	4	0.000	P	1	1		
Higginbotham, Milt	28	0.240	P	7	5	3.08	
Hoskins, Gerald	11	0.111	1B				
Hotard, Leo	5	0.000	P	0	1		
Howard, Tom	28	0.171	OF				
Isaacson, Herb	18	0.275	OF				
Koleff, Nick	11	0.000	P	3	6	5.60	
Leach, Dick	38	0.222	C				
Lockett, Bill	19	0.246	OF				
Loschke, Bob	29	0.102	P	10	5	2.64	
Lukosius, Justin	9	0.143					
MacCallum, Nelson	68	0.278	1B, 3B, SS, OF				
McNulty, Ed	28	0.170	P	6	10	4.25	
Melanson, Marv	29	0.159	P	14	11	2.63	
Meriwether, Al	38	0.222	1B				
Mizerock, John	31	0.241					
Moore, Morris	41	0.240	2B				
Mounts, Emory	43	0.159	OF				
Murray, Don	51	0.261	OF				
Neyen, Bill	40	0.242	1B				
Oneto, Francis	46	0.258	2B, SS				
Owen, Marv			M				
Pryor, Shapard	41	0.238	SS				
Reynolds, Bob	3	0.000	P	0	1		
Ryckman, Bill	47	0.257	SS				
Simmons, ---	4		P	0	2		
Sparks, Ferrell	30	0.192	C				
Spittle, Harry	11	0.227	P	3	6	6.11	
Stewart, Bob	122	0.284	1B, 3B				
Strichek, Ed	41	0.175	P	7	7	3.61	
Taliaferro, Ray	13	0.043	P	4	4	2.91	
Thomas, Gordon	20	0.163	1B				
Tsitouris, John	4	0.000	P	0	0	24.00	
Uzelatz, Max	6	0.000					
Viteretto, Pete	103	0.280	OF				
Wasiak, Stan	64	0.284	M, 2B, 3B, P	0	0		
Wenson, Ron	123	0.247	OF				
Wilson, Ward	10	0.308	P	2	1		
Wright, Bill	11	0.300	P	0	5		
Zeitler, Jack	24	0.247	SS				

Waycross, Georgia
Team Operated by Waycross Baseball Association, Inc.
Team President: J.C. Weldon
Vice President: W.C. Sweat
General Manager: Ray Martin
Manager(s): Paul Eames
Games played at Memorial Stadium
Season attendance: 36,854

Waycross Bears Team Roster

NAME	G	BA	POS	W	L	ERA	APF
Alden, Frank	46	0.289	SS				
Allen, Bill	13	0.172	P	5	4	3.53	
Altomer, Lou	4	0.000	P	1	1		

Augustoni, Bill	22	0.357	P	5	6	4.38
Baker, Earl	12	0.290	P	4	3	4.88
Baker, Floyd	44	0.303	P	17	8	2.92
Belladella, Bob	18	0.189	SS			
Bellamy, Perry	3	0.000				
Brewster, Charlie	65	0.277	2B, SS			
Cierniak, Don	29	0.071	P	6	11	4.17
Clifton, John	128	0.282	OF			
Cothran, Bob	50	0.306	2B			
Davis, Jack	60	0.179	OF			
Dean, Ray	2	0.000	P	0	0	
Dembek, Joe	120	0.273	OF, P	0	0	
Duval, Joe	9	0.100				
Eames, Paul	134	0.269	M, C, P	0	1	
Farmer, Dennis	3	0.100				
Foote, Ambrose	11	0.192	P	4	2	1.96
Gaston, Bob	1	0.000	P	0	0	
Hammon, Silas	2	0.000				
Harms, Lionel	4	0.000	P	0	1	
Hedin, Al	7	0.154	P	1	2	
Heffren, Ron	5	0.000	P	1	1	
Hoyal, Craig	5	0.500	P	0	2	
Jones, Lew	6	0.182				
Kowalski, Ed	62	0.228	2B, SS			
Mathison, Malcolm	6	0.176				
McColley, Bill"	136	0.237	1B, P	0	0	
Miller, Gerald	57	0.198	3B, SS			Albany
Moore, Lamar	11	0.207				
Mount, Ron	1	0.000	P	0	1	
Nesbihal, Ed	2	0.000				
O'Neill, John	29	0.167	P	6	6	3.53
Oster, Sandy	8	0.190				
Reckelhoff, Bob	3	0.083				
Reilly, Lou	6	0.111	P	1	0	
Rikard, Denver	131	0.293	OF			
Rowzee, Bob	9	0.000	P	0	3	
Sanson, Dick	2	0.000	P	0	0	
Scroggs, John	46	0.204	P	15	10	3.37
Server, Wallace	28	0.245	SS			
Tieken, Virgil	56	0.210	3B, C			
Vinson, Gene	3	0.250	P	1	0	
Walsh, Mike	76	0.243	3B			

1954 Georgia-Florida League Records
Batting
Highest Batting Average (minimum 100 at bats)
1. Edd Hartness – Tifton .364
2. Red Treadway – Fitzgerald .363
3. Kelvin Roberts – Tifton .331
4. Clarence Buheller – Brunswick .325
5. Don Williams – Thomasville .311

Most Hits
1. Clarence Buheller – Brunswick 184
2. Kelvin Roberts – Tifton 173
3. Bill Thompson – Fitzgerald 164
4. Red Treadway – Fitzgerald 158
5. Floyd Faust – Brunswick 153

Most Runs
1. Floyd Faust – Brunswick 143
2. Clarence Buheller – Brunswick 102
3. Larry Spinner – Tifton 95
4. Russ McGovern – Albany 88
5. Red Treadway – Fitzgerald 87

Most Total Bases
1. Clarence Buheller – Brunswick 284
2. Bill Thompson – Fitzgerald 257
3. Floyd Faust – Brunswick 242
4. Kelvin Roberts – Tifton 232
5. Larry Spinner – Tifton 230

Most Doubles
1. Denver Rikard – Waycross 40
2. Dick Wehman – Fitzgerald 38
3. Kelvin Roberts – Tifton 36
4. Bill Thompson – Fitzgerald 33
5. Charlie Brockell – Brunswick 29

Most Triples
1. Don Williams – Thomasville 12
2. Floyd Faust – Brunswick 10
   Red Treadway – Fitzgerald 10
   Bob Capone – Brunswick 10
5. Chuck Cottier – Americus-Cordele 9
   Pete Viteretto – Valdosta 9
   Floyd Hammen – Americus-Cordele 9

Most Home Runs
1. Clarence Buheller – Brunswick 19
   Larry Spinner – Tifton 19
3. Bill Thompson – Fitzgerald 16
4. Floyd Faust – Brunswick 14
5. Charlie Brockell – Americus-Cordele 12

Most Extra Base Hits
1. Bill Thompson – Fitzgerald 55
2. Clarence Buheller – Brunswick 54
3. Floyd Faust – Brunswick 51
4. Dick Wehman – Fitzgerald 49
5. Denver Rikard – Waycross 46

Most Runs Batted In
1. Bill Thompson – Fitzgerald 131
2. Clarence Buheller – Brunswick 119
3. Charlie Brockell – Brunswick 98
4. Larry Spinner – Tifton 96
5. Kelvin Roberts – Tifton 92

Most Stolen Bases
1. Floyd Faust – Brunswick 76
2. Ron Wenson – Valdosta 34
3. John Moriskiewicz – Brunswick 28
4. Earl Johnson – Albany 25
5. Bill Thompson – Fitzgerald 21
   John Clifton – Waycross 21
   Red Treadway – Fitzgerald 21

Fielding
Most Put-Outs
1. Bill Thompson 1B – Fitzgerald 1,105
2. Clarence Buheller 1B, OF – Brunswick 1,038
3. Bill McColley 1B, P – Waycross 1,036
4. Joe Canuso C – Brunswick 947
5. Ken Retzer C – Tifton 817

Most Assists
1. Chuck Cottier 2B – Americus-Cordele 398
2. Adrian Rechichar 2B – Brunswick 342
3. Charlie Brockell 3B, SS, P – Brunswick 298
4. Jack Poppell 2B – Albany 282
5. Enrique Salazar SS – Thom/Alba 266

Most Errors
1. Chuck Cottier 2B – Americus-Cordele 46
2. Adrian Rechichar 2B – Brunswick 45
3. Floyd Hammen 3B, SS – Americus-Cordele 43
4. Tom Dotterer 3B, SS – Fitzgerald 42
   Bill Batty 2B, 3B, SS – Albany 42

Walt Way 1B, 3B, OF, P – Albany 42

Pitching

Most Wins
1. Whammy Douglas – Brunswick 27
2. Bill Knox – Albany 20
   Earl Gearhart – Fitzgerald 20
4. Ron Gray – Brunswick 19
   John Claset – Fitzgerald 19

Most Losses
1. Harvey Tomter – Americus-Cordele 17
2. Jack Bunce – Americus-Cordele 15
3. Antonio Sarmiento – Tifton 13
4. Lane Martin – Albany 12
   Bob Schaffer – Albany 12

Highest Winning Percentage (10 game minimum)
1. Ron Gray – Brunswick .826
2. Whammy Douglas – Brunswick .818
3. Joe Greene – Valdosta .733
4. Bill Knox – Albany .690
   Earl Gearhart – Fitzgerald .690

Lowest Earned Run Average (100 inning minimum)
1. Joe Greene – Valdosta 1.70
2. Bill Knox – Albany 1.80
3. Whammy Douglas – Brunswick 2.06
4. Tom McMullen – Thomasville 2.18
5. Charles Lucabaugh – Americus-Cordele 2.25

Most Strikeouts
1. Whammy Douglas – Brunswick 273
2. John Claset – Fitzgerald 243
3. Marv Melanson – Valdosta 205
4. Bill Knox – Albany 187
5. Bob Schaffer – Albany 159

Most Bases on Balls
1. Lane Martin – Albany 139
2. Bill Augustoni – Waycross 131
3. Harvey Tomter – Americus-Cordele 130
4. Dick Hemmerle – Tifton 118
5. Whammy Douglas – Brunswick 116
   Wilbert Pender – Thomasville 116

Most Hits Allowed
1. Earl Gearhart – Fitzgerald 275
2. John Scroggs – Waycross 215
3. Floyd Baker – Waycross 211
4. John Claset – Fitzgerald 210
5. Tim Dinkelacker – Fitzgerald 205

Most Innings Pitched
1. Whammy Douglas – Brunswick 271
2. Earl Gearhart – Fitzgerald 258
3. John Claset – Fitzgerald 248
4. Bill Knox – Albany 240
5. Tim Dinkelacker – Fitzgerald 231

C Don Williams – Thomasville
C Ken Retzer – Tifton
UT Charlie Brockell – Brunswick
P Whammy Douglas – Brunswick
P Bill Knox – Albany
P Earl Gearhart – Fitzgerald
P Ron Gray – Brunswick
M Red Treadway – Fitzgerald

1954 Georgia-Florida League All-Star Team
1B Clarence Buheller – Brunswick
2B Adrian Rechichar – Brunswick
3B Bob Stewart – Valdosta
SS Phil Shartzer – Fitzgerald
OF Kelvin Roberts – Tifton
OF Floyd Faust – Brunswick
OF Sam Farless – Brunswick
OF Van Hill – Fitzgerald

1954

Georgia State League

League Office: Sylvania, Georgia
League President: Bill Estroff
Secretary: Charlie Odom
Salary Limit: $2,600 per month plus $600.
Player Rule: Each club was allowed a roster of sixteen players, not more than three veterans, not more than five limited service, and not less than eight rookies.

Georgia State League Final Standings

Team	W	L	Pct	GB	Affiliate
Vidalia Indians	85	44	.659	----	Unaffiliated
Douglas Trojans	85	45	.654	0.5	CIN-NL
Dublin Irish	82	48	.631	3.5	PIT-NL
Statesboro Pilots	57	73	.438	28.5	Unaffiliated
Hazlehurst-Baxley Cardinals	47	82	.364	38.0	STL-NL
Sandersville Wacos	33	97	.254	52.5	Unaffiliated

1954 Georgia State League Map

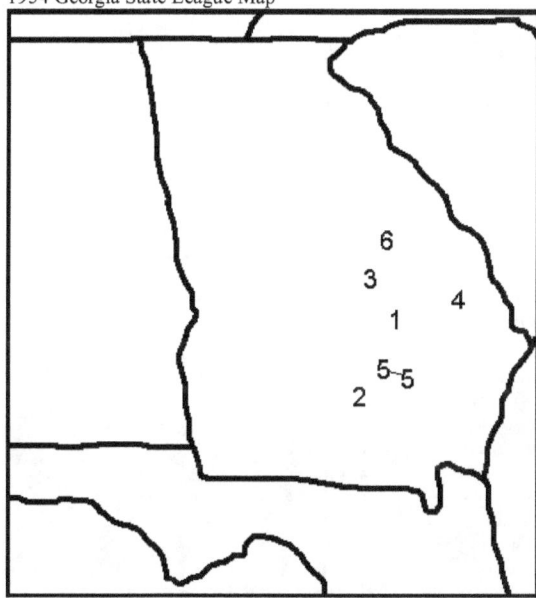

(numbers on map correspond to the place each team finished in regular season play)

The league downsized to a six-team loop after the 1953 season with Eastman and Jesup both quitting the circuit.

Dublin's Sam Buell set the all-time league single season record for the most runs scored with 150 during the season.

First place in the regular season went to Vidalia, who had the best record. A half game back was Douglas in second, and Dublin finished third by three and a half games. Statesboro took fourth place and was twenty-eight and a half games out of first place when the regular season wrapped up. In the Shaughnessy style playoffs, Vidalia defeated Statesboro four games to two, and Douglas eliminated Dublin four games to three. Vidalia made easy work of Douglas in the championship series sweeping the set in four consecutive games.

Douglas, Georgia

Team Operated by Douglas Trojans, Inc.
Team President: H.B. Chitty
Vice President-Secretary-Treasurer-General Manager: W.P. Ward, Jr.
Manager(s): Charles Bledsoe
Games played at Municipal Park
Season attendance: 35,589
Major League Affiliate: Cincinnati Reds – National League.

Douglas Trojans Team Roster

NAME	G	BA	POS	W	L	ERA	APF
Bastion, Marv	6	0.000	P	0	1		
Bledsoe, Charles	122	0.280	M, 3B, SS, C, P	0	0		
Bossard, Belasco	100	0.360	SS				
Bradberry, Buck	3	0.167	P	0	2		
Bumstead, Dan	4	0.429	P	2	0		
Crouch, Les	116	0.282	2B, 3B, SS				
Daidone, Joe	33	0.211	2B				
Davis, Van	123	0.322	1B				
Decker, Bob	69	0.301	2B, 3B				
Garcia, Manuel	16	0.167	P	5	3	4.81	
Gibson, Hammond	9	0.200	P	2	1		
Gilbert, Buddy	130	0.335	OF				
Green, Billy	39	0.179	P	16	10	2.37	
Hock, Bob	128	0.301	OF				
Holley, Jim	10	0.205	3B				
Jackson, John	7	0.111	P	6	0		
McLeod, George	19	0.138	P	2	4	7.39	
Meder, Dick	14	0.313	P	2	3	6.30	
Miller, Ed	9	0.143					
Monaco, Vince	76	0.238	3B, OF, P	11	4	4.25	
Peale, Anthony	1	0.500	P	0	1		
Robinette, Jimmie	83	0.301	OF				
Roth, Dick	1	0.000	P	0	0		
Rustin, Ted	34	0.213	P	20	8	4.04	
Schmidt, Haven	83	0.303	OF, C				
Smith, Jim	1	0.000					
Wells, Jack	24	0.164	P	11	4	2.81	
West, Ira	23	0.231	3B				
Whitson, Howard	9	0.375	P	2	1		
Whitzer, Mike	1	0.000	P	0	0		
Wright, Dick	11	0.216	P	3	1	3.75	
Wrona, Joe	10	0.143	P	3	2		

Dublin, Georgia

Team Operated by Dublin Baseball Association
Team President: W.A. Brewer
Vice President: W.W. Brinson
Secretary: A.O. Hadden
Treasurer: Louis Hatcher
Business Manager: W.W. Whaley, Jr.
Manager(s): George Kinnamon
Games played at Lovett Park
Season attendance: 57,945
Major League Affiliate: Pittsburgh Pirates – National League.

Dublin Irish Team Roster

NAME	G	BA	POS	W	L	ERA	APF
Arent, George	104	0.291	1B				
Baldwin, Robert	4	0.286	P	0	0		
Beheler, Ernest	14	0.114	1B				
Buell, Sam	127	0.259	OF				
Carter, Arlen	4	0.250	P	2	1		
Causion, Bill	129	0.326	OF				
Combs, Ralph	15	0.184	OF				
Fleming, Doug	120	0.269	2B				
Henkel, Ernest	1	0.000	P	0	0		

NAME	G	BA	POS	W	L	ERA	APF
Honkus, Stan	9	0.167	P	6	1	2.21	
Icenhour, Luther	53	0.308	SS				
Kinnamon, George	105	0.335	M, C, P	0	0		
Lakatosh, Dean	57	0.295	OF, P	21	6	4.02	
Lakatosh, Denton	74	0.262	C				
Leatherberry, John	24	0.094	P	9	2	3.21	
Long, Bob	21	0.265	P	9	6	5.09	
Meekins, Dennis	127	0.280	3B				
Moore, Willard	7	0.000	P	0	5		Sandersville
Morris, Milt	106	0.284	2B, SS, OF				
Pearce, Ernest	27	0.206	SS				
Pellarin, Anthony	1	0.000	P	1	0		
Perinis, Alex	5	0.143	P	0	2		
Powell, Duane	2	0.000	P	0	1		
Rich, Benny	6	0.083	P	2	0		
Sharpe, Corwin	2	0.000	P	0	0		
Shires, Bill	98	0.312	OF				
Stefanik, Ray	17	0.143	P	5	3	5.06	
Stewart, Bill	10	0.250	P	4	1	4.78	
Vanasse, Bob	17	0.194	P	3	5	6.56	
Vest, Milt	16	0.068	P	7	5	3.46	
Zimmerlink, Gene	43	0.212	P	13	12	4.61	

Hazlehurst-Baxley (Hazlehurst & Baxley), Georgia

Team Operated by Hazlehurst-Baxley Baseball Club, Inc.
Team President: Mack Aaron
Vice President: Dr. C.R. Youmans
Secretary: Kenneth S. Martin
General Manager: Charles A. Odom
Manager(s): Bill McGhee, Arnold Riesgo
Games played at Roland Cook Stadium
Season attendance: 18,121
Major League Affiliate: St. Louis Cardinals – National League.

Hazlehurst-Baxley Cardinals Team Roster

NAME	G	BA	POS	W	L	ERA	APF
Barrett, Garland	1	1.000					
Beaugez, Ray	3	0.083					
Bisesi, John	71	0.235	SS				
Bradley, Don	44	0.193	P	12	14	4.34	
Bryant, Ira	11	0.205	OF				
Cop, Milan	6	0.000	P	0	3		
Dal Porto, Angelo	57	0.301	SS				
Derry, Stan	42	0.262	OF				
Durant, Don	2	0.000	P	0	0		
Eckman, Ned	100	0.267	2B				
Edwards, Don	11	0.111	OF				
Elliott, Art	2	0.000	P	0	1		
Fleisch, Don	10	0.211	OF				
Ghelfi, Dick	9	0.000	P	0	1		
Hagar, Carl	60	0.247	3B, OF				
Hicks, Dick	18	0.125	P	1	9	7.53	
Hiland, Jimmie	42	0.238	P	13	10	3.39	
Keggereis, Bill	9	0.000	P	0	3		
Keller, Charles	19	0.260					
Kendig, Lawrence	17	0.094	P	6	7	4.00	
Kidd, Don	41	0.211	OF				
King, Bill	15	0.182	1B				
LaBar, Luther	17	0.080	3B				
Mahurin, Leman	46	0.257	P	7	12	4.77	
Mapes, Carl	6	0.000	P	0	1		
Mastracci, Bob	50	0.266	1B				
McGhay, Gerald	4	0.000	P	0	0		
McGhee, Bill			M				
McGhee, Bill	48	0.311	3B, P	0	0		
Miller, Bill	63	0.258	1B, P	0	1		
Otey, Dick	9	0.286	P	1	4		
Pendley, Jack	121	0.287	OF				
Pint, Don	78	0.248	OF				

NAME	G	BA	POS	W	L	ERA	APF
Reehoff, Ron	28	0.236	2B				
Riesgo, Arnold	63	0.275	M, C, P	0	0		
Scalici, Anthony	74	0.212	OF, C				
Schultis, Pete	5	0.400	P	0	2		
Thomas, Don	4	1.000	P	0	2		
Thornell, Bob	36	0.206	C				
Torres, Ed	24	0.264	3B				
Ulrich, Lawrence	14	0.286	P	2	4	5.79	
Waters, Rabun	26	0.103	P	5	8	6.73	
Wyatt, Gene	41	0.148	OF				

Sandersville, Georgia

Team Operated by Washington County Baseball Corporation
Team President: N.M. Jordan
Vice President: H.N. McMichael
Secretary-Treasurer: N.M. Jordan, Jr
General Manager-Travel Secretary: H.F. Blackburn
Manager(s): Dave Madison, Stan West
Games played at Sandersville Baseball Park
Season attendance: 25,600

Sandersville Wacos Team Roster

NAME	G	BA	POS	W	L	ERA	APF
Adams, Jerome	19	0.143	C				
Allegrucci, Don	38	0.176	2B				
Ambrose, Dick	12	0.053	P	1	8	4.22	
Arbogast, Ford	60	0.248	2B, C				
Baker, Jerry	7	0.238					
Bridges, Geneva	2	0.200	P	0	1		
Burg, Jerold	11	0.286	P	1	2		Vidalia
Caldwell, Wilbur	74	0.283	2B, 3B, P	8	4	3.32	Vidalia
Cimmino, Vince	24	0.044	P	2	11	5.89	
Collins, Jack	1	0.000					
Cook, John	34	0.263	OF, P	0	1		
Cooper, Bill	30	0.191	C				
Davis, Walter	4	0.400					
Dietrich, Bill	16	0.167	P	3	7	5.20	
Diez, Alfredo	35	0.157	P	6	14	6.37	
Falls, Tim	4	0.111					
Fasanaro, Dick	4	0.235					
Fisher, Stan	7	0.077	P	0	4		
Foster, Shelby	3	0.200					
Garcia, Jesus	40	0.242	2B				
Garmon, Ray	124	0.291	2B, 3B, OF, P	1	2		
Haber, Nate	9	0.200					
Hamlin, Nat	4	0.182	P	0	3		
Harrington, Lou	6	0.286	P	0	0		
Harris, Darrell	16	0.163	SS				
Hartley, Don	14	0.160	C				
Henderson, Bill	6	0.125	P	0	3		
Hite, Bob	10	0.273	P	0	7	5.65	
Holly, Joe	6	0.091					
Hood, Milt	9	0.242					
Hoyal, Craig	32	0.191	OF, P	3	2	5.36	
Jiminez, Dan	23	0.176	3B, P	0	0		Statesboro
Johnson, Myra	19	0.130					
Johnson, Sid	7	0.250	P	1	3		
Jones, Harvey	22	0.153	3B				
Kirincic, Don	1	0.000					
Koski, Bob	24	0.293	P	0	6	7.23	
Lazicky, Dick	1	0.000	P	0	0		
Leonard, Leon	1	0.000					
Madison, Dave	2	0.000	M, P	0	1		
May, Ted	1	0.000	P	0	0		
McDonald, Russ	8	0.067	P	0	2		
McGee, Bob	129	0.306	3B, OF				
McGraw, Willie	3	0.300					
McNeely, Bob	94	0.243	1B, OF				
Moore, Willard	7	0.000	P	0	5		Dublin
Morgan, Lucius	35	0.277	3B, SS				

Georgia Class-D Minor League Baseball Encyclopedia

NAME	G	BA	POS	W	L	ERA	APF	
Murphy, Dan	28	0.250	1B					
Owen, Bill	2	0.000	P	0	2			
Pardue, Larry	12	0.195	C					
Parent, Leo	1	0.500						
Reid, Bob	33	0.315	1B					
Ruark, Parnell	76	0.296	OF					Vidalia
Schurrer, Roland	15	0.050	P	4	4	6.71		
Tippett, Frank	13	0.150	P	4	6	4.65		
Warren, Rudy	90	0.281	OF					
West, Stan	33	0.286	M, P	3	4	4.60		
Whitmire, Glen	6	0.143						
Wilson, Jim	88	0.260	2B, 3B, SS, P	1	0			
Wulff, Clay	30	0.167	SS					
Zgraggen, Orlando	2	0.000	P	0	1			

Statesboro, Georgia
Team Operated by Statesboro Athletic Association, Inc.
Team President: C.B. McAllister
Vice President: Alfred Dorman
Secretary: R. Herbert Kingery
Treasurer: Herman E. Bray
Business Manager: R.F. Donaldson, Jr.
Manager(s): Jack Hines
Games played at Pilots Field
Season attendance: 18,532

Statesboro Pilots Team Roster

NAME	G	BA	POS	W	L	ERA	APF	
Bearden, Billy	43	0.134	OF, P	0	0			
Belladella, Bob	29	0.206	2B					
Bloom, Don	1	0.000	P	0	0			
Bolch, Bill	7	0.000						
Burnette, Tom	12	0.063	P	1	3	4.94		
Charette, Roger	6	0.000	P	0	1			
Cierniak, Don	10	0.083	P	3	4	3.88		
Dealing, Ephram	1	0.000	P	0	1			
Dodson, Sam	19	0.256	OF					
Duke, Bill	5	0.000						
Engel, Al	129	0.311	OF					
Farmer, Dennis	14	0.179	3B					
Ferrara, Tony	17	0.164	2B					
Ford, Bob	112	0.244	2B, OF, C, P	0	0			
Ghant, Roland	3	0.000	P	0	2			
Glaudi, Benjamin	12	0.071	P	1	2			
Hines, Jack			M					
Horton, Ralph	20	0.222						
Jiminez, Dan	23	0.176	3B, P	0	0			Sandersville
Johnson, Harry	5	0.000	P	2	2			
Kuykendall, Bob	48	0.261	OF, C, P	0	0			
Lane, Clyde	16	0.214	P	2	9	5.63		
Leachman, Don	1	0.000	P	0	1			
Lopez, Carlos	55	0.296	OF, P	12	12	3.86		
Lowery, Jason	70	0.294	OF					
Mallard, John	69	0.257	SS					
Mason, Max	2	0.000						
McCoy, Bob	14	0.133						
McMasters, Omer	4	0.000	P	0	0			
Parsons, Roger	7	0.111						
Peters, Gerald	130	0.270	1B, P	0	0			
Phillips, Gene	1	0.000	P	0	0			
Pilgrim, Arvie	110	0.241	3B, P	0	0			
Pompelia, Augie	19	0.262	2B					
Reeves, Herb	1	0.000	P	0	1			
Shaw, Steve	1	0.000	P	0	1			
Smith, Andy	1	0.250						
Tally, Hoover	6	0.111	P	1	3			
Thrasher, Cliff	118	0.299	OF, C, P	2	3	5.43		
Tidwell, Bruce	11	0.273	P					
Tidwell, Don	28	0.170	P	4	8	6.44		
Walters, Billy	12	0.222	2B					

NAME	G	BA	POS	W	L	ERA	APF
Warren, Jim	99	0.332	OF, P	15	7	3.19	
Whaley, Randy	38	0.122	P	11	11	4.22	
White, Curtis	2	0.000	P	1	1		
Willard, Miles	47	0.271	SS				

Vidalia, Georgia
Team Operated by Vidalia Baseball Association
Team President: G.H. Threlkeld
Vice President: H.B. Estroff
Secretary-Treasurer: G.H. Gibson
Business Manager: L.A. Levy
Manager(s): Jim Beavers
Games played at Vidalia Municipal Stadium
Season attendance: 53,334

Vidalia Indians Team Roster

NAME	G	BA	POS	W	L	ERA	APF
Adam, Dick	30	0.188	P	10	4	4.24	
Beavers, Jim	124	0.327	M, 1B, P	1	0		
Briggs, Clyde	43	0.241	OF				
Burg, Jerold	11	0.286	P	1	2		Sandersville
Caldwell, Wilbur	74	0.283	2B, 3B, P	8	4	3.32	Sandersville
Chance, Wendell	9	0.294	P	1	1		
Corley, Ray	2	0.000	P	0	1		
Deal, Bill	102	0.252	OF				
Dobbins, Mayes	25	0.191	2B				
Doke, Tom	31	0.152	P	11	8	4.42	
Draper, Dick	3	0.000	P	1	1		
Driggers, Bobby	122	0.337	1B, OF, C				
Duenas, Jose	105	0.334	SS				
Gilbert, Phil	44	0.239	P	22	6	2.23	
Green, Harold	128	0.245	3B				
Hinson, Bill	115	0.220	C				
Hughes, Norm	10	0.125	P	1	1		
Menna, Frank	81	0.276	OF				
Norris, Larry	4	0.333	P	3	0		
Pawlak, Walt	32	0.237	2B				
Plushanski, Fred	27	0.111	P	7	2	4.46	
Rice, Ron	18	0.286	2B				
Roberts, Art	7	0.077					
Ruark, Parnell	76	0.296	OF				Sandersville
Sacchetti, Charles	8	0.091					
Sedlack, Bob	4	0.167	P	0	1		
Sevier, John	3	0.000					
VanDerBeek, Jim	31	0.117	P	14	9	2.83	
Vaughn, Don	17	0.205	P	9	1	2.07	
Walker, Wiley	7	0.222	P	0	2		
Warren, Leon	2	0.000					
West, Ronnie	71	0.214	2B, SS, OF				

1954 Georgia State League Records
Batting
Highest Batting Average (minimum 100 at bats)
1. Belasco Bossard – Douglas   .360
2. Bobby Driggers – Vidalia   .337
3. Buddy Gilbert – Douglas   .335
   George Kinnamon – Dublin   .335
5. Jose Duenas – Vidalia   .334

Most Hits
1. Buddy Gilbert – Douglas   173
2. Bobby Driggers – Vidalia   169
3. Bill Causion – Dublin   164
4. Jim Beavers – Vidalia   162
5. Al Engel – Statesboro   156

Georgia Class-D Minor League Baseball Encyclopedia

Most Runs
1. Sam Buell – Dublin 150
2. Buddy Gilbert – Douglas 134
3. Bill Causion – Dublin 123
4. Van Davis – Douglas 120
5. Dennis Meekins – Dublin 111

Most Total Bases
1. Buddy Gilbert – Douglas 275
2. Bobby Driggers – Vidalia 274
3. Bill Causion – Dublin 269
   Van Davis – Douglas 269
5. Bob McGee – Sandersville 261

Most Doubles
1. Bobby Driggers – Vidalia 45
2. Bill Causion – Dublin 35
3. Buddy Gilbert – Douglas 34
4. Belasco Bossard – Douglas 33
5. Jim Beavers – Vidalia 31
   Al Engel – Statesboro 31

Most Triples
1. Bob McGee – Sandersville 17
2. Buddy Gilbert – Douglas 10
3. Jack Pendley - Hazlehurst-Baxley 9
   Les Crouch – Douglas 9
5. *four players tied with 8

Most Home Runs
1. Van Davis – Douglas 31
2. Jim Warren – Statesboro 30
3. George Arent – Dublin 21
4. Bill Causion – Dublin 18
   Sam Buell – Dublin 18

Most Extra Base Hits
1. Bobby Driggers – Vidalia 67
2. Bill Causion – Dublin 61
3. Buddy Gilbert – Douglas 60
4. Van Davis – Douglas 58
   Bob McGee – Sandersville 58

Most Runs Batted In
1. Van Davis – Douglas 135
2. Bill Causion – Dublin 116
3. Bob McGee – Sandersville 111
4. Bobby Driggers – Vidalia 105
5. Jim Warren – Statesboro 99

Most Stolen Bases
1. Gerald Peters – Statesboro 66
2. Sam Buell – Dublin 45
3. Dennis Meekins – Dublin 37
4. Charles Bledsoe – Douglas 30
5. Harold Green – Vidalia 29

Fielding
Most Put-Outs
1. Jim Beavers 1B, P – Vidalia 1,043
2. Gerald Peters 1B, P – Statesboro 1,039
3. Van Davis 1B – Douglas 985
4. George Arent 1B – Dublin 847
5. Bill Hinson C – Vidalia 744

Most Assists
1. Doug Fleming 2B – Dublin 301
2. Belasco Bossard SS – Douglas 287
3. Ned Eckman 2B - Hazlehurst-Baxley 267
4. Les Crouch 2B, 3B, SS – Douglas 266

5. Jose Duenas SS – Vidalia 265
   Dennis Meekins 3B – Dublin 265

Most Errors
1. Jim Wilson 2B, 3B, SS, P – Sandersville 69
2. Harold Green 3B – Vidalia 68
3. Jose Duenas SS – Vidalia 46
4. Arvie Pilgrim 3B, P – Statesboro 44
5. John Mallard SS – Statesboro 42

Pitching
Most Wins
1. Phil Gilbert – Vidalia 22
2. Dean Lakatosh – Dublin 21
3. Ted Rustin – Douglas 20
4. Billy Green – Douglas 16
5. Jim Warren – Statesboro 15

Most Losses
1. Don Bradley - Hazlehurst-Baxley 14
   Alfredo Diez – Sandersville 14
3. Gene Zimmerlink – Dublin 12
   Carlos Lopez – Statesboro 12
   Leman Mahurin - Hazlehurst-Baxley 12

Highest Winning Percentage (10 game minimum)
1. Don Vaughn – Vidalia .900
2. John Leatherberry – Dublin .818
3. Phil Gilbert – Vidalia .786
4. Dean Lakatosh – Dublin .778
   Fred Plushanski – Vidalia .778

Lowest Earned Run Average (100 inning minimum)
1. Phil Gilbert – Vidalia 2.23
2. Billy Green – Douglas 2.37
3. Jack Wells – Douglas 2.81
4. Jim VanDerBeek – Vidalia 2.83
5. Jim Warren – Statesboro 3.19

Most Strikeouts
1. Jimmie Hiland - Hazlehurst-Baxley 247
2. Billy Green – Douglas 218
3. Gene Zimmerlink – Dublin 200
4. Don Bradley - Hazlehurst-Baxley 175
5. Randy Whaley – Statesboro 173

Most Bases on Balls
1. Dean Lakatosh – Dublin 157
2. Gene Zimmerlink – Dublin 122
3. Randy Whaley – Statesboro 118
4. Leman Mahurin - Hazlehurst-Baxley 108
5. Billy Green – Douglas 100

Most Hits Allowed
1. Ted Rustin – Douglas 262
2. Don Bradley - Hazlehurst-Baxley 259
3. Leman Mahurin - Hazlehurst-Baxley 227
4. Alfredo Diez – Sandersville 221
5. Phil Gilbert – Vidalia 215

Most Innings Pitched
1. Phil Gilbert – Vidalia 258
2. Ted Rustin – Douglas 243
3. Don Bradley - Hazlehurst-Baxley 232
4. Billy Green – Douglas 228
5. Jimmy Hiland - Hazlehurst-Baxley 218

1954 Georgia State League All-Star Team
- 1B Van Davis – Douglas
- 2B Les Crouch – Douglas
- 3B Dennis Meekins – Dublin
- SS Belasco Bossard – Douglas
- OF Bobby Driggers – Vidalia
- OF Buddy Gilbert – Douglas
- OF Jim Warren – Statesboro
- C   Bill Hinson – Vidalia
- P   Phil Gilbert – Vidalia
- P   Jimmie Hiland - Hazlehurst-Baxley
- P   Billy Green – Douglas
- P   Don Vaughn – Vidalia

1955

Georgia-Florida League

League Office: Leslie, Georgia
League President: W.T. Anderson
League Vice President: Guy Connell
Salary Limit: $2,600 per month plus $600.
Player Rule: Each club was allowed a roster of sixteen players, not more than three veterans, not more than eight limited service, and not less than five rookies.

Georgia-Florida League Final Standings

Team	W	L	Pct	GB	Affiliate
Brunswick Pirates	87	52	.626	----	PIT-NL
Albany Cardinals	85	55	.607	2.5	STL-NL
Waycross Bears	72	65	.526	14.0	Unaffiliated
Valdosta Tigers	68	70	.493	18.5	DET-AL
Thomasville Dodgers	66	72	.478	20.5	BRK-NL
Cordele Orioles	63	74	.460	23.0	BAL-AL
Tifton Blue Sox	59	80	.424	28.0	Unaffiliated
Moultrie Redlegs	53	85	.384	33.5	CIN-NL

1955 Georgia-Florida League Map

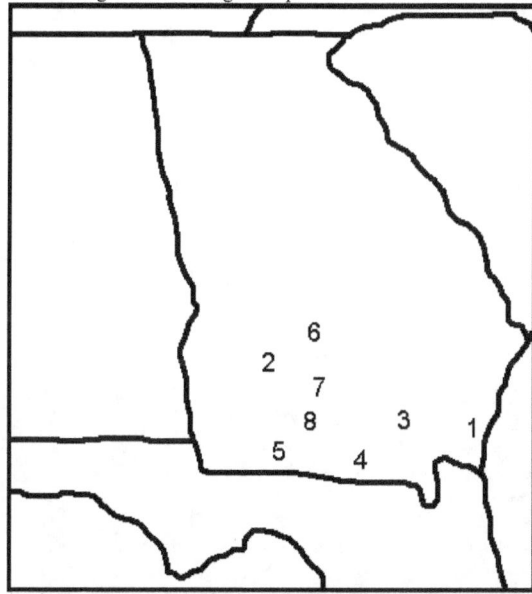

(numbers on map correspond to the place each team finished in regular season play)

Moultrie was once again part of the league after a one-year sabbatical replacing Fitzgerald, who filled the void when Moultrie departed previously. The combined Americus-Cordele team went defunct and was back to being just Cordele once again.

On April 21, Thomasville's Robert Spier pitched the season's first no-hitter against Waycross winning the game 6 to 0. Another no-hitter was tossed on May 10 by Brunswick hurler Alex Perinis in a 1 to 0 defeat of Cordele. And the season's third and final no-hitter came from the arm of Moultrie pitcher John Husich on May 23 in a 9 to 1 victory over Tifton.

Georgia Class-D Minor League Baseball Encyclopedia

The Brunswick Pirates finished the season atop the league standings followed in order by Albany, Waycross, and Valdosta. Valdosta took a three games to two loss from Brunswick in the first round of the post-season championship tournament, and Waycross defeated Albany in three straight contests. After the weather allowed only two games to be played, the championship series was declared a rainout for the second consecutive year in the league. Brunswick had won one of the games, and Waycross won the other. No champion was declared once again.

Albany, Georgia
Team Operated by Albany Baseball Club, Inc.
Team President: Morton M. Wiggins
Vice Presidents: August Busch, Jr., William Walsingham, Jr.
Secretary: Dolly Cockroft
General Manager: Sheldon A. "Chief" Bender
Manager(s): J.C. Dunn
Games played at Cardinal Park
Season attendance: 50,115
Major League Affiliate: St. Louis Cardinals – National League.

Albany Cardinals Team Roster

NAME	G	BA	POS	W	L	ERA	APF
Barton, Cecil	3	0.333	P	1	1		
Beatty, Arlin	8	0.286	P	1	3		
Bojorquez, Federico	19	0.163	SS				
Bone, Bill	124	0.262	SS				
Boyer, Lew	24	0.152	1B				
Calvetti, Lou	6	0.235	P	1	1		
Carmel, Duke	24	0.292	OF, P	0	0		
Cook, George	16	0.233	P	5	2	3.16	
Davis, Wayne	135	0.299	OF				
Deck, Ed	2	0.000	P	0	0		
Douglas, Ken	6	0.000	P	0	2		
Dunn, J.C.	138	0.300	M, 1B, OF, P	0	0		
Gilbert, Glenn	6	0.000	P	2	0		
Hanna, Vic	34	0.098	P	4	16	4.63	Tifton
Haverly, Karl	16	0.136	P	6	3	2.65	
Herring, Bob	5	0.118					
Hoffman, Charles	13	0.000	P	2	1		
Joyner, Julian	36	0.250	P	10	6	2.68	
Karczewski, Gerald	139	0.287	3B				
Keller, Gerald	7	0.083	P	2	0		
Kendig, Lawrence	23	0.086	P	11	6	2.75	
Kiser, Ron	48	0.230	1B				
Lackey, Bill	33	0.082	P	22	8	1.98	
Martin, Jim	15	0.237					
Nemeth, Frank	1	0.000	P	0	0		
O'Neill, John	19	0.087	P	1	3		
Proctor, Tom	9	0.000	P	2	3		
Rikard, Bob	114	0.274	OF, C				
Salcido, Carlos	13	0.154	OF				Tifton
Schieffer, John	32	0.141	P	16	8	3.14	
Smith, Fred	135	0.269	OF				
Stangel, Bob	11	0.279	OF				
Stokes, Bill	1	0.000	P	0	0		
Thompson, Bill	121	0.263	C				
Towich, Tom	1	0.000	P	0	0		
Tucker, Dwight	3	0.200	P	0	2		
Vaughn, Leroy	13	0.091	P	3	2	3.98	
Williams, Galen	132	0.319	2B				

Brunswick, Georgia
Team Operated by Brunswick Pirates, Inc.
Team President: Blanton Miller
Vice Presidents: Branch Rickey, Jr., Harold G. Roettger
Secretary: Walter Bunt
Treasurer: James A. Herron
General Manager: Jack Berger
Manager(s): Frank Oceak
Games played at Edo Miller Park
Season attendance: 41,743
Major League Affiliate: Pittsburgh Pirates – National League.

Brunswick Pirates Team Roster

NAME	G	BA	POS	W	L	ERA	APF
Beredino, Joe	22	0.239	OF				
Bowie, Don	33	0.248	OF				
Brockell, Charlie	129	0.269	1B, SS, OF, C, P	0	0		
Canuso, Joe	96	0.284	C				
Caputo, Lou	102	0.256	2B, 3B				Waycross
Douglas, Whammy	5	0.188	P	4	1	1.57	
Drotar, Joe	15	0.278	P	7	5	4.03	
Duffalo, Jim	38	0.181	P	17	4	2.64	
Duzyk, Bob	38	0.330	OF				
Fackler, Earl	132	0.314	1B				
Gilbert, Herb	47	0.224	OF				
Hartbarger, Jim	49	0.220	2B				
Hayden, Jim	40	0.158	P	13	9	3.02	
Hurst, Leon	14	0.270	P	7	5	3.15	
Jackson, Bill	123	0.206	2B, SS				Thomasville
Johnson, Ernest	5	0.231	P	1	3		
Koski, Bill	20	0.207	P	8	6	2.47	
McClenaghan, Russ	6	0.500					
Messina, Dino	70	0.191	OF				
Minjock, John	9	0.222	P	1	0		
Nisewonger, Jim	46	0.253	OF, P	2	2		
Oceak, Frank			M				
Patchell, Stan	8	0.071	P	2	1		
Perinis, Alex	23	0.171	P	6	4	2.04	
Perry, Joe	8	0.222	P	1	1		
Plaster, Buddy	5	0.000					
Ramsey, Frank	17	0.161	P	7	2	3.08	
Robertson, Bill	137	0.299	3B				
Serafini, Irv	21	0.087	P	3	5	5.26	
Shinnick, Dick	11	0.083	P	6	1	2.32	
Sisolak, Fred	99	0.243	2B, SS				
Sterns, Roland	2	0.429	P	0	2		
Vandiveer, Rod	2	0.000					
Waugh, Jim	3	0.000	P	2	1		
Weir, Gary	20	0.118	OF				
Wilson, Jack	140	0.349	OF				

Cordele, Georgia
Team Operated by Baseball Amusement Club, Inc.
Team President: J.W. Bridges
General Manager: Marvin A. Wilkinson
Manager(s): Gimpy Brown, Scoops Carey
Games played at City Park
Season attendance: 31,221
Major League Affiliate: Baltimore Orioles – American League.

Cordele Orioles Team Roster

NAME	G	BA	POS	W	L	ERA	APF
Berger, Fred	127	0.257	2B				
Bertrand, Art	2	0.000	P	0	0		
Bosse, Lou	26	0.225	OF				
Boyd, Warner	12	0.188	P	1	5	3.19	
Breeding, Marv	71	0.338	SS				
Brown, Gimpy	14	0.133	M, P	4	5	2.84	
Brown, Newton	99	0.267	1B				
Bunce, Jack	10	0.273	P	3	3		
Carey, Scoops			M				
Carpenter, Bill	4	0.000	P	0	1		
DeMont, Paul	84	0.323	2B, 3B				
Dennis, Harold	30	0.198	1B				

Georgia Class-D Minor League Baseball Encyclopedia

Name	G	BA	POS	W	L	ERA	APF
Domalik, Joe	4	0.200	P	0	0		
Ehnninger, Bob	1	0.000	P	0	0		
Fields, Howard	1	0.000	P	0	0		
Forrest, Dick	16	0.176	P	2	1	1.64	
Frazier, Lee	43	0.268	OF				
Garcia, Sergio	111	0.225	C				Moultrie
Gunning, Ed	11	0.286	P	4	3	3.70	
Guza, Mike	22	0.320	C				Thomasville
Hartman, Elmer	4	0.000	P	0	0		
Henrichsen, Gerald	116	0.267	OF, P	0	0		
Keuch, Warren	57	0.178	3B				
Kingsmore, Doug	5	0.100					
Kovach, Paul	18	0.233	P	3	4	4.72	
Kromy, Darwin	41	0.145	P	10	12	4.36	Valdosta
Lail, Jack	3	0.000					
Land, Curtis	6	0.200	P	0	1		
Lee, Joe	33	0.217	3B				
Lockwood, Howard	23	0.309	P	11	4	2.49	
Lubinski, Dick	123	0.292	OF				
McDonald, Russ	15	0.094	P	5	6	5.84	
McGarr, Dave	1	0.000	P	0	0		
Muskopf, Bob	4	0.000					
Pellagrini, Al	125	0.273	OF				
Phillips, Otis	4	0.000	P	0	1		
Powers, George	65	0.208	SS				
Ramey, Jerry	22	0.205	P	4	6	5.54	
Rodriguez, Angel	20	0.156	C				
Smith, George	19	0.119	P	7	7	4.08	
Stemper, Robb	26	0.211	C				
Tinsley, Art	17	0.048	P	8	8	3.28	
Tuck, Gerald	2	0.000					
Wartelle, Johnny	30	0.083	P	6	9	4.99	
Werner, Dan	4	0.000	P	0	1		
White, Bob	67	0.215	C				

Moultrie, Georgia

Team Operated by Moultrie Baseball Club, Inc.
Team President: J.L. Butler
Secretary-Business Manager: C.W. Vandiver
Treasurer: Dr. W.C. Arwood
Manager(s): Ken Polivka
Games played at Holmes Park
Season attendance: 30,451
Major League Affiliate: Cincinnati Reds – National League.

Moultrie Redlegs Team Roster

NAME	G	BA	POS	W	L	ERA	APF
Bettin, Bob	34	0.252	C				
Bullard, Henry	23	0.038	P	1	5	6.97	
Caudle, Jim	41	0.208	OF, P	1	0		
Condu, Phil	121	0.333	1B, OF				
Cook, Cliff	25	0.239	OF				
Crook, Don	18	0.296	P	2	3	6.00	
Crouch, Les	119	0.249	2B, 3B, SS, OF, P	0	0		
Daidone, Joe	65	0.235	2B				
Drostie, Carroll	8		P	2	2		
Fedak, Gene	24	0.096	P	6	12	4.10	
Fehrenbach, Floyd	126	0.297	3B				
Ferrara, Bernard	14	0.214					
Flowers, Bob	22	0.200					
Fogleman, Oliver	40	0.308	SS				
Folk, Dick	74	0.204	SS				
Garcia, Manuel	15	0.188	P	1	5	8.83	
Garcia, Sergio	111	0.225	C				Cordele
Green, Billy	39	0.160	P	8	11	5.79	
Hall, Morris	23	0.162	C				
Heckman, Ernie	48	0.201	1B				
Hill, Van	135	0.257	OF				
Howard, Tom	40	0.229	1B				
Husich, John	50	0.209	P	8	15	4.92	

Name	G	BA	POS	W	L	ERA	APF
Little, Elmer	23	0.108	P	4	9	6.34	
Lopez, Chino	20	0.160	P	1	4	5.20	
Myers, John	3	0.000	P	0	1		
Polivka, Ken	33	0.260	M, P	15	4	2.52	
Prince, Ralph	11	0.189					
Raisch, Charles	7	0.250	P	0	1		
Stone, Allan	11	0.333	P	0	2		
Tilley, Terry	9	0.083					
White, John	8	0.063	P	1	3		
Williams, Jim	19	0.283	1B				
Yarbrough, Dan	6	0.083	P	0	0		
Yarbrough, Jim	138	0.234	OF, C				
Zitek, Don	32	0.226	P	4	7	3.62	

Thomasville, Georgia

Team Operated by Thomasville Dodgers, Inc.
Team President: Heeth Varnedoe
Vice Presidents: Fresco Thompson, Dick Walsh
Secretary: Matthew A. Burns
Treasurer: William Gibson
General Manager: George E. Pfister
Manager(s): Pete Reiser
Games played at Municipal Stadium
Season attendance: 30,274
Major League Affiliate: Brooklyn Dodgers – National League.

Thomasville Dodgers Team Roster

NAME	G	BA	POS	W	L	ERA	APF
Anderson, Roger	31	0.172	1B				
Arellanes, Bill	42	0.235	3B				
Bayno, Joe	7	0.000	P	0	4		
Beiler, Carl	8	0.000					
Bova, Tom	5	0.000					
Brodsky, Sheldon	35	0.242	3B				
Carlson, Bob	10	0.200	SS				
Clancy, Bill	11	0.091	P	1	1		
Coleman, Bill	54	0.260	C				
Crawford, Jim	2	0.500	P	0	0		
Deal, Bill	137	0.284	OF				
Detmers, Larry	7	0.250	P	0	0		
Devlin, Conrad	34	0.248	3B, OF				
Dunn, Don	21	0.145	2B				
Erickson, Marlin	10	0.400	P	1	1		
Gershberg, Howard	6	0.368					
Green, Ray	12	0.214	3B				
Guza, Mike	22	0.320	C				Cordele
Heath, Harold	11	0.000	P	0	0		
Heinz, Martin	3	0.000	P	0	1		
Hejnosz, John	15	0.176	OF				
Henriquez, Julio	26	0.253	P				
Hire, Ashford	7	0.250	P	0	3		
Hughes, Jim	57	0.221	2B, 3B, SS				
Humbert, Jimmy	11	0.148	P	0	0		
Jackson, Bill	123	0.206	2B, SS				Brunswick
Jezek, Ed	5	0.250	P	0	1		
Jones, Fred	2	0.000	P	0	1		
Kopec, Don	12	0.111	C				
Langer, Jack	100	0.242	3B, SS, P	0	0		
Lavin, Tom	23	0.156	2B				
Lawlor, Bob	4	0.182					
Lopez, Victorino	2	0.000	P	0	0		
McMullin, Dale	124	0.287	1B				
Meyer, Bill	2	0.000	P	0	0		
Mills, Harvey	38	0.173	P	16	10	3.33	
Moore, Ed	8	0.000	P	0	1		
Nichols, Jim	18	0.108	OF				
Norris, Jim	134	0.245	OF				
Oster, Fred	8	0.167	P	1	3		
Pender, Wilbert	8	0.083	P	1	5		
Permeter, Harold	2	0.000	P	0	0		

NAME	G	BA	POS	W	L	ERA	APF
Priede, Nilo	9	0.148					
Reiser, Pete	1	0.000	M				
Ritchie, Ed	20	0.250	P	4	5	2.14	
Russell, Dave	47	0.216	3B, OF				
Salerno, Pasquale	94	0.306	OF				
Scannelli, Frank	74	0.230	C				
Sedlack, Bob	32	0.175	P	17	7	1.53	
Slezak, Francis	43	0.159	SS				
Smith, Jack	2	0.000	P	0	1		
Spier, Bob	56	0.299	P	15	8	3.05	
Steen, Bob	29	0.253	2B				
Virkstis, Bob	33	0.191	P	4	6	3.46	
Wells, Bill	27	0.185	P	6	13	3.39	

Tifton, Georgia

Team Operated by Tiftarea Baseball Club, Inc.
Team President: Dr. L.O. Shaw
Vice President-Treasurer: John Ford
Secretary: L.L. Kennedy
General Manager: Frank Raley
Manager(s): Paul Eames
Games played at Eve Park
Season attendance: 38,363

Tifton Blue Sox Team Roster

NAME	G	BA	POS	W	L	ERA	APF
Akins, Jack	5	0.063					
Barth, Jerry	5	0.000					
Bindschadler, Ben	31	0.213	P	7	10	3.53	
Bloom, Don	1	0.000	P	0	0		
Braziel, Dennis	93	0.292	1B, 2B, OF, C, P	0	0		
Burgess, Ted	38	0.120	P	10	9	2.20	
Campbell, Bob	9	0.179					
Carpenter, Max	5	0.429	P	1	1		
Chafin, Mark	<10						
Coffey, Herman	13	0.188	P	2	5	5.77	
Conrad, Bob	1	0.000	P	0	0		
Daniel, Bob	11	0.229	OF				
Doligale, John	83	0.298	OF				Waycross
Duncan, Jim	3	0.333					
Eames, Paul	135	0.289	M, 3B, C, P	0	1		
Englehart, Bill	71	0.260	OF, P	16	9	3.18	
Farmer, Dennis	21	0.129	3B				
Fauci, Tom	35	0.205	3B				
Forrest, Henry	5	0.000					
Fowler, Bob	2	0.000	P	0	1		
Gibbons, Bill	1	0.000	P	0	0		
Hanna, Vic	34	0.098	P	4	16	4.63	Albany
Hedin, Al	5	0.000	P	1	2		
Johnson, Lee	7	0.150	P	0	0		
Jones, Jerry	79	0.224	2B				
Kallas, Harry	139	0.273	2B, 3B, SS				
Longwello, Charles	67	0.233	3B, OF, P	1	3	3.72	
McGuire, Forrest	17	0.200					
Medlin, Jim	4	0.125					
Monterio, Dave	10	0.125	P	3	2		
Moore, Duke	3	0.000	P	0	2		
Morgan, Gordon	57	0.243	OF				
Parrish, Allen	11	0.222	P	1	3		
Pray, Don	12	0.341	1B				
Ray, George	2	0.000	P	0	1		
Robinson, Don	125	0.297	1B, OF, P	3	3	3.92	
Robinson, Jim	9	0.222	P	2	1		
Salcido, Carlos	13	0.154	OF				Albany
Salter, Fred	13	0.300					
Sarmiento, Antonio	24	0.133	P	5	12	3.65	
Smith, Dave	23	0.250	OF				
Spampinato, Tom	13	0.125	P	3	0		
Stutsman, Ed	50	0.246	1B				
Swain, Kurtis	12	0.229	C				
Thackston, John	2	0.000	P	0	1		
Watson, Art	8	0.000	P	0	1		
Willis, Bud	102	0.249	OF				
Wisniewski, John	97	0.281	SS				

Valdosta, Georgia

Team Operated by Valdosta Baseball Company, Inc.
Team President: Walter O. Briggs, Jr.
Vice President: John J. McHale
Secretary-Treasurer: H.M. Sisson
Director: T. Guy Connell
General Manager: R.B. "Bob" Bonifay
Manager(s): Stan Wasiak
Games played at Pendleton Park
Season attendance: 51,543
Major League Affiliate: Detroit Tigers – American League.

Valdosta Bears Team Roster

NAME	G	BA	POS	W	L	ERA	APF
Ainsworth, Harold	3	0.000	P	0	1		
Andrews, Chris	8	0.100					
Bays, Dick	20	0.143	P	6	8	2.11	
Beck, Dick	60	0.214	C				
Bowden, Russ	5	0.500	P	0	1		
Brill, Jim	36	0.247	C				
Carangelo, Ferdinand	29	0.229	OF				
Cartier, Dale	8	0.375	P	0	1		
Castille, Earl	13	0.000	P	2	2	2.83	
Caswell, Marv	4	0.333	P	0	1		
Chadwick, Reed	58	0.252	C				
Ciatto, Rosario	15	0.208	C				
Colone, Dick	139	0.265	1B, OF, P	0	0		
Daniels, Dick	45	0.335	1B				
Davis, Ned	12	0.162	OF				
Eaton, Gerald	6	0.143	P	1	1		
Fleshman, Elvin	12	0.222	P	2	4	5.03	
Green, Jim	9	0.184					
Griffy, Jim	79	0.307	3B, OF				
Hatcher, Marv	38	0.184	P	6	9	4.17	
Hayes, Tom	3	0.000					
Higginbotham, Milt	8	0.000	P	0	3		
Hinton, Dick	7	0.130					
Johnson, Bob	6	0.176					
Kardos, Jim	2	0.000	P	0	0		
Kromy, Darwin	41	0.145	P	10	12	4.36	Cordele
Kurth, Al	26	0.054	P	10	10	4.19	
Mauney, John	18	0.277	3B				
Mee, Joe	6	0.500	P	1	1		
Moore, Morris	101	0.195	2B, 3B				
Mounts, Emory	129	0.263	OF, P	0	0		
Pehanick, Al	19	0.095	P	10	5	1.87	
Powell, Hollis	5	0.316					
Robison, Ron	30	0.224	SS				
Siebert, Jim	9	0.125					
Smith, Charles	50	0.230	1B				
Strichek, Ed	26	0.088	P	12	7	2.01	
Tsitouris, John	31	0.107	P	10	9	3.07	
Vogt, Pete	16	0.289					
Walters, George	8	0.095	P	3	3	5.29	
Wasiak, Stan	96	0.306	M, 2B, P	0	0		
Wenson, Ron	125	0.287	OF				
Whetro, Ron	15	0.182					
Williams, Bob	107	0.231	SS				

Waycross, Georgia

Team Operated by Waycross Baseball Association, Inc.
Team President: Cecil Herrin
Vice President: M.M. Monroe, Jr.
Secretary-Treasurer: John Kopp

Business Manager: Claude Stone
Assistant Business Manager: W.C. Sweat
Manager(s): Jim Deery, Walt Widmayer
Games played at Memorial Stadium
Season attendance: 46,266

Waycross Bears Team Roster

NAME	G	BA	POS	W	L	ERA	APF
Barry, Willie	1	0.000	P	0	0		
Borrett, Curtis	29	0.242	OF				
Caputo, Lou	102	0.256	2B, 3B				Brunswick
Crowe, Charles	2	0.000					
Davis, Jack	107	0.223	OF				
Deery, Jim	103	0.304	M, 2B				
Doligale, John	83	0.298	OF				Tifton
Edgley, Joe	77	0.260	SS				
Ellis, Roy	18	0.100	P	3	3		
Engel, Al	133	0.263	OF				
Engel, Ray	125	0.215	C				
Farris, Jimmy	32	0.191	C				
Gunter, Carl	29	0.113	P	11	10	2.93	
Hoffman, Bob	13	0.094	P	4	7	2.48	
Hopkins, Joe	2	0.000	P	1	1		
Legursky, Carl	37	0.167	P	4	5	4.38	
MacConnell, Bob	132	0.294	1B, 2B, SS				
McKinstay, John	15	0.212	P	5	4	3.56	
Moore, Gayle	52	0.220	SS				
Morgan, George	112	0.280	1B, OF				
Pilgrim, Arvie	136	0.247	3B, OF				
Pyle, George	1	0.000	P	0	1		
Quigley, Jim	9	0.111	P	3	3	5.17	
Rakestraw, Don	11	0.000	P	0	1		
Rutter, Harry	27	0.179	OF				
Schlett, Bob	6	0.000	P	0	3		
Scranton, Dave	43	0.186	P	20	10	2.34	
Scroggs, John	30	0.143	P	11	8	2.90	
Smith, Paul	1	0.000	P	0	0		
Tidwell, Don	36	0.226	P	10	9	3.65	
Townley, Dave	9	0.000					
Widmayer, Walt	1	1.000	M				

1955 Georgia-Florida League Records
Batting
Highest Batting Average (minimum 100 at bats)
1. Jack Wilson – Brunswick .349
2. Marv Breeding – Cordele .338
3. Dick Daniels – Valdosta .335
4. Phil Condu – Moultrie .333
5. Bob Duzyk – Brunswick .330

Most Hits
1. Jack Wilson – Brunswick 175
2. Wayne Davis – Albany 164
3. Galen Williams – Albany 159
4. Bill Deal – Thomasville 155
5. J.C. Dunn – Albany 154

Most Runs
1. Jack Wilson – Brunswick 125
2. Fred Smith – Albany 120
3. Galen Williams – Albany 115
4. J.C. Dunn – Albany 109
5. Emory Mounts – Valdosta 106

Most Total Bases
1. Wayne Davis – Albany 267
2. J.C. Dunn – Albany 251
3. Bill Deal – Thomasville 236
4. Galen Williams – Albany 233
5. Bob MacConnell – Waycross 232

Most Doubles
1. Bob MacConnell – Waycross 37
2. Earl Fackler – Brunswick 34
3. Harry Kallas – Tifton 33
4. Jim Yarbrough – Moultrie 30
5. Bill Deal – Thomasville 29

Most Triples
1. Galen Williams – Albany 14
2. Bill Deal – Thomasville 11
   Van Hill – Moultrie 11
   Bob Rikard – Albany 11
5. Floyd Fehrenbach – Moultrie 10

Most Home Runs
1. Wayne Davis – Albany 20
   Dick Lubinski – Cordele 20
3. J.C. Dunn – Albany 17
   Bill Robertson – Brunswick 17
5. Joe Canuso – Brunswick 15

Most Extra Base Hits
1. Wayne Davis – Albany 54
   J.C. Dunn – Albany 54
   Bob MacConnell – Waycross 54
4. Jim Yarbrough – Moultrie 51
5. Bill Deal – Thomasville 50

Most Runs Batted In
1. J.C. Dunn – Albany 125
2. Wayne Davis – Albany 106
3. Jack Wilson – Brunswick 97
4. Joe Canuso – Brunswick 89
5. Bill Robertson – Brunswick 88

Most Stolen Bases
1. Arvie Pilgrim – Waycross 59
2. J.C. Dunn – Albany 48
3. Ron Wenson – Valdosta 47
4. Fred Smith – Albany 42
5. Galen Williams – Albany 27
   Gerald Karczewski – Albany 27
   Marv Breeding – Cordele 27

Fielding
Most Put-Outs
1. Earl Fackler 1B – Brunswick 1,067
2. Dale McMullin 1B – Thomasville 934
3. Bob MacConnell 1B, 2B, SS – Waycross 879
4. Newton Brown 1B – Cordele 860
5. Ray Engel C – Waycross 750

Most Assists
1. Fred Berger 2B – Cordele 393
2. Galen Williams 2B – Albany 356
3. Bill Jackson 2B, SS – Thom/Brun 342
4. Bob Williams SS – Valdosta 335
5. Jim Deery 2B – Waycross 319

Most Errors
1. Bob Williams SS – Valdosta 53
2. Joe Edgley SS – Waycross 50
   Floyd Fehrenbach 3B – Moultrie 50
4. Fred Sisolak 2B, SS – Brunswick 48
   Bill Robertson 3B – Brunswick 48
   Gerald Karczewski 3B – Albany 48

Pitching

Most Wins
1. Bill Lackey – Albany   22
2. Dave Scranton – Waycross   20
3. Bob Sedlack – Thomasville   17
   Jim Duffalo – Brunswick   17
5. John Schieffer – Albany   16
   Bill Englehart – Tifton   16
   Harvey Mills – Thomasville   16

Most Losses
1. Vic Hanna – Tift/Alba   16
2. John Husich – Moultrie   15
3. Bill Wells – Thomasville   13
4. Darwin Kromy – Vald/Cord   12
   Gene Fedak – Moultrie   12
   Antonio Sarmiento – Tifton   12

Highest Winning Percentage (10 game minimum)
1. Jim Duffalo – Brunswick   .810
2. Ken Polivka – Moultrie   .789
3. Frank Ramsey – Brunswick   .778
4. Bill Lackey – Albany   .733
   Howard Lockwood – Cordele   .733

Lowest Earned Run Average (100 inning minimum)
1. Bob Sedlack – Thomasville   1.53
2. Al Pehanick – Valdosta   1.87
3. Bill Lackey – Albany   1.98
4. Ed Strichek – Valdosta   2.01
5. Dick Bays – Valdosta   2.11

Most Strikeouts
1. Bill Lackey – Albany   222
2. Bob Sedlack – Thomasville   220
3. Dave Scranton – Waycross   206
4. Bill Englehart – Tifton   196
5. Harvey Mills – Thomasville   178

Most Bases on Balls
1. Bill Englehart – Tifton   155
2. Johnny Wartelle – Cordele   137
3. Bill Lackey – Albany   124
4. Billy Green – Moultrie   116
5. Jim Hayden – Brunswick   115

Most Hits Allowed
1. Bill Lackey – Albany   249
2. Darwin Kromy – Vald/Cord   218
3. John Schieffer – Albany   206
4. Dave Scranton – Waycross   202
5. John Husich – Moultrie   199

Most Innings Pitched
1. Bill Lackey – Albany   277
2. Dave Scranton – Waycross   258
3. Bob Sedlack – Thomasville   229
4. John Schieffer – Thomasville 212
   Bill Englehart – Tifton   212

C   Joe Canuso – Brunswick
C   Bill Thompson – Albany
UT Paul Demont – Cordele
P   Bill Lackey – Albany
P   Jim Duffalo – Brunswick
P   Dave Scranton – Waycross
P   Bob Sedlack – Thomasville
M   Frank Oceak – Brunswick

1955 Georgia-Florida League All-Star Team
1B Earl Fackler – Brunswick
2B Galen Williams – Albany
3B Bill Robertson – Brunswick
SS Marv Breeding – Cordele
OF Jack Wilson – Brunswick
OF Wayne Davis – Albany
OF Phil Condu – Moultrie
OF Dick Lubinski – Cordele

Georgia Class-D Minor League Baseball Encyclopedia

1955

Georgia State League

League Office: Dublin, Georgia
League President: W.H. Lovett
League Vice President: Howard Threlkeld
Secretary: A. Oswald Hadden
Salary Limit: $2,600 per month.
Player Rule: Each club was allowed a roster of sixteen players, not more than two veterans, not more than three limited service, and not less than eleven rookies.

Georgia State League Final Standings

Team	W	L	Pct	GB	Affiliate
Douglas Trojans	62	46	.574	----	CIN-NL
Sandersville Giants	56	51	.523	5.5	NY-NL
Hazlehurst-Baxley Cardinals	57	53	.518	6.0	STL-NL
Vidalia Indians	56	54	.509	7.0	CLE-AL
Dublin Irish	49	61	.445	14.0	PIT-NL
Statesboro Pilots	25	40	.385	N/A	Unaffiliated

1955 Georgia State League Map

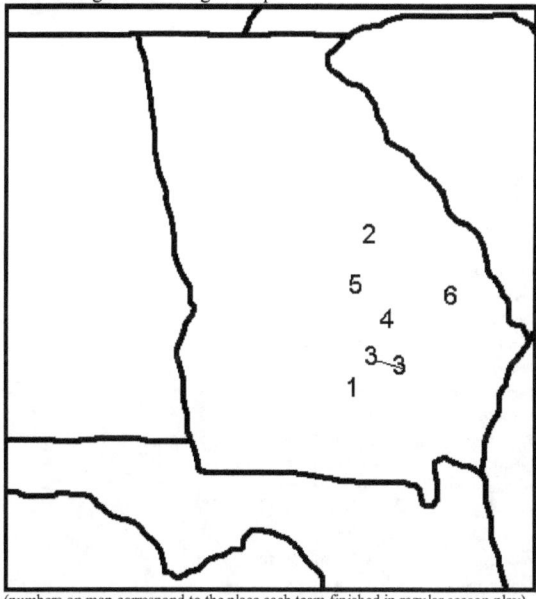

(numbers on map correspond to the place each team finished in regular season play)

The lineup of the league went unchanged from the previous season as all six clubs returned to the dirt. On July 1, Statesboro decided to call it quits and withdrew from the league. The five remaining teams adjusted their schedules and continued on with the baseball action.

It was on August 6, that Sandersville pitcher Leo Quatro pitched the season's only no-hitter as he and the Giants defeated Hazlehurst-Baxley 1 to 0.

Douglas took first place in regular season games followed in order by Sandersville, Hazlehurst-Baxley, and Vidalia. In the first round of playoffs, Douglas was victorious over Vidalia three games to one, and Sandersville ousted Hazlehurst-Baxley by the identical score. As the top two teams from the regular season squared off in the championship series, the rain began to fall with zeal. Douglas won three games, and Sandersville won one in the games that were played between the storms. The remainder of the series was called off, and both teams were declared to be co-champions.

Douglas, Georgia

Team Operated by Douglas Trojans, Inc.
Team President: E.E. Hilliard
Vice President: H.B. Chitty
General Manager: W.P. Ward, Jr.
Manager(s): Bob Wellman
Games played at Municipal Park
Season attendance: 32,925
Major League Affiliate: Cincinnati Reds – National League.

Douglas Trojans Team Roster

NAME	G	BA	POS	W	L	ERA	APF
Alomar, Rafael	105	0.303	OF				
Alvarez, Alberto	2	0.000					
Bumstead, Dan	5	0.300	P	0	2		
Caldwell, Wilbur	92	0.251	1B, 3B, OF, P	7	4	2.03	
Churlilla, Ed	9	0.250					
Cook, Cliff	86	0.300	OF				
Davis, Joe	100	0.253	3B, OF				
Diamond, Paul	6	0.000					
Dobzanski, Bob	25	0.283	P	12	8	3.35	
Dunlap, Don	2	0.000	P	0	0		
Falcone, Nick	9	0.133					
Fedak, Gene	5	0.100	P	0	3		
Folk, Dick	24	0.157	3B				
Goines, Jim	2	0.000	P	0	1		
Green, Billy	2	0.333	P	0	1		
Helmick, Julius	3	0.000	P	0	0		
Jackson, John	5	0.235	P	3	1		
Moreno, Heliodoro	11	0.143	P	2	3	4.29	
Nichols, Charles	6	0.500	P	1	1		
Salmonson, Lee	26	0.188	P	8	6	4.01	
Schmidt, Haven	104	0.250	C				
Sharp, Irv	108	0.275	2B, 3B				
Slaboszewski, Vince	19	0.140	OF				
Stasi, Rocco	2	0.000					
Tannreuther, Charles	19	0.088	P	6	5	5.76	
Thompson, Jim	3	0.000	P	0	0		
Torres, Felix	108	0.285	SS				
Valdez, Felipe	32	0.255	2B				
Welage, Dick	25	0.123	P	11	2	2.36	
Wellman, Bob	107	0.319	M, 1B, OF, P	1	1		
Wells, Jack	35	0.147	P	10	7	2.93	
Williams, Jim	14	0.186	1B				

Dublin, Georgia

Team Operated by Dublin Baseball Association
Team President: W.A. Brewer
Vice President: W.W. Brinson
Secretary: A. Oswald Hadden
Treasurer: Louis Hatcher
Business Manager: Huey Murphy
Manager(s): George Kinnamon
Games played at Lovett Park
Season attendance: 16,997
Major League Affiliate: Pittsburgh Pirates – National League.

Dublin Irish Team Roster

NAME	G	BA	POS	W	L	ERA	APF
Arent, George	103	0.294	1B				
Beane, Bill	14	0.048	P	4	5	5.80	
Beran, Lee	30	0.214	OF, P	1	4	7.62	

NAME	G	BA	POS	W	L	ERA	APF
Buell, Sam	56	0.254	OF				
Bush, Herb	30	0.292	OF				
Caputo, Lou	29	0.267	2B				
Dinan, Paul	43	0.222	3B				Statesboro
Edwards, Don	4	0.000	P	0	0		
Foss, Larry	23	0.250	P	4	4	5.51	
Garmon, Ray	14	0.235	OF				
Gaskins, Henry	12	0.217	SS				
Hardison, Jim	42	0.218	P	10	14	2.71	
Hill, Larry	2	0.000	P	0	0		
Hoenes, Ron	85	0.293	OF, C				
Honkus, Stan	6	0.200	P	0	2		
Hull, Tommy	20	0.159	P	10	3	2.49	
Johnson, Ernest	12	0.091	P	1	1	6.39	
Jordan, Albert	5	0.158					
Jordan, Joe	58	0.292	OF, P	0	2		Statesboro
Kenseith, Keith	3	0.500	P	0	0		
Kinnamon, George	97	0.248	M, C, P	5	2	3.60	
Kolaska, George	60	0.256	SS				
McClenaghan, Russ	60	0.318	OF, C				Statesboro
Meekins, Dennis	83	0.224	3B				
Minjock, John	15	0.192	P	5	7	3.38	
Morris, Milt	73	0.294	3B, SS, OF				Vidalia
Neeley, Bob	33	0.274	OF				
Perry, Joe	24	0.250	P	5	8	4.54	
Prescott, Andy	2	0.000					
Probitsky, Burke	85	0.255	OF				
Reider, Dave	61	0.297	2B				Statesboro
Runyan, Dick	7	0.111	P	1	3		
Schammel, George	18	0.250	P	0	3		
Shelton, Jim	6	0.364	P	1	2		
Smith, Tom	10	0.125	P	2	3	6.26	
Urbanski, Bill	54	0.229	2B				
Vandiveer, Rod	6	0.286					
Williams, Franklin	54	0.238	OF				

Hazlehurst-Baxley (Hazlehurst & Baxley), Georgia

Team Operated by Hazlehurst-Baxley Baseball Club, Inc.
Team President: W.W. Thompson
Vice President: J.B. Aycock
Secretary: Laura P. Bramblett
General Manager: Kenneth S. Martin
Manager(s): Sam Goody
Games played at Roland Cook Stadium
Season attendance: 10,397
Major League Affiliate: St. Louis Cardinals – National League.

Hazlehurst-Baxley Cardinals Team Roster

NAME	G	BA	POS	W	L	ERA	APF
Bradley, Don	34	0.156	P	9	9	2.47	
Cassell, Carl	6	0.176					
Dal Porto, Angelo	62	0.244	OF				
Davis, Al	99	0.307	OF, C				
Davis, Tom	27	0.162	P	6	5	5.42	
Duncan, Lindon	108	0.312	2B, SS, OF				
Dwyer, John	11	0.190					
Francis, Charles	15	0.243	OF, P	0	0		
Goody, Sam	106	0.265	M, 2B, 3B, SS, P	0	0		
Grammer, Jack	5	0.000					
Guenst, Charles	2	0.000					
Herring, Bob	21	0.200	C				
Hulsey, DeLane	12	0.000	P	1	7	5.43	
Jarvinen, Vern	5	0.154					
Knox, Al	68	0.276	OF, P	9	8	3.08	
Maguire, Paul	41	0.216	SS				
Mahurin, Leman	37	0.214	P	12	4	3.84	
Matthews, Jim	98	0.274	3B, OF				
McIntyre, Jim	11	0.121	3B				
Miller, Bill	47	0.210	1B				
Nemeth, Bob	19	0.194	P	4	5	4.14	
Payne, Charles	2	0.167					
Perlman, Bertram	9	0.083	P	2	2		
Phelps, Ray	3	0.667	P	0	0		
Proctor, Tom	1	0.000					
Quinn, Don	18	0.115	P	2	5	6.82	
Reed, Jack	27	0.229	P	11	5	3.33	
Sadowski, Bob	106	0.257	1B, 3B, SS, P	0	0		
Shalata, Bill	104	0.295	OF, P	0	0		
Siebold, John	16	0.167	SS				
Webber, Don	1	1.000	P	0	0		
Williams, Jim	39	0.223	C				
Wilson, Dick	4	0.000	P	1	2		
Woodall, Dick	3	0.000					
Young, Don	8	0.375	P	0	1		

Sandersville, Georgia

Team Operated by Washington County Baseball Club, Inc.
Team President: N.M. Jordan
Vice President: Clem Brown
Secretary-Treasurer: O.R. Hendricks
General Manager: T.C. Carr
Manager(s): Pete Pavlick
Games played at City Baseball Park
Season attendance: 31,005
Major League Affiliate: New York Giants – National League.

Sandersville Giants Team Roster

NAME	G	BA	POS	W	L	ERA	APF
Bell, Russ	22	0.115	OF				
Biassetti, Gil	28	0.152	P	6	7	5.11	
Butts, Bobby	19	0.190	OF				
Cali, Bill	4	0.167					
Camberari, Rocco	47	0.206	OF				
Carmichael, Dan	1	0.000					
Clements, Anthony	9	0.083	P	0	2		
Cockrell, Gene	59	0.211	3B, OF, P	0	0		
Crosby, Ralph	100	0.247	3B, SS				
Davis, Vic	42	0.241	P	14	9	3.44	
DeJesus, Bill	4	0.200	P	1	0		
Delida, Bob	3	0.000	P	0	0		
DeLuca, Ed	19	0.154	2B				Statesboro
Elias, Jack	96	0.332	SS, P	0	0		
Farris, Jimmy	22	0.239	OF, C				
Hatcher, Bill	89	0.229	OF, C				
Hinrichs, Donald	15	0.040	P	6	8	5.31	
Hoyal, Craig	5	0.000	P	0	0		
Kocak, George	4	0.000	P	0	2		
LaFaive, Dick	44	0.398	OF				
McCovey, Willie	107	0.305	1B				
Navarro, Julio	4	0.167	P	0	2		
Palmer, Bob	7	0.150					
Pavlick, Pete	96	0.281	M, 2B				
Pazienza, Bill	63	0.211	C				
Petriello, Joe	2	0.500	P	1	0		
Quatro, Leo	30	0.246	P	15	5	3.10	
Sager, Don	46	0.091	P	3	5	2.84	
Scott, Bob	27	0.186	OF				
Tally, Bill	1	0.000					
Walters, Jerry	25	0.192	OF				
Warren, Rudy	81	0.297	OF				
Yetsko, Andy	44	0.263	P	10	11	3.48	

Statesboro, Georgia

Team Operated by Statesboro Athletic Association, Inc.
Team President: C.B. McAllister
Secretary: R. Herbert Kingery
Treasurer: Herman E. Bray

Business Manager: R.F. Donaldson, Jr.
Manager(s): Gerald Peters, Jim Sosebee
Games played at Pilots Field
Season attendance: 8,750

Statesboro Pilots Team Roster

NAME	G	BA	POS	W	L	ERA	APF
Alexander, Tom	24	0.156	SS				
Bova, Tom	3	0.000					
Caldwell, Bob	50	0.218	3B, C, P	2	0		
DeLuca, Ed	19	0.154	2B				Sandersville
Dinan, Paul	43	0.222	3B				Dublin
Dobberstein, Charles	21	0.061	P	10	4	4.31	
Dyer, Vaughn	44	0.324	1B				
Farrar, Jim	6	0.211					
Fields, Howard	5	0.000	P	1	4		
Hutchins, Barry	21	0.053	P	6	7	5.15	
Icenhour, Luther	32	0.244	SS				
Johnson, Larry	3	0.000	P	0	1		
Jordan, Joe	58	0.292	OF, P	0	2		Dublin
Jungman, Lawrence	20	0.196	3B				
Keuch, Warren	6	0.150					
Kollin, Major	9	0.000	P	1	2		
Lavin, Tom	21	0.114					
MacFarlane, Morley	9	0.176	P	2	4		
Maxwell, John	2	0.000					
McClenaghan, Russ	60	0.318	OF, C				Dublin
Melbert, Bill	11	0.214	P	1	4	8.50	
Miller, Joe	64	0.320	OF, C				
Moss, Darvin	4	0.000	P	0	1		
Murray, Don	57	0.271	OF				
Nims, Keith	1	0.000	P	0	0		
Peters, Gerald	63	0.265	M, 1B, OF, P	0	0		
Reider, Dave	61	0.297	2B				Dublin
Sarmiento, Antonio	4	0.167	P	0	2		
Smith, Earl	3	0.000	P	0	0		
Smith, Larry	6	0.000	P	1	3		
Sosebee, Jim	31	0.265	M, SS, OF				
Spampinato, Tom	3	0.000	P	0	2		
Wagoner, Charles	8	0.143	P	1	0		
Wolfman, Cedric	10	0.303	P	0	4		

Vidalia, Georgia
Team Operated by Vidalia Baseball Association, Inc.
Team President: G.H. Threlkeld
Vice President: H.B. Estroff
Secretary-Treasurer: G.H. Gibson
Business Manager: L.A. Levy
Manager(s): Ed Levy
Games played at Municipal Stadium
Season attendance: 24,251
Major League Affiliate: Cleveland Indians – American League.

Vidalia Indians Team Roster

NAME	G	BA	POS	W	L	ERA	APF
Adam, Dick	4	0.500	P	0	2		
Bell, Gary	15	0.395	P	7	5	3.33	
Bennett, Gerald	6	0.000	P	0	1		
Cockroft, Joe	3	0.000	P	0	0		
Craven, Jim	13	0.375	P	1	3	17.00	
Deeds, Ray	33	0.134	P	7	11	4.58	
Deering, Verne	6	0.000	P	1	1		
Dillard, Don	27	0.247	OF				
Dolan, Lonnie	38	0.210	OF				
Drewiske, Roger	33	0.093	P	11	8	3.73	
Driggers, Bobby	84	0.321	OF				
Gerard, Ray	53	0.220	OF, P	2	0		
Gilbert, Phil	32	0.235	P	11	9	3.49	
Gongola, Pete	100	0.238	C				
Green, Harold	46	0.251	2B				
Hancock, Leroy	51	0.281	2B				
Henderson, Dave	46	0.171	SS				
Hodges, Jim	9	0.100					
Irby, Leroy	42	0.286	1B, OF				
Kindl, Bill	18	0.159	OF				
Kray, Vic	53	0.223	2B, SS, OF, P	0	3		
Levy, Ed	28	0.289	M, P	1	0		
McClaskey, Larry	23	0.340	P	9	2	4.38	
Morris, Milt	73	0.294	3B, SS, OF				Dublin
Odum, Bill	4	0.133					
Pereira, Andres	8	0.125					
Price, Charles	2	0.250	P	0	1		
Rediger, Glenn	103	0.296	1B, OF				
Swanson, Phil	5	0.143	P	2	1		
Tingle, Tom	110	0.304	SS, OF				
VanDerBeek, Jim	10	0.056	P	2	3		
Williams, Carl	8	0.105					
Wilson, Bob	105	0.308	3B				
Womack, Al	11	0.300	P	2	4	10.93	

1955 Georgia State League Records
Batting
Highest Batting Average (minimum 100 at bats)
1. Dick LaFaive – Sandersville   .398
2. Jack Elias – Sandersville   .332
3. Vaughn Dyer – Statesboro   .324
4. Bobby Driggers – Vidalia   .321
5. Joe Miller – Statesboro   .320

Most Hits
1. Bob Wilson – Vidalia   132
2. Rafael Alomar – Douglas   131
3. Bob Wellman – Douglas   130
4. Jack Elias – Sandersville   127
   Lindon Duncan - Hazlehurst-Baxley 127
   Felix Torres – Douglas   127

Most Runs
1. Felix Torres – Douglas   101
2. Jack Elias – Sandersville   96
3. Bob Wilson – Vidalia   87
   Bob Wellman – Douglas   87
5. Willie McCovey – Sandersville   82

Most Total Bases
1. Bob Wellman – Douglas   224
2. Felix Torres – Douglas   222
3. Willie McCovey – Sandersville   208
4. George Arent – Dublin   202
5. Jack Elias – Sandersville   194

Most Doubles
1. Felix Torres – Douglas   36
2. Bob Wellman – Douglas   31
3. Willie McCovey – Sandersville   24
   Bob Wilson – Vidalia   24
5. Bobby Driggers – Vidalia   23

Most Triples
1. Bill Shalata - Hazlehurst-Baxley 12
2. Bob Wilson – Vidalia   11
3. Haven Schmidt – Douglas   9
4. Rafael Alomar – Douglas   8
   Rudy Warren – Sandersville   8

Most Home Runs
1. Bob Wellman – Douglas   21

2. Cliff Cook – Douglas 20
3. Haven Schmidt – Douglas 19
   George Arent – Dublin 19
   Willie McCovey – Sandersville 19

Most Extra Base Hits
1. Felix Torres – Douglas 57
2. Bob Wellman – Douglas 52
3. Haven Schmidt – Douglas 49
4. Willie McCovey – Sandersville 44
5. Cliff Cook – Douglas 41
   George Arent – Dublin 41

Most Runs Batted In
1. Willie McCovey – Sandersville 113
2. Bob Wellman – Douglas 100
3. George Arent – Dublin 94
4. Felix Torres – Douglas 88
5. Rafael Alomar – Douglas 79

Most Stolen Bases
1. Bob Wilson – Vidalia 34
2. Jack Elias – Sandersville 31
3. Milt Morris – Vida/Dubl 22
4. Lindon Duncan - Hazlehurst-Baxley 16
5. Willie McCovey – Sandersville 15
   Bobby Driggers – Vidalia 15
   Burke Probitsky – Dublin 15

Fielding
Most Put-Outs
1. Willie McCovey 1B – Sandersville 897
2. Bob Wellman 1B, OF, P – Douglas 803
3. George Arent 1B – Dublin 774
4. Pete Gongola C – Vidalia 664
5. Glenn Rediger 1B, OF – Vidalia 651

Most Assists
1. Felix Torres SS – Douglas 319
2. Irv Sharp 2B, 3B – Douglas 292
3. Pete Pavlick 2B – Sandersville 279
4. Sam Goody 2B, 3B, SS, P - Hazlehurst-Baxley 258
5. Jack Elias SS – Sandersville 237

Most Errors
1. Felix Torres SS – Douglas 54
2. Lindon Duncan 2B, SS, OF - Hazlehurst-Baxley 52
3. Bob Sadowski 1B, 3B, SS, P - Hazlehurst-Baxley 41
4. Jack Elias SS, P – Sandersville 36
   Bob Wilson 3B – Vidalia 36
   Tom Tingle SS, OF – Vidalia 36

Pitching
Most Wins
1. Leo Quatro – Sandersville 15
2. Vic Davis – Sandersville 14
3. Leman Mahurin - Hazlehurst-Baxley 12
   Bob Dobzanski – Douglas 12
5. *four players tied with 11

Most Losses
1. Jim Hardison – Dublin 14
2. Andy Yetsko – Sandersville 11
   Ray Deeds – Vidalia 11
4. Vic Davis – Sandersville 9
   Phil Gilbert – Vidalia 9
   Don Bradley - Hazlehurst-Baxley 9

Highest Winning Percentage (10 game minimum)
1. Dick Welage – Douglas .846
2. Larry McClaskey – Vidalia .818
3. Tommy Hull – Dublin .769
4. Leo Quatro – Sandersville .750
   Leman Mahurin - Hazlehurst-Baxley .750

Lowest Earned Run Average (100 inning minimum)
1. Wilbur Caldwell – Douglas 2.03
2. Dick Welage – Douglas 2.36
3. Don Bradley - Hazlehurst-Baxley 2.47
4. Tommy Hull – Dublin 2.49
5. Jim Hardison – Dublin 2.71

Most Strikeouts
1. Vic Davis – Sandersville 189
2. Jim Hardison – Dublin 179
3. Leo Quatro – Sandersville 138
4. Roger Drewskie – Vidalia 129
5. Andy Yetsko – Sandersville 128

Most Bases on Balls
1. Vic Davis – Sandersville 112
2. Roger Drewiske – Vidalia 111
3. Harry Hutchins – Statesboro 104
4. Jim Hardison – Dublin 95
5. Larry Foss – Dublin 82

Most Hits Allowed
1. Jim Hardison – Dublin 193
2. Ray Deeds – Vidalia 188
3. Andy Yetsko – Sandersville 172
4. Phil Gilbert – Vidalia 168
5. Jack Wells – Douglas 165

Most Innings Pitched
1. Jim Hardison – Dublin 226
2. Vic Davis – Sandersville 196
3. Andy Yetsko – Sandersville 189
4. Leo Quatro – Sandersville 183
5. Phil Gilbert – Vidalia 178

Georgia Class-D Minor League Baseball Encyclopedia

1956

Georgia-Florida League

League Office: Leslie, Georgia
League President: W.T. Anderson
League Vice President: Guy Connell
Secretary: D.A. Osburn
Salary Limit: $2,600 per month plus $600.
Player Rule: Each club was allowed a roster of sixteen players, not more than two veterans, not more than eight limited service, and not less than six rookies.

Georgia-Florida League Final Standings

Team	W	L	Pct	GB	Affiliate
Valdosta Tigers	94	45	.676	----	DET-AL
Waycross Braves	79	59	.572	14.5	MIL-NL
Tifton Phillies	70	66	.515	22.5	PHI-NL
Albany Cardinals	70	68	.507	23.5	STL-NL
Moultrie Reds	68	71	.489	26.0	CIN-NL
Thomasville Dodgers	63	76	.453	31.0	BRK-NL
Brunswick Pirates	62	76	.449	31.5	PIT-NL
Fitzgerald A's	47	92	.338	47.0	KC-AL

1956 Georgia-Florida League Map

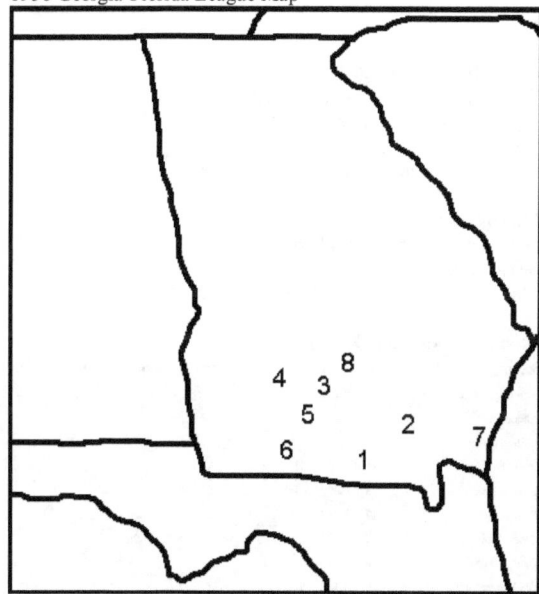

(numbers on map correspond to the place each team finished in regular season play)

There was one change in the lineup of the league from the prior season. Cordele dropped out, and Fitzgerald was admitted back into the league.

Albany moundsman Jere Hill threw a no-hitter on May 7 against Thomasville winning the game 2 to 1. On June 2, Fitzgerald pitcher Hank Szostak pitched a perfect game against Brunswick winning 3 to 0 in seven innings. Lou Souillard of Waycross hurled the third no-hitter of the season on August 23 to beat Fitzgerald 6 to 0. Moultrie slugger Bob Wellman set the league's all-time single season record for the most total bases with 296. He also set the all-time mark for the most extra base hits in a single season at 69. Albany's Chase Riddle also made history setting the all-time single season record in the league for the most runs batted in driving 142 base runners across the plate.

There was no playoff or post-season played at the end of the 1956 season.

Albany, Georgia
Team Operated by Albany Baseball Club
Team President: Morton M. Wiggins
Vice President: August A. Busch, Jr.
Secretary: Nadine Cravey
General Manager: Sheldon A. "Chief" Bender
Manager(s): Chase Riddle
Games played at Cardinal Park
Season attendance: 26,949
Major League Affiliate: St. Louis Cardinals – National League.

Albany Cardinals Team Roster

NAME	G	BA	POS	W	L	ERA	APF
Beane, Bill	15	0.192	P	5	4	5.93	
Boner, Billy	16	0.180	OF				
Brown, Don	27	0.221	OF				
Brown, Lou	30	0.209	OF				
Bruenjes, Allen	1	0.000	P	0	0		
Carmel, Duke	18	0.273	OF				
Carroll, Ray	51	0.176	OF				
Clark, Bob	66	0.253	SS				
Cloer, Burlon	12	0.176	P	5	2	2.89	
Cook, Dwight	105	0.234	2B, P	6	6	3.51	
Curl, Kedy	8	0.000	P	0	2		
Dreisbach, Ed	25	0.224	3B				
Dugan, Joe	67	0.252	OF				
Federico, Don	5	0.000					
Floyd, Bob	54	0.218	OF				Fitzgerald
Gabriel, Earl	10	0.208					
Gunn, Dick	48	0.255	3B				
Haverly, Karl	16	0.040	P	5	4	3.23	
Hickman, Jim	137	0.269	1B, SS, OF				
Hill, Jere	26	0.298	P	8	7	3.27	
Hurley, Don	13	0.043					
Keller, Gerald	2	0.000	P	0	1		
Kendig, Lawrence	51	0.120	P	20	10	2.45	
Kolson, Tom	19	0.192	P	3	1	5.37	
Latham, Don	12	0.000	P	2	2		
Lindsey, Charles	6	0.222	P	0	0		
MacIvor, Colin	11	0.167	P	2	0		
McDevitt, Tom	82	0.328	2B				
Meyer, Gary	13	0.194	OF				
O'Connor, Mike	16	0.053	P	3	6	5.53	
Oliver, Gene	9	0.250					
Orr, Billy	16	0.159	3B				
Perry, Ray	21	0.163	P	5	8	3.10	
Petty, Tom	21	0.077	P	5	8	3.53	
Poland, Bobby	15	0.167	P	1	3		
Pray, Don	84	0.260	1B				
Rice, Rollie	31	0.214	OF				
Riddle, Chase	137	0.353	M, 1B, 3B, C, OF, P	0	0		
Shultis, Pete	7	0.125	P	0	3		
Snyder, Dick	51	0.234	SS				
Squibb, Don	3	0.000	P	0	1		
Steele, Ron	43	0.235	OF, P	0	0		
Williams, Jim	127	0.252	C				

Brunswick, Georgia
Team Operated by Brunswick Pirates, Inc.
Team President: Blanton Miller
Vice President: Branch Rickey, Jr.
Secretary: Walter Bunt

Treasurer: James A. Herron
General Manager: John T. Helsel
Manager(s): Frank Oceak
Games played at Edo Miller Park
Season attendance: 30,714
Major League Affiliate: Pittsburgh Pirates – National League.

Brunswick Pirates Team Roster

NAME	G	BA	POS	W	L	ERA	APF
Anderton, Sherman	11	0.000	P	1	3		
Babich, Dick	138	0.289	1B, 3B				
Belinsky, Bo	11	0.083	P	2	3		
Brumbaugh, John	24	0.261	3B				
Cowan, Frank	3	0.000	P	0	0		
Davis, Bubba	47	0.250					
DeVany, Art	116	0.209	OF				
Douglas, Dan	18	0.232	OF				
Drapcho, Al	25	0.054	P	2	6	2.83	
Dworaczyk, Anthony	7	0.053					
Gray, Ron	6	0.167	P	1	2		
Hoenes, Ron	124	0.289	2B, C, OF				
Javier, Julian	18	0.180	3B				
Jordan, Ray	18	0.241					
Koski, Bob	82	0.270	OF, P	0	4		
Lipstas, Bob	55	0.202	OF, P	0	0		
Miller, Don	37	0.136	P	15	15	3.74	
Murillo, Jose	21	0.189	2B				
Oceak, Frank			M				
Perry, Joe	43	0.223	P	12	16	3.67	
Powell, Kelly	58	0.217	3B				
Recurt, Luis	97	0.232	2B				
Reiman, Ken	19	0.114	P	3	10	6.94	
Rich, Benny	36	0.163	P	19	9	2.64	
Richardson, Tom	8	0.000	P	0	3		
Rothgeb, John	3	0.000	P	0	0		
Sisolak, Fred	128	0.249	2B, 3B, SS, OF				
Stotler, Roy	80	0.214	SS				
Stubing, Moose	13	0.227	1B				
Torres, Guerry	17	0.077	P	7	5	1.80	
Whitcomb, Don	122	0.231	C				

Fitzgerald, Georgia

Team Operated by Colony City Baseball Club, Inc.
Team President: E.W. Mann, Jr.
Vice President-Treasurer: R.W. Jernigan, Jr.
Secretary-General Manager: Curtis Green
Manager(s): Red Treadway
Games played at Blue-Gray Stadium
Season attendance: 17,723
Major League Affiliate: Kansas City Athletics – American League.

Fitzgerald A's Team Roster

NAME	G	BA	POS	W	L	ERA	APF
Alexander, Grant	9	0.172					
Aylmer, Bob	21	0.088	P	4	6	3.44	
Babcock, Owen	43	0.193	2B				
Barone, Les	12	0.227	P	1	5	6.00	
Bernhardt, Virgil	11	0.087	C				
Bullock, Bruce	28	0.069	P	6	14	4.19	
Capps, Bill	39	0.226	SS				
Chance, Jesse	2	0.000	P	0	2		
Christie, John	37	0.118	P	12	15	3.75	
Cochran, Gene	13	0.040	P	1	6	4.18	
Correllas, Dick	12	0.200	SS				
Culbreth, Bud	2	0.167	P	1	1		
Dietz, Emmett	35	0.248	C, OF				
Farmer, Dave	11	0.175	3B				
Fields, Tom	3	0.000	P	0	0		
Floyd, Bob	54	0.218	OF				Albany
Fry, Bob	58	0.200	3B				
Garrison, Bill	23	0.162	SS				
George, Alex	138	0.268	SS, OF				
Gianelli, Ray	10	0.158	P	1	6	2.42	
Gilliam, Earl	9	0.158					
Graham, Lonnie	94	0.260	2B				
Halverson, Don	10	0.147	OF				
Harper, Cartha	4	0.182	P	0	1		
Howser, Tom	20	0.191	OF				
Kernica, Leo	6	0.000					
Knutson, Dick	10	0.000					
Krause, Bill	3	0.000					
Larimer, Stan	13	0.095	P	0	5	5.90	
Laudermilk, Joe	28	0.207	SS				
Maroney, John	18	0.309	3B				
McCaffrey, Tom	3	0.143	P	0	3		
Moore, Ray	2	0.500					
Morris, Clint	82	0.244	OF				
Niedzowieski, Ron	30	0.146	1B				
Patterson, Charles	10	0.125	P	0	4		Waycross
Rooks, Gerald	10	0.095	P	2	4		
Ruggerio, Pat	4	0.100					
Schamburg, Ted	64	0.300	3B, P	2	4		
Seagrave, DeMont	10	0.182	P	3	4	4.19	Moultrie
Sewell, Joe	3	0.000	P	0	2		
Smith, Charles	8	0.000	P	0	1		
Smith, Garry	53	0.215	1B				
Smithdeal, Sid	137	0.227	OF				
Stone, Dick	7	0.313	P	2	2		
Szostak, Henry	35	0.136	P	13	8	3.19	
Treadway, Red	70	0.333	M, 1B, OF, P	0	0		
Vaughn, Bobby	9	0.038					
Whitworth, Bob	13	0.046	C				

Moultrie, Georgia

Team Operated by Moultrie Baseball Club, Inc.
Team President: Dorcie E. Huffaker
Vice President: J.L. Butler
Secretary-General Manager: Reed Shank
Treasurer: Dr. W.C. Arwood
Manager(s): Bob Wellman
Games played at Holmes Park
Season attendance: 29,211
Major League Affiliate: Cincinnati Reds – National League.

Moultrie Reds Team Roster

NAME	G	BA	POS	W	L	ERA	APF
Amburgey, Conley	91	0.221	OF				
Azcue, Joe	2	0.333					
Bailey, Jim	15	0.143	P	6	6	3.17	
Beck, Bill	16	0.176	P	2	2	3.86	
Bossie, Ron	3	0.000	P	0	0		
Brown, Keith	17	0.088	P	6	9	4.64	
Crone, Bob	12	0.133	P	1	5	5.06	
Dauten, Fred	18	0.135	C				
Dobberstein, Charles	6	0.100	P	1	1		
Dodson, Sam	8	0.167					
Drane, Don	53	0.256	P	12	9	3.30	
Duncan, Fred	14	0.000	P	1	6	2.77	
Fenrick, Roger	4	0.000	P	0	0		
Flynn, Tom	12	0.100	P	3	3		
Fregin, Arnold	131	0.247	C				
Harris, Bob	78	0.257	OF				
Haury, John	70	0.246	2B				
Hinton, Terry	60	0.166	OF				
Isaacs, Cecil	23	0.203	P	9	6	3.19	
Jakubowski, Al	63	0.225	OF				
Kelly, Fred	12	0.000	P	1	1		
Leval, Al	60	0.215	2B				
Loftin, Jackie	3	0.000	P	0	1		

Georgia Class-D Minor League Baseball Encyclopedia

NAME	G	BA	POS	W	L	ERA	APF
Loveland, Jim	13	0.242					
McCune, Larry	25	0.106	P	8	5	4.04	
Nisewonger, Jim	13	0.281	P	8	2	2.86	
Passilla, Jim	139	0.248	SS				
Patriss, Bill	80	0.264	2B, 3B, OF				
Peeler, Tom	4	0.000	P	0	2		
Roberts, Bob	36	0.105	P	7	11	4.01	
Scercy, John	85	0.176	3B				
Seagrave, DeMont	10	0.182	P	3	4	4.19	Fitzgerald
Weddle, Billy	133	0.237	1B, 3B, OF				
Wellman, Bob	137	0.347	M, 1B, P	2	0	2.70	

Thomasville, Georgia

Team Operated by Thomasville Dodgers, Inc.
Team President: Heeth Varnedoe
Vice Presidents: Fresco Thompson, Dick Walsh
Secretary: Matthew A. Burns
Treasurer: William Gibson
General Manager: George E. Pfister
Manager(s): George Pfister
Games played at Municipal Stadium
Season attendance: 21,697
Major League Affiliate: Brooklyn Dodgers – National League.

Thomasville Dodgers Team Roster

NAME	G	BA	POS	W	L	ERA	APF
Arellanes, Bill	33	0.187	1B				
Bailey, Freddie	28	0.136	C				
Baldwin, Jack	26	0.209	OF				
Bergey, Jim	14	0.158	P	5	4	3.38	
Brio, Carl	27	0.215	OF				
Clancy, Bill	7	0.000	P	0	2		
Conquy, Gene	49	0.298	OF				
Coultas, Gary	22	0.083	C				
Craven, Jim	4	0.000	P	0	1		
DeFalco, Fred	113	0.255	OF				
Erickson, Marlin	14	0.083	P	0	3		
Fallon, Dick	39	0.223	3B				
Forsythe, Ron	50	0.074	P	7	7	3.71	
Glaser, Bob	118	0.205	1B				
Herring, Art	52	0.263	3B				
Horowitz, Ed	1	0.000					
Hurvitz, Bob	111	0.207	C				
Jackson, Bill	134	0.276	2B				
Johnson, Eric	15	0.176	P	1	5	4.22	
Koczwara, Bob	40	0.262	P	5	8	3.38	
Lawrence, Ralph	14	0.500	P	1	1		
Lee, Gene	2	1.000	P	0	0		
Mathis, Joe	24	0.093	P	9	8	2.71	
Merrigan, Walt	1	0.000	P	0	0		
Mixon, Art	139	0.264	SS				
Moss, Jim	6	0.000					
Murta, John	1	0.000	P	0	0		
Palmquist, Ed	38	0.275	OF				
Pfister, George			M				
Polk, Roy	32	0.209	P	13	10	2.55	
Rufer, Rudy	38	0.282	M, OF				
Scott, Dick	36	0.171	P	15	13	2.13	
Scott, George	47	0.237	3B				
Simpson, Warren	12	0.194	OF				
Slezak, Francis	12	0.194					
Smith, Arnie	31	0.232					
Steinhour, Jim	13	0.111	P	1	2		
Wexler, Jim	33	0.182	P	4	8	4.32	
Wilson, Francis	136	0.229	OF				
Wright, Jerry	5	0.375	P	1	3		
Wright, Jim	8	0.071					

Tifton, Georgia

Team Operated by Tiftarea Baseball Club, Inc.
Team President: John Ford
Vice President: John Orr
Secretary-Treasurer: H.L. Cartwright
General Manager: James Robertson
Manager(s): Wes Griffin, Eddie Miller
Games played at Eve Park
Season attendance: 20,794
Major League Affiliate: Philadelphia Phillies – National League.

Tifton Phillies Team Roster

NAME	G	BA	POS	W	L	ERA	APF
Brancato, Fred	4	0.000	P	1	1		
Corley, Stan	2	0.000	P	0	0		
Dale, Paul	12	0.238	C				
Davis, Bill	16	0.167	P	5	5	3.78	
Farnsworth, Fred	36	0.200	P	7	7	4.01	
Graham, Joe	33	0.127	P	8	7	2.86	
Grant, Melvin	21	0.133	P	2	4		
Griffin, Wes			M				
Hirst, Art	39	0.176	P	15	11	3.06	
Hopke, Fred	136	0.266	1B				
Hottell, Ed	20	0.143	P	5	9	5.05	
Hunt, Bob	134	0.277	OF				
Jacquin, Don	133	0.273	3B				
Kettle, Jerry	6	0.000	P	3	1		
Kucharski, Jerome	27	0.286	P	11	3	3.77	
Liddy, Jack	68	0.231	SS				
Marockie, Henry	53	0.232	OF				
Menkel, Ken	24	0.233	OF, P	0	3		
Miller, Eddie			M				
Miller, Glenn	136	0.247	2B				
Mowbray, Jim	2	0.000	P	0	0		
Pakes, Tom	1	0.000	P	0	0		
Penson, Paul	1	0.500	P	0	1		
Platt, Ralph	114	0.254	C				
Radzevich, Ed	35	0.090	P	9	8	3.35	
Robinson, Don	9	0.316	P	0	0		
Sampson, Mark	3	0.000	P	0	1		
Santoli, Carmen	53	0.216	OF				
Seecs, Henry	5	0.250	P	1	0		
Stopchuck, Mike	76	0.312	C, OF				
Thompson, Jessie	34	0.211	OF				
Tittl, Bob	9	0.231	P	3	3		
Tuttle, Bill	5	0.000	P	0	2		
Willis, Jim	103	0.233	OF				
Wyatt, Billy	66	0.193	SS				

Valdosta, Georgia

Team Operated by Valdosta Baseball Company, Inc.
Team President: Walter O. Briggs, Jr.
Vice President: John J. McHale
Secretary-Treasurer: H.M. Sisson
Director: T. Guy Connell
General Manager: John O'Neil
Manager(s): Bill Adair
Games played at Pendleton Park
Season attendance: 43,088
Major League Affiliate: Detroit Tigers – American League.

Valdosta Tigers Team Roster

NAME	G	BA	POS	W	L	ERA	APF
Adair, Bill	12	0.357	M				
Beck, Dick	25	0.247	C				
Caswell, Marv	2	0.000	P	0	0		
Cooke, Jay	139	0.273	1B				
Cross, Jim	139	0.270	3B				

Name	G	BA	POS	W	L	ERA
Dupon, Bart	133	0.296	OF			
Dustal, Bob	51	0.129	P	18	7	2.21
Fleshman, Elvin	22	0.159	P	11	4	2.90
Gilchrist, Jim	4	0.273				
Gladding, Fred	35	0.116	P	11	9	2.76
Grzenda, Joe	22	0.164	P	13	3	3.19
Johnson, Jim	1	0.000				
Jones, Ellis	3	0.000	P	0	1	
Justus, Dave	14	0.125	P	3	2	6.80
Kishner, Joseph	3	0.667				
Kushner, Joe	3		P	1	1	
Maupin, Bill	17	0.182				
McCue, George	123	0.231	OF			
McNeil, Bill	50	0.231	OF, P	20	4	2.70
Mendler, Dave	1	0.000				
Miner, Dean	46	0.232	OF			
Monson, Ron	17	0.240	OF			
Powell, Hollis	41	0.313	OF			
Powers, Ollie	1	0.000	P	0	1	
Ryckman, Bill	123	0.300	SS			
Scariato, Anthony	37	0.240	OF			
Sheppard, Ken	38	0.180	P	17	13	2.20
Sirota, Alex	114	0.220	C			
Stewman, Joe	3	0.167				
Trammel, Tom	2	0.000	P	0	0	
Welch, Ron	133	0.285	2B, SS			
White, Bob	22	0.289	OF			
Williams, Bob	7	0.130				
Williams, Fred	17	0.276	2B			

Waycross, Georgia

Team Operated by Waycross Baseball Association, Inc.
Team President: John R. Smith
Vice President: John Kopp
Secretary: Carlton Sweat
Treasurer: Ellie Royal
Business Manager: Charles Connor
Manager(s): Jim Deery
Games played at Memorial Stadium
Season attendance: 32,300
Major League Affiliate: Milwaukee Braves – National League.

Waycross Braves Team Roster

NAME	G	BA	POS	W	L	ERA	APF
Cahoon, Jim	21	0.130	P	8	8	4.03	
Dandurand, Tom	50	0.193	OF				
Deery, Jim	26	0.192	M, 2B				
D'Esposito, Dan	4	0.143	P	2	1		
Dorsey, Norris	12	0.158	P	3	2	2.88	
Engel, Ray	133	0.277	C				
Ford, Don	41	0.221	SS				
Gordon, Early	28	0.151					
Grissom, Herb	30	0.322	P	9	9	4.33	
Hoffman, Fred	15	0.111	P	2	5	4.65	
Johnson, Ivy	131	0.248	2B, 3B				
Lowry, John	137	0.280	OF				
Moore, Gayle	107	0.268	3B, SS				
Morgan, Roger	138	0.290	1B				
Patterson, Charles	10	0.125	P	0	4		Fitzgerald
Perez, Joaquin	135	0.264	2B, SS				
Pilgrim, Arvie	137	0.249	OF				
Roberts, John	3	0.000	P	0	0		
Sarmer, Joe	7	0.000	P	1	0		
Scranton, Dave	35	0.185	P	19	12	2.91	
Scroggs, John	49	0.218	P	9	5	2.79	
Souillard, Lou	22	0.111	P	9	6	2.20	
Stillings, Gerald	18	0.143	P	9	6	2.25	
Vroman, Larry	22	0.242	P	8	5	4.66	
White, Charles	3	0.300					
Zuccarini, Bob	81	0.255	OF				

1956 Georgia-Florida League Records

Batting

Highest Batting Average (minimum 100 at bats)
1. Chase Riddle – Albany   .353
2. Bob Wellman – Moultrie   .347
3. Red Treadway – Fitzgerald   .333
4. Tom McDevitt – Albany   .328
5. Hollis Powell – Valdosta   .313

Most Hits
1. Bob Wellman – Moultrie   165
2. Chase Riddle – Albany   164
3. Dick Babich – Brunswick   155
4. Roger Morgan – Waycross   151
5. Bill Ryckman – Valdosta   150

Most Runs
1. Chase Riddle – Albany   115
2. Glenn Miller – Tifton   113
3. Jim Cross – Valdosta   110
4. Bob Hunt – Tifton   104
5. Bob Wellman – Moultrie   101

Most Total Bases
1. Bob Wellman – Moultrie   296
2. Chase Riddle – Albany   281
3. Bart Dupon – Valdosta   242
4. Fred Hopke – Tifton   223
5. Roger Morgan – Waycross   219

Most Doubles
1. Chase Riddle – Albany   39
2. Bob Wellman – Moultrie   37
3. Dick Babich – Brunswick   31
4. Bart Dupon – Valdosta   29
5. Fred Sisolak – Brunswick   26

Most Triples
1. Art Mixon – Thomasville   13
2. Bob Hunt – Tifton   11
3. Sid Smithdeal – Fitzgerald   8
4. Bart Dupon – Valdosta   7
   Jim Hickman – Albany   7

Most Home Runs
1. Bob Wellman – Moultrie   30
2. Chase Riddle – Albany   24
3. Don Whitcomb – Brunswick   23
4. Fred Hopke – Tifton   20
5. Bart Dupon – Valdosta   17

Most Extra Base Hits
1. Bob Wellman – Moultrie   69
2. Chase Riddle – Albany   66
3. Bart Dupon – Valdosta   53
4. Fred Hopke – Tifton   44
   Jay Cooke – Valdosta   44

Most Runs Batted In
1. Chase Riddle – Albany   142
2. Bob Wellman – Moultrie   124
3. Bart Dupon – Valdosta   98
4. Jim Hickman – Albany   91
5. Dick Babich – Brunswick   90

Most Stolen Bases
1. Arvie Pilgrim – Waycross   62
2. Jim Cross – Valdosta   44

3. Chase Riddle – Albany — 35
4. Francis Wilson – Thomasville — 21
5. Art Mixon – Thomasville — 20
   Glenn Miller – Tifton — 20

Fielding

Most Put-Outs
1. Fred Hopke 1B – Tifton — 1,219
2. Roger Morgan 1B – Waycross — 1,196
3. Jay Cooke 1B – Valdosta — 1,135
4. Bob Wellman 1B, P – Moultrie — 1,000
5. Jim Williams C – Albany — 977

Most Assists
1. Joaquin Perez 2B, SS – Waycross — 376
2. Glenn Miller 2B – Tifton — 372
   Jim Passilla SS – Moultrie — 372
4. Bill Jackson 2B – Thomasville — 368
5. Art Mixon SS – Thomasville — 346

Most Errors
1. Art Mixon SS – Thomasville — 60
2. Jim Passilla SS – Moultrie — 54
3. Roy Stotler SS – Brunswick — 53
4. Bill Ryckman SS – Valdosta — 41
5. Glenn Miller 2B – Tifton — 39
   Jim Cross 3B – Valdosta — 39

Pitching

Most Wins
1. Bill McNeil – Valdosta — 20
   Lawrence Kendig – Albany — 20
3. Benny Rich – Brunswick — 19
   Dave Scranton – Waycross — 19
5. Bob Dustal – Valdosta — 18

Most Losses
1. Joe Perry – Brunswick — 16
2. Don Miller – Brunswick — 15
   John Christie – Fitzgerald — 15
4. Bruce Bullock – Fitzgerald — 14
5. Ken Sheppard – Valdosta — 13
   Dick Scott – Thomasville — 13

Highest Winning Percentage (10 game minimum)
1. Bill McNeil – Valdosta — .833
2. Joe Grzenda – Valdosta — .813
3. Jim Nisewonger – Moultrie — .800
4. Jerome Kucharski – Tifton — .786
5. Elvin Fleshman – Valdosta — .733

Lowest Earned Run Average (100 inning minimum)
1. Guerry Torres – Brunswick — 1.80
2. Dick Scott – Thomasville — 2.13
3. Ken Sheppard – Valdosta — 2.20
   Lou Souillard – Waycross — 2.20
5. Bob Dustal – Valdosta — 2.21

Most Strikeouts
1. Ken Sheppard – Valdosta — 271
2. Benny Rich – Brunswick — 257
3. Dick Scott – Thomasville — 251
4. Lawrence Kendig – Albany — 227
5. Don Miller – Brunswick — 203

Most Bases on Balls
1. Don Miller – Brunswick — 180
2. Benny Rich – Brunswick — 154
3. Joe Perry – Brunswick — 133
4. Roy Polk – Thomasville — 129
5. Ken Sheppard – Valdosta — 126
   John Christie – Fitzgerald — 126

Most Hits Allowed
1. John Christie – Fitzgerald — 219
2. Henry Szostak – Fitzgerald — 217
3. Joe Perry – Brunswick — 215
4. Dave Scranton – Waycross — 211
5. Don Miller – Brunswick — 210

Most Innings Pitched
1. Ken Sheppard – Valdosta — 262
2. Benny Rich – Brunswick — 256
3. Bob Dustal – Valdosta — 248
4. Dave Scranton – Waycross — 247
5. Lawrence Kendig – Albany — 242

1956 Georgia-Florida League All-Star Team

1B Fred Hopke – Tifton
2B Ron Welch – Valdosta
3B Jim Cross – Valdosta
SS Bill Ryckman – Valdosta
OF Jim Hickman – Albany
OF Bart Dupon – Valdosta
OF Arvie Pilgrim – Waycross
OF John Lowry – Waycross
C Ray Engel – Waycross
C Don Whitcomb – Brunswick
UT Fred Sisolak – Brunswick
P Benny Rich – Brunswick
P Dick Scott – Thomasville
P Dave Scranton – Waycross
P Ken Sheppard – Valdosta
M Bill Adair – Valdosta

1956

Georgia State League

League Office: Dublin, Georgia
League President: A. Oswald Hadden
League Vice President: Howard Threlkeld
Secretary: William A. Brewer
Salary Limit: $3,200 per month.
Player Rule: Each club was allowed a roster of sixteen players, not more than one veteran, not more than five limited service, and not less than ten rookies.

Georgia State League Final Standings

Team	W	L	Pct	GB	Affiliate
Douglas Reds	77	43	.642	----	CIN-NL
Sandersville Giants	70	50	.583	7.0	NY-NL
Vidalia Indians	63	57	.525	14.0	CLE-AL
Thomson Orioles	61	59	.508	16.0	BAL-AL
Hazlehurst-Baxley Tigers	49	71	.408	28.0	DET-AL
Dublin Irish	40	80	.333	37.0	PIT-NL

1956 Georgia State League Map

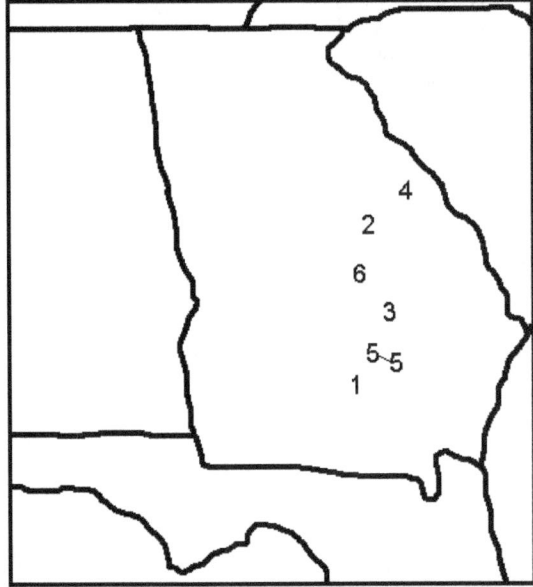

(numbers on map correspond to the place each team finished in regular season play)

In what would be the final year of baseball for the Georgia State League, another change in league cities was made prior to the start. Statesboro dropped out of the mix, and Thomson was added to keep an even number of clubs.

The new kid on the block provided the pitching for both of the season's no-hitters. On June 7, pitcher Ed Gunning hurled a no-hitter defeating Hazlehurst-Baxley in a 14 to 2 pounding. On August 7, another Thomson pitcher by the name of Jim Allison tossed a no-hitter against Douglas winning 9 to 0. Sandersville shortstop Harold Lanoux set the league's all-time single season record for the most errors as he booted 70 during the year.

Douglas came in first place in regular season action and was followed by Sandersville in second, Vidalia in third, and Thomson in fourth. First round playoff action saw Douglas defeat Vidalia three games to two, and Sandersville beat Thomson by the same final. The championship flag was garnered by Douglas in a three game to one defeat of Sandersville in the final series.

The Georgia State League did not return in the 1957 season or any time after falling by the way side as many of the small-town minor leagues did over the years.

Douglas, Georgia

Team Operated by Douglas Trojans, Inc.
Team President: E.E. Hilliard
Vice President: H.B. Chitty
General Manager: W.P. Ward, Jr.
Business Manager: Mrs. Ruth Hilliard
Manager(s): Johnny Vander Meer
Games played at Municipal Park
Season attendance: 32,316
Major League Affiliate: Cincinnati Reds – National League.

Douglas Reds Team Roster

NAME	G	BA	POS	W	L	ERA	APF
Alvarez, Alberto	112	0.263	C				
Amburgey, Conley	8	0.105					
Azcue, Joe	57	0.236	OF, C				
Bavoso, Tom	25	0.196	P	7	2	4.24	
Burtner, Hugh	5	0.100					
Clift, Frank	7	0.375	P	2	2		
Davis, Joe	89	0.249	1B, OF				
Davis, Van	46	0.324	1B				
Duran, Julio	116	0.281	2B				
Green, Bob	66	0.266	OF				
Helms, Larry	62	0.259	OF				
Hornsby, Jay	9	0.188					
Johnston, Jerry	25	0.229	P	10	4	3.07	
Kelley, Jim	40	0.067	P	7	5	5.32	
Maier, Ed	21	0.357	P	4	8	4.35	
Maples, Earl	116	0.266	3B				
Marquez, Humberto	37	0.138	P	16	8	3.28	
Micham, Jerry	114	0.275	OF				
Nordenhold, Henry	31	0.121	P	15	5	2.86	
Owen, Bill	6	0.000	P	1	1		
Phelan, Jim	41	0.263	P	14	7	3.72	
Pirela, Julio	119	0.252	SS				
Scercy, John	21	0.265					
Sizemore, Paul	4	0.000	P	1	0		
Tulner, Charles	40	0.228	1B				
Vander Meer, Johnny	4	0.250	M, P	0	0		
Wagner, Ted	6	0.222					
Yarbrough, Jim	25	0.283	OF, P	0	1		

Dublin, Georgia

Team Operated by Dublin Baseball Association
Team President: Bush Perry
Vice President: R.T. Gilder
Secretary: William Crowley
Treasurer: Louis Hatcher
General Manager-Travel Secretary: Huey Murphy
Manager(s): Wilbur Caldwell, Bob Clark, Wayne Wallace
Games played at Lovett Park
Season attendance: 20,577
Major League Affiliate: Pittsburgh Pirates – National League.

Georgia Class-D Minor League Baseball Encyclopedia

Dublin Irish Team Roster

NAME	G	BA	POS	W	L	ERA	APF
Anderson, Bill	74	0.287	1B, 2B				
Barron, Norm	31	0.222	P	6	12	4.33	
Beaman, George	26	0.268	P	3	7	5.05	
Bianchini, Ray	23	0.233	OF				
Caldwell, Wilbur	20	0.333	M, 3B, P	0	1		
Carson, Ray	65	0.247	1B				
Clark, Bob	59	0.260	M, 3B, SS, P	0	0		
Conrad, George	38	0.243	OF, C				
Cowan, Frank	3	0.250	P	0	2		
Davis, Bill	34	0.237	OF				
DeFoor, Max	7	0.143	P	1	2		
Douglas, Dan	70	0.297	OF				
Driggers, Bobby	12	0.216	OF				
Dworaczyk, Anthony	50	0.191	C				
Figueroa, Angel	51	0.284	OF				
Flynn, Bob	9	0.294	P	3	0		
Galloway, Oliver	1	0.000					
Gilbert, Herb	14	0.205	OF				
Glenn, ---	1	0.000					
Gorton, Ron	80	0.230	SS, P	0	0		
Hayden, Jim	18	0.279	P	4	7	4.29	
Honkus, Stan	4	0.143	P	2	1		
Hunt, Adrian	2	0.000	P	0	2		
Jessee, Frank	63	0.210	OF, C				
Kolar, John	38	0.194	3B				
Komara, Ray	2	0.333	P	0	0		
Maldonado, Ovidio	13	0.146	OF				
Messina, Dino	22	0.210	OF				
Micheli, Bob	47	0.212	C				
Minjock, John	41	0.083	P	13	6	3.10	
Moore, Billy Joe	47	0.245	OF				
Moran, Mike	8	0.063					
Ortiz, Felix	103	0.254	2B, 3B				
Perry, Harold	20	0.200	P	1	9	9.40	
Poulson, Gary	8	0.000	P	0	5		
Price, Charles	20	0.128					
Prozeralik, Nick	25	0.087	P	2	6	7.31	
Reimer, John	13	0.194	P	2	3		
Resavy, George	12	0.256	OF				
Robertson, Bill	30	0.320	OF				
Sarmer, Joe	11	0.091	P	0	5	6.60	
Serafini, Irv	10	0.278	P	2	4	6.89	
Shaffer, Frank	2	0.000	P	0	0		
Wallace, Wayne	110	0.284	M, 1B, P	0	0		Haz-Bax
Whaley, Charles	19	0.080	P	1	7	5.25	
Young, Wade	6	0.000	P	0	1		
Foster, Tom	8	0.200	P	1	2		
Graham, Homer	1	0.000	P	0	0		
Hubert, Stan	41	0.266	SS				
Huffman, Bill	96	0.326	2B				
Hurley, Don	31	0.220	3B, SS				
Jakosh, Lou	1	0.000	P	0	0		
Janeway, Gary	2	1.000	P	0	0		
Jezek, Nick	34	0.196	OF				
Johnson, Jim	26	0.177	OF				
King, Herman	5	0.308					
Kiser, Bob	6	0.190					
Knezevich, Ed	9	0.103					
Kosmicki, Michael	19	0.300	P	2	5	5.88	
Kovacic, Frank	18	0.205	OF, P	0	0		
LaMothe, Dennis	3	0.214					
Langlois, Paul	9	0.125	P	0	0		
Latham, Don	1	0.000	P	0	0		
Lindsey, Charles	22	0.127	3B				
Linnell, Gerald	17	0.194	OF				
Maxwell, Gordon	35	0.293	3B, OF				
McIntyre, Sam	34	0.243	P	10	14	4.29	
Merlob, Bob	12	0.091	P	2	3	3.34	
Meyer, Gary	15	0.164	OF				
Monson, Ron	52	0.211	OF				
Nelms, Charles	19	0.054	P	4	10	3.68	
Ott, Ron	43	0.241	C				
Page, Bill	13	0.118	P	2	2	4.41	
Palmitesso, Fred	2	0.000					
Peterson, Howard	24	0.167	P	10	7	2.64	
Pfander, John	3	0.111					
Riggs, Larry	3	0.000	P	0	0		
Ruggles, Raymond	51	0.189	SS				
Russo, Anthony	10	0.214	P	2	3	4.50	
Shalata, Bill	65	0.228	OF				
Sorrentino, John	39	0.120	P	5	12	5.01	
Spyhalski, Jim	22	0.302	OF				
Taliaferro, Ray	18	0.231	P	5	3	3.81	
Tasker, John	39	0.279	1B				
Verstraete, Don	4	0.000	P	1	1		
Wallace, Wayne	110	0.284	M, 1B, P	0	0		Dublin
Wasiak, Stan	28	0.288	M, 3B				
Whitmire, Glen	31	0.143	2B				
Williams, Bob	22	0.143	SS, P	4	2		
Willingham, John	61	0.245	C, P	0	2	4.29	Vidalia
Young, Don	4	0.250	P	0	2		

Hazlehurst-Baxley (Hazlehurst & Baxley), Georgia

Team Operated by Hazlehurst-Baxley Baseball Club, Inc.
Team President: W.W. Thompson
Vice President: J.B. Aycock
Secretary: Laura P. Bramblett
General Manager: Kenneth S. Martin
Manager(s): Wayne Wallace, Stan Wasiak
Games played at Roland Cook Stadium
Season attendance: 9,565
Major League Affiliate: Detroit Tigers – American League.

Hazlehurst-Baxley Tigers Team Roster

NAME	G	BA	POS	W	L	ERA	APF
Barna, Dick	37	0.164	3B				
Bruenjes, Allen	1	0.000	P	0	0		
Cincotta, Joe	20	0.230	C				
Colon, Joe	50	0.259	OF				
Cox, George	6	0.000	P	1	3		
Feller, Jack	42	0.235	C				
Flanagan, Jerome	58	0.276	OF				

Sandersville, Georgia

Team Operated by Washington County Baseball Club, Inc.
Team President: Ben J. Talbutton
Vice President: N.M. Jordan
Secretary-Treasurer: Leo Blackburn
General Manager: E.A. Bivins
Manager(s): Pete Pavlick
Games played at City Baseball Park
Season attendance: 21,287
Major League Affiliate: New York Giants – National League.

Sandersville Giants Team Roster

NAME	G	BA	POS	W	L	ERA	APF
Bassetti, Gil	45	0.177	P	21	8	2.26	
Bernsten, Ray	4	0.000	P	1	1		
Chandler, Bill	97	0.219	1B, OF, C				
Ennis, Emory	47	0.225	OF				
Francone, Nick	42	0.197	OF				
Ganzer, Bob	35	0.102	P	7	6	4.30	
Gershberg, Howard	10	0.125					
Hageman, John	23	0.167	P	6	3	4.32	
Higby, Lynn	3	0.000	P	0	2		
Hungate, Lew	120	0.236	OF, P	0	0		
Kochis, George	4	0.000	P	0	2		

Georgia Class-D Minor League Baseball Encyclopedia

NAME	G	BA	POS	W	L	ERA	APF
Lanoux, Harold	118	0.210	SS				
Maderis, Joe	28	0.167	P	7	6	4.57	
Marburger, Bob	8	0.241					
Milley, Al	113	0.280	1B				
Pavlick, Pete	113	0.292	M, 2B, 3B				
Reveira, Frank	102	0.332	C				
Sager, Don	38	0.176	P	7	3	2.55	
Sarver, Dan	118	0.251	3B, OF				
Shumate, Andy	118	0.212	2B, SS				
Slaughter, Frank	53	0.227	P	11	13	4.19	
Turbyfill, Harold	2	0.000	P	0	0		
White, Vern	4	0.667	P	0	1		
Williams, Jerry	76	0.236	OF, P	10	5	3.79	

Thomson, Georgia
Team Operated by Thomson Baseball Club, Inc.
Team President: G.B. Hartley
Vice President: Frank Hash
Secretary: J.A. Maxwell
Treasurer: Wilton Hinton
Manager(s): Gimpy Brown, Enid Drake
Games played at City Park
Season attendance: 40,849
Major League Affiliate: Baltimore Orioles – American League.

Thomson Orioles Team Roster

NAME	G	BA	POS	W	L	ERA	APF
Allison, Jim	21	0.074	P	4	4	4.76	
Brown, Gimpy			M				
Caradori, Jim	68	0.300	OF				
Cline, John	24	0.173	OF				
Conway, Alvin	99	0.281	OF				
Cowen, Gerald	4	0.000					
Del Monico, Gerald	72	0.272	SS				
Denny, Horace	5	0.500	P	0	1		
Drake, Enid	41	0.363	M, OF, C				
Duffy, Joe	28	0.105	OF				
Floyd, Charles	7	0.280					
Forrest, Dick	19	0.034	P	3	5	4.02	
Frazier, Clarence	19	0.164	OF				
Gaffney, George	7	0.118	P	1	2		
Geels, Bob	28	0.260	3B				
Gunning, Ed	31	0.250	P	14	9	2.74	
Kebler, Steve	1	0.000	P	0	1		
King, Rowland	3	0.500	P	0	1		
Lightfoot, Frank	13	0.222	1B				
Marquis, Roger	116	0.227	1B, P	2	2		
McCarthy, Frank	1	0.000	P	0	0		
McMillan, Bob	3	0.000					
Miles, Jerry	26	0.130	P	7	6	3.82	
Minch, Charles	15	0.158	C				
Morsberger, Charles	44	0.161	3B, SS				
Muir, Charles	11	0.143	P	3	2		
Myers, Ken	3	0.000	P	0	0		
Niemeier, Don	48	0.229	OF				
Nix, Tom	93	0.216	2B, 3B, SS, OF				
Saye, Charles	53	0.299	3B, OF				
Seeman, John	5	0.500	P	0	1		
Silbersack, Bob	21	0.237	2B				
Silva, Tom	35	0.219	3B				
Smith, George	83	0.326	2B, P	0	0		
Stocker, Ron	31	0.059	P	8	10	3.00	
Stowell, Doug	18	0.164	OF				
Strozyk, Ray	104	0.205	C				
Tinsley, Art	7	0.000	P	1	2		
Warren, Malcolm	36	0.169	P	10	7	2.80	
Welsh, Dan	29	0.205	P	8	6	5.00	
White, Glen	2	0.200					

Vidalia, Georgia
Team Operated by Vidalia Baseball Association, Inc.
Team President: G.H. Threlkeld
Vice President: H.B. Estroff
Secretary-Treasurer: G.H. Gibson
Business Manager: L.A. Levy
Manager(s): Mark Wylie
Games played at Municipal Stadium
Season attendance: 17,273
Major League Affiliate: Cleveland Indians – American League.

Vidalia Indians Team Roster

NAME	G	BA	POS	W	L	ERA	APF
Almeida, Dan	118	0.293	2B, 3B, P	0	0		
Belaj, Allen	38	0.189	SS				
Betsch, Dick	74	0.239	OF, P	5	6	4.40	
Brinkley, Lawrence	14	0.167	P	4	1	1.91	
Cailor, Howard	21	0.171	P	7	8	5.08	
Carrasquel, Manuel	75	0.264	SS				
Copeland, Cliff	7	0.000	P	0	1		
Dow, Bill	43	0.236	2B, 3B				
Dye, Cliff	8	0.000	P	0	1		
Engler, John	120	0.255	OF				
Gums, Marv	11	0.125	P	7	4	3.33	
Hardwick, Jim	47	0.279	OF				
Harms, Roger	5	0.167	P	2	1		
Henderson, Dave	11	0.273	SS				
Holdener, Lou	90	0.280	OF, C				
Keller, Harold	14	0.133	P	3	6	4.50	
Kowalczyk, Dick	43	0.177	2B, 3B, SS				
Morlan, Joe	53	0.266	OF, C				
Patterson, Ray	38	0.339	C				
Prescott, Howard	10	0.059	P	1	4	5.67	
Sims, Harold	29	0.026	P	4	10	5.26	
Smiley, Charles	119	0.293	1B, P	0	0		
Stigman, Dick	33	0.165	P	17	9	1.44	
Tingle, Tom	79	0.267	3B, OF				
Valesky, Don	57	0.248	OF				
Weiss, Dennis	10	0.308					
Willingham, John	61	0.245	C, P	0	2	4.29	Haz-Bax
Wylie, Mark	17	0.276	M, P	2	1	2.11	
Yurman, Frank	22	0.213	P	11	5	2.25	

1956 Georgia State League Records
Batting
Highest Batting Average (minimum 100 at bats)
1. Enid Drake – Thomson .363
2. Ray Patterson – Vidalia .339
3. Frank Reveira – Sandersville .332
4. George Smith – Thomson .326
   Bill Huffman - Hazlehurst-Baxley .326

Most Hits
1. Dan Almeida – Vidalia 145
2. Charles Smiley – Vidalia 125
3. Pete Pavlick – Sandersville 122
4. Julio Duran – Douglas 120
5. Frank Reveira – Sandersville 117
   Bill Huffman - Hazlehurst-Baxley 117

Most Runs
1. Pete Pavlick – Sandersville 95
   Dan Sarver – Sandersville 95
3. Julio Duran – Douglas 94
4. Dan Almeida – Vidalia 91
5. Charles Smiley – Vidalia 87

Georgia Class-D Minor League Baseball Encyclopedia

Most Total Bases
1. Al Milley – Sandersville 199
2. Charles Smiley – Vidalia 196
3. Lew Hungate – Sandersville 189
4. Frank Reveira – Sandersville 181
5. Dan Almeida – Vidalia 178

Most Doubles
1. Earl Maples – Douglas 28
2. Wayne Wallace – Haz-Bax/Dubl 25
3. Charles Smiley – Vidalia 22
   Frank Reveira – Sandersville 22
   Bill Huffman - Hazlehurst-Baxley 22

Most Triples
1. Charles Smiley – Vidalia 11
2. Alvin Conway – Thomson 10
3. Jerry Micham – Douglas 9
   Julio Pirela – Douglas 9
   George Smith – Thomson 9

Most Home Runs
1. Al Milley – Sandersville 21
2. Lew Hungate – Sandersville 19
3. Bill Anderson – Dublin 12
   Frank Reveira – Sandersville 12
   Dan Sarver – Sandersville 12

Most Extra Base Hits
1. Al Milley – Sandersville 44
2. Lew Hungate – Sandersville 43
3. Charles Smiley – Vidalia 42
4. Frank Reveira – Sandersville 37
   Wayne Wallace – Haz-Bax/Dubl 37

Most Runs Batted In
1. Al Milley – Sandersville 103
2. Frank Reveira – Sandersville 91
3. Lew Hungate – Sandersville 90
4. Wayne Wallace – Haz-Bax/Dubl 88
5. Jerry Micham – Douglas 77

Most Stolen Bases
1. Julio Duran – Douglas 32
2. Dan Almeida – Vidalia 27
3. Alberto Alvarez – Douglas 23
4. Dan Sarver – Sandersville 22
5. Andy Shumate – Sandersville 12
   Julio Pirela – Douglas 12

Fielding
Most Put-Outs
1. Wayne Wallace 1B, P – Haz-Bax/Dubl 927
2. Charles Smiley 1B, P – Vidalia 905
3. Al Milley 1B – Sandersville 899
4. Roger Marquis 1B, P – Thomson 799
5. Ray Strozyk C – Thomson 754

Most Assists
1. Julio Pirela SS – Douglas 344
2. Julio Duran 2B – Douglas 341
3. Dan Almeida 2B, 3B, P – Vidalia 314
4. Bill Huffman 2B - Hazlehurst-Baxley 275
5. Harold Lanoux SS – Sandersville 262

Most Errors
1. Harold Lanoux SS – Sandersville 70
2. Julio Pirela SS – Douglas 52
3. Dan Almeida 2B, 3B, P – Vidalia 51
4. Ron Gorton SS, P – Dublin 49
5. Earl Maples 3B – Douglas 48

Pitching
Most Wins
1. Gil Bassetti – Sandersville 21
2. Dick Stigman – Vidalia 17
3. Humberto Marquez – Douglas 16
4. Henry Nordenhold – Douglas 15
5. Ed Gunning – Thomson 14
   Jim Phelan – Douglas 14

Most Losses
1. Sam McIntyre - Hazlehurst-Baxley 14
2. Frank Slaughter – Sandersville 13
3. Norm Barron – Dublin 12
   John Sorrention - Hazlehurst-Baxley 12
5. Ron Stocker – Thomson 10
   Harold Sims – Vidalia 10
   Charles Nelms - Hazlehurst-Baxley 10

Highest Winning Percentage (10 game minimum)
1. Henry Nordenhold – Douglas .750
2. Gil Bassetti – Sandersville .724
3. Jerry Johnston – Douglas .714
4. Don Sager – Sandersville .700
5. Frank Yurman – Vidalia .688

Lowest Earned Run Average (100 inning minimum)
1. Dick Stigman – Vidalia 1.44
2. Frank Yurman – Vidalia 2.25
3. Gil Bassetti – Sandersville 2.26
4. Howard Peterson - Hazlehurst-Baxley 2.64
5. Ed Gunning – Thomson 2.74

Most Strikeouts
1. Dick Stigman – Vidalia 263
2. Gil Bassetti – Sandersville 219
3. Ed Gunning – Thomson 198
4. John Minjock – Dublin 151
5. Henry Nordenhold – Douglas 136

Most Bases on Balls
1. Frank Slaughter – Sandersville 136
2. Ed Gunning – Thomson 128
3. Sam McIntyre - Hazlehurst-Baxley 125
4. Harold Sims – Vidalia 111
5. Dick Stigman – Vidalia 97

Most Hits Allowed
1. Gil Bassetti – Sandersville 208
2. Humberto Marquez – Douglas 197
3. Sam McIntyre - Hazlehurst-Baxley 180
4. Jim Phelan – Douglas 171
5. Henry Nordenhold – Douglas 161

Most Innings Pitched
1. Gil Bassetti – Sandersville 247
2. Dick Stigman – Vidalia 213
3. Humberto Marquez – Douglas 195
4. John Minjock – Dublin 186
5. Ed Gunning – Thomson 184

1957

Georgia-Florida League

League Office: Leslie, Georgia
League President: W.T. Anderson
League Vice President: Guy Connell
Salary Limit: $2,600 per month plus $600.
Player Rule: Each club was allowed a roster of sixteen players, not more than two veterans, not more than eight limited service, and not less than six rookies.

Georgia-Florida League Final Standings

Team	W	L	Pct	GB	Affiliate
Albany Cardinals	84	55	.604	----	STL-NL
Valdosta Dodgers	77	62	.554	7.0	DET-AL
Thomasville Tigers	71	68	.511	13.0	BRK-NL
Fitzgerald Orioles	65	74	.468	19.0	BAL-AL
Moultrie/Brunswick Phillies	62	77	.446	22.0	PHI-NL
Waycross Braves	58	81	.417	26.0	MIL-NL

1957 Georgia-Florida League Map

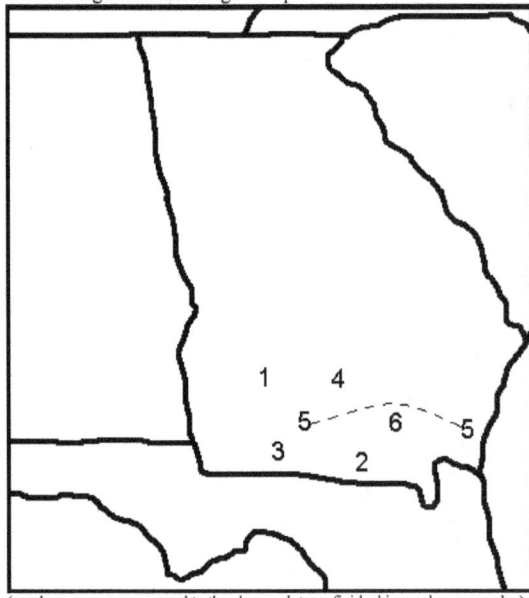

(numbers on map correspond to the place each team finished in regular season play)

Following the 1956 season, Brunswick and Tifton both quit the league and were not replaced. This transformed the league into a six-team loop. Another change in league cities came on June 1 when the Moultrie club moved its operations to Brunswick who had just dropped out of the league a few months prior.

On May 5, Waycross pitcher Fred Hoffman pitched the season's only no-hitter when he blanked Moultrie in the 1 to 0, eight-inning contest. Waycross's Mike Fandozzi set the all-time league single season record for the highest batting average with a .422 percentage.

Now trimmed down to a six-team circuit, the league abandoned the Shaughnessy playoff system and went with a split season format to determine which two teams would compete in the championship series. Valdosta and Thomasville tied for the top spot in the first half, but Valdosta earned the first championship series berth by winning a one-game playoff on July 19. Albany easily won the second half by an eight game margin over Waycross. Albany won the best of five games league championship series over Valdosta three games to two.

Albany, Georgia
Team Operated by Albany Baseball Club
Team President: Morton M. Wiggins
Vice President: August A. Busch, Jr.
Secretary: Nadine Cravey
General Manager: Sheldon A. "Chief" Bender
Manager(s): Chase Riddle
Games played at Cardinal Park
Season attendance: 38,174
Major League Affiliate: St. Louis Cardinals – National League.

Albany Cardinals Team Roster

NAME	G	BA	POS	W	L	ERA	APF
Bender, Chief	2	0.000	P	0	0		
Boner, Billy	14	0.171	C				
Boyer, Bob	68	0.306	3B				
Brown, Don	16	0.088	3B				
Brown, Lou	140	0.297	OF				
Carroll, Ray	60	0.264	OF				
Coy, Hugh	29	0.159	P	12	3	4.20	
DeGraaf, Bill	127	0.271	1B, C				
DeLuca, Tom	4	0.273					
Dexter, Dave	8	0.000	P	0	0		
Gunn, Dick	63	0.236	3B				
Hickman, Jim	138	0.287	1B, OF				
Huinker, Art	9	0.125	P	6	1	1.22	
Ingram, Clarence	36	0.231	P	17	7	2.29	
Kabbes, Ron	97	0.246	SS				
Kolson, Tom	22	0.065	P	5	3	3.77	
Lackey, Bill	1	0.000	P	0	0		
Leslie, Paul	90	0.331	OF				
Long, Joel	2	0.200					
McFadden, Ken	20	0.179	OF				
McIntyre, Sam	54	0.225	P	12	5	3.79	
Morris, Al	131	0.281	2B, SS				
Nelms, Charles	2	0.000	P	0	0		
Parker, Terry	7	0.448					
Passaro, Roland	13	0.346	P	4	4	3.63	
Perry, Charles	8	0.105	P	1	6	3.46	
Petty, Tom	8	0.000	P	1	2		
Richardson, Gordie	3	0.500	P	0	1		
Riddle, Chase	135	0.322	M, 1B, C, P	1	1		
Russell, Ken	1	0.000	P	0	0		
Shelley, Bill	10	0.222					
Shellnut, Wayne	21	0.160	P	3	5	4.26	
Shultis, Pete	30	0.245	P	8	8	3.99	
Smith, Jim	42	0.296	SS				
Stathos, Tony	21	0.237	P	9	3	3.42	
Thomas, Francis	9	0.333	P	0	2		
Wodka, Dick	14	0.286	P	4	2	3.36	
Wood, Tom	26	0.298	P	1	2	5.29	

Fitzgerald, Georgia
Team Operated by Fitzgerald Orioles
Team President: William Mann
Vice President-Treasurer: R.W. Jernigan, Jr.
Secretary: Curtis E. Green
General Manager: J.W. McDonald
Directors: Wiley Floyd, Raymond Harris, Harry Roberts, T.D. Boggus

Georgia Class-D Minor League Baseball Encyclopedia

Manager(s): Earl Weaver
Games played at Blue-Gray Stadium
Season attendance: 18,046
Major League Affiliate: Baltimore Orioles – American League.

Fitzgerald Orioles Team Roster

NAME	G	BA	POS	W	L	ERA	APF
Allison, Jim	8	0.118	P	2	5	4.59	
Barth, Al	80	0.332	1B, OF, P	1	4	3.42	
Bednar, Dave	134	0.246	1B				
Bird, Bob	129	0.245	3B				
Bishop, Danny	120	0.247	C				
Carpenter, Bill	23	0.261	P	3	7	4.96	
Cassidy, John	112	0.251	OF				
Curl, Kedy	35	0.162	P	15	9	2.51	
Fincher, Bill	37	0.243	P	15	12	3.90	
Frazier, Clarence	57	0.225	OF				
Gussin, Joe	20	0.000	P	0	1	11.70	
Heisler, Phil	48	0.139	P	8	14	4.27	
Jeanes, John	18	0.263	P	3	3	5.09	
Kolar, John	137	0.251	SS				
Kosak, Carl	17	0.171					
McCarron, Bob	6	0.000	P	0	0		
McMullen, Don	17	0.197	2B				
O'Donnell, Jim	10	0.167	P	0	2		
Pascoe, Ed	8	0.242					
Shosty, Bob	55	0.286	OF				
Sockman, Ron	138	0.279	2B, OF				
Stocker, Ron	32	0.155	P	9	10	3.34	
Strozyk, Ray	84	0.265	OF, C				
Tsatsa, Paul	33	0.107	P	6	3	4.10	
Weaver, Earl	112	0.288	M, 2B, P	1	0		
Werley, George	22	0.316	P	2	4	7.90	
Williams, Paul	1	0.000	P	0	0		

Moultrie/Brunswick, Georgia
Team Operated by Moultrie Baseball Club, Inc.
Team President: E.B. Beasley
Vice President: Jack King
Business Manager: C.W. Vandiver
Manager(s): Benny Zientara
Games played at Edgar Holmes Stadium (Moultrie) and Edo Miller Park (Brunswick)
Season attendance: 28,987
Major League Affiliate: Philadelphia Phillies – National League.

Moultrie/Brunswick Phillies Team Roster

NAME	G	BA	POS	W	L	ERA	APF
Aleshire, Jim	30	0.177	SS				
Anderson, Jim	78	0.264	2B, OF				
Balczac, Ed	5	0.000					
Bostwick, Bill	4	0.000	P	0	1		
Brancato, Fred	6	0.000	P	1	0		
Carrico, Edgar	20	0.163					
Colgan, Dick	21	0.094	P	6	8	5.58	
DeBruler, Ernest	27	0.071	P	2	8	5.05	
Diahl, Les	9	0.111					
Dutton, Dean	140	0.252	OF				
Dykstra, Leonard	41	0.114	P	9	10	3.66	
Farland, Jim	4	0.000	P	0	0		
Gemme, Bernie	38	0.214	OF				
Graham, Wayne	109	0.303	2B, 3B, SS				
Harrington, Fred	39	0.348	OF				
Hatfield, Jim	23	0.179	2B				
Heavener, Reggie	96	0.280	OF				
Hiedel, Dale	7	0.111					
Holcomb, Lou	79	0.178	SS				
Leber, Dick	27	0.221	C				
Lockhart, Ed	18	0.083	P	2	6	4.71	
McKee, Art	24	0.179	P	8	6	4.82	
Mowbray, Jim	9	0.429	P	1	1	5.21	
Nagy, Mike	48	0.249	OF				
Platt, Ralph	123	0.260	1B, OF, C, P	0	0		
Poholsky, John	20	0.077	P	4	7	5.44	
Pokorny, Joe	11	0.429	P	2	2	3.34	
Pontarelli, Lee	46	0.224	3B				
Powell, Chester	42	0.026	P	3	10	5.94	
Price, Paul	82	0.312	3B				
Shively, Jim	21	0.083	P	5	3	2.33	
Spence, Ed	13	0.296					
Stopchuck, Mike	109	0.323	1B				
Ullmann, John	11	0.111	OF				
Wallace, Mike	37	0.178	P	7	8	4.28	
Weilbacher, Dave	26	0.167	P	12	7	2.97	
Williams, Bill	20	0.188	2B				
Young, Phil	42	0.192	C				
Zientara, Benny	1	0.000	M, P	0	0		

Thomasville, Georgia
Team Operated by Thomasville Dodgers, Inc.
Team President: Heeth Varnedoe
Vice Presidents: Fresco Thompson, Richard Walsh
Secretary: Matthew A. Burns
Treasurer: William Gibson
Manager(s): Leon Hamilton, Roger Wright
Games played at Municipal Stadium
Season attendance: 25,438
Major League Affiliate: Brooklyn Dodgers - National League.

Thomasville Tigers Team Roster

NAME	G	BA	POS	W	L	ERA	APF
Anderson, Bill	1	0.333					
Aspromonte, Bob	53	0.263	3B, SS				
Barnhart, Lowell	95	0.206	OF				
Bean, Roger	77	0.241	C				
Booth, Bill	37	0.113	P	7	7	4.47	
Breeden, Jack	46	0.204	P	14	8	3.96	
Buhl, Larry	39	0.256	3B				
Burke, Don	103	0.221	C				
Burnell, Bob	17	0.333	OF				
Burnham, Al	1	0.000					
Burright, Possum	136	0.242	2B				
Capullo, Bob	7	0.000	P	0	2		
Chierichella, Carmine	17	0.167	P	2	2	4.12	
Christy, Jim	19	0.183	OF				
Clifton, Ralph	9	0.250	P	1	4		
Donovan, Tom	2	0.500	P	0	0		
Geesing, John	137	0.254	1B				
Hamilton, Leon			M				
Hopey, Anthony	21	0.200	P	2	5	6.60	
Jackson, Lendon	13	0.000	P	3	1	4.03	
Jones, Charles	10	0.067	P	0	0		
Leake, Darrell	6	0.182					
Martellani, Bob	7	0.000	P	0	1		
Melton, Gary	9	0.000					
Mills, Harvey	4	0.125	P	1	2		
Mote, Galen	88	0.255	3B				
Mullaney, Tom	5	0.000	P	0	1		
Pierce, Dick	10		P	3	4	2.90	
Pleau, Andre	3	0.000	P	0	1		
Ray, Matt	17	0.100	P	2	3	4.50	
Ready, Ken	4	0.333	P	1	1		
Rossi, Ron	138	0.321	OF				
Rufer, Rudy	83	0.359	M, OF, P	0	0		
Sasek, Dick	102	0.258	OF				
Scott, George	114	0.323	SS				
Scott, Siebert	66	0.163	P	20	9	3.29	
Steinhour, Jim	30	0.102	P	13	6	3.10	
Suto, Ray	6	0.000	P	0	1		

Teliszewski, Bernard	9	0.154				
Thurman, Clarence	5	0.000	P	0	0	
Wright, Jim	5	0.000				
Wright, Roger	2	0.000	M, P	0	0	
Young, Ford	25	0.188	P	2	10	5.14

Valdosta, Georgia
Team Operated by Valdosta Baseball Company, Inc.
Team President: Walter O. Briggs, Jr.
Vice President: John J. McHale
Secretary-Treasurer: Harry M. Sisson
Director: T. Guy Connell
General Manager: John O'Neil
Manager(s): Stan Wasiak
Games played at Pendleton Park
Season attendance: 35,910
Major League Affiliate: Detroit Tigers - American League.

Valdosta Dodgers Team Roster

NAME	G	BA	POS	W	L	ERA	APF
Bacque, Gene	6	0.000	P	0	2		
Bancroft, Charles	22	0.299	3B				
Bowen, Jack	126	0.303	C				
Bridges, Don	5	0.500	P	0	1		
Briner, Dan	132	0.311	OF				
Cross, Jim	130	0.269	3B, SS, P	0	0		
Duncan, Bob	32	0.200	OF				
Gladding, Fred	38	0.195	P	16	8	2.12	
Gonzalez, Tom	101	0.304	2B				
Graham, Bill	18	0.200	P	5	4	4.37	
Justus, Dave	38	0.115	P	9	13	4.08	
Kelsch, Rudy	29	0.182	OF				
Kliewer, Phil	29	0.115	P	14	7	2.71	
LoCicero, Dick	38	0.212	2B				
McCue, George	17	0.170	OF				
Meadows, Don	137	0.235	SS, OF				
Price, Nathan	27	0.241	OF				
Seiferlein, Don	6	0.000	P	0	0		
Sheldon, Dick	41	0.198	P	13	11	4.06	
Smith, Leo	82	0.286	OF, C				
Spyhalski, Jim	138	0.249	OF				
Swertfager, Fred	7	0.083	P	4	2	2.50	
Tasker, John	66	0.254	1B				
Walski, Pete	11	0.154	P	0	0		
Walter, Dick	28	0.211	P	12	6	2.49	
Wasiak, Stan	28	0.304	M, P	0	0		
White, Bob	74	0.283	1B				
Williams, Bob	24	0.156	P	4	7	5.11	
Yappel, August	2	0.000	P	0	1		

Waycross, Georgia
Team Operated by Waycross Baseball Association, Inc.
Team President: John R. Smith
Vice President: H.G. McClendon
Secretary: John Kopp
Treasurer: Ellie Royal
Manager(s): Mike Fandozzi
Games played at Memorial Stadium
Season attendance: 27,226
Major League Affiliate: Milwaukee Braves – National League.

Waycross Braves Team Roster

NAME	G	BA	POS	W	L	ERA	APF
Barfield, Frank	82	0.204	C				
Bass, Les	36	0.216	P	5	14	4.50	
Bergdoll, Charles	81	0.312	OF				
Biggs, MacDuff	31	0.108	1B				
Centi, Dave	35	0.210	OF, P	0	0		
Christoff, Ernie	24	0.226	P	10	5	3.85	
Fandozzi, Mike	134	0.422	M, 2B, P	0	0		
Farrar, Roger	27	0.180	SS				
Herzog, Tom	11	0.071					
Hoffman, Fred	25	0.409	P	1	8	4.97	
Kuczynski, Ed	6	0.100	P	1	3	4.38	
Lowry, John	58	0.272	OF				
Maricich, Eli	2	0.429					
McKeon, Bill	68	0.327	C				
Mihal, Ron	43	0.199	OF				
Morgan, George	58	0.261	1B				
Morzenti, Jerome	134	0.272	OF				
Nester, Jim	138	0.312	3B				
Powell, Jim	36	0.265	C				
Ramirez, Carlos	98	0.317	SS				
Ramont, Dick	5	0.333	P	1	3		
Scranton, Dave	33	0.197	P	10	8	2.90	
Souillard, Lou	15	0.080	P	3	7	3.51	
Stapp, John	67	0.186	2B, SS, OF, P	0	1		
Stein, Ed	10	0.250	P	1	1		
Stillings, Gerald	23	0.407	P	6	6	3.55	
Strock, Ray	19	0.222	P	0	4	4.57	
Taylor, Gene	6	0.100					
Thomas, Bill	67	0.276	3B, P	0	0		
Townsend, Charles	6	0.000	P	1	0		
Voboril, Bill	11	0.071					
Vroman, Larry	39	0.175	P	9	11	4.55	
Wasil, Andrew	19	0.190	P	2	5	4.24	
Weaver, Norm	19	0.129	1B				
Zeihen, Bernard	39	0.133	P	8	5	4.38	

1957 Georgia-Florida League Records
Batting
Highest Batting Average (minimum 100 at bats)
1. Mike Fandozzi – Waycross .422
2. Rudy Rufer – Thomasville .359
3. Fred Harrington – Brunswick .348
4. Al Barth – Fitzgerald .332
5. Paul Leslie – Albany .331

Most Hits
1. Mike Fandozzi – Waycross 189
2. Dan Briner – Valdosta 171
3. Ron Rossi – Thomasville 166
4. Lou Brown – Albany 160
   Ron Sockman – Fitzgerald 160

Most Runs
1. Possum Burright – Thomasville 115
2. Chase Riddle – Albany 107
3. Lou Brown – Albany 105
4. Ron Rossi – Thomasville 104
5. Dean Dutton – Brunswick 98

Most Total Bases
1. Jim Hickman – Albany 260
2. Chase Riddle – Albany 252
3. Al Morris – Albany 236
4. Mike Fandozzi – Waycross 228
5. Lou Brown – Albany 226

Most Doubles
1. Chase Riddle – Albany 27
   Mike Fandozzi – Waycross 27
3. Lou Brown – Albany 26
4. Jim Hickman – Albany 24
   Al Morris – Albany 24

Georgia Class-D Minor League Baseball Encyclopedia

Most Triples
1. Lou Brown – Albany 14
2. Mike Stopchuck – Brunswick 10
   Ron Rossi – Thomasville 10
4. George Scott – Thomasville 8
   Paul Leslie – Albany 8
   Jim Nester – Waycross 8

Most Home Runs
1. Jim Hickman – Albany 26
2. Al Morris – Albany 21
3. Chase Riddle – Albany 19
   Jim Spyhalski – Valdosta 19
5. John Geesing – Thomasville 15

Most Extra Base Hits
1. Jim Hickman – Albany 54
2. Chase Riddle – Albany 52
3. Al Morris – Albany 48
4. Lou Brown – Albany 44
5. Mike Stopchuck – Brunswick 42

Most Runs Batted In
1. Jim Hickman – Albany 113
2. John Geesing – Thomasville 102
3. Mike Stopchuck – Brunswick 92
4. Ron Rossi – Thomasville 91
5. Chase Riddle – Albany 89

Most Stolen Bases
1. Lou Brown – Albany 38
2. Rudy Rufer – Thomasville 37
3. Chase Riddle – Albany 32
4. Al Morris – Albany 28
5. Jim Cross – Valdosta 24

Fielding
Most Put-Outs
1. John Geesing 1B – Thomasville 1,083
2. Chase Riddle 1B, C, P – Albany 1,018
3. Dave Bednar 1B – Fitzgerald 1,002
4. Mike Stopchuck 1B – Brunswick 847
5. Bill DeGraaf 1B, C – Albany 799

Most Assists
1. Mike Fandozzi 2B, P – Waycross 387
2. Al Morris 2B, SS – Albany 378
3. Possum Burright 2B – Thomasville 371
4. John Kolar SS – Fitzgerald 357
5. George Scott SS – Thomasville 339

Most Errors
1. John Kolar – Fitzgerald 51
2. Lou Holcomb – Brunswick 41
3. Wayne Graham 2B, 3B, SS – Brunswick 40
4. Al Morris 2B, SS – Albany 38
5. Don Meadows SS, OF – Valdosta 37
   Ron Sockman 2B, OF – Fitzgerald 37

Pitching
Most Wins
1. Siebert Scott – Thomasville 20
2. Clarence Ingram – Albany 17
3. Fred Gladding – Valdosta 16
4. Kedy Curl – Fitzgerald 15
   Bill Fincher – Fitzgerald 15

Most Losses
1. Phil Heisler – Fitzgerald 14
   Les Bass – Waycross 14
3. Dave Justus – Valdosta 13
4. Bill Fincher – Fitzgerald 12
5. Dick Sheldon – Valdosta 11
   Larry Vroman – Waycross 11

Highest Winning Percentage (10 game minimum)
1. Hugh Coy – Albany .800
2. Tony Stathos – Albany .750
3. Clarence Ingram – Albany .708
4. Sam McIntyre – Albany .706
5. Siebert Scott – Thomasville .690

Lowest Earned Run Average (100 inning minimum)
1. Fred Gladding – Valdosta 2.12
2. Clarence Ingram – Albany 2.29
3. Dick Walter – Valdosta 2.49
4. Kedy Curl – Fitzgerald 2.51
5. Phil Kliewer – Valdosta 2.71

Most Strikeouts
1. Dick Sheldon – Valdosta 213
2. Fred Gladding – Valdosta 185
3. Bill Fincher – Fitzgerald 157
   Pete Shultis – Albany 157
5. Siebert Scott – Thomasville 144

Most Bases on Balls
1. Pete Shultis – Albany 154
2. Dave Scranton – Waycross 114
3. Larry Vroman – Waycross 110
4. Jack Breeden – Thomasville 107
5. Phil Heisler – Fitzgerald 106

Most Hits Allowed
1. Leonard Dykstra – Brunswick 229
2. Dick Sheldon – Valdosta 217
3. Larry Vroman – Waycross 198
4. Phil Heisler – Fitzgerald 195
5. Bill Fincher – Fitzgerald 188

Most Innings Pitched
1. Dick Sheldon – Valdosta 226
2. Fred Gladding – Valdosta 217
3. Siebert Scott – Thomasville 205
4. Leonard Dykstra – Brunswick 204
   Kedy Curl – Fitzgerald 204

1957 Georgia-Florida League All-Star Team
1B Mike Stopchuck – Brunswick
2B Al Morris – Albany
3B Jim Cross – Valdosta
SS George Scott – Thomasville
OF Jim Hickman – Albany
OF Ron Rossi – Thomasville
OF Dan Briner – Valdosta
OF Don Brown – Albany
C Jack Bowen – Valdosta
C Bill DeGraaf – Albany
UT Ron Sockman – Fitzgerald
P Fred Gladding – Valdosta
P Siebert Scott – Thomasville
P Clarence Ingram – Albany
P Bill Fincher – Fitzgerald
M Chase Riddle – Albany

1958

Georgia-Florida League

League Office: Leslie, Georgia
League President: W.T. Anderson
League Vice President: Guy Connell
Salary Limit: $3,200 per month.
Player Rule: Each club was allowed a roster of sixteen players, not more than three veterans, not more than seven limited service, and not less than six rookies.

Georgia-Florida League Final Standings

Team	W	L	Pct	GB	Affiliate
Albany Cardinals	86	41	.677	----	STL-NL
Valdosta Dodgers	75	52	.591	11.0	DET-AL
Dublin Orioles	72	56	.563	14.5	BAL-AL
Brunswick Phillies	64	64	.500	22.5	PHI-NL
Waycross Braves	47	80	.370	39.0	MIL-NL
Thomasville Tigers	39	89	.299	48.0	LA-NL

1958 Georgia-Florida League Map

(numbers on map correspond to the place each team finished in regular season play)

On again off again club Fitzgerald was off once again in the 1958 season. Dublin, another former Georgia State League club, was picked up to fill the void in the six-club circuit.

On July 23, Valdosta scored 16 runs in one inning to win a 20 to 16 slugfest against Thomasville. Bob Boyer of Albany set the all-time league mark for the most home runs hit in a single season with 32 long balls.

The league played a split season for the second year in a row with the winner of each half meeting in the league championship series at the end. Valdosta and Albany were tied at the top of the standings at the end of the first half. In a one-game playoff on July 9, Valdosta defeated Albany 7 to 6 to garner the first spot in the league championship series. Albany earned their position in the championship series at the end of the second half of play having the best record in the loop. Although Albany had the best cumulative record of both halves by eleven games over Valdosta, it was Valdosta who won the title of league champions by taking the final series three games to one.

Albany, Georgia

Team Operated by Albany Baseball Club
Team President: Morton M. Wiggins
Vice President: August A. Busch, Jr.
Secretary: Nadine Cravey
Business Manager: John Monfre
Manager(s): Mo Mozzali
Games played at Cardinal Park
Season attendance: 42,828
Major League Affiliate: St. Louis Cardinals – National League.

Albany Cardinals Team Roster

NAME	G	BA	POS	W	L	ERA	APF
Alvarez, Demetro	25	0.186	OF				
Arnitz, Pete	6	0.167	P	0	2		
Boyer, Bob	125	0.292	3B, OF, P	0	0		
Connell, Wes	8	0.000					
Dickerson, Jerry	32	0.218	P	12	5	3.94	
Dingus, Bill	127	0.219	SS, P	1	0		
Ebker, Bob	2	0.000	P	0	0		
Guymon, Darrell	2	0.750					
Haniak, Frank	33	0.210	2B				
Hernandez, Sam	116	0.264	2B, 3B, OF				
Hill, Don	7	0.231					
Hill, Jere	17	0.192	1B				
Johnson, Walt	17	0.239	OF, P	0	0		
Lackey, Bill	2	0.000	P	0	0		
Lock, Jerry	53	0.120	P	12	5	4.22	
Long, Joel	24	0.241	OF				
MacIvor, Colin	9	0.000	P	0	0		
Martin, Lane	10	0.111	P	6	0	6.12	
Miller, Ronald	118	0.283	3B				
Mitchell, Don	12	0.000	P	0	3	5.81	
Morton, Bill	126	0.266	C				
Mozzali, Mo	113	0.335	M, 1B, P	0	0		
Predovich, Walt	119	0.237	1B, OF				
Richardson, Gordie	22	0.214	P	13	4	2.93	
Roddenberry, Warren	44	0.333	P	11	7	3.69	
Scott, Frank	15	0.000	P	3	1	6.08	
Shannon, Mike	62	0.322	OF				
Smith, Harold	1	0.500					
Walker, Fred	50	0.167	P	13	8	5.52	
Wood, Tom	64	0.244	OF, P	14	4	3.31	
Worrell, Joe	7	0.125	P	1	2		
Zeleznock, John	53	0.278	OF, P	0	0		

Brunswick, Georgia

Team Operated by Brunswick Baseball Association, Inc.
Team President: Larry E. Brumit
Vice President: Blanton Miller
Secretary-Treasurer-Travel Secretary: Joseph C. Stewart
General Manager: James Wiche
Manager(s): Carlson Howerton
Games played at Edo Miller Memorial Park
Season attendance: 45,157
Major League Affiliate: Philadelphia Phillies – National League.

Brunswick Phillies Team Roster

NAME	G	BA	POS	W	L	ERA	APF
Baron, Vic	15	0.273	C				
Bonczek, Lonegan	60	0.261	SS				
Boozer, John	8	0.105	P	3	4	3.67	

Georgia Class-D Minor League Baseball Encyclopedia

NAME	G	BA	POS	W	L	ERA	
Campbell, Nolan	56	0.246	2B, OF				
Carmo, Bob	42	0.182	OF				
Colgan, Dick	11	0.154	P	2	5	3.79	
Contratto, George	60	0.319	1B				
Croge, Sam	33	0.244	P	15	8	4.10	
Farland, Jim	24	0.094	P	7	1	4.03	
Foreman, Dick	45	0.244	SS				
Hafner, Ron	11	0.294					
Hatfield, Jim	103	0.344	2B				Waycross
Hewitt, Phil	53	0.269	2B, OF, P	1	1		
Holcomb, Lou	16	0.188	SS				
Howerton, Carlson	34	0.302	M, 1B, 2B				
Jacoby, Brooks	2	0.000	P	0	0		
Johnson, Jerry	25	0.244	C				
Jonietz, Ben	61	0.255	OF				
Knutson, Larry	23	0.207	OF				
Kummer, Gerald	2	0.500	P	0	0		
Large, Don	25	0.325	P	3	8	4.78	
Leshock, Dave	6	0.333	P	0	1		
McGue, Don	7	0.125	P	0	2		
McKee, Art	34	0.302	P	4	5	4.50	
Mitchell, Steven	18	0.222	OF, P	1	2	4.09	
Pacholke, Al	4	0.000	P	0	0		
Platt, Ralph	66	0.268	C				
Pokorny, Joe	32	0.211	P	11	9	3.94	
Ramont, Terry	17	0.130	C				
Shima, Tom	19	0.167	P	8	4	2.89	
Simcich, John	119	0.358	3B				
Smith, Dick	2	0.000	P	0	1		
Stopchuck, Mike	114	0.316	1B, C, OF, P	0	0		
Tesmer, Warren	32	0.286	3B, OF				
Urrizola, Mike	31	0.088	P	8	13	4.61	
Walker, Ron	9	0.120					
Warren, Rudy	107	0.312	OF				Waycross
Wenrich, Dave	30	0.233	C				
Williams, John	11	0.125	P	2	3		
Williamson, Jim	61	0.302	2B				

Dublin, Georgia

Team Operated by Dublin Baseball Club, Inc.
Team President: J. Elmer Mackey
Vice President: Carlus Gay
Secretary: A.O. Hadden
Treasurer: L.P. Keen
General Manager: Norman C. Hughes
Manager(s): Earl Weaver
Games played at Lovett Park
Season attendance: 31,704
Major League Affiliate: Baltimore Orioles – American League.

Dublin Orioles Team Roster

NAME	G	BA	POS	W	L	ERA	APF
Barber, Steve	24	0.163	P	5	5	5.00	
Bednar, Dave	124	0.273	1B				
Bird, Bob	107	0.281	3B, SS, P	0	0		
Bolin, Joe	96	0.311	C, OF				
Breedlove, Ernest	21	0.211	P	3	3	5.87	
Bruns, Don	50	0.297	3B, OF, P	0	0		
Carver, Jim	13	0.240	C				
Dominy, Clint	15	0.000	P	1	3	10.50	
Ewin, Dick	56	0.351	OF				
Figueroa, Rodolfo	82	0.248	SS				
Hand, Dave	8	0.154					
Hughes, Norm	1	0.000	P	1	0		
Madaio, Gene	37	0.195	OF				
Malavase, Allie	5	0.000	P	1	1		
Mankovitch, Frank	48	0.202	P	12	9	4.41	
McClusky, Jim	11	0.209	C				
McGrath, Mike	10	0.125	P	2	1	4.64	
Menna, Frank	57	0.276	OF				

NAME	G	BA	POS	W	L	ERA	
Mitchell, Bill	10	0.000					
Nebinger, Dick	24	0.183	OF, P	0	0		
Nicholson, Dave	28	0.227	OF				
Pearson, Ron	37	0.141	P	15	13	3.95	
Phagan, Fred	30	0.315	C, OF				
Ryan, Tom	46	0.303	2B, 3B				
Semonik, Mike	82	0.206	2B				
Stocker, Ron	18	0.360	P	5	4	4.05	
Walker, Gary	37	0.301	SS				
Wartelle, Johnny	40	0.111	P	10	5	5.70	
Weaver, Earl	37	0.294	M, 2B, OF, P	0	0		
Werley, George	49	0.228	P	16	10	4.28	
White, Albert	18	0.276	2B				
White, Bob	62	0.242	C				
Williams, Dick	23	0.158	OF				
Zander, Ron	39	0.122	OF				

Thomasville, Georgia

Team Operated by Thomasville Dodgers Baseball Club
Team President: Heeth Varnedoe
Vice President: Fresco Thompson
Secretary: Matthew A. Burns
Treasurer: William Gibson
General Manager: George E. Pfister
Manager(s): Rudy Rufer, Sam Suplizio
Games played at Municipal Stadium
Season attendance: 17,451
Major League Affiliate: Los Angeles Dodgers – National League.

Thomasville Tigers Team Roster

NAME	G	BA	POS	W	L	ERA	APF
Allen, Ed	86	0.315	1B, OF				
Bergey, Francis	13	0.240	2B				
Bertschy, Bob	10	0.105					
Bonavia, Anthony	15	0.182	P	1	2	7.46	
Boone, Ron	18	0.118	C				
Booth, Bill	22	0.310	P	7	6	3.66	
Bozich, John	36	0.283	P	6	5	5.74	
Brady, Jim	10	0.000	P	1	3		
Breeden, Jack	1	0.000	P	0	1		
Britz, Greg	14	0.233	OF				
Buhl, Larry	9	0.133					
Burnham, Al	32	0.171	C				
Capullo, Bob	14	0.125	P	3	2	3.56	
Collins, Howard	30	0.075	P	4	13	5.62	
Crotty, John	8	0.000	P	0	0		
Cutter, Ron	59	0.279	2B, 3B				
Duckworth, Jim	15	0.167	P	2	5	6.00	
Dyer, Penhallow	3	0.143					
Ferrerra, Lee	18	0.185	3B				
Field, Gary	11	0.182	P	2	4	5.43	
Franklin, Hal	9	0.400	P	0	0		
Graf, Phil	30	0.125	P	0	4	6.96	
Hutchinson, Gordon	3	0.000	P	0	0		
Johnson, Marshall	4	0.000	P	0	2		
Johnston, Bob	7	0.600	P	0	2		
Joseph, Bill	12	0.154	P	4	6	4.35	
Julian, Charles	115	0.313	C				
Kalmes, Bill	25	0.107	P	0	8	6.55	
Kiesman, Bob	57	0.221	OF				
Klimkowski, Frank	6	0.000					
Lee, Gene	2	0.000	P	0	1		
Midgette, Dennis	16	0.261	P	2	7	11.34	
Miller, Rod	52	0.258	2B, 3B				
Motil, Bob	47	0.272	3B				
Muratore, Dick	16	0.217	2B				
Murray, Orlene	3	0.000	P	0	0		
Pagel, Vic	38	0.165	3B				
Parham, Dave	65	0.242	1B				

Georgia Class-D Minor League Baseball Encyclopedia

Name	G	BA	POS	W	L	ERA
Phillips, Dick	125	0.265	SS			
Pleau, Andre	16	0.250	P	5	4	4.42
Rouse, John	24	0.296	1B			
Rufer, Rudy			M			
Schultz, Stan	20	0.237	OF			
Shosty, Bob	91	0.280	OF			
Smith, Dick	124	0.274	OF, P	0	1	
Suplizio, Sam	38	0.318	M, OF, P	0	0	
Travers, Miles	4	0.000	P	0	3	
Tucker, Dick	13	0.208				
Yodhes, John	30	0.308	OF			
Zellner, Jerome	30	0.270	P	1	10	7.96

Valdosta, Georgia

Team Operated by Valdosta Baseball Company, Inc.
Team President: John J. McHale
Secretary-Treasurer: James A. Campbell
General Manager: John O'Neil
Manager(s): Stubby Overmire
Games played at Pendleton Park
Season attendance: 38,582
Major League Affiliate: Detroit Tigers – National League.

Valdosta Dodgers Team Roster

NAME	G	BA	POS	W	L	ERA	APF
Bancroft, Charles	115	0.287	2B				
Billingsley, Ray	62	0.283	OF				
Boger, Jim	24	0.075	P	10	5	4.13	
Burroughs, Gene	23	0.167	P	13	7	1.66	
Cummings, Vince	3	0.000	P	0	1		
Donatucci, John	25	0.173	SS				
Drake, John	20	0.132	P	4	7	6.03	
Exline, Bob	18	0.236	OF				
Gatza, Paul	8	0.211	P	6	1	3.38	
Jenkins, Reynolds	1	1.000	P	0	1		
Kahle, Huber	12	0.267	C				
Kebler, Steve	33	0.075	P	6	4	4.14	
Kimbrough, Charles	118	0.196	1B				
Laurie, Lawrence	54	0.172	C				
Lawrence, William	26	0.160	P	9	9	4.91	
LeBlanc, Carlton	33	0.167	P	8	6	4.92	
Lindgren, Lionel	125	0.243	OF				
Long, Clarence	105	0.269	OF				
McAuliffe, Dick	93	0.286	SS				
McDaniel, Joel	65	0.216	P	15	8	4.21	
Moore, Jackie	87	0.300	3B, C				
Myatt, Ralph	3	0.000	P	0	0		
Newton, Tom	29	0.259	OF				
Overmire, Stubby			M				
Ponte, Orville	2	0.000	P	0	0		
Ryan, Dean	14	0.143	P	4	2	4.64	
Smilee, Gary	3	0.333					
Webb, Tom	65	0.215	OF				
Weller, Jay	9	0.143	P	0	1		
Wert, Don	120	0.284	2B, 3B, P	0	0		

Waycross, Georgia

Team Operated by Waycross Baseball Association, inc.
Team President: Erin W. Johnson
Manager(s): Everett Robinson
Games played at Memorial Stadium
Season attendance: 26,512
Major League Affiliate: Milwaukee Braves – National League.

Waycross Braves Team Roster

NAME	G	BA	POS	W	L	ERA	APF
Bergstraesser, Bill	10	0.267	P	1	4	5.93	
Bolding, Billy	23	0.213	P	3	6	3.40	
Brewton, Byron	29	0.261	3B				
Butler, Cecil	31	0.230	P	14	6	2.39	
Cherek, LeRoy	2	0.000	P	0	0		
Duren, Jim	5	0.286	P	0	3		
Dyer, Leroy	32	0.185	P	6	11	5.62	
Fracaro, Dave	3	0.143	P	0	2		
Frioni, Alfonso	12	0.083	P	2	2	5.81	
Grace, John	12	0.258					
Grady, Bruce	54	0.242	3B				
Hagen, Dick	9	0.167	P	0	2		
Hatfield, Jim	103	0.344	2B				Brunswick
Healy, Dick	24	0.145	OF				
Henrichs, Russ	19	0.167	P	3	6	5.05	
Johnson, Lorne	43	0.276	OF, P	0	0		
Knoll, Dave	9	0.250	P	0	0		
Kuykendall, Jim	7	0.200	P	1	3		
Lewallen, Keith	19	0.217	OF				
MacLeod, Don	19	0.200	P	3	6	4.55	
Maxcy, Russ	68	0.253	SS				
McClenaghan, Russ	85	0.233	OF, P				
Moore, Jim	18	0.174	1B				
Nester, Jim	93	0.298	3B, OF, P	0	0		
Niles, Harry	20	0.239	2B				
Nisewonger, Jim	26	0.264	OF				
Norbert, Ted	106	0.312	1B, OF				
O'Mara, Larry	30	0.174	P	7	10	4.91	
Payne, Paul	1	0.000	P	0	0		
Poupore, Bernard	11	0.100	P	0	5	6.55	
Robinson, Everett			M				
Roesler, Ken	54	0.269	OF, P	0	0		
Ross, Ron	5	0.250	P	0	4		
Schmitz, John	43	0.202	SS				
Selph, Charles	46	0.210	2B, 3B				
Severson, Don	102	0.308	C				
Sosmer, Bernard	10	0.108					
Stapp, John	37	0.170	2B, SS, P	0	0		
Suarez, Rafael	12	0.200	C				
Tierney, Tom	63	0.261	OF				
Townsend, Charles	9	0.077	P	2	4	4.21	
Veinot, Ken	7	0.091					
Warren, Rudy	107	0.312	OF				Brunswick
Wilson, Lonnie	18	0.122	C				
Zeihen, Bernard	23	0.114	P	5	6	4.17	

1958 Georgia-Florida League Records

Batting

Highest Batting Average (minimum 100 at bats)
1. John Simcich – Brunswick .358
2. Dick Ewin – Dublin .351
3. Jim Hatfield – Wayc/Brun .344
4. Mo Mozzali – Albany .335
5. Mike Shannon – Albany .322

Most Hits
1. John Simcich – Brunswick 156
2. Mike Stopchuck – Brunswick 141
3. Jim Hatfield – Wayc/Brun 135
4. Bob Boyer – Albany 132
5. Don Wert – Valdosta 130

Most Runs
1. Sam Hernandez – Albany 118
2. Bob Boyer – Albany 107
3. John Simcich – Brunswick 104
4. Dave Bednar – Dublin 103
5. Mike Stopchuck – Brunswick 102
   Charles Bancroft – Valdosta 102

Georgia Class-D Minor League Baseball Encyclopedia

Most Total Bases
1. Bob Boyer – Albany   256
2. John Simcich – Brunswick   232
3. Mike Stopchuck – Brunswick   210
4. Dick Smith – Thomasville   199
5. Dave Bednar – Dublin   197
   Ted Norbert – Waycross   197

Most Doubles
1. Ted Norbert – Waycross   33
2. Lionel Lindgren – Valdosta   29
   Mo Mozzali – Albany   29
4. John Simcich – Brunswick   25
   Bill Morton – Albany   25

Most Triples
1. Dick Smith – Thomasville   18
2. Don Wert – Valdosta   11
3. Mike Stopchuck – Brunswick   7
4. Ronald Miller – Albany   6
   Dick Phillips – Thomasville 6
   Clarence Long – Valdosta   6

Most Home Runs
1. Bob Boyer – Albany   32
2. Bob Bird – Dublin   18
3. Dave Bednar – Dublin   16
4. John Simcich – Brunswick   15
5. Ted Norbert – Waycross   12

Most Extra Base Hits
1. Bob Boyer – Albany   56
2. Ted Norbert – Waycross   45
   Lionel Lindgren – Valdosta   45
4. John Simcich – Brunswick   43
5. Mike Stopchuck – Brunswick   40

Most Runs Batted In
1. Bob Boyer – Albany   121
2. Mike Stopchuck – Brunswick   105
3. John Simcich – Brunswick   104
4. Dave Bednar – Dublin   96
5. Ted Norbert – Waycross   86

Most Stolen Bases
1. Sam Hernandez – Albany   57
2. Dave Bednar – Dublin   32
3. Dick Smith – Thomasville   28
4. Ronald Miller – Albany   27
5. Bob Boyer – Albany   21

Fielding
Most Put-Outs
1. Dave Bednar 1B – Dublin   1,042
2. Charles Kimbrough 1B – Valdosta   1,011
3. Ted Norbert 1B, OF – Waycross   863
4. Bill Morton C – Albany   755
5. Mo Mozzali 1B, P – Albany   742

Most Assists
1. Dick Phillips SS – Thomasville   319
2. Sam Hernandez 2B, 3B, OF – Albany   318
3. Charles Bancroft 2B – Valdosta   298
4. Jim Hatfield 2B – Wayc/Brun   277
5. Bill Dingus SS, P – Albany   274

Most Errors
1. Bill Dingus SS, P – Albany   57
2. Dick Phillips SS – Thomasville   47
3. Dick McAuliffe SS – Valdosta   45
4. Rod Miller 2B, 3B – Thomasville   36
5. Jim Hatfield 2B – Wayc/Brun   31

Pitching
Most Wins
1. George Werley – Dublin   16
2. Ron Pearson – Dublin   15
   Sam Croge – Brunswick   15
   Joel McDaniel – Valdosta   15
5. Tom Wood – Albany   14
   Cecil Butler – Waycross   14

Most Losses
1. Ron Pearson – Dublin   13
   Mike Urrizola – Brunswick   13
   Howard Collins – Thomasville 13
4. Leroy Dyer – Waycross   11
5. George Werley – Dublin   10
   Larry O'Mara – Waycross   10
   Jerome Zellner – Thomasville 10

Highest Winning Percentage (10 game minimum)
1. Tom Wood – Albany   .778
2. Gordie Richardson – Albany   .765
3. Jerry Dickerson – Albany   .706
   Jerry Lock – Albany   .706
5. Cecil Butler – Waycross   .700

Lowest Earned Run Average (100 inning minimum)
1. Gene Burroughs – Valdosta   1.66
2. Cecil Butler – Waycross   2.39
3. Tom Shima – Brunswick   2.89
4. Gordie Richardson – Albany   2.93
5. Tom Wood – Albany   3.31

Most Strikeouts
1. Joe Pokorny – Brunswick   177
2. Ron Pearson – Dublin   139
3. Gene Burroughs – Valdosta   138
4. Frank Mankovitch – Dublin   137
5. George Werley – Dublin   133

Most Bases on Balls
1. Howard Collins – Thomasville 143
2. Mike Urrizola – Brunswick   141
3. Jerome Zellner – Thomasville 134
4. Fred Walker – Albany   128
5. Bill Kalmes – Thomasville   123

Most Hits Allowed
1. Ron Pearson – Dublin   251
2. Sam Croge – Brunswick   198
3. Joel McDaniel – Valdosta   192
4. Joe Pokorny – Brunswick   191
   George Werley – Dublin   191

Most Innings Pitched
1. Ron Pearson – Dublin   228
2. Sam Croge – Brunswick   213
3. George Werley – Dublin   208
4. Joe Pokorny – Brunswick   194
   Frank Mankovitch – Dublin   194

1958 Georgia-Florida League All-Star Team
1B Dave Bednar – Dublin
2B Jim Hatfield – Waycross
3B John Simcich – Brunswick
SS Dick McAuliffe – Valdosta
OF Bob Boyer – Albany

OF Mike Shannon – Albany
OF Mike Stopchuck – Brunswick
OF Dick Ewin – Dublin
C   Bill Morton – Albany
C   Charles Julian – Thomasville
P   Cecil Butler – Waycross
P   Ron Pearson – Dublin
P   Warren Roddenberry – Albany
P   Joel McDaniel – Valdosta
M   Mo Mozzali – Albany

1962

Georgia-Florida League

League Office: Brunswick, Georgia
League President: Larry E. Brumitt
League Vice President: Erin W. Johnson
Secretary: Richard A. Snyder
Player Rule: Each club was allowed a roster of twenty-two players, not more than eleven limited service, and not less than eleven rookies.

Georgia-Florida League Final Standings

Team	W	L	Pct	GB	Affiliate
Thomasville Tigers	76	41	.650	----	DET-AL
Dublin Braves	68	50	.576	8.5	MIL-NL
Brunswick Cardinals	47	70	.462	29.0	STL-NL
Moultrie Colt .22's	44	74	.373	32.5	HOU-NL

1962 Georgia-Florida League Map

(numbers on map correspond to the place each team finished in regular season play)

After a four-year hiatus, the slimmed-down Georgia-Florida League returned to the diamond with four familiar clubs: Brunswick, Dublin, Moultrie, and Thomasville.

Dublin pitcher Barry Miller pitched the season's only no-hitter on July 28, against Thomasville winning the shortened contest 2 to 0 in five innings. Pitcher Travis Martin, while playing for Moultrie and Thomasville during the season, set the league's all-time single season record for the highest winning percentage with .909 on a record of 10 wins and 1 loss.

No post-season was played by the small, four-club league.

Brunswick, Georgia
Team Operated by Brunswick Baseball Club
General Manager: Richard A. Snyder
Manager(s): Owen Friend
Games played at Edo Miller Park

Georgia Class-D Minor League Baseball Encyclopedia

Season attendance: 36,123
Major League Affiliate: St. Louis Cardinals – National League.

Brunswick Cardinals Team Roster

NAME	G	BA	POS	W	L	ERA	APF
Anders, Howard	21	0.136	P	3	6	5.40	
Ballard, Larry	39	0.202	OF				
Barty, Warren	107	0.280	OF, C				
Burchfield, Ken	84	0.194	OF				
Cade, Dane	2	0.286					
Coller, Jon	26	0.207	SS				
Cundiff, Bill	26	0.100	P	5	11	4.69	
Fann, Ernest	25	0.303	C				
Feldstein, Alan	10	0.176	2B				
Firek, Jan	34	0.248	OF				
Friend, Owen			M				
Green, Lee	35	0.283	OF				
Grimes, Jim	7	0.000	P	0	0	4.50	
Guthrie, Bill	22	0.120	P	7	6	5.01	
Holyfield, Harold	38	0.121	SS				
Hultzapple, Ken	12	0.000	P	0	1	5.29	
Johnson, Don	24	0.185	P	3	6	6.68	
Jones, Mike	20	0.077	P	3	2	7.29	
Kane, Ken	7	0.083					
Maddick, Russ	110	0.249	1B, OF				
Major, Tom	7	0.235	P	3	3	1.72	
Matchick, Tom	71	0.311	SS				
McAfee, Bud	5	0.300					
McDaniel, Kerry	75	0.233	1B, P	3	4	7.17	
Meyer, Russ	25	0.078	P	6	10	5.29	
Mills, Joe	9	0.000	P	1	3	7.83	
Morris, Charles	21	0.175	OF				
Musillo, John	13	0.286	P	0	2	4.50	
Neeley, Gary	20	0.241	3B				
Nelson, Don	25	0.182	P	2	1	3.82	
Newcomer, Jack	111	0.281	2B				
Norris, Bob	30	0.308	OF				
Romeo, Mike	28	0.050	P	2	5	4.85	
Seegmiller, Garth	91	0.236	3B				
Shuck, Larry	14	0.143	P	2	1	3.24	
Smith, Tommie	55	0.236	C				
Sullivant, Mickey	14	0.000	P	0	1	10.42	
Taylor, Jose	3	0.000					
Vingle, Dick	5	0.000	P	0	2	7.94	
Willis, Ron	57	0.251	OF, P	7	6	4.38	
Zackery, Rollie	40	0.272	OF				

Dublin, Georgia

Team Operated by Milwaukee National Baseball Club, Inc.
Team President: John J. McHale
Secretary-Treasurer: Ralph Delforge
Assistant Secretary: John Mullen
Business Manager: Bill Steinecke
Manager(s): Bill Steinecke
Games played at Lovett Park
Season attendance: 19,582
Major League Affiliate: Milwaukee Braves – National League.

Dublin Braves Team Roster

NAME	G	BA	POS	W	L	ERA	APF
Aguilar, Bob	68	0.306	1B				
Anderson, Dick	114	0.240	OF				
Botkin, Del	29	0.298	OF, C				
Branon, Mike	3	0.000					
Brown, Levi	33	0.319	OF				
Burns, Jim	2	1.000	P	0	0	10.50	
Clark, Glen	73	0.342	3B, OF				
Colvard, Herman	29	0.191	OF				
Cook, John	8	0.000	P	1	1	6.16	
Dairon, Wayne	4	0.143					
Driscoll, Jim	48	0.275	3B				
Flowers, John	13	0.067	P	3	1	6.07	
Hagen, Dick	40	0.133	P	7	3	2.27	
Hart, Dick	46	0.301	1B				
Haydel, Hal	17	0.077	P	7	4	3.53	
Hayworth, George	41	0.215	C				
Jenkins, Gary	14	0.115	P	5	2	4.19	
Kabat, John	5	0.000	P	0	0	9.00	
Kern, Dan	56	0.300	OF				
Kroll, Wayne	30	0.217	P	5	4	2.95	
Lowe, Macon	17	0.115	P	3	6	3.94	
Lubieski, Herman	36	0.267	OF				
Maust, Tom	91	0.206	2B, 3B, SS				
May, John	27	0.280	OF				
Miller, Barry	6	0.125	P	2	2	3.54	
Mullis, Don	71	0.245	2B				
Nesta, Nick	10	0.000	P	2	2	6.47	
Perez, Simon	37	0.093	P	11	7	4.71	
Pietrewicz, Alex	42	0.040	P	14	8	3.51	
Pirkel, Jim	56	0.190	OF				
Poitras, Bob	3	0.000	P	0	0	16.20	
Robinson, Bill	62	0.304	OF, P	0	0	15.00	
Rodriguez, Newton	11	0.308	P	1	2	3.69	
Rose, Wallace	8	0.000	P	0	2	5.19	
Rowe, Joe	28	0.271	OF				
Samuel, Manuel	119	0.269	SS				
Santmire, Glenn	9	0.333	P	1	0	6.12	
Sharp, Hubert	15	0.154	P	5	2	5.88	
Smith, Tom	73	0.243	C				
Steinecke, Bill			M				
Wyatt, John	10	0.077	P	1	4	4.95	

Moultrie, Georgia

Team Operated by Houston Sports Association, Inc.
Team President: Craig F. Cullinan
Business Manager: C.W. Vandiver
Director: James Walton
Manager(s): Jim Walton
Games played at Holmes Field
Season attendance: 18,560
Major League Affiliate: Houston Colt .45's – National League.

Moultrie Colt .22's Team Roster

NAME	G	BA	POS	W	L	ERA	APF
Ackerman, Bob	64	0.293	OF				
Aizupura, Nicomedes	94	0.229	2B				
Arcia, Jose	16	0.357	P	4	4	4.14	Thomasville
Booker, Bill	50	0.247	3B, SS				
Bridges, Barney	19	0.197	1B				
Bruno, Bob	17	0.208	OF				
Bukowski, John	23	0.115	P	4	5	4.93	
Carroll, Gerald	19	0.182	P	2	4	7.53	
Casanova, Rudy	36	0.195	SS, OF				
de la Torre, Albert	5	0.000					
Dembinsky, Charles	23	0.167	2B				
Fullen, Tom	27	0.128	P	6	8	4.57	
Gilmore, Bob	4	0.111					
Goldfield, Alan	15	0.091	P	8	4	3.15	
Heinze, Norm	66	0.251	C				
Hinkle, George	2	0.000	P	0	1	18.00	
Holbrook, Jim	25	0.082	P	6	12	3.61	
Holmquist, Doug	19	0.321	C				
Jacobus, Steve	110	0.271	1B, OF				
Johnson, Elijah	111	0.249	3B, OF				
Martin, Travis	17	0.233	P	10	1	2.97	Thomasville
Norris, Ron	4	0.111	P	1	2	1.96	
Palko, Bill	32	0.125	P	4	6	5.48	
Paris, Lester	9	0.162					
Partain, Jim	12	0.167	P	0	3	7.39	
Peterkin, Alfonso	66	0.259	OF				

Georgia Class-D Minor League Baseball Encyclopedia

NAME	G	BA	POS	W	L	ERA	APF
Ritter, Art	14	0.136	P	1	5	4.50	
Roberts, Wayne	8	0.000	P	0	3	11.77	
Rombach, Bob	64	0.214	OF				
Rouse, Bill	27	0.208	1B, P	0	1	11.25	
Sembera, Carroll	18	0.361	P	6	6	3.49	
Smith, Ron	41	0.211	3B, OF				
Staub, Ray	74	0.315	OF				
Taranto, Anthony	25	0.091	P	2	3	7.27	
Thaxton, Kent	13	0.133	P	1	5	6.07	
Torres, Miguel	47	0.178	SS				
Troy, Herb	62	0.267	C				
Walton, Jim	34	0.295	M, P	0	2	5.63	
Willett, Dennis	37	0.230	SS				
Wood, Ron	4	0.200	P	1	1	6.75	

Thomasville, Georgia
Team Operated by Thomasville Baseball Club, Inc.
Team President: Heeth Varnedoe
Vice Presidents: James A. Campbell, Richard B. Ferrell
Secretary-Treasurer: Harry M. Sisson
General Manager-Business Manager: John Q. Nolan
Manager(s): Gail Henley
Games played at Municipal Stadium
Season attendance: 18,610
Major League Affiliate: Detroit Tigers – American League

Thomasville Tigers Team Roster

NAME	G	BA	POS	W	L	ERA	APF
Arcia, Jose	16	0.357	P	4	4	4.14	Moultrie
Avery, Ken	9	0.120	P	6	2	2.88	
Barker, Tommy	50	0.305	3B				
Brunsberg, Arlo	15	0.327	C				
Campbell, George	103	0.276	OF				
Cawley, Gaynor	28	0.211	P	7	3	2.18	
Cressman, Bob	8	0.222	P	2	2	3.60	
Farington, Gerald	5	0.000	P	0	0	3.38	
Geminiani, Dick	26	0.122	P	8	7	5.18	
Grier, Harold	90	0.245	SS				
Hamrick, Connie	28	0.121	SS				
Hartman, John	32	0.248	OF				
Haygood, Charles	26	0.156	P	14	6	2.08	
Henley, Gail			M				
Hughes, Charles	14	0.184	3B				
Kuk, John	52	0.170	OF, P	1	0	0.00	
Kurt, Lyndon	4	0.222	P	1	0	1.80	
Lakeman, Charles	7	0.100					
Lange, Ron	18	0.147	P	7	3	4.92	
Lee, Tom	9	0.250	P	0	0	4.85	
Martin, Travis	17	0.233	P	10	1	2.97	Moultrie
McDaniel, Elmer	10	0.000	P	1	2	6.00	
Monkarsh, Bill	7	0.235					
Pallavicini, Vince	76	0.235	OF				
Parquet, Clyde	7	0.000	P	0	1	4.80	
Pavelko, Paul	112	0.250	OF				
Pennucci, Pat	2	0.375					
Pepper, Don	42	0.268	1B				
Ray, Jere	29	0.270	P	9	6	5.58	
Reese, Rich	73	0.328	1B				
Richardson, Marty	114	0.279	2B				
Schuler, Ron	8	0.263					
Schultz, Ken	96	0.291	3B				
Stoll, Max	33	0.188	P	8	7	4.73	
Thoele, Walt	24	0.237	SS				
Werking, Glenn	30	0.235	C				
Woods, Ralph	75	0.288	C				

1962 Georgia-Florida League Records
Batting
Highest Batting Average (minimum 100 at bats)
1. Glen Clark – Dublin .342
2. Rich Reese – Thomasville .328
3. Ray Staub – Moultrie .315
4. Tom Matchick – Brunswick .311
5. Bob Aguilar – Dublin .306

Most Hits
1. Manuel Samuel – Dublin 124
2. Marty Richardson – Thomasville 116
3. Jack Newcomer – Brunswick 110
4. Glen Clark – Dublin 100
5. Steve Jacobus – Moultrie 99
   Dick Anderson – Dublin 99

Most Runs
1. Manuel Samuel – Dublin 100
2. Marty Richardson – Thomasville 91
3. Paul Pavelko – Thomasville 84
4. Ken Schultz – Thomasville 79
5. Jack Newcomer – Brunswick 75

Most Total Bases
1. Glen Clark – Dublin 197
2. Jack Newcomer – Brunswick 172
3. Marty Richardson – Thomasville 171
4. Dick Anderson – Dublin 156
5. Warren Barty – Brunswick 146
   Steve Jacobus – Moultrie 146

Most Doubles
1. Dick Anderson – Dublin 22
2. George Campbell – Thomasville 20
3. Jack Newcomer – Brunswick 18
4. Steve Jacobus – Moultrie 17
   Bob Aguilar – Dublin 17

Most Triples
1. Marty Richardson – Thomasville 10
   Paul Pavelko – Thomasville 10
3. Dick Anderson – Dublin 7
4. Steve Jacobus – Moultrie 6
   Nicomedes Aizupura – Moultrie 6

Most Home Runs
1. Glen Clark – Dublin 26
2. Dan Kern – Dublin 15
3. Ken Burchfield – Brunswick 14
4. Garth Seegmiller – Brunswick 13
5. Jack Newcomer – Brunswick 12
   Dick Hart – Dublin 12

Most Extra Base Hits
1. Glen Clark – Dublin 43
2. Dick Anderson – Dublin 36
3. Jack Newcomer – Brunswick 34
4. Marty Richardson – Thomasville 31
5. Steve Jacobus – Moultrie 29

Most Runs Batted In
1. George Campbell – Thomasville 75
2. Glen Clark – Dublin 72
3. Paul Pavelko – Thomasville 66
4. Dick Anderson – Dublin 65
   Marty Richardson – Thomasville 65

Most Stolen Bases
1. Marty Richardson – Thomasville 35
2. Paul Pavelko – Thomasville 22
3. Russ Maddick – Brunswick 21
4. Elijah Johnson – Moultrie 18
5. Nicomedes Aizupura – Moultrie 14

Fielding
Most Put-Outs
1. Tom Smith C – Dublin 593
2. Rich Reese 1B – Thomasville 571
3. Steve Jacobus 1B, OF – Moultrie 550
4. Ralph Woods C – Thomasville 545
5. Russ Maddick 1B, OF – Brunswick 541

Most Assists
1. Marty Richardson 2B – Thomasville 277
2. Jack Newcomer 2B – Brunswick 268
3. Manuel Samuel SS – Dublin 245
4. Nicomedes Aizupura 2B – Moultrie 238
5. Harold Grier SS – Thomasville 228

Most Errors
1. Elijah Johnson 3B, OF – Moultrie 50
2. Tom Maust 2B, 3B, SS – Dublin 46
3. Jack Newcomer 2B – Brunswick 39
4. Manuel Samuel SS – Dublin 35
   Harold Grier SS – Thomasville 35

Pitching
Most Wins
1. Charles Haygood – Thomasville 14
   Alex Pietrewicz – Dublin 14
3. Simon Perez – Dublin 11
4. Travis Martin – Thom/Moul 10
5. Jere Ray – Thomasville 9

Most Losses
1. Jim Holbrook – Moultrie 12
2. Bill Cundiff – Brunswick 11
3. Russ Meyer – Brunswick 10
4. Alex Pietrewicz – Dublin 8
   Tom Fullen – Moultrie 8

Highest Winning Percentage (10 game minimum)
1. Travis Martin – Thom/Moul .909
2. Charles Haygood – Thomasville .700
   Dick Hagen – Dublin .700
   Gaynor Cawley – Thomasville .700
   Ron Lange – Thomasville .700

Lowest Earned Run Average (50 inning minimum)
1. Charles Haygood – Thomasville 2.08
2. Gaynor Cawley – Thomasville 2.18
3. Dick Hagen – Dublin 2.27
4. Ken Avery – Thomasville 2.88
5. Wayne Kroll – Dublin 2.95

Most Strikeouts
1. Alex Pietrewicz – Dublin 175
2. Charles Haygood – Thomasville 164
3. Jim Holbrook – Moultrie 138
4. Bill Cundiff – Brunswick 137
5. Simon Perez – Dublin 125

Most Bases on Balls
1. Jere Ray – Thomasville 124
2. Dick Geminiani – Thomasville 107
3. Jim Holbrook – Moultrie 90
4. Kerry McDaniel – Brunswick 80
5. Max Stoll – Thomasville 78

Most Hits Allowed
1. Alex Pietrewicz – Dublin 173
   Simon Perez – Dublin 173
3. Russ Meyer – Brunswick 152
4. Charles Haygood – Thomasville 145
5. Jere Ray – Thomasville 144

Most Innings Pitched
1. Charles Haygood – Thomasville 182
2. Alex Pietrewicz – Dublin 169
3. Simon Perez – Dublin 153
4. Jim Holbrook – Moultrie 147
5. Jere Ray – Thomasville 142

1962 Georgia-Florida League All-Star Team
1B Steve Jacobus – Moultrie
2B Jack Newcomer – Brunswick
3B Glen Clark – Dublin
SS Tom Matchick – Brunswick
OF Dick Anderson – Dublin
OF Ray Staub – Moultrie
OF Alfonso Peterkin – Moultrie
C Herb Troy – Moultrie
C Warren Barty – Brunswick
P Dick Hagen – Dublin
P Jim Holbrook – Moultrie
M Bill Steinecke – Dublin

Georgia Class-D Minor League Baseball Encyclopedia

1963

Georgia-Florida League

League Office: Brunswick, Georgia
League President: Larry E. Brumitt
League Vice President: Erin W. Johnson
Secretary: William P. Morton, Jr.
Player Rule: Each club was allowed a roster of twenty-two players, not more than one veteran, not more than ten limited service, and not less than eleven rookies.

Georgia-Florida League Final Standings

Team	W	L	Pct	GB	Affiliate
Thomasville Tigers	65	54	.546	----	DET-AL
Moultrie Colt .22's	62	54	.534	1.5	HOU-NL
Waycross Braves	56	63	.471	9.0	MIL-NL
Brunswick Cardinals	52	64	.448	11.5	STL-NL

1963 Georgia-Florida League Map

(numbers on map correspond to the place each team finished in regular season play)

Following the 1962 season, minor league baseball was reorganized eliminating classes B, C, and D. Having been a class-D league in every previous year of operation, the Georgia-Florida League was now stepped up to class-A. The league remained small with only four clubs, and one change was made during the off-season. Dublin dropped out, and familiar face Waycross stepped in to fill the position.

On July 25, Moultrie pitcher Jay Dahl pitched a no-hitter against Brunswick but lost the seven-inning game 0 to 1.

Again, no post-season games were played.

This was the final year of operation for the Georgia-Florida League. As interest in small-town minor league baseball waned, many such leagues faded away.

Brunswick, Georgia

Team Operated by St. Louis National Baseball Club, Inc.
General Manager: William P. Morton, Jr.
Manager(s): George Kissell
Games played at Edo Miller Park
Season attendance: 9,363
Major League Affiliate: St. Louis Cardinals – National League.

Brunswick Cardinals Team Roster

NAME	G	BA	POS	W	L	ERA	APF
Anthon, Fred	54	0.206	2B, 3B				
Apicella, Jim	17	0.245	2B				
Arnone, Bob	21	0.128	OF				
Bakenhaster, Dave	3	0.167	P	1	1	4.29	
Bowman, Clyde	34	0.198	OF, P	0	0	4.50	
Braddock, Ron	34	0.149	3B, OF				
Brayer, Dennis	41	0.148	1B				
Breeden, Danny	28	0.297	C				
Bukowski, John	5	0.091	P	4	1	2.45	
Byrd, Charles	49	0.302	OF				
Cecil, Ed	8	0.000	P	0	0	3.60	
Chambers, Jim	2	0.250					
Cosman, Jim	27	0.176	P	1	9	4.07	
Courser, Ron	44	0.210	OF				
Damaska, Bill	78	0.198	2B, 3B, OF				
Davis, Don	13	0.000	P	0	1	4.22	
Davis, Ernest	41	0.200	OF				
Davis, Vict	31	0.190	C				
Erickson, Dale	4	0.000	P	2	2	1.71	
Farrell, Dick	63	0.250	SS				
Finn, Francis	78	0.286	OF, P	1	1	4.50	
Franceck, Mike	12	0.040					
Guthrie, Bill	8	0.100	P	5	2	3.00	
Hamende, Joe	12	0.063	P	4	5	1.80	
Harris, Dick	34	0.160	OF				Waycross
Hester, Jim	1	1.000					
Holyfield, Harold	22	0.227	3B				
Hunter, Mike	58	0.269	1B, 3B				
Jacobus, Steve	23	0.286	1B				
Johnson, Don	2	0.000	P	0	0	18.00	
Jones, Mike	5	0.000	P	1	1	3.21	
Jusino, Ramon	5	0.000	P	0	0	5.00	
Kelley, Bill	19	0.000	P	3	2	4.33	
Kissell, George			M				
Maddick, Russ	29	0.219	1B				
McNamee, Bill	6	0.143	P	1	1	1.96	
Meyer, Russ	14	0.133	P	2	5	4.42	
Mills, Joe	9	0.235	P	0	0	7.71	
Miscisco, Dan	27	0.091	P	2	6	1.89	
Moore, Bob	4	0.000	P	0	0	9.00	
Newton, Leo	15	0.188	P	3	5	3.10	
Novak, Walt	40	0.241	OF				
Orsatti, Frank	12	0.212	OF				
Romeo, Mike	24	0.167	P	5	7	3.88	
Sloan, Mike	9	0.222	P	5	1	1.15	
Smith, Dennis	21	0.308	C				
Smith, Julius	56	0.232	OF				
Smith, Tommie	73	0.291	1B, C				
Spates, Larcus	65	0.250	2B				
Spencer, Roosevelt	48	0.163	C				
Spiezio, Ed	14	0.238	SS				
Stark, Clint	19	0.290	P	3	3	2.74	
Torres, Victor	49	0.312	SS				
Van, John	6	0.154	P	2	3	2.85	
Vingle, Dick	3	0.000	P	0	1	7.71	
Wall, Fred	7	0.182	P	4	1	3.89	
Wilson, Lonnie	31	0.200	OF, P	3	6	6.00	
Young, Don	16	0.280	OF				
Zeller, Bart	8	0.304					

Georgia Class-D Minor League Baseball Encyclopedia

Moultrie, Georgia
Team Operated by Houston National Baseball Club, Inc.
Team President: Roy Hofheinz
Vice President-General Manager: Paul Richards
Executive Vice President: George Kirksey
Business Manager: Stan Starrett
Manager(s): Jim Walton
Games played at Holmes Field
Season attendance: 11,402
Major League Affiliate: Houston Colt .45's – National League.

Moultrie Colt .22's Team Roster

NAME	G	BA	POS	W	L	ERA	APF
Aizupura, Nicomedes	61	0.238	2B				
Black, Bobby	20	0.111	P	10	5	2.69	
Brown, Jerome	3	0.000	P	0	1	0.00	
Canning, Bill	2	0.000	P	0	0	13.50	
Cawley, Gaynor	5	0.250	P	2	2	3.91	
Churn, Chuck	23	0.158	P	3	1	0.60	
Dahl, Jay	11	0.238	P	5	1	1.42	
de la Cruz, Ramon	68	0.192	3B, C				
Ellis, Jerry	59	0.137	2B				
Ferrand, Ray	53	0.306	3B				
Flood, Joe	7	0.083	P	3	4	2.06	
Goldfield, Alan	15	0.056	P	1	4	4.23	
Goodlett, Vince	2	0.000	P	0	0	5.40	
Green, Jim	89	0.226	C				
Howard, Larry	49	0.216	1B				
Marrujo, Jimmie	8	0.231	P	6	0	2.35	
Mello, Ed	21	0.077	P	2	5	4.20	
Murray, Charles	109	0.194	OF				
Murrell, Ivan	40	0.221	OF				
Palko, Bill	20	0.208	P	6	6	3.07	
Panella, Joe	82	0.223	OF				
Rivero, Freddy	10	0.000	P	0	0	6.55	
Robinson, Sammie	37	0.099	OF				
Rombach, Bob	97	0.175	3B, OF				
Ruck, Martin	16	0.000	P	2	1	4.67	
Sparks, Oliverio	58	0.226	OF				
Taranto, Anthony	11	0.182	P	0	6	5.40	
Thaxton, Kent	30	0.308	P	7	7	3.09	
Thomas, Frank	31	0.267	P	10	7	2.27	
Torppey, Kevin	8	0.000	P	3	3	4.26	
Tucker, Tom	9	0.125	P	2	1	1.73	
Walenczyk, Bob	99	0.236	1B, 3B, OF				
Walton, Jim			M				
Warden, Charles	25	0.151	C				
Willett, Dennis	111	0.292	SS				

Thomasville, Georgia
Team Operated by Thomasville Baseball Company, Inc.
Team President: Heeth Varnedoe
Vice Presidents: James A. Campbell, Richard B. Ferrell
General Manager-Business Manager: John Q. Nolan
Secretary-Treasurer: Harry M. Sisson
Manager(s): Whitey Federoff
Games played at Vardedoe Field
Season attendance: 7,342
Major League Affiliate: Detroit Tigers – American League.

Thomasville Tigers Team Roster

NAME	G	BA	POS	W	L	ERA	APF
Androsko, Steve	14	0.185	OF				
Barker, Tommy	17	0.250	3B				
Bly, John	96	0.262	OF				
Burger, Bob	17	0.200	P	8	5	2.62	
Campbell, George	78	0.236	OF				
Cernich, Joe	40	0.145	C				
Christino, Mike	28	0.284	1B				
Colvard, Herman	54	0.187	OF				Waycross
Devine, Mike	17	0.118	OF				
Federoff, Whitey			M				
Geminiani, Dick	3	0.000	P	0	0	13.50	
Glover, Jim	119	0.275	2B				
Hardin, Hugh	16	0.138	P	4	6	2.72	
Hart, Gary	23	0.091	P	2	5	2.34	
Hartman, John	100	0.193	OF				
Hughes, Charles	73	0.203	3B				
Ingram, Pete	13	0.125	P	2	0	3.09	
Johnson, Owen	13	0.346	P	3	1	2.53	
Laton, Bob	31	0.132	P	12	4	3.02	
Lazarewicz, Bob	14	0.077	P	2	6	2.61	
Lopez, Junior	9	0.192					
Miali, Jim	16	0.200	OF				
Miller, Bob	2	0.000	P	2	0	1.38	
Morowski, Gene	4	0.250	P	0	1	9.00	
Nichols, Bruce	111	0.247	1B, C				
O'Brien, Phil	21	0.103	P	6	6	2.97	
Pallavicini, Vince	7	0.333					
Pepper, Don	77	0.269	1B				
Perry, Walt	7	0.333	P	0	1	1.13	
Ross, Kent	15	0.211	OF				
Rudolph, Tom	19	0.061	P	6	8	2.31	
Smith, Leroy	6	0.231	P	4	0	1.35	
Steinbach, Bill	15	0.114	C				
Sterkenberg, Larry	23	0.183					
Symko, Anthony	84	0.188	3B, OF				
Thoele, Walt	116	0.209	SS				
Todtenhausen, Art	10	0.000	P	5	1	3.00	
Tuholski, Jim	27	0.136	P	8	8	2.53	
Vogel, Bill	5	0.182	P	1	2	3.55	
Young, Ken	3	0.400					

Waycross, Georgia
Team Operated by Milwaukee National Baseball Club, Inc.
Team President: John J. McHale
Secretary-Treasurer: Ralph Delforge
General Manager: Bill Steinecke
Manager(s): Bill Steinecke
Games played at Memorial Stadium
Season attendance: 21,560
Major League Affiliate: Milwaukee Braves – National League.

Waycross Braves Team Roster

NAME	G	BA	POS	W	L	ERA	APF
Alexander, Bob	10	0.188					
Anderson, Ken	68	0.235	OF				
Antonangeli, Don	3	0.000	P	0	1	10.13	
Bailey, John	8	0.182					
Ballard, Frank	7	0.000	P	0	1	4.24	
Barrett, Mike	13	0.000	P	2	2	4.50	
Breeden, Hal	116	0.330	1B				
Burns, Jim	27	0.114	P	8	11	3.45	
Colvard, Herman	54	0.187	OF				Thomasville
Cruz, Jose Ramon	30	0.212					
Davis, J.B.	97	0.232	OF				
Eiselstein, Bill	64	0.274	2B, 3B, SS				
Elmstrom, Carl	43	0.071	P	9	7	1.66	
Emmert, Dick	82	0.269	SS				
Gallo, Fred	19	0.105	C				
Garrett, Charles	57	0.276	2B				
Geter, Eldridge	35	0.114	P	8	7	2.95	
Giambelluca, Charles	12	0.111					
Harris, Dick	34	0.160	OF				Brunswick
Jensen, Dick	16	0.000	P	1	0	3.60	
Jinske, Wayne	114	0.310	C				
Koerner, Ted	17	0.065	P	3	5	1.80	
LeDuc, Carl	28	0.048	P	2	3	3.54	
Lubieski, Herman	3	0.000					

Georgia Class-D Minor League Baseball Encyclopedia

Lum, Mike	51	0.263	OF			
Maust, Tom	72	0.225	2B, 3B			
McEnroe, Jim	3	0.000	P	0	1	12.86
Meka, Mark	32	0.150	2B			
Mercier, Ron	40	0.176	3B			
Miller, Barry	19	0.200	P	5	8	3.54
Petersen, Charles	37	0.258	1B			
Robinson, Bill	113	0.316	OF			
Sharp, Hubert	21	0.200	P	7	4	2.76
Slivnik, Mike	14	0.118				
Steinecke, Bill			M			
Tarkington, Rondle	16	0.000	P	0	3	2.68
Then, Jose	6	0.000	P	2	2	8.10
Wallin, Ray	43	0.259	1B, OF			
Wells, Jim	53	0.216	2B, 3B			
West, Bill	32	0.208	P	9	8	3.00
Winchester, Joe	24	0.176	C			

1963 Georgia-Florida League Records

Batting

Highest Batting Average (minimum 100 at bats)
1. Hal Breeden – Waycross .330
2. Bill Robinson – Waycross .316
3. Victor Torres – Brunswick .312
4. Wayne Jinske – Waycross .310
5. Ray Ferrand – Moultrie .306

Most Hits
1. Bill Robinson – Waycross 132
2. Hal Breeden – Waycross 131
3. Dennis Willett – Moultrie 130
4. Jim Glover – Thomasville 122
5. Wayne Jinske – Waycross 110

Most Runs
1. Dennis Willett – Moultrie 73
2. Bill Robinson – Waycross 69
   Jim Glover – Thomasville 69
4. Charles Murray – Moultrie 57
5. John Bly – Thomasville 48

Most Total Bases
1. Bill Robinson – Waycross 200
2. Hal Breeden – Waycross 182
3. Jim Glover – Thomasville 171
4. Wayne Jinske – Waycross 151
5. Dennis Willett – Moultrie 147

Most Doubles
1. Bob Walenczyk – Moultrie 21
2. Bill Robinson – Waycross 18
3. Tommie Smith – Brunswick 17
4. Hal Breeden – Waycross 15
   Jim Glover – Thomasville 15

Most Triples
1. Bill Robinson – Waycross 10
2. Hal Breeden – Waycross 6
   Dick Emmert – Waycross 6
4. John Bly – Thomasville 5
   Walt Thoele – Thomasville 5
   Nicomedes Aizupura – Moultrie 5

Most Home Runs
1. Charles Murray – Moultrie 15
2. Mike Hunter – Brunswick 11
3. Bill Robinson – Waycross 10
   Jim Glover – Thomasville 10
5. Bruce Nichols – Thomasville 9

Most Extra Base Hits
1. Bill Robinson – Waycross 38
2. Charles Murray – Moultrie 30
3. Hal Breeden – Waycross 29
4. Bob Walenczyk – Moultrie 28
5. Jim Glover – Thomasville 27

Most Runs Batted In
1. Hal Breeden – Waycross 64
2. Bill Robinson – Waycross 62
3. Bob Walenczyk – Moultrie 53
4. Charles Murray – Moultrie 50
5. Jim Glover – Thomasville 47

Most Stolen Bases
1. Bill Robinson – Waycross 29
2. Dennis Willett – Moultrie 22
3. Larcus Spates – Brunswick 19
4. John Bly – Thomasville 14
5. Bob Rombach – Moultrie 13

Fielding

Most Put-Outs
1. Hal Breeden 1B – Waycross 892
2. Wayne Jinske C – Waycross 870
3. Bruce Nichols 1B, C – Thomasville 715
4. Jim Green C – Moultrie 701
5. Bob Walenczyk 1B, 3B, OF – Moultrie 578

Most Assists
1. Jim Glover 2B – Thomasville 312
2. Dennis Willett SS – Moultrie 261
3. Walt Thoele SS – Thomasville 258
4. Dick Emmert SS – Waycross 168
5. Bill Eiselstein 2B, 3B, SS – Waycross 149

Most Errors
1. Walt Thoele SS – Thomasville 44
2. Dick Emmert SS – Waycross 37
3. Tom Maust 2B, 3B – Waycross 32
4. Dennis Willett SS – Moultrie 31
5. Bill Eiselstein 2B, 3B, SS – Waycross 30

Pitching

Most Wins
1. Bob Laton – Thomasville 12
2. Frank Thomas – Moultrie 10
   Bobby Black – Moultrie 10
4. Bill West – Waycross 9
   Carl Elmstrom – Waycross 9

Most Losses
1. Jim Burns – Waycross 11
2. Jim Cosman – Brunswick 9
3. Bill West – Waycross 8
   Jim Tuholski – Thomasville 8
   Tom Rudolph – Thomasville 8
   Barry Miller – Waycross 8

Highest Winning Percentage (7 game minimum)
1. Bob Laton – Thomasville .750
2. Bill Guthrie – Brunswick .714
3. Bobby Black – Moultrie .667
4. Hubert Sharp – Waycross .636
5. Bob Burger – Thomasville .615

Lowest Earned Run Average (50 inning minimum)
1. Mike Sloan – Brunswick 1.15
2. Jay Dahl – Moultrie 1.42

3. Carl Elmstrom – Waycross 1.66
4. Joe Hamende – Brunswick 1.80
   Ted Koerner – Waycross 1.80

Most Strikeouts
1. Carl Elmstrom – Waycross 138
2. Frank Thomas – Moultrie 133
3. Jim Tuholski – Thomasville 131
4. Jim Burns – Waycross 130
5. Eldridge Geter – Waycross 117

Most Bases on Balls
1. Jim Burns – Waycross 75
2. Hugh Hardin – Thomasville 72
3. Carl Elmstrom – Waycross 65
4. Ed Mello – Moultrie 62
5. Bill Palko – Moultrie 59

Most Hits Allowed
1. Frank Thomas – Moultrie 130
2. Bill West – Waycross 129
3. Jim Tuholski – Thomasville 125
4. Bob Laton – Thomasville 124
5. Kent Thaxton – Moultrie 119

Most Innings Pitched
1. Frank Thomas – Moultrie 143
2. Jim Burns – Waycross 141
3. Jim Tuholski – Thomasville 139
4. Bill West – Waycross 138
5. Kent Thaxton – Moultrie 131

1963 Georgia-Florida League All-Star Team
1B Hal Breeden – Waycross
2B Jim Glover – Thomasville
3B Ray Ferrand – Moultrie
SS Dennis Willett – Moultrie
OF Bill Robinson – Waycross
OF John Bly - Thomasville
OF Oliverio Sparks – Moultrie
C Jim Green – Moultrie
C Bruce Nichols – Thomasville
P Carl Elmstrom – Waycross
P Jim Tuholski – Thomasville
M Bill Steinecke – Waycross

Georgia Class-D Minor League Baseball Encyclopedia

Georgia Class-D League All-Time Season Records

Georgia-Alabama League All-Time Single Season Records

Batting

Highest Batting Average (minimum 100 at bats)
1. George Rohe – Newnan – 1913 .435
2. Carl East – Carrollton – 1930 .434
3. Bernard Lewis – Lindale – 1930 .423
4. Woodrow Bottoms – Newnan – 1946 .421
5. Bernard Lewis – Talladega – 1929 .420
6. Gordon Pugh – Lindale – 1930 .416
7. Elmer Randall – Gadsden – 1913 .410
8. Clark Taliaferro – Carrollton – 1928 .392
9. Lou Finney – Carrollton – 1930 .389
10. Cliff McSwain – Huntsville – 1930 .388

Most Hits
1. Malvern Morgan – Valley – 1947 184
2. Bernard Lewis – Lindale – 1930 175
3. George Bailey – Opelika – 1948 174
4. Claude Shoemake – Rome – 1951 171
   Shorty Marshall – Carrollton – 1947 171
6. Claude Shoemake – Newnan – 1947 170
7. Fred Campbell – Griffin – 1948 168
   Gene Solt – Carrollton – 1950 168
   George Hughes – Valley – 1951 168
10. Delton Childs – Tallassee – 1948 166
    John Stowe – Rome – 1951 166

Most Runs
1. H.P. Mackie – Newnan – 1914 176
2. --- Smith – Newnan – 1914 165
3. Freddie DeSouza – Carrollton – 1950 149
4. Jack Shipley – Cedartown – 1930 131
5. Bernard Lewis – Lindale – 1930 128
6. Ted Browing – Newnan – 1947 122
7. Jake Daniel – Vall/LaGr – 1946 118
8. George Kelly – Cedartown – 1930 116
9. Bob Edwards – Valley – 1948 114
10. Leon Carter – LaGrange – 1950 113

Most Total Bases
1. Gene Solt – Carrollton – 1950 311
2. Bernard Lewis – Lindale – 1930 303
3. Claude Shoemake – Rome – 1951 290
4. Jake Daniel – Vall/LaGr – 1946 285
5. Carl Franson – Newnan – 1949 264
6. George Kelly – Cedartown – 1930 263
7. Malvern Morgan – Valley – 1947 259
8. Red Howell – Carrollton – 1928 256
   Luther Gunnells – Carrollton – 1946 256
10. Jack Bearden – Griffin – 1950 254

Most Doubles
1. John Stowe – Rome – 1951 39
2. Ray Clark – Carrollton – 1950 38
3. Eddie Reese – Huntsville – 1930 37
   Claude Shoemake – Rome – 1951 37
5. Bernard Lewis – Lindale – 1930 35
   J.H. Hammond – Huntsville – 1930 35
7. *eight players tied with 34

Most Triples
1. Earl Persons – Gadsden – 1929 17
2. Bob Edwards – Valley – 1948 16
   John Krochina – LaGrange – 1949 16
4. Ray Treadway – Cedartown – 1928 15
   Cliff Verner – Talladega – 1929 15
   Joe Chambers – Valley – 1946 15
   John Millard – Newnan – 1948 15
   Bill Hudson – Opelika – 1949 15
9. Bernard Lewis – Talladega – 1929 14
   Marlin Hathcock – Tallassee – 1946 14
   George Hughes – Valley – 1951 14

Most Home Runs
1. Gene Solt – Carrollton – 1950 38
2. Carl Franson – Newnan – 1950 31
3. Jake Daniel – Vall/LaGr – 1946 30
4. Carl Franson – Newnan – 1949 28
5. Jo-Jo White – Carrollton – 1928 27
6. George Kelly – Cedartown – 1930 26
   Claude Shoemake – Rome – 1951 26
8. Charles Knowles – Cedartown – 1929 25
   Bernard Lewis – Lindale – 1930 25
   Ken Guettler – Griffin – 1947 25

Most Extra Base Hits
1. Bernard Lewis – Lindale – 1930 69
2. Carl Franson – Newnan – 1949 68
3. Gene Solt – Carrollton – 1950 66
4. Claude Shoemake – Rome – 1951 65
5. Jake Daniel – Vall/LaGr – 1946 63
   Freddie DeSouza – Carrollton – 1950 63
7. Red Howell – Carrollton – 1928 61
8. J.H. Hammond – Huntsville – 1930 58
9. --- Higginbotham – Anniston – 1930 57
10. Joe Langdon – Anniston – 1930 56
    Eddie Reese – Huntsville – 1930 56
    Jack Bearden – Griffin – 1950 56

Most Runs Batted In
1. Gene Solt – Carrollton – 1950 151
2. Claude Shoemake – Rome – 1951 135
3. Jack Bearden – Griffin – 1951 127
4. Jake Daniel – Vall/LaGr – 1946 122
5. Jim Stoyle – Griffin – 1950 121
6. Joe Schmidt – Newnan – 1949 108
7. Claude Shoemake – Newnan – 1946 107
   Bill Hudson – Opelika – 1949 107
9. Bill Brown - Alexander City – 1950 106
   Bob Adams – LaGrange – 1951 106

Most Stolen Bases
1. Jack Huesman - Alexander City – 1949 — 80
2. Bill Rucker – Carrollton – 1949 — 75
3. Bob Edwards – Valley – 1948 — 67
4. Delton Childs – Tallassee – 1948 — 50
5. Al Julian – Opelika – 1949 — 47
6. George Liddy – LaGrange – 1948 — 44
7. --- Lamar – Anniston – 1914 — 43
8. Ted Browning – Newnan – 1947 — 42
9. Jack Huesman - Alexander City – 1948 — 41
   Eli Maricich – Valley – 1951 — 41

Fielding
Most Put-Outs
1. Henry Zich 1B – Tallassee – 1948 — 1,143
2. Yancy Senn 1B – Gadsden – 1929 — 1,124
3. Jake Daniel 1B, P – Vall/LaGr – 1946 — 1,108
4. Bill Brown 1B - Alexander City – 1948 — 1,102
5. Wheeler Flemming 1B – Opelika – 1947 — 1,088
6. Bill Jones 1B – Tallassee – 1946 — 1,066
7. Jim Lewis 1B – Valley – 1948 — 1,058
8. Alton McAfee 1B – Newnan – 1948 — 1,057
9. Harold Pinson 1B – Tallassee – 1949 — 1,025
10. Alton McAfee 1B – Newnan – 1949 — 991

Most Assists
1. Bob Adams SS – Tallassee – 1949 — 401
2. John Millard SS – Newnan – 1948 — 395
3. Maurice Wright SS – Tallassee – 1947 — 389
4. George Noga SS – Griffin – 1950 — 371
5. Joe Chambers 2B – Valley – 1946 — 370
6. Frank Costa SS – Gadsden – 1929 — 368
7. Joe Chambers 2B – Valley – 1948 — 364
8. Luther Gunnells SS – Opelika – 1947 — 362
   Ray Clark SS – Valley – 1948 — 362
   Jack Huesman 2B, SS - Alexander City – 1949 — 362

Most Errors
1. --- Cleveland SS – Cedartown – 1930 — 74
   Paul Flores SS – Opelika – 1949 — 74
3. --- Spitznagle SS – Opelika – 1914 — 61
   John Millard SS – Newnan – 1949 — 61
5. Maurice Wright SS – Tallassee – 1947 — 58
6. Vince Bosarge SS – Valley – 1946 — 57
   Luther Gunnells SS – Opelika – 1947 — 57
8. Dick Kelly 3B – Carrollton – 1947 — 53
   Luther Gunnells SS – Opel/Alex – 1948 — 53
   Fred Campbell SS, C – Griffin – 1948 — 53
   Bob McAndrew 2B – Griffin – 1949 — 53

Pitching
Most Wins
1. Paul Brock – Newnan – 1947 — 23
   Bill Kallaher – Opelika – 1948 — 23
   Gene Doerfliniter – Carrollton – 1948 — 23
4. Bill Webb – Carrollton – 1947 — 22
   Jesse Danna – Valley – 1948 — 22
   Don Bessent – LaGrange – 1950 — 22
7. Paul Fittery – Carrollton – 1928 — 21
   John McFadden – Newnan – 1949 — 21
   Bill Bustle – Newnan – 1950 — 21
   Marv Chappell – LaGrange – 1951 — 21

Most Losses
1. Jesse Danna – Valley – 1947 — 18
2. Claude Jackson – Opelika – 1949 — 17
3. Bob Matthews – Carr/Newn – 1947 — 16
   Bill Heisig – LaGrange – 1948 — 16
   Jimmy Sparks – Rome – 1950 — 16

6. Jim Vickers – Opelika – 1946 — 15
   Elmer Copeland – LaGrange – 1947 — 15
   Ed Chitwood - Alexander City – 1947 — 15
   Claude Jackson – Opelika – 1948 — 15
   Jim Magnatta – LaGrange – 1948 — 15
   Carlos Lopez – Griffin – 1949 — 15
   Hy Cohen – LaGrange – 1949 — 15
   Tom O'Barr – Rome – 1951 — 15

Highest Winning Percentage (10 game minimum)
1. Jack Nabors – Tall/Newn – 1915 — .923
2. Paul Fittery – Carrollton – 1928 — .913
3. Bob Devaney – Newnan – 1948 — .909
4. Paul Fittery – Carrollton – 1929 — .889
5. Sherry Smith – Cedartown – 1930 — .875
6. Charles Harrison – LaGrange – 1951 — .864
7. Rufus Nolly – LaGrange – 1916 — .857
8. Paul Brock – Carrollton – 1946 — .833
9. Bill Kallaher – Opelika – 1948 — .821
10. Elmer Wallace – Newnan – 1949 — .818

Lowest Earned Run Average (100 inning minimum)
1. Paul Fittery – Carrollton – 1928 — 1.60
2. Paul Fittery – Carrollton – 1929 — 1.81
3. Ben Frakes – Gads/Carr – 1928 — 1.85
4. John Lindsey - Alexander City – 1948 — 2.00
5. Elmer Wallace – Newnan – 1949 — 2.02
6. Jesse Danna – Valley – 1948 — 2.06
7. Bill Kallaher – Opelika – 1948 — 2.08
   Floyd Shaw – Valley – 1946 — 2.08
9. Gene Doerflinger – Carrollton – 1948 — 2.13
10. Jesse Danna – Valley – 1947 — 2.15

Most Strikeouts
1. Gene Doerflinger – Carrollton – 1948 — 233
2. Don Bessent – LaGrange – 1950 — 229
3. Bill Bustle – Newnan – 1950 — 228
4. Paul Brock – Newnan – 1947 — 220
5. Mickey Mihalik – Newnan – 1948 — 214
6. John O'Donnell – Griffin – 1948 — 191
7. Bill Kallaher – Opelika – 1948 — 181
8. John McFadden – Newnan – 1949 — 180
9. John Lindlsey - Alexander City – 1950 — 168
10. Marv Chappell - Alexander City – 1949 — 162

Most Bases on Balls
1. Mickey Mihalik – Newnan – 1948 — 149
2. John O'Donnell – Griffin – 1948 — 143
3. Bill Kilgore – Opelika – 1949 — 140
4. Carlos Lopez – Griffin – 1949 — 135
   Marv Chappell – Alex/LaGr – 1950 — 135
6. Claude Jackson – Opelika – 1948 — 132
   Tom O'Barr – Rome – 1951 — 132
8. Marv Chappell - Alexander City – 1949 — 129
9. Marv Chappell – LaGrange – 1951 — 128
   Clem Kelecava – Griffin – 1951 — 128

Most Hits Allowed
1. Paul Brock – Newnan – 1947 — 282
2. Bill Stolte – Griffin – 1951 — 273
3. Elmer Copeland – LaGrange – 1947 — 268
4. George Granger – Lindale – 1930 — 264
5. Paul Crain – Carr/Vall – 1947 — 255
6. Ralph Stanfield – Lindale – 1928 — 245
7. Abe White – Griffin – 1947 — 244
8. Marcus McWhorter – Valley – 1948 — 242
9. Lefty Hockette – Anniston – 1930 — 239
10. John Lindlsey - Alexander City – 1950 — 233

Most Innings Pitched
1. Paul Brock – Newnan – 1947 — 313
2. John Lindsey - Alexander City – 1948 — 275
3. Paul Crain – Carr/Vall – 1947 — 261
4. Gene Doerflinger – Carrollton – 1948 — 253
5. Bill Kallaher – Opelika – 1948 — 251
   Marv Chappell – LaGrange – 1951 — 251
7. John Barger – Newnan – 1948 — 249
8. Bob Matthews – Carr/Newn – 1947 — 248
9. Elmer Copeland – LaGrange – 1947 — 244
   John McFadden – Newnan – 1949 — 244

Georgia-Florida League All-Time Single Season Records

Batting

Highest Batting Average (minimum 100 at bats)
1. Mike Fandozzi – Waycross – 1957 — .422
2. Beattie Feathers – Americus – 1936 — .396
3. Emil Restaino – Thomasville – 1949 — .388
   Moose Alexander – Thomasville – 1940 — .388
5. Walt Bremer – Waycross – 1950 — .384
6. Ducky Detweiler – Cordele – 1951 — .381
7. Eddie Kazak – Albany – 1941 — .378
   Sherwood McKenzie – Thomasville – 1940 — .378
9. Joe Kwiatkowski – Valdosta – 1948 — .371
10. Rocco Ippolito – Moultrie – 1948 — .370

Most Hits
1. Eddie Kazak – Albany – 1941 — 221
2. Ralph Ellis – Thomasville – 1940 — 203
3. Paul Smith – Tallahassee – 1950 — 196
4. Pete Thomassie – Waycross – 1940 — 193
5. Bubba Phillips – Thomasville – 1949 — 192
6. Hal Schultz – Tallahassee – 1940 — 190
7. Howard Henkel – Thomasville – 1948 — 189
   Mike Fandozzi – Waycross – 1957 — 189
9. Charles Farrar – Waycross - 1940 — 187
10. Cy Lowery – Tallahassee – 1940 — 186

Most Runs
1. Davey Williams – Waycross – 1947 — 147
2. Hubert Rose – Moultrie – 1950 — 145
3. Floyd Faust – Brunswick – 1954 — 143
4. Ed Trojanowski – Americus – 1949 — 141
5. Bob Lyons – Waycross – 1949 — 135
6. Harold Shiles – Waycross – 1949 — 134
7. Eddie Kazak – Albany – 1941 — 133
   Russ McGovern – Albany – 1953 — 133
9. Russ Leach – Albany – 1940 — 131
10. John McCullough – Americus – 1947 — 130
    Charles Perchak – Moultrie – 1950 — 130

Most Total Bases
1. Bob Wellman – Moultrie – 1956 — 296
2. Eddie Kazak – Albany – 1941 — 290
   Rocco Ippolito – Moultrie – 1948 — 290
4. Tom Corbett – Thomasville – 1937 — 289
5. Ralph Ellis – Thomasville – 1940 — 285
6. Clarence Buheller – Brunswick – 1954 — 284
7. Chase Riddle – Albany – 1956 — 281
8. Charles Farrar – Waycross – 1940 — 279
9. Ken Rhyne – Moultrie – 1947 — 273
   Frank Thomas – Tallahassee – 1948 — 273

Most Doubles
1. Marv Leib – Valdosta – 1948 — 47
2. Jim Stoyle – Fitzgerald – 1953 — 46
3. Eddie Kazak – Albany – 1941 — 45
4. Fred Marolewski – Albany – 1948 — 43
5. Carl Bethman – Moultrie – 1939 — 41
   Norris Strickland – Cordele – 1948 — 41
7. Denver Rikard – Waycross – 1954 — 40
8. Frank Thomas – Tallahassee – 1948 — 39
   Harold Stamey – Americus – 1949 — 39
   Chase Riddle – Albany – 1956 — 39

Most Triples
1. Dave Pluss – Valdosta – 1942 — 23
2. Casey Kimbrell – Tallahassee – 1940 — 22

3. Eddie Robinson – Valdosta – 1940   21
   Ultus Alvarez – Thomasville – 1953   21
5. Lee Jenkins – Valdosta – 1948   20
6. Glenn Murray – Tallahassee – 1935   18
   Bill Glynn – Americus – 1946   18
   Doug Johnson – Tallahassee – 1946   18
   Charlie Weathers – Waycross – 1948   18
   Harry Geis – Cordele – 1949   18
   Bert Hamric – Valdosta – 1950   18
   Dick Smith – Thomasville – 1958   18

Most Home Runs
1. Bob Boyer – Albany – 1958   32
2. Bob Wellman – Moultrie – 1956   30
3. Glenn Eury – Moultrie – 1951   29
4. Ken Rhyne – Moultrie – 1948   27
5. Tom Corbett – Thomasville – 1937   26
   Jim Hickman – Albany – 1957   26
   Glen Clark – Dublin – 1962   26
8. Ken Rhyne – Moultrie – 1947   24
   Chase Riddle – Albany – 1956   24
10. Don Whitcomb – Brunswick – 1956   23

Most Extra Base Hits
1. Bob Wellman – Moultrie – 1956   69
2. Bill Glynn – Americus – 1946   67
3. Chase Riddle – Albany – 1956   66
4. Marv Leib – Valdosta – 1948   64
5. Carl Bethman – Moultrie – 1939   62
   Harold Stamey – Americus – 1949   62
7. Tom Corbett – Thomasville – 1937   61
   Frank Thomas – Tallahassee – 1948   61
9. Russell Rac – Albany – 1949   59
   Ultus Alvarez – Thomasville – 1953   59

Most Runs Batted In
1. Chase Riddle – Albany – 1956   142
2. Ken Rhyne – Moultrie – 1947   141
3. Russell Rac – Albany – 1949   134
4. Frank Thomas – Tallahassee – 1948   132
5. Charles Farrar – Waycross – 1940   131
   Harold Ivy – Moultrie – 1950   131
   Bill Thompson – Fitzgerald – 1954   131
8. Ken Rhyne – Moultrie – 1946   129
9. J.C. Dunn – Albany – 1955   125
10. Bob Wellman – Moultrie – 1956   124

Most Stolen Bases
1. Floyd Faust – Brunswick – 1954   76
2. Ed Trojanowski – Americus – 1949   69
3. Arvie Pilgrim – Waycross – 1956   62
4. George Fisher – Waycross – 1948   60
   Bubba Phillips – Thomasville – 1949   60
6. Arvie Pilgrim – Waycross – 1955   59
7. Sam Hernandez – Albany – 1958   57
8. Gene Depperschmidt – Valdosta – 1949   54
   Floyd Faust – Brunswick – 1953   54
10. J.C. Dunn – Albany – 1955   48

Fielding
Most Put-Outs
1. Ed Davis IF – Panama City – 1935   1,391
2. Eddie Hoffman 1B – Americus – 1940   1,376
3. Paul Swoboda 1B – Thomasville – 1939   1,300
4. Neal Hertweck 1B – Albany – 1949   1,273
5. Ken Robinett 1B – Thomasville – 1952   1,262
6. Ralph Weeks 1B – Thomasville – 1947   1,260
7. Bernard Brockelman 1B – Americus – 1941   1,243
8. Eddie Robinson 1B – Valdosta – 1940   1,239
9. Harry Hughes 1B – Waycross – 1940   1,234
10. Eddie Robinson 1B – Valdosta – 1939   1,227

Most Assists
1. Lew Quinn UT – Americus – 1936   677
2. Monty Basgall 2B – Valdosta – 1942   502
3. Ray Hamrick SS – Americus – 1941   486
4. Charlie Brewster SS – Waycross – 1940   475
5. John Sullivan SS – Thomasville – 1941   471
6. Henry Navarro SS – Thomasville – 1949   468
7. George Wopinek SS – Tallahassee – 1948   463
8. Frank Pelat 2B – Moultrie – 1940   461
9. Andrew Laumann SS – Moultrie – 1947   460
   Gene Merandi SS – Albany – 1952   460

Most Errors
1. Ray Hamrick SS – Americus – 1941   100
2. Percy Hassler SS – Thomasville – 1948   96
3. Charlie Brewster SS – Waycross – 1940   88
   Tom Hurd SS – Cordele – 1946   88
5. Bill Broukal SS – Cordele – 1949   86
6. John Sullivan SS – Thomasville – 1941   83
7. George Wopinek SS – Tallahassee – 1948   82
8. Bernie Wenitski SS – Americus – 1949   81
9. Everett Tysinger SS – Cordele – 1941   80
10. Don McNally SS – Tallahassee – 1950   77

Pitching
Most Wins
1. Whammy Douglas – Brunswick – 1954   27
2. Ace Adams – Cordele – 1937   26
   Elwood Lawson – Waycross – 1940   26
4. John Asmer – Americus – 1946   24
5. Mel Bosser – Thomasville – 1940   23
   Irv Peterman – Albany – 1941   23
   Ray Seidel – Waycross – 1948   23
7. Jim McClure – Americus – 1936   22
   Lloyd Gross – Moultrie – 1939   22
   Morris Frank – Albany – 1949   22
   John Hushebeck – Americus – 1950   22
   Harry Raulerson – Waycross – 1951   22
   Bill Lackey – Albany – 1955   22

Most Losses
1. John Lindstrom – Moultrie – 1940   22
2. Ray Scheidt – Moultrie – 1952   21
3. Calvin Kirksey – Tallahassee – 1941   20
4. Walt Purcey – Cordele – 1940   19
   Stan Wysocki – Cordele – 1940   19
   Mel Nicolai – Cordele – 1946   19
7. Calvin Kirksey – Tallahassee – 1942   18
   Dick Childs – Waycross – 1950   18
   Charles Kott – Moultrie – 1952   18
   Anthony Fabrizio – Cordele – 1953   18

Highest Winning Percentage (10 game minimum)
1. Travis Martin – Moul/Thom – 1962   .909
2. Leon Scherer – Tallahassee – 1935   .900
   Norm Smith – Cordele – 1937   .900
4. Bob Koczwara – Thomasville – 1953   .882
5. George Wasconis – Thomasville – 1953   .875
6. Harry Raulerson – Waycross – 1949   .857
7. Woody Davis – Cordele – 1936   .850
8. Red McColl – Americus – 1938   .842
   Antonio Sarmiento – Tifton – 1952   .842
10. Herb Moore – Albany – 1946   .833
    John Herbik – Moultrie – 1947   .833
    Bill McNeil – Valdosta – 1956   .833

Lowest Earned Run Average (100 inning minimum)
1. Antonio Sarmiento – Tifton – 1952   1.26
2. Taylor Phillips – Waycross – 1952   1.39
3. Kip Sauerbrun – Thom/Moul – 1941   1.40
4. Herb Moore – Albany – 1946   1.44
5. Bob Sedlack – Thomasville – 1955   1.53
6. Gene Burroughs – Valdosta – 1958   1.66
   Carl Elmstrom – Waycross – 1963   1.66
8. Joe Greene – Valdosta – 1954   1.70
9. Bill Knox – Albany – 1954   1.80
   Guerry Torres – Brunswick – 1956   1.80

Most Strikeouts
1. Art Ceccarelli – Valdosta – 1949   294
2. Gaylord Lemish – Moultrie – 1946   278
3. Jack Frisinger – Albany – 1947   274
4. Whammy Douglas – Brunswick – 1954   273
5. Ken Sheppard – Valdosta – 1956   271
6. Taylor Phillips – Waycross – 1952   265
   Fred Green – Brunswick – 1952   265
8. Ray Burnett – Americus – 1947   262
9. Benny Rich – Brunswick – 1956   257
10. Morris Frank – Albany – 1949   254

Most Bases on Balls
1. Fred Green – Brunswick – 1952   190
2. John Byrne – Valdosta – 1948   185
3. Taylor Phillips – Waycross – 1952   182
4. Don Miller – Brunswick – 1956   180
5. Ray Burnett – Americus – 1947   179
6. Jim Burns – Americus – 1942   174
7. Wes Breschini – Thomasville – 1950   166
   Courtney Stempel – Cordele – 1950   166
9. Rolf Moeller – Tallahassee – 1950   162
   Roberto Betancourt – Tifton – 1951   162
   Taylor Phillips – Waycross – 1951   162

Most Hits Allowed
1. Krim Bess – Albany – 1938   360
2. Walt Purcey – Cordele – 1940   326
3. John Lindstrom – Moultrie – 1940   321
4. Henry Weaver – Albany – 1940   319
5. Mel Bosser – Thomasville – 1940   316
6. Stan Wysocki – Cordele – 1940   314
7. Ray Seidel – Waycross – 1948   303
8. Lloyd Gross – Moultrie – 1939   293
   Kerr Williams – Moultrie – 1940   293
10. Ace Adams – Cordele – 1937   287
    John Barnett – Waycross – 1941   287

Most Innings Pitched
1. Ace Adams – Cordele – 1937   339
2. Calvin Kirksey – Tallahassee – 1942   310
3. Lloyd Gross – Moultrie – 1939   303
4. Wally Deal – Valdosta – 1940   299
5. Taylor Phillips – Waycross – 1952   297
6. Lefty West – Americus – 1939   294
7. Walt Purcey – Cordele – 1940   291
8. Krim Bess – Albany – 1936   290
   Harry Raulerson – Waycross – 1951   290
10. Stan Ferens – Albany – 1940   289

Georgia State League All-Time Single Season Records

Batting
Highest Batting Average (minimum 100 at bats)
1. Ollie Tucker – Cedartown – 1921   .438
2. Don Brennan – Dublin – 1951   .420
3. Ike Boone – Cedartown – 1920   .412
   --- Thrasher – Cordele – 1914   .412
5. Jim Stoyle – Sparta – 1949   .400
   Edd Hartness – Eastman – 1950   .400
7. Dick LaFaive – Sandersville – 1955   .398
8. C.M. Chancey – Americus – 1913   .386
   Walt Sowers – Baxley – 1950   .386
10. George Thrasher – LaGrange – 1921   .385

Most Hits
1. Alvin Jenkins – Jesup – 1951   207
2. Edd Hartness – Eastman – 1950   201
3. Jim Stoyle – Sparta – 1949   191
   Jim Beavers - Hazlehurst-Baxley – 1952   191
5. Ted Patterson – Sparta – 1949   189
6. Jim Sosebee – Jesup – 1953   186
7. Charlie Ridgeway – Fitzgerald – 1950   183
   Ray Warzyniak – Eastman – 1953   183
9. Fred Tschudin – Douglas – 1949   182
   Cotton Chafin – Eastman – 1949   182
   Jim Smith – Vidalia – 1949   182

Most Runs
1. Sam Buell – Dublin – 1954   150
2. Eli Maricich – Eastman – 1953   139
3. Edd Hartness – Eastman – 1950   137
4. Alvin Jenkins – Jesup – 1951   135
5. Buddy Gilbert – Douglas – 1954   134
6. Bob Zuccarini - Hazlehurst-Baxley – 1953   131
7. Jim Martin – Douglas – 1930   130
   Parnell Ruark – Dublin – 1951   130
   Van Davis – Douglas – 1953   130
10. Charlie Ridgeway – Fitzgerald – 1950   129

Most Total Bases
1. Edd Hartness – Eastman – 1950   331
2. Jim Stoyle – Sparta – 1949   319
3. Jim Beavers - Hazlehurst-Baxley – 1952   310
4. Van Davis – Douglas – 1953   308
5. John Tidwell – Dublin – 1950   292
   Parnell Ruark – Dublin – 1950   292
   Parnell Ruark – Dublin – 1951   292
8. Ray Warzyniak – Eastman – 1953   291
9. Jim Caudle – Eastman – 1953   290
10. Eli Maricich – Eastman – 1953   289

Most Doubles
1. Edd Hartness – Eastman – 1950   48
2. Jim Burns – Vidalia – 1952   47
3. Jim Beavers – Hazlehurst-Baxley – 1952   46
4. Bobby Driggers – Vidalia – 1954   45
5. Chet Kanavage – Baxley – 1949   43
   Dan Hoard – Eastman – 1952   43
7. Bill Barnes – Tifton – 1949   42
   Jim Sosebee – Jesup – 1953   42
9. Edd Hartness – Eastman – 1949   41
   Bill Crago – Fitzgerald – 1950   41
   Ray Warzyniak – Eastman – 1953   41

Georgia Class-D Minor League Baseball Encyclopedia

Most Triples
1. Ted Patterson – Sparta – 1949   24
2. Chuck Oertel – Baxley – 1950   19
   Ted Patterson – Sand/East – 1953   19
4. Jim Stoyle – Sparta – 1949   18
5. Parnell Ruark – Sparta – 1949   17
   Bob McGee – Sandersville – 1954   17
7. Cotton Chafin – Eastman – 1949   15
8. Everett Bankston – Cordele – 1914   14
9. *six players tied with   12

Most Home Runs
1. Van Davis – Douglas – 1953   44
2. Parnell Ruark – Dublin – 1950   39
3. Parnell Ruark – Dublin – 1951   32
4. Everett Bankston – Cordele – 1914   31
   Chuck Quimby – Statesboro – 1952   31
   Van Davis – Douglas – 1954   31
7. Van Davis – Douglas – 1950   30
   Jim Warren – Statesboro – 1954   30
9. Van Davis – Douglas – 1951   29
10. Eli Maricich – Eastman – 1953   29

Most Extra Base Hits
1. Edd Hartness – Eastman – 1950   79
2. Jim Stoyle – Sparta – 1949   74
3. Jim Burns – Vidalia – 1952   72
   Jim Beavers – Hazlehurst-Baxley – 1952   72
5. Van Davis – Douglas – 1953   69
6. Earl Hartman – Tifton – 1949   67
   Parnell Ruark – Dublin – 1950   67
   Bill McGhee – Hazlehurst-Baxley – 1952   67
   Ray Warzyniak – Eastman – 1953   67
   Bobby Driggers – Vidalia – 1954   67

Most Runs Batted In
1. Van Davis – Douglas – 1953   159
2. Jim Burns – Vidalia – 1952   155
3. Parnell Ruark – Dublin – 1951   140
   Ray Warzyniak – Eastman – 1953   140
5. Van Davis – Douglas – 1951   139
6. Edd Hartness – Eastman – 1949   136
7. Van Davis – Douglas – 1954   135
8. Earl Hartman – Tifton – 1949   134
   Edd Hartness – Eastman – 1950   134
   Jim Caudle – Eastman – 1953   134

Most Stolen Bases
1. Charlie Ridgeway – Fitzgerald – 1948   80
2. Gerald Peters – Statesboro – 1954   66
3. Charlie Ridgeway – Fitzgerald – 1950   63
   Jim Martin – Douglas – 1950   63
5. Wilbur Caldwell – Eastman – 1952   58
6. Jim Martin – Douglas – 1949   54
7. Bill Henderson – Fitzgerald – 1950   52
   Charlie Ridgeway – Fitzgerald – 1952   52
9. Cotton Chafin – Eastman – 1949   51
10. Hector Faberlle – Douglas – 1952   49

Fielding
Most Put-Outs
1. Edd Hartness 1B – Eastman – 1950   1,307
2. Van Davis 1B – Douglas – 1950   1,274
3. Sam Robertson 1B – Douglas – 1949   1,271
4. Earl Hartman 1B – Tifton – 1949   1,255
5. Van Davis 1B – Douglas – 1951   1,228
6. Jerome Silverman 1B – Vidalia – 1949   1,224
7. Edd Hartness 1B – Eastman – 1949   1,212
8. Bob Reid 1B – Eastman – 1952   1,198
9. Tom Duga 1B – Tifton – 1950   1,138
10. Bill Enos 1B – Baxley – 1950   1,128

Most Assists
1. Emil Rey SS – Douglas – 1950   449
2. Emil Rey SS – Douglas – 1949   446
3. Lew Hallford SS – Jesup – 1950   442
4. Jim Morrison SS – Tifton – 1950   434
5. Roy Baker 2B – Douglas – 1950   423
6. Bill Barnes 2B – Tifton – 1949   415
7. Orestes Perada 2B – Douglas – 1949   410
8. Ralph Fall SS – Dubl/Jesu – 1951   392
9. Emil Rey SS – Douglas – 1952   386
10. John Mallard 2B, SS – Jesup – 1953   381

Most Errors
1. Harold Lanoux SS – Sandersville – 1956   70
2. Jim Wilson 2B, 3B, SS, P – Sandersville – 1954   69
3. Bob Shawver SS – Hazlehurst-Baxley – 1952   68
   Harold Green 3B – Vidalia – 1954   68
5. Bobby Howard SS – Fitzgerald – 1950   65
6. Bryce Carmichael 2B – Baxley – 1949   62
7. Jim Smith 3B, SS – Vidalia-Lyons – 1948   61
   Lew Hallford SS – Jesup – 1950   61
9. Ralph Fall SS – Vidalia – 1950   60
10. Fred Weaver SS – Fitzgerald – 1952   59

Pitching
Most Wins
1. Don Rudolph – Jesup – 1951   28
2. Mike Rossi – Vidalia – 1949   25
3. Charles Smalley – Dublin – 1950   23
   Jim Harp – Eastman – 1951   23
5. Phil Gilbert – Vidalia – 1954   22
6. Paul Brock – Sparta – 1948   21
   Luis Fernandez – Tifton – 1949   21
   George Cook – Sparta – 1949   21
   Dario Jiminez – Fitzgerald – 1950   21
   Dean Lakatosh – Dublin – 1954   21
   Gil Bassetti – Sandersville – 1956   21

Most Losses
1. Raul Villamea – Dublin – 1952   20
2. Noel Oquendo – Fitzgerald – 1949   19
3. John Merget – Vidalia – 1950   18
4. Joe Grasso – Douglas – 1949   17
5. --- Hall – Cordele – 1913   16
   Fred Plushanski – Vidalia – 1953   16
7. Rudy Belakovy – Douglas – 1948   15
   Ed Sherman – Vidalia – 1950   15
   Noel Oquendo – Fitzgerald – 1950   15
   Bill Hopkins – Baxley – 1950   15
   Fred Pippin – Fitzgerald – 1952   15

Highest Winning Percentage (10 game minimum)
1. Jim Harden – Eastman – 1948   .929
2. Don Quinn – Douglas – 1953   .917
3. Wilbur Osthoff – Dublin – 1949   .900
   Don Vaughn – Vidalia – 1954   .900
5. Jerry Jones – Douglas – 1952   .857
6. Dick Welage – Douglas – 1955   .846
7. Sid Leon – Sparta – 1948   .833
8. John Leatherberry – Dublin – 1954   .818
   Larry McClaskey – Vidalia – 1955   .818
10. Frank Clements – Eastman – 1952   .813

Lowest Earned Run Average (100 inning minimum)
1. Jim Harden – Eastman – 1948   1.36
2. Paul Brock – Sparta – 1948   1.38
3. Dick Stigman – Vidalia – 1956   1.44
4. Sid Leon – Sparta – 1948   1.48

5. Kermit Schmidt – Fitzgerald – 1948   1.78
6. Wilbur Caldwell – Douglas – 1955   2.03
7. John McCormick – Sparta – 1948   2.11
8. Lefty Guise – Douglas – 1951   2.16
9. Julian Morgan – Vidalia-Lyons – 1948   2.23
    Phil Gilbert – Vidalia – 1954   2.23

Most Strikeouts
1. Paul Brock – Sparta – 1948   270
2. Dick Stigman – Vidalia – 1956   263
3. Jimmie Hiland - Hazlehurst-Baxley – 1954   247
4. Noel Oquendo – Dublin – 1952   245
5. Charles Smalley – Dublin – 1950   237
6. Bob Scalisi – Fitzgerald – 1950   236
7. Noel Oquendo – Fitzgerald – 1949   224
8. Gil Bassetti – Sandersville – 1956   219
9. Billy Green – Douglas – 1954   218
10. Ralph Hisey – Dubl/East – 1949   203

Most Bases on Balls
1. Ralph Hisey – Dubl/East – 1949   187
2. Fred Pippin – Fitzgerald – 1952   183
3. Don Vaughn – Dublin – 1952   173
4. Noel Oquendo – Fitzgerald – 1949   171
5. Marcelo Fernandez – Vidalia – 1950   170
6. Dean Lakatosh – Dublin – 1954   157
7. John Sullivan – Fitz/East – 1951   153
8. Joe Grasso – Douglas – 1949   150
9. Noel Oquendo – Fitzgerald – 1950   148
10. Noel Oquendo – Dublin – 1952   147

Most Hits Allowed
1. Raul Villamea – Dublin – 1952   288
2. Bob Scalisi – Fitzgerald – 1950   273
3. Fred Pippin – Fitzgerald – 1952   269
4. Ted Patterson – Douglas – 1954   262
5. Don Bradley - Hazlehurst-Baxley – 1954   259
6. Paul Gehringer – Baxley – 1950   258
7. Dario Jiminez – Douglas – 1950   252
8. Jim Harp – Eastman – 1951   250
9. Ed Sherman – Vidalia – 1950   248
10. Fred Plushanski – Vidalia – 1953   247

Most Innings Pitched
1. Mike Rossi – Vidalia – 1949   325
2. Noel Oquendo – Fitzgerald – 1949   297
3. Don Rudolph – Jesup – 1951   285
4. George Cook – Sparta – 1949   276
5. Bob Scalisi – Fitzgerald – 1950   274
6. Luis Fernandez – Tifton – 1949   271
7. Noel Oquendo – Dublin – 1952   269
8. Jerry Simon – Dubl/Tift – 1949   268
9. Jim Harp – Eastman – 1949   267
    Higgins Duncan – Douglas – 1950   267

Georgia Class-D League Player/Pitcher Register

Register Listing Example

YR	TEAM	LG	G	AB	R	H	2B	3B	HR	RBI	SB	BB	SO	BA	POS	PO	A	E	FA	GP	W	L	ERA	IP	H	SO	BB
Blackburn, James Ray "Jim"			BR TR 6'4" 175 lbs. b. 06/19/1924 Warsaw, KY d. 10/26/1969 Cincinnati, OH																								
1941	Cordele	GFL	12	23	0	4	2	0	0	3	0	1	4	0.174	P	1	5	0	1.000	11	1	3	7.16	49	66	13	15
1942	Cordele	GFL	24	62	6	18	4	0	0	5	0	3	15	0.290	P	5	28	5	0.868	23	8	11	3.76	153	160	83	63

The above register listing example is to be used as a guide for reading the player/pitcher register. Each part of the register is defined as follows.

Each player's name is in bold in order of last name, first name, middle name, and nickname listed in quotes. In the example above, **Blackburn** is the last name, **James** is the first name, **Ray** is the middle name, and **Jim** is the player's nickname.

To the right of the player's name, on the same line, is the player's vital information. **BR** indicicates that the player batted right-handed, and **TR** indicates that the player threw right-handed. **BL** is listed for left-handed batting players, and **TL** for left-handed throwing players. Switch-hitting players are listed as **BS**. The player's height and weight are listed next as **6'4" 175 lbs.** Next is **b. 06/19/1924 Warsaw, KY**, the player's birthdate and birthplace. If the player is deceased and his date and place of death are known, this information is listed next. In the example, it's listed as **d. 10/26/1969 Cincinnati, OH**. Not all of the vital information was available for all players. What was available is listed in the register.

Across the top of each page of the register are abbreviated column headings for each statistic that is listed for each player. Here are the definitions for each column heading in the order they appear left to right at the top of each page.

YR = Year that the player played in a Georgia Class-D league.
TEAM = Team that the player played for.
LG = Georgia league that the player played for. Abbreviations for each league are:
    GAL = Georgia-Alabama League
    GFL = Georgia-Florida League
    GSL = Georgia State League
    ESL = Empire State League (Georgia State League)
    FLAG = Florida-Alabama-Georgia League (Georgia State League)
G = Games player appeared in.
AB = At Bats.
R = Runs scored.
H = Hits.
2B = Doubles hit.
3B = Triples hit.
HR = Home runs hit.
RBI = Runs Batted In.
SB = Stolen Bases.
BB = Bases on Balls player was issued by opposing pitchers.
SO = Strikeouts player was issued by opposing pitchers.
BA = Batting Average. Calculated as H/AB.
POS = Position(s) player played on defense.
PO = Put Outs made while playing defense.
A = Assists of put outs made while playing defense.
E = Errors committed while playing defense.
FA = Fielding Average. Calculated as (PO+A)/(PO+A+E).
GP = Games player appeared in as a pitcher.
W = Games won by player as pitcher of record.
L = Games lost by player as pitcher of record.
ERA = Earned Run Average. Calculated as (Earned Runs/IP)x9
IP = Innings pitched by pitcher.
H = Hits allowed by pitcher.
SO = Strikeouts issued by pitcher.
BB = Baseball on Balls issued by pitcher.

Not all of this information was available for all players. What was available is listed in the register.

Georgia Class-D Minor League Baseball Encyclopedia

YR	TEAM	LG	G	AB	R	H	2B	3B	HR	RBI	SB	BB	SO	BA	POS	PO	A	E	FA	GP	W	L	ERA	IP	H	SO	BB
Aaron, W.M.																											
1914	Rome	GAL	29	94	6	21				0				0.223	P	12	69	6	0.931	29							
1915	Rome	GAL	20	56	5	7	0	0	0					0.125	P	3	41	5	0.898	18	9	8					
Aase, Kermit																											
1938	Cordele	GFL	10	23	1	6	0	0	0	4	0	0	9	0.261	P	3	14	0	1.000	8	2	5	5.00	54	61	20	28
1939	Thomasville	GFL													P								<45				
Abadie, Benjamin "Ben"		BR TR																									
1949	Waycross	GFL	76	289	45	84	14	5	5	57	7	21	47	0.291	OF	121	7	12	0.914								
Abbott, ---																											
1914	Gadsden	GAL	31	86	5	11				0				0.128	P	83	42	11	0.919	31							
1914	Anniston	GAL	86	330	35	69				12				0.209	3B	378	172	40	0.932								
Abell, ---																											
1928	Gadsden - Lindale	GAL	39	144	14	38	4	1	0	3	8	10		0.264	1B	332	12	7	0.980								
Abercrombie, ---																											
1915	Griffin	GAL	<6												P					<6							
Abrams, Norman "Norm"		BL TR																									
1953	Cordele	GFL	137	522	81	125	13	4	0	44	12	65	51	0.239	2B, 3B, SS	219	296	70	0.880								
Abreu, Joseph "Joe"		BR TR																									
1947	Newnan	GAL	104	396	84	115	28	2	8	91	22	66	29	0.290	M, 2B	321	333	22	0.967								
Ackerman, Robert "Bob"		BR TR																									
1962	Moultrie	GFL	64	229	35	67	13	2	1	33	0	38	24	0.293	OF	74	6	8	0.909								
Acree, John T.																											
1949	Sparta	GSL	15	46	14	15	3	0	0	1	0	0	9	0.326	OF	12	0	4	0.750								
Acton, James "Jim"		BR TR																									
1948	LaGrange	GAL	97	344	70	114	19	4	14	80	10	69	43	0.331	M, 1B, OF, C	457	46	25	0.953								
Adair, Hubert P.		BR TR																									
1953	Waycross	GFL	21	56	10	8	1	0	0	2	1	10	7	0.143	OF	18	1	2	0.905								
Adair, Marion Danne "Bill"		BR TR b. 02/10/1913 d. 06/17/2002 Minette, AL																									
1956	Valdosta	GFL	12	14	4	5	1	0	2	9	1	5	1	0.357	M												
Adair, Thomas "Tommy"		BR TR																									
1939	Americus	GFL	50	99	12	32	0	0	0	3	1	9	9	0.323	UT, P	16	50	7	0.904	35	8	13	3.47	192	196	71	97
1940	Americus	GFL	60	196	26	62	1	1	0	20	4	18	7	0.316	P, IF					31	10	13	3.61	222	245	89	66
1946	Americus	GFL	29	58	8	14	1	0	0	2	0	9	6	0.241	P	4	62	2	0.971	26	12	8	2.72	169	157	96	53
1948	Americus	GFL	17	49	3	12	2	0	0	6	0	1	4	0.245	P	11	18	0	1.000	16	7	6	4.19	118	136	51	28
Adam, Richard "Dick"		BR TR																									
1954	Vidalia	GSL	30	48	6	9	0	0	0	7	0	9	12	0.188	P	11	21	0	1.000	29	10	4	4.24	140	126	49	54
1955	Vidalia	GSL	4	4		2								0.500	P					3	0	2					
Adamcewicz, Erwin		BR TL																									
1948	Albany	GFL	140	549	92	153	29	5	1	68	8	57	94	0.279	OF	205	12	15	0.935								
1949	Albany	GFL	27	107	17	29	8	1	1	19	1	16	21	0.271	OF	44	1	2	0.957								
Adams, Ace Townsend "Ace"		BR TR 5'10" 182 lbs. b. 04/02/1912 Willows, CA																									
1937	Cordele	GFL	66	196	23	48	9	2	3	34	0	18	17	0.245	P	31	69	9	0.917	45	26	13	2.34	339	287	218	100
1952	Fitzgerald	GSL	10	7	1	4	1	0	0	3	0	2	1	0.571	M												
Adams, Carl		BR TR																									
1950	Thomasville	GFL	21	50	9	11	2	0	0	1	0	4	18	0.220	P	5	19	2	0.923	21	12	6	3.66	128	150	76	37
Adams, Henry																											
1939	Waycross	GFL	10	29	3	8	2	1	0	7	0	1	4	0.276	OF	10	2	0	1.000								
Adams, Jerome		BR TR																									
1953	Tifton	GFL	22	51	3	5	2	0	0	1	0	4	30	0.098	C	62	5	1	0.985								
1954	Sandersville	GSL	19	56	2	8	0	0	0	4	0	7	15	0.143	C	80	11	4	0.958								
Adams, John E.		BL TL																									
1953	Waycross	GFL	30	69	7	15	2	0	0	6	0	4	13	0.217	P	9	32	5	0.891	25	8	10	3.57	169	164	86	71
Adams, Kenneth E. "Ken"		BR TR																									
1952	Fitzgerald	GSL	42	100	16	28	3	1	0	7	0	6	11	0.280	OF, P	20	22	2	0.955	22	5	9	3.73	147	161	77	48
1953	Fitzgerald	GFL	28	59	8	11	1	0	0	5	0	12	11	0.186	P					12	3	3	4.65	62	78	22	21
Adams, Marvin R.																											
1929	Cedartown	GAL	14	11	0	2	0	0	0		1	2		0.182	P					8	1	3		26	34	14	6
1930	Cedartown	GAL	6												P					6	0	2	12.86	21	37	12	12
Adams, Phil C.																											
1948	Valdosta	GFL	<10																									
Adams, Robert Eugene "Bob"		BR TR																									
1947	LaGrange	GAL	14	49	12	14	0	0	0	5	2	6	13	0.286	SS	34	33	4	0.944								
1948	LaGrange	GAL	122	437	94	101	23	2	2	45	8	96	86	0.231	2B, SS	281	342	44	0.934								
1951	LaGrange	GAL	111	475	102	158	28	7	6	106	25	41	58	0.333	2B, 3B, SS	273	315	47	0.926								
Adams, Robert G. "Bob"		BR TR																									
1948	Tallassee	GAL	101	395	68	118	21	10	1	39	10	38	35	0.299	2B, 3B, SS, OF	239	218	24	0.950								
1949	Tallassee	GAL	121	501	73	126	29	9	4	52	7	31	60	0.251	SS	218	401	37	0.944								
1950	Alexander City	GAL	126	492	86	138	30	6	7	91	21	53	68	0.280	2B, 3B, SS	240	312	32	0.945								
Adams, Thomas "Tom"		BL																									
1948	Valdosta	GFL	11	39	2	9	0	1	0	2	1	2	12	0.231													
Adcock, Robert H. "Bob"		BR TR																									
1949	Griffin	GAL	92	315	80	109	20	13	6	69	13	83	52	0.346	OF	176	20	16	0.925								
1949	Thomasville	GFL	25	89	17	25	3	1	2	13	2	18	24	0.281	OF	37	2	3	0.929								
1951	Eastman	GSL	40	145	22	53	11	2	1	29	4	31	9	0.366	OF	96	6	3	0.971								
Addison, George		BL TR																									
1940	Americus	GFL	19	70	12	24	6	0	0	13	1	9	10	0.343	OF	22	4	6	0.813								

Georgia Class-D Minor League Baseball Encyclopedia

YR	TEAM	LG	G	AB	R	H	2B	3B	HR	RBI	SB	BB	SO	BA	POS	PO	A	E	FA	GP	W	L	ERA	IP	H	SO	BB
Aaron, W.M.																											
1914	Rome	GAL	29	94	6	21					0			0.223	P	12	69	6	0.931	29							
1915	Rome	GAL	20	56	5	7	0	0	0					0.125	P	3	41	5	0.898	18	9	8					
Aase, Kermit																											
1938	Cordele	GFL	10	23	1	6	0	0	0	4	0	0	9	0.261	P	3	14	0	1.000	8	2	5	5.00	54	61	20	28
1939	Thomasville	GFL													P									<45			
Abadie, Benjamin "Ben"		BR TR																									
1949	Waycross	GFL	76	289	45	84	14	5	5	57	7	21	47	0.291	OF	121	7	12	0.914								
Abbott, ---																											
1914	Gadsden	GAL	31	86	5	11					0			0.128	P	83	42	11	0.919	31							
1914	Anniston	GAL	86	330	35	69				12				0.209	3B	378	172	40	0.932								
Abell, ---																											
1928	Gadsden - Lindale	GAL	39	144	14	38	4	1	0	3	8	10	0.264		1B	332	12	7	0.980								
Abercrombie, ---																											
1915	Griffin	GAL	<6												P					<6							
Abrams, Norman "Norm"		BL TR																									
1953	Cordele	GFL	137	522	81	125	13	4	0	44	12	65	51	0.239	2B, 3B, SS	219	296	70	0.880								
Abreu, Joseph "Joe"		BR TR																									
1947	Newnan	GAL	104	396	84	115	28	2	8	91	22	66	29	0.290	M, 2B	321	333	22	0.967								
Ackerman, Robert "Bob"		BR TR																									
1962	Moultrie	GFL	64	229	35	67	13	2	1	33	0	38	24	0.293	OF	74	6	8	0.909								
Acree, John T.																											
1949	Sparta	GSL	15	46	14	15	3	0	0	1	0	0	9	0.326	OF	12	0	4	0.750								
Acton, James "Jim"		BR TR																									
1948	LaGrange	GAL	97	344	70	114	19	4	14	80	10	69	43	0.331	M, 1B, OF, C	457	46	25	0.953								
Adair, Hubert P.		BR TR																									
1953	Waycross	GFL	21	56	10	8	1	0	0	2	1	10	7	0.143	OF	18	1	2	0.905								
Adair, Marion Danne "Bill"		BR TR b. 02/10/1913 d. 06/17/2002 Minette, AL																									
1956	Valdosta	GFL	12	14	4	5	1	0	2	9	1	5	1	0.357	M												
Adair, Thomas "Tommy"		BR TR																									
1939	Americus	GFL	50	99	12	32	0	0	0	3	1	9	9	0.323	UT, P	16	50	7	0.904	35	8	13	3.47	192	196	71	97
1940	Americus	GFL	60	196	26	62	1	1	0	20	4	18	7	0.316	P, IF					31	10	13	3.61	222	245	89	66
1946	Americus	GFL	29	58	8	14	1	0	0	2	0	9	6	0.241	P	4	62	2	0.971	26	12	8	2.72	169	157	96	53
1948	Americus	GFL	17	49	3	12	2	0	0	6	0	1	4	0.245	P	11	18	0	1.000	16	7	6	4.19	118	136	51	28
Adam, Richard "Dick"		BR TR																									
1954	Vidalia	GSL	30	48	6	9	0	0	0	7	0	9	12	0.188	P	11	21	0	1.000	29	10	4	4.24	140	126	49	54
1955	Vidalia	GSL	4	4		2								0.500	P					3	0	2					
Adamcewicz, Erwin		BR TL																									
1948	Albany	GFL	140	549	92	153	29	5	1	68	8	57	94	0.279	OF	205	12	15	0.935								
1949	Albany	GFL	27	107	17	29	8	1	1	19	1	16	21	0.271	OF	44	1	2	0.957								
Adams, Ace Townsend "Ace"		BR TR 5'10" 182 lbs. b. 04/02/1912 Willows, CA																									
1937	Cordele	GFL	66	196	23	48	9	2	3	34	0	18	17	0.245	P	31	69	9	0.917	45	26	13	2.34	339	287	218	100
1952	Fitzgerald	GSL	10	7	1	4	1	0	0	3	0	2	1	0.571	M												
Adams, Carl		BR TR																									
1950	Thomasville	GFL	21	50	9	11	2	0	0	1	0	4	18	0.220	P	5	19	2	0.923	21	12	6	3.66	128	150	76	37
Adams, Henry																											
1939	Waycross	GFL	10	29	3	8	2	1	0	7	0	1	4	0.276	OF	10	2	0	1.000								
Adams, Jerome		BR TR																									
1953	Tifton	GFL	22	51	3	5	2	0	0	1	0	4	30	0.098	C	62	5	1	0.985								
1954	Sandersville	GSL	19	56	2	8	0	0	0	4	0	7	15	0.143	C	80	11	4	0.958								
Adams, John E.		BL TL																									
1953	Waycross	GFL	30	69	7	15	2	0	0	6	0	4	13	0.217	P	9	32	5	0.891	25	8	10	3.57	169	164	86	71
Adams, Kenneth E. "Ken"		BR TR																									
1952	Fitzgerald	GSL	42	100	16	28	3	1	0	7	0	6	11	0.280	OF, P	20	22	2	0.955	22	5	9	3.73	147	161	77	48
1953	Fitzgerald	GFL	28	59	8	11	1	0	0	5	0	12	11	0.186	P					12	3	3	4.65	62	78	22	21
Adams, Marvin R.																											
1929	Cedartown	GAL	14	11	0	2	0	0	0		1	2	0	0.182	P					8	1	3		26	34	14	6
1930	Cedartown	GAL	6												P					6	0	2	12.86	21	37	12	12
Adams, Phil C.																											
1948	Valdosta	GFL	<10																									
Adams, Robert Eugene "Bob"		BR TR																									
1947	LaGrange	GAL	14	49	12	14	0	0	0	5	2	6	13	0.286	SS	34	33	4	0.944								
1948	LaGrange	GAL	122	437	94	101	23	2	2	45	8	96	86	0.231	2B, SS	281	342	44	0.934								
1951	LaGrange	GAL	111	475	102	158	28	7	6	106	25	41	58	0.333	2B, 3B, SS	273	315	47	0.926								
Adams, Robert G. "Bob"		BR TR																									
1948	Tallassee	GAL	101	395	68	118	21	10	1	39	10	38	35	0.299	2B, 3B, SS, OF	239	218	24	0.950								
1949	Tallassee	GAL	121	501	73	126	29	9	4	52	7	31	60	0.251	SS	218	401	37	0.944								
1950	Alexander City	GAL	126	492	86	138	30	6	7	91	21	53	68	0.280	2B, 3B, SS	240	312	32	0.945								
Adams, Thomas "Tom"		BL																									
1948	Valdosta	GFL	11	39	2	9	0	1	0	2	1	2	12	0.231													
Adcock, Robert H. "Bob"		BR TR																									
1949	Griffin	GAL	92	315	80	109	20	13	6	69	13	83	52	0.346	OF	176	20	16	0.925								
1949	Thomasville	GFL	25	89	17	25	3	1	2	13	2	18	24	0.281	OF	37	2	3	0.929								
1951	Eastman	GSL	40	145	22	53	11	2	1	29	4	31	9	0.366	OF	96	6	3	0.971								
Addison, George		BL TR																									
1940	Americus	GFL	19	70	12	24	6	0	0	13	1	9	10	0.343	OF	22	4	6	0.813								

Georgia Class-D Minor League Baseball Encyclopedia

YR	TEAM	LG	G	AB	R	H	2B	3B	HR	RBI	SB	BB	SO	BA	POS	PO	A	E	FA	GP	W	L	ERA	IP	H	SO	BB
Allen, Edwin "Ed"		BL TR																									
1958	Thomasville	GFL	86	314	59	99	17	3	5	49	6	72	57	0.315	1B, OF	326	34	12	0.968								
Allen, Frank Leon "Frank"		BR TR 5'9" 175 lbs. b. 08/26/1889 Newbern, AL d. 07/30/1933 Gainesville, AL																									
1928	Gadsden	GAL	38	108	11	28	7	0	1		0	6	19	0.259	OF, P	27	29	2	0.966	20	12	6	2.46	150	153	40	19
1929	Gadsden	GAL	6												P					6	0	1		7	13	2	11
1930	Talladega	GAL	12	48	9	12	0	0	1		5	12	5	0.250	1B	144	6	5	0.968								
Allen, Harry K.																											
1920	Carrollton	GSL		93	5	10	2	0	0		0			0.108	P, OF												
1921	Carrollton	GSL		28	2	1								0.036	P												
Allen, James W. "Jim"		BL TL																									
1953	Hazlehurst-Baxley	GSL	8											0.167	P						1	1		<45			
Allen, Joel		BL TR																									
1950	Douglas	GSL	66	241	41	53	4	0	0	12	0	43	26	0.220	OF	88	7	5	0.950								
Allen, John R. "Johnny"		BR TR																									
1946	LaGrange	GAL	129	495	76	127	15	7	3	42	10	59	56	0.257	2B, 3B, OF, P	210	82	20	0.936	1	0	0	0.00	3			
1947	LaGrange(57) - Carrollton(26)	GAL	83	310	55	75	12	8	1	23	6	65	37	0.242	2B, OF	172	44	11	0.952								
1948	Griffin	GAL	23	66	9	17	2	0	0	7	2	7	25	0.258	3B	19	20	8	0.830								
1951	Valley(2) - Alex City(60)	GAL	62	220	40	63	14	0	3	41	3	35	33	0.286	2B, 3B, OF	87	61	13	0.919								
Allen, L.																											
1939	Valdosta	GFL													P									<45			
Allen, William D. "Bill"		BR TL																									
1950	Waycross	GFL	38	59	4	6	0	0	0	1	0	6	28	0.102	P	4	45	9	0.845	37	6	14	5.08	170	174	135	144
1953	Waycross	GFL	59	122	11	21	2	0	0	6	4	6	34	0.172	OF, P	25	50	6	0.926	36	9	17	3.28	225	200	161	128
1953	Sandersville	GSL	10	24	1	3	1	0	0	0	0	0	5	0.125	P						0	2		<45			
1954	Waycross	GFL	13	29	4	5	0	0	0	0	0	0	3	9 0.172	P	2	9	2	0.846	10	5	4	3.53	74	70	49	43
Alleruzo, Larry																											
1936	Thomasville	GFL													P									<30			
Allison, E.B.																											
1915	LaGrange	GAL	58	221	17	42	6	0	0					0.190	2B	118	118	26	0.901								
Allison, James "Jim"		BR TR																									
1956	Thomson	GSL	21	27	1	2	1	0	0	2	0	1	10	0.074	P	4	11	2	0.882	21	4	4	4.76	68	57	51	44
1957	Fitzgerald	GFL	8	17		2								0.118	P					8	2	5	4.59	51	51	23	22
Allman, Frank		BL																									
1954	Albany	GFL	23	42	8	9	1	0	0	2	0	7	6	0.214													
Almeida, Daniel "Dan"		BR TR																									
1956	Vidalia	GSL	118	495	91	145	20	5	1	53	27	43	36	0.293	2B, 3B, P	248	314	51	0.917	1	0	0					
Almon, ---																											
1928	Gadsden	GAL	11	44	4	12	2	0	0		2	3	10	0.273	OF	31	2	0	1.000								
Alomar, Rafael		BR TR																									
1955	Douglas	GSL	105	433	70	131	22	8	8	79	8	26	56	0.303	OF	228	14	18	0.931								
Alonso, John		BR TR																									
1949	Alexander City	GAL	72	229	37	58	6	6	0	25	7	23	40	0.253	OF	96	3	6	0.943								
1950	Douglas	GSL	29	104	14	28	4	1	0	15	3	16	20	0.269	OF	43	1	8	0.846								
Alperman, Charles Augustus "Whitey"		BR TR 5'10" 180 lbs. b. 11/11/1879 Etna, PA d. 12/25/1942 Pittsburgh, PA																									
1913	Waycross	ESL	14	56	4	14	0	0	0					0.250	OF	24	10	2	0.944								
Alrick, Edward "Ed"																											
1949	Vidalia-Lyons - Sparta	GSL	13	9	0	3	0	0	0	1	0	0	5	0.333	P					13	2	6	9.55	49	64	25	61
Altomare, John		BR TR																									
1952	Jesup	GSL	42	66	6	9	1	0	0	3	0	13	20	0.136	P	3	14	0	1.000	36	11	8	4.72	143	150	73	71
Altomer, Louis "Lou"		BR TR																									
1953	Sandersville	GSL	8											0.308	P						2	2		<45			
1954	Waycross	GFL	4	5		0								0.000	P					4	1	1		<45			
Alvares, Ramon L.																											
1949	Fitzgerald	GSL	38	147	17	35	2	1	1	22	3	27	32	0.238	1B	318	20	7	0.980								
Alvarez, Alberto		BR TR																									
1955	Douglas	GSL	2	2		0								0.000													
1956	Douglas	GSL	112	395	78	104	18	5	3	60	23	79	37	0.263	C	553	71	21	0.967								
Alvarez, Demetro		BR TR																									
1958	Albany	GFL	25	43	8	8	3	0	1	4	0	10	15	0.186	OF	7	1	1	0.889								
Alvarez, Luis		BR TR																									
1951	Alexander City	GAL	32	66	5	9	1	0	0	3	0	4	16	0.136	P	6	35	1	0.976	30	8	10	4.95	151	181	63	81
Alvarez, Ultus		BR TR																									
1953	Thomasville	GFL	139	547	113	164	26	21	12	123	12	60	104	0.300	SS, OF	351	70	20	0.955								
Alves, Joseph "Joe"		BR TR																									
1953	Cordele	GFL	57	214	16	39	3	1	0	4	1	29	34	0.182	2B	165	174	30	0.919								
Amadee, Joe																											
1930	Talladega	GAL	16	40	6	9	1	3	0		2	2	11	0.225	P	0	19	2	0.905	13	7	3	5.91	67	115	31	27
Amaral, Dan																											
1936	Cordele	GFL	68	244	48	90	16	10	5	27	7			0.369	OF	136	5	5	0.966								
1937	Cordele	GFL	107	406	80	138	19	11	3	78	10	54	35	0.340	OF	162	10	6	0.966								
Amazon, H.W.																											
1914	LaGrange	GAL	75	241	15	44					10			0.183	1B	683	45	8	0.989								
1915	LaGrange	GAL	58	206	20	30	5	1	0					0.146	1B	555	24	10	0.983								
Ambrose, Richard "Dick"		BR TR																									
1953	Dublin	GSL	24	25	3	2	0	0	0	0	0	4	12	0.080	P	4	13	3	0.850	23	2	4	6.23	78	88	60	57
1954	Sandersville	GSL	12	19	1	1	0	0	0	0	0	0	12	0.053	P	1	9	0	1.000	12	1	8	4.22	49	47	27	16

Georgia Class-D Minor League Baseball Encyclopedia

YR	TEAM	LG	G	AB	R	H	2B	3B	HR	RBI	SB	BB	SO	BA	POS	PO	A	E	FA	GP	W	L	ERA	IP	H	SO	BB
Amburgey, Conley		BL TR																									
1956	Moultrie	GFL	91	308	61	68	11	5	3	28	6	59	57	0.221	OF	125	8	16	0.893								
1956	Douglas	GSL	8	19		2								0.105													
Ammon, Walter "Walt"																											
1935	Albany	GFL	39	98	9	19	4	1	0	1		6	27	0.194	P					39	21	12		263	253	63	65
1936	Albany	GFL	34	80	7	18	1	0	0	8	1			0.225	P					34	12	10	4.90	202		96	99
Ammons, Dewey		BL																									
1953	Thomasville	GFL	2											0.500													
Ammons, S.L. "Bud"																											
1928	Anniston	GAL	83	300	61	112	17	3	13		3	42	13	0.373	M, 1B	684	52	12	0.984								
1929	Anniston	GAL	37	140	27	43	10	0	1		7	26	7	0.307	M, 1B	330	29	5	0.986								
Amoroso, Dante		BR TR																									
1946	Valdosta	GFL	3												P					3	0	1	0.00	4	7	1	3
Anders, Howard		BL TL																									
1962	Brunswick	GFL	21	22	1	3	1	0	0	3	0	2	12	0.136	P	2	14	2	0.889	20	3	6	5.40	70	46	78	70
Anderson, ---																											
1913	Waycross	ESL	85	302	36	91	12	2	3					0.301	SS, OF	131	168	23	0.929								
1914	Waycross	GSL		315	35	73	6	2	0	24				0.232													
1915	Thomasville	FLAG	46												SS, OF	114	130	26	0.904								
Anderson, ---																											
1914	Valdosta	GSL		108	6	15	0	0	0	0				0.139													
Anderson, ---																											
1917	Tri-Cities	GAL	16	64	11	17	5	1	0	1				0.266	1B	156	7	1	0.994								
Anderson, ---																											
1930	Lindale	GAL	5												P					5	1	0	9.00	16	25	2	8
Anderson, ---		BR TR																									
1946	Carrollton	GAL	<10																								
Anderson, Carl Jr.		BL TR																									
1952	Vidalia	GSL	95	334	36	86	5	1	0	41	3	45	46	0.257	C	508	44	12	0.979								
Anderson, Frank M.																											
1935	Thomasville	GFL	9												P					9	2	4		56	51	29	19
1936	Thomasville	GFL	65	159	18	40	5	2	0	19	1			0.252	P					65	17	10	2.61	259		134	75
Anderson, Harrison		BR TR																									
1947	Waycross	GFL	11	47	10	12	4	0	1	7	0	4	2	0.255	1B	89	2	11	0.892								
Anderson, Jack																											
1941	Thomasville	GFL	102	387	51	111	11	6	5	57	4	34	70	0.287	1B	883	36	16	0.983								
Anderson, James D. "Jim"		BL TR																									
1957	Brunswick	GFL	78	258	44	68	17	0	5	45	7	72	42	0.264	2B, OF	247	122	19	0.951								
Anderson, Kenneth "Ken"		BR TR																									
1963	Waycross	GFL	68	226	26	53	7	1	3	16	9	24	48	0.235	OF	76	6	2	0.976								
Anderson, Marion																											
1929	Carrollton	GAL	74	274	41	96	20	6	0		3	29	14	0.350	2B	167	224	21	0.949								
1935	Americus	GFL	57	199	29	52	11	2	0	11		47	15	0.261	IF	150	173	5	0.985								
Anderson, Martin		BL TL																									
1947	Valley	GAL	22	49	8	15	0	1	0	6	0	4	21	0.306	P	4	17	2	0.913	18	8	6	3.71	119	118	93	64
Anderson, Richard A. "Dick"		BR TR																									
1947	Griffin	GAL	30	94	8	12	1	0	4	10	3	6	36	0.128	C	123	21	10	0.935								
Anderson, Richard K. "Dick"		BR TR																									
1962	Dublin	GFL	114	413	72	99	22	7	7	65	12	50	98	0.240	OF	174	14	14	0.931								
Anderson, Roger		BR TR																									
1955	Thomasville	GFL	31	93	14	16	5	1	1	7	1	13	17	0.172	1B	219	14	10	0.959								
Anderson, T.P.		BR TR																									
1950	Eastman	GSL	97	397	85	113	8	5	0	37	19	76	49	0.285	OF	199	22	15	0.936								
Anderson, Victor																											
1915	Griffin	GAL	16	44	1	3	0	0	0					0.068	P	3	37	3	0.930	13	5	4					
1916	Griffin	GAL	19	49	4	10				0				0.204	P												
Anderson, Walter "Walt"																											
1949	Fitzgerald	GSL	13	29	3	3	2	0	0	3	0	6	9	0.103	P	9	10	1	0.950	11	0	4	5.00	72	51	22	35
Anderson, William "Bill"		BL TR																									
1949	Tifton	GSL	11	26	4	4	1	0	0	0	0	2	11	0.154	P	1	13	0	1.000	11	4	1	4.19	58	36	23	37
1956	Dublin	GSL	74	261	44	75	19	4	12	47	1	39	64	0.287	1B, 2B	259	107	26	0.934								
1957	Thomasville	GFL	1	3		1								0.333													
Anderton, Sherman		BR TR																									
1956	Brunswick	GFL	11	10	0	0	0	0	0	0	0	1	7	0.000	P	3	5	0	1.000	11	1	3		<45			
Andres, Robert "Bob"		BR TR																									
1948	Thomasville	GFL	15	25	2	5	2	0	0	2	0	2	3	0.200	P	1	14	0	1.000	14	3	5	4.21	62	54	50	60
1949	Thomasville	GFL	12	16	1	4	1	0	0	0	0	1	5	0.250	P	2	8	1	0.909	11	2	3	2.60	52	45	32	28
Andrews, Chris		BR																									
1955	Valdosta	GFL	8	10		1								0.100													
Androsko, Stephen "Steve"		BR TR																									
1963	Thomasville	GFL	14	27	1	5	0	0	0	2	1	5	20	0.185	OF	7	1	2	0.800								
Androvich, Joseph A. "Joe"		BR																									
1952	Dublin	GSL	14	39	4	6	0	0	1	3	1	9	10	0.154													
Angeli, Joseph "Joe"		BR TR																									
1946	Tallahassee	GFL	125	465	79	119	22	9	6	79	16	60	73	0.256	OF	184	20	12	0.944								

Georgia Class-D Minor League Baseball Encyclopedia

YR	TEAM	LG	G	AB	R	H	2B	3B	HR	RBI	SB	BB	SO	BA	POS	PO	A	E	FA	GP	W	L	ERA	IP	H	SO	BB
Angelone, John		BR TR																									
1952	Valdosta	GFL	127	455	63	117	9	6	0	55	15	111	29	0.257	M, SS	296	407	30	0.959								
1953	Thomasville	GFL	131	465	101	142	15	7	0	79	13	111	23	0.305	M, SS, P	227	343	26	0.956		0	0	<45				
1954	Thomasville	GFL	13	43	4	10	1	0	0	2	0	2	4	0.233	M, 3B, P	11	26	3	0.925	1	0	0	<45				
Anile, Joseph "Joe"		BR TR																									
1953	Brunswick	GFL	9											0.263													
Anjeski, Elmer		BR TR																									
1946	Tallahassee	GFL	63	243	39	79	9	7	1	34	15	25	57	0.325	OF	120	12	8	0.943								
1947	Tallahassee	GFL	141	558	116	177	16	12	7	83	25	83	73	0.317	OF	308	16	16	0.953								
Annino, Alfio		BR TR																									
1935	Albany	GFL	87	312	53	92	21	6	0		9	26	44	0.295	IF	108	12	2	0.984								
1936	Albany	GFL	112	418	87	119	11	8	3	50	13			0.285	OF	291	12	9	0.971								
Annunziato, Alfred "Al"		BR TR 5'11" 170 lbs. b. 05/15/1915 Stamford, CT																									
1937	Americus	GFL	59	173	22	40	6	0	6	22	2	32	27	0.231	C	224	34	10	0.963								
1938	Americus	GFL	99	306	45	75	16	0	3	44	4	49	62	0.245	C	328	59	13	0.968								
Annunzio, Joe																											
1936	Thomasville	GFL	55	194	20	46	4	3	2	30	5			0.237	C	233	34	7	0.974								
Ansley, ---																											
1915	Brunswick	FLAG	<10																								
Anthon, Fred		BR TR																									
1963	Brunswick	GFL	54	155	12	32	9	0	2	13	2	27	40	0.206	2B, 3B	55	81	16	0.895								
Anthony, ---																											
1906	Albany	GSL													P												
Anthony, George W.		BR TR																									
1953	Thomasville	GFL	2											0.000	P						0	0	<45				
Anthony, Stanley "Stan"		BR TR																									
1950	Opelika	GAL	23	67	6	7	0	0	1	3	2	15	27	0.104	2B	62	51	3	0.974								
Antley, ---																											
1914	Waycross	GSL		117	12	21	5	0	1		0			0.179													
1915	Waycross	FLAG	38	100	6	19	1	0	0		3			0.190	OF, P	31	65	7	0.932	20	10	9		169	103	99	59
Antolick, Joseph "Joe"		BR TR 6'0" 185 lbs. b. 04/11/1916 Hokendauqua, PA																									
1948	Moultrie	GFL	98	297	36	76	14	1	1	48	7	31	25	0.256	M, C	381	42	11	0.975								
Antonangeli, Donald "Don"		BR TR																									
1963	Waycross	GFL	3	3	0	0	0	0	0	0	0	0	2	0.000	P					3	0	1	10.13	8	9	7	9
Apicella, James "Jim"		BR TR																									
1963	Brunswick	GFL	17	53	5	13	1	0	0	6	0	4	9	0.245	2B	34	25	6	0.908								
Appleby, Ellis																											
1942	Dothan	GFL	33	106	16	20	1	1	0	5	1	30	20	0.189	3B	52	84	18	0.883								
Appling, Horace																											
1936	Moultrie	GFL	10	39	4	11	2	1	0	1	0			0.282	OF	17	5	3	0.880								
Arbogast, Ford		BR TR																									
1954	Sandersville	GSL	60	222	22	55	7	6	3	32	4	9	25	0.248	2B, C	293	69	17	0.955								
Archaumbault, Charles		BR TR																									
1953	Valdosta	GFL	15	50	5	12	1	1	0	5	2	8	14	0.240	OF	11	6	2	0.895								
Archer, James William "Jim"		BR TL 6'0" 190 lbs. b. 05/25/1932 Max Meadows, VA																									
1951	LaGrange	GAL	9												P					9	2	3	7.24	46	58	34	28
Archer, Richard H. "Dick"		BR TR																									
1953	Dublin	GSL	4											0.000	P						0	0	<45				
Archipoli, Andrew "Andy"		TR																									
1940	Americus	GFL	84	351	59	91	14	3	1	35	10	33	50	0.259	2B	189	278	17	0.965								
1941	Valdosta	GFL	101	371	71	112	15	5	3	58	13	59	47	0.302	3B	194	183	45	0.893								
Arcia, Jose Raimundo "Jose" (Orta)		BR TR 6'3" 170 lbs. b. 08/22/1943 Havana, Cuba																									
1962	Moultrie(12) - Thomasville(4)	GFL	16	14	0	5	0	0	0	2	0	1	3	0.357	P	2	15	0	1.000	16	4	4	4.14	50	49	31	24
Arcoleo, Frank		BR TR																									
1948	Baxley	GSL	118	476	67	119	10	0	0	35	20	46	12	0.250	SS	219	253	54	0.897								
Ard, Thomas "Tom"		BL TL																									
1950	Valley	GAL	10	15	1	3	0	0	0	2	0	0	3	0.200	P	1	7	0	1.000								
Ardis, ---																											
1920	Carrollton	GSL	3	0	0	0	0	0	0																		
Arduini, Salvatore "Sal"		BR TR																									
1948	Thomasville	GFL	137	548	90	144	23	7	5	82	11	66	97	0.263	3B	129	268	45	0.898								
Arellanes, William "Bill"		BR TR																									
1955	Thomasville	GFL	42	166	19	39	7	1	1	16	1	19	53	0.235	3B	26	62	15	0.854								
1956	Thomasville	GFL	33	107	13	20	2	1	2	12	1	15	35	0.187	1B	223	13	3	0.987								
Arent, George		BR TR																									
1954	Brunswick	GFL	24	86	10	21	7	0	1	10	0	4	21	0.244	1B	44	9	5	0.914								
1954	Dublin	GSL	104	443	78	129	24	1	21	90	4	24	76	0.291	1B	847	62	25	0.973								
1955	Dublin	GSL	103	411	68	121	20	2	19	94	0	31	40	0.294	1B	774	63	26	0.970								
Arlitt, Adolph "Buzz"																											
1941	Moultrie	GFL	132	497	102	172	33	8	7	92	5	87	51	0.346	M, 1B, P	1169	92	31	0.976	9	1	0	5.00	27	25	15	15
Armstrong, Carl																											
1941	Americus - Thomasville	GFL	93	321	44	67	7	1	0	28	1	60	72	0.209	3B	99	186	39	0.880								
Arnitz, Peter "Pete"		BR TR																									
1958	Albany	GFL	6	6		1								0.167	P					6	0	2	<30				
Arnold, Merrill "Mel"		BL TL																									
1939	Cordele	GFL	139	537	78	163	22	7	4	63	13	67	56	0.304	OF	336	10	10	0.972								
1940	Cordele	GFL	97	378	71	125	16	9	2	54	13	56	28	0.331	OF	247	7	2	0.992								

Georgia Class-D Minor League Baseball Encyclopedia

YR	TEAM	LG	G	AB	R	H	2B	3B	HR	RBI	SB	BB	SO	BA	POS	PO	A	E	FA	GP	W	L	ERA	IP	H	SO	BB
Arnone, Robert "Bob"		BL TR																									
1963	Brunswick	GFL	21	47	7	6	0	0	0	1	0	8	6	0.128	OF	18	0	1	0.947								
Arroyo, Blas M. "Yaya"		BL TR 5'10" 155 lbs b. 10/08/1924 Cuba																									
1948	Carrollton	GAL	65	214	35	45	7	1	0	28	13	29	48	0.210	3B, OF, P	77	43	16	0.882	7	2	2	3.00	48	49	24	20
1950	Carrollton	GAL	33	71	15	20	3	0	2	10	0	7	6	0.282	P	6	12	1	0.947	18	9	7	5.37	104	105	52	72
Arterburn, Harry		BR TR																									
1951	Cordele	GFL	109	406	46	104	13	3	4	54	11	45	69	0.256	1B	840	44	11	0.988								
Asbill, Joseph "Joe"		BR																									
1952	Moultrie	GFL	12	20	0	3	0	0	0	0	0	0	3	0.150													
Ash, George		BR TR																									
1951	Americus	GFL	26	73	6	14	0	0	0	6	0	6	13	0.192	P	3	21	3	0.889	14	0	8	4.98	85	80	24	71
Ashcraft, William B. "Bill"																											
1950	Hazlehurst-Baxley	GSL													P					0	0						
Ashton, Andrew		BR TL																									
1953	Tifton	GFL	2											0.000	P					0	0		<45				
Ashworth, Johnny																											
1942	Dothan	GFL	6	13	0	3	0	0	0	1	0	4	2	0.231	P	0	9	0	1.000	5	1	2	7.31	32	52	7	11
Asinof, Eliot		BL TL 5'10" 180 lbs b. 07/13/1919 New York, NY																									
1940	Moultrie	GFL	15	54	8	16	2	0	0	7	1	8	10	0.296	1B	144	10	4	0.975								
Askew, ---																											
1913	Anniston	GAL	68	246	39	79					19			0.321	OF	114	13	12	0.914								
1914	Gadsden	GAL	59	219	22	54				4				0.247	1B, OF	239	58	9	0.971								
1915	Dothan	FLAG	<10																								
Asmer, John		BR TR																									
1946	Americus	GFL	46	113	19	26	5	1	0	16	1	9	8	0.230	P	13	53	4	0.943	35	24	6	2.81	240	209	132	99
1947	Americus	GFL	39	83	4	14	1	0	0	6	0	9	2	0.169	OF, P	18	24	3	0.933	25	7	11	6.02	127	151	80	68
1949	Moultrie	GFL	25	49	10	11	0	0	0	6	3	0.224	P	3	25	4	0.875	24	11	4	4.14	126	138	69	70
Aspromonte, Robert Thomas "Bob"		BR TR 6'2" 185 lbs b. 06/19/1938 Brooklyn, NY																									
1957	Thomasville	GFL	53	198	35	52	5	3	1	21	0	24	14	0.263	3B, SS	91	115	16	0.928								
Astin, Robert W. "Bob"		BR TR																									
1946	Newnan	GAL	3												P					3	1	0	0.00	9	13	5	6
1947	Newnan	GAL	32	97	11	28	2	0	0	8	1	8	13	0.289	OF	43	7	4	0.926								
Atchison, John		BR TR																									
1946	Thomasville	GFL	3												P					3	1	2	0.00	22	31	9	16
Atchley, Loy																											
1928	Ann - Car - Ced	GAL	61	185	29	59	8	2	4	4	8	20	0.319	OF, P	82	31	4	0.966	17	3	6	3.52	92	98	29	19
Atkinson, Don		BL TL																									
1939	Americus	GFL	10	17	1	0	0	0	0	0	0	2	7	0.000	P	2	11	0	1.000	0	4	6.89	47	63	17	18	
1940	Americus	GFL	<10												P					9	4	2	7.00	54	89	27	31
Attaway, Robert "Bob"		BL TR																									
1948	Albany	GFL	133	470	75	135	28	4	1	84	9	99	47	0.287	C	815	88	22	0.976								
Attride, ---																											
1915	Dothan	FLAG	27	99	9	24	3	0	1		1			0.242	C	171	30	5	0.976								
Atwater, Charles "Charlie"		BR TR																									
1939	Waycross	GFL	11	20	3	2	0	0	0	3	0	6	6	0.100	P	6	18	2	0.923	8	3	5	3.74	65	71	35	19
1940	Waycross	GFL	23	63	10	13	2	0	0	5	0	5	11	0.206	P					21	14	4	2.62	158	142	70	65
1941	Waycross - Thomasville	GFL	16	35	10	11	4	1	0	4	0	9	9	0.314	P	4	11	1	0.938	14	6	5	5.58	92	119	30	45
Atzert, George		BR TR																									
1948	Moultrie	GFL	13	16	2	2	0	0	0	1	0	1	5	0.125	P	3	11	0	1.000								
1949	Moultrie	GFL	25	54	6	11	0	0	0	0	0	4	22	0.204	P	4	36	3	0.930	25	9	6	3.00	153	171	64	65
Aucoin, Alvin J. "Al"		BR TR																									
1953	Waycross	GFL	82	258	39	82	20	0	8	27	3	39	6	0.318	M, OF, C, P	249	32	7	0.976	13	3	1	5.75	61	74	17	36
August, Joseph "Joe"		BR TR																									
1946	Tallahassee	GFL	13	51	9	11	1	0	1	7	3	6	12	0.216	OF	11	2	0	1.000								
Augustoni, William "Bill"		BL TL																									
1954	Waycross	GFL	22	42	9	15	2	0	0	5	1	12	12	0.357	P	6	19	3	0.893	17	5	6	4.38	115	68	124	131
Aurelio, Edward "Ed"		BR TR																									
1947	Tallassee	GAL	48	157	21	39	2	2	1	26	5	10	26	0.248	1B	288	9	5	0.983								
1948	Douglas	GSL	13	43	3	8	2	0	1	4	0	4	4	0.186	OF	7	3	4	0.714								
Austin, Alvin		BL TR																									
1948	Waycross	GFL	94	330	68	90	14	3	3	53	4	56	45	0.273	OF	122	11	6	0.957								
1949	Waycross	GFL	122	453	93	116	19	8	1	69	9	91	60	0.256	OF	200	11	10	0.955								
1950	Waycross	GFL	128	472	82	129	22	5	3	63	6	95	46	0.273	3B, OF	276	18	16	0.948								
Austin, Forrest E.																											
1942	Dothan	GFL	56	212	30	62	9	2	2	50	1	31	28	0.292	OF	68	19	7	0.926								
Austin, Robert E. "Bob"																											
1942	Dothan	GFL	8												P					8	3	5	5.57	63	77	42	35
Avera, James "Jim"		BR TR																									
1940	Cordele	GFL	58	187	25	40	11	0	3	23	4	16	43	0.214	P, IF					14	2	11	3.45	107	106	72	61
Averette, ---																											
1906	Americus	GSL													OF												
Averette, David "Dave"																											
1936	Cordele	GFL	23	88	17	26	4	2	2	15	2			0.295	OF	25	5	2	0.938								
Avery, ---																											
1928	Carrollton	GAL		21	1	4								0.190													
Avery, Kenneth "Ken"		BR TL																									
1962	Thomasville	GFL	9	25	0	3	1	0	0	4	0	2	7	0.120	P					9	6	2	2.88	72	67	58	17

Georgia Class-D Minor League Baseball Encyclopedia

YR	TEAM	LG	G	AB	R	H	2B	3B	HR	RBI	SB	BB	SO	BA	POS	PO	A	E	FA	GP	W	L	ERA	IP	H	SO	BB
Avinger, J. Frank		BL TR																									
1952	Fitzgerald	GSL	62	241	37	74	13	0	0	35	3	26	5	0.307	1B, OF	349	23	11	0.971								
Ayers, Lonzo		BR TR																									
1947	Newnan(15) - Griffin(32)	GAL	47	86	20	18	1	0	2	6	1	10	21	0.209	P	5	24	1	0.967	32	5	4	3.20	107	109	45	72
Ayers, W.F.																											
1939	Cordele	GFL													P											<45		
Aylmer, Robert "Bob"		BR TR																									
1956	Fitzgerald	GFL	21	34	4	3	1	1	0	3	0	2	11	0.088	P	2	13	1	0.938	17	4	6	3.44	81	79	69	33
Azcue, Jose Joaquin (Lopez) "Joe"		BR TR 6'0" 200 lbs. b. 08/18/1939 Cienfuegos, Cuba																									
1956	Moultrie	GFL	2	6		2								0.333													
1956	Douglas	GSL	57	140	16	33	8	1	0	23	1	12	25	0.236	OF, C	114	11	8	0.940								
Azzarello, Frank		BL TL																									
1950	Opelika	GAL	23	89	9	16	2	0	1	16	0	13	23	0.180	1B	197	8	3	0.986								
Babcock, Harry		BR TR																									
1953	Sandersville	GSL	27	104	18	29	4	5	1	13	6	12	17	0.279	OF	77	2	3	0.963								
Babcock, Owen		BR TR																									
1956	Fitzgerald	GFL	43	181	21	35	2	1	0	7	5	16	29	0.193	2B	114	144	17	0.938								
Babich, Richard "Dick"		BR TR																									
1956	Brunswick	GFL	138	537	65	155	31	1	3	90	3	53	43	0.289	1B, 3B	972	94	19	0.982								
Bach, Phillip "Phil"		BR TR																									
1953	Brunswick	GFL	10	20	6	4	1	0	0	0	0	6	8	0.200	P	3	17	1	0.952	10	4	2	4.09	55	47	27	36
Bacha, William "Bill"		BR TR																									
1947	Americus	GFL	98	379	55	93	18	4	1	39	9	31	52	0.245	3B	94	167	25	0.913								
Bachars, John "Medar"		BR TR																									
1953	Statesboro	GSL	20	62	7	13	0	1	0	4	0	7	7	0.210	OF	26	3	0	1.000								
1953	Waycross	GFL	50	177	13	38	0	0	1	17	1	22	33	0.215	OF	86	9	7	0.931								
Bachelor, Harry																											
1920	Rome	GSL		46	9	7	0	0	0		0			0.152	OF												
Bacque, Gene		BR TR																									
1957	Valdosta	GFL	6	5		0								0.000	P					6	0	2	<30				
Badia, Armenio		BR TR																									
1954	Tifton	GFL	99	345	51	86	11	3	11	57	6	38	94	0.249	OF, P	198	13	18	0.921	6	0	0	<45				
Badour, Robert "Bob"		BR TR																									
1953	Tifton	GFL	7											0.000	P						0	0	<45				
1953	Vidalia	GSL	10	18	2	5	0	0	0	2	1	3	3	0.278	P	3	12	0	1.000	10	1	3	6.85	46	53	21	32
Baggens, ---																											
1914	Americus - Valdosta	GSL		55	4	14	3	0	0		6			0.255													
Baglivi, Bill																											
1937	Thomasville	GFL	107	374	60	82	4	2	1	32	7	70	45	0.219	SS	197	341	50	0.915								
Bagwell, E.S.																											
1906	Valdosta	GSL													M, OF												
1913	Newnan	GAL													M												
Bagwell, James "Jim"		BR TR																									
1950	Thomasville	GFL	50	176	30	40	4	2	1	24	2	35	46	0.227	OF	109	6	7	0.943								
Bahnson, Richard "Dick"		BR TR																									
1952	Dublin	GSL	47	182	26	33	7	0	2	19	6	22	30	0.181	3B	38	92	11	0.922								
Bailey, ---																											
1917	Talladega	GAL	3	9	1	0	0	0	0		0			0.000	3B	3	3	1	0.857								
Bailey, ---																											
1928	Carrollton - Anniston	GAL	5												P					5	0	0	12.00	9	23	2	8
Bailey, ---		BR																									
1946	Tallahassee	GFL	<10																								
Bailey, Donald "Don"		BL TL																									
1946	Opelika	GAL	94	352	45	114	18	1	7	56	5	28	22	0.324	1B, OF, P	420	16	17	0.962	3	0	1	0.00	13	15	5	3
1947	Opelika	GAL	126	503	91	160	14	6	2	77	23	60	26	0.318	OF	200	11	15	0.934								
1950	Opelika	GAL													M												
1951	Opelika	GAL													M												
Bailey, Freddie		BS TR																									
1956	Thomasville	GFL	28	66	6	9	2	0	0	4	0	13	21	0.136	C	148	7	8	0.951								
Bailey, George D.		BL TL																									
1948	Opelika	GAL	125	488	88	174	22	6	1	76	17	72	16	0.357	OF	157	9	11	0.938								
Bailey, James Hopkins "Jim"		BS TL 6'2" 210 lbs. b. 09/10/1959 Strawberry Plains, TN																									
1956	Moultrie	GFL	15	35	5	5	0	0	0	2	0	5	11	0.143	P	2	16	5	0.783	15	6	6	3.17	88	86	75	41
Bailey, John J.		BR																									
1963	Waycross	GFL	8	22	2	4	0	1	0	2	0	1	3	0.182													
Bailey, Paul		BR TR																									
1940	Albany	GFL	20	83	13	26	2	2	0	9	0	11	21	0.313	2B	46	39	11	0.885								
Baines, Alfred																											
1928	Cedartown	GAL	77	265	27	63	5	2	0		2	18	53	0.238	SS	148	230	30	0.926								
Bakay, John																											
1941	Albany	GFL	111	409	88	108	17	4	0	56	2	83	40	0.264	OF	194	20	10	0.955								
1942	Albany	GFL	126	473	84	163	26	11	0	94	10	68	43	0.345	OF	394	45	18	0.961								
Bakenhaster, David Lee "Dave"		BR TR 5'10" 168 lbs. b. 06/20/1964 Columbus, OH																									
1963	Brunswick	GFL	3	6	1	1	1	0	0	0	0	2	2	0.167	P					3	1	1	4.29	21	14	25	14

218

Georgia Class-D Minor League Baseball Encyclopedia

YR	TEAM	LG	G	AB	R	H	2B	3B	HR	RBI	SB	BB	SO	BA	POS	PO	A	E	FA	GP	W	L	ERA	IP	H	SO	BB
Baker, ---																											
1915	Thomasville	FLAG				0								0.000													
1915	Valdosta	FLAG	9												P					9	4	3		66	51	24	15
Baker, Allen		BR TR																									
1950	Opelika	GAL	52	169	16	37	9	1	2	21	2	25	48	0.219	C	271	31	14	0.956								
Baker, Earl		BR TR																									
1954	Waycross	GFL	12	31	7	9	3	1	1	4	0	3	8	0.290	P	6	16	1	0.957	10	4	3	4.88	72	76	37	31
Baker, Floyd		BR TR																									
1954	Waycross	GFL	44	122	18	37	4	1	0	20	4	10	17	0.303	P	12	65	4	0.951	30	17	8	2.92	216	211	111	71
Baker, George																											
1938	Americus	GFL	87	307	43	81	13	6	0	35	1	35	43	0.264	OF	148	10	11	0.935								
1939	Americus	GFL	13	51	5	7	0	0	0	5	2	10	2	0.137	OF	20	1	2	0.913								
Baker, Gerald E. "Jerry"		BR TR																									
1953	Cordele	GFL	19	63	7	11	2	0	1	8	0	3	12	0.175	C	48	8	4	0.933								
1953	Sandersville	GSL	2											0.000														
1954	Sandersville	GSL	7	21		5								0.238														
Baker, Howard Francis "Howard"		BR TR 5'11" 175 lbs. b. 03/01/1888 Bridgeport, CT d. 01/16/1964 Bridgeport, CT																									
1914	Talladega	GAL	78	321	29	87					5			0.271	M, C	506	86	15	0.975								
1915	Talladega	GAL	61	227	27	67	14	1	3					0.295	C	345	65	11	0.974								
Baker, James G. "Jake"																											
1929	Lindale	GAL	23	57	6	11	2	0	0		0	1	13	0.193	P	5	23	1	0.966	22	10	8		153	138	91	52
1930	Lindale	GAL	37	86	12	19	3	1	0		2	5	6	0.221	P	11	46	5	0.919	32	15	9	4.04	185	210	102	75
Baker, Oscar																											
1915	Dothan - Ame-Gains	FLAG	28	87	9	16	5	0	0		1			0.184	M, OF, P	20	34	1	0.982	12	5	3		81	68	54	18
Baker, Ray																											
1949	Hazlehurst-Baxley	GSL													M													
Baker, Roy E.		BR TR																									
1949	Douglas	GSL	75	240	34	62	10	3	0	26	4	38	33	0.258	3B	82	126	34	0.860								
1950	Douglas	GSL	134	476	52	116	13	3	0	58	12	79	63	0.244	2B	322	423	30	0.961								
Baker, Royal		BR TR																									
1948	Moultrie	GFL	29	80	8	15	2	2	0	7	1	7	14	0.188	OF	25	1	4	0.867								
Baker, Winford		BR																									
1952	Waycross	GFL	19	55	6	8	2	0	0	5	4	16	15	0.145													
Baktis, John "Simon"		BR TR																									
1951	Americus	GFL	69	223	32	59	9	3	6	50	0	47	35	0.265	C	335	34	8	0.979								
Bakunas, Al		BR																									
1946	Cordele	GFL	<10																								
Balais, Alex		BR																									
1947	LaGrange	GAL	11	14	1	3	0	1	0	1	0	0	5	0.214													
Balczac, Edward "Ed"		BR																									
1957	Brunswick	GFL	5	11		0								0.000													
Baldwin, Jack		BR TL																									
1956	Thomasville	GFL	26	91	11	19	5	0	2	18	1	8	23	0.209	OF	37	2	5	0.886								
Baldwin, Lamar		BR TR																									
1950	Douglas	GSL	75	178	27	37	3	1	0	14	5	23	26	0.208	OF, C	107	9	7	0.943								
1951	Tifton	GFL	64	181	31	50	5	2	1	21	10	32	21	0.276	OF, C	135	10	10	0.935								
1951	Douglas	GSL	10	27	6	9	2	1	0	5	1	2	2	0.333													
Baldwin, Robert		BR TR																									
1954	Dublin	GSL	4	7		2								0.286	P					3	0	0		<45			
Balen, John		BL																									
1946	Albany	GFL	<10																								
Bales, ---																											
1914	Americus	GSL		92	12	31	8	4	4		4			0.337													
1915	Valdosta	FLAG	30	114	15	27	3	0	0		7			0.237	3B	34	67	9	0.918								
1916	Griffin	GAL	40	142	16	43					3			0.303	3B												
1920	Carrollton	GSL		60	3	16	3	0	0		1			0.267													
Bales, Jack		BL TR																									
1949	Thomasville	GFL	69	208	29	50	8	2	1	16	0	20	46	0.240	C	368	38	19	0.955								
Ball, James A. "Jim"		BL TR																									
1947	Opelika	GAL	122	475	93	145	19	11	7	70	39	74	31	0.305	OF	246	11	21	0.924								
1948	Opelika	GAL	117	448	85	149	13	6	2	76	37	74	8	0.333	M, OF	249	10	14	0.949								
1949	Opelika	GAL	115	419	82	143	12	4	4	68	14	68	24	0.341	M, OF	219	10	10	0.958								
Ball, John W.		BL TR																									
1946	Newnan	GAL	67	240	43	78	6	3	0	31	13	32	14	0.325	2B, P	123	145	12	0.957	1	0	1	0.00	2	3	0	1
1953	Hazlehurst-Baxley	GSL	33	65	6	11	1	1	0	3	0	17	14	0.169	P	7	44	6	0.895	30	15	8	3.34	194	186	124	108
Ball, Robert "Bob"																											
1941	Moultrie	GFL	18	39	4	6	1	1	0	3	0	5	7	0.154	C	50	3	2	0.964								
Balla, John		BR TR																									
1952	Moultrie	GFL	66	250	36	50	9	3	1	15	15	52	45	0.200	OF	136	12	16	0.902								
Ballard, Frank		BL TR																									
1963	Waycross	GFL	7	3	0	0	0	0	0	0	0	0	3	0.000	P					7	0	1	4.24	17	21	13	3
Ballard, Larry		BR TR																									
1962	Brunswick	GFL	39	99	16	20	5	0	3	11	1	9	27	0.202	OF	24	1	3	0.893								
Ballentine, Curtis																											
1942	Tallahassee	GFL	103	364	38	85	11	8	1	38	2	46	53	0.234	1B, OF	531	23	17	0.970								

Georgia Class-D Minor League Baseball Encyclopedia

YR	TEAM	LG	G	AB	R	H	2B	3B	HR	RBI	SB	BB	SO	BA	POS	PO	A	E	FA	GP	W	L	ERA	IP	H	SO	BB
Ballou, Don																											
1939	Thomasville - Valdosta	GFL	36	71	5	10	1	0	0	2	0	4	28	0.141	P	12	32	3	0.936	25	7	12	3.31	185	207	38	33
Balogh, Steve		BR TR																									
1952	Eastman	GSL	37	143	21	29	1	0	0	11	1	22	28	0.203	2B	83	104	7	0.964								
Ban, Richard "Dick"		BL TL																									
1951	Albany	GFL	34	61	5	13	2	1	0	5	0	7	13	0.213	P	6	14	5	0.800	30	12	3	3.17	139	109	94	108
1952	Albany	GFL	42	75	10	10	0	0	0	9	0	20	25	0.133	P	10	33	4	0.915	30	12	9	3.10	177	152	103	129
Banas, George A.																											
1949	Hazlehurst-Baxley	GSL	68	252	36	61	11	1	0	32	3	46	45	0.242	OF	140	8	10	0.937								
Bancroft, Charles		BL TR																									
1957	Valdosta	GFL	22	77	13	23	1	1	0	6	1	11	7	0.299	3B	23	32	4	0.932								
1958	Valdosta	GFL	115	415	102	119	19	2	0	35	13	122	22	0.287	2B	285	298	23	0.962								
Bandini, Philip "Phil"																											
1949	Hazlehurst-Baxley	GSL	11	46	12	18	0	0	0	3	3	7	11	0.391	OF	22	1	1	0.958								
Bandoch, Edward "Ed"		BR TR																									
1947	Tallahassee	GFL	73	209	26	47	10	1	0	19	0	48	47	0.225	3B, C	321	54	13	0.966								
1948	Tallahassee	GFL	22	60	10	15	1	1	0	8	3	17	13	0.250	C	126	14	4	0.972								
1949	Tallahassee	GFL	26	80	11	14	4	0	0	10	1	20	22	0.175	C	123	18	7	0.953								
Banks, Gerald		BR TR																									
1954	Ame-Cor(20) - Fitzgerald(1)	GFL	21	12	2	2	0	0	0	1	0	2	4	0.167	P	2	5	1	0.875	20	2	5	5.76	50	49	31	25
Bankston, Wilborn Everett "Everett"		BL TR 5'11" 180 lbs. b. 05/25/1893 Barnesville, GA d. 02/26/1970 Griffin, GA																									
1914	Cordele	GSL		401	82	144	14	14	31		8			0.359													
Bannister, ---																											
1913	LaGrange	GAL	36	110	14	32					4			0.291	P, OF	32	25	5	0.919	11	5	6					
1914	LaGrange	GAL	78	270	35	73					9			0.270	OF	104	34	8	0.945								
Banta, Sterling		BR TR																									
1940	Moultrie	GFL	35	142	19	40	6	1	0	33	3	12	7	0.282	OF	64	4	2	0.971								
Banville, ---																											
1917	LaGrange	GAL	15	51	4	13	2	2	0		2			0.255	OF, 1B	75	0	3	0.962								
Barath, David "Dave"		BL TR																									
1951	Valley	GAL	47	146	31	45	7	2	2	19	2	27	12	0.308	OF	59	1	3	0.952								
Barbare, P.																											
1930	Talladega	GAL	19	59	6	20	6	0	0		3	7	7	0.339	2B, OF	64	44	5	0.956								
Barbare, Walter Lawrence "Walt"		BR TR 6'0" 162 lbs. b. 08/11/1891 Greenville, SC d. 10/28/1965 Greenville, SC																									
1930	Talladega	GAL	19	54	9	15	0	0	0		2	4	1	0.278													
Barbella, Victor "Vic"		BR TR																									
1948	Valdosta	GFL	12	18	4	5	0	0	0	3	0	2	4	0.278	P	3	12	5	0.750								
Barber, ---																											
1906	Valdosta	GSL													P												
Barber, ---																											
1915	Waycross	FLAG	75	254	23	51	9	1	2		4			0.201	1B	733	33	17	0.978								
Barber, ---																											
1921	Carrollton	GSL		319	62	108								0.339	OF												
Barber, Stephen David "Steve"		BL TL 6'0" 200 lbs. b. 04/21/1939 Takoma Park, MD																									
1958	Dublin	GFL	24	49	6	8	3	0	0	6	0	5	18	0.163	P	8	37	5	0.900	22	5	5	5.00	108	88	85	103
Barbero, Frank L.																											
1937	Tallahassee	GFL		49	1	15				0	4	1		0.306	1B	122	9	4	0.970								
Barberra, Clement "Clem"		BL TL																									
1953	Cordele	GFL	20	59	4	14	5	0	0	9	0	11	12	0.237	OF	19	2	4	0.840								
Barbier, John		BR TR																									
1952	Cordele	GFL	41	83	10	8	0	0	0	4	0	14	33	0.096	P	15	54	5	0.932	39	16	14	2.64	235	233	115	95
1954	Thomasville	GFL	28	64	5	15	3	1	0	6	0	1	10	0.234	P	9	29	3	0.927	27	9	9	3.14	152	177	80	47
Barbieri, Fernando		BR TR																									
1951	Valdosta	GFL	23	66	10	16	5	0	0	7	1	12	4	0.242	2B	32	33	7	0.903								
Barclay, Robert M.																											
1914	Rome	GAL	16	49	3	9					0			0.184	P	5	23	3	0.903	16							
Barfield, Frank		BR TR																									
1957	Waycross	GFL	82	201	14	41	7	1	2	17	0	33	77	0.204	C	281	28	16	0.951								
Bargas, John		BR TR																									
1947	Moultrie	GFL	34	117	12	24	5	0	0	12	0	23	21	0.205	C	219	27	6	0.976								
Barger, John		BR TR																									
1948	Newnan	GAL	47	108	19	29	1	2	1	27	0	24	15	0.269	P	11	38	2	0.961	38	20	9	2.17	249	228	153	55
Barker, George		BR TR																									
1950	Valdosta	GFL	27	56	10	12	0	0	0	5	0	9	8	0.214	P	2	30	1	0.970	25	10	7	4.07	148	162	69	70
Barker, Norbert "Norb"		BR TR																									
1950	Alexander City	GAL	24	96	29	31	3	2	3	23	0	20	8	0.323	2B	54	52	1	0.991								
Barker, Tommy K.		BL TR																									
1962	Thomasville	GFL	50	141	24	43	6	1	1	20	3	15	17	0.305	3B	17	26	11	0.796								
1963	Thomasville	GFL	17	52	8	13	1	0	0	5	2	12	5	0.250	3B	11	21	4	0.889								
Barkley, ---		BR TR																									
1946	Carrollton	GAL	4												P					4	2	1	0.00	31	24	16	5
Barlam, Barnett		BR TR																									
1946	Valdosta	GFL	24	43	1	5	0	1	0	2	0	5	27	0.116	P	4	14	2	0.900	24	4	6	4.69	121	120	101	51
Barna, Michael "Mike"		BR TR																									
1954	Valdosta	GFL	22	49	9	9	2	0	0	4	1	10	14	0.184	2B	33	27	6	0.909								

Georgia Class-D Minor League Baseball Encyclopedia

YR	TEAM	LG	G	AB	R	H	2B	3B	HR	RBI	SB	BB	SO	BA	POS	PO	A	E	FA	GP	W	L	ERA	IP	H	SO	BB
Barna, Richard "Dick"		BR TR																									
1956	Hazlehurst-Baxley	GSL	37	128	18	21	3	1	1	10	1	21	41	0.164	3B	28	48	20	0.792								
Barnard, ---																											
1915	Thomasville	FLAG	<10																								
Barnes, ---																											
1906	Americus	GSL													3B												
Barnes, ---																											
1921	Carrollton	GSL	<10												P												
Barnes, ---																											
1930	Huntsville	GAL	15	52	5	10	1	0	0		2	6	16	0.192	3B	22	19	3	0.932								
Barnes, Duge		BR TR																									
1940	Cordele	GFL	14	45	5	7	2	0	0	2	0	5	7	0.156	OF	34	0	2	0.944								
Barnes, Irv F.																											
1935	Americus	GFL	95	392	39	78	15	3	7		4	20	41	0.199	IF	182	211	28	0.933								
Barnes, Luther		BR TR																									
1948	Douglas	GSL	39	156	13	30	5	3	1	14	4	12	25	0.192	3B, OF	56	32	9	0.907								
Barnes, Robert E. "Bob"		BR TR																									
1950	Tifton	GSL	47	98	16	20	3	1	0	9	0	12	17	0.204	P	7	24	0	1.000	31	11	9	4.92	150	181	56	49
Barnes, William W. "Bill"		BL TR																									
1946	Moultrie	GFL	21	82	16	25	3	2	2	13	2	5	15	0.305	3B	23	36	5	0.922								
1947	Moultrie	GFL	89	350	73	103	12	2	4	37	10	31	36	0.294	3B	69	168	23	0.912								
1948	Moultrie	GFL	40	159	22	40	7	1	0	12	1	12	23	0.252	3B	33	85	13	0.901								
1948	Douglas	GSL	39	150	18	41	5	4	0	20	6	16	14	0.273	M, 3B	45	102	10	0.936								
1949	Tifton	GSL	147	605	111	175	42	6	9	105	10	54	44	0.289	2B	384	415	31	0.963								
1950	Tifton	GSL	92	357	60	96	19	3	6	66	15	17	29	0.269	M, 2B	269	253	16	0.970								
Barnett, ---																											
1913	Thomasville	ESL	97	339	31	76	19	0	1					0.224	OF	119	18	9	0.938								
1914	Thomasville	GSL		115	12	27	3	0	0		5			0.235													
Barnett, Byron		BR TR																									
1952	Vidalia	GSL	11	12	2	3	0	0	0	3	0	6	7	0.250	P	1	8	0	1.000								
1953	Fitzgerald	GFL	1											0.000	P					0	0		<45				
1953	Eastman	GSL	13	24	2	4	0	0	0	2	0	3	8	0.167	P	6	4	0	1.000	13	3	2	6.86	59	72	27	24
Barnett, John F.		BR TR																									
1940	Moultrie	GFL	23	76	6	13	2	0	0	11	0	6	16	0.171	SS	191	373	36	0.940								
1941	Waycross	GFL	43	107	16	18	5	1	1	14	0	16	25	0.168	P	14	37	0	1.000	43	18	9	2.51	237	287	75	45
Barnett, Lowell		BL TR																									
1940	Thomasville	GFL	112	441	98	141	17	2	1	41	22	85	30	0.320	P					14	6	7	2.89	106	105	30	27
Barnhart, ---																											
1921	LaGrange	GSL													C												
Barnhart, Lowell																											
1957	Thomasville	GFL	95	262	34	54	13	2	2	29	3	42	62	0.206	OF	134	12	6	0.961								
Barnhart, Robert "Bob"																											
1939	Valdosta	GFL	26	92	14	20	2	0	0	6	1	11	18	0.217	3B	33	64	12	0.890								
Baron, Victor "Vic"		BR TR																									
1958	Brunswick	GFL	15	33	3	9	1	0	0	5	0	4	11	0.273	C	49	5	1	0.982								
Barone, Anthony		BR TR																									
1950	Hazlehurst-Baxley	GSL	108	329	54	77	12	6	0	22	1	107	65	0.234	SS	197	283	40	0.923								
1953	Hazlehurst-Baxley	GSL	4											0.200													
Barone, Frank		BR TR																									
1952	Douglas	GSL	13	44	5	12	0	1	0	5	1	9	11	0.273	3B	22	33	9	0.859								
Barone, Lester "Les"																											
1956	Fitzgerald	GFL	12	22	2	5	0	1	0	2	0	0	7	0.227	P					9	1	5	6.00	45	59	23	26
Barrett, Francis Joseph "Red"		BR TR 6'2" 173 lbs. b. 07/31/1913 Ft. Lauderdale, FL d. 03/06/1998 Leesburg, FL																									
1935	Albany	GFL	19	45	5	4	0	0	0		0	2	13	0.089	P					25	8	10		130	134	102	58
1936	Albany	GFL	11	29	2	5	0	0	0	0	1			0.172	P					11	5	4	4.06	71		38	60
Barrett, Garland		BR TR																									
1953	Hazlehurst-Baxley	GSL	2											0.000	P					0	0	1	<45				
1954	Hazlehurst-Baxley	GSL	1	1		1								1.000													
Barrett, Michael "Mike"		BR TR																									
1963	Waycross	GFL	13	5	0	0	0	0	0	0	0	0	1	0.000	P	0	3	1	0.750	12	2	2	4.50	18	19	13	7
Barron, Norman "Norm"		BL TL																									
1956	Dublin	GSL	31	54	6	12	1	0	0	3	0	3	13	0.222	P	7	23	5	0.857	25	6	12	4.33	133	120	90	95
Barrow, Raymond "Ray"		BL TL																									
1947	Americus	GFL	16	25	0	4	1	0	0	3	0	1	11	0.160	P	1	16	3	0.850	15	1	4	7.42	57	87	38	36
Barry, Eugene "Gene"																											
1942	Albany	GFL	19	64	12	15	3	1	0	7	3	7	16	0.234	OF	32	0	2	0.941								
Barry, Jeremiah "Berry"																											
1937	Tallahassee	GFL	52	174	16	29	2	1	0	12	3	19	34	0.167	C	167	41	9	0.959								
Barry, Willie Clifford "Willie"		BR TR																									
1955	Waycross	GFL	1	0										0.000	P					1	0	0	<45				
Bartell, ---																											
1915	Valdosta - Ame-Gains	FLAG	17	22	1	5	0	1	0		2			0.227													
Barth, Albert "Al"		BR TR																									
1957	Fitzgerald	GFL	80	259	43	86	11	3	10	50	2	46	67	0.332	1B, OF, P	187	28	9	0.960	15	1	4	3.42	71	73	47	26
Barth, Jerry		BR																									
1955	Tifton	GFL	5	8	0									0.000													

221

Georgia Class-D Minor League Baseball Encyclopedia

YR	TEAM	LG	G	AB	R	H	2B	3B	HR	RBI	SB	BB	SO	BA	POS	PO	A	E	FA	GP	W	L	ERA	IP	H	SO	BB
Bartholomew, ---																											
1942	Americus	GFL	7												P					7	0	3	2.37	19	31	8	15
Bartholomew, John "Jack"		BR TR																									
1949	Carrollton	GAL	25	64	16	14	0	0	0	4	3	20	8	0.219	2B	30	37	7	0.905								
1953	Cordele	GFL	7											0.208													
1953	Jesup	GSL	4											0.313													
Bartley, Boyd Owen "Boyd"		BR TR 5'8" 165 lbs. b. 02/11/1920 Chicago, IL																									
1954	Thomasville	GFL													M												
Bartley, Don L.		BR TR																									
1952	Brunswick	GFL	10	7	3	3	0	0	0	1	0	1	2	0.429	P	2	3	2	0.714								
Bartolozzi, Ralph		BL TL																									
1947	Tallahassee	GFL	133	433	87	102	14	8	2	71	17	115	64	0.236	1B	1097	58	36	0.970								
Barton, Cecil		BL TL																									
1954	Albany	GFL	6	14		0								0.000	P					5	1	1	<45				
1955	Albany	GFL	3	6		2								0.333	P					3	1	1	<45				
Bartula, Matthew		BR TR																									
1946	Valley	GAL	2												P					2	0	0	0.00	5			
Barty, Harley W. "Warren"		BR TR																									
1962	Brunswick	GFL	107	339	68	95	14	2	11	55	9	47	87	0.280	OF, C	449	29	21	0.958								
Basgall, Romanus "Monty"		BR TR 5'10" 175 lbs. b. 02/08/1922 Pfeifer, KS																									
1942	Valdosta	GFL	126	502	71	127	14	7	1	65	10	48	69	0.253	2B	427	502	35	0.964								
Baskin, Percy Allen "Al"		BR TR																									
1947	Valdosta	GFL	37	57	5	4	3	0	0	1	0	5	45	0.070	P	8	18	5	0.839	37	6	11	3.83	169	168	76	108
1949	Tifton	GSL	15	50	6	4	1	0	0	5	0	7	16	0.080	P	8	9	3	0.850	13	5	5	5.48	92	60	65	53
1950	Tifton	GSL	20	32	1	3	1	0	0	3	0	4	22	0.094	P	11	35	4	0.920	19	2	5	5.46	84	83	45	71
Bass, Daniel "Danny"		BL TL																									
1950	Albany	GFL	17	62	19	14	1	3	2	12	2	11	11	0.226	OF	27	1	3	0.903								
Bass, Leslie "Les"		BR TR																									
1957	Waycross	GFL	36	51	3	11	2	0	1	7	0	7	13	0.216	P	8	16	1	0.960	32	5	14	4.50	146	162	83	81
Bassett, A. Grady																											
1929	Anniston	GAL	7												P					7	3	2		44	41	15	13
1930	Lindale	GAL	3												P					3	1	1	9.56	16	27	11	9
Bassetti, Gilbert "Gil"		BR TR																									
1956	Sandersville	GSL	45	79	6	14	1	0	0	4	0	9	20	0.177	P	10	41	7	0.879	44	21	8	2.26	247	208	219	72
Bassignani, Albert "Al"																											
1949	Hazlehurst-Baxley	GSL	88	361	34	78	13	2	7	39	3	24	54	0.216	1B	801	33	27	0.969								
Bastion, Marvin "Marv"																											
1950	Alexander City	GAL	30	43	3	7	0	0	0	4	0	1	14	0.163	P	3	17	1	0.952	29	3	6	4.59	104	108	38	67
1951	Douglas	GSL	26	50	9	10	1	0	0	1	0	11	13	0.200	P	10	28	8	0.826	25	6	9	3.51	136	146	44	73
1954	Douglas	GSL	6	4		0								0.000	P					6	0	1	<45				
Batchko, Joseph "Joe"		BL TL																									
1946	Moultrie(17) - Thomasville(9)	GFL	26	84	10	14	1	0	3	11	0	9	14	29 0.167	OF, P	16	1	2	0.895	1	0	0	0.00	2			
Bateman, Edward "Ed"		BL TR																									
1953	Cordele	GFL	14	43	7	11	3	0	0	5	1	14	10	0.256	OF	17	3	3	0.870								
Bates, ---																											
1921	Griffin	GSL													P												
Battistelli, Angelo		BR TR																									
1949	Griffin	GAL	18	59	8	11	3	0	0	7	1	10	15	0.186	SS	37	43	13	0.860								
1950	Griffin	GAL	14	45	9	5	0	0	0	0	1	12	16	0.111	3B	13	29	7	0.857								
Battle, Donald "Don"		BR																									
1954	Thomasville	GFL	11	24	3	5	0	0	0	0	1	7		0.208													
Battson, Cecil																											
1913	Anniston	GAL	11												P					11	8	3					
1914	Anniston	GAL	29	73	6	5				1				0.068	P	6	49	6	0.902	29							
Batty, Thomas "Tom"		BR TR																									
1950	Tifton	GSL	15	50	10	8	0	0	0	8	3	12	19	0.160	OF	29	1	6	0.833								
Batty, William "Bill"		BR TR																									
1954	Albany	GFL	112	403	64	106	18	5	3	45	16	85	47	0.263	2B, 3B, SS	136	174	42	0.881								
Bauer, Edward A. "Ed"		BL TL																									
1946	Valdosta	GFL	24	77	4	17	1	0	1	7	3	7	17	0.221	OF	32	10	4	0.913								
1953	Vidalia	GSL	38	154	24	48	10	6	2	23	2	20	22	0.312	OF	59	7	4	0.943								
Bauman, Walter "Walt"		BL TL																									
1952	Hazlehurst-Baxley	GSL	31	82	7	19	1	0	0	5	0	10	17	0.232	P	13	25	2	0.950	30	20	5	2.75	213	184	108	96
Baumgardner, ---																											
1914	Gadsden	GAL	75	260	32	63				8				0.242	3B	122	69	22	0.897								
Bavoso, Thomas "Tom"		BR TR																									
1956	Douglas	GSL	25	46	7	9	3	0	0	4	0	2	13	0.196	P	1	11	3	0.800	19	7	2	4.24	87	98	68	38
Bayno, Joseph "Joe"		BL TL																									
1955	Thomasville	GFL	7	6		0								0.000	P					7	0	4	<45				
Bays, Richard "Dick"		BL TL																									
1955	Valdosta	GFL	20	42	5	6	0	0	0	3	0	5	16	0.143	P	10	28	1	0.974	19	6	8	2.11	128	111	74	64
Bazner, Henry																											
1935	Panama City	GFL	58	179	19	38	4	2	4		3	12	51	0.212	P					30	9	16		275	142	180	60
Beach, Edward "Ed"		BL TR																									
1949	Valley	GAL	32	58	6	9	0	0	0	1	0	6	18	0.155	P	7	35	3	0.933	32	13	9	2.29	177	140	120	89

Georgia Class-D Minor League Baseball Encyclopedia

YR	TEAM	LG	G	AB	R	H	2B	3B	HR	RBI	SB	BB	SO	BA	POS	PO	A	E	FA	GP	W	L	ERA	IP	H	SO	BB
Beagle, H.E.																											
1929	Talledega	GAL	54	227	34	65	7	3	1		2	14	20	0.286	3B	76	136	17	0.926								
Beaird, Richard "Dick"		BL TR																									
1949	LaGrange	GAL	<10																								
1950	Eastman	GSL	<10																								
1951	Waycross	GFL	21	60	11	11	3	0	2	8	0	12	10	0.183	OF	19	0	1	0.950								
Beal, William "Bill"		BR TR																									
1953	Vidalia	GSL	7											0.167	P						0	4		<45			
Beall, ---																											
1917	LaGrange	GAL	3	12	0	1	0	0	0		0			0.083	2B	2	6	1	0.889								
1917	Talladega	GAL	8	32	0	8	2	0	0		0			0.250	1B	83	4	2	0.978								
Beaman, George		BL TR																									
1956	Dublin	GSL	26	41	4	11	3	0	0	2	0	2	16	0.268	P	5	14	2	0.905	25	3	7	5.05	98	97	62	54
Bean, Roger		BR TR																									
1957	Thomasville	GFL	77	253	24	61	10	0	1	31	0	43	32	0.241	C	392	32	14	0.968								
Beane, Edward "Ed"																											
1942	Albany	GFL	7	23	0	2	0	0	0	0	0	0	9	0.087	P	1	17	0	1.000	8	2	3	3.63	62	52	37	39
Beane, William "Bill"		BL TR																									
1955	Dublin	GSL	14	21	4	1	0	0	0	4	0	13	9	0.048	P	1	9	4	0.714	13	4	5	5.80	76	82	54	49
1956	Albany	GFL	15	26	5	5	1	0	0	0	0	8	8	0.192	P	4	8	1	0.923	15	5	4	5.93	85	102	65	54
Bearden, Henry Eugene "Gene"		BL TL 6'3" 204 lbs. b. 09/05/1920 Lexa, AR																									
1939	Moultrie	GFL	29	65	4	12	1	0	0	4	0	2	21	0.185	P	6	49	2	0.965	27	5	11	3.48	168	192	106	91
Bearden, John R. "Jack"		BR TR																									
1949	Dublin	GSL	43	158	38	49	11	1	14	41	0	28	14	0.310	OF	99	8	4	0.964								
1950	Griffin	GAL	121	435	108	154	31	6	19	98	12	87	28	0.354	M, OF	266	13	8	0.972								
1951	Griffin	GAL	115	435	96	139	27	5	19	127	3	106	33	0.320	M, OF	286	9	6	0.980								
1952	Jesup(100) - Dublin(26)	GSL	126	479	92	142	31	1	20	100	5	90	43	0.296	M, OF	308	18	8	0.976								
1953	Fitzgerald	GFL	15	51	10	15	3	0	1	10	0	11	4	0.294	OF	33	3	1	0.973								
Bearden, William "Billy"		BR TR																									
1952	Waycross	GFL	17	30	5	1	1	0	0	3	0	5	11	0.033	OF	22	0	0	1.000								
1953	Waycross	GFL	31	106	13	22	2	1	3	16	0	15	31	0.208	OF	60	1	9	0.871								
1954	Statesboro	GSL	43	112	18	15	5	0	3	19	2	16	45	0.134	OF, P	42	2	1	0.978	2	0	0	<45				
Beasley, ---																											
1913	LaGrange	GAL	46	142	14	29					2			0.204	P					24	10	14					
Beasley, ---		BR																									
1946	Carrollton	GAL	<10																								
Beasley, John		BR TR																									
1950	Rome(35) - Carrollton(4)	GAL	39	130	19	26	6	0	0	13	4	16	41	0.200	SS	48	95	13	0.917								
Beatty, Arlin		BR TR																									
1955	Albany	GFL	8	7		2								0.286	P					8	1	3	<45				
Beaty, Frank A.																											
1949	Eastman	GSL	26	69	8	17	2	1	0	11	0	4	7	0.246	P	14	31	2	0.957	27	7	7	5.02	129	97	100	89
Beauchamp, Walter J. "Walt"		BR TR																									
1949	Vidalia-Lyons	GSL	75	290	64	77	16	6	0	28	3	62	36	0.266	2B	185	189	25	0.937								
1950	Carrollton	GAL	27	89	18	27	7	3	0	11	2	31	13	0.303	2B	43	32	10	0.882								
1950	Vidalia-Lyons	GSL	92	334	73	88	12	3	1	45	20	84	55	0.263	2B	247	254	32	0.940								
1951	Douglas	GSL	37	152	46	39	6	4	0	14	6	33	17	0.257	2B	108	130	20	0.922								
Beaugez, Raymond "Ray"		BR																									
1954	Hazlehurst-Baxley	GSL	3	12		1								0.083													
Beavers, James "Jim"		BR TR																									
1947	Tallassee	GAL	26	56	6	7	1	1	0	2	0	5	17	0.125	P	7	23	3	0.909	25	10	9	4.75	142	130	84	108
1948	Opelika	GAL	23	60	8	16	2	0	2	9	1	7	11	0.267	P	4	18	3	0.880	20	5	12	3.44	136	129	96	80
1952	Hazlehurst-Baxley	GSL	122	526	119	191	46	5	21	108	27	41	36	0.363	1B	975	46	28	0.973								
1954	Vidalia	GSL	124	495	105	162	31	5	16	84	23	35	36	0.327	M, 1B, P	1043	89	24	0.979	9	1	0	<45				
Beazley, John Andrew "Johnny"		BR TR 190 lbs. b. 05/25/1918 Nashville, TN d. 04/21/1990 Nashville, TN																									
1937	Tallahassee	GFL	13												P					13	1	7	4.50	74	91	29	38
Beck, ---																											
1920	Carrollton	GSL		43	9	5								0.116	P, OF												
Beck, ---																											
1928	Cedartown - Talladega	GAL	23	94	15	27	2	3	0		3	3	9	0.287	1B, OF	104	6	4	0.965								
Beck, Dale		BR TR																									
1951	LaGrange	GAL	37	141	35	43	10	1	2	29	1	26	19	0.305	OF	61	4	10	0.867								
Beck, Richard "Dick"		BR TR																									
1955	Valdosta	GFL	60	159	16	34	4	0	2	11	1	26	38	0.214	C	252	31	8	0.973								
1956	Valdosta	GFL	25	81	18	20	2	0	1	14	1	15	14	0.247	C	141	10	1	0.993								
Beck, Theodore A. "Ted"		BR TR																									
1948	Albany	GFL	43	116	14	40	9	4	1	23	1	12	7	0.345	2B, P	29	42	12	0.855	20	8	8	3.80	128	135	73	81
Beck, William "Bill"		BR TR																									
1956	Moultrie	GFL	16	17	1	3	0	0	0	0	0	2	5	0.176	P	2	5	1	0.875	14	2	2	3.86	49	48	30	33
Bedingfield, J.R.																											
1920	LaGrange	GSL													P												
Bednar, David "Dave"		BL TL																									
1957	Fitzgerald	GFL	134	467	72	115	17	1	9	71	12	66	92	0.246	1B	1002	54	10	0.991								
1958	Dublin	GFL	124	469	103	128	17	2	16	96	32	90	80	0.273	1B	1042	71	17	0.985								
Beecher, Robert "Bob"		BR TR																									
1951	Haz-Bax(6) - Eastman(29)	GSL	35	100	24	22	4	1	1	15	1	47	27	0.220	OF	78	8	3	0.966								
Beheler, Ernest		BL TR																									

Georgia Class-D Minor League Baseball Encyclopedia

YR	TEAM	LG	G	AB	R	H	2B	3B	HR	RBI	SB	BB	SO	BA	POS	PO	A	E	FA	GP	W	L	ERA	IP	H	SO	BB
1954	Dublin	GSL	14	44	9	5	0	1	0	5	1	13	11	0.114	1B	94	4	4	0.961								
Behrends, Albert "Al"		BR TR																									
1940	Moultrie	GFL	138	547	92	179	29	11	4	90	0	68	55	0.327	OF	230	13	17	0.935								
Behrens, Edwin "Ed"		BR TR																									
1950	Albany	GFL	141	536	94	147	17	6	8	88	10	85	54	0.274	1B	842	66	22	0.976								
Behrman, Henry Bernard "Hank"		BR TR 5'11" 174 lbs. b. 06/27/1921 Brooklyn, NY d. 01/20/1987 New York, NY																									
1941	Valdosta	GFL	44	109	9	18	3	1	1	13	0	6	26	0.165	P	18	51	6	0.920	37	18	10	3.11	252	226	175	118
Beiler, Carl		BL TR																									
1954	Thomasville	GFL	33	98	14	26	0	2	0	8	1	14	20	0.265	OF	33	0	5	0.868								
1955	Thomasville	GFL	8	10		0								0.000													
Belaj, Allen		BR TR																									
1956	Vidalia	GSL	38	132	14	25	1	2	0	16	1	11	24	0.189	SS	43	52	13	0.880								
Belakovy, Rudy		BL TL																									
1948	Douglas	GSL	41	83	5	14	2	1	0	1	1	13	23	0.169	P	4	30	4	0.895	33	9	15	3.73	188	196	76	67
Belcher, Neil		BR TR																									
1946	Thomasville	GFL	2												P					2	0	0	0.00	4			
Belinsky, Robert "Bo"		BL TL 6'2" 191 lbs. b. 12/07/1936 New York, NY d. 11/23/2001 Las Vegas, NV																									
1956	Brunswick	GFL	11	12	1	1	0	0	0	1	0	1	8	0.083	P	2	4	2	0.750	11	2	3	<45				
Belknap, Lyle																											
1939	Cordele	GFL													P								<45				
Bell, Charles J. "Charlie"																											
1920	Carrollton	GSL		343	68	109	19	6	4		22			0.318	M, SS, 2B, 3B, P												
Bell, Gary		BR TR 6'1" 198 lbs. b. 11/17/1936 San Antonio, TX																									
1955	Vidalia	GSL	15	38	4	15	5	0	0	3	0	2	1	0.395	P	5	16	2	0.913	14	7	5	3.33	100	67	126	70
Bell, Jefferson		BR TR																									
1946	Albany	GFL	127	510	85	136	19	11	2	74	22	42	69	0.267	2B, 3B	200	249	55	0.891								
1947	Albany	GFL	32	111	8	20	1	1	2	8	1	11	19	0.180	2B	73	93	10	0.943								
1948	Waycross	GFL	135	513	95	137	21	4	6	86	14	88	56	0.267	3B	158	244	48	0.893								
Bell, John		BL TL																									
1951	Griffin	GAL	13	17	1	2	0	0	0	0	0	3	2	0.118	P	3	16	0	1.000	12	1	4	9.39	46	72	22	41
Bell, Russell "Russ"		BR TR																									
1955	Sandersville	GSL	22	61	4	7	2	1	0	2	0	7	13	0.115	OF	24	2	3	0.897								
Belladella, Robert "Bob"		BR TR																									
1954	Waycross	GFL	18	37	1	7	1	0	0	1	0	3	10	0.189	SS	13	19	3	0.914								
1954	Statesboro	GSL	29	97	10	20	4	0	1	10	1	9	13	0.206	2B	59	83	14	0.910								
Bellamy, Perry		BR																									
1954	Waycross	GFL	3	3	0									0.000													
Bender, Sheldon A. "Chief"		BR TR																									
1949	Albany	GFL	41	86	13	19	1	0	0	11	1	6	18	0.221	M, P	9	26	2	0.946	26	11	3	2.42	119	114	54	25
1950	Albany	GFL	39	64	10	16	1	0	0	7	2	11	8	0.250	M, P	16	30	2	0.958	33	12	5	2.78	152	135	61	33
1951	Albany	GFL	27	44	4	10	1	0	0	4	0	1	3	0.227	M, P	3	27	2	0.938	26	10	4	2.51	111	99	38	29
1957	Albany	GFL	2	2	0									0.000	P					2	0	0	<30				
Benedict, ---																											
1917	Rome-Lindale	GAL	16	52	4	9	0	0	0		1			0.173	OF, C	27	5	3	0.914								
Benedict, Cletus		BL TL																									
1954	Albany	GFL	52	154	18	26	3	2	2	16	5	31	36	0.169	1B	378	23	5	0.988								
Benedict, Hoyt		BR TR																									
1950	Albany	GFL	30	56	8	5	0	0	0	4	1	5	19	0.089	P	5	25	1	0.968	29	10	8	3.45	159	159	123	91
Benezue, ---		BR TR																									
1946	Valley	GAL	1												P					1	0	0	0.00	1			
Benish, Robert "Bob"		BL TL																									
1950	Thomasville	GFL	83	200	33	53	3	0	8	38	1	33	13	0.265	M, 1B, OF, P	163	32	7	0.965	17	4	5	4.80	75	93	23	22
Benjamin, Alfred Stanley "Stan"		BR TR 6'2" 194 lbs. b. 05/05/1914 Framingham, MA																									
1937	Thomasville	GFL	123	494	64	153	25	13	1	61	28	26	62	0.310	3B	153	321	56	0.894								
1938	Thomasville	GFL	97	391	75	134	32	12	3	77	19	32	45	0.343	3B	107	198	28	0.916								
Bennett, ---																											
1917	Tri-Cities	GAL	4	10	1	2	0	1	0		0			0.200	P	0	14	0	1.000	4	2	1		27	23	9	14
Bennett, Charles L.		BR TR																									
1946	LaGrange	GAL	3												P					3	1	0	0.00	16	22	13	11
1952	Moultrie	GFL	14	19	2	4	0	0	0	1	0	3	5	0.211													
1952	Vidalia	GSL	12	26	1	6	1	0	0	1	0	2	5	0.231	P					12	0	6	8.17	65	81	26	58
Bennett, Craig		BR TR																									
1946	Tallahassee	GFL	26	32	3	5	0	0	0	4	0	1	9	0.156	P	3	26	1	0.967	25	5	6	5.05	98	118	61	52
Bennett, Frank		BR TL																									
1939	Waycross	GFL	25	63	4	12	1	0	0	4	0	2	22	0.190	P	2	25	0	1.000	24	8	9	3.73	157	154	69	71
1940	Waycross	GFL	31	89	4	11	0	0	0	6	0	6	44	0.124	P					30	16	6	2.86	230	250	98	53
Bennett, Gerald		BR TR																									
1955	Vidalia	GSL	6	9		0								0.000	P					6	0	1					
Benson, Gene																											
1942	Moultrie	GFL	21	72	10	18	2	1	0	5	0	8	14	0.250	OF	31	4	2	0.946								
Benson, John		BR																									
1953	Vidalia	GSL	2												0.125													
Beran, Leon "Lee"		BR TR																									
1951	Brunswick	GFL	46	63	12	10	0	0	0	2	1	1	12	0.159	P					32	9	5	5.27	152	135	101	126
1955	Dublin	GSL	30	70	8	15	3	0	1	7	1	1	11	0.214	OF, P	22	9	4	0.886	11	1	4	7.62	26	31	15	24
Beredino, Joseph "Joe"		BR TR																									
1955	Brunswick	GFL	22	67	9	16	1	2	0	7	0	6	26	0.239	OF	31	0	1	0.969								

Georgia Class-D Minor League Baseball Encyclopedia

YR	TEAM	LG	G	AB	R	H	2B	3B	HR	RBI	SB	BB	SO	BA	POS	PO	A	E	FA	GP	W	L	ERA	IP	H	SO	BB
Berg, Edward "Ed"		BR TR																									
1948	Tallassee	GAL	80	258	22	47	9	0	0	17	2	14	61	0.182	2B	189	208	22	0.947								
1949	Tallassee	GAL	117	436	55	102	13	1	0	40	11	49	75	0.234	2B	307	321	24	0.963								
Bergdoll, Charles		BR TR																									
1957	Waycross	GFL	81	279	47	87	16	4	1	35	0	60	45	0.312	OF	190	5	5	0.975								
Berger, Fred		BL TR																									
1955	Cordele	GFL	127	448	86	115	9	8	0	39	15	97	86	0.257	2B	299	393	33	0.954								
Bergey, Francis		BL TR																									
1958	Thomasville	GFL	13	50	6	12	0	0	1	0	5	3	6	7	0.240	2B	32	33	6	0.915								
Bergey, James "Jim"		BR TR																									
1956	Thomasville	GFL	14	19	3	3	0	0	0	3	0	8	5	0.158	P	3	20	3	0.885	13	5	4	3.38	72	66	50	44
Bergstraesser, William "Bill"		BR TR																									
1958	Waycross	GFL	10	15	3	4	0	0	0	3	0	1	3	0.267	P	3	11	0	1.000	10	1	4	5.93	44	38	23	46
Beringhele, Basil																											
1942	Valdosta	GFL	53	222	31	56	13	2	0	24	0	24	15	0.252	1B	518	47	15	0.974								
Berman, Norman "Norm" "Buddy"		BS TR																									
1946	Valdosta	GFL	<10																								
1949	Carrollton	GAL	112	396	69	90	12	0	0	22	9	71	76	0.227	2B	306	252	21	0.964								
1950	Alex City(15) - Carrollton(3)	GAL	18	62	13	20	1	1	0	8	4	13	9	0.323	2B	38	35	4	0.948								
Bernat, Walter "Walt"																											
1941	Tallahassee	GFL	8	29	5	6	0	0	0	3	0	4	2	0.207	SS	9	20	11	0.725								
Bernhardt, Virgil		BL TR																									
1956	Fitzgerald	GFL	11	23	2	2	1	0	0	2	0	7	14	0.087	C	36	3	1	0.975								
Bernier, William "Bill"		BR TR																									
1951	Americus	GFL	26	59	4	5	0	1	0	2	0	9	10	0.085	P					22	9	10	2.76	163	124	97	65
Bernstein, ---																											
1913	Americus	ESL	27	108	15	30	6	0	0					0.278	SS	63	73	17	0.889								
Bernsten, Raymond "Ray"		BR TR																									
1956	Sandersville	GSL	4	3	0									0.000	P					4	1	1					
Berry, George																											
1935	Americus	GFL	91	313	37	94	9	4	6		5	25	13	0.300	C	665	73	8	0.989								
1936	Americus	GFL	47	156	27	46	7	0	4	28	0			0.295	M, C	209	18	5	0.978								
Berry, John																											
1935	Panama City	GFL	30	83	5	14	2	0	0		0	5	7	0.169	P					21	10	7		148	168	53	56
1938	Thomasville	GFL	4												P					4	1	2	5.63	32	35	13	15
Berry, Lawrence "Larry"		BR TR																									
1939	Valdosta	GFL	127	406	37	88	13	0	1	44	7	32	79	0.217	C	574	78	13	0.980								
1940	Valdosta	GFL	24	85	5	15	2	0	0	7	2	4	11	0.176	C	106	13	4	0.967								
1941	Cordele	GFL	78	249	23	51	9	1	0	27	0	36	28	0.205	C	335	66	13	0.969								
Berry, Samuel "Sam"		BR TR																									
1951	Hazlehurst-Baxley	GSL	50	201	35	49	6	1	2	21	8	23	39	0.244	OF	122	6	6	0.955								
Bertha, Elmer "Bates"		BR TR 6'1" 135 lbs b. 10/29/1927 Jessup, PA																									
1948	Carrollton	GAL	37	126	13	23	2	0	1	8	0	15	28	0.183	1B	278	7	6	0.979								
Bertrand, Arthur "Art"		BR TR																									
1955	Cordele	GFL	2	1	0									0.000	P					2	0	0	<45				
Bertschy, Robert "Bob"		BR																									
1958	Thomasville	GFL	10	19	1	2	1	0	0	0	0	1	10	0.105													
Berzonski, John																											
1952	Statesboro	GSL	16	34	4	5	0	0	0	0	1	5	13	0.147	P	4	6	0	1.000	16	5	6	5.89	81	87	40	52
1953	Statesboro	GSL	12	14	2	3	0	0	0	0	0	2	7	0.214	P	2	15	0	1.000	12	0	4	5.44	48	65	17	27
Bess, Frank "Krim"																											
1935	Albany	GFL	51	137	19	31	9	1	1		0	2	20	0.226	P					40	19	10		240	250	112	80
1936	Albany	GFL	62	159	14	25	4	0	1	16	1			0.157	P					62	21	15	3.48	290		117	68
1938	Albany	GFL	35	91	3	15	1	2	0	5	1	3	20	0.165	P	9	41	1	0.980	36	18	6	3.23	231	360	91	56
1939	Albany	GFL													P					5	1	4	5.49	41	63	20	19
Bess, Robert "Bob"		BR TR																									
1948	Douglas(3) - Vid-Lyo(21)	GSL	24	32	0	1	0	0	0	0	0	2	13	0.031	P	1	15	3	0.842	24	2	6	5.00	90	97	20	39
Bessent, Fred Donald "Don"		BR TR 6'0" 175 lbs b. 03/13/1931 Jacksonville, FL d. 07/07/1990 Jacksonville, FL																									
1950	LaGrange	GAL	43	120	22	33	1	2	3	11	1	11	15	0.275	P	6	49	8	0.873	29	22	7	2.23	242	190	229	92
Betancourt, Roberto		BR TR																									
1950	Tifton	GSL	31	101	17	24	5	0	1	11	1	5	24	0.238	3B, P	17	39	8	0.875	11	3	4	4.80	75	73	49	55
1951	Tifton	GFL	74	166	29	35	11	0	2	21	7	26	42	0.211	3B, P	32	60	5	0.948	41	18	14	2.87	279	200	201	162
Betcher, George		BR TR																									
1951	Cordele	GFL	59	227	46	73	12	3	1	43	7	46	23	0.322	3B	71	115	20	0.903								
Betcher, Ralph "Froggie"		BR TR																									
1952	Cordele	GFL	121	434	79	133	17	4	1	63	5	108	40	0.306	3B	145	203	22	0.941								
Bethea, George		BR TR																									
1951	Waycross	GFL	19	27	4	3	0	0	0	3	0	2	6	0.111	P	5	22	0	1.000	20	5	5	4.03	76	82	29	44
Bethman, Carl																											
1939	Moultrie	GFL	139	568	92	175	41	12	9	111	22	41	90	0.308	3B	168	255	35	0.924								
Betsch, Richard "Dick"		BL TL																									
1956	Vidalia	GSL	74	205	35	49	5	3	0	13	1	41	47	0.239	OF, P	64	15	7	0.919	19	5	6	4.40	86	78	56	58
Bettin, Robert "Bob"		BL TR																									
1953	Dublin	GSL	54	223	43	68	13	3	5	38	4	42	31	0.305	OF, C	194	23	8	0.964								
1955	Moultrie	GFL	34	115	13	29	3	0	0	17	0	25	30	0.252	C	197	22	8	0.965								

Georgia Class-D Minor League Baseball Encyclopedia

YR	TEAM	LG	G	AB	R	H	2B	3B	HR	RBI	SB	BB	SO	BA	POS	PO	A	E	FA	GP	W	L	ERA	IP	H	SO	BB
Bettineschi, Frank		BR TR																									
1952	Vidalia	GSL	78	268	36	78	9	1	2	62	7	34	42	0.291	3B	76	119	17	0.920								
1953	Vidalia	GSL	29	110	20	30	4	1	0	18	0	21	11	0.273	3B	38	54	10	0.902								
Bettison, ---																											
1930	Carrollton	GAL	<10												C												
Bettleyon, Robert "Bob"		BR TR																									
1951	Cordele	GFL	108	386	43	84	3	4	0	39	8	49	64	0.218	1B, 2B, 3B	229	191	30	0.933								
Betts, ---																											
1915	Americus-Gainesville	FLAG	40	67	5	15	2	0	0		3			0.224													
Betz, Robert J. "Bob"		BR TR																									
1948	Tallassee	GAL	30	112	9	26	6	1	1	12	1	15	24	0.232	OF	37	4	1	0.976								
Bevell, Pat		BR TR																									
1940	Waycross	GFL	50	143	15	34	2	0	0	20	1	7	14	0.238	C	143	24	3	0.982								
Beverly, Charles		BR TR																									
1949	Waycross	GFL	12	41	9	9	1	0	0	8	1	13	9	0.220	2B	29	26	2	0.965								
Beverly, Jack																											
1948	Tallahassee	GFL	<10												P						0	0					
Bevil (Bevilacqua), Louis Eugene "Lou"		BR TR 5'11" 190 lbs. b. 11/27/1922 Nelson, IL d. 02/01/1973 Dixon, IL																									
1941	Thomasville	GFL	54	129	14	21	3	3	0	10	1	3	34	0.163	P	24	51	6	0.926	43	17	15	3.80	256	247	182	143
Beyrer, Harold																											
1939	Americus	GFL	16	59	9	15	2	0	0	3	0	9	8	0.254	2B	32	33	1	0.985								
Bianchi, Frank		BR TR																									
1949	Griffin	GAL	17	15	1	3	0	0	0	1	1	2	4	0.200	P	3	8	2	0.846	17	2	4	7.53	49	57	20	54
Bianchini, Raymond "Ray"		BR TR																									
1956	Dublin	GSL	23	73	13	17	5	1	0	12	3	21	20	0.233	OF	11	1	2	0.857								
Biassetti, Gilbert "Gil"		BR TR																									
1955	Sandersville	GSL	28	33	6	5	0	0	0	3	0	7	7	0.152	P	5	16	5	0.808	28	6	7	5.11	104	115	57	68
Biel, ---																											
1915	Waycross	FLAG	12	34	3	5	0	0	0		0			0.147	2B	24	24	5	0.906								
Bieser, Fred		BR TR																									
1946	Carrollton	GAL	24	54	8	6	1	0	1	6	0	5	19	0.111	OF	10	1	1	0.917								
Biggerstaff, Jack																											
1949	Eastman	GSL	22	73	9	16	3	0	0	11	1	7	12	0.219	OF	33	1	2	0.944								
Biggs, MacDuff		BL TR																									
1957	Waycross	GFL	31	111	7	12	5	0	0	7	0	12	24	0.108	1B	251	16	10	0.964								
Billingsley, ---																											
1913	LaGrange	GAL	80	285	32	81					7			0.284	P, C	493	127	23	0.964								
Billingsley, Raymond "Ray"		BL TR																									
1958	Valdosta	GFL	62	240	51	68	14	1	0	27	7	52	19	0.283	OF	95	5	0	1.000								
Bindschadler, Benjamin "Ben"		BR TR																									
1955	Tifton	GFL	31	47	8	10	0	0	0	5	0	10	12	0.213	P	9	22	5	0.861	29	7	10	3.53	148	127	79	92
Birchfield, Gilbert "Frog"																											
1941	Americus	GFL	40	74	10	11	2	0	0	5	0	9	32	0.149	P	7	40	8	0.855	38	12	15	4.28	202	218	98	122
Bird, James William "Jim"		BL TR																									
1950	Eastman	GSL	20	61	12	12	3	1	1	10	2	9	11	0.197	2B	28	34	2	0.969								
Bird, Robert "Bob"		BL TR																									
1957	Fitzgerald	GFL	129	425	89	104	18	3	12	61	2	122	86	0.245	3B	150	231	27	0.934								
1958	Dublin	GFL	107	302	65	85	19	0	18	77	1	150	55	0.281	3B, SS, P	117	228	18	0.950	3	0	0		<30			
Bisesi, John E.		BR TR																									
1953	Albany	GFL	132	474	76	107	8	3	1	42	10	87	54	0.226	SS	234	320	66	0.894								
1954	Hazlehurst-Baxley	GSL	71	260	50	61	6	8	0	21	11	64	40	0.235	SS	146	157	41	0.881								
Bishop, Charles Tuller "Charlie"		BR TR 6'2" 195 lbs. b. 01/01/1924 Atlanta, GA d. 07/05/1993 Lawrenceville, GA																									
1946	Albany	GFL	33	92	13	21	4	3	0	11	0	10	34	0.228	OF, P	21	30	7	0.879	15	8	4	2.93	123	94	98	74
Bishop, Danny		BS TR																									
1957	Fitzgerald	GFL	120	364	50	90	18	4	4	53	1	80	66	0.247	C	658	63	18	0.976								
Bishop, Patrick "Pat"		BR TR																									
1948	Cordele	GFL	13	7	0	0	0	0	0	0	0	3	1	0.000	P	0	2	0	1.000								
Bitting, Earl																											
1913	Waycross	ESL	35	141	19	37	0	0	0					0.262	3B	50	73	15	0.891								
1914	Brunswick - Americus	GSL		316	46	97	17	3	5		20			0.307	M												
Black, ---																											
1914	Talladega	GAL	12	37	5	8					1			0.216	P	3	29	0	1.000	12							
1921	Lindale	GSL													P												
Black, Bobby		BR TR																									
1963	Moultrie	GFL	20	36	3	4	2	0	1	5	0	0	25	0.111	P	4	12	0	1.000	20	10	5	2.69	107	80	88	55
Black, Eugene "Gene"		BR TR																									
1951	Valley	GAL	38	84	7	14	2	0	1	9	1	4	38	0.167	P	5	30	8	0.814	36	10	11	4.64	194	224	104	96
Black, Loyd																											
1941	Americus	GFL	3	12	1	1	0	0	0	0	1	0	3	0.083	OF	4	1	0	1.000								
Black, Ralph E.		BR TR																									
1950	Eastman	GSL	11	20	4	2	0	0	0	0	1	5	9	0.100	P	2	3	4	0.556	11	3	4	7.17	54	46	53	66
Black, Wayne																											
1935	Moultrie	GFL	90	350	34	91	16	1	1		8	24	24	0.260	IF	165	245	45	0.901								

Georgia Class-D Minor League Baseball Encyclopedia

YR	TEAM	LG	G	AB	R	H	2B	3B	HR	RBI	SB	BB	SO	BA	POS	PO	A	E	FA	GP	W	L	ERA	IP	H	SO	BB
Blackburn, James Ray "Jim"		BR TR 6'4" 175 lbs. b. 06/19/1924 Warsaw, KY d. 10/26/1969 Cincinnati, OH																									
1941	Cordele	GFL	12	23	0	4	2	0	0	3	0	1	4	0.174	P	1	5	0	1.000	11	1	3	7.16	49	66	13	15
1942	Cordele	GFL	24	62	6	18	4	0	0	5	0	3	15	0.290	P	5	28	5	0.868	23	8	11	3.76	153	160	83	63
Blackburn, Thomas "Tom"		BL TR																									
1947	Valley	GAL	100	371	55	106	11	3	1	40	6	36	55	0.286	3B, OF	181	15	21	0.903								
1949	Valley	GAL	119	465	72	121	19	3	0	42	17	48	58	0.260	OF	186	16	13	0.940								
Blackman, Donald "Don"		BR TR																									
1947	Valdosta	GFL	27	70	3	13	2	0	0	6	1	24	32	0.186	2B	52	38	5	0.947								
Blackmon, Grover		BL																									
1946	Waycross	GFL	<10																								
Blackstock, Harold "Hal"		BR TR																									
1936	Cordele	GFL	110	475	78	130	16	4	4	46	16			0.274	SS	213	377	56	0.913								
1946	Valley	GAL	47	165	16	45	13	1	0	26	1	9	11	0.273	3B	46	75	6	0.953								
1947	Valley(14) - Griffin (100)	GAL	114	443	80	140	34	6	1	51	18	37	28	0.316	3B, SS	186	328	47	0.916								
Blackwell, ---																											
1913	Opelika	GAL	90	338	48	105					17			0.311	2B	176	155	30	0.917								
1914	Opelika	GAL	88	338	53	97					10			0.287	3B	138	102	19	0.927								
1915	Dothan - Ame-Gains	FLAG	39	144	13	39	11	0	0		1			0.271	2B, OF	60	34	10	0.904								
Blackwell, Dan																											
1941	Tallahassee	GFL	62	245	28	58	12	6	1	38	5	20	44	0.237	OF	138	6	9	0.941								
Blackwell, Kenneth "Ken"		BR TR																									
1953	Cordele	GFL	28	45	1	3	0	0	0	3	0	4	18	0.067	P	2	17	1	0.950	27	5	6	4.88	120	122	48	68
Blackwell, Thomas "Tom"		BR TR																									
1946	Moultrie	GFL	99	387	49	94	12	0	3	52	5	19	25	0.243	3B	94	186	35	0.889								
1947	Griffin	GAL	118	456	57	112	13	2	0	42	15	25	35	0.246	3B	154	240	36	0.916								
1948	Griffin	GAL	50	196	21	55	8	1	0	18	3	13	12	0.281	2B, 3B	114	102	19	0.919								
Blackwell, Verne																											
1939	Americus	GFL	111	435	75	121	12	12	5	48	3	45	58	0.278	OF	217	16	10	0.959								
Blackwell, William "Bill"		BL TR																									
1949	Tallassee	GAL	115	412	62	119	10	5	2	38	23	38	52	0.289	M, OF	251	20	14	0.951								
Blansit, ---																											
1915	Americus-Gainesville	FLAG	4		0									0.000	P					4	2	1		22	11	8	9
Blanton, ---																											
1906	Waycross	GSL													OF, 3B												
Blanton, E. Hugh		BR TR																									
1950	Dublin	GSL	89	264	50	72	6	2	19	60	2	52	44	0.273	1B, OF, P	322	66	16	0.960	29	12	7	5.05	173	165	105	112
1951	Dublin	GSL	67	162	28	35	6	0	4	18	4	29	22	0.216	1B, OF, P	94	75	11	0.939	30	12	10	4.20	195	168	91	114
Blasco, Pete																											
1939	Waycross	GFL	11	45	7	6	1	0	0	3	0	6	7	0.133	SS	16	22	7	0.844								
Blaze, Frank		BR TR																									
1946	Valley	GAL	<10																								
Bledsoe, Charles		BS TR																									
1951	Waycross	GFL	125	448	61	117	14	4	2	53	9	52	43	0.261	C	648	89	21	0.972								
1952	Waycross	GFL	140	506	70	121	16	6	2	52	16	73	36	0.239	C	888	85	24	0.976								
1953	Douglas	GSL	123	503	99	162	24	4	5	91	19	66	32	0.322	M, C, P	728	68	14	0.983		0	0	<45				
1954	Douglas	GSL	122	472	99	132	19	1	7	82	30	54	46	0.280	M, 3B, SS, C, P	640	131	24	0.970	1	0	0	<45				
Bledsoe, William "Billy"		BL TR																									
1949	Valdosta	GFL	30	34	3	5	0	0	0	2	0	4	8	0.147	P	5	16	1	0.955	29	8	2	3.00	96	94	45	53
1950	Valdosta	GFL	40	91	12	18	4	1	0	12	0	11	24	0.198	P	12	35	5	0.904	34	16	13	3.54	229	212	120	124
1953	Thomasville	GFL	12	19	1	4	0	0	0	2	0	1	5	0.211	P						3	2	<45				
Bleidistel, Wally																											
1936	Albany	GFL													P								<30				
Blevins, Jesse																											
1942	Albany	GFL	2	6	2	2	0	0	0	1	0	2	1	0.333	C	10	0	2	0.833								
Blewster, Davis "Dave"		BR TR																									
1939	Thomasville	GFL													P								<45				
1940	Moultrie	GFL	<10												P					8	1	6	5.91	35	41	13	34
Bloodworth, Charles		BR TR																									
1949	Waycross	GFL	95	298	53	77	11	4	1	41	6	47	61	0.258	OF	148	13	4	0.976								
1950	Waycross	GFL	18	50	9	14	2	0	0	4	1	6	9	0.280	OF	15	2	1	0.944								
Bloodworth, James Henry "Jimmy"		BR TR 5'11" 180 lbs. b. 07/26/1917 Tallahassee, FL																									
1935	Panama City	GFL	55	200	21	61	10	3	4		0	13	19	0.305	OF	82	117	26	0.884								
Bloom, Donald "Don"		BL TL																									
1954	Statesboro	GSL	1	1		0								0.000	P					1	0	0	<45				
1955	Tifton	GFL	1	0										0.000	P					1	0	0	<45				
Blume, James "Jim"		BR TR																									
1953	Douglas(16) - Jesup(1)	GSL	17	32	6	8	1	0	0	5	0	6	11	0.250	P						0	1	<45				
Bly, John		BR TR																									
1963	Thomasville	GFL	96	347	48	91	13	5	2	38	14	27	63	0.262	OF	204	5	9	0.959								
Boatman, James "Jim"		BL TR																									
1947	Alexander City	GAL	37	99	17	21	2	0	0	16	4	18	28	0.212	SS, OF	26	31	15	0.792								
Boatwright, John		BR TR																									
1949	Moultrie	GFL	24	94	14	23	3	0	2	15	3	6	39	0.245	OF	32	3	6	0.854								
Bobo, William "Bill"		BR TR																									
1940	Cordele	GFL	29	58	3	10	2	0	0	5	1	7	20	0.172	P					26	6	11	5.18	146	188	81	70

Georgia Class-D Minor League Baseball Encyclopedia

YR	TEAM	LG	G	AB	R	H	2B	3B	HR	RBI	SB	BB	SO	BA	POS	PO	A	E	FA	GP	W	L	ERA	IP	H	SO	BB
Bobowski, Edward "Ed"		BR TR																									
1948	LaGrange	GAL	22	34	4	5	1	0	0	1	0	4	9	0.147	P	1	12	0	1.000	13	2	4	4.64	66	79	17	28
1949	LaGrange(13) - Carrollton(20)	GAL	33	67	8	16	1	1	0	5	1	9	20	0.239	P	12	29	2	0.953	33	10	13	3.51	187	187	74	112
1950	Carrollton	GAL	32	83	12	14	2	0	1	7	0	7	31	0.169	P	10	28	2	0.950	27	17	7	4.96	176	182	100	118
Bodan, Joseph "Joe"																											
1942	Valdosta	GFL	86	325	54	84	13	5	2	37	4	28	54	0.258	OF	127	11	11	0.926								
Boddy, Robert "Bob"		BR TR																									
1950	Eastman(28) - Dublin(9)	GSL	37	144	41	46	11	3	2	25	9	22	15	0.319	2B, SS	81	96	17	0.912								
Bodnar, Elmer		BS TR																									
1949	Albany	GFL	132	488	73	113	15	4	3	59	8	78	97	0.232	2B	275	334	38	0.941								
Boehme, Kenneth "Ken"		BR TR																									
1952	Dublin	GSL	48	135	25	34	5	2	2	16	5	23	10	0.252	C	243	20	10	0.963								
Bogardus, Earl		BR TR																									
1952	Moultrie	GFL	20	52	3	6	0	0	0	5	0	6	17	0.115	C	83	7	0	1.000								
Bogart, Eugene "Gene"																											
1941	Tallahassee	GFL	57	244	41	57	6	2	0	16	5	25	26	0.234	3B	93	171	40	0.868								
Boger, James "Jim"		BR TR																									
1958	Valdosta	GFL	24	40	5	3	0	0	0	2	0	7	22	0.075	P	8	10	2	0.900	21	10	5	4.13	122	109	121	69
Boggan, George		BL TR																									
1949	Albany	GFL	28	66	8	10	2	0	0	7	0	13	20	0.152	P	6	33	4	0.907	28	15	5	3.52	189	155	113	81
Boggs, Patrick "Pat"		BR																									
1953	Sandersville	GSL	13	39	2	4	0	0	0	5	0	7	5	0.103													
Bohn, Lloyd		BR TR																									
1954	Americus-Cordele	GFL	15	16	1	3	0	0	0	3	0	1	10	0.188	P					8	2	3	<45				
Bohonko, John																											
1939	Cordele	GFL	20	67	15	18	6	0	1	6	1	8	11	0.269	3B	29	50	10	0.888								
Bojorquez, Federico		BR TR																									
1955	Albany	GFL	19	43	7	7	0	1	0	5	2	10	11	0.163	SS	22	35	9	0.864								
Bolam, Robert "Bob"		BL TR																									
1951	Brunswick	GFL	76	285	56	77	19	2	2	31	10	60	27	0.270	2B, OF	134	60	14	0.933								
Bolch, William "Bill"		BR TR																									
1950	Hazlehurst-Baxley	GSL	27	83	8	17	2	1	1	9	0	16	11	0.205	OF	30	2	4	0.889								
1954	Statesboro	GSL	7	11		0								0.000													
Bolding, Billy		BL TR																									
1958	Waycross	GFL	23	47	2	10	3	0	0	3	0	3	16	0.213	P	6	18	1	0.960	13	3	6	3.40	82	86	47	43
Bolin, J.B. "Pete"		BL TR																									
1953	Brunswick	GFL	84	363	85	115	16	3	1	36	15	34	40	0.317	OF	151	8	13	0.924								
Bolin, Joe N.		BR TR																									
1958	Dublin	GFL	96	341	70	106	24	0	9	78	1	68	42	0.311	C, OF	260	12	11	0.961								
Boling, Edward																											
1929	Talledega	GAL	90	316	64	78	10	4	0		16	41	33	0.247	1B	779	33	8	0.990								
1930	Talladega	GAL	33	133	24	43	4	1	1		4	22	14	0.323	1B	292	7	4	0.987								
Bollman, William "Bill"		BR TR																									
1949	Tallahassee	GFL	130	493	70	116	20	0	4	48	6	65	59	0.235	1B, 2B, 3B, SS	274	313	65	0.900								
Bolster, Harvey																											
1941	Tallahassee	GFL	30	107	9	18	3	0	2	11	0	6	46	0.168	OF	45	0	4	0.918								
Bolt, ---																											
1921	Lindale	GSL													P												
Bonaparte, Robert "Bob"		BR TR																									
1951	Brunswick	GFL	126	496	87	150	25	7	16	87	27	49	82	0.302	1B, OF	823	34	34	0.962								
Bonavia, Anthony		BR TR																									
1958	Thomasville	GFL	15	11	1	2	0	0	0	2	0	0	3	0.182	P	4	4	2	0.800	15	1	2	7.46	35	44	41	23
Bonczek, Lonegan		BR TR																									
1958	Brunswick	GFL	60	245	33	64	13	1	5	45	1	21	34	0.261	SS	111	133	21	0.921								
Bonds, Kenneth "Ken"		BR TR																									
1949	Americus	GFL	42	119	14	21	1	0	0	9	3	19	22	0.176	C	226	33	11	0.959								
Bone, ---																											
1913	Opelika	GAL	62	217	19	50					6			0.230	C	345	60	7	0.983								
Bone, William "Bill"		BR TR																									
1955	Albany	GFL	124	412	51	108	9	4	0	43	12	82	64	0.262	SS	206	291	44	0.919								
Boner, Byrns "Billy"		BR TR																									
1956	Albany	GFL	16	50	7	9	2	0	0	5	1	12	14	0.180	OF	18	2	1	0.952								
1957	Albany	GFL	14	41	3	7	1	0	1	4	1	3	11	0.171	C	68	12	1	0.988								
Bonet, Hector		BR TR																									
1953	Valdosta	GFL	31	100	13	30	3	0	0	3	2	11	12	0.300	OF	27	2	3	0.906								
Bongard, Ed "Eddie"		BR																									
1940	Moultrie	GFL	<10																								
Bonifay, Albert L.		BL TL																									
1920	Carrollton	GSL		71	6	15	3	0	0		0			0.211	P												
1920	LaGrange	GSL													P												
Bonnett, Luther		BR TR																									
1950	Cordele	GFL	13	44	5	9	0	0	0	4	1	9	7	0.205	OF	23	1	3	0.889								
Bonowitz, John Joe		BR TR 5'10" 165 lbs b. 08/12/1899 Columbus, OH d. 09/04/1969 Hollywood, FL																									
1936	Americus	GFL	48	200	46	72	15	4	8	40	3			0.360	M, OF	86	6	4	0.958								

228

Georgia Class-D Minor League Baseball Encyclopedia

YR	TEAM	LG	G	AB	R	H	2B	3B	HR	RBI	SB	BB	SO	BA	POS	PO	A	E	FA	GP	W	L	ERA	IP	H	SO	BB
Booker, John		BL TR																									
1948	Alexander City	GAL	25	88	16	14	3	0	0	8	5	16	14	0.159	SS	30	68	13	0.883								
1950	Opelika	GAL	24	81	8	12	1	0	0	4	0	11	11	0.148	SS	35	77	15	0.882								
Booker, William G. "Bill"		BR TR																									
1962	Moultrie	GFL	50	154	28	38	7	1	0	11	1	28	16	0.247	3B, SS	37	49	21	0.804								
Boone, Isaac Morgan "Ike"		BL TR 6'0" 195 lbs. b. 02/17/1897 Samantha, AL d. 08/01/1958 Northport, AL																									
1920	Cedartown	GSL		274	62	113								0.412													
Boone, Ronald "Ron"		BR TR																									
1958	Thomasville	GFL	18	34	7	4	1	0	0	2	1	7	9	0.118	C	57	9	2	0.971								
Boos, Wendell		BR TR																									
1947	Alexander City	GAL	35	62	4	9	1	0	0	6	0	11	19	0.145	P	4	40	9	0.830	32	11	14	4.38	187	209	66	76
Boote, ---																											
1914	Rome	GAL	13	37	3	3				1				0.081	P	4	26	0	1.000	13							
Booth, James J. "Jim"																											
1949	Sparta	GSL	20	65	9	16	4	1	0	11	1	10	3	0.246	C	86	7	4	0.959								
Booth, Wayne		BR TR																									
1946	Thomasville	GFL	1												P					1	0	0	0.00	3			
Booth, William "Bill"		BR TR																									
1957	Thomasville	GFL	37	53	5	6	1	0	0	2	0	5	22	0.113	P	6	24	1	0.968	37	7	7	4.47	175	187	116	95
1958	Thomasville	GFL	22	42	4	13	1	0	0	5	0	5	7	0.310	P	8	16	1	0.960	20	7	6	3.66	118	108	98	55
Boozer, John Morgan "John"		BR TR 6'3" 205 lbs. b. 07/22/1938 Columbia, SC d. 01/24/1986 Lexington, SC																									
1958	Brunswick	GFL	8	19		2								0.105	P					8	3	4	3.67	49	26	52	43
Boozer, Wesley "Wes"																											
1939	Cordele	GFL	28	51	2	5	1	1	0	3	0	4	18	0.098	P	4	22	0	1.000	23	4	7	4.98	121	135	45	73
Bope, George																											
1915	Brunswick	FLAG	74	265	38	74	11	2	3	13				0.279	1B, P	630	33	21	0.969	0							
1916	Anniston	GAL	42	150	19	33				9				0.220	1B												
1917	Anniston	GAL	5	13	0	2				0				0.154	1B, 3B	40	3	0	1.000								
Borden, Wallace "Wallie"		BR TR																									
1940	Waycross	GFL	133	534	102	150	16	5	2	51	12	69	112	0.281	OF	245	23	18	0.937								
1941	Waycross	GFL	138	554	109	158	20	6	1	63	21	77	92	0.285	OF	323	19	18	0.950								
Borders, Aubrey																											
1946	Newnan(13) - Carrollton(16)	GAL	29	60	7	16	6	0	0	7	0	8	9	0.267	P	4	24	2	0.933	25	7	6	3.82	132	115	84	34
Borom, Edward Jones "Red"		BL TR 5'10" 175 lbs. b. 10/30/1916 Spartanburg, SC																									
1935	Tallahassee	GFL	7	21	3	5	0	0	0		1	1	1	0.238	IF	22	26	2	0.960								
Borrett, Curtis		BL TL																									
1955	Waycross	GFL	29	99	16	24	4	2	0	14	2	20	13	0.242	OF	32	0	3	0.914								
Bosarge, Vincent "Vince"		BS TR																									
1946	Valley	GAL	120	501	53	110	15	3	0	51	24	32	62	0.220	SS	115	326	57	0.886								
1947	Valley	GAL	48	189	34	46	2	2	0	18	8	22	19	0.243	SS	83	126	29	0.878								
Bosch, Ortelio		BR TR																									
1953	Waycross	GFL	74	291	55	77	9	4	0	29	10	45	28	0.265	SS	137	211	24	0.935								
Bossard, Belasco		BR TR																									
1954	Douglas	GSL	100	431	107	155	33	4	9	65	18	36	17	0.360	SS	188	287	40	0.922								
Bosse, Louis "Lou"		BR TR																									
1955	Cordele	GFL	26	80	18	18	3	4	0	12	8	24	23	0.225	OF	31	4	4	0.897								
Bosser, Melvin Edward "Mel"		BR TR 6'0" 173 lbs. b. 02/08/1914 Johnstown, PA d. 03/26/1986 Crossville, TN																									
1939	Thomasville	GFL	30	69	7	27	2	1	0	5	0	0	9	0.391	P	11	25	4	0.900	25	7	12	3.32	149	154	50	48
1940	Thomasville	GFL	49	134	17	33	3	0	0	15	4	5	13	0.246	P					38	23	11	3.58	274	316	118	90
1946	Carrollton	GAL	4												P					4	1	2	0.00	18	20	3	7
Bossie, Ronald "Ron"		BR TR																									
1956	Moultrie	GFL	3	2		0								0.000	P					2	0	0		<45			
Bostwick, ---																											
1914	Selma	GAL	9	26	1	2				0				0.077	P	4	16	3	0.870	9							
1915	Griffin	GAL	10												P	1	20	1	0.955	8	2	4					
Bostwick, William "Bill"		BR TR																									
1957	Brunswick	GFL	4	3		0								0.000	P					4	0	1		<30			
Boswell, Brant																											
1928	Carrollton	GAL	88	357	79	97	19	2	12		14	52	38	0.272	2B	201	269	28	0.944								
Boswell, John		BR TR																									
1953	Sandersville	GSL	1												0.000	P					1	0			<45			
Botkin, Delmer "Del"		BR TL																									
1962	Dublin	GFL	29	57	13	17	1	0	2	9	0	10	8	0.298	OF, C	57	3	2	0.968								
Bottoms, Woodrow		BL TR																									
1946	Newnan	GAL	80	292	77	123	22	6	1	49	13	50	9	0.421	3B, SS	86	65	22	0.873								
1947	Newnan	GAL	48	208	50	70	11	5	1	26	15	25	13	0.337	3B, SS	60	126	20	0.903								
1948	Sparta	GSL	99	371	78	139	20	6	0	58	10	69	30	0.375	M, SS	141	287	34	0.926								
1949	Valley	GAL	20	65	15	20	1	0	0	4	6	21	6	0.308	M, 3B	31	17	4	0.923								
1949	Sparta	GSL	50	186	36	47	7	4	1	32	1	45	11	0.253	M, SS	97	156	24	0.913								
1950	Opelika	GAL	18	69	17	19	0	0	0	8	0	15	8	0.275	M												
Bottone, Louis "Lou"																											
1939	Tallahassee	GFL	57	217	20	54	5	3	1	35	2	18	19	0.249	OF	94	4	4	0.961								
Bottorff, Thomas "Tom"		BL TR																									
1949	Opelika	GAL	21	55	5	14	0	0	0	8	0	13	6	0.255	1B	135	10	9	0.942								
1949	Dublin	GSL	<10																									

Georgia Class-D Minor League Baseball Encyclopedia

YR	TEAM	LG	G	AB	R	H	2B	3B	HR	RBI	SB	BB	SO	BA	POS	PO	A	E	FA	GP	W	L	ERA	IP	H	SO	BB
Bourell, Roy																											
1935	Albany	GFL	22	51	4	6	1	0	1		0	4	28	0.118	P					24	5	7		128	161	62	63
1936	Albany	GFL													P					<30							
Bourgeois, Joseph A. "Joe"		BL TR																									
1953	Albany	GFL	49	105	13	22	4	0	0	7	1	8	25	0.210	P	9	38	6	0.887	34	16	7	3.16	185	169	131	69
Bova, Tom		BR																									
1955	Thomasville	GFL	5	6	0									0.000													
1955	Statesboro	GSL	3	6	0									0.000													
Bowden, ---																											
1913	Cordele	ESL	59	217	31	62	11	2	2					0.286	C, OF	193	31	20	0.918								
1914	Brunswick	GSL		63	16	20	7	1	5		2			0.317													
1915	Americus-Gainesville	FLAG	5												P					5	2	3		24	30	8	5
1915	Waycross	FLAG	6												P					6	2	2		30	28	13	17
Bowden, David Timon "Tim"		BL TR 5'10" 175 lbs. b. 08/15/1891 McDonough, GA d. 10/25/1949 Emory, GA																									
1920	Rome	GSL		291	37	106	15	12	1		23			0.364	M, OF												
Bowden, Raymond "Ray"		BR TR																									
1947	Thomasville	GFL	88	321	48	89	9	2	0	29	5	40	45	0.277	2B	233	220	9	0.981								
Bowden, Russell "Russ"		BL TL																									
1955	Valdosta	GFL	5	2		1								0.500	P					5	0	1		<45			
Bowdoin, Lawrence H.																											
1915	Griffin	GAL	44	169	20	43	12	2	1					0.254	3B	42	67	5	0.956								
1916	Grif - New - Ann	GAL	66	231	17	37					3			0.160	P, 3B												
1917	Tri-Cities	GAL	16	62	8	15	3	2	0		3			0.242	3B	10	23	7	0.825								
1920	Griffin	GSL													2B												
Bowen, ---																											
1906	Waycross	GSL													1B, C												
Bowen, Grady																											
1913	Americus	ESL	96	364	57	118	10	2	3					0.324	3B	146	201	25	0.933								
1914	Newnan	GAL	67	265	34	71					12			0.268	SS	127	180	29	0.914								
1914	Americus	GSL		241	25	67	9	0	0		10			0.278													
1916	LaGrange	GAL	70	231	38	65					11			0.281	M, 3B												
Bowen, Harold																											
1942	Albany	GFL	70	261	23	65	6	4	0	25	0	14	26	0.249	OF	114	3	4	0.967								
Bowen, Howard		BR TR																									
1950	Tifton	GSL	10	16	0	0	0	0	0	0	0	1	5	0.000	P	1	6	1	0.875								
Bowen, Jack		BR TR																									
1957	Valdosta	GFL	126	413	72	125	22	3	3	61	12	69	40	0.303	C	793	91	16	0.982								
Bowen, Rex																											
1935	Albany	GFL	118	421	88	121	27	3	5		14	48	38	0.287	IF	256	340	13	0.979								
1936	Albany	GFL	62	245	39	60	17	2	4	42	6			0.245	2B	178	153	8	0.976								
Bowers, Stewart Cole Jr. "Stew"		BS TR 6'0" 170 lbs. b. 02/26/1915 New Freedom, PA																									
1939	Thomasville	GFL	33	69	13	13	1	1	0	7	1	12	19	0.188	P	15	34	1	0.980	28	14	9	3.57	194	172	82	56
1940	Thomasville	GFL	11	28	3	8	1	0	0	2	0	3	8	0.286	P					10	4	6	4.71	65	88	45	14
Bowie, Donald "Don"		BL TR																									
1955	Brunswick	GFL	33	105	16	26	6	1	4	24	2	20	18	0.248	OF	52	2	2	0.964								
Bowland, Arthur English Jr. "Art"		BL TR 6'0" 180 lbs b. 05/09/1923 Pawtucket, RI																									
1942	Valdosta	GFL	126	493	100	149	20	4	0	57	26	99	25	0.302	OF	231	13	9	0.964								
Bowman, Clyde		BR TL																									
1963	Brunswick	GFL	34	86	7	17	4	0	1	8	2	10	16	0.198	OF, P	27	6	1	0.971	1	0	0	4.50	4	4	5	4
Box, ---		BR TR																									
1952	Jesup	GSL	11												P	2	13	2	0.882								
Boxer, Seymour		BR TR																									
1950	Jesup	GSL	37	70	8	11	3	0	0	3	0	10	11	0.157	P	5	69	4	0.949	36	13	12	3.54	211	215	92	97
1953	Jesup	GSL	37	96	13	22	3	0	0	9	1	5	15	0.229	P	14	48	3	0.954	34	18	11	3.82	217	204	116	128
Boyce, George		BR TR																									
1952	Brunswick	GFL	96	305	27	65	10	0	0	22	4	45	46	0.213	C	515	65	23	0.962								
Boyce, Kenneth "Ken"		BR																									
1953	Tifton	GFL	3											0.000													
1953	Vidalia	GSL	8											0.105													
Boyd, J.S.																											
1913	Talladega	GAL		44	3	17					0			0.386	P					5	2	3					
1915	Newnan	GAL	60	238	40	72	12	3	1					0.303	OF	118	9	4	0.969								
1916	Newnan	GAL	70	260	40	63					22			0.242	OF												
Boyd, Smith																											
1906	Albany	GSL													P, OF, 3B												
Boyd, Warner		BR TR																									
1955	Cordele	GFL	12	16	1	3	2	0	0	2	0	2	6	0.188	P	2	6	6	0.571	12	1	5	3.19	48	41	28	27
Boyer, Kenneth "Ken"		BR TR																									
1952	Vidalia	GSL	87	309	44	69	8	0	1	36	13	37	62	0.223	3B, OF, C	224	54	11	0.962								
Boyer, Louis "Lew"		BR TL																									
1955	Albany	GFL	24	79	9	12	1	1	1	4	3	9	20	0.152	1B	179	4	5	0.973								
Boyer, Milton "Milt"		BL TL																									
1946	Opelika	GAL	5												P					5	0	1	0.00	23	31	6	24
1948	Tallassee	GAL	52	127	12	34	2	1	1	14	1	22	17	0.268	OF, P	38	38	0	1.000	25	8	10	4.66	137	138	82	103
Boyer, Robert "Bob"		BR TR																									
1957	Albany	GFL	68	255	35	78	13	3	7	52	7	24	54	0.306	3B	69	128	20	0.908								
1958	Albany	GFL	125	452	107	132	20	4	32	121	21	96	78	0.292	3B, OF, P	202	27	20	0.920	2	0	0	<30				

Georgia Class-D Minor League Baseball Encyclopedia

YR	TEAM	LG	G	AB	R	H	2B	3B	HR	RBI	SB	BB	SO	BA	POS	PO	A	E	FA	GP	W	L	ERA	IP	H	SO	BB
Boykin, Gayle N.		BR TR																									
1953	Thomasville	GFL	19	17	1	1	0	0	0	0	0	4	4	0.059	P	0	5	1	0.833	19	0	2	5.40	55	51	44	47
Boykin, Roma																											
1915	Anniston	GAL	45	149	11	28	3	1	0					0.188	OF	30	3	3	0.917								
Bozeman, James "Jim"		BR TR																									
1946	Thomasville	GFL	1												P					1	0	0	0.00	3			
Bozich, John		BR TR																									
1958	Thomasville	GFL	36	53	6	15	4	0	1	10	0	8	14	0.283	P	5	23	1	0.966	23	6	5	5.74	94	106	44	76
Bozzuto, Albert "Bert"		BL TL 5'9" 160 lbs b. 03/07/1927 Hamden, CT																									
1947	Carrollton	GAL	26	62	2	7	0	0	0	3	0	0	26	0.113	P	0	11	3	0.786	24	10	6	3.09	140	137	99	33
1948	Carrollton	GAL	14	30	4	3	1	0	0	1	0	1	12	0.100	P					14	5	5	3.84	82	78	56	29
1949	Carrollton(9) - Alex City(17)	GAL	26	43	1	8	0	0	0	1	0	2	12	0.186	P	4	13	2	0.895	26	5	14	5.12	137	159	78	70
Bradberry, J. Don "Buck"																											
1954	Fitzgerald	GFL	12	20	1	5	3	0	0	6	0	4	10	0.250	P	2	10	2	0.857	11	1	6	5.64	59	69	28	31
1954	Douglas	GSL	3	6		1								0.167	P					3	0	2	<45				
Braddock, Ronald "Ron"		BR TR																									
1963	Brunswick	GFL	34	67	9	10	3	1	0	3	2	11	27	0.149	3B, OF	15	21	7	0.837								
Bradley, Donald E. "Don"																											
1954	Hazlehurst-Baxley	GSL	44	83	11	16	4	1	0	9	0	10	21	0.193	P	11	53	7	0.901	38	12	14	4.34	232	259	175	94
1955	Hazlehurst-Baxley	GSL	34	64	5	10	2	0	0	3	0	4	17	0.156	P	8	30	7	0.844	31	9	9	2.47	164	152	115	42
Bradley, Eugene P.																											
1915	Talladega	GAL	18	57	6	12	0	1	0					0.211	OF	20	2	2	0.917								
1921	Cedartown	GSL		279	59	94								0.337	OF												
Bradley, Robert "Bob"																											
1936	Thomasville	GFL	57	207	20	46	6	1	1	18	5			0.222	UT	122	143	15	0.946								
Bradshaw, George Thomas "George"		BR TR 6'2" 185 lbs. b. 09/12/1924 Salisbury, NC d. 11/04/1994 Hendersonville, NC																									
1947	Valdosta	GFL	18	71	9	19	3	0	1	8	0	3	12	0.268	C	102	12	4	0.966								
Bradshaw, Hugh		BR TR																									
1949	Tallahassee	GFL	25	76	3	17	2	0	1	6	0	8	17	0.224	C	107	17	7	0.947								
1950	Newnan	GAL	45	143	17	42	7	0	2	20	0	13	16	0.294	C	240	18	7	0.974								
Brady, ---																											
1942	Albany	GFL	8												P					8	2	2	6.27	33	41	17	26
Brady, James Joseph "Jim"		BL TL 6'2" 185 lbs. b. 03/02/1936 Jersey City, NJ																									
1958	Thomasville	GFL	10	7	1	0	0	0	0	0	0	2	4	0.000	P	2	2	2	0.667	10	1	3	<30				
Brady, Kenneth "Ken"																											
1941	Cordele	GFL	33	104	9	18	1	0	0	5	1	13	24	0.173	OF	51	7	11	0.841								
Braganca, Joseph "Joe"		BR TR																									
1949	LaGrange	GAL	47	110	14	23	1	0	0	6	0	24	26	0.209	C	204	17	16	0.932								
1950	LaGrange	GAL	67	187	24	37	4	1	1	20	1	45	46	0.198	C	241	31	11	0.961								
1951	Americus	GFL	52	151	14	27	5	0	1	23	1	31	44	0.179													
Brakefield, William O.																											
1915	Valdosta	FLAG				0								0.000	P		0										
Brancato, Frederick "Fred"		BL TL																									
1956	Tifton	GFL	4	7		0								0.000	P					4	1	1	<45				
1957	Brunswick	GFL	6	2		0								0.000	P					6	1	0	<30				
Brancato, James "Jim"		BL TL																									
1946	Valdosta	GFL	28	81	6	12	2	0	0	3	4	11	28	0.148	OF	41	5	3	0.939								
Brand, Clarence		BR TR																									
1946	Albany	GFL	35	131	20	19	4	0	0	9	1	17	34	0.145	3B, OF	32	22	16	0.771								
Brande, Ralph																											
1939	Americus	GFL	118	447	48	124	17	4	2	67	6	32	20	0.277	3B, OF	149	114	25	0.913								
Brandenburg, Charles		BR TR																									
1954	Americus-Cordele	GFL	47	148	23	38	8	4	1	29	3	37	39	0.257	OF, C	182	25	7	0.967								
Brandon, C.N. "Goat"																											
1920	Carrollton	GSL		284	52	87	16	6	3	11				0.306	OF												
Brandt, Frederick H. "Fred"		BR TR																									
1954	Thomasville	GFL	8	4		0								0.000	P					8	1	0	<45				
Brannan, Charles		BR TR																									
1946	Tallahassee	GFL	112	384	72	112	10	5	2	49	12	64	45	0.292	1B, OF	843	54	27	0.971								
1947	Tallahassee	GFL	10	26	10	7	2	0	0	5	1	4	1	0.269													
Brannen, ---																											
1913	LaGrange	GAL	65	226	33	59				6				0.261	P, OF	111	173	22	0.928	8	4	4					
Brannon, ---																											
1930	Talladega	GAL	80	296	44	88	14	9	0		5	19	22	0.297	C	298	67	16	0.958								
Brannon, Shaw																											
1942	Dothan	GFL	23	52	6	8	0	0	0	3	0	15	14	0.154	C	91	5	2	0.980								
Branon, Michael "Mike"		BL																									
1962	Dublin	GFL	3	4	0	0	0	0	0	0	0	0	1	0.000													
Braun, Kenneth "Ken"		BL TL																									
1946	Valdosta	GFL	64	140	24	36	8	2	0	27	0	20	34	0.257	OF, P	20	20	6	0.870	23	10	6	2.28	150	145	87	68
Braun, Leon		BR TR																									
1953	Tifton	GFL	3											0.000	P						0	1	<45				
1953	Sandersville - Statesboro	GSL	2											0.000	P						0	1	<45				
Brawner, Ralph		BL TR																									
1947	Tallassee	GAL	36	152	22	41	7	3	1	13	9	12	34	0.270	OF	74	8	3	0.965								

YR	TEAM	LG	G	AB	R	H	2B	3B	HR	RBI	SB	BB	SO	BA	POS	PO	A	E	FA	GP	W	L	ERA	IP	H	SO	BB
Bray, ---																											
1914	Rome	GAL	75	360	52	88					7			0.244	2B	274	277	38	0.935								
Bray, Clarence Wilbur "Buster"		BL TL 6'0" 170 lbs. b. 04/01/1913 Birmingham, AL d. 09/04/1982 Evansville, IN																									
1939	Waycross	GFL													P									<45			
Brayer, Dennis		BL TL																									
1963	Brunswick	GFL	41	88	1	13	1	0	0	4	2	4	18	0.148	1B	173	8	7	0.963								
Braze, ---																											
1915	Valdosta	FLAG	<10												P		0										
Braziel, Dennis		BL TR																									
1955	Tifton	GFL	93	349	48	102	15	1	5	47	7	52	32	0.292	1B, 2B, OF, C, P	365	57	16	0.963	1	0	0	<45				
Brazier, ---																											
1913	Cordele	ESL	102	393	58	121	14	5	4					0.308	OF	155	11	17	0.907								
1915	Thomasville	FLAG	40	155	19	41	6	0	1		3			0.265	OF	62	6	5	0.932								
1915	Griffin	GAL	26	89	16	25	6	1	0					0.281	OF	55	2	3	0.950								
Breaux, Clifford "Cliff"		BR TR																									
1950	Thomasville	GFL	56	211	31	52	7	1	2	35	10	37	57	0.246	OF	97	10	8	0.930								
Breeden, Danny Richard "Danny"		BR TR 6'1" 185 lbs. b. 06/27/1942 Albany, GA																									
1963	Brunswick	GFL	28	74	15	22	4	0	1	10	0	14	10	0.297	C	162	6	2	0.988								
Breeden, Harold Noel "Hal"		BR TR 6'2" 200 lbs. b. 06/28/1944 Albany, GA																									
1963	Waycross	GFL	116	397	45	131	15	6	8	64	5	28	69	0.330	1B	892	41	10	0.989								
Breeden, Jack		BR TL																									
1957	Thomasville	GFL	46	54	11	11	1	0	0	2	0	10	10	0.204	P	10	29	1	0.975	40	14	8	3.96	150	136	141	107
1958	Thomasville	GFL	1	1	0									0.000	P					1	0	1	<30				
Breeding, Marvin Eugene "Marv"		BR TR																									
1955	Cordele	GFL	71	266	47	90	11	9	4	48	27	18	38	0.338	SS	133	211	35	0.908								
Breedlove, Ernest		BL TR																									
1958	Dublin	GFL	21	19	6	4	3	0	0	4	0	10	4	0.211	P	1	10	0	1.000	18	3	3	5.87	46	42	31	38
Breidt, Robert "Bob"		BR TR																									
1953	Sandersville	GSL	65	226	31	49	5	2	0	24	0	30	33	0.217	C	232	45	15	0.949								
Brelich, Mike		BR																									
1940	Moultrie	GFL	<10																								
Bremer, Walter "Walt"		BR TR																									
1947	Waycross	GFL	133	506	103	144	26	8	10	115	9	76	97	0.285	3B	129	286	52	0.889								
1948	Waycross	GFL	53	183	39	56	10	2	3	27	5	41	21	0.306	OF	73	3	5	0.938								
1949	Waycross	GFL	102	370	70	87	21	5	4	88	8	64	43	0.235	3B	111	181	33	0.898								
1950	Waycross	GFL	62	211	46	81	16	4	4	45	8	68	30	0.384	3B, OF	107	28	9	0.938								
1951	Waycross	GFL	44	150	29	47	10	2	2	28	1	29	12	0.313	3B	42	73	12	0.906								
1952	Waycross	GFL	137	486	84	150	26	5	4	95	6	107	32	0.309	3B	135	290	42	0.910								
Brennan, Donald "Don"		BR TR																									
1951	Dublin	GSL	83	207	82	87	20	1	12	54	8	62	33	0.420	2B	195	225	25	0.944								
1952	Eastman	GSL	30	111	15	30	5	0	2	17	8	14	10	0.270	2B	72	86	13	0.924								
Brennan, Wilbert		BR TR																									
1949	Moultrie	GFL	18	44	7	6	1	0	0	3	2	10	9	0.136	OF	13	0	2	0.867								
Brenner, ---																											
1906	Americus	GSL													2B												
Brenner, Herbert																											
1920	Lindale	GSL													1B												
1921	Lindale	GSL		166	28	53								0.319	1B												
Breschini, Wes		BR TL																									
1950	Thomasville	GFL	31	73	4	16	2	0	0	10	0	7	27	0.219	P	4	26	2	0.938	30	14	14	3.64	205	152	209	166
Brewer, ---																											
1915	Valdosta	FLAG	10	35	5	12	3	3	0		0			0.343	OF	18	0	1	0.947								
Brewer, George W.		BR TR																									
1950	Douglas	GSL	26	60	7	16	0	0	0	8	0	5	17	0.267	P	5	25	3	0.909	24	9	7	5.13	142	141	51	82
Brewer, Henry																											
1921	Griffin	GSL																									
Brewer, Orbie L.		BR TR																									
1947	Moultrie	GFL	72	275	47	72	7	3	0	19	4	29	25	0.262	OF	99	5	14	0.881								
Brewster, Charles Lawrence "Charlie"		BR TR 5'8" 175 lbs. b. 12/27/1916 Marthaville, LA																									
1940	Waycross	GFL	140	584	114	178	23	9	12	98	35	32	69	0.305	SS	272	475	88	0.895								
1941	Waycross	GFL	78	297	71	98	13	5	8	53	41	35	36	0.330	SS	172	279	32	0.934								
1948	Waycross	GFL	92	352	70	104	26	0	10	90	19	51	29	0.295	SS	188	244	40	0.915								
1954	Waycross	GFL	65	231	38	64	14	0	2	35	15	30	15	0.277	2B, SS	135	145	29	0.906								
Brewster, William "Bill"																											
1941	Tallahassee	GFL	20	72	9	19	1	0	1	7	1	3	18	0.264	OF	30	2	5	0.865								
Brewton, Byron		BR TR																									
1958	Waycross	GFL	29	88	11	23	5	0	1	9	1	25	29	0.261	3B	26	43	8	0.896								
Brick, Jerome		BR TR																									
1954	Valdosta	GFL	25	65	6	12	2	0	0	2	1	9	9	0.185	OF	34	3	1	0.974								
Bricker, Cy		BL TL																									
1947	Albany	GFL	9												P					9	0	3	2.54	46	38	27	24
Brickner, Walter "Walt"		BL TL																									
1940	Moultrie	GFL	117	462	76	147	21	7	1	53	8	41	47	0.318	1B	952	54	28	0.973								
1941	Moultrie	GFL	132	508	95	171	31	9	4	82	12	79	47	0.337	OF	372	13	22	0.946								
Bridges, Barney		BL TL																									
1962	Moultrie	GFL	19	61	8	12	3	1	0	8	0	7	20	0.197	1B	136	3	5	0.965								

Georgia Class-D Minor League Baseball Encyclopedia

YR	TEAM	LG	G	AB	R	H	2B	3B	HR	RBI	SB	BB	SO	BA	POS	PO	A	E	FA	GP	W	L	ERA	IP	H	SO	BB
Bridges, Donald "Don"		BR TR																									
1957	Valdosta	GFL	5	2		1								0.500	P					5	0	1	<30				
Bridges, Floyd		BR TR																									
1952	Jesup	GSL	18	36	2	6	0	0	0	3	0	5	20	0.167	P	0	15	1	0.938	18	6	4	4.46	101	106	51	64
Bridges, Franklin "Frank"		BR TR																									
1951	Albany(16) - Brunswick(54)	GFL	70	235	41	60	16	0	4	34	12	55	41	0.255	OF	154	10	5	0.970								
Bridges, Geneva		BR TR																									
1954	Sandersville	GSL	2	5		1								0.200	P					2	0	1	<45				
Bridges, Harold		BL TL																									
1946	LaGrange(13) - Valley(3)	GAL	16	32	5	2	1	0	0	1	1	3	15	0.063	P	2	10	3	0.800	12	3	5	6.52	58	72	24	22
Briggs, Clyde		BL TR																									
1954	Vidalia	GSL	43	174	26	42	4	0	0	22	4	10	18	0.241	OF	99	0	2	0.980								
Briggs, Harold		BL TL																									
1947	LaGrange	GAL	13	19	1	3	0	0	0	1	0	0	5	0.158	P	6	15	1	0.955	13	1	5	6.71	55	71	16	32
Brightwell, William "Bill"		BR TR																									
1946	Valdosta	GFL	24	37	1	5	0	0	0	0	0	1	6	0.135	P	13	12	3	0.893	19	4	6	2.57	91	75	83	59
Brill, James "Jim"		BR TR																									
1955	Valdosta	GFL	36	93	15	23	4	0	0	10	3	15	15	0.247	C	129	20	8	0.949								
Brill, Stanley "Stan"		BR TR																									
1949	Moultrie	GFL	137	568	91	149	18	4	0	53	28	72	64	0.262	2B	438	421	34	0.962								
Briner, Daniel "Dan"		BL TL																									
1957	Valdosta	GFL	132	550	97	171	15	5	2	45	14	55	43	0.311	OF	272	19	10	0.967								
Brinkley, Lawrence		BR TR																									
1956	Vidalia	GSL	14	12	2	2	0	0	0	1	0	2	2	0.167	P	5	14	1	0.950	14	4	1	1.91	47	42	25	17
Brinkman, Frank		BR TR																									
1948	Griffin	GAL	77	286	32	75	8	2	0	27	2	29	43	0.262	OF	110	7	13	0.900								
Brinson, ---																											
1920	Carrollton	GSL	<10												SS												
Brinson, Luther		BR TR																									
1951	Waycross	GFL	114	411	76	109	12	2	1	50	23	58	46	0.265	3B, SS, OF	119	114	30	0.886								
1952	Waycross	GFL	105	380	64	110	16	6	1	47	19	59	34	0.289	2B, SS, OF	175	211	31	0.926								
Brio, Carl		BL TL																									
1956	Thomasville	GFL	27	65	15	14	0	1	0	3	5	14	7	0.215	OF	31	1	1	0.970								
Briscoe, Bertram		BR TR																									
1953	Vidalia	GSL	34	133	14	38	8	3	1	28	3	16	20	0.286	3B, OF	74	23	5	0.951								
Brisson, Virgil		BR TR																									
1952	Cordele	GFL	20	35	3	4	1	0	0	1	0	4	12	0.114	P	5	21	6	0.813	20	5	8	3.50	108	97	79	74
Britchet, Jackson Jr.																											
1942	Albany	GFL	34	69	4	13	3	0	0	4	0	4	31	0.188	P	8	40	5	0.906	37	8	10	2.51	172	160	83	73
Brittian, ---																											
1915	Anniston	GAL	28	93	5	24	2	1	0					0.258	2B	55	48	15	0.873								
Britz, Gregory "Greg"		BR TR																									
1958	Thomasville	GFL	14	43	2	10	0	0	0	5	0	4	4	0.233	OF	18	1	2	0.905								
Brock, ---																											
1917	LaGrange	GAL	12	43	5	13	2	0	0	4				0.302	2B, SS	15	31	8	0.852								
Brock, Edward "Ed"		BR TR																									
1940	Albany	GFL	10	25	5	9	1	0	0	6	0	8	3	0.360	2B	16	19	3	0.921								
Brock, Leon Paul "Paul"		BR TR																									
1946	Carrollton	GAL	12	36	8	12	2	0	0	7	0	1	9	0.333	P	7	22	1	0.967	12	10	2	3.46	91	92	56	32
1947	Newnan	GAL	67	182	20	41	1	3	2	14	0	8	32	0.225	OF, P	34	65	4	0.961	43	23	11	2.33	313	282	220	72
1948	Sparta	GSL	46	120	15	39	8	4	0	16	0	8	25	0.325	P	7	53	4	0.938	37	21	10	1.38	260	171	270	73
1949	Sparta	GSL	15	47	8	13	2	1	2	14	0	2	8	0.277	P	6	21	2	0.931	14	9	4	2.29	102	33	87	22
1953	Fitzgerald	GFL	17	25	0	1	0	0	0	0	0	1	7	0.040	P	3	12	3	0.833	17	2	6	6.20	74	86	43	45
Brockell, Charles "Charlie"		BR TR																									
1954	Brunswick	GFL	134	457	63	123	29	4	12	98	1	52	66	0.269	3B, SS, P	177	298	38	0.926	5	0	1	<45				
1955	Brunswick	GFL	129	487	63	131	17	0	12	68	3	49	51	0.269	1B, SS, OF, C, P	571	140	20	0.973	2	0	0	<45				
Brockelman, Bernard																											
1941	Americus	GFL	138	520	80	147	19	4	0	81	17	65	29	0.283	1B	1243	90	22	0.984								
Brodsky, Sheldon		BR TR																									
1955	Thomasville	GFL	35	120	11	29	6	0	3	13	0	9	18	0.242	3B	25	49	14	0.841								
Brodzinski, James "Jim"		BR TR																									
1947	Tallassee(27) - Griffin(4)	GAL	31	58	5	10	0	2	1	4	2	3	21	0.172	P	2	25	3	0.900	31	9	9	4.44	158	146	58	108
1948	Alexander City	GAL	11	12	1	1	0	0	0	1	0	4	5	0.083	P	0	8	1	0.889								
Brogden, Otis		BR TR																									
1946	Opelika	GAL	52	193	29	43	5	1	1	13	3	22	50	0.223	2B	108	108	23	0.904								
Brooks, Floyd		BS TR																									
1946	Moultrie	GFL	103	370	104	116	13	1	0	36	31	81	47	0.314	2B	235	231	39	0.923								
Brooks, R.																											
1914	Selma	GAL	27	63	10	25					0			0.397	P	23	20	5	0.896	27							
1915	Griffin	GAL	14	31	6	9	5	0	0					0.290	P					10	5	5					

233

Georgia Class-D Minor League Baseball Encyclopedia

YR	TEAM	LG	G	AB	R	H	2B	3B	HR	RBI	SB	BB	SO	BA	POS	PO	A	E	FA	GP	W	L	ERA	IP	H	SO	BB
Brooks, Warren P.		BR TR																									
1941	Moultrie	GFL	95	372	58	97	17	7	1	46	5	25	35	0.261	SS	134	344	44	0.916								
1942	Moultrie	GFL	104	410	79	117	7	4	1	43	13	42	22	0.285	SS	200	308	59	0.896								
1946	Moultrie	GFL	15	46	10	20	4	1	0	11	0	7	4	0.435	2B	20	23	2	0.956								
1947	Griffin	GAL	75	285	51	94	10	7	0	42	6	23	16	0.330	2B	180	180	17	0.955								
1947	Moultrie	GFL	24	83	15	30	6	2	0	9	0	17	5	0.361	2B	66	69	12	0.918								
Brophy, James "Jim"		BR TR																									
1947	Valdosta	GFL	13	56	9	11	1	1	1	7	0	7	18	0.196	OF	21	1	1	0.957								
Brosnan, John Patrick "Pat"		BS TR																									
1950	Moultrie	GFL	16	28	4	5	1	0	0	5	0	4	9	0.179	P	2	11	2	0.867	16	4	5	5.10	67	74	26	47
1954	Tifton	GFL	9	7		2								0.286	P					9	1	2		<45			
Broukal, William "Bill"		BR TR																									
1949	Cordele	GFL	137	525	105	138	23	14	7	60	19	103	121	0.263	SS	249	425	86	0.887								
Brouthers, Walt																											
1913	Waycross - Americus	ESL	100	360	48	97	10	2	3					0.269	OF	312	138	29	0.939								
1914	Cordele	GSL		394	87	104	8	2	4	41				0.264													
Brown, ---																											
1915	Anniston - LaGrange	GAL	22	76	9	15	4	0	1					0.197	OF	36	1	2	0.949								
Brown, ---																											
1941	Moultrie	GFL	3												P					3	1	0	5.54	13	12	10	16
Brown, ---		BR TR																									
1946	Thomasville	GFL	1												P					1	0	0	0.00	6			
Brown, ---		BR TR																									
1951	Hazlehurst-Baxley	GSL	9												P					9	1	2	5.12	51	61	17	35
Brown, Albert R. "Al"		BL TR																									
1949	Cordele	GFL	36	69	9	9	2	0	0	1	1	6	25	0.130	P	2	30	0	1.000	28	5	9	4.57	122	147	75	70
1950	Rome	GAL	37	82	10	20	3	1	3	14	0	8	20	0.244	OF, P	19	16	1	0.972	18	3	8	6.64	84	108	52	61
Brown, Arles		BR TR																									
1947	Cordele	GFL	14	35	1	4	1	0	0	1	0	4	8	0.114	P	3	11	0	1.000	11	3	4	2.70	70	86	37	29
Brown, Ben																											
1935	Thomasville	GFL	116	425	82	143	8	7	10		11	54	45	0.336	OF	241	12	17	0.937								
1936	Thomasville	GFL	49	181	28	46	7	1	6	29	5			0.254	OF	106	3	7	0.940								
Brown, Bobby E.		BR TR																									
1954	Thomasville	GFL	102	344	54	79	7	5	1	30	13	27	74	0.230	OF	164	9	16	0.915								
Brown, C. Lamar		BL TR																									
1952	Waycross	GFL	115	406	71	115	10	7	0	35	15	96	56	0.283	OF	148	8	9	0.945								
1953	Douglas	GSL	90	358	88	111	11	3	4	42	15	84	33	0.310	OF	177	10	5	0.974								
Brown, Donald "Don"		BR TR																									
1951	Albany	GFL	101	341	58	76	18	7	2	46	14	55	101	0.223	3B	107	196	52	0.854								
1956	Albany	GFL	27	86	10	19	2	0	3	15	0	12	17	0.221	OF	10	2	6	0.667								
1957	Albany	GFL	16	34	4	3	1	0	0	1	1	5	12	0.088	3B	3	31	1	0.971								
Brown, Eugene "Gene"		BR TR																									
1949	Americus	GFL	76	238	27	51	9	2	0	33	2	35	46	0.214	3B, OF	90	43	10	0.930								
Brown, Hubert		BR TL																									
1946	Newnan	GAL	10	22	2	3	0	0	0	0	0	3	4	0.136	OF, P	19	16	2	0.946	10	3	5	4.36	64	70	26	17
Brown, Jerome		BR TR																									
1963	Moultrie	GFL	3	1	0	0	0	0	0	0	0	0	1	0.000	P					3	0	1	0.00	6	7	6	1
Brown, John		BR																									
1953	Vidalia	GSL	5											0.050														
Brown, Keith		BR TR																									
1956	Moultrie	GFL	17	34	0	3	0	0	0	2	0	4	16	0.088	P	7	24	3	0.912	17	6	9	4.64	97	102	55	73
Brown, Levi		BR TR																									
1962	Dublin	GFL	33	94	21	30	7	1	6	35	3	12	11	0.319	OF	37	2	4	0.907								
Brown, Lloyd Andrew "Gimpy"		BL TL 5'9" 170 lbs. b. 12/25/1904 Beeville, TX d. 01/14/1974 Opa-Locka, FL																										
1946	Newnan	GAL	38	98	15	21	4	1	2	17	6	12	12	0.214	M, P	10	39	3	0.942	20	9	8	2.17	149	133	110	25
1955	Cordele	GFL	14	45	0	6	3	0	0	3	0	3	13	0.133	M, P	3	12	0	1.000	10	4	5	2.84	73	80	34	12
1956	Thomson	GSL													M												
Brown, Louis "Lou"		BL TR																									
1956	Albany	GFL	30	91	22	19	2	2	2	11	2	24	32	0.209	OF	58	2	3	0.952								
1957	Albany	GFL	140	539	105	160	26	14	4	67	38	112	117	0.297	OF	206	6	16	0.930								
Brown, Martin E.																											
1937	Americus	GFL	36	99	11	19	2	0	0	6	2	10	11	0.192	OF	72	1	4	0.948								
Brown, Newton		BL TL																									
1955	Cordele	GFL	99	386	68	103	14	8	6	52	4	28	84	0.267	1B	860	38	20	0.978								
Brown, Norman Ladelle "Norm"		BS TR 6'3" 180 lbs. b. 02/01/1919 Evergreen, NC d. 05/31/1995 Bennetsville, SC																										
1937	Moultrie	GFL	43	94	8	18	2	0	1	6	0	8	13	0.191	P	17	38	5	0.917	32	10	13	3.52	202	197	105	95
1938	Moultrie	GFL	33	91	18	26	4	2	0	5	0	10	20	0.286	P	12	38	2	0.962	29	16	12	3.49	209	208	152	102
Brown, Roger		BR TR																									
1950	Valdosta	GFL	10	27	6	4	3	0	0	5	0	6	9	0.148	SS	17	25	5	0.894								
Brown, William C. Jr. "Bill"		BR TR																									
1948	Alexander City	GAL	126	422	69	103	16	6	5	74	8	85	90	0.244	1B	1102	58	21	0.982								
1949	Alexander City	GAL	112	408	49	121	15	2	3	79	5	44	25	0.297	1B	872	61	34	0.965								
1950	Alexander City	GAL	126	452	91	148	28	6	10	106	5	82	38	0.327	1B	969	43	14	0.986								
1951	Alexander City	GAL	78	282	58	83	12	4	9	61	3	63	24	0.294	M, 1B	723	43	9	0.988								
Brown, Xenophon Jr.		BR TR																									
1940	Moultrie	GFL	<10												P									<35			

Georgia Class-D Minor League Baseball Encyclopedia

YR	TEAM	LG	G	AB	R	H	2B	3B	HR	RBI	SB	BB	SO	BA	POS	PO	A	E	FA	GP	W	L	ERA	IP	H	SO	BB
Browning, Douglas C. "Doug"		BR TR																									
1953	Statesboro	GSL	2											1.000	P						1	0		<45			
Browning, Theodore "Ted"		BR TR																									
1946	Newnan	GAL	123	512	90	154	23	9	2	61	15	19	45	0.301	OF, P	278	10	8	0.973	1	0	0	0.00	1			
1947	Newnan	GAL	123	521	122	162	24	9	5	46	42	54	36	0.311	OF	269	11	5	0.982								
Brownslow, ---																											
1914	Gadsden	GAL	23	82	4	18				7				0.220	OF	54	52	4	0.964								
Bruce, Paul E. "Buster"																											
1936	Thomasville	GFL	47	105	12	22	4	0	0	8	0			0.210	P					47	14	17	3.37	259		138	150
1937	Cordele	GFL	34	83	11	20	0	2	1	12	0	8	19	0.241	P	9	39	2	0.960	35	12	11	2.96	225	225	109	109
Bruenjes, Allen		BR TR																									
1956	Albany	GFL	1	0										0.000	P					1	0	0	<45				
1956	Hazlehurst-Baxley	GSL	1	2		0								0.000	P					1	0	0					
Brumbaugh, John		BR TR																									
1953	Brunswick	GFL	41	149	20	32	7	0	1	18	3	10	26	0.215	SS	66	99	23	0.878								
1953	Dublin	GSL	56	231	31	45	8	2	4	21	4	13	34	0.195	SS	111	156	32	0.893								
1954	Brunswick	GFL	9	24		5								0.208													
1956	Brunswick	GFL	24	92	15	24	5	1	0	12	0	3	16	0.261	3B	23	54	8	0.906								
Bruner, Bruce E.																											
1921	Carrollton	GSL		104	7	14								0.135	SS												
1928	Talladega	GAL	19	75	12	15	0	0	0		2	7	10	0.200	M, SS	33	59	8	0.920								
Bruner, Walter Roy "Roy"		BR TR 6'0" 165 lbs. b. 02/10/1917 Cecilia, KY d. 11/30/1986 St. Matthews, KY																									
1937	Thomasville	GFL	28	73	10	18	4	0	0	2	1	12	17	0.247	P	11	31	1	0.977	26	12	8	3.24	197	192	81	96
1938	Thomasville	GFL	36	92	8	23	5	0	0	6	0	7	21	0.250	P	8	39	7	0.870	35	19	8	3.87	237	249	132	67
Brunner, Sheldon																											
1936	Thomasville	GFL													P									<30			
Bruno, Robert "Bob"		BR TR																									
1948	Eastman(27) - Sparta(2)	GSL	29	109	9	21	5	0	0	9	3	14	27	0.193	OF	62	3	2	0.970								
1962	Moultrie	GFL	17	53	7	11	3	1	0	7	0	7	14	0.208	OF	26	4	3	0.909								
Bruns, Donald "Don"		BR TR																									
1958	Dublin	GFL	50	192	33	57	14	2	5	48	1	21	39	0.297	3B, OF, P	55	18	9	0.890	5	0	0	<30				
Brunsberg, Arlo Adolph "Arlo"		BL TR 6'0" 195 lbs. b. 08/15/1940 Fertile, MN																									
1962	Thomasville	GFL	15	52	6	17	2	1	2	13	0	7	18	0.327	C	91	7	2	0.980								
Brunson, Marion		BL TL																									
1948	Tallassee	GAL	11	22	2	2	0	0	0	0	0	3	4	0.091	P	2	11	3	0.813	10	1	7	4.17	54	49	40	62
Bryant, Chic																											
1936	Tallahassee	GFL	18	43	5	8	0	0	0	2	0			0.186	P					18	5	8	5.06	112		28	72
Bryant, Harold		BR TR																									
1947	Moultrie	GFL	65	210	27	46	8	4	0	24	6	36	43	0.219	3B, OF	65	103	27	0.862								
1948	Moultrie	GFL	65	200	25	39	4	0	0	18	6	32	38	0.195	2B, 3B	134	155	31	0.903								
1948	Douglas	GSL	49	184	18	39	4	1	0	9	5	23	37	0.212	3B	66	102	15	0.918								
1950	Hazlehurst-Baxley	GSL	55	206	23	44	6	0	0	14	1	27	37	0.214	3B, SS	74	109	17	0.915								
Bryant, Ira		BL TL																									
1954	Hazlehurst-Baxley	GSL	11	39	2	8	1	0	0	3	1	5	7	0.205	OF	15	0	2	0.882								
Bryant, Irwin		BR TR																									
1950	Opelika	GAL	10	30	6	5	0	1	0	6	1	4	15	0.167	OF	12	1	1	0.929								
Bryant, James "Jim"		BR TR																									
1950	Rome	GAL	57	146	23	32	2	0	1	15	4	35	37	0.219	C	219	35	21	0.924								
Bryant, James T. Jr. "Jim"																											
1942	Waycross	GFL	13	37	4	13	2	0	0	3	0	1	3	0.351	P	5	16	1	0.955	12	7	2	2.60	90	93	53	42
Bryant, William "Bill"																											
1939	Valdosta	GFL	18	70	5	17	2	0	0	9	2	4	9	0.243	OF	50	0	4	0.926								
Brydon, Robert "Bob"																											
1941	Valdosta	GFL	78	285	45	94	9	5	1	50	7	30	41	0.330	OF	171	4	8	0.956								
Bryson, Hoyle																											
1938	Tallahassee	GFL	32	75	9	16	4	1	0	10	0	7	13	0.213	P	5	38	1	0.977	30	16	10	3.52	220	222	100	50
1939	Tallahassee	GFL	33	66	2	8	0	1	0	5	0	4	17	0.121	P	7	40	3	0.940	32	7	15	3.76	177	199	80	41
Bryson, Jesse "Joe"		BR TR																									
1946	Opelika	GAL	8												P					8	2	2	0.00	37	36	14	18
Brzowsky, Emil		BL TR																									
1940	Valdosta	GFL	15	18	2	3	1	0	0	1	0	2	8	0.167	P					13	2	4	5.94	50	72	17	20
Bubeck, Robert "Bob"		BL TR																									
1950	Vidalia-Lyons	GSL	32	124	16	35	2	0	3	11	0	25	25	0.282	OF	68	2	4	0.946								
Bucco, Richard "Dick"		BR TR																									
1949	Americus	GFL	27	94	19	24	1	1	1	8	6	8	34	0.255	OF	44	1	4	0.918								
Bucek, John		BR TR																									
1946	Newnan	GAL	98	363	59	109	13	3	7	68	4	30	57	0.300	3B, OF, P	138	24	6	0.964	3	0	0	0.00	8			
Bucha, Anthony		BR TR																									
1948	Americus	GFL	51	149	15	33	8	1	0	16	3	26	23	0.221	C	195	26	15	0.936								
Buchanan, ---																											
1906	Valdosta	GSL													P												
Buck, Joseph "Joe"		BR TR																									
1946	Tallassee	GAL	<10																								
Buckles, James G. "Jim"		BR TR																									
1952	Thomasville	GFL	38	46	2	4	1	0	0	3	0	4	17	0.087	P	5	27	1	0.970	35	7	3	3.07	129	118	57	60

Georgia Class-D Minor League Baseball Encyclopedia

YR	TEAM	LG	G	AB	R	H	2B	3B	HR	RBI	SB	BB	SO	BA	POS	PO	A	E	FA	GP	W	L	ERA	IP	H	SO	BB
Buddhu, Charles																											
1936	Thomasville	GFL	20	61	7	12	2	1	0	9	2			0.197	SS	18	43	17	0.782								
Buell, Samuel "Sam"		BL TL																									
1954	Dublin	GSL	127	478	150	124	22	6	18	75	45	125	152	0.259	OF	292	21	11	0.966								
1955	Dublin	GSL	56	173	36	44	5	0	7	22	8	57	46	0.254	OF	130	9	4	0.972								
Buesse, Carlton "Carl"																											
1906	Waycross	GSL													M, P												
Buesse, F.																											
1906	Waycross	GSL													3B, SS												
Buffington, Jack																											
1941	Moultrie	GFL	9	31	10	10	1	1	1	7	0	8	6	0.323	3B	7	19	8	0.765								
Buffington, Rex																											
1941	Thomasville	GFL	31	81	11	12	1	0	0	5	0	8	30	0.148	P	7	43	2	0.962	29	14	11	3.32	214	240	84	79
Buheller, Clarence		BR TR																									
1953	Dublin	GSL	50	198	23	51	10	3	5	23	3	16	18	0.258	2B, OF	89	68	12	0.929								
1954	Brunswick	GFL	141	567	102	184	27	8	19	119	15	45	53	0.325	1B, OF	1038	47	19	0.983								
Buhl, Larry		BR TR																									
1957	Thomasville	GFL	39	117	17	30	4	2	0	10	2	18	32	0.256	3B	25	53	3	0.963								
1958	Thomasville	GFL	9	15		2								0.133													
Buie, ---																											
1915	Ame-Gains - Thomasville	FLAG	<10																								
Bukowski, John		BR TL																									
1962	Moultrie	GFL	23	26	2	3	0	0	0	2	0	9	9	0.115	P	3	22	1	0.962	23	4	5	4.93	95	100	104	58
1963	Brunswick	GFL	5	11	0	1	0	0	0	0	0	0	6	0.091	P					5	4	1	2.45	33	32	35	14
Bullard, Henry		BR TR																									
1955	Moultrie	GFL	23	26	1	1	0	0	0	0	0	1	8	0.038	P	1	18	3	0.864	23	1	5	6.97	71	87	41	64
Bullock, Bruce		BR TR																									
1956	Fitzgerald	GFL	28	58	4	4	0	0	0	1	0	4	18	0.069	P	3	27	6	0.833	27	6	14	4.19	159	172	81	84
Bumstead, Daniel "Dan"		BL TL																									
1953	Fitzgerald	GFL	2											0.000	P						0	0	<45				
1954	Douglas	GSL	4	7		3								0.429	P					4	2	0	<45				
1955	Douglas	GSL	5	10		3								0.300	P					4	0	2					
Bunce, John "Jack"		BR TR																									
1954	Americus-Cordele	GFL	46	69	9	18	1	0	0	6	0	13	19	0.261	P	11	46	4	0.934	41	9	15	3.96	216	203	108	102
1955	Cordele	GFL	10	11	2	3	1	0	0	3	0	0	2	0.273	P					9	3	3	<45				
Bunch, Jake																											
1936	Cordele	GFL													P								<30				
Bundrick, Clinton		BR TR																									
1946	Tallassee	GAL	14	49	7	11	0	0	0	5	2	8	7	0.224	SS	20	29	11	0.817								
Bundy, ---																											
1913	Brunswick	ESL	37	147	16	31	0	0	0					0.211	2B	56	66	18	0.871								
Burbank, ---																											
1929	Anniston	GAL	19	66	12	19	3	0	1		1	4	7	0.288	OF	33	9	4	0.913								
Burcham, Thomas "Tom"		BL TR																									
1952	Thomasville	GFL	90	330	43	95	18	4	1	40	2	49	46	0.288	3B	110	194	29	0.913								
1953	Valdosta	GFL	93	336	53	107	14	9	3	48	0	52	22	0.318	3B	97	85	29	0.863								
Burchfield, Boyd																											
1939	Waycross	GFL													P								<45				
Burchfield, Kenneth Wayne "Ken"		BR TR																									
1962	Brunswick	GFL	84	263	52	51	9	2	14	29	3	49	82	0.194	OF	111	9	12	0.909								
Burden, ---																											
1906	Valdosta	GSL													C, 1B												
Burford, Lamar		BR TR																									
1953	Valdosta	GFL	122	450	81	136	19	7	4	74	4	77	100	0.302	OF	144	15	15	0.914								
Burford, Larry		BR TR																									
1954	Americus-Cordele	GFL	138	493	74	123	13	7	6	66	7	18	36	0.249	OF	224	10	17	0.932								
Burford, Red																											
1929	Carrollton	GAL		13	0	1								0.077	OF												
Burg, Jerold		BL TL																									
1954	Vidalia(3) - Sandersville(8)	GSL	11	14	3	4	0	0	0	1	0	0	1	0.286	P	1	6	2	0.778	11	1	2	<45				
Burgamy, Ralph R.		BR TR																									
1949	Eastman - Dublin	GSL	131	496	102	157	31	7	28	123	4	85	52	0.317	3B	145	176	37	0.897								
1950	Eastman	GSL	141	525	127	160	28	9	15	106	8	113	54	0.305	3B, OF	168	94	23	0.919								
1952	Eastman	GSL	18	73	8	16	3	0	0	6	0	9	0	0.219	OF	37	0	1	0.974								
Burger, Robert "Bob"		BS TR																									
1963	Thomasville	GFL	17	30	5	6	0	1	0	2	0	4	14	0.200	P	3	29	3	0.914	16	8	5	2.62	86	71	83	56
Burgess, ---																											
1915	Newnan	GAL	27	96	15	25	7	0	1					0.260	3B	27	56	4	0.954								
1916	Griffin	GAL	70	249	28	65					15			0.261	SS, 3B												
1917	Griffin	GAL	10	31	10	9	5	0	0		5			0.290	2B, 3B, OF	9	22	3	0.912								
1920	Griffin	GSL													2B												
Burgess, Jay		BR TR																									
1950	Fitzgerald	GSL	13	41	5	10	2	0	0	4	0	9	12	0.244	1B	84	4	5	0.946								
Burgess, Ted		BL TR																									
1955	Tifton	GFL	38	83	11	10	0	0	2	8	1	3	49	0.120	P	11	41	2	0.963	25	10	9	2.20	172	150	119	61

Georgia Class-D Minor League Baseball Encyclopedia

YR	TEAM	LG	G	AB	R	H	2B	3B	HR	RBI	SB	BB	SO	BA	POS	PO	A	E	FA	GP	W	L	ERA	IP	H	SO	BB
Burk, Ronald "Ron"		BR TR																									
1949	LaGrange	GAL	48	166	31	38	7	3	0	14	8	30	19	0.229	2B	119	111	22	0.913								
Burke, ---																											
1914	Selma	GAL	21												OF	43	13	1	0.982								
1915	Waycross	FLAG	75	273	34	69	14	2	0		21			0.253	OF	134	6	5	0.966								
Burke, Donald "Don"		BR TR																									
1957	Thomasville	GFL	103	299	35	66	10	1	6	35	4	43	89	0.221	C	548	49	15	0.975								
Burke, Joseph "Joe"		BR TR																									
1948	Carrollton	GAL	15	35	5	9	1	0	0	2	0	3	7	0.257	P					9	3	3	2.39	49	52	23	33
Burkey, Melvin		BR TL																									
1948	Americus	GFL	27	38	2	4	2	0	0	0	0	7	17	0.105	P	6	16	6	0.786	24	5	9	6.49	111	125	74	68
Burkhardt, John		BR																									
1947	Moultrie	GFL	12	23	4	7	0	0	0	2	0	6	7	0.304													
Burkholder, John																											
1941	Cordele	GFL	13	31	4	3	0	0	0	1	0	3	15	0.097	OF, P	7	7	2	0.875	5	1	0	4.71	21	34	6	14
Burkwitt, Irwin		BR TR																									
1946	Cordele(104) - Moultrie(1)	GFL	105	382	52	94	10	12	1	50	11	75	71	0.246	OF	184	15	21	0.905								
Burleson, Art																											
1915	Rome	GAL	10	25	3	3	2	0	0					0.120	M, P	1	7	1	0.889	8	3	2					
Burlick, William "Bill"																											
1939	Americus	GFL	91	342	53	101	12	3	0	35	9	32	23	0.295	3B	159	236	44	0.900								
Burnell, Robert "Bob"		BL TR																									
1957	Thomasville	GFL	17	39	3	13	2	1	0	4	0	7	5	0.333	OF	16	3	2	0.905								
Burnett, Edward "Ed"		BR TR																									
1946	Opelika	GAL	58	175	17	49	9	2	0	16	2	16	16	0.280	1B, 3B, P	158	58	15	0.935	16	4	6	5.14	105	133	19	30
Burnett, Gerald		BL TR																									
1952	Hazlehurst-Baxley	GSL	16	42	3	10	0	2	0	4	0	1	4	0.238	OF	14	1	1	0.938								
Burnett, L.W.																											
1936	Americus	GFL	10	33	12	7	2	0	0	1	0			0.212	2B	15	27	7	0.857								
Burnett, Raymond "Ray"		BL TL																									
1947	Americus	GFL	64	135	14	25	4	2	2	19	0	18	22	0.185	P	9	34	2	0.956	40	21	10	3.81	253	225	262	179
Burnette, Etheridge		BR TR																									
1947	Opelika	GAL	64	192	34	53	6	3	0	18	2	27	18	0.276	3B, P	54	64	16	0.881	16	5	3	3.21	84	93	31	18
Burnette, Tommy Lee "Tom"		BR TL																									
1954	Statesboro	GSL	12	16	1	1	0	0	0	0	0	2	7	0.063	P	1	5	1	0.857	11	1	3	4.94	51	52	32	39
Burnham, Alonzo "Al"		BR																									
1957	Thomasville	GFL	1	4	0									0.000													
1958	Thomasville	GFL	32	70	11	12	2	0	0	10	1	15	32	0.171	C	101	9	3	0.973								
Burns, ---			0																								
1915	Valdosta	FLAG	<10																								
Burns, James E. "Jim"		BL TL																									
1952	Vidalia	GSL	125	485	92	162	47	0	25	155	10	81	32	0.334	OF	198	14	6	0.972								
1953	Vidalia	GSL	120	461	105	160	29	3	21	99	1	93	38	0.347	OF	200	12	11	0.951								
Burns, James F. "Jim"		BR TL																									
1940	Moultrie	GFL	100	292	28	76	8	4	2	40	7	16	63	0.260	P, IF					31	5	12	7.18	148	84	94	125
1941	Moultrie	GFL	73	175	23	53	6	2	1	26	1	17	21	0.303	P	42	45	8	0.916	34	12	13	3.77	222	209	144	149
1942	Moultrie	GFL	73	212	22	51	7	1	0	13	2	15	34	0.241	P	77	67	13	0.917	33	15	15	3.46	255	226	246	174
Burns, James F. "Jim"		BL TL																									
1962	Dublin	GFL	2	3	0	3	1	0	0	2	0	0	0	1.000	P					2	0	0	10.50	6	2	10	8
1963	Waycross	GFL	27	44	9	5	0	0	0	5	1	5	14	0.114	P	6	23	5	0.853	26	8	11	3.45	141	112	130	75
Burns, James W. "Jim"		BL TR																									
1940	Albany	GFL	47	188	32	53	4	1	0	15	8	25	14	0.282	2B	110	129	9	0.964								
1941	Albany	GFL	121	533	121	167	13	8	2	61	29	74	37	0.313	SS	245	371	75	0.891								
Burns, Robert "Bob"																											
1936	Albany	GFL	8	12	0	3	0	0	0	3	0			0.250	P								<30				
Burns, William H. "Bill"		BR TR																									
1948	Eastman	GSL	10	29	3	5	1	0	0	2	0	1	5	0.172	P					9	3	5	3.63	67	66	58	27
1949	Sparta	GSL	19	50	8	10	0	0	0	5	1	6	11	0.200	P	3	15	2	0.900	22	5	8	5.79	115	89	39	72
Burnstein, Leonard		BR TR																									
1949	Carrollton	GAL	17	41	7	10	1	0	0	2	0	6	2	0.244	OF	17	0	0	1.000								
Burpo, Howard																											
1941	Valdosta	GFL	43	132	11	25	3	1	0	22	1	15	6	0.189	P	190	19	9	0.959	12	2	4	5.14	70	57	46	54
Burress, ---																											
1914	Cordele	GSL		364	14	95	6	6	2		3			0.261													
Burright, Larry Allen "Possum"		BR TR 5'11" 170 lbs. b. 07/10/1937 Roseville, IL																									
1957	Thomasville	GFL	136	521	115	126	19	7	3	30	22	128	132	0.242	2B	331	371	36	0.951								
Burroughs, Eugene "Gene"		BR TR																									
1958	Valdosta	GFL	23	60	4	10	0	0	1	0	1	17	0.167	P	7	28	1	0.972	22	13	7	1.66	168	96	138	86	
Burrows, John		BR TL 5'10" 200 lbs. b. 10/30/1913 Winnfield, LA d. 04/27/1987 Coal Run, OH																									
1941	Moultrie	GFL	6												P					6	1	3	9.00	17	27	1	8
Burruss, ---																											
1915	Dothan	FLAG	71	253	33	43	7	0	2		7			0.170	SS	135	184	30	0.914								
Burt, Richard "Dick"		BR TR																									
1950	Thomasville	GFL	34	64	1	9	1	1	0	5	0	7	28	0.141	C	60	5	9	0.878								

Georgia Class-D Minor League Baseball Encyclopedia

YR	TEAM	LG	G	AB	R	H	2B	3B	HR	RBI	SB	BB	SO	BA	POS	PO	A	E	FA	GP	W	L	ERA	IP	H	SO	BB
Burt, Thomas "Tommy"		BL TL																									
1939	Tallahassee	GFL	13	43	3	9	1	0	0	4	0	1	12	0.209	P	3	17	3	0.870	9	5	1	3.22	67	70	22	18
1940	Tallahassee - Thomasville	GFL	40	96	6	13	3	0	0	8	0	5	30	0.135	P					33	9	16	4.29	216	262	106	79
1941	Thomasville	GFL	2												P					2	0	2	8.00	9	13	3	5
Burtner, Hugh		BL																									
1956	Douglas	GSL	5	20		2								0.100													
Burtner, Lewis "Lou"		GFL																									
1937	Moultrie	GFL	87	335	44	75	11	3	1	25	6	55	59	0.224	3B	103	182	31	0.902								
Burton, ---																											
1928	Lindale	GAL	17	59	2	12	2	0	0		0	3	14	0.203													
Burton, James M. "Jim"		BR TR																									
1952	Hazlehurst-Baxley	GSL	89	268	42	56	9	1	2	33	0	44	60	0.209	C	379	39	18	0.959								
Burton, Leonard																											
1941	Tallahassee	GFL	11	25	1	4	0	0	0	1	0	1	6	0.160	P	0	12	2	0.857	11	2	6	4.13	61	54	66	40
Busa, Albert "Al"		BR TR																									
1948	Moultrie	GFL	41	57	4	8	1	0	0	5	0	10	14	0.140	P	8	23	0	1.000	34	9	4	3.88	153	163	123	97
1949	Moultrie	GFL	19	19	3	2	0	0	0	1	0	4	8	0.105	P	5	13	1	0.947	16	2	6	3.76	67	76	64	39
Busch, George		BR TR																									
1950	Rome(16) - Griffin(18)	GAL	34	45	5	6	0	0	0	6	0	20	23	0.133	P	3	27	2	0.938	33	11	11	4.56	158	162	73	111
Bush, Carl		BL																									
1946	Tallassee	GAL	<10																								
Bush, Herbert "Herb"		BL TL																									
1955	Dublin	GSL	30	113	27	33	5	1	6	23	5	10	17	0.292	OF	56	3	5	0.922								
Bush, Ray		BR TR																									
1953	Tifton	GFL	4											0.000	P					0	0		<45				
Bussan, Donald "Don"		BR TR																									
1952	Brunswick	GFL	58	210	22	51	15	1	2	55	10	26	27	0.243	OF	88	5	4	0.959								
Bustle, William "Bill"		BR TL																									
1950	Newnan	GAL	79	199	27	57	10	0	3	26	4	28	17	0.286	1B, OF, P	109	60	3	0.983	32	21	10	3.49	237	228	228	113
Butchko, Steve		BR																									
1951	Brunswick	GFL	10	14	0	3	1	0	0	0	1	0	3	0.214													
Butkus, Carl																											
1942	Moultrie	GFL	15	60	11	15	0	2	0	10	0	10	10	0.250	C	80	5	6	0.934								
Butler, C.L.																											
1929	Talledega	GAL	26	107	15	26	5	5	0		0	3	17	0.243	2B	108	57	9	0.948								
Butler, Cecil Dean "Slewfoot"		BR TR 6'4" 195 lbs. b. 10/23/1937 Dallas, GA																									
1958	Waycross	GFL	31	61	10	14	3	0	0	7	0	7	21	0.230	P	10	38	1	0.980	26	14	6	2.39	177	151	115	43
Buttice, Louis "Lou"		BR TR																									
1952	Eastman	GSL	42	126	20	25	5	0	1	18	1	20	24	0.198	3B, OF	50	27	8	0.906								
1953	Eastman	GSL	11	27	7	6	3	0	0	2	0	11	10	0.222													
Butts, ---																											
1928	Carrollton	GAL		15	6	7								0.467	1B												
Butts, Bobby		BR TR																									
1955	Sandersville	GSL	19	63	15	12	2	0	0	1	1	23	11	0.190	OF	44	2	2	0.958								
Butts, Eugene "Gene"		BR																									
1950	Jesup	GSL	11	12	4	1	0	0	0	0	1	5	4	0.083													
Byrd, Charles		BL TR																									
1963	Brunswick	GFL	49	149	26	45	10	0	0	21	4	12	18	0.302	OF	71	9	2	0.976								
Byrd, Walter "Walt"		BR TR																									
1950	Griffin	GAL	16	59	9	11	2	0	0	7	0	15	18	0.186	OF	22	2	2	0.923								
Byrne, John F.		BR TR																									
1948	Valdosta	GFL	38	69	7	12	2	0	1	6	0	6	31	0.174	P	6	29	11	0.761	37	15	10	3.21	182	144	138	185
Cabaniss, Gerald		BR TR																									
1949	Tallahassee	GFL	71	299	36	85	11	3	2	41	13	7	18	0.284	M, 2B	195	212	21	0.951								
Cabera, ---																											
1915	Americus-Gainesville	FLAG	<10																								
Cacciola, James "Jim"		BR TR																									
1950	LaGrange	GAL	11	49	12	14	3	0	2	4	1	4	12	0.286	OF	16	0	2	0.889								
Cade, Dane		BR																									
1962	Brunswick	GFL	2	7	1	2	0	0	0	1	0	1	2	0.286													
Cagle, Lamar		BR																									
1946	Tallahassee	GFL	<10																								
Cahill, Norman "Norm"		BL TR																									
1946	Valdosta	GFL	12	33	4	8	1	0	0	4	0	5	8	0.242	OF	8	0	4	0.667								
Cahoon, Jim		BR TR																									
1956	Waycross	GFL	21	46	4	6	0	,0	0	3	0	8	16	0.130	P	5	18	4	0.852	21	8	8	4.03	134	118	99	60
Cailor, Howard		BR TL																									
1956	Vidalia	GSL	21	41	6	7	0	0	0	4	0	4	23	0.171	P	1	9	3	0.769	20	7	8	5.08	101	99	58	86
Cain, Charles		BR TR																									
1951	Douglas	GSL	19	38	4	5	1	0	0	2	0	5	12	0.132	P	5	20	2	0.926	19	4	8	6.17	108	110	32	85
Cain, George		BR TL																									
1946	Carrollton	GAL	7												P					7	1	1	0.00	20	26	7	10
1948	Carrollton	GAL	25	52	2	8	0	0	0	5	0	3	11	0.154	P	4	21	3	0.893	22	8	6	4.29	128	141	55	54

Georgia Class-D Minor League Baseball Encyclopedia

YR	TEAM	LG	G	AB	R	H	2B	3B	HR	RBI	SB	BB	SO	BA	POS	PO	A	E	FA	GP	W	L	ERA	IP	H	SO	BB
Cain, Merritt Patrick "Sugar"		BL TR 5'11" 190 lbs. b. 04/05/1907 Macon, GA d. 04/03/1975 Atlanta, GA																									
1930	Carrollton	GAL	35	106	14	30	5	0	0		0	9	24	0.283	P	13	23	2	0.947	21	8	10	4.80	163	185	103	58
1948	Vidalia-Lyons	GSL													M												
Calabrese, Joseph "Joe"		BR TR																									
1950	Fitzgerald	GSL	114	421	55	112	11	4	0	44	3	66	60	0.266	OF	190	11	13	0.939								
Caldara, ---																											
1930	Carrollton	GAL	1												P					1	0	1	18.00	2	6	2	1
Calder, ---																											
1906	Albany	GSL													P												
Caldwell, ---																											
1915	Waycross	FLAG	26	85	10	18	4	0	0		11			0.212	OF	46	5	1	0.981								
Caldwell, ---																											
1917	Griffin	GAL	5	10	0	1	0	0	0		0			0.100	P	1	6	1	0.875	5	3	1		37	29	14	9
Caldwell, ---																											
1929	Anniston	GAL	27	101	16	24	1	3	2		6	9	9	0.238	OF	44	5	4	0.925								
Caldwell, F. Calvin		BL TR																									
1951	Fitzgerald	GSL	20	68	7	18	2	0	0	10	1	12	12	0.265	OF	36	2	1	0.974								
Caldwell, James A. "Jim"		BR TR																									
1954	Thomasville	GFL	22	76	9	16	2	0	0	7	1	13	8	0.211	SS	41	37	12	0.867								
Caldwell, Maurice		BR TR																									
1953	Eastman	GSL	1											0.000													
Caldwell, Robert E. "Bob"		BR TR																									
1955	Statesboro	GSL	50	179	26	39	4	0	0	18	1	18	30	0.218	3B, C, P	117	55	16	0.915	6	2	0					
Caldwell, Wilbur "Ears"		BR TR																									
1948	Eastman	GSL	99	357	45	87	9	2	0	29	13	28	57	0.244	3B, SS, OF	101	177	25	0.917								
1949	Eastman	GSL	116	459	90	119	26	1	5	58	17	55	57	0.259	3B	141	217	33	0.916								
1950	Eastman	GSL	138	554	101	154	34	8	12	120	23	51	65	0.278	3B, SS, P	162	304	49	0.905	17	2	6	4.62	78	90	45	46
1951	Eastman	GSL	126	506	104	143	22	8	4	57	35	70	42	0.283	1B, 3B, SS, OF, P	418	253	32	0.954	13	5	3	3.52	69	73	23	24
1952	Eastman	GSL	121	453	118	136	32	2	13	56	58	89	42	0.300	3B, P	146	230	22	0.945	27	9	7	3.67	125	121	84	39
1953	Eastman	GSL	122	481	108	143	36	4	7	62	38	84	59	0.297	3B, OF, P	151	220	27	0.932	34	13	6	4.43	136	152	61	57
1954	Sandersville(32) - Vidalia(42)	GSL	74	300	58	85	18	4	3	45	17	42	43	0.283	2B, 3B, P	121	157	19	0.936	16	8	4	3.32	114	113	87	30
1955	Douglas	GSL	92	338	74	85	16	2	4	35	7	57	68	0.251	1B, 3B, OF, P	175	125	17	0.946	17	7	4	2.03	102	86	88	23
1956	Dublin	GSL	20	69	17	23	1	0	1	10	5	21	6	0.333	M, 3B, P	18	17	4	0.897	5	0	1					
Cali, William "Bill"		BR																									
1955	Sandersville	GSL	4	12		2								0.167													
Calkins, Dick																											
1949	Carrollton	GAL	1												OF												
Callahan, Michael "Mike"		BR TR																									
1953	Vidalia	GSL	24	43	4	7	1	0	0	3	0	10	9	0.163	P	5	21	3	0.897	23	7	10	4.36	128	98	97	90
Callaway, Charles		BR																									
1954	Thomasville	GFL	5	13		3								0.231													
Callaway, William "Bill"		BL TL																									
1947	Cordele	GFL	12	22	4	9	1	1	0	7	0	6	8	0.409	P												
1948	Cordele	GFL	12	28	3	6	1	0	0	3	0	2	7	0.214	P	1	8	0	1.000	10	5	4	6.16	57	72	31	42
Callen, Jim			0																								
1949	Carrollton	GAL	4												OF												
Calloway, Don G.		BR																									
1953	Fitzgerald	GFL	3											0.000													
Calobrisi, Francis "Frank"		BR TR																									
1952	Statesboro	GSL	12	47	10	12	0	1	0	5	1	7	2	0.255	SS	25	30	7	0.887								
1953	Tifton	GFL	128	502	79	129	12	4	0	59	18	46	35	0.257	2B, 3B, SS, OF	224	242	43	0.916								
Calvetti, Louis "Lou"		BL TL																									
1955	Albany	GFL	6	17		4								0.235	P					4	1	1	<45				
Camberari, Rocco		BL TL																									
1955	Sandersville	GSL	47	160	30	33	7	0	6	31	4	35	17	0.206	OF	55	7	2	0.969								
Camp, Henry Loy "Loy"		BR TR																									
1946	LaGrange	GAL	39	98	9	16	3	0	0	7	0	8	16	0.163	P	17	36	2	0.964	26	10	14	4.16	188	187	112	54
1947	LaGrange	GAL	11	23	4	5	0	0	0	2	0	2	1	0.217	P					9	3	3	2.70	60	55	40	23
Camp, Howard Lee "Howie" "Red"		BL TR 5'9" 169 lbs. b. 07/01/1893 Munsford, AL d. 05/08/1960 Eastaboga, AL																									
1913	Talladega	GAL	90	347	44	109				17				0.314	OF	155	20	11	0.941								
1914	Talladega	GAL	57	300	35	85				11				0.283	OF	86	17	12	0.896								
1915	Talladega	GAL	57	209	35	68	14	4	1					0.325	OF	71	7	2	0.975								
1916	Talladega	GAL	59	230	34	71	12	2	2	17				0.309	OF												
1928	Anniston	GAL	91	360	53	109	16	3	3	5	16	16		0.303	OF	135	7	3	0.979								
1929	Talledega	GAL	85	306	60	100	25	8	9	22	27	20		0.327	M, OF	203	17	5	0.978								
Campbell, Benjamin "Ben"		BL TR																									
1948	Newnan	GAL	69	177	11	38	5	1	1	20	2	19	15	0.215	OF, C, P	204	18	10	0.957	26	8	5	3.69	122	122	99	70
Campbell, Clifford "Cliff"		BR TR																									
1946	Thomasville	GFL	6												P					6	2	2	0.00	30	49	7	14
1951	Moultrie	GFL	15	28	1	3	0	0	0	1	0	1	6	0.107	P	3	17	4	0.833	15	4	4	5.09	69	74	19	48
Campbell, Douglas D. "Doug"		BR TR																									
1953	Valdosta	GFL	122	370	53	89	7	0	0	55	3	82	41	0.241	3B, SS	222	309	48	0.917								
Campbell, Earl		BR																									
1947	Tallahassee	GFL	12	41	6	11	2	0	1	6	0	2	14	0.268													

Georgia Class-D Minor League Baseball Encyclopedia

YR	TEAM	LG	G	AB	R	H	2B	3B	HR	RBI	SB	BB	SO	BA	POS	PO	A	E	FA	GP	W	L	ERA	IP	H	SO	BB
Campbell, Fred G.		BR TR																									
1948	Griffin	GAL	123	471	98	168	34	6	3	105	20	61	31	0.357	SS, C	270	295	53	0.914								
1951	Griffin	GAL	102	405	111	132	26	10	3	75	28	77	36	0.326	M, SS	194	321	40	0.928								
Campbell, George		BR TR																									
1962	Thomasville	GFL	103	340	60	94	20	1	7	75	5	46	87	0.276	OF	112	2	8	0.934								
1963	Thomasville	GFL	78	225	43	53	6	3	6	34	7	51	50	0.236	OF	88	4	7	0.929								
Campbell, Joseph V. "Joe"		BR TR																									
1951	Griffin	GAL	77	317	69	120	21	6	13	94	4	47	14	0.379	2B	185	238	21	0.953								
Campbell, Lem																											
1936	Cordele	GFL	110	432	58	102	12	6	5	48	24			0.236	2B	358	318	39	0.945								
1937	Cordele	GFL	90	343	48	86	5	3	0	24	8	31	23	0.251	SS	218	312	42	0.927								
Campbell, Nolan		BR TR																									
1958	Brunswick	GFL	56	203	46	50	6	2	2	20	7	47	39	0.246	2B, OF	93	38	13	0.910								
Campbell, Paul																											
1948	Griffin	GAL													M												
Campbell, Robert "Bob"		BR																									
1955	Tifton	GFL	9	28		5								0.179													
Campo, Raymond "Ray"		BR TR																									
1947	Tallassee	GAL	41	125	19	32	4	0	0	17	1	29	18	0.256	C	208	13	4	0.982								
Cann, William "Bill"		BL TL																									
1948	Thomasville	GFL	27	36	4	5	0	0	0	0	0	4	17	0.139	P	3	25	4	0.875	27	4	6	5.05	107	129	59	67
Canning, William "Bill"		BR TR																									
1963	Moultrie	GFL	2	0	0	0	0	0	0	0	0	0	0	0.000	P					2	0	0	13.50	2	4	5	2
Cannon, D.T. "Shorty"																											
1921	Carrollton	GSL		195	37	59								0.303	OF, SS												
Cannon, Harry S.																											
1935	Americus	GFL	29	72	4	17	4	2	1		0	4	19	0.236	P					33	12	7		179	197	87	48
Cannon, Robert "Bob"		BR TL																									
1950	Hazlehurst-Baxley	GSL	17	34	3	4	1	0	0	1	0	2	5	0.118	P	3	10	1	0.929	15	4	6	4.10	90	80	62	42
1951	Hazlehurst-Baxley	GSL	35	82	4	15	1	1	0	7	0	10	11	0.183	P	2	22	3	0.889	32	13	12	3.95	198	193	101	82
Cannon, William "Bill"																											
1936	Cordele	GFL	34	81	7	16	3	2	1	7	0			0.198	P					34	8	8	5.01	201		61	61
Canteley, Maxie		BR TR																									
1939	Cordele	GFL	19	35	1	1	0	0	0	0	1	2	12	0.029	P	2	20	4	0.846	18	6	6	4.03	105	113	49	56
1940	Cordele	GFL	13	18	0	2	1	0	0	3	0	0	6	0.111	P					13	2	5	7.02	41	62	11	29
Cantler, Donald "Don"		BL TL																									
1948	Moultrie	GFL	21	71	5	20	1	1	0	9	0	8	15	0.282	OF	32	4	1	0.973								
Cantley, John																											
1913	Opelika	GAL	37	113	7	29				3				0.257	P	29	106	3	0.978	23	10	13					
1914	Opelika	GAL	33	121	13	33				2				0.273	P	24	67	4	0.958	33							
Canuso, Joseph "Joe"		BR TR																									
1954	Brunswick	GFL	131	461	54	104	20	2	2	51	3	30	64	0.226	C	947	92	11	0.990								
1955	Brunswick	GFL	96	363	66	103	21	0	15	89	4	22	30	0.284	C	518	56	15	0.975								
Capone, Robert A. "Bob"		BL TR																									
1953	Brunswick	GFL	128	502	71	131	19	3	0	46	14	36	48	0.261	3B	158	242	43	0.903								
1954	Brunswick	GFL	118	449	86	115	18	10	1	47	14	44	39	0.256	3B, OF	76	126	29	0.874								
Cappel, Louis "Lou"		BR TR																									
1940	Tallahassee	GFL	14	40	5	9	1	0	0	5	0	4	7	0.225	1B	72	4	3	0.962								
Capps, William T. "Bill"		BR TR																									
1956	Fitzgerald	GFL	39	155	22	35	4	0	0	9	6	10	16	0.226	SS	43	69	18	0.862								
Capullo, Robert "Bob"		BL TL																									
1957	Thomasville	GFL	7	0										0.000	P					7	0	2		<30			
1958	Thomasville	GFL	14	16	1	2	1	0	0	2	0	2	4	0.125	P	4	9	2	0.867	13	3	2	3.56	43	46	27	28
Caputo, Louis "Lou"		BR TR																									
1955	Brunswick(32) - Waycross(70)	GFL	102	383	57	98	17	0	3	44	5	60	40	0.256	2B, 3B	121	203	22	0.936								
1955	Dublin	GSL	29	120	19	32	9	0	2	20	0	17	15	0.267	2B	66	90	10	0.940								
Caradori, James "Jim"		BL TR																									
1956	Thomson	GSL	68	220	56	66	12	6	0	20	7	63	52	0.300	OF	106	8	15	0.884								
Carangelo, Ferdinand		BR TR																									
1955	Valdosta	GFL	29	83	10	19	2	0	1	8	3	14	17	0.229	OF	24	5	0	1.000								
Carel, Paul		BR TR																									
1940	Americus	GFL	<10												P									<35			
Carey, Elwood		BL TR																									
1948	Moultrie	GFL	52	101	12	23	3	0	0	12	0	7	26	0.228	P	8	38	0	1.000	38	13	13	3.40	212	214	133	80
Carey, Max George "Scoops"		BS TR 5'11" 170 lbs. b. 01/11/1890 Terre Haute, IN d. 05/30/1976 Miami, FL																									
1955	Cordele	GFL													M												
Carlesi, Vincent "Vince"		BL TL																									
1952	Tifton	GFL	116	400	46	73	5	3	0	28	1	80	58	0.183	1B	925	52	16	0.984								
Carlin, James J. "Jim"		0																									
1938	Cordele	GFL	40	148	9	31	4	0	0	14	2	12	27	0.209	SS	74	121	15	0.929								
Carlson, Lesley "Les"		BL TL																									
1946	Albany	GFL	4												P					4	0	3	0.00	9	9	8	21
Carlson, Ray		0																									
1942	Americus	GFL	40	140	25	32	3	1	0	17	4	26	10	0.229	OF	78	1	6	0.929								

240

Georgia Class-D Minor League Baseball Encyclopedia

YR	TEAM	LG	G	AB	R	H	2B	3B	HR	RBI	SB	BB	SO	BA	POS	PO	A	E	FA	GP	W	L	ERA	IP	H	SO	BB
Carlson, Robert E. "Bob"		BR TR																									
1951	Brunswick	GFL	35	111	8	23	6	1	0	6	0	18	29	0.207	SS	59	83	20	0.877								
1953	Fitzgerald	GFL	44	170	26	49	7	0	1	18	0	24	17	0.288	M, SS	81	138	22	0.909								
1955	Thomasville	GFL	10	30	2	6	1	1	0	3	0	9	11	0.200	SS	18	20	10	0.792								
Carlson, Robert J. "Bob"			0																								
1942	Americus	GFL	67	256	44	60	8	3	0	25	2	53	38	0.234	2B	164	173	28	0.923								
Carlyle, Roy Edward "Roy"		BL TR 6'2" 195 lbs. b. 12/10/1900 Buford, GA d. 11/22/1956 Norcross, GA																									
1921	Griffin	GSL		48	11	22								0.458													
Carmel, Leon James "Duke"		BL TL 6'3" 202 lbs. b. 04/23/1937 New York, NY																									
1955	Albany	GFL	24	65	10	19	2	0	1	4	0	7	15	0.292	OF, P	28	1	1	0.967	1	0	0	<45				
1956	Albany	GFL	18	55	9	15	4	0	0	10	3	12	16	0.273	OF	26	3	6	0.829								
Carmichael, ---			0																								
1921	Carrollton	GSL		14	1	8								0.571													
Carmichael, Dan		BR																									
1955	Sandersville	GSL	1	1		0								0.000													
Carmichael, Edward "Ed"		BR TR																									
1939	Valdosta	GFL	15	51	11	16	3	0	0	3	3	8	10	0.314	OF	19	2	0	1.000								
1947	Tallassee(87) - Alex City (37)	GAL	124	466	72	151	23	3	3	77	7	52	42	0.324	OF	191	8	12	0.943								
Carmichael, Walter B. "Bryce"		BR TR																									
1948	Baxley	GSL	121	439	42	109	14	7	10	63	12	33	86	0.248	2B	236	262	42	0.922								
1949	Hazlehurst-Baxley	GSL	137	550	116	172	28	11	15	113	17	57	82	0.313	2B	345	303	62	0.913								
Carmo, Robert "Bob"		BR TR																									
1958	Brunswick	GFL	42	159	23	29	3	1	1	19	1	19	33	0.182	OF	65	1	4	0.943								
Carn, Irving "Irv"		BR TR																									
1952	Statesboro	GSL	124	522	86	148	33	2	1	58	4	58	39	0.284	OF	229	10	12	0.952								
1953	Tifton	GFL	2											0.125													
1953	Statesboro	GSL	13	49	11	12	2	0	0	2	1	9	4	0.245	OF	23	2	1	0.962								
Caro, Jack		BR TR																									
1951	Waycross	GFL	115	426	56	127	23	3	0	52	9	52	56	0.298	SS	221	361	55	0.914								
Carolan, Joseph "Joe"		BR TR																									
1952	Thomasville	GFL	134	495	72	123	15	6	15	93	5	78	130	0.248	OF	241	12	12	0.955								
1954	Albany	GFL	15	55	9	12	1	2	1	3	1	10	18	0.218	OF	22	0	1	0.957								
Carpenter, John		BL TL																									
1946	Newnan	GAL	2												P					2	1	0	0.00	12	14	9	8
Carpenter, Max		BR TL																									
1953	Douglas	GSL	29	66	9	11	3	0	1	9	1	7	23	0.167	P	8	25	3	0.917	27	11	6	5.13	158	172	102	123
1955	Tifton	GFL	5	7		3								0.429	P					4	1	1	<45				
Carpenter, William "Bill"		BR TR																									
1955	Cordele	GFL	4	1		0								0.000	P					3	0	1	<45				
1957	Fitzgerald	GFL	23	46	3	12	2	0	0	3	1	1	10	0.261	P	6	15	3	0.875	17	3	7	4.96	78	95	67	57
Carr, William G. "Bill"		BR TR																									
1949	Moultrie		53	194	25	39	7	2	1	21	3	23	37	0.201	SS, OF	89	124	24	0.899								
Carrasquel, Manuel		BR TR																									
1956	Vidalia	GSL	75	288	42	76	10	4	3	51	4	13	49	0.264	SS	123	160	33	0.896								
Carrico, Edgar		BL																									
1957	Brunswick	GFL	20	49	7	8	0	0	1	10	1	5	12	0.163													
Carroll, Dorsey Lee "Dixie"		BL TR 5'11" 165 lbs. b. 05/09/1891 Paducah, KY d. 10/13/1984 Jacksonville, FL																									
1928	Talladega	GAL	14	53	12	1	1	0		0	3	5		0.226	OF	27	1	0	1.000								
1929	Anniston	GAL	30	120	9	35	7	1	2		3	7	27	0.292	OF	69	4	2	0.973								
1930	Huntsville	GAL													M												
Carroll, Gerald		BL TL																									
1962	Moultrie	GFL	19	22	3	4	2	0	1	5	0	1	9	0.182	P	2	13	2	0.882	16	2	4	7.53	43	52	51	47
Carroll, Ray		BR TR																									
1956	Albany	GFL	51	148	19	26	6	4	0	13	1	10	51	0.176	OF	61	3	8	0.889								
1957	Albany	GFL	60	178	22	47	4	4	2	28	2	18	41	0.264	OF	89	3	9	0.911								
Carroll, William "Bill"		BL TL																									
1948	Griffin	GAL	13	41	8	7	2	0	0	4	2	11	17	0.171	1B	92	3	3	0.969								
Carson, Raymond "Ray"		BL TR																									
1956	Dublin	GSL	65	231	37	57	15	1	3	30	8	42	54	0.247	1B	454	22	20	0.960								
Carter, ---																											
1914	Anniston	GAL	14	46	2	9				4				0.196	OF	27	2	5	0.853								
1917	Talladega	GAL	2	5	1	1	0	0	0	0				0.200	OF	6	0	1	0.857								
Carter, ---																											
1921	Cedartown	GSL													C												
Carter, Arlen		BR TR																									
1953	Dublin	GSL	20	26	4	3	0	1	0	2	0	5	10	0.115	P	4	14	1	0.947	17	3	10	7.54	74	87	73	67
1954	Dublin	GSL	4	8		2								0.250	P					4	2	1	<45				
Carter, Emil		BR TR																									
1946	LaGrange	GAL	<10																								
1951	Tifton	GFL	123	454	42	105	15	3	0	48	6	40	45	0.231	2B	304	295	30	0.952								
1952	Tifton	GFL	133	549	67	121	5	5	0	50	1	43	60	0.220	2B	353	386	27	0.965								
Carter, Homer A.																											
1928	Carrollton - Gadsden	GAL	28	71	8	18	3	1	1	0	4	8		0.254	P, OF	11	25	4	0.900	19	9	8	4.00	126	151	47	23
1930	Carrollton	GAL		20		3								0.150	P												
1930	Anniston	GAL	20	43	5	4	0	0	0	0	2	6		0.093	P	0	31	1	0.969	20	6	6	5.46	112	137	41	26
1930	Huntsville	GAL	27	69	7	15	1	0	0	1	6	15		0.217	P	6	26	4	0.889	24	8	11	6.37	164	222	69	74

Georgia Class-D Minor League Baseball Encyclopedia

YR	TEAM	LG	G	AB	R	H	2B	3B	HR	RBI	SB	BB	SO	BA	POS	PO	A	E	FA	GP	W	L	ERA	IP	H	SO	BB
Carter, Lawrence E. "Larry"																											
1942	Moultrie	GFL	125	476	77	142	26	5	1	67	18	50	37	0.298	1B	1107	56	23	0.981								
Carter, Leon		BR TR																									
1950	LaGrange	GAL	122	497	113	162	28	7	16	105	15	52	28	0.326	3B	117	216	28	0.922								
Carter, Mack																											
1938	Cordele	GFL	95	364	41	91	13	6	0	43	6	24	39	0.250	1B	814	44	13	0.985								
1939	Cordele	GFL	95	347	38	87	8	1	0	40	11	25	33	0.251	1B	853	55	16	0.983								
Carter, Robert G. "Bob"		BR TR																									
1953	Thomasville	GFL	59	198	36	56	5	3	1	39	3	24	21	0.283	OF, C	100	9	5	0.956								
Carter, Russ B.																											
1920	Cedartown	GSL													OF												
1920	Carrollton	GSL	<10												OF												
Carter, Steve S.		BL TR																									
1947	Tallassee(14) - Alex City(12)	GAL	26	95	14	22	5	1	3	16	1	4	31	0.232	3B, OF	25	24	12	0.803								
Cartier, Dale		BL TL																									
1954	Valdosta	GFL	11	6	0	0	0	0	0	0	0	3	3	0.000	P					4	0	1		<45			
1955	Valdosta	GFL	8	16		6								0.375	P					2	0	1		<45			
Cartwright, Donald "Don"		BR TR																									
1954	Americus-Cordele	GFL	6	14		0								0.000	P					6	0	3		<45			
Cartwright, James P.																											
1928	Lindale	GAL	69	264	58	98	20	1	10		6	27	18	0.371	1B, OF	301	22	17	0.950								
Caruso, Enrico		BL TL																									
1950	Rome	GAL	18	27	4	11	2	0	0	2	0	2	6	0.407	P	3	10	1	0.929	17	3	2	6.53	62	82	40	60
Carver, James "Jim"		BR TR																									
1958	Dublin	GFL	13	50	10	12	3	0	2	7	0	7	13	0.240	C	63	1	2	0.970								
Casanega, David "Dave"		BL TR																									
1954	Tifton	GFL	26	91	9	20	6	0	1	8	1	12	21	0.220	SS	34	38	4	0.947								
Casanova, Rudy		BR TR																									
1962	Moultrie	GFL	36	128	23	25	7	0	1	13	4	37	26	0.195	SS, OF	49	33	9	0.901								
Case, S.E.																											
1928	Anniston	GAL	86	320	44	95	13	12	3		10	23	21	0.297	C	330	85	15	0.965								
Casey, Charles		BR TR																									
1946	Valley	GAL	25	64	9	11	3	0	0	7	0	4	9	0.172	C	81	11	2	0.979								
1949	Valley	GAL	15	30	3	5	1	0	0	5	1	3	4	0.167	C	42	3	4	0.918								
Cash, ---																											
1928	Lindale	GAL	14	56	9	12	3	1	0		3	4	2	0.214	SS	23	38	5	0.924								
Cash, A. Jackson "Al"		BR TR																									
1952	Waycross	GFL	45	174	30	48	8	3	0	23	3	23	17	0.276	2B	93	108	7	0.966								
1953	Waycross	GFL	112	425	43	108	19	4	0	43	6	41	42	0.254	2B, SS	210	238	17	0.963								
Cash, John "Jack"		BR TR																									
1951	Rome	GAL	111	467	103	143	24	6	5	64	13	57	53	0.306	2B	320	274	21	0.966								
1952	Douglas	GSL	28	107	19	31	4	2	0	11	10	18	6	0.290	2B	76	62	8	0.945								
Cash, Paul		BL TR																									
1939	Albany	GFL	10	19	2	8	1	0	0	2	0	2	2	0.421	P	9	5	1	0.933	6	3	2	4.50	38	31	12	27
1940	Albany	GFL	73	170	17	47	6	3	0	20	0	22	30	0.276	P, IF					30	17	6	3.26	196	192	92	59
Cash, Sewell		BR TR																									
1953	Douglas	GSL	7											0.063	P						1	2		<45			
Cashion, ---																											
1917	Anniston	GAL	13	47	6	15	2	1	0		4			0.319	1B, C	122	3	2	0.984								
Cassell, Carl		BR TR																									
1954	Albany	GFL	43	96	5	16	0	0	1	11	1	11	37	0.167	C	179	21	12	0.943								
1955	Hazlehurst-Baxley	GSL	6	17		3								0.176													
Cassidy, ---																											
1906	Valdosta	GSL													P												
Cassidy, John		BR TR																									
1957	Fitzgerald	GFL	112	443	61	111	23	4	5	53	5	62	91	0.251	OF	228	11	10	0.960								
Castaing, ---																											
1917	LaGrange	GAL	3	9	1	0	0	0	0		0			0.000	1B	26	2	0	1.000								
Castalado, Jerry		BR TR																									
1953	Sandersville	GSL	6											0.000	P						1	0		<45			
Castaneda (Blomberg), James "Jim"		BR TL																									
1954	Americus-Cordele	GFL	79	255	31	63	12	2	0	32	0	59	41	0.247	1B	625	35	11	0.984								
Castelgrande, Vito		BR TR																									
1946	Tallahassee	GFL	113	410	77	103	17	7	0	44	18	83	56	0.251	OF	213	17	13	0.947								
Castelli, Anthony		BR																									
1954	Thomasville	GFL	6	17		1								0.059													
Castiglione, Peter Paul "Pete"		BR TR 5'11" 175 lbs. b. 2/13/1921 Greenwich, CT																									
1941	Moultrie	GFL	92	403	68	113	20	4	0	42	1	26	23	0.280	3B	94	197	23	0.927								
Castille, Earl		BR TR																									
1955	Valdosta	GFL	13	11	0	0	0	0	0	0	0	1	7	0.000	P	2	5	1	0.875	12	2	2	2.83	54	40	35	22
Castillo, Celido																											
1935	Tallahassee	GFL	57	214	33	52	8	4	0		7	25	8	0.243	IF	129	165	16	0.948								
Castillo, Sergio		BR TR																									
1952	Jesup	GSL	15	63	11	12	1	0	1	5	0	12	12	0.190	2B	28	24	3	0.945								

Georgia Class-D Minor League Baseball Encyclopedia

YR	TEAM	LG	G	AB	R	H	2B	3B	HR	RBI	SB	BB	SO	BA	POS	PO	A	E	FA	GP	W	L	ERA	IP	H	SO	BB
Caswell, Marvin "Marv"		BR TR																									
1955	Valdosta	GFL	4	9	3									0.333	P					4	0	1	<45				
1956	Valdosta	GFL	2	1	0									0.000	P					1	0	0	<45				
Catalano, Peter "Pete"		BR TR																									
1950	Douglas	GSL	33	133	22	46	7	2	5	18	2	10	19	0.346	OF	38	3	4	0.911								
1951	Douglas	GSL	125	494	81	135	15	3	1	56	9	66	54	0.273	OF	188	8	17	0.920								
1952	Douglas(72) - Fitzgerald(19)	GSL	91	355	56	93	22	3	3	60	12	38	30	0.262	OF	183	10	8	0.960								
Cataldo, J. Thomas "Tom"		BR TR																									
1951	Alexander City	GAL	37	137	20	41	5	3	0	16	4	17	8	0.299	3B	36	86	7	0.946								
Catchings, Benjamin "Ben"		BL TR																									
1948	Alexander City	GAL	93	307	50	64	2	6	0	32	36	82	27	0.208	M, 3B, SS	136	232	34	0.915								
Catchpole, James "Jim"		BR TL																									
1946	Thomasville	GFL	5												P					5	0	2	0.00	14	19	5	14
Cater, James "Jim"		BL TL																									
1948	Valdosta	GFL	33	48	6	7	1	0	0	3	0	9	33	0.146	P	3	13	2	0.889	33	10	8	4.02	132	139	99	74
1949	Valdosta	GFL	31	46	6	7	4	0	0	3	1	7	21	0.152	P	4	25	4	0.879	31	9	4	2.85	142	103	151	96
1952	Tifton	GFL	16	43	10	12	2	0	0	4	0	7	9	0.279	P	3	21	5	0.828	15	6	9	3.60	115	98	101	77
1953	Tifton	GFL	36	100	13	19	3	1	0	8	0	12	39	0.190	P	12	36	5	0.906	35	21	10	2.66	254	195	251	155
Cates, Eli Eldo "Eli"		BR TR 5'9" 175 lbs. b. 01/26/1877 Greens Fork, IN d. 05/29/1964 Anderson, IN																									
1913	Brunswick	ESL	34	96	11	23	5	1	0					0.240	P, OF	20	48	2	0.971	22	11	11					
1916	Rome	GAL	25	66	9	21					1			0.318	P												
Cathey, Hardin Abner Jr. "Lil Abner"		BR TR 6'4" 190 lbs. b. 07/06/1919 Burns, TX d. 07/27/1997 Nashville, TN																									
1940	Thomasville	GFL	38	103	10	20	1	2	0	8	0	1	15	0.194	P					31	20	8	3.27	237	250	186	82
Cathey, John		BR TL																									
1951	Douglas	GSL	19	43	7	7	1	0	2	8	0	5	9	0.163	P	4	24	1	0.966	16	7	4	5.57	84	89	39	72
1953	Douglas	GSL	14	40	5	8	2	1	0	5	0	1	12	0.200	P	4	21	2	0.926	13	5	6	4.88	83	94	38	43
Cathey, Robert "Bob"		BR TR																									
1949	Moultrie	GFL	70	272	36	64	12	1	1	35	5	33	40	0.235	1B	586	28	18	0.972								
Cato, Roy Frank "Roy"		BL TR																									
1952	Douglas	GSL	101	340	40	80	17	3	0	52	1	55	36	0.235	C	471	41	15	0.972								
1953	Waycross	GFL	127	444	62	113	17	8	3	53	6	76	70	0.255	3B, C	494	98	20	0.967								
Catterton, J. Franklin "Frank"		BL TR																									
1951	Griffin	GAL	59	137	30	34	5	0	0	13	3	18	20	0.248	P	7	48	1	0.982	34	12	11	5.07	167	209	85	55
Caudle, James "Jim"		BL TR																									
1952	Eastman	GSL	69	245	33	75	15	2	9	39	0	18	57	0.306	OF	80	12	6	0.939								
1953	Eastman	GSL	125	505	92	167	26	8	27	134	6	48	79	0.331	1B, OF, P	286	19	12	0.962		0	0	<45				
1955	Moultrie	GFL	41	125	10	26	6	1	2	17	0	14	34	0.208	OF, P	32	0	2	0.941	1	1	0	<45				
Causion, William "Bill"		BL TL																									
1954	Dublin	GSL	129	503	123	164	35	8	18	116	19	83	106	0.326	OF	200	14	18	0.922								
Cavallaro, Ferdinand "Fred"		BR TR																									
1951	Moultrie	GFL	18	73	4	19	2	0	0	10	0	10	16	0.260	OF	47	4	2	0.962								
1953	Fitzgerald	GFL	47	171	23	42	9	0	0	18	2	17	22	0.246	OF	87	6	14	0.869								
1953	Douglas	GSL	20	75	11	19	0	0	2	9	2	6	10	0.253	3B	17	40	3	0.950								
Cavaness, James H. "Jim"		GFL																									
1942	Albany	GFL	14	45	5	10	0	2	0	3	1	2	8	0.222	3B	13	17	2	0.938								
Cawley, Gaynor		BS TL																									
1962	Thomasville	GFL	28	19	4	4	1	0	0	3	0	5	4	0.211	P	1	11	1	0.923	24	7	3	2.18	66	52	75	29
1963	Moultrie	GFL	5	8	0	2	1	0	0	1	0	0	3	0.250	P					5	2	2	3.91	23	24	24	15
Cearley, Wilbur																											
1939	Cordele	GFL	126	480	66	147	24	10	5	78	8	41	44	0.306	OF	282	32	21	0.937								
Ceccarelli, Arthur Edward "Art" "Chic"		BR TL 6'0" 190 lbs. b. 04/02/1930 New Haven, CT																									
1949	Valdosta	GFL	34	72	8	9	0	0	0	4	0	11	34	0.125	P	8	27	1	0.972	34	17	8	3.21	210	152	294	149
Cecil, Edward "Ed"		BR TR																									
1963	Brunswick	GFL	8	4	0	0	0	0	0	0	0	0	0	0.000	P					6	0	0	3.60	15	8	21	8
Celardo, Edward F. "Ed"		BR TR																									
1952	Tifton	GFL	118	412	36	98	13	2	0	44	1	47	55	0.238	C	537	80	17	0.973								
1953	Tifton	GFL	127	394	48	95	12	3	0	52	4	58	51	0.241	C	706	74	16	0.980								
Celiberti, Frank		BR TR																									
1951	Fitzgerald	GSL	15	23	4	4	0	0	0	1	0	5	3	0.174	OF	10	1	1	0.917								
Celozzi, Joseph "Joe"		BR TR																									
1953	Sandersville	GSL	8											0.077	P						0	2	<45				
Center, Marvin Earl "Pete"		BR TR 6'4" 190 lbs. b. 04/22/1912 Hazel Green, KY																									
1937	Americus	GFL	19	40	3	10	3	1	0	3	0	6	14	0.250	P	12	12	5	0.828	13	1	8	4.38	72	78	36	54
Centi, David "Dave"		BR TR																									
1957	Waycross	GFL	35	124	11	26	7	1	1	14	0	8	34	0.210	OF, P	41	1	4	0.913	2	0	0	<30				
Ceran, ---		BR TR																									
1951	Brunswick	GFL	32												P	7	33	1	0.976								
Ceravolo, Joseph "Joe"		BR TR																									
1948	Vidalia-Lyons	GSL	23	83	9	14	1	1	0	3	2	10	25	0.169	2B	33	32	2	0.970								
Cercek, Edward "Ed"		BL TR 6'3" 185 lbs. 05/21/1927 Cleveland, OH																									
1950	Americus	GFL	60	220	28	53	6	1	4	29	2	30	46	0.241	OF	76	6	9	0.901								
Cernich, Joseph "Joe"		BL TR																									
1963	Thomasville	GFL	40	83	3	12	1	0	0	8	0	6	25	0.145	C	96	6	2	0.981								
Chadner, Richard "Dick"		BL TL																									
1954	Brunswick	GFL	7	2		1								0.500	P					7	0	0	<45				

Georgia Class-D Minor League Baseball Encyclopedia

YR	TEAM	LG	G	AB	R	H	2B	3B	HR	RBI	SB	BB	SO	BA	POS	PO	A	E	FA	GP	W	L	ERA	IP	H	SO	BB
Chadwick, ---																											
1930	Talladega	GAL	18	74	9	18	2	3	1		0	2	16	0.243	OF	35	2	3	0.925								
Chadwick, W. Reed		BR TR																									
1952	Fitzgerald(52) - Eastman(3)	GSL	55	212	31	65	14	2	1	44	3	27	34	0.307	C	241	33	15	0.948								
1955	Valdosta	GFL	58	206	21	52	6	0	1	27	2	18	24	0.252	C	349	32	10	0.974								
Chafin, Loran "Cotton"		BL TR																									
1949	Eastman	GSL	135	548	128	182	36	15	8	97	51	61	43	0.332	OF	203	22	20	0.918								
1953	Tifton	GFL	133	532	109	166	20	13	0	72	38	59	41	0.312	2B, 3B, OF	249	226	38	0.926								
1954	Tifton	GFL	59	228	52	65	12	6	1	23	11	26	31	0.285	2B	166	151	19	0.943								
Chafin, Mark																											
1955	Tifton	GFL	<10																								
Chafin, Robert "Bobbie"		BR TR																									
1949	Griffin	GAL	17	32	5	3	0	0	0	1	0	9	11	0.094	P	3	13	1	0.941	17	1	4	5.57	63	59	39	65
Chaillot, Emil		BL TL																									
1953	Dublin	GSL	54	197	46	56	11	1	9	39	0	38	18	0.284	1B, P	318	19	14	0.960	11	5	4	5.48	69	67	30	31
Chalker, A.G.																											
1916	Griffin - LaGrange	GAL	61	189	14	36				7				0.190	C												
Chambers, ---																											
1913	Opelika	GAL	91	335	52	99					15			0.296	3B, OF	109	116	32	0.875								
1914	Opelika	GAL	93	348	56	93					8			0.267	OF	145	87	32	0.879								
1915	Dothan	FLAG	75	273	44	67	17	1	1		15			0.245	1B	696	13	22	0.970								
Chambers, ---																											
1921	Cedartown	GSL													P												
Chambers, Inman		BL TR																									
1942	Waycross	GFL	34	78	14	20	1	0	0	3	0	15	23	0.256	P	5	38	5	0.896	35	13	13	3.08	213	225	78	48
1946	Waycross	GFL	25	42	5	6	1	0	0	3	0	5	8	0.143	P	1	32	1	0.971	25	7	5	3.05	127	112	90	48
Chambers, James "Jim"		BL																									
1963	Brunswick	GFL	2	4	1	1	0	0	0	0	0	0	2	0.250													
Chambers, Joseph P. "Joe"		BL TR																									
1946	Valley	GAL	128	475	95	138	14	15	7	59	21	55	44	0.291	2B	300	370	21	0.970								
1947	Valley	GAL	126	480	102	152	14	13	5	96	21	87	37	0.317	2B	317	345	32	0.954								
1948	Valley	GAL	125	431	86	141	23	12	3	99	12	106	30	0.327	2B	299	364	24	0.965								
1949	Dublin	GSL	100	338	64	89	18	4	5	46	15	77	17	0.263	M, 2B	264	290	15	0.974								
1951	Griffin	GAL	34	141	36	34	4	0	1	19	8	48	18	0.241	2B	94	104	11	0.947								
Chambers, Robert "Bob"		BR TR																									
1952	Brunswick	GFL	32	100	7	18	4	0	1	12	0	10	21	0.180	3B	21	38	8	0.881								
Champlain, ---																											
1913	Thomasville	ESL	97	335	37	79	11	0	4					0.236	3B	148	212	32	0.918								
1914	Thomasville	GSL		359	46	110	19	4	1		14			0.306													
Chance, Jesse		BL TL																									
1956	Fitzgerald	GFL	2	2		0								0.000	P					2	0	2		<45			
Chance, Wendell		BR TR																									
1954	Vidalia	GSL	9	17		5								0.294	P					6	1	1		<45			
Chancey, C.M.																											
1913	Americus	ESL	102	368	68	142	32	4	10					0.386	OF	133	14	7	0.955								
1921	LaGrange	GSL		39	7	13								0.333													
Chandler, David "Dave"		BR TR																									
1947	LaGrange	GAL	20	27	8	5	0	2	0	2	0	6	5	0.185	P	6	14	1	0.952	19	3	4	5.45	76	95	25	27
Chandler, Jack W.		BR TR																									
1946	Tallassee	GAL	105	378	50	91	17	3	4	48	13	18	57	0.241	OF	123	6	11	0.921								
Chandler, Norman "Norm"		BR TL																									
1952	Waycross	GFL	30	55	3	8	0	0	0	4	0	7	13	0.145	P	10	28	6	0.864	30	13	8	1.99	176	151	146	73
Chandler, Raymond "Ray"		BL																									
1950	Opelika	GAL	15	36	4	5	0	0	0	3	0	6	11	0.139													
Chandler, William J. "Bill"		BL TR																									
1956	Sandersville	GSL	97	274	26	60	7	0	3	33	2	30	59	0.219	1B, OF, C	279	13	17	0.945								
Chandler, William L. "Billy"		BR TR																									
1952	Thomasville	GFL	35	92	6	27	3	0	0	6	0	1	12	0.293	P	8	41	3	0.942	28	13	12	3.71	204	179	105	139
1953	Thomasville	GFL	15	35	3	5	0	0	0	3	0	3	5	0.143	P	0	17	1	0.944	15	7	4	4.16	80	83	44	52
Chaplin, Bert Edgar "Ed"		BL TR 5'7" 158 lbs. b. 09/25/1893 Pelzer, SC d. 08/15/1978 Sanford, FL																									
1920	Carrollton	GSL		281	73	87	13	8	3		19			0.310	OF, C												
Chaplin, Melvin "Mel"		BR TR																									
1952	Albany	GFL	34	76	8	14	5	0	0	9	0	16	8	0.184	P	7	45	1	0.981	27	15	6	2.18	202	197	73	56
Chapman, ---																											
1914	Waycross	GSL		103	14	16	2	2	0		5			0.155													
1915	Waycross	FLAG	<10																								
Chapman, Joel "Herb"		BL TR																									
1949	Valley	GAL	83	316	56	111	19	2	8	74	12	41	15	0.351	1B, OF	237	8	4	0.984								
Chappell, Marvin "Marv"		BR TR																									
1947	Alexander City	GAL	61	150	22	34	4	1	1	10	3	10	43	0.227	OF, P	61	47	7	0.939	30	7	13	3.42	150	151	70	67
1948	Alexander City	GAL	75	199	26	43	7	2	0	19	3	12	48	0.216	M, OF, P	71	50	5	0.960	32	9	12	4.38	150	152	78	89
1949	Alexander City	GAL	89	235	36	74	10	4	2	22	2	9	57	0.315	OF, P	64	49	6	0.950	51	20	7	2.34	235	180	162	129
1950	Alex City(68) - LaGrange(6)	GAL	74	175	16	33	4	3	0	15	2	8	30	0.189	OF, P	33	29	2	0.969	37	17	10	3.49	222	215	144	135
1951	LaGrange	GAL	62	127	18	29	6	1	1	15	1	9	29	0.228	P	16	34	10	0.833	45	21	8	2.55	251	225	120	128
Chaptman, Devon		BL TR																									
1948	Newnan	GAL	16	33	1	4	0	0	0	3	0	3	8	0.121	P	2	17	2	0.905	16	6	5	3.03	92	95	57	33

Georgia Class-D Minor League Baseball Encyclopedia

YR	TEAM	LG	G	AB	R	H	2B	3B	HR	RBI	SB	BB	SO	BA	POS	PO	A	E	FA	GP	W	L	ERA	IP	H	SO	BB
Charette, Donald "Don"		BR TR																									
1953	Jesup	GSL	21	28	5	3	1	0	0	3	0	0	9	0.107	P	1	15	0	1.000	17	3	2	5.69	68	86	36	48
Charette, Roger		BL TL																									
1954	Statesboro	GSL	6	4		0								0.000	P					3	0	1	<45				
Charles, James F. "Jim"		BR TR																									
1949	LaGrange	GAL	24	48	10	11	2	0	1	10	0	6	17	0.229	P	7	25	4	0.889	24	13	5	4.10	147	132	108	93
Charmolue, Jules																											
1938	Tallahassee	GFL	47	171	27	36	7	2	1	16	1	15	19	0.211	1B	443	17	12	0.975								
Chase, Kendall Fay "Ken" "Lefty"		BL TL 6'2" 210 lbs. b. 10/06/1913 Oneonta, NY d. 01/16/1985 Oneonta, NY																									
1935	Panama City	GFL	31	89	8	23	7	0	0		1	3	18	0.258	P					27	11	11		184	192	220	92
Chastant, ---																											
1915	Anniston - Newnan	GAL	58	204	31	49	9	0	4					0.240	2B, OF	111	106	10	0.956								
1917	Tri-Cities	GAL	15	54	6	12	4	0	0		1			0.222	OF	33	3	2	0.947								
Chatham, C.B. "Happy"																											
1915	Valdosta	FLAG	21	80	14	22	2	0	0	8				0.275	SS	38	62	14	0.877								
1920	Carrollton	GSL		109	12	28								0.257	3B, SS, 2B												
Chechile, William "Bill"		BR TR																									
1949	Griffin(32) - Newnan(89)	GAL	121	436	72	120	18	13	5	80	17	57	80	0.275	OF	233	18	9	0.965								
1950	Newnan	GAL	122	460	95	124	24	6	9	82	29	65	74	0.270	OF	263	17	14	0.952								
Cheney, ---																											
1913	Thomasville	ESL	25	76	6	18	3	0	0					0.237	P	12	48	2	0.968	16	10	6					
1916	Griffin - Talladega	GAL	35	106	5	24				0				0.226	P												
Cheney, Thomas Edgar "Tom"		BR TR 6'0" 180 lbs. b. 10/14/1934 Morgan, GA d. 11/01/2001 Rome, GA																									
1952	Albany	GFL													P						0	1	27.00				
1953	Albany	GFL	36	65	8	13	2	0	0	11	0	6	16	0.200	P	8	37	3	0.938	35	9	12	3.61	172	147	122	85
Cherek, LeRoy		BL TR																									
1958	Waycross	GFL	2	1		0								0.000	P					2	0	0	<30				
Chergey, Paul		BR TR																									
1951	Brunswick	GFL	20	30	5	4	0	0	0	0	0	2	5	0.133	P	5	22	6	0.818	19	4	8	4.55	87	99	60	47
1953	Douglas	GSL	16	26	4	3	1	0	0	1	0	6	7	0.115	P	0	13	1	0.929	13	5	5	4.14	74	69	30	35
Chernetsky, Anthony		BR TR																									
1946	Cordele	GFL	90	336	42	91	11	1	0	40	3	24	54	0.271	OF, C	480	47	24	0.956								
Cherry, Richard "Dick"		BR TR																									
1946	Waycross	GFL	2												P					2	0	0	0.00	11			
1947	Waycross	GFL	12	21	4	3	0	0	0	1	0	6	6	0.143	P	1	11	0	1.000	12	4	3	4.37	68	81	32	24
Chestnut, H.C.																											
1921	LaGrange	GSL													C												
Chetaitis, Stanley "Stan"																											
1941	Thomasville	GFL	12	44	3	8	1	0	0	5	0	3	5	0.182	C	62	7	3	0.958								
Chew, Norman "Ray"																											
1941	Moultrie	GFL	4	12	0	2	0	0	0	1	0	2	4	0.167	C	17	3	3	0.870								
Chiado, Robert "Bob"																											
1938	Moultrie	GFL	28	112	17	37	9	4	1	19	3	8	10	0.330	OF	128	4	6	0.957								
Chierichella, Carmine		BR TR																									
1957	Thomasville	GFL	17	18	1	3	0	0	0	4	0	1	4	0.167	P	3	11	2	0.875	17	2	2	4.12	59	59	30	34
Childers, James C. "Jimmy"		BR																									
1953	Valdosta	GFL	1											0.000													
1953	Jesup	GSL	4											0.167													
Childs, Delton		BL TR																									
1948	Tallassee	GAL	126	477	100	166	20	12	2	58	50	98	58	0.348	OF	281	21	13	0.959								
1949	Albany	GFL	113	443	109	152	24	6	0	47	35	81	61	0.343	OF	167	8	8	0.956								
Childs, Frank		BR TR																									
1946	Newnan(36) - Carrollton(3)	GAL	39	129	6	23	3	1	0	11	1	3	13	0.178	OF, P	48	2	3	0.943	7	0	3	0.00	20	30	16	25
1947	Griffin	GAL	61	143	8	33	6	4	0	11	2	5	25	0.231	OF, P	31	36	5	0.931	34	11	11	4.83	166	171	125	92
Childs, Richard "Dick"		BR TR																									
1949	Waycross	GFL	20	49	2	5	0	0	0	1	0	3	20	0.102	P	3	32	2	0.946	20	9	6	2.91	127	99	71	64
1950	Waycross	GFL	33	60	7	9	0	0	0	2	0	8	20	0.150	P	18	53	10	0.877	33	7	18	5.78	179	204	83	94
Chilton, Warren																											
1949	Eastman	GSL	51	175	31	36	4	0	0	18	15	44	28	0.206	SS	69	135	18	0.919								
Chipman, A.B.																											
1920	LaGrange	GSL													C												
Chitwood, Edgar "Ed"		BR TR																									
1947	Alexander City	GAL	27	44	2	4	1	0	0	3	0	6	23	0.091	P	0	38	3	0.927	27	5	15	6.10	146	186	66	87
Chitwood, Ken E.																											
1929	Cedartown	GAL	24	60	13	20	3	0	1		0	1	5	0.333	P	19	49	3	0.958	18	9	5		109	116	47	38
1930	Cedartown	GAL	32	100	18	36	4	0	2		0	6	12	0.360	P	7	56	7	0.900	27	13	6	6.19	189	227	103	58
Chlebek, Stanley "Stan"		BR TL																									
1954	Brunswick	GFL	6	3		0								0.000	P					6	1	1	<45				
Cholakian, Edward "Ed"		BR TR																									
1952	Thomasville	GFL	45	188	31	53	8	3	0	15	11	25	14	0.282	2B	117	136	20	0.927								
Chredar, Stephen "Steve"		BR TR																									
1947	Cordele(8) - Tallahassee(18)	GFL	26	33	4	6	0	0	0	1	0	4	3	0.182	P	1	20	4	0.840	23	3	3	5.23	93	102	43	53
Christakis, George																											
1941	Tallahassee	GFL	8	29	5	5	0	0	0	2	0	5	4	0.172	2B	14	13	3	0.900								

Georgia Class-D Minor League Baseball Encyclopedia

YR	TEAM	LG	G	AB	R	H	2B	3B	HR	RBI	SB	BB	SO	BA	POS	PO	A	E	FA	GP	W	L	ERA	IP	H	SO	BB
Christenbury, Lloyd Reid "Low"		BL TR 5'7" 165 lbs. b. 10/19/1893 Mecklenburg County, NC d. 12/13/1944 Birmingham, AL																									
1916	Newnan - Anniston	GAL	59	220	42	65					20			0.295	SS, OF												
1917	Anniston	GAL	16	62	16	23	4	3	0		3			0.371	SS	29	55	6	0.933								
Christiansen, ---																											
1929	Carrollton	GAL		34	6	11								0.324													
1929	Cedartown	GAL	43	142	23	40	6	0	1	1	13		6	0.282	OF	116	5	1	0.992								
Christie, Frank		BR TR																									
1949	Tifton	GSL	28	62	4	16	3	0	0	11	8	0	11	0.258	P	4	21	2	0.926	27	12	7	5.74	127	100	69	94
1950	Tifton	GSL	25	69	8	13	1	0	0	3	0	6	11	0.188	P	3	29	1	0.970	25	12	7	3.76	170	180	74	85
1951	Tifton	GFL	9												P					9	3	5	3.40	53	62	23	17
1952	Fitzgerald	GSL	14	21	2	8	1	0	0	4	0	3	0	0.381	P	4	10	3	0.824	10	2	4	5.60	45	52	12	42
Christie, John		BR TL																									
1956	Fitzgerald	GFL	37	85	7	10	0	1	0	5	0	7	30	0.118	P	15	31	6	0.885	35	12	15	3.75	221	219	147	126
Christie, Lew W. "Jake"																											
1939	Moultrie	GFL													P								<45				
Christino, Michael "Mike"		BL TL																									
1963	Thomasville	GFL	28	81	11	23	2	0	0	13	1	20	11	0.284	1B	222	16	4	0.983								
Christoff, Ernest "Ernie"		BR TR																									
1957	Waycross	GFL	24	53	11	12	3	0	0	1	0	4	17	0.226	P	3	21	3	0.889	21	10	5	3.85	131	123	109	66
Christopher, Leo		BR TR																									
1950	Haziehurst-Baxley	GSL	38	125	15	27	3	4	0	12	1	17	29	0.216	3B, OF	52	30	15	0.845								
Christy, James "Jim"		BR TR																									
1957	Thomasville	GFL	19	60	5	11	2	1	0	8	0	6	17	0.183	OF	19	4	3	0.885								
Chulick, William "Bill"		BR																									
1946	Cordele	GFL	<10																								
Chumbris, Nicholas "Nick"		BR TR																									
1952	Waycross	GFL	36	138	9	41	13	0	1	21	1	5	14	0.297	OF	34	1	5	0.875								
Churlilla, Edward "Ed"		BR																									
1955	Douglas	GSL	9	12		3								0.250													
Churn, Clarence Nottingham "Chuck"		BR TR 6'3" 205 lbs. b. 02/01/1930 Bridgetown, VA																									
1963	Moultrie	GFL	23	19	0	3	1	0	0	0	0	2	2	0.158	P	7	3	1	0.909	12	3	1	0.60	30	15	27	6
Ciani, Nicholas "Nick"		BL TL																									
1949	Tallassee	GAL	117	393	88	91	17	4	15	66	10	103	42	0.232	OF	152	9	7	0.958								
Ciatto, Rosario		BR TR																									
1954	Valdosta	GFL	9	31		7								0.226													
1955	Valdosta	GFL	15	48	2	10	3	0	1	7	0	8	16	0.208	C	91	11	3	0.971								
Cibrowski, Marion		BR TR																									
1940	Americus	GFL	100	416	50	117	17	5	2	61	4	10	26	0.281	OF	201	28	7	0.970								
1941	Valdosta	GFL	129	514	103	166	29	6	2	82	31	49	18	0.323	OF, P	252	64	13	0.960	4	0	1	1.13	16	14	6	3
Cibulski, Floyd		BR TR																									
1952	Statesboro	GSL	43	104	9	17	1	1	0	13	0	5	16	0.163	OF, P	8	40	3	0.941	33	14	11	4.10	204	217	78	83
Ciccimarro, John																											
1942	Dothan	GFL	33	110	11	18	7	0	0	9	0	17	42	0.164	SS	48	77	19	0.868								
Ciccone, Nicholas "Nick"		BR																									
1946	Cordele	GFL	<10																								
Ciccone, Remo		BL TL																									
1940	Cordele	GFL	110	421	65	116	15	6	1	30	8	51	55	0.276	OF, IF, P	395	29	19	0.957				<35				
Cichon, Frank		BL TR																									
1948	Carrollton	GAL	108	410	67	109	13	9	12	66	12	30	67	0.266	OF	182	12	28	0.874								
1949	Carrollton	GAL	55	196	41	54	5	3	1	29	8	26	23	0.276	OF	86	12	6	0.942								
Cielesz, Walter "Walt"		BL TR																									
1939	Moultrie	GFL	113	432	73	124	15	11	4	77	12	66	26	0.287	OF	220	14	10	0.959								
1940	Moultrie	GFL	23	84	10	21	2	3	0	11	4	11	9	0.250	OF	45	3	3	0.941								
Cierniak, Donald "Don"		BL TL																									
1954	Waycross	GFL	29	42	2	3	0	0	0	0	0	5	22	0.071	P	4	33	3	0.925	28	6	11	4.17	123	119	91	67
1954	Statesboro	GSL	10	24	1	2	0	0	0	0	1	7		0.083	P	0	6	1	0.857	10	3	4	3.88	51	57	29	17
Cimmino, Vincent "Vince"		BR TR																									
1954	Sandersville	GSL	24	45	0	2	0	0	0	4	4	16		0.044	P	2	22	4	0.857	24	2	11	5.89	136	161	103	75
Cincotta, Joseph "Joe"		BR TR																									
1956	Haziehurst-Baxley	GSL	20	61	8	14	5	0	1	8	1	17	20	0.230	C	98	12	9	0.924								
Clair, Thomas "Tom"		BR TR																									
1946	Americus	GFL	1												P					1	0	0	0.00	3			
Clancey, ---																											
1913	Waycross	ESL	29	78	7	11	0	0	0					0.141	SS	41	31	10	0.878								
Clancy, John William "Bud"		BL TL 6'0" 170 lbs. b. 09/15/1900 Odell, IL d. 09/26/1968 Ottumwa, IA																									
1942	Valdosta	GFL	48	167	36	48	10	3	0	31	5	32	11	0.287	1B	374	38	7	0.983								
Clancy, William "Bill"		BR TR																									
1955	Thomasville	GFL	11	11	1	1	0	0	0	1	0	3	6	0.091	P	3	5	1	0.889	11	1	1	<45				
1956	Thomasville	GFL	7	4		0								0.000	P					7	0	2	<45				
Clapham, Bradley "Brad"		BL TL																									
1952	Tifton	GFL	48	115	7	17	1	0	0	5	1	8	12	0.148	P	10	55	5	0.929	37	18	12	2.33	243	240	108	105
1953	Tifton	GFL	59	121	16	31	4	4	2	20	1	6	15	0.256	P	13	50	3	0.955	38	15	11	3.78	231	230	179	117
Clapp, Charles																											
1915	Anniston - Talladega	GAL	37	129	13	29	4	0	0					0.225	OF	72	2	1	0.987								
1916	Talladega	GAL	62	213	30	67					12			0.315	OF												

Georgia Class-D Minor League Baseball Encyclopedia

YR	TEAM	LG	G	AB	R	H	2B	3B	HR	RBI	SB	BB	SO	BA	POS	PO	A	E	FA	GP	W	L	ERA	IP	H	SO	BB
Clarich, James "Jim"		BR TR																									
1949	Tallahassee	GFL	12	17	2	6	1	0	0	1	0	0	3	0.353	P	3	16	0	1.000	10	1	4	3.83	54	42	22	58
Clark, ---																											
1913	Gadsden	GAL	19	66	11	20				4				0.303	2B	52	60	1	0.991								
1913	LaGrange	GAL	81	320	44	72				11				0.225	3B, SS	127	192	42	0.884								
1915	Waycross	FLAG	75	289	39	68	6	1	0	15				0.235													
1916	Anniston	GAL	21	77	13	27				3				0.351	SS												
Clark, Glen Ester "Glen"		BS TR 6'1" 190 lbs. b. 03/07/1941 Austin, TX																									
1962	Dublin	GFL	73	292	71	100	15	2	26	72	4	37	68	0.342	3B, OF	76	91	31	0.843								
Clark, Langdon "Wild Bill"																											
1914	Waycross	GSL													M												
Clark, Louis "Lou"		BR TR																									
1951	Brunswick	GFL	24	27	6	4	0	0	2	6	0	6	10	0.148	P	1	5	1	0.857	16	3	1	4.08	53	45	46	38
Clark, Philip James "Phil"		BR TR 6'3" 210 lbs. b. 10/03/1932 Albany, GA																									
1951	Albany	GFL	38	94	8	17	2	1	0	11	1	7	21	0.181	P	13	40	3	0.946	34	18	7	2.96	219	164	135	103
1953	Albany	GFL	8											0.083	P						1	3		<45			
Clark, R.H.																											
1928	Cedartown	GAL	89	351	70	129	21	3	4		15	18	5	0.368	2B, OF, C	224	75	20	0.937								
1929	Cedartown	GAL	90	371	65	121	18	4	10		18	23	5	0.326	OF	161	43	19	0.915								
1930	Cedartown	GAL	94	376	59	129	21	10	3		4	21	8	0.343	OF, C, P	228	35	9	0.967	2	1	1	6.75	16	25	3	5
Clark, Raymond "Ray"		BR TR																									
1948	Valley	GAL	112	405	50	95	15	3	0	44	2	34	62	0.235	SS	175	362	51	0.913								
1949	Valley	GAL	44	158	16	39	8	2	0	23	2	15	15	0.247	SS	72	95	25	0.870								
1950	Carrollton	GAL	119	459	82	155	38	2	12	77	6	56	48	0.338	SS	152	253	38	0.914								
Clark, Robert G. "Bob"		BL TR																									
1956	Albany	GFL	66	237	43	60	9	2	2	24	3	61	11	0.253	SS	138	176	14	0.957								
1956	Dublin	GSL	59	196	26	51	7	0	3	28	1	34	8	0.260	M, 3B, SS, P	79	118	20	0.908	2	0	0					
Clark, Roy																											
1949	Dublin	GSL	79	297	35	62	17	2	5	29	4	25	37	0.209	SS	108	170	36	0.885								
Clark, Walter "Walt"																											
1937	Thomasville	GFL	42	108	14	30	4	0	1	15	0	6	7	0.278	P	25	34	5	0.922	34	13	9	3.57	209	219	59	81
1938	Thomasville	GFL	40	117	14	30	3	0	0	10	0	4	7	0.256	P	33	24	4	0.934								
Clark, William																											
1913	Waycross	ESL	47	116	9	22	2	1	0					0.190	M, P, OF	18	66	8	0.913	25	16	9					
Clarke, William "Bill"		BL TR																									
1952	Dublin	GSL	16	45	6	7	1	0	0	2	2	5	8	0.156	OF	19	0	2	0.905								
Clary, Ellis "Cat"		BR TR 5'8" 160 lbs. b. 09/11/1916 Valdosta, GA d. 06/02/2000 Valdosta, GA																									
1935	Americus	GFL	89	334	57	72	14	1	1		9	40	45	0.216	IF	184	261	49	0.901								
1936	Americus	GFL	21	85	11	16	1	3	0	8	13			0.188	SS	51	72	13	0.904								
Claset, John L.		BL TL																									
1953	Fitzgerald	GFL	32	82	9	12	2	0	0	2	0	12	38	0.146	P	5	27	5	0.865	35	13	15	3.75	228	222	186	155
1954	Fitzgerald	GFL	42	79	11	14	3	0	0	11	1	16	35	0.177	P	3	28	1	0.969	42	19	11	2.90	248	210	243	79
Clawson, Charles		BR TR																									
1946	Tallahassee	GFL	5												P					5	1	3	0.00	21	27	11	14
Claypool, James Samuel "Jim"		BL TR																									
1950	Vidalia-Lyons	GSL	89	314	50	95	18	5	2	41	0	34	44	0.303	OF, C	337	39	15	0.962								
1951	Fitzgerald	GSL	124	488	68	155	37	8	3	73	3	49	49	0.318	OF, C	407	59	30	0.940								
Clemens, Chester Spurgeon "Chet"		BR TR 6'0" 175 lbs. B. 05/10/1917 San Fernando, CA																									
1937	Tallahassee	GFL	34	125	19	29	5	3	0	15	6	20	31	0.232	OF	78	5	4	0.954								
Clement, Ed S.		BL TR																									
1940	Waycross	GFL	<10												P					5	2	3	1.13	48	37	14	11
Clements, Anthony		BL TL																									
1955	Sandersville	GSL	9	12		1								0.083	P					8	0	2					
Clements, Frank		BR TR																									
1952	Eastman	GSL	20	55	4	9	1	0	0	2	0	5	25	0.164	P	7	24	1	0.969	20	13	3	3.25	155	143	52	57
1953	Eastman	GSL	17	41	5	5	4	0	0	2	0	6	11	0.122	P	6	12	1	0.947	16	8	3	4.22	111	109	48	29
Clements, Mason		BR TR																									
1950	Rome	GAL	31	85	9	20	2	0	0	6	5	15	7	0.235	3B	23	55	13	0.857								
1951	Jesup	GSL	111	418	83	119	16	0	1	80	22	69	35	0.285	3B	122	252	53	0.876								
Clements, Ralph		BL TL																									
1949	Tallassee	GAL	36	73	4	22	1	0	0	10	0	5	10	0.301	P	4	25	0	1.000	28	14	7	2.21	187	148	114	76
Cleveland, ---																											
1930	Cedartown	GAL	96	396	97	114	19	3	3		2	31	35	0.288	SS	166	290	74	0.860								
Click, James Waldren "Jim"																											
1942	Dothan	GFL	39	150	20	47	8	1	3	32	0	13	21	0.313	OF	45	4	9	0.845								
Clifford, Ernest		BR TR																									
1952	Thomasville	GFL	37	60	4	4	0	0	0	1	0	8	41	0.067	P	3	20	1	0.958	35	9	15	3.57	189	205	78	47
Clift, Frank		BR TR																									
1956	Douglas	GSL	7	8		3								0.375	P					6	2	2					
Clifton, Henry E.		BR TL																									
1950	Dublin	GSL	102	348	59	93	19	0	4	34	2	53	44	0.267	1B, P	619	61	21	0.970	25	13	7	3.83	169	166	107	116
1952	Dublin	GSL	18	53	8	12	1	0	2	6	0	5	3	0.226	P	3	17	1	0.952	10	2	4	6.95	57	58	34	43
1953	Dublin	GSL	94	289	55	84	8	1	8	39	0	46	36	0.291	1B, OF, P	301	68	16	0.958	29	14	8	5.07	174	190	93	131

Georgia Class-D Minor League Baseball Encyclopedia

YR	TEAM	LG	G	AB	R	H	2B	3B	HR	RBI	SB	BB	SO	BA	POS	PO	A	E	FA	GP	W	L	ERA	IP	H	SO	BB
Clifton, John H.		BR TR																									
1953	Waycross	GFL	82	306	45	82	14	4	2	45	4	38	38	0.268	OF	147	14	8	0.953								
1953	Douglas	GSL	1											0.000													
1954	Waycross	GFL	128	485	74	137	27	7	3	66	21	48	47	0.282	OF	253	14	10	0.964								
Clifton, Ralph		BL TL																									
1957	Thomasville	GFL	9	8		2								0.250	P					9	1	4	<30				
Cline, John		BL TR																									
1956	Thomson	GSL	24	75	9	13	1	2	0	12	0	15	29	0.173	OF	36	0	2	0.947								
Cline, Leonard		BR TR																									
1951	Brunswick	GFL	50	171	28	36	6	0	1	20	6	34	20	0.211	SS	57	128	7	0.964								
Cloer, Burlon		BR TR																									
1956	Albany	GFL	12	17	3	3	0	0	0	2	0	5	5	0.176	P	1	9	0	1.000	11	5	2	2.89	53	62	23	19
Cloninger, Al		BL																									
1940	Cordele	GFL	<10																								
Clonts, Ray																											
1936	Cordele	GFL	26	101	15	24	4	2	0	14	1			0.238	C	136	22	4	0.975								
Cloude, William "Bill"		BR TR																									
1951	Waycross	GFL	30	112	17	33	3	2	0	15	0	9	4	0.295	OF	40	3	4	0.915								
Cluley, Michael "Mike"		BR TL																									
1949	Cordele	GFL	31	46	8	4	1	0	0	1	2	1	15	0.087	P	9	24	2	0.943	25	4	5	5.63	104	128	72	72
Coapland, Bernis		BR TR																									
1946	Valdosta	GFL	3												P					3	0	2	0.00	15	17	8	3
Coates, Richard "Dick"		BR TR																									
1946	Waycross	GFL	13	48	8	11	5	1	0	8	1	3	16	0.229	1B	99	2	1	0.990								
Coats, Glenn		BR																									
1946	Moultrie	GFL	<10																								
Cobb, James "Jim"		BR TR																									
1953	Waycross	GFL	5											0.333	P						0	2	<45				
Cobb, Joe		BR TR																									
1954	Tifton	GFL	6	3		0								0.000	P					6	0	1	<45				
Cobb, Neal																											
1948	Cordele	GFL	<10																								
Cobiella, Ricardo		BR TR																									
1950	Carrollton	GAL	21	66	10	14	1	0	0	6	0	16	8	0.212	2B	60	48	4	0.964								
Coble, David Lamar "Dave"		BR TR 6'1" 183 lbs. b. 12/24/1912 Monroe, NC d. 10/15/1971 Orlando, FL																									
1936	Moultrie	GFL	91	309	43	77	11	6	4	49	3			0.249	C	353	66	10	0.977								
1949	Douglas	GSL													M												
1950	Douglas - Tifton	GSL													M												
Coccetti, Allen "Al"																											
1942	Moultrie	GFL	125	427	66	117	22	6	4	63	4	58	55	0.274	OF	208	16	10	0.957								
Cochran, Gene		BR TR																									
1956	Fitzgerald	GFL	13	25	2	1	0	0	0	2	0	2	5	0.040	P	6	8	3	0.824	13	1	6	4.18	71	72	51	41
Cochran, John																											
1915	Rome	GAL	60	213	47	71	15	2	11					0.333	OF	74	8	6	0.932								
Cochran, William "Bill"		BR TR																									
1951	Brunswick	GFL	11	21	1	4	1	0	0	1	0	3	8	0.190	P	4	15	1	0.950	11	2	5	3.99	70	81	13	21
Cockrell, Gene		BR TR																									
1955	Sandersville	GSL	59	194	23	41	3	1	3	17	3	21	45	0.211	3B, OF, P	74	49	6	0.953	1	0	0					
Cockroft, Joseph "Joe"		BR TR																									
1955	Vidalia	GSL	3	0										0.000	P					3	0	0					
Coffey, ---																											
1915	Valdosta	FLAG	18	56	6	14	2	2	0		2			0.250	1B	140	7	3	0.980								
Coffey, Herman		BR TL																									
1955	Tifton	GFL	13	16	3	3	1	0	0	0	0	2	3	0.188	P	0	5	1	0.833	11	2	5	5.77	53	60	49	34
Cohen, Arnold																											
1935	Albany	GFL	24	92	24	29	4	3	0		2	10	9	0.315	OF	44	1	4	0.918								
Cohen, Hyman "Hy"		BR TR 6'5" 220 lbs. b. 01/29/1931 Brooklyn, NY																									
1948	LaGrange	GAL	28	35	5	6	0	0	0	3	0	7	7	0.171	P	1	18	1	0.950	22	7	5	5.50	72	75	43	79
1949	LaGrange	GAL	40	55	3	12	0	0	0	2	0	8	8	0.218	P	10	16	4	0.867	40	11	15	3.33	192	173	148	89
Cohick, Harry		BR TR																									
1940	Americus	GFL	52	156	15	40	8	3	0	31	2	9	19	0.256	P, IF					31	12	12	2.61	217	202	82	61
1941	Americus	GFL	15	28	2	4	0	0	0	0	0	5	7	0.143	P	5	7	3	0.800	10	1	3	3.71	51	57	24	16
Coho, Russell "Russ"		BS TR																									
1954	Americus-Cordele	GFL	72	217	33	48	6	1	0	26	2	56	54	0.221	C	386	48	16	0.964								
Coker, E.R.																											
1929	Talledega	GAL	39	89	9	27	4	0	1		1	6	11	0.303	P	28	38	1	0.985	22	12	8		173	193	54	31
1930	Carrollton	GAL		37		9								0.243	SS												
Coker, Jack D.		BR TL																									
1947	Waycross	GFL	33	80	9	20	5	0	0	5	0	1	8	0.250	P	5	51	13	0.812	33	12	10	3.95	205	169	198	159
Coker, James "Jim"		BR TR																									
1947	Cordele	GFL	21	78	5	17	1	1	1	14	0	5	15	0.218	C	115	6	10	0.924								
1948	Alexander City	GAL	50	145	12	22	3	1	0	17	0	24	34	0.152	C	235	27	8	0.970								
1949	Alexander City	GAL	10	37	3	9	0	0	0	4	0	3	2	0.243	1B	90	3	0	1.000								
Colangelo, Stanley "Stan"		BR TR																									
1953	Vidalia	GSL	3											0.000	P						0	0	<45				

Georgia Class-D Minor League Baseball Encyclopedia

YR	TEAM	LG	G	AB	R	H	2B	3B	HR	RBI	SB	BB	SO	BA	POS	PO	A	E	FA	GP	W	L	ERA	IP	H	SO	BB
Colcolough, Thomas Bernard "Tom"		BR TR 5'10" 180 lbs. b. 10/08/1870 Charleston, SC d. 12/10/1919 Charleston, SC																									
1915	Americus-Gainesville	FLAG				0								0.000	P					0							
Cole, ---																											
1913	Newnan	GAL	57	205	39	62					4			0.302	SS	100	159	40	0.866								
Cole, Harold		BL TR																									
1950	Rome	GAL	103	355	77	107	20	3	5	50	13	43	38	0.301	OF	172	12	10	0.948								
Cole, Herman C. "Sam"																											
1935	Americus	GFL	112	455	66	153	29	5	1		24	30	15	0.336	OF	224	12	6	0.975								
1936	Americus	GFL	117	500	82	153	17	5	9	81	9			0.306	OF	232	14	12	0.953								
1937	Americus	GFL	49	181	25	47	12	1	3	28	2	18	10	0.260	OF	99	5	6	0.945								
Cole, Jack		BS TR																									
1951	Rome	GAL	99	365	58	112	10	3	5	49	13	45	37	0.307	OF	211	10	15	0.936								
Cole, Joseph "Joe"																											
1937	Cordele	GFL													P					1	0			15	15	6	2
Cole, Kenneth "Ken"		BR TR																									
1947	Opelika	GAL	28	109	7	18	0	0	0	10	0	7	15	0.165	C	139	24	11	0.937								
Coleman, Malcolm		BR TR																									
1949	Vidalia-Lyons	GSL	13	47	7	10	0	0	0	1	1	7	6	0.213	SS	17	31	8	0.857								
1950	Vidalia-Lyons	GSL	16	54	3	10	2	0	0	5	0	6	6	0.185													
1951	Fitzgerald(44) - Douglas(10)	GSL	54	214	30	47	7	0	0	28	6	24	18	0.220	2B, 3B	95	120	31	0.874								
Coleman, Sidney "Sid"																											
1935	Panama City	GFL	117	434	84	117	24	5	9		9	48	52	0.270	IF	191	329	73	0.877								
1936	Thomasville	GFL	95	347	45	83	11	5	4	40	1			0.239	SS	185	353	46	0.921								
Coleman, William "Bill"		BR TR																									
1955	Thomasville	GFL	54	173	20	45	2	2	0	10	0	27	28	0.260	C	369	22	17	0.958								
Coles, Charles Edward "Chuck"		BL TL 5'9" 180 lbs. b. 06/27/1931 Fredericktown, PA d. 01/25/1996 Myrtle Beach, SC																									
1950	Valdosta	GFL	111	454	116	161	19	14	14	75	32	63	42	0.355	OF	243	17	9	0.967								
Colflesh, John "Jack"		BR TR																									
1949	Americus	GFL	22	89	12	18	3	0	0	6	3	6	17	0.202	OF	36	3	8	0.830								
1952	Cordele	GFL	39	144	17	30	3	0	0	9	1	16	11	0.208	SS, OF	67	32	7	0.934								
Colgan, Richard "Dick"		BR TR																									
1957	Brunswick	GFL	21	32	4	3	0	0	1	2	0	1	13	0.094	P	4	17	3	0.875	21	6	8	5.58	92	116	67	86
1958	Brunswick	GFL	11	13	2	2	1	0	0	0	0	1	5	0.154	P	3	7	3	0.769	11	2	5	3.79	38	42	23	23
Colgan, William "Bill"		BR TR																									
1940	Thomasville	GFL	<10																								
1941	Waycross	GFL	72	241	31	60	8	3	1	29	3	29	54	0.249	OF	99	2	8	0.927								
1946	Thomasville	GFL	113	424	40	100	13	3	0	62	7	44	71	0.236	3B, OF	184	73	35	0.880								
1947	Waycross	GFL	18	58	6	14	5	0	0	11	0	6	6	0.241	OF	20	1	1	0.955								
Colina, Eddie																											
1941	Cordele	GFL	35	152	27	41	5	3	0	5	3	9	24	0.270	2B	101	92	14	0.932								
Coller, Jon A.		BL TR																									
1962	Brunswick	GFL	26	87	10	18	2	3	1	6	2	14	23	0.207	SS	38	66	6	0.945								
Colley, Owen		BR TR																									
1946	Valley	GAL	11	37	3	3	0	0	0	5	1	4	11	0.081	3B	7	20	7	0.794								
Collier, ---																											
1906	Albany	GSL													P												
Collier, ---																											
1930	Huntsville	GAL	6												P					6	2	1	7.71	21	32	19	16
Collins, Charles "Charlie"		BR TR																									
1935	Tallahassee	GFL	42	154	30	47	7	3	2		2	17	22	0.305	OF	48	9	12	0.826								
1948	Opelika	GAL	15	28	1	3	0	0	0	3	1	2	11	0.107	P	6	12	0	1.000	13	3	5	6.65	65	87	35	38
1950	Alexander City	GAL	63	145	24	35	3	1	1	16	0	17	31	0.241	OF, P	20	17	6	0.860	27	16	6	3.52	184	153	91	114
Collins, James "Jim"		BR																									
1953	Douglas	GSL	2											0.000													
Collins, John H. "Howard"		BR TR																									
1958	Thomasville	GFL	30	40	4	3	0	0	0	2	1	9	19	0.075	P	2	21	2	0.920	28	4	13	5.62	133	118	93	143
Collins, John N. "Jack"		BS TR																									
1948	Sparta	GSL	119	519	83	145	10	4	0	37	17	27	38	0.279	3B	110	258	36	0.911								
1949	Sparta	GSL	137	627	104	173	20	4	2	46	16	27	36	0.276	3B	159	287	46	0.907								
1950	Dublin	GSL	138	610	85	173	26	4	18	98	17	24	61	0.284	3B	139	261	57	0.875								
1951	Dublin	GSL	28	111	14	38	7	0	1	17	1	4	4	0.342	3B	40	51	6	0.938								
1954	Sandersville	GSL	1	3		0								0.000													
Collins, Lee		BR TR																									
1947	Ta(13) - Ca(4) - Ne(7) - AC(23)	GAL	47	164	14	33	7	0	1	22	0	19	21	0.201	OF	58	2	4	0.938								
Collins, Robert D. "Bob"		BR TL																									
1949	Thomasville	GFL	13	29	1	4	0	0	0	1	0	2	13	0.138	P	7	26	1	0.971	13	2	9	3.52	87	64	72	64
1950	Griffin	GAL	15	17	2	0	0	0	0	0	0	7	8	0.000	P	4	9	1	0.929	14	2	5	6.24	49	46	40	40
1950	Thomasville	GFL	14	15	3	3	1	0	0	0	0	2	5	0.200	P	1	15	5	0.762	14	1	3	5.63	48	58	48	29
Collins, Steven C. "Steve"		BR TR																									
1950	Moultrie	GFL	28	102	19	26	4	1	0	12	0	20	5	0.255	M, 3B	25	40	10	0.867								
Collins, William "Bill"																											
1938	Tallahassee	GFL	15	40	2	2	0	0	0	0	0	8	22	0.050	P	3	20	1	0.958	15	3	8	3.56	124	155	24	22
Collins, William E. "Bill"		BR TR																									
1942	Americus	GFL	7	17	10	8	4	0	0	3	0	9	2	0.471	OF	17	1	2	0.900								
1951	Hazlehurst-Baxley	GSL	48	153	39	37	9	1	4	30	1	56	29	0.242	OF	123	4	6	0.955								
1952	Vidalia	GSL	112	379	111	109	24	0	16	80	0	121	44	0.288	OF	193	7	4	0.980								
1953	Eastman	GSL	39	137	23	37	4	0	4	24	2	35	23	0.270	OF	67	3	4	0.946								

Georgia Class-D Minor League Baseball Encyclopedia

YR	TEAM	LG	G	AB	R	H	2B	3B	HR	RBI	SB	BB	SO	BA	POS	PO	A	E	FA	GP	W	L	ERA	IP	H	SO	BB
Collum, Ambrose			BR TR																								
1946	Newnan	GAL	1												P					1	0	0	0.00	1			
Colombatto, Peter "Pete"			BR TR																								
1947	Moultrie	GFL	104	385	70	101	14	2	0	35	8	55	59	0.262	2B	279	271	30	0.948								
Colon, Joseph "Joe"			BL TR																								
1956	Hazlehurst-Baxley	GSL	50	166	33	43	5	2	0	12	6	46	29	0.259	OF	77	3	10	0.889								
Colone, Richard "Dick"			BL TL																								
1955	Valdosta	GFL	139	544	79	144	19	5	9	72	12	65	79	0.265	1B, OF, P	529	30	24	0.959	1	0	0		<45			
Colson, Rodney "Rod"			BL TR																								
1949	Valley	GAL	38	122	10	28	4	1	0	10	3	17	14	0.230	OF	73	5	6	0.929								
Colter, ---			BR TR																								
1946	Carrollton	GAL	1												P					1	0	0	0.00	2			
Columbano, Aldo			BR TR																								
1950	Rome(2) - Griffin(13)	GAL	15	53	7	7	0	0	0	3	2	13	11	0.132	3B	7	24	7	0.816								
Colvard, Herman			BL TR																								
1962	Dublin	GFL	29	47	10	9	1	2	0	3	2	8	21	0.191	OF	10	0	1	0.909								
1963	Waycross(34) - Thomasville(20)	GFL	54	123	17	23	4	0	0	6	2	22	37	0.187	OF	42	6	6	0.889								
Colvin, John "Jack"			BL																								
1953	Fitzgerald	GFL	6											0.500													
1953	Sandersville	GSL	7											0.364													
Combs, ---																											
1915	Griffin	GAL	<6												P					<6							
Combs, Ralph			BR TR																								
1953	Dublin	GSL	79	293	43	87	14	4	5	42	1	39	46	0.297	3B, OF	115	72	20	0.903								
1954	Dublin	GSL	15	49	10	9	1	0	1	8	1	6	8	0.184	OF	18	2	3	0.870								
Comegys, Clarence Jr.			BR TR																								
1951	Cordele	GFL	25	39	7	5	1	0	1	1	0	3	10	0.128	P	0	15	0	1.000	14	4	3	4.68	75	86	40	47
Comegys, Howard			BR TR																								
1953	Cordele	GFL	13	13	4	3	0	0	0	0	0	5	3	0.231	P	3	11	2	0.875	13	1	5	6.66	50	70	18	37
Comiskey, Robert "Bob"			BR TR																								
1948	Tallassee	GAL	64	194	20	63	5	0	3	35	0	25	4	0.325	M, C	219	35	5	0.981								
1949	Tallassee	GAL	80	225	13	56	11	1	1	20	0	36	10	0.249	M, C	323	27	9	0.975								
Commisso, Domenick "Dom"			BR TR																								
1952	Moultrie	GFL	52	193	24	48	4	1	0	6	2	33	13	0.249	2B, 3B, SS	111	151	23	0.919								
Comolli, Victor "Vic"			BL TR																								
1948	Americus	GFL	92	330	45	84	11	6	4	55	9	40	49	0.255	1B, C	576	51	22	0.966								
1949	Americus	GFL	100	322	49	99	17	2	5	54	17	49	46	0.307	C	526	64	24	0.961								
Comotti, Elmo			BR TR																								
1946	Thomasville	GFL	25	70	5	11	0	0	0	4	0	6	16	0.157	P	12	40	1	0.981	25	14	8	2.02	192	168	133	70
Company, Ronald "Ron"			BR TR																								
1954	Tifton	GFL	90	346	66	90	20	2	6	50	3	37	54	0.260	OF	133	13	13	0.918								
Condit, ---			BR TR																								
1946	Opelika(11) - Carrollton(7)	GAL	18	48	2	8	0	0	0	1	0	3	7	0.167	P	5	24	0	1.000	18	8	7	3.02	134	119	70	42
Condu, Phillip "Phil"			BL TL																								
1955	Moultrie	GFL	121	454	69	151	20	8	4	77	5	48	34	0.333	1B, OF	251	23	14	0.951								
Conhenney, James "Jim"			BR TR																								
1949	Carrollton	GAL	94	294	56	64	7	3	0	32	15	59	70	0.218	3B	85	174	26	0.909								
Coniff, E.P.																											
1906	Americus	GSL													M												
Conley, ---																											
1915	Thomasville	FLAG	71	248	33	54	7	0	0		10			0.218	2B, OF	97	44	13	0.916								
Conn, Robert "Bob"			BR TR																								
1953	Douglas	GSL	122	467	97	142	28	3	7	70	15	74	44	0.304	2B	318	285	28	0.956								
Connell, Truman			BR TR																								
1948	Vidalia-Lyons	GSL	118	408	82	146	24	7	11	82	10	94	78	0.358	M, OF	228	3	18	0.928								
1949	Fitzgerald	GSL	35	103	25	23	8	2	3	20	0	49	18	0.223	OF	156	7	7	0.959								
Connell, Wesley "Wes"			BL																								
1958	Albany	GFL	8	13		0								0.000													
Conner, James "Jim"			BR TR																								
1950	Hazlehurst-Baxley	GSL	10	22	2	3	0	0	0	1	0	1	9	0.136	P					8	3	5	4.17	54	46	15	47
Conner, John			BR TR																								
1948	Cordele	GFL	136	584	111	170	31	10	1	58	21	60	80	0.291	2B, 3B, SS, OF	283	125	50	0.891								
Connor, ---			BR																								
1946	LaGrange	GAL	<10																								
Conovan, Tillman "Mike"			BR TL																								
1948	Tallassee(7) - Opelika(27)	GAL	34	40	5	5	0	1	0	5	0	8	23	0.125	P	5	28	6	0.846	34	3	14	6.15	136	134	121	121
Conquy, Eugene "Gene"			BR TR																								
1956	Thomasville	GFL	49	188	31	56	8	1	6	35	7	14	23	0.298	OF	52	3	8	0.873								
Conrad, George			BR TR																								
1956	Dublin	GSL	38	111	11	27	2	1	3	14	0	14	14	0.243	OF, C	109	6	2	0.983								
Conrad, Robert "Bob"			BR TL																								
1955	Tifton	GFL	1	1		0								0.000	P					1	0	0		<45			
Conte, Michael																											
1951	Griffin	GAL													M												

Georgia Class-D Minor League Baseball Encyclopedia

YR	TEAM	LG	G	AB	R	H	2B	3B	HR	RBI	SB	BB	SO	BA	POS	PO	A	E	FA	GP	W	L	ERA	IP	H	SO	BB
Conti, Louis "Lou"		BR																									
1954	Tifton	GFL	3	11		1								0.091													
Contini, Robert "Bobby"		BR TR																									
1939	Thomasville - Valdosta	GFL	125	451	65	118	14	10	2	47	7	43	66	0.262	OF	259	12	13	0.954								
1940	Valdosta	GFL	16	61	8	19	1	2	0	12	0	6	4	0.311	OF	23	6	1	0.967								
Contratto, George		BS TL																									
1958	Brunswick	GFL	60	226	47	72	14	4	0	40	3	51	17	0.319	1B	475	36	0	1.000								
Conway, Alvin		BR TR																									
1956	Thomson	GSL	99	359	60	101	12	10	5	76	6	75	58	0.281	OF	216	14	11	0.954								
Cook, ---																											
1921	Cedartown	GSL													OF, P													
Cook, ---		BL TL																									
1952	Jesup	GSL	6												P					6	3	3	3.31	49	55	19	17
Cook, Don Richard "Don"		BR TR																									
1951	Valdosta	GFL	17	34	4	7	1	1	0	3	0	3	2	0.206	P	4	15	3	0.864	16	6	2	3.70	90	84	53	44
Cook, Dwight		BR TR																									
1956	Albany	GFL	105	304	67	71	13	3	4	44	15	50	68	0.234	2B, P	172	151	17	0.950	18	6	6	3.51	118	85	104	85
Cook, George E.		BL TL																									
1948	Sparta	GSL	24	56	3	4	0	0	0	1	0	12	23	0.071	P	8	38	2	0.958	22	12	7	2.56	169	153	105	59
1949	Sparta	GSL	34	103	9	20	3	1	0	8	0	13	39	0.194	P	13	70	4	0.954	36	21	12	3.07	276	137	184	109
1951	Dublin	GSL	20	38	3	4	0	0	0	1	0	6	19	0.105	P	2	43	3	0.938	20	10	3	5.24	127	159	44	52
1955	Albany	GFL	16	30	6	7	3	1	1	3	1	4	12	0.233	P	4	7	1	0.917	10	5	2	3.16	57	52	25	25
Cook, John		BR TR																									
1962	Dublin	GFL	8	5	1	0	0	0	0	0	0	2	4	0.000	P					8	1	1	6.16	19	23	20	17
Cook, John Ray "John"		BL TL																									
1953	Brunswick	GFL	25	77	12	20	4	1	1	10	0	7	9	0.260	OF	28	3	1	0.969								
1954	Sandersville	GSL	34	118	15	31	3	1	1	11	0	16	18	0.263	OF, P	75	7	8	0.911	2	0	1	<45				
Cook, Raymond Clifford "Cliff"		BR TR 6'0" 188 lbs. b. 08/20/1936 Dallas, TX																									
1955	Moultrie	GFL	25	88	20	21	7	2	3	15	1	19	32	0.239	OF	45	1	4	0.920								
1955	Douglas	GSL	86	340	62	102	19	2	20	66	4	29	67	0.300	OF	134	13	8	0.948								
Cook, Robert "Bob"		BL TL																									
1948	Waycross	GFL	21	27	6	2	0	0	0	3	0	4	10	0.074	P	3	19	1	0.957	21	3	4	4.30	69	71	33	17
Cook, Roland E. "Ron"		BR																									
1946	Tallahassee	GFL	5												P					5	0	2	0.00	18	18	8	13
Cook, W. Hugh		BR TR																									
1950	Valley	GAL	106	382	50	106	12	3	0	47	4	17	21	0.277	1B, 3B, OF, P	285	45	14	0.959	15	0	3	6.75	52	57	24	34
Cook, William "Bill"		BR TR																									
1948	Eastman	GSL	28	73	4	13	1	2	0	6	1	2	33	0.178	P	1	16	4	0.810	26	8	11	3.55	180	172	95	85
Cooke, Jay		BL TL																									
1956	Valdosta	GFL	139	477	88	130	22	6	16	82	7	122	92	0.273	1B	1135	84	23	0.981								
Coombs, ---																											
1921	Carrollton	GSL	<10												P												
Coombs, Woodfin "Woody"		BL TL																									
1935	Thomasville	GFL	109	387	66	88	20	2	3		9	93	71	0.227	IF	153	245	39	0.911								
Cooper, ---																											
1913	Gadsden	GAL	59	214	30	57				8				0.266	OF	116	108	29	0.885								
Cooper, ---																											
1915	Brunswick	FLAG	<10												P					0							
Cooper, Carl E.		BL TR																									
1949	LaGrange	GAL	112	373	85	114	14	2	20	94	6	72	34	0.306	M, 1B, OF	285	17	6	0.981								
1950	LaGrange	GAL	108	373	77	124	17	0	22	99	7	71	20	0.332	M, OF	146	17	5	0.970								
1951	LaGrange	GAL	92	314	82	116	17	4	17	90	8	71	7	0.369	OF	135	14	3	0.980								
Cooper, Frank D.		BL TR																									
1950	Tifton	GSL	11	19	2	5	1	0	0	0	0	7	6	0.263													
1952	Tifton	GFL	133	487	58	111	16	1	0	55	5	65	50	0.228	OF	322	28	12	0.967								
1953	Tifton	GFL	136	477	82	135	30	2	0	71	13	90	49	0.283	OF	308	26	15	0.957								
Cooper, Robert "Bob"		BL TL																									
1953	Sandersville	GSL	4											0.250	P						0	1	<45				
Cooper, Stewart		BR TR																									
1947	Cordele	GFL	20	90	12	29	3	0	0	20	0	7	10	0.322	OF	36	1	4	0.902								
Cooper, William "Bill"		BL TL																									
1951	LaGrange	GAL	39	137	13	29	6	0	0	22	3	10	13	0.212	M, 1B	291	11	5	0.984								
Cooper, William A. "Bill"		BR TR																									
1954	Sandersville	GSL	30	94	12	18	0	1	0	5	0	21	21	0.191	C	141	17	7	0.958								
Cooper, William E. "Bill"		BR TR																									
1948	Cordele	GFL	33	89	6	18	1	1	1	11	1	3	21	0.202	P	8	22	5	0.857	29	16	9	3.25	202	232	118	58
1953	Fitzgerald	GFL	1											0.000	P					0	0		<45				
Cop, Milan		BR TL																									
1953	Hazlehurst-Baxley	GSL	36	61	4	2	0	0	0	4	0	11	26	0.033	P	8	24	5	0.865	36	16	4	4.58	179	167	130	129
1954	Hazlehurst-Baxley	GSL	6	7		0								0.000	P					6	0	3	<45				
Copeland, Clifford "Cliff"		BL TR																									
1956	Vidalia	GSL	7	7		0								0.000	P					7	0	1					
Copeland, Elmer		BR TR																									
1946	LaGrange	GAL	36	81	3	10	0	0	0	4	0	4	15	0.123	P	4	32	1	0.973	33	14	10	4.50	196	189	101	49
1947	LaGrange	GAL	41	101	7	15	2	0	0	2	2	9	20	0.149	P	11	33	4	0.917	37	13	15	3.95	244	268	108	46

251

Georgia Class-D Minor League Baseball Encyclopedia

YR	TEAM	LG	G	AB	R	H	2B	3B	HR	RBI	SB	BB	SO	BA	POS	PO	A	E	FA	GP	W	L	ERA	IP	H	SO	BB
Copeland, James L. "Jim"		BR TR																									
1952	Eastman	GSL	17	37	2	7	0	0	0	0	0	4	7	0.189	P	11	19	3	0.909	17	3	9	5.73	99	96	54	81
Coppola, Herbert "Herb"		BR TR																									
1946	Waycross	GFL	10	19	1	1	1	0	0	1	0	1	7	0.053	P	3	9	0	1.000	10	4	2	5.00	45	50	26	34
Corbett, ---																											
1915	Valdosta - Thomasville	FLAG	47	173	16	34	5	1	0		9			0.197	2B, OF	57	14	15	0.826								
Corbett, Eugene Louis "Gene"		BL TR 6'1" 190 lbs. b. 10/25/1913 Winona, MN																									
1952	Albany	GFL	12	35	3	5	2	0	0	3	0	7	1	0.143	M, 1B	102	7	0	1.000								
Corbett, Thomas "Tom"																											
1936	Thomasville	GFL	65	238	30	75	10	6	4	32	3			0.315	OF	121	10	6	0.956								
1937	Thomasville	GFL	124	475	97	166	25	10	26	113	13	67	40	0.349	OF	231	21	6	0.977								
Corder, Robert Darrell "Bob"		BR TR																									
1952	Moultrie	GFL	80	304	29	54	8	3	0	16	2	38	55	0.178	SS	201	231	42	0.911								
1953	Vidalia	GSL	51	188	15	48	10	0	1	28	3	23	21	0.255	SS	103	147	25	0.909								
Cordero, Manuel		BL TL																									
1951	Dublin	GSL	77	293	60	88	18	4	3	54	7	40	48	0.300	1B	726	38	7	0.991								
Corley, Arthur "Art"		BR TR																									
1947	Tallassee	GAL	10	23	1	2	1	0	0	2	0	3	8	0.087	P	2	19	0	1.000	10	7	2	2.25	72	50	27	44
Corley, Earl		BR TR																									
1950	Griffin	GAL	17	61	1	15	2	0	0	6	0	6	5	0.246	C	64	10	4	0.949								
Corley, Furman																											
1941	Cordele	GFL	22	30	1	8	1	0	0	4	0	1	4	0.267	P	1	18	4	0.826	23	1	11	4.82	84	104	43	50
Corley, Harold		BL TR																									
1948	Albany	GFL	35	134	24	23	4	0	2	15	3	27	24	0.172	SS	53	104	29	0.844								
Corley, Kenneth "Ken"		BR TR																									
1946	Americus	GFL	116	473	81	150	24	6	4	82	12	19	55	0.317	OF	129	19	6	0.961								
Corley, Raymond "Ray"		BR TR																									
1954	Vidalia	GSL	2	1		0								0.000	P					2	0	1	<45				
Corley, Stan		BR TR																									
1956	Tifton	GFL	2	0										0.000	P					2	0	0	<45				
Cornelius, Rusty																											
1920	Lindale	GSL													P												
1921	Carrollton	GSL	<10												P												
1921	Lindale	GSL													P												
Cornett, Homer		BR TR																									
1953	Jesup	GSL	2											0.000	P					0	0		<45				
Cornwell, John		BR TR																									
1954	Tifton	GFL	25	95	20	21	2	1	0	9	1	16	15	0.221	2B	58	50	9	0.923								
Corrales, Reinaldo "Reggie"		BR TR																									
1950	Carrollton	GAL	32	95	24	27	6	0	0	15	0	31	16	0.284	C	62	6	6	0.919								
Correllas, Richard "Dick"		BR TR																									
1956	Fitzgerald	GFL	12	45	5	9	4	0	0	3	0	7	18	0.200	SS	15	24	16	0.709								
Corso, Eugene "Gene"		BR TR																									
1951	Brunswick	GFL	23	80	19	19	3	0	3	18	6	20	15	0.238	OF	45	2	3	0.940								
Corthell, Richard "Dick"		BR TR																									
1954	Thomasville	GFL	15	49	10	13	3	0	0	6	4	6	5	0.265	3B	15	23	6	0.864								
Cosby, ---																											
1928	Carrollton - Lindale	GAL	15	58	7	17	4	0	0		0	5	10	0.293	SS	19	26	6	0.882								
Cosman, James Henry "Jim"		BR TR 6'4" 211 lbs. b. 02/19/1943 Brockport, NY																									
1963	Brunswick	GFL	27	17	2	3	1	0	0	1	0	2	9	0.176	P	4	11	3	0.833	27	1	9	4.07	73	66	84	52
Coss, Royden		BR TR																									
1948	Tallassee	GAL	31	52	4	9	1	0	0	1	0	7	16	0.173	P	8	42	3	0.943	31	7	8	5.16	157	171	51	120
Costa, Frank																											
1929	Gadsden	GAL	98	339	39	74	8	8	1		3	38	39	0.218	SS	212	368	33	0.946								
1930	Lindale	GAL	93	367	77	124	26	8	11		14	42	49	0.338	SS	231	316	46	0.922								
Costa, Tony																											
1929	Gadsden	GAL	89	349	48	101	20	6	1		5	29	23	0.289	2B	199	294	18	0.965								
Costello, Daniel Francis "Dan"		BL TR 6'0" 185 lbs. b. 09/09/1891 Jessup, PA d. 03/26/1936 Pittsburgh, PA																									
1917	Anniston	GAL	16	51	13	12	3	1	0		10			0.235	OF	23	4	0	1.000								
Costello, Daniel P. "Dan"		BS TL																									
1949	Tallahassee	GFL	46	112	9	19	2	1	0	6	2	18	40	0.170	1B, P	99	37	5	0.965	23	6	11	3.20	138	135	88	74
1950	Tallahassee	GFL	21	32	5	5	1	0	0	2	0	3	18	0.156	P	4	15	0	1.000	19	3	3	6.04	73	88	51	56
Costello, Thomas "Tom"		BR TR																									
1951	Cordele	GFL	28	76	10	10	3	1	1	7	1	25	30	0.132													
Cothran, Robert "Bob"		BR TR																									
1954	Waycross	GFL	50	216	40	66	10	3	1	22	15	17	17	0.306	2B	122	139	7	0.974								
Cotney, Vernon "Vern"		BR TR																									
1952	Jesup	GSL	67	240	45	58	12	1	0	18	7	38	30	0.242	2B, OF	144	101	19	0.928								
Cottengim, Charles																											
1949	Tifton	GSL	22	79	15	21	3	0	0	16	1	12	8	0.266	C	90	7	9	0.915								
Cotter, James "Jim"		BR TR																									
1954	Americus-Cordele	GFL	19	67	8	15	1	0	1	10	2	11	20	0.224	OF	35	6	6	0.872								
Cottier, Charles Keith "Chuck"		BR TR 5'10" 175 lbs. b. 01/08/1936 Delta, CO																									
1954	Americus-Cordele	GFL	138	507	71	127	22	9	2	49	7	59	77	0.250	2B	370	398	46	0.943								

Georgia Class-D Minor League Baseball Encyclopedia

YR	TEAM	LG	G	AB	R	H	2B	3B	HR	RBI	SB	BB	SO	BA	POS	PO	A	E	FA	GP	W	L	ERA	IP	H	SO	BB
Coulling, Stanley H. "Stan"		BR TR 6'3" 190 lbs. b. 06/04/1921 Rocky Mount, NC																									
1941	Moultrie	GFL	35	65	8	9	2	0	0	4	0	12	22	0.138	P	5	44	3	0.942	36	11	11	4.04	185	232	77	48
1942	Moultrie	GFL	26	72	3	11	2	1	0	6	0	2	16	0.153	P	8	36	2	0.957	28	10	9	2.75	193	181	90	37
1950	Carrollton	GAL	14	33	4	6	0	0	1	3	0	7	4	0.182	P					8	3	3	4.59	51	66	27	8
Coultas, Gary		BR TR																									
1956	Thomasville	GFL	22	48	4	4	0	0	0	3	0	9	11	0.083	C	116	11	4	0.969								
Courser, Ronald "Ron"		BR TR																									
1963	Brunswick	GFL	44	100	11	21	4	1	2	7	1	15	34	0.210	OF	47	3	8	0.862								
Courtney, James		BL																									
1949	Tallassee	GAL	11	26	7	5	0	1	1	3	2	6		3 0.192													
Courtney, William "Bill"		BR TR																									
1950	Moultrie	GFL	139	534	76	135	26	5	1	64	22	59	107	0.253	SS	299	419	75	0.905								
Coveney, John Patrick "Jack"		BR TR 5'9" 175 lbs. b. 06/10/1880 South Natick, MA d. 03/28/1961 Wayland, MA																									
1913	Waycross	ESL	29	89	7	15	0	0	0					0.169	C	111	23	3	0.978								
1914	Waycross	GSL		217	31	50	12	0	1		9			0.230	M												
Cowan, E.																											
1914	Selma	GAL	69	261	43	74				19				0.284	3B	154	145	14	0.955								
Cowan, Frank		BR TR																									
1956	Brunswick	GFL	3	2		0								0.000	P					3	0	0	<45				
1956	Dublin	GSL	3	4		1								0.250	P					3	0	2					
Cowan, James "Jim"		BR TR																									
1951	Moultrie	GFL	58	155	21	29	8	0	0	16	0	21	27	0.187	C	116	26	14	0.910								
Cowan, W. W.																											
1914	Selma	GAL	67	171	52	54				27				0.316	2B	93	106	18	0.917								
Cowen, Gerald		BL																									
1956	Thomson	GSL	4	4		0								0.000													
Cox, ---																											
1914	Thomasville	GSL		356	43	90	16	3	2	19				0.253													
Cox, Francis A. "Frank"		BR TR																									
1952	Albany	GFL	28	54	4	12	1	1	0	5	0	0	7	0.222	P	10	30	2	0.952	27	10	4	2.23	137	87	93	111
Cox, George		BL TL																									
1956	Hazlehurst-Baxley	GSL	6	7		0								0.000	P					6	1	3					
Cox, James H. "Jim"		BR TR																									
1935	Thomasville	GFL	78	299	38	77	14	7	1		8	38	28	0.258	IF	103	52	35	0.816								
1937	Tallahassee	GFL	39	149	22	42	4	3	0	13	4	20	8	0.282	SS	85	133	25	0.897								
Cox, Max		BR TR																									
1946	LaGrange	GAL	7												P					7	0	3	0.00	19	18	5	6
Coy, Hugh		BR TR																									
1957	Albany	GFL	29	44	8	7	0	0	0	3	0	5	17	0.159	P	6	22	3	0.903	26	12	3	4.20	135	136	92	92
Cozart, Paul		BR TR																									
1954	Thomasville	GFL	111	453	57	123	16	5	3	57	10	37	81	0.272	3B, SS, OF	135	115	16	0.940								
Cozens, John		BR TR																									
1951	Fitzgerald	GSL	28	104	11	25	2	0	0	7	1	18	13	0.240	OF	43	8	2	0.962								
Craddock, ---																											
1920	Cedartown	GSL													SS												
Craft, Maurice Montague "Molly"		BR TR 6'2" 165 lbs. b. 11/28/1895 Portsmouth, VA d. 10/25/1978 Los Angeles, CA																									
1928	Anniston - Lindale	GAL	14	50	11	21	3	0	1		1	2	6	0.420	1B	79	3	0	1.000								
Crago, William E. "Bill"		BL TL																									
1948	Fitzgerald	GSL	105	381	58	85	6	9	0	33	10	66	58	0.223	OF	263	14	8	0.972								
1949	Fitzgerald	GSL	137	502	125	139	23	7	4	69	29	141	55	0.277	OF	357	18	13	0.966								
1950	Fitzgerald	GSL	140	510	112	165	41	5	10	93	24	136	50	0.324	OF	336	15	12	0.967								
Craig, Myron		BR TR																									
1950	Thomasville	GFL	14	29	8	6	3	0	0	3	2	13	14	0.207	2B	25	17	5	0.894								
Craig, Roger Lee "Roger"		BR TR 6'4" 191 lbs. b. 02/17/1930 Durham, NC																									
1950	Valdosta	GFL	25	66	8	8	1	0	1	2	0	9	20	0.121	P	8	24	2	0.941	23	14	7	3.13	167	136	152	150
Craig, Royal		BL TR																									
1954	Albany	GFL	1	0										0.000	P					1	0	0	<45				
Craig, Steven M. "Steve"		BR TR																									
1948	Tallahassee	GFL	40	113	10	21	5	0	0	15	0	22	23	0.186	C	82	12	6	0.940								
Crain, Paul		BR TR																									
1947	Carrollton(3) - Valley(38)	GAL	41	112	10	23	6	0	0	10	0	8	13	0.205	P	19	48	5	0.931	33	19	14	2.93	261	255	152	54
Crandall, John "Johnny"		BR																									
1940	Tallahassee	GFL	<10																									
Cranston, ---																											
1906	Columbus	GSL													C												
Craven, James "Jim"		BR TR																									
1955	Vidalia	GSL	13	8	1	3	0	0	0	1	0	1	3	0.375	P	2	4	1	0.857	12	1	3	17.00	18	43	12	17
1956	Thomasville	GFL	4	2		0								0.000	P					4	0	1	<45				
Craven, Jesse C. "Jess"																											
1913	Newnan	GAL	90	345	9	121				24				0.351	OF	96	17	8	0.934								
1914	Newnan	GAL	27	96	12	24				4				0.250	OF	29	14	3	0.935								
1915	LaGrange	GAL	29	102	10	31	4	0	0					0.304	OF	46	3	2	0.961								
1920	Carrollton	GSL		325	52	87	10	4	1	4				0.268	OF, 1B												
Craven, Robert A. "Bob"		BL TL																									
1950	Jesup	GSL	17	16	1	1	0	0	0	1	0	5	7	0.063	P	2	11	0	1.000	17	3	3	2.47	51	53	22	25
1951	Jesup	GSL	41	65	7	14	2	0	0	4	0	20	24	0.215	P	11	34	2	0.957	37	14	6	2.82	182	148	129	113

Georgia Class-D Minor League Baseball Encyclopedia

YR	TEAM	LG	G	AB	R	H	2B	3B	HR	RBI	SB	BB	SO	BA	POS	PO	A	E	FA	GP	W	L	ERA	IP	H	SO	BB
Craven, Tommy																											
1920	Carrollton	GSL		9	1	3								0.333													
Crawford, James "Jim"		BR TR																									
1955	Thomasville	GFL	2	2		1								0.500	P					2	0	0		<45			
Crawford, James Jr. "Jim"		BR TR																									
1952	Jesup	GSL	112	419	46	105	15	1	0	38	7	48	49	0.251	3B	164	215	45	0.894								
Crawford, Wayne		BL TR																									
1950	Rome	GAL	102	336	52	82	13	4	5	48	10	54	25	0.244	OF, C	413	51	26	0.947								
Crawley, ---																											
1906	Americus	GSL													OF												
Creager, Bill																											
1939	Waycross	GFL	79	321	53	83	19	10	7	40	5	30	92	0.259	2B	213	221	20	0.956								
Creamer, Brice H.		BR TR																									
1948	Griffin	GAL	14	35	4	9	0	0	0	6	0	2	8	0.257	P	5	15	1	0.952	13	3	7	5.85	80	95	29	61
Creel, C. Scobie		BR TR																									
1950	Opelika	GAL	67	155	22	40	3	3	1	17	1	28	22	0.258	2B, OF, P	62	47	7	0.940	22	2	6	5.46	56	68	38	32
Creel, James Aubrey "Jim"		BR TR																									
1950	Opelika	GAL	47	134	13	37	4	1	1	20	0	14	18	0.276	OF, P	31	15	4	0.920	19	8	8	4.07	115	110	70	87
1951	Opelika	GAL	29	70	10	20	5	1	0	11	0	10	7	0.286	P	4	12	3	0.842	16	8	6	4.38	109	105	68	67
Creighton, Joseph "Joe"		BL TR																									
1952	Dublin	GSL	60	208	28	45	10	0	4	28	7	17	19	0.216	SS	92	133	31	0.879								
Cressman, Robert "Bob"		BL TL																									
1962	Thomasville	GFL	8	9	1	2	0	0	0	0	0	3	5	0.222	P					8	2	2	3.60	35	27	36	28
Crews, ---																											
1906	Americus	GSL														P												
Crisler, Joseph "Joe"																											
1935	Moultrie	GFL	41	131	15	24	2	3	0		4	5	17	0.183	P					29	11	10		190	172	123	68
1936	Moultrie	GFL	50	98	12	21	0	0	3	14	1			0.214	P					50	13	10	3.68	181		81	82
Crisp, Ransom		BR TR																									
1954	Thomasville	GFL	24	47	3	11	0	0	0	4	0	1	12	0.234	C	64	6	4	0.946								
Croge, Sam		BR TR																									
1958	Brunswick	GFL	33	82	9	20	5	0	0	17	0	7	8	0.244	P	6	48	4	0.931	33	15	8	4.10	213	198	115	99
Cromartie, Hendrick "Henry"		BL TR																									
1949	Cordele	GFL	31	100	14	20	3	1	1	11	0	21	26	0.200	1B	247	7	7	0.973								
1949	Hazlehurst-Baxley	GSL	41	149	29	30	6	5	0	14	2	31	39	0.201	1B	362	19	5	0.987								
Cromartie, William "Bill"		BR TR																									
1948	Tallahassee	GFL	39	113	24	30	2	1	0	21	0	24	15	0.265	P	3	29	9	0.780	24	10	7	4.95	169	195	149	101
Crone, Robert "Bob"		BR TR																									
1956	Moultrie	GFL	12	15	1	2	0	0	0	0	0	4	4	0.133	P	3	9	3	0.800	10	1	5	5.06	48	55	38	26
Cronic, George T.		BR TR																									
1951	Fitzgerald	GSL	21	50	8	11	1	0	0	1	0	7	13	0.220	P	5	15	3	0.870	17	4	10	6.09	102	142	16	52
Cronic, Guin		BL TL																									
1946	Waycross	GFL	31	67	5	19	4	0	0	6	0	5	19	0.284	P	5	38	3	0.935	29	12	9	3.27	165	147	143	57
1947	Waycross	GFL	14	24	5	6	1	1	1	5	0	2	4	0.250	P	1	14	1	0.938	11	4	4	5.34	64	81	37	45
Cronin, Francis M. "Frank"																											
1941	Waycross	GFL	10	20	5	4	0	0	0	0	0	6	4	0.200	P	0	8	1	0.889	10	6	2	2.28	67	51	40	30
1942	Waycross	GFL	18	55	7	11	1	0	0	6	0	6	13	0.200	P	1	21	1	0.957	18	9	5	4.29	126	162	67	55
Cronin, James T. "Jim"		BL TR																									
1947	Thomasville	GFL	130	483	82	141	27	7	5	79	10	42	68	0.292	OF	197	18	15	0.935								
Crook, Robert "Don"		BR TR																									
1955	Moultrie	GFL	18	27	5	8	2	0	0	4	0	2	5	0.296	P	3	11	5	0.737	14	2	3	6.00	57	67	28	40
Crosby, Ralph		BR TR																									
1955	Sandersville	GSL	100	364	61	90	14	1	5	38	5	45	74	0.247	3B, SS	114	144	34	0.884								
Crosley, Umpire																											
1906	Albany	GSL														P, OF												
Cross, Donald "Don"		BR TR																									
1937	Cordele	GFL	36	118	28	32	5	2	0	12	5	19	9	0.271	SS	53	90	11	0.929								
1938	Thomasville	GFL	116	447	73	115	22	6	1	62	13	68	29	0.257	2B	262	362	38	0.943								
1953	Vidalia	GSL	28	78	11	23	2	0	0	7	1	16	9	0.295	M, SS, P	17	29	2	0.958		0	0		<45			
Cross, James "Jim"		BR TR																									
1956	Valdosta	GFL	139	549	110	148	16	3	4	61	44	94	67	0.270	3B	134	279	39	0.914								
1957	Valdosta	GFL	130	501	85	135	18	4	5	72	24	95	52	0.269	3B, SS, P	155	240	32	0.925	3	0	0		<30			
Crosslin, ---																											
1930	Huntsville	GAL	39	167	40	50	5	4	4		3	8	17	0.299	SS	55	86	24	0.855								
Crotty, John		BR TR																									
1958	Thomasville	GFL	8	1		0								0.000	P					8	0	0		<30			
Crouch, ---																											
1917	Rome-Lindale	GAL	16	62	7	15	1	1	0		4			0.242	3B	18	26	4	0.917								
Crouch, Lester "Les"		BR TR																									
1947	Cordele	GFL	10	40	3	12	0	0	0	4	0	4	9	0.300	SS	16	25	5	0.891								
1948	Cordele	GFL	135	455	89	106	15	4	0	41	12	97	80	0.233	2B, SS	292	352	62	0.912								
1953	Statesboro(67) - Douglas(13)	GSL	80	278	55	82	22	1	4	47	15	62	29	0.295	SS	139	252	33	0.922								
1954	Douglas	GSL	116	465	106	131	16	9	8	69	20	86	55	0.282	2B, 3B, SS	240	266	39	0.928								
1955	Moultrie	GFL	119	450	69	112	19	6	4	61	9	46	64	0.249	2B, 3B, SS, OF, P	245	252	29	0.945	3	0	0		<45			

Georgia Class-D Minor League Baseball Encyclopedia

YR	TEAM	LG	G	AB	R	H	2B	3B	HR	RBI	SB	BB	SO	BA	POS	PO	A	E	FA	GP	W	L	ERA	IP	H	SO	BB
Crow, Lee																											
1914	Talladega	GAL	68	217	20	54					12			0.249	2B, 3B	199	270	34	0.932								
1915	Talladega	GAL	61	241	40	53	15	0	0					0.220	3B	88	109	19	0.912								
Crow, Paul		BL TR																									
1946	Valley	GAL	80	261	30	70	10	1	2	44	2	30	32	0.268	OF	100	6	7	0.938								
Crowder, ---																											
1906	Valdosta	GSL													SS												
Crowder, ---		BR																									
1946	Valley	GAL	<10																								
Crowder, H.F.																											
1929	Gadsden	GAL	28	67	11	22	4	0	0		1	8	12	0.328	P	6	30	2	0.947	21	7	8		124	147	36	37
1930	Cedartown	GAL	34	95	12	29	3	1	0		1	6	12	0.305	P	2	39	2	0.953	22	9	6	6.00	144	182	63	55
1930	Anniston	GAL	2												P					2	0	1	9.00	6	11	2	2
Crowe, Charles		BR																									
1955	Waycross	GFL	2	2		0								0.000													
Crowe, Hoyt																											
1928	Lindale	GAL	31	86	11	20	4	0	0		0	2	9	0.233	OF, P	15	22	2	0.949	18	6	11	2.49	152	154	59	24
1929	Carrollton	GAL	21	53	2	10	2	0	0		1	2	5	0.189	P	6	33	0	1.000	22	8	7		135	145	49	35
Crowl, Ernest		BR TR																									
1950	Rome	GAL	19	28	6	6	1	0	0	9	0	1	4	0.214	P	4	10	2	0.875	19	4	4	4.68	77	84	29	48
Crowley, ---																											
1906	Americus	GSL													2B												
Crowley, Walter "Walt"		BL TR																									
1949	Tallahassee	GFL	75	143	16	28	4	3	1	16	0	12	34	0.196	P	20	32	12	0.813	35	14	14	3.54	244	215	195	134
Crowson, Marvin "Marv"		BR TR																									
1946	Carrollton	GAL	6												P					6	3	1	0.00	35	26	18	16
Crucitti, Anthony "Tony"		BR TR																									
1947	Americus	GFL	11	35	3	4	1	0	0	4	0	2	16	0.114	SS	17	28	10	0.818								
Crum, McPherson		BR TR																									
1951	Dublin	GSL	16	41	4	7	2	0	0	1	0	2	8	0.171	P	4	16	2	0.909	16	8	5	5.47	97	90	76	98
Crumley, John		BR																									
1951	Valdosta	GFL	119	448	72	121	20	8	5	70	20	62	58	0.270													
Crumly, Ivan		BR TR																									
1946	Valdosta	GFL	125	482	89	133	18	14	3	89	17	55	52	0.276	1B	988	70	24	0.978								
Crutchfield, Eugene "Gene"		BR TR																									
1953	Dublin	GSL	7											0.125	P						0	1	<45				
Cruthers, Hal																											
1939	Americus	GFL	42	164	18	38	4	3	0	15	5	16	18	0.232	2B	100	115	19	0.919								
Cruz, Jose Ramon		BR																									
1963	Waycross	GFL	30	33	3	7	1	0	1	8	0	4	11	0.212													
Cruze, Robert "Bob"		BR TL																									
1948	Thomasville	GFL	39	64	8	14	2	1	0	5	0	9	13	0.219	P	7	37	3	0.936	37	10	11	4.34	166	156	213	135
Cudemo, Michael "Mike"		BR TR																									
1950	Newnan	GAL	60	195	25	40	6	1	0	30	2	32	22	0.205	C	349	47	8	0.980								
1950	Dublin	GSL	29	105	14	27	0	1	1	12	1	12	15	0.257	OF, C	128	7	7	0.951								
1951	Rome	GAL	105	364	52	101	10	3	0	59	1	59	39	0.277	C	468	45	8	0.985								
Cudillo, Joe																											
1937	Tallahassee	GFL	71	261	33	61	13	4	2	26	5	32	53	0.234	1B	701	30	16	0.979								
Culberson, Delbert Leon "Leon"		BR TR 5'11" 180 lbs. b. 08/06/1919 Halls, GA d. 09/11/1989 Rome, GA																									
1951	Rome	GAL	103	370	83	118	23	1	14	80	7	78	15	0.319	M, 3B, SS, OF	159	211	32	0.920								
Culbreth, Bud		BR TR																									
1956	Fitzgerald	GFL	2	6		1								0.167	P					2	1	1	<45				
Culp, ---																											
1921	Cedartown	GSL													P												
Culpepper, J.E.																											
1920	LaGrange	GSL		41	3	14								0.341	M, P												
Culpepper, William "Bill"		BR TR																									
1947	Alexander City	GAL	65	249	44	82	18	5	2	34	6	19	32	0.329	3B, OF	74	101	25	0.875								
1948	Alexander City	GAL	116	414	62	109	15	2	11	75	14	52	50	0.263	OF	236	6	7	0.972								
1949	Vidalia-Lyons	GSL	24	93	15	28	5	0	1	11	0	13	14	0.301	OF	56	6	6	0.912								
1951	Alexander City	GAL	21	75	13	24	2	1	0	8	0	7	8	0.320													
Cummings, ---																											
1906	Cordele	GSL													OF												
Cummings, Clarence "Polly"																											
1939	Americus	GFL	42	96	13	24	4	2	0	12	0	4	28	0.250	P	18	88	5	0.955	37	13	17	6.17	143	250	135	108
Cummings, Vincent "Vince"		BR TR																									
1958	Valdosta	GFL	3	3		0								0.000	P					3	0	1	<30				
Cumpson, William "Bill"		BR TR																									
1950	Vidalia-Lyons(14) - Jesup(20)	GSL	34	106	19	25	5	0	2	18	2	22	23	0.236	OF	37	2	4	0.907								
Cundiff, William "Bill"		BR TL																									
1962	Brunswick	GFL	26	40	2	4	1	0	0	1	0	5	19	0.100	P	9	22	1	0.969	26	5	11	4.69	121	116	137	74
Cunningham, Ed		BR TR																									
1951	Brunswick	GFL	18	51	5	7	1	0	1	5	0	9	8	0.137	OF	20	3	3	0.885								
Cunningham, Lawrence "Larry"		BR TR																									
1950	Vid-Lyo(82) - Haz-Bax(18)	GSL	100	381	63	95	9	0	2	45	3	65	66	0.249	OF	112	7	7	0.944								

Georgia Class-D Minor League Baseball Encyclopedia

YR	TEAM	LG	G	AB	R	H	2B	3B	HR	RBI	SB	BB	SO	BA	POS	PO	A	E	FA	GP	W	L	ERA	IP	H	SO	BB
Cuoco, Albert "Al"		BR TR																									
1950	Valdosta	GFL	88	292	48	80	12	6	0	46	8	58	30	0.274	3B	97	21	23	0.837								
Cuomo, Mario Matthew "Mario"		BR TR 6'0" 190 lbs. b. 06/15/1932 Queens, NY																									
1952	Brunswick	GFL	81	254	31	62	10	2	1	26	7	54	55	0.244	OF	170	10	6	0.968								
Curl, Kedy A.		BS TR																									
1954	Albany	GFL	1	1	0									0.000	P					1	0	0	<45				
1956	Albany	GFL	8	4	0									0.000	P					8	0	2	<45				
1957	Fitzgerald	GFL	35	74	10	12	4	0	0	7	0	10	38	0.162	P	10	26	4	0.900	34	15	9	2.51	204	187	123	77
Curley, James B. "Jim"																											
1942	Waycross	GFL	17	64	11	12	0	0	0	1	0	13	11	0.188	SS	26	53	12	0.868								
Currie, Frank																											
1929	Lindale	GAL	82	306	53	97	16	2	1		3	32	15	0.317	3B	110	173	17	0.943								
Currie, William Cleveland "Bill"		BR TR 6'0" 175 lbs. b. 11/29/1928 Leary, GA																									
1950	Waycross	GFL	46	124	9	30	4	1	2	17	0	3	26	0.242	P	17	32	10	0.831	39	15	11	3.77	272	245	240	129
Curry, ---																											
1930	Huntsville	GAL	20	42	5	7	2	0	0		0	4	17	0.167	P	4	30	1	0.971	15	4	3	5.28	87	102	21	50
Curtis, Ira																											
1948	Thomasville	GFL	13	31	3	4	1	0	0	4	0	3	10	0.129	P	0	11	3	0.786	13	7	3	2.89	84	81	59	44
Curtis, Vernon Eugene "Vern" "Turk"		BR TR 6'0" 170 lbs. b. 05/24/1920 Cairo, IL d. 06/24/1992 Cairo, IL																									
1942	Waycross	GFL	3	11	0	3	0	0	0	0	0	1	2	0.273	P	0	8	0	1.000	3	3	0	0.33	27	11	36	5
Cusick, John Peter "Jack"		BR TR 6'0" 170 lbs. b. 06/12/1928 Weehawken, NJ d. 11/17/1989 Englewood, NJ																									
1946	Americus	GFL	93	338	51	92	11	5	0	67	10	30	46	0.272	3B	100	167	33	0.890								
Cusick, Joseph "Joe"		BR TR																									
1940	Albany	GFL	108	421	36	118	21	0	0	65	0	15	12	0.280	M, C	620	43	7	0.990								
1941	Albany	GFL	123	506	63	157	27	2	0	93	0	30	12	0.310	M, C	8			1.000								
1942	Albany	GFL	96	330	48	103	26	1	1	38	1	22	5	0.312	M, C	453	51	6	0.988								
Cutcliff, Thomas "Tom"		BR TR																									
1949	Cordele	GFL	134	468	51	93	13	6	0	56	8	80	95	0.199	2B	355	361	46	0.940								
Cutter, Ronald "Ron"		BR TR																									
1958	Thomasville	GFL	59	222	48	62	10	2	1	24	4	42	37	0.279	2B, 3B	130	120	22	0.919								
Cyrus, David "Dave"		BL TR																									
1947	Albany	GFL	70	131	18	42	7	0	0	18	2	23	9	0.321	OF, P	15	38	4	0.930	35	13	13	3.31	226	242	147	70
1948	Albany	GFL	55	111	15	29	2	0	0	18	1	22	11	0.261	P	7	28	7	0.833	32	15	12	3.74	214	252	147	97
1949	Americus(40) - Albany(7)	GFL	47	99	18	24	5	1	0	10	1	13	12	0.242	P	6	32	6	0.864	38	18	7	3.42	234	241	203	122
Dabbs, Chester		BL TR																									
1946	Tallassee	GAL	20	80	9	14	3	0	0	7	0	7	18	0.175	3B	25	31	8	0.875								
1948	Americus	GFL	31	101	16	19	5	0	1	8	2	23	41	0.188	OF	45	4	7	0.875								
1949	Vidalia-Lyons	GSL	15	63	10	11	3	0	1	6	0	19	16	0.175	OF	43	3	2	0.958								
Dacey, Red																											
1913	Americus	ESL	55	172	16	27	0	0	0					0.157	P, OF	87	37	7	0.947	12	9	3					
Dacus, Joseph "Joe"		BR TR																									
1951	Rome	GAL	87	282	41	70	8	1	1	31	5	33	35	0.248	SS, OF, P	104	179	44	0.865	15	5	3	3.63	67	47	62	88
1953	Waycross	GFL	79	309	44	89	8	2	1	36	2	23	32	0.288	3B, OF, P	96	105	22	0.901		0	0	<45				
1953	Douglas	GSL	21	90	16	26	1	0	0	2	0	6	9	0.289	OF	52	2	1	0.982								
Dahl, Jay Steven "Jay"		BS TL 5'10" 183 lbs. b. 12/06/1945 San Bernardino, CA d. 06/20/1965 Salisbury, NC																									
1963	Moultrie	GFL	11	21	1	5	1	1	0	3	0	1	2	0.238	P	2	8	0	1.000	11	5	1	1.42	57	32	71	18
Daidone, Joseph "Joe"		BR TR																									
1954	Douglas	GSL	33	128	25	27	7	0	0	20	3	31	20	0.211	2B	70	88	13	0.924								
1955	Moultrie	GFL	65	238	40	56	4	2	0	26	4	42	24	0.235	2B	170	125	21	0.934								
Dairon, Wayne		BL																									
1962	Dublin	GFL	4	14	4	2	0	0	0	0	1	3	8	0.143													
Dal Porto, Angelo		BR TR																									
1953	Hazlehurst-Baxley	GSL	124	459	80	125	19	7	7	76	12	69	66	0.272	SS	191	279	58	0.890								
1954	Hazlehurst-Baxley	GSL	57	216	43	65	9	3	2	19	5	39	43	0.301	SS	113	129	38	0.864								
1955	Hazlehurst-Baxley	GSL	62	213	41	52	8	3	6	29	1	31	42	0.244	OF	82	3	5	0.944								
Dale, Paul		BL TR																									
1956	Tifton	GFL	12	42	4	10	3	0	0	3	0	6	7	0.238	C	87	10	2	0.980								
Daley, ---																											
1913	Waycross	ESL	17	66	1	13	0	0	0					0.197	3B	32	26	4	0.935								
Daley, Gilbert "Gil"		BL TR																									
1949	Tifton	GSL	167	426	70	128	15	3	8	63	26	37	39	0.300	OF	188	8	8	0.961								
1950	Tifton	GSL	125	497	87	157	32	9	12	99	35	44	50	0.316	OF	248	18	16	0.943								
1951	Albany	GFL	110	437	100	141	24	9	11	71	32	37	30	0.323	OF	166	15	16	0.919								
Dalton, Elroy		BL TL																									
1948	Cordele	GFL	53	172	31	46	8	1	2	18	3	38	38	0.267	1B	349	8	15	0.960								
Daly, Hugh		BR TR																									
1950	Cordele	GFL	76	194	28	38	6	2	1	22	5	23	48	0.196	OF, C	222	23	12	0.953								
1951	Cordele	GFL	42	126	20	24	5	2	0	9	1	17	31	0.190	C	172	20	8	0.960								
1953	Cordele	GFL	66	191	18	34	4	0	0	16	3	16	31	0.178	OF, C	209	35	16	0.938								
Damaska, William "Bill"		BR TR																									
1963	Brunswick	GFL	78	232	26	46	10	0	1	14	11	21	53	0.198	2B, 3B, OF	129	95	17	0.929								
Dan, Virgil		BR TR																									
1948	LaGrange	GAL	10												1B	87	4	3	0.968								
Dance, John		BL TL																									
1946	Albany	GFL	77	293	40	69	9	2	0	42	0	25	58	0.235	OF	116	11	14	0.901								
1947	Albany	GFL	13	37	4	6	1	0	0	1	2	1	9	0.162	OF	14	2	0	1.000								

Georgia Class-D Minor League Baseball Encyclopedia

YR	TEAM	LG	G	AB	R	H	2B	3B	HR	RBI	SB	BB	SO	BA	POS	PO	A	E	FA	GP	W	L	ERA	IP	H	SO	BB
Dandurand, Thomas "Tom"		BR TR																									
1956	Waycross	GFL	50	150	15	29	7	0	2	23	1	24	62	0.193	OF	72	5	7	0.917								
Daniel, Douglas "Doug"		BR TR																									
1950	Hazlehurst-Baxley	GSL	23	103	27	29	0	2	0	7	8	11	11	0.282	OF	27	0	2	0.931								
1951	Jesup	GSL	11	37	13	8	0	0	0	8	5	16	3	0.216	OF	16	3	0	1.000								
1952	Jesup	GSL	24	98	16	25	2	1	0	10	10	14	3	0.255	OF	46	1	1	0.979								
1953	Jesup	GSL	4											0.750													
Daniel, Handley Jacob "Jake"		BL TL 5'11" 175 lbs. b. 04/22/1911 Roanoke, AL d. 04/23/1996 LaGrange, GA																									
1946	Valley(33) - LaGrange(96)	GAL	129	446	118	159	30	3	30	122	15	98	64	0.357	M, 1B, P	1108	62	18	0.985	5	0	0	0.00	9			
1947	LaGrange(74) - Newnan(21)	GAL	95	294	63	92	13	7	13	68	6	103	55	0.313	1B	788	59	16	0.981								
1950	Valley	GAL	36	130	28	45	16	0	4	39	0	29	9	0.346	1B	724	17	10	0.987								
1952	Vidalia	GSL	44	143	34	34	6	0	7	26	0	50	15	0.238	1B	363	16	3	0.992								
1953	Vidalia	GSL	37	141	26	40	7	0	3	31	2	29	19	0.284	M, 1B	331	19	6	0.983								
Daniel, Robert "Bob"		BR TR																									
1955	Tifton	GFL	11	35	4	8	0	1	0	2	0	3	10	0.229	OF	21	1	3	0.880								
Daniel, Stewart		BR TR																									
1950	Jesup	GSL	83	274	39	59	8	2	0	21	2	32	17	0.215	OF	100	3	7	0.936								
Daniels, Richard "Dick"		BL TL																									
1952	Fitzgerald	GSL	99	375	55	102	17	1	1	42	8	62	71	0.272	1B, OF	602	44	36	0.947								
1955	Valdosta	GFL	45	164	33	55	9	5	0	35	5	40	16	0.335	1B	373	17	7	0.982								
Danielson, Dan																											
1941	Valdosta	GFL	88	371	85	106	9	9	1	28	20	45	63	0.286	2B	59	22	20	0.802								
Danish, Christopher "Chris"		BR TR																									
1947	LaGrange	GAL	73	228	40	68	7	7	1	34	6	42	46	0.298	C	375	28	19	0.955								
Danna, Charles		BR TR																									
1947	Valley	GAL	110	412	63	131	16	2	0	57	11	40	25	0.318	C	618	80	12	0.983								
1948	Valley	GAL	115	379	32	109	12	6	0	55	3	50	18	0.288	C	539	68	17	0.973								
Danna, Jesse		BL TL																									
1947	Valley	GAL	51	129	17	22	4	2	1	22	1	25	17	0.171	OF, P	38	37	3	0.962	27	17	18	2.15	188	164	98	31
1948	Valley	GAL	61	170	23	47	6	1	3	20	0	32	19	0.276	M, OF, P	43	44	7	0.926	30	22	6	2.06	236	213	99	45
1949	Valley	GAL	10	15	4	4	0	0	0	3	0	7	2	0.267	M												
Danowski, William "Bill"		BR TR																									
1953	Eastman	GSL	39	67	12	19	1	1	0	8	0	9	9	0.284	P	6	17	1	0.958	22	4	6	5.28	109	121	61	69
D'Antonio, Joe																											
1939	Waycross	GFL	41	170	22	41	5	5	0	19	0	23	26	0.241	2B	87	107	16	0.924								
Darden, William "Bill"		BR TR																									
1948	Valdosta	GFL	36	80	9	8	1	0	0	6	1	3	30	0.100	P	7	58	5	0.929	34	12	7	3.47	187	185	129	95
Dardes, Nicholas "Nick"		BR TR																									
1949	Hazlehurst-Baxley	GSL	59	211	28	35	2	0	0	10	9	41	64	0.166	SS	140	139	23	0.924								
Darr, Donald "Don"		BL TL																									
1951	Americus	GFL	27	47	8	10	2	0	0	13	0	13	13	0.213	P	5	26	3	0.912	23	11	5	3.49	116	90	65	99
Daugherty, Michael "Mike"		BR TR																									
1946	Newnan	GAL	13	49	8	12	2	0	0	2	3	6	7	0.245	OF	23	3	1	0.963								
Daugherty, Norman L. "Norm"																											
1935	Thomasville	GFL	21	51	2	7	1	0	0		0	1	14	0.137	P					24	7	8		137	136	79	68
Dauten, Fred		BR TR																									
1956	Moultrie	GFL	18	37	3	5	0	0	0	3	0	9	11	0.135	C	43	2	2	0.957								
Davenport, ---																											
1906		GSL													P, OF												
Davenport, ---																											
1913	Cordele	ESL	13	50	3	11	1	0	0					0.220	OF	23	0	2	0.920								
1913	Thomasville	ESL	60	244	26	68	11	2	5					0.279	1B	616	36	14	0.979								
1914	Thomasville	GSL		360	60	101	16	1	2		19			0.281													
Davenport, ---																											
1921	Carrollton	GSL		103	10	24								0.233	2B												
1921	Griffin	GSL													2B												
1930	Carrollton	GAL		10		1								0.100													
Davenport, Nevil		BR TR																									
1948	Vidalia-Lyons	GSL	34	128	16	29	2	0	0	15	5	10	38	0.227	3B	19	29	1	0.980								
1949	Valley	GAL	22	65	7	13	2	2	0	4	3	10	10	0.200	2B	23	27	8	0.862								
1949	Dublin - Eastman	GSL	35	130	21	26	5	0	5	18	4	13	27	0.200	OF	75	25	7	0.935								
Davids, W. Roland																											
1942	Tallahassee	GFL	42	107	9	15	4	0	0	7	0	9	23	0.140	P	22	41	3	0.955	31	7	13	5.16	178	217	91	59
Davidson, Robert L. "Bob"		BL TR																									
1952	Cordele	GFL	112	390	61	118	7	6	0	38	5	60	46	0.303	2B, OF	205	68	13	0.955								
Davis, ---																											
1914	Waycross - Valdosta	GSL		51	2	6	3	1	1		1			0.118													
Davis, ---		BR TR																									
1946	LaGrange	GAL	1												P					1	0	1	0.00	8	8	7	4
Davis, Alfred L. "Al"		BR TR																									
1955	Hazlehurst-Baxley	GSL	99	323	65	99	19	3	11	61	7	72	66	0.307	OF, C	381	36	15	0.965								
Davis, Alton		BL TL																									
1953	Tifton	GFL	24	38	3	7	1	0	0	5	0	3	14	0.184	P	2	21	1	0.958	23	6	5	3.12	98	109	31	35
Davis, Arthur "Art"		BL TL																									
1946	Moultrie	GFL	1												P					1	0	0	0.00	3			

Georgia Class-D Minor League Baseball Encyclopedia

YR	TEAM	LG	G	AB	R	H	2B	3B	HR	RBI	SB	BB	SO	BA	POS	PO	A	E	FA	GP	W	L	ERA	IP	H	SO	BB
Davis, Bubba		BR																									
1956	Brunswick	GFL	47	148	23	37	9	0	4	23	3	10	34	0.250													
Davis, C. Victor "Vic"		BR TR																									
1955	Sandersville	GSL	42	87	11	21	2	1	0	13	0	5	17	0.241	P	10	39	7	0.875	31	14	9	3.44	196	153	189	112
Davis, Carl																											
1929	Carrollton	GAL		19	3	2								0.105	P												
1930	Carrollton	GAL	<10												P												
1930	Talladega	GAL													P						0	1	9.90				
Davis, Carl A.		BL TL																									
1953	Sandersville	GSL	4											0.222	P						0	4		<45			
Davis, Clarence		BL																									
1946	Tallassee	GAL	<10																								
Davis, Donald "Don"		BR TR																									
1963	Brunswick	GFL	13	9	0	0	0	0	0	0	0	1	7	0.000	P	1	9	1	0.909	13	0	1	4.22	32	25	20	25
Davis, Edward E. "Ed"																											
1935	Panama City	GFL	108	377	49	102	25	6	6		4	32	65	0.271	IF	1391	45	25	0.983								
Davis, Ernest		BL TL																									
1963	Brunswick	GFL	41	90	10	18	0	1	3	9	2	17	39	0.200	OF	44	2	1	0.979								
Davis, Eugene "Gene"		BR TR																									
1953	Albany	GFL	131	532	90	148	30	14	5	89	8	53	106	0.278	3B	164	171	39	0.896								
Davis, Fred		BR TR																									
1947	Alexander City	GAL	12	15	2	2	1	0	0	0	0	1	5	0.133	P	1	8	1	0.900	12	0	4	5.09	53	69	29	24
1948	Alexander City	GAL	22	42	4	6	0	1	0	4	0	1	12	0.143	P	1	22	0	1.000	22	7	6	4.21	109	117	68	45
Davis, H. Thurman																											
1951	Dou(19) - Fit(55) - Dub(37)	GSL	111	421	43	99	12	1	1	27	3	28	34	0.235	3B, SS	200	300	54	0.903								
1952	Fitzgerald	GSL	121	493	75	131	16	2	1	63	11	44	30	0.266	3B	169	300	35	0.931								
1954	Fitzgerald	GFL	130	464	74	117	11	1	0	44	4	70	55	0.252	3B	141	236	25	0.938								
Davis, Hargrove																											
1941	Valdosta	GFL	8	25	4	5	0	1	0	3	0	0	5	0.200	OF	4	0	3	0.571								
Davis, Hazen		BR TR																									
1954	Tifton	GFL	6	9		2								0.222	P					6	1	4		<45			
Davis, Homer																											
1938	Americus	GFL	32	70	5	16	1	2	0	9	0	0	22	0.229	P	2	23	2	0.926	31	12	9	4.60	182	206	66	70
1939	Americus	GFL													P									<45			
Davis, Howard F.																											
1938	Americus	GFL	13	30	1	8	1	0	0	4	0	1	4	0.267	P	1	20	0	1.000	11	6	3	3.26	69	80	18	19
Davis, Howard T.		BR TR																									
1950	Fitzgerald(25) - Dublin(53)	GSL	78	274	35	58	13	1	4	31	1	19	44	0.212	SS, OF	107	77	14	0.929								
1953	Fitzgerald	GFL	135	498	53	123	15	2	0	48	7	58	41	0.247	3B	171	248	33	0.927								
Davis, J.B.		BR TR																									
1963	Waycross	GFL	97	267	27	62	8	4	2	28	2	51	78	0.232	OF	93	7	7	0.935								
Davis, Jack H.		BR TR																									
1954	Waycross	GFL	60	117	16	21	4	2	0	9	2	21	21	0.179	OF	69	10	4	0.952								
1955	Waycross	GFL	107	346	40	77	14	1	2	42	8	47	64	0.223	OF	161	16	6	0.967								
Davis, James "Jim"		BR TR																									
1946	Opelika	GAL	4												P					4	0	1	0.00	8	14	2	7
1949	Tallassee		17	15	9	5	0	0	0	1	1	1	3	0.333	P	3	9	0	1.000								
Davis, John Wilbur "Bud"		BL TR 6'0" 207 lbs. b. 12/07/1896 Merry Point, VA d. 05/26/1967 Williamsburg, VA																									
1914	Opelika	GAL	14	42	2	6				0				0.143	P	57	42	5	0.952	14							
1914	Talladega	GAL	38	111	11	23				4				0.207	P	6	22	5	0.848	38							
1916	Newnan	GAL	52	173	33	52	7	0	16	7	8			0.301	OF, P												
Davis, Joseph "Joe"		BL TR																									
1952	Douglas	GSL	83	336	47	102	17	1	4	51	15	40	19	0.304	1B, OF	264	12	5	0.982								
1955	Douglas	GSL	100	388	65	98	20	2	4	45	9	78	40	0.253	3B, OF	207	19	7	0.970								
1956	Douglas	GSL	89	317	56	79	11	2	6	51	6	64	29	0.249	1B, OF	280	12	12	0.961								
Davis, Lisle																											
1941	Americus	GFL	24	109	22	29	6	2	2	17	3	7	17	0.266	OF	43	0	3	0.935								
Davis, Ned		BR TR																									
1955	Valdosta	GFL	12	37	6	6	1	0	0	4	0	6	8	0.162	OF	14	2	0	1.000								
Davis, Ralph		BL TR																									
1947	Alexander City	GAL	30	105	11	26	4	0	1	4	1	23	10	0.248	2B, 3B	57	72	10	0.928								
Davis, Spencer "Onion"		BL TL																									
1947	Cordele	GFL	12	28	4	6	0	1	2	3	0	3	9	0.214	P					8	1	4	4.79	47	61	12	34
Davis, Sterling		BR TR																									
1952	Brunswick	GFL	30	105	9	17	0	0	0	2	1	10	23	0.162	3B, OF	36	19	9	0.859								
Davis, Thomas "Tom"		BR TR																									
1955	Hazlehurst-Baxley	GSL	27	37	3	6	0	0	0	5	1	3	16	0.162	P	0	8	4	0.667	27	6	5	5.42	103	120	49	68
Davis, Van		BR TR																									
1950	Douglas	GSL	138	474	119	140	27	2	30	103	7	135	96	0.295	1B	1274	49	24	0.982								
1951	Douglas	GSL	129	450	101	150	30	2	29	139	10	118	83	0.333	1B	1228	68	22	0.983								
1952	Douglas	GSL	100	340	80	111	19	1	22	87	11	100	28	0.326	M, 1B	811	49	15	0.983								
1953	Douglas	GSL	126	441	130	150	24	1	44	159	4	145	43	0.340	1B, P	973	59	13	0.988		0	1		<45			
1954	Douglas	GSL	123	453	120	146	24	3	31	135	4	129	74	0.322	1B	985	62	15	0.986								
1956	Douglas	GSL	46	170	31	55	10	0	7	44	1	34	31	0.324	1B	372	23	6	0.985								
Davis, Victor "Vic"		BR TR																									
1963	Brunswick	GFL	31	63	8	12	1	0	1	5	1	7	15	0.190	C	199	10	5	0.977								

Georgia Class-D Minor League Baseball Encyclopedia

YR	TEAM	LG	G	AB	R	H	2B	3B	HR	RBI	SB	BB	SO	BA	POS	PO	A	E	FA	GP	W	L	ERA	IP	H	SO	BB
Davis, Virgil Max "Max"		BL TL																									
1947	Alexander City	GAL	120	439	58	129	18	12	4	67	3	45	31	0.294	1B, OF	543	20	18	0.969								
1948	Alexander City	GAL	59	196	24	59	11	2	1	30	4	32	8	0.301	OF	102	12	4	0.966								
Davis, W.C.																											
1928	Cedartown	GAL	42	132	9	37	7	1	1		0	2	16	0.280	1B, P	156	13	0	1.000	17	11	3	2.65	112	98	34	20
1929	Cedartown	GAL	29	63	6	16	2	0	0		0	4	10	0.254	P	2	24	0	1.000								
1930	Talladega	GAL	2												P					2	0	1	9.90	10	21	1	1
Davis, Walter		BR																									
1954	Sandersville	GSL	4	10		4								0.400													
Davis, Wayne		BR TR																									
1951	Moultrie(29) - Waycross(2)	GFL	31	131	17	28	7	1	2	15	0	7	18	0.214	OF	68	4	11	0.867								
1955	Albany	GFL	135	549	101	164	25	9	20	106	4	51	72	0.299	OF	190	14	21	0.907								
Davis, Wendell E.		BL TR																									
1950	Moultrie	GFL	71	259	40	79	11	4	3	43	3	33	26	0.305	1B, 3B	127	103	8	0.966								
1951	Moultrie	GFL	119	466	88	160	30	6	22	96	2	58	28	0.343	1B, OF	530	37	13	0.978								
Davis, Wendell J.																											
1949	Dublin	GSL	13	39	4	9	1	0	0	3	0	0	3	0.231	M, P	7	10	0	1.000	9	3	1	4.00	45	22	28	14
Davis, William "Bill"		BR TR																									
1956	Tifton	GFL	16	30	0	5	2	0	0	0	0	5	12	0.167	P	3	14	2	0.895	15	5	5	3.78	81	70	33	49
Davis, William "Bill"		BR TR																									
1956	Dublin	GSL	34	131	12	31	7	0	2	10	3	10	41	0.237	OF	74	2	7	0.916								
Davis, William H. "Bill"		BR TR																									
1948	Fitzgerald	GSL	13	16	6	4	0	0	0	1	0	2	3	0.250	P	2	7	0	1.000								
Davis, Woodrow Wilson "Woody"		BL TR 6'1" 200 lbs. b. 04/25/1913 Nicholls, GA																									
1936	Cordele	GFL	27	52	4	3	1	0	0	7	0			0.058	P					27	17	3	1.87	159		124	55
1939	Valdosta	GFL	84	234	26	61	13	4	1	34	4	9	18	0.261	UT, P	269	77	4	0.989	34	13	11	3.27	215	207	123	76
1940	Valdosta	GFL	<10												P					8	3	4	5.10	60	68	32	22
Dawkins, Robert A. "Bob"		BL TL																									
1950	LaGrange	GAL	15	20	2	3	0	0	0	3	0	1	6	0.150	P	0	6	7	0.462	13	1	3	6.89	47	41	29	57
Dawson, Ronald D. "Ron"		BR TR																									
1953	Vidalia	GSL	2											0.000	P					0	0	0		<45			
Day, ---																											
1913	Thomasville	ESL	24	60	10	17	1	0	0					0.283	P	9	36	1	0.978	22	16	6					
1914	Thomasville	GSL		104	10	24	0	0	0		1			0.231													
Day, ---																											
1913	Cordele	ESL	93	328	47	87	20	4	1					0.265	1B	768	63	38	0.956								
Day, ---		BR TR																									
1946	Opelika	GAL	5												P					5	0	2	0.00	22	36	4	7
Day, Donald F. "Don"		BL TR																									
1951	Cordele	GFL	120	458	84	136	16	6	5	62	15	80	35	0.297	OF	251	13	21	0.926								
1952	Cordele	GFL	133	506	75	152	10	10	0	54	9	92	32	0.300	OF	273	14	23	0.926								
Day, Dwight		BR TR																									
1950	Moultrie	GFL	12	19	1	1	0	0	0	0	0	2	9	0.053	P	2	8	2	0.833	12	2	6	6.10	59	79	20	14
de la Cruz, Ramon		BR TR																									
1963	Moultrie	GFL	68	193	16	37	6	2	0	19	0	12	54	0.192	3B, C	165	58	13	0.945								
de la Torre, Albert		BR																									
1962	Moultrie	GFL	5	12	0	0	0	0	0	1	0	4	5	0.000													
Deal, ---																											
1930	Talladega	GAL	38	127	22	40	8	4	3		4	19	18	0.315	2B	66	54	5	0.960								
Deal, Marvin "Marv"		BR TR																									
1952	Brunswick	GFL	26	44	8	10	0	1	0	4	0	8	10	0.227	P	3	18	0	1.000	26	8	12	4.27	139	136	86	76
1953	Brunswick	GFL	22	47	8	13	1	0	0	7	0	6	12	0.277	P	7	21	2	0.833	21	9	5	4.34	114	97	115	80
Deal, Nip		BR																									
1946	LaGrange	GAL	<10																								
Deal, Silas																											
1939	Tallahassee	GFL													P									<45			
Deal, Wallace "Wally"		BR TR																									
1939	Valdosta	GFL	47	93	5	11	0	1	0	9	0	9	31	0.118	P	10	63	4	0.948	45	18	11	2.95	259	263	129	64
1940	Valdosta	GFL	52	115	14	23	5	3	0	5	1	9	40	0.200	P					51	18	15	3.07	299	282	157	84
Deal, William "Bill"		BR TR																									
1954	Thomasville	GFL	22	63	12	11	0	0	0	4	5	10	16	0.175	OF	37	5	1	0.977								
1954	Vidalia	GSL	102	405	75	102	17	8	13	65	16	51	67	0.252	OF	217	11	12	0.950								
1955	Thomasville	GFL	137	545	83	155	29	11	10	80	9	43	63	0.284	OF	275	22	15	0.952								
Dealing, Ephram		BL TL																									
1954	Statesboro	GSL	1	0										0.000	P					1	0	1		<45			
Dean, Charles		BR TR																									
1946	LaGrange	GAL	59	189	39	47	10	1	3	43	8	41	39	0.249	3B, OF, P	93	20	7	0.942	2	0	0	0.00	8			
Dean, James Harry "Harry"		BR TR 6'4" 185 lbs. b. 05/12/1915 Rockmart, GA d. 06/01/1960 Rockmart, GA																									
1946	Carrollton	GAL	2												P					2	1	0	0.00	9	10	7	2
Dean, Ray		BR TR																									
1954	Waycross	GFL	2	2		0								0.000	P					2	0	0		<45			
Dean, Theodore "Ted"		BR TR																									
1949	Valdosta	GFL	89	318	50	72	11	8	0	51	16	42	62	0.226	2B, 3B, SS	181	163	32	0.915								

Georgia Class-D Minor League Baseball Encyclopedia

YR	TEAM	LG	G	AB	R	H	2B	3B	HR	RBI	SB	BB	SO	BA	POS	PO	A	E	FA	GP	W	L	ERA	IP	H	SO	BB
DeArman, H.P																											
1928	Cedartown	GAL	88	322	62	93	14	5	12		9	19	43	0.289	1B, P	785	24	17	0.979	5	1	1	5.25	24	37	6	3
1929	Anniston	GAL	83	300	40	78	17	3	3		6	14	19	0.260	1B	699	53	25	0.968								
1930	Anniston	GAL	10	34	6	8	1	1	0		1	2	6	0.235	1B	100	4	3	0.972								
DeArmond, Hollis		BR TR																									
1947	Valdosta	GFL	43	153	23	48	6	2	1	22	4	15	32	0.314	OF	70	6	5	0.938								
DeBosky, Edward																											
1921	Cedartown	GSL																									
DeBruler, Ernest John "Ernest"		BL TL																									
1957	Brunswick	GFL	27	28	2	2	0	1	0	1	0	5	10	0.071	P	2	16	6	0.750	26	2	8	5.05	107	89	92	103
Decatur, Arthur Rue "Art"		BR TR 6'1" 190 lbs. b. 01/14/1894 Cleveland, OH d. 04/25/1966 Talladega, AL																									
1914	Talladega	GAL	20	55	3	10					0			0.182	OF	14	18	3	0.914								
1915	Talladega	GAL	22	61	1	3	0	0	0					0.049	P	11	34	2	0.957	21	11	8					
Deck, Edward "Ed"		BR TR																									
1955	Albany	GFL	2	1		0								0.000	P					2	0	0	<45				
Decker, Robert "Bob"		BR TR																									
1954	Douglas	GSL	69	259	59	78	16	3	1	35	8	57	26	0.301	2B, 3B	118	146	24	0.917								
DeCosta, ---																											
1906	Albany - Americus	GSL													C, 1B												
Dedon, ---																											
1914	Valdosta - Brunswick	GSL		47	10	9	1	1	0		7			0.191													
Deeds, Ray Edward "Ray"		BR TR																									
1955	Vidalia	GSL	33	67	2	9	0	0	0	5	0	3	15	0.134	P	4	21	6	0.806	33	7	11	4.58	167	188	101	58
Deering, Vernon "Verne"		BR TL																									
1954	Tifton	GFL	15	21	3	2	0	0	0	2	0	5	13	0.095	P	6	20	2	0.929	15	2	7	5.29	68	82	47	35
1955	Vidalia	GSL	6	4		0								0.000	P					6	1	1					
Deery, James "Jim"		BR TR																									
1955	Waycross	GFL	103	368	72	112	25	2	2	32	16	75	32	0.304	M, 2B	233	319	14	0.975								
1956	Waycross	GFL	26	78	8	15	4	1	0	9	1	15	11	0.192	M, 2B	46	74	3	0.976								
DeFalco, Ferdinand "Fred"		BR TR																									
1956	Thomasville	GFL	113	372	52	95	14	6	4	53	5	71	84	0.255	OF	190	15	7	0.967								
DeFeo, Robert "Bob"		BR TR																									
1949	Tallassee(10) - Griffin(33)	GAL	43	145	22	44	9	2	0	23	3	16	24	0.303	3B	52	79	14	0.903								
1949	Moultrie	GFL	17	68	4	13	1	0	1	7	0	6	15	0.191	3B	12	38	6	0.893								
1950	Opelika	GAL	11	41	2	7	1	0	0	5	2	5	7	0.171	3B	8	20	7	0.800								
DeFoor, Max																											
1956	Dublin	GSL	7	7		1								0.143	P					7	1	2					
DeFore, Edward "Ed"		BR TR																									
1951	Albany	GFL	34	122	20	27	9	1	3	22	7	14	33	0.221	OF	66	1	5	0.931								
1951	Hazlehurst-Baxley	GSL	27	93	6	18	1	1	2	9	2	2	21	0.194	OF	47	1	4	0.923								
1953	Tifton	GFL	17	43	7	8	4	0	0	5	0	4	7	0.186	OF	12	0	0	1.000								
1953	Eastman	GSL	6											0.120													
DeGourscey, Joseph "Joe"		BR TR																									
1950	LaGrange	GAL	26	34	2	2	0	0	0	1	0	2	15	0.059	P	3	12	2	0.882	26	3	6	3.77	86	59	52	77
DeGraaf, William "Bill"		BR TR																									
1957	Albany	GFL	127	447	68	121	9	2	9	68	4	68	64	0.271	1B, C	799	96	24	0.974								
DeGregorio, Syl																											
1938	Moultrie	GFL	38	155	30	33	7	1	1	20	2	25	15	0.213	2B	100	140	12	0.952								
Deibler, Mason		BR TR																									
1948	Tallassee	GAL	24	45	1	5	0	0	0	3	0	2	16	0.111	P	3	16	5	0.792	22	7	5	2.68	114	94	52	68
1948	Albany	GFL	11	12	1	0	0	0	0	0	0	2	4	0.000	P	0	1	1	0.500								
1949	Alex City(4) - Tallassee(9)	GAL	13	10	0	0	0	0	0	0	0	0	3	0.000	P	2	8	0	1.000	13	3	4	4.50	46	57	32	23
Deleso, Vinny																											
1952	Tifton	GFL	15	60	5	10	0	0	0	2	0	3	10	0.167	OF	23	8	3	0.912								
Deitch, Elliott		BR TR																									
1950	Cordele	GFL	26	31	5	4	1	0	0	3	0	10	11	0.129	P	9	17	2	0.929	26	3	9	6.25	108	145	62	53
1950	Vidalia-Lyons	GSL	10	19	1	3	1	0	0	1	0	1	4	0.158	P					9	1	8	6.33	54	82	21	21
Deitch, Michael "Mike"		BR TR																									
1949	Moultrie	GFL	27	42	6	6	0	0	0	4	0	13	19	0.143	P	14	20	2	0.944	28	5	8	4.96	136	135	85	72
DeJesus, William "Bill"		BR TR																									
1955	Sandersville	GSL	4	5		1								0.200	P					4	1	0					
DeJohn, John		BR TR																									
1940	Waycross	GFL	140	563	118	174	31	11	7	68	11	65	58	0.309	2B	355	390	29	0.963								
DeKoning, William Callahan "Bill"		BR TR 5'11" 185 lbs. b. 12/19/1918 Brooklyn, NY d. 07/26/1979 Palm Harbor, FL																									
1939	Americus	GFL	32	110	8	22	5	0	0	9	1	6	24	0.200	C	177	30	6	0.972								
Del Isola, Salvatore "Sal"		BR TR																									
1948	Tallahassee	GFL	13	32	8	7	1	0	0	4	0	2	2	0.219	P	0	23	4	0.852	13	4	5	3.88	72	80	36	38
Del Monico, Gerald		BR TR																									
1956	Thomson	GSL	72	276	45	75	18	3	0	26	4	49	32	0.272	SS	116	153	27	0.909								
Del Papa, Frank		BL TL																									
1946	Moultrie	GFL	104	380	53	104	14	4	10	73	7	31	49	0.274	OF	113	9	7	0.946								
Del Piano, Michael "Mike"		BR TR																									
1950	Moultrie	GFL	60	51	6	5	0	0	0	3	0	7	12	0.098	P	9	40	5	0.907	60	9	6	4.24	140	140	63	72
1951	Moultrie	GFL	29	84	8	19	5	0	0	7	0	10	12	0.226	P	5	31	3	0.923	17	6	6	4.34	112	136	49	44
Delich, William "Bill"		BR TR																									
1950	Valdosta	GFL	20	80	18	21	4	1	1	13	8	11	19	0.263	SS	46	69	16	0.878								

Georgia Class-D Minor League Baseball Encyclopedia

YR	TEAM	LG	G	AB	R	H	2B	3B	HR	RBI	SB	BB	SO	BA	POS	PO	A	E	FA	GP	W	L	ERA	IP	H	SO	BB
Delida, John Robert "Bob"		BR TR																									
1955	Sandersville	GSL	3	3	0									0.000	P					3	0	0					
Delo, Lawrence		BR TR																									
1949	Tallahassee	GFL	27	32	5	4	2	0	0	2	0	3	14	0.125	P	6	12	3	0.857	26	3	8	5.91	96	130	38	64
DeLuca, Edward "Ed"		BR TR																									
1955	Statesboro(16) - Sandersville(3)	GSL	19	65	8	10	2	1	0	5	0	13	18	0.154	2B	42	41	4	0.954								
DeLuca, Thomas "Tom"		BR																									
1957	Albany	GFL	4	11		3								0.273													
DeLucia, Pasquale		BR TR																									
1948	Valdosta	GFL	14	55	7	12	0	1	0	4	3	9	11	0.218	OF	22	3	1	0.962								
DeMatteis, John		BR TR																									
1950	Rome	GAL	16	47	7	11	0	0	0	3	1	5	8	0.234	OF	17	2	2	0.905								
DeMatteis, Salvatore "Sal"		BR TR																									
1950	Rome	GAL	106	357	86	94	12	4	3	41	28	113	40	0.263	OF	217	16	14	0.943								
Dembek, Joseph "Joe"		BR TR																									
1951	Waycross	GFL	66	246	56	58	13	8	2	28	9	42	38	0.236	OF	143	6	6	0.961								
1954	Waycross	GFL	120	400	84	109	22	2	1	37	13	95	84	0.273	OF, P	225	15	12	0.952	1	0	0	<45				
Dembinski, Daniel "Dan"		BR TR																									
1949	LaGrange	GAL	17	47	5	8	2	1	1	7	0	8	12	0.170	C	107	7	4	0.966								
Dembinsky, Charles		BR TR																									
1962	Moultrie	GFL	23	84	5	14	6	1	0	13	6	11	22	0.167	2B	41	37	8	0.907								
Demchuk, Bill																											
1942	Valdosta	GFL	4												P					4	1	0	3.18	17	12	12	18
Demma, Salvatore "Sam"		BR TR																									
1941	Waycross - Moultrie	GFL	79	277	25	58	3	1	1	29	0	22	60	0.209	C	405	32	24	0.948								
1951	Alexander City	GAL	45	156	20	36	13	1	4	27	0	29	14	0.231	M, C	188	27	6	0.973								
Demont, Paul		BR TR																									
1949	Moultrie	GFL	103	389	59	97	11	3	0	40	19	32	39	0.249	3B, SS	133	227	32	0.918								
1950	Cordele	GFL	138	560	75	145	15	6	0	85	27	39	31	0.259	2B, 3B	195	261	33	0.933								
1952	Cordele	GFL	128	519	82	156	16	10	0	48	20	65	37	0.301	2B	384	333	28	0.962								
1955	Cordele	GFL	84	322	53	104	11	4	1	43	8	29	29	0.323	2B, 3B	99	145	17	0.935								
Dempsey, Frank																											
1949	Hazlehurst-Baxley	GSL	32	123	17	29	4	0	0	16	1	23	17	0.236	OF	61	4	7	0.903								
Dendinger, Jacob "Dick"		BR TR																									
1947	Carrollton	GAL	23	77	16	20	6	1	2	12	2	18	14	0.260	OF	26	0	2	0.929								
1948	Carrollton	GAL	16	46	4	13	5	0	0	8	3	12	6	0.283	OF	23	0	2	0.920								
Dendy, Robert "Bob"		BR TR																									
1949	Hazlehurst-Baxley	GSL	23	77	15	15	3	0	0	6	1	25	19	0.195	2B	56	53	9	0.924								
1950	Valdosta	GFL	45	143	23	34	10	1	3	29	4	32	45	0.238	3B	48	54	19	0.843								
Deneau, Belmont		BL TL																									
1953	Valdosta	GFL	17	25	2	4	0	0	0	2	0	1	10	0.160	P	4	25	2	0.935	17	3	6	5.55	73	83	40	55
Denison, Jack		BL TR																									
1952	Valdosta	GFL	75	280	51	89	16	4	0	40	23	55	28	0.318	OF	159	6	4	0.976								
Dennany, Robert "Bob"		BL TL																									
1947	Opelika	GAL	29	67	5	6	1	0	0	4	0	5	23	0.090	P	11	25	1	0.973	23	8	5	3.70	141	143	84	62
1948	Opelika	GAL	25	58	10	12	1	0	0	5	1	7	14	0.207	P	6	35	4	0.911	20	9	9	3.73	140	124	95	76
Dennis, C.T.		BR TR																									
1946	Opelika	GAL	1												P					1	0	0	0.00	4			
Dennis, Harold		BL TL																									
1955	Cordele	GFL	30	111	26	22	3	1	2	9	0	28	40	0.198	1B	255	14	9	0.968								
Dennis, Jack		BR																									
1950	Carrollton	GAL	10	12	3	4	0	0	0	2	0	3	2	0.333													
Denny, Fred		BL																									
1946	Albany	GFL	4												P					4	0	2	0.00	15	18	12	9
Denny, Horace		BL TL																									
1946	Newnan	GAL	<10																								
1956	Thomson	GSL	5	5		3								0.500	P					5	0	1					
Denton, Malcolm																											
1930	Huntsville	GAL	3												P					3	0	2	11.25	8	12	0	0
DePillo, George		BR TR																									
1947	Newnan	GAL	22	93	10	28	5	1	0	8	0	4	14	0.301	2B	63	56	3	0.975								
Deporto, Jesse		BR																									
1949	Moultrie	GFL	10	22	4	2	1	0	0	2	0	6	12	0.091													
Depperschmidt, Eugene "Gene"		BR TR																									
1949	Valdosta	GFL	128	471	105	159	29	9	10	91	54	84	81	0.338	OF	179	13	9	0.955								
DeRieux, Robert "Bob"		BR TR																									
1950	Thomasville	GFL	129	481	60	96	19	4	3	62	9	72	147	0.200	3B	144	241	62	0.861								
Dernback, Allen "Al"		BR TR																									
1938	Albany	GFL	124	451	73	106	21	4	1	74	11	63	91	0.235	2B	261	359	64	0.906								
1939	Albany	GFL	134	460	76	114	23	5	2	58	15	59	63	0.248	2B	363	398	56	0.931								
1940	Albany	GFL	73	279	42	67	20	4	0	39	2	40	57	0.240	2B	182	214	35	0.919								
Derry, Stanley "Stan"		BL TR																									
1954	Hazlehurst-Baxley	GSL	42	149	17	39	4	3	1	22	6	24	35	0.262	OF	54	8	8	0.886								
DeShong, James Brooklyn "Jimmie"		BR TR 5'11" 165 lbs. b. 11/30/1909 Harrisburg, PA d. 10/16/1993 Lower Paxton Township, PA																									
1951	Cordele	GFL													M												

Georgia Class-D Minor League Baseball Encyclopedia

YR	TEAM	LG	G	AB	R	H	2B	3B	HR	RBI	SB	BB	SO	BA	POS	PO	A	E	FA	GP	W	L	ERA	IP	H	SO	BB
Desmuke, Harry		BL TL																									
1946	Albany	GFL	7												P					7	1	2	0.00	29	34	20	16
DeSousa, John		BR																									
1954	Americus-Cordele	GFL	10	14	2	3	1	0	0	2	0	1	1	0.214													
DeSouza, Federico "Freddie"		BR TR																									
1950	Carrollton	GAL	122	421	149	126	33	6	24	92	6	165	92	0.299	3B	137	239	27	0.933								
DeSpirito, Joseph "Joe"		BR TR																									
1953	Cordele	GFL	4											0.000	P					0	0	0	<45				
D'Esposito, Dan		BL TL																									
1956	Waycross	GFL	4	7		1								0.143	P					4	2	1	<45				
DeStafano, Louis "Lou"		BR TR																									
1953	Douglas	GSL	17	43	5	8	2	0	0	6	0	15	7	0.186	C	85	6	5	0.948								
1954	Fitzgerald	GFL	13	25	5	4	0	0	0	1	0	2	4	0.160	C	24	1	2	0.926								
DeStefano, Michael "Mike"		BR TR																									
1954	Tifton	GFL	18	48	14	7	1	0	1	4	2	7	16	0.146	OF	18	1	2	0.905								
Detmers, Larry "Larry"		BR TR																									
1955	Thomasville	GFL	7	8		2								0.250	P					7	0	0	<45				
Detweiler, Robert Sterling "Ducky"		BR TR 5'11" 178 lbs. b. 02/15/1919 Trumbauersville, PA																									
1951	Cordele	GFL	38	113	20	43	14	2	1	28	3	22	9	0.381	M, 2B	64	69	5	0.964								
Deutch, Morris																											
1937	Cordele	GFL	22	86	18	24	2	0	2	13	4	8	11	0.279	OF	34	2	3	0.923								
Devaney, Robert "Bob"		BR TR																									
1948	Newnan	GAL	23	39	4	5	0	0	0	3	0	4	14	0.128	P	6	22	1	0.966	23	10	1	2.63	120	104	60	30
DeVany, Arthur "Art"		BR TR																									
1956	Brunswick	GFL	116	388	50	81	10	0	14	51	4	46	190	0.209	OF	153	14	16	0.913								
Deveney, James "Jim"		BR																									
1954	Brunswick	GFL	6	9		2								0.222													
Devine, Michael "Mike"		BR TR																									
1963	Thomasville	GFL	17	51	2	6	1	0	0	2	0	10	20	0.118	OF	18	3	1	0.955								
DeViveiros, Bernard John "Bernie"		BR TR 5'7" 160 lbs. b. 04/19/1901 Oakland, CA d. 07/05/1994 Oakland, CA																									
1940	Americus	GFL	44	139	24	37	6	1	0	17	5	17	9	0.266	M, 3B	62	95	13	0.924								
Devlin, Conrad		BR TR																									
1955	Thomasville	GFL	34	121	29	30	4	2	1	15	4	27	8	0.248	3B, OF	44	23	2	0.971								
DeWeese, Malcolm "Mal"																											
1935	Moultrie	GFL	50	161	12	47	8	1	1		3	11	16	0.292	C	227	45	5	0.982								
1936	Moultrie	GFL	106	402	73	111	17	9	12	74	15			0.276	3B	239	4	22	0.917								
Dews, Robert P. "Barefoot Bobby"																											
1937	Tallahassee	GFL	78	275	39	83	13	3	2	44	6	31	14	0.302	C	283	48	11	0.968								
Dexter, David "Dave"		BR TR																									
1957	Albany	GFL	8	5		0								0.000	P					8	0	0	<30				
Deyo, ---																											
1906	Cordele	GSL													OF												
Dezik, John																											
1937	Thomasville	GFL	123	469	63	130	17	8	4	81	9	58	38	0.277	OF	204	18	11	0.953								
Diahl, Lester "Les"		BL																									
1957	Brunswick	GFL	9	9		1								0.111													
Diamond, Paul		BR																									
1955	Douglas	GSL	6	1		0								0.000													
DiBello, Donald "Don"		BR TR																									
1951	LaGrange	GAL	99	349	59	91	19	4	7	63	4	50	76	0.261	OF	161	10	8	0.955								
Dickerman, Edmond "Ed"		BR TR																									
1949	Tallassee	GAL	34	115	11	30	9	1	0	16	0	16	19	0.261	3B	43	46	7	0.927								
1950	Tifton	GSL	40	161	32	49	12	0	3	35	3	22	11	0.304	2B	94	108	9	0.957								
1951	Tifton	GFL	108	411	64	124	28	9	1	82	9	65	20	0.302	3B, SS	133	178	36	0.896								
1952	Tifton	GFL	137	497	76	139	26	5	5	82	9	89	31	0.280	M, 3B	192	256	27	0.943								
Dickerson, ---																											
1915	Ame-Gains - Valdosta	FLAG	18	47	5	13	0	1	0		0			0.277	P	6	18	3	0.889	12	5	7		82	57	40	31
Dickerson, ---		BR TR																									
1946	LaGrange	GAL	2												P					2	0	0	0.00	3			
Dickerson, Jerry		BR TR																									
1958	Albany	GFL	32	55	7	12	0	0	0	8	0	5	15	0.218	P	10	25	2	0.946	31	12	5	3.94	153	159	59	98
Dickinson, John		BR TR																									
1946	Newnan	GAL	5												P					5	2	2	0.00	27	25	5	7
Dickson, ---																											
1930	Huntsville	GAL	5												P					5	1	1	7.80	15	21	3	10
Dickson, Edwin G. "Ed"		BL TR																									
1949	Newnan	GAL	63	236	50	55	10	0	0	20	4	46	23	0.233	OF	83	8	2	0.978								
Dickson, Robin																											
1935	Panama City	GFL	69	151	23	50	6	0	0		1	20	29	0.331	C	370	63	9	0.980								
DiCola, Charles																											
1949	Fitzgerald	GSL													M												
Didier, Melvin "Mel"		BR TR																									
1949	Thomasville	GFL	32	55	6	11	0	0	1	6	0	7	7	0.200	P	5	16	0	1.000	25	7	11	6.35	139	168	77	83
Diehl, Leonard		BR TR																									
1950	Newnan	GAL	67	260	37	49	9	1	0	19	2	54	43	0.188	SS	109	147	32	0.889								

Georgia Class-D Minor League Baseball Encyclopedia

YR	TEAM	LG	G	AB	R	H	2B	3B	HR	RBI	SB	BB	SO	BA	POS	PO	A	E	FA	GP	W	L	ERA	IP	H	SO	BB
Diering, Charles Edward Allen "Chuck"		BR TR 5'10" 165 lbs. b. 02/05/0923 St. Louis, MO																									
1942	Albany	GFL	126	472	102	144	25	6	3	64	8	85	74	0.305	OF	268	19	17	0.944								
Dietrich, Bill J.		BR TR																									
1954	Sandersville	GSL	16	36	5	6	0	0	0	6	0	6	16	0.167	P	3	15	1	0.947	16	3	7	5.20	90	88	83	77
Dietz, Bill																											
1941	Moultrie	GFL	39	88	10	17	2	0	0	2	0	8	18	0.193	P	5	36	5	0.891	36	14	12	4.44	225	213	177	127
Dietz, Emmett		BR TR																									
1956	Fitzgerald	GFL	35	117	16	29	6	0	4	21	1	18	27	0.248	C, OF	76	13	11	0.890								
Diez, Alfredo		BR TR																									
1954	Sandersville	GSL	35	70	4	11	1	1	0	0	0	2	39	0.157	P	8	26	4	0.895	32	6	14	6.37	164	221	99	90
Diffly, Peter		BR TR																									
1948	Opelika	GAL	42	130	15	29	6	2	0	14	1	13	33	0.223	SS	35	70	9	0.921								
DiFranco, Sam J.		BR TR																									
1949	Fitzgerald	GSL	84	317	40	81	12	7	1	38	5	28	62	0.256	SS	153	193	35	0.908								
1950	Fitzgerald	GSL	25	106	15	30	7	0	0	20	0	11	17	0.283	3B	22	41	10	0.863								
DiGirolomo, Alfred "Al"		BR TR																									
1951	Waycross	GFL	22	52	10	14	2	0	0	6	0	9	8	0.269	3B	10	21	9	0.775								
DiGirolomo, Rocco		BR TR																									
1951	Valley	GAL	17	34	5	10	0	0	0	7	0	2	3	0.294	C	32	2	0	1.000								
Dillard, ---																											
1906	Columbus	GSL													3B												
Dillard, David Donald "Don"		BL TR 6'1" 200 lbs. b. 01/08/1937 Greenville, SC																									
1955	Vidalia	GSL	27	93	9	23	2	1	1	9	1	8	19	0.247	OF	42	2	6	0.880								
Dillard, Rudolph "Rudy"		BR TR																									
1950	Jesup	GSL	34	70	4	11	2	1	0	9	0	1	18	0.157	P	8	15	1	0.958	33	10	11	4.87	159	154	90	129
Dillon, Charles		BR																									
1951	Brunswick	GFL	12	22	1	9	1	0	0	2	0	0	6	0.409													
Dillon, J.T.R.																											
1920	Griffin	GSL																									
1921	Griffin	GSL																									
DiLullo, Ralph																											
1949	Thomasville	GFL													M												
DiMare, Dominick "Dom"		BR																									
1953	Statesboro	GSL	9											0.037													
DiMartino, Joseph "Joe"		BR TR																									
1946	Albany	GFL	91	303	36	82	16	4	0	42	2	26	46	0.271	C	440	76	25	0.954								
DiMasi, Joseph "Joe"		BL TL																									
1947	Carrollton	GAL	17	57	11	14	3	1	1	12	3	12	14	0.246	OF	20	2	1	0.957								
Dimitriadis, James "Jim"		BL TL																									
1947	Thomasville	GFL	28	53	3	12	2	0	0	4	0	0	9	0.226	P	2	31	1	0.971	26	6	10	4.06	133	143	82	72
DiMott, Donald "Don"		BL TL																									
1954	Thomasville	GFL	75	261	57	73	18	5	5	38	4	56	30	0.280	1B, OF	314	32	17	0.953								
Dinan, Paul		BR TR																									
1955	Dublin(24) - Statesboro(19)	GSL	43	126	24	28	9	1	3	14	3	27	25	0.222	3B	33	74	17	0.863								
DiNecci, Alfred "Al"		BR TR																									
1951	Cordele	GFL	42	149	36	32	4	2	0	9	6	24	25	0.215	2B	106	98	15	0.932								
Dingler, George		BR TR																									
1950	Cordele	GFL	84	280	28	61	11	1	0	25	2	35	32	0.218	C	326	36	19	0.950								
Dingus, William "Bill"		BR TR																									
1958	Albany	GFL	127	416	84	91	14	3	9	66	10	114	104	0.219	SS, P	227	274	57	0.898	2	1	0		<30			
Dinkelacker, Timothy "Tim"		BR TR																									
1954	Fitzgerald	GFL	36	92	12	21	2	0	0	9	0	5	23	0.228	P	8	29	2	0.949	35	16	8	3.16	231	205	150	109
DiRoberto, John		BL TR																									
1953	Tifton	GFL	20	56	15	14	2	0	0	1	1	12	7	0.250	3B	8	23	15	0.674								
1953	Eastman	GSL	93	303	67	89	16	1	2	35	8	88	55	0.294	SS, OF	136	40	11	0.941								
Dispenziere, Carmen		BR TR																									
1940	Moultrie	GFL	26	91	14	28	1	0	0	12	7	1	13	0.308	C	109	20	9	0.935								
1941	Moultrie	GFL	8	25	3	7	1	0	0	3	0	5	7	0.280	OF	17	2	0	1.000								
Dittmer, Charles		BL TL																									
1953	Dublin	GSL	106	372	56	97	16	0	9	62	2	60	48	0.261	OF, C	286	22	8	0.975								
Dittus, George																											
1942	Cordele	GFL	41	166	26	38	6	0	0	16	1	22	34	0.229	1B	377	14	9	0.978								
Dixon, ---																											
1930	Anniston	GAL	13	47	10	17	4	0	2		0	4	6	0.362	3B	14	25	6	0.867								
Dixon, Percy		BR TR																									
1940	Moultrie	GFL	<10												P									<35			
Dixon, Stokely		BR TR																									
1940	Albany	GFL	14	25	1	1	0	0	0	0	0	1	16	0.040	P					13	4	4	3.43	76	78	23	20
1941	Albany	GFL	19	50	5	12	3	2	0	12	0	3	22	0.240	P	2	13	3	0.833	19	4	6		115	129	54	43
1942	Tallahassee	GFL	29	75	7	11	1	2	0	3	1	4	31	0.147	P	7	8	1	0.938	22	10	8	3.69	127	145	43	49
Dixon, William R. "Bill"		BR TR																									
1953	Thomasville	GFL	136	450	70	104	13	4	6	74	3	104	63	0.231	C	723	59	15	0.981								
Doane, Carlton "Carl"		BR TR																									
1946	Waycross	GFL	13	29	3	6	0	0	0	5	0	3	3	0.207	P	2	18	1	0.952	13	6	2	3.89	74	78	58	17
1947	Waycross	GFL	13	10	2	3	0	0	0	1	0	2	1	0.300	P	0	11	1	0.917								

Georgia Class-D Minor League Baseball Encyclopedia

YR	TEAM	LG	G	AB	R	H	2B	3B	HR	RBI	SB	BB	SO	BA	POS	PO	A	E	FA	GP	W	L	ERA	IP	H	SO	BB
Dobberstein, Charles		BR TR																									
1955	Statesboro	GSL	21	49	5	3	0	0	0	1	0	3	20	0.061	P	8	26	6	0.850	19	10	4	4.31	119	134	72	42
1956	Moultrie	GFL	6	10		1								0.100	P					6	1	1	<45				
Dobbins, Howard																											
1929	Lindale	GAL	57	201	33	64	14	1	1		2	28	11	0.318	OF	131	6	1	0.993								
Dobbins, Ralph		BR TR																									
1948	Baxley	GSL	48	140	15	32	3	0	1	15	2	29	34	0.229	OF	61	3	5	0.928								
1949	Tifton - Vidalia-Lyons	GSL	139	507	71	111	22	2	8	86	11	81	90	0.219	OF	385	12	22	0.947								
1950	Vidalia-Lyons	GSL	136	512	64	109	15	1	11	76	2	79	125	0.213	OF	318	20	15	0.958								
Dobbins, William Mayes "Mayes"		BL TR																									
1951	Opelika(23) - Valley(14)	GAL	37	132	24	33	8	1	1	16	1	26	18	0.250	2B	79	74	12	0.927								
1950	Eastman	GSL	120	462	91	119	18	3	1	64	11	110	55	0.258	2B, SS	314	366	36	0.950								
1952	Vidalia	GSL	122	455	100	117	15	3	0	40	22	135	90	0.257	2B	326	320	34	0.950								
1953	Vidalia	GSL	105	371	90	96	11	2	2	33	18	134	42	0.259	2B	295	294	21	0.966								
1954	Vidalia	GSL	25	89	22	17	2	0	0	6	4	33	7	0.191	2B	60	62	7	0.946								
Dobbs, Gilbert "Gil"		BR TR																									
1940	Albany	GFL	29	106	8	31	2	1	2	16	0	10	11	0.292	C	130	22	8	0.950								
Dobek, John		BL TL																									
1953	Sandersville	GSL	63	210	46	56	13	1	13	53	4	66	54	0.267	1B	496	25	7	0.987								
Dobernic, John L.																											
1935	Moultrie	GFL	29	73	1	9	0	0	0		0	2	21	0.123	P					35	9	17		217	128	127	86
1936	Moultrie	GFL													P									<30			
Dobias, John E.		BL TL																									
1953	Cordele	GFL	67	269	44	79	11	10	0	36	7	26	26	0.294	OF, P	140	1	4	0.972		0	0	<45				
Dobner, Charles A.																											
1937	Albany	GFL		12	1	3			0	0	0			0.250	P	1	7	1	0.889								
Dobzanski, Robert "Bob"		BR TR																									
1955	Douglas	GSL	25	53	8	15	3	0	0	4	0	2	14	0.283	P	3	14	2	0.895	23	12	8	3.35	121	116	79	49
Dodgin, James C. "Jim"		BL TL																									
1949	Douglas	GSL	135	547	93	143	16	9	5	90	18	79	44	0.261	OF	321	12	6	0.982								
1951	Tifton	GFL	108	400	93	131	20	9	2	62	24	88	20	0.328	OF	243	9	14	0.947								
1952	Tifton(59) - Moultrie(6)	GFL	65	237	55	64	10	5	1	27	11	66	19	0.270	OF	99	7	7	0.938								
Dodson, ---																											
1928	Lindale	GAL	13	22	2	5	2	0	1		0	2	3	0.227	P	3	15	5	0.783	12	5	2	3.65	69	57	37	13
Dodson, Richard A. "Dick"		BL TR																									
1950	Jesup	GSL	24	35	2	3	2	0	0	5	0	1	8	0.086	P	2	11	2	0.867	18	5	3	5.32	71	63	47	69
1950	Waycross	GFL	14	23	2	4	0	1	0	5	1	1	1	0.174	P	1	6	2	0.778	14	3	3	7.09	47	38	19	50
Dodson, Samuel "Sam"		BL TR																									
1954	Statesboro	GSL	19	39	6	10	1	1	0	2	0	5	15	0.256	OF	14	0	0	1.000								
1956	Moultrie	GFL	8	24		4								0.167													
Doehler, Charles		BL TR																									
1953	Sandersville	GSL	31	85	18	20	1	1	0	9	0	16	16	0.235	OF	59	4	3	0.955								
Doerflinger, Eugene "Gene"		BR TR																									
1947	Alexander City	GAL	25	54	8	12	2	1	0	6	0	9	11	0.222	P	4	29	1	0.971	21	8	7	3.47	140	125	105	68
1948	Carrollton	GAL	41	88	9	16	1	0	0	6	0	14	14	0.182	P	14	35	2	0.961	37	23	11	2.13	253	180	233	123
Doherty, ---																											
1914	Waycross	GSL		180	16	31	4	1	0		9			0.172													
Doke, Ted Joe "Ted"		BR TR																									
1954	Albany	GFL	2	2		0								0.000	P					2	0	0	<45				
Doke, Thomas "Tom"		BL TL																									
1954	Vidalia	GSL	31	66	9	10	2	0	0	3	0	1	26	0.152	P	6	27	2	0.943	31	11	8	4.42	159	167	124	77
Dolan, Lonnie		BL TR																									
1953	Sandersville	GSL	3											0.000													
1955	Vidalia	GSL	38	81	6	17	1	0	0	6	3	19	24	0.210	OF	48	0	4	0.923								
Dolhrman, Paul																											
1938	Tallahassee	GFL	58	217	32	55	9	7	0	27	8	29	41	0.253	OF	111	2	10	0.919								
Doligale, John		BL TR																									
1955	Waycross(16) - Tifton(67)	GFL	83	315	48	94	8	4	6	51	5	37	59	0.298	OF	127	9	10	0.932								
Doll, Arthur James "Art" "Moose"		BR TR 6'1" 190 lbs. b. 05/07/1913 Chicago, IL d. 04/28/1978 Calumet City, IL																									
1946	Tallahassee	GFL	63	138	17	40	9	2	0	32	1	14	15	0.290	M, C, P	90	23	3	0.974	24	6	6	2.75	121	141	66	24
Dollard, Robert "Bob"																											
1941	Americus	GFL	5	9	4	3	0	0	0	0	0	2	4	0.333	P	3	2	1	0.833	5	1	1	7.04	23	28	5	24
Domalik, Joseph "Joe"		BR TR																									
1955	Cordele	GFL	4	5		1								0.200	P					4	0	0	<45				
Dominy, Clinton C. "Clint"		BR TR																									
1958	Dublin	GFL	15	10	0	0	0	0	0	1	0	3	3	0.000	P	1	3	0	1.000	15	1	3	10.50	30	43	17	25
Dommer, Charles "Chuck"		BR TR																									
1946	Americus	GFL	38	86	12	13	1	2	1	5	2	2	40	0.151	P	9	50	7	0.894	33	17	5	2.15	222	165	182	69
Donahue, Matt																											
1928	Gadsden	GAL	38	131	17	33	3	1	1		2	16	12	0.252	OF	74	0	2	0.974								

Georgia Class-D Minor League Baseball Encyclopedia

YR	TEAM	LG	G	AB	R	H	2B	3B	HR	RBI	SB	BB	SO	BA	POS	PO	A	E	FA	GP	W	L	ERA	IP	H	SO	BB
Donaldson, Earl																											
1913	Anniston	GAL	79	299	53	83					25			0.278	SS	150	214	42	0.897								
1914	Anniston	GAL	99	373	70	87					27			0.233	SS	190	283	47	0.910								
1915	Brunswick	FLAG	<10																								
1915	Anniston	GAL	56	201	30	49	8	1	2					0.244	SS	129	154	27	0.913								
1916	Rome	GAL	67	257	38	58					14			0.226	SS												
1917	Rome-Lindale	GAL	16	63	13	11	1	0	0		5			0.175	2B, SS, OF	26	51	3	0.963								
1920	Lindale	GSL													SS												
1921	Lindale	GSL													SS												
1928	Lindale	GAL	67	254	41	64	13	2	1		4	30	22	0.252	M, 2B	159	178	18	0.949								
Donaldson, George M.		BL TR																									
1950	Cordele	GFL	10	41	9	17	2	1	1	8	3	6	10	0.415	1B	73	2	3	0.962								
Donaldson, Jack																											
1913	LaGrange	GAL	78	325	54	111					22			0.342	SS	295	70	25	0.936								
1914	Opelika - LaGrange	GAL	76	299	45	48					13			0.161	OF	146	11	6	0.963								
1914	LaGrange	GAL	50	262	54	80					19			0.305	SS	120	211	27	0.925								
1915	Newnan	GAL	33	127	15	31	9	0	3					0.244	OF	32	6	0	1.000								
1915	LaGrange	GAL	58	224	20	56	3	0	0					0.250	SS	90	159	39	0.865								
Donatucci, John		BR TR																									
1958	Valdosta	GFL	25	81	15	14	2	0	1	7	0	21	20	0.173	SS	32	66	9	0.916								
Donnelly, Robert L. "Bob"		BR TR																									
1953	Cordele	GFL	22	51	5	10	1	1	0	5	2	6	16	0.196	P					9	2	5	5.26	53	69	27	30
Donofry, Donald A. "Don"		BR TR																									
1953	Cordele	GFL	126	408	50	96	13	3	0	48	8	58	74	0.235	OF, P	196	13	7	0.968		0	0		<45			
Donovan, Thomas "Tom"		BR TL																									
1957	Thomasville	GFL	2	2		1								0.500	P					2	0	0		<30			
Dorin, Henry																											
1941	Cordele	GFL	5	12	1	2	0	0	0	0	0	0	4	0.167	P	2	4	1	0.857	5	1	3	5.52	31	45	17	8
Dorough, John		BR																									
1946	Cordele	GFL	<10																								
Dorsey, Norris		BR TR																									
1956	Waycross	GFL	12	19	0	3	0	0	0	2	0	2	9	0.158	P	1	8	0	1.000	12	3	2	2.88	50	43	34	18
Dorsky, Manuel "Mike"		BR TR																									
1948	Opelika(25) - Alex City(55)	GAL	80	272	29	56	10	4	0	26	3	33	57	0.206	OF	171	6	16	0.917								
1950	Opelika	GAL	38	144	24	34	4	1	2	16	8	24	24	0.236	OF	94	2	8	0.923								
Dorwin, Rodney "Rod"		BL TL																									
1948	Moultrie	GFL	132	362	61	92	15	5	4	49	10	91	79	0.254	OF, P	185	33	27	0.890	18	7	9	4.36	97	103	52	64
1949	Waycross	GFL	77	247	56	60	6	6	3	36	6	85	55	0.243	OF, P	159	8	7	0.960	9	2	6	7.60	45	61	19	37
1949	Tifton	GSL	66	231	56	66	12	3	2	22	2	62	41	0.286	OF	136	13	11	0.931								
Dotlich, Joe																											
1936	Tallahassee	GFL	121	448	62	114	13	2	4	60	8			0.254	1B	1177	53	22	0.982								
Dotson, Eugene "Gene"		BR TR																									
1949	Moultrie	GFL	122	397	58	84	8	1	0	39	8	67	66	0.212	C	465	84	25	0.956								
1950	Cordele	GFL	15	46	8	9	0	1	1	6	1	18	10	0.196	C	101	8	1	0.991								
Dotterer, Thomas "Tom"		BR TR																									
1954	Fitzgerald	GFL	97	305	41	64	11	1	0	29	11	50	75	0.210	3B, SS	137	186	42	0.885								
Dougan, John		BR TR																									
1948	Fitzgerald(23) - Sparta(60)	GSL	83	285	30	66	14	3	4	37	7	42	84	0.232	OF	116	5	7	0.945								
Dougan, Stanley "Stan"		BR TR																									
1948	Fitzgerald(9) - Sparta(5)	GSL	14	24	2	1	1	0	0	1	0	2	5	0.042	P	3	19	1	0.957	13	4	3	3.82	66	68	22	35
Douglas, Charles William "Whammy"		BR TR 6'2" 185 lbs. b. 02/17/1935 Carrboro, NC																									
1954	Brunswick	GFL	39	102	10	18	1	0	2	8	0	6	55	0.176	P	4	49	9	0.855	37	27	6	2.06	271	195	273	116
1955	Brunswick	GFL	5	16		3								0.188	P					5	4	1	1.57	46	39	34	13
Douglas, Daniel "Dan"		BR TR																									
1956	Brunswick	GFL	18	56	6	13	3	0	1	8	0	8	11	0.232	OF	22	3	7	0.781								
1956	Dublin	GSL	70	256	49	76	15	3	8	42	0	45	44	0.297	OF	159	4	9	0.948								
Douglas, David Hal		BR TR																									
1942	Waycross	GFL	26	103	12	24	6	0	0	11	2	7	1	0.233	OF	51	5	1	0.982								
Douglas, Kenneth "Ken"		BR TL																									
1955	Albany	GFL	6	4		0								0.000	P					6	0	2		<45			
Douglas, Leroy		BL TR																									
1954	Valdosta	GFL	23	71	9	15	1	2	0	8	3	6	6	0.211	OF	32	1	8	0.805								
Dove, Patrick "Pat"		BL TR																									
1938	Thomasville	GFL	20	46	12	17	5	1	1	8	0	6	7	0.370	P	11	14	3	0.893	13	4	3	5.05	73	98	17	36
1939	Thomasville	GFL	115	403	60	107	18	1	3	42	3	28	30	0.266	UT, P	223	46	17	0.941	11	2	5	4.81	58	71	23	30
1940	Thomasville	GFL	121	448	87	141	27	7	2	55	13	15	42	0.315	P, 2B	406	210	48	0.928	20	4	4	6.11	81	113	37	37
1941	Thomasville	GFL	64	291	64	98	22	6	0	46	8	10	14	0.337	3B	88	104	31	0.861								
1946	Thomasville(62) - Cordele(49)	GFL	111	455	66	133	24	4	2	69	7	30	31	0.292	1B, 2B, 3B	461	128	40	0.936								
1951	Moultrie	GFL	34	125	9	37	4	0	1	11	0	10	4	0.296	C	139	24	6	0.964								
Dow, William "Bill"		BR TR																									
1956	Vidalia	GSL	43	148	34	35	2	7	1	20	11	36	30	0.236	2B, 3B	68	88	15	0.912								
Dowdy, ---																											
1917	Tri-Cities	GAL	16	47	8	14	4	2	0		0			0.298	SS	21	44	11	0.855								
Downs, Wilburn		BR TR																									
1946	Tallassee	GAL	22	70	5	9	2	0	0	7	0	7	13	0.129	2B	43	45	8	0.917								

Georgia Class-D Minor League Baseball Encyclopedia

YR	TEAM	LG	G	AB	R	H	2B	3B	HR	RBI	SB	BB	SO	BA	POS	PO	A	E	FA	GP	W	L	ERA	IP	H	SO	BB
Doyle, ---																											
1914	Talladega	GAL	20	71	6	13				0				0.183	1B	109	12	16	0.883								
Dozier, ---																											
1915	Americus-Gainesville	FLAG	<10												P					0							
Dragotto, Ralph		BR TR																									
1950	Valley	GAL	86	307	49	85	12	7	5	41	13	52	55	0.277	OF	130	6	15	0.901								
Drake, J. Enid		BL TR																									
1956	Thomson	GSL	41	102	18	37	9	3	4	24	0	16	17	0.363	M, OF, C	119	9	3	0.977								
Drake, Jay		BR TR																									
1950	Albany	GFL	111	355	56	88	17	4	7	61	11	41	53	0.248	OF, C	513	53	12	0.979								
Drake, John		BR TR																									
1958	Valdosta	GFL	20	38	2	5	1	0	0	3	0	2	15	0.132	P	1	16	0	1.000	17	4	7	6.03	91	86	67	90
Drane, Donald "Don"		BL TL																									
1956	Moultrie	GFL	53	86	12	22	1	4	0	12	0	8	27	0.256	P	13	35	8	0.857	31	12	9	3.30	180	166	142	71
Drapcho, Al		BR TR																									
1956	Brunswick	GFL	25	37	2	2	0	0	1	1	0	3	15	0.054	P	5	15	5	0.800	25	2	6	2.83	108	101	62	41
Draper, Lovell																											
1914	Talladega	GAL													M												
Draper, Richard "Dick"		BS TR																									
1954	Thomasville	GFL	9	4	0									0.000	P					9	0	1		<45			
1954	Vidalia	GSL	3	3	0									0.000	P					3	1	1		<45			
Dravecky, Andrew		BR TR																									
1946	Tallahassee	GFL	83	263	38	59	2	2	1	35	3	35	45	0.224	C	468	59	22	0.960								
1947	Tallahassee	GFL	100	303	60	78	13	8	2	44	7	69	52	0.257	C	555	50	20	0.968								
1948	Tallahassee	GFL	117	372	62	102	9	3	1	53	4	94	35	0.274	C	587	76	21	0.969								
Dreisbach, Edward "Ed"		BR TR																									
1956	Albany	GFL	25	85	6	19	2	0	1	15	0	7	14	0.224	3B	18	30	8	0.857								
Drew, J. Richard "Dick"		BR TR																									
1952	Fitzgerald	GSL	14	17	2	0	0	0	0	2	0	3	11	0.000	P	1	3	2	0.667								
Drewiske, Roger		BR TR																									
1955	Vidalia	GSL	33	54	5	5	0	0	0	2	0	2	14	0.093	P	6	34	3	0.930	32	11	8	3.73	169	149	129	111
Drews, Roy		BR TR																									
1951	Griffin	GAL	107	416	82	132	20	5	12	99	12	56	24	0.317	OF, C	447	29	28	0.944								
Driggers, Robert "Bobby"		BL TR																									
1953	Vidalia	GSL	82	328	60	102	16	7	8	64	12	36	58	0.311	OF, C	291	12	15	0.953								
1954	Vidalia	GSL	122	502	90	169	45	6	16	105	9	60	65	0.337	1B, OF, C	319	21	17	0.952								
1955	Vidalia	GSL	84	315	60	101	23	3	13	74	15	38	30	0.321	OF	207	7	10	0.955								
1956	Dublin	GSL	12	37	6	8	1	0	0	6	1	14	2	0.216	OF	19	2	0	1.000								
Driscoll, ---																											
1920	Lindale	GSL													OF												
1921	Lindale	GSL													OF												
Driscoll, James Bernard "Jim"		BL TR 5'11" 175 lbs. b. 05/14/1944 Medford, MA																									
1962	Dublin	GFL	48	120	29	33	6	1	3	21	6	24	39	0.275	3B	17	45	17	0.785								
Driskell, Roy		BR TR																									
1947	Alexander City	GAL	36	130	10	24	1	0	1	12	2	8	40	0.185	OF	78	2	7	0.920								
Drostie, Carroll		BR TR																									
1954	Fitzgerald	GFL	13	23	1	4	0	0	0	2	0	5	15	0.174	P	3	12	0	1.000	13	4	6	5.16	61	65	35	40
1955	Moultrie	GFL	8												P					8	2	2		<45			
Drotar, Joseph "Joe"		BR TR																									
1955	Brunswick	GFL	15	36	6	10	1	0	0	3	0	3	8	0.278	P	4	17	0	1.000	15	7	5	4.03	96	93	83	50
Druga, Thomas "Tom"		BL TL																									
1950	Tifton	GSL	133	484	75	114	22	2	3	53	7	83	72	0.236	1B	1138	56	29	0.976								
Duay, Theodore "Ted"																											
1935	Tallahassee	GFL	55	188	23	50	8	1	1		0	17	9	0.266	C	319	35	14	0.962								
Dubbs, Clayton		BR TR																									
1949	Americus	GFL	16	49	3	10	2	0	0	5	1	9	11	0.204	3B	18	18	9	0.800								
Duberstein, Edward "Ed"																											
1935	Moultrie	GFL	57	199	31	52	10	4	2		3	36	28	0.261	IF	540	36	16	0.973								
1936	Moultrie	GFL	102	359	42	109	14	7	4	53	5			0.304	1B	900	38	17	0.982								
Duby, Robert W. "Bob"		BL TL																									
1953	Albany	GFL	4											0.000	P					0	0			<45			
Duckworth, James Raymond "Jim"		BR TR 6'4" 194 lbs. b. 05/24/1939 National City, CA																									
1958	Thomasville	GFL	15	18	0	3	1	0	0	2	0	0	9	0.167	P	1	5	0	1.000	15	2	5	6.00	45	43	47	47
Duda, John		BL TL																									
1942	Albany	GFL	18	46	9	10	3	0	1	4	0	3	12	0.217	P, OF	4	24	2	0.933	15	5	7	4.50	108	105	74	83
1946	Albany	GFL	13	21	4	6	1	0	0	3	0	4	8	0.286	P					9	1	1	0.00	28	46	9	17
Dudas, Albert "Al"																											
1941	Albany	GFL	15	62	13	16	2	3	0	13	1	7	7	0.258	OF	29	1	2	0.938								
Dudley, ---																											
1906	Albany - Americus	GSL													OF, 1B												
Dudley, John H.		BR TR																									
1953	Cordele	GFL	97	374	54	77	5	1	0	21	12	38	57	0.206	3B, SS	145	149	36	0.891								

Georgia Class-D Minor League Baseball Encyclopedia

YR	TEAM	LG	G	AB	R	H	2B	3B	HR	RBI	SB	BB	SO	BA	POS	PO	A	E	FA	GP	W	L	ERA	IP	H	SO	BB
Dudley, Martin																											
1913	Thomasville	ESL	76	278	33	70	9	1	3					0.252	M, C	538	66	10	0.984								
1914	Thomasville	GSL		374	44	82	12	2	2		3			0.219	M												
1917	Tri-Cities	GAL	15	52	3	11	0	0	0		0			0.212	M, C	88	7	2	0.979								
Duenas, Jose		BR TR																									
1954	Vidalia	GSL	105	425	84	142	27	7	4	77	7	53	21	0.334	SS	175	265	46	0.905								
Duff, ---																											
1928	Lindale	GAL	12	43	2	8	0	0	0		0	0	10	0.186	OF	22	0	2	0.917								
Duff, Arthur "Art"																											
1941	Albany	GFL	123	466	95	122	28	7	11	80	6	75	91	0.262	OF	256	13	15	0.947								
Duffalo, James Francis "Jim"		BR TR 6'1" 175 lbs. b. 11/25/1935 Helvetia, PA																									
1955	Brunswick	GFL	38	94	2	17	4	1	0	8	0	2	13	0.181	P	11	42	3	0.946	29	17	4	2.64	201	178	124	67
Duffy, Joseph "Joe"		BR TR																									
1956	Thomson	GSL	28	76	3	8	2	0	0	8	0	14	26	0.105	OF	35	0	2	0.946								
Dugan, ---																											
1920	Carrollton	GSL	<10												P												
Dugan, Joseph "Joe"		BR TR																									
1956	Albany	GFL	67	230	51	58	5	3	3	30	9	44	56	0.252	OF	87	4	6	0.938								
Dugger, Charles		BR TR																									
1950	Cordele	GFL	27	87	6	15	4	0	0	11	0	11	41	0.172	2B	16	23	4	0.907								
Duke, Willard "Willie"		BR																									
1948	Tallassee	GAL	10	26	0	5	0	0	0	0	0	1	6	0.192													
Duke, William "Bill"		BR																									
1954	Statesboro	GSL	5	11		0								0.000													
Dukovich, ---																											
1942	Moultrie	GFL	11												P					11	1	5	6.64	42	36	19	43
Dulancy, C.A. Jr.																											
1942	Tallahassee	GFL	13	41	1	5	0	0	0	3	0	9	16	0.122	OF	15	3	2	0.900								
Dulick, Pete																											
1939	Moultrie	GFL	12	12	0	2	0	0	0	3	0	0	0	0.167	P	2	2	0	1.000				<45				
Dull, Robert "Bob"		BL																									
1946	Thomasville	GFL	<10																								
Dumas, ---																											
1921	Cedartown	GSL													SS												
Dumas, Otto B.																											
1928	Carrollton	GAL	20	84	7	25	9	0	1		2	4	10	0.298	OF	27	3	3	0.909								
Duncan, Charles		BR TR																									
1948	Tallassee	GAL	23	35	3	5	0	0	0	3	0	3	10	0.143	P	1	23	1	0.960	20	4	12	4.03	105	97	45	70
Duncan, Frank																											
1941	Americus	GFL	24	52	3	7	1	0	0	2	0	5	25	0.135	P	14	16	9	0.769	18	2	8	4.88	94	94	37	67
Duncan, Fred		BR TR																									
1956	Moultrie	GFL	14	15	2	0	0	0	0	0	0	0	11	0.000	P	5	7	1	0.923	14	1	6	2.77	52	43	30	30
Duncan, Higgins		BR TR																									
1950	Douglas	GSL	42	96	5	12	1	1	0	3	0	6	37	0.125	P	8	46	3	0.947	39	19	12	3.13	267	217	133	96
Duncan, James "Jim"		BL																									
1955	Tifton	GFL	3	6		2								0.333													
Duncan, John W.		BS TR																									
1946	Tallassee	GAL	11	21	1	4	0	0	0	4	0	3	3	0.190	P	6	11	9	0.654	11	2	5	6.47	57	75	21	20
1951	Fitzgerald	GSL													M												
Duncan, Lindon		BL TR																									
1955	Hazlehurst-Baxley	GSL	108	407	67	127	17	5	6	62	16	43	44	0.312	2B, SS, OF	256	209	52	0.899								
Duncan, Richard L. "Dick"		BR TR																									
1952	Brunswick	GFL	24	92	15	18	0	0	0	5	7	10	15	0.196	OF	42	0	1	0.977								
Duncan, Robert T. "Bob"		BR TR																									
1957	Valdosta	GFL	32	90	6	18	3	0	2	16	1	11	35	0.200	OF	47	0	1	0.979								
Duncan, Troy		BR																									
1946	LaGrange	GAL	<10																								
Dundee, Patrick "Pat"		BR TR																									
1952	Hazlehurst-Baxley	GSL	23	71	7	14	1	0	0	9	4	18	5	0.197	3B	26	34	9	0.870								
Dunham, ---																											
1915	Thomasville	FLAG				0								0.000													
Dunlap, Donald "Don"		BL TL																									
1955	Douglas	GSL	2	0										0.000	P					2	0	0					
Dunlap, Robert "Bob"		BR TR																									
1953	Sandersville	GSL	3											0.500	P					2	1		<45				
Dunlevy, Harry		BR TR																									
1940	Moultrie	GFL	16	23	4	5	2	0	0	3	0	1	7	0.217	P					14	1	4	5.67	54	75	25	28
Dunn, Donald "Don"		BR TR																									
1955	Thomasville	GFL	21	62	8	9	0	1	0	2	1	10	16	0.145	2B	28	35	5	0.926								
Dunn, Edward G. "Ed"		BL TL																									
1942	Valdosta	GFL	7												P					7	2	4	2.80	45	44	19	27
1948	Newnan	GAL	8												P					8	2	4	3.96	50	50	42	33
1950	Jesup	GSL	25	40	4	6	0	0	0	3	0	9	17	0.150	P	6	13	1	0.950	25	5	10	5.81	113	120	82	91
Dunn, J.C.		BR TR																									
1955	Albany	GFL	138	514	109	154	28	9	17	125	48	71	54	0.300	M, 1B, OF, P	582	42	19	0.970	2	0	0	<45				

Georgia Class-D Minor League Baseball Encyclopedia

YR	TEAM	LG	G	AB	R	H	2B	3B	HR	RBI	SB	BB	SO	BA	POS	PO	A	E	FA	GP	W	L	ERA	IP	H	SO	BB
Dunning, Guy H.																											
1915	Americus-Gainesville	FLAG	74	316	58	100	14	5	1	21				0.316	OF	167	7	9	0.951								
Dupon, Barton "Bart"		BL TL																									
1956	Valdosta	GFL	133	500	83	148	29	7	17	98	5	86	68	0.296	OF	221	15	21	0.918								
Duran, Julio		BR TR																									
1956	Douglas	GSL	116	427	94	120	20	1	0	33	32	72	32	0.281	2B	306	341	36	0.947								
Durant, Donald "Don"		BR TR																									
1954	Hazlehurst-Baxley	GSL	2	3	0									0.000	P					2	0	0		<45			
Duren, James "Jim"		BR TR																									
1958	Waycross	GFL	5	7		2								0.286	P					5	0	3		<30			
Durham, J.C.																											
1920	Cedartown	GSL																									
Durheim, Harry																											
1937	Tallahassee	GFL													P						1	2		26	38	7	13
Durkin, James "Jim"		BR TR																									
1950	LaGrange	GAL	53	181	31	47	7	1	3	23	2	20	23	0.260	C	277	29	18	0.944								
Durley, George																											
1913	Thomasville	ESL													M												
Dusak, Ervin Frank "Erv"		BR TR 6'2" 185 lbs. b. 07/29/1920 Chicago, IL d. 11/06/1994 Glendale Heights, IL																									
1939	Albany	GFL	134	508	85	157	29	7	1	78	11	57	45	0.309	OF	274	27	10	0.968								
1940	Albany	GFL	141	544	125	182	37	13	6	98	9	84	57	0.335	OF, P	305	28	12	0.965					<35			
Dustal, Robert Andrew "Bob"		BR TR 6'0" 172 lbs. b. 09/28/1935 Sayreville, NJ																									
1956	Valdosta	GFL	51	85	8	11	1	0	0	2	0	9	30	0.129	P	14	48	4	0.939	47	18	7	2.21	248	199	150	89
Dutton, Charles		BL																									
1954	Albany	GFL	8	10		0								0.000													
Dutton, Dean		BL TR																									
1957	Brunswick	GFL	140	519	98	131	10	5	2	33	12	128	61	0.252	OF	241	26	17	0.940								
Duval, ---																											
1921	Griffin	GSL													OF												
Duval, Joe		BR																									
1954	Waycross	GFL	9	10		1								0.100													
Duzyk, Robert "Bob"		BL TL																									
1955	Brunswick	GFL	38	115	16	38	7	0	2	22	1	14	26	0.330	OF	46	2	6	0.889								
Dvorak, Ray		BR TR																									
1940	Albany	GFL	13	42	8	10	1	0	0	3	2	8	6	0.238	2B	15	31	3	0.939								
Dworaczyk, Anthony		BR TR																									
1956	Brunswick	GFL	7	19		1								0.053													
1956	Dublin	GSL	50	173	21	33	9	0	5	26	0	30	66	0.191	C	262	25	8	0.973								
Dwyer, John		BR																									
1955	Hazlehurst-Baxley	GSL	11	21	1	4	0	0	0	0	1	1	8	0.190													
Dwyer, William "Bill"		BR TR																									
1946	Waycross	GFL	124	508	87	139	12	5	1	43	24	60	49	0.274	2B	310	338	45	0.935								
1947	Waycross	GFL	119	480	104	134	14	6	0	53	30	69	33	0.279	1B, 2B, SS, OF	518	98	34	0.948								
Dye, Benjamin "Ben"		BL TR																									
1951	Americus	GFL	107	369	62	88	11	9	0	42	4	72	66	0.238	SS, OF, C	198	67	22	0.923								
Dye, Clifford "Cliff"		BR TR																									
1956	Vidalia	GSL	8	7		0								0.000	P					8	0	1					
Dye, Hoyle		BR																									
1946	Newnan	GAL	<10																								
Dyer, Leroy		BR TL																									
1958	Waycross	GFL	32	54	4	10	2	0	0	2	0	8	12	0.185	P	9	22	6	0.838	30	6	11	5.62	149	148	110	106
Dyer, Penhallow		BL																									
1958	Thomasville	GFL	3	7		1								0.143													
Dyer, Vaughn		BL TL																									
1953	Statesboro	GSL	100	384	75	136	22	6	4	78	14	47	12	0.354	1B	874	58	11	0.988								
1955	Statesboro	GSL	44	170	27	55	5	2	2	29	2	21	13	0.324	1B	326	25	7	0.980								
Dykes, Charles "Charlie"		BR TR																									
1946	Americus	GFL	123	457	93	120	16	9	3	57	23	68	79	0.263	2B	282	308	70	0.894								
Dykstra, Leonard		BR TR																									
1957	Brunswick	GFL	41	70	7	8	0	0	0	2	0	9	35	0.114	P	8	31	1	0.975	39	9	10	3.66	204	229	114	101
Dyser, Bill		BL TL																									
1948	LaGrange	GAL	8												P					8	4	0	4.50	48	59	28	18
Dziedzic, Walter "Walt"		BR																									
1951	Valdosta	GFL	12	29	4	5	1	1	0	10	0	7	6	0.172													
Eames, Paul		BL TR																									
1950	Albany	GFL	97	276	45	70	8	1	7	55	8	63	19	0.254	OF, C	450	68	9	0.983								
1951	Albany	GFL	37	130	16	30	5	0	1	17	2	13	25	0.231	C	128	31	3	0.981								
1952	Thomasville	GFL	133	467	76	148	22	7	12	83	6	88	31	0.317	C	535	107	24	0.964								
1954	Waycross	GFL	134	442	64	119	24	1	3	60	6	86	30	0.269	M, C, P	790	100	21	0.977	10	0	1		<45			
1955	Tifton	GFL	135	495	69	143	23	0	5	62	13	66	27	0.289	M, 3B, C, P	736	129	19	0.979	7	0	1		<45			
Earl, Leslie "Les"		BR TR																									
1950	Moultrie	GFL	23	70	15	17	3	1	1	10	2	9	13	0.243	C	87	17	5	0.954								
Earley, Jerry		BR TR																									
1952	Albany	GFL	11	44	4	9	2	0	0	2	0	8	10	0.205	1B	102	7	8	0.932								

Georgia Class-D Minor League Baseball Encyclopedia

YR	TEAM	LG	G	AB	R	H	2B	3B	HR	RBI	SB	BB	SO	BA	POS	PO	A	E	FA	GP	W	L	ERA	IP	H	SO	BB
Early, ---																											
1928	Lindale	GAL	79	307	50	92	19	2	10		3	7	13	0.300	OF, C	236	31	17	0.940								
Earp, Whitfield																											
1921	Lindale	GSL													C												
East, Carlton William "Carl"		BL TR 6'2" 178 lbs. b. 08/27/1894 Marietta, GA d. 01/15/1953 Whitesburgh, GA																									
1914	Thomasville	GSL		61	10	17	4	2	2			0		0.279													
1930	Carrollton	GAL	64	226	60	98	23	2	16		1	60	7	0.434	M, OF	85	7	2	0.979								
1947	LaGrange	GAL													M												
East, Gordon Hugh "Hugh"		BR TR 6'2" 185 lbs. b. 07/07/1919 Birmingham, AL d. 11/02/1981 Charleston, SC																									
1948	Tallassee	GAL													M												
Easterling, Eugene "Gene"		BL TR																									
1951	Douglas	GSL	34	71	4	12	3	0	0	3	0	0	15	0.169	P	9	29	2	0.950	25	5	13	4.75	142	130	116	123
Easterling, Paul		BR TR 5'11" 180 lbs. b. 09/28/1905 Reidsville, GA d. 03/15/1993 Reidsville, GA																									
1951	Hazlehurst-Baxley	GSL	32	124	20	35	6	0	3	24	5	21	9	0.282	OF	44	3	0	1.000								
Eaton, Gerald		BR TR																									
1955	Valdosta	GFL	6	7		1								0.143	P					6	1	1		<45			
Eaton, Joe																											
1941	Tallahassee	GFL	132	501	55	127	11	9	2	53	7	37	100	0.253	1B	1140	72	25	0.980								
Eaton, Richard "Dick"		BL TL																									
1949	Thomasville	GFL	108	393	67	101	23	8	11	45	14	58	90	0.257	1B	867	64	38	0.961								
Ebel, Walter "Wally"																											
1936	Tallahassee	GFL	122	473	94	139	22	8	2	58	13			0.294	OF	318	51	13	0.966								
1937	Tallahassee	GFL	48	178	23	42	9	4	0	13	2	31	35	0.236	2B	115	107	14	0.941								
Ebetino, John		BR TR																									
1949	Griffin	GAL	37	47	5	6	0	0	0	4	0	11	12	0.128	P	7	36	3	0.935	37	5	11	4.47	157	186	80	65
1950	Griffin	GAL	40	95	16	25	5	0	0	11	1	10	10	0.263	P	12	32	2	0.957	29	9	4	3.93	135	145	71	32
Ebker, Robert "Bob"		BR TR																									
1958	Albany	GFL	2	2		0								0.000	P					2	0	0		<30			
Eckenroth, Leroy																											
1942	Tallahassee	GFL	21	69	10	14	0	0	0	4	0	16	16	0.203	3B	35	52	9	0.906								
Eckenroth, Willard "Bill"		BR TR																									
1940	Cordele	GFL	<10												P									<35			
Ecklund, William "Bill"		BL TL																									
1948	Baxley	GSL	10	20	2	2	0	0	0	1	0	4	9	0.100	P	6	7	1	0.929	10	4	4	2.91	65	64	43	39
Eckman, Ned		BR TR																									
1954	Hazlehurst-Baxley	GSL	100	420	47	112	15	3	0	36	5	26	45	0.267	2B	215	267	38	0.927								
Edelstein, Jacob		BR TR																									
1952	Valdosta	GFL	140	514	82	136	15	3	0	55	12	91	56	0.265	1B	1210	62	22	0.983								
Edge, Harvey		BR TR																									
1948	Valley	GAL	22	14	3	3	1	0	0	0	0	5	4	0.214	P	2	12	1	0.933	20	2	5	4.68	50	61	30	23
1949	Valley	GAL	37	51	5	6	0	0	0	5	0	4	13	0.118	P	11	36	3	0.940	31	6	10	3.87	114	140	60	58
Edge, Roy		BR																									
1946	Thomasville	GFL	<10																								
Edgley, Joseph "Joe"		BR TR																									
1955	Waycross	GFL	77	262	53	68	9	2	7	37	11	56	50	0.260	SS	133	219	50	0.876								
Edmondson, Lee		BR TR																									
1946	LaGrange	GAL	<10																								
1948	Valley	GAL	19	53	10	10	2	1	0	4	0	3	8	0.189	C	71	10	4	0.953								
Edmondson, W.C.																											
1914	Newnan	GAL	74	259	29	59				4				0.228	3B	169	114	22	0.928								
1915	Newnan	GAL	25	82	14	14	4	0	3					0.171	3B	32	56	5	0.946								
Edwards, Donald K. "Don"		BR TR																									
1955	Dublin	GSL	4	0										0.000	P					4	0	0					
1954	Albany	GFL	45	96	7	18	6	0	1	5	0	11	41	0.188	OF	49	1	5	0.909								
1954	Hazlehurst-Baxley	GSL	11	36	3	4	1	0	0	0	0	4	18	0.111	OF	17	0	1	0.944								
Edwards, Elmer		BR TR																									
1946	Americus(15) - Cordele(105)	GFL	120	482	66	114	20	4	2	50	10	33	82	0.237	3B, OF	158	37	19	0.911								
Edwards, Hoyt		BR TR																									
1948	Newnan(6) - Carrollton(22)	GAL	28	33	1	3	0	0	0	2	0	4	11	0.091	P	6	22	3	0.903	27	8	6	4.34	110	120	50	49
Edwards, Malcolm "Mac"																											
1935	Americus	GFL	8	25	3	4	1	1	0		0	1	6	0.160	P					9	4	3		55	46	25	12
1936	Americus	GFL	30	51	5	8	1	0	0	5	0			0.157	P					30	8	9	4.17	151		53	76
Edwards, Raymond "Ray"		BR TR																									
1947	Tallassee	GAL	125	490	75	134	26	5	5	70	16	54	52	0.273	3B, OF	208	160	16	0.958								
1948	Tallassee	GAL	78	353	64	90	14	3	2	62	24	61	58	0.255	3B	118	200	27	0.922								
1949	Alexander City	GAL	117	376	59	79	14	1	4	45	13	70	54	0.210	3B	160	210	25	0.937								
Edwards, Robert Earl "Bob"		BL TR																									
1947	Valley	GAL	116	476	101	145	19	10	2	48	35	50	65	0.305	OF, P	293	20	21	0.937								
1948	Valley	GAL	125	489	114	156	31	16	5	52	67	65	53	0.319	OF	350	11	14	0.963								
Ehnninger, Robert "Bob"		BR TR																									
1955	Cordele	GFL	1	0										0.000	P					1	0	0		<45			
Eidson, Lewis		BL TL																									
1947	Newnan	GAL	18	44	4	5	0	0	0	3	1	1	9	0.114	P	4	22	1	0.963	17	10	4	2.92	117	97	59	32
Eilbacher, Leo		BL TL																									
1954	Americus-Cordele	GFL	92	378	52	102	9	4	2	32	5	57	62	0.270	OF	219	13	14	0.943								

Georgia Class-D Minor League Baseball Encyclopedia

YR	TEAM	LG	G	AB	R	H	2B	3B	HR	RBI	SB	BB	SO	BA	POS	PO	A	E	FA	GP	W	L	ERA	IP	H	SO	BB
Eilstrop, ---		BR TR																									
1947	Americus	GFL	30												OF	33	6	3	0.929								
Eiselstein, William "Bill"		BR TR																									
1963	Waycross	GFL	64	208	24	57	11	4	0	22	3	41	55	0.274	2B, 3B, SS	71	149	30	0.880								
Elder, Eugene "Gene"		BR TR																									
1954	Thomasville	GFL	116	413	58	108	25	4	3	52	8	53	46	0.262	2B, OF	239	263	37	0.931								
Eldrid, Henry																											
1906	Albany	GSL													2B												
Elenchin, John		BR TR																									
1946	Cordele	GFL	97	330	44	84	10	2	0	32	4	46	61	0.255	OF, P	139	24	5	0.970	12	1	1	5.60	45	61	18	32
Elias, Jack		BR TR																									
1955	Sandersville	GSL	96	382	96	127	21	5	12	70	31	52	56	0.332	SS, P	146	237	36	0.914	1	0	0					
Elkins, Bobby U.		BL TR																									
1953	Thomasville	GFL	82	290	45	73	14	5	3	42	2	48	46	0.252	3B	87	152	28	0.895								
Ellington, ---																											
1920	Griffin	GSL													P												
Ellington, Paul		BR																									
1946	Valley	GAL	<10																								
Elliott, Albert W. "Buck"		BR TR																									
1940	Moultrie	GFL	50	195	30	51	8	1	0	15	0	30	33	0.262	SS	89	138	34	0.870								
Elliott, Arthur J. "Art"		BR TR																									
1953	Albany	GFL	4											1.000	P					0	0		<45				
1953	Statesboro	GSL	38	57	3	9	1	0	0	4	0	5	13	0.158	P	6	32	2	0.950	29	6	12	5.49	141	140	66	86
1954	Albany	GFL	5	3	0									0.000	P					4	0	3		<45			
1954	Hazlehurst-Baxley	GSL	2	4	0									0.000	P					2	0	1		<45			
Ellis, ---																											
1914	Americus	GSL		325	41	103	22	8	15		3			0.317													
Ellis, ---																											
1917	Talladega	GAL	16	62	6	19	4	1	2		3			0.306	OF	30	2	4	0.889								
Ellis, ---																											
1921	Cedartown	GSL													2B												
Ellis, George		BL TR																									
1950	Opelika	GAL	11	13	3	2	0	0	0	1	0	3	6	0.154	P	0	2	0	1.000								
Ellis, Gerhart		BR TR																									
1948	Griffin	GAL	13	21	3	2	0	0	0	2	0	4	6	0.095	P	3	11	1	0.933	13	2	5	3.09	64	57	40	41
Ellis, Jerry		BR TR																									
1963	Moultrie	GFL	59	168	12	23	8	0	0	8	2	12	31	0.137	2B	79	86	7	0.959								
Ellis, Ralph		BL TR																									
1940	Thomasville	GFL	125	551	115	203	35	16	5	82	25	29	46	0.368	OF	212	7	6	0.973								
Ellis, Roy		BR TR																									
1951	Waycross	GFL	14	14	0	0	0	0	0	0	0	1	1	0.000	P	2	13	7	0.682	13	1	6	4.98	47	42	18	36
1952	Waycross	GFL	15	13	4	0	0	0	0	0	0	4	2	0.000	P	1	10	2	0.846	14	3	4	6.26	46	44	38	27
1955	Waycross	GFL	18	10	2	1	0	0	0	0	0	4	6	0.100	P	1	5	0	1.000	18	3	3	<45				
Ellison, Lee		BR TR																									
1947	Alexander City	GAL	19	33	1	7	2	0	0	2	0	2	10	0.212	P	5	22	3	0.900	18	2	10	5.57	84	108	37	26
Ello, James "Jim"		BR TR																									
1947	Carrollton(3) - Griffin(86)	GAL	89	281	26	63	11	2	1	30	5	20	47	0.224	C	378	56	14	0.969								
1948	Griffin(57) - Alex City(46)	GAL	103	354	29	104	7	1	1	35	6	27	40	0.294	C	455	79	18	0.967								
1949	Alexander City	GAL	115	371	41	85	3	2	1	34	12	29	27	0.229	C	464	60	11	0.979								
Elmore, Verdo Wilson "Ellie"		BL TR 5'11" 185 lbs. b. 12/10/1899 Gordo, AL d. 08/05/1969 Birmingham, AL																									
1929	Anniston	GAL	52	169	28	61	5	4	4		0	8	5	0.361	M, 1B	303	9	10	0.969								
Elmstrom, Carl		BR TR																									
1963	Waycross	GFL	43	28	6	2	0	0	0	2	0	13	7	0.071	P	8	16	2	0.923	43	9	7	1.66	125	87	138	65
Elrod, ---																											
1913	Thomasville - Valdosta	ESL	10												P					10	5	5					
1915	Americus-Gainesville	FLAG													P					0							
Elston, Richard A. "Dick"		BR TR																									
1935	Albany	GFL	13	38	3	6	0	0	0		0	1	10	0.158	P					14	7	2		91	69	79	27
Embler, Jack		BR TR																									
1940	Waycross	GFL	40	101	6	20	1	0	0	12	0	5	17	0.198	P					40	18	9	3.11	252	262	94	71
Embry, Harry		0																									
1936	Moultrie	GFL	21	70	7	15	2	0	1	5	1			0.214	OF	40	2	4	0.913								
Embry, Joel		BR TR																									
1948	Valley	GAL	27	53	6	12	0	0	0	3	1	7	19	0.226	P	6	29	1	0.972	25	8	6	3.24	136	128	60	72
Emmert, Richard "Dick"		BR TR																									
1963	Waycross	GFL	82	286	37	77	8	6	1	29	4	41	61	0.269	SS	119	168	37	0.886								
Endicott, William Franklin "Bill"		BL TL 5'11" 175 lbs. b. 09/04/1918 Acorn, MO																									
1937	Albany	GFL	102	441	64	131	15	2	1	26	12	29	25	0.297	OF	184	8	8	0.960								
1938	Albany	GFL	108	441	96	156	28	4	0	62	40	46	18	0.354	OF	244	8	5	0.981								
Engel, Albert "Al"		BL TL																									
1954	Statesboro	GSL	129	501	91	156	31	5	4	34	10	66	79	0.311	OF	309	10	18	0.947								
1955	Waycross	GFL	133	518	78	136	25	3	1	35	13	82	54	0.263	OF	306	9	7	0.978								
Engel, Raymond "Ray"		BL TR																									
1955	Waycross	GFL	125	400	44	86	20	0	5	63	6	76	75	0.215	C	750	111	20	0.977								
1956	Waycross	GFL	133	458	73	127	22	1	11	73	3	74	56	0.277	C	882	78	21	0.979								

Georgia Class-D Minor League Baseball Encyclopedia

YR	TEAM	LG	G	AB	R	H	2B	3B	HR	RBI	SB	BB	SO	BA	POS	PO	A	E	FA	GP	W	L	ERA	IP	H	SO	BB
England, James R. "Jim"		BL TR																									
1953	Valdosta	GFL	40	133	19	30	3	0	0	18	0	16	11	0.226	2B, P	95	95	18	0.913	0	0	0	<45				
Engle, Robert "Bob"		BR TR																									
1948	Thomasville	GFL	59	129	17	32	5	2	0	19	2	34	13	0.248	M, OF	25	7	2	0.941								
Englehart, William "Bill"		BL TL																									
1955	Tifton	GFL	71	146	22	38	6	0	1	10	2	22	32	0.260	OF, P	46	34	4	0.952	33	16	9	3.18	212	158	196	155
Engler, John		BR TR																									
1956	Vidalia	GSL	120	443	72	113	13	3	7	68	5	55	63	0.255	OF	216	9	12	0.949								
English, Edgar																											
1941	Thomasville	GFL	14	27	4	3	1	0	0	1	0	4	12	0.111	P	5	8	2	0.867	14	3	3	5.01	70	77	33	35
Ennis, ---																											
1920	Lindale	GSL													2B												
Ennis, Emory		BL TR																									
1956	Sandersville	GSL	47	138	16	31	6	0	0	12	4	22	30	0.225	OF	67	1	3	0.958								
Enos, William "Bill"		BL TL																									
1950	Hazlehurst-Baxley	GSL	134	536	44	155	23	3	1	87	2	44	9	0.289	M, 1B	1128	69	17	0.986								
Enquist, Richard "Ernest"		BR TR																									
1953	Jesup	GSL	44	165	22	44	8	2	1	25	1	28	16	0.267	3B, SS	43	71	9	0.927								
Ensley, Leon "Jim"		BL TR																									
1952	Waycross	GFL	75	147	15	42	6	1	0	23	2	22	15	0.286	P	12	67	2	0.975	35	18	9	2.36	259	212	126	88
Epps, George		BL TR																									
1947	Americus	GFL	17	63	5	17	0	0	0	6	0	1	11	0.270	OF	17	0	2	0.895								
Erickson, Dale		BR TR																									
1963	Brunswick	GFL	4	5	0	0	0	0	0	0	0	0	3	0.000	P					4	2	2	1.71	21	14	19	11
Erickson, Marlin		BR TR																									
1955	Thomasville	GFL	10	5	1	2	0	0	0	2	0	1	2	0.400	P	0	5	1	0.833	10	1	1	<45				
1956	Thomasville	GFL	14	12	2	1	0	0	0	0	0	3	4	0.083	P					9	0	3	<45				
Ermisch, Howard		BR TR																									
1947	LaGrange	GAL	62	237	35	65	8	1	0	12	9	18	6	0.274	M, 3B, SS	125	144	25	0.915								
Ery, Ed W.																											
1913	Opelika	GAL		231	31	66					5			0.286	M, OF, P	138	48	8	0.959	24	19	5					
1914	Opelika	GAL	53	177	21	45					2			0.254	P	52	49	6	0.944	53							
1915	Valdosta	FLAG	51	154	10	26	5	0	1		4			0.169	OF, P	37	54	8	0.919	24	13	8		203	160	87	24
Eskridge, James "Jim"		BR TR																									
1946	Waycross	GFL	24	85	21	16	6	0	0	9	1	18	35	0.188	SS	42	55	19	0.836								
Esposito, Anthony		BL TL																									
1950	Vidalia-Lyons	GSL	136	479	72	124	20	3	4	48	4	68	58	0.259	1B, OF	1100	51	31	0.974								
Esser, William Clark "Bill"																											
1937	Albany	GFL	97	341	41	74	12	3	4	37	4	50	57	0.217	OF	145	15	4	0.976								
Estep, Virgil		BR TR																									
1954	Valdosta	GFL	54	197	18	56	12	3	7	34	0	9	56	0.284	C	311	47	16	0.957								
Etchison, Clarence Hampton "Buck"		BL TL 6'1" 190 lbs. b. 01/27/1915 Baltimore, MD d. 01/24/1980 East New Market, MD																									
1949	Griffin	GAL	44	169	33	46	14	0	2	25	4	26	4	0.272	M, 1B	357	25	4	0.990								
Eubanks, ---																											
1913	Cordele	ESL	91	308	46	87	17	1	3					0.282	C	648	96	14	0.982								
1914	Cordele	GSL		350	48	108	12	6	3		10			0.309													
Euliss, Wallis M. Jr. "Walt"		BR TR																									
1942	Americus	GFL	5	6	0	1	0	0	0	0	0	2	4	0.167	P	0	5	1	0.833	6	0	4	9.00	22	27	20	27
1946	Waycross	GFL	2												P					2	0	0	0.00	5			
Eure, Carlton																											
1941	Tallahassee	GFL	130	502	68	135	17	10	1	77	12	53	62	0.269	OF, P	184	19	18	0.919	9	0	0	4.22	32	34	20	34
Eury, Glenn		BR TR																									
1951	Moultrie	GFL	111	462	66	118	20	0	29	86	2	32	145	0.255	OF	217	16	16	0.936								
Eustice, Willard "Willis"		BL TL																									
1948	Valley	GAL	44	99	9	28	5	0	1	9	1	6	18	0.283	P	5	23	3	0.903	29	10	8	3.76	153	163	120	74
Evans, Dean T.																											
1936	Americus	GFL	55	235	38	70	11	3	0	23	9			0.298	2B	97	78	20	0.897								
1938	Cordele	GFL	111	439	75	138	14	8	4	66	18	52	63	0.314	OF	280	14	21	0.933								
1939	Waycross	GFL	107	404	67	109	15	9	1	61	22	48	48	0.270	OF	273	10	7	0.976								
Evans, Frank		BL TR																									
1949	Americus	GFL	38	133	20	32	2	1	2	11	0	20	26	0.241	3B	34	81	31	0.788								
Evans, James A. "Jim"		BL TR																									
1953	Valdosta	GFL	132	464	68	117	11	3	0	57	7	97	62	0.252	2B, 3B	261	320	35	0.943								
Evans, Millard		BR TR																									
1946	Newnan	GAL	32	63	9	13	1	0	0	3	1	1	13	0.206	P	9	36	5	0.900	31	5	13	3.99	167	153	115	81
Evans, Robert																											
1942	Cordele	GFL	31	117	17	43	9	3	0	29	0	2	18	0.368	OF	49	5	4	0.931								
Evans, Willard M.		BR TR																									
1948	Sparta	GSL	9												P					9	9	0	1.50	78	44	55	37
1949	Sparta	GSL	28	84	11	22	0	2	1	9	0	4	8	0.262	P	10	35	2	0.957	29	14	10	3.45	193	91	144	87
Everette, ---																											
1906	Americus	GSL													P												
Evernham, George		BR TR																									
1951	Cordele	GFL	19	33	2	3	0	0	0	0	0	6	9	0.091	C	29	4	3	0.917								

Georgia Class-D Minor League Baseball Encyclopedia

YR	TEAM	LG	G	AB	R	H	2B	3B	HR	RBI	SB	BB	SO	BA	POS	PO	A	E	FA	GP	W	L	ERA	IP	H	SO	BB
Evins, John		BL TR																									
1948	Griffin	GAL	22	68	9	16	5	1	0	4	0	15	23	0.235	OF	36	7	2	0.956								
Ewaniak, John		BR TR																									
1947	Albany	GFL	140	519	95	167	32	8	11	99	5	92	72	0.322	OF	206	14	12	0.948								
Ewer, Seaborn																											
1941	Moultrie	GFL	6	25	3	6	0	0	0	3	0	3	5	0.240	OF	6	3	4	0.692								
Ewin, Donley "Dick"		BL TL																									
1958	Dublin	GFL	56	225	62	79	12	3	7	43	0	47	49	0.351	OF	116	9	5	0.962								
Exline, Robert "Bob"		BR TR																									
1958	Valdosta	GFL	18	55	6	13	2	1	0	3	0	13	11	0.236	OF	43	1	3	0.936								
Ezzell, Robert A. "Bob"																											
1929	Carrollton	GAL	95	355	82	131	32	5	13		15	40	21	0.369	1B	961	27	15	0.985								
1930	Carrollton	GAL	84	346	75	108	20	5	20		18	36	24	0.312	1B	835	28	15	0.983								
Fabbio, Anthony T.		BR TR																									
1953	Fitzgerald	GFL	134	427	56	98	15	2	0	55	3	64	58	0.230	C	706	83	37	0.955								
Faberlle, Hector		BS TR																									
1952	Waycross	GFL	58	189	48	51	7	5	0	15	37	59	20	0.270	OF	114	12	10	0.926								
1952	Douglas	GSL	55	203	53	63	11	4	0	28	49	58	19	0.310	OF	129	4	9	0.937								
Fabrizio, Anthony		BR TR																									
1953	Cordele	GFL	45	52	8	10	2	0	1	3	0	17	22	0.192	P	8	31	5	0.886	31	6	18	6.55	132	174	54	101
Fackler, Earl		BL TR																									
1952	Brunswick	GFL	110	389	43	96	27	4	3	45	8	40	53	0.247	1B, OF	323	22	14	0.961								
1955	Brunswick	GFL	132	487	97	153	34	6	6	69	10	61	77	0.314	1B	1067	62	23	0.980								
Factor, Leonard		BR TR																									
1940	Moultrie	GFL	10	29	2	4	0	0	0	0	0	1	4	0.138	C	49	3	1	0.981								
Faehr, Al																											
1951	Hazlehurst-Baxley	GSL													M												
Fahan, Edward "Ed"																											
1941	Americus	GFL	80	313	45	91	10	4	0	44	5	31	36	0.291	2B	165	207	33	0.919								
Fain, Stanley "Stan"		BL TR																									
1946	Tallahassee	GFL	10	19	2	2	1	1	0	1	0	2	10	0.105	P	2	10	2	0.857	10	3	5	3.84	61	65	57	39
Fair, Paul																											
1942	Dothan	GFL	53	84	22	31	2	2	0	11	3	27	50	0.369	2B	107	169	32	0.896								
Faircloth, ---																											
1913	Waycross	ESL	8												P	7	20	5	0.844	5	2	3					
Fairley, Florian		BR TR																									
1946	Thomasville	GFL	15	12	1	3	2	0	0	0	0	0	1	0.250	P	1	7	0	1.000	14	1	2	0.00	35	31	14	34
Falcigno, Harry		BR TR																									
1950	Alexander City	GAL	117	420	52	108	15	5	4	62	5	54	72	0.257	OF	187	12	17	0.921								
1951	Alexander City	GAL	78	316	39	88	9	3	2	52	7	33	39	0.278	OF	133	5	11	0.926								
1951	Dublin(6) - Fitzgerald(39)	GSL	45	152	16	38	8	0	2	28	5	20	24	0.250	OF	78	4	3	0.965								
Falcione, Andrew		BR																									
1953	Jesup(6) - Dublin(14)	GSL	20	42	8	5	1	0	0	2	1	13	5	0.119													
Falcone, Nicholas "Nick"		BR																									
1953	Fitzgerald	GFL	7											0.222													
1955	Douglas	GSL	9	15		2								0.133													
Falconi, Frank																											
1936	Cordele	GFL	44	173	21	40	5	3	0	10	5			0.231	OF	81	26	5	0.955								
Fall, Ralph E.		BR TR																									
1949	Vidalia-Lyons	GSL	76	282	30	69	5	3	1	35	3	27	38	0.245	SS	123	168	32	0.901								
1950	Vidalia-Lyons	GSL	96	365	49	84	18	3	5	57	2	30	73	0.230	SS	173	267	60	0.880								
1951	Dublin(99) - Jesup(28)	GSL	127	491	93	115	16	0	9	63	7	72	64	0.234	SS	223	392	53	0.921								
Fallon, Richard "Dick"		BR TR																									
1956	Thomasville	GFL	39	130	10	29	6	0	0	18	3	10	45	0.223	3B	45	73	12	0.908								
Falls, Tim		BR																									
1954	Sandersville	GSL	4	9		1								0.111													
Falter, Thomas F. "Tom"		BR TR																									
1952	Valdosta	GFL	101	398	58	106	8	6	0	40	9	60	42	0.266	2B, 3B	193	220	33	0.926								
Fandozzi, Michael "Mike"		BR TR																									
1957	Waycross	GFL	134	448	90	189	27	6	0	66	10	109	25	0.422	M, 2B, P	320	387	21	0.971	2	0	0	<30				
Fann, Ernest		BR TR																									
1962	Brunswick	GFL	25	66	13	20	6	1	0	8	1	10	21	0.303	C	156	13	7	0.960								
Fanning, Rip		BR TR																									
1929	Anniston	GAL	84	281	28	64	10	2	0		1	19	24	0.228	C	362	68	19	0.958								
1930	Lindale	GAL	94	340	40	82	10	2	3		3	27	28	0.241	C	425	55	11	0.978								
Fantasia, Salvatore "Sal"		BR TR																									
1952	Fitzgerald	GSL	26	88	24	18	4	1	2	13	1	26	16	0.205	OF	31	0	0	1.000								
Fappiano, Eugene "Gene"		BR TR																									
1951	Valley	GAL	106	420	68	120	21	3	2	53	5	40	39	0.286	2B	246	272	42	0.925								
Farington, Gerald		BR TR																									
1962	Thomasville	GFL	5	2	0	0	0	0	0	0	0	0	1	0.000	P					5	0	0	3.38	8	6	7	5
Farland, James "Jim"		BL TL																									
1957	Brunswick	GFL	4	2		0								0.000	P					4	0	0	<30				
1958	Brunswick	GFL	24	32	2	3	1	0	0	3	0	8	19	0.094	P	6	14	1	0.952	24	7	1	4.03	96	95	88	87

Georgia Class-D Minor League Baseball Encyclopedia

YR	TEAM	LG	G	AB	R	H	2B	3B	HR	RBI	SB	BB	SO	BA	POS	PO	A	E	FA	GP	W	L	ERA	IP	H	SO	BB
Farless, Samuel "Sam"		BL TR																									
1953	Brunswick	GFL	53	200	27	55	3	0	1	26	1	20	24	0.275	OF	64	4	6	0.919								
1954	Brunswick	GFL	127	495	86	141	13	7	4	74	19	42	38	0.285	OF	177	17	10	0.951								
Farmer, ---																											
1914	Selma	GAL	69	272	51	82						18		0.301	SS	134	158	37	0.888								
Farmer, David "Dave"		BR TR																									
1956	Fitzgerald	GFL	11	40	5	7	3	1	0	5	2	2	10	0.175	3B	9	23	11	0.744								
Farmer, Jonathan Dennis "Dennis"		BR TR																									
1954	Waycross	GFL	3	10		1								0.100													
1954	Tifton	GFL	56	192	19	46	6	0	0	12	0	13	27	0.240	2B, SS	78	101	14	0.927								
1954	Statesboro	GSL	14	39	2	7	1	0	0	3	1	1	7	0.179	3B	9	14	4	0.852								
1955	Tifton	GFL	21	70	5	9	2	0	0	4	1	6	4	0.129	3B	10	24	3	0.919								
Farnsworth, Fred		BR TR																									
1956	Tifton	GFL	36	75	3	15	3	0	1	10	0	7	16	0.200	P	5	19	0	1.000	20	7	7	4.01	137	159	72	41
Farr, Curtis "Red"		BR																									
1946	Carrollton	GAL	<10																								
Farrar, Charles		BR TR																									
1939	Waycross	GFL	56	205	24	61	7	5	2	33	0	17	32	0.298	OF	98	1	3	0.971								
1940	Waycross	GFL	140	585	110	187	34	14	10	131	2	48	73	0.320	OF	278	11	16	0.948								
1941	Waycross	GFL	48	188	27	57	7	1	1	27	1	23	31	0.303	OF	94	7	4	0.962								
1946	Waycross	GFL	31	99	20	31	6	0	3	21	0	9	11	0.313	OF	36	2	5	0.884								
1948	Eastman(40) - Fitzgerald(72)	GSL	112	438	59	124	20	5	3	57	3	47	39	0.283	M, OF	193	11	8	0.962								
1949	Tifton	GSL	136	469	90	144	35	0	17	103	7	85	34	0.307	M, OF	258	8	10	0.964								
Farrar, James "Jim"		BR																									
1955	Statesboro	GSL	6	19		4								0.211													
Farrar, Roger		BL TR																									
1957	Waycross	GFL	27	89	9	16	1	0	1	8	2	14	18	0.180	SS	30	75	10	0.913								
Farrar, William "Bill"		BR TR																									
1948	Alexander City	GAL	16	40	11	4	0	0	0	2	2	8	13	0.100	OF	15	2	4	0.810								
Farrell, Richard "Dick"		BR TR																									
1963	Brunswick	GFL	63	208	26	52	3	1	4	20	3	18	32	0.250	SS	76	121	23	0.895								
Farris, James "Jimmy"		BR TR																									
1955	Waycross	GFL	32	68	2	13	0	1	0	1	0	5	6	0.191	C	59	9	2	0.971								
1955	Sandersville	GSL	22	71	5	17	1	0	0	8	2	3	15	0.239	OF, C	64	6	4	0.946								
Fasanaro, Richard "Dick"		BR																									
1954	Sandersville	GSL	4	17		4								0.235													
Fasano, Benjamin "Benny"		BR TL																									
1949	Hazlehurst-Baxley	GSL	104	396	55	94	12	7	4	51	7	42	56	0.237	OF, P	182	60	13	0.949	24	7	10	4.65	155	97	72	89
1951	Americus	GFL	60	154	28	33	8	1	1	25	1	24	26	0.214	OF, P	66	52	7	0.944	25	13	4	3.83	167	170	62	61
Fatui, Charles																											
1935	Moultrie	GFL	93	338	48	97	17	4	1		14	34	38	0.287	IF	100	194	38	0.886								
Faucette, Lew		BR																									
1946	Newnan	GAL	<10																								
Fauci, Thomas "Tom"		BR TR																									
1955	Tifton	GFL	35	127	17	26	6	1	3	15	0	19	22	0.205	3B	34	55	7	0.927								
Faulk, Leon		BR																									
1953	Sandersville	GSL	5											0.286													
Faust, Floyd H. "Dynamite"		BR TR																									
1953	Brunswick	GFL	126	436	123	122	18	4	9	61	54	26	85	0.280	OF	228	9	14	0.944								
1954	Brunswick	GFL	141	560	143	153	27	10	14	67	76	89	96	0.273	OF	247	17	21	0.926								
Feaster, ---																											
1936	Moultrie	GFL													P						2	3	5.34	32		15	30
Feathers, William Beattie "Beattie"		BR TR 5'10" 185 lbs. b. 08/04/1908 Bristol, VA d. 03/11/1979 Winston-Salem, NC																									
1936	Americus	GFL	61	240	58	95	11	4	9	52	4			0.396	OF	111	14	7	0.947								
Fedak, Eugene "Gene"		BR TR																									
1955	Moultrie	GFL	24	52	5	5	0	0	0	2	0	2	22	0.096	P	8	32	3	0.930	24	6	12	4.10	158	155	94	114
1955	Douglas	GSL	5	10		1								0.100	P					5	0	3					
Federico, Donald "Don"																											
1956	Albany	GFL	5	2		0								0.000													
Federoff, Alfred "Whitey"		BR TR 5'10" 165 lbs. b. 07/11/1924 Bairdford, PA																									
1963	Thomasville	GFL													M												
Federow, Emil		BR TR																									
1948	LaGrange	GAL	25	38	7	9	1	1	0	6	2	5	9	0.237	P	7	16	2	0.920	18	4	5	5.49	82	81	75	64
Feeley, ---																											
1929	Anniston	GAL	15	45	4	9	1	0	0		2	5	5	0.200	OF	21	2	3	0.885								
Fehrenbach, Floyd		BL TR																									
1955	Moultrie	GFL	126	481	75	143	21	10	1	56	9	69	65	0.297	3B	175	203	50	0.883								
Feie, Bill																											
1942	Cordele	GFL	12												P					12	4	1	4.65	60	69	39	29
Feinstien, Joseph "Joe"		BL TR																									
1949	LaGrange	GAL	22	29	5	8	0	0	0	7	0	3	4	0.276	P	6	12	1	0.947	22	6	1	5.51	67	75	61	69
Felaz, John		BR																									
1951	Brunswick	GFL	14	29	1	2	0	0	0	1	0	1	4	0.069													
Feldman, Nathan		BL TL																									
1951	LaGrange	GAL	11	12	1	2	0	0	0	0	0	7	2	0.167	P	1	13	0	1.000	10	2	2	4.04	49	54	23	19

Georgia Class-D Minor League Baseball Encyclopedia

YR	TEAM	LG	G	AB	R	H	2B	3B	HR	RBI	SB	BB	SO	BA	POS	PO	A	E	FA	GP	W	L	ERA	IP	H	SO	BB
Feldstein, Alan		BR TR																									
1962	Brunswick	GFL	10	34	6	6	0	0	1	2	0	5	4	0.176	2B	21	14	2	0.946								
Feller, Jack Leland "Jack"		BR TR 5'10" 185 lbs. b. 12/10/1936 Adrian, MI																									
1956	Hazlehurst-Baxley	GSL	42	149	19	35	7	0	4	27	3	15	9	0.235	C	211	27	5	0.979								
Fenrick, Roger		BR TR																									
1956	Moultrie	GFL	4	5	0									0.000	P					4	0	0	<45				
Fenster, Aaron		BR TR																									
1953	Valdosta	GFL	75	248	28	58	16	1	2	45	1	22	26	0.234	C	350	46	26	0.938								
Fenton, ---																											
1913	Waycross	ESL	98	336	36	87	16	1	7					0.259	OF	258	16	7	0.975								
Feola, Charles		BR TR																									
1953	Vidalia	GSL	3											0.000	P					0	0	0	<45				
Ferens, Stanley "Stan" "Lefty"		BS TL 5'11" 170 lbs. b. 03/05/1915 Wendel, PA d. 10/07/1994 Hempfield Township, PA																									
1940	Albany	GFL	39	114	6	19	2	0	0	3	0	6	32	0.167	P					39	20	11	2.34	289	263	253	50
Ferguson, ---																											
1917	Talladega	GAL	6	21	3	6	2	1	0		0			0.286	OF	12	0	0	1.000								
Ferguson, ---		BR																									
1946	Valley	GAL	<10																								
Ferguson, Arthur "Art"		BL TR																									
1950	Albany	GFL	64	228	66	52	10	3	2	19	17	55	27	0.228	2B, 3B, OF	117	98	21	0.911								
Ferguson, James M. "Jim"		BR TR																									
1954	Americus-Cordele	GFL	95	208	23	51	7	2	0	25	3	23	69	0.245	3B, OF, C	316	62	25	0.938								
Ferko, Robert "Bob"		BR																									
1951	Hazlehurst-Baxley	GSL	10	14	0	3	0	0	0	0	0	1	7	0.214													
Fernandez, Cecil																											
1935	Thomasville	GFL	86	284	36	83	12	3	2		4	22	33	0.292	C	355	54	10	0.976								
1936	Thomasville	GFL	37	130	13	34	7	2	1	25	6			0.262	C	157	29	6	0.969								
Fernandez, Jose B.		BR TR																									
1953	Sandersville	GSL	6											0.364	P						1	1	<45				
Fernandez, Luis E.		BR TR																									
1949	Tifton	GSL	36	97	11	13	2	0	0	9	0	13	28	0.134	P	9	44	6	0.898	38	21	11	3.12	271	108	108	114
1950	Tifton	GSL	28	64	8	12	4	0	1	10	0	9	15	0.188	P	2	34	3	0.923	28	9	9	4.61	168	177	91	75
Fernandez, Marcelo		BR TR																									
1949	Vidalia-Lyons	GSL	29	81	13	23	3	0	1	3	0	4	23	0.284	P, IF	6	36	2	0.955	28	14	9	3.26	196	98	131	108
1950	Vidalia-Lyons	GSL	36	85	16	21	2	1	1	7	0	2	17	0.247	P	8	46	6	0.900	34	14	10	3.47	200	146	168	170
Fernandez, Miguel "Mike"		BR TR																									
1950	Carrollton	GAL	4												P					4	1	3		29			
Fernandez, Rafael A.																											
1948	Valdosta	GFL	<10																								
Ferra, Joseph "Joe"		BR TR																									
1946	Thomasville	GFL	16	47	7	6	2	1	0	3	0	10	24	0.128	1B	125	2	7	0.948								
1949	LaGrange	GAL	32	113	25	37	5	5	6	30	0	14	29	0.327	OF	50	1	1	0.981								
Ferrand, Raymond "Ray"		BR TR																									
1963	Moultrie	GFL	53	170	29	52	9	3	3	26	9	41	16	0.306	3B	75	86	11	0.936								
Ferrara, Anthony "Tony"		BR TR																									
1954	Statesboro	GSL	17	61	7	10	0	2	0	7	0	5	9	0.164	2B	36	38	2	0.974								
Ferrara, Bernard		BR																									
1955	Moultrie	GFL	14	28	5	6	2	0	1	3	0	8	4	0.214													
Ferrell, Beverly "Red"																											
1935	Thomasville	GFL	115	407	83	122	29	7	11		6	64	69	0.300	OF	255	20	14	0.952								
1936	Thomasville	GFL	112	402	86	139	19	11	14	77	31			0.346	OF	248	20	13	0.954								
Ferrerra, Lee		BR TR																									
1958	Thomasville	GFL	18	65	10	12	2	0	1	8	0	9	14	0.185	3B	8	14	7	0.759								
Fetner, Charles		BL TL																									
1950	Carrollton	GAL	16	59	2	16	1	1	0	11	3	4	4	0.271	1B	127	1	3	0.977								
Fetter, Kenneth "Ken"		BR TR																									
1948	Americus	GFL	24	65	11	11	0	0	0	6	0	18	16	0.169	C	110	20	2	0.985								
Field, William "Gary"		BR TL																									
1958	Thomasville	GFL	11	22	0	4	0	0	0	2	0	0	6	0.182	P	7	12	1	0.950	10	2	4	5.43	53	55	27	36
Fields, Conrad																											
1917	LaGrange	GAL	8	17	2	5	0	0	0		1			0.294	P, 2B	0	18	1	0.947	7	2	3		52	30	47	12
Fields, Howard		BR TR																									
1955	Cordele	GFL	1	0										0.000	P					1	0	0	<45				
1955	Statesboro	GSL	5	9		0								0.000	P					5	1	4					
Fields, Thomas "Tom"		BR TR																									
1956	Fitzgerald	GFL	3	3	0									0.000	P					3	0	0	<45				
Fields, Walter "Walt"		BR TR																									
1946	Valdosta	GFL	20	67	6	14	2	0	0	8	0	4	17	0.209	OF	30	4	0	1.000								
Figueroa, Angel		BR TR																									
1956	Dublin	GSL	51	208	42	59	5	2	0	15	9	20	18	0.284	OF	128	13	4	0.972								
Figueroa, Rodolfo		BL TR																									
1958	Dublin	GFL	82	318	59	79	6	1	0	21	5	63	29	0.248	SS	130	226	29	0.925								
Fillingim, Dana		BL TR 5'10" 175 lbs. b. 11/06/1893 Columbus, GA d. 02/03/1961 Tuskegee, AL																									
1913	Cordele	ESL	34	106	5	16	0	0	0					0.151	P	14	89	6	0.945	25	15	10					
1914	Cordele	GSL		96	2	14	0	0	0		0			0.146													

Georgia Class-D Minor League Baseball Encyclopedia

YR	TEAM	LG	G	AB	R	H	2B	3B	HR	RBI	SB	BB	SO	BA	POS	PO	A	E	FA	GP	W	L	ERA	IP	H	SO	BB
Filo, Ed		BL TR																									
1940	Albany	GFL	124	493	81	158	28	9	10	103	9	35	43	0.320	OF, C	281	20	20	0.938								
Finch, ---		BR TR																									
1953	Sandersville	GSL	4											0.000	P					0	0		<45				
Fincher, Robert "Bob"		BR																									
1946	Carrollton	GAL	10	33	3	8	0	0	1	4	1	2	7	0.242													
Fincher, William "Bill"		BR TL																									
1957	Fitzgerald	GFL	37	74	7	18	0	1	0	8	0	6	14	0.243	P	3	25	2	0.933	37	15	12	3.90	201	188	157	104
Fingers, M.																											
1939	Albany	GFL													P								<45				
Fink, James "Jim"		BR TR																									
1946	Tallahassee	GFL	90	291	45	71	6	5	0	40	4	34	64	0.244	3B, SS	92	146	26	0.902								
1947	Tallahassee	GFL	12	50	10	12	1	0	0	8	5	6	8	0.240	3B	18	17	5	0.875								
Finley, Douglas "Doug"		BR TR																									
1948	Baxley	GSL	121	482	37	109	8	7	4	48	12	45	87	0.226	OF	235	8	10	0.960								
1949	Tifton		134	539	99	154	31	5	4	80	11	41	46	0.286	OF	292	20	21	0.937								
Finley, Robert Edward "Bob"		BR TR 6'1" 200 lbs. b. 11/25/1915 Ennis, TX d. 01/02/1986 West Covina, CA																									
1937	Moultrie	GFL	36	140	13	33	6	2	1	23	3	8	17	0.236	C	155	22	8	0.957								
Finn, Francis		BR TL																									
1963	Brunswick	GFL	78	217	37	62	10	2	3	36	6	40	32	0.286	OF, P	105	17	1	0.992	14	1	1	4.50	30	19	22	22
Finney, Louis Klopsche "Lou"		BL TR 6'0" 180 lbs. b. 08/13/1910 Buffalo, AL d. 04/22/1966 Lafayette, AL																									
1928	Talladega	GAL	70	257	30	79	5	5	2		3	6	18	0.307	C	158	32	10	0.950								
1929	Gadsden	GAL	81	288	37	96	15	6	3		13	11	16	0.333	C	349	69	17	0.961								
1930	Carrollton	GAL	55	234	43	91	17	2	7		7	4	14	0.389	OF	124	8	6	0.957								
1946	Opelika(39) - Valley(6)	GAL	45	164	28	49	6	5	5	24	2	25	5	0.299	1B, OF	331	15	12	0.966								
Finney, Robert "Bob"		BR TR																									
1946	Valley	GAL	23	68	6	11	1	0	0	10	1	5	5	0.162	C	94	7	4	0.962								
Fiori, Benjamin "Ben"		BR																									
1949	Tallahassee	GFL	16	14	1	1	0	0	0	0	0	2	6	0.071													
Firek, Jan		BR TR																									
1962	Brunswick	GFL	34	117	26	29	5	1	5	23	1	13	30	0.248	OF	34	7	13	0.759								
Fish, Hamilton																											
1921	Griffin	GSL		182	32	56								0.308	1B												
Fisher, ---																											
1930	Carrollton	GAL	19	67	13	19	1	0	1		1	6	3	0.284	2B	34	56	13	0.874								
Fisher, George D.		BS TR																									
1948	Waycross	GFL	133	505	123	155	19	6	2	82	60	101	77	0.307	2B, OF	235	126	23	0.940								
1949	Waycross	GFL	61	230	52	77	13	2	1	37	15	45	23	0.335	1B	490	34	12	0.978								
Fisher, Harry Devereaux "Harry"		BL TR 6'0" 180 lbs. b. 01/03/1926 Newbury, ON, CAN d. 09/20/1981 Waterloo, ON, CAN																									
1947	Tallahassee	GFL	39	85	9	27	6	0	1	21	0	4	17	0.318	P	4	32	0	1.000	32	16	9	3.15	197	153	209	131
Fisher, Robert Taylor "Bob"		BR TR 5' 10" 170 lbs b. 11/03/1886 Nashville, TN d. 08/04/1963 Jacksonville, FL																									
1906	Columbus	GSL													SS												
Fisher, Ronald "Ron"		BR TR																									
1948	Tallassee	GAL	62	196	22	53	9	2	1	18	1	20	23	0.270	C	224	37	12	0.956								
Fisher, Stanley "Stan"		BR TR																									
1954	Sandersville	GSL	7	13		1								0.077	P					7	0	4	<45				
Fisher, Vernon "Vern"		BR TR																									
1953	Valdosta	GFL	38	85	6	16	3	1	0	7	0	3	19	0.188	P	12	60	5	0.935	34	15	13	3.67	223	242	126	80
Fisher, W.A.		BR TR																									
1938	Moultrie	GFL	35	124	17	26	5	2	0	16	1	19	31	0.210	OF	93	20	4	0.966								
Fittery, Paul Clarence "Paul"		BR TL 5'8" 156 lbs. b. 10/10/1887 Lebanon, PA d. 01/28/1974 Cartersville, GA																									
1928	Carrollton	GAL	66	222	35	54	6	0	2		2	35	51	0.243	M, OF, P	85	73	6	0.963	28	21	2	1.60	225	194	137	29
1929	Carrollton	GAL	39	108	16	23	2	3	2		1	16	23	0.213	M, P	45	58	3	0.972	23	16	2	1.81	174	165	89	30
1930	Anniston	GAL	27	68	10	14	1	1	0		0	9	9	0.206	M, P	4	23	1	0.964	17	11	4	3.52	128	154	45	17
Fitzgerald, ---																											
1915	Americus-Gainesville	FLAG	<10																									
Fitzgerald, H. Louie "Lou"		b. 08/25/1920 Cleveland, TN																									
1942	Americus	GFL	25	96	20	23	3	2	0	7	0	19	13	0.240	3B, SS	26	67	9	0.912								
Fitzgerald, John M.		BR TR																									
1949	Tallahassee	GFL	32	61	11	16	3	1	0	2	0	6	21	0.262	P	10	25	6	0.854	23	5	15	5.90	122	117	78	104
Flaherty, Christopher "Chris"		BR TR																									
1949	LaGrange	GAL	98	334	45	89	15	6	5	52	2	48	68	0.266	1B, 3B	329	97	22	0.951								
Flair, Albert Dell "Al" "Broadway"		BL TL 6'4" 195 lbs. b. 07/24/1916 New Orleans, LA d. 07/25/1988 New Orleans, LA																									
1937	Moultrie	GFL	109	431	46	125	14	5	3	68	6	21	27	0.290	1B	1015	56	24	0.978								
1938	Moultrie	GFL	66	264	38	91	13	7	0	45	4	20	9	0.345	1B	642	30	6	0.991								
Flair, Elmer																											
1942	Waycross	GFL	44	164	19	41	5	1	1	27	1	20	18	0.250	OF	58	7	7	0.903								
Flanagan, Jerome		BR TR																									
1956	Hazlehurst-Baxley	GSL	58	214	39	59	9	3	4	21	5	31	36	0.276	OF	82	5	10	0.897								
Flanagan, William "Bill"		BR TR																									
1952	Moultrie	GFL	29	22	1	4	1	0	0	2	0	2	7	0.182	P	4	20	5	0.828	29	3	9	5.82	82	92	70	75
Flanigan, Cheri Jim		BR TR																									
1953	Albany	GFL	10	16	2	3	1	0	0	0	0	2	2	0.188	P	1	10	3	0.786		3	4	<45				

Georgia Class-D Minor League Baseball Encyclopedia

YR	TEAM	LG	G	AB	R	H	2B	3B	HR	RBI	SB	BB	SO	BA	POS	PO	A	E	FA	GP	W	L	ERA	IP	H	SO	BB
Fleisch, Donald "Don"		BL TR																									
1949	Griffin	GAL	14	44	3	5	0	0	0	1	2	8	14	0.114	SS	31	21	10	0.839								
1953	Albany	GFL	49	141	23	30	2	3	0	11	3	42	35	0.213	OF	51	6	2	0.966								
1954	Albany	GFL	26	77	9	20	5	2	0	11	1	11	11	0.260	OF	41	3	3	0.936								
1954	Hazlehurst-Baxley	GSL	10	38	3	8	3	0	0	1	1	6	13	0.211	OF	9	1	2	0.833								
Fleischer, Herbert "Herb"		BL TL																									
1953	Dublin	GSL	8											0.000	P						2	3		<45			
Fleming, Douglas "Doug"		BL TR																									
1953	Brunswick	GFL	38	136	18	27	4	0	0	11	1	20	32	0.199	2B	83	86	18	0.904								
1954	Dublin	GSL	120	465	78	125	27	5	4	79	6	41	64	0.269	2B	308	301	26	0.959								
Flemming, Redmond "Wheeler"		BR TR																									
1947	Opelika	GAL	125	498	70	119	16	8	0	54	12	45	81	0.239	1B	1088	67	19	0.984								
1948	Opelika	GAL	104	367	65	102	14	4	1	50	12	65	35	0.278	1B	933	81	17	0.984								
1949	Opelika	GAL	111	401	53	103	16	3	0	59	12	46	34	0.257	1B	913	53	16	0.984								
1950	Opelika	GAL	91	316	36	71	9	1	1	49	6	45	45	0.225	M, 1B	735	49	11	0.986								
1951	Opelika	GAL	55	196	24	45	3	0	0	20	3	42	15	0.230	M, 1B	426	24	13	0.972								
Fleshman, Elvin		BL TL																									
1955	Valdosta	GFL	12	18	3	4	0	0	0	2	0	3	7	0.222	P	4	10	0	1.000	12	2	4	5.03	59	41	54	59
1956	Valdosta	GFL	22	44	5	7	1	0	0	3	0	8	17	0.159	P	10	32	0	1.000	21	11	4	2.90	121	78	110	123
Flohr, ---																											
1920	Lindale	GSL													3B												
Flood, Joseph "Joe"		BR TR																									
1963	Moultrie	GFL	7	12	3	1	0	0	1	2	0	2	3	0.083	P					7	3	4	2.06	48	35	41	8
Flora, William "Bill"																											
1935	Thomasville	GFL	23	57	3	3	0	0	0		0	3	17	0.053	P					24	13	6		159	144	94	73
1936	Thomasville	GFL	11	13	1	2	1	0	0	2	0			0.154	P					11	4	4	3.73	41		24	39
Flores, Paul		BR TR																									
1949	Opelika	GAL	119	399	78	122	19	9	8	70	22	75	63	0.306	SS	217	314	74	0.878								
Flowers, ---																											
1917	Talladega	GAL	17	65	8	19	3	4	1		3			0.292	OF	25	6	0	1.000								
Flowers, B.																											
1914	Rome	GAL	33	112	7	21					0			0.188	P	4	25	3	0.906	33							
Flowers, Burnice		BR																									
1946	Carrollton	GAL	<10																								
Flowers, H.																											
1914	Rome	GAL	10	35	12	12					0			0.343	P	26	26	2	0.963	10							
Flowers, John		BL TL																									
1962	Dublin	GFL	13	15	3	1	0	0	0	0	1	4	11	0.067	P	2	18	4	0.833	12	3	1	6.07	46	48	38	35
Flowers, Robert J. "Bob"		BR																									
1955	Moultrie	GFL	22	60	4	12	0	0	1	9	1	5	12	0.200													
Floyd, Buck																											
1928	Anniston - Gadsden	GAL	21	42	4	7	2	0	0		0	3	9	0.167	P	3	15	2	0.900	20	5	9	4.90	112	143	35	40
Floyd, Charles		BL																									
1956	Thomson	GSL	7	25		7								0.280													
Floyd, Robert "Bob"		BL TR																									
1956	Albany(34) - Fitzgerald(20)	GFL	54	165	20	36	4	2	0	19	7	35	25	0.218	OF	77	1	8	0.907								
Flynn, Don R.																											
1915	Newnan	GAL	58	212	43	76	16	1	15					0.358	OF	94	11	3	0.972								
1916	Newnan	GAL	68	241	52	88					8			0.365	OF												
1917	Griffin	GAL	15	60	8	20	6	0	2		5			0.333	OF, P	25	16	6	0.872	4	2	0		31	27	30	5
Flynn, Robert "Bob"		BR TR																									
1956	Dublin	GSL	9	17		5								0.294	P					5	3	0					
Flynn, Thomas "Tom"		BL TL																									
1956	Moultrie	GFL	12	10	2	1	0	0	0	0	0	1	2	0.100	P	3	5	0	1.000	11	3	3	<45				
Foell, George		BL TR																									
1951	LaGrange	GAL	37	150	35	34	3	0	0	10	10	22	19	0.227	3B, SS	73	102	21	0.893								
Fogg, William "Bill"		BR TR																									
1948	Americus	GFL	30	65	5	12	0	0	0	5	0	7	19	0.185	P	6	40	8	0.852	30	11	14	4.70	182	184	168	132
Fogleman, Oliver		BL TR																									
1955	Moultrie	GFL	40	133	16	41	2	0	1	9	1	17	19	0.308	SS	54	98	20	0.884								
Foley, Walter "Walt"																											
1937	Moultrie	GFL	89	304	38	72	18	3	1	39	3	34	41	0.237	OF	164	6	11	0.939								
Folk, Richard "Dick"		BR TR																									
1955	Moultrie	GFL	74	225	28	46	4	5	0	25	8	47	82	0.204	SS	84	198	42	0.870								
1955	Douglas	GSL	24	70	17	11	3	1	0	5	1	7	19	0.157	3B	17	35	6	0.897								
Folson, ---		BR																									
1946	Valley	GAL	<10																								
Foltmer, Harold		BR TR																									
1950	Waycross	GFL	80	242	24	49	11	0	2	24	0	20	46	0.202	3B, C	250	38	13	0.957								
Foote, Ambrose		BR TR																									
1954	Waycross	GFL	11	26	3	5	1	0	0	2	0	3	3	0.192	P					7	4	2	1.96	55	50	32	30
Forbes, John		BL																									
1949	Tallahassee	GFL	10	34	6	9	2	2	2	6	2	4	6	0.265													
Ford, Donald L. "Don"		BR TR																									
1956	Waycross	GFL	41	140	17	31	0	1	0	11	3	22	33	0.221	SS	63	118	13	0.933								

Georgia Class-D Minor League Baseball Encyclopedia

YR	TEAM	LG	G	AB	R	H	2B	3B	HR	RBI	SB	BB	SO	BA	POS	PO	A	E	FA	GP	W	L	ERA	IP	H	SO	BB
Ford, Donald T. "Don"		BR TR																									
1947	Tallassee(8) - LaGrange(29)	GAL	37	113	11	23	6	0	0	8	5	11	19	0.204	C	157	33	9	0.955								
1950	Waycross	GFL	84	309	37	79	12	1	1	41	2	31	43	0.256	C	468	41	15	0.971								
Ford, Leonard																											
1937	Moultrie	GFL	24	44	6	9	1	0	0	3	0	7	4	0.205	P	5	37	2	0.955	20	4	9	3.86	105	103	45	59
Ford, Lonnie		BR TR																									
1950	Albany	GFL	12	23	3	6	0	0	0	2	0	2	5	0.261	P	1	14	2	0.882	12	4	4	4.22	64	54	77	51
Ford, Robert "Bob"		BR TR																									
1953	Tifton	GFL	46	183	17	44	4	1	0	21	1	11	25	0.240	SS	82	111	18	0.915								
1953	Sandersville	GSL	87	379	62	100	16	4	3	40	7	24	33	0.264	SS	136	243	39	0.907								
1954	Thomasville	GFL	2	8	0									0.000													
Ford, Robert W. "Bob"		BR TR																									
1953	Statesboro	GSL	89	291	28	76	10	0	0	44	2	19	31	0.261	3B, OF	82	72	9	0.945								
1954	Statesboro	GSL	112	401	49	98	22	1	3	51	5	29	44	0.244	2B, OF, C, P	260	134	21	0.949	4	0	0	<45				
Foreman, Donald "Don"		BR TR																									
1949	Albany	GFL	25	93	11	20	4	0	1	4	2	3	26	0.215	OF	29	3	6	0.842								
Foreman, Richard "Dick"		BR TR																									
1958	Brunswick	GFL	45	156	28	38	8	2	5	29	1	20	46	0.244	SS	54	95	25	0.856								
Forrest, Henry		BR																									
1955	Tifton	GFL	5	6	0									0.000													
Forrest, Jim		BL TL																									
1940	Valdosta	GFL	<10												P									<35			
Forrest, Richard "Dick"																											
1955	Cordele	GFL	16	17	1	3	1	0	0	1	0	1	8	0.176	P	3	10	0	1.000	16	2	1	1.64	55	30	32	32
1956	Thomson	GSL	19	29	0	1	0	0	0	2	0	2	7	0.034	P	3	18	4	0.840	19	3	5	4.02	85	70	71	49
Forrester, Franklin "Frank"		BR TR																									
1947	Griffin	GAL	115	443	62	104	16	3	2	32	9	54	49	0.235	OF	251	9	10	0.963								
1949	Griffin	GAL	43	131	13	30	0	0	0	16	2	20	19	0.229	OF	84	4	4	0.957								
Forsythe, Ronald "Ron"		BR TR																									
1956	Thomasville	GFL	50	27	2	2	0	0	0	1	0	5	11	0.074	P	2	25	0	1.000	50	7	7	3.71	119	126	81	64
Fortner, ---																											
1921	LaGrange	GSL													SS												
1921	Rome	GSL													2B												
Fortuna, Walter																											
1941	Thomasville	GFL	9	18	3	3	1	0	0	1	2	2	10	0.167	OF	6	2	1	0.889								
Foss, George Dueward "Deeby"		BR TR 5'10" 170 lbs. b. 06/13/1897 Register, GA d. 11/10/1969 Brandon, FL																									
1915	Thomasville	FLAG	12	39	6	10	1	0	0					0.256	SS, P	22	24	13	0.780	0							
Foss, Larry Curtis "Larry"		BR TR 6'2" 187 lbs. b. 04/18/1936 Castleton, KS																									
1955	Dublin	GSL	23	28	1	7	0	0	0	3	0	0	9	0.250	P	2	16	2	0.900	23	4	4	5.51	80	72	63	82
Foster, ---																											
1906	Columbus	GSL													P, OF												
Foster, ---		BR																									
1946	Carrollton	GAL	<10																								
Foster, Duell		BL TL																									
1952	Douglas	GSL	26	58	6	14	2	0	0	7	1	5	8	0.241	P	9	22	2	0.939	24	5	7	3.83	141	146	80	45
1953	Waycross	GFL	35	79	10	17	2	0	0	5	0	6	18	0.215	P	8	40	7	0.873	31	13	12	2.79	203	189	94	56
Foster, R.A.																											
1920	LaGrange	GSL													P												
Foster, Ralph																											
1949	Eastman	GSL	13	30	2	2	0	0	1	2	0	4	7	0.067	P	3	9	2	0.857	11	2	1	5.48	46	31	30	48
Foster, Richard "Dick"		BR TR																									
1951	LaGrange	GAL	47	213	49	65	7	3	0	18	11	23	23	0.305	SS	101	147	34	0.879								
Foster, Shelby		BR																									
1954	Sandersville	GSL	3	10		2								0.200													
Foster, Thomas "Tom"		BR TR																									
1956	Hazlehurst-Baxley	GSL	8	10		2								0.200	P					8	1	2					
Fountain, Harvey		BL TL																									
1951	Hazlehurst-Baxley	GSL	17	21	2	3	1	0	0	1	0	2	12	0.143	P	1	6	2	0.778	17	1	8	7.50	60	62	35	92
Fountain, Ronald "Ron"		BR TR																									
1952	Valdosta	GFL	129	480	63	121	21	2	3	58	6	56	103	0.252	OF	321	23	12	0.966								
Fouts, Paul		BR TR																									
1947	Cordele	GFL	71	300	44	87	20	4	3	40	2	16	34	0.290	2B	217	225	30	0.936								
Fowler, ---																											
1929	Cedartown	GAL	15	30	1	7	1	0	1		0	1	4	0.233	P	12	9	1	0.955	8	1	2		26	30	15	17
Fowler, Cecil William "Cecil"																											
1941	Tallahassee	GFL	4	12	2	2	0	0	0	0	0	2	3	0.167	OF	11	1	2	0.857								
Fowler, Lincoln																											
1949	Tifton	GSL	17	32	4	6	1	0	1	4	0	3	7	0.188	P	5	18	2	0.920	15	3	6	6.91	69	59	38	69
Fowler, Robert "Bob"		BR TR																									
1955	Tifton	GFL	2	1		0								0.000	P					2	0	1	<45				
Fowler, Ted		BR TR																									
1954	Tifton	GFL	21	20	0	1	1	0	0	0	0	0	15	0.050	P	7	12	3	0.864	19	2	5	4.77	66	73	36	44
Fowler, Wheeler		BR TR																									
1951	Hazlehurst-Baxley	GSL	87	316	28	75	14	5	2	35	3	27	67	0.237	3B	85	171	36	0.877								

Georgia Class-D Minor League Baseball Encyclopedia

YR	TEAM	LG	G	AB	R	H	2B	3B	HR	RBI	SB	BB	SO	BA	POS	PO	A	E	FA	GP	W	L	ERA	IP	H	SO	BB
Fox, Jim																											
1921	Rome	GSL		78	11	24								0.308	M, 1B												
Foytack, Paul Eugene "Paul"		BR TR 5'11" 180 lbs. b. 11/16/1930 Scranton, PA																								
1949	Thomasville	GFL	35	76	7	9	2	0	0	2	0	9	36	0.118	P	9	29	5	0.884	35	14	10	3.29	208	167	207	133
Fracaro, David "Dave"		BR TR																									
1958	Waycross	GFL	3	7		1								0.143	P					4	0	2	<30				
Frady, Herbert "Herb"		BR TR																									
1950	Rome	GAL	69	215	42	57	8	1	4	31	10	56	38	0.265	3B	59	97	29	0.843								
Frady, William "Bill"		BR TL																									
1953	Statesboro	GSL	8											0.080	P					8	5	3	4.50	60	64	25	24
Fragela, Alberto		BR TR																									
1952	Waycross	GFL	12	35	4	6	0	0	0	1	0	1	9	0.171	SS	19	26	5	0.900								
Fraker, Richard "Dick"		BR TR																									
1942	Dothan	GFL	34	111	19	20	3	2	0	11	0	34	12	0.180	OF	75	4	4	0.952								
1946	Carrollton	GAL	38	137	19	36	3	0	0	9	3	10	7	0.263	OF	63	2	2	0.970								
Frakes, Ben																											
1928	Gadsden - Carrollton	GAL	20	49	4	4	0	0	0		0	1	14	0.082	P	10	29	1	0.975	17	5	9	1.85	117	152	35	32
Fraley, Carroll		BR TR																									
1954	Albany	GFL	7	5		0								0.000	P					7	0	1	<45				
Francek, Michael "Mike"		BR																									
1963	Brunswick	GFL	12	25	1	1	0	0	0	1	1	2	12	0.040													
Francis, Charles		BR TR																									
1955	Hazlehurst-Baxley	GSL	15	37	7	9	3	0	2	9	3	7	9	0.243	OF, P	7	1	1	0.889	4	0	0					
Francis, Edwin "Ed"		BL TL																									
1948	Americus	GFL	24	78	7	15	2	1	0	3	2	8	23	0.192	OF	31	4	6	0.854								
Francoline, James "Jim"		BR																									
1938	Tallahassee	GFL	41	141	26	42	9	4	0	24	3	38	24	0.298	3B	67	35	14	0.879								
1951	Americus	GFL	108	380	71	97	20	6	3	90	2	113	43	0.255													
Francone, Nicholas "Nick"		BR TR																									
1956	Sandersville	GSL	42	137	20	27	3	1	1	6	6	18	36	0.197	OF	86	1	6	0.935								
Frank, Morris		BR TR																									
1948	Albany	GFL	11	23	2	1	0	0	0	0	0	0	10	0.043	P	1	4	0	1.000	10	4	4	2.45	66	54	66	31
1949	Albany	GFL	39	88	6	13	4	0	1	7	0	6	36	0.148	P	6	21	3	0.900	38	22	9	1.94	236	170	254	93
Franklin, Harold "Hal"		BR TR																									
1958	Thomasville	GFL	9	5		2								0.400	P					9	0	0	<30				
Franks, ---																											
1913	Brunswick - Valdosta	ESL	88	319	30	77	12	4	1					0.241	OF	133	15	5	0.967								
Franks, Paul J.		BL TL																									
1954	Valdosta	GFL	1	3		0								0.000	P					1	0	1	<45				
Franson, Carl		BL TR																									
1948	Newnan	GAL	123	475	73	113	18	9	13	67	8	46	62	0.238	3B	122	202	40	0.890								
1949	Newnan	GAL	124	498	106	134	34	6	28	104	4	68	70	0.269	3B	122	250	37	0.910								
1950	Newnan	GAL	121	429	111	105	15	0	31	96	7	107	64	0.245	3B	105	256	27	0.930								
1951	Moultrie	GFL	88	340	75	100	13	3	15	46	1	69	33	0.294	3B	70	185	34	0.882								
Frantell, Donald "Don"		BR TR																									
1949	Valdosta(20) - Albany(12)	GFL	32	94	12	12	4	0	0	10	0	26	29	0.128	2B	61	47	6	0.947								
Franz, William "Bill"		BL TL																									
1948	Albany	GFL	15	15	6	6	0	0	0	2	0	3	4	0.400	P	7	8	4	0.789								
Frazee, ---																											
1930	Huntsville	GAL	3												P					3	1	0	8.10	10	22	0	3
Frazier, Andrew "Andy"		BR TR																									
1949	Thomasville	GFL	130	529	62	133	16	1	11	78	17	11	81	0.251	2B	320	321	42	0.939								
Frazier, Carey "Lance"		BR TR																									
1946	Valley	GAL	29	100	19	22	1	1	0	6	2	8	8	0.220	1B, C	226	16	6	0.976								
1947	Valley	GAL	14	41	5	16	0	0	0	5	0	13	5	0.390	C	63	8	0	1.000								
1949	Valley	GAL	10	37	4	9	2	0	0	3	0	2	1	0.243	C	74	6	2	0.976								
Frazier, Clarence		BR TR																									
1956	Thomson	GSL	19	73	7	12	1	0	0	5	1	14	15	0.164	OF	34	4	8	0.826								
1957	Fitzgerald	GFL	57	236	25	53	12	3	1	23	5	22	75	0.225	OF	123	8	7	0.949								
Frazier, Daniel "Dan"		BL TR																									
1951	Valley	GAL	21	55	11	15	3	2	0	11	1	8	4	0.273	OF	11	0	2	0.846								
Frazier, John		BR TR																									
1948	Valley	GAL	35	153	23	30	5	1	1	13	1	12	23	0.196	OF	62	2	4	0.941								
Frazier, Lee		BR TR																									
1955	Cordele	GFL	43	138	15	37	2	0	0	16	7	16	42	0.268	OF	52	2	5	0.915								
Frazier, Ralph		BL TL																									
1946	Valley	GAL	102	368	69	96	11	6	4	48	9	57	36	0.261	OF	127	12	9	0.939								
1947	Valley	GAL	12	45	6	11	0	1	1	6	0	5	0	0.244	1B	98	5	2	0.981								
Frazier, William C. "Bill"		BL TR																									
1951	Moultrie	GFL	49	126	20	28	3	1	2	8	1	11	39	0.222	OF, P	26	44	4	0.946	28	11	9	3.86	184	175	79	105
Frederick, William "Bill"		BR																									
1946	Opelika	GAL	3												P					3	2	1	0.00	13	14	11	9
Fredericks, Harry		BR TR																									
1950	Americus	GFL	25	90	15	25	6	2	1	15	5	16	9	0.278	OF	37	1	1	0.974								

Georgia Class-D Minor League Baseball Encyclopedia

YR	TEAM	LG	G	AB	R	H	2B	3B	HR	RBI	SB	BB	SO	BA	POS	PO	A	E	FA	GP	W	L	ERA	IP	H	SO	BB
Freedman, Benny																											
1929	Gadsden	GAL	12	47	6	13	1	1	1		0	1	3	0.277	OF, P	21	3	0	1.000	7	1	0		9	11	3	1
1929	Carrollton	GAL	88	333	67	104	14	2	15		9	37	46	0.312	OF	189	13	15	0.931								
Freeland, John		BR TR																									
1947	Cordele	GFL	75	234	34	58	8	4	0	28	0	41	10	0.248	C	145	27	1	0.994								
Freeman, Harold																											
1939	Americus	GFL	35	136	22	30	2	1	0	8	1	13	41	0.221	SS	39	96	24	0.849								
Freeman, James L. "Jim"		BR TR																									
1951	Tifton	GFL	11	12	0	2	0	0	0	0	0	1	3	0.167	P	3	7	1	0.909								
1953	Sandersville	GSL	42	60	11	16	1	0	0	5	0	11	7	0.267	P	1	5	2	0.750	12	3	5	7.74	50	64	22	26
Freese, Eugene Lewis "Gene" "Augie"		BR TR 5'11" 175 lbs. b. 01/08/1934 Wheeling, WV																									
1953	Brunswick	GFL	117	460	94	142	28	7	9	89	18	47	36	0.309	2B, SS, P	257	316	39	0.936	0	0		<45				
Fregin, Arnold		BL TR																									
1954	Fitzgerald	GFL	54	176	34	38	7	1	4	28	0	41	39	0.216	OF	76	3	6	0.929								
1956	Moultrie	GFL	131	421	67	104	20	6	3	54	4	100	49	0.247	C	776	76	19	0.978								
Freis, Clayton																											
1939	Americus	GFL	37	94	10	15	3	0	0	5	2	6	24	0.160	P	7	43	4	0.926	27	10	15	3.71	194	179	137	98
Frentz, ---																											
1913	Gadsden	GAL	13												P					13	10	3					
Freund, Norman "Norm"																											
1937	Moultrie	GFL	41	161	25	38	5	4	0	15	2	17	16	0.236	3B	51	97	13	0.919								
Frew, William "Bill"		BL TL																									
1947	Thomasville	GFL	32	62	7	10	0	2	0	6	0	2	18	0.161	P	2	35	7	0.841	27	6	12	3.88	146	142	81	87
Frey, ---																											
1930	Huntsville	GAL	10	37	10	4	0	0	0		1	7	7	0.108	SS	15	34	11	0.817								
Frey, Larry																											
1941	Tallahassee	GFL	9	7	4	2	1	0	0	1	0	4	1	0.286	P	1	5	0	1.000	6	1	1	6.86	21	35	10	12
Friar, Delbert "Del"																											
1936	Tallahassee	GFL	77	243	25	58	11	2	3	33	2			0.239	C	248	32	5	0.982								
Fricano, Marion John "Marion"		BR TR 6'0" 170 lbs. b. 07/15/1923 Brant, NY d. 05/18/1976 Tijuana, Mexico																									
1948	Valdosta	GFL	39	80	12	16	2	0	0	5	0	14	21	0.200	P	10	44	4	0.931	32	13	7	3.13	178	200	94	48
Friedman, Stanley "Stan"		BR TR																									
1948	Fitzgerald	GSL	60	169	16	41	7	1	1	27	2	24	25	0.243	C	230	7	1	0.996								
1949	Fitzgerald	GSL	18												C	98	2	3	0.971								
Friend, Owen Lacey "Red"		BR TR 6'1" 180 lbs. b. 03/21/1927 Granite City, IL																									
1962	Brunswick	GFL													M												
Frioni, Alfonso		BR TR																									
1958	Waycross	GFL	12	12	0	1	1	0	0	1	0	0	5	0.083	P	0	5	1	0.833	12	2	2	5.81	31	36	14	14
Frisinger, Jack		BL TL																									
1947	Albany	GFL	34	87	13	18	2	2	0	5	0	3	27	0.207	P	2	28	3	0.909	33	20	7	2.18	219	136	274	137
Frost, Robert F. "Bob"																											
1939	Americus	GFL	31	104	7	27	4	1	0	13	0	17	23	0.260	C	182	21	4	0.981								
Froug, Melvin "Mel"		BL TL																									
1949	Cordele	GFL	53	184	29	54	16	0	0	35	1	37	47	0.293	1B	326	14	12	0.966								
Fry, Robert "Bob"		BR TR																									
1956	Fitzgerald	GFL	58	215	25	43	7	1	2	20	0	12	60	0.200	3B	70	137	19	0.916								
Fryman, Howard		BR TR																									
1953	Albany	GFL	5											0.125	P						3	0	<45				
Fucci, Dominic "Dom"		BR TR																									
1951	LaGrange	GAL	23	81	18	24	2	2	2	16	3	13	11	0.296	OF	37	2	5	0.886								
Fullen, Thomas "Tom"		BR TR																									
1962	Moultrie	GFL	27	47	2	6	0	0	0	4	0	2	12	0.128	P	3	28	2	0.939	27	6	8	4.57	124	125	113	68
Fuller, ---																											
1930	Cedartown	GAL	4												P					4	1	1	5.54	13	13	6	6
Fuller, Bertram																											
1920	Carrollton	GSL		45	6	9								0.200	SS												
Fullington, ---																											
1949	Carrollton	GAL	4	2	0	1	0	0	0	0	0	0	0	0.500													
Fulton, Robert "Bob"		BL TR																									
1949	Newnan	GAL	113	347	56	98	13	2	13	63	7	86	27	0.282	OF, C	629	61	30	0.958								
1950	Thomasville	GFL	129	412	82	119	19	6	15	96	3	119	58	0.289	C	827	104	21	0.978								
Fultz, Charles "George"		BL TR																									
1948	Waycross	GFL	11	21	3	4	1	0	0	2	0	5	8	0.190	P	2	18	3	0.870	11	6	3	2.32	62	57	26	21
Fulwiler, Harold																											
1941	Cordele	GFL	8	31	2	9	1	0	0	5	1	4	5	0.290	OF	7	1	0	1.000								
Funk, Ernest "Ernie"		BR TR																									
1948	Thomasville	GFL	43	92	14	19	2	0	0	13	1	11	17	0.207	P	2	53	6	0.902	39	19	13	2.43	230	223	160	81
Fuqua, Roger																											
1928	Anniston	GAL	61	220	26	62	8	1	1		4	3	9	0.282	SS	137	171	22	0.933								
1929	Anniston	GAL	92	370	63	137	20	5	8		17	11	11	0.370	SS	181	261	46	0.906								
1930	Anniston	GAL	95	400	74	140	25	4	4		19	17	9	0.350	2B, SS	206	302	22	0.958								
Futcher, John		BS TR																									
1948	Fitzgerald	GSL	12	40	4	10	0	0	0	1	1	1	8	0.250	SS	22	25	9	0.839								
1949	Waycross	GFL	13	53	8	15	3	0	0	10	0	2	12	0.283													

Georgia Class-D Minor League Baseball Encyclopedia

YR	TEAM	LG	G	AB	R	H	2B	3B	HR	RBI	SB	BB	SO	BA	POS	PO	A	E	FA	GP	W	L	ERA	IP	H	SO	BB
Gabriel, Earl		BL																									
1956	Albany	GFL	10	24	6	5	0	0	0	1	1	5	5	0.208													
Gaddy, John Wilson "Sheriff"		BR TR 6'0" 182 lbs. b. 02/05/1914 Wadesboro, NC d. 05/03/1966 Albemarle, NC																									
1939	Albany	GFL													P									<45			
Gaffney, George		BR TR																									
1956	Thomson	GSL	7	17		2								0.118	P					7	1	2					
Gagnon, Russell "Russ"		BR TR																									
1948	Eastman	GSL	78	259	39	55	7	8	2	28	16	36	67	0.212	2B	218	197	24	0.945								
1949	Eastman	GSL	121	421	75	108	32	2	12	61	8	65	104	0.257	SS	252	315	55	0.912								
Gaidzis, John R.		BR																									
1953	Cordele	GFL	15	38	3	4	1	0	0	3	0	3	8	0.105													
Gaillard, Mel																											
1941	Thomasville	GFL	54	207	37	59	5	4	1	30	4	28	14	0.285	OF	59	9	9	0.883								
Gaillard, Theodore "Ted"		BR TR																									
1950	LaGrange	GAL	13	33	2	4	1	0	0	2	0	6	16	0.121	P	0	6	1	0.857	13	5	4	4.50	84	83	54	43
Gaines (Ginzberg), Samuel "Sam"		BR TR																									
1950	Jesup	GSL	15	31	7	8	1	0	1	4	0	1	7	0.258	P	6	10	5	0.762	11	3	5	6.87	55	67	46	65
Gaines, R.H.																											
1921	Griffin	GSL													1B												
Gaisford, Jerry		BR TR																									
1953	Valdosta	GFL	16	51	3	8	1	0	0	9	2	3	13	0.157	OF	17	0	2	0.895								
Gaisser, Roy																											
1941	Thomasville	GFL	5												P					5	0	0	13.50	10	21	5	4
Galasso, Louis "Lou"		BR TR																									
1948	Albany	GFL	26	94	18	23	5	0	0	10	1	23	17	0.245	3B	34	39	8	0.901								
Galen, Joseph "Joe"		BR TR																									
1952	Moultrie	GFL	42	142	12	37	4	1	0	21	2	18	27	0.261	3B, SS	56	83	20	0.874								
Galey, Robert "Bob"		BR TR																									
1947	Waycross	GFL	41	101	16	28	3	1	1	6	0	5	17	0.277	P	4	22	3	0.897	31	18	8	4.11	219	218	223	117
1949	Waycross	GFL	21	50	7	12	2	0	1	6	0	3	9	0.240	P	5	15	3	0.870	15	5	3	3.87	93	79	68	67
Galinkin, Norman "Norm"		BL TL																									
1948	Waycross	GFL	93	310	63	92	16	2	5	64	6	74	60	0.297	1B	684	42	25	0.967								
Gall, William "Bill"		BR TR																									
1949	Cordele	GFL	30	56	8	13	2	0	0	5	0	6	26	0.232	P	14	25	2	0.951	29	7	11	4.47	153	178	88	62
Gallagher, ---																											
1914	Americus - Brunswick	GSL		79	9	16	3	0	0		0			0.203													
Gallagher, ---																											
1921	Carrollton	GSL	<10												OF												
Gallagher, Charles		BR TR																									
1928	Talladega	GAL	98	375	86	115	21	12	14		17	39	29	0.307	1B, OF, P	364	34	13	0.968	16	4	1	3.60	75	73	45	27
1940	Thomasville	GFL	12	42	3	11	1	0	0	8	0	3	5	0.262	3B	20	23	4	0.915								
Gallart, Armando		BR TR																									
1946	Newnan	GAL	76	259	43	75	5	3	3	37	3	23	39	0.290	3B, SS, P	109	190	28	0.914	1	0	0		1			
Gallegos, N.F.																											
1936	Cordele	GFL	18	69	12	19	4	1	1	14	0			0.275	OF	38	3	2	0.953								
Gallivan, Philip, Joseph "Phil"		BR TR 6'0" 170 lbs. b. 05/29/1907 Seattle, WA d. 11/24/1969 St. Paul, MN																									
1930	Carrollton	GAL	7												P					7	1	2	4.05	60	51	10	11
Gallo, Frederick "Fred"		BR TR																									
1963	Waycross	GFL	19	19	1	2	2	0	0	4	0	2	10	0.105	C	19	3	0	1.000								
Galloway, Oliver		BR TR																									
1948	Tallassee	GAL	27	72	4	20	1	1	0	7	0	14	8	0.278	C	165	23	8	0.959								
1949	Valley	GAL	63	215	28	62	9	3	0	34	2	31	4	0.288	C	340	26	6	0.984								
1950	Dublin	GSL	89	334	49	92	18	0	2	40	1	34	18	0.275	C	535	40	9	0.985								
1951	Dublin	GSL	125	492	47	140	28	2	2	79	5	36	6	0.285	C	619	52	25	0.964								
1956	Dublin	GSL	1	2	0	0								0.000													
Gallucci, Frank		BR TR																									
1951	Hazlehurst-Baxley	GSL	65	218	33	63	17	5	1	39	5	50	18	0.289	SS, OF	111	32	9	0.941								
Galoffin, Jose																											
1948	Vidalia-Lyons(8) - Fitzgerald(3)	GSL	11	14	0	0	0	0	0	0	1	1	10	0.000	P	4	10	0	1.000	11	2	3	4.78	49	54	14	37
Gandy, Robert Brinkley "Bob" "String"		BL TR 6'3" 180 lbs. b. 08/25/1893 Jacksonville, FL d. 06/19/1945 Jacksonville, FL																									
1915	Waycross - Brunswick	FLAG	74	281	37	77	12	1	3		18			0.274	2B, OF, P	69	33	18	0.850	0							
Ganong, ---																											
1915	Anniston	GAL	13	44	4	12	3	0	0					0.273													
Ganss, Robert "Bob"																											
1942	Moultrie	GFL	83	258	48	62	11	2	0	30	10	51	34	0.240	C	394	35	10	0.977								
Ganzer, Robert "Bob"		BR TR																									
1956	Sandersville	GSL	35	49	5	5	0	0	0	1	0	3	16	0.102	P	9	27	8	0.818	33	7	6	4.30	136	133	90	86
Garcia, David		BR																									
1953	Albany	GFL	2												0.286													
Garcia, Jesus		BR TR																									
1952	Douglas	GSL	37	143	35	43	10	0	2	18	5	29	28	0.301	2B	101	79	15	0.923								
1953	Sandersville	GSL	60	232	38	60	9	2	0	25	4	30	34	0.259	2B	154	127	13	0.956								
1954	Sandersville	GSL	40	128	14	31	5	1	0	18	2	37	23	0.242	2B	80	95	11	0.941								
Garcia, Jose Ramon (Valdez) "Jose"		BL TL																									
1950	Douglas	GSL	15	53	4	9	0	0	0	5	3	9	9	0.170	OF	29	1	4	0.882								

Georgia Class-D Minor League Baseball Encyclopedia

YR	TEAM	LG	G	AB	R	H	2B	3B	HR	RBI	SB	BB	SO	BA	POS	PO	A	E	FA	GP	W	L	ERA	IP	H	SO	BB
Garcia, Manuel		BR TR																									
1954	Douglas	GSL	16	24	1	4	0	0	0	5	0	0	11	0.167	P	3	7	1	0.909	15	5	3	4.81	58	54	43	38
1955	Moultrie	GFL	15	16	3	3	0	0	0	1	0	2	7	0.188	P	1	7	2	0.800	14	1	5	8.83	52	67	47	60
Garcia, Sergio		BR TR																									
1955	Cordele(47) - Moultrie(64)	GFL	111	373	41	84	9	1	5	50	3	38	52	0.225	C	590	77	10	0.985								
Gardecki, Stanley "Stan"		BR																									
1940	Moultrie	GFL	<10																								
Gardner, ---																											
1915	Waycross	FLAG	20												P	4	45	2	0.961	20	12	7		171	162	92	20
Gardner, Joel C.																											
1949	Dublin	GSL	75	247	28	65	11	4	3	44	0	31	14	0.263	OF	75	13	4	0.957								
Garmon, Raymond "Ray"		BL TR																									
1953	Sandersville	GSL	19	36	5	12	1	1	0	3	0	2	7	0.333	P	1	13	0	1.000	12	3	4	4.35	62	76	16	24
1954	Sandersville	GSL	124	525	80	153	21	5	6	48	5	34	58	0.291	2B, 3B, OF, P	148	66	38	0.849	8	1	2	<45				
1955	Dublin	GSL	14	51	6	12	3	0	0	2	1	4	5	0.235	OF	36	0	3	0.923								
Garner, ---																											
1928	Gadsden	GAL	67	231	26	58	3	2	1		4	12	16	0.251	OF, C	206	14	4	0.982								
Garner, Homer		BR TR																									
1949	Newnan	GAL	20	48	2	9	1	1	0	1	0	4	6	0.188	P	4	21	1	0.962	17	7	9	4.50	120	118	73	45
Garner, Robert P. "Bob"		BR TR																									
1946	Carrollton	GAL	67	210	31	59	11	0	12	35	4	19	35	0.281	OF, P	81	7	7	0.926	10	3	4	6.10	59	73	29	31
Garner, William W. "Bill"		BR TR																									
1948	Moultrie	GFL	27	27	4	4	0	0	0	2	0	6	12	0.148	P	3	14	7	0.708	27	5	6	5.14	91	119	44	44
1949	Moultrie	GFL	35	68	3	6	0	0	0	1	0	3	15	0.088	P	7	32	13	0.750	36	10	12	3.10	186	179	93	80
1950	Moultrie	GFL	13	35	4	9	1	0	0	1	0	1	9	0.257	P	8	26	4	0.895	13	5	6	3.75	84	87	45	48
Garone, Michael "Mike"		BR TR																									
1948	LaGrange	GAL	10	32	0	3	0	1	0	1	0	5	14	0.094	OF	13	2	0	1.000								
Garrecht, Robert "Bob"		BR TR																									
1949	Thomasville	GFL	35	51	2	10	1	0	0	6	0	3	12	0.196	P	6	32	5	0.884	35	7	12	3.91	159	157	106	54
Garrett, ---		BR																									
1946	Waycross	GFL	<10																								
Garrett, Charles		BL TR																									
1963	Waycross	GFL	57	163	25	45	6	1	0	10	5	46	36	0.276	2B	94	119	12	0.947								
Garrett, H.L. "Tige"																											
1914	Talladega	GAL	39	131	11	28				0				0.214	M, 1B	362	22	7	0.982								
1915	Talladega	GAL	53	205	30	53	15	1	2					0.259	M, 1B	516	17	20	0.964								
1916	Talladega	GAL	69	238	21	54				12				0.227	M, 1B												
1920	Griffin	GSL													M, 1B												
1928	Carrollton	GAL	30	124	21	24	6	0	1	3	7	14	0.194	3B	45	44	9	0.908								
Garrison, ---																											
1914	Talladega	GAL	6	18	2	2				0				0.111	OF	6	1	0	1.000								
Garrison, Lyle		BR TR																									
1946	Albany(20) - Cordele(18)	GFL	38	53	5	11	0	0	0	5	0	9	6	0.208	P	4	32	3	0.923	37	6	12	4.08	150	160	111	130
Garrison, William "Bill"		BR TR																									
1956	Fitzgerald	GFL	23	68	7	11	2	2	0	8	1	21	16	0.162	SS	41	62	16	0.866								
Garton, Edward D. "Ed"		BR TR																									
1953	Brunswick	GFL	17	25	4	7	3	0	1	5	0	4	8	0.280	P	0	9	2	0.818	14	4	4	4.58	57	59	54	49
Garvey, ---																											
1921	Carrollton	GSL	<10												P												
Gary, Louis "Lou"		BR																									
1953	Albany	GFL	4											0.056													
Gaskins, Henry		BR TR																									
1955	Dublin	GSL	12	23	3	5	0	0	0	0	1	12	8	0.217	SS	15	22	8	0.822								
Gassoway, Paul		BR																									
1940	Thomasville	GFL	<10																								
1941	Thomasville	GFL	55	198	21	45	5	1	1	27	1	20	38	0.227	C	288	14	15	0.953								
Gast, Lawrence "Mike"		GFL																									
1942	Americus	GFL	8	24	2	2	0	0	0	0	0	4	11	0.083	P	2	13	4	0.789	8	6	2	2.73	66	60	43	44
Gaston, Robert "Bob"		BR TR																									
1954	Waycross	GFL	1	0										0.000	P					1	0	0	<45				
Gaston, William "Dave"																											
1914	Americus	GSL		382	75	117	24	12	10		38			0.306	M												
Gates, ---		BL TL																									
1951	Valdosta	GFL	8												P					8	4	2	2.52	50	52	17	20
Gatza, Paul		BR TR																									
1958	Valdosta	GFL	8	19		4								0.211	P					7	6	1	3.38	48	43	34	21
Gault, Pat																											
1929	Cedartown	GAL	46	118	24	27	0	2	8		0	13	10	0.229	P	58	65	1	0.992	24	8	10		150	157	63	60
1930	Cedartown	GAL	6												P					6	1	1	4.34	29	33	13	8
Gautreaux, Joseph Jr. "Joe"		BR TR																									
1942	Waycross	GFL	22	68	2	7	2	0	0	4	0	2	21	0.103	P	5	39	3	0.936	21	7	12	3.27	165	147	89	66
1946	Waycross	GFL	20	39	2	3	0	0	0	1	0	6	13	0.077	P	6	29	5	0.875	20	8	7	3.46	125	120	66	44
Gavaghan, Thomas "Tom"		BL TL																									
1948	Moultrie	GFL	11	12	1	2	0	0	0	0	0	5	0.167		P	0	6	2	0.750								

Georgia Class-D Minor League Baseball Encyclopedia

YR	TEAM	LG	G	AB	R	H	2B	3B	HR	RBI	SB	BB	SO	BA	POS	PO	A	E	FA	GP	W	L	ERA	IP	H	SO	BB
Gay, William "Bill"		BR TR																									
1954	Brunswick	GFL	24	56	3	9	3	0	0	6	0	7	12	0.161	C	86	9	3	0.969								
Gearhart, Earl		BR TR																									
1954	Fitzgerald	GFL	48	114	14	28	7	1	1	15	1	9	36	0.246	P	11	48	1	0.983	40	20	9	3.07	258	275	118	66
Geary, Eugene Francis Joseph "Huck"		BL TR 5'10" 170 lbs. b. 01/22/1917 Buffalo, NY d. 01/27/1981 Cuba, NY																									
1938	Thomasville	GFL	74	295	44	72	18	4	2	28	7	26	31	0.244	SS	149	232	18	0.955								
Geary, Henry		BL TR																									
1951	Valdosta	GFL	124	447	103	120	24	3	5	70	14	110	38	0.268	OF	212	22	16	0.936								
1953	Jesup	GSL	29	102	30	32	6	0	4	18	6	28	12	0.314	3B	15	44	20	0.747								
Geary, Robert Norton "Bob"		BR TR 5'11" 168 lbs. b. 05/10/1891 Cincinnati, OH d. 01/03/1980 Cincinnati, OH																									
1914	Americus	GSL		237	35	73	11	6	0		5			0.308													
Geehring, Donald "Don"		BR TR																									
1948	Americus	GFL	46	154	18	36	6	1	1	13	7	19	32	0.234	2B, 3B	72	72	21	0.873								
Geels, Robert "Bob"		BR TR																									
1956	Thomson	GSL	28	104	19	27	6	1	1	18	3	22	11	0.260	3B	19	48	12	0.848								
Geesing, John		BL TL																									
1957	Thomasville	GFL	137	485	82	123	21	2	15	102	6	100	111	0.254	1B	1083	72	31	0.974								
Gehringer, Paul		BR TR																									
1950	Hazlehurst-Baxley	GSL	61	106	18	22	4	1	3	13	0	18	46	0.208	P	17	56	2	0.973	47	13	12	3.84	253	258	117	129
1953	Hazlehurst-Baxley	GSL	18	30	1	3	1	0	0	1	0	1	21	0.100	P	10	16	3	0.897	15	4	4	2.82	67	65	15	25
Geis, Harry		BR TR																									
1948	Cordele	GFL	85	329	48	88	21	2	6	51	3	21	46	0.267	1B, OF	337	9	11	0.969								
1949	Cordele	GFL	118	497	92	160	25	18	7	95	14	29	75	0.322	1B, OF	425	32	26	0.946								
Geminiani, Richard "Dick"		BR TR																									
1962	Thomasville	GFL	26	41	1	5	0	0	0	1	0	3	21	0.122	P	9	20	4	0.879	26	8	7	5.18	113	85	78	107
1963	Thomasville	GFL	3	1	0	0	0	0	0	0	0	0	1	0.000	P					3	0	0	13.50	4	3	7	11
Gemme, Bernard "Bernie"		BL TR																									
1957	Brunswick	GFL	38	140	15	30	8	2	2	28	0	15	25	0.214	OF	60	9	2	0.972								
Gendreau, Ronald "Ron"		BR TR																									
1951	Moultrie	GFL	123	450	61	110	19	2	8	59	3	69	93	0.244	SS	282	434	71	0.910								
Genevrino, Michael Angelo "Mike"		BL TL																									
1950	Americus	GFL	70	250	34	71	15	1	1	38	1	38	46	0.284	1B	571	33	2	0.997								
1951	Tifton(38) - Americus(57)	GFL	95	310	46	83	17	0	3	37	0	74	30	0.268	1B	883	36	10	0.989								
1952	Statesboro	GSL	63	240	33	70	14	1	2	39	1	33	23	0.292	1B	492	34	8	0.985								
Gentile, Samuel Christopher "Sam"		BL TR 5'11" 180 lbs. b. 10/12/1916 Charlestown, MA d. 05/04/1998 Everett, MA																									
1937	Moultrie	GFL	124	515	84	157	20	9	3	68	14	28	45	0.305	OF	278	13	11	0.964								
Gentle, ---																											
1915	Newnan	GAL	10	24	1	2	1	0	0					0.083	P					6-							
Gentry, Richard L. "Dick"		BR TR																									
1954	Tifton	GFL	44	159	25	30	5	4	2	13	5	37	36	0.189	SS	92	133	22	0.911								
Gentry, W.E. "Ed"																											
1928	Gadsden	GAL	75	285	43	91	12	2	2		11	29	5	0.319	2B, 3B, SS	135	224	15	0.960								
1929	Cedartown	GAL	87	352	51	96	15	4	7		5	19	16	0.273	3B	124	207	21	0.940								
1930	Cedartown	GAL	84	347	68	117	27	8	10		3	20	9	0.337	3B	81	292	18	0.954								
George, Alex Thomas M. "Alex"		BL TR 5'11" 170 lbs. b. 09/27/1938 Kansas City, MO																									
1956	Fitzgerald	GFL	138	421	68	113	15	2	2	42	9	127	114	0.268	SS, OF	277	97	14	0.964								
George, Charles Peter "Greek"		BR TR 6'2" 200 lbs. b. 12/25/1912 Waycross, GA d. 08/15/1999 Metairie, LA																									
1951	Americus(8) - Tifton(29)	GFL	37	135	15	36	5	1	1	18	0	22	13	0.267	1B	231	16	4	0.984								
1952	Tifton	GFL	31	121	22	40	5	3	0	19	7	25	9	0.331	M, 1B, C	204	18	5	0.978								
George, John D. "Johnny"		BR TR																									
1942	Americus	GFL	6	22	0	2	0	0	0	3	0	1	8	0.091	C	31	1	2	0.941								
1949	Dublin	GSL	24	104	22	5	1	0	12	2	3	7		0.212	C	139	12	3	0.981								
1953	Dublin	GSL	44	159	20	37	9	1	3	28	1	12	15	0.233	M, C, P	76	13	6	0.937	11	1	2	9.40	45	68	16	20
George, Milton "Milt"		BR																									
1946	Newnan	GAL	<10																								
Gerace, John		BR TR																									
1951	Americus	GFL	31	64	8	9	0	0	0	3	0	4	18	0.141	P	2	43	4	0.918	31	11	7	3.23	167	157	116	83
Gerard, Raymond "Ray"		BR TR																									
1955	Vidalia	GSL	53	164	23	36	7	1	5	24	0	19	40	0.220	OF, P	77	4	6	0.931	3	2	0					
Gergely, William "Bill"		BL TR																									
1951	Valdosta	GFL	125	472	88	138	22	6	3	74	10	83	35	0.292	3B, OF	200	32	20	0.921								
1952	Valdosta	GFL	11	40	5	10	2	0	0	3	1	7	6	0.250	OF	18	1	2	0.905								
German, Preston		BR TR																									
1946	Albany	GFL	103	414	65	119	14	1	0	36	16	43	44	0.287	2B	240	221	35	0.929								
Gershberg, Howard		BR																									
1955	Thomasville	GFL	6	19		7								0.368													
1956	Sandersville	GSL	10	32	5	4	1	0	1	2	2	6	10	0.125													
Geter, Eldridge		BR TR																									
1963	Waycross	GFL	35	35	3	4	1	0	0	2	0	1	14	0.114	P	3	11	4	0.778	32	8	7	2.95	113	83	117	49
Ghant, Roland		BR TR																									
1954	Statesboro	GSL	3	2		0								0.000	P					3	0	2		<45			
Ghelfi, Richard "Dick"		BR TR																									
1953	Hazlehurst-Baxley	GSL	22	48	4	10	5	0	0	6	0	4	19	0.208	P	3	21	1	0.960	22	11	4	3.23	128	121	69	81
1954	Hazlehurst-Baxley	GSL	9	6		0								0.000	P					9	0	1		<45			
Giambelluca, Charles		BR																									
1963	Waycross	GFL	12	18	8	2	0	0	0	0	0	8	2	0.111													

Georgia Class-D Minor League Baseball Encyclopedia

YR	TEAM	LG	G	AB	R	H	2B	3B	HR	RBI	SB	BB	SO	BA	POS	PO	A	E	FA	GP	W	L	ERA	IP	H	SO	BB
Gianelli, Ray		BR TR																									
1956	Fitzgerald	GFL	10	19	3	3	0	0	0	0	0	2	6	0.158	P					8	1	6	2.42	52	45	38	33
Giaquinto, Frank		BR TR																									
1950	Valdosta	GFL	13	28	4	4	1	0	0	1	0	8	15	0.143	P	2	14	2	0.889	12	7	2	3.14	83	75	56	43
Giavedoni, Nilo		BR																									
1951	Albany	GFL	14	25	3	5	1	0	0	5	0	3	7	0.200													
Gibbons, William "Bill"		BR TR																									
1952	Tifton	GFL	11	13	1	1	0	0	0	0	0	0	5	0.077	P	1	6	2	0.778								
1955	Tifton	GFL	1	2		0								0.000	P					1	0	0	<45				
Gibson, ---																											
1917	Tri-Cities	GAL	1	0	0	0	0	0	0		0			0.000	P	0	0	0		1	0	0		1	4	0	1
Gibson, ---																											
1921	Griffin	GSL													OF												
Gibson, Charles F. "Charlie"																											
1941	Moultrie	GFL	128	508	77	135	22	3	4	76	6	37	76	0.266	OF, P	224	14	13	0.948	3	1	1	4.71	21	20	10	13
1942	Moultrie	GFL	122	480	79	134	26	10	2	88	7	28	59	0.279	OF, P	217	95	30	0.912	4	2	2	4.50	28	30	11	11
Gibson, Hammond		BR TR																									
1954	Douglas	GSL	9	15		3								0.200	P					9	2	1		<45			
Gibson, Samuel Braxton "Sam"		BL TR 6'2" 198 lbs. b. 08/05/1899 King, NC d. 01/31/1983 High Point, NC																									
1949	Griffin	GAL	<10												M, P						0	2					
Giglio, Joe																											
1930	Talladega	GAL	1												P					1	0	1	45.00	2	8	0	3
Giglio, Joseph "Joe"		BR TR																									
1947	Valley	GAL	10	17	1	1	1	0	0	1	0	0	3	0.059	P	2	6	2	0.800	10	3	2	3.63	52	50	38	13
Gilbert, Arthur "Art"		BR TR																									
1946	Valley	GAL	38	90	8	18	2	0	1	8	0	4	21	0.200	P	4	53	2	0.966	38	15	12	4.52	233	226	123	80
Gilbert, Clarence																											
1949	Hazlehurst-Baxley	GSL	17	63	17	11	2	0	0	1	3	18	23	0.175	OF	40	1	2	0.953								
Gilbert, Drew Edward "Buddy"		BL TR 6'3" 195 lbs. b. 07/26/1935 Knoxville, TN																									
1954	Douglas	GSL	130	516	134	173	34	10	16	96	14	86	105	0.335	OF	299	9	14	0.957								
Gilbert, Glenn		BL TL																									
1955	Albany	GFL	6	6		0								0.000	P					6	2	0	<45				
Gilbert, Harry J.		BR TR																									
1953	Brunswick	GFL	3											0.000	P					0	0		<45				
Gilbert, Herbert E. "Herb"		BL TR																									
1955	Brunswick	GFL	47	147	15	33	3	0	0	12	1	24	21	0.224	OF	53	10	8	0.887								
1956	Dublin	GSL	14	39	6	8	1	0	1	9	3	5	5	0.205	OF	11	2	0	1.000								
Gilbert, John "Jack"		BS TR																									
1948	Baxley	GSL	28	72	10	15	1	1	0	3	1	10	14	0.208	P	3	31	1	0.971	25	16	8	2.64	208	173	124	50
1950	Dublin(3) - Jesup(7)	GSL	10	14	0	3	1	0	0	0	0	0	4	0.214													
Gilbert, Lewis																											
1920	Griffin	GSL													OF												
Gilbert, Philip "Phil" "Chicken"																											
1951	Hazlehurst-Baxley	GSL	19	27	5	6	0	0	0	2	0	6	4	0.222	P	0	17	0	1.000	17	2	6	5.92	76	104	42	65
1952	Eastman	GSL	28	68	7	16	0	0	0	9	1	6	16	0.235	P	7	21	3	0.903	27	17	6	2.97	182	142	150	94
1954	Vidalia	GSL	44	92	14	22	1	0	1	10	0	18	11	0.239	P	23	40	3	0.955	40	22	6	2.23	258	215	168	74
1955	Vidalia	GSL	32	68	6	16	2	0	0	8	1	4	10	0.235	P	10	38	2	0.960	28	11	9	3.49	178	168	118	71
Gilchrist, James "Jim"		BR																									
1956	Valdosta	GFL	4	11		3								0.273													
Gill, Audis		BR TR																									
1946	Opelika	GAL	52	189	37	50	5	3	1	23	5	21	20	0.265	3B, OF	84	59	16	0.899								
Gill, William H. "Bill"		BR TR																									
1949	Valdosta	GFL	129	432	62	115	12	8	1	50	17	58	43	0.266	C	1169	102	26	0.980								
Gillespie, ---																											
1913	Cordele	ESL	30	79	3	15	3	0	0					0.190	P	12	58	5	0.933	15	5	10					
Gillespie, Frank																											
1949	Eastman	GSL	14	39	4	9	0	0	0	5	0	4	10	0.231	P	6	19	1	0.962	17	5	6	6.25	95	86	55	53
Gillet, Albert "Al"		BS TR																									
1947	Valdosta	GFL	21	64	8	9	1	0	0	3	0	9	7	0.141	C	93	15	5	0.956								
Gilliam, Earl		BR TR																									
1953	Waycross	GFL	38	117	9	21	2	1	0	3	0	16	29	0.179	2B, SS	75	81	15	0.912								
1956	Fitzgerald	GFL	9	19		3								0.158													
Gilliland, ---																											
1917	Tri-Cities	GAL	2	7	0	3	0	0	0		0			0.429	OF	1	0	0	1.000								
Gillis, Grant		BR TR 5'10" 165 lbs. b. 01/24/1901 Grove Hill, AL d. 02/04/1981 Thomasville, AL																									
1936	Moultrie	GFL	92	340	51	88	15	4	1	41	8			0.259	M, 2B	203	241	14	0.969								
1937	Moultrie	GFL	90	339	51	98	14	5	1	26	2	52	13	0.289	M, 2B	201	293	11	0.978								
1938	Moultrie	GFL	27	114	12	35	2	1	0	11	4	13	4	0.307	3B	23	57	6	0.930								
Gilmore, Donald E. "Don"		BS TR																									
1946	Albany	GFL	35	51	4	10	0	0	0	3	0	9	24	0.196	P	10	34	6	0.880	34	5	11	4.58	159	173	94	108
Gilmore, John		BR TR																									
1948	Opelika	GAL	115	427	77	77	4	1	0	27	10	89	74	0.180	2B	239	303	34	0.941								
Gilmore, Robert "Bob"		BR																									
1962	Moultrie	GFL	4	9	1	1	0	0	0	0	0	0	2	0.111													

283

Georgia Class-D Minor League Baseball Encyclopedia

YR	TEAM	LG	G	AB	R	H	2B	3B	HR	RBI	SB	BB	SO	BA	POS	PO	A	E	FA	GP	W	L	ERA	IP	H	SO	BB
Gilmore, Russell "Russ"		BR																									
1953	Valdosta	GFL	6											0.125													
Gilson, John		BR TR																									
1946	LaGrange	GAL	12	19	2	6	0	1	0	2	0	4	3	0.316	P	2	13	1	0.938	10	0	4	5.14	49	49	25	33
Gilstrap, John		BR																									
1940	Thomasville	GFL	<10																								
1947	Americus	GFL	34	108	12	26	3	1	0	16	1	8	17	0.241													
Ginn, Stark																											
1916	LaGrange	GAL	60	203	24	47					12			0.232	OF												
Giombetti, Edward "Eddie"		BR TR 5'8" 160 lbs. b. 10/24/1923 Jessup, PA																									
1948	Carrollton	GAL	1												P					1	0	0		4			
Giordano, Alphonse "Al"		BR TR																									
1951	Valdosta	GFL	50	159	25	39	6	4	2	26	3	23	27	0.245	C	282	33	7	0.978								
1952	Valdosta	GFL	53	137	22	32	7	0	0	24	6	54	27	0.234	C	247	32	16	0.946								
Gisclair, Clyde		BR TR																									
1954	Thomasville	GFL	35	104	11	29	4	0	1	13	0	14	18	0.279	OF	56	4	0	1.000								
Givens, William "Bill"																											
1935	Moultrie	GFL	50	187	20	42	5	1	0		0	7	38	0.225	C	283	45	10	0.970								
Gladding, Fred Earl "Fred"		BL TR 6'0" 225 lbs. b. 06/28/1936 Flat Rock, MI																									
1956	Valdosta	GFL	35	69	4	8	2	0	0	4	0	1	29	0.116	P	8	29	4	0.902	35	11	9	2.76	199	166	167	86
1957	Valdosta	GFL	38	77	6	15	2	1	0	8	0	7	20	0.195	P	7	50	3	0.950	37	16	8	2.12	217	185	185	93
Gladich, Frank S.		BR TR																									
1950	Tallahassee	GFL	49	111	21	26	5	0	1	16	0	18	27	0.234	1B	202	7	7	0.968								
1953	Brunswick	GFL	36	92	9	21	3	0	1	15	0	8	14	0.228	P	6	48	1	0.982	31	14	13	3.13	213	202	96	50
Glamp, Francis		BR TR																									
1952	Brunswick	GFL	39	124	23	29	5	1	3	16	19	34	43	0.234	3B	53	70	22	0.848								
Glaser, Robert "Bob"		BL TL																									
1956	Thomasville	GFL	118	404	54	83	10	4	0	24	7	54	89	0.205	1B	802	42	21	0.976								
Glass, ---																											
1913	Talladega	GAL	89	344	55	97				33				0.282	2B	152	151	35	0.896								
Glass, ---																											
1928	Cedartown	GAL	31	86	9	19	4	0	2		0	3	9	0.221	P	11	47	2	0.967	23	11	9	4.73	154	166	68	60
1930	Cedartown	GAL	2												P					2	0	2	9.90	10	15	7	4
Glass, Richard "Dick"		BR																									
1946	Albany	GFL	<10																								
Glaudi, Benjamin		BR TR																									
1954	Statesboro	GSL	12	14	1	1	0	0	0	0	0	1	5	0.071	P	0	4	1	0.800	12	1	2	<45				
Glaze, Claude		BL TR																									
1947	Opelika	GAL	20	35	1	8	3	0	0	5	0	0	11	0.229	P	0	17	3	0.850	18	5	5	4.19	86	81	52	44
1948	Opelika - Alex City	GAL	22	46	1	14	5	1	0	7	0	1	6	0.304	P	4	16	3	0.870	15	2	8	4.30	90	99	47	68
Glaze, Hugh		BR TR																									
1947	LaGrange	GAL	66	244	47	68	8	1	1	21	21	27	27	0.279	SS	132	171	27	0.918								
Glazner, Charles Franklin "Whitey"		BR TR 5'9" 165 lbs. b. 09/17/1893 Sycamore, AL d. 06/06/1989 Orlando, FL																									
1913	Anniston	GAL	10												P					10	6	4					
1914	Anniston	GAL	22	62	5	10				0				0.161	P	25	36	5	0.924	22							
1915	Anniston	GAL	25	63	3	8	1	0	0					0.127	P	11	48	2	0.967	19	8	9					
1930	Cedartown	GAL	14	33	2	3	0	0	0		0	1	3	0.091	P	2	23	1	0.962	14	4	3	5.72	85	115	23	37
Glenn, ---		BR																									
1956	Dublin	GSL	1	1		0								0.000													
Glover, Charles		BL TL																									
1951	Tifton	GFL	32	144	23	38	2	0	1	20	4	10	16	0.264	OF	55	6	4	0.938								
Glover, James "Jim"		BR TR																									
1940	Moultrie	GFL	<10												P								<35				
1963	Thomasville	GFL	119	443	69	122	15	2	10	47	10	35	61	0.275	2B	301	312	22	0.965								
Glover, Omer Lee "Omer"		BR TR																									
1948	Alex City(27) - Carrollton(22)	GAL	49	116	9	20	1	1	0	8	2	16	25	0.172	C	165	26	8	0.960								
1952	Jesup	GSL	10	39	2	8	2	0	0	3	0	1	5	0.205	C	37	4	3	0.932								
Glynn, William "Bill"		BL TL 6'0" 190 lbs. b. 07/30/1925 Sussex, NJ																									
1946	Americus	GFL	114	470	88	154	34	18	15	101	8	39	73	0.328	1B	1037	67	28	0.975								
Godbold, Gus S.		BR TR																									
1948	Moultrie	GFL	135	528	122	148	10	2	1	39	22	50	100	0.280	2B, SS, OF	337	331	59	0.919								
Godwin, Charles William "Bill"		BR TR																									
1946	Opelika	GAL	40	149	13	41	6	1	1	13	0	3	13	0.275	3B	38	72	17	0.866								
1947	Opelika	GAL	91	366	46	111	24	7	2	54	10	14	31	0.303	3B	78	165	15	0.942								
1951	Opelika	GAL	66	271	36	82	19	4	6	57	4	26	34	0.303	3B, OF, C	176	133	17	0.948								
Goeken, Donald "Don"		BL TR																									
1951	Rome	GAL	68	162	25	46	11	0	8	27	1	31	30	0.284	OF, C	135	12	13	0.919								
Goen, ---																											
1915	Thomasville	FLAG	2												P					2	1	1		17	9	19	6
Goetz, Arthur "Art"		BL TR																									
1939	Albany	GFL													P								<45				
1940	Albany	GFL	24	58	8	14	1	1	0	2	1	2	11	0.241	P					23	8	9	3.28	140	152	104	57
Goff, James R. "Jim"		BR TR																									
1949	LaGrange	GAL	84	286	53	69	11	6	6	46	0	39	72	0.241	OF	98	9	5	0.955								
1950	LaGrange	GAL	113	402	69	111	18	7	21	82	1	65	92	0.276	1B, OF	653	37	23	0.968								

Georgia Class-D Minor League Baseball Encyclopedia

YR	TEAM	LG	G	AB	R	H	2B	3B	HR	RBI	SB	BB	SO	BA	POS	PO	A	E	FA	GP	W	L	ERA	IP	H	SO	BB
Goff, Jim F.																											
1939	Thomasville	GFL													P									<45			
Goggans, Bryant		BR TR																									
1948	Sparta	GSL	44	120	13	21	5	0	0	7	0	11	23	0.175	OF, P	26	12	6	0.864	18	5	8	5.01	88	90	34	49
Goggans, G.E. "Cheese"																											
1928	Carrollton	GAL	87	340	53	105	24	1	14		4	6	26	0.309	C	302	67	19	0.951								
1929	Carrollton	GAL	92	335	37	96	12	2	6		6	12	24	0.287	C	374	60	13	0.971								
1930	Anniston	GAL	86	345	58	116	26	3	7		5	10	19	0.336	C	356	53	13	0.969								
1930	Carrollton	GAL	<10												C												
Gohl, Vincent "Vince"		BL TL																									
1948	Moultrie	GFL	15	20	4	3	0	0	0	2	0	2	5	0.150	P	1	15	1	0.941	11	3	2	3.98	52	54	34	30
Goicoechea, Leonardo "Leo"		BL TL																									
1947	Carrollton	GAL	12	25	2	4	0	0	0	3	0	3	3	0.160	P	2	5	3	0.700	12	5	2	3.46	65	59	65	35
Goines, James "Jim"		BR TR																									
1955	Douglas	GSL	2	1		0								0.000	P					2	0	1					
Goins, Preston		BR TR																									
1953	Eastman	GSL	15	23	5	2	0	0	0	1	1	4	6	0.087	P					0	0		<45				
Goldasich, Paul																											
1938	Tallahassee	GFL	61	206	24	46	11	4	1	25	5	20	34	0.223	UT	191	19	17	0.925								
Golden, ---																											
1915	Newnan	GAL	7												P	1	18	1	0.950	7	3	2					
Goldfield, Alan		BR TL																									
1962	Moultrie	GFL	15	33	1	3	0	0	0	1	0	5	15	0.091	P	6	17	2	0.920	15	8	4	3.15	103	80	120	46
1963	Moultrie	GFL	15	18	0	1	0	0	0	1	0	1	8	0.056	P	3	16	5	0.792	15	1	4	4.23	66	51	74	46
Goldsmith, Ralph		BR TR																									
1940	Cordele	GFL	15	31	2	6	0	0	0	4	0	1	3	0.194	2B	23	15	2	0.950								
Golembiewski, Marion S.		BR TR																									
1947	Albany	GFL	107	386	57	107	27	4	2	61	1	17	59	0.277	1B, OF, P	184	18	12	0.944	16	8	3	4.50	84	97	65	28
1950	Moultrie	GFL	101	363	54	100	22	1	3	70	3	45	39	0.275	1B, OF, P	582	31	14	0.978	15	4	3	4.89	46	48	37	21
Gondolfi, Arthur "Art"																											
1916	Newnan	GAL	70	254	44	64					23			0.252	SS												
1917	Griffin	GAL	14	55	12	10	1	0	0		4			0.182	SS	27	28	9	0.859								
Gonet, William T. "Bill"		BR TR																									
1953	Thomasville	GFL	39	138	13	30	4	0	1	18	0	13	23	0.217	OF	60	3	2	0.969								
Gongola, Peter "Pete"		BR TR																									
1955	Vidalia	GSL	100	362	52	86	12	1	3	39	6	28	49	0.238	C	664	59	19	0.974								
Gonzales, Oscar		BR																									
1954	Americus-Cordele	GFL	25	75	12	8	0	1	1	5	3	19	26	0.107													
Gonzalez, Cotayo		BL TL																									
1950	Carrollton	GAL	8												P					8	4	2	4.19	58	66	27	24
Gonzalez, Thomas Jr. "Tom"		BR TR																									
1957	Valdosta	GFL	101	395	64	120	14	7	3	51	1	38	36	0.304	2B	208	270	32	0.937								
Gooch, John Beverly "Johnny"		BS TR 5'11" 175 lbs. b. 11/09/1897 Smyrna, TN d. 05/15/1975 Nashville, TN																									
1916	Talladega	GAL	70	232	18	41					3			0.177	C												
Good, Wilbur David Jr. "Bill"		BR TR																									
1948	Fitzgerald	GSL	114	440	62	139	16	5	1	65	9	54	25	0.316	M, 3B, SS, OF, P	182	274	38	0.923	15	5	2	3.91	76	82	33	23
1949	Fitzgerald	GSL	64	234	38	59	4	0	0	43	1	47	13	0.252	M, SS	124	137	20	0.929								
Good, Wilbur David Sr. "Will"		BL TL 5'6" 165 lbs. b. 09/28/1885 Punxsutawney, PA d. 12/30/1963 Brooksville, FL																									
1942	Tallahassee	GFL													M												
Goode, ---																											
1930	Carrollton	GAL	19	76	7	14	5	0	0		1	7	11	0.184	SS	44	55	11	0.900								
Goode, Noah		BL TR																									
1948	Americus	GFL	54	214	23	54	4	2	1	15	5	17	45	0.252	3B	55	108	31	0.840								
Goodlett, William "Vince"		BL TL																									
1963	Moultrie	GFL	2	2	0	0	0	0	0	0	0	0	1	0.000	P					2	0	0	5.40	5	3	2	5
Goodrich, ---																											
1906	Columbus	GSL													OF												
Goodwin, Fred		BL																									
1951	Opelika	GAL	51	147	22	40	8	0	1	20	4	21	10	0.272													
Goodwin, Gervin		BR																									
1946	Tallahassee	GFL	14	40	4	10	0	1	0	5	1	2	6	0.250													
Goodwin, Gilbert "Gil"																											
1941	Americus	GFL	11	44	5	8	1	0	0	5	0	4	10	0.182	2B, P	32	32	4	0.941	8	1	3	9.00	32	52	17	20
Goodwin, T. Hoyt		BR TR																									
1951	Valley	GAL	63	231	31	61	7	2	0	31	7	21	17	0.264	OF	105	7	5	0.957								
Goodwin, Troy																											
1949	Fitzgerald	GSL	11	36	2	9	2	0	0	1	0	1	4	0.250	3B	11	18	5	0.853								
Goody (Goodsoozian), Samuel "Sam"		BR TR																									
1952	Albany	GFL	141	597	95	167	26	6	1	47	18	57	24	0.280	2B	401	455	20	0.977								
1955	Hazlehurst-Baxley	GSL	106	408	65	108	10	2	1	48	12	42	16	0.265	M, 2B, 3B, SS, P	167	258	24	0.947	3	0	0					
Goosetree, Ed																											
1917	Talladega	GAL	16	64	8	15	4	0	0		0			0.234	M, 3B, SS	31	40	11	0.866								
Gordey, Alexander "Alex"		BR TR																									
1952	Jesup	GSL	16	31	0	2	0	0	0	2	0	4	10	0.065	P	0	15	3	0.833	15	3	6	6.08	74	86	41	51

Georgia Class-D Minor League Baseball Encyclopedia

YR	TEAM	LG	G	AB	R	H	2B	3B	HR	RBI	SB	BB	SO	BA	POS	PO	A	E	FA	GP	W	L	ERA	IP	H	SO	BB
Gordon, ---																											
1914	Brunswick	GSL		121	9	23	1	0	5		6			0.190													
Gordon, Early		BR																									
1956	Waycross	GFL	28	53	6	8	1	0	0	6	1	5	20	0.151													
Gordon, Jerry		BR TR																									
1953	Dublin	GSL	24	87	26	22	6	1	2	11	2	16	21	0.253	OF	33	3	3	0.923								
Gordon, Melvin																											
1941	Valdosta	GFL	27	62	3	3	0	1	1	2	0	6	29	0.048	P	4	22	1	0.963	27	16	7	1.98	177	148	103	31
Gordon, Robert E. "Bob"		BR TR																									
1952	Statesboro	GSL	49	197	31	54	8	1	0	21	2	14	20	0.274	2B, OF	121	72	10	0.951								
Gore, Jack		BR TR																									
1952	Douglas	GSL	94	348	46	72	11	3	5	47	5	37	77	0.207	3B	100	168	34	0.887								
Gormish, Michael "Mike"		BL TL																									
1948	Tallahassee	GFL	25	66	5	11	1	0	0	10	0	8	25	0.167	P	4	27	4	0.886	22	6	8	4.43	122	140	70	100
Gorton, Ronald "Ron"		BR TR																									
1956	Dublin	GSL	80	318	29	73	7	3	2	27	2	28	73	0.230	SS, P	150	219	49	0.883	1	0	0					
Gottesman, Bert		BL TL																									
1948	Waycross	GFL	11	6	1	0	0	0	0	0	0	4	3	0.000	P	0	5	2	0.714								
Gould, ---																											
1920	LaGrange	GSL													P												
Gould, Peter "Pete"		BR TR																									
1949	Americus(46) - Waycross(56)	GFL	102	366	71	101	7	1	0	48	14	37	47	0.276	3B, SS, C	209	120	28	0.922								
Gounaris, Alexander "Alex"		BR TR																									
1949	LaGrange	GAL	33	38	1	6	1	0	0	4	0	4	7	0.158	P	3	20	3	0.885	33	5	8	4.15	115	108	106	93
Gowan, Reid																											
1947	Moultrie	GFL	14	47	7	14	1	1	0	7	1	1	5	0.298	P					8	4	2	3.50	54	54	44	14
Grabert, Herman		BR TR																									
1953	Albany	GFL	131	496	98	148	26	5	9	70	21	77	59	0.298	1B	1015	50	23	0.979								
Grace, John		BR																									
1958	Waycross	GFL	12	31	8	8	2	0	2	10	1	9	3	0.258													
Graddick, John		BL TL																									
1948	Cordele	GFL	24	35	3	5	1	1	0	5	0	8	19	0.143	P	2	23	2	0.926	24	3	6	5.20	97	110	48	57
Grady, Bruce		BR TR																									
1958	Waycross	GFL	54	211	26	51	9	1	1	26	2	17	24	0.242	3B	56	73	21	0.860								
Graf, Phillip "Phil"		BR TR																									
1958	Thomasville	GFL	30	24	4	3	0	0	0	2	0	4	13	0.125	P	4	5	2	0.818	29	0	4	6.96	75	77	63	96
Graffeo, John		BR TR																									
1946	Cordele	GFL	12	46	5	11	1	1	0	2	0	3	12	0.239	OF	14	0	3	0.824								
Graham, Alvin																											
1937	Americus	GFL	32	57	1	5	0	0	0	1	0	8	15	0.088	P	7	26	1	0.971	27	8	9	5.14	168	199	81	89
Graham, Bernard		BL TL																									
1954	Brunswick	GFL	16	13	2	2	0	0	0	0	1	4	8	0.154	P	4	6	1	0.909	15	2	3	6.28	53	52	59	59
Graham, H. Thomas "Tom"		BR TR																									
1951	Douglas	GSL	13	12	1	0	0	0	0	0	0	4	7	0.000	P	0	4	1	0.800								
Graham, Homer		BR TR																									
1956	Hazlehurst-Baxley	GSL	1	0										0.000	P					1	0	0					
Graham, Joseph "Joe"		BL TL																									
1956	Tifton	GFL	33	55	4	7	1	1	0	2	0	7	36	0.127	P	4	29	4	0.892	33	8	7	2.86	154	140	133	65
Graham, Lonnie		BL TR																									
1956	Fitzgerald	GFL	94	308	54	80	9	4	0	31	5	90	57	0.260	2B	229	209	22	0.952								
Graham, Thomas "Tom"																											
1942	Dothan	GFL	15	42	6	6	0	1	0	4	0	7	13	0.143	P	2	36	2	0.950	16	7	8	2.52	125	96	115	60
Graham, Wayne Leon "Wayne"		BR TR 6'0" 200 lbs. b. 04/06/1937 Yoakum, TX																									
1957	Brunswick	GFL	109	449	75	136	18	3	8	58	11	41	31	0.303	2B, 3B, SS	267	240	40	0.927								
Graham, William Albert "Bill"		BR TR 6'3" 217 lbs. b. 01/21/1937 Flemingsburg, KY																									
1957	Valdosta	GFL	18	30	5	6	2	0	1	2	0	3	5	0.200	P	2	12	1	0.933	12	5	4	4.37	68	58	66	53
Grammer, Jack		BR																									
1955	Hazlehurst-Baxley	GSL	5	6		0								0.000													
Granger, George																											
1930	Lindale	GAL	51	123	19	40	11	4	3		0	11	30	0.325	P	5	40	4	0.918	29	14	11	5.03	204	264	90	56
Granger, Gerald		BR TR																									
1950	Hazlehurst-Baxley	GSL	19	21	5	3	1	0	0	1	0	4	4	0.143	P	2	12	1	0.933								
Grant, Charles H. "Charlie"																											
1941	Moultrie - Tallahassee	GFL	46	187	19	41	5	4	1	25	1	13	35	0.219	2B	112	137	16	0.940								
1942	Dothan	GFL	70	295	61	85	15	5	0	45	11	29	39	0.288	2B	189	211	28	0.935								
Grant, Cy																											
1935	Albany	GFL	13	48	8	16	0	1	1		2	5	3	0.333	OF	21	2	0	1.000								
Grant, Melvin		BR TR																									
1956	Tifton	GFL	21	15	3	2	0	0	0	2	0	1	8	0.133	P	0	8	1	0.889	18	2	4	<45				
Grant, Perley "Gabby"		BR TR																									
1951	Valley	GAL	108	402	62	128	30	6	3	75	12	32	31	0.318	M, C	478	58	16	0.971								
1953	Sandersville	GSL	53	189	30	55	12	4	1	35	3	20	6	0.291	M, C, P	215	16	4	0.983		0	2	<45				
Grasso, Joseph "Joe"																											
1949	Douglas	GSL	32	100	6	15	4	1	0	7	0	17	29	0.150	P	28	64	2	0.979	38	13	17	3.65	264	122	144	150

Georgia Class-D Minor League Baseball Encyclopedia

YR	TEAM	LG	G	AB	R	H	2B	3B	HR	RBI	SB	BB	SO	BA	POS	PO	A	E	FA	GP	W	L	ERA	IP	H	SO	BB
Graves, ---																											
1914	Talladega	GAL	8	19	1	4				0				0.211	3B	7	10	3	0.850								
Graves, Millard																											
1939	Tallahassee	GFL													P									<45			
Gravino, Frank John "Frank"		BR TR 5'9" 186 lbs. b. 01/29/1923 Newark, NJ d. 04/05/1994 Rochester, NY																									
1942	Albany	GFL	52	131	13	26	8	2	0	15	1	21	48	0.198	P	49	31	17	0.825	28	13	9	3.52	184	147	127	139
Gravino, Joseph P. "Joe"		BR																									
1953	Thomasville	GFL	2											0.143													
Gray, ---																											
1913	Cordele	ESL	22	85	11	27	0	0	0					0.318	SS	31	45	14	0.844								
Gray, ---																											
1928	Lindale - Anniston	GAL	58	175	20	42	10	0	0		4	3	16	0.240	OF, P	76	40	9	0.928	22	8	2	4.86	137	158	57	43
1929	Talledega	GAL	31	118	11	29	6	11	1		3	0	7	0.246	SS	68	91	12	0.930								
1930	Huntsville	GAL	71	207	13	49	6	2	1		1	4	19	0.237	1B, 2B, OF, P	208	64	12	0.958	24	2	6	6.49	97	143	31	53
Gray, Milton Marshall "Milt"		BR TR 6'1" 170 lbs. b. 02/21/1914 Louisville, KY d. 06/30/1969 Quincy, FL																									
1935	Thomasville	GFL	95	315	46	94	12	4	1		18	41	19	0.298	C	452	64	19	0.964								
Gray, Richard Benjamin "Dick"		BR TR 5'11" 165 lbs. b. 07/11/1937 Jefferson, PA																									
1951	Valdosta	GFL	110	463	118	140	21	12	6	71	31	49	37	0.302	3B	238	325	30	0.949								
Gray, Ronald "Ron"		BL TL																									
1954	Brunswick	GFL	34	72	10	9	0	0	0	3	0	11	33	0.125	P	8	39	6	0.887	31	19	4	2.71	209	187	116	101
1956	Brunswick	GFL	6	6		1								0.167	P					6	1	2	<45				
Grayston, Ed D. "Eddie"		d. 1995																									
1935	Americus	GFL	109	424	68	118	16	4	10		1	25	26	0.278	M, IF	1004	44	19	0.982								
1936	Americus	GFL	116	465	82	155	33	3	10	96	13			0.333	1B	1069	59	18	0.984								
1937	Americus	GFL	120	448	73	134	12	5	12	78	5	57	28	0.299	1B	1076	53	10	0.991								
Greco, Alfred "Al"																											
1949	Douglas	GSL	12	11	2	1	0	0	0	0	1	2	4	0.091	P	1	14	2	0.882	20	2	6	6.67	54	43	27	37
Greek, William "Bill"																											
1936	Albany	GFL	22	82	10	25	2	0	0	11	0			0.305	UT	39	30	11	0.863								
Green, ---																											
1921	LaGrange	GSL		170	41	53								0.312	SS, 2B												
Green, ---																											
1941	Waycross	GFL	4												OF	4	1	0	1.000								
Green, ---		BR TR																									
1946	LaGrange	GAL	1												P					1	0	0	0.00	2			
1946	Valley	GAL	<10																								
Green, Claude		BR TR																									
1951	Moultrie	GFL	12	49	7	15	1	0	0	9	0	3	9	0.306	1B	99	7	4	0.964								
Green, Fred Allen "Fred"		BR TL 6'4" 190 lbs. b. 09/14/1933 Titusville, NJ d. 12/22/1996 Titusville, NJ																									
1952	Brunswick	GFL	40	101	13	15	5	0	2	6	0	13	25	0.149	P	12	46	2	0.967	34	20	12	2.54	269	187	265	190
Green, Harold		BR TR																									
1954	Vidalia	GSL	128	469	89	115	11	5	7	57	29	102	55	0.245	3B	147	262	68	0.857								
1955	Vidalia	GSL	46	175	44	44	7	0	0	14	12	30	20	0.251	2B	92	102	11	0.946								
Green, James "Jim"		BL TR																									
1954	Valdosta	GFL	13	33	1	4	0	0	0	7	0	3	15	0.121	OF	8	0	1	0.889								
1955	Valdosta	GFL	9	38		7								0.184													
1963	Moultrie	GFL	89	257	28	58	10	1	1	29	4	54	49	0.226	C	701	45	18	0.976								
Green, Lee		BL TL																									
1962	Brunswick	GFL	35	120	28	34	9	0	4	21	1	23	19	0.283	OF	65	0	6	0.915								
Green, Paul		BR TR																									
1949	Griffin	GAL	12	42	3	7	0	0	0	7	1	5	9	0.167	SS	30	34	15	0.810								
Green, Ray C.																											
1930	Huntsville	GAL	30	104	16	30	4	4	1		2	15	31	0.288	OF, C	64	11	6	0.926								
Green, Raymond "Ray"		BR TR																									
1952	Valdosta	GFL	88	324	39	82	15	3	1	39	5	50	68	0.253	3B, SS	113	174	31	0.903								
1955	Thomasville	GFL	12	42	6	9	0	1	0	4	0	5	8	0.214	3B	12	10	5	0.815								
Green, Robert "Bob"		BL TL																									
1946	Tallahassee	GFL	30	72	6	11	0	0	0	6	0	6	14	0.153	P	8	37	5	0.900	29	14	8	2.75	193	177	115	82
Green, Robert L. "Bob"		BL TR																									
1956	Douglas	GSL	66	229	54	61	10	7	11	42	6	58	28	0.266	OF	105	4	10	0.916								
Green, William Rae "Billy"		BL TL																									
1954	Douglas	GSL	39	78	12	14	1	1	0	13	0	19	29	0.179	P	11	25	4	0.900	34	16	10	2.37	228	157	218	100
1955	Moultrie	GFL	39	50	11	8	1	0	0	3	0	6	7	0.160	P	6	12	1	0.947	33	8	11	5.79	154	150	105	116
1955	Douglas	GSL	2	3		1								0.333	P					2	0	1					
Greenamoyer, William "Bill"		TR TR																									
1949	Thomasville	GFL	13	22	3	6	1	0	0	3	0	2	3	0.273	P	6	7	0	1.000	12	4	3	7.44	52	68	24	32
Greenan, William "Bill"		BR																									
1954	Valdosta	GFL	3	13		1								0.077													
Greene, ---																											
1929	Talledega	GAL	8												P					8	1	3		37	54	9	7
Greene, Joseph E. "Joe"		BR TR																									
1954	Valdosta	GFL	21	45	3	11	0	0	0	2	0	7	13	0.244	P	6	22	0	1.000	18	11	4	1.70	122	103	107	30
Greene, Ray C.																											
1928	Gadsden - Lindale	GAL	30	96	7	22	3	0	0		0	9	12	0.229	C	122	16	7	0.952								
1928	Gadsden	GAL	68	255	29	77	12	2	6		3	11	12	0.302	C	191	59	11	0.958								

Georgia Class-D Minor League Baseball Encyclopedia

YR	TEAM	LG	G	AB	R	H	2B	3B	HR	RBI	SB	BB	SO	BA	POS	PO	A	E	FA	GP	W	L	ERA	IP	H	SO	BB
Greener, Andrew		BR TR																									
1951	Valdosta	GFL	14	33	3	2	0	0	0	1	3	8	9	0.061	OF	15	0	3	0.833								
Greer, Elwyn		BR TR																									
1940	Cordele	GFL	23	72	2	7	1	0	0	5	0	4	22	0.097	P					20	8	8	3.42	150	196	60	63
Gregg, Fred		BR TR																									
1947	Cordele	GFL	105	402	65	131	16	13	2	61	9	45	44	0.326	3B, SS	203	322	66	0.888								
1948	Cordele	GFL	121	475	93	148	22	17	1	61	28	66	51	0.312	3B	143	221	43	0.894								
Gregg, James "Jim"																											
1949	Eastman	GSL	18	61	10	17	2	0	1	11	1	5	9	0.279	OF	29	3	1	0.970								
Gregory, Bob G.		BR TR																									
1948	Tallassee	GAL	7												P					7	4	1	2.68	47	45	5	12
Gremp, Lewis Edward "Buddy"		BR TR 6'1" 175 lbs. b. 08/05/1919 Denver, CO d. 01/30/1995 Manteca, CA																									
1936	Albany	GFL	60	197	28	41	8	2	1	15	0			0.208	SS	99	117	29	0.882								
1937	Albany	GFL	113	376	58	91	10	8	1	37	5	37	47	0.242	2B	296	209	30	0.944								
Grice, John		BR TR																									
1947	Thomasville	GFL	137	536	110	182	29	11	3	99	15	57	43	0.340	OF	264	22	10	0.966								
Grieger, Russell "Russ"																											
1937	Tallahassee	GFL	34	125	19	32	3	1	0	14	2	15	7	0.256	OF	56	11	4	0.944								
1938	Tallahassee	GFL	27	95	19	25	6	1	0	8	6	12	14	0.263	C	95	31	3	0.977								
Grier, Harold		BR TR																									
1962	Thomasville	GFL	90	339	67	83	11	1	1	33	4	57	62	0.245	SS	136	228	35	0.912								
Griffin, ---																											
1913	Newnan	GAL	83	314	42	83					11			0.264	1B	675	38	8	0.989								
1914	Cordele	GSL		246	41	73	16	2	2		8			0.297													
Griffin, Alva L.		BR TR																									
1953	Cordele	GFL	33	84	8	12	3	0	0	4	0	18	24	0.143	C	91	11	4	0.962								
Griffin, Edsel "Ed"		BR TR																									
1947	LaGrange	GAL	89	309	42	61	6	1	0	20	6	44	49	0.197	3B, OF, C	143	91	25	0.903								
1948	LaGrange	GAL	12	27	2	6	1	0	0	4	2	3	5	0.222													
Griffin, H.																											
1906	Waycross	GSL													OF												
Griffin, Hal																											
1913	Americus	ESL	101	377	44	100	21	0	1					0.265	M, 1B	983	77	21	0.981								
1915	Newnan	GAL	60	218	18	45	4	0	2					0.206	1B	663	45	13	0.982								
1916	Newnan	GAL	70	249	29	66					9			0.265	1B												
1917	Griffin	GAL	16	61	12	14	3	0	0		2			0.230	1B	158	21	4	0.978								
Griffin, Ivy Moore "Ivy"		BL TR 5'11" 180 lbs. b. 11/16/1896 Thomasville, AL d. 08/25/1957 Gainesville, FL																									
1936	Cordele	GFL	113	432	67	125	17	3	4	63	12			0.289	M, 1B	900	47	10	0.990								
1937	Cordele	GFL	118	424	83	130	17	6	2	62	6	82	30	0.307	M, 1B	1043	65	7	0.994								
Griffin, T.																											
1906	Waycross	GSL													2B												
Griffin, Wes																											
1956	Tifton	GFL													M												
Griffith, Ralph																											
1929	Lindale	GAL	33	84	9	18	4	1	0		0	4	2	0.214	P	11	46	2	0.966	30	11	11		188	212	64	45
1930	Carrollton	GAL	19	48	12	11	1	0	1		0	0	9	0.229	P	3	30	3	0.917	15	5	5	7.07	98	136	30	32
Griffith, Richard D. "Dick"		BR TR																									
1952	Tifton	GFL	26	49	5	12	1	0	0	7	0	10	8	0.245	P	4	23	3	0.900	22	5	5	2.52	100	76	38	61
Griffy, James "Jim"		BR TR																									
1951	Griffin	GAL	29	53	8	15	1	0	1	8	0	9	17	0.283	3B, P	9	24	5	0.868								
1955	Valdosta	GFL	79	290	48	89	13	4	9	50	15	40	56	0.307	3B, OF	95	108	30	0.871								
Grigg, William "Bill"																											
1949	Dublin	GSL	12	16	1	1	0	0	0	1	0	1	5	0.063													
Griggs, William E. "Bill"		BR TR																									
1946	LaGrange	GAL	1												P					1	0	1	0.00	2	3	0	1
1949	Valley	GAL	16	16	0	0	0	0	0	0	0	3	10	0.000	P	3	10	1	0.929	16	2	4	3.70	56	60	29	19
1950	Eastman	GSL	27	50	6	8	2	0	0	11	0	13	24	0.160	P	5	29	1	0.971	27	11	6	2.83	140	119	86	83
1951	Eastman	GSL	33	71	6	12	0	0	0	8	0	8	23	0.169	P	10	36	4	0.920	28	13	10	3.44	191	184	91	89
Grilliot, William "Bill"		BR TR																									
1951	LaGrange	GAL	45	159	19	38	9	0	1	19	1	10	16	0.239	3B, C	111	49	4	0.976								
Grimes, ---																											
1928	Carrollton - Lindale	GAL	10	42	6	16	5	0	0		1	1	4	0.381	SS	15	16	9	0.775								
Grimes, David "Dave"		BR																									
1946	Newnan	GAL	<10																								
Grimes, Glenn																											
1936	Tallahassee	GFL	25	91	12	24	4	3	0	17	2			0.264	OF	39	1	3	0.930								
Grimes, James "Jim"		BL TL																									
1962	Brunswick	GFL	7	4	0	0	0	0	0	0	0	0	1	0.000	P					7	0	0	4.50	10	7	14	10
Grimes, Marion																											
1939	Waycross	GFL													P									<45			
Grimes, Michael "Mike"																											
1941	Thomasville	GFL	23	90	7	17	5	0	0	4	0	5	26	0.189	C	116	7	4	0.969								
Grimsley, Weldon		BR TR																									
1952	Moultrie	GFL	17	63	3	10	3	0	0	3	2	14	14	0.159	OF	14	0	2	0.875								
Grinnells, Harold		BR TR																									
1951	Opelika	GAL	13	28	3	10	0	0	0	3	0	0	1	0.357	P	6	16	1	0.957	13	1	6	6.35	68	83	26	37

Georgia Class-D Minor League Baseball Encyclopedia

YR	TEAM	LG	G	AB	R	H	2B	3B	HR	RBI	SB	BB	SO	BA	POS	PO	A	E	FA	GP	W	L	ERA	IP	H	SO	BB
Grish, Steve																											
1942	Albany	GFL	118	467	76	128	18	13	2	51	7	50	60	0.274	3B	133	228	47	0.885								
Grissom, Herbert "Herb"		BL TR																									
1956	Waycross	GFL	30	59	3	19	3	0	0	6	0	4	14	0.322	P	6	22	0	1.000	27	9	9	4.33	133	147	91	55
Grizzell, Robert "Bob"		BL TR																									
1951	Opelika	GAL	14	52	8	12	1	0	1	7	0	8	10	0.231	OF	20	1	1	0.955								
Groat, Clarence																											
1942	Tallahassee	GFL	104	400	89	120	13	9	0	34	10	84	43	0.300	OF	284	23	11	0.965								
Grobar, James "Jim"		BR TR																									
1954	Fitzgerald	GFL	72	272	54	73	15	6	5	42	9	42	62	0.268	OF	129	6	4	0.971								
Grogei, Donald "Don"		BR TR																									
1950	Americus	GFL	61	230	30	51	6	6	2	28	7	16	51	0.222	OF	172	8	4	0.978								
Gronsky, Steve		BR TR																									
1952	Cordele	GFL	38	40	6	5	0	0	0	2	0	10	18	0.125	P	2	26	3	0.903	37	9	4	3.16	131	136	64	73
Groome, J.L.																											
1915	Griffin - LaGrange	GAL	41	153	11	35	8	1	2					0.229	3B	33	31	7	0.901								
Gross, ---																											
1914	Brunswick	GSL		94	8	29	6	2	3	2				0.309													
Gross, ---																											
1920	Rome	GSL		268	41	63	10	1	1	2				0.235	OF												
Gross, Donald "Don"		BR TR																									
1947	Cordele	GFL	101	384	64	85	7	0	1	39	6	48	52	0.221	2B, 3B, C	229	150	32	0.922								
1948	Waycross	GFL	107	375	50	96	4	4	0	51	5	34	43	0.256	1B, OF, C	597	49	19	0.971								
1949	Waycross	GFL	20	73	17	21	1	0	0	7	2	10	6	0.288													
Gross, J.F.																											
1921	Rome	GSL													P													
Gross, Jerrold		BR TR																									
1952	Moultrie	GFL	15	24	3	2	0	0	0	1	0	2	11	0.083	P	2	10	1	0.923	15	2	5	2.57	63	46	25	45
Gross, Lloyd																											
1939	Moultrie	GFL	48	102	14	17	4	0	0	7	0	15	32	0.167	P	9	64	3	0.961	42	22	10	2.76	303	293	168	71
Grote, Harold		BR TR																									
1949	Valdosta	GFL	125	428	82	118	26	3	5	65	24	93	75	0.276	3B, OF	120	174	39	0.883								
Groves, ---		BR																									
1946	Valley	GAL	<10																								
Gruber, Robert "Bob"		BR TR																									
1948	Moultrie	GFL	44	154	17	41	1	1	0	15	3	11	22	0.266	3B	22	48	8	0.897								
Grupposo, Vincent "Vince"		BR TR																									
1946	Waycross	GFL	20	62	6	11	1	0	0	7	1	9	9	0.177	3B	23	45	4	0.944								
Grzenda, Joseph Charles "Joe"		BR TL 6'2" 180 lbs. b. 06/08/1937 Scanton, PA																									
1956	Valdosta	GFL	22	55	5	9	2	0	0	4	0	5	23	0.164	P	8	22	4	0.882	22	13	3	3.19	144	94	129	114
Guenst, Charles		BL TR																									
1953	Hazlehurst-Baxley	GSL	13	57	14	17	2	2	0	17	1	8	5	0.298	OF	17	1	1	0.947								
1955	Hazlehurst-Baxley	GSL	2	5		0								0.000													
Guerriero, ---																											
1942	Albany	GFL	4												P					4	2	1	5.25	24	23	6	10
Guess, ---																											
1915	Americus-Gainesville	FLAG	67	237	33	65	15	0	1		11			0.274	1B	625	23	19	0.972								
Guettler, Kenneth Adam "Ken"		BR TR 5'11" 190 lbs b. 05/29/1927 Bay City, MI d. 12/25/1977 Jacksonville, FL																									
1947	Griffin	GAL	109	404	80	135	18	6	25	103	12	49	53	0.334	OF	172	19	12	0.941								
Guido, Edward "Ed"		BR TR																									
1948	LaGrange	GAL	35	119	19	21	2	1	0	11	8	35	32	0.176	3B, OF	39	21	6	0.909								
Guinn, James K. "Jim"																											
1936	Americus	GFL	118	498	91	161	20	8	7	72	10			0.323	3B	161	225	23	0.944								
1937	Americus	GFL	125	489	78	146	18	4	4	49	9	50	17	0.299	3B	192	284	24	0.952								
1938	Americus	GFL	124	511	80	158	19	6	1	59	15	42	20	0.309	3B	185	260	43	0.912								
Guinty, Charles		BL TL 6'2" 172 lbs. b. 09/18/1909 Driggs, AR d. 08/13/1968 Little Rock, AR																									
1948	Americus	GFL	15	32	3	6	0	0	0	1	0	6	21	0.188	P	3	22	2	0.926	14	3	6	5.85	80	98	50	69
Guise, Witt Orison "Lefty"		BL TL 6'2" 172 lbs. b. 09/18/1909 Driggs, AR d. 08/13/1968 Little Rock, AR																									
1951	Douglas	GSL	23	63	10	17	2	0	0	5	1	5	18	0.270	M, P	8	24	0	1.000	23	14	6	2.16	154	147	127	29
Guitterez, W.																											
1913	LaGrange	GAL	55	209	24	49				8				0.234	2B	59	129	21	0.900								
1914	Selma	GAL	62	215	20	48				6				0.223	M, C	317	80	11	0.973								
1916	Newnan	GAL	16	62	7	16				1				0.258	OF												
Gula, Peter "Pete"		BR TR																									
1948	Sparta	GSL	108	408	65	127	20	9	3	64	4	47	51	0.311	OF	235	11	9	0.965								
1949	Sparta	GSL	107	467	101	163	29	9	2	77	10	74	54	0.349	OF	326	11	14	0.960								
Gulliver, Clark		BR TR																									
1946	Carrollton	GAL	90	344	52	69	12	2	1	20	8	31	75	0.201	OF, P	193	8	3	0.985	1	0	0	0				
Gulvas, Joseph W. "Joe"		BR TR																									
1953	Thomasville	GFL	56	195	37	52	8	3	1	33	10	23	20	0.267	3B, OF	72	66	8	0.945								
Gums, Marvin "Marv"		BR TR																									
1956	Vidalia	GSL	11	32	1	4	1	0	0	4	0	2	10	0.125	P	3	19	2	0.917	11	7	4	3.33	92	78	72	55
Gunn, Richard "Dick"		BL TR																									
1956	Albany	GFL	48	184	26	47	4	0	0	21	4	25	26	0.255	3B	28	71	12	0.892								
1957	Albany	GFL	63	267	38	63	9	6	0	23	9	15	18	0.236	3B	56	112	21	0.889								

Georgia Class-D Minor League Baseball Encyclopedia

YR	TEAM	LG	G	AB	R	H	2B	3B	HR	RBI	SB	BB	SO	BA	POS	PO	A	E	FA	GP	W	L	ERA	IP	H	SO	BB
Gunnells, Luther		BR TR																									
1946	Carrollton	GAL	117	402	89	153	27	2	24	96	31	46	26	0.381	M, SS, P	180	326	40	0.927	3	0	1	0.00	5	8	1	1
1947	Opelika	GAL	123	458	90	144	30	2	21	94	27	68	44	0.314	M, SS	201	362	57	0.908								
1948	Opelika(106) - Alex City(11)	GAL	117	371	79	120	18	3	13	91	28	86	32	0.323	M, SS	242	301	53	0.911								
Gunning, Edward "Ed"		BR TR																									
1955	Cordele	GFL	11	28	4	8	2	0	0	3	0	3	7	0.286	P	4	12	2	0.889	11	4	3	3.70	73	52	58	46
1956	Thomson	GSL	31	64	11	16	2	1	0	6	0	6	12	0.250	P	5	36	5	0.891	29	14	9	2.74	184	137	198	128
Gunter, Carl		BL TL																									
1955	Waycross	GFL	29	62	1	7	0	0	0	4	1	0	26	0.113	P	2	22	3	0.889	29	11	10	2.93	175	168	139	82
Gunter, Raymond "Ray"		BR TR																									
1953	Statesboro	GSL	7											0.000	P					0	0	2		<45			
Gupton, Harry		BR TR																									
1952	Dublin	GSL	41	167	29	49	10	1	0	16	11	16	12	0.293	SS	64	121	22	0.894								
Gurdy, ---		BR TR																									
1946	Carrollton	GAL	1												P					1	0	0	0.00	2			
Gurri, Anibal		BR TR																									
1952	Valdosta	GFL	48	148	21	31	2	4	2	24	7	17	39	0.209	3B, OF	42	31	10	0.880								
1952	Statesboro	GSL	44	145	31	40	5	1	9	25	4	17	44	0.276	3B	31	52	12	0.874								
1953	Statesboro	GSL	93	346	49	94	16	5	6	56	6	31	65	0.272	OF, P	122	12	8	0.944	2	4		<45				
Gusak, Tony		BR																									
1939	Americus	GFL	99	367	64	111	20	9	3	63	3	44	40	0.302	2B	227	259	40	0.924								
1940	Americus	GFL	<10																								
Gussin, Joseph "Joe"		BR TR																									
1957	Fitzgerald	GFL	20	10	0	0	0	0	0	0	0	0	6	0.000	P	2	1	0	1.000	20	0	1	11.70	30	54	19	32
Gustavson, Carl		BR TR																									
1948	Valley	GAL	34	85	12	14	3	3	0	5	1	7	14	0.165	P	10	39	2	0.961	29	15	8	2.88	194	196	96	64
Guth, Gene R.		BR TR																									
1942	Americus	GFL	33	83	8	12	1	0	0	2	0	9	18	0.145	P	12	31	3	0.935	30	10	14	3.83	214	204	144	97
Guthrie, ---																											
1915	Griffin - Newnan	GAL	14	37	1	5	2	1	1					0.135	P					12	5	6					
Guthrie, William David "Bill"		BR TR																									
1962	Brunswick	GFL	22	25	2	3	0	0	0	6	0	9	4	0.120	P	6	28	2	0.944	22	7	6	5.01	97	88	71	64
1963	Brunswick	GFL	8	20	1	2	0	0	0	2	0	3	14	0.100	P					8	5	2	3.00	57	38	75	27
Guymon, Darrell		BR																									
1958	Albany	GFL	2	4		3								0.750													
Guyton, ---		BR TR																									
1946	Carrollton	GAL	24	69	9	12	3	0	0	6	1	9	11	0.174	3B	9	19	4	0.875								
Guza, Michael "Mike"		BR TR																									
1955	Cordele(20) - Thomasville(2)	GFL	22	50	10	16	2	1	0	7	2	5	8	0.320	C	52	3	3	0.948								
Haber, Nathan "Nate"		BL TL																									
1949	Dublin	GSL	20	31	18	8	2	0	0	13	0	25	13	0.258	OF	32	2	3	0.919								
1950	Jesup	GSL	111	368	81	86	15	1	1	36	7	144	48	0.234	OF	177	10	6	0.969								
1951	Alexander City	GAL	37	100	20	27	4	0	0	13	2	36	18	0.270	OF	60	2	5	0.925								
1954	Sandersville	GSL	9	30		6								0.200													
Haddican, Harold		BR TR																									
1946	Tallahassee	GFL	85	321	58	88	14	3	0	31	34	46	69	0.274	OF, C	283	29	11	0.966								
Haden, Stanley "Stan"		BR TR																									
1938	Tallahassee	GFL	44	151	25	41	8	1	0	11	4	24	12	0.272	2B	85	116	14	0.935								
Hader, George																											
1936	Albany	GFL	10	22	3	5	2	0	1	3	0			0.227	P					10	2	2	3.07	44		18	26
Hadley, Harry		BR																									
1940	Albany	GFL	<10																								
Haefner, Milton Arnold "Mickey"		BL TL 5'8" 160 lbs. b. 10/09/1912 Lenzburg, IL d. 01/03/1995 New Athens, IL																									
1938	Tallahassee	GFL	82	202	30	53	10	3	0	28	2	41	34	0.262	P	57	59	8	0.935	35	15	10	3.27	234	248	107	66
Hafey, Will		BL TR																									
1940	Waycross	GFL	13	49	10	12	0	0	1	3	0	13	6	0.245	1B	133	6	4	0.972								
Hafner, Ronald "Ron"		BR																									
1958	Brunswick	GFL	11	34	6	10	2	0	0	3	1	6	9	0.294													
Hagan, ---		BR TR																									
1952	Jesup	GSL	7												P					7	1	6	3.05	62	62	19	32
Hagar, Carl		BR TR																									
1954	Hazlehurst-Baxley	GSL	60	219	18	54	12	0	2	30	3	21	48	0.247	3B, OF	77	64	16	0.898								
Hageman, John		BR TR																									
1956	Sandersville	GSL	23	24	2	4	1	1	1	2	0	0	13	0.167	P	3	11	2	0.875	22	6	3	4.32	73	66	50	60
Hagen, Richard "Dick"		BR TR																									
1958	Waycross	GFL	9	6		1								0.167	P					8	0	2		<30			
1962	Dublin	GFL	40	45	2	6	1	0	0	3	0	2	13	0.133	P	3	13	1	0.941	32	7	3	2.27	95	75	123	25
Hager, Fred																											
1921	LaGrange	GSL		166	31	52								0.313	M, C												
Hagle, Donald "Don"		BL																									
1948	Cordele	GFL	14	37	4	5	0	1	0	4	0	4	11	0.135													
Hahn, ---																											
1930	Huntsville	GAL	15	57	6	9	2	2	0		0	0	11	0.158	2B	44	39	9	0.902								
Hahn, Earl																											
1937	Cordele	GFL		36	10	11				0	9	1		0.306	OF	33	0	1	0.971								

Georgia Class-D Minor League Baseball Encyclopedia

YR	TEAM	LG	G	AB	R	H	2B	3B	HR	RBI	SB	BB	SO	BA	POS	PO	A	E	FA	GP	W	L	ERA	IP	H	SO	BB
Hahn, Louis "Lou"		BR TR																									
1952	Cordele	GFL	18	66	11	20	1	3	0	9	0	8	8	0.303	OF	23	2	2	0.926								
Hair, William G. "Bill"																											
1942	Dothan	GFL	40	111	13	18	3	0	0	4	0	8	25	0.162	P	19	48	6	0.918	35	12	11	3.36	214	189	148	115
Halden, Joe																											
1939	Moultrie	GFL													M												
Hale, Donald "Don"		BR TR																									
1948	Griffin	GAL	22	34	2	5	1	0	0	0	0	0	9	0.147	P	6	20	0	1.000	21	2	7	5.29	80	95	43	68
Hall, ---																											
1906	Cordele	GSL													P												
Hall, ---																											
1913	Cordele	ESL	38	117	12	28	1	0	0					0.239	P, OF	14	25	4	0.907	28	12	16					
1914	Cordele	GSL		108	7	28	0	0	4		0			0.259													
1917	Rome-Lindale	GAL	2	7	0	0	0	0	0		0			0.000	P	1	2	1	0.750	2	0	2		18	23	7	3
1920	Rome	GSL		33	4	8	0	0	0		3			0.242													
Hall, ---																											
1936	Albany	GFL													P										<30			
Hall, Carl		BL TL																									
1946	Tallassee	GAL	23	46	4	6	2	0	0	4	0	1	11	0.130	P	4	20	1	0.960	18	4	8	3.68	110	89	106	44
Hall, Floyd		BL TR																									
1946	Valley	GAL	44	132	23	26	2	0	1	16	7	23	27	0.197	OF	61	1	7	0.899								
Hall, G.H.		0																									
1915	Dothan	FLAG	27	90	5	24	0	0	0		4			0.267	P	12	56	4	0.944	21	14	5		173	146	78	18
Hall, Jack R.		BR TR																									
1952	Moultrie	GFL	16	40	1	9	1	0	0	3	0	3	8	0.225	C	52	6	3	0.951								
Hall, Jesse		BL TR																									
1946	Moultrie	GFL	<10																								
1948	Valley	GAL	42	172	28	47	5	1	0	12	6	12	26	0.273	OF	70	2	4	0.947								
Hall, Morris R.		BL TR																									
1954	Thomasville	GFL	8	21		4								0.190													
1955	Moultrie	GFL	23	74	10	12	2	1	1	10	0	13	18	0.162	C	134	10	8	0.947								
Hall, Robert "Bob"		BL TL																									
1947	LaGrange	GAL	64	233	33	59	6	3	0	19	7	18	35	0.253	1B, OF	285	15	9	0.971								
1948	LaGrange	GAL	36	147	26	40	2	1	1	28	3	15	17	0.272	1B	298	14	3	0.990								
Hall, Robert "Bob"		BR TR																									
1951	Waycross	GFL	40	116	24	26	5	0	0	11	3	35	18	0.224	OF	62	4	2	0.971								
1952	Waycross	GFL	30	95	16	27	3	0	0	5	6	27	20	0.284	2B, OF	46	36	4	0.953								
Hallford, Lewis "Lew"		BR TR																									
1950	Jesup	GSL	133	514	103	163	35	10	6	91	20	73	39	0.317	SS	340	442	61	0.928								
1951	Jesup	GSL	107	422	100	113	18	5	2	86	28	69	18	0.268	SS	217	343	28	0.952								
Hallman, George		BR TR																									
1952	Dublin	GSL	16	54	6	11	2	0	0	4	1	7	10	0.204	OF	30	2	1	0.970								
Halsall, Walter B. "Walt"																											
1949	Dublin	GSL	40	170	43	55	9	4	3	19	12	22	3	0.324	SS	70	135	18	0.919								
Halter, Richard "Dick"		BR TR																									
1954	Valdosta	GFL	1	1		0								0.000	P					1	0	0	<45				
Halverson, Donald "Don"		BL TL																									
1956	Fitzgerald	GFL	10	34	5	5	1	0	0	1	0	10	6	0.147	OF	11	3	2	0.875								
Ham, ---																											
1906	waycross	GSL													P, OF												
Hamende, Joseph "Joe"		BL BR																									
1963	Brunswick	GFL	12	16	2	1	0	0	0	0	0	2	6	0.063	P	4	11	1	0.938	12	4	5	1.80	65	45	49	22
Hamilton, ---																											
1906	Americus	GSL													P												
Hamilton, George		BL TR																									
1950	Opelika	GAL	39	155	33	42	5	1	2	10	4	22	18	0.271	2B	107	95	12	0.944								
Hamilton, Leon																											
1957	Thomasville	GFL													M												
Hamilton, William V. "Bill"		BR TR																									
1951	Eastman	GSL	31	121	12	20	4	1	0	9	0	15	11	0.165	1B	304	13	5	0.984								
Hamlin, Nat		BR TR																									
1951	Fitzgerald	GSL	20	51	4	10	2	1	0	6	0	3	8	0.196	P	6	26	1	0.970	19	6	10	4.65	120	129	33	67
1952	Eastman	GSL	15	47	3	10	1	1	0	8	0	4	8	0.213	P	3	15	3	0.857	15	8	5	4.77	115	102	43	46
1953	Eastman	GSL	25	66	7	11	6	1	0	6	0	7	16	0.167	P	6	27	6	0.846	25	13	8	4.52	185	186	67	77
1954	Sandersville	GSL	4	11		2								0.182	P					4	0	3	<45				
Hamlin, William "Bill"		BR TR																									
1951	Cordele	GFL	18	20	4	2	0	0	1	7		9	0.100		P	2	11	3	0.813	14	2	6	5.12	58	64	14	43
Hamm, Francis		BR TR																									
1946	Cordele	GFL	19	41	2	4	0	0	0	3	0	2	26	0.098	P	3	14	3	0.850	19	1	9	3.86	112	115	49	66
Hammack, Marion "Shurley"		BR TR																									
1947	LaGrange	GAL	78	287	23	54	7	4	0	28	5	21	75	0.188	2B	205	197	20	0.953								
1949	LaGrange	GAL	99	343	49	89	15	5	4	42	1	66	45	0.259	2B, SS	235	245	35	0.932								
Hammel, Wayne		BR TR																									
1948	Douglas	GSL	76	253	27	63	9	2	0	33	3	50	20	0.249	OF, C	141	9	8	0.949								

Georgia Class-D Minor League Baseball Encyclopedia

YR	TEAM	LG	G	AB	R	H	2B	3B	HR	RBI	SB	BB	SO	BA	POS	PO	A	E	FA	GP	W	L	ERA	IP	H	SO	BB
Hammen, Floyd		BR TR																									
1953	Valdosta	GFL	130	510	100	120	18	3	1	34	16	85	50	0.235	SS, OF	203	108	31	0.909								
1954	Americus-Cordele	GFL	95	341	58	81	11	9	1	40	6	71	54	0.238	3B, SS	153	234	43	0.900								
Hammett, Miles		BR TR																									
1948	Griffin	GAL	18	34	0	3	0	0	0	1	0	0	16	0.088	P	3	29	5	0.865	17	1	6	3.03	86	85	43	64
Hammock, William "Bill"		BR TR																									
1946	Tallassee	GAL	34	97	10	17	1	0	0	5	1	8	16	0.175	C	106	10	1	0.991								
Hammon, Silas		BR																									
1954	Waycross	GFL	2	1		0								0.000													
Hammond, J.H.																											
1930	Huntsville	GAL	103	417	83	148	35	10	13		11	35	43	0.355	1B, OF	666	29	37	0.949								
Hammons, Herbert "Herb"		BL																									
1948	Valley	GAL	14	53	4	10	1	1	1	2	0	4	4	0.189													
Hamner, R.L.																											
1928	Anniston	GAL	62	224	26	64	8	4	4		3	15	16	0.286	OF	146	7	3	0.981								
Hamons, Frank L. "Bull"																											
1952	Vidalia	GSL													M												
1953	Fitzgerald	GFL													M												
1953	Vidalia	GSL													M												
Hampshire, Larry		BL TR																									
1953	Thomasville	GFL	139	482	112	139	20	9	3	50	16	97	47	0.288	OF	238	14	6	0.977								
Hamric, Odbert Herman "Bert"		BL TL 6'0" 165 lbs. b. 03/01/1928 Clarksburg, WV d. 08/08/1984 Springboro, OH																									
1950	Valdosta	GFL	138	557	119	174	25	18	10	96	25	66	72	0.312	OF	264	20	28	0.910								
Hamrick, Charles		BR TR																									
1947	LaGrange(23) - Newnan(18)	GAL	41	139	32	34	3	2	1	22	3	26	24	0.245	OF	70	5	3	0.962								
Hamrick, Connie		BL TR																									
1962	Thomasville	GFL	28	66	8	8	1	0	0	7	1	12	19	0.121	SS	20	35	10	0.846								
Hamrick, Raymond Bernard "Ray"		BR TR 5'11" 160 lbs. b. 08/01/1921 Nashville, TN																									
1941	Americus	GFL	138	558	106	152	33	6	0	58	5	89	70	0.272	SS	289	486	100	0.886								
1948	Vidalia-Lyons	GSL	40	128	18	35	6	5	0	17	1	12	22	0.273	1B, C	172	6	11	0.942								
Hamrick, Roy S.		BR TR																									
1947	LaGrange	GAL	21	70	10	20	6	2	1	20	1	7	7	0.286	1B	147	3	9	0.943								
1949	Vidalia-Lyons	GSL	124	442	67	119	15	0	7	65	5	61	80	0.269	C	522	73	40	0.937								
Hancock, Leroy		BR TR																									
1955	Vidalia	GSL	51	196	41	55	5	1	1	21	3	34	8	0.281	2B	123	127	16	0.940								
Hand, David "Dave"		BR																									
1958	Dublin	GFL	8	26		4								0.154													
Hand, Dewey E.																											
1930	Anniston	GAL	14	42	10	18	2	3	0		0	2	7	0.429	P	3	18	3	0.875	13	4	6	5.88	75	124	38	15
1935	Thomasville	GFL	6												P					6	1	3		27	47	13	7
Handel, Henry		BR TR																									
1949	Tallahassee	GFL	19	35	3	5	0	0	0	5	0	4	11	0.143	P	2	26	1	0.966	15	4	7	4.39	84	98	29	46
1950	Tallahassee	GFL	19	36	4	5	1	0	0	2	0	3	13	0.139	P	8	18	2	0.929	19	9	6	4.05	91	99	52	44
Haney, Clayton "Clay"		BR TR																									
1953	Vidalia	GSL	29	47	6	12	1	0	1	3	0	6	9	0.255	P	0	15	4	0.789	22	3	6	7.64	73	80	39	86
Haney, Joe T.		BR TR																									
1954	Tifton	GFL	34	48	8	10	0	0	0	0	0	6	12	0.208	P	5	17	1	0.957	23	3	4	3.81	85	88	53	39
Haniak, Frank		BR TR																									
1958	Albany	GFL	33	100	21	21	3	0	0	8	2	18	21	0.210	2B	76	84	7	0.958								
Hanna, ---																											
1916	Rome	GAL	34	114	14	26					10			0.228	OF												
Hanna, John																											
1942	Albany	GFL	5												P					5	0	3	6.83	29	30	23	30
Hanna, Perry		BR TR																									
1953	Vidalia	GSL	10	8	2	3	2	0	0	0	0	2	3	0.375	P	2	4	3	0.667	10	0	4	<45				
Hanna, Victor "Vic"		BR TR																									
1954	Albany	GFL	8	6		2								0.333	P					8	0	0	<45				
1955	Albany(5) - Tifton(29)	GFL	34	51	4	5	0	0	0	5	0	6	9	0.098	P	9	18	1	0.964	32	4	16	4.63	144	126	86	94
Hannon, Chick																											
1913	Anniston	GAL													M												
Hansen, Henry																											
1941	Valdosta	GFL	9	24	2	3	0	0	0	1	0	2	16	0.125	P	3	13	0	1.000	9	4	3	3.49	67	67	26	34
Hanson, C.W.																											
1921	Rome	GSL		70	11	22								0.314													
Hanson, Harry Francis "Harry"		BR TR 5'11" b. 01/17/1896 Elgin, IL d. 10/05/1966 Savannah, GA																									
1913	Newnan	GAL	17	56	6	14				5				0.250	C	72	12	0	1.000								
1916	Griffin	GAL	70	240	21	59				6				0.246	OF, C												
1917	Griffin	GAL	15	48	1	7	3	0	0	1				0.146	OF, C	12	8	1	0.952								
Hanson, J.W.		BR TR																									
1950	Valley(31) - Alex City(5)	GAL	36	109	23	21	3	0	0	5	6	21	19	0.193	3B, SS	39	69	15	0.878								
Harbison, Douglas																											
1916	Griffin	GAL	17	58	5	8				1				0.138	OF												
Hardage, ---																											
1913	Opelika	GAL	31	132	17	35				7				0.265	OF	51	1	2	0.963								

292

Georgia Class-D Minor League Baseball Encyclopedia

YR	TEAM	LG	G	AB	R	H	2B	3B	HR	RBI	SB	BB	SO	BA	POS	PO	A	E	FA	GP	W	L	ERA	IP	H	SO	BB
Hardegree, William "Bill"		BL TR																									
1946	Albany	GFL	<10																								
1948	Waycross	GFL	48	161	28	37	7	4	1	22	1	40	55	0.230	OF	73	5	10	0.886								
1948	Eastman	GSL	74	250	27	52	7	3	1	25	11	46	86	0.208	OF	133	7	11	0.927								
1949	Griffin	GAL	16	64	10	10	0	0	0	4	3	12	13	0.156	OF	39	3	1	0.977								
1949	Eas - Dub - Fit	GSL	38	139	25	35	6	3	4	30	1	35	33	0.252	OF	66	7	6	0.924								
Harden, James W. "Jim"		BR TR																									
1948	Eastman	GSL	16	42	5	8	2	0	0	8	0	5	9	0.190	P	5	15	1	0.952	16	13	1	1.36	132	105	67	14
1949	Eastman	GSL	27	81	12	20	5	0	0	12	0	16	21	0.247	P	12	47	3	0.952	28	20	5	2.62	234	86	136	32
1950	Eastman	GSL	31	86	5	17	2	0	0	5	0	11	23	0.198	P	9	53	3	0.954	31	14	14	2.96	225	213	128	37
1951	Eastman	GSL	28	65	6	11	3	0	0	8	0	13	12	0.169	P	9	26	0	1.000	28	15	7	3.02	188	203	64	34
Hardin, Doyle "Henry"		BR TR																									
1940	Albany	GFL	71	291	46	85	18	1	0	44	5	27	30	0.292	OF	177	14	7	0.965								
Hardin, Hugh R.		BR TL																									
1963	Thomasville	GFL	16	29	3	4	1	0	0	2	0	7	11	0.138	P	2	13	2	0.882	16	4	6	2.72	96	66	113	72
Hardish, Richard "Dick"		BR TR																									
1952	Cordele	GFL	21	21	0	1	0	0	0	0	0	0	6	0.048	P	0	10	4	0.714	21	1	5	4.94	51	55	23	52
Hardison, James "Jim"		BL TR																									
1955	Dublin	GSL	42	87	17	19	2	1	0	9	0	8	16	0.218	P	7	56	5	0.926	37	10	14	2.71	226	193	179	95
Hardwick, George																											
1929	Lindale	GAL	25	56	4	13	3	0	1	0	1		12	0.232	P	8	17	2	0.926	20	8	4		122	164	37	23
1930	Carrollton	GAL	12	36	6	12	1	0	0	0	1		3	0.333	P	7	9	1	0.941	11	3	5	6.46	71	104	23	24
Hardwick, James "Jim"		BL TR																									
1956	Vidalia	GSL	47	197	37	55	9	4	3	33	5	16	23	0.279	OF	82	2	2	0.977								
Hare, Bernard		BL TL																									
1949	Thomasville	GFL	52	178	25	48	5	3	1	25	3	28	25	0.270	OF	60	8	5	0.932								
Hargis, ---																											
1930	Huntsville	GAL	10	38	2	6	1	0	0		0	1	7	0.158													
Hargis, James "Jim"		BR TR																									
1949	Newnan(7) - Griffin(10)	GAL	17	53	7	14	2	0	0	9	0	4	1	0.264	OF	18	1	0	1.000								
Hargrove, Woodrow "Woody"																											
1936	Cordele	GFL	19	50	4	15	1	0	0	6	0			0.300	P					19	2	2	3.19	48		17	19
1937	Cordele	GFL	69	172	17	39	7	4	1	12	3	12	26	0.227	P	92	39	10	0.929	34	17	10	3.88	209	210	99	70
1938	Cordele	GFL	110	419	47	135	22	7	3	78	10	28	46	0.322	UT, P	293	51	16	0.956	16	5	5	3.56	101	113	50	33
1941	Thomasville	GFL	46	177	28	57	6	2	6	36	3	13	21	0.322	OF, P	120	9	11	0.921	2	2	0	1.50	18	14	7	8
Harjo, Fesser																											
1941	Moultrie	GFL	7	13	0	2	0	0	0	1	0	0	7	0.154	P	1	6	1	0.875	7	0	2	7.64	33	42	13	18
Harkness, Jean																											
1937	Tallahassee	GFL	17	43	1	5	2	0	0	3	0	2	9	0.116	P	10	10	1	0.952	10	0	8	10.19	53	79	18	51
Harms, Carl																											
1942	Albany	GFL	14	30	3	4	3	0	0	4	0	3	17	0.133	P	0	20	2	0.909	12	2	5	5.31	78	79	33	56
Harms, Lionel		BR TR																									
1954	Waycross	GFL	4	6	0									0.000	P					2	0	1	<45				
Harms, Roger		BR TR																									
1956	Vidalia	GSL	5	12		2								0.167	P					5	2	1					
Harp, James "Jim"		BR TR																									
1949	Eastman	GSL	35	109	14	21	1	0	0	13	0	16	20	0.193	P	20	59	3	0.963	36	20	11	3.07	267	124	148	81
1950	Eastman	GSL	30	60	7	5	1	0	0	4	1	14	26	0.083	P					28	13	6	3.53	176	185	85	49
1951	Eastman	GSL	45	112	13	30	3	2	0	17	2	16	21	0.268	P	16	55	4	0.947	36	23	12	2.30	254	250	115	57
1952	Eastman	GSL	48	116	16	26	3	0	0	8	1	17	15	0.224	1B, P	72	59	4	0.970	34	15	10	2.40	229	190	103	36
1953	Eastman	GSL	51	96	14	21	1	0	0	14	1	15	21	0.219	P	16	34	5	0.909	35	19	11	3.33	227	228	102	42
Harper, ---																											
1906	Cordele	GSL													SS												
Harper, Cartha		BR TR																									
1956	Fitzgerald	GFL	4	11		2								0.182	P					1	0	1	<45				
Harper, Charles B.		BR TR																									
1950	Americus	GFL	13	36	0	8	3	0	0	4	0	1	10	0.222	P	3	17	2	0.909	13	4	6	3.70	90	70	44	70
Harper, Dean		BR TL																									
1952	Tifton	GFL	22	67	9	10	3	1	0	5	1	12	13	0.149	OF	29	1	2	0.938								
Harper, Luther		BR TR																									
1951	Hazlehurst-Baxley	GSL	15	67	8	10	2	0	0	7	2	7	12	0.149	2B	38	47	3	0.966								
Harper, William "Bill"		BR TR																									
1946	LaGrange	GAL	14	59	7	11	1	0	0	4	0	3	10	0.186	3B	10	12	5	0.815								
Harrell, Benjamin "Ben"		BR TR																									
1946	Opelika	GAL	42	90	8	18	1	0	0	8	1	2	17	0.200	P	5	35	1	0.976	23	5	12	4.14	126	115	70	71
1947	Newnan	GAL	12	19	1	1	0	0	0	0	0	4	2	0.053													
Harrell, Joseph "Joe"		BR TR																									
1947	Alexander City	GAL	56	193	14	41	5	2	1	19	6	16	30	0.212	SS	82	177	41	0.863								
Harrell, Raymond James "Ray"		BR TR 6'1" 185 lbs b. 02/16/1912 Petrolia, TX d. 01/28/1984 Alexandria, LA																									
1950	Fitzgerald	GSL	28	67	7	16	3	0	2	13	0	14	17	0.239	M, P	1	27	3	0.903	27	15	10	4.17	203	226	108	67
Harrelson, Cleveland		BR TR																									
1950	Alexander City	GAL	22	31	8	4	0	0	0	4	1	12	13	0.129	2B	15	15	2	0.938								
Harrelson, John		BR TL																									
1947	Griffin	GAL	34	82	9	17	1	1	0	9	0	4	21	0.207	P	13	32	4	0.918	27	12	12	4.15	169	196	83	71
Harrigan, W.L.																											
1906	Americus	GSL													M, OF												

Georgia Class-D Minor League Baseball Encyclopedia

YR	TEAM	LG	G	AB	R	H	2B	3B	HR	RBI	SB	BB	SO	BA	POS	PO	A	E	FA	GP	W	L	ERA	IP	H	SO	BB
Harrington, Charles F. "Fred"		BR TR																									
1957	Brunswick	GFL	39	164	33	57	14	1	9	47	2	7	18	0.348	OF	57	4	3	0.953								
Harrington, Hayes																											
1935	Albany	GFL	103	335	71	109	30	3	4		11	43	34	0.325	C	444	50	15	0.971								
Harrington, Louis "Lou"		BR TR																									
1954	Sandersville	GSL	6	21		6								0.286	P					1	0	0	<45				
Harrington, Walter																											
1939	Cordele	GFL	23	100	10	29	7	1	0	7	0	3	12	0.290	1B	221	14	7	0.971								
Harris, ---		BR TR																									
1946	Newnan	GAL	1												P					1	0	0	0				
Harris, C.																											
1929	Cedartown	GAL	16	54	11	15	4	0	0		2	5	4	0.278	2B	40	46	5	0.945								
1930	Huntsville	GAL	10	39	6	12	0	0	1		0	2	3	0.308	2B, P	27	29	4	0.933	2	0	2	14.00	9	22	2	2
Harris, Darrell		BR TR																									
1954	Sandersville	GSL	16	49	4	8	1	0	0	6	0	5	17	0.163	SS	22	41	13	0.829								
Harris, H. Dick		BL TR																									
1963	Waycross(20) - Brunswick(14)	GFL	34	100	12	16	6	0	2	13	0	22	21	0.160	OF	41	4	2	0.957								
Harris, Jack																											
1929	Talledega	GAL	54	198	31	49	6	6	4		10	18	52	0.247	2B	151	142	14	0.954								
Harris, Joe																											
1928	Anniston	GAL	13	24	3	5	0	0	0		1	1	3	0.208	P	6	19	4	0.862	11	3	4	4.04	69	28	18	41
1929	Lindale	GAL	16	23	1	4	0	0	0		0	2	3	0.174	P	4	11	2	0.882	16	2	6		75	95	23	29
Harris, L. Mercer		BL TR																									
1947	Cordele	GFL	55	167	31	50	5	3	0	19	2	38	6	0.299	M, 1B, 3B	258	37	7	0.977								
Harris, Oliver J.		BL TL																									
1953	Dublin	GSL	44	138	13	26	1	1	1	8	0	34	29	0.188	1B	317	26	16	0.955								
Harris, Reese		BR																									
1940	Moultrie	GFL	<10																								
Harris, Robert "Bob"		BL																									
1950	Opelika	GAL	10	19	0	1	0	0	0	0	0	2	11	0.053													
Harris, Robert D. "Bob"		BR TR																									
1956	Moultrie	GFL	78	272	58	70	14	3	3	36	13	55	61	0.257	OF	148	8	9	0.945								
Harris, William E. "Bill"		BR TR																									
1948	Baxley	GSL	84	297	29	73	4	0	1	31	7	21	30	0.246	C	506	37	25	0.956								
1950	Hazlehurst-Baxley	GSL	98	352	35	96	14	4	3	48	2	18	28	0.273	OF, C	171	11	13	0.933								
1951	Hazlehurst-Baxley	GSL	126	483	76	147	20	5	2	56	9	42	32	0.304	OF, C	464	54	24	0.956								
Harris, William Thomas "Bill"		BL TR 5'8" 187 lbs b. 12/03/1931 Duguayville, NB, CAN																									
1951	Valdosta	GFL	40	88	19	25	2	2	0	19	1	8	9	0.284	P	10	31	2	0.953	32	18	9	2.19	201	126	189	66
Harrison, ---																											
1929	Carrollton	GAL	16	55	8	17	2	1	1		1	4	12	0.309	OF	33	1	1	0.971								
Harrison, Charles L.		BR TR																									
1951	LaGrange	GAL	28	65	8	14	2	0	0	7	0	12	12	0.215	P	4	32	5	0.878	28	19	3	3.73	186	185	114	101
Harrison, Dennis "Dennie"		BR TR																									
1939	Valdosta	GFL	115	424	90	126	14	3	0	38	38	75	33	0.297	OF	271	26	14	0.955								
1940	Valdosta	GFL	81	316	75	85	10	1	0	22	20	65	32	0.269	3B	95	159	31	0.891								
Harrison, L.H.		BR TR																									
1953	Tifton	GFL	50	161	38	33	4	0	0	9	2	34	21	0.205	SS	67	103	21	0.890								
Harrison, Randy		BL																									
1954	Americus-Cordele	GFL	10	34	4	9	0	1	0	6	0	5	3	0.265													
Harrison, William "Bill"		BR TR																									
1949	Valley	GAL	13	51	10	9	1	1	0	2	2	3	9	0.176	2B	37	30	7	0.905								
Harrod, Jerrel		BR TR																									
1952	Waycross	GFL	84	300	31	74	10	2	0	25	2	24	24	0.247	OF	126	4	12	0.915								
Harrow, Herbert "Herb"		BR TR																									
1953	Sandersville	GSL	36	118	29	27	5	2	1	18	2	37	20	0.229	2B	66	71	10	0.932								
Hart, ---																											
1906	Cordele	GSL													C												
Hart, Clarence																											
1930	Huntsville	GAL													M												
Hart, Gary		BR TL																									
1963	Thomasville	GFL	23	11	3	1	0	0	0	0	0	2	5	0.091	P	0	7	0	1.000	23	2	5	2.34	50	46	49	24
Hart, Norman "Norm"		BL TL																									
1949	Griffin	GAL	10	16	4	2	0	0	0	0	1	1	7	0.125	P	3	11	1	0.933								
Hart, Richard "Dick"		BR TR																									
1962	Dublin	GFL	46	173	39	52	7	3	12	46	1	23	58	0.301	1B	316	14	14	0.959								
Hartbarger, James "Jim"		BR TR																									
1955	Brunswick	GFL	49	191	20	42	4	0	0	12	2	13	49	0.220	2B	126	152	23	0.924								
Hartlein, William "Bill"		BR TR																									
1947	Valley	GAL	97	370	45	110	12	2	1	49	6	21	49	0.297	OF	141	5	10	0.936								
Hartley, Donald "Don"		BL TR																									
1954	Sandersville	GSL	14	50	6	8	2	0	0	3	0	5	4	0.160	C	120	8	4	0.970								
Hartley, Donald Lee "Lee"		BR TR																									
1948	Sparta	GSL	35	136	18	29	3	1	0	15	4	8	21	0.213	OF	43	3	1	0.979								
1949	Sparta	GSL	117	427	41	104	18	4	0	60	3	42	41	0.244	OF	277	23	21	0.935								

Georgia Class-D Minor League Baseball Encyclopedia

YR	TEAM	LG	G	AB	R	H	2B	3B	HR	RBI	SB	BB	SO	BA	POS	PO	A	E	FA	GP	W	L	ERA	IP	H	SO	BB
Hartley, James E. "Jim"		BR TR																									
1951	Jesup	GSL	34	71	11	14	3	0	0	8	2	13	23	0.197	P	9	55	2	0.970	34	13	5	2.95	192	171	67	76
Hartley, Travis		BR TR																									
1938	Cordele	GFL	44	116	8	21	2	2	0	8	0	5	19	0.181	P	22	23	4	0.918	21	6	9	3.24	139	148	52	68
1939	Valdosta	GFL	39	65	2	12	3	0	0	4	0	2	10	0.185	P	5	37	6	0.875	34	9	4	3.05	168	170	70	60
1940	Valdosta	GFL	30	69	11	19	2	0	0	7	0	2	10	0.275	P					26	9	3	4.72	122	150	34	42
Hartman, Earl		BL TL																									
1946	Albany	GFL	112	412	64	111	18	9	4	63	7	58	56	0.269	1B	927	50	26	0.974								
1947	Griffin	GAL	117	437	89	129	26	11	15	76	14	57	67	0.295	1B	949	42	22	0.978								
1948	Sparta	GSL	60	183	43	54	8	8	6	47	2	47	42	0.295	1B	458	10	8	0.983								
1949	Tifton	GSL	146	524	116	157	40	4	23	134	9	88	53	0.300	1B	1255	53	20	0.985								
Hartman, Elmer		BL TL																									
1955	Cordele	GFL	4	1		0								0.000	P					4	0	0	<45				
Hartman, John		BL TR																									
1962	Thomasville	GFL	32	109	19	27	2	1	3	16	0	9	25	0.248	OF	39	2	1	0.976								
1963	Thomasville	GFL	100	269	30	52	4	4	3	22	5	37	83	0.193	OF	121	8	8	0.942								
Hartman, Richard "Dick"		BR TR																									
1949	Alexander City	GAL	39	93	9	15	0	0	0	4	3	9	13	0.161	C	166	19	2	0.989								
1950	Alexander City	GAL	16	53	9	14	2	1	0	11	2	3	2	0.264	C	75	10	0	1.000								
Hartner, ---																											
1913	Brunswick	ESL	43	132	20	35	4	0	2					0.265	P, OF	29	50	2	0.975	23	15	8					
1914	Waycross	GSL		60	3	6	0	0	1		0			0.100													
Hartness, Edgar Clifford "Edd"		BL TL 5'11" 180 lbs b. 03/12/1920 Murphy, NC																									
1938	Americus	GFL	108	443	66	123	16	14	8	69	2	24	45	0.278	1B	1029	38	31	0.972								
1939	Americus	GFL	129	491	89	175	27	9	1	69	20	47	29	0.356	OF	314	17	17	0.951								
1949	Eastman	GSL	139	486	119	177	41	12	13	136	27	104	16	0.364	M, 1B	1212	65	19	0.985								
1950	Eastman	GSL	142	503	137	201	48	11	20	134	25	121	19	0.400	M, 1B	1307	64	24	0.983								
1953	Tifton	GFL	135	491	94	158	25	6	6	83	15	76	21	0.322	M, 1B	1074	45	13	0.989								
1954	Tifton	GFL	113	365	68	133	27	2	4	56	6	53	22	0.364	M, 1B, OF	560	32	10	0.983								
Hartz, John																											
1941	Waycross	GFL	27	65	10	12	1	1	0	7	0	10	20	0.185	P	5	28	5	0.868	27	17	8	3.70	180	205	83	105
Harvey, ---																											
1915	Brunswick	FLAG				0								0.000													
Harvey, Eugene "Gene"		BR TR																									
1950	Vidalia-Lyons	GSL	79	279	34	55	4	1	1	26	2	19	61	0.197	2B, SS	123	156	25	0.918								
Harvey, Joseph S. "Joe"		BR TR																									
1953	Jesup	GSL	5											0.167	P					1	1		<45				
Harwood, ---																											
1906	Cordele	GSL													C												
Harwood, Donald "Don"		BR TR																									
1947	Waycross	GFL	32	72	11	16	7	1	1	12	0	8	26	0.222	P	3	33	6	0.857	31	13	10	3.67	179	173	165	119
1948	Waycross	GFL	19	38	10	11	3	0	2	5	0	3	13	0.289	P	2	13	1	0.938	17	6	6	5.13	93	97	70	78
Haschak, Bill		BR																									
1946	Cordele	GFL	<10																								
Hassler, Percy A.		BR TR																									
1947	Thomasville	GFL	50	175	32	39	9	0	0	24	8	27	36	0.223	3B, SS	97	133	37	0.861								
1948	Thomasville	GFL	136	568	114	148	26	5	1	52	17	74	64	0.261	SS	283	419	96	0.880								
Hasty, Robert Keller "Bob"		BR TR 6'3" 210 lbs b. 05/03/1896 Canton, GA d. 05/28/1972 Dallas, GA																									
1921	Carrollton	GSL	<10												P												
1938	Cordele	GFL	28	62	3	6	2	0	0	1	0	1	9	0.097	M, P	6	30	4	0.900								
Hatcher, Jerry		BR TR																									
1950	Valdosta	GFL	21	41	3	7	0	0	0	4	0	2	14	0.171	P	2	20	1	0.957	16	7	3	4.72	103	113	45	59
Hatcher, Marvin "Marv"		BR TR																									
1950	Moultrie	GFL	17	39	6	6	0	0	0	4	0	8	11	0.154	P	5	11	1	0.941	17	8	5	4.46	101	89	46	58
1951	Moultrie	GFL	60	100	8	18	2	1	0	6	0	19	35	0.180	P	7	47	6	0.900	51	14	9	2.71	256	235	115	105
1955	Valdosta	GFL	38	49	3	9	5	0	0	2	0	1	14	0.184	P	10	22	0	1.000	38	6	9	4.17	136	138	84	54
Hatcher, William "Bill"		BR TR																									
1955	Sandersville	GSL	89	315	46	72	10	2	4	31	5	20	44	0.229	OF, C	427	33	23	0.952								
Hatfield, James "Jim"		BL TR																									
1957	Brunswick	GFL	23	84	12	15	3	0	0	4	0	10	18	0.179	2B	34	28	13	0.827								
1958	Brunswick(36) - Waycross(67)	GFL	103	393	77	135	17	2	10	58	8	54	36	0.344	2B	260	277	31	0.945								
Hathaway, R.H.																											
1921	Carrollton	GSL		110	20	18								0.164	P												
Hathcock, Marlin		BR TR																									
1946	Tallassee	GAL	117	513	86	141	20	14	5	48	8	21	79	0.275	2B, SS	256	310	40	0.934								
1948	Tallassee	GAL	11	33	7	7	0	0	0	2	2	6	9	0.212	2B	29	17	5	0.902								
Haury, John		BR TR																									
1956	Moultrie	GFL	70	284	45	70	4	0	3	24	4	43	44	0.246	2B	113	150	12	0.956								
Hausfeld, Walter "Walt"		BR TR																									
1948	Douglas	GSL	15	41	2	6	0	1	0	4	1	7	8	0.146	OF	19	0	0	1.000								
Haverly, Karl		BR TR																									
1955	Albany	GFL	16	22	4	3	0	0	0	6	0	8	10	0.136	P	6	13	0	1.000	15	6	3	2.65	78	63	48	37
1956	Albany	GFL	16	25	1	1	0	0	0	0	0	2	12	0.040	P	4	19	1	0.958	15	5	4	3.23	78	77	47	33
Hawkins, ---																											
1906	Americus	GSL													P												
Hawkins, E.J.																											
1921	Cedartown	GSL													P												

Georgia Class-D Minor League Baseball Encyclopedia

YR	TEAM	LG	G	AB	R	H	2B	3B	HR	RBI	SB	BB	SO	BA	POS	PO	A	E	FA	GP	W	L	ERA	IP	H	SO	BB
Hawkins, G.B.																											
1913	Valdosta - Brunswick	ESL	60	229	33	76	10	3	0					0.332	OF	96	24	7	0.945								
1913	Opelika	GAL	36	94	7	26				4				0.277	P					20	10	10					
1913	Newnan	GAL	19												P					19	7	12					
1914	Opelika	GAL	26	85	11	15				0				0.176	P	8	38	10	0.821	26							
1915	Brunswick	FLAG	33	92	5	15	4	1	1	3				0.163	OF, P	18	39	5	0.919	18	8	8		143	125	82	52
1915	Griffin	GAL	11	35	6	10	6	2	0					0.286	P					<6							
1916	Anniston	GAL	25	71	3	10					1			0.141	OF, P												
1920	Griffin	GSL													P												
Hawkins, H.E. "Cy"																											
1920	Rome	GSL		248	22	75	6	5	3		2			0.302	C												
1921	Carrollton	GSL		108	7	23								0.213	M, OF												
1921	Griffin	GSL													OF, C												
1928	Talladega - Lindale	GAL	5												M, P					5	0	3	10.29	21	39	9	5
Hawkins, Jack																											
1913	Waycross	ESL													M												
Hawley, Rondell		BR TR																									
1949	Albany	GFL	15	20	4	5	2	0	0	4	0	0	1	0.250	P	1	11	0	1.000	14	1	4	5.10	60	57	44	36
Hay, Derl		BL TL																									
1948	Americus	GFL	10	9	1	1	0	0	0	0	0	0	3	7 0.111	P	2	4	0	1.000								
Hay, Robert C. "Bob"		BR TR																									
1950	Jesup	GSL	110	398	62	104	14	1	0	40	3	78	25	0.261	2B	262	324	36	0.942								
1951	Jesup	GSL	123	446	82	100	12	1	0	33	3	87	32	0.224	2B	351	328	15	0.978								
1952	Jesup	GSL	51	199	44	56	8	1	0	11	0	51	15	0.281	SS	86	162	17	0.936								
Hay, Seaborn H. "Howard"		BR TR																									
1953	Statesboro	GSL	4											0.250	P						0	1		<45			
Haydel, John Harold "Hal"		BR TR 6'0" 190 lbs b. 07/09/1944 Houma, LA																									
1962	Dublin	GFL	17	26	2	2	0	0	0	2	0	6	13	0.077	P	3	11	4	0.778	17	7	4	3.53	74	59	80	52
Hayden, James "Jim"		BL TL																									
1954	Brunswick	GFL	26	25	1	3	0	0	0	3	0	0	6	0.120	P	2	12	4	0.778	23	1	3	7.50	60	52	63	77
1955	Brunswick	GFL	40	95	7	15	2	1	0	5	0	3	22	0.158	P	9	32	4	0.911	30	13	9	3.02	185	168	134	115
1956	Dublin	GSL	18	43	4	12	2	0	0	2	0	1	7	0.279	P	5	12	3	0.850	16	4	7	4.29	84	78	69	44
Hayden, John		BR TR																									
1949	LaGrange	GAL	16	27	7	3	1	0	0	3	0	3	6	0.111	P	3	4	0	1.000	14	2	4	4.50	64	49	60	58
Hayes, Bruce																											
1914	Gadsden	GAL													M												
Hayes, Edwin "Ed"		BL TR																									
1951	Brunswick	GFL	51	122	14	28	3	2	0	14	2	27	19	0.230	C	216	25	1	0.996								
Hayes, Frank		BR TR																									
1946	Opelika	GAL	5												P					5	0	1	0.00	17	21	4	10
Hayes, Thomas J. "Tom"		BR TR																									
1954	Brunswick	GFL	5	4		1								0.250	P					5	1	0		<45			
1955	Valdosta	GFL	3	4		0								0.000													
Haygood, Charles		BL TL																									
1962	Thomasville	GFL	26	64	6	10	2	1	0	10	1	3	22	0.156	P	10	27	9	0.804	26	14	6	2.08	182	145	164	69
Haynes, Bill																											
1942	Albany	GFL	3												P					3	0	1	4.85	13	12	3	13
Haynes, Hoover		BR TR																									
1949	Valley	GAL	32	45	7	8	1	0	0	6	1	18	14	0.178	P	6	19	1	0.962	32	12	6	3.11	159	172	80	43
Haynes, Willard		BR TR																									
1948	Alexander City	GAL	13	19	3	2	0	0	0	0	0	5	9	0.105	P	2	8	1	0.909	11	1	5	5.74	47	68	14	14
1950	Valley	GAL	24	42	8	5	1	0	0	4	0	12	15	0.119	P	7	27	6	0.850	24	11	5	5.44	134	168	58	58
Hayworth, George		BR TR																									
1962	Dublin	GFL	41	107	10	23	1	0	0	14	1	27	25	0.215	C	278	16	9	0.970								
Head, Ralph		BR TR 5'10" 175 lbs b. 08/30/1893 Tallapoosa, GA d. 10/08/1962 Muskadine, AL																									
1913	LaGrange	GAL	14												P					14	8	6					
1914	LaGrange	GAL	28	77	6	9				0				0.117	P	14	41	5	0.917	28							
1915	LaGrange	GAL	21	65	3	4	2	0	1					0.062	P	12	42	7	0.885	15	6	9					
Headen, Ray																											
1939	Tallahassee	GFL	61	224	33	56	7	4	2	22	12	28	33	0.250	OF	104	5	9	0.924								
Heagerty, L.E.																											
1938	Moultrie	GFL	37	133	19	36	1	4	0	19	0	22	11	0.271	C	180	23	7	0.967								
Healy, Francis		BR TR																									
1947	Americus	GFL	35	72	7	10	0	0	0	8	1	11	27	0.139	P	6	47	14	0.791	32	12	15	3.57	212	222	130	105
Healy, Richard "Dick"																											
1958	Waycross	GFL	24	83	6	12	2	1	0	2	1	11	25	0.145	OF	55	6	2	0.968								
Hearn, George		BR TR																									
1952	Dublin	GSL	100	352	60	98	16	1	4	51	23	37	43	0.278	M, 1B, C	635	39	13	0.981								
Hearn, Joshua		BL TL																									
1952	Valdosta	GFL	28	37	2	5	0	0	0	1	0	3	10	0.135	P	7	21	3	0.903	28	7	5	2.88	122	123	38	65
1953	Thomasville	GFL	5											0.167	P						1	1		<45			
Hearn, Philip Bernard "Barnie"		BL TR 5'11" 198 lbs b. 10/13/1912 Savannah, SC																									
1936	Thomasville	GFL	63	265	58	82	10	5	5	30	36			0.309	OF	159	14	6	0.966								
1937	Tallahassee	GFL		43	2	9			0	5	0			0.209	OF	20	1	0	1.000								
Heath, Harold		BR TR																									
1955	Thomasville	GFL	11	1	0	0	0	0	0	0	0	0	1	0.000	P	0	5	0	1.000	11	0	0		<45			

Georgia Class-D Minor League Baseball Encyclopedia

YR	TEAM	LG	G	AB	R	H	2B	3B	HR	RBI	SB	BB	SO	BA	POS	PO	A	E	FA	GP	W	L	ERA	IP	H	SO	BB
Heath, Norman "Norm"		BR TR																									
1950	Newnan	GAL	63	240	37	57	11	2	1	37	2	37	42	0.238	SS	90	151	23	0.913								
Heathcock, Ennis		BR TR																									
1952	Thomasville	GFL	17	25	4	6	1	1	0	4	0	0	5	0.240	P	2	22	2	0.923	12	2	5	6.00	60	62	30	57
Heaton, Ralph		BR TR																									
1952	Vidalia	GSL	34	93	10	18	2	0	2	12	1	8	26	0.194	P	8	48	2	0.966	31	16	5	4.03	219	229	93	93
1953	Vid(6) - Sta(3) - Eas(2)	GSL	11	21	1	7	0	0	0	2	0	1	2	0.333	P	1	18	1	0.950	11	3	7	7.35	60	77	14	33
Heavener, Reginald "Reggie"		BL TR																									
1957	Brunswick	GFL	96	343	47	96	16	3	6	46	2	61	64	0.280	OF	169	12	12	0.938								
Heavner, James "Jim"		BL TR																									
1950	Jesup	GSL	24	83	9	17	1	0	0	9	0	16	14	0.205	1B	154	4	4	0.975								
Hebert, Walter		BR TR																									
1947	Alexander City	GAL	15	52	4	7	0	1	0	4	1	5	14	0.135	3B	18	25	8	0.843								
Heck, ---																											
1915	Dothan	FLAG	74	280	31	70	5	1	0		12			0.250	3B	102	118	19	0.921								
Heck, ---		BR TR																									
1946	Tallahassee	GFL	78	221	42	59	6	1	0	25	11	38	49	0.267	2B, SS	110	131	27	0.899								
Heckman, Ernie		BR TR																									
1955	Moultrie	GFL	48	164	23	33	6	1	4	23	3	42	40	0.201	1B	387	32	12	0.972								
Hedin, Allen "Al"		BR TR																									
1954	Waycross	GFL	7	13		2								0.154	P					7	1	2	<45				
1955	Tifton	GFL	5	5		0								0.000	P					5	1	2	<45				
Heffline, Bob		BR TR																									
1946	Cordele	GFL	65	250	28	71	10	10	2	32	3	30	42	0.284	OF	93	11	4	0.963								
Heffren, Ronald "Ron"		BR TR																									
1954	Waycross	GFL	5	3		0								0.000	P					4	1	1	<45				
Heflin, Phillip "Phil"		BL TL																									
1951	Tifton(54) - Americus(68)	GFL	122	424	75	95	10	4	0	39	9	102	69	0.224	1B	1122	54	28	0.977								
Heft, Arnold																											
1938	Thomasville	GFL													P						0	0	<45				
Hegedorn, Gary		BL TR																									
1949	Tallahassee	GFL	25	67	12	12	4	1	1	10	1	32	30	0.179	1B	205	5	5	0.977								
Heidlebach, ---																											
1929	Gadsden	GAL	28	62	3	12	0	0	0		0	4	13	0.194	P	6	26	4	0.889	29	10	11		175	188	71	50
Heidt, ---																											
1913	Cordele	ESL	43	144	7	30	3	0	1					0.208	SS	54	84	12	0.920								
Heins, Robert "Bob"		BR TR																									
1951	Albany	GFL	17	33	1	5	0	0	0	1	0	0	4	0.152	P	4	18	1	0.957	17	4	5	3.97	93	84	51	76
1952	Albany	GFL	41	77	8	9	0	0	0	3	0	3	18	0.117	P	18	33	4	0.927	41	11	10	2.47	204	167	106	109
Heinz, Charles																											
1938	Tallahassee	GFL	9	18	2	5	1	0	0	2	0	1	4	0.278	UT	8	1	0	1.000								
Heinz, Martin		BR TR																									
1954	Thomasville	GFL	11	12	0	2	0	0	0	1	0	0	1	0.167	P	1	7	2	0.800	10	1	2	<45				
1955	Thomasville	GFL	3	3		0								0.000	P					3	0	1	<45				
Heinze, Norman "Norm"		BR TR																									
1962	Moultrie	GFL	66	191	32	48	5	3	0	27	3	27	34	0.251	C	302	25	13	0.962								
Heisig, William "Bill"		BR TR																									
1948	LaGrange	GAL	44	63	6	8	1	0	0	3	0	7	24	0.127	P	4	28	3	0.914	44	7	16	5.20	180	222	89	92
Heisler, Allen		BR TR																									
1953	Vidalia	GSL	7												0.167	P					1	0		<45				
Heisler, Phillip "Phil"		BR TR																									
1957	Fitzgerald	GFL	48	72	1	10	3	0	0	7	0	6	32	0.139	P	5	43	3	0.941	46	8	14	4.27	192	195	100	106
Heistand, Charles		BR TR																									
1952	Thomasville	GFL	11	12	1	4	0	0	0	3	0	1	6	0.333	P	0	5	1	0.833								
Hejnosz, John		BR TR																									
1955	Thomasville	GFL	15	51	6	9	2	0	1	4	2	9	14	0.176	OF	27	1	1	0.966								
Helbig, James "Anthony"		BR TR																									
1951	Moultrie	GFL	104	426	80	120	14	3	1	35	8	73	49	0.282	2B	269	322	41	0.935								
Heller, Harry		BR TR																									
1940	Cordele	GFL	40	176	35	49	3	5	1	21	4	16	32	0.278	2B	95	125	16	0.932								
Heller, Ronald "Ron"		BR TR																									
1954	Valdosta	GFL	4	2		0								0.000	P					4	1	1	<45				
Helmick, Julius		BR TR																									
1955	Douglas	GSL	3	0										0.000	P					3	0	0					
Helms, Lawrence "Larry"		BR TR																									
1956	Douglas	GSL	62	197	29	51	5	2	3	28	9	21	44	0.259	OF	80	5	6	0.934								
Helvey, Robert "Bob"																											
1935	Tallahassee	GFL	25	60	3	11	3	0	0		0	0	31	0.183	P					31	9	9		156	176	46	41
Hemings, Fay		BR																									
1952	Hazlehurst-Baxley	GSL	10	32	1	5	0	0	0	0	1		6	0.156													
Hemmerle, Richard "Dick"		BR TR																									
1954	Tifton	GFL	30	69	8	10	0	1	0	5	0	8	26	0.145	P	12	41	3	0.946	30	13	10	3.45	198	189	146	118
Henderson, Charles "Chuck"																											
1942	Valdosta	GFL	81	322	84	106	17	5	1	34	19	69	35	0.329	3B	88	179	26	0.911								

Georgia Class-D Minor League Baseball Encyclopedia

YR	TEAM	LG	G	AB	R	H	2B	3B	HR	RBI	SB	BB	SO	BA	POS	PO	A	E	FA	GP	W	L	ERA	IP	H	SO	BB
Henderson, David "Dave"		BR TR																									
1955	Vidalia	GSL	46	164	20	28	2	1	0	10	2	9	28	0.171	SS	69	131	13	0.939								
1956	Vidalia	GSL	11	33	8	9	1	0	0	6	0	6	6	0.273	SS	21	36	7	0.891								
Henderson, H.L. "Hap"																											
1920	Carrollton	GSL		40	7	8								0.200	P, OF												
Henderson, Robert "Bob"		BR TR																									
1948	Thomasville	GFL	39	80	11	15	0	0	0	4	0	12	13	0.188	P	5	45	4	0.926	38	12	11	3.47	223	214	141	76
Henderson, William "Bill"		BR TR																									
1954	Brunswick(9) - Albany(4)	GFL	13	16	0	1	0	0	0	1	0	0	11	0.063	P	1	11	1	0.923	13	2	2	4.89	46	49	26	27
1954	Sandersville	GSL	6	8		1								0.125	P					5	0	3		<45			
Henderson, William A. "Bill"		BR TR																									
1950	Fitzgerald	GSL	82	327	79	121	17	4	2	41	52	43	15	0.370	OF	160	8	11	0.939								
Henegar, Russell "Russ"		BL TR																									
1949	Valley	GAL	28	40	3	14	0	0	0	9	0	3	4	0.350	P	4	19	2	0.920	20	6	5	4.07	84	84	35	55
Henkel, Ernest		BL TR																									
1953	Dublin	GSL	14	24	0	5	0	0	0	1	0	4	10	0.208	P	9	20	4	0.879	14	2	5	6.04	73	79	39	46
1954	Dublin	GSL	1	0										0.000	P					1	0	0		<45			
Henkel, Howard		BL TR																									
1947	Thomasville	GFL	40	180	36	59	8	1	0	17	4	20	22	0.328	2B	82	208	16	0.948								
1948	Thomasville	GFL	138	561	103	189	20	6	1	56	17	80	24	0.337	2B	368	389	43	0.946								
Henley, Gail Curtice "Gail"		BL TR 5'9" 180 lbs b. 10/15/1928 Wichata, KS																									
1962	Thomasville	GFL													M												
Henley, Howard		BR TR																									
1949	Albany	GFL	33	57	5	14	4	1	0	6	0	10	14	0.246	P	8	36	6	0.880	30	13	7	2.51	165	161	105	67
Henne, Bob																											
1952	Thomasville	GFL	<10																								
Henrichs, Russell "Russ"		BR TR																									
1958	Waycross	GFL	19	24	7	4	0	0	2	6	0	7	6	0.167	P	5	11	1	0.941	18	3	6	5.05	73	88	50	34
Henrichsen, Gerald		BR TR																									
1955	Cordele	GFL	116	427	62	114	20	2	8	84	10	37	72	0.267	OF, P	163	7	15	0.919	3	0	0		<45			
Henrickson, Edward "Ed"		BL TL																									
1948	Vid-Lyo(10) - Fitzgerald(109)	GSL	119	480	63	122	21	12	2	60	13	55	67	0.254	OF	232	9	7	0.972								
1949	Fitzgerald	GSL	18												OF	25	5	1	0.968								
Henriquez, Julio		BR TR																									
1955	Thomasville	GFL	26	83	9	21	5	0	1	10	1	7	26	0.253	1B	73	5	2	0.975								
Henry, ---																											
1906	Columbus	GSL													P, OF												
Henry, ---																											
1913	Anniston	GAL	89	332	48	78				18				0.235	OF	182	13	7	0.965								
Henry, Wilbur C.																											
1935	Americus	GFL	51	188	34	59	7	3	4		3	21	33	0.314	OF	86	8	7	0.931								
Hensley, Paul		BR TR																									
1954	Brunswick	GFL	4	2		0								0.000	P					4	1	1		<45			
Herald, Ray		BL TR																									
1951	Brunswick	GFL	25	102	16	28	5	1	1	15	1	7	7	0.275	OF	22	1	2	0.920								
Herbert, Bentley		BR TR																									
1952	Waycross	GFL	13	28	2	5	0	0	0	2	0	1	10	0.179	P	4	10	1	0.933	13	5	5	2.37	76	59	27	46
Herbert, Donald "Don"		BR TR																									
1949	Thomasville	GFL	41	120	8	23	3	0	0	6	0	11	24	0.192	C	187	27	10	0.955								
Herbik, John		BR TR																									
1947	Moultrie	GFL	46	101	11	17	2	1	0	10	0	7	11	0.168	P	5	24	1	0.967	33	15	3	3.58	171	184	86	61
1948	Moultrie	GFL	11	13	1	2	0	0	0	0	0	0	5	0.154													
1951	Moultrie	GFL	34	93	8	14	4	0	0	4	2	13	14	0.151	P	8	22	5	0.857	23	8	11	4.32	154	176	60	56
Herbison, James "Jim"		BR TR																									
1947	Albany	GFL	140	542	103	138	25	4	0	42	26	81	99	0.255	2B, SS	353	377	51	0.935								
Herdt, Donald 'Don"		BR TR																									
1949	Tallassee	GAL	94	319	34	70	8	2	5	35	6	23	72	0.219	3B, C	139	129	40	0.870								
Hernandez, John																											
1941	Valdosta	GFL	48	186	37	54	6	8	2	25	4	22	31	0.290	1B	386	41	12	0.973								
Hernandez, Samuel "Sam"		BR TR																									
1953	Statesboro	GSL	125	506	108	150	29	7	4	56	36	45	35	0.296	2B	359	376	31	0.960								
1958	Albany	GFL	116	439	118	116	23	4	8	67	57	100	44	0.264	2B, 3B, OF	316	318	30	0.955								
Herndon, Hardin																											
1920	Lindale	GSL		171	34	52								0.304	M, OF												
1921	Lindale	GSL		144	45	48								0.333	M, 1B, OF												
Herndon, Roy																											
1939	Cordele	GFL	18	72	6	18	4	0	0	6	0	6	12	0.250	2B	59	44	9	0.920								
Herold, Joe																											
1914	Valdosta	GSL		369	54	93	12	1	0		6			0.252	M												
Herrell, Donald "Don"																											
1942	Tallahassee	GFL	68	260	42	61	12	4	3	41	11	34	58	0.235	1B	651	33	13	0.981								
Herrera, Raymond "Ray"		BR TR																									
1953	Hazlehurst-Baxley	GSL	122	467	96	123	24	8	7	108	20	81	64	0.263	3B	158	233	21	0.949								
Herring, ---																											
1913	Waycross	ESL	18	57	4	10	0	0	0					0.175	P	7	25	2	0.941	13	5	8					

Georgia Class-D Minor League Baseball Encyclopedia

YR	TEAM	LG	G	AB	R	H	2B	3B	HR	RBI	SB	BB	SO	BA	POS	PO	A	E	FA	GP	W	L	ERA	IP	H	SO	BB
Herring, Arthur D. "Art"		BR TR																									
1956	Thomasville	GFL	52	171	32	45	4	1	0	18	5	38	19	0.263	3B	48	93	12	0.922								
Herring, Earl		BR TR																									
1950	Alexander City	GAL	44	113	9	16	2	1	1	9	1	30	47	0.142	C	217	16	6	0.975								
1950	Waycross	GFL	18	65	7	13	3	0	1	14	0	11	21	0.200	C	115	11	9	0.933								
Herring, Robert "Bob"		BR TR																									
1955	Albany	GFL	5	17		2								0.118													
1955	Hazlehurst-Baxley	GSL	21	65	10	13	3	1	0	4	0	0	21	0.200	C	96	12	6	0.947								
Herring, William P. "Bill"		BR																									
1946	Valley	GAL	<10																								
Herringdine, M. Cecil		BL TR																									
1950	Jesup	GSL	24	104	19	29	3	1	9	28	0	5	18	0.279	OF	47	2	1	0.980								
1951	Dublin	GSL	113	401	71	107	20	2	13	79	15	56	37	0.267	OF	211	10	9	0.961								
1952	Eastman	GSL	89	367	51	108	11	1	6	60	1	22	29	0.294	OF	169	13	9	0.953								
1953	Sandersville	GSL	122	476	78	137	23	2	21	102	4	53	39	0.288	OF, C	327	13	12	0.966								
Herrington, George		BL TR																									
1951	Waycross	GFL	11	23	3	3	1	0	0	0	1	6	9	0.130	OF	5	2	2	0.778								
Hersimaki, Frederic "Fred"		BL TR																									
1948	Tallahassee	GFL	58	182	35	57	2	1	1	22	1	30	31	0.313	OF	51	3	15	0.783								
Hertweck, Neal Charles "Neal"		BL TL 6'1" 157 lbs b. 11/22/1931 St. Louis, MO																									
1949	Albany	GFL	139	539	96	137	17	10	12	109	14	67	74	0.254	1B	1273	73	19	0.986								
Herzog, Thomas "Tom"		BL																									
1957	Waycross	GFL	11	14	1	1	0	0	0	0	0	0	3	0.071													
Hession, William "Bill"		BR TR																									
1951	Americus	GFL	20	74	13	19	3	1	0	11	0	9	15	0.257	OF	45	5	2	0.962								
Hessler, Bill																											
1906	Columbus	GSL													M, 2B, C												
Hester, James "Jim"		BR																									
1963	Brunswick	GFL	1	1	0	1	0	0	2	0	0	0	0	1.000													
Heughens, Ronald "Ron"		BR TR																									
1952	Dublin	GSL	11	40	3	5	0	0	0	1	2	5	13	0.125	C	62	9	2	0.973								
1953	Statesboro	GSL	3											0.250													
Heving, John Aloysius "Johnnie"		BR TR 6'0" 175 lbs b. 04/29/1896 Covington, KY d. 12/24/1968 Salisbury, NC																									
1946	Tallassee	GAL	11	22	1	8	0	0	0	3	0	3	2	0.364	M												
1949	Tallahassee	GFL													M												
Hewitt, Phillip "Phil"		BR TR																									
1958	Brunswick	GFL	53	182	36	49	10	0	2	29	2	53	25	0.269	2B, OF, P	114	54	13	0.928	4	1	1	<30				
Heyer, Richard "Dick"		BR TR																									
1951	Valley(3) - Rome(9)	GAL	12	10	3	2	0	0	0	0	0	2	6	0.200	P	2	4	0	1.000								
Hickey, James Robert "Jim" "Sid"		BR TR 6'1" 204 lbs b. 10/22/1920 North Abington, MA d. 09/20/1997 Manchester, CT																									
1935	Moultrie	GFL	17	42	3	6	2	0	0		0	1	12	0.143	P					23	6	7		114	120	43	29
Hickman, James Lucius "Jim"		BR TR 6'4" 205 lbs b. 05/10/1937 Henning, TN																									
1956	Albany	GFL	137	536	94	144	17	7	14	91	13	77	117	0.269	1B, SS, OF	349	43	23	0.945								
1957	Albany	GFL	138	522	94	150	24	4	26	113	9	99	116	0.287	1B, OF	425	29	10	0.978								
Hicks, Elroy		BR TR																									
1947	Opelika	GAL	15	23	0	3	1	0	0	1	0	1	10	0.130	P	2	11	4	0.765								
Hicks, R.E.																											
1921	Carrollton	GSL		56	7	14								0.250	1B, P												
1921	Griffin	GSL													1B												
Hicks, Richard N. "Dick"		BL TL																									
1954	Hazlehurst-Baxley	GSL	18	24	1	3	2	0	0	1	0	2	8	0.125	P	2	9	8	0.579	17	1	9	7.53	55	68	33	53
Hicks, Robah		BR TR																									
1952	Brunswick	GFL	11	43	5	11	0	0	0	2	1	1	9	0.256	OF	16	3	3	0.864								
Hiedel, Dale		BR																									
1957	Brunswick	GFL	7	18		2								0.111													
Higby, Lynn		BR TR																									
1956	Sandersville	GSL	3	5		0								0.000	P					3	0	2					
Higgenbottom, Dizzy Dean		BL TL																									
1954	Fitzgerald	GFL	12	13	2	1	0	0	0	2	0	4	8	0.077	P	3	9	2	0.857	12	1	2	<45				
Higginbotham, ---																											
1930	Anniston	GAL	90	354	91	121	30	4	23		5	39	63	0.342	OF	138	9	15	0.907								
Higginbotham, Milton Wallace "Milt"		BR TR																									
1954	Valdosta	GFL	28	50	8	12	1	2	0	4	1	3	12	0.240	P	7	34	2	0.953	25	7	5	3.08	149	134	101	67
1955	Valdosta	GFL	8	7		0								0.000	P					8	0	3	<45				
Higginbotham, Morris		BR																									
1946	Tallassee	GAL	<10																								
High, Andrew Aird "Andy" "Knee"		BL TR 5'6" 155 lbs b. 11/21/1897 Ava, IL d. 02/22/1981 Toledo, OH																									
1941	Cordele	GFL	4	15	2	6	7	0	1	3	1	1	0	0.400	2B	8	7	3	0.833								
Hightower, Eugene "Gene"		BR TL																									
1950	Moultrie	GFL	11	18	1	1	1	0	0	1	0	0	10	0.056	P	2	13	3	0.833								
Hiland, Jimmie L.		BR TR																									
1954	Hazlehurst-Baxley	GSL	42	80	14	19	3	0	1	11	0	13	31	0.238	P	9	27	3	0.923	35	13	10	3.39	218	191	247	84
Hill, ---																											
1915	Brunswick	FLAG			0									0.000													
1915	Waycross	FLAG			0									0.000	P					0							

Georgia Class-D Minor League Baseball Encyclopedia

YR	TEAM	LG	G	AB	R	H	2B	3B	HR	RBI	SB	BB	SO	BA	POS	PO	A	E	FA	GP	W	L	ERA	IP	H	SO	BB
Hill, ---																											
1930	Anniston	GAL	2												P					2	1	0	5.63	8	6	2	9
Hill, Donald "Don"		BR																									
1958	Albany	GFL	7	13	3									0.231													
Hill, George		BR TR																									
1951	Opelika	GAL	12	19	2	1	0	0	0	0	0	2	7	0.053	P	1	6	1	0.875								
Hill, James William "Jim"		BR TR																									
1946	Carrollton	GAL	121	401	45	103	9	1	0	50	3	36	31	0.257	C	553	61	22	0.965								
1947	Carrollton	GAL	90	308	41	91	20	4	0	47	0	8	18	0.295	C	459	35	7	0.986								
1948	Carrollton	GAL	95	330	30	79	4	0	0	54	1	23	12	0.239	C	503	44	20	0.965								
Hill, Jere		BR TR																									
1956	Albany	GFL	26	47	3	14	4	1	0	8	0	10	8	0.298	P	6	33	1	0.975	17	8	7	3.27	110	82	108	61
1958	Albany	GFL	17	26	1	5	1	0	0	3	0	13	9	0.192	1B	63	4	3	0.957								
Hill, Larry		BR TR																									
1955	Dublin	GSL	2	1	0									0.000	P					2	0	0					
Hill, Marion		BR TR																									
1948	Vidalia-Lyons	GSL	26	62	8	16	4	0	0	11	0	4	15	0.258	P	10	22	6	0.842	20	5	9	4.89	116	116	60	89
Hill, Oliver Clinton "John"		BL TR 5'11" 178 lbs b. 10/16/1909 Powder Springs, GA d. 09/20/1970 Decatur, GA																									
1946	Tallassee	GAL	97	355	51	121	23	1	8	70	9	36	7	0.341	3B	106	153	14	0.949								
1947	Tallassee(47) - Newnan(78)	GAL	125	507	73	146	27	3	10	101	6	37	13	0.288	M, 3B	120	256	26	0.935								
1948	Carrollton	GAL	12	47	2	8	3	0	0	4	0	3	1	0.170	M, 3B	12	28	4	0.909								
Hill, Robert A. "Bob" "Tiny"		BL TL																									
1941	Cordele	GFL	40	98	2	13	2	0	0	6	0	3	32	0.133	P	7	37	4	0.917	40	18	12	7.06	125	260	150	83
1942	Waycross	GFL	27	87	16	28	4	0	0	6	1	9	18	0.322	P	11	47	1	0.983	26	19	4	2.03	200	172	154	36
1946	Waycross	GFL	7												P					7	3	1	0.00	43	49	13	12
1947	Americus	GFL	103	371	70	105	18	7	7	72	7	75	86	0.283	1B	807	46	17	0.980								
Hill, Van		BL TL																									
1953	Fitzgerald	GFL	70	232	36	61	9	3	0	20	11	34	36	0.263	OF, P	141	5	8	0.948		0	0		<45			
1954	Fitzgerald	GFL	133	430	62	114	16	3	1	67	8	70	64	0.265	OF	245	15	14	0.949								
1955	Moultrie	GFL	135	510	91	131	22	11	2	43	4	97	67	0.257	OF	346	9	19	0.949								
Hilliard, Grady		BR TL																									
1950	Waycross	GFL	92	208	38	58	15	2	5	41	3	33	42	0.279	1B, P	206	35	12	0.953	31	16	10	4.55	198	200	117	124
Hilyer, Kenneth "Ken"		BR TR																									
1953	Albany	GFL	136	512	118	171	30	5	15	116	24	97	49	0.334	2B	321	350	38	0.946								
Hines, ---																											
1906	Americus	GSL													P, OF												
Hines, ---		BR TR																									
1952	Valdosta	GFL	10												C	57	3	4	0.938								
Hines, Jack																											
1953	Statesboro	GSL													M												
1954	Statesboro	GSL													M												
Hinges, ---																											
1917	Talladega	GAL	1	5	0	1	0	0	0		1			0.200	SS	1	3	0	1.000								
Hink, William "Bill"		BR TR																									
1940	Thomasville - Tallahassee	GFL	93	364	39	90	13	2	0	25	7	35	34	0.247	2B	229	295	40	0.929								
1941	Thomasville - Albany	GFL	121	483	112	116	14	8	2	53	7	109	53	0.240	3B	131	207	39	0.897								
Hinkle, Charles L. "Leon"		BR TR																									
1949	Tallassee	GAL	23	26	2	3	0	0	0	0	1	2	5	0.115	P	4	5	2	0.818	15	3	4	4.66	58	68	23	31
Hinkle, Gaston "Jack"		BR TR																									
1948	Albany	GFL	<10																									
1949	Albany	GFL	33	128	29	29	3	2	0	10	5	35	24	0.227	SS	55	96	17	0.899								
Hinkle, George R.		BL TL																									
1962	Moultrie	GFL	2	2	0	0	0	0	0	0	0	0	2	0.000	P					2	0	1	18.00	5	13	2	2
Hinrichs, Donald		BR TR																									
1955	Sandersville	GSL	15	25	6	1	0	0	0	1	0	4	4	0.040	P	4	22	1	0.963	15	6	8	5.31	78	84	34	39
Hinrichs, Wayne		BR TR																									
1941	Tallahassee	GFL	36	88	10	16	2	1	0	7	2	2	19	0.182	P	10	34	5	0.898	34	10	14	3.82	205	255	90	81
Hinson, William B. "Bill"		BR TR																									
1954	Vidalia	GSL	115	410	69	90	24	3	6	64	3	56	55	0.220	C	744	74	19	0.977								
Hinton, Richard "Dick"		BR																									
1955	Valdosta	GFL	7	23		3								0.130													
Hinton, Terry		BR TR																									
1956	Moultrie	GFL	60	211	23	35	6	1	4	18	2	24	79	0.166	OF	109	4	11	0.911								
Hire, Ashford		BR TR																									
1955	Thomasville	GFL	7	4		1								0.250	P					7	0	3	<45				
Hirst, Arthur "Art"		BL TL																									
1956	Tifton	GFL	39	74	11	13	1	0	1	9	1	6	30	0.176	P	8	47	2	0.965	38	15	11	3.06	218	173	179	115
Hisey, Ralph		BR TR																									
1940	Tallahassee	GFL	56	185	21	33	4	4	0	12	1	11	25	0.178	P, IF					28	9	14	4.63	214	195	104	142
1949	Dublin - Eastman	GSL	42	138	15	28	5	0	1	13	1	12	7	0.203	P, IF	108	34	3	0.979	32	17	8	3.78	212	109	203	187
Hitchcock, James Franklin "Jim"		BR TR 5'11" 175 lbs b. 06/28/1911 Inverness, AL d. 06/23/1959 Montgomery, AL																									
1946	Opelika	GAL	66	190	25	46	7	2	2	26	2	16	13	0.242	M, 2B, SS, P	97	122	14	0.940	1	0	0	0.00	1			
Hite, Bob Lou "Bob"		BR TL																									
1954	Sandersville	GSL	10	22	3	6	1	0	0	0	0	0	4	0.273	P	3	4	1	0.875	10	0	7	5.65	51	59	27	34
Hitson, John		BL TR																									
1946	Opelika	GAL	44	164	21	39	6	0	0	15	5	9	31	0.238	SS	62	83	36	0.801								

Georgia Class-D Minor League Baseball Encyclopedia

YR	TEAM	LG	G	AB	R	H	2B	3B	HR	RBI	SB	BB	SO	BA	POS	PO	A	E	FA	GP	W	L	ERA	IP	H	SO	BB
Hitt, Ray "Jack"		BR TR																									
1946	Newnan	GAL	2												P					2	0	0	0.00	4			
Hoag, Myril Oliver "Myril"		BR TR 5'11" 180 lbs b. 03/09/1908 Davis, CA d. 07/28/1971 High Springs, FL																									
1950	Valley(28) - Rome(28)	GAL	56	107	15	31	6	0	1	18	10	14	7	0.290	M, P	17	43	3	0.952	36	15	11	2.60	208	191	137	73
Hoak, Donald Albert "Don" "Tiger"		BR TR 6'0" 175 lbs b. 02/05/1928 Roulette, PA d. 10/09/1969 Pittsburgh, PA																									
1947	Valdosta	GFL	134	485	71	143	16	12	5	68	12	87	100	0.295	3B	166	236	42	0.905								
Hoard, ---																											
1915	Griffin	GAL	20	77	6	19	7	1	2					0.247	SS	49	58	11	0.907								
Hoard, Floyd Daniel "Dan"		BL TR																									
1950	Eastman	GSL	39	170	24	45	13	1	1	20	0	4	11	0.265	OF	52	2	2	0.964								
1951	Eastman	GSL	123	511	63	170	34	0	3	80	2	30	12	0.333	OF	231	14	9	0.965								
1952	Eastman	GSL	119	476	62	165	43	1	1	111	2	17	15	0.347	OF, C	279	20	8	0.974								
Hobbs, ---		BR TR																									
1950	Newnan	GAL	7												P					7	3	2	4.76	51	47	25	29
Hobbs, Tigner		BR TR																									
1950	Tifton	GSL	56	225	34	53	7	2	0	14	3	28	31	0.236	3B	57	94	18	0.893								
Hocevar, Joe		BR TR																									
1940	Tallahassee	GFL	<10												P					8	1	5	6.83	54	58	20	40
Hoch, ---																											
1913	Talladega	GAL	37	147	23	42						3		0.286	1B	316	18	8	0.977								
Hock, Robert "Bob"		BL TR																									
1954	Douglas	GSL	128	499	74	150	27	1	0	63	5	44	43	0.301	OF	191	5	10	0.951								
Hockette, George Edward "Lefty"		BL TL 6'0" 174 lbs b. 04/07/1908 Perth, MS d. 01/20/1974 Plantation, FL																									
1928	Gadsden	GAL	57	171	18	55	10	2	1		5	8	0.322		OF, P	53	28	0	1.000	23	6	10	3.95	148	160	37	25
1929	Gadsden	GAL	26	65	6	13	1	2	0		0	3	15	0.200	P	6	36	2	0.955	22	8	9		139	145	45	16
1930	Anniston	GAL	29	81	14	18	0	3	0		0	5	7	0.222	P	4	54	1	0.983	26	11	8	4.63	177	239	68	30
Hoderlein, Melvin Anthony "Mel"		BS TR 5'10" 185 lbs b. 06/24/1923 Mount Carmel, OH																									
1942	Cordele	GFL	87	354	56	88	15	5	0	28	8	25	61	0.249	SS	127	266	64	0.860								
Hodge, ---																											
1914	Talladega	GAL	15	51	5	14				2				0.275	SS	25	38	4	0.940								
1914	Americus - Brunswick	GSL		92	5	25	1	1	0	1				0.272													
1915	Americus-Gainesville	FLAG	62	231	28	57	6	0	3	11				0.247	SS	129	132	39	0.870								
1916	Talladega	GAL	13	46	7	11				1				0.239	SS												
Hodge, Clarence		BR TR																									
1946	Albany	GFL	32	122	11	19	3	0	0	12	2	8	28	0.156	OF	48	2	5	0.909								
Hodge, Clarence Clemet "Shovel"		BL TR 6'4" 190 lbs b. 07/06/1893 Mount Andrew, AL d. 12/31/1967 Ft. Walton Beach, FL																									
1915	Dothan	FLAG	23	78	6	22	2	1	0	0				0.282	P	6	71	5	0.939								
Hodges, James "Jim"		BR																									
1955	Vidalia	GSL	9	10		1								0.100													
Hodgin, W.H.																											
1921	Rome	GSL		284	40	89								0.313	OF												
Hodkey, Aloysius Joseph "Eli"		BL TL 6'4" 185 lbs b. 11/03/1917 Lorain, OH																									
1938	Moultrie	GFL	21	39	3	6	0	1	0	1	0	3	10	0.154	P	2	12	3	0.824	19	4	4	3.31	106	85	105	60
Hoellman, ---																											
1930	Huntsville	GAL	6												P					6	0	4	10.61	28	47	1	21
Hoenes, Ronald "Ron"		BL TR																									
1955	Dublin	GSL	85	246	42	72	12	2	0	26	7	37	21	0.293	OF, C	314	40	15	0.959								
1956	Brunswick	GFL	124	436	54	126	22	4	1	59	6	87	48	0.289	2B, C, OF	285	61	20	0.945								
Hofferth, Stewart Edward "Stew"		BR TR 6'2" 195 lbs b. 01/27/1913 Logansport, IN d. 03/07/1994 Valparaiso, IN																									
1936	Tallahassee	GFL	102	350	60	117	20	4	1	64	8			0.334	C	303	43	15	0.958								
1940	Americus	GFL	71	249	37	64	12	4	2	38	1	27	11	0.257	M, C	335	37	7	0.982								
1941	Valdosta	GFL	132	506	71	171	32	6	1	92	2	52	10	0.338	M, C	822	71	12	0.987								
1942	Valdosta	GFL	62	249	43	91	17	12	3	53	1	19	4	0.365	M, C	573	40	5	0.992								
Hoffman, Charles		BR TR																									
1955	Albany	GFL	13	9	1	0	0	0	0	0	0	2	6	0.000	P	0	8	0	1.000	13	2	1		<45			
Hoffman, Ed "Eddie"		BS TL																									
1939	Americus	GFL	129	481	74	120	15	4	7	53	11	67	65	0.249	1B	1153	95	13	0.990								
1940	Americus	GFL	139	539	87	160	26	6	3	80	16	69	41	0.297	1B	1376	61	18	0.988								
1941	Valdosta	GFL	57	189	28	48	8	5	1	27	6	42	27	0.254	1B	468	31	10	0.980								
Hoffman, Ed R.		0																									
1941	Americus	GFL	30	82	5	22	1	0	0	10	0	4	15	0.268	P	31	47	9	0.897	15	3	7	5.88	75	81	36	36
Hoffman, Edward Adolph "Tex"		BL TR 5'9" 195 lbs b. 11/30/1893 San Antonio, TX d. 05/19/1947 New Orleans, LA																									
1935	Tallahassee	GFL	62	185	34	46	7	4	1		0	31	33	0.249	M, IF	407	36	22	0.953								
1936	Tallahassee	GFL													M													
1937	Tallahassee	GFL													M													
Hoffman, Frederick "Fred"		BL TL																									
1956	Waycross	GFL	15	18	0	2	0	0	0	1	0	1	4	0.111	P	2	11	3	0.813	15	2	5	4.65	60	54	46	53
1957	Waycross	GFL	25	44	4	18	2	0	0	4	0	1	9	0.409	P	2	19	4	0.840	17	1	8	4.97	76	71	59	61
Hoffman, Karl																											
1938	Moultrie	GFL	23	59	4	8	0	0	0	1	1	6	5	0.136	P	6	29	5	0.875	18	6	10	3.88	130	119	81	69
Hoffman, Myron		BR TR																									
1949	Thomasville	GFL	41	63	5	13	1	0	0	2	0	3	16	0.206	P	5	44	5	0.907	41	9	8	3.10	177	174	82	88
1950	Thomasville	GFL	14	7	2	3	0	0	0	0	0	1	1	0.429	P	0	7	0	1.000								
Hoffman, Robert "Bob"		BR TR																									
1955	Waycross	GFL	13	32	1	3	0	0	0	0	0	3	17	0.094	P	1	12	0	1.000	13	4	7	2.48	80	67	72	51

Georgia Class-D Minor League Baseball Encyclopedia

YR	TEAM	LG	G	AB	R	H	2B	3B	HR	RBI	SB	BB	SO	BA	POS	PO	A	E	FA	GP	W	L	ERA	IP	H	SO	BB
Hoffman, Robert C. "Bob"		BR TR																									
1951	Valdosta	GFL	25	75	11	12	3	1	0	4	0	3	18	0.160	P	2	25	2	0.931	25	17	4	2.38	189	136	111	97
Hoffman, Robert W. "Bob"		BL TR																									
1946	Albany	GFL	46	108	11	25	5	0	0	9	3	9	22	0.231	P	7	62	7	0.908	34	15	14	3.06	244	132	154	90
Hoflac, Joseph "Joe"		BR TR																									
1946	LaGrange	GAL	26	64	8	16	0	1	2	6	1	5	13	0.250	OF	26	1	2	0.931								
Hoflack, Daniel "Dan"		BR TR																									
1946	Americus	GFL	11	35	8	9	2	1	0	4	0	2	9	0.257	OF	11	1	1	0.923								
1947	LaGrange	GAL	40	148	6	36	3	3	0	23	0	7	28	0.243	OF	70	1	0	1.000								
Hogarth, L. Arthur "Art"		BR TR																									
1952	Cordele	GFL	124	480	58	119	19	8	0	54	1	54	81	0.248	1B	1050	55	14	0.987								
Holbrook, James "Jim"		BR TR																									
1962	Moultrie	GFL	25	49	3	4	0	1	0	3	0	4	28	0.082	P	1	35	4	0.900	25	6	12	3.61	147	140	138	90
Holbrook, James Marbury "Sammy"		BR TR 5'11" 189 lbs b. 07/17/1910 Meridian, MS d. 04/10/1991 Jackson, MS																									
1929	Talladega	GAL	81	290	44	80	8	10	4		7	35	35	0.276	C	333	57	25	0.940								
Holcomb, E.																											
1930	Huntsville	GAL	10	22	4	6	2	1	0		0	1	0	0.273	P	0	8	1	0.889	9	2	4	6.85	46	70	14	15
Holcomb, Hot																											
1930	Carrollton	GAL	2												P					2	1	1	7.71	14	27	3	6
Holcomb, Louis "Lou"		BR TR																									
1957	Brunswick	GFL	79	287	15	51	5	2	3	27	0	21	68	0.178	SS	122	184	41	0.882								
1958	Brunswick	GFL	16	69	10	13	3	0	0	7	0	5	6	0.188	SS	27	40	5	0.931								
Holden, Joseph Francis "Joe"		BL TR 5'8" 175 lbs b. 06/04/1913 St. Clair, PA d. 05/10/1996 St. Clair, PA																									
1939	Moultrie	GFL	64	139	15	30	5	0	1	18	0	24	12	0.216	C	153	18	4	0.977								
1940	Moultrie	GFL	39	125	17	34	6	0	1	21	2	5	9	0.272	M, C	142	14	3	0.981								
1946	Cordele	GFL	<10												M												
Holdener, Louis "Lou"		BR TR																									
1956	Vidalia	GSL	90	321	44	90	15	2	7	57	1	20	50	0.280	OF, C	567	53	21	0.967								
Holder, Charles		BR TR																									
1947	Tallahassee	GFL	129	530	81	142	25	9	1	77	14	49	29	0.268	SS	207	399	57	0.914								
Holderfield, Harold		BR TR																									
1954	Thomasville	GFL	78	267	35	74	11	6	1	29	4	11	55	0.277	OF	136	5	6	0.959								
Holiday, ---																											
1913	Waycross	ESL	27	96	9	15	0	0	0					0.156	1B	275	20	6	0.980								
Holland, Fred																											
1937	Americus	GFL	32	93	12	20	2	2	3	12	0	11	14	0.215	C	98	9	5	0.955								
Holland, Sid																											
1914	LaGrange	GAL	94	334	42	94				13				0.281	2B	304	209	24	0.955								
1915	LaGrange	GAL	19	73	12	16	1	3	0					0.219	2B	50	43	12	0.886								
Hollenkamp, Richard "Dick"		BR TR																									
1953	Valdosta	GFL	24	65	9	12	1	0	0	6	0	11	12	0.185	C	92	13	4	0.963								
1952	Thomasville	GFL	71	129	9	19	4	0	0	7	1	28	28	0.147	OF, 1B	106	17	3	0.976								
Holley, James "Jim"		BR TR																									
1954	Douglas	GSL	10	39	6	8	0	1	0	7	1	7	10	0.205	3B	5	20	2	0.926								
Holliday, ---																											
1917	Anniston	GAL	1	1	0	0	0	0	0		0			0.000	P	0	0	1	0.000	1	0	0		1	3	1	1
Holliday, Hugh		BR																									
1947	Valdosta	GFL	26	35	5	9	0	1	0	7	0	2	0	0.257	M												
Hollingsworth, ---																											
1917	LaGrange	GAL	7	17	2	2	0	0	0		1			0.118	OF, P	3	17	0	1.000	5	2	3		41	34	27	14
Hollingsworth, Charles		BR TR																									
1952	Albany	GFL	18	45	5	10	3	0	0	5	0	2	15	0.222	P	1	27	2	0.933	15	7	4	2.88	100	68	60	59
Hollis, Grady		BR TR																									
1953	Vidalia	GSL	60	228	31	56	12	1	3	33	5	32	49	0.246	OF	105	6	13	0.895								
Holloman, Alva Lee "Bobo"		BR TR 6'2" 207 lbs b. 03/07/1925 Thomaston, GA d. 05/01/1987 Athens, GA																									
1946	Moultrie	GFL	44	99	18	21	0	1	1	9	0	7	31	0.212	P	7	67	7	0.914	37	20	5	2.33	216	154	184	114
Holloran, ---																											
1929	Anniston	GAL	37	149	24	51	10	5	3		4	11	18	0.342	2B	100	113	13	0.942								
1930	Lindale	GAL	86	347	90	118	18	9	21		8	28	31	0.340	1B, 2B	537	122	23	0.966								
Holloway, James N. "Jim"																											
1937	Cordele	GFL	24	87	8	22	5	1	0	12	0	3	12	0.253	OF	38	0	3	0.927								
Holly, Joseph "Joe"		BR																									
1954	Sandersville	GSL	6	22		2								0.091													
Holmes, James "Jim"		BR TR																									
1946	LaGrange	GAL	2												P					2	1	0	0.00	10	12	2	2
Holmes, Jeptha		BR TR																									
1952	Fitzgerald	GSL	74	277	39	71	11	2	2	39	9	46	40	0.256	C	399	47	10	0.978								
Holmes, William "Ducky"		0																									
1913	LaGrange	GAL													M												
Holmquist, Douglas "Doug"		BR TR																									
1962	Moultrie	GFL	19	56	7	18	1	1	0	7	0	5	10	0.321	C	110	10	1	0.992								
Holsomback, Leonard "Squirt"																											
1928	Lindale	GAL	56	197	32	61	14	4			4	23	38	0.310	3B	72	45	22	0.842								
1929	Carrollton	GAL	98	405	59	109	17	1	8		11	46	58	0.269	3B	111	196	28	0.916								
1930	Carrollton	GAL	84	348	78	105	20	6	7		7	48	27	0.302	3B	104	170	23	0.923								

Georgia Class-D Minor League Baseball Encyclopedia

YR	TEAM	LG	G	AB	R	H	2B	3B	HR	RBI	SB	BB	SO	BA	POS	PO	A	E	FA	GP	W	L	ERA	IP	H	SO	BB
Holt, ---																											
1915	Thomasville	FLAG	2												P					2	1	0		7	6	3	4
1915	Anniston	GAL	40	164	8	32	2	0	0					0.195	3B	34	64	12	0.891								
Holt, Douglas "Doug"																											
1939	Tallahassee	GFL	15	57	2	11	2	0	0	5	0	3	14	0.193	C	83	16	4	0.961								
Holt, William E. "Bill"		BL TR																									
1950	Jesup	GSL	18	71	9	16	3	0	0	9	1	6	16	0.225	OF	24	0	3	0.889								
Holtz, Red																											
1920	Carrollton	GSL		13	3	4								0.308	1B												
Holyfield, Harold		BR TR																									
1962	Brunswick	GFL	38	99	11	12	3	0	0	6	1	16	31	0.121	SS	43	48	18	0.835								
1963	Brunswick	GFL	22	75	9	17	4	2	2	9	2	8	19	0.227	3B	21	27	10	0.828								
Hominsky, Ivan		BR TR																									
1949	Douglas	GSL	25	92	12	12	2	1	0	12	1	14	16	0.130	3B	31	41	12	0.857								
1950	Douglas	GSL	135	511	58	103	13	5	1	47	3	55	87	0.202	3B	154	238	42	0.903								
Hondzinski, Fred		BR TR																									
1953	Fitzgerald	GFL	17	55	7	11	1	0	0	2	0	6	12	0.200	OF	29	5	2	0.944								
Honkus, Stanley "Stan"		BR TR																									
1954	Brunswick	GFL	26	46	5	12	2	0	0	8	0	1	11	0.261	P	3	20	3	0.885	24	9	6	3.36	107	101	77	67
1954	Dublin	GSL	9	24		4								0.167	P					8	6	1	2.21	61	49	47	33
1955	Dublin	GSL	6	5		1								0.200	P					6	0	2					
1956	Dublin	GSL	4	7		1								0.143	P					4	2	1					
Hood, Milton "Milt"		BR TR																									
1949	Eastman - Fitzgerald	GSL	43	141	10	23	4	0	0	10	1	8	17	0.163	C	224	21	4	0.984								
1954	Sandersville	GSL	9	33		8								0.242													
Hooks, David "Dave"		BL TR																									
1950	Newnan	GAL	44	156	27	53	8	1	2	28	2	16	14	0.340	OF	45	5	4	0.926								
Hopey, Anthony		BL TL																									
1957	Thomasville	GFL	21	25	3	5	0	0	0	1	0	1	9	0.200	P	1	14	0	1.000	19	2	5	6.60	75	87	53	68
Hopke, Fred		BL TL																									
1956	Tifton	GFL	136	512	86	136	21	3	20	89	8	81	85	0.266	1B	1219	70	32	0.976								
Hopkins, Joseph Jr. "Joe"		BR TR																									
1955	Waycross	GFL	2	2		0								0.000	P					2	1	1	<45				
Hopkins, Robert N. "Bob"		BL TL																									
1953	Waycross	GFL	13	18	2	2	0	0	0	0	0	2	8	0.111	P	2	4	4	0.600	13	2	7	5.67	54	65	24	42
Hopkins, William Robert "Bill"		BR TR																									
1950	Hazlehurst-Baxley	GSL	44	64	4	9	0	0	0	1	0	3	15	0.141	P	3	37	6	0.870	44	4	15	6.11	159	181	92	137
Hopper, ---																											
1913	Anniston	GAL	29	89	14	28				10				0.315	1B	181	16	8	0.961								
Horine, Lawrence		BR TR																									
1953	Cordele	GFL	70	257	41	68	6	3	2	26	10	43	53	0.265	OF	105	9	12	0.905								
Horn, Vernon "Vern"																											
1939	Albany	GFL	32	76	5	12	0	0	0	6	0	5	15	0.158	P	41	3	1	0.978	28	18	6	2.19	197	157	132	67
Horne, Armine		BR TR																									
1953	Hazlehurst-Baxley	GSL	3											0.167	P					1	0		<45				
Horne, Thomas O. "Tom"		BR TR																									
1953	Valdosta	GFL	19	38	1	4	0	0	0	0	0	3	16	0.105	P	4	20	2	0.923	19	4	5	5.14	105	107	51	76
1954	Americus-Cordele	GFL	22	28	1	3	0	0	0	2	0	7	14	0.107	P	3	20	0	1.000	22	5	6	3.48	101	111	56	32
Hornsberg, Arthur "Art"		BR TR																									
1946	Valley	GAL	10	12	2	2	0	0	0	1	0	5	3	0.167	P					7	1	1	0.00	33	39	10	8
Hornsby, Jay		BR																									
1956	Douglas	GSL	9	32		6								0.188													
Hornsby, Leonard		BL TL																									
1946	Tallassee	GAL	1												P					1	0	1	0.00	1	1	0	2
Horowitz, Edward "Ed"		BR																									
1956	Thomasville	GFL	1	1		0								0.000													
Horton, Marvin "Marv"		BL TR																									
1939	Waycross	GFL	12	40	7	12	3	2	0	1	0	1	3	0.300	3B	8	25	3	0.917								
1940	Waycross	GFL	136	547	86	165	19	8	4	78	7	31	58	0.302	3B	96	270	64	0.851								
1941	Waycross	GFL	78	306	54	96	12	1	2	38	2	27	21	0.314	3B	84	129	34	0.862								
Horton, Ralph		BR																									
1954	Statesboro	GSL	20	63	6	14	2	0	0	4	1	7	13	0.222													
Horton, Roger		BR TR																									
1948	Waycross	GFL	22	62	18	7	0	0	0	4	2	25	9	0.113													
1948	Eastman	GSL	10	39	2	8	2	0	0	3	1	8	10	0.205	SS	18	40	3	0.951								
Hoskiewicz, ---																											
1936	Cordele	GFL													P						1	4	5.23	43		13	18
Hoskins, Gerald		BL TL																									
1954	Valdosta	GFL	11	18	1	2	0	0	0	1	1	4	5	0.111	1B	46	2	4	0.923								
Hotard, Leo		BR TR																									
1954	Valdosta	GFL	5	3		0								0.000	P					5	0	1	<45				
Hottell, Edwin "Ed"		BL TL																									
1956	Tifton	GFL	20	35	2	5	0	0	0	3	0	4	16	0.143	P	5	17	1	0.957	19	5	9	5.05	98	90	80	79
Houck, Fred		BR TR																									
1940	Moultrie	GFL	19	80	16	28	2	1	0	15	0	5	10	0.350	3B	11	29	9	0.816								

Georgia Class-D Minor League Baseball Encyclopedia

YR	TEAM	LG	G	AB	R	H	2B	3B	HR	RBI	SB	BB	SO	BA	POS	PO	A	E	FA	GP	W	L	ERA	IP	H	SO	BB
Hovell, Robert "Bob"		BR TR																									
1949	Alexander City	GAL	123	491	58	123	21	4	3	68	19	21	79	0.251	OF	202	27	26	0.898								
1950	Alexander City	GAL	106	396	65	106	16	6	10	63	29	26	64	0.268	OF	167	10	7	0.962								
Howard, Alton		BR TR																									
1952	Vidalia	GSL	120	458	75	93	16	1	1	45	21	45	84	0.203	OF	298	14	5	0.984								
1953	Vidalia(28) - Eastman(87)	GSL	115	426	71	116	16	4	9	73	10	59	85	0.272	OF	309	16	8	0.976								
Howard, Crawford		BR TR																									
1946	Americus	GFL	82	284	45	66	15	4	3	50	11	45	45	0.232	OF	131	7	3	0.979								
1947	Americus	GFL	139	558	102	169	31	4	3	113	28	57	58	0.303	OF	279	18	19	0.940								
1948	Americus	GFL	140	548	122	174	34	7	8	111	22	77	61	0.318	OF	303	10	14	0.957								
Howard, Lawrence Rayford "Larry"		BR TR 6'3" 200 lbs b. 06/06/1945 Columbus, OH																									
1963	Moultrie	GFL	49	148	11	32	5	1	1	15	2	13	30	0.216	1B	315	21	11	0.968								
Howard, Robert R. "Bobby"		BR TR																									
1950	Fitzgerald	GSL	136	567	111	163	18	8	5	84	30	56	43	0.287	SS	247	332	65	0.899								
Howard, Thomas Q. "Tom"		BR TL																									
1954	Valdosta	GFL	28	82	13	14	4	0	1	8	0	16	32	0.171	OF	22	1	2	0.920								
1955	Moultrie	GFL	40	131	14	30	4	1	0	8	2	18	28	0.229	1B	301	17	5	0.985								
Howe, F.E.		BR TR																									
1951	Moultrie	GFL	17	50	4	8	0	0	0	1	0	11	7	0.160	3B	29	43	14	0.837								
Howe, Robert A. "Bob"		BR TR																									
1951	Valley	GAL	16	39	6	7	0	0	0	1	0	3	6	0.179	P	4	20	1	0.960	16	7	3	3.28	107	110	41	52
Howell, Bryan		BL TR																									
1942	Waycross	GFL	127	510	81	160	22	11	2	66	11	50	32	0.314	OF	274	16	12	0.960								
1952	Waycross	GFL	17	61	7	16	2	0	1	9	1	4	3	0.262	OF	28	1	0	1.000								
Howell, C.L. "Lloyd"																											
1913	Newnan	GAL	89	266	63	102				0				0.383	2B	234	232	29	0.941								
1914	Newnan	GAL	82	340	60	113				12				0.332	1B	857	46	11	0.988								
1915	Griffin	GAL	25	96	20	39	14	1	0					0.406	OF	24	4	2	0.933								
1928	Gadsden - Lindale	GAL	42	155	27	39	5	2	4	5	12		32	0.252	OF	48	4	1	0.981								
Howell, Francis M.		BR TR																									
1953	Dublin(95) - Eastman(29)	GSL	124	446	83	120	26	3	4	71	6	114	24	0.269	2B, 3B, OF, C, P	231	178	23	0.947		0	0	<45				
Howell, Homer Elliott "Dixie"		BR TR 5'11" 195 lbs b. 04/24/1920 Louisville, KY d. 10/05/1990 Birmingham, NY																									
1938	Thomasville	GFL	81	276	42	74	8	8	0	31	3	36	33	0.268	C	388	53	17	0.963								
Howell, James "Jim"		BR TR																									
1947	Cordele	GFL	16	68	10	12	2	0	0	8	1	3	15	0.176	3B	19	13	8	0.800								
1949	Dublin	GSL	87	356	42	94	22	2	9	53	11	26	67	0.264	OF	193	6	10	0.952								
Howell, Millard D. "Dixie"																											
1942	Dothan	GFL	32	116	22	40	6	1	1	22	1	23	3	0.345	SS	90	110	12	0.943								
Howell, Murray Donald "Red" "Porky"		BR TR 6'0" 215 lbs b. 01/29/1909 Atlanta, GA d. 10/01/1950 Travelers Rest, SC																									
1928	Carrollton	GAL	95	409	87	152	34	11	16		7	21	18	0.372	OF	139	21	3	0.982								
Howell, Peter "Pete"		BL TR																									
1949	Cordele	GFL	31	118	14	21	3	0	1	11	0	2	41	0.178	OF	35	3	2	0.950								
Howerton, Carlson		BL TR																									
1958	Brunswick	GFL	34	126	25	38	2	0	2	15	3	20	14	0.302	M, 1B, 2B	197	25	3	0.987								
Howig, Donald		BL																									
1946	Valdosta	GFL	<10																								
Howser, Thomas "Tom"		BL TL																									
1956	Fitzgerald	GFL	20	68	9	13	2	0	0	7	1	15	13	0.191	OF	31	2	1	0.971								
Howton, Frank		BR TR																									
1949	Opelika	GAL	24	50	4	5	0	0	0	5	0	7	10	0.100	P	3	16	2	0.905	24	11	6	2.94	144	149	82	63
Howton, George																											
1936	Americus	GFL	8	12	1	1	0	0	0	1	0			0.083	P					8	2	0	4.35	31		7	11
Hoyal, Craig		BR TR																									
1953	Sandersville	GSL	48	104	13	15	1	2	0	11	0	20	35	0.144	OF, P	69	12	3	0.964	14	2	4	6.30	60	75	30	28
1954	Waycross	GFL	5	2		1								0.500	P					5	0	2	<45				
1954	Sandersville	GSL	32	94	13	18	3	0	4	7	0	13	36	0.191	OF, P	39	7	6	0.885	13	3	2	5.36	47	56	17	21
1955	Sandersville	GSL	5	2		0								0.000	P					2	0	0					
Hoyle, Alex		BR TR																									
1950	Americus	GFL	33	93	10	18	2	1	2	11	0	4	30	0.194	P	14	58	4	0.947	31	12	13	2.68	218	197	116	74
Hubbard, Carl		BR TR																									
1946	LaGrange	GAL	1												P					1	0	0	0.00	5			
Hubbard, Charles		BR																									
1949	Americus	GFL	10	4	0	0	0	0	0	0	0	1	1	0.000													
Hubbard, Herman																											
1941	Americus	GFL	19	68	9	17	0	0	0	6	0	14	8	0.250	2B	34	52	10	0.896								
Huber, Ray																											
1939	Valdosta	GFL	32	99	9	26	2	0	0	8	2	10	11	0.263	SS	60	79	15	0.903								
Hubert, Stanley "Stan"		BR TR																									
1956	Hazlehurst-Baxley	GSL	41	143	26	38	4	1	0	15	8	26	15	0.266	SS	63	104	17	0.908								
Hudson, ---																											
1906	Americus	GSL													P												
Hudson, Frank																											
1937	Americus	GFL	26	65	9	17	0	0	0	6	0	4	15	0.262	P	5	26	8	0.795	20	8	10	4.38	154	151	76	73

Georgia Class-D Minor League Baseball Encyclopedia

YR	TEAM	LG	G	AB	R	H	2B	3B	HR	RBI	SB	BB	SO	BA	POS	PO	A	E	FA	GP	W	L	ERA	IP	H	SO	BB
Hudson, William B. "Bill"		BR TR																									
1948	Opelika	GAL	90	315	59	94	12	10	6	46	5	41	55	0.298	OF	138	8	6	0.961								
1949	Opelika	GAL	113	411	88	133	21	15	8	107	20	78	78	0.324	OF	160	6	12	0.933								
1950	Griffin	GAL	105	404	93	106	12	2	13	69	16	55	82	0.262	OF	131	9	9	0.940								
1950	Dublin	GSL	22	82	19	19	1	0	3	17	0	15	19	0.232	OF	26	3	2	0.935								
Hudson, William C. "Bill"		BR TR																									
1949	Carrollton	GAL	24	62	12	20	3	2	1	14	0	5	19	0.323	1B	70	1	2	0.973								
Hudson, William G. "Bill"																											
1939	Thomasville	GFL	23	52	6	11	0	1	0	6	0	5	13	0.212	P	15	16	2	0.939	11	3	6	3.41	66	64	35	31
Huelfer, Dennis C.		BR TR																									
1952	Brunswick	GFL	48	110	12	24	6	0	2	15	1	16	33	0.218	OF, P	46	12	3	0.951	13	0	4	5.82	51	61	16	51
1953	Brunswick	GFL	49	98	10	21	3	0	1	18	0	18	21	0.214	OF, P	16	1	1	0.944	25	10	8	2.91	133	118	75	112
Huesman, John "Jack"		BR TR																									
1947	Alexander City	GAL	62	229	45	62	6	2	0	18	6	34	24	0.271	2B	158	198	28	0.927								
1948	Alexander City	GAL	123	443	81	116	16	7	0	34	41	105	41	0.262	2B	362	339	20	0.972								
1949	Alexander City	GAL	126	430	108	114	9	5	0	42	80	128	28	0.265	2B, SS	337	362	30	0.959								
Huey, O.D.																											
1936	Moultrie	GFL	12	11	2	2	0	0	0	0	0			0.182	P									<30			
Huffaker, Wayne																											
1937	Americus	GFL	34	69	2	7	0	0	0	1	0	5	23	0.101	P	8	49	2	0.966	31	7	15	4.27	211	211	72	89
Huffman, Robert "Bob"		BR TR																									
1947	Alexander City	GAL	59	178	15	26	7	3	0	11	1	15	61	0.146	C	240	36	20	0.932								
Huffman, William "Bill"		BL TR																									
1956	Hazlehurst-Baxley	GSL	96	359	63	117	22	6	1	54	9	49	14	0.326	2B	253	275	16	0.971								
Huggins, Miller																											
1928	Gadsden - Carrollton	GAL	79	304	41	76	4	1	1		9	13	16	0.250	3B	98	162	25	0.912								
1929	Cedartown	GAL	21	84	12	26	3	2	1		0	3	4	0.310	3B	17	49	18	0.786								
Hughes, ---																											
1920	Cedartown	GSL													P												
Hughes, Charles		BL TR																									
1962	Thomasville	GFL	14	38	11	7	1	0	1	4	0	11	12	0.184	3B	8	22	2	0.938								
1963	Thomasville	GFL	73	237	28	48	10	1	5	21	3	38	63	0.203	3B	54	123	12	0.937								
Hughes, George T.		BL TR																									
1950	Valley	GAL	100	379	75	126	23	5	3	72	23	56	33	0.332	OF	236	13	5	0.980								
1951	Valley	GAL	115	468	110	168	27	14	0	62	12	60	24	0.359	OF	314	6	9	0.973								
Hughes, Harry		BL TL																									
1940	Waycross	GFL	127	456	77	154	24	7	2	79	9	83	27	0.338	1B	1234	59	25	0.981								
Hughes, James "Jim"		BR TL																									
1951	Opelika	GAL	13	32	6	7	0	0	0	2	0	2	12	0.219	P	4	10	2	0.875	13	4	1	5.61	77	83	24	43
Hughes, James C. "Jim"		BL TR																									
1952	Valdosta	GFL	22	71	9	10	1	0	0	3	1	13	16	0.141	OF	14	1	1	0.938								
1952	Vidalia	GSL	13	27	1	5	1	0	0	3	0	3	4	0.185													
1953	Thomasville	GFL	22	93	21	31	7	0	0	10	3	16	11	0.333	2B	61	57	5	0.959								
1955	Thomasville	GFL	57	199	32	44	3	3	3	26	9	34	42	0.221	2B, 3B, SS	96	128	30	0.882								
Hughes, Norman G. "Norm"		BR TR																									
1953	Tifton	GFL	1											0.000	P					0	0			<45			
1953	Eastman	GSL	31	54	3	9	0	0	0	2	0	7	15	0.167	P	9	21	2	0.938	31	12	5	4.70	157	161	84	86
1954	Vidalia	GSL	10	16	3	2	1	0	0	0	0	3	4	0.125	P					3	1	1		<45			
1958	Dublin	GFL	1	4	0									0.000	P					1	1	0		<30			
Hughson, Cecil Carlton "Tex"		BR TR 6'3" 198 lbs b. 02/09/1916 Buda, TX d. 08/06/1993 San Marcos, TX																									
1937	Moultrie	GFL	32	66	4	11	4	1	0	5	0	3	12	0.167	P	3	13	2	0.889	19	8	6	2.38	121	133	76	38
Huinker, Arthur "Art"		BR TL																									
1957	Albany	GFL	9	16		2								0.125	P					9	6	1	1.22	59	39	40	23
Huisking, Charles																											
1935	Tallahassee	GFL	15	39	4	9	1	1	0		0	2	21	0.231	P					13	4	4		91	69	54	39
Hulet, Fred		BR TR																									
1950	Moultrie	GFL	12	19	1	2	0	0	0	0	0	4	7	0.105	P	1	10	3	0.786	12	1	4	9.00	46	68	28	52
Hull, Tommy		BR TR																									
1955	Dublin	GSL	20	44	7	7	0	0	0	2	0	1	15	0.159	P	3	17	2	0.909	20	10	3	2.49	123	109	80	52
Hulsey, DeLane		BL TR																									
1955	Hazlehurst-Baxley	GSL	12	16	0	0	0	0	0	0	0	0	7	0.000	P	2	11	0	1.000	12	1	7	5.43	53	59	27	29
Hultzapple, Kenneth "Ken"		BR TR																									
1962	Brunswick	GFL	12	4	0	0	0	0	0	0	0	0	2	0.000	P	0	5	1	0.833	12	0	1	5.29	17	24	18	8
Humberson, Bob "Roxie"		BR																									
1946	LaGrange	GAL	<10																								
Humbert, Jimmy		BR TR																									
1955	Thomasville	GFL	11	27	4	4	0	0	0	2	1	9	6	0.148	P					1	0	0		<45			
Humbracht, Harold "Hal"		BR TR																									
1946	Opelika	GAL	12	40	1	4	0	0	0	1	0	3	5	0.100	1B, P	98	2	1	0.990	1	0	0	0.00	2			
Humphries, ---																											
1913	Cordele	ESL	44	158	17	32	0	0	0					0.203	3B	54	47	14	0.878								
Humphries, ---																											
1921	Lindale	GSL													P												
Humphries, John William "Johnny"		BR TR 6'1" 185 lbs b. 06/23/1915 Clifton Forge, VA d. 06/24/1965 New Orleans, LA																									
1948	Douglas	GSL	11	27	3	5	2	0	0	2	0	1	6	0.185	M, P	2	11	1	0.929	10	3	2	3.16	57	58	39	10

Georgia Class-D Minor League Baseball Encyclopedia

YR	TEAM	LG	G	AB	R	H	2B	3B	HR	RBI	SB	BB	SO	BA	POS	PO	A	E	FA	GP	W	L	ERA	IP	H	SO	BB
Humphries, Roy																											
1930	Carrollton	GAL	<10												OF												
1935	Americus	GFL	53	221	36	63	16	2	3		4	24	33	0.285	OF	104	10	5	0.958								
Hungate, E. Lewis "Lew"		BL TR																									
1956	Sandersville	GSL	120	444	76	105	21	3	19	90	11	71	52	0.236	OF, P	194	11	16	0.928	1	0	0					
Hunnicutt, ---																											
1929	Talledega	GAL	28	102	11	18	4	3	1		3	9	13	0.176	3B	23	53	7	0.916								
Hunnicutt, Warner		BR TR																									
1953	Eastman	GSL	4											0.000	P						0	2	<45				
Hunt, Adrian		BR TR																									
1956	Dublin	GSL	2	2		0								0.000	P					2	0	2					
Hunt, Raymond A. "Ray"		BR TR																									
1946	Newnan	GAL	34	98	13	23	4	1	0	16	1	19	18	0.235	C	130	9	2	0.986								
Hunt, Robert "Bob"		BR TR																									
1956	Tifton	GFL	134	516	104	143	22	11	7	77	13	82	93	0.277	OF	289	21	11	0.966								
Hunter, ---																											
1928	Gadsden	GAL	10	27	7	8	2	0	0		2	10	7	0.296	OF	20	1	2	0.913								
Hunter, Bob																											
1921	Griffin	GSL																									
1921	Rome	GSL													2B												
Hunter, H.C.																											
1920	Cedartown	GSL													3B												
Hunter, Michael "Mike"																											
1963	Brunswick	GFL	58	186	25	50	6	0	11	34	3	18	46	0.269	1B, 3B	173	58	7	0.971								
Hurd, Thomas Carr "Tom" "Whitey"		BR TR 5'9" 155 lbs b. 05/27/1924 Danville, VA d. 09/05/1982 Waterloo, IA																									
1946	Cordele	GFL	122	502	80	114	17	10	0	50	2	73	86	0.227	SS	278	382	88	0.882								
Hurley, ---																											
1913	Valdosta	ESL	89	350	55	109	14	8	3					0.311	1B, OF	325	42	12	0.968								
1914	Valdosta	GSL		330	2	104	10	6	1		12			0.315													
Hurley, ---		BR TR																									
1946	Carrollton	GAL	1												P					1	0	0	0.00	3			
Hurley, Gerald Don "Don"		BR TR																									
1956	Albany	GFL	13	23	3	1	0	0	0	2	0	4	10	0.043													
1956	Hazlehurst-Baxley	GSL	31	109	9	24	5	0	1	10	1	8	31	0.220	3B, SS	32	54	14	0.860								
Hurst, ---																											
1930	Anniston	GAL	13	44	4	14	0	0	0		0	4	1	0.318	C	64	5	3	0.958								
Hurst, John		BR TR																									
1950	Thomasville	GFL	104	392	56	92	11	4	3	30	8	43	78	0.235	2B	212	317	44	0.923								
Hurst, Leon		BR TR																									
1955	Brunswick	GFL	14	37	2	10	3	0	0	2	0	3	8	0.270	P	8	13	4	0.840	13	7	5	3.15	97	91	55	44
Hurvitz, Robert "Bob"		BR TR																									
1956	Thomasville	GFL	111	343	36	71	13	4	4	38	3	40	20	0.207	C	773	80	28	0.968								
Hushebeck, John		BR TR																									
1950	Americus	GFL	35	87	16	19	4	0	0	4	0	9	17	0.218	P	9	53	1	0.984	35	22	8	3.22	221	195	131	121
Husich, John		BL TL																									
1953	Fitzgerald	GFL	38	69	8	14	1	0	0	9	0	8	11	0.203	P	8	29	4	0.902	29	13	8	2.90	180	163	101	109
1954	Fitzgerald	GFL	50	78	11	20	3	0	0	6	0	6	21	0.256	P	6	13	3	0.864	40	9	10	4.23	151	150	94	82
1955	Moultrie	GFL	50	86	7	18	0	2	0	12	0	7	22	0.209	P	12	31	4	0.915	38	8	15	4.92	181	199	124	104
Hutcherson, William "Billy"																											
1941	Cordele	GFL	14	47	6	12	2	0	0	4	1	7	8	0.255	2B	16	16	6	0.842								
1942	Cordele	GFL	34	124	25	32	4	5	0	11	6	25	19	0.258	OF	72	45	19	0.860								
Hutchins, ---																											
1914	Rome	GAL	30	122	11	25				4				0.205	OF	52	2	6	0.900								
1915	Rome	GAL	55	207	30	51	6	0	0					0.246	1B	436	35	23	0.953								
Hutchins, Barry		BR TR																									
1953	Douglas	GSL	8											0.286	P						1	2	<45				
1955	Statesboro	GSL	21	38	3	2	0	0	0	0	0	12	20	0.053	P	4	22	6	0.813	19	6	7	5.15	117	116	117	104
Hutchins, Robert L. "Bob"		BL TL																									
1949	Carrollton	GAL	7												P					7	4	3	2.33	54	51	34	19
1950	Rome(15) - Carrollton(9)	GAL	24	40	8	9	1	0	0	2	0	5	5	0.225	P	5	10	0	1.000	24	9	3	5.21	102	129	60	49
1951	Rome	GAL	10	8	1	1	0	0	0	1	0	2	2	0.125	P	1	5	0	1.000								
Hutchinson, Gordon		BR TR																									
1958	Thomasville	GFL	3	0										0.000	P					3	0	0	<30				
Hutchinson, James "Jim"		BL TR																									
1948	Baxley	GSL	104	319	41	52	2	3	0	19	16	53	58	0.163	1B, OF	220	13	5	0.979								
Hutchison, ---																											
1915	Brunswick	FLAG			0									0.000													
Huthmaker, Frederick "Fred"		BR TR																									
1952	Hazlehurst-Baxley	GSL	21	40	4	8	0	0	0	5	0	9	17	0.200	P	4	23	0	1.000	21	7	4	3.69	117	125	67	48
1953	Hazlehurst-Baxley	GSL	41	91	8	16	4	1	0	15	0	6	25	0.176	P	8	25	2	0.943	41	19	9	4.02	217	216	110	99
Hutson, Cecil		BR TR																									
1953	Jesup	GSL	75	91	9	16	3	0	0	6	0	10	14	0.176	P	4	42	1	0.979	75	17	12	3.46	265	246	156	98
Hydringer, ---																											
1928	Cedartown	GAL	21	47	1	7	0	0	0		0	3	14	0.149	P	3	56	2	0.967	21	7	8	4.03	134	129	55	48

Georgia Class-D Minor League Baseball Encyclopedia

YR	TEAM	LG	G	AB	R	H	2B	3B	HR	RBI	SB	BB	SO	BA	POS	PO	A	E	FA	GP	W	L	ERA	IP	H	SO	BB
Icenhour, Luther		BR TR																									
1954	Dublin	GSL	53	195	26	60	13	1	2	28	2	27	25	0.308	SS	72	150	18	0.925								
1955	Statesboro	GSL	32	127	18	31	5	1	0	11	6	16	16	0.244	SS	45	91	13	0.913								
Icenhour, Phillip "Phil"		BL TR																									
1947	Moultrie	GFL	43	156	16	39	5	3	1	23	1	15	29	0.250	OF	59	5	7	0.901								
Ingalls, John "Jack"		BL TR																									
1948	Waycross	GFL	35	74	7	16	2	0	2	11	0	5	23	0.216	P	2	16	3	0.857	34	12	9	5.23	186	181	197	148
1949	Waycross	GFL	15	31	1	3	0	0	0	2	0	1	10	0.097	P	5	9	2	0.875	13	4	5	7.89	57	64	55	82
Ingram, Clarence		BR TR																									
1952	Albany	GFL	37	45	8	6	0	0	0	2	0	5	17	0.133	P	4	26	4	0.882	36	4	9	3.60	135	129	66	75
1957	Albany	GFL	36	65	7	15	3	0	0	6	0	5	10	0.231	P	15	25	3	0.930	34	17	7	2.29	189	167	70	58
Ingram, Jimmy																											
1920	Carrollton	GSL		7	1	1								0.143	P												
Ingram, Peter "Pete"		BR TR																									
1963	Thomasville	GFL	13	8	1	1	0	0	0	1	0	1	4	0.125	P	1	6	1	0.875	12	2	0	3.09	32	34	11	8
Ippolito, Rocco		BR TR																									
1948	Moultrie	GFL	124	495	121	183	28	8	21	102	30	62	60	0.370	OF, P	186	40	18	0.926	14	8	6	2.81	96	94	69	49
Irby, Leroy		BL TR																									
1955	Vidalia	GSL	42	133	27	38	8	0	6	30	1	25	17	0.286	1B, OF	137	13	11	0.932								
Irons, Edward "Ed"		BR TR																									
1950	Opelika	GAL	55	200	44	72	12	5	12	57	4	34	18	0.360	3B, C	198	55	11	0.958								
Irvin, James "Jim"		BR TR																									
1948	Opelika	GAL	33	77	5	17	1	0	0	9	0	12	15	0.221	C	99	20	7	0.944								
Isaacs, Cecil		BL TR																									
1956	Moultrie	GFL	23	59	9	12	4	0	0	7	0	3	16	0.203	P	2	20	5	0.815	19	9	6	3.19	144	123	99	44
Isaacson, Herbert "Herb"		BL TL																									
1954	Valdosta	GFL	18	69	5	19	2	5	0	11	0	5	7	0.275	OF	20	0	1	0.952								
Isbell, Maurice																											
1936	Americus	GFL	15	29	1	6	0	0	0	5	1			0.207	P					15	4	2	3.27	66		22	26
Isert, Fred J.																											
1937	Thomasville	GFL	33	100	7	12	4	0	0	5	0	7	27	0.120	P	9	44	6	0.898	32	20	8	2.45	250	219	136	85
Isert, Louis "Lou"		BR TR																									
1940	Thomasville - Albany	GFL	36	155	15	29	4	0	0	5	1	17	28	0.187	SS	58	108	27	0.860								
Israel, William "Bill"		BR TR																									
1946	Carrollton	GAL	30	62	3	15	2	0	0	5	0	1	10	0.242	P	3	23	3	0.897	24	12	8	3.96	134	149	60	54
Itkin, Alfred "Al"		BR TR																									
1950	Vidalia-Lyons	GSL	37	68	12	9	1	0	0	4	0	19	15	0.132	P	11	61	14	0.837	36	11	14	5.10	210	211	124	133
1951	Cordele	GFL	14	36	4	7	2	0	0	5	0	8	6	0.194	P	3	25	2	0.933	12	6	6	3.75	96	103	59	50
Ivester, Neal B.																											
1949	Hazlehurst-Baxley	GSL	85	321	24	79	8	1	0	32	6	18	25	0.246	C	348	39	13	0.968								
Ivey, Douglas "Doug"		BL TL																									
1937	Americus	GFL	30	58	4	10	1	0	0	5	0	13	15	0.172	P	11	29	1	0.976	25	10	11	3.34	148	165	43	37
1940	Thomasville	GFL	<10												P								<35				
Ivey, Robert H. "Bob"																											
1938	Cordele	GFL	63	242	32	57	11	2	0	30	5	26	30	0.236	UT	147	130	32	0.896								
Ivey, Robert W. "Bob"																											
1949	Dublin	GSL	45	130	14	27	5	1	0	15	6	19	10	0.208	P, C	78	68	15	0.907	44	12	12	4.05	220	123	122	117
Ivey, William M. "Bill"		BR TR																									
1953	Albany	GFL	19	63	9	12	1	1	0	7	0	12	18	0.190	OF	23	0	3	0.885								
Ivy, Harold		BL TR																									
1950	Moultrie	GFL	118	424	94	135	13	8	13	131	9	110	69	0.318	OF	218	9	14	0.942								
Izzo, John		BR TR																									
1946	Thomasville	GFL	3												P					3	0	1	0.00	5	6	1	10
Jack, Richard W. "Dick"		BR TR																									
1953	Fitzgerald	GFL	11	15	0	0	0	0	0	0	0	0	5	0.000	P	5	6	2	0.846		2	4		<45			
Jackimchuk, Nick																											
1941	Albany	GFL	34	135	22	40	4	1	0	20	2	21	30	0.296	SS	69	89	19	0.893								
Jackson, Charles R.																											
1914	LaGrange	GAL	10	36	4	9					1			0.250	OF	19	11	1	0.968								
1915	Talladega	GAL	50	187	22	51	16	1	1					0.273	OF	164	8	5	0.972								
Jackson, Claude		BR TR																									
1946	Opelika	GAL	1												P					1	0	0	0.00	1			
1948	Opelika	GAL	51	121	16	18	3	0	0	14	2	17	27	0.149	P	10	53	2	0.969	39	13	15	4.28	223	224	106	132
1949	Opelika	GAL	48	104	12	26	4	0	1	13	0	15	16	0.250	P	11	34	3	0.938	41	16	17	3.35	234	226	128	118
1950	Opelika	GAL	23	67	8	12	0	0	0	6	0	2	12	0.179	P	6	35	1	0.976	19	13	3	2.46	139	125	75	67
1951	Opelika	GAL	19	42	4	8	1	0	0	3	0	7	10	0.190	P	1	11	1	0.923	13	1	9	6.55	66	78	35	50
Jackson, Frank		BR TR																									
1949	Griffin	GAL	12	26	3	3	1	0	0	1	0	2	9	0.115	OF	7	3	0	1.000								
Jackson, Gene		BR TR																									
1940	Valdosta	GFL	45	160	26	37	6	2	0	12	2	30	37	0.231	OF	112	4	6	0.951								
Jackson, Harold S.		BR TR																									
1953	Jesup	GSL	34	81	9	12	0	0	0	5	3	10	7	0.148	3B, P	23	47	6	0.921	14	2	4	3.81	52	53	28	31
Jackson, John		BR TR																									
1954	Douglas	GSL	7	18		2								0.111	P					6	6	0	<45				
1955	Douglas	GSL	5	17		4								0.235	P					4	3	1					

Georgia Class-D Minor League Baseball Encyclopedia

YR	TEAM	LG	G	AB	R	H	2B	3B	HR	RBI	SB	BB	SO	BA	POS	PO	A	E	FA	GP	W	L	ERA	IP	H	SO	BB
Jackson, Joseph Earl "Earl"																											
1942	Tallahassee	GFL	99	378	37	104	8	3	1	43	2	45	20	0.275	3B	143	189	27	0.925								
Jackson, Lendon		BR TR																									
1957	Thomasville	GFL	13	15	0	0	0	0	0	0	0	1	10	0.000	P	1	5	1	0.857	13	3	1	4.03	38	38	27	38
Jackson, William T. "Bill"		BR TR																									
1955	Brunswick - Thomasville	GFL	123	465	62	96	16	4	0	40	4	51	80	0.206	2B, SS	317	342	38	0.945								
1956	Thomasville	GFL	134	508	70	140	10	6	1	46	12	62	52	0.276	2B	380	368	36	0.954								
Jacob, Vincent "Vince"		BR TR																									
1951	Brunswick	GFL	57	136	15	31	3	0	0	14	0	27	42	0.228	C	259	20	6	0.979								
Jacobs, George																											
1940	Moultrie	GFL													M												
Jacobs, Ottis		BR TR																									
1949	Tallassee	GAL	12	13	1	1	0	0	0	0	0	2	4	0.077	P	5	8	0	1.000								
1951	Tifton	GFL	47	110	11	15	2	0	0	9	0	14	34	0.136	P	13	49	6	0.912	33	20	12	3.12	251	217	190	128
Jacobs, William F. "Will"		BR TL																									
1951	Brunswick	GFL	20	51	5	6	0	0	0	1	0	6	14	0.118	P	5	26	4	0.886	17	9	8	2.57	133	103	81	77
Jacobsen, Edward A. "Ed"		BL TR																									
1951	Brunswick	GFL	110	421	66	110	19	5	5	54	20	80	37	0.261	OF	178	8	15	0.925								
Jacobus, Stephen "Steve"		BL TL																									
1962	Moultrie	GFL	110	365	49	99	17	6	6	48	2	63	91	0.271	1B, OF	550	31	28	0.954								
1963	Brunswick	GFL	23	56	10	16	4	0	1	11	0	4	16	0.286	1B	62	2	1	0.985								
Jacoby, Brooks		BR TR																									
1958	Brunswick	GFL	2	0										0.000	P					2	0	0		<30			
Jacquin, Donald "Don"		BR TR																									
1956	Tifton	GFL	133	488	77	133	24	3	7	73	8	73	76	0.273	3B	158	285	32	0.933								
Jacquot, James "Jim"		BR TR																									
1947	Albany	GFL	12	34	3	5	1	0	0	0	0	4	12	0.147	OF	12	1	0	1.000								
Jaeckel, Roy		BR TR																									
1939	Cordele	GFL	72	255	28	66	10	2	0	29	1	24	43	0.259	UT	317	143	27	0.945								
1940	Cordele - Tallahassee	GFL	118	448	65	131	17	4	1	60	13	57	39	0.292	OF, IF	292	114	17	0.960								
1941	Tallahassee	GFL	50	171	17	33	5	0	0	14	1	23	26	0.193	OF	98	20	4	0.967								
1942	Cordele	GFL	92	346	66	87	14	3	0	26	12	48	33	0.251	2B	256	314	27	0.955								
Jakosh, Louis "Lou"		BL TL																									
1956	Hazlehurst-Baxley	GSL	1	0										0.000	P					1	0	0					
Jakowczyk, Wallace "Wally"		BL TR																									
1950	Americus	GFL	109	404	70	113	18	7	9	83	10	81	44	0.280	OF	277	13	13	0.957								
Jakubov, John																											
1949	Eastman	GSL	27	64	5	6	0	0	0	5	0	9	29	0.094	P	3	21	2	0.923	29	15	9	3.84	204	104	77	81
Jakubowski, Alfred "Al"		BR TR																									
1956	Moultrie	GFL	63	218	25	49	5	3	0	17	2	27	60	0.225	OF	141	6	8	0.948								
James, Forrest Hood "Fob"																											
1928	Carrollton	GAL	73	305	44	89	13	0	1		3	20	20	0.292	1B	733	29	12	0.984								
1929	Lindale	GAL	49	180	26	51	7	1	4		2	9	14	0.283	1B	478	16	6	0.988								
James, R.E.																											
1921	Rome	GSL													OF, P												
Jameson, Don																											
1942	Americus	GFL	86	332	52	101	15	6	1	56	5	24	30	0.304	C, OF	228	12	16	0.938								
Jamison, Thomas E. "Tom"		BR TR																									
1951	Fitzgerald	GSL	18	31	2	4	0	0	0	1	0	2	11	0.129	P	0	11	3	0.786	17	2	4	6.25	72	89	13	56
Janci, Fred		BL TR																									
1940	Tallahassee	GFL	45	164	20	40	2	1	1	19	2	18	15	0.244	1B	392	18	16	0.962								
Janelle, Ray		BR TR																									
1951	Albany	GFL	15	31	5	2	0	0	0	0	1	4	14	0.065	P	2	21	0	1.000	14	6	6	4.55	87	92	31	58
Janeway, Gary		BR TR																									
1956	Hazlehurst-Baxley	GSL	2	1		1								1.000	P					2	0	0					
Jarvinen, Vernon "Vern"		BL																									
1955	Hazlehurst-Baxley	GSL	5	13		2								0.154													
Jarvis, Robert Glenn "Bob"		BR TR																									
1948	Opelika	GAL	123	442	86	122	19	7	4	55	13	74	51	0.276	3B	135	240	40	0.904								
1949	Opelika	GAL	113	398	62	106	19	4	5	79	13	55	49	0.266	3B	120	220	35	0.907								
1950	Valley(52) - Griffin(31)	GAL	83	307	58	73	9	3	9	51	25	47	45	0.238	3B, SS	95	160	27	0.904								
Javier, Manuel Julian (Liranzo) "Julian" BR TR 6'1" 175 lbs b. 08/09/1936 San Francisco De Macoris, Dominican Republic																											
1956	Brunswick	GFL	18	50	5	9	0	1	0	0	0	2	18	0.180	3B	16	25	6	0.872								
Jay, Paul		BR TR																									
1949	Waycross	GFL	60	135	25	29	5	1	2	25	1	11	18	0.215	OF, P	29	41	4	0.946	38	21	8	3.30	237	232	158	76
Jeakle, Edwin "Ed"		BR TR																									
1950	LaGrange	GAL	89	350	55	96	25	4	8	68	5	44	40	0.274	OF	185	7	13	0.937								
Jeanes, John		BR TR																									
1957	Fitzgerald	GFL	18	19	3	5	1	0	0	3	0	2	2	0.263	P	1	4	2	0.714	15	3	3	5.09	46	64	24	27
Jeffcoat, William		BR TR																									
1946	Tallahassee	GFL	1												P					1	0	0	0.00	2			
Jefferson, Ernest																											
1941	Albany	GFL	18	58	6	11	1	2	0	11	0	2	13	0.190	P	3	24	2	0.931	17	12	3	2.54	124	115	119	47

Georgia Class-D Minor League Baseball Encyclopedia

YR	TEAM	LG	G	AB	R	H	2B	3B	HR	RBI	SB	BB	SO	BA	POS	PO	A	E	FA	GP	W	L	ERA	IP	H	SO	BB
Jefts, Virgil Robert "Virgil"		BR TR																									
1948	Carrollton	GAL	12	32	3	11	1	0	0	2	0	2	3	0.344	C	62	5	1	0.985								
1949	Carrollton	GAL	114	377	48	91	18	1	2	40	0	71	47	0.241	C	550	71	26	0.960								
1951	Jesup	GSL	120	454	49	123	16	2	3	68	0	60	31	0.271	C	577	49	11	0.983								
Jenkins, Gary		BR TR																									
1962	Dublin	GFL	14	26	0	3	0	0	0	0	0	2	11	0.115	P	5	19	6	0.800	14	5	2	4.19	73	66	53	35
Jenkins, L. Alvin		BL TR																									
1951	Jesup	GSL	125	551	135	207	35	11	3	50	41	56	40	0.376	OF	289	17	17	0.947								
Jenkins, Lee		BL TR																									
1948	Valdosta	GFL	126	516	95	178	16	20	1	77	27	78	75	0.345	OF	189	15	11	0.949								
1949	Valdosta	GFL	81	310	53	103	14	12	2	46	15	22	27	0.332	OF	103	14	5	0.959								
Jenkins, Reynolds		BR TR																									
1958	Valdosta	GFL	1	1		1								1.000	P					1	0	1		<30			
Jenkins, Robert H. "Bob"		BR TR																									
1950	Valdosta	GFL	35	81	6	17	3	0	0	12	1	9	19	0.210	C	116	11	3	0.977								
Jenkins, Thomas Griffith "Tom" "Tut"		BL TR 6'1" 174 lbs b. 04/10/1898 Camden, AL d. 05/03/1979 Weymouth, MA																									
1916	Griffin	GAL	37	126	24	42				7				0.333	OF												
1917	Griffin	GAL	14	47	5	13	6	0	0	2				0.277	OF, 3B	21	2	4	0.852								
Jensen, Richard "Dick"		BR TR																									
1963	Waycross	GFL	16	9	0	0	0	0	0	0	0	1	4	0.000	P	1	2	0	1.000	15	1	0	3.60	30	28	22	15
Jesmer, W.H.																											
1920	Rome	GSL		267	27	61	11	0	0		5			0.228	1B												
1921	Carrollton	GSL		142	17	40								0.282	1B												
Jessee, Frank		BR TR																									
1956	Dublin	GSL	63	205	30	43	4	1	3	18	0	27	27	0.210	OF, C	193	17	7	0.968								
Jeter, Cleo		BR TR																									
1946	Opelika(7) - LaGrange(38)	GAL	45	126	15	36	9	0	1	21	0	9	28	0.286	P, OF	28	25	2	0.964	26	14	11	3.86	182	179	103	48
1947	Opelika	GAL	13	16	2	4	1	0	0	0	0	3	4	0.250													
Jezek, Edward "Ed"		BR TR																									
1953	Thomasville	GFL	26	53	7	11	3	0	0	1	0	7	20	0.208	P	6	31	5	0.881	26	11	5	2.61	152	109	118	88
1955	Thomasville	GFL	5	4		1								0.250	P					4	0	1		<45			
Jezek, Richard "Nick"		BL TR																									
1956	Hazlehurst-Baxley	GSL	34	97	13	19	4	0	6	2	18		38	0.196	OF	67	3	5	0.933								
Jimenez, Felipe		BR TR																									
1952	Statesboro	GSL	66	236	34	57	9	0	2	23	3	27	12	0.242	3B, OF, C, P	135	66	24	0.893	6	1	1	3.45	47	44	30	32
Jiminez, Daniel R. "Dan"		BR TR																									
1951	Tifton	GFL	13	20	0	1	0	0	0	0	0	4	2	0.050													
1951	Fitzgerald	GSL	45	154	15	23	4	1	0	12	2	32	23	0.149	3B, OF	66	35	13	0.886								
1953	Statesboro	GSL	85	261	32	74	9	0	1	26	17	46	26	0.284	3B, OF, P	72	74	15	0.907	26	4	3	5.16	89	103	31	40
1954	Statesboro(10) - Sandersville(13)	GSL	23	74	7	13	3	0	0	6	0	11	6	0.176	3B, P	11	20	7	0.816	5	0	0		<45			
Jiminez, Dario		BR TR																									
1950	Douglas	GSL	70	120	14	17	3	0	0	8	0	10	14	0.142	P	12	70	2	0.976	44	21	10	2.93	240	252	88	53
Jinske, Wayne		BR TR																									
1963	Waycross	GFL	114	355	47	110	13	2	8	39	6	56	34	0.310	C	870	68	17	0.982								
Jobe, Lewis "Lew"		BR TR																									
1946	Cordele	GFL	30	70	7	20	4	1	0	9	0	2	11	0.286	P	5	31	2	0.947	25	5	12	3.75	151	135	89	80
1947	Cordele	GFL	28	74	9	16	4	1	0	2	0	2	8	0.216	P	1	17	2	0.900	15	2	8	4.70	88	117	51	38
Joergen, Jim																											
1952	Moultrie	GFL	<10																									
Johannsen, ---																											
1916	Anniston	GAL	64	219	24	43					5			0.196	OF, 2B												
1920	Griffin	GSL													3B													
Johengen, George		BL TL																									
1950	LaGrange	GAL	33	69	10	17	1	0	0	10	0	11	11	0.246	1B, P	75	15	1	0.989	19	9	3	2.66	105	89	69	58
Johns, James "Jim"		BR TR																									
1951	Opelika	GAL	29	93	14	22	3	1	2	8	2	19	32	0.237	2B	61	74	11	0.925								
Johnsen, Tor																											
1935	Moultrie	GFL	52	189	27	56	10	5	3		4	9	36	0.296	OF	91	2	4	0.959								
Johnson, ---																											
1920	Griffin	GSL														P												
Johnson, ---																											
1942	Moultrie	GFL	4												P					4	0	3	6.38	24	30	17	17
Johnson, Charles		BR TR																									
1949	Thomasville	GFL	137	488	59	103	12	2	0	48	6	70	108	0.211	3B	152	241	60	0.868								
Johnson, Clyde M.		BR TR																									
1953	Douglas	GSL	2											0.000	P					0	1		<45				
Johnson, Donald "Don"		BR TL																									
1962	Brunswick	GFL	24	27	8	5	0	0	0	3	0	3	8	0.185	P	13	20	5	0.868	24	3	6	6.68	93	111	90	61
1963	Brunswick	GFL	2	0	0	0	0	0	0	0	0	0	0	0.000	P					2	0	0	18.00	1	1	0	3
Johnson, Douglas "Doug"		BR TR																									
1946	Tallahassee	GFL	124	450	90	136	11	18	2	83	15	82	83	0.302	3B, SS, P	176	281	74	0.861	1	0	0	0.00	1			
Johnson, Earl		TR BR 6'0" 185 lbs b. 11/01/1896 Fairmont, WV																									
1920	Cedartown	GSL													P					36	20	8		252	238	124	40
Johnson, Earl A.		BR TR																									
1953	Hazlehurst-Baxley	GSL	82	252	47	74	8	4	4	42	3	42	36	0.294	C	434	36	13	0.973								
1954	Albany	GFL	131	440	80	122	22	3	2	70	25	76	64	0.277	OF, C	736	93	17	0.980								

Georgia Class-D Minor League Baseball Encyclopedia

YR	TEAM	LG	G	AB	R	H	2B	3B	HR	RBI	SB	BB	SO	BA	POS	PO	A	E	FA	GP	W	L	ERA	IP	H	SO	BB
Johnson, Eli																											
1941	Cordele	GFL	9	23	2	9	1	0	0	0	0	0	4	0.391	2B	5	11	4	0.800								
Johnson, Elijah T.		BR TR																									
1962	Moultrie	GFL	111	385	70	96	13	1	11	59	18	39	108	0.249	3B, OF	125	98	50	0.817								
Johnson, Emmitt H.																											
1941	Tallahassee	GFL	64	244	37	69	9	2	0	41	8	38	10	0.283	3B	70	157	28	0.890								
Johnson, Eric		BL TL																									
1956	Thomasville	GFL	15	17	0	3	0	0	0	0	0	2	6	0.176	P	0	5	1	0.833	15	1	5	4.22	49	47	24	29
Johnson, Ernest		BR TR																									
1955	Brunswick	GFL	5	13		3								0.231	P					5	1	3	<45				
1955	Dublin	GSL	12	11	1	1	0	0	0	2	0	1	4	0.091	P	2	6	1	0.889	12	1	1	6.39	31	41	24	22
Johnson, George M.		BR TR																									
1946	Waycross	GFL	<10																								
1948	Alexander City	GAL	71	256	46	62	10	3	0	15	18	29	49	0.242	3B	79	119	32	0.861								
1949	Valley	GAL	14	50	6	10	0	0	0	8	4	3	9	0.200	2B	30	26	4	0.933								
Johnson, Harold W.		BR TR																									
1948	Vidalia-Lyons	GSL	35	94	6	15	0	1	0	7	0	5	18	0.160	P	5	41	6	0.885	34	17	13	3.35	226	210	150	97
Johnson, Harry		BR TR																									
1952	Tifton	GFL	40	109	8	20	2	0	0	8	1	8	23	0.183	P	13	59	2	0.973	36	19	12	2.54	262	240	91	84
1953	Tifton	GFL	38	70	9	17	4	1	0	5	1	4	13	0.243	P	18	39	3	0.950	37	16	10	3.24	222	225	97	97
1954	Statesboro	GSL	5	8		0								0.000	P					5	2	2	<45				
Johnson, Howard "Howie"		BR TR																									
1949	Waycross	GFL	27	88	16	14	4	0	2	9	1	12	21	0.159	C	162	24	3	0.984								
Johnson, Ivy		BL TR																									
1953	Tifton	GFL	27	63	6	11	0	0	0	3	2	10	17	0.175	3B	18	17	6	0.854								
1956	Waycross	GFL	131	460	62	114	18	5	2	55	15	59	76	0.248	2B, 3B	142	251	33	0.923								
Johnson, James "Jim"		BR TR																									
1956	Valdosta	GFL	1	1		0								0.000													
1956	Hazlehurst-Baxley	GSL	26	79	10	14	2	0	0	8	0	12	21	0.177	OF	35	0	8	0.814								
Johnson, James J. "Jim"		BR TR																									
1952	Moultrie	GFL	16	44	2	8	2	0	0	2	0	3	10	0.182	OF	12	2	0	1.000								
Johnson, Jerry M.		BR TR																									
1958	Brunswick	GFL	25	78	10	19	3	0	0	6	0	8	8	0.244	C	142	7	7	0.955								
Johnson, Jim																											
1938	Moultrie	GFL	73	302	36	71	13	5	0	24	4	13	32	0.235	OF	133	17	10	0.938								
Johnson, John B.		BR TR																									
1946	Newnan	GAL	32	82	10	15	3	0	2	9	2	6	21	0.183	P	10	42	0	1.000	32	20	8	2.92	231	228	138	41
Johnson, Joseph "Joe"		BR TR																									
1946	Valley(21) - LaGrange(79)	GAL	100	338	44	77	13	5	1	53	5	27	48	0.228	OF, P	193	4	9	0.956	1	0	0	0.00	2			
Johnson, Lawrence "Larry"		BR TR																									
1955	Statesboro	GSL	3	2		0								0.000	P					3	0	1					
Johnson, Lawrence Owen "Owen"		BR TR																									
1963	Thomasville	GFL	13	26	5	9	1	0	1	7	0	5	5	0.346	P					5	3	1	2.53	32	26	22	9
Johnson, Lee		BR TR																									
1951	Tifton	GFL	22	35	6	7	1	0	0	2	0	2	9	0.200													
1951	Dublin(1) - Douglas(10)	GSL	11	40	3	7	1	0	0	0	2	5	17	0.175	SS	12	24	6	0.857								
Johnson, Lee		BR TR																									
1955	Tifton	GFL	7	20		3								0.150	P					3	0	0	<45				
Johnson, Lee H.																											
1936	Albany	GFL	113	437	66	120	27	5	16	84	9			0.275	1B	1029	52	21	0.981								
1937	Albany	GFL	123	474	65	149	29	3	3	67	24	54	58	0.314	1B	1043	60	20	0.982								
Johnson, Lorne		BL TL																									
1958	Waycross	GFL	43	152	32	42	5	3	2	24	2	42	20	0.276	OF, P	79	3	1	0.988	1	0	0	<30				
Johnson, Marion																											
1938	Thomasville	GFL	25	121	24	35	4	2	1	15	2	16	12	0.289	2B	64	98	9	0.947								
1939	Cordele	GFL	14	54	3	9	1	0	0	1	1	2	10	0.167	2B	30	41	7	0.910								
1942	Dothan	GFL	32	130	24	37	7	4	0	23	14	48	14	0.285	3B	45	84	13	0.908								
Johnson, Marshall		BR TR																									
1958	Thomasville	GFL	4	3		0								0.000	P					4	0	2	<30				
Johnson, Myra Lee "Myra"		BR																									
1954	Sandersville	GSL	19	54	6	7	0	0	0	3	0	20	14	0.130													
Johnson, Norman "Norm"		BR																									
1940	Americus	GFL	<10																								
Johnson, Oscar		BL TR																									
1949	Cordele	GFL	38	75	4	16	2	0	0	6	1	3	19	0.213	P	4	38	5	0.894	30	8	14	4.22	177	197	114	94
Johnson, Robert "Bob"																											
1941	Waycross	GFL	29	110	14	28	2	2	0	11	0	14	22	0.255	SS	63	90	17	0.900								
Johnson, Robert Wallace "Bob"		BR TR 5'10" 175 lbs b. 03/04/1936 Omaha, NE																									
1955	Valdosta	GFL	6	17		3								0.176													
Johnson, Roy		BL TR																									
1951	Alexander City	GAL	23	32	7	6	0	0	0	3	0	4	6	0.188	C	39	8	2	0.959								
Johnson, Rudolph V.		BL TR																									
1950	Dublin	GSL	103	397	65	105	13	2	2	41	12	58	33	0.264	OF	207	8	6	0.973								
1951	Dublin(89) - Fitzgerald(39)	GSL	128	512	100	143	10	5	0	43	16	95	16	0.279	2B, OF	328	88	22	0.950								

Georgia Class-D Minor League Baseball Encyclopedia

YR	TEAM	LG	G	AB	R	H	2B	3B	HR	RBI	SB	BB	SO	BA	POS	PO	A	E	FA	GP	W	L	ERA	IP	H	SO	BB
Johnson, Sidney L. "Sid"		BR TR																									
1953	Sandersville	GSL	27	101	16	32	4	3	0	17	3	15	10	0.317	SS	20	25	5	0.900								
1954	Sandersville	GSL	7	12		3								0.250	P					5	1	3	<45				
Johnson, Thomas "Tom"		BR TR																									
1954	Tifton	GFL	12	37	6	6	0	0	0	4	1	6	4	0.162	2B	24	28	5	0.912								
Johnson, Thomas L. "Red"																											
1941	Americus	GFL	117	503	95	157	27	9	9	69	5	29	59	0.312	OF	228	8	19	0.925								
1942	Americus	GFL	97	389	62	105	21	8	9	64	1	32	49	0.270	OF	307	15	17	0.950								
Johnson, Walter H. "Walt"		BL TL																									
1958	Albany	GFL	17	46	11	11	2	0	0	5	1	5	12	0.239	OF, P	15	2	1	0.944	2	0	0	<30				
Johnson, Wilbur L.		BR TR																									
1954	Tifton	GFL	27	62	7	14	5	0	1	6	0	6	12	0.226	P	7	28	7	0.833	25	7	10	4.20	137	137	120	99
Johnson, William E. "Bill"		BL BR																									
1952	Dublin	GSL	11	13	2	1	0	0	0	0	0	4	3	0.077	P	3	6	1	0.900								
Johnston, James G. "Jim"		BR TR																									
1950	Dublin	GSL	85	318	69	80	11	2	6	37	11	70	67	0.252	2B	207	233	32	0.932								
1951	Eastman	GSL	129	492	89	127	22	0	4	53	22	103	42	0.258	2B	355	310	31	0.955								
1952	Douglas	GSL	36	128	21	22	6	0	0	9	5	30	14	0.172	2B	97	84	13	0.933								
Johnston, Jerry		BR TL																									
1956	Douglas	GSL	25	48	10	11	1	1	0	9	0	8	8	0.229	P	8	17	2	0.926	23	10	4	3.07	138	101	107	87
Johnston, Robert "Bob"		BR TR																									
1958	Thomasville	GFL	7	5		3								0.600	P					7	0	2	<30				
Johnston, Robert L. "Bob"		BR TR																									
1953	Tifton	GFL	40	146	16	30	5	0	1	12	3	18	26	0.205	2B	100	85	12	0.939								
Johnston, Robert N. "Bob"		BR TR																									
1950	Waycross	GFL	42	166	33	39	5	5	0	19	5	25	31	0.235	3B	54	51	15	0.875								
Jones, ---																											
1913	Waycross	ESL	42	150	18	39	7	0	0					0.260	1B	359	29	7	0.982								
1914	Waycross	GSL		251	39	62	8	3	2		14			0.247													
Jones, ---		BR TR																									
1949	Thomasville	GFL	8												P					8	2	5	4.88	48	52	30	39
Jones, Barry		BR TR																									
1947	Valley	GAL	57	221	45	53	5	2	0	21	6	33	21	0.240	SS	106	169	38	0.879								
Jones, Billy Joe		BR TR																									
1953	Fitzgerald	GFL	4											0.000	P					0	0		<45				
Jones, C. Rudolph "Rudy"		BL TL																									
1947	Waycross	GFL	108	459	94	153	27	10	0	48	22	63	56	0.333	1B, OF	388	19	20	0.953								
Jones, Charles		BR																									
1946	Albany	GFL	10	24	3	2	0	0	0	1	0	1	5	0.083													
Jones, Charles		BL TR																									
1957	Thomasville	GFL	10	15	0	1	0	0	0	0	0	1	7	0.067	P					1	0	0	<30				
Jones, D.																											
1920	Cedartown	GSL		63	14	19								0.302	M, C												
Jones, Ellis		BR TR																									
1956	Valdosta	GFL	3	0										0.000	P					3	0	1	<45				
Jones, Frederick "Fred"		BR TR																									
1955	Thomasville	GFL	2	4		0								0.000	P					2	0	1	<45				
Jones, Harry		BR																									
1953	Sandersville	GSL	8											0.308													
Jones, Harvey		BR TR																									
1954	Sandersville	GSL	22	72	12	11	2	0	0	9	0	17	16	0.153	3B	19	32	9	0.850								
Jones, Isom "Heisman"																											
1917	LaGrange	GAL	3	11	0	1	0	0	0		0			0.091	M, OF	1	1	1	0.667								
Jones, Jack		BR TR																									
1953	Vidalia	GSL	7											0.250	P					2	2		<45				
Jones, Jack E.		BR TR																									
1954	Tifton	GFL	26	74	18	15	4	0	0	4	4	22	18	0.203	SS	24	44	10	0.872								
Jones, James "Jim"		BR TR																									
1946	Newnan	GAL	3												P					3	1	0	0.00	7	10	2	2
Jones, Jerry		BR TR																									
1955	Tifton	GFL	79	304	43	68	8	3	1	24	4	37	21	0.224	2B	196	187	17	0.958								
Jones, Jerry W.		BL TL																									
1952	Douglas	GSL	46	71	13	23	1	0	0	8	1	18	15	0.324	P	5	17	2	0.917	28	12	2	3.64	163	154	109	90
1953	Waycross	GFL	2											0.000	P					1	0		<45				
Jones, Lawrence C.		BL TL																									
1950	Tallahassee	GFL	10	19	1	2	0	0	0	2	0	1	8	0.105	P	0	7	2	0.778	10	1	4	3.46	52	56	26	44
Jones, Lewis "Lew"		BR																									
1954	Waycross	GFL	6	22		4								0.182													
Jones, Louis "Lou"		BR TR																									
1950	Valley(55) - Griffin(31)	GAL	86	304	37	80	12	4	2	44	3	20	34	0.263	3B, OF	19	18	2	0.949								
Jones, Michael "Mike"		BR TR																									
1962	Brunswick	GFL	20	13	2	1	0	0	0	0	0	0	4	0.077	P	1	14	3	0.833	20	3	2	7.29	42	46	41	37
1963	Brunswick	GFL	5	4	0	0	0	0	0	0	0	0	1	0.000	P					4	1	1	3.21	14	9	12	11
Jones, Murray		BR																									
1946	Opelika	GAL	<10																									

Georgia Class-D Minor League Baseball Encyclopedia

YR	TEAM	LG	G	AB	R	H	2B	3B	HR	RBI	SB	BB	SO	BA	POS	PO	A	E	FA	GP	W	L	ERA	IP	H	SO	BB
Jones, R.E.																											
1916	LaGrange	GAL	21	43	4	9					0			0.209	P												
Jones, Ray F.		BR TR																									
1952	Douglas(1) - Vidalia(15)	GSL	16	31	3	3	0	0	0	1	0	2	7	0.097	P	7	13	2	0.909	16	5	5	4.92	75	75	28	49
Jones, Richard H. "Dick"		BR TR																									
1948	Valdosta	GFL	27	95	12	20	3	0	0	10	5	5	26	0.211	OF	40	2	1	0.977								
1949	Valdosta	GFL	123	499	93	163	33	2	5	52	37	36	68	0.327	3B, OF	197	43	17	0.934								
Jones, Ronald "Ron"		BR																									
1954	Tifton	GFL	27	87	5	15	1	0	1	9	0	5	31	0.172													
Jones, Roscoe G.																											
1937	Albany	GFL	20	73	14	16	1	0	1	7	0	13	9	0.219	OF	50	5	4	0.932								
Jones, Roser D.		BR TR																									
1947	Griffin(6) - LaGrange(25)	GAL	31	121	20	34	4	5	1	13	3	6	13	0.281	OF	36	2	2	0.950								
Jones, Roy L. "Casey"		BR TR																									
1949	Carrollton	GAL	22	22	3	3	0	0	0	1	0	5	10	0.136	P	5	20	3	0.893	21	4	3	2.57	77	65	48	39
1950	Newnan(21) - Carrollton(13)	GAL	34	51	4	7	0	0	0	3	1	9	21	0.137	C, P	259	69	20	0.943	32	11	7	5.12	137	162	78	78
1951	Douglas	GSL	28	67	5	9	2	0	0	4	1	8	22	0.134	P	5	36	0	1.000	27	10	12	4.96	176	194	92	65
Jones, Stanton "Stan"		BR TR																									
1950	Dublin	GSL	23	30	5	2	1	0	0	2	0	4	13	0.067	P	5	13	1	0.947	23	4	7	4.50	92	115	19	25
Jones, Thomas J. "Tom"		BR TR																									
1947	Opelika	GAL	32	85	10	19	4	0	0	9	0	4	12	0.224	P	15	41	5	0.918	30	12	11	4.04	196	214	77	56
1950	Opelika	GAL	16	23	2	4	0	0	0	1	0	4	3	0.174	P	2	13	2	0.882	15	3	7	5.18	66	72	31	27
Jones, Vernon "Vern"		BR TR																									
1947	Albany	GFL	12	16	6	4	1	0	0	2	2	3	0	0.250	P	9	11	2	0.909	10	1	4	6.51	47	61	32	36
Jones, Ward		BR TR																									
1946	Newnan	GAL	52	182	28	45	8	3	0	17	7	12	35	0.247	2B	107	117	17	0.929								
Jones, Willard M. "Bill"		BL TR																									
1951	Moultrie	GFL	42	151	26	44	3	3	1	18	7	20	20	0.291	OF, P	51	8	5	0.922	24	2	11	6.23	65	80	40	55
1952	Tifton	GFL	137	511	87	135	18	4	1	42	15	92	57	0.264	3B, SS, OF	128	146	44	0.862								
Jones, William "Bill"		BR TR																									
1946	Tallassee	GAL	124	430	73	117	16	2	8	58	10	52	45	0.272	1B	1066	49	27	0.976								
Jones, William C. "Bill"		BR TR																									
1946	Newnan	GAL	21	43	5	13	2	0	0	5	0	1	10	0.302	P	9	32	1	0.976	20	7	6	2.57	112	83	50	47
1947	Newnan(54) - Carrollton(16)	GAL	70	203	31	56	6	3	0	27	0	11	24	0.276	OF, P	44	41	5	0.944	36	14	11	3.41	232	210	130	76
Jones, William H. "Bill"		BL TR																									
1951	Moultrie	GFL	22	19	0	1	0	0	0	2	0	6	3	0.053	3B	23	42	9	0.878								
Jonietz, Bernard "Ben"		BL TR																									
1958	Brunswick	GFL	61	188	38	48	8	1	3	28	2	48	50	0.255	OF	97	6	6	0.945								
Jonnard, Clarence James "Bubber"		BR TR 6'1" 185 lbs b. 11/23/1897 Nashville, TN d. 08/23/1977 New York, NY																									
1917	Talladega	GAL	16	52	2	12	3	0	0		0			0.231	C	76	26	2	0.981								
Jonnard, Claude Alfred "Claude"		BR TR 6'1" 165 lbs b. 11/23/1897 Nashville, TN d. 08/27/1959 Nashville, TN																									
1917	Talladega	GAL	3	7	0	0	0	0	0		0			0.000	P	0	3	1	0.750	3	2	0		31	17	21	9
Joratz, Robert "Bob"																											
1937	Albany	GFL	95	385	61	116	27	3	9	51	4	35	38	0.301	OF	226	13	7	0.972								
1938	Albany	GFL	99	381	76	132	20	9	0	72	19	63	24	0.346	OF	230	7	7	0.971								
Jorda, ---																											
1913	Gadsden	GAL	78	284	35	88				17				0.310	C	416	72	18	0.964								
Jordan, ---																											
1915	Brunswick	FLAG	69	245	30	73	13	0	1		15			0.298	3B, C, P	291	42	6	0.982	0							
Jordan, Adolf Otto "Dutch"		BR TR 5'10" 185 lbs b. 01/05/1880 Pittsburgh, PA d. 12/23/1972 West Allegheny, PA																									
1913	Valdosta	ESL	96	378	69	130	34	2	2					0.344	M, 2B	291	262	16	0.972								
1914	Brunswick	GSL		246	22	69	14	6	5		14			0.280	M												
1915	Valdosta	FLAG	60	229	26	51	10	0	1		5			0.223	M, 1B, 2B	267	139	11	0.974								
Jordan, Albert		BR																									
1955	Dublin	GSL	5	19		3								0.158													
Jordan, Joseph "Joe"		BL TR																									
1955	Dublin(25) - Statesboro(33)	GSL	58	212	27	62	11	0	5	36	3	17	17	0.292	OF, P	90	5	6	0.941	6	0	2					
Jordan, Kirby		BL TR																									
1940	Thomasville	GFL	52	198	33	63	11	4	5	31	8	17	21	0.318	OF	137	4	11	0.928								
Jordan, Louis																											
1914	Gadsden	GAL	68	230	28	66					1			0.287	M, C	367	48	16	0.963								
Jordan, Nance																											
1937	Tallahassee	GFL	38	133	10	33	3	2	3	13	0	20	25	0.248	1B	375	20	13	0.968								
Jordan, Ray		BR																									
1956	Brunswick	GFL	18	54	7	13	3	0	1	5	0	5	21	0.241													
Jorgenson, Merlin		BL TL																									
1952	Brunswick	GFL	34	48	2	4	0	0	0	0	0	5	9	0.083	P	3	13	3	0.842	25	3	10	3.88	109	87	74	75
Joseph, William "Bill"		BR TR																									
1958	Thomasville	GFL	12	26	1	4	1	0	0	0	0	0	4	0.154	P	3	7	1	0.909	11	4	6	4.35	62	64	32	69
Josephs, Albert "Al"		BR TR																									
1953	Cordele	GFL	15	26	2	6	0	0	0	1	0	5	12	0.231	P	8	13	1	0.955	15	3	4	5.61	77	79	39	78
Joyce, Arnold		BR TR																									
1948	Newnan	GAL	32	63	5	17	0	0	0	6	1	2	10	0.270	OF, P	18	13	2	0.939	14	3	5	8.63	49	60	24	53
1950	Rome	GAL	16	30	3	5	0	0	0	2	0	4	6	0.167	P	2	12	0	1.000	10	3	5	3.90	67	62	39	64

Georgia Class-D Minor League Baseball Encyclopedia

YR	TEAM	LG	G	AB	R	H	2B	3B	HR	RBI	SB	BB	SO	BA	POS	PO	A	E	FA	GP	W	L	ERA	IP	H	SO	BB
Joyner, ---																											
1929	Cedartown	GAL	7												P					7	0	4		21	30	8	15
Joyner, Julian		BL TR																									
1949	Tallassee	GAL	31	56	4	7	2	0	1	5	1	6	24	0.125	P	3	33	0	1.000	26	7	10	3.77	172	176	86	64
1950	Albany	GFL	40	82	10	16	3	0	0	9	0	7	23	0.195	P	10	34	2	0.957	39	16	6	3.21	213	216	134	70
1952	Albany	GFL	41	86	8	11	1	0	0	9	0	8	26	0.128	P	14	36	2	0.962	38	19	9	2.15	222	174	137	75
1953	Albany	GFL	23	44	8	9	1	0	0	8	0	6	13	0.205	P	5	30	2	0.946	22	7	10	2.20	131	124	81	47
1954	Albany	GFL	40	42	3	5	0	0	0	4	0	10	14	0.119	P	4	31	2	0.946	39	10	9	2.64	133	111	99	48
1955	Albany	GFL	36	48	6	12	3	0	0	2	1	5	12	0.250	P	3	20	2	0.920	31	10	6	2.68	121	106	100	34
Judy, George		BR TL																									
1947	Tallahassee	GFL	24	49	2	12	4	0	0	3	0	1	11	0.245	P	5	34	5	0.886	20	7	8	2.50	133	115	85	70
1948	Tallahassee	GFL	28	73	6	14	1	0	0	9	0	6	19	0.192	P	5	48	5	0.914	27	14	10	4.11	184	195	127	87
Julian, Alfred "Al"		BR TR																									
1949	Opelika	GAL	119	491	87	141	13	0	1	31	47	52	28	0.287	OF	190	33	15	0.937								
1950	Opelika	GAL	14	54	7	11	2	0	0	4	1	6	4	0.204	OF	20	2	1	0.957								
1951	Opelika	GAL	52	217	46	59	10	1	1	20	7	35	15	0.272	OF	121	8	9	0.935								
Julian, Charles		BR TR																									
1958	Thomasville	GFL	115	374	73	117	17	4	7	80	2	98	37	0.313	C	660	64	26	0.965								
Julian, Robert "Bob"		BR TR																									
1949	Opelika	GAL	113	447	83	106	13	3	3	38	25	54	49	0.237	2B	264	295	39	0.935								
1950	Opelika	GAL	126	508	87	120	21	3	0	38	38	46	54	0.236	3B, SS	190	303	32	0.939								
1951	Opelika	GAL	61	239	48	57	8	1	0	21	18	31	27	0.238	SS	135	194	20	0.943								
Jumonville, George Benedict "George"		BR TR 6'0" 175 lbs b. 05/16/1917 Mobile, AL d. 12/12/1996 Mobile, AL																									
1936	Cordele	GFL	17	49	7	11	1	0	1	11	0			0.224	SS	18	40	6	0.906								
1937	Cordele	GFL	124	444	56	125	20	5	5	63	9	48	48	0.282	3B	152	294	47	0.905								
1938	Cordele	GFL	115	421	54	97	16	1	2	46	3	35	51	0.230	3B	153	250	46	0.898								
1939	Thomasville	GFL	135	541	95	152	25	6	2	51	5	51	76	0.281	3B	166	320	41	0.922								
Jungman, Lawrence		BR TR																									
1955	Statesboro	GSL	20	46	13	9	3	0	0	2	0	23	14	0.196	3B	10	14	6	0.800								
Jurkovic, Bill																											
1938	Moultrie	GFL	45	151	18	34	5	2	1	21	5	21	34	0.225	UT	164	38	10	0.953								
Jusino, Ramon Luis "Ramon"		BR TR																									
1963	Brunswick	GFL	5	1	0	0	0	0	0	0	0	0	1	0.000	P					5	0	0	5.00	9	11	4	3
Justiss, L.L. "Red"																											
1929	Carrollton	GAL	29	71	9	16	7	0	0		0	7	8	0.225	P	3	35	3	0.927	26	10	12		184	211	95	53
1930	Carrollton	GAL		52		15								0.288	P												
1930	Anniston	GAL	22	53	13	16	6	0	0		1	6	13	0.302	P	5	29	6	0.850	22	10	9	4.43	138	154	82	47
Justus, David "Dave"		BR TR																									
1956	Valdosta	GFL	14	24	1	3	0	0	0	0	0	1	12	0.125	P	1	6	0	1.000	13	3	2	6.80	49	41	51	51
1957	Valdosta	GFL	38	61	6	7	2	0	0	6	0	10	21	0.115	P	7	30	5	0.881	29	9	13	4.08	159	137	129	88
Kabat, John		BR TR																									
1962	Dublin	GFL	5	1	2	0	0	0	0	0	0	1	0	0.000	P					4	0	0	9.00	5	9	2	5
Kabbes, Ronald "Ron"		BR TR																									
1957	Albany	GFL	97	338	49	83	12	3	1	39	5	60	55	0.246	SS	157	256	30	0.932								
Kahle, Huber		BR TR																									
1958	Valdosta	GFL	12	30	2	8	0	0	0	1	0	3	11	0.267	C	40	2	2	0.955								
Kahn, Louis "Lou"																											
1937	Albany	GFL	67	262	33	66	17	2	1	31	5	16	27	0.252	C	325	65	17	0.958								
Kalena, ---																											
1915	Thomasville	FLAG	<10												P					0							
Kallaher, William "Bill"		BL TL																									
1947	Opelika	GAL	38	97	11	26	3	0	0	15	0	2	18	0.268	P	9	44	2	0.964	26	16	10	3.09	192	176	143	73
1948	Opelika	GAL	82	199	26	50	4	3	4	47	0	25	26	0.251	1B, P	153	84	6	0.975	35	23	5	2.08	251	212	181	85
Kallas, Harry		BR TR																									
1951	Cordele	GFL	35	127	9	24	2	1	0	8	1	10	20	0.189	SS	77	122	17	0.921								
1954	Americus-Cordele	GFL	59	245	48	63	9	1	3	21	6	32	25	0.257	SS	111	186	30	0.908								
1955	Tifton	GFL	139	531	70	145	33	1	8	81	6	2	58	0.273	2B, 3B, SS	195	273	34	0.932								
Kalmes, William "Bill"		BR TL																									
1958	Thomasville	GFL	25	28	2	3	1	0	0	0	0	2	10	0.107	P	5	14	2	0.905	23	0	8	6.55	77	49	62	123
Kamenski, Bernard		BL TL																									
1953	Hazlehurst-Baxley	GSL	125	492	112	152	27	9	3	65	15	87	71	0.309	1B	941	65	22	0.979								
Kanavage, Chester B. "Chet"		BR TR																									
1948	Baxley	GSL	84	273	35	65	11	4	3	28	12	15	18	0.238	1B, C	498	29	10	0.981								
1949	Hazlehurst-Baxley	GSL	127	499	78	181	43	1	17	101	13	44	16	0.363	C	379	77	21	0.956								
1951	Hazlehurst-Baxley	GSL	103	389	74	132	28	0	11	58	15	61	16	0.339	2B	289	275	19	0.967								
Kane, ---																											
1920	Rome	GSL		262	50	81	11	3	2		14			0.309	3B												
1921	Rome	GSL		288	56	100								0.347	3B												
Kane, Henry		BL TL																									
1948	Griffin	GAL	126	475	95	159	21	10	6	89	29	73	71	0.335	OF	202	14	19	0.919								
Kane, Kenneth "Ken"		BR																									
1962	Brunswick	GFL	7	12	2	1	0	0	0	0	0	1	4	0.083													
Kane, Murray		BR TR																									
1946	Valdosta	GFL	7												P					7	2	2	0.00	18	22	15	20
1947	Valdosta	GFL	16	18	3	4	0	1	0	3	0	2	7	0.222	P	1	9	2	0.833	16	4	3	2.57	63	53	57	52
Karczewski, Gerald		BR TR																									
1955	Albany	GFL	139	495	96	142	27	8	6	72	27	89	58	0.287	3B	149	198	48	0.878								

Georgia Class-D Minor League Baseball Encyclopedia

YR	TEAM	LG	G	AB	R	H	2B	3B	HR	RBI	SB	BB	SO	BA	POS	PO	A	E	FA	GP	W	L	ERA	IP	H	SO	BB
Kardos, James "Jim"		BR TR																									
1955	Valdosta	GFL	2	0										0.000	P					2	0	0		<45			
Karpel, Herbert "Herb" "Lefty"		BL TL 5'9" 180 lbs b. 12/27/1917 Brooklyn, NY d. 01/24/1995 San Diego, CA																									
1938	Thomasville	GFL	13	28	3	10	1	1	1	6	0	3	5	0.357	P	4	7	1	0.917	9	8	1	1.54	76	65	51	24
Karpinec, Everett		BR TR																									
1948	Eastman	GSL	96	373	51	102	14	2	1	40	12	40	24	0.273	SS	196	302	43	0.921								
Karpoe, John																											
1939	Albany	GFL	27	103	20	27	5	2	0	17	1	10	18	0.262	OF	40	5	1	0.978								
Kash, Leslie "Les"		BR TR																									
1948	Fitzgerald	GSL	28	76	4	10	2	0	0	1	0	6	26	0.132	P	4	39	6	0.878	28	13	8	2.77	192	168	166	78
Katalinic, John		BR TR																									
1949	LaGrange	GAL	22	33	3	5	0	0	0	3	0	1	7	0.152	P	7	16	3	0.885	22	6	5	4.55	85	81	47	77
Kates, ---																											
1913	Thomasville	ESL	28	104	11	24	0	0	0					0.231	1B	57	6	7	0.900								
Katkaveck, Stanley "Stan" "Mickey"		BR TR																									
1946	Albany	GFL	57	192	15	45	11	0	0	20	1	28	34	0.234	C	381	47	10	0.977								
1947	Albany	GFL	102	313	42	70	10	2	0	37	4	42	48	0.224	M, C	630	51	13	0.981								
1948	Waycross	GFL	109	351	68	84	14	1	0	46	4	67	24	0.239	M, C	664	51	10	0.986								
1949	Waycross	GFL	95	308	51	73	11	0	2	39	3	68	59	0.237	M, C	561	77	14	0.979								
Kaye, Charles		BL TR																									
1949	Cordele	GFL	25	77	7	12	2	0	0	3	1	17	21	0.156	OF	42	1	1	0.977								
Kazak (Tkaczuk), Edward Terrance "Eddie"		BR TR 6'0" 175 lbs b. 07/18/1920 Steubenville, OH d. 12/15/1999 Austin, TX																									
1940	Valdosta	GFL	130	528	83	154	38	8	4	101	7	34	56	0.292	2B	342	387	48	0.938								
1941	Albany	GFL	135	584	133	221	45	9	2	113	5	59	40	0.378	2B	318	383	66	0.914								
Keane, John "Johnny"		b. 11/03/1911 d. 01/06/1967																									
1938	Albany	GFL	115	425	85	127	23	8	0	70	29	56	25	0.299	M, 3B	156	231	30	0.928								
1939	Albany	GFL	121	423	83	133	27	5	0	70	9	60	17	0.314	M, 3B	174	225	32	0.926								
Kearns, John																											
1935	Americus	GFL	33	92	16	25	5	0	0		0	7	24	0.272	P					33	17	7		202	229	147	57
Kebler, Stephen "Steve"		BS TR																									
1956	Thomson	GSL	1	2	0									0.000	P					1	0	1					
1958	Valdosta	GFL	33	53	4	4	1	0	0	1	0	1	31	0.075	P	4	22	1	0.963	33	6	4	4.14	137	137	69	87
Keen, Elmer		BL TR																									
1951	Moultrie	GFL	12	10	2	1	0	0	0	1	0	3	3	0.100	P	1	6	0	1.000								
Keggereis, William "Bill"		BL TL																									
1953	Albany	GFL	21	25	1	3	0	0	0	1	0	0	10	0.120	P	0	9	0	1.000	21	4	1	5.48	69	54	49	60
1954	Albany	GFL	7	11	0									0.000	P					7	1	2		<45			
1954	Hazlehurst-Baxley	GSL	9	11	0									0.000	P					9	0	3		<45			
Keister, Harry		BL TL																									
1954	Albany	GFL	111	409	58	117	17	4	6	60	7	48	57	0.286	OF	156	7	17	0.906								
Kelecava, Clement P. "Clem"		BS TL																									
1950	Griffin	GAL	46	82	7	15	4	0	0	8	0	6	26	0.183	P	11	24	1	0.972	36	10	10	5.35	165	185	88	98
1951	Griffin	GAL	34	80	9	16	2	0	1	10	0	12	25	0.200	P	7	33	2	0.952	32	12	12	4.62	189	197	107	128
Keleher, Oscar		BR																									
1953	Sandersville	GSL	6											0.095													
Kell, Everett Lee "Skeeter"		BR TR 5'9" 160 lbs b. 10/11/1929 Swifton, AR																									
1949	Moultrie	GFL	82	299	54	86	9	6	3	35	15	46	33	0.288	SS	153	218	31	0.923								
1950	Cordele	GFL	122	451	88	159	30	4	2	67	17	78	32	0.353	2B	319	359	40	0.944								
Keller, Bob																											
1937	Americus	GFL	126	470	71	133	23	8	9	68	5	55	46	0.283	2B	279	321	30	0.952								
Keller, Charles		BL																									
1954	Hazlehurst-Baxley	GSL	19	77	6	20	2	1	2	10	0	3	0	0.260													
Keller, Edwin H. "Ed"		BR TR																									
1953	Valdosta	GFL	9											0.429	P						0	4		<45			
1953	Jesup	GSL	1											0.500	P						0	0		<45			
Keller, George Edward "George"		BR																									
1948	Opelika(6) - Alex City(9)	GAL	15	10	1	1	0	0	0	0	0	0	4	0.100													
Keller, Gerald		BR TR																									
1955	Albany	GFL	7	12		1								0.083	P					7	2	0		<45			
1956	Albany	GFL	2	1		0								0.000	P					2	0	1		<45			
Keller, Harold		BR TR																									
1956	Vidalia	GSL	14	30	2	4	0	2	0	0	0	0	3	0.133	P	3	9	2	0.857	13	3	6	4.50	66	54	68	61
Keller, Kenneth "Ken"		BR																									
1950	Thomasville	GFL	14	26	2	7	0	0	0	2	0	2	11	0.269													
Kelley, ---																											
1914	Valdosta	GSL		101	11	26	2	0	0		3			0.257													
1917	Anniston	GAL	15	47	8	11	5	1	0		3			0.234	OF	19	1	1	0.952								
Kelley, James "Jim"		BR TR																									
1956	Douglas	GSL	40	30	5	2	0	0	0	1	0	4	14	0.067	P	8	20	0	1.000	39	7	5	5.32	115	97	75	92
Kelley, William A. "Bill"		BR TR																									
1963	Brunswick	GFL	19	16	0	0	0	0	0	0	0	1	13	0.000	P	1	7	3	0.727	18	3	2	4.33	52	54	23	32
Kelly, Arthur "Art"		BL TR																									
1947	Americus	GFL	123	452	71	127	32	9	2	68	9	76	57	0.281	3B, OF	163	53	27	0.889								
Kelly, F.H. "George"																											
1929	Cedartown	GAL	97	402	71	121	20	9	16		3	14	22	0.301	1B	752	29	11	0.986								
1930	Cedartown	GAL	96	424	116	152	19	7	26		4	19	32	0.358	1B	982	41	13	0.987								

Georgia Class-D Minor League Baseball Encyclopedia

YR	TEAM	LG	G	AB	R	H	2B	3B	HR	RBI	SB	BB	SO	BA	POS	PO	A	E	FA	GP	W	L	ERA	IP	H	SO	BB
Kelly, Fred A.																											
1956	Moultrie	GFL	12	5	0	0	0	0	0	0	0	0	4	0.000	P	0	5	2	0.714	11	1	1		<45			
Kelly, Harold																											
1929	Anniston	GAL	22	56	4	8	3	1	0	0	0	14	0.143		P	4	37	1	0.976	21	11	4		139	142	54	27
1930	Anniston	GAL	10	16	4	5	1	0	0	0	0	0	0.313		P	1	13	4	0.778	10	3	5	4.62	39	48	14	14
Kelly, Howard																											
1939	Albany	GFL	12	36	4	5	0	1	0	2	0	7	5	0.139	1B	77	6	3	0.965								
Kelly, Jesse		BR TR																									
1950	Moultrie	GFL	75	218	39	45	5	0	1	22	4	46	40	0.206	2B, 3B	72	124	17	0.920								
Kelly, John J. "Jack"																											
1941	Waycross	GFL	138	523	71	127	16	9	0	61	8	82	65	0.243	2B	334	377	40	0.947								
1942	Waycross	GFL	123	441	70	108	13	4	3	41	7	92	40	0.245	2B	436	357	36	0.957								
Kelly, Joseph F. "Joe"																											
1937	Moultrie	GFL	55	184	30	52	8	2	0	27	10	37	13	0.283	SS	108	195	19	0.941								
Kelly, Kenneth L. "Ken"		BR TR																									
1953	Brunswick	GFL	25	89	12	20	1	0	0	9	2	7	14	0.225	SS	41	57	20	0.831								
Kelly, Mason		BR TR																									
1950	Carrollton	GAL	1	0	0	0	0	0	0	0	0	0	0	0.000	P					1	0	0		1	1	1	0
Kelly, Oliver																											
1941	Waycross	GFL	112	476	71	142	18	14	0	59	9	27	54	0.298	SS	185	207	47	0.893								
Kelly, Richard W. "Dick"		BL TR																									
1947	Carrollton	GAL	122	524	95	159	15	5	9	84	16	17	28	0.303	3B	132	251	53	0.878								
Kelsch, Rudolph "Rudy"		BR TR																									
1957	Valdosta	GFL	29	77	8	14	1	1	0	9	1	13	13	0.182	OF	22	3	1	0.962								
Kelton, Wiley F.																											
1920	Cedartown	GSL		291	43	88								0.302	1B												
1921	Cedartown	GSL		285	47	86								0.302	OF, 1B												
1928	Cedartown	GAL	58	222	43	72	9	0	9		7	15	24	0.324	M, OF	51	15	3	0.957								
Kemmerer, Nathaniel		BR TR																									
1949	Griffin	GAL	31	57	8	12	2	0	0	9	0	5	7	0.211	P	9	16	2	0.926	31	11	11	4.69	169	187	85	88
1950	Griffin(16) - Valley(4)	GAL	20	41	4	5	1	0	0	3	0	1	8	0.122	P	6	15	3	0.875	19	5	9	5.45	99	118	40	59
Kemp, Roy Maxwell "Roy"		BR TL																									
1953	Cordele	GFL	36	52	3	6	0	0	0	4	20	0.115		P	6	34	4	0.909	35	4	14	5.25	151	162	91	133
1953	Douglas	GSL	3											0.000	P					0	0		<45				
Kendall, George		BR TR																									
1951	Valdosta	GFL	120	461	91	150	25	14	5	79	11	59	59	0.325	1B, OF	875	45	21	0.978								
Kendig, Lawrence		BR TR																									
1954	Hazlehurst-Baxley	GSL	17	32	0	3	0	0	0	2	0	1	16	0.094	P	2	10	2	0.857	16	6	7	4.00	90	87	60	37
1955	Albany	GFL	23	58	3	5	0	0	0	0	0	3	23	0.086	P	2	14	0	1.000	22	11	6	2.75	154	128	123	53
1956	Albany	GFL	51	83	8	10	1	0	0	4	0	9	35	0.120	P	15	28	2	0.956	51	20	10	2.45	242	196	227	74
Kenmore, ---		BR																									
1946	Opelika	GAL	<10																								
Kennedy, ---																											
1917	Talladega	GAL	1	2	0	0	0	0	0		0			0.000	OF	1	0	0	1.000								
Kennedy, Joseph R. "Joe"																											
1949	Tifton	GSL	22	84	22	19	4	1	1	2	4	19	24	0.226	SS	39	60	16	0.861								
Kenny, Kenneth "Ken"																											
1936	Cordele	GFL	14	27	0	1	0	0	0	0	0			0.037	P					14	3	6	4.85	78		35	50
Kenny, Sherman		BL TR																									
1953	Sandersville	GSL	36	128	25	34	5	0	1	25	5	31	13	0.266	OF	66	6	10	0.878								
Kenseith, Keith		BR TR																									
1955	Dublin	GSL	3	2		1								0.500	P					3	0	0					
Kent, Otis		BR TR																									
1946	Opelika(1) - Valley(25)	GAL	26	62	3	11	0	0	0	7	0	0	6	0.177	P	5	26	4	0.886	26	9	5	3.77	136	45	54	36
Keough, John																											
1941	Valdosta	GFL	51	198	35	48	6	3	2	25	3	35	37	0.242	3B	49	111	26	0.860								
Kerce, Robert "Bob"		BR TR																									
1948	Albany	GFL	22	47	7	9	0	1	0	4	0	7	24	0.191	P	4	42	7	0.868	22	9	7	3.26	127	109	99	114
Kern, Daniel "Dan"		BL TR																									
1962	Dublin	GFL	56	217	55	65	10	0	15	56	1	25	55	0.300	OF	79	2	2	0.976								
Kernica, Leo		BR																									
1956	Fitzgerald	GFL	6	11		0								0.000													
Kerr, James McDonald "Jim"																											
1938	Thomasville	GFL	33	89	10	19	4	1	1	8	0	3	30	0.213	P	14	38	9	0.852	28	13	11	3.28	211	185	143	120
Kerr, Thomas E. "Tom"		BR TR																									
1946	Americus	GFL	5												P					5	1	2	0.00	29	30	14	13
1947	Americus	GFL	9												P					9	4	4	4.13	48	64	32	21
Kerr, William B. "Bill"		BL TR																									
1950	Jesup	GSL	24	75	15	14	2	0	0	11	3	29	19	0.187	2B	43	33	5	0.938								
Kettle, Gerald "Jerry"		BL TL																									
1956	Tifton	GFL	6	15		0								0.000	P					6	3	1		<45			
Keuch, Warren		BR TR																									
1955	Cordele	GFL	57	180	26	32	3	1	0	17	1	42	34	0.178	3B	59	86	14	0.912								
1955	Statesboro	GSL	6	20		3								0.150													

Georgia Class-D Minor League Baseball Encyclopedia

YR	TEAM	LG	G	AB	R	H	2B	3B	HR	RBI	SB	BB	SO	BA	POS	PO	A	E	FA	GP	W	L	ERA	IP	H	SO	BB
Kidd, Donald "Don"		BR TR																									
1954	Hazlehurst-Baxley	GSL	41	142	26	30	4	6	5	22	2	20	59	0.211	OF	60	6	3	0.957								
Kienle, Fred		BR TR																									
1940	Americus	GFL	19	35	4	10	1	1	0	4	0	2	3	0.286	P					19	4	7	7.18	79	89	53	65
Kiesman, Robert "Bob"		BL TL																									
1958	Thomasville	GFL	57	181	29	40	7	1	4	32	7	34	61	0.221	OF	122	13	4	0.971								
Kiker, B.																											
1906	Americus	GSL													OF												
Kildoo, Donald "Don"		BR TL																									
1953	Brunswick	GFL	17	35	4	5	0	0	0	0	0	6	13	0.143	P	1	18	3	0.864	16	9	5	2.25	112	87	113	61
Kilgore, William "Bill"		BR TR																									
1946	LaGrange	GAL	<10																								
1948	Opelika	GAL	12	26	2	7	1	0	0	5	1	1	1	0.269	P	5	9	1	0.933	10	5	2	3.75	60	55	18	40
1949	Opelika	GAL	38	83	5	19	3	2	1	6	1	10	14	0.229	P	18	31	0	1.000	37	17	8	3.00	219	182	116	140
Killian, C.L.		BR TR																									
1940	Cordele	GFL	90	317	33	77	10	0	0	32	2	41	27	0.243	SS	141	225	28	0.929								
Killingsworth, ---																											
1914	Anniston	GAL	31	90	6	8					0			0.089	P	16	64	6	0.930	31							
Kimball, ---																											
1914	Selma	GAL	18	65	11	11					0			0.169	OF	17	28	3	0.938								
1914	Rome	GAL	90	318	29	93					10			0.292	C	528	106	16	0.975								
Kimber, Ray		BR TR																									
1950	Tallahassee	GFL	32	48	11	7	1	1	0	4	0	7	14	0.146	P	5	15	1	0.952	32	10	8	4.76	136	150	63	97
Kimbrell, James W. "Casey"		BL TR																									
1938	Tallahassee	GFL	41	157	31	50	7	6	1	16	4	23	14	0.318	OF	78	3	7	0.920								
1939	Tallahassee	GFL	130	478	95	148	12	8	6	83	37	89	44	0.310	OF	255	7	17	0.939								
1940	Tallahassee	GFL	139	551	121	164	28	22	4	74	19	100	49	0.298	OF	303	6	22	0.934								
Kimbrell, Wilbur																											
1942	Dothan	GFL	11	42	8	10	4	1	0	6	1	9	11	0.238	SS	15	29	9	0.830								
Kimbrough, Charles		BL TR																									
1958	Valdosta	GFL	118	387	57	76	16	0	6	69	3	90	94	0.196	1B	1011	42	23	0.979								
Kinard, Guilford "Buster"		BR TR																									
1947	Moultrie	GFL	33	135	28	39	10	0	2	28	7	21	8	0.289	M, OF	48	5	5	0.914								
Kinard, James "Jim"		BR TR																									
1952	Cordele	GFL	31	75	12	19	1	0	0	10	2	18	13	0.253	3B, OF	39	23	6	0.912								
Kindl, William "Bill"		BR TR																									
1955	Vidalia	GSL	18	69	8	11	1	0	1	10	1	5	7	0.159	OF	23	3	3	0.897								
King, ---																											
1913	Gadsden	GAL	23												P					23	12	11					
1914	Gadsden	GAL	27	80	4	14					0			0.175	P	9	45	6	0.900	27							
1915	Anniston - Rome	GAL	18	46	2	5	0	0	0					0.109	P	1	34	4	0.897	16	4	8					
King, ---																											
1929	Gadsden	GAL	10	19	0	4	0	0	0		0	0	5	0.211	P					8	1	4		35	47	21	14
King, Claude		BR TR																									
1947	Griffin	GAL	11	27	0	6	0	0	0	3	0	0	4	0.222	P					7	2	4	6.45	53	63	13	24
King, Herman		BL																									
1956	Hazlehurst-Baxley	GSL	5	13		4								0.308													
King, Kenneth R. "Ken"		BR TR																									
1953	Statesboro	GSL	17	68	16	18	3	0	0	9	3	19	14	0.265	3B	12	27	1	0.975								
King, Rowland		BR TR																									
1956	Thomson	GSL	3	4		2								0.500	P					3	0	1					
King, William "Bill"		BL TL																									
1954	Hazlehurst-Baxley	GSL	15	55	7	10	1	0	0	3	0	3	25	0.182	1B	101	5	6	0.946								
Kingery, ---																											
1915	Waycross	FLAG	16	59	5	10	0	0	0		0			0.169	2B	44	48	6	0.939								
Kingsmore, Douglas "Doug"		BR																									
1955	Cordele	GFL	5	10		1								0.100													
Kinnamon, George		BR TR																									
1952	Brunswick	GFL	28	106	9	25	5	0	1	11	0	13	10	0.236	M, C	166	11	6	0.967								
1954	Dublin	GSL	105	370	67	124	15	3	6	77	6	59	36	0.335	M, C, P	616	66	12	0.983	4	0	0	<45				
1955	Dublin	GSL	97	282	30	70	12	0	5	34	4	22	37	0.248	M, C, P	431	64	9	0.982	20	5	2	3.60	55	57	9	6
Kinnamon, William "Bill"		BR TR																									
1949	Tallahassee	GFL	34	107	19	24	3	0	1	10	0	14	15	0.224	C	163	23	14	0.930								
Kinnas, Christ		BR TR																									
1946	Moultrie	GFL	12	15	4	3	0	0	0	4	0	3	5	0.200	P	1	12	1	0.929	11	2	4	5.17	47	63	29	20
1951	Fitzgerald	GSL	18	36	2	6	1	1	0	3	0	5	8	0.167	P	6	14	4	0.833	17	4	5	3.82	92	98	33	48
Kinney, William "Bill"		BR TR																									
1946	Thomasville	GFL	11	22	2	1	0	0	0	1	0	5	6	0.045	P	1	6	0	1.000	11	3	4	5.10	67	81	18	29
Kinsel, William "Bill"																											
1935	Albany	GFL	14	31	5	6	2	0	0		0	2	13	0.194	P					18	4	6		87	96	30	50
Kipp, ---																											
1906	Valdosta	GSL													3B												
1914	Valdosta - Waycross	GSL		182	27	39	2	0	0		6			0.214													
Kirby, Bob		BL TL																									
1953	Sandersville	GSL	5											0.083	P						1	1	<45				

Georgia Class-D Minor League Baseball Encyclopedia

YR	TEAM	LG	G	AB	R	H	2B	3B	HR	RBI	SB	BB	SO	BA	POS	PO	A	E	FA	GP	W	L	ERA	IP	H	SO	BB
Kirby, Howard																											
1937	Tallahassee	GFL	8												P					8	1	5	7.04	46	57	13	29
Kirby, James D. "Jim"		BR TR																									
1953	Brunswick	GFL	68	183	25	38	6	3	0	23	1	25	21	0.208	OF, C, P	211	18	8	0.966		0	0	<45				
Kirby, James E. "Jim"																											
1942	Cordele	GFL	61	232	33	59	12	4	0	25	9	22	31	0.254	OF	177	15	4	0.980								
Kirincic, Donald "Don"		BR																									
1954	Sandersville	GSL	1	4		0								0.000													
Kirk, Walter "Walt"		BR TR																									
1948	Valdosta	GFL	21	75	12	25	6	0	1	13	3	17	10	0.333	2B	34	45	9	0.898								
1949	Valdosta	GFL	18	65	13	17	4	2	0	15	4	15	11	0.262	2B	28	32	1	0.984								
Kirke, M.M.																											
1915	Griffin	GAL	49	173	34	47	9	3	1					0.272	SS	79	92	27	0.864								
1916	Griffin	GAL	62	207	25	51					12			0.246	OF, SS												
Kirkland, Dan																											
1942	Tallahassee	GFL	43	169	26	43	4	0	1	24	2	15	26	0.254	OF	79	1	3	0.964								
Kirkland, William "Bill"		BR																									
1947	Griffin	GAL	10	18	2	4	1	0	0	1	0	0	2	0.222													
Kirksey, William "Calvin"		BL TR																									
1940	Tallahassee	GFL	23	69	4	7	0	1	0	4	0	2	24	0.101	P					22	12	8	3.03	175	171	74	80
1941	Tallahassee	GFL	35	72	7	19	2	1	0	8	0	8	13	0.264	P	14	26	1	0.976								
1941	Tallahassee	GFL	88	274	25	67	5	0	0	25	9	15	20	0.245	OF, P	180	43	16	0.933	33	9	20	4.66	193	263	131	113
1942	Tallahassee	GFL	45	121	10	24	1	1	0	12	0	12	30	0.198	P	14	59	4	0.948	45	20	18	2.82	310	266	183	111
1946	Valley(7) - LaGrange(14)	GAL	21	48	7	10	0	1	0	4	1	4	13	0.208	P	6	20	0	1.000	21	8	9	4.16	132	131	60	43
Kirksey, William J. "Bill"																											
1942	Tallahassee	GFL	50	183	21	34	1	1	0	11	5	6	17	0.186	C	266	24	8	0.973								
Kirschner, George		BR TR																									
1946	Carrollton	GAL	1												P					1	0	0	0.00	4			
Kiser, Robert "Bob"		BR																									
1956	Hazlehurst-Baxley	GSL	6	21		4								0.190													
Kiser, Ronald "Ron"		BL TL																									
1955	Albany	GFL	48	165	30	38	11	2	4	19	3	20	39	0.230	1B	367	16	11	0.972								
Kish, Alex																											
1938	Americus	GFL	23	46	6	9	0	0	0	5	0	2	13	0.196	P	8	16	2	0.923	16	4	5	6.22	94	111	22	62
1939	Americus	GFL													P								<45				
Kishner, Joseph		BR																									
1956	Valdosta	GFL	3	3		2								0.667													
Kissell, George																											
1963	Brunswick	GFL													M												
Kite, Bert																											
1913	Brunswick	ESL	47	152	16	37	6	0	1					0.243	M, C	309	44	9	0.975								
1914	Brunswick	GSL													M												
Kittrell, Edward "Ed"		BR TR																									
1949	Opelika - Alex City	GAL	15	26	1	4	0	0	0	2	0	2	10	0.154	P	4	19	1	0.958	15	3	5	5.03	68	77	59	81
Kitts, Claude																											
1921	Carrollton	GSL		56	9	9								0.161	P												
Kivett, William "Bill"		BL TR																									
1946	Moultrie	GFL	77	239	37	63	8	1	1	37	4	25	41	0.264	C	440	36	10	0.979								
Klaus, Richard "Dick"		BR TR																									
1952	Moultrie	GFL	130	465	80	134	27	3	2	39	3	102	31	0.288	M, 2B, SS, OF, P	328	371	42	0.943								
Kleine, George																											
1941	Albany	GFL	38	105	11	21	1	0	0	7	0	17	25	0.200	P	16	63	4	0.952	36	20	9	2.57	259	283	149	52
Klemme, Stanley "Stan"		BL TR																									
1952	Moultrie	GFL	118	426	45	96	14	2	8	60	5	58	60	0.225	OF	160	15	12	0.936								
Kliewer, Phillip "Phil"		BR TL																									
1957	Valdosta	GFL	29	61	8	7	0	0	0	0	0	7	25	0.115	P	14	44	6	0.906	29	14	7	2.71	186	172	121	104
Klimash, Walter "Walt"		BR TR																									
1949	Thomasville	GFL	12	13	2	4	2	0	0	3	0	2	1	0.308	P	2	6	3	0.727								
Klimkowski, Franklin "Frank"		BR																									
1958	Thomasville	GFL	6	12		0								0.000													
Klingert, John		BR TR																									
1951	Valdosta	GFL	20	60	18	16	3	0	1	8	2	9	15	0.267	1B	115	4	4	0.967								
Klobe, Ray		BL TL																									
1949	Albany	GFL	23	39	9	11	1	0	0	4	1	2	9	0.282	P	9	17	0	1.000	22	7	1	5.61	85	92	61	41
Kloss, Walter "Walt"		BR TR																									
1951	Americus	GFL	37	139	27	31	5	3	0	12	2	20	24	0.223	3B, SS	33	104	7	0.951								
1952	Eastman	GSL	79	298	31	64	14	0	0	24	1	26	35	0.215	2B, 3B, SS	138	232	13	0.966								
1953	Eastman	GSL	123	455	55	110	23	1	9	70	1	42	61	0.242	2B	282	343	21	0.967								
Klump, ---																											
1914	Thomasville	GSL		396	72	88	4	0	1		8			0.222													
Knabe, Richard "Dick"		BR TR																									
1948	Thomasville	GFL	32	42	2	5	1	0	0	4	0	8	22	0.119	P	4	31	5	0.875	32	2	9	5.41	128	159	105	100
1949	Thomasville	GFL	34	64	6	11	1	1	0	4	0	15	24	0.172	P	6	33	3	0.929	33	11	11	3.23	181	181	134	91
Knapp, Roy																											
1942	Dothan	GFL	82	336	73	81	12	1	0	25	24	64	48	0.241	OF	179	9	9	0.954								

Georgia Class-D Minor League Baseball Encyclopedia

YR	TEAM	LG	G	AB	R	H	2B	3B	HR	RBI	SB	BB	SO	BA	POS	PO	A	E	FA	GP	W	L	ERA	IP	H	SO	BB
Knappe, John		BR TR																									
1946	Thomasville	GFL	3												P					3	0	1	0.00	13	22	5	10
Knezevich, Edward "Ed"		BL																									
1956	Hazlehurst-Baxley	GSL	9	29		3								0.103													
Knight, ---																											
1914	Rome	GAL	27	91	4	14				0				0.154	P	7	82	5	0.947	27							
1915	Rome - Newnan	GAL	15	36	0	2	0	0	0					0.056	P	4	31	2	0.946	15	6	6					
Knight, Harold		BR TR																									
1951	LaGrange	GAL	19	28	4	6	2	0	0	4	0	8	9	0.214	P	2	20	1	0.957	19	7	5	5.93	88	115	27	42
Knoblauch, Raymond "Ray"		BR TR																									
1948	Albany	GFL	27	32	4	7	1	0	0	3	0	4	13	0.219	P	5	7	4	0.750	20	4	5	5.04	84	86	32	82
Knodel, Leonard "Len"		BR TR																									
1953	Fitzgerald	GFL	18	15	1	0	0	0	0	0	0	2	7	0.000	P	1	7	0	1.000	16	1	6	4.67	52	61	23	36
1953	Douglas	GSL	13	30	6	7	0	0	0	3	0	6	7	0.233	P	9	16	2	0.926	13	6	4	4.12	83	76	48	53
Knoke, John		BR TR																									
1948	Griffin	GAL	14	21	4	3	1	1	0	4	0	2	5	0.143	P	4	16	1	0.952	12	2	6	4.85	52	55	26	39
Knoll, David "Dave"		BR TR																									
1958	Waycross	GFL	9	8		2								0.250	P					9	0	0		<30			
Knoll, Frank Jr.																											
1942	Americus	GFL	19	74	14	13	3	1	0	7	0	6	21	0.176	OF	30	1	1	0.969								
Knopp, Melvin "Mel"		BR TR																									
1948	Griffin	GAL	45	137	23	29	3	0	0	11	0	25	28	0.212	2B	91	97	18	0.913								
Knowles, Charles																											
1928	Cedartown	GAL	86	298	64	99	15	1	21		7	36	17	0.332	OF, C	322	44	5	0.987								
1929	Cedartown	GAL	99	359	92	113	16	1	25		7	46	24	0.315	C	428	67	21	0.959								
1930	Cedartown	GAL	95	364	89	123	27	3	16		5	57	22	0.338	OF, C	333	45	7	0.982								
Knowles, Earl		BR TR																									
1946	Tallassee	GAL	116	431	56	113	16	7	4	54	9	26	34	0.262	OF, P	235	9	8	0.968	1	0	0	0.00	1			
1947	Tallassee	GAL	69	273	32	85	13	2	2	43	3	13	23	0.311	OF	148	6	6	0.963								
Knowles, Lowe		BR TR																									
1950	Rome	GAL	99	371	80	131	26	3	23	98	3	63	25	0.353	1B	749	33	14	0.982								
Knox, ---																											
1914	Talladega	GAL	23	85	13	30					1			0.353	OF	32	12	0	1.000								
1916	Talladega	GAL	14	56	5	5					2			0.089	OF												
Knox, Alfred "Al"		BR TR																									
1955	Hazlehurst-Baxley	GSL	68	192	23	53	9	2	0	29	5	12	11	0.276	OF, P	69	26	6	0.941	24	9	8	3.08	114	102	83	42
Knox, Fred																											
1935	Moultrie	GFL	62	231	36	62	8	4	1		11	23	32	0.268	OF	145	6	7	0.956								
Knox, William "Bill"		BR TR																									
1954	Albany	GFL	43	100	9	20	1	1	0	14	0	8	23	0.200	P	14	50	4	0.941	32	20	9	1.80	240	185	187	67
Knutson, Larry		BR TR																									
1958	Brunswick	GFL	23	92	9	19	5	0	1	13	0	4	19	0.207	OF	62	4	7	0.904								
Knutson, Richard "Dick"		BR																									
1956	Fitzgerald	GFL	10	16	0	0	0	0	0	0	0	1	6	0.000													
Knutson, Ronald "Ron"		BL																									
1949	Tallahassee	GFL	10	14	1	3	0	1	0	1	0	3	2	0.214													
Koart, William "Bill"		BR TR																									
1949	Tallahassee	GFL	34	83	4	16	4	0	0	11	0	10	19	0.193	C	102	19	7	0.945								
Koby, Richard "Dick"		BR TR																									
1949	Cordele	GFL	103	375	72	95	15	2	4	48	5	55	74	0.253	3B	101	176	34	0.891								
Kocak, George		BR TR																									
1955	Sandersville	GSL	4	4		0								0.000	P					4	0	2					
Koch, Arthur "Art"		BR TR																									
1941	Valdosta	GFL	31	73	5	9	0	1	0	2	0	7	45	0.123	P	6	19	2	0.926	29	14	10	4.04	185	205	136	93
1942	Valdosta	GFL	22	60	3	6	2	0	0	1	0	9	26	0.100	P	3	24	5	0.844	26	14	7	2.61	176	146	116	108
1946	Valdosta	GFL	25	51	7	3	0	0	0	2	2	13	31	0.059	P	7	30	3	0.925	25	7	9	3.82	172	171	103	88
1947	Valdosta	GFL	35	45	5	2	0	0	0	3	0	15	32	0.044	P	4	31	6	0.854	35	9	9	3.65	180	170	138	136
Kochis, George		BR TR																									
1956	Sandersville	GSL	4	5		0								0.000	P					4	0	2					
Koczwara, Robert L. "Bob"		BR TR																									
1953	Thomasville	GFL	47	77	8	11	2	0	0	7	0	10	29	0.143	P	10	31	1	0.976	41	15	2	2.28	142	104	58	85
1956	Thomasville	GFL	40	65	10	17	3	1	1	10	0	8	21	0.262	P	8	28	4	0.900	29	5	8	3.38	125	122	78	55
Koellmer, William E. "Bill"		BR TR																									
1948	Americus	GFL	18	59	16	10	2	0	0	8	1	16	22	0.169	OF	15	3	1	0.947								
1948	Douglas	GSL	78	294	41	63	18	3	2	27	8	29	88	0.214	OF	174	6	8	0.957								
1949	Douglas - Fitzgerald	GSL	49	168	19	44	17	1	1	31	3	20	21	0.262	OF, 1B	181	7	2	0.989								
1950	Fitzgerald	GSL	50	175	26	31	6	2	1	24	2	35	48	0.177	1B, OF	257	13	9	0.968								
Koenig, Herman																											
1915	Talladega	GAL	46	170	23	42	5	2	1					0.247	2B	107	113	15	0.936								
1916	Talladega	GAL	70	250	18	50					8			0.200	2B												
Koenig, Leon																											
1947	Valdosta	GFL	120	432	45	109	11	7	0	41	10	34	84	0.252	OF	168	17	15	0.925								
Koenigsmark, Theodore "Ted"		BR TR																									
1953	Valdosta	GFL	19	46	2	6	1	0	0	1	0	1	19	0.130	P	10	36	0	1.000	19	8	8	3.51	123	101	81	90
Koerner, Theodore "Ted"		BR TR																									
1963	Waycross	GFL	17	31	2	2	0	0	0	1	1	1	12	0.065	P	5	18	4	0.852	17	3	5	1.80	85	63	75	49

Georgia Class-D Minor League Baseball Encyclopedia

YR	TEAM	LG	G	AB	R	H	2B	3B	HR	RBI	SB	BB	SO	BA	POS	PO	A	E	FA	GP	W	L	ERA	IP	H	SO	BB
Kolar, John		BR TR																									
1956	Dublin	GSL	38	134	13	26	2	0	1	14	0	10	32	0.194	3B	36	63	10	0.908								
1957	Fitzgerald	GFL	137	521	67	131	23	6	2	53	3	54	89	0.251	SS	222	357	51	0.919								
Kolaska, George		BR TR																									
1955	Dublin	GSL	60	234	32	60	10	4	2	26	7	33	19	0.256	SS	104	171	20	0.932								
Koleff, Nicholas "Nick"		BR TR																									
1954	Valdosta	GFL	11	14	1	0	0	0	0	0	0	2	12	0.000	P	5	14	2	0.905	10	3	6	5.60	53	52	57	33
Kollin, Major		BR TR																									
1955	Statesboro	GSL	9	8	0									0.000	P					9	1	2					
Kolson, Thomas "Tom"		BR TR																									
1956	Albany	GFL	19	26	4	5	1	0	0	1	0	0	14	0.192	P	1	10	2	0.846	18	3	1	5.37	62	66	36	37
1957	Albany	GFL	22	31	3	2	0	0	0	1	0	6	13	0.065	P	3	25	1	0.966	22	5	3	3.77	98	90	60	63
Koltz, Theodore Leo "Ted"		BR TR																									
1942	Americus	GFL	9	23	1	2	0	0	0	0	0	0	6	0.087	P	2	17	0	1.000	9	3	5	3.00	63	58	28	37
Komara, Raymond "Ray"		BR TR																									
1956	Dublin	GSL	2	3		1								0.333	P					2	0	0					
Komisarek, Edward "Ed"		BR TR																									
1948	Thomasville	GFL	136	478	92	127	23	2	7	70	5	108	76	0.266	OF, C	359	35	16	0.961								
Konek, Peter "Pete"																											
1949	Newnan	GAL	10	29	3	8	1	0	0	6	0	4	6	0.276													
1952	Brunswick	GFL	15	28	4	3	0	0	0	0	0	2	6	0.107	P	4	17	3	0.875	12	4	4	2.51	79	75	22	34
Konneman, W.H.																											
1920	LaGrange	GSL													P												
1921	LaGrange	GSL													P, OF												
Kopacz, Edward "Ed"		BR TR																									
1953	Vidalia	GSL	35	133	23	28	3	4	6	23	3	9	48	0.211	1B, OF	184	3	10	0.949								
Kopec, Donald "Don"		BR TR																									
1955	Thomasville	GFL	12	27	3	3	0	0	0	0	0	5	14	0.111	C	47	3	1	0.980								
Kopp, Carlyle "Clyde"		BR TR																									
1941	Albany	GFL	19	83	15	16	2	3	0	9	4	17	14	0.193	OF	49	2	3	0.944								
Koppenhaver, Robert "Bob"		BR TR																									
1949	Albany	GFL	93	357	94	104	7	2	0	32	31	81	51	0.291	SS	166	274	49	0.900								
Kops, Willard B.																											
1949	Hazlehurst-Baxley	GSL	26	66	11	17	1	0	0	6	0	11	11	0.258	P	9	32	4	0.911	23	6	10	5.24	139	100	61	102
Koranda, James B. "Jim"		BR TR																									
1953	Thomasville	GFL	65	243	47	65	14	2	5	57	4	38	43	0.267	OF	96	7	5	0.954								
Korcheck, Michael "Mike"		BR TR																									
1949	Valdosta	GFL	89	308	58	78	12	10	0	38	14	62	55	0.253	SS	110	234	48	0.878								
1950	Valdosta	GFL	88	335	51	87	10	13	1	54	8	44	35	0.260	SS	171	265	39	0.918								
Kosak, Carl		BR																									
1957	Fitzgerald	GFL	17	41	2	7	0	0	0	5	0	7	10	0.171													
Kosar, Joe																											
1937	Thomasville	GFL	23	47	5	8	1	0	0	4	0	3	15	0.170	P	12	20	5	0.865	17	4	7	4.08	108	129	42	48
Koski, Robert "Bob"		BL TL																									
1954	Sandersville	GSL	24	41	5	12	1	1	0	2	0	3	10	0.293	P	1	14	3	0.833	16	0	6	7.23	66	45	65	99
1956	Brunswick	GFL	82	267	25	72	10	3	0	28	4	31	78	0.270	OF, P	117	11	10	0.928	12	0	4	<45				
Koski, William John "Bill" "T-Bone"		BR TR 6'4" 185 lbs b. 02/06/1932 Madera, CA																									
1955	Brunswick	GFL	20	29	4	6	1	0	0	0	0	5	6	0.207	P	1	25	2	0.929	18	8	6	2.47	102	89	54	42
Kosmicki, Michael		BR TR																									
1956	Hazlehurst-Baxley	GSL	19	20	2	6	2	0	0	2	0	0	1	0.300	P	2	10	3	0.800	17	2	5	5.88	49	49	35	53
Koss, Edward "Ed"		BR TR																									
1950	Fitzgerald	GSL	51	140	9	31	4	0	0	11	6	17	12	0.221	1B	203	10	9	0.959								
Kossuth, Otto																											
1950	Moultrie	GFL	12	27	6	6	1	0	0	4	0	3	7	0.222	P	3	11	2	0.875	12	5	4	4.71	65	71	21	34
Kostner, Richard "Dick"		BR TR																									
1952	Douglas	GSL	63	171	25	38	4	1	0	20	2	33	27	0.222	2B, 3B, P	72	89	6	0.964	21	9	5	3.42	113	98	74	61
1953	Waycross	GFL	4											0.200	P					0	0	0	<45				
1953	Douglas	GSL	87	250	49	74	13	4	3	37	2	59	39	0.296	SS, P	102	141	20	0.924	28	16	6	3.07	182	166	111	77
Koszenski, Stanley "Stan"		BR TL																									
1954	Tifton	GFL	13	19	5	3	0	0	0	0	0	4	9	0.158	P	4	16	0	1.000	12	2	3	4.58	55	56	37	31
Kott, Charles		BR TR																									
1952	Moultrie	GFL	39	81	5	10	0	3	0	9	0	7	34	0.123	P	9	72	8	0.910	33	9	18	2.82	233	211	116	151
Kovach, Paul		BR TR																									
1955	Cordele	GFL	18	30	7	7	2	1	1	5	0	4	11	0.233	P	6	14	1	0.952	13	3	4	4.72	61	62	35	33
Kovacic, Frank		BR TR																									
1956	Hazlehurst-Baxley	GSL	18	39	8	8	0	3	0	3	1	12	14	0.205	OF, P	14	1	1	0.938	2	0	0					
Koval, George		BR TR																									
1940	Moultrie	GFL	<10												P								<35				
Kovaleski, John		BR TR																									
1952	Brunswick	GFL	127	460	74	136	6	2	0	38	19	99	49	0.296	2B	358	345	39	0.947								
1953	Jesup	GSL	67	248	62	76	12	2	0	29	14	71	27	0.306	2B	179	166	16	0.956								
Kovaluk, Theodore "Ted"																											
1949	Sparta	GSL	11	42	7	4	0	0	0	3	0	6	7	0.095	OF	22	0	2	0.917								
Kowalczyk, Richard "Dick"		BR TR																									
1956	Vidalia	GSL	43	147	17	26	2	0	0	15	0	18	28	0.177	2B, 3B, SS	72	88	16	0.909								

Georgia Class-D Minor League Baseball Encyclopedia

YR	TEAM	LG	G	AB	R	H	2B	3B	HR	RBI	SB	BB	SO	BA	POS	PO	A	E	FA	GP	W	L	ERA	IP	H	SO	BB
Kowalski, Edward "Ed"		BR TR																									
1954	Waycross	GFL	62	228	27	52	5	1	0	14	7	18	40	0.228	2B, SS	130	154	35	0.890								
Kozimer, Harry		BR TR																									
1949	Cordele	GFL	13	51	8	8	1	1	0	4	0	7	15	0.157	3B	5	17	11	0.667								
Kozubal, Alexander "Alex"		BL TL																									
1950	Newnan	GAL	115	421	83	113	25	3	3	55	9	77	28	0.268	OF	168	7	6	0.967								
Kracher, Joseph Peter "Joe" "Jug"		BR TR 5'11" 185 lbs b. 11/04/1915 Philadelphia, PA d. 12/24/1981 San Angelo, TX																									
1936	Thomasville	GFL	45	177	21	46	7	5	0	19	9			0.260	OF	117	27	5	0.966								
1937	Thomasville	GFL	92	322	44	91	11	6	1	42	7	30	38	0.283	UT	392	79	14	0.971								
1938	Thomasville	GFL	115	430	72	120	21	10	1	59	11	47	37	0.279	UT	407	134	31	0.946								
Kramer, Robert "Bob"		BR TR																									
1948	LaGrange	GAL	108	359	45	84	4	2	1	42	13	66	38	0.234	3B, OF, C	196	80	31	0.899								
Kranitzky, Charles "Chuck"		BR TR d. 11/26/1992 Norristown, PA																									
1948	Americus	GFL	11	30	7	3	0	0	0	8	0	9	9	0.100	C	41	5	4	0.920								
Krankie, ---																											
1921	LaGrange	GSL																									
Krapp, Eugene Hamlet "Gene"		BR TR 5'5" 165 lbs b. 05/12/1887 Rochester, NY d. 04/13/1923 Detroit, MI																									
1916	Talladega	GAL	13	34	10	11				3				0.324	P												
Kratzer, Duane																											
1936	Albany	GFL	113	429	101	130	20	4	5	48	46			0.303	UT	326	138	36	0.928								
1937	Albany	GFL	23	96	19	23	3	0	1	6	5	15	8	0.240	OF	32	2	2	0.944								
Kraus, James "Jim"		BR TR																									
1948	Tallahassee	GFL	26	70	5	15	3	0	0	7	0	5	24	0.214	P	5	28	5	0.868	26	10	12	5.52	176	209	69	120
Krause, William "Bill"		BR																									
1956	Fitzgerald	GFL	3	11		0								0.000													
Krauss, Bernard																											
1949	Douglas	GSL	29	54	5	10	0	0	0	2	0	14	12	0.185	P	13	42	3	0.948	33	14	10	2.98	187	73	68	65
Krausse, Lewis Bernard Sr. "Lew"		BR TR 6'0" 167 lbs b. 06/08/1912 Media, PA d. 09/06/1988 Sarasota, FL																									
1947	Americus	GFL													M													
Kray, Victor "Vic"		BR TR																									
1955	Vidalia	GSL	53	179	29	40	14	2	0	23	3	24	31	0.223	2B, SS, OF, P	90	73	14	0.921	3	0	3					
Kreamcheck, Edward "Ed"		BL TL																									
1946	Opelika	GAL	113	380	63	98	9	7	11	48	4	44	99	0.258	1B, OF, P	257	10	5	0.982	1	0	0	0.00	5			
Krebs, ---																											
1915	Thomasville	FLAG				0								0.000													
Kreider, Jesse		BR TR																									
1947	Waycross	GFL	26	93	14	32	5	1	3	19	1	11	13	0.344	OF	34	1	8	0.814								
Kreitner, Albert Joseph "Mickey"		BR TR 6'3" 190 lbs b. 10/10/1922 Nashville, TN																									
1941	Americus	GFL	100	284	23	66	9	0	0	25	1	29	48	0.232	C	356	32	14	0.965								
Kremer, George		BR TR																									
1947	Americus	GFL	65	228	24	39	5	1	0	21	7	35	47	0.171	SS	127	229	50	0.877								
Kreshka, Emil "Mike"		BR TR																									
1950	Vidalia-Lyons	GSL	82	302	57	87	11	5	3	54	17	70	19	0.288	M, OF	120	1	3	0.976								
Kress, Charles Steven "Charlie"		BL TL 6'0" 190 lbs b. 12/09/1921 Philadelphia, PA																									
1941	Cordele	GFL	104	421	84	137	28	17	4	50	15	43	29	0.325	1B	909	40	22	0.977								
Kret, Anthony		BR TR																									
1950	Americus	GFL	139	510	105	129	21	7	2	69	14	122	55	0.253	3B	137	166	59	0.837								
Kriczky, Michael "Mike"		BR TR																									
1953	Brunswick	GFL	11	23	5	5	0	0	0	3	0	5	1	0.217	P	4	13	0	1.000	11	5	3	1.80	70	57	46	47
Krings, David "Dave"		BR TR																									
1949	LaGrange	GAL	48	186	21	41	8	4	0	26	7	16	26	0.220	SS	56	60	21	0.847								
1950	LaGrange	GAL	116	476	108	152	23	9	3	38	30	60	59	0.319	OF	178	12	4	0.979								
Krinsky, Robert																											
1942	Tallahassee	GFL	60	183	23	36	3	1	0	18	2	23	43	0.197	C	212	18	10	0.958								
Kritsky, Walter "Walt"		BR TR																									
1946	Opelika	GAL	9												P					9	1	4	6.40	45	49	28	35
Krochina, John		BR TR																									
1949	LaGrange	GAL	107	391	78	108	18	16	5	50	9	55	82	0.276	OF	246	14	4	0.985								
Krohn, Duane		BL TL																									
1947	Newnan	GAL	20	32	0	5	0	0	0	2	0	2	12	0.156	P	1	10	2	0.846	19	4	3	3.68	88	78	69	44
Krohn, Layton		BR TR																									
1950	Alexander City	GAL	35	84	11	17	0	1	0	7	0	5	27	0.202	P	2	43	4	0.918	33	15	11	3.06	218	203	155	74
1951	Alexander City	GAL	21	40	3	10	1	1	0	6	0	8	15	0.250	P	9	27	4	0.900	20	9	7	3.78	138	166	68	55
Kroll, James "Jim"		BR TR																									
1940	Valdosta	GFL	68	275	29	65	8	4	2	33	3	18	30	0.236	OF	115	7	12	0.910								
1941	Americus	GFL	134	503	70	131	19	11	4	66	7	73	55	0.260	3B	169	176	41	0.894								
Kroll, Wayne		BR TR																									
1962	Dublin	GFL	30	23	1	5	1	0	0	4	0	5	10	0.217	P	3	16	1	0.950	27	5	4	2.95	64	41	74	50
Kromy, Darwin		BR TR																									
1955	Cordele(18) - Valdosta(23)	GFL	41	76	7	11	2	0	0	4	0	5	38	0.145	P	13	37	1	0.980	39	10	12	4.36	198	218	68	100
Kruppa, Paul		BR TL																									
1953	Vidalia	GSL	4											0.000	P					0	0		<45				
Kucharski, Jerome		BR TL																									
1956	Tifton	GFL	27	42	9	12	1	0	2	8	0	7	17	0.286	P	9	23	0	1.000	25	11	3	3.77	124	88	140	102

Georgia Class-D Minor League Baseball Encyclopedia

YR	TEAM	LG	G	AB	R	H	2B	3B	HR	RBI	SB	BB	SO	BA	POS	PO	A	E	FA	GP	W	L	ERA	IP	H	SO	BB
Kucinski, Michael "Mickey"																											
1939	Americus	GFL	19	49	4	10	2	2	0	10	0	4	6	0.204	C	66	11	2	0.975								
Kuczynski, Edward "Ed"		BR TR																									
1957	Waycross	GFL	6	10		1								0.100	P					6	1	3	4.38	39	41	38	28
Kuhlman, William																											
1913	Americus	ESL	73	273	31	79	9	1	0					0.289	M, 2B	170	194	20	0.948								
1914	Cordele	GSL		281	82	82	8	1	0		12			0.292													
Kuhn, George																											
1949	Dublin	GSL	14	61	13	12	2	2	0	8	1	3	9	0.197	3B	24	26	5	0.909								
Kuk, John		BR TR																									
1962	Thomasville	GFL	52	153	21	26	4	2	4	19	0	26	68	0.170	OF, P	38	2	7	0.851	1	1	0	0.00	5	3	3	4
Kulesa, John		BR TR																									
1950	Griffin	GAL	23	43	9	9	1	0	0	8	1	10	6	0.209	P	1	13	0	1.000	11	3	3	6.62	53	78	23	31
Kulig, Alphonse A. "Al"		BR TR																									
1948	Griffin	GAL	31	82	11	20	1	1	0	8	0	8	15	0.244	P	8	58	2	0.971	30	18	9	3.28	217	204	137	103
Kummer, Gerald		BR TR																									
1958	Brunswick	GFL	2	2		1								0.500	P					2	0	0	<30				
Kunigonis, John																											
1939	Moultrie	GFL	24	58	7	9	1	0	0	3	0	4	21	0.155	P	4	27	0	1.000	23	7	8	4.27	158	159	65	80
Kuppin, ---																											
1913	Talladega	GAL	4												P					4	2	2					
Kuras, Walter "Walt"		BL TL																									
1949	Carrollton	GAL	27	64	11	17	0	0	0	7	0	6	12	0.266	P	6	21	2	0.931	25	12	8	2.77	159	144	101	92
Kurt, Lyndon		BR TL																									
1962	Thomasville	GFL	4	9	0	2	1	0	0	4	0	0	4	0.222	P					4	1	0	1.80	20	8	31	20
Kurth, Albert "Al"		BR TR																									
1955	Valdosta	GFL	26	56	2	3	0	0	0	1	0	4	28	0.054	P	3	31	1	0.971	26	10	10	4.19	146	141	124	72
Kushner, Joe		BR TR																									
1956	Valdosta	GFL	3												P					3	1	1	<45				
Kushta, William "Bill"		BR TR																									
1950	Hazlehurst-Baxley	GSL	114	380	44	106	24	3	2	47	3	83	27	0.279	C	537	85	16	0.975								
1951	Haz-Bax(81) - Dublin(37)	GSL	118	441	86	131	20	3	2	59	16	74	26	0.297	M, 2B, 3B, SS, OF, C, P	342	134	21	0.958	20	0	2	6.51	47	76	12	16
Kusmierski, Richard "Dick"		BR TL																									
1954	Albany	GFL	4	0										0.000	P					4	0	0	<45				
Kuwala, Edward "Ed"																											
1942	Americus	GFL	5	21	0	2	0	0	0	2	0	1	4	0.095	2B	13	7	4	0.833								
Kuykendall, James Jr. "Jim"		BR TL																									
1958	Waycross	GFL	7	10		2								0.200	P					5	1	3	<30				
Kuykendall, Robert "Bob"		BR TR																									
1954	Statesboro	GSL	48	161	21	42	6	1	5	31	3	23	25	0.261	OF, C, P	110	14	5	0.961	1	0	0	<45				
Kwiatkowski, Joseph "Joe"		BR TR																									
1948	Valdosta	GFL	118	474	101	176	30	11	2	90	19	53	66	0.371	OF	268	27	13	0.958								
Kyle, Leon																											
1937	Tallahassee	GFL	24	54	9	5	3	0	1	4	1	8	27	0.093	P	4	46	3	0.843	21	14	3	2.69	144	143	50	63
LaBar, Luther		BR TR																									
1954	Hazlehurst-Baxley	GSL	17	50	4	4	0	1	0	1	0	7	12	0.080	3B	20	21	7	0.854								
LaCarter, Raymond "Ray"																											
1949	Tifton	GSL	22	45	3	4	0	0	0	2	0	6	18	0.089	P	7	19	1	0.963	18	5	4	4.76	138	84	37	62
Lacey, ---																											
1928	Carrollton	GAL	6	15	3	2								0.133	P					6	4	2	3.68	44	41	13	12
1929	Carrollton	GAL		18	3	4								0.222	P												
1929	Talladega	GAL	13	35	4	7	0	0	0		0	1	3	0.200	P	1	24	2	0.926	13	4	6		81	76	15	24
1930	Carrollton	GAL	<10												P												
Lackey, Wilfred "Bill"		BR TR																									
1955	Albany	GFL	33	98	7	8	2	0	0	6	0	11	41	0.082	P	9	40	2	0.961	33	22	8	1.98	277	249	222	124
1957	Albany	GFL	1	0										0.000	P					1	0	0	<30				
1958	Albany	GFL	2	2		0								0.000	P					2	0	0	<30				
Lacy, Osceola Guy Jr. "Guy"																											
1938	Americus	GFL	33	110	16	23	3	0	1	15	0	19	24	0.209	2B	119	50	10	0.944								
Lacy, Osceola Guy Sr. "Guy"		BR TR 5'11" 170 lbs b. 06/12/1897 Cleveland, TN d. 11/19/1953 Cleveland, TN																									
1916	Anniston	GAL	49	186	21	42				2				0.226	2B												
1917	Anniston	GAL	16	65	17	22	5	2	0	9				0.338	OF, 3B	20	7	2	0.931								
1937	Americus	GFL	21	58	15	20	2	0	1	5	0	16	3	0.345	M, 1B	118	10	2	0.985								
LaFaive, Richard "Dick"		BL TR																									
1955	Sandersville	GSL	44	191	50	76	13	4	5	37	10	15	21	0.398	OF	93	5	8	0.925								
LaFaive, Verne																											
1935	Panama City	GFL	27	78	4	17	1	1	1		0	2	10	0.218	P					19	5	6		109	136	54	30
LaFitte, Edward Francis "Ed" "Doc"		BR TR 6'2" 188 lbs b. 04/07/1886 New Orleans, LA d. 04/12/1971 Jenkintown, PA																									
1914	LaGrange	GAL	95	338	45	94				6				0.278	M, C	611	92	13	0.982								
1915	LaGrange	GAL	55	196	14	48	9	0	3					0.245	M, C	289	87	11	0.972								
1916	LaGrange	GAL													M												
LaFrance, William "Bill"		BR TR																									
1946	Moultrie	GFL	72	267	28	85	20	3	5	61	2	53	49	0.318	OF	130	5	10	0.931								
1947	Moultrie	GFL	138	503	83	153	33	7	18	111	10	101	81	0.304	OF, P	278	37	21	0.938	19	6	3	3.46	112	103	88	53

Georgia Class-D Minor League Baseball Encyclopedia

YR	TEAM	LG	G	AB	R	H	2B	3B	HR	RBI	SB	BB	SO	BA	POS	PO	A	E	FA	GP	W	L	ERA	IP	H	SO	BB
Lagan, John		BL TL																									
1951	Americus	GFL	13	32	1	5	0	0	0	2	0	4	9	0.156	P	5	21	2	0.929	13	3	4	3.69	83	86	34	38
Lageman, Ralph		BL TL																									
1950	Albany	GFL	142	513	116	160	29	9	5	79	46	132	76	0.312	OF	307	12	22	0.935								
Lagorio, George		BR																									
1949	Thomasville	GFL	13	24	6	6	1	0	0	4	0	9	6	0.250													
Lail, Jack		BR																									
1955	Cordele	GFL	3	8		0								0.000													
Laird, Green Flake "Red"		GAL																									
1928	Carrollton	GAL	32	101	9	24	4	1	1		0	8	13	0.238	OF, P	26	20	3	0.939	15	9	4	4.80	120	149	30	20
Lakatosh, Dean		BR TR																									
1954	Dublin	GSL	57	132	24	39	8	0	1	16	4	9	16	0.295	OF, P	28	40	5	0.932	35	21	6	4.02	215	190	142	157
Lakatosh, Denton		BR TR																									
1954	Dublin	GSL	74	202	25	53	10	2	3	25	3	8	57	0.262	C	292	30	11	0.967								
Lakeman, Charles		BL																									
1962	Thomasville	GFL	7	10	0	1	0	0	0	1	0	0	4	0.100													
Lamar, ---																											
1913	Anniston	GAL	88	328	47	93					30			0.284	2B	221	208	45	0.905								
1914	Anniston	GAL	98	385	63	113					43			0.294	2B	216	217	46	0.904								
Lamar, Nick																											
1906	Americus	GSL													1B, P												
Lamb, ---		BR TR																									
1946	Tallassee	GAL	1												P					1	0	1	0.00	2	2	4	0
Lambert, ---																											
1930	Huntsville	GAL	46	103	18	30	7	1	2		0	5	10	0.291	P	3	43	4	0.920	22	6	9	5.97	110	151	27	33
Lamey, Walter "Walt"		BL																									
1949	Albany	GFL	11	26	8	5	1	1	0	0	0	9	7	0.192													
Laminack, ---																											
1928	Anniston - Talladega	GAL	77	311	55	78	7	4	0		13	20	26	0.251	3B	78	136	24	0.899								
1929	Talladega	GAL	44	162	26	37	3	1	4		6	26	24	0.228	3B	86	107	16	0.923								
LaMothe, Dennis		BR																									
1956	Hazlehurst-Baxley	GSL	3	14		3								0.214													
LaMotte, ---																											
1906	Valdosta	GSL													OF												
Lampley, William "Bill"																											
1941	Americus	GFL	42	76	6	8	0	0	0	5	0	3	11	0.105	P	6	39	4	0.918	42	8	13	5.48	189	239	87	71
Land, Curtis Jr.		BR TR																									
1955	Cordele	GFL	6	5		1								0.200	P					6	0	1		<45			
Land, Richard "Dick"		BR TR																									
1946	Tallassee	GAL	11	17	2	3	0	0	0	0	0	6	7	0.176	P					7	1	2	0.00	40	32	21	23
Land, William Gilbert "Doc"		BL TL 5'11" 165 lbs b. 05/14/1903 Binnsville, MS d. 04/14/1986 Livingston, AL																									
1929	Gadsden	GAL	84	315	52	109	12	7	3		32	18	20	0.346	OF	141	7	7	0.955								
1930	Lindale	GAL	57	227	39	74	9	3	3		16	17	14	0.326	1B, OF	229	11	6	0.976								
Lande, Gilbert "Gil"		BL TL																									
1951	Brunswick	GFL	27	99	10	21	4	0	1	16	0	9	10	0.212	OF	51	5	1	0.982								
Landers, Kenneth "Ken"		BL																									
1953	Jesup	GSL	2											0.286													
Landis, John L. "Jack"		BR TR																									
1954	Americus-Cordele	GFL	74	261	38	56	11	1	4	34	3	46	40	0.215	M, 1B, 3B	179	104	20	0.934								
Landis, Richard "Dick"		BR TR																									
1940	Cordele	GFL	<10												P									<35			
Lane, ---																											
1906	Americus	GSL													3B, 2B, SS												
Lane, Clyde		BR TR																									
1953	Statesboro	GSL	31	57	5	8	1	0	0	2	0	6	24	0.140	P	6	21	2	0.931	30	9	12	5.32	159	145	110	88
1954	Statesboro	GSL	16	28	4	6	0	0	0	2	0	1	11	0.214	P	4	10	1	0.933	14	2	9	5.63	80	105	35	38
Lane, David R. "Dave"		BR																									
1953	Statesboro	GSL	4											0.300													
Lane, Eli		BR																									
1946	Valdosta	GFL	<10																								
Lane, Lefty																											
1928	Talladega	GAL	42	122	14	35	3	1	0		2	6	7	0.287	OF, P	23	56	8	0.908	30	17	9	2.84	212	198	90	35
1929	Talladega	GAL	11	25	0	4	0	0	0		0	0	1	0.160	P	4	16	2	0.909	10	2	6		59	91	18	12
1930	Talladega	GAL	15	44	9	15	0	0	1		0	2	1	0.341	P	5	15	1	0.952	13	5	6	7.20	85	138	43	33
Lane, Leon D.		BR TR																									
1940	Cordele - Tallahassee	GFL	15	45	5	9	0	0	0	5	0	0	13	0.200	P					10	4	4	4.83	82	96	43	40
Laney, Floyd		BR TR																									
1949	Griffin	GAL	51	134	12	31	4	0	0	14	3	16	17	0.231	3B, C	75	27	22	0.823								
Laney, Joyce Lee "Lee"		BL TL																									
1950	Newnan	GAL	101	358	61	99	20	6	1	34	8	62	44	0.277	1B	705	35	22	0.971								
Langdon, Joe																											
1929	Anniston	GAL	53	200	40	59	10	4	5		3	19	27	0.295	OF	100	11	3	0.974								
1930	Anniston	GAL	104	429	80	142	32	9	15		7	23	41	0.331	2B, OF	212	47	14	0.949								
Langdon, Joseph "Joe"		BR TR																									
1949	Valley	GAL	35	57	6	9	1	0	0	3	0	7	24	0.158	P	7	23	3	0.909	35	8	9	4.80	165	166	139	70

Georgia Class-D Minor League Baseball Encyclopedia

YR	TEAM	LG	G	AB	R	H	2B	3B	HR	RBI	SB	BB	SO	BA	POS	PO	A	E	FA	GP	W	L	ERA	IP	H	SO	BB
Lange, Ronald "Ron"		BR TR																									
1962	Thomasville	GFL	18	34	3	5	0	0	1	6	0	4	16	0.147	P	7	12	0	1.000	18	7	3	4.92	86	84	82	33
Langemeier, Paul		BR TR																									
1947	Moultrie	GFL	29	37	9	5	0	0	0	2	0	8	14	0.135	P	3	25	4	0.875	27	9	5	5.06	96	115	38	65
1948	Moultrie	GFL	17	25	5	3	1	0	0	3	1	6	8	0.120	P	2	12	1	0.933	15	7	5	4.68	77	75	67	52
1949	Carrollton	GAL	14	17	2	1	0	0	0	4	0	9	4	0.059	P	5	18	3	0.885	14	4	4	3.13	69	62	31	32
Langer, Jack		BR TR																									
1955	Thomasville	GFL	100	298	55	72	11	3	0	26	6	64	64	0.242	3B, SS, P	115	198	33	0.905	1	0	0	<45				
Langley, Buddy		BL TL																									
1953	Waycross - Cordele	GFL	34	107	4	8	0	0	0	3	0	15	52	0.075	1B	286	12	10	0.968								
Langley, James D. "Jim"		BR TL																									
1946	Carrollton	GAL	19	68	7	17	1	0	0	10	5	1	13	0.250	1B	96	3	1	0.990								
1947	Carrollton	GAL	89	346	73	96	19	3	18	64	17	34	58	0.277	1B	771	34	17	0.979								
1950	Alexander City	GAL	10	37	7	13	3	2	0	5	1	5	4	0.351													
Langlois, Paul		BR TR																									
1956	Hazlehurst-Baxley	GSL	9	8		1								0.125	P					9	0	0					
Langston, Howard		BR																									
1954	Tifton	GFL	3	9		2								0.222													
Langston, James "Jim"		BR TR																									
1951	Rome	GAL	16	34	5	11	2	0	0	3	0	1	7	0.324	P	3	11	1	0.933	15	4	6	6.51	76	107	31	47
Langston, Joe		BR TR																									
1940	Tallahassee	GFL	12	33	8	6	1	2	2	4	0	1	14	0.182	P					9	5	3	2.06	70	59	29	34
1941	Tallahassee	GFL	36	83	11	14	1	1	0	5	0	11	30	0.169	P	13	27	6	0.870	39	5	16	4.73	215	237	122	148
Lanier, Joseph "Joe"		BR TR																									
1935	Panama City	GFL	27	58	8	3	1	0	0		2	12	23	0.052	P					29	10	13		207	184	83	62
Lankford, Jerry		BR TR																									
1952	Moultrie	GFL	22	24	1	2	0	0	0	0	0	2	11	0.083	P	3	8	4	0.733	21	2	2	4.56	71	73	35	33
Lanoux, J. Harold		BL TR																									
1956	Sandersville	GSL	118	357	62	75	11	1	1	37	7	85	70	0.210	SS	125	262	70	0.847								
Lantrip, William "Bill"		BL TL																									
1946	Tallassee	GAL	27	57	6	16	1	0	0	4	0	6	8	0.281	P	4	25	2	0.935	26	11	9	4.59	153	149	83	76
LaPadula, Nicholas "Nick"		BR TR																									
1951	Rome	GAL	35	101	16	35	4	1	3	17	0	31	21	0.347	OF	40	3	4	0.915								
LaPiana, Peter		BR TR																									
1940	Cordele - Moultrie	GFL	27	84	13	13	2	0	0	5	0	14	25	0.155	3B	24	38	10	0.861								
Lapovicy, Frank		BL TL																									
1948	Eastman	GSL	44	145	20	29	4	3	2	16	1	21	27	0.200	1B, OF	242	9	10	0.962								
Large, Donald "Don"		BR TR																									
1958	Brunswick	GFL	25	40	2	13	1	1	0	7	0	5	14	0.325	P	8	16	2	0.923	18	3	8	4.78	79	80	57	53
Large, George		BR TR																									
1951	Valdosta	GFL	13	54	9	12	0	1	0	4	1	9	13	0.222	SS	18	21	6	0.867								
Larimer, Roger																											
1941	Tallahassee	GFL	17	39	1	5	0	0	0	1	0	1	11	0.128	P	8	15	0	1.000	16	7	7	3.06	103	87	76	61
Larimer, Stanley "Stan"		BR TR																									
1956	Fitzgerald	GFL	13	21	0	2	0	0	0	0	0	1	6	0.095	P	3	11	2	0.875	12	0	5	5.90	61	59	39	45
Larivee, Armand		BR																									
1946	Valdosta	GFL	20	75	13	21	2	0	0	12	3	5	8	0.280													
Larned, Harold T.		BS TL																									
1954	Tifton	GFL	18	32	2	1	0	0	0	2	0	5	17	0.031	P	0	24	2	0.923	17	6	5	2.57	98	85	84	65
Lary, Frank Strong "Frank" "Mule"		BR TR 5'11" 180 lbs b. 04/10/1930 Northport, AL																									
1950	Thomasville	GFL													P						4	0	3.00				
Lasry, Jack		BR TR																									
1951	Brunswick	GFL	15	16	1	3	0	0	0	0	1	2	3	0.188	C	34	2	2	0.947								
Lassetter, Donald O'Neal "Don"		BR TR 6'3" 200 lbs b. 03/27/1933 Newnan, GA																									
1952	Albany	GFL	13	50	6	11	2	0	1	4	0	2	1	0.220	OF	24	2	3	0.897								
Lassetter, Roy																											
1920	Carrollton	GSL		8	1	2								0.250													
1920	Lindale	GSL		49	6	17								0.347													
1921	Lindale	GSL																									
Lassiter, Robert "Bob"		BR TR																									
1948	Newnan	GAL	11	20	2	7	1	0	0	2	0	5	6	0.350	P	5	12	0	1.000	10	3	4	3.26	58	59	31	19
Lastres, Danilo		BR TR																									
1951	Tifton	GFL	47	180	43	42	6	3	1	33	9	47	37	0.233	SS	98	152	24	0.912								
Latham, Donald "Don"		BL TL																									
1956	Albany	GFL	12	10	2	0	0	0	0	0	0	1	2	0.000	P	0	9	1	0.900	12	2	2	<45				
1956	Hazlehurst-Baxley	GSL	1	0										0.000	P					1	0	0					
Laton, Robert "Bob"		BR TR																									
1963	Thomasville	GFL	31	38	4	5	0	0	0	2	0	8	13	0.132	P	6	20	1	0.963	28	12	4	3.02	125	124	85	28
Latsko, George																											
1942	Tallahassee	GFL	122	469	90	144	19	8	1	65	16	56	24	0.307	OF	218	7	14	0.941								
Latta, John		BR																									
1946	Tallassee	GAL	11	30	3	4	0	0	0	1	0	3	11	0.133													
Laubach, Carl																											
1949	Carrollton	GAL	<10												1B												

Georgia Class-D Minor League Baseball Encyclopedia

YR	TEAM	LG	G	AB	R	H	2B	3B	HR	RBI	SB	BB	SO	BA	POS	PO	A	E	FA	GP	W	L	ERA	IP	H	SO	BB
Lauderdale, Thomas "Tom"		BR																									
1954	Thomasville	GFL	2	3		0								0.000													
Laudermilk, Joseph "Joe"		BL TR																									
1956	Fitzgerald	GFL	28	111	13	23	4	0	1	19	0	16	9	0.207	SS	35	105	17	0.892								
Laumann, Andrew		BR TR																									
1946	Moultrie	GFL	103	342	90	75	6	0	3	35	6	82	30	0.219	SS	202	272	37	0.928								
1947	Moultrie	GFL	137	510	128	140	21	2	4	67	9	122	63	0.275	SS	288	460	57	0.929								
1948	Moultrie	GFL	96	323	59	85	18	5	1	48	5	88	61	0.263	SS	187	304	39	0.926								
Lauria, Cosmo		BR TR																									
1946	Waycross	GFL	46	181	22	35	5	0	0	13	3	19	38	0.193	3B	46	109	10	0.939								
Laurie, Lawrence		BL TR																									
1958	Valdosta	GFL	54	169	25	29	5	0	0	24	1	30	21	0.172	C	294	26	6	0.982								
Lavender, ---																											
1906	Cordele	GSL													P												
Lavin, Thomas "Tom"		BR TR																									
1955	Thomasville	GFL	23	77	14	12	1	1	1	10	1	14	24	0.156	2B	36	34	1	0.986								
1955	Statesboro	GSL	21	44	14	5	0	0	0	6	1	23	18	0.114													
Law, Gordon		BR TR																									
1948	Thomasville	GFL	27	52	2	7	1	0	0	5	0	10	17	0.135	OF	21	0	2	0.913								
Lawhon, Sid																											
1939	Albany	GFL													P									<45				
Lawlor, Robert "Bob"		BR																									
1955	Thomasville	GFL	4	11		2								0.182													
Lawman, Gerald		BR TR																									
1954	Tifton	GFL	13	57	11	10	0	0	0	9	2	18	11	0.175	SS	81	43	3	0.976								
Lawrence, Ralph		BL TL																									
1956	Thomasville	GFL	14	4	0	2	0	0	0	2	0	2	1	0.500	P	0	1	0	1.000	14	1	1	<45				
Lawrence, William		BR TR																									
1958	Valdosta	GFL	26	50	4	8	0	0	0	1	0	3	12	0.160	P	1	12	0	1.000	26	9	9	4.91	132	144	64	84
Lawson, Elwood		BR TR																									
1939	Waycross	GFL	23	43	8	14	1	0	0	4	0	5	7	0.326	P	3	11	2	0.875	19	8	5	4.31	117	120	56	62
1940	Waycross	GFL	43	109	16	19	0	1	0	12	0	10	34	0.174	P					38	26	6	3.16	251	233	157	147
Lawson, Leroy		BL TL																									
1949	LaGrange	GAL	30	112	14	28	5	2	2	16	1	18	20	0.250	1B, OF	142	5	7	0.955								
1949	Fitzgerald	GSL	36	130	19	35	2	5	1	25	6	26	17	0.269	1B	267	18	10	0.966								
Layne, Ivoria Hillis "Hillis" "Tony"		BL TR 6'0" 170 lbs b. 02/23/1918 Whitwell, TN																									
1938	Americus	GFL	112	447	85	141	22	12	6	70	1	45	32	0.315	2B	251	372	27	0.958								
Layton, Fred		BR TR																									
1952	Jesup	GSL	46	148	13	30	3	2	1	20	3	17	15	0.203	OF	71	5	2	0.974								
1953	Eastman - Sandersville	GSL	4											0.273													
Lazar, Stephen "Steve"																											
1942	Albany	GFL	80	322	49	87	12	4	0	35	2	19	35	0.270	2B	188	197	19	0.953								
Lazarewicz, Robert "Bob"		BR TL																									
1963	Thomasville	GFL	14	13	1	1	0	0	0	0	0	4	9	0.077	P	5	14	2	0.905	14	2	6	2.61	62	60	39	33
Lazaro, Joseph "Joe"																											
1949	Hazlehurst-Baxley	GSL	10	38	8	11	3	0	1	7	6	0	4	0.289	OF	35	3	1	0.974								
Lazicky, Richard J. "Dick"		BL TL																									
1950	Valley	GAL	31	29	6	2	0	0	1	1	8	18	0.069	P	4	15	8	0.704	27	4	5	6.55	103	117	77	102
1951	Valley	GAL	31	40	9	9	1	0	0	6	0	16	15	0.225	P	1	22	2	0.920	24	10	5	3.46	125	109	87	80
1954	Sandersville	GSL	1	0										0.000	P					1	0	0	<45				
Lazor, John Paul "Johnny"		BL TR 5'9" 180 lbs b. 09/09/1912 Taylor, WA																									
1937	Moultrie	GFL	115	455	89	143	25	6	6	61	10	43	38	0.314	OF	210	17	7	0.970								
Lazzari, James "Jim"		BR TR																									
1949	Newnan	GAL	36	135	25	27	8	2	0	10	7	28	25	0.200	OF	70	3	3	0.961								
Leach, Richard "Dick"		BR TR																									
1954	Valdosta	GFL	38	108	11	24	7	1	0	13	3	22	20	0.222	C	246	17	9	0.967								
Leach, Russell "Russ"		BL TL																									
1939	Albany	GFL	116	481	72	137	27	3	0	52	6	31	29	0.285	1B	860	69	33	0.966								
1940	Albany	GFL	134	516	131	174	19	5	0	65	13	69	47	0.337	1B	1201	44	36	0.972								
1941	Albany	GFL	136	565	128	184	28	9	3	117	18	78	25	0.326	1B	1161	84	37	0.971								
Leachman, Donald "Don"		BR TR																									
1954	Statesboro	GSL	1	0										0.000	P					1	0	1	<45				
Leake, Darrell		BR																									
1957	Thomasville	GFL	6	11		2								0.182													
Leaman, ---																											
1915	Anniston - Griffin	GAL	23	94	6	12	1	1	0					0.128	2B	46	57	14	0.880								
Leamon, James "Jim"																											
1936	Cordele	GFL	44	87	16	18	2	0	0	17	1			0.207	UT	78	21	6	0.943								
Leary, Bill		BR TR																									
1946	Cordele - Waycross	GFL	17	21	3	5	0	1	0	7	0	9	6	0.238	P	1	15	5	0.762	17	2	10	6.64	80	113	46	36
Leatherberry, John		BR TR																									
1954	Dublin	GSL	24	32	1	3	0	0	0	1	0	1	9	0.094	P	3	17	2	0.909	24	9	2	3.21	98	82	53	56
Leatherwood, Gilbert "Gil"		BL TL																									
1939	Valdosta	GFL	54	207	22	37	1	4	0	28	0	13	37	0.179	1B	466	28	7	0.986								
1947	Waycross	GFL	39	146	18	28	6	0	0	16	0	13	21	0.192	1B	306	17	1	0.997								

Georgia Class-D Minor League Baseball Encyclopedia

YR	TEAM	LG	G	AB	R	H	2B	3B	HR	RBI	SB	BB	SO	BA	POS	PO	A	E	FA	GP	W	L	ERA	IP	H	SO	BB
Leber, Richard "Dick"		BR TR																									
1957	Brunswick	GFL	27	86	12	19	3	0	5	16	0	13	33	0.221	C	125	16	4	0.972								
LeBlanc, Carlton		BR TR																									
1958	Valdosta	GFL	33	54	8	9	1	0	2	6	0	1	14	0.167	P	4	25	3	0.906	27	8	6	4.92	117	112	86	81
LeBlanc, Roland "Rollie"		BR TR																									
1941	Albany	GFL	116	488	91	155	29	8	4	114	10	38	52	0.318	OF	254	18	26	0.913								
Lechtansky, Edward "Ed"		BR TR																									
1952	Cordele	GFL	52	124	7	27	4	0	0	20	0	30	24	0.218	C	135	17	3	0.981								
Ledbetter, Robert "Bob"		BR TR																									
1930	Anniston	GAL	29	96	9	30	5	1	2		1	1	12	0.313	P	8	55	0	1.000	27	11	7	3.93	206	227	85	58
LeDuc, Carl		BR TR																									
1963	Waycross	GFL	28	21	2	1	0	0	0	0	0	5	13	0.048	P	7	22	3	0.906	28	2	3	3.54	94	94	58	25
Lee, Eugene "Gene"		BR TR																									
1956	Thomasville	GFL	2	1		1								1.000	P					1	0	0	<45				
1958	Thomasville	GFL	2	0										0.000	P					2	0	1	<30				
Lee, Frank		BR TR																									
1947	Cordele	GFL	14	46	2	14	2	0	0	4	1	5	13	0.304	OF	15	1	3	0.842								
1948	Valley	GAL	32	125	20	25	2	0	0	9	5	16	15	0.200	OF	59	1	5	0.923								
Lee, George		BR TR																									
1939	Waycross	GFL	7												P					7	3	2	5.20	45	53	17	24
1940	Waycross	GFL	<10												P								<35				
Lee, Harold Burnham "Hal" "Sheriff"		BR TR 5'11" 180 lbs b. 02/15/1905 Ludlow, MS d. 09/04/1989 Pascagoula, MS																									
1947	Cordele	GFL	35	114	18	29	6	1	0	25	1	19	10	0.254	3B	18	56	12	0.860								
1948	Cordele	GFL	107	402	66	125	16	5	1	83	11	51	27	0.311	M, 1B, 2B	389	110	15	0.971								
1949	Cordele	GFL	71	197	32	62	9	1	1	28	6	36	11	0.315	M, 1B, 3B	150	45	17	0.920								
Lee, Harold R.																											
1938	Thomasville	GFL	95	395	53	119	24	9	1	47	11	34	58	0.301	OF	194	19	14	0.938								
Lee, James "Jim"		BR TR																									
1946	Albany	GFL	20	29	3	7	0	0	0	3	0	5	7	0.241	P	4	20	1	0.960	20	2	8	4.87	85	98	61	46
Lee, Joseph "Joe"																											
1955	Cordele	GFL	33	92	11	20	5	0	1	6	2	25	29	0.217	3B	18	34	14	0.788								
Lee, L. Fred		BL TR																									
1950	Carrollton	GAL	108	384	68	100	23	3	10	65	3	54	64	0.260	OF	143	4	10	0.936								
1951	Douglas(5) - Eastman(39)	GSL	44	163	23	44	11	3	2	26	4	19	21	0.270	OF	68	2	1	0.986								
Lee, Norman "Norm"		BR																									
1953	Statesboro	GSL	7											0.313													
Lee, Richard J. "Dick"		BR TR																									
1953	Albany	GFL	8											0.000	P					1	1		<45				
Lee, Rick C.		BR TR																									
1953	Valdosta	GFL	37	79	10	14	1	0	0	8	0	7	10	0.177	P	12	39	3	0.944	29	5	10	5.37	139	150	74	106
Lee, Roy Edwin "Roy"		BL TL 175 lbs b. 09/28/1917 Elmira, NY d. 11/11/1985 St. Louis, MO																									
1938	Thomasville	GFL	121	456	65	93	14	5	2	48	1	71	91	0.204	1B	1161	60	21	0.983								
Lee, Thomas E. "Tom"		BR TR																									
1962	Thomasville	GFL	9	4	0	1	0	0	0	0	0	0	2	0.250	P					9	0	0	4.85	13	12	17	5
Leeper, Mason		BL TL																									
1946	Waycross	GFL	12	15	4	6	2	0	0	5	0	1	2	0.400	P	0	5	0	1.000	11	2	4	0.00	39	27	68	51
1947	Waycross	GFL	7												P					7	3	1	4.50	46	20	87	72
Lefevre, Leroy		BR TR																									
1950	Tallahassee	GFL	138	481	126	152	25	6	6	91	28	122	76	0.316	2B	352	428	41	0.950								
Lefler, Henry		BR TR																									
1947	Cordele	GFL	113	395	65	107	17	4	1	61	7	75	57	0.271	1B, 3B, SS	515	126	47	0.932								
Leftridge, Walter L. "Lee"		BL TR																									
1950	Albany	GFL	123	493	93	150	17	10	6	61	26	38	49	0.304	OF	204	22	14	0.942								
Legursky, Carl		BL TL																									
1955	Waycross	GFL	37	48	2	8	1	0	0	6	0	4	14	0.167	P	6	13	3	0.864	34	4	5	4.38	115	122	56	56
Lehman, Kenneth Karl "Ken"		BL TL 6'0" 186 lbs b. 06/10/1928 Seattle, WA																									
1947	Valdosta	GFL	25	55	8	12	0	0	0	5	0	2	7	0.218	P	10	18	4	0.875	21	5	11	2.49	130	102	92	90
Lehman, Otto																											
1921	Carrollton	GSL		20	1	2								0.100	P												
1921	Cedartown	GSL													P												
Lehmann, Chauncey		BR																									
1952	Vidalia	GSL	16	36	4	5	0	0	0	0	0	4	6	0.139													
Lehner, Collis		BL TR																									
1951	Opelika(24) - Valley(1)	GAL	25	63	11	13	6	1	1	9	0	4	10	0.206	P	2	25	1	0.964	20	4	9	6.03	106	109	45	77
Lehrman, Charles		BR TR																									
1950	Thomasville	GFL	34	75	2	9	0	0	0	0	0	4	21	0.120	P	10	43	10	0.841	35	4	14	4.26	184	164	119	133
Leib (Leibovitz), Marvin "Marv"		BR TR																									
1948	Valdosta	GFL	138	534	83	175	47	12	5	77	1	71	120	0.328	1B	1165	47	34	0.973								
Leili, Joseph "Joe"		BR TR																									
1946	Americus	GFL	65	194	23	49	12	0	1	24	0	21	40	0.253	C	322	48	11	0.971								
Leininger, ---																											
1913	Valdosta - Brunswick	ESL	94	332	41	62	0	0	0					0.187	3B	132	188	45	0.877								
Leistritz, Harold																											
1936	Albany	GFL	32	108	16	21	0	0	0	4	1			0.194	3B	70	95	12	0.932								

Georgia Class-D Minor League Baseball Encyclopedia

YR	TEAM	LG	G	AB	R	H	2B	3B	HR	RBI	SB	BB	SO	BA	POS	PO	A	E	FA	GP	W	L	ERA	IP	H	SO	BB
Leitz, Albert "Al"		BR TR																									
1939	Waycross	GFL	111	318	38	99	19	3	1	59	2	43	9	0.311	M, C, 3B	371	79	9	0.980								
1940	Waycross	GFL	121	449	48	144	18	9	1	78	7	33	9	0.321	M, C	555	76	8	0.987								
1941	Waycross	GFL	128	492	69	155	25	5	4	98	4	40	6	0.315	M, C	560	93	11	0.983								
1942	Waycross	GFL	107	368	53	116	18	4	0	57	4	44	14	0.315	M, C	459	73	7	0.987								
1946	Tallassee	GAL	<10																								
Lemish, Gaylord		BR TR																									
1946	Moultrie	GFL	38	90	13	17	4	0	0	5	0	8	26	0.189	P	19	49	3	0.958	38	14	13	3.33	238	175	278	140
1947	Moultrie	GFL	20	48	5	9	3	0	0	9	0	4	14	0.188	P	5	9	1	0.933	19	8	6	3.82	106	90	130	73
Lemons, Carol		BL TR																									
1953	Valdosta	GFL	37	123	22	28	11	1	1	29	0	42	18	0.228	OF, P	85	8	8	0.921	0	0		<45				
Lenn, Edwin "Ed"																											
1942	Albany	GFL	126	519	60	143	26	6	1	86	10	27	44	0.276	1B	1069	55	27	0.977								
Lenn, Wayne																											
1941	Moultrie	GFL	3												P					3	0	0	20.25	4	8	2	3
Lentz, Walter "Walt"		BR TR																									
1947	Moultrie	GFL	33	65	5	14	0	0	0	4	0	9	13	0.215	P	3	20	6	0.793	29	12	7	2.95	174	160	142	65
Leon, ---																											
1914	Valdosta - Brunswick	GSL		66	8	14	3	0	1		6			0.212													
1915	Rome	GAL	47	171	13	39	7	0	0					0.228	3B	50	103	22	0.874								
Leon, Isidoro (Becerra) "Sid" "Izzy"		BR TR 5'10" 160 lbs b. 01/04/1911 Cruces, Cuba																									
1948	Sparta	GSL	29	97	13	23	2	3	0	17	0	12	9	0.237	P	9	40	3	0.942	28	20	4	1.48	244	186	173	50
Leonard, ---																											
1914	Americus	GSL		342	55	91	18	2	2		15			0.266													
1916	LaGrange	GAL	61	223	28	48					12			0.215	2B												
Leonard, Leon		BR																									
1954	Sandersville	GSL	1	2		0								0.000													
Leshock, Dave		BR TR																									
1958	Brunswick	GFL	6	3		1								0.333	P					5	0	1	<30				
Leslie, Paul A.		BR TR																									
1950	Fitzgerald	GSL	32	55	8	4	1	0	0	3	0	12	38	0.073	P	3	33	5	0.878	32	9	10	4.65	180	206	78	78
Leslie, Paul W.		BL TR																									
1957	Albany	GFL	90	341	63	113	14	8	5	54	10	38	21	0.331	OF	150	16	7	0.960								
Lessley, John C.																											
1929	Cedartown	GAL	39	152	15	50	8	1	1		0	6	7	0.329	OF	73	0	3	0.961								
1930	Cedartown	GAL	94	417	90	161	16	8	16		1	9	14	0.386	OF	175	13	4	0.979								
Letchas, Charlie		BR TR 5'10" 150 lbs b. 10/03/1915 Thomasville, GA d. 03/14/1995 Tampa, FL																									
1935	Thomasville	GFL	116	440	69	126	20	2	5		6	26	52	0.286	IF	289	322	42	0.936								
1936	Thomasville	GFL	89	331	47	94	16	2	0	37	9			0.284	3B	166	209	38	0.908								
1937	Thomasville	GFL	121	498	98	154	17	12	7	53	7	46	22	0.309	2B	375	424	45	0.947								
Letlow, Lewis "Lou"		BL TL																									
1950	Opelika	GAL	29	102	13	19	4	4	0	11	1	13	19	0.186	OF	25	0	0	1.000								
Leval, Alfred "Al"		BR TR																									
1956	Moultrie	GFL	60	242	29	52	5	0	1	15	1	23	37	0.215	2B	177	149	24	0.931								
Leveille, Roland		BR																									
1946	Valdosta	GFL	<10																								
Levison, ---																											
1915	Brunswick	FLAG				0								0.000													
Levy (Whitner), Edward Clarence "Ed"		BR TR 6'5" 190 lbs b. 10/28/1916 Birmingham, AL																									
1955	Vidalia	GSL	28	45	7	13	1	0	1	7	3	6	3	0.289	M, P					5	1	0					
Lewallen, Keith		BR TR																									
1958	Waycross	GFL	19	69	11	15	4	2	0	6	3	11	19	0.217	OF	32	2	0	1.000								
Lewetag, Albert "Al"		BR TR																									
1948	Moultrie	GFL	18	57	9	11	0	0	1	3	0	12	16	0.193	3B	15	24	11	0.780								
Lewis, Donald A. "Don"		BR TR																									
1950	Hazlehurst-Baxley	GSL	127	540	113	174	32	12	11	90	23	50	76	0.322	OF	338	24	18	0.953								
Lewis, Dudley D.																											
1906	Columbus	GSL													M, OF												
Lewis, J. Ames "Bernard"		BR TR 6'1" 185 lbs b. 02/14/1904 Wetupea, AL																									
1928	Talladega	GAL	94	369	73	134	26	13	12		8	20	22	0.363	OF	145	6	8	0.950								
1929	Talladega	GAL	92	379	78	159	27	14	8		23	16	31	0.420	OF	190	17	6	0.972								
1930	Lindale	GAL	96	414	128	175	35	9	25		18	32	26	0.423	OF	198	11	7	0.968								
Lewis, James "Jim"		BR TR																									
1946	Valley	GAL	93	329	54	108	21	5	4	49	4	23	25	0.328	1B	813	26	9	0.989								
1947	Valley	GAL	90	334	39	107	18	4	1	63	3	51	34	0.320	1B	747	65	6	0.993								
1948	Valley	GAL	121	454	79	142	19	5	3	102	5	88	26	0.313	1B	1058	42	9	0.992								
Lewis, Ralph		BR TR																									
1950	Tallahassee	GFL	33	121	19	25	4	0	0	17	2	20	11	0.207	3B	37	53	15	0.857								
Lewis, Robert "Bob"		BR TR																									
1954	Tifton	GFL	28	89	15	15	1	0	4	17	1	16	40	0.169	OF	33	1	5	0.872								
Lewis, William E. "Bill"		BR TR																									
1948	Newnan	GAL	104	350	73	114	26	3	10	66	6	47	18	0.326	C	555	50	17	0.973								
Lewison, William "Bill"		BR TR																									
1949	Moultrie	GFL	33	128	16	23	0	0	0	13	2	19	23	0.180	3B	37	69	17	0.862								
L'Hommedieu, F.E.																											
1915	Brunswick	FLAG	1												P					1	1	0		9	8	9	4

Georgia Class-D Minor League Baseball Encyclopedia

YR	TEAM	LG	G	AB	R	H	2B	3B	HR	RBI	SB	BB	SO	BA	POS	PO	A	E	FA	GP	W	L	ERA	IP	H	SO	BB
Licata, Vincent "Vince"		BR TR																									
1953	Jesup	GSL	24	88	11	20	3	0	0	11	0	9	5	0.227	3B	32	41	10	0.880								
Lichti, Russell		BR																									
1950	Tallahassee	GFL	10	30	3	1	0	0	0	4	0	2	7	0.033													
Liddy, George		BL TR																									
1948	LaGrange	GAL	108	425	92	141	17	4	5	44	44	76	40	0.332	OF	256	12	20	0.931								
Liddy, John "Jack"		BR TR																									
1956	Tifton	GFL	68	255	35	59	10	0	2	37	5	1	45	0.231	SS	104	180	34	0.893								
Liedtke, Clyde		BR TR																									
1949	Dublin - Tifton	GSL	20	29	3	4	0	0	0	2	0	6	8	0.138	P	2	24	0	1.000	21	4	5	6.68	97	84	40	74
1950	Opelika	GAL	12	16	2	1	0	0	0	1	0	7	9	0.063	P	0	10	1	0.909	11	5	4	5.08	62	79	33	44
Lightfoot, Frank		BL TL																									
1954	Thomasville	GFL	9	28		5								0.179													
1956	Thomson	GSL	13	45	7	10	2	0	0	4	1	11	9	0.222	1B	102	12	5	0.958								
Liles, Tommy																											
1942	Cordele	GFL	71	234	31	61	2	1	0	24	2	50	31	0.261	1B	620	28	14	0.979								
Lillie, James "Jim"		BR TR																									
1946	Thomasville	GFL	1												P					1	0	0	0.00	1			
Liming, James "Jim"		BR TR																									
1946	Albany	GFL	12	21	1	2	0	0	0	2	0	4	9	0.095	P	2	12	2	0.875	11	3	3	2.91	68	60	36	36
Linderman, Robert "Bob"		BR TR																									
1940	Cordele	GFL	111	400	52	104	10	2	0	41	4	38	39	0.260	C	335	62	18	0.957								
Lindermuth, Glen		BL TL																									
1950	Tallahassee	GFL	135	480	119	135	17	12	8	97	15	120	47	0.281	1B, OF	334	23	20	0.947								
Lindermuth, Richard "Dick"		BL TL																									
1950	Tallahassee	GFL	132	466	104	151	27	16	6	105	13	73	51	0.324	OF, C	687	103	28	0.966								
Lindgren, Lionel		BR TR																									
1958	Valdosta	GFL	125	456	81	111	29	5	11	80	13	76	128	0.243	OF	182	12	10	0.951								
Lindley, Jack																											
1936	Americus	GFL	30	111	25	34	6	3	3	16	8			0.306	OF	51	6	1	0.983								
Lindquist, Carl Emil "Carl"		BR TR 6'2" 185 lbs b. 05/09/1919 Morris Run, PA																									
1941	Valdosta	GFL	4												P					4	1	1	3.86	21	24	6	3
Lindsey, Charles B.		BL TR																									
1956	Albany	GFL	6	9		2								0.222	P					1	0	0	<45				
1956	Hazlehurst-Baxley	GSL	22	71	9	9	1	0	1	6	0	13	27	0.127	3B	20	39	6	0.908								
Lindsey, John		BR TR																									
1948	Alexander City	GAL	48	86	10	8	0	0	1	8	0	14	40	0.093	P	6	27	1	0.971	48	19	12	2.00	275	217	156	51
Lindsley, Leon "John"		BR TR																									
1950	Alexander City	GAL	35	82	8	9	0	0	0	3	1	11	35	0.110	P	8	25	5	0.868	35	18	8	2.43	241	233	168	59
Lindstrom, John		BL TR																									
1939	Moultrie	GFL	37	58	4	4	0	0	0	3	0	10	20	0.069	P	5	45	2	0.962	35	9	10	3.78	174	175	95	81
1940	Moultrie	GFL	48	106	3	16	0	0	0	6	0	3	31	0.151	P, IF					45	8	22	4.69	261	321	158	100
Lineberger, Donald "Don"		BL TR																									
1952	Thomasville	GFL	69	265	32	65	6	2	0	20	1	29	70	0.245	OF	143	6	11	0.931								
Lines, Donald "Don"		BR																									
1952	Valdosta	GFL	18	44	9	13	1	0	2	6	0	2	11	0.295													
Linnell, Gerald		BR TR																									
1956	Hazlehurst-Baxley	GSL	17	67	4	13	1	1	2	8	0	1	20	0.194	OF	34	0	1	0.971								
Linneman, Joe Jr.																											
1942	Albany	GFL	11	19	0	2	0	0	0	0	0	4	12	0.105	P	1	13	3	0.824	13	3	6	6.25	59	58	31	54
Lipetri, Michael Angelo "Angelo"		BR TR 6'1" 180 lbs b. 07/06/1930 Brooklyn, NY																									
1950	Americus	GFL	18	58	9	14	1	0	0	10	0	14	12	0.241	SS	34	39	12	0.859								
Lippold, Gregory "Greg"																											
1936	Tallahassee	GFL	16	38	6	8	2	0	1	7	0			0.211	P					16	9	4	3.26	102		37	32
Lipsey, ---																											
1914	Valdosta	GSL		96	4	23	1	0	0		2			0.240													
Lipstas, Robert "Bob"		BR TR																									
1951	Brunswick	GFL	24	54	2	6	2	0	0	3	0	5	26	0.111	OF	33	3	3	0.923								
1956	Brunswick	GFL	55	178	29	36	6	1	1	18	4	42	50	0.202	OF, P	96	18	10	0.919	1	0	0	<45				
Liptak, William "Bill"		BR TR																									
1951	Americus	GFL	71	279	54	75	7	8	0	27	21	48	28	0.269	OF	147	6	7	0.956								
Lisinski, Donald "Don"		BR TR																									
1948	Cordele	GFL	12	16	0	1	0	0	0	1	0	3	9	0.063	P	1	5	2	0.750	11	3	3	4.70	46	58	31	23
Liszewski, Joseph "Joe"		BR TR																									
1952	Brunswick	GFL	33	71	10	13	3	0	0	5	0	10	28	0.183	P	10	75	2	0.977	32	13	13	5.04	125	189	82	118
Littell, Don		BL TL																									
1948	Douglas	GSL	20	61	1	11	1	0	0	5	0	4	6	0.180	P	8	16	2	0.923	11	3	6	5.04	75	83	35	34
Little, ---																											
1921	Carrollton	GSL	<10												SS												
Little, Elmer		BR TR																									
1955	Moultrie	GFL	23	37	5	4	0	0	1	3	0	4	11	0.108	P	4	20	3	0.889	18	4	9	6.34	88	93	46	64
Little, James M. "Jim"		BR TR																									
1953	Tifton	GFL	39	118	19	21	3	0	0	10	3	11	17	0.178	3B, C	119	37	9	0.945								
Little, Keith Edwin "Keith"		BR TR 6'2" 210 lbs b. 08/16/1929 Grandville, MI																									
1948	Thomasville	GFL	131	500	67	133	16	8	7	73	2	37	86	0.266	1B	1063	55	44	0.962								

Georgia Class-D Minor League Baseball Encyclopedia

YR	TEAM	LG	G	AB	R	H	2B	3B	HR	RBI	SB	BB	SO	BA	POS	PO	A	E	FA	GP	W	L	ERA	IP	H	SO	BB
Little, Walter "Walt"		BR TR																									
1946	Carrollton	GAL	2												P					2	1	1	0.00	17	19	8	4
1947	Carrollton	GAL	10	31	4	4	0	0	0	1	0	1	9	0.129	P	0	7	2	0.778	10	7	3	3.60	80	75	68	24
1948	Carrollton	GAL	27	62	1	11	1	1	0	9	0	7	15	0.177	P	1	12	3	0.813	27	13	7	3.92	154	151	99	85
1949	Carrollton(10) - Alex City(2)	GAL	12	24	1	2	0	0	0	0	0	2	7	0.083	P	1	9	0	1.000	12	4	6	5.12	58	63	53	39
Livingston, ---																											
1920	Griffin	GSL													C												
Livingston, Douglas "Doug"		BR																									
1953	Jesup	GSL	3											0.500													
Livingston, F.S.																											
1915	Brunswick	FLAG	<10												P					0							
1915	LaGrange	GAL	21	54	1	7	2	0	0					0.130	P	1	27	2	0.933	16	5	9					
1916	LaGrange - Rome	GAL	22	59	6	10					0			0.169	P												
1917	Tri-Cities	GAL	6	11	1	3	0	0	1		0			0.273	P	4	15	1	0.950	4	2	2		28	34	14	5
Lloyd, ---																											
1913	Waycross	ESL	33	116	13	29	5	0	0					0.250	2B	68	71	16	0.897								
Lloyd, Robert A. "Bob"		BR TR																									
1952	Moultrie	GFL	17	42	5	11	0	0	0	1	0	4	13	0.262	P	2	19	2	0.913	14	4	7	3.77	93	73	68	68
LoCicero, Richard "Dick"		BR TR																									
1957	Valdosta	GFL	38	118	15	25	2	0	0	16	1	20	30	0.212	2B	71	76	14	0.913								
Lock, Jerry		BR TR																									
1958	Albany	GFL	53	50	3	6	0	0	0	2	0	1	8	0.120	P	14	23	2	0.949	53	12	5	4.22	143	148	90	75
Lockett, William "Bill"		BR TR																									
1954	Valdosta	GFL	19	57	6	14	1	1	0	5	0	6	3	0.246	OF	19	2	0	1.000								
Lockhart, Edward "Ed"		BR TR																									
1957	Brunswick	GFL	18	12	1	1	0	0	0	1	0	3	5	0.083	P	0	5	1	0.833	18	2	6	4.71	42	45	42	33
Lockman, Charles		BR																									
1940	Moultrie	GFL	<10																								
Lockwood, Howard		BR TR																									
1955	Cordele	GFL	23	55	7	17	3	2	0	5	0	1	9	0.309	P	4	25	4	0.879	20	11	4	2.49	134	107	86	62
Loehr, David "Dave"		BL TR																									
1951	Albany	GFL	51	181	33	52	16	2	0	21	6	23	21	0.287	C	223	36	7	0.974								
Loeser, Richard "Dick"		BR TR																									
1948	Albany	GFL	114	464	85	131	18	1	0	47	10	71	68	0.282	3B	117	153	37	0.879								
Loftin, Jackie		BR TR																									
1956	Moultrie	GFL	3	2		0								0.000	P					3	0	1		<45			
Lohr, Lawrence "Larry"		BR TR																									
1946	Tallassee	GAL	34	69	4	7	0	1	0	0	0	3	39	0.101	P	10	31	5	0.891	33	15	10	3.56	197	189	114	80
1947	Talla(11) - New(1) - Grif(10)	GAL	22	38	4	5	1	1	0	4	0	3	21	0.132	P	4	15	2	0.905	21	6	8	4.67	104	107	51	62
Lokey, George		BR TR																									
1940	Cordele - Moultrie	GFL	57	202	32	47	7	3	3	28	5	35	38	0.233	OF, IF	105	24	15	0.896								
Lomas, Wayne		BR TR																									
1939	Moultrie	GFL	27	58	6	10	1	1	0	1	0	4	24	0.172	P	7	25	3	0.914	26	7	11	4.97	145	154	97	88
Lomberger, John		BR TR																									
1947	LaGrange	GAL	68	257	35	67	6	6	3	52	2	21	44	0.261	OF	91	9	6	0.943								
Long, Chester																											
1936	Moultrie	GFL	29	63	6	7	2	0	0	3	0			0.111	P					29	7	7	4.01	155		58	43
Long, Clarence		BL TL																									
1958	Valdosta	GFL	105	401	48	108	11	6	1	60	1	36	74	0.269	OF	222	7	17	0.931								
Long, H.L.																											
1914	Newnan	GAL	25	89	13	29				3				0.326	P	31	36	8	0.893	25							
1917	Tri-Cities	GAL	7	15	1	3	0	0	0	0				0.200	P	4	31	3	0.921	6	3	2		48	38	27	15
1920	Carrollton	GSL		29	6	0	0	0	0	0				0.000	P												
1921	Carrollton	GSL		6	0	1								0.167	P												
1929	Anniston	GAL	5												P					5	2	2		27	34	9	11
Long, Horace "Hoke"																											
1935	Americus	GFL	21	68	8	21	7	0	0		0	2	2	0.309													
Long, Howard		BL TL																									
1946	Waycross	GFL	2												P					2	0	0	0.00	7			
Long, James B. "Jim"		BR TR																									
1953	Dub - San - Eas	GSL	39	78	8	15	2	0	0	6	0	8	14	0.192	P	10	20	1	0.968	33	11	6	4.88	153	162	67	84
Long, James M. "Jim"		BR TR																									
1940	Cordele	GFL	40	154	18	31	3	2	0	20	1	10	45	0.201	SS	77	115	34	0.850								
1948	Eastman	GSL	13	39	4	5	0	0	0	2	2	6	4	0.128													
1948	Douglas	GSL	29	106	7	23	3	0	0	6	1	13	3	0.217	2B	78	66	4	0.973								
Long, Joel		BL TR																									
1957	Albany	GFL	2	5		1								0.200													
1958	Albany	GFL	24	79	10	19	0	1	1	9	1	5	15	0.241	OF	30	2	8	0.800								
Long, Robert R. "Bob"		BR TR																									
1954	Dublin	GSL	21	49	11	13	0	0	1	4	0	8	21	0.265	P	7	16	5	0.821	20	9	6	5.09	129	128	118	94
Long, Wallace		BL TL																									
1950	Thomasville	GFL	79	295	49	84	7	7	3	34	11	38	33	0.285	OF	117	3	9	0.930								
Long, William L. "Bill"		BR TR																									
1948	Albany	GFL	135	522	92	159	31	6	3	83	19	61	54	0.305	OF	287	28	16	0.952								
Longwello, Charles		BR TR																									
1955	Tifton	GFL	67	163	20	38	6	0	3	22	4	21	40	0.233	3B, OF, P	61	35	5	0.950	20	1	3	3.72	58	49	53	45

Georgia Class-D Minor League Baseball Encyclopedia

YR	TEAM	LG	G	AB	R	H	2B	3B	HR	RBI	SB	BB	SO	BA	POS	PO	A	E	FA	GP	W	L	ERA	IP	H	SO	BB
Lonzano, Manuel P.		BR TR																									
1951	Dublin(6) - Fitzgerald(15)	GSL	21	60	4	14	2	0	0	8	0	11	10	0.233	3B	22	34	3	0.949								
Looney, Russell "Russ"		BL TR																									
1937	Americus	GFL	23	85	14	24	2	1	0	8	5	9	6	0.282	OF	45	4	0	1.000								
1940	Valdosta	GFL	24	104	18	30	6	1	1	9	3	11	9	0.288	OF, IF	59	7	4	0.943								
1941	Cordele	GFL	64	236	44	62	11	0	1	12	9	41	30	0.263	OF	221	7	6	0.974								
Looney, William "Bill"		BL TR																									
1952	Albany	GFL	37	144	21	39	7	2	2	24	1	12	11	0.271	OF	61	1	3	0.954								
Lopez, ---																											
1929	Carrollton	GAL	19	70	18	17	2	0	1		4	13	10	0.243	OF	32	5	1	0.974								
Lopez, Carlos E.		BL TL																									
1949	Griffin	GAL	43	88	13	18	1	1	0	4	0	12	33	0.205	P	20	52	13	0.847	42	12	15	4.04	223	213	123	135
1950	Griffin(41) - Alex City(24)	GAL	65	137	35	42	3	3	2	25	5	23	22	0.307	OF, P	51	25	8	0.905	35	8	8	6.60	150	177	95	92
1953	Tifton	GFL	8											0.133	P		0	3		<45							
1953	Statesboro	GSL	36	96	11	24	7	0	0	9	2	7	15	0.250	OF, P	26	40	6	0.917	20	10	4	2.37	129	113	88	59
1954	Statesboro	GSL	55	115	18	34	9	0	1	13	1	8	5	0.296	OF, P	34	48	9	0.901	38	12	12	3.86	210	214	144	99
Lopez, Emerito R. "Junior"		BR																									
1963	Thomasville	GFL	9	26	3	5	0	0	1	2	1	6	10	0.192													
Lopez, Rafael "Chino"		BR TR																									
1955	Moultrie	GFL	20	50	3	8	1	2	0	2	1	1	9	0.160	P					8	1	4	5.20	45	40	24	20
Lopez, Victorino		BR TR																									
1955	Thomasville	GFL	2	0										0.000	P					2	0	0		<45			
Lorenz, Marvin "Marv"																											
1939	Tallahassee	GFL	16	62	4	10	3	0	0	1	0	2	20	0.161	1B	126	12	3	0.979								
Loschke, Leo		BR TR																									
1946	Valdosta	GFL	31	47	6	7	1	0	0	2	0	9	24	0.149	P	8	32	7	0.851	28	10	7	4.89	138	145	75	107
Loschke, Robert "Bob"		BL TL																									
1954	Valdosta	GFL	29	59	9	6	2	0	1	8	0	12	27	0.102	P	13	32	2	0.957	20	10	5	2.64	126	91	82	55
Lott, Edgar D.																											
1929	Lindale	GAL	59	203	57	72	6	3	4		19	34	19	0.355	OF	109	6	5	0.958								
1930	Anniston	GAL	68	278	56	85	15	12	2		21	37	25	0.306	OF	153	6	7	0.958								
Lott, F.O.																											
1929	Talledega	GAL	38	94	12	25	3	0	1		2	1	14	0.266	P	11	31	0	1.000	27	16	5		185	182	99	41
1930	Anniston	GAL	25	64	6	17	3	0	0		0	10	15	0.266	P	3	38	4	0.911	25	7	14	4.91	174	212	61	52
Loudermilk, Joseph "Joe"		BL TR																									
1950	Eastman	GSL	73	250	31	43	2	1	0	21	3	46	36	0.172	SS	108	233	26	0.929								
1951	Eastman	GSL	94	315	58	88	8	2	0	44	4	49	22	0.279	SS	121	285	34	0.923								
Louis, Robert J. "Bob"		BR TR																									
1948	Albany	GFL	102	373	71	112	28	7	3	57	11	60	49	0.300	SS	172	313	50	0.907								
Lourik, Alexander "Alex"		BR																									
1951	LaGrange	GAL	10	38	5	4	2	0	0	2	2	9	5	0.105													
Love, ---		BR TR																									
1951	Hazlehurst-Baxley	GSL	8												P					8	0	4	5.43	53	45	14	55
Love, B.L.																											
1916	Anniston	GAL	64	208	15	48				8				0.231	OF												
Lovelace, ---																											
1906	Albany	GSL													3B												
Lovelady, Willard		BR TL																									
1948	Carrollton	GAL	15	16	0	3	0	0	0	2	0	0	3	0.188	P	1	8	0	1.000	15	2	1	3.56	48	40	18	31
Loveland, James "Jim"		BR																									
1956	Moultrie	GFL	13	33	9	8	0	0	0	1	1	7	9	0.242													
Loveless, Deason		BR TR																									
1940	Thomasville	GFL	127	508	86	143	30	10	4	90	8	30	52	0.281	3B	200	250	34	0.930								
Lovell, Charles		BL TL																									
1952	Moultrie	GFL	30	44	2	9	1	0	0	2	0	8	15	0.205	P	3	18	3	0.875	20	0	9	6.04	79	85	36	63
Lovell, Hugh		BR																									
1948	Douglas	GSL	12	18	3	3	0	0	0	0	0	3	4	0.167													
Lovett, ---																											
1913	Newnan	GAL	13												P					13	9	4					
1914	Newnan	GAL	6	18	1	3					0			0.167	P	3	8	0	1.000	6							
Lovett, Willie T. Jr. "Bill"		BR TR																									
1948	Griffin	GAL	37	134	17	26	4	1	0	8	3	12	22	0.194	2B, OF	60	22	7	0.921								
1949	Eastman	GSL	11	44	7	8	2	1	0	1	1	8	7	0.182	SS	19	26	4	0.918								
1950	Dublin(11) - Fitzgerald(106)	GSL	117	401	56	79	17	3	3	47	8	71	64	0.197	3B	105	174	34	0.891								
Loveys, William "Bill"		BR TR																									
1948	Douglas	GSL	27	47	3	4	0	0	0	3	2	4	24	0.085	P	1	12	1	0.929	26	3	12	4.99	119	135	46	61
1949	Douglas	GSL	33	79	11	9	2	1	0	7	1	8	47	0.114	P	9	32	1	0.976	33	15	7	3.90	226	113	108	135
Lowe, ---																											
1914	Valdosta	GSL		111	9	35	4	1	0		3			0.315													
Lowe, ---		BR																									
1946	LaGrange	GAL	<10																								
Lowe, John																											
1949	Dublin	GSL	19	60	12	13	2	0	1	5	0	13	5	0.217	OF	21	2	1	0.958								
Lowe, Louis "Lou"		BR TR																									
1940	Tallahassee	GFL	18	77	12	17	5	0	0	3	0	3	4	0.221	3B	22	15	4	0.902								

Georgia Class-D Minor League Baseball Encyclopedia

YR	TEAM	LG	G	AB	R	H	2B	3B	HR	RBI	SB	BB	SO	BA	POS	PO	A	E	FA	GP	W	L	ERA	IP	H	SO	BB
Lowe, Macon		BL TR																									
1962	Dublin	GFL	17	26	0	3	0	0	0	1	0	2	12	0.115	P	8	9	0	1.000	16	3	6	3.94	64	60	77	31
Lowell, ---		BR TR																									
1946	Tallassee	GAL	1												P					1	0	0	0.00	1			
Lowery, Cy		BL TR																									
1938	Cordele	GFL	14	39	4	6	3	0	0	1	0	4	5	0.154	SS	26	30	1	0.982								
1939	Tallahassee	GFL	134	523	55	139	22	4	0	63	12	33	21	0.266	SS	180	226	60	0.871								
1940	Tallahassee	GFL	140	562	81	186	23	12	0	71	11	48	23	0.331	3B	197	295	39	0.927								
1941	Tallahassee	GFL	81	334	66	104	10	5	2	32	8	35	22	0.311	OF	153	117	20	0.931								
Lowery, D.D.																											
1915	Rome	GAL	<10												P					<6							
1916	Newnan	GAL	16	40	6	6					2			0.150	P												
1920	Rome	GSL		109	9	19	2	0	0		1			0.174	P, OF												
1921	Rome	GSL													P												
Lowery, Jason L.		BL TR																									
1953	Statesboro	GSL	38	128	22	37	7	1	3	22	5	14	12	0.289	OF	69	3	8	0.900								
1954	Statesboro	GSL	70	252	44	74	13	1	10	46	9	26	27	0.294	OF	115	8	8	0.939								
Lowery, Lester "Les"																											
1936	Tallahassee	GFL	41	108	12	19	2	1	0	8	0			0.176	P					41	15	10	4.11	252		71	74
1937	Tallahassee	GFL	41	99	13	14	3	1	0	8	0	11	20	0.141	P	26	37	3	0.955	28	6	13	4.64	200	235	59	72
Lowman, Carroll "Cal"																											
1937	Thomasville	GFL	71	248	26	57	12	2	2	35	2	19	45	0.230	C	263	46	11	0.966								
Lown, Omar Joseph "Turk"		BR TR 6'1" 185 lbs b. 05/30/1924 Brooklyn, NY																									
1942	Valdosta	GFL	29	85	14	21	0	0	0	9	0	5	13	0.247	P	4	42	4	0.920	30	18	8	1.94	232	170	204	113
Lowry, ---																											
1928	Gadsden	GAL	73	275	42	65	7	2	2		15	23	31	0.236	2B, 3B, SS	235	200	28	0.940								
Lowry, John		BR TR																									
1956	Waycross	GFL	137	450	73	126	23	2	10	78	16	92	102	0.280	OF	226	11	14	0.944								
1957	Waycross	GFL	58	206	42	56	11	2	8	44	8	41	39	0.272	OF	127	6	9	0.937								
Lowther, ---																											
1915	Brunswick	FLAG	<10												P					0							
Luberto, Santo		BR TR																									
1948	Valdosta	GFL	124	486	102	152	24	10	1	88	11	94	90	0.313	3B	143	230	38	0.908								
Lubieski, Herman		BR TR																									
1962	Dublin	GFL	36	60	13	16	5	0	1	9	1	9	23	0.267	OF	16	0	2	0.889								
1963	Waycross	GFL	3	1	0	0	0	0	0	0	0	1	1	0.000													
Lubinski, Richard "Dick"		BR TR																									
1955	Cordele	GFL	123	424	97	124	21	3	20	87	18	84	104	0.292	OF	168	14	24	0.883								
Luby, Jim		BR TR																									
1946	Cordele	GFL	12	44	12	9	0	0	0	2	5	9	5	0.205	OF	21	2	0	1.000								
Lucabaugh, Charles		BL TL																									
1954	Americus-Cordele	GFL	118	420	48	96	15	8	6	55	5	82	40	0.229	OF, P	211	35	15	0.943	18	5	6	2.25	108	94	78	21
Lucarella, Rinaldo H.																											
1949	Hazlehurst-Baxley	GSL	56	206	36	46	5	7	2	22	3	29	39	0.223	OF	124	10	3	0.978								
Lucchesi, Frank		b. 04/24/1927 San Francisco, CA																									
1952	Thomasville	GFL	138	524	87	161	29	3	1	59	31	78	36	0.307	M, OF	339	17	1	0.997								
Luce, Arthur "Art"		BR TR																									
1947	Valley	GAL	18	70	6	14	6	0	1	14	3	5	9	0.200	M, OF	38	3	1	0.976								
Luchetta, Frank		BL TL																									
1950	Waycross	GFL	72	259	38	62	3	1	1	14	2	59	32	0.239	OF	96	10	7	0.938								
Luciano, Michael "Mike"		BR TR																									
1954	Albany	GFL	12	24	7	5	1	0	0	0	0	5	10	0.208	OF	21	5	2	0.929								
Luckey, George "Dick"																											
1941	Americus	GFL	102	320	42	77	15	1	0	64	1	49	9	0.241	M, C, P	403	42	7	0.985	15	1	1	4.83	41	49	15	13
Luckman, John "Jack"		BR TR																									
1946	Albany	GFL	16	55	3	10	1	1	0	2	0	10	21	0.182	SS	19	23	9	0.824								
Lucus, ---																											
1920	Rome	GSL		41	7	7	1	0	0		0			0.171	P												
Luddy, Harold		BL																									
1953	Sandersville	GSL	3											0.200													
Lugo, Louis "Lou"		BR TR																									
1953	Fitzgerald	GFL	1											0.000	P					0	0		<45				
1953	Dublin	GSL	2											0.000	P					0	0		<45				
Lukasiuk (Lucas), Louis "Lou"																											
1938	Albany	GFL	101	387	73	110	21	8	1	56	19	38	42	0.284	SS	220	272	35	0.934								
1939	Albany	GFL	134	572	85	166	34	6	1	77	4	37	58	0.290	SS	266	422	63	0.916								
Luker, John		BR TR																									
1953	Dublin	GSL	8											0.000	P					2	0		<45				
Lukon, Edward Paul "Eddie" "Mongoose"		BL TL 5'10" b. 08/05/1920 Burgettstown, PA d. 11/07/1996 Canonsburg, PA																									
1939	Valdosta	GFL	137	516	86	155	24	17	3	104	28	39	48	0.300	OF	217	13	8	0.966								
Lukon, John		BR TR																									
1940	Valdosta	GFL	116	452	74	102	8	5	1	40	19	46	53	0.226	OF	203	182	25	0.939								
1941	Americus - Cordele	GFL	126	498	86	133	20	12	1	43	24	65	44	0.267	2B	264	292	71	0.887								
Lukosius, Justin		BR																									
1954	Valdosta	GFL	9	21		3								0.143													

Georgia Class-D Minor League Baseball Encyclopedia

YR	TEAM	LG	G	AB	R	H	2B	3B	HR	RBI	SB	BB	SO	BA	POS	PO	A	E	FA	GP	W	L	ERA	IP	H	SO	BB
Lum, Michael Ken-Wai "Mike"		BL TL 6'0" 180 lbs b. 10/27/1945 Honolulu, HI																									
1963	Waycross	GFL	51	114	17	30	3	2	0	12	3	12	32	0.263	OF	47	2	4	0.925								
Luna, C.W.																											
1915	Anniston	GAL	35	121	1	24	1	0	0					0.198	C	186	33	5	0.978								
Lunger, ---																											
1913	Anniston	GAL	27	99	7	23				3				0.232	3B	51	44	8	0.922								
Lutes, James "Jim"		BR																									
1946	Newnan	GAL	<10																								
Lutes, William "Bill"		BL TL																									
1947	Tallahassee	GFL	126	455	96	128	19	11	8	76	10	74	51	0.281	OF	186	14	13	0.939								
Luttrell, ---																											
1913	Newnan	GAL	13												P					13	9	4					
Lutz, David "Dave"		BR TR																									
1954	Americus-Cordele	GFL	14	28	4	7	1	0	0	3	0	3	11	0.250	P	0	20	1	0.952	12	2	3	5.09	76	86	39	49
Lynch, Wayne		BR TR																									
1948	Cordele	GFL	27	58	10	12	2	0	0	4	2	4	16	0.207	P	11	40	5	0.911	27	10	12	3.13	167	190	96	75
1949	Cordele	GFL	33	83	11	12	0	0	0	6	3	14	21	0.145	P	14	46	3	0.952	32	11	15	3.45	211	251	100	64
Lynn, Frederick "Fred"		BL TL																									
1946	Valdosta	GFL	25	41	1	5	0	0	0	3	0	1	16	0.122	P	2	18	0	1.000	24	7	6	4.67	104	107	69	80
1947	Valdosta	GFL	22	31	0	2	0	0	0	0	0	2	15	0.065	P	3	10	5	0.722	22	6	5	5.13	86	99	41	59
Lyons, Donald W. "Don"		BL																									
1954	Americus-Cordele	GFL	9	30		6								0.200													
Lyons, John I.		BR TR																									
1953	Jesup	GSL	2											0.000	P						0	1	<45				
Lyons, Patrick "Pat"		BR TR																									
1949	LaGrange	GAL	19	65	9	13	2	1	1	6	2	4	14	0.200	OF	30	3	1	0.971								
Lyons, Raymond "Ray"		BR																									
1946	LaGrange	GAL	<10																								
Lyons, Robert D. "Bob"		BR TR																									
1948	Waycross	GFL	119	447	118	136	12	5	0	50	21	120	42	0.304	2B, SS	263	314	55	0.913								
1949	Waycross	GFL	116	453	135	131	25	5	0	56	7	105	36	0.289	2B	291	310	32	0.949								
Lyons, Thomas "Tom"		BR																									
1950	Thomasville	GFL	11	22	5	5	0	0	0	2	1	3	7	0.227													
MacCallum, Nelson		BR TR																									
1954	Valdosta	GFL	68	237	43	66	13	2	3	30	5	36	24	0.278	1B, 3B, SS, OF	221	82	24	0.927								
MacConnell, Robert S. "Bob"		BR TR																									
1955	Waycross	GFL	132	514	87	151	37	7	10	87	13	55	62	0.294	1B, 2B, SS	879	178	31	0.972								
MacDonald, Donald "Don"		BL TL																									
1952	Dublin	GSL	23	85	12	23	4	1	3	13	0	12	15	0.271	1B	173	6	1	0.994								
MacFarlane, Morley		BL TL																									
1955	Statesboro	GSL	9	17		3								0.176	P					6	2	4					
MacIvor, Colin		BL TL																									
1956	Albany	GFL	11	12	0	2	0	0	0	1	0	0	2	0.167	P	7	9	1	0.941	11	2	0	<45				
1958	Albany	GFL	9	7	0	0								0.000	P					9	0	0	<30				
Mack, Jerome		BR TR																									
1947	Valdosta	GFL	23	84	8	20	2	2	0	10	0	6	35	0.238	OF	29	5	2	0.944								
Mackey, John																											
1941	Cordele	GFL	17	30	4	9	2	0	0	6	0	2	7	0.300	P	6	11	0	1.000	13	1	3	5.17	47	61	26	29
Mackie, H.P.																											
1914	Newnan	GAL	93	354	176	94					24			0.266	2B	298	253	32	0.945								
1915	Newnan	GAL	43	161	30	47	5	0	0					0.292	2B	105	127	10	0.959								
1916	Newnan	GAL	66	233	39	71					14			0.305	2B												
MacLeod, Donald "Don"		BR TR																									
1958	Waycross	GFL	19	25	3	5	1	0	0	1	0	9	10	0.200	P	10	23	3	0.917	16	3	6	4.55	83	64	70	81
Macli, Al		BR TR																									
1946	Thomasville	GFL	77	213	21	42	3	0	0	20	4	38	30	0.197	C	212	41	10	0.962								
Macrinotis, Lou																											
1942	Americus	GFL	126	492	74	136	21	5	1	49	11	35	60	0.276	3B	131	258	43	0.900								
Madaio, Eugene "Gene"		BL TL																									
1958	Dublin	GFL	37	133	23	26	3	1	1	12	0	30	28	0.195	OF	72	2	3	0.961								
Maddick, Russell "Russ"		BL TL																									
1962	Brunswick	GFL	110	354	51	88	11	1	4	53	21	57	77	0.249	1B, OF	541	28	22	0.963								
1963	Brunswick	GFL	29	96	17	21	5	0	0	12	5	17	20	0.219	1B	190	12	6	0.971								
Maddox, Delma		BR TR																									
1950	Opelika	GAL	40	91	9	13	2	1	0	5	0	4	16	0.143	P	13	42	2	0.965	34	10	12	4.36	198	197	101	108
Maderis, Joseph "Joe"		BR TR																									
1956	Sandersville	GSL	28	42	2	7	1	0	0	2	0	2	13	0.167	P	10	18	3	0.903	27	7	6	4.57	126	119	97	90
Madison, David Pledger "Dave"		BR TR 6'3" 190 lbs b. 02/01/1921 Brooksville, MS d. 12/08/1985 Macon, MS																									
1954	Sandersville	GSL	2	2	0	0								0.000	M, P					2	0	1	<45				
Maelwig, ---		BR																									
1946	Cordele	GFL	<10																								
Maggi, Ernest		BR TR																									
1950	Jesup	GSL	30	133	21	31	9	0	3	16	2	6	35	0.233	OF	45	3	6	0.889								
Magnatta, James "Jim"		BR TR																									
1948	LaGrange	GAL	37	65	8	6	2	0	0	5	0	15	31	0.092	P	5	40	4	0.918	37	9	15	4.16	186	230	87	81

Georgia Class-D Minor League Baseball Encyclopedia

YR	TEAM	LG	G	AB	R	H	2B	3B	HR	RBI	SB	BB	SO	BA	POS	PO	A	E	FA	GP	W	L	ERA	IP	H	SO	BB
Maguire, Paul		BR TR																									
1955	Hazlehurst-Baxley	GSL	41	139	12	30	2	2	3	17	1	16	38	0.216	SS	69	117	30	0.861								
Mahaffey, James "Jim"																											
1935	Americus	GFL	9												P					9	2	4		49	64	43	13
Mahoney, ---		BR TR																									
1946	Tallassee	GAL	1												P					1	0	0	0.00	1			
Mahurin, Leman		BS TR																									
1954	Hazlehurst-Baxley	GSL	46	105	11	27	8	1	2	11	0	1	23	0.257	P	13	37	7	0.877	35	7	12	4.77	215	227	128	108
1955	Hazlehurst-Baxley	GSL	37	70	10	15	1	2	2	15	0	5	17	0.214	P	3	18	3	0.875	26	12	4	3.84	136	133	91	57
Maiden, John		BL TL																									
1950	Tallahassee	GFL	102	355	63	89	15	4	2	59	7	75	71	0.251	1B	768	40	27	0.968								
Maier, Edward "Ed"		BR TR																									
1956	Douglas	GSL	21	28	5	10	0	0	0	1	0	4	3	0.357	P	3	17	2	0.909	21	4	8	4.35	89	88	60	59
Major, Thomas "Tom"		BR TR																									
1962	Brunswick	GFL	7	17	0	4	0	0	0	1	0	0	4	0.235	P					7	3	3	1.72	47	41	50	15
Malavase, Allie		BR TR																									
1958	Dublin	GFL	5	3	0									0.000	P					5	1	1		<30			
Malcolm, W. Lewis "Lew"		BR																									
1946	LaGrange	GAL	12	21	3	3	0	0	0	2	0	2	4	0.143													
Maldonado, Ovidio		BR TR																									
1956	Dublin	GSL	13	48	2	7	1	0	0	5	2	6	12	0.146	OF	37	1	2	0.950								
Mallard, John		BR TR																									
1953	Jesup	GSL	122	456	86	131	14	3	2	46	14	68	60	0.287	2B, SS	231	381	43	0.934								
1954	Statesboro	GSL	69	268	42	69	8	1	1	25	12	39	36	0.257	SS	102	159	42	0.861								
Malone, Frank																											
1942	Cordele	GFL	22	82	8	14	3	1	0	9	0	8	15	0.171	2B	49	55	16	0.867								
Maloney, Patrick "Pat"		BR TR																									
1946	Valdosta	GFL	3												P					3	0	0	0.00	6			
Maloof, Joseph "Joe"		BR TR																									
1949	Carrollton	GAL	11	16	1	3	0	0	0	0	0	1	4	0.188	P	1	10	1	0.917								
Maltby, ---																											
1915	Valdosta	FLAG	12	47	4	11	0	0		4				0.234	OF	29	0	1	0.967								
Manahan, Gerald		BR																									
1954	Americus-Cordele	GFL	2	5	0									0.000													
Manchester, Richard C. "Dick"																											
1913	Americus	ESL	98	310	39	84	14	3	0					0.271	C	510	134	34	0.950								
1914	Americus	GSL		260	38	62	9	1	4		6			0.238													
1915	Americus-Gainesville	FLAG	31	108	12	30	7	2	1		2			0.278	C	142	37	8	0.957								
1915	Griffin	GAL	28	97	12	18	4	0	1					0.186	C	164	30	4	0.980								
Mancini, Herbert "Herb"		BR TR																									
1949	LaGrange	GAL	53	181	34	41	2	3	0	14	8	27	40	0.227	3B	51	97	19	0.886								
Manes, Jerry		BR																									
1953	Sandersville	GSL	3												0.000													
Manfredi, Ralph J.		BR																									
1951	Valdosta	GFL	113	394	80	110	14	7	2	58	17	84	35	0.279													
Manheim, Francis		BS TR																									
1946	Tallassee	GAL	16	44	7	6	2	0	0	3	0	2	12	0.136	P	6	19	5	0.833	16	6	7	4.38	111	114	73	52
Mankovitch, Frank		BR TR																									
1958	Dublin	GFL	48	109	12	22	6	0	2	16	0	3	35	0.202	P	11	45	6	0.903	31	12	9	4.41	194	182	137	92
Mann, J. Elbert		BR																									
1947	Alexander City	GAL	10	28	3	9	1	0	0	0	1	1	8	0.321													
Mann, Thomas "Tom"		BR TR																									
1946	Thomasville	GFL	27	97	12	20	4	0	0	9	0	14	21	0.206	OF	38	1	6	0.867								
Manning, ---																											
1930	Carrollton	GAL	2												P					2	0	1	6.75	8	9	1	4
1938	Moultrie	GFL	3												P					3	1	2	7.31	16	20	5	12
Manning, Tommy																											
1941	Americus	GFL	35	130	15	22	2	0	1	7	4	16	25	0.169	OF	62	4	3	0.957								
Manning, William F. "Bill"		BL TL																									
1948	Tallahassee	GFL	65	234	37	62	8	3	0	29	5	61	26	0.265	1B	536	9	12	0.978								
Manno, Donald D. "Don"		BR TR 6'1" 190 lbs b. 05/04/1915 Williamsport, PA d. 03/11/1995 Williamsport, PA																									
1950	Waycross	GFL	77	231	57	66	11	1	9	52	14	84	34	0.286	M, 1B, 3B, SS, OF	204	62	18	0.937								
1950	Tifton	GSL	50	170	35	49	13	0	6	37	2	51	13	0.288	2B, OF	101	29	12	0.915								
Mansfield, Clifford "Cliff"		BL TL																									
1953	Jesup	GSL	124	498	84	151	21	5	2	62	35	57	63	0.303	1B	1118	37	25	0.979								
Manson, ---																											
1915	Brunswick	FLAG			0									0.000	P					0							
Manush, Frank Benjamin "Frank"		BR TR 175 lbs b. 09/18/1883 Tuscumbia, AL d. 01/05/1965 Laguna Beach, CA																									
1916	Rome	GAL	65	240	48	72				25				0.300	M, 3B												
1920	Griffin	GSL		166	24	50								0.301	2B												
Mapes, Carl		BR TR																									
1951	Hazlehurst-Baxley	GSL	58	123	10	27	3	0	0	12	1	9	27	0.220	OF, P	20	54	10	0.881	47	14	4	2.88	206	214	62	87
1952	Hazlehurst-Baxley	GSL	12	22	2	2	0	0	0	0	0	3	7	0.091	P					9	2	4	4.06	51	60	13	15
1954	Hazlehurst-Baxley	GSL	6	4	0									0.000	P					6	0	1		<45			

Georgia Class-D Minor League Baseball Encyclopedia

YR	TEAM	LG	G	AB	R	H	2B	3B	HR	RBI	SB	BB	SO	BA	POS	PO	A	E	FA	GP	W	L	ERA	IP	H	SO	BB
Maples, Earl		BR TR																									
1956	Douglas	GSL	116	403	79	107	28	2	6	60	9	76	90	0.266	3B	110	194	48	0.864								
Maratowski, Fred																											
1937	Moultrie	GFL	93	273	33	65	7	4	1	25	6	71	37	0.238	OF	174	7	9	0.953								
Marbet, Otto																											
1920	LaGrange	GSL													1B												
Marburger, Robert "Bob"		BR																									
1956	Sandersville	GSL	8	29		7								0.241													
Marcello, Anthony																											
1949	Douglas - Tifton	GSL	13	12	4	1	0	0	0	2	0	8	7	0.083	P					13	5	2	6.13	47	36	14	26
Marhoover, Gary		BR TR																									
1953	Dublin	GSL	6											0.000	P						0	3	<45				
Maricich, Elijah "Eli"		BR TR																									
1950	Valley	GAL	84	326	91	100	18	8	14	56	24	54	61	0.307	2B, SS	136	254	48	0.890								
1951	Valley	GAL	111	416	103	118	25	6	14	75	41	83	61	0.284	SS	234	337	47	0.924								
1953	Eastman	GSL	124	505	139	163	27	6	29	117	47	74	74	0.323	3B, SS	202	335	44	0.924								
1954	Fitzgerald	GFL	31	118	25	33	7	0	3	18	2	15	22	0.280	SS, OF	40	33	6	0.924								
1957	Waycross	GFL	2	7		3								0.429													
Marino, Emil		BR TR																									
1950	Cordele	GFL	16	56	9	10	1	2	1	9	3	11	13	0.179	OF	22	1	3	0.885								
Marion, J.W.																											
1915	Griffin - Talladega	GAL	61	208	26	58	6	0	0					0.279	SS	94	144	21	0.919								
1921	Griffin	GSL													2B												
Marion, John Wyeth "Red"		BR TR 6'2" 175 lbs b. 03/14/1914 Richburg, SC d. 03/13/1975 San Jose, CA																									
1936	Americus	GFL	66	262	61	88	13	8	8	41	15			0.336	OF	169	12	6	0.968								
Markham, Kenneth "Ken"		BR TR																									
1946	Thomasville	GFL	33	64	10	13	3	1	0	5	0	5	11	0.203	P	7	48	7	0.887	27	5	11	5.39	142	175	73	74
1947	Thomasville	GFL	41	85	8	19	4	0	0	10	0	11	18	0.224	P	9	48	6	0.905	35	13	12	4.00	218	205	102	118
Markham, Richard "Dick"		BR TR																									
1948	Thomasville	GFL	23	67	6	15	0	2	0	9	0	6	15	0.224	OF	18	3	4	0.840								
1949	Fitzgerald	GSL	34	107	7	17	6	0	0	7	1	13	29	0.159	OF	50	3	4	0.930								
Markland, John		BR TR																									
1950	Moultrie	GFL	34	111	13	36	6	0	0	25	3	20	20	0.324	C	118	12	8	0.942								
Markle, Lewis "Lou"		BL TR																									
1951	Americus	GFL	22	62	12	16	4	1	1	7	0	26	8	0.258	OF	38	2	2	0.952								
Marks, Max																											
1928	Cedartown - Talladega	GAL	45	135	14	31	1	1	0		3	8	20	0.230	3B, P	22	97	5	0.960	19	5	8	3.51	136	145	38	57
1929	Carrollton	GAL		4	0	1								0.250	P												
1929	Anniston	GAL	42	92	6	16	2	0	0		4	7	7	0.174	P	25	44	5	0.932	25	8	8		119	146	29	55
Marlow, Walter "Walt"		BR TR																									
1948	Albany	GFL	11	15	1	0	0	0	0	0	0	2	5	0.000	P	4	9	0	1.000	11	2	3	6.13	47	52	26	42
Marnie, Harry Sylvester "Hal"		BR TR 6'1" 178 lbs b. 07/06/1918 Philadelphia, PA d. 01/07/2002 Philadelphia, PA																									
1939	Moultrie	GFL	119	489	81	140	11	6	0	31	6	55	47	0.286	2B	342	384	34	0.955								
Marockie, Henry																											
1956	Tifton	GFL	53	194	26	45	7	3	1	28	5	33	37	0.232	OF	77	2	5	0.940								
Marolewski, Fred Daniel "Fred" "Fritz"		BR TR 205 lbs b. 10/06/1928 Chicago, IL																									
1948	Albany	GFL	140	546	96	148	43	8	6	89	9	76	130	0.271	1B	1084	86	42	0.965								
Maroney, John		BR TR																									
1956	Fitzgerald	GFL	18	68	10	21	2	0	1	9	2	8	6	0.309	3B	24	20	11	0.800								
Marotta, Daniel "Dan"		BR																									
1950	Jesup	GSL	28	67	4	9	3	0	0	6	0	5	20	0.134													
Marquez, Humberto		BR TR																									
1956	Douglas	GSL	37	65	14	9	4	0	0	7	1	16	32	0.138	P	6	29	6	0.854	29	16	8	3.28	195	197	94	55
Marquis, Roger Julian "Roger" "Noonie"		BL TL 6'0" 190 lbs b. 04/05/1937 Holyoke, MA																									
1956	Thomson	GSL	116	384	59	87	12	5	4	64	1	89	89	0.227	1B, P	799	52	17	0.980	6	2	2					
Marrero, Leonilo		BR TR																									
1950	Dublin	GSL	17	60	4	11	2	0	0	2	1	3	2	0.183	C	100	9	4	0.965								
Marrochi, Hugo J.		BR TR																									
1953	Thomasville	GFL	14	48	8	11	2	0	0	4	0	8	11	0.229	1B	94	1	3	0.969								
Marrujo, Jimmie		BR TR																									
1963	Moultrie	GFL	8	26	2	6	0	0	0	4	1	3	8	0.231	P					8	6	0	2.35	65	62	71	26
Marsh, Jim E.		BR TR																									
1938	Cordele	GFL	27	58	8	15	2	1	1	5	0	12	9	0.259	P	9	38	6	0.887	22	7	7	3.37	139	136	54	79
1939	Waycross	GFL	23	48	5	9	1	0	0	3	0	4	9	0.188	P	6	46	7	0.881	18	7	10	3.50	131	128	47	58
1940	Waycross	GFL	19	43	2	9	1	1	0	1	1	2	10	0.209	P					12	3	5	4.24	68	84	39	32
Marshall, ---																											
1915	Talladega	GAL	<6												P					<6							
Marshall, ---		BR TR																									
1946	Valley	GAL	1												P					1	1	0	0.00	7	5	7	2
Marshall, Herbert R. "Shorty"		BR TR 5'6" 135 lbs b. 03/31/0921 Washington County, GA																									
1946	Carrollton	GAL	128	524	88	143	28	3	8	54	20	29	38	0.273	2B	306	316	27	0.958								
1947	Carrollton	GAL	121	518	99	171	29	7	7	76	16	38	20	0.330	2B, SS	285	305	33	0.947								
1948	Carrollton	GAL	121	495	99	152	32	3	13	52	20	60	16	0.307	2B	360	334	38	0.948								
1950	Carrollton	GAL	80	305	70	108	19	3	10	64	4	30	14	0.354	M, 2B	117	121	13	0.948								
1952	Jesup	GSL	66	273	44	77	12	0	6	36	4	24	9	0.282	SS	118	170	25	0.920								

Georgia Class-D Minor League Baseball Encyclopedia

YR	TEAM	LG	G	AB	R	H	2B	3B	HR	RBI	SB	BB	SO	BA	POS	PO	A	E	FA	GP	W	L	ERA	IP	H	SO	BB
Marshall, Reavis																											
1949	Dublin	GSL	10	43	4	6	1	0	1	6	2	3	8	0.140	OF	30	3	1	0.971								
Marshall, Richard R. "Dick"		BL TR																									
1950	LaGrange	GAL	30	54	3	10	1	0	0	1	1	1	13	0.185	P	11	36	5	0.904	29	9	8	4.78	130	122	85	116
Marsilisi, Michael "Mike"		BR																									
1952	Brunswick	GFL	10	29	2	6	1	0	0	0	1	5	5	0.207													
Martellani, Robert "Bob"		BS TR																									
1957	Thomasville	GFL	7	4	0									0.000	P					7	0	1		<30			
Martin, Amos																											
1930	Carrollton	GAL	27	117	22	39	6	0	5		2	6	7	0.333	SS	37	80	11	0.914								
Martin, Archie																											
1935	Panama City	GFL	17	59	8	12	3	0	0		0	5	15	0.203	C	94	10	4	0.963								
1936	Moultrie	GFL	42	112	14	27	5	0	2	14	1			0.241	C	118	16	9	0.937								
Martin, Charles B.																											
1935	Tallahassee	GFL	88	302	29	63	7	4	0		6	21	22	0.209	C	412	53	13	0.973								
Martin, Edwin																											
1938	Americus	GFL	61	255	40	70	11	3	0	42	0	17	12	0.275	OF	130	15	2	0.986								
Martin, Fred		BL TR																									
1951	Brunswick	GFL	60	92	10	27	2	1	0	9	1	5	8	0.293	P	14	49	2	0.969	22	13	5	3.07	161	128	111	87
Martin, Harold																											
1939	Cordele	GFL	39	137	35	32	0	2	0	17	1	36	19	0.234	2B	107	93	19	0.913								
Martin, James "Jim"		BR																									
1955	Albany	GFL	15	38	6	9	1	1	1	5	0	5	8	0.237													
Martin, James C. "Jim"		BR TR																									
1948	Douglas	GSL	95	320	49	78	10	3	2	29	10	54	84	0.244	OF	151	12	6	0.964								
1949	Douglas	GSL	130	530	130	144	22	9	10	64	54	83	114	0.272	3B, OF	169	137	37	0.892								
1950	Douglas	GSL	135	533	107	134	20	6	3	47	63	100	92	0.251	OF	329	14	17	0.953								
Martin, John R.		BL TL																									
1953	Statesboro	GSL	19	30	3	8	0	0	1	5	0	0	12	0.267	P	2	14	2	0.889	17	2	6	6.08	74	78	68	63
Martin, Lane		BL TL																									
1954	Albany	GFL	33	39	3	6	0	0	1	4	0	4	16	0.154	P	4	29	8	0.805	32	10	12	4.76	138	127	120	139
1958	Albany	GFL	10	18	5	2	0	0	0	1	0	5	15	0.111	P	1	13	1	0.933	10	6	0	6.12	50	55	35	40
Martin, S.R.																											
1920	LaGrange	GSL																									
1921	Carrollton	GSL		101	11	25								0.248													
Martin, Travis		BR TR																									
1962	Moultrie(7) - Thomasville(10)	GFL	17	30	5	7	0	0	0	3	0	7	9	0.233	P	8	25	1	0.971	16	10	1	2.97	91	79	73	22
Martin, W.P.																											
1915	Griffin	GAL	18	62	3	9	0	0	0					0.145	M, OF	14	4	0	1.000								
Martin, William F. "Billie"		BL TR																									
1949	Opelika	GAL	30	59	9	10	0	0	0	4	0	9	13	0.169	P	13	19	1	0.970	20	6	7	4.54	119	116	84	59
1950	Opelika	GAL	38	65	5	12	0	0	0	3	0	10	15	0.185	P	3	18	1	0.955	25	3	10	4.80	133	144	57	108
Martinez, Fred "Freddie"		BR TR																									
1940	Americus	GFL	36	122	21	23	4	0	1	13	4	24	17	0.189	2B	89	98	11	0.944								
Martini, Fernando		BR TR																									
1948	Tallassee(58) - Valley(27)	GAL	85	319	42	88	17	5	6	61	10	23	35	0.276	OF	154	3	13	0.924								
Martini, Paul		BR TR																									
1950	Waycross	GFL	140	568	80	145	21	8	2	57	15	47	45	0.255	2B, SS	340	433	45	0.945								
Martinich, Antonio "Tony"		BR TR																									
1949	Tallahassee	GFL	87	339	61	96	12	6	1	59	14	45	34	0.283	OF	140	20	5	0.970								
Martz, ---																											
1928	Gadsden	GAL	14	44	3	10	2	0	0		1	0	2	0.227	SS	12	35	9	0.839								
Maruschak, Nicholas "Nick"		BL TL																									
1951	Griffin	GAL	113	441	55	119	15	4	0	60	6	61	19	0.270	1B	988	49	23	0.978								
Masatto, Frank		BR																									
1953	Statesboro	GSL	1											0.250													
Mashburn, Ernest		BR TL																									
1946	LaGrange	GAL	19	65	7	12	1	1	0	3	2	2	15	0.185	OF, P	20	3	5	0.821	2	0	2	0.00	10	15	1	10
1946	Cordele	GFL	<10												OF												
1947	Cordele	GFL	33	125	24	22	1	2	0	2	2	25	32	0.176	OF	93	8	9	0.918								
Mason, George		BR TR																									
1947	Tallassee(39) - Newnan(13)	GAL	52	186	35	45	12	2	0	14	10	29	43	0.242	OF	76	8	7	0.923								
1947	Thomasville	GFL	11	35	4	6	0	2	0	3	2	4	16	0.171	OF	9	1	2	0.833								
Mason, J.																											
1928	Lindale	GAL	10	28	2	3	0	0	0		0	5	0	0.107													
Mason, John		BR TR																									
1949	Valley	GAL	57	133	17	32	3	2	0	11	3	17	16	0.241	OF, C	178	12	7	0.964								
Mason, Max		BR																									
1954	Statesboro	GSL	2	5	0									0.000													
Mason, S.																											
1928	Cedartown	GAL	66	248	42	69	10	0	8		10	18	31	0.278	OF	66	7	2	0.973								
Massey, Horace		BR TR																									
1948	Americus	GFL	38	137	18	38	3	2	0	12	8	18	22	0.277	OF	43	2	2	0.957								
Massey, Terrance																											
1941	Thomasville	GFL	8	27	4	8	0	1	1	3	0	0	5	0.296	OF	11	0	1	0.917								

Georgia Class-D Minor League Baseball Encyclopedia

YR	TEAM	LG	G	AB	R	H	2B	3B	HR	RBI	SB	BB	SO	BA	POS	PO	A	E	FA	GP	W	L	ERA	IP	H	SO	BB
Masterson, William "Bill"		BR																									
1946	Moultrie	GFL	<10																								
Mastracci, Robert "Bob"		BL TR																									
1954	Hazlehurst-Baxley	GSL	50	188	26	50	7	2	2	34	4	18	41	0.266	1B	319	22	21	0.942								
Matchick, John Thomas "Tom"		BL TR 6'0" 175 lbs b. 09/07/1943 Hazleton, PA																									
1962	Brunswick	GFL	71	264	53	82	14	3	1	31	9	27	51	0.311	SS	99	159	30	0.896								
Matesich, Jose "Joe"		BR TR																									
1953	Cordele	GFL	26	75	4	16	2	0	0	8	1	9	23	0.213	OF	24	1	3	0.893								
Mathes, Edward "Ed"		BS																									
1954	Brunswick	GFL	13	27	6	4	0	0	0	2	0	12	13	0.148													
Mathewson, ---																											
1928	Carrollton	GAL		12	2	3								0.250													
Mathey, Maurice "Bud"		BR																									
1949	Tallassee	GAL	20	57	10	20	2	0	1	4	2	3	12	0.351													
Mathieson, Robert "Bob"		BR																									
1949	Vidalia-Lyons	GSL	11	19	1	1	0	0	0	3	0	4	8	0.053	P	1	14	1	0.938	11	4	4	5.68	57	42	34	29
Mathis, Joseph "Joe"		BR TR																									
1956	Thomasville	GFL	24	54	5	5	0	0	0	0	0	7	22	0.093	P	5	31	2	0.947	24	9	8	2.71	173	153	139	51
Mathis, Willie Ed																											
1942	Waycross	GFL	103	404	66	15	19	5	3	54	25	48	36	0.037	3B	132	265	46	0.896								
Mathison, Malcolm		BL																									
1954	Waycross	GFL	6	17		3								0.176													
Matican, Marvin "Marv"		BR TR																									
1950	Vidalia-Lyons	GSL	14	51	10	12	2	0	3	12	2	7	23	0.235	OF	26	1	1	0.964								
Matt, J.W.																											
1935	Panama City	GFL	13	46	7	10	2	1	0		1	5	17	0.217	C	17	0	2	0.895								
Matthews, Harry																											
1915	Newnan	GAL	58	188	18	50	5	1	4					0.266	M, C	326	74	6	0.985								
1916	Newnan	GAL	67	219	14	49					6			0.224	M, C												
1917	Tri-Cities	GAL	11	38	4	8	1	0	0		3			0.211	OF	23	3	1	0.963								
1921	Griffin	GSL		16	2	5								0.313	M												
Matthews, James "Jim"		BL TR																									
1955	Hazlehurst-Baxley	GSL	98	351	58	96	21	3	1	47	10	39	31	0.274	3B, OF	179	34	15	0.934								
Matthews, Luther		BR TR																									
1949	Carrollton	GAL	8												P					8	3	3	2.52	50	57	19	9
Matthews, Matty																											
1917	Griffin	GAL	16	60	3	14	4	0	0		3			0.233	M, C	89	13	3	0.971								
Matthews, Robert "Bob"		BR TR																									
1946	Carrollton	GAL	35	75	8	8	0	0	0	3	0	6	9	0.107	P	4	52	1	0.982	35	16	13	6.88	123	227	111	50
1947	Carrollton(23) - Newnan(17)	GAL	40	99	15	18	1	1	0	3	0	8	14	0.182	P	7	52	2	0.967	38	18	16	2.54	248	229	114	45
Mauldin, Mason W.		BR TR																									
1948	Eastman	GSL	76	305	36	73	4	1	0	16	15	22	22	0.239	OF	133	6	5	0.965								
1949	Eastman - Sparta	GSL	110	418	55	102	18	2	0	29	20	24	36	0.244	OF	152	16	11	0.939								
Mauney, John		BR TR																									
1955	Valdosta	GFL	18	65	11	18	5	0	0	12	0	8	12	0.277	3B	15	35	7	0.877								
Maupin, William E. "Bill"		BR																									
1956	Valdosta	GFL	17	44	6	8	1	0	0	1	0	5	8	0.182													
Maurer, Ray		BR TR																									
1951	LaGrange	GAL	16	61	10	14	4	0	0	5	0	8	7	0.230	3B	4	12	3	0.842								
Maurer, Walter "Walt"		BR TR																									
1951	LaGrange	GAL	20	63	10	9	1	0	0	6	1	17	9	0.143	OF	18	1	0	1.000								
Maust, Thomas "Tom"		BL TR																									
1962	Dublin	GFL	91	272	54	56	5	2	5	22	8	71	118	0.206	2B, 3B, SS	145	163	46	0.870								
1963	Waycross	GFL	72	187	25	42	1	0	2	10	7	35	57	0.225	2B, 3B	57	74	32	0.804								
Maxcy, Russell "Russ"		BR TR																									
1958	Waycross	GFL	68	237	27	60	18	0	2	28	2	30	40	0.253	SS	123	200	23	0.934								
Maxwell, Elmo																											
1947	Tallahassee	GFL	<10																								
Maxwell, Gordon		BL TR																									
1956	Hazlehurst-Baxley	GSL	35	140	29	41	6	5	1	18	4	19	20	0.293	3B, OF	52	34	11	0.887								
Maxwell, John		BR TR																									
1953	Sandersville	GSL	4											0.333	P						0	2		<45			
1955	Statesboro	GSL	2	6		0								0.000													
Maxwell, Robert "Bob"																											
1942	Dothan	GFL	72	201	24	43	5	1	2	27	7	29	56	0.214	P	45	85	3	0.977	41	18	12	2.89	277	280	116	48
May, John C.		BL TR																									
1962	Dublin	GFL	27	75	12	21	4	0	2	13	3	16	7	0.280	OF	29	0	6	0.829								
May, Ted		BR TR																									
1954	Sandersville	GSL	1	2		0								0.000	P					1	0	0		<45			
Mayorquinn, Ernesto		BR TR																									
1951	Tifton	GFL	16	28	5	4	0	1	0	0	0	4	3	0.143	P	2	18	0	1.000	15	6	5	6.04	82	92	35	54
Mays, ---																											
1914	Newnan	GAL	34	112	16	30				1				0.268	P	17	65	9	0.901	34							
1915	Thomasville	FLAG	11	34	0	5	1	0	0	2				0.147	P					5	1	4		46	46	22	16

Georgia Class-D Minor League Baseball Encyclopedia

YR	TEAM	LG	G	AB	R	H	2B	3B	HR	RBI	SB	BB	SO	BA	POS	PO	A	E	FA	GP	W	L	ERA	IP	H	SO	BB
Mays, W. Everett		BL TR																									
1952	Dublin	GSL	125	469	93	135	26	9	17	90	20	87	89	0.288	OF	205	13	18	0.924								
Mazak (Mierzejek), Leonard "Leo"		BL TL																									
1948	Douglas	GSL	27	61	5	10	3	2	0	9	0	5	10	0.164	P, OF	5	14	4	0.826	21	6	9	4.54	109	97	67	69
1949	Douglas	GSL	32	80	9	14	2	0	0	10	1	14	22	0.175	P	25	45	3	0.959	32	12	11	5.66	183	131	90	111
1950	Carrollton	GAL	26	77	8	16	5	0	0	6	0	2	13	0.208	P	7	15	4	0.846	19	4	9	6.24	124	157	53	61
Maze, John																											
1939	Thomasville	GFL													P					5	2	3	4.62	39	38	13	12
Mazer, Alphonse "Al"																											
1938	Moultrie	GFL	82	325	59	87	12	9	1	54	14	46	27	0.268	2B	202	292	19	0.963								
Mazzone, ---		BR TR																									
1946	Cordele(35) - Moultrie(6)	GFL	41	138	21	24	1	0	0	10	1	25	37	0.174	3B	40	57	14	0.874								
McAdams, Ralph																											
1938	Tallahassee	GFL	66	252	36	84	16	4	1	45	1	13	20	0.333	C	292	34	9	0.973								
1939	Tallahassee	GFL	49	169	23	47	5	1	0	23	1	14	8	0.278	M, C	154	48	14	0.935								
McAfee, Alton		BL TL																									
1948	Newnan	GAL	124	458	87	134	29	6	6	94	8	52	54	0.293	1B	1057	44	14	0.987								
1949	Newnan	GAL	121	434	73	112	22	3	4	68	12	67	29	0.258	1B	991	53	19	0.982								
1950	Newnan	GAL	10	31	4	8	3	0	1	4	3	7	2	0.258	1B	76	5	2	0.976								
McAfee, Bernard "Bud"		BR																									
1962	Brunswick	GFL	5	10	2	3	0	0	0	1	0	4	3	0.300													
McAndrew, Robert "Bob"		BR TR																									
1949	Griffin	GAL	111	398	45	101	10	4	0	54	3	45	38	0.254	2B	296	247	53	0.911								
1950	Griffin	GAL	118	472	72	113	10	1	0	39	6	77	40	0.239	2B	316	314	29	0.956								
McArthur, Donald "Don"		BR TR																									
1949	Americus	GFL	98	368	51	98	16	5	3	47	5	38	42	0.266	3B, OF	150	75	17	0.930								
McAuliffe, ---																											
1921	Cedartown	GSL													2B												
1921	LaGrange	GSL													SS, 2B												
1921	Rome	GSL													2B												
McAuliffe, Richard John "Dick"		BL TR 5'11" 176 lbs b. 11/29/1939 Hartford, CT																									
1958	Valdosta	GFL	93	336	70	96	17	5	8	62	9	82	39	0.286	SS	173	262	45	0.906								
McBride, ---																											
1917	Anniston	GAL	2	6	1	1	0	1	0		0			0.167	P	0	1	0	1.000	2	2	0		15	7	11	6
McBride, Delton		BL																									
1949	Alexander City	GAL	12	25	3	4	1	0	0	1	0	3	4	0.160													
McBride, Harold																											
1941	Valdosta	GFL	3												P					3	1	0	3.21	14	13	9	12
1942	Valdosta	GFL	16	41	4	7	1	0	0	4	1	2	22	0.171	P	7	22	2	0.935	16	7	5	2.94	104	95	57	61
McBride, Tom R.		BR TR																									
1948	Newnan	GAL	29	43	2	9	3	0	1	6	0	6	13	0.209	P	3	8	0	1.000								
McBryde, Warren		BR TR																									
1940	Cordele	GFL	27	86	6	20	3	1	0	13	0	4	18	0.233	OF	29	1	4	0.882								
1946	Thomasville	GFL	88	336	60	113	16	9	4	61	8	43	32	0.336	OF	131	10	18	0.887								
McCaffrey, Thomas "Tom"		BR TR																									
1956	Fitzgerald	GFL	3	7		1								0.143	P					3	0	3		<45			
McCain, Samuel "Sam"		BL TL																									
1949	Americus	GFL	126	448	86	123	17	4	7	63	27	84	102	0.275	1B, OF	752	38	38	0.954								
McCall, Maurice Gordon "Gordon"		BR TR																									
1954	Thomasville	GFL	10	14	1	2	0	0	0		0	2	4	0.143	P					9	2	3		<45			
McCallum, Richard "Dick"		BR TL																									
1948	Tallahassee	GFL	11	16	1	1	0	0	0	0	0	2	6	0.063	P	1	9	0	1.000	11	0	6	7.09	47	53	15	41
1950	Tallahassee	GFL	12	23	1	6	0	1	0	4	0	0	7	0.261	P	0	14	2	0.875	12	3	2	2.77	52	43	23	31
McCalman, Jack																											
1950	Hazlehurst-Baxley	GSL													P					0	0						
McCann, Clifford "Cliff"																											
1942	Valdosta	GFL	20	49	3	5	0	1	0	2	0	9	15	0.102	P	6	31	2	0.949	20	6	8	3.63	114	129	49	36
McCarnes, James "Jim"		BL TR																									
1946	Waycross	GFL	125	503	111	169	34	6	1	72	14	72	40	0.336	OF	204	16	6	0.973								
McCarron, Robert "Bob"		BR TR																									
1957	Fitzgerald	GFL	6	5	0	0								0.000	P					6	0	0		<30			
McCarthy, ---																											
1928	Talladega	GAL	27	90	8	17	1	2	0		2	9	24	0.189	C	64	22	5	0.945								
McCarthy, Franklin D. "Frank"		BL TL																									
1956	Thomson	GSL	1	1		0								0.000	P					1	0	0					
McCarthy, John J.		BL TR																									
1952	Vidalia(9) - Fitzgerald(6)	GSL	15	16	2	4	1	0	0	0	0	3	2	0.250	P	6	9	5	0.750	15	2	3	5.83	54	64	24	31
McCarthy, Richard "Dick"		BL TL																									
1946	Americus	GFL	1												P					1	0	0	0.00	2			
McCasland, Stanley "Stan"		BR TR																									
1954	Thomasville	GFL	7	7		3								0.429	P					7	2	0		<45			
McClaskey, Larry		BR TR																									
1955	Vidalia	GSL	23	53	10	18	3	0	1	8	0	3	5	0.340	P	8	13	1	0.955	19	9	2	4.38	109	108	83	73
McClatchey, Robert "Bob"		BR TL																									
1949	Moultrie	GFL	99	350	44	83	13	2	4	35	6	40	70	0.237	OF	183	13	11	0.947								

Georgia Class-D Minor League Baseball Encyclopedia

YR	TEAM	LG	G	AB	R	H	2B	3B	HR	RBI	SB	BB	SO	BA	POS	PO	A	E	FA	GP	W	L	ERA	IP	H	SO	BB
McClellan, Harvey McDowell "Harvey"		BR TR 5'9" 143 lbs b. 12/22/1894 Cynthiana, KY d. 11/06/1925 Cynthiana, KY																									
1917	Talladega	GAL	16	65	10	21	4	0	0		3			0.323	3B	47	52	5	0.952								
McClenaghan, Russell "Russ"		BL TR																									
1954	Brunswick	GFL	5	10		2								0.200													
1955	Brunswick	GFL	6	12		6								0.500													
1955	Dublin(23) - Statesboro(37)	GSL	60	211	32	67	21	1	1	24	5	15	33	0.318	OF, C	206	18	16	0.933								
1958	Waycross	GFL	85	253	29	59	15	2	1	30	1	32	39	0.233	OF, P	89	4	9	0.912	1	0	0		<30			
McClinton, Eugene Leon "Gene"		BR TR																									
1953	Hazlehurst-Baxley	GSL	25	51	10	11	3	0	1	7	0	4	15	0.216	P	3	22	0	1.000	19	8	3	4.50	102	109	72	68
McCloskey, Frank																											
1941	Moultrie	GFL	7	27	4	5	0	1	0	7	0	5	8	0.185	OF	10	1	2	0.846								
McClure, James C. "Jim"																											
1936	Americus	GFL	51	124	30	35	2	1	0	19	1			0.282	P					51	22	9	3.92	266		179	95
McClure, Oscar																											
1939	Tallahassee	GFL	132	486	84	134	22	4	0	48	7	90	60	0.276	2B	349	353	31	0.958								
McCluskey, Austin		BR TR																									
1953	Vidalia	GSL	14	20	2	5	0	0	0	3	0	2	3	0.250	P						0	5		<45			
McClusky, James "Jim"		BR TR																									
1958	Dublin	GFL	11	43	5	9	1	0	1	6	0	5	7	0.209	C	66	4	4	0.946								
McClusky, LeRoy																											
1941	Thomasville	GFL	5	20	1	1	0	0	0	0	0	0	7	0.050	OF	7	1	1	0.889								
McColl, Alexander Boyd "Red"		BS TR 6'1" 178 lbs b. 03/29/1894 Eagleville, OH d. 02/06/1991 Kingsville, OH																									
1938	Americus	GFL	37	65	8	8	3	0	0	1	0	9	16	0.123	M, P	6	56	3	0.954	34	16	3	2.04	190	158	83	33
McColley, William "Bill"		BL TL																									
1954	Waycross	GFL	136	447	50	106	15	0	0	52	10	76	68	0.237	1B, P	1036	43	20	0.982	1	0	0		<45			
McCollum, ---																											
1928	Lindale	GAL	6												P					6	1	5	5.73	44	64	12	6
McCombie, Charles		BR TR																									
1953	Thomasville	GFL	18	46	2	4	0	0	0	6	0	2	19	0.087	P	5	20	1	0.962	18	9	6	2.82	115	84	88	73
McConnell, Edward "Ed"		BR																									
1946	Opelika	GAL	<10																									
McCord, Norman "Norm"		BR TR																									
1948	Tallahassee	GFL	30	92	10	14	1	2	0	5	0	17	23	0.152	1B	229	12	5	0.980								
McCorkle, Robert Lee "Bob"																											
1942	Valdosta	GFL	14	50	10	13	1	0	0	7	0	7	12	0.260	C	47	17	3	0.955								
McCormack, ---																											
1906	Albany	GSL													C												
McCormack, Thomas "Tom"		BL TL																									
1953	Statesboro	GSL	3											0.667													
1954	Americus-Cordele	GFL	51	200	35	42	3	1	0	13	4	22	19	0.210	1B	409	18	7	0.984								
McCormick, John		BR TR																									
1948	Sparta	GSL	19	55	3	11	1	1	0	7	0	8	8	0.200	P	8	21	3	0.906	18	10	6	2.11	145	111	98	62
McCormick, Richard "Dick"		BR TR																									
1947	Cordele	GFL	21	73	7	11	2	1	0	5	0	9	26	0.151	2B	54	64	12	0.908								
McCorry, ---																											
1941	Cordele - Thomasville	GFL	4												P					4	0	3	5.29	17	16	2	10
McCovey, Willie Lee "Willie"		BL TL 6'4" 210 lbs b. 01/10/1938 Mobile, AL																									
1955	Sandersville	GSL	107	410	82	125	24	1	19	113	15	56	89	0.305	1B	897	51	23	0.976								
McCoy, ---																											
1914	Waycross	GSL		226	36	71	9	1	3		16			0.314													
McCoy, Robert "Bob"		BR																									
1954	Statesboro	GSL	14	15	2	2	1	1	0	3	0	1	2	0.133													
McCraney, ---																											
1913	Talladega	GAL	48	176	20	38					8			0.216	3B	64	73	16	0.895								
McCraney, Wayne		BR TL																									
1948	Alexander City	GAL	37	58	13	13	0	0	1	5	0	10	16	0.224	P	7	33	4	0.909	31	9	11	3.85	166	144	83	123
1949	Alexander City	GAL	25	61	4	14	5	0	0	8	0	4	11	0.230	P	6	20	1	0.963	19	7	10	4.57	130	131	43	90
McCrary, James E. "Jim"		BR TR																									
1948	Moultrie	GFL	31	101	17	19	3	2	0	12	1	23	15	0.188	3B	36	63	9	0.917								
1953	Cordele	GFL	48	171	32	41	4	1	0	20	2	36	10	0.240	SS	95	118	29	0.880								
McCravy, Charles		BR TR																									
1946	Newnan	GAL	2												P					2	0	1	0.00	4	4	2	1
1947	Newnan(10) - Valley(6)	GAL	16	33	1	4	0	0	0	0	0	1	7	0.121	P	3	5	0	1.000	16	3	8	6.00	78	105	56	27
McCrone, Thomas "Tom"		BR TR																									
1952	Brunswick	GFL	109	344	52	80	13	1	0	37	15	31	38	0.233	3B, OF, C	215	100	29	0.916								
McCue, George		BL TL																									
1956	Valdosta	GFL	123	476	88	110	15	5	4	44	13	61	60	0.231	OF	242	12	10	0.962								
1957	Valdosta	GFL	17	47	8	8	2	0	1	8	2	8	6	0.170	OF	20	2	3	0.880								
McCulley, Melvin		BR TR																									
1947	Albany	GFL	48	170	28	44	6	3	0	25	3	36	25	0.259	OF	70	3	10	0.880								
McCulloch, Robert "Bob"		BR TR																									
1949	Newnan	GAL	54	118	19	25	5	0	1	15	0	29	45	0.212	C	174	20	2	0.990								
McCullough, John		BR TR																									
1947	Americus	GFL	139	517	130	150	31	6	4	51	42	111	79	0.290	2B	408	352	47	0.942								

Georgia Class-D Minor League Baseball Encyclopedia

YR	TEAM	LG	G	AB	R	H	2B	3B	HR	RBI	SB	BB	SO	BA	POS	PO	A	E	FA	GP	W	L	ERA	IP	H	SO	BB
McCune, Larry		BR TR																									
1956	Moultrie	GFL	25	47	1	5	1	0	0	4	0	4	19	0.106	P	9	23	2	0.941	25	8	5	4.04	136	142	92	63
McDaniel, Dan		BR TR																									
1953	Fitzgerald	GFL	6											0.150	P						0	1		<45			
McDaniel, Elmer		BR TR																									
1962	Thomasville	GFL	10	4	0	0	0	0	0	0	0	1	2	0.000	P	0	9	0	1.000	10	1	2	6.00	21	30	15	4
McDaniel, Ernest		BR TR																									
1942	Cordele	GFL	38	100	10	16	0	0	0	6	0	14	13	0.160	P	11	45	4	0.933	33	11	13	4.73	230	269	96	102
McDaniel, Joel		BL TR																									
1958	Valdosta	GFL	65	116	12	25	5	1	0	17	0	9	38	0.216	P	8	37	1	0.978	39	15	8	4.21	184	192	102	100
McDaniel, Kerry D.		BL TL																									
1962	Brunswick	GFL	75	215	31	50	7	1	9	37	3	32	71	0.233	1B, P	363	43	13	0.969	12	3	4	7.17	64	64	44	80
McDaniels, Donald "Don"		BR TR																									
1953	Douglas	GSL	22	78	11	15	1	2	0	10	0	17	17	0.192	3B	24	28	4	0.929								
McDermid, Douglas "Doug"		BR TR																									
1952	Vidalia	GSL	19	31	2	2	0	1	0	2	0	0	7	0.065	P	3	22	2	0.926	19	5	7	6.16	73	67	51	67
McDevitt, Daniel Eugene "Danny"		BL TL 5'10" 175 lbs b. 11/18/1932 New York, NY																									
1951	LaGrange	GAL	12	16	1	4	0	0	0	3	1	1	6	0.250	P	1	5	6	0.500								
McDevitt, Thomas "Tom"		BR TR																									
1956	Albany	GFL	82	314	70	103	14	3	2	41	7	65	30	0.328	2B	228	203	13	0.971								
McDonald, ---																											
1916	Anniston	GAL	35	136	10	31				1				0.228	C												
McDonald, ---																											
1929	Cedartown	GAL	9												P					9	3	2		54	64	12	24
1930	Talladega	GAL	2												P					2	0	1	6.75	8	15	6	2
McDonald, John		BL																									
1953	Cordele	GFL	3											0.091													
McDonald, Robert L. "Bob"		BR TR																									
1947	Cordele	GFL	33	134	23	43	7	1	0	16	0	11	9	0.321	2B	59	54	23	0.831								
1948	Douglas	GSL	46	171	12	40	2	0	0	14	0	2	4	0.234	2B, P	71	82	12	0.927	17	5	8	4.10	90	84	45	47
McDonald, Russell "Russ"		BR TR																									
1954	Americus-Cordele	GFL	6	8	0									0.000	P					6	0	4	<45				
1954	Sandersville	GSL	8	15		1								0.067	P					6	0	2	<45				
1955	Cordele	GFL	15	32	1	3	0	0	0	2	0	4	12	0.094	P	2	14	3	0.842	15	5	6	5.84	94	109	77	75
McDonough, ---																											
1929	Gadsden	GAL	12	42	4	15	3	0	0		1	5	8	0.357	2B	33	47	5	0.941								
McDougald, Julius		BS TR																									
1950	Tifton	GSL	33	99	34	22	1	1	1	5	7	50	27	0.222	3B	38	52	13	0.874								
McDuff, ---																											
1917	Anniston	GAL	5	20	2	6	0	1	0		0			0.300	3B, C	6	9	3	0.833								
McDuffie, ---																											
1915	Anniston	GAL	10	29	2	4	1	0	0					0.138	P	3	19	1	0.957	8	3	4					
McEnroe, James "Jim"		BR TR																									
1963	Waycross	GFL	3	2	0	0	0	0	0	0	0	0	2	0.000	P					3	0	1	12.86	7	9	2	8
McFadden, John		BR TR																									
1949	Newnan	GAL	37	87	9	16	1	0	0	9	1	5	15	0.184	P	4	31	4	0.897	37	21	9	2.55	244	196	180	99
McFadden, Ken		BR TR																									
1957	Albany	GFL	20	67	4	12	1	0	0	5	1	8	21	0.179	OF	22	4	1	0.963								
McFarland, ---																											
1914	Waycross	GSL		75	5	15	0	0	0		0			0.200													
McFarland, William "Bill"		BR TR																									
1947	Newnan	GAL	20	71	7	19	2	0	0	14	0	9	13	0.268	1B	188	6	4	0.980								
McFarlane, Alex																											
1936	Cordele	GFL	111	417	58	112	14	8	9	64	8			0.269	3B	129	230	42	0.895								
1937	Tallahassee	GFL	69	235	25	52	4	1	3	24	4	35	36	0.221	SS	99	164	34	0.886								
McFarlin, ---																											
1915	Brunswick	FLAG	32	91	3	15	1	0	0		1			0.165	OF, P	12	38	5	0.909	19	12	5		147	133	86	25
McGarity, Leslie "Les"		BL TR																									
1946	Tallassee(14) - Opelika(35)	GAL	49	182	18	54	6	0	5	27	0	11	12	0.297	C, P	218	32	4	0.984	3	1	0	0.00	16	14	11	8
1948	Vidalia-Lyons	GSL	68	245	37	63	10	0	0	29	2	31	22	0.257	C	314	44	19	0.950								
McGarr, David "Dave"		BL TL																									
1955	Cordele	GFL	1	0										0.000	P					1	0	0	<45				
McGee, Bob G.		BL TR																									
1954	Sandersville	GSL	129	504	99	154	25	17	16	111	9	55	57	0.306	3B, OF	266	36	27	0.918								
McGee, Wilson		BL TL																									
1941	Waycross	GFL	3												P					3	1	0	1.64	11	10	3	5
1942	Moultrie	GFL	26	62	6	13	1	0	0	7	0	2	13	0.210	P	1	31	3	0.914	27	9	8	4.34	141	195	55	48
1946	Newnan	GAL	29	70	2	11	1	0	0	4	1	1	9	0.157	P	9	33	1	0.977	29	13	10	4.06	186	196	117	44
McGhay, Gerald D.		BL TL																									
1954	Hazlehurst-Baxley	GSL	4	5		0								0.000	P					3	0	0	<45				
McGhee, Richard B. "Dick"																											
1949	Douglas	GSL	103	395	70	105	18	7	10	69	10	47	75	0.266	OF	152	13	10	0.943								
McGhee, Thomas "Tom"		BR TR																									
1950	Tallahassee	GFL	21	51	9	13	2	1	2	6	0	8	16	0.255	OF	25	3	2	0.933								

Georgia Class-D Minor League Baseball Encyclopedia

YR	TEAM	LG	G	AB	R	H	2B	3B	HR	RBI	SB	BB	SO	BA	POS	PO	A	E	FA	GP	W	L	ERA	IP	H	SO	BB
McGhee, William Mac "Bill" "Fibber"		BL TL 5'10" 185 lbs b. 09/05/1905 Shawmut, AL d. 03/10/1984 Decatur, GA																									
1929	Carrollton	GAL	61	222	26	69	9	2	0		2	14	19	0.311	OF	165	12	7	0.962								
1930	Carrollton	GAL	19	61	5	11	5	0	2		0	5	7	0.180	SS	24	26	12	0.806								
1930	Anniston	GAL	96	387	66	127	22	9	2		16	26	24	0.328	1B	976	25	11	0.989								
1951	Fitzgerald	GSL													M												
1954	Hazlehurst-Baxley	GSL													M												
McGhee, William Richard "Bill"		BR TR																									
1948	Douglas	GSL	54	194	14	55	20	1	0	30	0	11	34	0.284	3B, OF	67	20	9	0.906								
1950	Douglas(9) - Fitzgerald(87)	GSL	96	379	79	113	28	5	16	102	9	58	56	0.298	1B, OF	457	13	13	0.973								
1951	Fitzgerald(63) - Haz-Bax(64)	GSL	127	491	98	158	27	3	18	77	9	72	47	0.322	1B, OF	736	32	27	0.966								
1952	Hazlehurst-Baxley	GSL	115	463	112	156	37	5	25	118	27	63	53	0.337	OF	213	17	6	0.975								
1954	Hazlehurst-Baxley	GSL	48	167	40	52	14	3	5	32	5	41	14	0.311	3B, P	48	76	21	0.855	1	0	0	<45				
McGlade, ---																											
1917	Tri-Cities	GAL	16	57	12	16	3	2	2		1			0.281	2B	45	38	10	0.892								
McGovern, Russell D. "Russ"		BL TR																									
1947	Albany	GFL	128	428	74	106	16	10	1	38	24	99	64	0.248	OF	263	17	12	0.959								
1953	Albany	GFL	132	479	133	131	22	6	0	52	23	131	34	0.273	M, OF	322	17	6	0.983								
1954	Albany	GFL	134	474	88	122	18	6	1	39	15	87	45	0.257	M, OF	331	12	8	0.977								
McGowan, Frank		BR																									
1953	Vidalia	GSL	7											0.154													
McGowen, Tullis Earl "Mickey"		BL TL 6'2" 200 lbs b. 11/26/1921 Dothan, AL																									
1941	Waycross	GFL	32	95	6	15	1	0	0	7	1	6	40	0.158	P	7	37	4	0.917	31	14	14	2.73	251	211	180	75
McGrath, John		BL TR																									
1950	Tallahassee	GFL	32	52	9	10	0	0	0	4	0	10	19	0.192	P	3	38	3	0.932	29	9	4	4.80	122	106	89	94
McGrath, Michael "Mike"		BR TR																									
1958	Dublin	GFL	10	8	0	1	0	0	0	0	0	1	5	0.125	P	0	3	0	1.000	10	2	1	4.64	33	29	25	18
McGravy, Hoyt		BL TL																									
1952	Waycross	GFL	94	346	43	95	16	6	5	46	2	23	64	0.275	OF	130	6	8	0.944								
1953	Waycross	GFL	79	281	28	70	12	3	1	37	2	31	51	0.249	OF	102	3	11	0.905								
1953	Douglas	GSL	38	147	23	49	9	0	3	25	2	13	16	0.333	OF	49	5	8	0.871								
McGraw, Willie		BR																									
1954	Sandersville	GSL	3	10		3								0.300													
McGreal, James "Jimmy"		BR																									
1940	Albany	GFL	<10																								
McGue, Donald "Don"		BR TR																									
1958	Brunswick	GFL	7	8		1								0.125	P					4	0	2	<30				
McGuire, Edward P. "Ed"		BR TR																									
1953	Brunswick	GFL	5											0.000	P					0	0		<45				
McGuire, Forrest		BR																									
1955	Tifton	GFL	17	35	6	7	0	0	1	3	0	1	10	0.200													
McIntyre, James "Jim"		BR TR																									
1955	Hazlehurst-Baxley	GSL	11	33	1	4	0	0	1	6	1	2	19	0.121	3B	21	12	8	0.805								
McIntyre, Samuel "Sam"		BR TR																									
1956	Hazlehurst-Baxley	GSL	34	70	7	17	2	2	0	4	0	5	26	0.243	P	8	46	8	0.871	31	10	14	4.29	174	180	110	125
1957	Albany	GFL	54	102	17	23	3	1	0	12	1	10	32	0.225	P	3	23	2	0.929	31	12	5	3.79	107	90	64	75
McKay, F.S.																											
1929	Talladega	GAL	11	31	1	5	1	0	0		0	1	3	0.161	P	2	17	2	0.905	11	4	7		82	98	21	25
1930	Talladega	GAL	15	33	1	5	1	0	0		0	3	6	0.152	P	4	28	1	0.970	15	5	6	4.59	100	122	36	32
McKay, Richard "Dick"		BR TR																									
1949	Americus	GFL	39	68	7	8	0	0	0	3	0	6	44	0.118	P	6	29	6	0.854	39	7	8	5.59	174	199	121	127
McKay, Roy		BR TL																									
1953	Douglas	GSL	33	70	6	11	3	0	0	10	0	1	18	0.157	P	4	21	4	0.862	32	11	6	6.08	154	148	140	140
McKee, Arthur "Art"		BL TL																									
1957	Brunswick	GFL	24	39	7	7	0	0	0	2	0	6	9	0.179	P	2	14	5	0.762	19	8	6	4.82	97	89	83	67
1958	Brunswick	GFL	34	53	8	16	2	0	0	5	0	4	8	0.302	P	8	21	3	0.906	24	4	5	4.50	94	115	64	56
McKenna, Robert "Bob"		BR TR																									
1950	Tifton	GSL	27	88	6	19	3	0	1	8	1	6	20	0.216	3B	18	28	6	0.885								
McKenney, William "Bill"		BR TR																									
1948	Albany(32) - Moultrie(4)	GFL	36	124	14	23	5	2	2	16	2	17	27	0.185	OF	47	3	0	1.000								
McKenzie, Sherwood		BL TL																									
1935	Thomasville	GFL	71	246	39	71	10	1	1		6	17	13	0.289	P					31	9	12		183	161	101	97
1936	Thomasville	GFL	27	95	13	30	1	1	1	8	6			0.316	1B	210	12	8	0.965								
1937	Thomasville	GFL	80	292	32	84	8	3	1	40	1	33	13	0.288	1B, P	704	43	10	0.987	7	3	3	3.42	50	55	13	15
1938	Thomasville	GFL	119	475	70	146	20	6	2	89	4	36	25	0.307	1B, P	145	25	7	0.960	8	4	0	4.73	40	50	12	17
1939	Thomasville	GFL	136	551	73	167	23	5	6	75	9	42	18	0.303	OF, P	163	15	10	0.947	6	2	3	5.08	39	46	20	11
1940	Thomasville	GFL	112	460	82	174	23	7	4	97	16	39	18	0.378	OF	182	20	13	0.940								
McKenzie, William																											
1935	Thomasville	GFL	32	77	2	13	2	0	0		0	0	30	0.169	IF	440	32	10	0.979								
McKenzie, William J. "Bill"																											
1936	Tallahassee	GFL	16	38	3	4	1	0	1	6	0			0.105	P					16	3	5	3.97	93		37	50
McKeon, William J. "Bill"		BR TR																									
1957	Waycross	GFL	68	254	35	83	16	0	3	45	1	14	35	0.327	C	326	31	9	0.975								
McKinley, Peter "Pete"																											
1935	Panama City	GFL	13	31	1	6	1	0	0		0	2	11	0.194	P					14	5	5		75	88	29	40
McKinley, Thomas M. "Tom"																											
1937	Albany	GFL	24	69	6	15	1	0	0	10	0	13	9	0.217	C	103	12	3	0.975								

Georgia Class-D Minor League Baseball Encyclopedia

YR	TEAM	LG	G	AB	R	H	2B	3B	HR	RBI	SB	BB	SO	BA	POS	PO	A	E	FA	GP	W	L	ERA	IP	H	SO	BB
McKinney, ---																											
1928	Lindale - Carrollton	GAL	41	148	17	42	9	1	2		5	4	10	0.284	C	174	27	9	0.957								
McKinney, Clarence		BR TR																									
1950	Tifton	GSL	106	439	63	116	28	6	2	84	4	27	25	0.264	OF	221	5	6	0.974								
McKinney, Heaford		BR TR																									
1953	Albany	GFL	137	480	98	152	28	12	4	95	13	138	76	0.317	OF	286	13	13	0.958								
McKinney, William "Bill"		BR TR																									
1947	Alexander City	GAL	34	111	6	15	1	0	0	4	0	2	32	0.135	C	141	19	3	0.982								
McKinnon, Bill																											
1920	Carrollton	GSL		25	4	7	0	0	0		0			0.280	P												
McKinstay, John		BR TR																									
1955	Waycross	GFL	15	33	8	7	0	0	0	1	0	4	8	0.212	P	1	16	0	1.000	15	5	4	3.56	86	86	24	25
McKnight, ---																											
1906	Americus	GSL													P												
McLaughlin, ---																											
1928	Talladega	GAL	15	39	4	8	0	1	0		0	1	10	0.205	P	20	28	4	0.923	13	6	5	3.45	94	100	31	22
1929	Gadsden	GAL	19	35	1	2	0	1	0		0	0	10	0.057	P	4	19	1	0.958	16	1	7		77	103	23	29
McLaughlin, Edward																											
1920	Griffin	GSL													SS												
1921	Griffin	GSL													SS												
McLaughlin, Patrick "Pat"		BL TR																									
1952	Dublin	GSL	49	175	35	44	10	2	5	31	9	26	29	0.251	OF	63	5	5	0.932								
McLean, Charles		BS TL																									
1948	Albany	GFL	103	405	74	106	21	13	2	55	5	44	133	0.262	OF	167	14	12	0.938								
McLean, Harvey		BR																									
1953	Eastman	GSL	4											0.000													
McLean, John D.		BR TL																									
1953	Thomasville	GFL	23	41	2	3	0	0	0	0	0	4	22	0.073	P	10	19	3	0.906	23	9	6	4.11	116	97	48	103
1954	Thomasville	GFL	6	4		0								0.000	P					6	0	3	<45				
McLemore, Roy		BR TR																									
1952	Thomasville	GFL	46	116	17	23	1	0	0	10	0	8	9	0.198	P	5	35	4	0.909	37	20	11	2.14	273	271	99	77
1953	Valdosta	GFL	21	35	6	5	1	0	0	4	0	8	6	0.143	P	5	15	1	0.952	21	3	10	4.43	138	148	57	31
McLendon, ---																											
1913	Cordele	ESL	64	238	15	59	8	2	0					0.248	3B	100	133	30	0.886								
McLennan, Donald "Don"		BL TR																									
1953	Hazlehurst-Baxley	GSL	97	350	63	121	14	4	5	71	11	38	19	0.346	OF, P	132	22	10	0.939	16	5	5	4.82	84	89	55	56
McLeod, George		BR TR																									
1953	Fitzgerald	GFL	14	27	2	8	0	0	1	4	0	1	9	0.296	P					9	1	7	6.45	53	59	28	46
1954	Douglas	GSL	19	29	4	4	0	0	2	2	0	0	16	0.138	P	3	12	2	0.882	17	2	4	7.39	67	67	38	73
McLeod, James William "Jim"		BR TR																									
1948	LaGrange	GAL	23	43	4	7	0	0	0	6	1	2	10	0.163	P	7	14	0	1.000	21	6	6	4.19	101	81	86	109
McLeod, Peter "Pete"		BR TR																									
1948	Newnan	GAL	30	106	14	28	3	0	0	17	2	22	10	0.264	OF	53	1	5	0.915								
McLin, ---																											
1914	Opelika	GAL	50												OF	94	14	11	0.908								
McMahon, James "Jim"		BR TR																									
1946	Cordele	GFL	42	71	6	9	0	0	0	4	0	2	24	0.127	P	11	63	4	0.949	42	5	15	4.01	202	221	101	83
McMahon, Michael "Mike"		BR TR																									
1951	Fitzgerald	GSL	11	12	1	2	0	0	0	0	0	2	6	0.167	P	2	9	2	0.846								
McMannus, ---																											
1913	Waycross	ESL	25	53	2	13	0	0	0					0.245	P	11	44	2	0.965	11	5	6					
McManus, Joseph "Joe"		BR TR																									
1951	Rome	GAL	41	98	18	28	2	0	1	12	0	9	10	0.286	P	6	42	1	0.980	31	16	5	5.77	184	215	75	78
McMasters, Omer		BR TR																									
1954	Statesboro	GSL	4	4		0								0.000	P					4	0	0	<45				
McMillan, Frank V.		BR TR																									
1946	Moultrie	GFL	60	240	47	67	12	6	0	34	2	40	29	0.279	OF	99	11	6	0.948								
McMillan, Norman Alexis "Norm" "Bub"		BR TR 6'0" 175 lbs b. 10/05/1895 Latta, SC d. 09/28/1969 Marion, SC																									
1914	Valdosta	GSL		106	14	32	6	3	0		6			0.302													
1915	Valdosta	FLAG	60	226	32	68	14	2	5		13			0.301	OF	126	9	3	0.978								
McMillan, Robert "Bob"		BR																									
1956	Thomson	GSL	3	4		0								0.000													
McMullen, Donald "Don"		BR TR																									
1957	Fitzgerald	GFL	17	61	5	12	1	0	2	11	2	14	24	0.197	2B	28	22	3	0.943								
McMullen, G.																											
1939	Albany	GFL													P								<45				
McMullen, Tom E.		BL TR																									
1954	Thomasville	GFL	21	46	5	9	0	0	0	2	0	5	11	0.196	P	6	31	0	1.000	20	8	8	2.18	136	102	103	57
McMullin, Dale		BL TR																									
1955	Thomasville	GFL	124	435	67	125	24	2	12	79	4	84	43	0.287	1B	934	61	30	0.971								
McNair, Ralph																											
1937	Moultrie	GFL	76	265	31	74	8	1	2	32	4	26	33	0.279	C	320	50	11	0.971								

Georgia Class-D Minor League Baseball Encyclopedia

YR	TEAM	LG	G	AB	R	H	2B	3B	HR	RBI	SB	BB	SO	BA	POS	PO	A	E	FA	GP	W	L	ERA	IP	H	SO	BB
McNally, Donald J. "Don"		BR TR																									
1950	Tallahassee	GFL	138	513	104	127	24	8	6	64	17	107	107	0.248	SS	225	368	77	0.885								
1951	Brunswick	GFL	95	348	81	93	19	4	2	33	18	102	42	0.267	2B, SS	207	279	37	0.929								
1953	Brunswick	GFL	30	95	15	17	2	0	1	6	0	19	15	0.179	SS, P	38	63	9	0.918		1	0	<45				
1954	Brunswick	GFL	82	304	47	66	15	2	3	40	6	46	45	0.217	2B, SS, P	145	217	30	0.923	7	1	1	<45				
McNally, James W. "Jim"																											
1936	Thomasville	GFL	29	88	10	20	2	1	1	5	4			0.227	1B	184	3	6	0.969								
McNamara, Charles																											
1949	Hazlehurst-Baxley	GSL	19	72	10	12	2	0	1	6	0	10	16	0.167	OF	31	5	4	0.900								
McNamee, William "Bill"		BR TL																									
1963	Brunswick	GFL	6	7	0	1	0	0	0	0	0	0	6	0.143	P					5	1	1	1.96	23	11	22	4
McNease, Harry																											
1949	Fitzgerald	GSL	12	43	3	7	3	0	0	1	1	8	14	0.163	2B	27	21	4	0.923								
McNeely, Robert "Bob"		BR TR																									
1954	Sandersville	GSL	94	354	53	86	19	3	6	50	2	36	40	0.243	1B, OF	578	24	24	0.962								
McNeil, William "Bill"		BL TR																									
1956	Valdosta	GFL	50	91	25	21	4	0	0	12	0	33	23	0.231	OF, P	30	26	4	0.933	28	20	4	2.70	190	155	139	57
McNulty, Edwin A. "Ed"		BR TR																									
1954	Valdosta	GFL	28	47	5	8	0	0	0	4	2	11	18	0.170	P	8	29	1	0.974	26	6	10	4.25	127	127	66	48
McNulty, James E. "Jim"		BR TR																									
1947	Valdosta	GFL	125	457	63	111	9	8	0	36	9	54	110	0.243	2B, SS	372	441	24	0.971								
McNulty, John S.		BR TR																									
1947	Waycross	GFL	114	466	80	129	28	2	4	63	9	59	32	0.277	SS	177	264	53	0.893								
McPartland, Douglas "Doug"		BR TR																									
1953	Tifton	GFL	7											0.286	P						0	1	<45				
1953	Statesboro - Sandersville	GSL	3											0.000	P						0	1	<45				
McPherson, Roger		BR TR																									
1952	Vidalia	GSL	81	307	33	70	13	1	1	39	4	28	59	0.228	1B	654	40	21	0.971								
McPherson, Ronald "Ron"		BR TR																									
1952	Eastman	GSL	20	73	10	19	2	1	0	3	2	5	10	0.260	OF	32	3	4	0.897								
McPherson, Thurman "Tom"																											
1939	Cordele	GFL	16	27	2	6	0	0	0	2	0	2	11	0.222	P	0	14	4	0.778	12	5	3	4.62	76	93	21	43
McQuaig, Gerald Joseph "Jerry"		BR TR 5'11" 183 lbs b. 01/31/1912 Douglas, GA d. 02/05/2001 Buford, GA																									
1935	Americus	GFL	29	105	20	30	11	0	2		2	19	13	0.286	OF	46	1	2	0.959								
1936	Moultrie	GFL	42	148	28	40	5	3	3	20	10			0.270	OF	115	5	3	0.976								
McQuillen, Jack W.																											
1942	Americus	GFL	73	290	42	63	12	5	0	25	10	34	22	0.217	OF	164	36	9	0.957								
McRae, James "Jim"		BR TR																									
1946	Thomasville	GFL	31	89	6	18	3	1	0	10	0	7	22	0.202	OF	21	3	4	0.857								
McRae, William "Bill"		BR TR																									
1946	LaGrange(17) - Newnan(21)	GAL	38	116	12	16	4	0	1	6	0	7	35	0.138	3B	18	25	5	0.896								
McSwain, Cliff																											
1930	Huntsville	GAL	34	147	43	57	12	5	4		3	7	8	0.388	OF	65	12	5	0.939								
McTaggert, Charles		BR TR																									
1948	Alexander City	GAL	22	32	1	5	0	0	0	2	0	3	9	0.156	P	6	15	0	1.000	23	8	3	3.86	84	80	38	47
1949	Alexander City	GAL	28	59	4	8	0	0	0	1	1	1	18	0.136	P	4	28	1	0.970	26	9	7	3.16	154	160	76	80
McVay, Francis M. "Frosty"		BR TR																									
1938	Tallahassee	GFL	121	493	72	137	19	8	4	82	14	30	41	0.278	3B	182	199	56	0.872								
1939	Cordele	GFL	132	510	74	134	14	2	0	59	13	44	59	0.263	SS	222	325	42	0.929								
1940	Tallahassee	GFL	106	460	62	114	14	10	2	62	7	33	29	0.248	2B	284	251	38	0.934								
1941	Thomasville	GFL	127	529	82	170	29	10	1	87	9	37	40	0.321	2B	322	373	55	0.927								
1942	Moultrie	GFL	120	442	68	130	30	3	2	73	7	39	39	0.294	M, 2B	282	360	37	0.946								
McWhorter, Marcus		BR TL																									
1947	Griffin	GAL	22	44	2	5	1	0	0	1	0	0	13	0.114	P	6	16	2	0.917	21	8	7	4.15	115	140	55	39
1948	Valley	GAL	35	91	11	16	0	0	0	6	0	12	24	0.176	P	1	13	3	0.824	34	14	13	3.01	221	242	88	38
McWhorter, Pierce		BR TR																									
1947	Waycross	GFL	96	292	57	73	15	2	2	49	3	54	47	0.250	C	560	58	14	0.978								
Meaders, Elden		BR																									
1940	Moultrie	GFL	<10																								
Meador, Robert J. "Bob"		BR TR																									
1951	Waycross	GFL	68	269	52	75	11	4	2	35	39	24	49	0.279	OF	159	8	10	0.944								
Meadows, Donald G. "Don"		BR TR																									
1957	Valdosta	GFL	137	460	74	108	15	1	8	88	16	103	55	0.235	SS, OF	246	273	37	0.933								
Meadows, Herman		BR TR																									
1948	Fitzgerald	GSL	9												P					9	5	1	3.24	50	46	18	17
1949	Fitzgerald - Sparta	GSL	33	71	11	15	1	0	0	11	0	20	19	0.211	P	13	25	0	1.000	35	10	14	5.45	180	134	77	79
Meadows, John		BR TR																									
1951	Rome	GAL	21	51	10	12	1	1	0	6	1	2	4	0.235	P	8	27	2	0.946	19	8	4	4.42	114	108	55	79
Meads, Charles		BR TR																									
1950	Opelika	GAL	24	67	11	12	0	0	0	3	0	23	21	0.179	2B	41	32	2	0.973								
Meagher, Robert D. "Bob"		BR TR																									
1953	Cordele	GFL	32	55	2	6	1	0	0	4	0	4	23	0.109	P	13	30	8	0.843	32	3	15	9.69	170	173	88	147
Meder, Richard "Dick"		BR TR																									
1954	Douglas	GSL	14	16	3	5	1	0	0	0	0	2	2	0.313	P	3	7	1	0.909	14	2	3	6.30	50	62	31	24

Georgia Class-D Minor League Baseball Encyclopedia

YR	TEAM	LG	G	AB	R	H	2B	3B	HR	RBI	SB	BB	SO	BA	POS	PO	A	E	FA	GP	W	L	ERA	IP	H	SO	BB
Mediamolle, Frank		BL																									
1940	Albany	GFL	<10																								
1942	Waycross	GFL	126	474	63	117	14	7	0	82	9	80	32	0.247	1B	1186	67	10	0.992								
Medley, Carl		BR TR																									
1953	Jesup	GSL	124	511	97	154	29	4	23	129	6	42	50	0.301	OF, C	254	24	15	0.949								
Medlin, James "Jim"		BR																									
1955	Tifton	GFL	4	8		1								0.125													
Medlock, ---																											
1913	Waycross - Valdosta	ESL	79	279	36	70	16	3	4					0.251	OF	141	24	9	0.948								
1914	Valdosta	GSL		381	48	116	26	10	6		14			0.304													
1915	Valdosta	FLAG	59	214	32	67	9	7	2		3			0.313	OF	108	6	5	0.958								
Medlock, Frank		BR TR																									
1946	Opelika	GAL	<10																								
1947	Tallassee	GAL	64	206	25	37	8	1	1	19	3	34	29	0.180	C	277	52	5	0.985								
Mee, Joseph "Joe"		BR TR																									
1955	Valdosta	GFL	6	6		3								0.500	P					6	1	1		<45			
Meekins, Dennis		BR TR																									
1954	Dublin	GSL	127	507	111	142	21	5	8	83	37	79	57	0.280	3B	159	265	31	0.932								
1955	Dublin	GSL	83	313	38	70	9	0	1	37	14	38	36	0.224	3B	105	137	17	0.934								
Meeres, Gordon		BR																									
1950	Valdosta	GFL	25	66	5	14	1	0	0	3	0	3	12	0.212													
Mehrens, Wallace																											
1941	Americus	GFL	16	28	5	5	0	0	0	1	0	2	10	0.179	P	3	20	1	0.958	16	3	6	5.14	77	89	57	36
Meier, John R.		BR TR																									
1953	Dublin	GSL	13	53	7	10	1	0	0	4	1	6	3	0.189	1B	116	7	2	0.984								
Meka, Mark		BR TR																									
1963	Waycross	GFL	32	107	9	16	2	0	1	8	1	8	24	0.150	2B	50	55	8	0.929								
Melanson, Marvin "Marv"		BR TR																									
1954	Valdosta	GFL	29	69	11	11	1	1	0	6	0	12	18	0.159	P	8	32	6	0.870	28	14	11	2.63	205	174	205	88
Melbert, William "Bill"		BR TR																									
1955	Statesboro	GSL	11	14	3	3	1	0	0	2	0	2	5	0.214	P	2	5	0	1.000	10	1	4	8.50	36	47	18	32
Mellinger, James "Jim"		BL TL																									
1948	Tallassee	GAL	48	116	12	34	5	0	2	21	1	9	26	0.293	P	12	32	4	0.917	26	9	8	3.70	163	163	100	100
Mello, Edward "Ed"		BL TL																									
1963	Moultrie	GFL	21	26	3	2	0	0	0	0	0	1	15	0.077	P	2	11	4	0.765	21	2	5	4.20	75	76	74	62
Melton, Clifford George "Cliff"		BL TL 6'5" 203 lbs b. 01/03/1912 Brevard, NC d. 07/28/1986 Baltimore, MD																									
1954	Americus-Cordele	GFL	17	16	0	6	2	0	0	2	0	0	4	0.375	M												
Melton, Gary		BL																									
1957	Thomasville	GFL	9	18		0								0.000													
Melton, Raymond "Ray"		BR TR																									
1938	Cordele	GFL	15	44	4	8	0	0	0	3	0	5	13	0.182	3B	16	38	2	0.964								
1939	Waycross	GFL	23	45	4	3	0	0	0	1	1	5	17	0.067	C	43	9	5	0.912								
1946	LaGrange	GAL	<10																								
1947	LaGrange	GAL	48	166	23	39	3	2	0	23	9	21	29	0.235	3B	55	84	19	0.880								
Melton, Reuben Franklin "Rube"		BR TR 6'5" 205 lbs b. 02/27/1917 Cramerton, NC d. 09/11/1971 Greer, SC																									
1937	Albany	GFL	27	64	6	18	4	0	1	10	0	5	11	0.281	P	6	29	1	0.972	25	6	11	4.01	166	164	97	89
Melvin, ---		BR																									
1946	Newnan	GAL	<10																								
Mena, Ignacio M.		BR TR																									
1953	Dublin(13) - Sandersville(51)	GSL	64	228	47	66	10	3	6	40	2	50	43	0.289	3B, OF	99	29	11	0.921								
Menapace, Edwin "Ed"		BR TR																									
1952	Statesboro	GSL	47	168	23	53	5	1	8	40	1	20	13	0.315	C	237	35	8	0.971								
1953	Tifton	GFL	3											0.333													
1953	Statesboro(17) - Vidalia(55)	GSL	72	262	39	67	15	2	8	40	1	35	24	0.256	3B, C	214	51	17	0.940								
Mendillo, Anthony		BR																									
1946	Thomasville	GFL	<10																								
Mendler, David "Dave"		BR																									
1956	Valdosta	GFL	1	1		0								0.000													
Mendoza, Raymond "Ray"																											
1949	Dublin	GSL	105	400	73	102	23	7	7	59	12	53	75	0.255	1B	894	58	25	0.974								
Menig, Samuel "Sam"		BL TR																									
1948	Moultrie	GFL	98	258	36	65	4	1	0	34	4	68	43	0.252	C	429	41	17	0.965								
Menkel, Kenneth "Ken"		BL TL																									
1956	Tifton	GFL	24	43	7	10	4	0	1	10	0	8	6	0.233	OF, P	27	4	4	0.886	5	0	3		<45			
Menna, Frank		BL TL																									
1954	Vidalia	GSL	81	261	52	72	14	4	5	52	3	59	48	0.276	OF	102	8	9	0.924								
1958	Dublin	GFL	57	185	26	51	11	2	3	34	9	45	32	0.276	OF	79	3	3	0.965								
Merandi, Eugene "Gene"		BR TR																									
1952	Albany	GFL	139	514	61	117	27	5	4	62	12	58	68	0.228	SS	261	460	61	0.922								
Mercer, ---																											
1906	Columbus	GSL													P, OF												
Mercier, Ronald "Ron"		BR TR																									
1963	Waycross	GFL	40	91	11	16	2	0	1	11	0	13	23	0.176	3B	30	46	11	0.874								

Georgia Class-D Minor League Baseball Encyclopedia

YR	TEAM	LG	G	AB	R	H	2B	3B	HR	RBI	SB	BB	SO	BA	POS	PO	A	E	FA	GP	W	L	ERA	IP	H	SO	BB
Merget, John		BR TR																									
1950	Vidalia-Lyons	GSL	36	77	5	12	4	0	0	8	0	7	27	0.156	P	10	43	4	0.930	36	7	18	4.85	204	236	82	95
1951	Cordele	GFL	24	46	2	10	3	0	0	2	0	3	13	0.217	P	1	29	1	0.968	24	6	9	4.01	119	114	67	62
Meriwether, Conklyn Wells "Al"		BL TL 6'0" 189 lbs b. 06/19/1918 Island Grove, FL																									
1954	Valdosta	GFL	38	135	19	30	3	1	6	26	1	22	18	0.222	1B	299	27	6	0.982								
Merlob, Robert "Bob"		BL TL																									
1956	Hazlehurst-Baxley	GSL	12	11	0	1	0	0	0	0	0	0	4	0.091	P	1	8	0	1.000	12	2	3	3.34	35	36	24	29
Merrigan, Walter "Walt"		BR TR																									
1956	Thomasville	GFL	1	1		0								0.000	P					1	0	0	<45				
Mertz, James Verlin "Jim"		BR TR 5'10" 170 lbs b. 08/10/1916 Lima, OH																									
1939	Waycross	GFL	29	50	6	8	0	0	0	0	0	10	17	0.160	P	7	27	5	0.872	26	8	7	3.00	168	155	107	89
Messina, Dino		BR TR																									
1955	Brunswick	GFL	70	256	29	49	1	1	0	15	9	24	34	0.191	OF	88	6	4	0.959								
1956	Dublin	GSL	22	81	17	17	2	1	0	4	5	17	4	0.210	OF	23	3	3	0.897								
Metheny, Arthur Beauregard "Bud"		BL TL 5'11" 190 lbs b. 06/01/1915 St. Louis, MO																									
1948	Baxley	GSL	85	291	44	91	20	3	7	48	5	50	8	0.313	M, 1B	610	30	9	0.986								
Methvin, ---																											
1915	Newnan	GAL	<6												P					<6							
1916	Griffin	GAL	4	10	0	2					0			0.200													
Meyer, Gary		BR TR																									
1956	Albany	GFL	13	36	2	7	0	0	0	3	0	2	13	0.194	OF	5	0	0	1.000								
1956	Hazlehurst-Baxley	GSL	15	55	4	9	0	0	0	1	1	4	16	0.164	OF	13	1	4	0.778								
Meyer, Russell J. "Russ"		BR TR																									
1962	Brunswick	GFL	25	51	2	4	0	0	0	4	0	3	21	0.078	P	10	17	3	0.900	24	6	10	5.29	131	152	103	72
1963	Brunswick	GFL	14	15	2	2	0	0	0	0	0	1	8	0.133	P	3	3	2	0.750	14	2	5	4.42	53	53	43	18
Meyer, William "Bill"		BR TR																									
1955	Thomasville	GFL	2	1		0								0.000	P					2	0	0	<45				
Miali, James "Jim"		BL TL																									
1963	Thomasville	GFL	16	55	12	11	1	0	1	3	4	12	17	0.200	OF	34	3	0	1.000								
Miarka, Stanley "Stan"		BR TR																									
1953	Fitzgerald(4) - Tifton(23)	GFL	27	79	12	15	3	1	0	9	2	13	21	0.190	3B	19	38	7	0.891								
Michael, J.E.																											
1950	Opelika	GAL	16	63	11	15	0	1	0	6	1	4	9	0.238	OF	25	2	3	0.900								
Michaels, William "Bill"		BR TR																									
1946	Albany	GFL	3												P					3	0	0	0.00	9			
Micham, Jerry		BR TR																									
1956	Douglas	GSL	114	422	65	116	15	9	4	77	6	47	64	0.275	OF	225	11	21	0.918								
Michel, Harold		BR TR																									
1938	Albany	GFL	110	408	74	133	23	3	1	66	8	26	14	0.326	C	528	83	9	0.985								
1939	Albany	GFL	70	231	28	73	7	1	0	29	8	24	7	0.316	C	331	36	10	0.973								
Micheli, Robert "Bob"		BR TR																									
1956	Dublin	GSL	47	137	12	29	0	0	1	7	0	25	32	0.212	C	260	48	13	0.960								
Michelson, Warren		BR TR																									
1950	Valdosta	GFL	13	11	0	2	0	0	0	1	0	1	2	0.182	P	0	12	1	0.923								
Mickle, ---																											
1917	Anniston	GAL	10	24	4	7	0	0	0		1			0.292	OF, P	4	11	0	1.000	7	2	2		32	31	16	6
Middiknight (Mitternacht), ---																											
1914	Americus	GSL		154	24	29	2	3	2		12			0.188													
1915	Americus-Gainesville	FLAG	19	63	5	16	1	0	0		4			0.254	2B, P	43	32	5	0.938	0							
1915	Rome	GAL	14	48	2	5	2	0	0					0.104	3B	14	28	7	0.857								
Middlebrooks, ---																											
1906	Americus	GSL													OF												
Midgette, W. Dennis		BR TR																									
1958	Thomasville	GFL	16	23	4	6	2	0	0	2	0	2	8	0.261	P	1	9	2	0.833	16	2	7	11.34	50	62	30	78
Miehoff, Sol																											
1939	Cordele	GFL	118	471	60	134	22	6	1	44	11	42	64	0.285	OF	203	16	7	0.969								
Mihal, Ronald "Ron"		BS TL																									
1957	Waycross	GFL	43	146	23	29	4	1	1	8	7	36	37	0.199	OF	81	6	3	0.967								
Mihalik, Michael "Mickey"		BR TR																									
1946	Tallassee	GAL	13	20	1	1	0	0	0	0	0	1	9	0.050	P	0	10	0	1.000	12	2	4	3.88	58	53	36	37
1948	Newnan	GAL	37	90	7	11	2	0	0	4	0	7	24	0.122	P	6	32	3	0.927	34	15	14	3.47	223	201	214	149
Mikesell, Maurice		BR TR																									
1948	Americus	GFL	12	42	8	7	0	1	0	3	1	12	7	0.167	SS	25	33	3	0.951								
Mikulski, Robert "Stan"		BR TR																									
1952	Dublin	GSL	20	74	6	15	4	0	0	9	0	8	27	0.203	3B	21	33	7	0.885								
Milam, Lawrence		BL																									
1947	Cordele	GFL	10	30	3	4	1	0	0	0	0	5	9	0.133													
Milcsik, Ray																											
1941	Cordele	GFL	28	88	10	16	1	3	0	8	1	19	26	0.182	SS	44	87	18	0.879								
1942	Cordele	GFL	12	48	5	5	1	1	0	2	1	7	6	0.104	SS	20	42	7	0.899								
Miles, Jerry		BL TR																									
1956	Thomson	GSL	26	46	4	6	0	0	0	0	9	12	0.130	P	3	27	3	0.909	26	7	6	3.82	125	127	69	69	
Miles, R.L.																											
1916	Anniston	GAL	19	66	0	11					0			0.167	C												

Georgia Class-D Minor League Baseball Encyclopedia

YR	TEAM	LG	G	AB	R	H	2B	3B	HR	RBI	SB	BB	SO	BA	POS	PO	A	E	FA	GP	W	L	ERA	IP	H	SO	BB
Millard, John		BR TR																									
1948	Newnan	GAL	126	456	80	120	21	15	4	62	12	68	79	0.263	SS	266	395	47	0.934								
1949	Newnan	GAL	124	462	80	135	20	8	5	81	9	70	41	0.292	SS	258	326	61	0.905								
Miller, ---																											
1914	Waycross	GSL		19	2	3	0	0	0		0			0.158													
Miller, ---																											
1916	Griffin	GAL	21	83	13	28				4				0.337													
1917	Griffin	GAL	16	62	8	16	3	0	0	8				0.258	OF, 3B	20	17	2	0.949								
Miller, Barry		BL TL																									
1962	Dublin	GFL	6	8	1	1	0	0	0	0	0	0	6	0.125	P					6	2	2	3.54	28	22	24	19
1963	Waycross	GFL	19	30	3	6	0	0	0	3	1	5	17	0.200	P	5	15	1	0.952	19	5	8	3.54	94	83	63	43
Miller, Charles E.		BR TR																									
1948	Alexander City	GAL	15	56	10	12	4	0	0	11	2	3	7	0.214	C	68	6	2	0.974								
Miller, Dan																											
1920	LaGrange	GSL													2B												
Miller, Dean R.		BR TR																									
1953	Brunswick	GFL	35	113	19	30	4	0	1	19	0	19	11	0.265	2B, P	60	46	7	0.938		0	0	<45				
Miller, Donald "Don"		BR TR																									
1956	Brunswick	GFL	37	88	8	12	0	0	0	6	0	7	26	0.136	P	11	51	7	0.899	35	15	15	3.74	238	210	203	180
Miller, Edward "Eddie"																											
1956	Tifton	GFL													M												
Miller, Edward A. "Ed"		BR																									
1954	Douglas	GSL	9	35		5								0.143													
Miller, Francis "Frank"		BR TR																									
1935	Tallahassee	GFL	47	162	23	40	14	4	2		1	18	25	0.247	IF	431	19	7	0.985								
1940	Americus	GFL	79	300	36	93	15	6	0	47	3	25	34	0.310	OF, IF	144	34	9	0.952								
Miller, Franklin "Frank"		BR TR																									
1952	Vidalia	GSL	13	17	2	4	1	0	0	2	0	0	7	0.235	P	0	6	0	1.000								
Miller, Gerald		BR TR																									
1954	Albany(29) - Waycross(28)	GFL	57	172	27	34	5	3	0	17	2	24	40	0.198	3B, SS	59	85	17	0.894								
Miller, Gibbs		BR																									
1947	Moultrie	GFL	14	33	6	8	2	0	1	2	0	5	4	0.242													
Miller, Glenn E.		BL TR																									
1956	Tifton	GFL	136	515	113	127	22	4	4	58	20	129	59	0.247	2B	308	372	39	0.946								
Miller, Harold																											
1941	Cordele	GFL	57	123	12	22	0	2	0	10	1	10	37	0.179	P	14	45	9	0.868	36	13	15	4.26	228	253	93	109
Miller, Howard																											
1941	Americus	GFL	6	14	0	2	0	0	0	0	0	0	5	0.143	P	3	11	1	0.933	6	3	1	3.41	37	35	16	10
Miller, Joseph "Joe"		BR TR																									
1955	Statesboro	GSL	64	244	50	78	16	3	12	60	5	39	25	0.320	OF, C	190	18	13	0.941								
Miller, Kenneth E. "Ken"																											
1936	Albany	GFL	108	403	47	99	13	8	4	43	28			0.246	OF	206	28	22	0.914								
Miller, Pinkie																											
1939	Americus	GFL	53	185	26	59	7	1	1	29	1	19	20	0.319	OF	79	1	1	0.988								
Miller, Ray																											
1942	Albany	GFL	44	191	26	44	9	1	0	19	2	17	35	0.230	2B	128	101	21	0.916								
Miller, Richard "Dick"		BR TR																									
1951	Waycross	GFL	16	22	5	3	0	0	0	1	0	1	5	0.136	P	2	10	2	0.857	15	2	3	4.98	47	47	22	48
Miller, Robert C. "Bob"		BL TR																									
1950	Tifton	GSL	21	74	7	20	2	0	0	11	4	13	18	0.270	OF	28	2	2	0.938								
Miller, Robert S. "Bob"		BR TL																									
1963	Thomasville	GFL	2	4	0	0	0	0	0	0	0	1	1	0.000	P					2	2	0	1.38	13	8	6	6
Miller, Rodney Carter "Rod"		BL TR 5'10" 160 lbs b. 01/16/1940 Portland, OR																									
1958	Thomasville	GFL	52	178	50	46	8	4	2	21	5	55	31	0.258	2B, 3B	118	136	36	0.876								
Miller, Ronald		BR TR																									
1958	Albany	GFL	118	424	97	120	19	6	2	58	27	96	43	0.283	3B	133	212	30	0.920								
Miller, Stanley A. "Stan"		BL TR																									
1953	Jesup	GSL	27	50	8	13	2	0	1	7	0	8	13	0.260	P	4	10	2	0.875	22	11	3	4.17	121	108	62	61
Miller, William "Bill"		BR TR																									
1954	Hazlehurst-Baxley	GSL	63	217	45	56	10	4	14	54	9	39	70	0.258	1B, P	472	40	16	0.970	1	0	1	<45				
1955	Hazlehurst-Baxley	GSL	47	162	32	34	5	0	10	40	2	38	54	0.210	1B	363	20	9	0.977								
Milley, Allan "Al"		BL TR																									
1956	Sandersville	GSL	113	396	79	111	21	2	21	103	11	89	53	0.280	1B	899	60	10	0.990								
Mills, ---																											
1913	Thomasville	ESL	14												2B	34	5	6	0.867								
Mills, ---																											
1915	Americus-Gainesville	FLAG	<10												P					0							
1915	Valdosta	FLAG	<10												P					0							
Mills, Gilbert "Gil"		BR TR																									
1947	Valdosta	GFL	84	227	31	58	9	4	1	27	3	37	57	0.256	OF, P	62	25	11	0.888	16	5	11	4.36	99	95	74	86
Mills, Harvey		BL TL																									
1955	Thomasville	GFL	38	81	8	14	2	0	0	3	0	3	10	0.173	P	5	33	4	0.905	30	16	10	3.33	192	177	178	84
1957	Thomasville	GFL	4	8		1								0.125	P					4	1	2	<30				

Georgia Class-D Minor League Baseball Encyclopedia

YR	TEAM	LG	G	AB	R	H	2B	3B	HR	RBI	SB	BB	SO	BA	POS	PO	A	E	FA	GP	W	L	ERA	IP	H	SO	BB
Mills, Joseph "Joe"		BR TR																									
1962	Brunswick	GFL	9	7	0	0	0	0	0	0	0	1	3	0.000	P					8	1	3	7.83	23	28	27	29
1963	Brunswick	GFL	9	17	1	4	1	0	0	1	0	0	10	0.235	P					3	0	0	7.71	7	10	4	6
Mills, L.																											
1914	Gadsden	GAL	59	219	22	54				4				0.247	M, 1B	262	11	9	0.968								
Mills, Richard C. "Dick"		BR TL																									
1950	Cordele	GFL	48	81	8	10	0	0	0	3	0	14	34	0.123	P	13	38	6	0.895	43	10	12	3.48	207	210	111	64
1952	Cordele	GFL	28	57	5	7	3	0	0	2	0	8	21	0.123	P	7	34	3	0.932	23	7	10	2.82	169	159	89	56
Milner, Bloomer Holt "Cat"		BR TR 5'9" 162 lbs b. 1900																									
1920	LaGrange	GSL		236	43	71								0.301	SS												
1921	LaGrange	GSL		57	11	20								0.351	3B												
1930	Carrollton	GAL	<10																								
1942	Dothan	GFL	110	402	48	118	21	4	0	75	3	63	7	0.294	M, 1B	1022	42	17	0.984								
Milner, Bruce		BR TR																									
1947	Valley	GAL	23	82	7	18	2	0	0	6	1	6	10	0.220	OF	29	9	2	0.950								
Milner, Charlie		b. 08/23/1891																									
1950	Valley	GAL	1												P					1	0	0	2.25	4	4		
Milner, James R. "Jim"																											
1942	Dothan	GFL	108	465	86	147	27	5	2	62	19	46	13	0.316	OF	328	12	13	0.963								
Milner, Walter "Walt"		BR TR																									
1946	Valley	GAL	19	36	2	8	2	1	0	3	0	0	6	0.222	M, P	7	31	1	0.974	19	7	7	3.67	103	108	62	20
Milo, ---		BR																									
1946	Carrollton	GAL	<10																								
Milosevich, Michael "Mike" "Mollie"		BR TR 5'10" 172 lbs b. 01/13/1915 Zeigler, IL d. 02/03/1966 East Chicago, IN																									
1949	Hazlehurst-Baxley	GSL	75	273	52	79	26	3	8	49	5	53	14	0.289	M, 3B	87	183	23	0.922								
1951	Americus	GFL	105	375	53	85	18	1	1	55	1	86	24	0.227	M, 2B, SS	231	345	26	0.957								
Milster, Jack		BR TR																									
1950	Hazlehurst-Baxley	GSL	11	33	11	8	1	1	0	3	0	17	10	0.242	SS	22	32	8	0.871								
Minarck, William "Bill"		BR TR																									
1947	Valley	GAL	14	48	8	5	2	1	0	3	2	8	11	0.104	SS	22	36	10	0.853								
Minch, Charles		BR TR																									
1956	Thomson	GSL	15	38	3	6	2	0	0	3	0	1	10	0.158	C	68	3	2	0.973								
Mincy, Russell Thomas "Red"		BL TL 5'10" 188 lbs b. 12/23/1916 Hickory, NC																									
1949	Douglas	GSL	146	564	113	165	34	2	8	98	30	88	14	0.293	OF	332	4	6	0.982								
Miner, Dean		BR TR																									
1956	Valdosta	GFL	46	155	19	36	6	1	0	12	4	19	26	0.232	OF	50	4	5	0.915								
Minjock, John Ray "John"		BR TR																									
1953	Brunswick	GFL	11	7	3	0	0	0	0	0	0	4	4	0.000	P	1	6	2	0.778		2	0	<45				
1955	Brunswick	GFL	9	9		2								0.222	P					9	1	0	<45				
1955	Dublin	GSL	15	26	3	5	0	0	0	1	0	4	11	0.192	P	9	12	3	0.875	15	5	7	3.38	88	84	46	37
1956	Dublin	GSL	41	72	7	6	1	0	1	4	0	3	28	0.083	P	6	27	2	0.943	40	13	6	3.10	186	143	151	75
Mink, Deane I. Jr.		BS TL																									
1952	Valdosta	GFL	15	25	2	4	1	0	0	3	0	7	8	0.160	P	2	21	0	1.000	15	5	4	3.38	88	67	39	53
1953	Thomasville	GFL	18	29	3	4	1	1	0	3	0	3	9	0.138	P	2	17	1	0.950	16	8	3	3.00	75	53	47	51
Mink, Joseph "Joe"		BR TR																									
1948	Fitzgerald(5) - Douglas(5)	GSL	10	27	3	5	1	0	0	1	1	2	5	0.185	OF	8	2	0	1.000								
1949	Alex City(3) - Newnan(12)	GAL	15	43	4	14	2	0	2	4	0	3	5	0.326	OF	13	3	1	0.941								
Minner, Paul Edison "Paul" "Lefty"		BL TL 6'5" 210 lbs b. 06/30/1923 New Wilmington, PA																									
1941	Thomasville	GFL	3												P					3	0	2	6.43	14	21	6	8
Minor, Howard		BR																									
1946	LaGrange	GAL	<10																								
Mintz, Dwain		BR TR																									
1949	Valdosta	GFL	43	148	25	35	7	2	0	21	5	35	30	0.236	SS	52	88	18	0.886								
Mirande, Anthony		BR																									
1953	Jesup	GSL	9											0.185													
Miscisco, Daniel "Dan"		BR TL																									
1963	Brunswick	GFL	27	11	1	1	0	0	0	0	0	2	6	0.091	P	4	10	1	0.933	27	2	6	1.89	57	45	48	23
Miskulin, John		BL TL																									
1948	Baxley	GSL	30	67	6	7	1	1	0	4	0	9	19	0.104	P	9	34	5	0.896	28	12	12	2.49	217	173	187	89
Mitchell, ---																											
1906	Valdosta	GSL													2B												
Mitchell, Donald "Don"		BL TR																									
1958	Albany	GFL	12	9	1	0	0	0	0	0	0	2	4	0.000	P	1	6	2	0.778	12	0	3	5.81	31	27	15	46
Mitchell, Ed																											
1939	Valdosta	GFL	20	71	10	16	3	1	0	5	4	12	23	0.225	OF	35	0	4	0.897								
Mitchell, Joe Bob		BR																									
1941	Cordele	GFL	85	297	73	105	23	2	12	84	20	54	43	0.354	OF, P	255	40	26	0.919	4	1	1	6.00	30	22	32	29
1947	Alexander City	GAL	17	44	6	12	4	1	0	3	0	3	10	0.273													
Mitchell, Mervyn "Merv"																											
1936	Thomasville	GFL	19	70	9	17	4	0	2	7	1			0.243	1B, P	168	13	2	0.989				<30				
Mitchell, Steven		BL TL																									
1958	Brunswick	GFL	18	54	11	12	0	0	3	1	14	11	0.222	OF, P	24	3	1	0.964	9	1	2	4.09	33	27	17	31	
Mitchell, William "Bill"		BR																									
1958	Dublin	GFL	10	8	2	0	0	0	0	0	0	5	5	0.000													

Georgia Class-D Minor League Baseball Encyclopedia

YR	TEAM	LG	G	AB	R	H	2B	3B	HR	RBI	SB	BB	SO	BA	POS	PO	A	E	FA	GP	W	L	ERA	IP	H	SO	BB
Mitskavich, Nestor		BR TR																									
1948	Cordele	GFL	32	75	6	10	3	0	1	5	0	13	41	0.133	P	4	22	4	0.867	31	10	12	3.50	206	224	110	122
Mittewede, Walter																											
1920	Lindale	GSL		272	45	82								0.301	3B												
1921	Lindale	GSL		219	40	70								0.320	3B												
Mittleman, Richard "Dick"																											
1935	Americus	GFL	109	390	49	99	16	4	2		17	28	33	0.254	OF	243	126	19	0.951								
Mixon, Arthur "Art"		BR TR																									
1956	Thomasville	GFL	139	474	73	125	14	13	1	60	20	78	95	0.264	SS	186	346	60	0.899								
Mixon, Clark		BL TR																									
1953	Thomasville	GFL	11	13	3	5	0	0	0	0	0	5	2	0.385	P	1	11	0	1.000		2	1	<45				
1954	Thomasville	GFL	9	6		2								0.333	P					9	0	2	<45				
Mize, Michael "Mike"		BR																									
1946	Valdosta	GFL	<10																								
Mize, Pope																											
1938	Cordele	GFL	19	74	11	23	3	1	2	11	0	3	7	0.311	OF	22	0	0	1.000								
Mizell, Wilmer David "Vinegar Bend"		BR TL 6'3" 205 lbs b. 08/13/1930 Vinegar Bend, AL d. 02/21/1999 Kerrville, TX																									
1949	Albany	GFL	23	59	2	6	2	0	0	1	0	2	27	0.102	P	3	20	3	0.885	23	12	3	1.98	141	85	175	65
Mizerock, John		BR																									
1954	Valdosta	GFL	31	79	8	19	4	0	0	11	1	9	10	0.241													
Mlynarek, Anthony		BR TR																									
1948	Griffin	GAL	70	232	30	62	4	1	3	23	2	22	22	0.267	C	392	39	19	0.958								
Mlynarek, Lawrence		BR TR																									
1949	Thomasville	GFL	46	146	16	36	3	0	2	19	5	20	25	0.247	OF	35	3	2	0.950								
Mock, ---		BR																									
1953	Sandersville	GSL	1											0.500													
Mock, George		BR TR																									
1946	Waycross	GFL	106	414	75	105	10	3	0	40	14	69	37	0.254	3B, SS	142	235	38	0.908								
Moeller, George		BR TR																									
1949	Valdosta	GFL	115	390	65	112	17	4	6	76	7	52	46	0.287	OF, P	175	28	15	0.931	12	5	2	2.53	64	45	27	36
Moeller, Rolf		BR TR																									
1950	Tallahassee	GFL	37	53	3	9	0	0	0	1	0	2	17	0.170	P	6	30	7	0.837	36	9	8	4.53	147	121	116	162
Moffett, Frank																											
1914	Valdosta	GSL													M												
Molck, Larry		BR TR																									
1952	Thomasville	GFL	20	75	7	16	2	1	0	7	2	5	15	0.213	OF	29	4	2	0.943								
Molinder, Wallace "Walt"																											
1942	Americus	GFL	6	15	1	1	0	0	0	1	0	2	5	0.067	P	0	4	1	0.800	7	1	4	5.65	43	52	18	32
Molokie, Leon		BR TR																									
1951	Cordele	GFL	87	354	42	111	15	2	2	61	8	34	19	0.314	2B, OF	200	46	21	0.921								
Monaco, Frank		BR TR																									
1948	Tallassee	GAL	92	341	73	76	8	2	2	15	8	78	61	0.223	SS	149	257	45	0.900								
Monaco, Vincent "Vince"		BR TR																									
1954	Douglas	GSL	76	244	37	58	6	0	5	46	3	24	34	0.238	3B, OF, P	74	35	6	0.948	15	11	4	4.25	106	105	81	54
Monahan, James E. "Jim"		BR TR																									
1952	Brunswick	GFL	43	146	24	48	8	3	3	20	5	27	17	0.329	3B, OF	75	37	9	0.926								
Monarchi, Eugene L. "Gene"		BR TR 5'7" 150 lbs b. 06/11/1925 Jessup, PA																									
1948	Carrollton	GAL	111	322	55	76	9	0	0	38	1	88	48	0.236	SS	154	264	44	0.905								
Monarchi, Peter A. "Pete"		BR TR 5'10" 170 lbs b. 02/13/1927 Jessup, PA																									
1947	Carrollton	GAL	70	230	42	62	16	3	5	44	0	47	48	0.270	2B, OF	100	42	6	0.959								
1948	Carrollton	GAL	<10												2B												
1948	Vidalia-Lyons	GSL	72	237	28	43	7	1	1	26	3	46	49	0.181	1B	111	2	4	0.966								
Monasterio, Eduardo		BR TR																									
1954	Tifton	GFL	42	151	25	37	6	3	0	23	8	11	24	0.245	3B	31	59	9	0.909								
Monkarsh, William "Bill"		BR																									
1962	Thomasville	GFL	7	17	3	4	1	0	1	5	0	5	5	0.235													
Monroe, Raymond "Ray"		BR TR																									
1951	Douglas	GSL	120	469	54	97	15	2	1	49	5	40	56	0.207	3B	111	269	37	0.911								
Monson, Ronald "Ron"		BR TR																									
1956	Valdosta	GFL	17	50	14	12	4	0	0	8	0	16	7	0.240	OF	18	1	2	0.905								
1956	Hazlehurst-Baxley	GSL	52	147	17	31	3	1	3	18	1	29	47	0.211	OF	53	7	8	0.882								
Montalvo, Jose B.		BR TR																									
1946	Valley	GAL	67	184	30	53	10	1	2	29	1	28	41	0.288	OF, C, P	193	34	14	0.942	2	0	0	0.00	3			
Monterio, David "Dave"		BR TR																									
1955	Tifton	GFL	10	16	0	2	0	0	0	2	0	0	2	0.125	P					8	3	2	<45				
Montgomery, Robert "Bob"																											
1949	Hazlehurst-Baxley	GSL	11	13	1	4	0	0	0	1	0	2	4	0.308													
Montgomery, Walter "Walt"		BR TL																									
1950	Albany	GFL	30	50	5	8	0	0	0	3	0	1	10	0.160	P	5	20	4	0.862	30	7	9	4.73	139	125	169	133
Moody, Frank																											
1935	Americus	GFL	114	439	77	117	17	4	2		5	49	46	0.267	IF	144	259	34	0.922								
Moody, Joseph "Joe"		BR TR																									
1946	Waycross	GFL	122	470	102	147	27	7	5	98	3	72	62	0.313	OF	228	15	9	0.964								
Moon, Eulas																											
1920	LaGrange	GSL																									

Georgia Class-D Minor League Baseball Encyclopedia

YR	TEAM	LG	G	AB	R	H	2B	3B	HR	RBI	SB	BB	SO	BA	POS	PO	A	E	FA	GP	W	L	ERA	IP	H	SO	BB
Moore, ---																											
1914	Waycross	GSL		61	14	21	2	1	4		1			0.344													
Moore, Charles M.		BR TR																									
1950	Thomasville	GFL	33	139	22	30	2	0	0	11	9	22	22	0.216	2B	70	76	9	0.942								
Moore, Earl		BR TR																									
1946	Thomasville	GFL	4												P					4	0	1	0.00	16	16	5	12
Moore, Ed																											
1942	Dothan	GFL	7	23	4	5	0	0	0	3	3	4	2	0.217	OF	11	1	0	1.000								
Moore, Edward Jr. "Ed"		BR TR																									
1949	Valdosta	GFL	32	46	7	7	0	1	0	7	0	3	9	0.152	P	6	16	3	0.880	31	8	6	4.11	127	134	104	63
1955	Thomasville	GFL	8	2		0								0.000	P					8	0	1		<45			
Moore, Eugene C. "Gene"		BR TR																									
1950	Americus	GFL	21	65	11	14	6	0	0	6	0	7	12	0.215	OF	10	1	0	1.000								
Moore, Gayle		BL TR																									
1955	Waycross	GFL	52	177	23	39	7	2	0	12	5	24	17	0.220	SS	73	127	11	0.948								
1956	Waycross	GFL	107	366	45	98	15	1	2	42	2	38	42	0.268	3B, SS	121	206	35	0.903								
Moore, H. Clem																											
1920	Griffin	GSL													OF												
1921	Carrollton	GSL		95	21	38								0.400	OF												
Moore, H.H.																											
1928	Gadsden	GAL	64	253	41	74	9	9	3		11	12	15	0.292	2B, SS	95	206	29	0.912								
Moore, Herbert H. "Herb"		BL TL																									
1946	Albany	GFL	116	365	50	118	25	4	2	76	4	58	33	0.323	M, 1B, OF, P	269	43	12	0.963	29	15	3	1.44	175	89	214	83
Moore, Hugh		BR TR																									
1940	Albany	GFL	98	378	47	91	13	4	0	35	6	29	47	0.241	SS	145	275	37	0.919								
1941	Cordele	GFL	18	60	6	12	1	0	0	10	1	9	4	0.200	3B	11	41	9	0.852								
1942	Albany	GFL	1	5	0	1	0	0	0	2	0	0	0	0.200	SS	0	1	1	0.500								
Moore, J.																											
1928	Carrollton	GAL	8												P					8	1	2	5.85	40	45	14	21
Moore, Jackie Spencer "Jackie"		BR TR 6'0" 180 lbs b. 02/19/1939 Jay, FL																									
1958	Valdosta	GFL	87	333	61	100	20	3	9	78	5	51	32	0.300	3B, C	445	75	11	0.979								
Moore, James																											
1914	Talladega	GAL	29	98	8	16					3			0.163	OF	54	4	1	0.983								
1915	Talladega	GAL	51	177	32	56	8	1	4					0.316	OF	103	5	4	0.964								
Moore, James "Jim"		BL TR																									
1958	Waycross	GFL	18	69	5	12	3	0	1	11	0	7	15	0.174	1B	140	8	5	0.967								
Moore, James L. "Jim"		BR TR																									
1951	Fitzgerald(91) - Dublin(37)	GSL	128	513	87	163	29	11	16	104	10	50	52	0.318	1B, OF	869	44	18	0.981								
Moore, Jewell		BR																									
1946	Opelika	GAL	11	39	7	11	0	2	1	6	0	7	5	0.282													
Moore, John "Jack"																											
1949	Dublin	GSL	12	42	9	10	2	0	2	8	0	12	11	0.238	2B	39	41	13	0.860								
Moore, John D.		BL TL																									
1953	Statesboro	GSL	19	20	2	2	0	0	0	1	2	9		0.100	P	1	12	0	1.000	19	2	6	6.32	74	86	43	50
Moore, Lamar		BL																									
1954	Waycross	GFL	11	29	6	6	3	0	0	3	0	6	11	0.207													
Moore, Lloyd E.		BR TR																									
1951	Albany	GFL	27	51	7	12	2	0	0	3	1	7	13	0.235	P	5	22	2	0.931	27	9	5	3.92	124	129	32	55
Moore, M. Duke		BR TR																									
1955	Tifton	GFL	3	4		0								0.000	P					3	0	2		<45			
Moore, Morris		BL TR																									
1954	Valdosta	GFL	41	121	16	29	3	0	1	9	1	16	27	0.240	2B	63	95	17	0.903								
1955	Valdosta	GFL	101	313	50	61	12	2	1	33	8	67	70	0.195	2B, 3B	139	215	19	0.949								
Moore, Ray		BR																									
1956	Fitzgerald	GFL	2	2		1								0.500													
Moore, Robert "Bob"		BL TL																									
1963	Brunswick	GFL	4	1	1	0	0	0	0	0	0	0	1	0.000	P					3	0	0	9.00	3	6	2	4
Moore, Vernon "Vern"		BR TR																									
1947	Americus	GFL	38	122	24	29	4	2	3	15	1	24	26	0.238	OF	76	8	0	1.000								
Moore, Willard		BR TR																									
1953	Sandersville	GSL	19	26	3	4	0	0	0	2	0	2	13	0.154	P	2	14	2	0.889	18	3	7	7.20	80	103	53	60
1954	Sandersville - Dublin	GSL	7	6		0								0.000	P					7	0	5		<45			
Moore, William "Billy Joe"		BR TR																									
1956	Dublin	GSL	47	192	26	47	3	2	4	17	3	21	54	0.245	OF	61	3	8	0.889								
Moore, William L. "Bill"		BL TL																									
1954	Americus-Cordele	GFL	20	28	3	4	0	0	0	2	0	2	9	0.143	P	7	5	3	0.800	19	4	7	4.74	76	93	34	57
Moorefield, ---																											
1914	Rome	GAL	50	189	35	67					5			0.354	OF	90	4	5	0.949								
Moorehead, Richard "Dick"		BL TL																									
1950	Cordele	GFL	83	304	44	83	14	3	1	42	11	33	60	0.273	OF	128	9	3	0.979								
Moran, ---																											
1917	LaGrange	GAL	8	26	0	4	0	0	0		1			0.154	OF, P	4	17	0	1.000	3	2	1		27	18	13	9
Moran, Charles																											
1913	Brunswick	ESL													M												

Georgia Class-D Minor League Baseball Encyclopedia

YR	TEAM	LG	G	AB	R	H	2B	3B	HR	RBI	SB	BB	SO	BA	POS	PO	A	E	FA	GP	W	L	ERA	IP	H	SO	BB
Moran, Michael "Mike"		BR																									
1956	Dublin	GSL	8	16		1								0.063													
Morelli, James "Jim"		BL TR																									
1949	Carrollton	GAL	107	401	86	104	16	3	13	52	15	71	41	0.259	OF	257	11	14	0.950								
1950	Carrollton	GAL	113	422	112	123	19	5	14	70	10	109	38	0.291	OF	228	15	8	0.968								
1951	Douglas	GSL	90	357	86	127	25	9	3	38	23	63	10	0.356	OF	226	10	17	0.933								
Moreno, Heliodoro		BR TR																									
1955	Douglas	GSL	11	14	0	2	0	1	0	3	0	2	4	0.143	P	3	7	1	0.909	11	2	3	4.29	42	40	14	12
Morgan, Billy		BR TR																									
1940	Waycross	GFL	15	26	0	0	0	0	0	0	0	0	2	11 0.000	P					15	5	3	3.08	79	75	23	46
1941	Waycross	GFL	4	9	0	2	0	0	0	1	0	1	1	0.222	P	1	5	0	1.000	4	0	2	1.64	22	19	7	8
Morgan, Fred																											
1942	Valdosta	GFL	43	137	22	36	2	2	1	20	0	12	35	0.263	P	17	28	4	0.918	28	16	6	2.80	206	187	73	67
Morgan, George		BL TL																									
1955	Waycross	GFL	112	375	45	105	12	0	1	49	2	51	43	0.280	1B, OF	587	18	21	0.966								
1957	Waycross	GFL	58	207	33	54	5	2	2	31	0	48	42	0.261	1B	482	41	9	0.983								
Morgan, Gordon		BR TR																									
1955	Tifton	GFL	57	181	30	44	7	1	2	21	3	27	48	0.243	OF	132	12	12	0.923								
Morgan, Julian		BR TR																									
1948	Vidalia-Lyons	GSL	15	41	2	9	0	0	0	6	0	0	7	0.220	P	4	12	3	0.842	15	7	4	2.23	109	100	45	33
1949	Vidalia-Lyons	GSL													M												
1953	Sandersville	GSL													M												
Morgan, Lucius		BL TR																									
1953	Sandersville	GSL	105	394	81	130	24	7	16	88	8	69	24	0.330	M, 2B, 3B, SS, P	168	257	36	0.922		0	0	<45				
1954	Sandersville	GSL	35	137	33	38	13	1	8	33	2	15	9	0.277	3B, SS	52	94	12	0.924								
Morgan, Malvern		BR TR																									
1946	Valley	GAL	96	345	54	103	25	2	5	48	2	27	17	0.299	3B, OF, P	109	114	15	0.937	2	2	0	0.00	12	16	3	0
1947	Valley	GAL	126	505	96	184	34	7	9	90	13	55	22	0.364	1B, 3B	320	205	24	0.956								
1949	Valley	GAL	77	283	56	106	27	1	8	79	17	43	8	0.375	M, 1B, 2B	512	82	15	0.975								
1951	Valley	GAL	116	451	83	144	32	1	6	105	6	69	10	0.319	1B, 3B	647	116	15	0.981								
Morgan, Roger		BR TR																									
1956	Waycross	GFL	138	520	93	151	25	5	11	83	7	71	93	0.290	1B	1196	58	35	0.973								
Morgan, William Cy "Cy"																											
1937	Thomasville	GFL	109	438	82	140	19	5	2	41	3	41	34	0.320	M, OF	240	15	8	0.970								
1938	Thomasville	GFL	114	439	90	132	19	9	0	49	12	58	24	0.301	M, OF	210	6	10	0.956								
1939	Thomasville	GFL	96	334	35	104	12	0	0	46	2	33	26	0.311	M, OF	176	8	7	0.963								
Moriarity, Dean		BL TR																									
1952	Thomasville	GFL	22	87	9	17	5	0	0	7	0	8	14	0.195	2B	42	36	13	0.857								
Moriskiewicz, John		BR TR																									
1954	Brunswick	GFL	117	366	78	93	21	4	6	57	28	93	101	0.254	OF	157	19	15	0.921								
Morlan, Joseph "Joe"		BR TR																									
1956	Vidalia	GSL	53	188	16	50	11	0	2	24	0	17	18	0.266	OF, C	243	17	6	0.977								
Morowski, Gene		BR TR																									
1963	Thomasville	GFL	4	4	1	1	0	0	1	1	0	0	1	0.250	P					4	0	1	9.00	8	5	8	17
Morrell, Willard Blackmer "Bill"		BR TR 6'0" 172 lbs b. 04/09/1893 Hyde Park, MA d. 08/05/1975 Birmingham, AL																									
1939	Valdosta	GFL	14	10	2	2	1	0	0	3	0	7	1	0.200	M, P	0	6	0	1.000				<45				
1940	Valdosta	GFL	<10												M, P					5	2	2	6.35	34	54	13	2
1941	Cordele	GFL	8	15	0	2	0	0	0	0	0	2	4	0.133	M, P	2	1	1	0.750	8	2	3	8.29	38	61	11	16
Morris, Albert "Al"		BR TR																									
1957	Albany	GFL	131	509	97	143	24	3	21	80	28	75	112	0.281	2B, SS	349	378	38	0.950								
Morris, Charles B.		BR TR																									
1962	Brunswick	GFL	21	63	8	11	2	0	1	4	2	8	25	0.175	OF	14	2	1	0.941								
Morris, Clinton "Clint"		BR TR																									
1956	Fitzgerald	GFL	82	312	35	76	4	1	1	27	6	26	49	0.244	OF	118	9	6	0.955								
Morris, David "Dave"		BR TR																									
1947	Newnan	GAL	18	55	9	10	0	0	1	8	0	5	12	0.182	OF	21	1	3	0.880								
Morris, Ed "Eddie"		BR TR																									
1939	Albany	GFL	106	386	55	105	16	9	0	48	8	29	57	0.272	UT	350	17	27	0.931								
Morris, Milton "Milt"		BL TR																									
1954	Dublin	GSL	106	334	71	95	15	7	9	44	16	77	62	0.284	2B, SS, OF	137	147	36	0.888								
1955	Dublin(49) - Vidalia(24)	GSL	73	265	62	78	15	1	5	47	22	66	40	0.294	3B, SS, OF	112	102	33	0.866								
Morris, Raymond "Ray"		BR TR																									
1946	Opelika	GAL	5												P					5	0	1	0.00	18	32	5	16
Morris, Taras A. "Ted"		BR TR																									
1953	Brunswick	GFL	10	14	0	6	0	0	0	3	0	4	2	0.429	P						1	4	<45				
Morris, Teddy R.																											
1941	Waycross	GFL	27	81	5	17	2	1	0	4	1	3	20	0.210	P	6	32	2	0.950	26	11	10	3.88	195	221	67	84
Morris, Willard																											
1936	Cordele	GFL	22	30	6	10	1	1	0	1	0			0.333	P					22	2	6	3.93	87		37	35
Morrison, Dean		BL TL																									
1946	Valley	GAL	19	23	4	4	0	0	0	2	0	3	5	0.174	P					19	4	5	4.69	71	56	68	59
Morrison, James "Harry"																											
1914	Selma	GAL	22	68	5	7					0			0.103	P	7	50	0	1.000	22							
1915	Anniston	GAL	<6												P					<6							
1916	Anniston	GAL	24	60	3	13					0			0.217	P												
1917	Anniston	GAL	5	10	1	1	1	0	0		0			0.100	P	3	17	1	0.952	4	1	1		24	22	11	3

Georgia Class-D Minor League Baseball Encyclopedia

YR	TEAM	LG	G	AB	R	H	2B	3B	HR	RBI	SB	BB	SO	BA	POS	PO	A	E	FA	GP	W	L	ERA	IP	H	SO	BB
Morrison, James W. "Jim"		BR TR																									
1949	Waycross	GFL	10	40	7	11	2	1	0	4	0	4	10	0.275	SS	15	26	9	0.820								
1949	Tifton	GSL	89	346	73	99	20	3	1	47	12	54	41	0.286	SS	160	241	25	0.941								
1950	Tifton	GSL	130	513	123	150	22	5	0	48	15	92	65	0.292	SS	264	434	50	0.933								
Morrison, Ronald "Ron"		BR																									
1953	Douglas	GSL	1											0.000													
Morrongiello, Michael "Mike"		BR TR																									
1949	LaGrange	GAL	35	131	26	45	9	5	2	24	7	30	13	0.344	2B	73	76	7	0.955								
Morrow, ---																											
1921	Rome	GSL		274	40	96								0.350	C												
Morsberger, Charles		BR TR																									
1956	Thomson	GSL	44	155	17	25	6	0	0	7	1	24	50	0.161	3B, SS	63	82	38	0.792								
Morse, Whitey																											
1913	Valdosta - Brunswick	ESL	101	361	45	114	12	0	0					0.316	M, 1B	873	79	17	0.982								
1914	Valdosta - Brunswick	GSL		211	29	55	7	0	0		3			0.261	M												
Morton, ---																											
1915	Anniston	GAL	17	62	5	11	1	1	0					0.177	OF, P	10	1	1	0.917	6-							
Morton, William "Bill"		BR TR																									
1958	Albany	GFL	126	440	79	117	25	0	8	66	5	79	49	0.266	C	755	67	11	0.987								
Morzenti, Jerome		BL TR																									
1957	Waycross	GFL	134	482	55	131	18	6	5	65	1	50	105	0.272	OF	229	15	19	0.928								
Moseley, ---																											
1915	Dothan - Ame-Gains	FLAG	25	76	7	16	1	0	0		2			0.211	P	3	51	6	0.900	17	8	7		139	126	71	35
1915	Americus-Gainesville	FLAG	2												P					2	2	0		18	12	11	8
Mosley, C.S.																											
1921	Griffin	GSL													SS												
Mosley, Robert "Bob"		BL TL																									
1953	Douglas	GSL	1											0.000	P						0	1		<45			
Moss, Darvin		BR TR																									
1955	Statesboro	GSL	4	5		0								0.000	P					1	0	1					
Moss, James "Jim"		BR																									
1956	Thomasville	GFL	6	1		0								0.000													
Moss, John Lester "Les"		BR TR 5'11" 205 lbs b. 05/14/1925 Tulsa, OK																									
1942	Americus	GFL	109	391	46	117	23	2	3	58	1	30	57	0.299	C	502	46	17	0.970								
Moss, Joseph F. "Joe"		BL TR																									
1950	Alex City(7) - Opelika(12)	GAL	19	59	12	18	3	0	0	14	3	11	11	0.305	OF	24	0	1	0.960								
1951	Opelika	GAL	41	166	19	40	4	0	0	20	2	9	27	0.241	OF	83	8	7	0.929								
Mote, Galen		BL TR																									
1957	Thomasville	GFL	88	318	59	81	12	6	4	40	1	79	44	0.255	3B	98	146	26	0.904								
Mote, John		BR TR																									
1951	Fitzgerald	GSL	31	49	3	5	0	0	0	2	1	17	18	0.102	P	2	26	4	0.875	31	5	12	5.43	159	172	61	139
Motil, Robert "Bob"		BR TR																									
1958	Thomasville	GFL	47	184	29	50	11	3	3	32	0	18	29	0.272	3B	45	93	10	0.932								
Mott, Elisha Matthew "Bitsy"		BR TR 5'8" 155 lbs b. 06/12/1918 Arcadia, FL																									
1939	Americus	GFL	77	315	48	88	14	2	1	21	3	37	39	0.279	SS	161	194	29	0.924								
1940	Americus	GFL	137	547	76	133	12	2	0	41	14	49	46	0.243	SS	270	409	73	0.903								
1941	Cordele	GFL	6	22	1	3	0	0	0	2	0	2	4	0.136	OF	6	12	4	0.818								
Mottler, Ernest																											
1949	Vidalia-Lyons - Dublin	GSL	34	110	13	21	4	0	1	11	2	21	36	0.191	C	148	13	6	0.964								
Moulder, Glen Hubert "Glen"		BR TR 6'0" 180 lbs b. 09/28/1917 Cleveland, OK d. 11/27/1994 Decatur, GA																									
1940	Americus	GFL	36	106	10	21	3	0	0	4	1	2	15	0.198	P					34	20	9	2.65	251	214	164	94
Moulton, E.R. "Jack"																											
1929	Lindale	GAL	86	308	63	98	22	7	12		12	20	46	0.318	M, 1B, P	459	79	9	0.984	14	5	4		75	89	26	28
1930	Lindale	GAL	59	201	48	61	16	1	12		11	17	30	0.303	M, 1B, OF, P	238	17	16	0.941	9	1	0	6.57	37	52	9	16
Mount, Ronald "Ron"		BR TR																									
1954	Waycross	GFL	1	1		0								0.000	P					1	0	1		<45			
Mounts, Emory		BL TL																									
1954	Valdosta	GFL	43	132	18	21	3	2	1	11	6	35	40	0.159	OF	52	8	2	0.968								
1955	Valdosta	GFL	129	472	106	124	16	1	4	43	25	123	107	0.263	OF, P	217	14	10	0.959	1	0	0		<45			
Mowbray, James "Jim"		BR TR																									
1956	Tifton	GFL	2	2		0								0.000	P					2	0	0		<45			
1957	Brunswick	GFL	9	14		6								0.429	P					9	1	1	5.21	38	44	42	21
Mozzali, Maurice Joseph "Mo"		BL TL																									
1958	Albany	GFL	113	328	100	110	29	1	3	63	10	94	11	0.335	M, 1B, P	742	58	9	0.989	5	0	0		<30			
Mueninghoff, Dick																											
1939	Thomasville	GFL	135	485	52	122	14	4	0	56	7	54	99	0.252	SS	238	441	55	0.925								
Muhlenbein, Henry		BL TL																									
1940	Albany	GFL	<10												P									<35			
Muir, Charles		BR TR																									
1956	Thomson	GSL	11	21	2	3	0	0	0	2	0	1	4	0.143	P					7	3	2					
Mulkin, ---																											
1928	Gadsden	GAL	12	47	5	11	0	1	0		0	1	2	0.234	OF	21	0	0	1.000								
Mullaney, Tom		BL TL																									
1957	Thomasville	GFL	5	2		0								0.000	P					5	0	1		<30			

Georgia Class-D Minor League Baseball Encyclopedia

YR	TEAM	LG	G	AB	R	H	2B	3B	HR	RBI	SB	BB	SO	BA	POS	PO	A	E	FA	GP	W	L	ERA	IP	H	SO	BB
Mullen, Vincent "Moon"		BR TR																									
1946	Thomasville	GFL	90	268	58	87	18	6	0	71	4	101	27	0.325	M, 2B, 3B	126	176	30	0.910								
1947	Thomasville	GFL	54	159	27	44	9	1	0	28	0	41	18	0.277	M, 2B, 3B, SS	53	83	20	0.872								
Mulligan, ---																											
1915	Valdosta	FLAG	<10																								
Mullin, ---																											
1913	Brunswick	ESL	78	297	32	69	18	0	2					0.232	SS	150	160	40	0.886								
Mullis, Donald "Don"		BR TR																									
1962	Dublin	GFL	71	245	29	60	1	0	0	27	8	35	19	0.245	2B	133	157	17	0.945								
Munch, William "Bill"		BR TR																									
1947	Tallahassee	GFL	12	15	5	8	0	2	0	4	0	1	4	0.533	P	0	3	0	1.000								
Munday, Charles		BR TR																									
1950	Moultrie	GFL	46	144	19	33	7	0	2	32	0	28	34	0.229	C	181	30	7	0.968								
Mundo, James "Jim"																											
1937	Albany	GFL	22	81	12	14	6	0	1	10	0	10	9	0.173	2B	67	64	5	0.963								
Munford, ---																											
1921	Cedartown	GSL													SS												
Munroe, Kenneth "Ken"		BR TR																									
1951	Waycross	GFL	25	30	2	7	1	0	0	2	0	2	6	0.233	P	6	16	1	0.957	24	6	4	2.69	77	65	30	37
Muratore, Richard "Dick"		BR TR																									
1958	Thomasville	GFL	16	46	10	10	2	1	0	4	1	30	10	0.217	2B	48	50	8	0.925								
Murch, Red																											
1913	Thomasville	ESL	80	302	42	86	11	0	4					0.285	2B	274	184	22	0.954								
1914	Thomasville	GSL		287	62	71	6	0	0		12			0.247													
1915	Thomasville	FLAG	46	150	17	34	4	0	0		9			0.227	M, 2B	123	132	16	0.941								
Murchison, Thomas Malcolm "Tim"		BR TL 6'0" 185 lbs b. 10/08/1896 Liberty, NC d. 10/20/1962 Liberty, NC																									
1938	Tallahassee	GFL													M												
Murillo, Jose M.		BR TR																									
1956	Brunswick	GFL	21	74	11	14	2	1	0	5	1	23	29	0.189	2B	49	36	7	0.924								
Murphee, William "Bill"		BL TL																									
1947	Carrollton	GAL	39	112	23	34	2	3	1	15	1	31	22	0.304	1B	315	13	6	0.982								
Murphy, ---																											
1913	Thomasville	ESL	73	281	55	95	18	8	4					0.338	SS	147	177	47	0.873								
Murphy, Daniel J. "Dan"		BL TL																									
1951	LaGrange	GAL	110	428	105	138	27	4	12	66	7	89	60	0.322	1B	950	51	35	0.966								
1954	Sandersville	GSL	28	100	10	25	4	0	1	19	0	12	25	0.250	1B	199	10	8	0.963								
Murphy, Daniel O. "Dan"		BR TR																									
1952	Statesboro	GSL	36	145	37	42	8	2	0	12	12	19	7	0.290	SS	65	136	10	0.953								
Murphy, Edward Joseph "Ed"		BR TR 5'11" 190 lbs b. 08/23/1918 Joliet, IL d. 12/10/1991 Joliet, IL																									
1938	Albany	GFL	125	512	88	164	33	13	3	113	15	39	63	0.320	1B	1084	61	17	0.985								
1948	Americus	GFL	14	31	4	4	0	0	0	2	0	6	8	0.129	M												
1949	Americus	GFL	49	154	38	53	10	3	4	39	9	15	11	0.344	M, 1B	333	15	2	0.994								
1950	Americus	GFL	42	85	18	26	5	4	1	19	2	9	6	0.306	M, 1B	141	6	3	0.980								
Murphy, James "Jim"		BR TR																									
1947	Griffin	GAL	112	410	62	113	19	9	2	65	30	53	33	0.276	OF	285	11	12	0.961								
Murphy, P. Lamar		BL TR																									
1951	Alexander City	GAL	69	244	43	80	4	3	3	47	3	54	6	0.328	OF	159	2	6	0.964								
Murphy, Robert "Bob"		BR TR																									
1951	Opelika	GAL	41	157	21	52	9	1	5	27	0	21	11	0.331	OF	85	3	4	0.957								
Murphy, Robert E. "Bob"		BR TR																									
1952	Albany	GFL	95	365	44	100	16	0	6	44	6	26	22	0.274	OF	154	16	12	0.934								
Murphy, William E. "Bill"		BR TR																									
1951	Albany	GFL	126	469	95	141	27	6	9	100	6	76	74	0.301	1B	1138	54	25	0.979								
Murray, Charles		BL TR																									
1963	Moultrie	GFL	109	382	57	74	11	4	15	50	8	42	148	0.194	OF	136	9	7	0.954								
Murray, Charles "Charlie"																											
1939	Thomasville	GFL	29	112	13	22	3	0	1	10	1	9	16	0.196	OF	51	6	8	0.877								
Murray, Donald G. "Don"		BL TR																									
1953	Douglas	GSL	123	498	75	143	27	3	4	72	7	34	43	0.287	OF	226	23	15	0.943								
1954	Valdosta	GFL	51	184	23	48	6	0	0	19	6	9	13	0.261	OF	70	5	9	0.893								
1955	Statesboro	GSL	57	207	28	56	12	2	2	42	2	20	25	0.271	OF	101	4	8	0.929								
Murray, Francis L.		BL TL																									
1946	Waycross	GFL	14	42	2	7	1	0	0	3	0	2	18	0.167	P	7	28	3	0.921	14	8	3	3.96	100	90	66	79
Murray, Glenn Dale "Glenn"																											
1935	Tallahassee	GFL	115	572	71	140	23	18	8		14	38	75	0.245	OF	202	22	14	0.941								
1936	Tallahassee	GFL	62	254	51	93	15	9	7	61	4			0.366	OF	127	11	7	0.952								
1938	Tallahassee	GFL	52	185	27	54	5	4	3	34	2	22	13	0.292	OF	96	3	2	0.980								
Murray, Milton "Milt"		BR TR																									
1948	Vidalia-Lyons	GSL	36	125	24	28	2	0	0	9	12	28	30	0.224	SS	61	109	11	0.939								
1949	Vidalia-Lyons	GSL	42	168	37	49	8	2	0	20	7	39	24	0.292	SS	84	125	18	0.921								
Murray, Orlene		BR TR																									
1958	Thomasville	GFL	3	2		0								0.000	P					3	0	0		<30			
Murray, Ralph		BR TR																									
1946	LaGrange	GAL	27	93	13	14	2	0	0	3	1	12	32	0.151	3B	21	35	4	0.933								

Georgia Class-D Minor League Baseball Encyclopedia

YR	TEAM	LG	G	AB	R	H	2B	3B	HR	RBI	SB	BB	SO	BA	POS	PO	A	E	FA	GP	W	L	ERA	IP	H	SO	BB
Murray, Robert Hayes "Bob"		BL TR 5'7" 155 lbs b. 07/04/1894 St. Albans, VT d. 01/04/1979 Nashua, NH																									
1935	Moultrie	GFL													M												
Murray, Thomas "Tom"		BR TR																									
1946	LaGrange	GAL	24	52	6	13	0	1	0	0	0	2	9	0.250	P	2	18	3	0.870	13	6	3	5.04	75	72	53	33
1947	LaGrange	GAL	27	68	11	18	1	1	1	11	1	4	11	0.265	P	3	11	0	1.000	14	5	5	4.45	83	97	45	29
Murray, Walter "Walt"		BR																									
1947	LaGrange	GAL	10	12	1	1	0	0	0	0	1	2	7	0.083													
Murray, William "Bill"		BR TR																									
1946	Americus	GFL	33	85	19	12	0	0	0	8	0	15	17	0.141	P	7	62	6	0.920	33	21	6	3.22	232	249	142	80
Murrell, Ivan Augustus (Peters) "Ivan"		BR TR 6'2" 196 lbs b. 04/24/1945 Almirante, Panama																									
1963	Moultrie	GFL	40	140	21	31	8	0	4	18	7	8	51	0.221	OF	69	6	3	0.962								
Murta, John		BR TL																									
1956	Thomasville	GFL	1	0										0.000	P					1	0	0	<45				
Muse, Donald "Don"		BR TR																									
1948	LaGrange	GAL	79	274	42	79	6	4	2	39	10	32	34	0.288	3B, C	335	62	29	0.932								
1949	LaGrange	GAL	112	378	65	109	12	3	4	44	9	63	45	0.288	SS, C	548	146	36	0.951								
Musial, Edward "Ed"		BL TL																									
1950	Waycross	GFL	47	142	33	39	6	3	0	24	5	59	27	0.275	OF	85	0	2	0.977								
Musillo, John		BR TR																									
1962	Brunswick	GFL	13	7	1	2	1	0	0	2	0	0	3	0.286	P	0	2	1	0.667	13	0	2	4.50	18	32	22	14
Muskopf, Robert "Bob"		BR																									
1955	Cordele	GFL	4	10		0								0.000													
Muskulin, John		BL TL																									
1946	Tallahassee	GFL	4												P					4	0	1	0.00	9	13	4	6
Musser, Richard "Dick"		BR TR																									
1953	Tifton	GFL	7											0.150													
1953	Vidalia	GSL	18	60	6	14	4	0	2	9	1	4	9	0.233	OF	18	1	1	0.950								
Musumeci, John		BR TR																									
1951	Americus	GFL	76	318	61	97	19	6	0	52	11	36	27	0.305	3B	81	209	23	0.927								
Muth, Richard "Dick"		BR TR																									
1935	Panama City	GFL	110	427	44	100	13	7	8		6	21	94	0.234	OF	220	32	9	0.966								
Muti, Nicholas "Nick"		BR																									
1946	Tallassee	GAL	<10																									
Myatt, Charles		BL TR																									
1954	Americus-Cordele	GFL	17	66	5	19	1	0	0	5	0	7	6	0.288	3B	19	25	6	0.880								
Myatt, Ralph		BR TR																									
1958	Valdosta	GFL	3	5		0								0.000	P					3	0	0	<30				
Myers, Donald "Don"		BR TR																									
1946	Valdosta	GFL	25	99	14	30	3	0	0	9	2	5	20	0.303	OF	34	4	6	0.864								
Myers, James "Jim"		BR TR																									
1942	Moultrie	GFL	126	515	73	121	14	5	1	44	17	50	61	0.235	OF	315	12	16	0.953								
Myers, John L.		BL TR																									
1955	Moultrie	GFL	3	5		0								0.000	P					3	0	1	<45				
Myers, Kenneth "Ken"		BR TR																									
1956	Thomson	GSL	3	0										0.000	P					3	0	0					
Myers, Richard L. "Dick"		BR TR																									
1950	Tifton	GSL	11	23	0	4	0	0	0	1	0	1	7	0.174	P	3	5	5	0.615	11	3	4	5.37	67	63	45	56
Myers, Robert "Bob"		BR TL																									
1950	Moultrie	GFL	21	31	3	3	0	0	0	3	0	3	15	0.097	P	4	16	1	0.952	21	5	4	4.89	81	75	49	65
Myers, William F. "Bill"		BR TR																									
1953	Vidalia	GSL	17	66	8	18	1	1	1	6	0	7	8	0.273	OF	52	0	0	1.000								
Mytrysak, John "Lefty"		BL TL 6'0" 200 lbs b. 06/27/1926 Homer City, PA																									
1951	Americus	GFL	8												P					8	1	7	5.33	54	61	26	35
Nabors, Herman John "Jack"		BR TR 6'3" 185 lbs b. 11/19/1887 Montevallo, AL d. 11/20/1923 Wilton, AL																									
1915	Talladega - Newnan	GAL	15	50	4	9	2	0	0					0.180	P					15	12	1					
Nafus, Virgil																											
1941	Moultrie	GFL	28	63	0	9	0	1	0	4	0	4	12	0.143	P	3	30	0	1.000	26	9	10	2.92	148	105	121	110
Nagle, Robert H. "Bob"		BL TR																									
1948	Carrollton	GAL	32	79	11	15	1	0	1	6	2	15	19	0.190	3B	19	46	11	0.855								
Nagy, Michael "Mike"		BR TR																									
1957	Brunswick	GFL	48	185	22	46	8	1	2	16	1	28	41	0.249	OF	86	5	7	0.929								
Najour, George		BR TR																									
1946	Newnan	GAL	24	85	9	18	3	2	0	11	3	4	9	0.212	3B	30	32	9	0.873								
Nakunas, Steve																											
1939	Thomasville	GFL	68	198	17	43	3	0	0	30	2	8	19	0.217	C	155	29	16	0.920								
Nance, ---																											
1915	Brunswick	FLAG	74	258	27	69	9	1	0		11			0.267	3B, C, P	163	136	15	0.952	0							
Nance, Hoover		BR TR																									
1949	Valley	GAL	15	47	12	5	0	0	0	3	4	10	18	0.106	OF	27	1	0	1.000								
Naphole, John F.																											
1949	Hazlehurst-Baxley	GSL	26	73	10	17	5	0	0	9	3	3	24	0.233	P	13	18	3	0.912	25	8	9	5.00	153	99	88	87
Narieka, Joe																											
1941	Moultrie - Americus	GFL	15	37	1	4	0	0	0	0	0	0	13	0.108	P	6	17	2	0.920	15	5	8	4.97	96	114	48	43

Georgia Class-D Minor League Baseball Encyclopedia

YR	TEAM	LG	G	AB	R	H	2B	3B	HR	RBI	SB	BB	SO	BA	POS	PO	A	E	FA	GP	W	L	ERA	IP	H	SO	BB
Narron, Samuel "Sam"		BR TR 5'10" 180 lbs b. 08/25/1913 Middlesex, NC d. 12/31/1996 Middlesex, NC																									
1935	Albany	GFL	93	361	69	126	24	3	16		3	28	16	0.349	OF	253	128	18	0.955								
Nasworthy, Luther		BR TR																									
1948	Carrollton	GAL	10	25	0	3	1	0	0	1	0	1	9	0.120													
1949	Carrollton	GAL	93	320	43	78	13	1	11	47	5	27	87	0.244	SS, OF	152	156	27	0.919								
Navarro, Henry		BR TR																									
1949	Thomasville	GFL	141	515	100	125	29	8	8	69	23	100	109	0.243	SS	227	468	76	0.901								
Navarro, Ignatius John "Ignatius"		BR TR																									
1953	Brunswick	GFL	3											0.500	P						0	1	<45				
Navarro, Julio (Ventura) "Julio" "Whiplash"		BR TR 5'11" 190 lbs b. 01/09/1936 Vieques, PR																									
1955	Sandersville	GSL	4	6		1								0.167	P					4	0	2					
Naylor, Richard J. "Dick"		BR TR																									
1953	Thomasville	GFL	15	32	5	8	1	0	0	7	0	3	8	0.250	P						2	1	<45				
Nazzaro, Carman		BR TR																									
1948	LaGrange	GAL	11	42	4	11	3	0	1	8	0	5	11	0.262	OF	13	2	2	0.882								
Nebinger, Richard Jr. "Dick"		BR TR																									
1958	Dublin	GFL	24	71	9	13	2	1	3	9	1	12	28	0.183	OF, P	29	2	0	1.000	1	0	0	<30				
Neborak, William "Bill"		BR																									
1940	Moultrie	GFL	<10																								
Nedelco, Alex		BR TL																									
1947	Thomasville	GFL	17	36	3	5	1	1	0	0	0	1	12	0.139	P	2	11	1	0.929	12	6	3	3.49	80	70	64	26
Nee, Dan																											
1936	Moultrie	GFL	19	68	8	16	4	1	2	10	0			0.235	1B	120	3	5	0.961								
Needles, ---																											
1913	Gadsden	GAL	6												P					6	3	3					
Neeley, Gary		BR TR																									
1962	Brunswick	GFL	20	54	13	13	3	1	4	18	1	13	15	0.241	3B	15	24	9	0.813								
Neeley, Robert "Bob"		BR TR																									
1955	Dublin	GSL	33	113	18	31	5	1	4	14	5	11	29	0.274	OF	52	4	2	0.966								
Neely, Jesse "Jess"		BR TR																									
1950	Americus	GFL	31	90	14	14	2	2	0	7	2	21	29	0.156	2B	25	46	9	0.888								
Negray, Ronald Alvin "Ron"		BR TR 6'1" 185 lbs b. 02/26/1930 Akron, OH																									
1949	Valdosta	GFL	36	81	10	14	0	1	0	10	0	13	15	0.173	P	6	33	5	0.886	34	21	6	2.17	228	183	242	79
Neigefind, Victor "Vic"																											
1935	Thomasville	GFL	6												P					6	2	2		31	32	24	7
Nelms, Charles		BL TL																									
1956	Hazlehurst-Baxley	GSL	19	37	3	2	0	0	0	0	0	3	10	0.054	P	5	22	1	0.964	19	4	10	3.68	110	105	73	61
1957	Albany	GFL	2	1		0								0.000	P					2	0	0	<30				
Nelson, ---																											
1913	LaGrange	GAL	80	294	45	78					11			0.265	OF, P	74	37	11	0.910	8	2	6					
1917	LaGrange	GAL	2	6	1	2	0	0	0		1			0.333	OF	5	0	0	1.000								
Nelson, Burel		BR TR																									
1946	Tallassee	GAL	7												P					7	1	2	0.00	32	41	23	14
1947	Tallassee	GAL	37	100	4	16	0	0	0	11	0	0	22	0.160	P	10	41	7	0.879	32	13	14	3.26	232	220	161	85
1949	Carrollton	GAL	22												P					22	5	8			108	51	
Nelson, Charles E.		BR TL																									
1951	Douglas	GSL	17	39	3	3	0	0	0	0	0	2	9	0.077	P	6	23	2	0.935	14	3	7	2.56	95	88	36	29
1952	Douglas	GSL	17	47	10	11	1	0	0	0	0	8	12	0.234	P					9	3	3	4.58	55	66	14	17
Nelson, Charles O.		BL TR																									
1952	Valdosta	GFL	12	37	3	5	2	0	0	0	1	7	11	0.135	OF	7	0	2	0.778								
Nelson, Donald Selby "Don"		BR TR																									
1962	Brunswick	GFL	25	44	8	8	1	0	1	2	0	0	13	0.182	P	1	6	2	0.778	12	2	1	3.82	33	27	22	16
Nelson, Eugene C. "Gene"		BR TR																									
1950	Moultrie	GFL	17	22	1	4	1	1	0	3	0	3	10	0.182	P	5	2	1	0.875	15	4	3	5.61	61	83	27	43
Nelson, James "Jim"		BR TR																									
1946	Opelika	GAL	37	132	11	37	6	1	0	16	1	1	11	0.280	C	127	20	6	0.961								
1947	Opelika	GAL	88	323	45	81	9	3	0	38	10	19	11	0.251	C	510	46	14	0.975								
1948	Thomasville	GFL	101	362	49	107	13	1	0	45	0	47	19	0.296	C	720	72	26	0.968								
1951	Opelika	GAL	38	142	15	32	4	0	0	14	1	15	1	0.225	C	156	19	6	0.967								
Nelson, Richard "Dick"		BR TR																									
1948	Eastman	GSL	23	53	3	8	2	0	0	5	0	1	13	0.151	P	5	14	0	1.000	23	4	13	4.40	135	144	76	69
1949	Carrollton	GAL	26	33	4	7	1	1	1	1	0	1	6	0.212	P	1	9	1	0.909	26	5	5	4.60	88	85	32	61
Nelson, Robert "Bob"																											
1941	Moultrie	GFL	24	101	14	27	1	1	0	6	4	5	11	0.267													
Nemeth, Frank		BR TR																									
1955	Albany	GFL	1	1		0								0.000	P					1	0	0	<45				
Nemeth, Robert "Bob"		BR TR																									
1955	Hazlehurst-Baxley	GSL	19	36	5	7	2	1	0	4	0	4	9	0.194	P	3	18	0	1.000	17	4	5	4.14	87	88	55	55
Nemier, ---																											
1942	Tallahassee	GFL	4	13	2	4	0	1	0	0	0	1	4	0.308	C	14	1	0	1.000								
Nesbihal, Edward "Ed"		BR																									
1954	Waycross	GFL	2	0										0.000													
Nesta, Nicholas "Nick"		BR TR																									
1962	Dublin	GFL	10	9	0	0	0	0	0	0	0	2	4	0.000	P	0	7	2	0.778	10	2	2	6.47	32	32	33	33

Georgia Class-D Minor League Baseball Encyclopedia

YR	TEAM	LG	G	AB	R	H	2B	3B	HR	RBI	SB	BB	SO	BA	POS	PO	A	E	FA	GP	W	L	ERA	IP	H	SO	BB
Nester, James "Jim"		BR TR																									
1957	Waycross	GFL	138	503	71	157	10	8	5	76	4	64	43	0.312	3B	99	133	30	0.885								
1958	Waycross	GFL	93	342	54	102	8	2	1	48	3	51	24	0.298	3B, OF, P	115	50	15	0.917	1	0	0		<30			
Nettles, Hoke																											
1929	Carrollton	GAL	6	18	7	10								0.556	OF												
Newcomb, ---																											
1936	Albany	GFL													P									<30			
Newcomb, Walter "Tete"		BL TR																									
1935	Tallahassee	GFL	97	369	57	108	16	2	3		12	34	29	0.293	OF	168	20	7	0.964								
1936	Tallahassee	GFL	122	476	70	141	16	7	5	85	10			0.296	OF	202	17	9	0.961								
1937	Tallahassee	GFL	87	337	39	89	9	3	2	30	11	32	14	0.264	OF	203	16	11	0.952								
1938	Americus	GFL	58	200	24	60	9	2	0	37	1	15	13	0.300	UT	156	50	16	0.928								
1939	Cordele	GFL	49	159	11	34	8	0	0	20	2	20	11	0.214	UT	180	39	14	0.940								
1940	Tallahassee	GFL	127	472	57	136	20	2	1	68	7	50	18	0.288	1B, UT, P	613	63	29	0.959					<35			
Newcomer, Jack		BR TR																									
1962	Brunswick	GFL	111	392	75	110	18	4	12	56	12	62	85	0.281	2B	235	268	39	0.928								
Newell, Kirk																											
1914	Opelika	GAL	91	349	62	90					30			0.258	M, 2B	232	261	33	0.937								
1915	Rome	GAL	13	48	4	7	1	0	0					0.146	3B	33	25	4	0.935								
Newell, Robert W. "Bob"		BL TL																									
1949	Thomasville	GFL	33	131	27	21	6	0	1	15	5	34	27	0.160	1B	280	10	8	0.973								
1950	Thomasville	GFL	125	443	81	111	21	3	5	47	8	87	54	0.251	1B	992	62	21	0.980								
Newhall, Robert "Bob"		BL TL																									
1946	Opelika	GAL	84	259	33	59	9	2	0	25	3	32	35	0.228	2B, C, P	185	147	20	0.943	2	0	0	0.00	5			
Newkirk, ---																											
1906	Americus	GSL													SS, 2B												
Newkirk, ---																											
1913	LaGrange	GAL	91	319	58	77					35			0.241	1B	862	28	30	0.967								
Newlin, Bob																											
1941	Tallahassee	GFL	3												P					3	0	0	12.00	9	11	3	7
Newmarch, Ronald "Ron"		BR TR																									
1953	Fitzgerald	GFL	8											0.000	P					2	1			<45			
1953	Haz-Bax - Sandersville	GSL	26	54	6	5	0	0	0	3	0	11	23	0.093	P	6	19	0	1.000	24	8	10	4.28	164	186	78	72
Newsome, Arthur "Art"		BL TL																									
1946	Valley	GAL	12	15	2	6	1	0	0	0	0	2	1	0.400	P					5	1	3	0.00	20	21	12	12
Newsome, Lamar Ashby "Skeeter"		BR TR 5'9" 170 lbs b. 10/18/1910 Phenix City, AL d. 08/31/1989 Columbus, GA																									
1930	Talladega	GAL	83	352	63	100	18	4	5		14	21	21	0.284	SS	197	309	47	0.915								
Newton, Doc																											
1928	Gadsden	GAL	16	38	6	8	2	0	1	0	0		10	0.211	M, P					6	2	3	4.83	41	61	8	6
Newton, L. Doin "Leo"		BR TR																									
1963	Brunswick	GFL	15	16	1	3	0	0	0	3	0	5	9	0.188	P	3	13	0	1.000	15	3	5	3.10	61	63	63	32
Newton, Thomas "Tom"		BR TR																									
1958	Valdosta	GFL	29	116	22	30	7	1	2	10	0	13	7	0.259	OF	31	3	3	0.919								
Newton, W. Cash																											
1915	Newnan	GAL	58	189	22	46	5	0	0					0.243	SS	103	177	25	0.918								
1916	Talladega	GAL	20	63	7	9					0			0.143	SS												
Neyen, William "Bill"		BL TL																									
1954	Valdosta	GFL	40	124	16	30	3	1	1	6	3	17	21	0.242	1B	320	22	9	0.974								
Nicholas, Alvin																											
1936	Thomasville	GFL	35	119	25	37	4	3	3	25	4			0.311	1B	286	10	13	0.958								
1937	Thomasville	GFL	42	143	24	28	6	1	4	19	2	31	36	0.196	1B	428	17	8	0.982								
Nichols, Bruce		BR TR																									
1963	Thomasville	GFL	111	348	41	86	13	0	9	43	1	49	86	0.247	1B, C	715	59	14	0.982								
Nichols, Charles R.		BR TR																									
1955	Douglas	GSL	6	6		3								0.500	P					6	1	1					
Nichols, Fred		BR TR																									
1947	Alexander City	GAL	62	226	39	57	9	1	9	31	10	30	54	0.252	OF	101	6	17	0.863								
Nichols, James E. "Jim"		BS TR																									
1949	Moultrie	GFL	11	16	2	2	0	0	0	1	0	0	6	0.125													
1955	Thomasville		18	37	2	4	1	2	0	3	2	9	14	0.108	OF	8	0	5	0.615								
Nicholson, David Lawrence "Dave"		BR TR 6'2" 215 lbs b. 08/29/1939 St. Louis, MO																									
1958	Dublin	GFL	28	110	19	25	7	2	3	21	0	17	41	0.227	OF	52	2	3	0.947								
Nichting, Raymond "Ray"		BR TR																									
1951	Fitzgerald	GSL	74	273	45	75	5	5	1	31	9	37	25	0.275	OF	141	17	19	0.893								
1952	Fitzgerald	GSL	126	466	84	144	15	10	8	80	15	109	52	0.309	OF	323	21	22	0.940								
Nickerson, Frank		BR TR																									
1948	Douglas(14) - Vidalia-Lyons(1)	GSL	15	21	2	3	0	0	0	1	0	3	8	0.143	P	2	11	0	1.000	15	1	6	5.95	62	77	19	54
Nicolai, Melvin "Mel"		BR TR																									
1946	Cordele	GFL	39	79	4	10	1	0	0	3	0	4	33	0.127	P	12	38	5	0.909	38	10	19	3.53	214	219	157	95
Niedowicz, Frank		BR TR																									
1949	Moultrie	GFL	111	428	61	135	20	9	4	77	19	43	50	0.315	1B, OF	284	13	11	0.964								
Niedzowieski, Ronald "Ron"		BL TL																									
1956	Fitzgerald	GFL	30	96	6	14	2	0	0	5	0	15	38	0.146	1B	230	6	8	0.967								
Niemeier, Donald "Don"		BR TR																									
1956	Thomson	GSL	48	175	22	40	8	0	0	14	6	22	39	0.229	OF	75	7	6	0.932								

Georgia Class-D Minor League Baseball Encyclopedia

YR	TEAM	LG	G	AB	R	H	2B	3B	HR	RBI	SB	BB	SO	BA	POS	PO	A	E	FA	GP	W	L	ERA	IP	H	SO	BB
Nierpoetter, William "Billy"		BR TR																									
1949	Newnan	GAL	34	63	4	10	0	0	0	7	0	8	19	0.159	P	5	18	0	1.000	34	15	12	4.26	184	189	142	116
1950	Valley(11) - Alex City(6)	GAL	17	21	0	3	1	0	0	2	0	2	3	0.143	P	6	17	1	0.958	17	2	8	6.18	67	84	27	54
Niklas, Roger		BR TR																									
1950	Waycross	GFL	11	34	7	9	1	0	0	3	0	4	9	0.265	OF	19	1	2	0.909								
Niles, Harry		BR TR																									
1958	Waycross	GFL	20	71	15	17	2	1	2	6	0	17	18	0.239	2B	48	41	4	0.957								
Nims, Keith		BR TR																									
1955	Statesboro	GSL	1	0										0.000	P					1	0	0					
Nisewonger, James B. "Jim"		BR TR																									
1953	Brunswick	GFL	48	103	13	23	4	0	1	12	1	10	19	0.223	P	11	53	4	0.941	31	18	6	1.99	213	189	115	106
1955	Brunswick	GFL	46	162	33	41	5	2	2	27	4	9	37	0.253	OF, P	64	17	6	0.931	8	2	2	<45				
1956	Moultrie	GFL	13	32	3	9	2	0	0	5	0	4	5	0.281	P	7	19	2	0.929	13	8	2	2.86	85	75	53	33
1958	Waycross	GFL	26	91	20	24	5	0	2	11	6	23	13	0.264	OF	43	3	3	0.939								
Nitram, ---																											
1920	LaGrange	GSL													SS												
Nix, George		BR																									
1946	Newnan	GAL	<10												M												
Nix, Henry		BL TR																									
1946	Albany(26) - Cordele(18)	GFL	44	144	16	33	3	0	0	11	4	17	31	0.229	2B, OF	73	49	16	0.884								
1951	Jesup	GSL	105	360	45	87	16	1	2	44	1	33	40	0.242	1B, OF	276	11	7	0.976								
Nix, Thomas "Tom"		BL TR																									
1956	Thomson	GSL	93	352	49	76	8	5	5	45	6	46	101	0.216	2B, 3B, SS, OF	150	127	27	0.911								
Njirich, Gildo		BR TR																									
1946	Waycross	GFL	40	131	14	31	5	1	0	22	0	17	25	0.237	OF, C	122	9	7	0.949								
1947	Waycross	GFL	82	297	36	73	7	1	1	45	3	23	42	0.246	OF, C	507	44	18	0.968								
Noah, Harold		BL TR																									
1947	Valdosta	GFL	47	170	23	41	5	6	0	23	5	18	66	0.241	OF	90	9	10	0.908								
1950	Tifton	GSL	25	88	17	23	3	2	1	10	4	27	19	0.261	OF	67	2	6	0.920								
Nobles, ---																											
1929	Cedartown	GAL	6												P					6	1	0		17	28	2	8
Nobles, Julian		BR TR																									
1946	Americus(1) - Thomasville(28)	GFL	29	44	8	11	0	0	0	1	0	4	6	0.250	P	10	27	4	0.902	28	6	11	4.60	135	154	52	52
Noga, George		BR TR																									
1948	Griffin	GAL	98	370	48	104	10	8	2	42	2	36	55	0.281	3B	103	158	21	0.926								
1949	Griffin	GAL	122	458	71	121	21	4	7	72	11	54	58	0.264	3B, SS	207	272	31	0.939								
1950	Griffin	GAL	120	484	106	144	17	8	12	80	21	63	56	0.298	SS	252	371	44	0.934								
Nojunas, Albert "Al"		BL																									
1948	Moultrie	GFL	10	9	1	2	1	0	0	2	0	2	5	0.222													
Nolley, ---																											
1906	Albany	GSL													OF												
Nolly, Rufus																											
1916	LaGrange	GAL	14	45	5	8					0			0.178	P					14	12	2					
1917	Anniston		4	11	1	3	0	0	0		0			0.273	P	1	11	2	0.857	4	1	0		26	27	19	8
Norbert, Theodore Jr. "Ted"		BR TR																									
1958	Waycross	GFL	106	410	55	128	33	0	12	86	4	51	48	0.312	1B, OF	863	48	13	0.986								
Nordenhold, Henry		BL TL																									
1956	Douglas	GSL	31	66	7	8	1	0	0	7	0	5	23	0.121	P	11	13	3	0.889	29	15	5	2.86	176	161	136	85
Norman, Jesse																											
1915	Talladega	GAL	18	60	4	12	6	1	0					0.200	P	4	37	1	0.976	18	10	4					
Norris, James R. "Jim"		BL TR																									
1953	Thomasville	GFL	4											0.286														
1955	Thomasville	GFL	134	494	75	121	16	5	4	61	23	79	59	0.245	OF	202	14	10	0.956								
Norris, Larry		BL TL																									
1954	Vidalia	GSL	4	12		4								0.333	P					4	3	0	<45				
Norris, Robert "Bob"		BR TR																									
1962	Brunswick	GFL	30	78	13	24	3	1	2	8	2	11	18	0.308	OF	31	0	2	0.939								
Norris, Ronald "Ron"		BR TR																									
1962	Moultrie	GFL	4	9	2	1	0	0	0	1	0	0	1	0.111	P					4	1	2	1.96	23	15	13	8
North, Lamar		BR TR																									
1948	Eastman	GSL	105	373	47	101	14	4	0	36	9	24	55	0.271	OF	184	7	12	0.941								
1949	Eastman	GSL	117	450	74	145	27	7	1	80	17	22	20	0.322	C	541	29	10	0.983								
North, Robert E. "Bob"		BR TR																									
1952	Jesup	GSL	22	66	8	15	3	0	1	8	3	16	9	0.227	2B	39	30	13	0.841								
Norton, Harold N.		BR TL																									
1953	Valdosta	GFL	118	466	75	132	18	3	0	36	10	35	42	0.283	OF	226	11	23	0.912								
Noto, Philip "Phil"		BR TR																									
1946	Opelika	GAL	40	127	13	23	2	0	0	8	0	7	29	0.181	SS	76	128	20	0.911								
1947	Opelika(10) - Tallassee(14)	GAL	24	58	2	12	1	0	0	4	2	5	14	0.207	2B	22	19	0	1.000								
1949	Opelika	GAL	100	312	37	90	8	2	0	52	0	34	40	0.288	C	511	64	23	0.962								
Novak, Walter "Walt"		BL TR																									
1963	Brunswick	GFL	40	116	22	28	5	0	1	3	9	10	33	0.241	OF	47	6	3	0.946								
Nowak, Edmund "Ed"																											
1936	Albany	GFL	11	20	1	8	1	0	0	2	0			0.400	P					11	3	1	4.70	46		14	15
1937	Albany	GFL	26	65	5	14	2	0	0	4	0	1	9	0.215	P	18	21	5	0.886	16	5	7	6.03	97	117	35	53
1941	Valdosta	GFL	2												P					2	0	2	54.00	1	1	0	7

Georgia Class-D Minor League Baseball Encyclopedia

YR	TEAM	LG	G	AB	R	H	2B	3B	HR	RBI	SB	BB	SO	BA	POS	PO	A	E	FA	GP	W	L	ERA	IP	H	SO	BB
Nowak, Henry E. "Hank"																											
1937	Albany	GFL	39	78	12	17	2	1	0	7	0	12	16	0.218	P	15	45	6	0.909	34	11	13	4.19	217	193	134	130
1938	Albany	GFL	39	91	19	22	1	4	1	13	0	8	8	0.242	P	12	58	2	0.972	33	20	11	3.78	243	226	165	137
Nunley, ---																											
1906	Albany	GSL													P												
Nunn, ---																											
1920	Lindale	GSL													C												
Nunnally, ---																											
1921	Rome	GSL													OF												
O'Barr, Thomas B. "Tom"																											
1949	Sparta	GSL	12	30	3	4	0	1	0	2	0	1	5	0.133	P	2	13	4	0.789	13	2	3	5.71	63	53	27	54
1950	Albany	GFL	12	8	0	0	0	0	0	0	0	0	4	0.000	P	1	4	0	1.000								
1951	Rome	GAL	48	107	16	20	2	1	0	11	2	5	17	0.187	P	13	54	6	0.918	39	13	15	3.89	208	232	107	132
1952	Douglas	GSL	43	105	18	35	5	0	0	12	3	11	11	0.333	OF, P	31	34	6	0.915	19	9	7	2.89	134	112	73	66
1953	Douglas	GSL	1											0.000	P					0	0	1		<45			
O'Brien, ---																											
1914	Valdosta - Brunswick	GSL		350	28	90	18	0	3		4			0.257													
1915	Brunswick	FLAG		0										0.000													
O'Brien, James J. "Jim"		BR TR																									
1946	Cordele	GFL	9												P					9	0	2	0.00	27	38	10	12
O'Brien, Phillip "Phil"		BR TL																									
1963	Thomasville	GFL	21	29	0	3	0	0	0	1	0	1	15	0.103	P	0	15	1	0.938	21	6	6	2.97	100	87	85	28
O'Brien, William J. "Bill"		BR TR																									
1948	Tallahassee	GFL	24	91	11	23	2	2	0	9	2	6	16	0.253	OF	37	1	4	0.905								
1949	Tallahassee	GFL	90	337	48	95	17	4	3	37	9	54	46	0.282	OF	196	16	15	0.934								
O'Bryant, Oscar		BR TR																									
1951	Eastman	GSL	17	23	1	1	0	0	0	2	0	3	10	0.043	P	0	7	0	1.000	17	1	3	4.73	59	66	29	37
O'Callaghan, Thomas "Tom"		BR TR																									
1950	Waycross	GFL	32	79	5	18	1	1	1	3	0	4	24	0.228	P	6	11	0	1.000	19	4	6	4.70	90	112	50	51
Oceak, Frank John "Frank"		b. 09/08/1912 Pocahantas, VA d. 03/19/1983 Johnstown, PA																									
1953	Dublin	GSL													M												
1954	Brunswick	GFL													M												
1955	Brunswick	GFL													M												
1956	Brunswick	GFL													M												
O'Coine, Marshall		BR TR																									
1949	Waycross	GFL	22	39	5	12	2	0	0	6	0	3	10	0.308	P	4	10	1	0.933	21	8	4	3.86	91	93	51	45
O'Connell, Robert J. "Joe"		BR																									
1953	Dublin	GSL	8											0.250													
O'Connell, Thomas A. "Tom"		BR																									
1946	Newnan	GAL	<10																								
O'Connor, Michael "Mike"		BR TR																									
1956	Albany	GFL	16	19	0	1	0	0	0	0	0	2	12	0.053	P	1	11	2	0.857	16	3	6	5.53	57	47	65	61
Odell, Clancy																											
1942	Valdosta	GFL													M												
Odom, Lilburn																											
1936	Cordele	GFL	115	421	69	113	13	9	13	90	9			0.268	OF	295	12	19	0.942								
O'Donnell, Harry Herman "Harry"		BR TR 5'8" 175 lbs b. 04/02/1894 Philadelphia, PA d. 01/31/1958 Philadelphia, PA																									
1935	Thomasville	GFL													M												
O'Donnell, James "Jim"		BL TR																									
1957	Fitzgerald	GFL	10	12	2	2	0	0	0	1	0	1	7	0.167	P					9	0	2		<30			
O'Donnell, John J.		BL TL																									
1948	Griffin	GAL	68	164	23	51	5	1	1	27	1	11	22	0.311	OF, P	29	48	5	0.939	35	15	12	3.23	234	187	191	143
Odum, William "Bill"		BR																									
1955	Vidalia	GSL	4	15		2								0.133													
Oehler, Victor "Vic"																											
1935	Albany	GFL	14	56	14	19	7	0	1		0	6	10	0.339	OF	48	2	0	1.000								
Oertel, Charles Frank "Chuck"		BL TR 5'8" 165 lbs b. 03/12/1931 Coffeyville, KS																									
1950	Hazlehurst-Baxley	GSL	92	398	71	140	14	19	3	59	4	25	30	0.352	3B, SS	139	157	47	0.863								
Ogiego, Walter "Walt"																											
1939	Tallahassee	GFL	39	94	11	19	1	1	0	8	0	5	14	0.202	P	22	73	2	0.979	31	17	8	3.19	220	220	136	81
Ogier, T.L.		BR TR																									
1939	Cordele	GFL	67	244	25	64	6	0	0	14	7	29	49	0.262	3B	79	118	24	0.891								
1940	Cordele	GFL	54	201	22	44	4	2	1	27	2	17	39	0.219	SS	140	102	27	0.900								
Ogle, Fred																											
1937	Tallahassee	GFL	27	77	5	10	0	1	0	6	1	7	17	0.130	P	22	41	4	0.940	16	7	5	2.14	118	97	35	40
Ogle, Hugh																											
1929	Lindale	GAL	13	30	6	5	1	0	0		2	6	9	0.167	P	14	13	1	0.964								
Oglesby, Alexander "Alex"		BR TR																									
1950	Tallahassee	GFL	16	23	1	3	1	0	0	6	0	3	6	0.130	C	29	1	1	0.968								
1951	Griffin	GAL	40	99	10	16	0	0	0	6	0	17	17	0.162	C	121	17	3	0.979								
1952	Jesup	GSL	67	254	23	54	4	0	1	24	2	24	18	0.213	C	330	43	12	0.969								
Oglesby, Hugh		BR TR																									
1946	Carrollton	GAL	26	87	9	13	1	1	1	5	0	8	22	0.149	OF	35	2	4	0.902								
O'Higgins, Dennis																											
1936	Thomasville	GFL	20	42	5	8	1	0	1	6	0			0.190	P					20	3	8	4.45	99		42	65

355

Georgia Class-D Minor League Baseball Encyclopedia

YR	TEAM	LG	G	AB	R	H	2B	3B	HR	RBI	SB	BB	SO	BA	POS	PO	A	E	FA	GP	W	L	ERA	IP	H	SO	BB
Ohr, Clifford "Cliff"		BR TR																									
1954	Thomasville	GFL	4	2	0									0.000	P					3	0	0	<45				
O'Kelley, Clyde		BL TR																									
1946	Opelika	GAL	22	63	11	10	1	0	0	5	0	7	20	0.159	C	98	19	5	0.959								
Okey, Kene																											
1942	Americus	GFL	7												P					7	3	4	4.81	43	61	10	12
O'Kronley, Pete																											
1938	Thomasville	GFL	10	28	3	6	1	0	0	1	0	0	7	0.214	P	10	0	0	1.000	9	5	3	3.88	72	78	23	16
Olayko, Alexander "Alex"		BR TR																									
1948	Opelika	GAL	99	335	48	70	6	3	2	41	9	42	74	0.209	C	543	78	15	0.976								
Oldershaw, Howard		BR TR																									
1948	Baxley	GSL	16	32	1	5	2	0	0	2	0	2	10	0.156	P	4	18	2	0.917	16	5	6	3.78	88	82	47	43
1949	Hazlehurst-Baxley	GSL	52	132	12	28	1	0	2	15	4	17	32	0.212	P, OF	42	47	8	0.918	35	10	13	6.09	195	157	94	104
Oldfield, Pat																											
1928	Anniston	GAL	21	75	8	18	4	0	0		3	5	6	0.240	3B	19	29	5	0.906								
1929	Anniston	GAL	97	365	57	103	10	6	4		12	32	15	0.282	3B	238	60	28	0.914								
1930	Cedartown	GAL	58	214	31	70	5	1	3		2	9	5	0.327	2B, 3B, C	84	57	10	0.934								
Oliver, Ben		BR TR																									
1946	Tallahassee	GFL	27	48	6	7	0	0	0	4	1	8	10	0.146	P	4	30	2	0.944	24	7	7	4.94	124	146	61	60
Oliver, Eugene George "Gene"		BR TR 6'2" 225 lbs b. 03/22/1935 Moline, IL																									
1956	Albany	GFL	9	16		4								0.250													
Oliveri, Fred																											
1949	Fitzgerald	GSL	14												1B	79	3	7	0.921								
Olmstead, Paul		BR TR																									
1949	Waycross	GFL	28	50	8	11	1	1	0	1	0	5	11	0.220	P	3	38	3	0.932	27	6	5	5.21	121	149	80	78
Olmstead, Theodore "Ted"		BL TL																									
1946	Albany	GFL	8												P					8	1	4	0.00	27	28	33	33
O'Malley, Daniel "Dan"		BR TR																									
1950	Hazlehurst-Baxley	GSL	17	46	5	14	2	0	0	2	0	2	12	0.304	OF	13	2	0	1.000								
O'Mara, Laurence "Larry"		BR TR																									
1958	Waycross	GFL	30	46	6	8	1	0	0	3	0	4	16	0.174	P	17	21	4	0.905	27	7	10	4.91	141	152	77	50
O'Neal, ---																											
1917	Talladega	GAL	10	41	5	8	3	0	0		1			0.195	3B, SS, OF	23	4	11	0.711								
O'Neal, S. Thomas "Tom"		BR TR																									
1953	Vidalia	GSL	10	18	3	4	0	0	0	4	0	1	8	0.222	P					2	2		<45				
O'Neil, George Michael "Mickey"		BR TR 5'10" 185 lbs b. 04/12/1900 St. Louis, MO d. 04/08/1964 St. Louis, MO																									
1951	Brunswick	GFL													M												
1952	Brunswick	GFL													M												
O'Neil, John Francis "John"		BR TR 5'9" 155 lbs b. 04/19/1920 Shelbiana, KY																									
1939	Tallahassee	GFL	13	43	5	8	0	0	0	2	0	8	5	0.186	SS	22	41	8	0.887								
O'Neill, John J.		BL TL																									
1954	Waycross	GFL	29	54	5	9	1	1	0	5	0	3	22	0.167	P	5	27	1	0.970	24	6	6	3.53	120	100	97	66
1955	Albany	GFL	19	23	0	2	0	0	0	0	0	0	11	0.087	P	4	13	1	0.944	14	1	3	<45				
Oneto, Francis		BR TR																									
1954	Valdosta	GFL	46	159	18	41	10	0	0	11	3	22	27	0.258	2B, SS	111	130	18	0.931								
Oquendo, Noel		BR TR																									
1949	Fitzgerald	GSL	54	178	29	40	13	1	4	30	5	24	46	0.225	P, OF	41	58	6	0.943	41	17	19	4.06	297	175	224	171
1950	Fitzgerald	GSL	40	77	13	16	4	0	2	7	0	11	16	0.208	P	11	36	8	0.855	31	9	15	5.29	187	191	122	148
1951	Dublin	GSL	44	94	15	29	5	1	2	12	0	12	15	0.309	P	8	29	2	0.949	36	13	9	3.56	172	150	109	110
1952	Dublin	GSL	86	231	39	63	24	0	5	45	5	37	39	0.273	OF, P	68	60	7	0.948	33	20	10	3.68	269	223	245	147
O'Quinn, ---																											
1906	Valdosta	GSL													P												
Orlandi, Ronald "Ron"		BR TR																									
1949	Fitzgerald	GSL	78	240	33	49	13	2	1	20	3	43	53	0.204	C, P	144	79	27	0.892	18	5	9	6.05	110	88	52	71
1950	Fitzgerald	GSL	128	484	51	137	21	0	5	86	8	60	66	0.283	C	781	82	22	0.975								
Orner, Charles		BR TR																									
1950	Vidalia-Lyons	GSL	82	251	27	69	8	2	3	28	3	43	41	0.275	C	353	58	15	0.965								
O'Rourke, James Francis "Frank"		BR TR 5'10" 165 lbs b. 11/28/1894 Hamilton, ON, CAN d. 05/14/1986 Chatham, NJ																									
1942	Cordele	GFL													M												
O'Rourke, Thomas J. "Tom"		BL TL																									
1953	Dublin	GSL	16	63	16	20	4	1	0	11	3	13	5	0.317													
Orr, Albert F. "Dick"																											
1937	Albany	GFL	37	125	18	27	6	1	2	13	2	19	33	0.216	2B	92	83	11	0.941								
Orr, Billy J.		BR TR																									
1956	Albany	GFL	16	44	6	7	1	0	0	3	1	6	16	0.159	3B	14	31	6	0.882								
Orsatti, Frank		BL TL																									
1963	Brunswick	GFL	12	33	3	7	2	0	0	1	1	4	7	0.212	OF	15	0	0	1.000								
Ortiz, Felix		BR TR																									
1956	Dublin	GSL	103	378	49	96	14	3	0	27	3	33	52	0.254	2B, 3B	168	215	44	0.897								
Ortiz, Otoniel		BR TR																									
1948	Newnan	GAL	109	450	82	135	19	4	6	66	8	70	56	0.300	2B	222	264	39	0.926								
Osborne, E. Peter "Pete"		BL TR																									
1946	Waycross	GFL	63	173	18	48	5	1	1	33	1	22	21	0.277	OF, P	30	42	5	0.935	32	18	8	3.95	196	217	115	75

Georgia Class-D Minor League Baseball Encyclopedia

YR	TEAM	LG	G	AB	R	H	2B	3B	HR	RBI	SB	BB	SO	BA	POS	PO	A	E	FA	GP	W	L	ERA	IP	H	SO	BB
Osborne, Ernest Preston "Tiny"			BL TR 6'4" 215 lbs b. 04/09/1893 Porterdale, GA d. 01/05/1969 Atlanta, GA																								
1920	Griffin	GSL													P, OF												
1921	Griffin	GSL	47	9	17									0.362	P												
Osborne, Wilson		BR																									
1953	Jesup	GSL	8											0.400													
Osburn, Herman		BR TR																									
1953	Cordele	GFL	21	35	0	3	0	0	0	2	1	4	11	0.086	P	3	23	2	0.929	21	2	8	3.55	109	114	67	56
Oscher, Robert "Bob"																											
1935	Tallahassee	GFL	18	50	5	9	0	0	0	0		7	23	0.180	P					23	6	10		149	140	104	69
Osment, ---																											
1906	Cordele	GSL													OF												
Osteen, Frank		BR TR																									
1947	Alexander City	GAL	17	38	2	5	0	0	0	1	0	5	9	0.132	OF	32	2	4	0.895								
Osteen, W.J.																											
1916	Newnan - Anniston	GAL	36	65	5	11				0				0.169	OF, P												
Osteen, William "Bill"		BR TR																									
1947	Alexander City	GAL	10	20	2	6	1	0	0	2	0	1	2	0.300													
1949	Albany	GFL	81	252	45	82	11	6	1	38	8	32	22	0.325	C	405	41	9	0.980								
Ostendorf, Frederick K. "Fred"		BL TL 6'0" 169 lbs b. 08/05/1890 Baltimore, MD d. 03/02/1965 Kecoughtan, VA																									
1915	Thomasville	FLAG	10	24	0	4	0	0	0	1				0.167													
1915	Griffin	GAL	<6												P					<6							
Oster, Frederick "Fred"		BR TR																									
1955	Thomasville	GFL	8	6		1								0.167	P					8	1	3		<45			
Oster, Sandy		BR																									
1954	Waycross	GFL	8	21		4								0.190													
Osthoff, Wilbur S.																											
1949	Dublin	GSL	114	457	84	121	18	4	5	52	13	31	52	0.265	SS, P	232	244	44	0.915	14	9	1	2.48	80	28	47	36
Ostopchuck, Joseph "Joe"		BR TR																									
1953	Albany	GFL	27	49	4	9	2	1	0	4	1	2	19	0.184	P	4	15	1	0.950	27	11	3	3.09	128	92	94	85
Otey, Richard "Dick"		BL TL																									
1954	Hazlehurst-Baxley	GSL	9	7		2								0.286	P					8	1	4		<45			
O'Toole, Daniel "Dan"																											
1942	Cordele	GFL	15	37	4	7	0	0	0	1	0	5	8	0.189	P	24	7	3	0.912	14	5	8	7.50	66	70	17	40
O'Toole, James P. "Jim"		BR TR																									
1950	Fitzgerald	GSL	27	54	13	14	1	0	0	9	3	18	11	0.259	C	84	8	3	0.968								
Ott, Ronald "Ron"		BL TR																									
1956	Hazlehurst-Baxley	GSL	43	141	18	34	7	2	0	12	0	16	34	0.241	C	238	28	3	0.989								
Otten, Donald "Don"		BR TR																									
1947	Valdosta	GFL	22	45	4	8	1	0	0	3	0	2	12	0.178	P	8	22	4	0.882	21	6	10	4.33	129	134	68	74
Ouchterloney, Donald "Don"		BR																									
1946	Valdosta	GFL	12	47	7	9	1	0	0	9	1	6	10	0.191													
Overland, John		BR TL																									
1948	Tallahassee(17) - Valdosta(20)	GFL	37	141	29	45	7	1	1	20	1	18	17	0.319	1B	265	8	8	0.972								
Overmire, Frank W. "Stubby"		BR TL 5'7" 170 lbs b. 05/16/1919 Moline, MI d. 03/03/1977 Lakeland, FL																									
1958	Valdosta	GFL													M												
Overstreet, Charles		BR TL																									
1948	Douglas	GSL	20	34	2	4	1	0	0	3	0	3	7	0.118	P	6	8	1	0.933	18	3	6	3.58	83	76	51	53
Overton, Dannie																											
1917	Rome-Lindale	GAL	9	28	6	10	1	0	0	4				0.357	M, OF, SS	16	18	6	0.850								
Overton, H.A.																											
1914	Selma	GAL	46	174	32	32				13				0.184	SS	96	150	22	0.918								
1915	Rome	GAL	44	159	17	36	4	1	1					0.226	SS	73	126	26	0.884								
1920	Rome	GSL		244	57	63	10	2	3	28				0.258	2B												
1921	Lindale			172	44	53								0.308	2B												
Owen, Marvin James "Marv" "Freck"		BR TR 6'1" 175 lbs b. 03/22/1906 Agnew, CA d. 06/22/1991 Mountain View, CA																									
1954	Valdosta	GFL													M												
Owen, Maurice		BR TR																									
1949	Tallassee	GAL	22	45	1	4	2	0	0	3	0	5	12	0.089	P	6	28	3	0.919	22	9	9	2.20	139	108	57	76
Owen, William Lee "Bill"		BR TR																									
1953	Dublin(10) - Jesup(10)	GSL	20	40	4	9	2	0	1				7	0.225	P	2	10	0	1.000	15	1	6	8.39	59	57	30	69
1954	Sandersville	GSL	2	4		0								0.000	P					2	0	2		<45			
1956	Douglas	GSL	6	3		0								0.000	P					6	1	1					
Owens, D.L.																											
1935	Panama City	GFL	105	433	61	99	15	0	1		21	37	55	0.229	IF	170	155	23	0.934								
Oyler, Richard "Dick"																											
1936	Thomasville	GFL	14	26	4	8	2	0	1	1	0			0.308	P					14	2	2	4.98	56		19	39
Ozburn, ---																											
1930	Cedartown	GAL	82	313	51	73	14	3	3		4	21	46	0.233	2B	188	273	46	0.909								
Pacanowski, Albert "Art"		BR																									
1951	Waycross	GFL	12	36	5	9	0	0	0	3	0	3	9	0.250													
Pace, Carl																											
1914	Talladega	GAL													M												
Pacholke, Albert "Al"		BR TR																									
1958	Brunswick	GFL	4	1		0								0.000	P					4	0	0		<30			

Georgia Class-D Minor League Baseball Encyclopedia

YR	TEAM	LG	G	AB	R	H	2B	3B	HR	RBI	SB	BB	SO	BA	POS	PO	A	E	FA	GP	W	L	ERA	IP	H	SO	BB
Padgett, Charles		BR TR																									
1946	Newnan(47) - LaGrange(1)	GAL	48	165	22	32	4	0	1	10	2	18	33	0.194	SS	71	116	17	0.917								
1947	Carrollton	GAL	17	68	9	11	1	0	0	5	1	5	13	0.162	SS	23	53	12	0.864								
1950	Rome	GAL	15	49	10	12	2	0	0	3	1	9	6	0.245	SS	29	36	2	0.970								
1950	Jesup	GSL	99	372	39	101	14	3	4	60	7	38	50	0.272	3B	94	158	22	0.920								
Padgett, Thomas W. "Tom"		BR TR																									
1953	Douglas	GSL	2											0.000	P						0	1	<45				
Padgett, Travis																											
1939	Moultrie	GFL	26	96	11	24	3	0	0	12	1	14	13	0.250	OF	35	5	3	0.930								
Padgett, William D. "Bill"		BR TR																									
1950	Rome(25) - Griffin(4)	GAL	29	34	1	2	0	0	0	1	0	14	19	0.059	P	1	26	4	0.871	29	2	9	5.81	113	123	66	107
1951	Griffin	GAL	34	67	7	9	1	0	0	1	0	14	35	0.134	P	3	25	2	0.933	34	13	9	3.75	199	222	90	110
Paepke, Jack		BR TR																									
1953	Brunswick	GFL	115	374	80	119	32	1	21	109	4	82	30	0.318	M, C, P	604	38	16	0.976		4	1	<45				
Page, Glen		BL TR																									
1947	Tallahassee	GFL	57	109	12	26	5	1	0	16	1	15	15	0.239	P	4	47	4	0.927	33	15	6	2.63	202	192	121	83
Page, William "Bill"		BR TL																									
1956	Hazlehurst-Baxley	GSL	13	17	3	2	0	0	0	2	0	3	8	0.118	P	1	10	0	1.000	11	2	2	4.41	51	57	25	33
Pagel, Victor "Vic"		BR TR																									
1958	Thomasville	GFL	38	133	11	22	4	2	1	12	0	20	42	0.165	3B	35	62	17	0.851								
Paisley, William "Bill"		BR																									
1946	Tallahassee	GFL	<10																									
Paison, Bob		BR																									
1946	Cordele	GFL	<10																									
Pakes, Thomas "Tom"		BR TR																									
1956	Tifton	GFL	1	0										0.000	P					1	0	0	<45				
Palantino, Robert "Bob"		BL TL 5'11" 190 lbs b. 07/30/1922 Utica, NY																									
1946	Americus	GFL	19	19	1	2	0	0	0	1	0	2	6	0.105	P	1	10	1	0.917	19	4	3	3.57	63	62	51	31
Palko, William "Bill"		BR TL																									
1962	Moultrie	GFL	32	24	4	3	0	1	1	4	0	4	8	0.125	P	4	13	5	0.773	28	4	6	5.48	69	61	65	64
1963	Moultrie	GFL	20	24	2	5	0	0	0	1	0	2	12	0.208	P	7	13	2	0.909	19	6	6	3.07	88	69	91	59
Pallavicini, Vincent "Vince"		BL TR																									
1962	Thomasville	GFL	76	260	40	61	12	1	2	47	0	44	51	0.235	OF	59	7	8	0.892								
1963	Thomasville	GFL	7	9	0	3	1	0	0	1	0	1	1	0.333													
Palmantier, A.B.																											
1920	Rome	GSL		296	34	90	11	2	1		9			0.304	OF												
Palmer, Max		BR TR																									
1950	Waycross	GFL	25	86	5	13	1	0	2	9	1	18	22	0.151	OF	42	2	6	0.880								
Palmer, Robert D. "Bob"		BL																									
1955	Sandersville	GSL	7	20		3								0.150													
Palmitesso, Frederick "Fred"		BR																									
1956	Hazlehurst-Baxley	GSL	2	4		0								0.000													
Palmquist, Edwin Lee "Ed"		BR TR 6'3" 195 lbs b. 06/10/1933 Los Angeles, CA																									
1956	Thomasville	GFL	38	109	17	30	3	1	0	15	5	31	23	0.275	OF	61	4	5	0.929								
Palumbo, ---		BR TR																									
1946	Tallahassee	GFL	1												P					1	0	0	0.00	4			
Palumbo, William "Bill"		BR TR																									
1948	Valdosta	GFL	131	497	122	146	22	10	2	70	10	147	98	0.294	2B, 3B	300	315	32	0.951								
Pancoe, Joseph "Joe"		BR TR																									
1948	Moultrie	GFL	19	69	18	25	5	2	1	15	1	14	13	0.362	OF	21	1	2	0.917								
Panek, Ed																											
1939	Valdosta	GFL	32	117	18	32	3	1	1	21	2	6	16	0.274	OF	76	1	3	0.963								
Panella, ---																											
1915	Griffin	GAL	7												P					7	1	3					
Panella, Joseph "Joe"		BL TL																									
1963	Moultrie	GFL	82	247	45	55	13	1	4	20	10	40	44	0.223	OF	115	7	2	0.984								
Pappas, Nicholas "Nick"		BR TR																									
1949	Valley	GAL	21	56	9	11	2	0	0	6	0	3	14	0.196	P	8	17	1	0.962	18	8	4	4.58	120	107	97	89
1951	Hazlehurst-Baxley	GSL	35	79	8	14	2	0	1	4	0	9	11	0.177	P	4	38	3	0.933	27	12	11	4.58	163	164	95	103
Pardue, Larry		BR TR																									
1954	Sandersville	GSL	12	41	2	8	1	0	0	3	0	2	12	0.195	C	81	5	3	0.966								
Pare, Albert "Al"		BR TR																									
1954	Tifton	GFL	31	107	21	16	5	0	0	3	2	17	18	0.150	OF	59	6	8	0.890								
Pare, John		BR TR																									
1948	Eastman	GSL	97	309	41	77	7	2	1	38	16	54	30	0.249	M, C	573	47	19	0.970								
Parent, Leo		BR																									
1954	Sandersville	GSL	1	4		2								0.500													
Parente, Greg		BR TR																									
1946	Cordele	GFL	49	93	13	30	4	6	3	22	1	8	11	0.323	P	5	25	5	0.857	23	6	11	4.29	147	146	131	119
Parham, David "Dave"		BL TL																									
1958	Thomasville	GFL	65	240	34	58	8	2	1	25	0	43	76	0.242	1B	430	29	19	0.960								
Parilla, ---																											
1920	Lindale	GSL		39	5	12								0.308													
Paris, Lester		BR																									
1962	Moultrie	GFL	9	37	9	6	0	0	1	3	0	4	8	0.162													

Georgia Class-D Minor League Baseball Encyclopedia

YR	TEAM	LG	G	AB	R	H	2B	3B	HR	RBI	SB	BB	SO	BA	POS	PO	A	E	FA	GP	W	L	ERA	IP	H	SO	BB
Park, Loyal		BR TR																									
1953	Fitzgerald	GFL	88	289	49	84	14	4	4	43	6	60	32	0.291	OF	134	20	9	0.945								
Park, Maynard		BL TL																									
1947	Cordele	GFL	21	49	10	8	1	0	0	1	0	6	19	0.163	P	7	20	1	0.964	20	10	8	3.63	139	163	41	60
Parker, ---																											
1913	Thomasville	ESL	23	84	13	27	3	0	1					0.321	2B	67	27	4	0.959								
1913	Brunswick	ESL	85	327	41	84	11	1	1					0.257	2B	171	148	28	0.919								
1914	Brunswick	GSL		401	58	110	10	2	0	13				0.274													
1915	Thomasville	FLAG	70	276	34	61	4	3	0	16				0.221	3B	104	119	31	0.878								
1917	LaGrange	GAL	8	27	2	6	0	0	0	2				0.222	2B	24	22	0	1.000								
Parker, ---																											
1915	Valdosta	FLAG	<10												P					0							
1917	Griffin	GAL	1	3	0	1	0	0	0	0				0.333	P	2	3	0	1.000	1	0	1		8	9	6	6
Parker, ---																											
1930	Huntsville	GAL	35	136	18	50	10	4	1		1	3	3	0.368	1B	203	10	5	0.977								
Parker, Charles W.																											
1949	Eastman	GSL	125	454	68	124	26	3	8	104	6	57	55	0.273	2B	266	358	30	0.954								
Parker, Douglas Woolley "Dixie"		BL TR 5'11" 160 lbs b. 04/24/1895 Forest Home, AL d. 05/15/1972 Tuscaloosa, AL																										
1936	Americus	GFL	17	53	4	10	1	0	0	5	0			0.189	M, C	63	9	2	0.973								
1937	Americus	GFL	25	79	8	23	0	1	0	5	0	2	1	0.291	M, C	100	17	5	0.959								
Parker, Dudley																											
1938	Cordele	GFL	82	302	62	89	15	2	2	19	6	51	30	0.295	2B	161	121	36	0.887								
1939	Waycross	GFL	80	313	48	75	8	8	2	39	8	37	36	0.240	3B	78	165	25	0.907								
Parker, Ray		BR TR																									
1951	Waycross	GFL	31	108	12	29	2	1	0	13	0	14	9	0.269	OF	36	1	0	1.000								
Parker, Terry		BR																									
1957	Albany	GFL	7	29		13								0.448													
Parker, W. Newton "Gashouse"		BR TR																									
1946	LaGrange	GAL	27	90	12	25	5	0	1	16	2	14	17	0.278	M, 1B, P	177	10	4	0.979	1	0	0	0.00	7			
Parks, ---																											
1915	Dothan	FLAG	62	270	34	88	15	1	0	15				0.326	OF	75	13	5	0.946								
Parks, ---																											
1928	Cedartown - Anniston	GAL	20	44	3	6	0	0	0	0	0		7	0.136	P	5	17	1	0.957	19	10	6	4.54	113	141	26	34
Parks, Jack W.		BL TR																									
1946	Tallassee	GAL	87	261	37	65	12	1	8	45	3	30	52	0.249	C	431	41	26	0.948								
Parks, James																											
1920	Cedartown	GSL		58	11	25								0.431													
1921	Griffin	GSL		181	44	68								0.376	OF												
Parks, Woodford		BR TR																									
1946	Tallassee	GAL	7												P					7	6	1	2.75	59	60	22	15
Parnell, H. Eugene "Gene"		BR TR																									
1950	Douglas(11) - Tifton(16)	GSL	27	24	2	3	0	0	0	1	0	5	16	0.125	P	1	11	0	1.000	27	4	4	5.38	87	87	48	58
Parnell, M.R.																											
1921	Rome	GSL																									
Parquet, Clyde		BS TR																									
1962	Thomasville	GFL	7	4	0	0	0	0	0	0	0	2	1	0.000	P					6	0	1	4.80	15	7	25	20
Parri, Carlo		BR TR																									
1948	Baxley	GSL	16	7	0	0	0	0	0	0	0	0	3	0.000	P	5	5	1	0.909								
Parrish, Allen		BR TR																									
1955	Tifton	GFL	11	9	1	2	0	0	0	1	0	3	2	0.222	P	1	4	0	1.000	11	1	3		<45			
Parrish, Ronald "Ron"		BR TR																									
1951	Jesup	GSL	57	125	11	17	5	1	0	4	0	24	36	0.136	OF, P	27	49	6	0.927	35	15	11	3.48	217	198	102	138
1953	Jesup	GSL	2											0.500	P					1	0			<45			
Parrott, William "Willie"		BR TR																									
1953	Sandersville	GSL	26	55	6	13	0	0	0	6	0	3	7	0.236	P	6	23	3	0.906	22	5	8	5.76	100	125	81	63
Parsons, Edward Dixon "Dixie"		BR TR 6'2" 180 lbs b. 05/12/1916 Talladega, AL d. 10/31/1991 Longview, TX																										
1946	Waycross(22) - Moultrie(65)	GFL	87	262	45	94	19	3	7	61	4	28	32	0.359	M, OF, C	218	14	6	0.975								
Parsons, Harold		BR TR																									
1952	Statesboro	GSL	24	35	2	4	0	0	0	1	0	4	9	0.114	P	2	19	3	0.875	21	3	5	3.87	79	77	20	47
Parsons, Roger		BR																									
1954	Statesboro	GSL	7	18		2								0.111													
Partain, James "Jim"		BL TL																									
1962	Moultrie	GFL	12	6	0	1	0	0	0	0	0	2	5	0.167	P	0	3	0	1.000	12	0	3	7.39	28	33	17	23
Pasch, Allan		BL TR																									
1948	Americus	GFL	39	151	23	39	4	0	0	15	3	24	27	0.258	3B	34	50	9	0.903								
Paschal, Benjamin Edward "Ben"		BR TR 5'11" 185 lbs b. 10/13/1895 Enterprise, AL d. 11/10/1974 Charlotte, NC																										
1915	Dothan	FLAG	64	259	41	75	13	6	7	23				0.290	OF	115	3	4	0.967								
Pascoe, Edward "Ed"		BR																									
1957	Fitzgerald	GFL	8	33		8								0.242													
Passarella, Robert E. "Bob"		BR TR																									
1951	Americus(36) - Cordele(84)	GFL	120	452	52	100	18	4	1	52	6	51	85	0.221	3B, SS	214	306	59	0.898								
Passaro, Roland		BR TR																									
1957	Albany	GFL	13	26	8	9	2	0	2	6	0	3	7	0.346	P	4	9	0	1.000	11	4	4	3.63	67	61	59	39
Passilla, James "Jim"		BR TR																									
1956	Moultrie	GFL	139	475	58	118	14	1	3	53	4	65	72	0.248	SS	190	372	54	0.912								

Georgia Class-D Minor League Baseball Encyclopedia

YR	TEAM	LG	G	AB	R	H	2B	3B	HR	RBI	SB	BB	SO	BA	POS	PO	A	E	FA	GP	W	L	ERA	IP	H	SO	BB
Patchell, Stanley "Stan"		BR TR																									
1954	Brunswick	GFL	17	32	2	5	1	0	0	1	0	4	11	0.156	P	2	17	6	0.760	16	3	9	3.64	99	87	75	82
1955	Brunswick	GFL	8	14		1								0.071	P					7	2	1	<45				
Patchin, Art																											
1939	Waycross	GFL	26	61	12	18	4	0	0	11	0	4	11	0.295	P	4	25	4	0.879	24	8	11	3.04	148	169	70	47
Pate, Robert E. "Bob"		BL TR																									
1952	Fitzgerald	GSL	63	228	29	42	4	3	1	30	5	25	43	0.184	2B, OF	93	18	10	0.917								
Patriss, William "Bill"		BR TR																									
1953	Vidalia	GSL	64	228	32	51	8	1	2	38	4	20	52	0.224	3B, SS	68	135	36	0.849								
1956	Moultrie	GFL	80	296	38	78	16	6	4	56	1	29	49	0.264	2B, 3B, OF	142	63	11	0.949								
Patrow, Ed "Eddie"																											
1939	Cordele	GFL	72	259	33	73	12	5	0	26	4	36	41	0.282	SS	134	236	33	0.918								
Patten, Roger		BL TR																									
1953	Dublin	GSL	8											0.222	P						1	2	<45				
Patterson, ---																											
1917	Tri-Cities	GAL	16	56	11	7	2	0	1		1			0.125	OF	24	1	1	0.962								
Patterson, ---																											
1930	Huntsville	GAL	71	268	40	100	15	4	3		2	11	5	0.373	C	234	50	21	0.931								
Patterson, Britt																											
1939	Tallahassee	GFL													P								<45				
1942	Americus	GFL	11												P					11	1	4	5.95	62	67	48	42
Patterson, Charles		BL TL																									
1956	Waycross(2) - Fitzgerald(8)	GFL	10	16	1	2	1	0	0	2	0	2	2	0.125	P	1	3	1	0.800	10	0	4	<45				
Patterson, Derward		BR TR																									
1947	Alexander City	GAL	19	50	0	11	1	0	0	3	0	5	5	0.220													
1950	Rome(4) - Valley(8)	GAL	12	27	3	5	2	0	0	4	0	6	3	0.185													
Patterson, Joe H.		BR TR																									
1939	Valdosta	GFL	37	57	2	5	0	0	0	0	0	2	10	0.088	P	10	42	3	0.945	33	9	15	3.99	169	181	96	76
1940	Valdosta	GFL	54	113	16	31	4	1	0	9	1	8	28	0.274	P, IF					42	17	12	3.57	265	265	158	92
Patterson, Raymond "Ray"		BR TR																									
1956	Vidalia	GSL	38	118	23	40	4	0	9	26	1	23	20	0.339	C	152	22	8	0.956								
Patterson, Theodore "Ted"		BR TR																									
1948	Sparta	GSL	101	418	65	128	15	10	1	41	35	26	30	0.306	2B	221	233	28	0.942								
1949	Sparta	GSL	135	616	118	189	38	24	2	62	35	41	49	0.307	2B	357	367	48	0.938								
1951	Jesup	GSL	22	105	27	36	3	1	0	17	9	9	5	0.343	OF	19	0	2	0.905								
1952	Jesup	GSL	50	220	32	73	17	2	2	26	4	11	19	0.332	2B	149	129	13	0.955								
1953	Sandersville(42) - Eastman(7)	GSL	49	219	45	80	21	19	2	47	13	11	14	0.365	1B	329	9	6	0.983								
Patterson, William E. "Bill"		BL TR																									
1946	Carrollton	GAL	<10																								
1947	Carrollton	GAL	81	197	34	49	7	0	3	30	6	61	38	0.249	OF, C	282	26	9	0.972								
1948	Vidalia-Lyons	GSL	39	133	17	33	3	1	0	18	6	26	12	0.248	C	184	98	8	0.972								
1950	Ca(1) - Gr(88) - Va(4) - AC(16)	GAL	109	322	44	75	11	0	1	68	3	80	48	0.233	C	469	50	15	0.972								
Patton, M. Henry																											
1929	Carrollton	GAL	99	379	84	108	30	5	12		17	58	51	0.285	OF	198	8	7	0.967								
1930	Cedartown	GAL	96	365	81	105	25	5	18		11	54	52	0.288	OF	121	12	7	0.950								
Paulick, Frank		BR TR																									
1946	Moultrie	GFL	71	220	28	59	10	1	2	21	8	33	30	0.268	OF, C	413	42	13	0.972								
1947	Waycross	GFL	53	190	34	52	11	1	0	40	4	31	29	0.274	OF	63	1	2	0.970								
1949	Fitzgerald	GSL	20	67	8	11	4	0	1	10	0	9	19	0.164	C	107	16	6	0.953								
Pavelko, Paul		BL TR																									
1962	Thomasville	GFL	112	380	84	95	5	10	0	66	22	81	60	0.250	OF	188	5	11	0.946								
Pavlick, Peter "Pete"		BR TR																									
1955	Sandersville	GSL	96	324	61	91	9	2	2	50	14	78	21	0.281	M, 2B	222	279	18	0.965								
1956	Sandersville	GSL	113	418	95	122	9	3	2	56	8	86	23	0.292	M, 2B, 3B	128	212	30	0.919								
Pavone, Nicholas "Nick"		BL TL																									
1946	Albany	GFL	14	51	9	12	1	0	0	6	1	8	12	0.235	OF	16	1	4	0.810								
Pavuk, Thomas "Tom"		BR																									
1954	Thomasville	GFL	14	44	7	14	5	0	1	5	1	3	11	0.318													
Pawlak, Walter "Walt"		BR TR																									
1954	Thomasville	GFL	52	184	21	44	2	0	0	13	3	21	43	0.239	2B	86	99	11	0.944								
1954	Vidalia	GSL	32	131	18	31	4	1	0	19	4	13	35	0.237	2B	72	87	3	0.981								
Pawlick, John		BR TR																									
1949	Fitzgerald	GSL	93	327	52	80	17	1	4	47	7	48	63	0.245	M, OF	223	17	8	0.968								
1953	Jesup	GSL	109												C	397	52	14	0.970								
Payne, Charles																											
1955	Hazlehurst-Baxley	GSL	2	6		1								0.167													
Payne, George Washington "George"		BR TR 5'11" 172 lbs b. 05/23/1890 Mount Vernon, KY d. 01/24/1959 Bellflower, CA																									
1914	Brunswick	GSL		46	7	6	0	0	0		0			0.130	P					23	12	6	2.36	160	127	100	41
Payne, John H.		BR TR																									
1954	Albany	GFL	32	45	3	7	0	0	0	2	0	11	14	0.156	P	9	25	2	0.944	32	10	8	3.85	159	149	119	83
Payne, Paul		BR TR																									
1958	Waycross	GFL	1	0										0.000	P					1	0	0	<30				
Payne, Richard "Dick"		BR TR																									
1954	Brunswick	GFL	44	54	14	7	2	0	0	4	0	25	20	0.130	P	8	34	2	0.955	41	14	8	3.48	194	179	143	99
Pazienza, William "Bill"		BR TR																									
1955	Sandersville	GSL	63	152	27	32	2	2	4	27	1	35	44	0.211	C	246	28	10	0.965								

Georgia Class-D Minor League Baseball Encyclopedia

YR	TEAM	LG	G	AB	R	H	2B	3B	HR	RBI	SB	BB	SO	BA	POS	PO	A	E	FA	GP	W	L	ERA	IP	H	SO	BB
Peacock, Arlen		BR TR																									
1952	Thomasville	GFL	10	22	1	0	0	0	0	0	0	4	16	0.000	P	2	13	2	0.882	10	2	4	3.36	59	62	24	29
Peacock, Cecil E.		BR TR																									
1946	Opelika	GAL	15	29	1	3	0	0	0	0	0	1	7	0.103	P	1	12	4	0.765	15	3	9	6.55	77	92	37	33
Peacock, T.D.																											
1937	Cordele	GFL	36	116	19	26	1	0	0	12	4	25	14	0.224	2B	122	102	18	0.926								
Peake, ---		BR TR																									
1946	Opelika	GAL	4												P					4	1	3	0.00	24	32	12	9
Peale, Anthony		BR TR																									
1954	Douglas	GSL	1	2		1								0.500	P					1	0	1	<45				
Pearce, Ernest		BR TR																									
1954	Dublin	GSL	27	97	13	20	2	0	0	10	1	12	22	0.206	SS	48	75	15	0.891								
Pearson, ---																											
1915	Thomasville	FLAG	31	97	6	15	1	0	0		1			0.155	OF, P	16	1	1	0.944	19	8	11		169	143	98	44
Pearson, Ronald "Ron"		BR TL																									
1958	Dublin	GFL	37	85	10	12	2	1	0	5	1	6	32	0.141	P	12	33	5	0.900	36	15	13	3.95	228	251	139	104
Pearson, Thomas "Tom"		BL TL																									
1948	Fitzgerald	GSL	78	272	25	67	12	0	0	35	2	43	46	0.246	1B	660	26	12	0.983								
Peddy, ---																											
1915	Americus-Gainesville	FLAG	23	62	9	22	4	0	0		2			0.355	P	8	30	5	0.884	17	5	8		111	142	32	15
Peele, Sanford																											
1937	Americus	GFL		44	3	14				9	12	1		0.318	C	42	10	2	0.963								
Peeler, ---																											
1917	Griffin	GAL	2	6	1	2	0	0	0		0			0.333	P	1	6	0	1.000	2	0	1		15	21	2	4
Peeler, Thomas H. "Tom"		BL TL																									
1956	Moultrie	GFL	4	2		0								0.000	P					4	0	2	<45				
Peeples, ---																											
1917	Rome-Lindale	GAL	6	16	0	1	0	0	0		0			0.063	P	2	11	1	0.929	6	2	2		44	34	14	8
Pegram, George		BL																									
1946	Tallahassee	GFL	<10																								
Pehanick, Al		BR TR																									
1955	Valdosta	GFL	19	42	3	4	1	0	0	3	0	7	26	0.095	P	4	34	3	0.927	19	10	5	1.87	135	89	118	49
Pelat, Frank		BR TR																									
1936	Tallahassee	GFL	121	432	70	118	12	10	1	61	8			0.273	2B	312	324	27	0.959								
1937	Tallahassee	GFL	115	437	52	111	17	8	2	61	17	54	37	0.254	2B	311	336	31	0.954								
1939	Moultrie	GFL	135	474	113	130	25	8	3	45	11	117	46	0.274	SS	294	380	45	0.937								
1940	Moultrie	GFL	136	529	88	128	29	5	1	53	6	88	53	0.242	2B	369	461	33	0.962								
Pelham, William "Bill"																											
1936	Moultrie	GFL	12	19	1	0	0	0	0	0	0			0.000													
Pellagrini, Albert "Al"		BL TL																									
1955	Cordele	GFL	125	436	80	119	16	2	1	41	13	103	59	0.273	OF	271	27	13	0.958								
Pellarin, Anthony		BR TR																									
1954	Dublin	GSL	1	4		0								0.000	P					1	1	0	<45				
Pellicier, ---																											
1929	Anniston	GAL	13	47	4	10	1	0	0		0	3	4	0.213	OF	24	3	0	1.000								
Pelot, Harold		BR TR																									
1947	Thomasville	GFL	13	16	3	3	1	0	0	0	0	0	6	0.188	P	0	7	1	0.875								
Penczak, Joseph "Joe"		BR TR																									
1950	Albany	GFL	35	136	20	33	8	1	4	19	7	13	20	0.243	3B	31	70	8	0.927								
Pender, Marcus		BR TR																									
1950	Eastman	GSL	18	26	2	3	1	0	0	4	0	4	12	0.115	P	1	14	4	0.789	18	3	6	7.39	67	74	51	84
Pender, Wilbert		BR TL																									
1954	Thomasville	GFL	26	53	6	12	2	1	0	12	0	9	19	0.226	P	1	33	5	0.872	25	9	11	4.35	151	134	156	116
1955	Thomasville	GFL	8	12		1								0.083	P					8	1	5	<45				
Pendergraft, James "Jim"																											
1949	Dublin	GSL	19	35	6	8	2	0	0	4	1	2	3	0.229	P	10	17	0	1.000	23	6	6	4.89	81	59	25	25
Pendley, Horace J. "Jack"		BR TR																									
1954	Hazlehurst-Baxley	GSL	121	505	100	145	18	9	5	39	24	42	84	0.287	OF	307	21	18	0.948								
Pennington, Joseph "Joe"		BL TL																									
1951	Valley	GAL	37	64	13	13	3	0	0	7	4	18	8	0.203	P	11	37	3	0.941	34	13	9	2.45	165	165	94	37
Pennucci, Patrick "Pat"		BR																									
1962	Thomasville	GFL	2	8	2	3	1	0	0	3	0	0	3	0.375													
Pensky, Stanley "Stan"		BR TR																									
1936	Moultrie	GFL	74	299	42	69	8	3	5	33	12			0.231	OF	134	59	13	0.937								
1937	Moultrie	GFL	28	111	10	26	4	2	1	13	2	14	12	0.234	2B	54	67	12	0.910								
1940	Cordele	GFL	44	159	12	40	8	0	0	24	0	12	18	0.252	2B	154	124	14	0.952								
Penso, John																											
1937	Moultrie	GFL		60	9	15		1		6	3			0.250	2B	40	36	7	0.916								
Penson, Paul Eugene "Paul"		BR TR 6'1" 185 lbs b. 07/21/1931 Kansas City, KS																									
1956	Tifton	GFL	1	2		1								0.500	P					1	0	1	<45				
Penton, Henry		BL TL																									
1949	Moultrie	GFL	50	80	8	16	2	1	0	2	0	9	8	0.200	P	13	26	5	0.886	32	9	9	5.30	168	193	62	95
Pepitone, John		BL																									
1946	Valdosta	GFL	<10																								

Georgia Class-D Minor League Baseball Encyclopedia

YR	TEAM	LG	G	AB	R	H	2B	3B	HR	RBI	SB	BB	SO	BA	POS	PO	A	E	FA	GP	W	L	ERA	IP	H	SO	BB
Pepper, Donald Hoyte "Don"		BL TR 6'4" 215 lbs b. 10/08/1943 Saratoga, Springs, NY																									
1962	Thomasville	GFL	42	149	24	40	8	0	3	27	0	13	22	0.268	1B	299	33	6	0.982								
1963	Thomasville	GFL	77	275	27	74	13	0	3	37	1	33	36	0.269	1B	567	32	15	0.976								
Peppers, Dorsey		BR																									
1940	Valdosta	GFL	<10																								
1941	Cordele	GFL	7	20	2	4	1	0	0	0	0	2	4	0.200	OF	11	1	0	1.000								
Perada, Orestes		BR TR																									
1949	Douglas	GSL	132	553	95	165	19	3	1	81	22	47	40	0.298	2B	360	410	32	0.960								
1951	Douglas	GSL	80	291	31	64	8	2	0	17	5	27	21	0.220	2B	191	240	17	0.962								
Perchak, Charles		BL TL																									
1950	Moultrie	GFL	139	512	130	148	29	3	11	116	21	142	61	0.289	OF	331	13	10	0.972								
Perdue, Glenn		BS TL																									
1949	Opelika	GAL	17	35	4	6	0	0	0	1	0	2	8	0.171	P	4	14	2	0.900	16	3	4	3.80	71	68	48	64
Pereira, Andres		BR																									
1955	Vidalia	GSL	8	24		3								0.125													
Perello, Amedio D. "Dave"		BR TR																									
1948	Eastman	GSL	63	251	38	62	7	2	0	27	27	17	19	0.247	3B, OF	110	92	15	0.931								
1949	Fitzgerald	GSL	82	330	70	81	13	0	0	31	20	42	14	0.245	3B	115	142	39	0.868								
Perez, Joaquin		BR TR																									
1956	Waycross	GFL	135	527	95	139	18	3	1	40	10	90	61	0.264	2B, SS	265	376	33	0.951								
Perez, Simon R.		BR TR																									
1962	Dublin	GFL	37	54	6	5	0	0	0	2	0	10	24	0.093	P	10	34	3	0.936	35	11	7	4.71	153	173	125	46
Perez, Thomas J. "Tom"		BR TR																									
1951	Brunswick	GFL	39	129	18	27	3	1	0	11	3	20	14	0.209	1B	329	21	5	0.986								
Perinis, Alexander "Alex"		BR TR																									
1954	Dublin	GSL	5	7		1								0.143	P					5	0	2		<45			
1955	Brunswick	GFL	23	35	6	6	0	1	0	2	0	1	13	0.171	P	1	11	2	0.857	22	6	4	2.04	97	50	79	95
Perkins, David "Dave"																											
1954	Thomasville	GFL	4	4		1								0.250	P					1	0	1		<45			
Perlman, Bertram		BL TL																									
1955	Hazlehurst-Baxley	GSL	9	12		1								0.083	P					9	2	2					
Permeter, Harold		BR TR																									
1955	Thomasville	GFL	2	1		0								0.000	P					2	0	0		<45			
Perna, Frank		BL TL																									
1953	Cordele	GFL	3											0.000	P						0	2		<45			
Perry, ---																											
1906	Americus	GSL													OF												
Perry, ---																											
1915	Thomasville	FLAG	<10																								
Perry, Charles		BR TR																									
1957	Albany	GFL	8	19		2								0.105	P					8	1	6	3.46	52	53	52	33
Perry, Harold		BR TR																									
1956	Dublin	GSL	20	20	2	4	0	1	0	0	0	1	7	0.200	P	3	10	1	0.929	19	1	9	9.40	45	60	31	46
Perry, Joseph "Joe"		BL TR																									
1955	Brunswick	GFL	8	9		2								0.222	P					8	1	1		<45			
1955	Dublin	GSL	24	32	1	8	1	1	0	1	0	2	7	0.250	P	2	14	1	0.941	23	5	8	4.54	105	105	60	59
1956	Brunswick	GFL	43	94	10	21	2	0	0	4	0	9	33	0.223	P	12	40	15	0.776	35	12	16	3.67	233	215	189	133
Perry, Ray		BS TR																									
1956	Albany	GFL	21	43	6	7	1	0	0	4	0	2	10	0.163	P	8	21	6	0.829	20	5	8	3.10	119	90	86	85
Perry, Robert "Bob"		BL TL																									
1950	Thomasville	GFL	21	66	15	16	1	3	0	11	6	8	26	0.242	OF	37	4	2	0.953								
Perry, Robert D. "Bob"		BR TR																									
1950	Valley	GAL	62	236	33	58	12	1	0	30	3	32	37	0.246	3B	81	113	18	0.915								
Perry, Thomas E. "Tom"																											
1936	Albany	GFL	23	58	6	10	0	1	0	4	0			0.172	P					23	7	5	2.70	110		51	41
Perry, Walter "Walt"		BR TR																									
1963	Thomasville	GFL	7	18	1	6	0	1	0	1	0	0	5	0.333	P					2	0	1	1.13	8	5	4	4
Perryman, Everett Key "Parson"		BR TR 6'4" 193 lbs b. 10/24/1888 Everett Springs, GA d. 09/12/1966 Starke, FL																									
1928	Lindale	GAL	30	110	22	38	6	2	2		3	7	26	0.345	OF	27	4	5	0.861								
Persons, Earl																											
1929	Gadsden	GAL	101	420	66	157	18	17	8		23	13	23	0.374	OF	186	44	11	0.954								
Persons, James "Jim"		BR TR																									
1947	Alexander City	GAL	32	100	10	21	1	0	0	16	1	15	18	0.210	3B, C	88	44	15	0.898								
Persoskie, Metro																											
1941	Valdosta	GFL	45	113	12	22	4	0	0	9	1	15	14	0.195	P	47	25	6	0.923	25	9	7	3.82	158	156	133	94
Pescitelli, Pasquale		BS TR																									
1950	LaGrange	GAL	22	71	12	19	1	1	0	3	2	6	8	0.268	2B	29	41	6	0.921								
Petchulat, George		BR TR																									
1948	Tallahassee	GFL	12	19	1	3	0	0	0	0	0	0	7	0.158	P	0	15	1	0.938	12	1	3	4.67	52	47	36	41
Peterkin, Alfonso		BR TR																									
1962	Moultrie	GFL	66	212	40	55	8	2	6	27	7	21	64	0.259	OF	95	1	6	0.941								
Peterman, Irwin "Irv"																											
1941	Albany	GFL	38	110	18	24	2	0	0	9	0	12	46	0.218	P	12	45	4	0.934	33	23	8	2.92	262	261	151	74

Georgia Class-D Minor League Baseball Encyclopedia

YR	TEAM	LG	G	AB	R	H	2B	3B	HR	RBI	SB	BB	SO	BA	POS	PO	A	E	FA	GP	W	L	ERA	IP	H	SO	BB
Peterman, William David "Bill"		BR TR 6'2" 185 lbs b. 03/20/1921 Philadelphia, PA d. 03/13/1999 Philadelphia, PA																									
1949	Moultrie	GFL	31	76	19	17	2	0	0	9	3	17	6	0.224	M, C	52	5	0	1.000								
1950	Cordele	GFL													M												
Peters, Charles		BR TR																									
1946	Valley	GAL	1												P					1	0	0	0.00	5			
Peters, Genie																											
1939	Waycross	GFL	23	93	14	20	3	1	1	11	4	11	12	0.215	OF	52	8	4	0.938								
Peters, Gerald C.		BL TL																									
1952	Statesboro	GSL	71	280	60	82	12	1	2	29	32	50	48	0.293	OF	101	7	6	0.947								
1953	Statesboro	GSL	126	502	93	126	27	4	4	49	44	76	77	0.251	1B, OF	425	27	29	0.940								
1954	Statesboro	GSL	130	486	108	131	22	8	4	52	66	114	63	0.270	1B, P	1039	44	36	0.968	4	0	0	<45				
1955	Statesboro	GSL	63	234	57	62	18	2	0	29	13	54	28	0.265	M, 1B, OF, P	232	13	5	0.980	6	0	0					
Petersen, Charles		BL TL																									
1963	Waycross	GFL	37	66	7	17	4	0	2	9	0	8	30	0.258	1B	109	7	3	0.975								
Peterson, ---																											
1917	LaGrange	GAL	1	3	0	0	0	0	0		0			0.000	OF	1	0	0	1.000								
Peterson, Gerald "Jerry"																											
1941	Thomasville	GFL	21	66	12	16	4	0	0	7	1	9	21	0.242	P	11	10	2	0.913	7	1	1	8.70	30	40	23	27
Peterson, Harding William "Hardy"		BR TR 6'0" 205 lbs b. 10/17/1929 Perth Amboy, NJ																									
1950	Tallahassee	GFL	45	138	19	38	5	1	2	18	1	15	9	0.275	C	225	35	6	0.977								
Peterson, Howard		BR TL																									
1956	Hazlehurst-Baxley	GSL	24	54	11	9	1	0	0	1	0	9	21	0.167	P	8	22	1	0.968	20	10	7	2.64	143	127	99	38
Peterson, Thomas "Tom"		BR TR																									
1954	Albany	GFL	13	42	6	11	1	0	0	4	0	5	14	0.262	SS	18	23	6	0.872								
Peterson, Wright		BR TR																									
1946	Thomasville	GFL	8												P					8	1	5	0.00	31	45	15	30
Petraglia, Joseph "Joe"		BR TR																									
1949	Tallahassee	GFL	52	135	18	30	2	1	0	6	5	16	36	0.222	2B, 3B	42	68	21	0.840								
Petrella, Joe																											
1936	Thomasville	GFL	55	202	26	49	2	0	1	15	3			0.243	2B	153	155	13	0.960								
Petrick, John		BR TR																									
1953	Dublin	GSL	56	230	49	74	15	1	11	57	7	35	16	0.322	OF	142	8	5	0.968								
Petriello, Joseph "Joe"		BR TR																									
1955	Sandersville	GSL	2	4		2								0.500	P					2	1	0					
Petrolongo, Joseph "Joe"		BR TR																									
1949	Thomasville	GFL	45	131	22	29	3	0	0	16	4	25	24	0.221	C	249	27	12	0.958								
Petrosky, Mike																											
1939	Waycross	GFL	64	147	24	44	14	1	2	16	0	9	26	0.299	P, OF	40	51	7	0.929	36	15	11	2.33	228	211	83	52
Petrovich, Ronald "Ron"		BR TR																									
1954	Thomasville	GFL	8	8		0								0.000	P					8	1	4	<45				
Petroziello, Carl																											
1942	Moultrie	GFL	125	464	67	116	17	12	1	52	8	54	77	0.250	3B	169	221	46	0.894								
Pettis, Thomas "Tom"		BL TL																									
1947	Cordele	GFL	12	40	9	6	0	0	0	0	0	14	14	0.150	1B	107	3	2	0.982								
Petty, Eugene T. "Gene"		BL TL																									
1950	Waycross	GFL	14	44	8	10	3	0	0	8	0	12	5	0.227	OF	28	2	1	0.968								
Petty, Fred K.		BR TR																									
1953	Hazlehurst-Baxley	GSL	27	106	29	28	3	3	2	24	4	26	15	0.264	OF	74	2	3	0.962								
Petty, James "Jim"		BL TL																									
1946	Tallahassee	GFL	21	84	11	25	2	2	1	13	1	6	11	0.298	1B	158	12	11	0.939								
Petty, Thomas "Tom"		BR TL																									
1956	Albany	GFL	21	39	4	3	0	0	0	1	0	8	8	0.077	P	6	7	4	0.765	20	5	8	3.53	107	79	97	104
1957	Albany	GFL	8	3		0								0.000	P					8	1	2	<30				
Petty, Vernon "Vern"																											
1942	Cordele	GFL	97	390	75	131	38	4	1	66	2	43	27	0.336	3B	103	202	30	0.910								
Petty, Virgil		BR TR																									
1953	Douglas(23) - Jesup(8)	GSL	31	100	18	24	5	1	2	17	0	10	26	0.240	OF	23	0	3	0.885								
Pezold, Lorenz Johannes "Larry"		BR TR 5'9" 175 lbs b. 06/22/1893 New Orleans, LA d. 10/22/1957 Baton Rouge, LA																									
1913	Gadsden	GAL	86	299	76	91				18				0.304	OF,	111	21	9	0.936								
Pfander, John		BR																									
1956	Hazlehurst-Baxley	GSL	3	9		1								0.111													
Pfeifer, Cyril "Cy"		BL TL																									
1952	Dublin	GSL	84	289	65	95	22	2	4	51	21	65	8	0.329	M, 1B	513	31	14	0.975								
Pfeifer, Fred																											
1936	Albany	GFL	18	76	13	20	2	3	0	8	2			0.263	SS	44	58	17	0.857								
Pfeifer, Tony		BL TR																									
1952	Tifton	GFL	24	35	3	3	0	0	0	1	0	4	20	0.086	P	0	12	1	0.923	23	7	6	3.17	105	82	47	57
Pfeiffer, Harry		BR TR																									
1946	Albany	GFL	21	86	9	11	2	0	1	11	1	13	32	0.128	OF	35	1	3	0.923								
Pfister, George Edward "George"		BR TR 6'0" 200 lbs b. 09/04/1918 Bound Brook, NJ d. 08/14/1997 St. Joseph, MO																									
1956	Thomasville	GFL													M												
Pfund, Le Roy Herbert "Lee"		BR TR 6'1" 185 lbs b. 10/10/1918 Oak Park, IL																									
1941	Albany	GFL	29	67	13	16	7	0	0	13	0	6	16	0.239	P	3	21	6	0.800	27	10	10	5.16	157	186	84	94
Phagan, Fred		BR TR																									
1958	Dublin	GFL	30	111	19	35	8	0	4	23	0	14	11	0.315	C, OF	89	5	7	0.931								

363

Georgia Class-D Minor League Baseball Encyclopedia

YR	TEAM	LG	G	AB	R	H	2B	3B	HR	RBI	SB	BB	SO	BA	POS	PO	A	E	FA	GP	W	L	ERA	IP	H	SO	BB
Phebus, Raymond William "Bill"		BR TR 5'9" 170 lbs b. 08/02/1909 Cherryvale, KS d. 10/11/1989 Bartow, FL																									
1949	Dublin	GSL													M												
Pheister, Paul		BL TR																									
1948	LaGrange	GAL	67	258	40	70	11	3	3	39	7	35	30	0.271	1B, 3B, OF	270	33	21	0.935								
Phelan, ---																											
1906	Cordele	GSL													P												
Phelan, James "Jim"		BR TR																									
1956	Douglas	GSL	41	80	8	21	3	1	0	7	1	7	13	0.263	P	10	34	4	0.917	25	14	7	3.72	167	171	98	58
Phelps, Raymond "Ray"		BR TR																									
1955	Hazlehurst-Baxley	GSL	3	3		2								0.667	P					3	0	0					
Phillips, ---																											
1917	LaGrange	GAL	5	15	1	4	0	0	0		2			0.267	OF	14	0	1	0.933								
Phillips, David "Dave"		BR TR																									
1942	Americus	GFL	23	55	1	4	0	0	0	1	0	3	23	0.073	P	6	30	3	0.923	23	6	12	4.38	150	154	62	94
Phillips, Dick		BR TR																									
1958	Thomasville	GFL	125	453	83	120	19	6	1	59	12	110	71	0.265	SS	241	319	47	0.923								
Phillips, Gene		BR TR																									
1954	Statesboro	GSL	1	2	0									0.000	P					4	0	0	<45				
Phillips, John Melvin "Bubba"		BR TR 5'9" 180 lbs b. 02/24/1928 West Point, MS d. 06/22/1993 Hattiesburg, MS																									
1949	Thomasville	GFL	138	583	114	192	17	11	12	75	60	32	70	0.329	OF	312	29	16	0.955								
Phillips, Otis Glen "Otis"		BL TR																									
1955	Cordele	GFL	4	3	0									0.000	P					4	0	1	<45				
Phillips, Randolph		BR TL																									
1950	Cordele	GFL	44	88	6	15	3	0	0	8	0	8	29	0.170	P	6	34	3	0.930	43	17	11	2.92	216	180	162	117
Phillips, Raymond "Ray"		BR TR																									
1946	Thomasville	GFL	52	220	33	63	7	2	0	18	2	11	18	0.286	OF	72	8	3	0.964								
1947	Thomasville	GFL	119	498	83	150	30	3	0	41	16	41	47	0.301	OF	247	14	14	0.949								
Phillips, Sam M.		BR TR																									
1953	Cordele	GFL	4											0.000	P		0	1	<45								
Phillips, William Taylor "Taylor" "T-Bone"		BL TL 5'11" 185 lbs b. 06/18/1933 Atlanta, GA																									
1951	Waycross	GFL	32	53	7	5	1	0	0	6	0	10	28	0.094	P	12	39	0	1.000	32	10	8	4.26	167	110	125	162
1952	Waycross	GFL	47	97	11	12	0	0	0	3	0	12	39	0.124	P	26	80	12	0.898	46	21	10	1.39	297	202	265	182
Philpott, Carey		BR TR																									
1948	Opelika	GAL	18	47	7	7	0	0	0	2	1	9	8	0.149	C	81	4	2	0.977								
1950	Valley	GAL	87	252	34	50	5	1	1	24	4	34	43	0.198	C	259	42	20	0.938								
Pickel, Oliver																											
1939	Tallahassee	GFL	37	91	5	14	0	1	0	2	4	5	14	0.154	P	10	45	5	0.917	36	13	14	3.82	238	239	134	115
Pickering, Chris																											
1935	Thomasville	GFL	97	329	41	87	17	2	5		8	17	54	0.264	P					9	2	2		29	17	38	63
Pickett, ---																											
1917	Anniston	GAL	10	40	6	11	1	0	0		3			0.275	3B, C	33	16	3	0.942								
Pickett, Fred																											
1935	Moultrie	GFL	93	335	51	85	18	4	0		5	35	27	0.254	IF	202	269	31	0.938								
Picklesimer, ---																											
1930	Talladega	GAL	59	223	45	69	8	8	4		9	30	39	0.309	3B, OF	90	51	20	0.876								
Piepho, Harry																											
1906	Valdosta	GSL													M												
Pierce, ---																											
1913	Valdosta - Brunswick	ESL	85	299	39	75	2	0	0					0.251	C	450	96	15	0.973								
Pierce, Dick		BR TR																									
1957	Thomasville	GFL	10												P	4	7	1	0.917	10	3	4	2.90	59	48	37	34
Pierce, Jerome		BR TR																									
1953	Fitzgerald	GFL	95	310	49	61	7	3	0	25	11	58	96	0.197	SS	143	211	52	0.872								
1954	Fitzgerald	GFL	32	128	39	26	3	1	1	13	0	24	29	0.203	2B	97	95	24	0.889								
Pierce, Peter "Pete"		BR TR																									
1939	Waycross	GFL	30	114	15	28	4	0	0	16	2	10	10	0.246	3B	36	62	17	0.852								
Pierre, Bill																											
1914	Brunswick - Americus	GSL		166	21	46	14	2	11		1			0.277													
1916	Rome	GAL	66	240	19	62					12			0.258	C												
1917	Anniston	GAL	5	16	3	6	2	0	0		2			0.375	M, C	23	7	1	0.968								
1930	Huntsville	GAL	1												M, P					1	0	1	10.80	5	13	0	2
Pierro, William Leonard "Bill"		BR TR 6'1" 155 lbs b. 04/15/1926 Brooklyn, NY																									
1947	Tallahassee	GFL	14	13	0	0	0	0	0	0	0	0	8	0.000	P	1	4	1	0.833								
Pierson, Argyle																											
1938	Tallahassee	GFL	9	29	0	2	0	0	0	1	0	0	11	0.069	P	2	9	0	1.000	9	6	3	3.43	63	71	29	20
1939	Tallahassee	GFL	39	116	10	27	3	2	1	17	0	5	32	0.233	P	20	46	4	0.943	32	18	9	2.42	257	219	149	81
Piet, Ernest "Ernie"		BR TR 6'1" 161 lbs b. 01/31/1930 Chicago, IL																									
1950	Americus	GFL	36	83	11	18	4	0	0	8	0	4	18	0.217	P	12	64	4	0.950	34	11	9	4.14	198	183	121	138
Pietrewicz, Alexander "Alex"		BL TL																									
1962	Dublin	GFL	42	50	9	2	0	0	1	2	0	14	27	0.040	P	15	30	3	0.938	42	14	8	3.51	169	173	175	73
Pignatano, Joseph Benjamin "Joe"		BR TR 5'10" 180 lbs b. 08/04/1929 Brooklyn, NY																									
1950	Valdosta	GFL	127	424	102	121	17	17	4	77	22	127	53	0.285	OF, C	732	80	18	0.978								

Georgia Class-D Minor League Baseball Encyclopedia

YR	TEAM	LG	G	AB	R	H	2B	3B	HR	RBI	SB	BB	SO	BA	POS	PO	A	E	FA	GP	W	L	ERA	IP	H	SO	BB
Pilgrim, Arvie		BR TR																									
1954	Statesboro	GSL	110	411	72	99	11	2	0	39	14	63	60	0.241	3B, P	123	238	44	0.891	1	0	0	<45				
1955	Waycross	GFL	136	539	79	133	14	2	1	61	59	61	42	0.247	3B, OF	184	128	27	0.920								
1956	Waycross	GFL	137	527	84	131	12	1	0	31	62	52	45	0.249	OF	288	13	17	0.947								
Pillar, William J. "Bill"		BR TR																									
1953	Brunswick	GFL	6											0.167	P					2	0		<45				
Pillow, Clarence		BR TR																									
1954	Thomasville	GFL	114	413	68	94	16	7	10	67	13	72	85	0.228	1B, 3B	646	129	29	0.964								
Pine, Kenneth "Ken"		BR TR																									
1940	Americus	GFL	17	53	5	8	0	0	0	2	0	5	17	0.151	P, IF					11	5	5	2.78	81	89	22	15
Pinion, Willis		BR TL																									
1952	Hazlehurst-Baxley	GSL	17	34	2	5	0	0	0	5	0	4	6	0.147	P	5	21	1	0.963	16	4	4	4.80	90	89	58	70
Pinkston, Ewell		BR																									
1947	Valdosta		21	57	8	14	1	0	0	4	5	13	9	0.246													
Pinner, Ted																											
1942	Waycross	GFL	69	236	28	57	7	1	0	22	0	40	36	0.242	SS	116	212	27	0.924								
Pinson, Harold		BL TR																									
1949	Tallassee	GAL	115	402	52	103	12	6	3	35	12	63	50	0.256	1B	1025	48	17	0.984								
Pinson, John		BS TR																									
1950	Rome	GAL	81	289	57	90	9	9	0	43	13	61	30	0.311	2B	202	169	14	0.964								
1950	Eastman	GSL	26	77	12	24	6	0	0	14	2	15	8	0.312	SS	23	27	9	0.847								
Pint, Donald "Don"		BL TR																									
1954	Hazlehurst-Baxley	GSL	78	266	33	66	11	6	9	51	3	34	85	0.248	OF	101	7	4	0.964								
Pippin, Fred		BL TR																									
1952	Fitzgerald	GSL	57	124	21	30	5	1	0	10	2	13	22	0.242	P	11	38	1	0.980	42	16	15	4.29	258	289	112	183
Pirela, Julio		BR TR																									
1956	Douglas	GSL	119	441	69	111	14	9	4	36	12	59	63	0.252	SS	194	344	52	0.912								
Pirkel, James "Jim"		BR TR																									
1962	Dublin	GFL	56	174	23	33	5	2	5	29	3	20	49	0.190	OF	37	5	2	0.955								
Pittman, ---																											
1915	Thomasville	FLAG	18	67	7	15	5	0	0		2			0.224	OF	26	0	3	0.897								
Pittman, Al		BR TR																									
1946	Carrollton	GAL	12	25	1	3	0	0	0	0	0	2	4	0.120	P	4	13	0	1.000	12	4	4	4.43	69	89	26	22
Pizzitola, Vincent "Vince"		BR TR																									
1951	Waycross	GFL	34	92	12	22	1	1	0	11	2	18	11	0.239	OF	36	3	2	0.951								
Pizzo, Joseph "Joe"		BR TR																									
1948	Americus	GFL	28	131	22	40	13	2	0	27	0	11	6	0.305	3B	28	45	10	0.880								
Place, Paul		BR TR																									
1946	Valley	GAL	24	77	13	23	2	2	0	8	1	13	9	0.299	C	96	11	1	0.991								
Plaia, Bernard "Benny"		BR TR																									
1942	Cordele	GFL	28	81	5	12	0	0	0	3	0	2	23	0.148	P	4	38	11	0.792	30	9	15	3.36	198	198	102	98
Plante, ---		BR																									
1946	Cordele	GFL	<10																								
Plaster, B. Arlen "Buddy"		BR																									
1955	Brunswick	GFL	5	19	0									0.000													
Platt, Ralph		BL TR																									
1956	Tifton	GFL	114	342	73	87	14	2	6	47	11	88	87	0.254	C	623	69	6	0.991								
1957	Brunswick	GFL	123	416	72	108	21	3	7	59	4	77	74	0.260	1B, OF, C, P	748	91	23	0.973	2	0	0	<30				
1958	Brunswick	GFL	66	250	43	67	13	1	4	48	1	28	26	0.268	C	396	31	14	0.968								
Plaza, Ronald "Ron"		BS TR																									
1952	Albany	GFL	135	497	75	105	11	3	9	47	3	72	69	0.211	3B	167	260	28	0.938								
Pleau, Andre		BL TR																									
1957	Thomasville	GFL	3	1	0									0.000	P					3	0	1	<30				
1958	Thomasville	GFL	16	20	5	5	3	0	0	4	0	7	4	0.250	P	2	7	0	1.000	16	5	4	4.42	55	71	31	24
Pliszka, Matthew "Matt"		BL TR																									
1947	Americus	GFL	112	361	61	85	15	6	1	48	10	47	50	0.235	1B, OF, C	525	50	25	0.958								
Ploszaj, Chester		BL TR																									
1951	Hazlehurst-Baxley	GSL	35	152	28	29	4	0	0	11	3	25	10	0.191	SS	59	81	19	0.881								
1952	Hazlehurst-Baxley	GSL	120	453	101	107	12	0	0	44	5	121	37	0.236	2B	359	293	38	0.945								
Plushanski, Fred		BL TR																									
1952	Vidalia	GSL	15	36	4	6	0	0	0	3	0	3	2	0.167	P	3	16	1	0.950	15	5	5	4.35	89	109	27	20
1953	Vidalia	GSL	46	86	8	16	2	0	0	7	0	6	5	0.186	P	7	45	3	0.945	43	6	16	4.23	217	247	88	55
1954	Vidalia	GSL	27	36	6	4	0	0	0	1	0	5	6	0.111	P	5	26	3	0.912	27	7	2	4.46	109	143	48	22
Pluss, Dave																											
1942	Valdosta	GFL	118	456	94	139	16	23	9	105	17	68	45	0.305	OF	256	9	12	0.957								
Plyn, Percy S.		BR TR																									
1946	Opelika	GAL	23	91	9	18	3	0	1	8	0	10	20	0.198	SS	33	57	19	0.826								
1948	Moultrie	GFL	58	211	44	46	6	1	0	16	8	53	25	0.218	SS, OF	79	56	20	0.871								
Podein, George		BR TR																									
1939	Valdosta	GFL	25	47	3	6	2	1	0	2	1	7	7	0.128	UT	45	7	3	0.945								
1940	Valdosta	GFL	89	327	63	85	15	7	8	44	12	39	61	0.260	C, OF	319	40	9	0.976								
1941	Cordele	GFL	114	421	69	100	18	10	2	66	13	63	61	0.238	3B	294	42	18	0.949								
Podgajny, John Sigmund "Johnny" "Specs"		BR TR 6'2" 173 lbs b. 06/10/1920 Chester, PA d. 03/02/1971 Chester, PA																									
1939	Moultrie	GFL	48	69	7	9	2	0	0	2	0	6	22	0.130	P	9	46	4	0.932	38	15	10	2.92	194	190	116	76

Georgia Class-D Minor League Baseball Encyclopedia

YR	TEAM	LG	G	AB	R	H	2B	3B	HR	RBI	SB	BB	SO	BA	POS	PO	A	E	FA	GP	W	L	ERA	IP	H	SO	BB
Podolski, Richard "Dick"		BR TR																									
1953	Fitzgerald	GFL	34	47	7	8	1	0	0	10	0	10	16	0.170	P	6	22	7	0.800	33	7	7	4.20	150	171	47	58
Podowski, Philip "Phil"		BR TR																									
1954	Albany	GFL	2	1		0								0.000	P					2	0	0	<45				
Poholsky, John		BR TR																									
1957	Brunswick	GFL	20	26	1	2	0	0	0	0	0	4	11	0.077	P	4	15	1	0.950	19	4	7	5.44	81	92	50	57
Pohutsky, Chester		BL TL																									
1954	Thomasville	GFL	19	44	8	10	0	0	0	7	1	20	17	0.227	1B	118	12	5	0.963								
Poindexter, R.C.																											
1929	Lindale	GAL	80	266	35	84	12	3	7		1	19	14	0.316	C	270	29	5	0.984								
Poitras, Robert "Bob"		BL TR																									
1962	Dublin	GFL	3	1	0	0	0	0	0	0	0	0	0	0.000	P					3	0	0	16.20	5	10	5	3
Pokorny, Joseph "Joe"		BR TR																									
1957	Brunswick	GFL	11	7	3	3	0	0	0	0	0	1	2	0.429	P	3	8	1	0.917	11	2	2	3.34	35	34	24	15
1958	Brunswick	GFL	32	76	7	16	0	1	1	11	0	7	23	0.211	P	10	37	2	0.959	32	11	9	3.94	194	191	177	88
Poland, Bobby		BR TL																									
1956	Albany	GFL	15	12	2	2	0	0	0	2	1	2	3	0.167	P	6	4	0	1.000	13	1	3	<45				
Poland, Eugene F.																											
1915	Valdosta	FLAG	<10																								
1915	LaGrange	GAL	58	202	39	60	12	2	1					0.297	OF	110	10	7	0.945								
1916	LaGrange	GAL	70	249	36	68					19			0.273	OF												
1917	LaGrange	GAL	6	22	2	6	1	0	0		1			0.273	OF	11	0	0	1.000								
Poland, P.																											
1916	LaGrange	GAL	12	37	2	9				0				0.243	OF												
Polivka, Kenneth Lyle "Ken" "Soup"		BL TL 5'10" 175 lbs b. 01/21/1921 Chicago, IL d. 07/23/1988 Aurora, IL																									
1955	Moultrie	GFL	33	50	3	13	3	0	0	5	0	4	5	0.260	M, P	5	19	2	0.923	30	15	4	2.52	132	112	106	40
Polk, Roy B.		BL TR																									
1956	Thomasville	GFL	32	67	9	14	2	1	0	10	1	12	17	0.209	P	10	34	3	0.936	29	13	10	2.55	198	132	176	129
Pollack, Leonard		BR TR																									
1948	Baxley	GSL	30	59	8	9	1	0	0	6	0	5	7	0.153	P	9	33	1	0.977	23	10	5	3.79	145	155	96	68
1949	Tifton	GSL	30	102	22	22	5	0	0	15	0	2	7	0.216	P	19	32	8	0.864	25	9	13	5.01	167	108	113	91
Pollard, A. Eugene "Gene"		BL TL																									
1949	Griffin	GAL	73	260	51	65	7	0	0	24	12	62	20	0.250	1B, OF	419	4	13	0.970								
1949	Dublin	GSL	48	176	32	43	6	1	0	22	2	39	12	0.244	1B	403	15	7	0.984								
1951	Hazlehurst-Baxley	GSL	55	207	40	71	12	0	1	41	2	46	6	0.343	1B	439	26	5	0.989								
Pollock, Stanley "Stan"		BR																									
1954	Fitzgerald	GFL	1	1		0								0.000													
Polly, Henry																											
1939	Albany	GFL	11	33	0	2	1	0	0	1	0	1	13	0.061	P	5	17	1	0.957	9	8	1	1.57	86	66	60	30
Pompelia, August "Augie"		BR TR																									
1952	Statesboro	GSL	77	302	41	84	10	1	0	26	4	34	24	0.278	2B, SS	170	186	21	0.944								
1954	Statesboro	GSL	19	65	4	17	2	0	0	9	1	14	1	0.262	2B	54	64	5	0.959								
Pompelia, Emmett "Gene"		BR TR																									
1947	Cordele	GFL	98	368	62	97	8	8	1	37	11	51	72	0.264	OF	247	16	18	0.936								
Pomykala, James "Jim"		BR TR																									
1950	Tallahassee	GFL	17	37	4	7	0	0	0	3	0	0	8	0.189	P	3	16	3	0.864	16	4	8	3.80	97	100	45	47
Ponce, Catarino		BR TR																									
1953	Hazlehurst-Baxley	GSL	14	17	3	2	1	0	0	0	0	1	5	0.118	P	1	7	0	1.000	13	2	0	<45				
Pond, ---																											
1916	Rome	GAL	68	236	29	59				10				0.250	1B, OF												
1917	Rome-Lindale	GAL	17	58	10	18	5	1	0	4				0.310	2B, C	62	43	11	0.905								
Pontarelli, Lee		BR TR																									
1957	Brunswick	GFL	46	156	25	35	5	0	10	31	2	35	38	0.224	3B	37	69	18	0.855								
Ponte, Orville		BR TR																									
1958	Valdosta	GFL	2	0										0.000	P					2	0	0	<30				
Poole, ---																											
1906	Albany - Americus	GSL													3B, OF												
Poole, ---																											
1906	Cordele	GSL													2B												
Poole, Benny O.		BR TL																									
1954	Thomasville	GFL	10	9	2	1	0	0	0	0	0	2	4	0.111	P					9	0	2	<45				
Poole, Buddy		BR TR																									
1949	Carrollton	GAL	12	15	2	3	0	0	0	0	0	1	7	0.200	P	5	7	2	0.857	12	1	3	4.78	49	36	29	52
Poole, Edward																											
1915	Dothan	FLAG	23	65	8	14	1	0	0		0			0.215	P	17	51	5	0.932	22	13	7		185	124	119	71
Poole, James Robert Jr. "Jim"		BR TR																									
1946	Moultrie	GFL	49	192	35	52	9	2	0	20	2	29	16	0.271	2B, SS	69	96	16	0.912								
Poole, James Robert Sr. "Jim" "Easy"		BL TR 6'0" 175 lbs b. 05/12/1895 Taylorsville, NC d. 01/02/1975 Hickory, NC																									
1946	Moultrie	GFL	22	49	13	14	3	1	2	16	0	10	6	0.286	M, 1B	105	3	2	0.982								
1947	Moultrie	GFL													M												
1951	Moultrie	GFL													M												
Poole, Ralph		BR TR																									
1946	Tallassee	GAL	31	80	6	14	2	0	0	6	0	3	15	0.175	P	6	35	1	0.976	31	19	6	2.80	215	182	107	44

Georgia Class-D Minor League Baseball Encyclopedia

YR	TEAM	LG	G	AB	R	H	2B	3B	HR	RBI	SB	BB	SO	BA	POS	PO	A	E	FA	GP	W	L	ERA	IP	H	SO	BB
Pope, Ashley F.																											
1915	Griffin	GAL	54	200	27	58	20	1	3					0.290	1B	510	21	23	0.958								
1916	Griffin	GAL	70	240	29	56					6			0.233	1B, OF, P												
Pope, C.		BR TR																									
1946	Opelika	GAL	9												P					9	2	4	0.00	32	44	10	11
Pope, James Ray "Jim"		BR TR																									
1953	Waycross	GFL	23	50	4	10	0	0	0	6	0	5	3	0.200	C	70	7	7	0.917								
Popovich, Charles		BR TR																									
1948	Tallassee	GAL	<10																								
1948	Albany	GFL	16	37	8	10	1	0	0	1	3	8	11	0.270	OF	22	2	1	0.960								
Poppell, Jack		BR TR																									
1953	Hazlehurst-Baxley	GSL	112	501	100	133	19	3	0	45	19	51	30	0.265	2B	322	292	24	0.962								
1954	Albany	GFL	103	379	60	92	10	5	0	39	13	55	43	0.243	2B	259	282	25	0.956								
Popwell, Julius		BR																									
1953	Fitzgerald	GFL	8											0.348													
Porco, Frank		BR																									
1948	Griffin	GAL	14	40	4	6	1	0	0	4	0	6	14	0.150													
Porreca, Frank		BR TR																									
1947	Albany	GFL	134	491	53	133	16	10	1	70	5	62	87	0.271	1B	1089	46	23	0.980								
Porter, Bill																											
1937	Americus	GFL													M												
Porterfield, Lee		BL TL																									
1946	Tallassee	GAL	1												P					1	1	0	0.00	5	10	4	5
Portomene, Angelo		BR TR																									
1952	Dou(3) - Sta(40) - Dub(7)	GSL	50	146	17	27	4	0	0	13	2	30	29	0.185	SS	85	127	21	0.910								
Posey, ---																											
1906	Albany	GSL													P, OF												
Posey, ---																											
1929	Anniston	GAL	19	67	9	21	2	4	1		1	4	2	0.313	OF	27	1	2	0.933								
Posey, Walter "Walt"		BR TR																									
1946	Tallassee	GAL	74	252	34	66	14	3	4	41	5	39	43	0.262	OF	128	6	5	0.964								
Potocnik, Elmer		BR TR																									
1948	Americus	GFL	16	31	3	4	1	0	0	4	0	0	17	0.129	P	3	12	1	0.938	16	3	5	6.60	75	99	32	42
Potts, Clifford "Cliff"																											
1938	Tallahassee	GFL	25	55	6	11	2	0	0	5	0	12	12	0.200	P	2	15	2	0.895	24	8	8	3.58	146	153	64	51
Poulas, Nicholas "Nick"		BR																									
1948	LaGrange	GAL	14	29	5	6	0	0	0	4	1	3	10	0.207													
Poulson, Gary		BR TR																									
1956	Dublin	GSL	8	12		0								0.000	P					8	0	5					
Pounds, J.P.																											
1921	Griffin	GSL		61	12	23								0.377	OF												
Pounds, Leroy "Roy"		BR TL																									
1950	Albany	GFL	41	76	9	12	2	0	0	7	0	8	29	0.158	P	6	43	7	0.875	40	15	5	2.58	199	166	132	121
Poupore, Bernard		BR TR																									
1958	Waycross	GFL	11	20	1	2	0	0	0	1	0	1	7	0.100	P	2	10	0	1.000	11	0	5	6.55	44	50	29	55
Powell, ---																											
1921	Lindale	GSL													C												
Powell, Chester		BR TR																									
1957	Brunswick	GFL	42	39	2	1	0	0	0	0	0	4	21	0.026	P	9	22	2	0.939	41	3	10	5.94	109	139	69	94
Powell, Clifford "Cliff"		BR TR																									
1953	Waycross	GFL	37	128	23	33	4	2	0	12	1	17	19	0.258	OF	49	2	4	0.927								
Powell, Duane		BR TR																									
1954	Dublin	GSL	2	2		0								0.000	P					2	0	1	<45				
Powell, Hollis		BR TR																									
1955	Valdosta	GFL	5	19		6								0.316													
1956	Valdosta	GFL	41	144	28	45	9	2	2	31	0	18	31	0.313	OF	67	2	2	0.972								
Powell, James "Jim"		BR TR																									
1957	Waycross	GFL	36	117	10	31	5	1	1	22	0	26	14	0.265	C	203	15	7	0.969								
Powell, John		BR TR																									
1948	Alexander City	GAL	49	138	16	37	1	0	0	14	4	11	19	0.268	SS, P	32	60	17	0.844								
Powell, John S. "Jack"		BL TR																									
1950	Waycross	GFL	66	242	25	70	5	2	1	40	0	20	22	0.289	1B	410	30	12	0.973								
Powell, Joseph R. "Joe"		BL																									
1952	Tifton	GFL	11	34	1	5	0	0	0	2	0	1	5	0.147													
Powell, Kelly		BR TR																									
1956	Brunswick	GFL	58	207	17	45	7	2	2	18	0	11	52	0.217	3B	45	83	18	0.877								
Powell, O.T. "Harry"																											
1906	Americus	GSL													M												
Powell, Quincie		BL TR																									
1953	Dublin	GSL	15	30	2	6	1	0	0	1	0	3	10	0.200	P	0	6	1	0.857	11	2	3	5.88	49	69	9	24
Powers, ---																											
1913	Talladega	GAL	24	86	9	29				3				0.337	SS	35	63	11	0.899								
1915	Americus-Gainesville	FLAG	21	79	11	26	1	1	1	0				0.329	2B	41	67	15	0.878								
1921	Carrollton	GSL	<10												SS												

Georgia Class-D Minor League Baseball Encyclopedia

YR	TEAM	LG	G	AB	R	H	2B	3B	HR	RBI	SB	BB	SO	BA	POS	PO	A	E	FA	GP	W	L	ERA	IP	H	SO	BB
Powers, Fred		BR																									
1949	Opelika(10) - Newnan(2)	GAL	12	43	4	9	1	0	0	2	2	3	14	0.209													
Powers, George		BR TR																									
1955	Cordele	GFL	65	231	25	48	9	1	0	27	3	26	48	0.208	SS	117	186	39	0.886								
Powers, John Calvin "John"		BL TR 6'0" 190 lbs b. 07/08/1929 Birmingham, AL																									
1949	Valley	GAL	62	226	60	72	14	4	6	36	12	42	31	0.319	OF	141	3	9	0.941								
Powers, Ollie		BR TR																									
1956	Valdosta	GFL	1	1		0								0.000	P					1	0	1		<45			
Powers, Thomas "Tom"		BR TR																									
1947	Newnan - Tallassee	GAL	15	51	6	7	1	0	0	5	1	9	13	0.137	SS	22	46	9	0.883								
Prados, Robert "Bob"		BR TR																									
1948	Eastman	GSL	25	89	13	2	3	4	1	16	2	6	18	0.022	3B	27	31	16	0.784								
Prappas, James "Jim"		BL TL																									
1951	LaGrange	GAL	85	307	87	98	15	1	16	70	14	78	65	0.319	OF	233	7	8	0.968								
Pratt, ---																											
1913	Americus	ESL	19	55	4	7	0	0	0					0.127	P	8	32	2	0.952	15	9	6					
1914	Americus	GSL		109	8	27	1	2	0		1			0.248													
1915	Americus-Gainesville	FLAG	<10																								
Pratt, Arthur "Art"		BR TR																									
1952	Eastman	GSL	53	215	23	48	5	0	0	16	6	21	32	0.223	OF	94	8	6	0.944								
Pratt, Francis Bruce "Frank"		BL TR 5'10" 155 lbs b. 08/24/1897 Blocton, AL d. 03/08/1974 Centreville, AL																									
1917	Anniston	GAL	5	11	2	2	0	0	0		0			0.182	P	1	6	1	0.875								
1920	Carrollton	GSL		205	29	60	12	2	0		3			0.293	P, OF, SS												
Pratt, George																											
1952	Brunswick	GFL													M												
Pratt, Thomas "Tom"		BL TL																									
1946	LaGrange	GAL	45	148	19	43	9	3	0	15	2	19	37	0.291	OF	54	6	4	0.938								
Pray, Donald "Don"		BL TL																									
1955	Tifton	GFL	12	44	7	15	4	0	1	4	1	8	3	0.341	1B	93	4	3	0.970								
1956	Albany	GFL	84	311	54	81	17	2	4	43	10	61	31	0.260	1B	655	42	9	0.987								
Predovich, Walter "Walt"		BR TR																									
1958	Albany	GFL	119	431	82	102	23	0	7	69	6	71	85	0.237	1B, OF	334	22	14	0.962								
Prescott, Andrew D. "Andy"		BR																									
1955	Dublin	GSL	2	7		0								0.000													
Prescott, Howard		BR TL																									
1956	Vidalia	GSL	10	17	2	1	0	0	0	1	0	3	5	0.059	P	1	4	2	0.714	10	1	4	5.67	46	41	46	43
Pressley, Omer V. "Babe"																											
1920	Carrollton	GSL		112	20	35								0.313	UT												
Prezina, John																											
1937	Moultrie	GFL													P						2	1		17	16	9	11
Price, ---																											
1915	Dothan	FLAG	31	101	14	29	10	0	3		3			0.287	C, P	106	44	8	0.949	11	7	3		81	62	50	30
1915	Thomasville	FLAG	<10																								
Price, Charles		BR TR																									
1952	Vidalia	GSL	31	69	7	13	1	1	1	8	0	5	12	0.188	P	3	27	3	0.909	31	12	7	3.69	166	173	119	78
1953	Vidalia	GSL	16	40	8	6	1	0	0	2	0	4	14	0.150	P	3	13	1	0.941	16	7	7	4.78	98	102	68	55
1955	Vidalia	GSL	2	4		1								0.250	P					2	0	1					
1956	Dublin	GSL	20	39	3	5	1	0	0	3	0	8	10	0.128													
Price, Jake																											
1938	Americus	GFL	27	65	4	9	1	0	0	7	0	4	11	0.138	P	11	29	5	0.889	25	6	16	5.41	168	220	48	64
Price, Louis "Lou"																											
1949	Fitzgerald	GSL	40	112	19	13	1	2	0	8	3	35	43	0.116	2B	95	94	15	0.926								
Price, Nathan		BR TR																									
1957	Valdosta	GFL	27	83	16	20	6	0	4	15	1	16	26	0.241	OF	32	2	2	0.944								
Price, Paul		BR TR																									
1957	Brunswick	GFL	82	263	72	82	20	4	7	38	4	85	64	0.312	3B	87	166	25	0.910								
Price, Ronald "Ron"		BR TR																									
1954	Tifton	GFL	2	0										0.000	P					2	0	0		<45			
Pride, Jude																											
1942	Dothan	GFL	53	202	25	44	12	1	0	14	0	28	37	0.218	SS	93	141	18	0.929								
Priede, Nilo		BR																									
1955	Thomasville	GFL	9	27		4								0.148													
Prince, ---																											
1920	Rome	GSL													SS												
Prince, Howard		BL TL																									
1948	Douglas	GSL	109	423	55	106	11	4	2	40	15	50	58	0.251	1B	1006	54	12	0.989								
Prince, Jim T.		BL TR																									
1940	Cordele	GFL	85	338	53	107	17	7	2	53	2	19	43	0.317	3B	181	106	35	0.891								
Prince, Ralph		BR																									
1955	Moultrie	GFL	11	37	9	7	0	0	0	1	1	8	7	0.189													
Prince, William "Bill"																											
1936	Moultrie	GFL	42	164	24	51	12	2	0	26	1			0.311	3B	44	106	7	0.955								
Pritchett, Douglas "Doug"		BR TR																									
1946	LaGrange	GAL	12	28	3	5	0	0	0	2	1	4	8	0.179	SS	7	24	9	0.775								

368

Georgia Class-D Minor League Baseball Encyclopedia

YR	TEAM	LG	G	AB	R	H	2B	3B	HR	RBI	SB	BB	SO	BA	POS	PO	A	E	FA	GP	W	L	ERA	IP	H	SO	BB
Probitsky, Burke		BL TL																									
1955	Dublin	GSL	85	302	52	77	6	0	1	32	15	67	45	0.255	OF	177	10	15	0.926								
Probst, ---																											
1917	LaGrange	GAL	16	59	6	17	3	0	0		5			0.288	3B	23	31	5	0.915								
Procopio, Andrew		BR TR																									
1951	Fitzgerald	GSL	13	44	3	9	1	0	0	6	1	10	12	0.205	SS	22	42	9	0.877								
Proctor, ---																											
1920	Griffin	GSL													P													
Proctor, Louis																											
1913	Anniston	GAL	42	144	21	48					8			0.333	OF	67	6	2	0.973								
1914	Anniston	GAL	54	288	27	48					6			0.167	M, OF	129	6	1	0.993								
Proctor, Thomas "Tom"		BR TR																									
1954	Albany	GFL	18	26	3	8	1	0	0	3	0	1	7	0.308	P	5	11	1	0.941	17	3	3	2.76	75	59	34	30
1955	Albany	GFL	9	11	0	0								0.000	P					9	2	3	<45				
1955	Hazlehurst-Baxley	GSL	1	0										0.000													
Prozeralik, Nicholas "Nick"		BR TR																									
1956	Dublin	GSL	25	46	3	4	0	0	0	3	0	5	16	0.087	P	3	10	8	0.619	19	2	6	7.31	64	96	31	55
Pruett, John		BR TR																									
1948	Tallassee	GAL	23	74	9	19	2	1	0	5	0	10	11	0.257	SS	31	61	9	0.911								
Pruett, Milton		BR TR																									
1948	Eastman	GSL	100	349	46	84	6	3	0	36	14	48	22	0.241	1B	676	17	27	0.963								
Pruitt, ---																											
1930	Cedartown	GAL	25	66	9	15	2	0	2		0	2	12	0.227	P	10	32	3	0.933	22	9	7	7.03	137	170	71	84
Pryor, Shapard		BR TR																									
1954	Valdosta	GFL	41	130	29	31	5	1	2	13	2	46	26	0.238	SS	79	97	28	0.863								
Przeworski, Theodore "Ted"		BR TR																									
1948	LaGrange(77) - Carrollton(46)	GAL	123	406	84	100	18	5	11	90	7	107	118	0.246	3B, OF	157	51	19	0.916								
Puckett, Vearel																											
1937	Moultrie	GFL	34	81	6	12	0	0	1	4	0	8	25	0.148	P	7	48	4	0.932	29	14	7	3.97	197	197	103	119
Puent, Lawrence "Larry"		BL TL																									
1946	Albany	GFL	15	16	0	3	0	0	0	2	0	3	7	0.188	P	0	10	1	0.909	15	0	7	6.24	49	55	34	29
Puffer, Gerald		BR TR																									
1948	Fitzgerald	GSL	58	138	19	29	4	1	0	12	0	22	16	0.210	OF, P	36	33	8	0.896	31	14	11	2.66	193	166	96	78
1950	Valley	GAL	45	91	12	21	1	0	0	7	1	12	13	0.231	P	6	42	3	0.941	25	11	8	3.81	144	157	81	61
1951	Valley	GAL	88	320	70	88	13	2	0	26	6	60	39	0.275	3B, P	98	168	20	0.930	13	3	5	4.50	64	81	27	33
Pugh, Earl		BL TL																									
1940	Thomasville	GFL	<10												P								<35				
Pugh, Gordon																											
1929	Lindale	GAL	29	109	18	39	3	1	3		2	11	12	0.358	OF	49	4	1	0.981								
1930	Lindale	GAL	94	380	105	158	34	6	12		12	50	24	0.416	OF	132	21	5	0.968								
Pulcini, John		BL TL																									
1947	Valdosta	GFL	96	357	44	71	7	5	1	36	9	58	97	0.199	1B	799	37	18	0.979								
Pulliam, J.C.																											
1920	Carrollton	GSL		33	6	4								0.121	SS												
Punyko, Arthur "Art"		BR TR																									
1950	Newnan	GAL	51	199	48	60	16	2	8	42	4	27	19	0.302	OF	65	2	2	0.971								
Purcell, E.E.																											
1921	Griffin	GSL																									
Purcell, George																											
1939	Cordele	GFL	7												P					8	2	5	3.54	56	66	23	12
Purcey, Walter "Walt"		BL TL																									
1938	Cordele	GFL	4												P					4	2	2	2.18	33	31	23	5
1939	Cordele	GFL	48	120	8	18	1	2	0	6	0	5	22	0.150	P	29	49	5	0.940	30	6	14	2.92	179	188	68	53
1940	Cordele	GFL	49	128	8	30	5	0	0	16	0	7	24	0.234	P, IF					41	15	19	3.00	291	326	129	72
Purdy, John		BL																									
1946	Valdosta	GFL	<10																								
Puro, Ray		BR TR																									
1950	Albany	GFL	94	332	47	73	7	1	1	33	9	30	57	0.220	2B, 3B	184	193	34	0.917								
Putnam, Basil		BL TL																									
1946	LaGrange	GAL	13	51	6	8	4	0	0	1	1	3	12	0.157	OF	17	1	2	0.900								
Puttman, Frank																											
1935	Albany	GFL	120	444	71	150	28	4	18		5	32	83	0.338	IF	422	59	26	0.949								
Pyle, George		BR TR																									
1955	Waycross	GFL	1	1		0								0.000	P					1	0	1	<45				
Quackenbush, Mark																											
1936	Cordele	GFL	13	57	8	12	0	0	0	3	1			0.211	OF	31	2	3	0.917								
Quartuci, Ray		BR TR																									
1951	Americus	GFL	34	123	13	14	2	1	0	4	1	18	32	0.114	2B	105	94	19	0.913								
Quatro, Leo		BR TR																									
1955	Sandersville	GSL	30	57	13	14	4	0	0	7	0	9	11	0.246	P	7	32	10	0.796	29	15	5	3.10	183	160	138	63
Quattrini, Rino		BL TL																									
1951	Tifton	GFL	28												P	9	44	1	0.981	28	8	13	4.35	176	190	94	84
Quattrone, Joseph "Joe"		BR TR																									
1950	Tallahassee	GFL	32	411	92	109	19	2	11	69	8	136	76	0.265	OF	189	11	11	0.948								
Query, D.D. "Wray"																											
1929	Talledega	GAL	59	177	30	47	4	6	4		8	9	32	0.266	P	93	34	6	0.955	21	10	7		125	138	56	60
1930	Talladega	GAL	45	168	24	44	2	5	1		2	6	22	0.262	OF, P	49	8	2	0.966	4	0	3	7.20	15	23	9	4

Georgia Class-D Minor League Baseball Encyclopedia

YR	TEAM	LG	G	AB	R	H	2B	3B	HR	RBI	SB	BB	SO	BA	POS	PO	A	E	FA	GP	W	L	ERA	IP	H	SO	BB
Quick, James Harold "Hal" "Blondie"		BR TR 5'10" 163 lbs b. 10/04/1917 Rome, GA d. 03/09/1974 Swansea, IL																									
1936	Americus	GFL	116	462	74	133	12	6	1	48	8			0.288	SS	296	319	40	0.939								
1937	Americus	GFL	121	455	51	102	14	7	4	51	6	44	30	0.224	SS	243	402	53	0.924								
1938	Americus	GFL	118	470	74	126	18	5	1	60	7	47	38	0.268	SS	248	409	48	0.932								
Quick, John H.		BR																									
1946	Opelika	GAL	105	385	58	112	21	6	4	46	5	31	64	0.291	OF	100	6	3	0.972								
Quigley, James "Jim"		BL TL																									
1955	Waycross	GFL	9	18		2								0.111	P					9	3	3	5.17	47	40	15	36
Quilici, Gabe		BR TR																									
1950	Tallahassee	GFL	15	20	1	1	0	0	0	0	0	3	11	0.050	P	1	4	0	1.000	13	6	1	4.22	49	51	54	47
Quimby, Charles "Chuck"		BR TR																									
1952	Statesboro	GSL	122	436	116	145	25	1	31	126	5	115	29	0.333	M, 1B, 2B, 3B, OF	357	156	23	0.957								
Quinlan, Bud		BR TR																									
1946	Tallahassee	GFL	4												P					4	0	3	0.00	13	17	10	12
Quinn, Donald G. "Don"		BR TL																									
1952	Hazlehurst-Baxley	GSL	38	57	7	8	0	0	0	2	0	4	13	0.140	P	7	31	3	0.927	35	12	9	4.65	149	169	58	65
1953	Douglas	GSL	27	51	6	0	0	0	0	3	0	7	30	0.000	P	4	24	4	0.875	27	11	1	4.81	129	148	42	77
1955	Hazlehurst-Baxley	GSL	18	26	2	3	0	0	0	1	0	1	6	0.115	P	2	17	2	0.905	18	2	5	6.82	66	91	32	28
Quinn, Lewis "Lew"																											
1936	Americus	GFL	109	432	55	111	17	3	4	45	9			0.257	UT	243	677	61	0.938								
1937	Moultrie	GFL	36	153	18	38	7	2	1	30	1	8	19	0.248	SS	91	123	19	0.918								
Quinn, Paul H.		BR TR																									
1953	Brunswick	GFL	5											1.000	P		0	0						<45			
Raburn, Charles "Charley" "Big Indian"																											
1915	LaGrange	GAL	21	58	2	8	0	1	0					0.138	P	5	41	3	0.939	17	2	13					
1916	Talladega	GAL	22	50	2	9				0				0.180	P												
1917	Talladega	GAL	6	13	0	3	0	0	0	0				0.231	OF, P	1	12	0	1.000	5	0	4		27	29	11	10
Rac, Russell		BR TR																									
1949	Albany	GFL	136	519	103	164	31	12	16	134	16	79	89	0.316	OF	236	9	14	0.946								
Rackley, Marvin Eugene "Marv"		BL TL 5'10" 170 lbs b. 07/25/1921 Seneca, SC																									
1941	Valdosta	GFL	133	568	113	183	19	15	6	83	19	42	33	0.322	OF	273	14	22	0.929								
Rada, Roger		BL TR																									
1952	Brunswick	GFL	115	437	45	125	25	6	2	65	7	34	16	0.286	1B	895	73	5	0.995								
Radney, Joe		BR TR																									
1940	Tallahassee	GFL	31	76	3	8	1	0	0	1	0	5	19	0.105	P					32	10	15	2.60	218	212	139	82
1941	Tallahassee	GFL	44	100	10	20	1	0	0	10	0	8	31	0.200	P	6	45	3	0.944	44	12	16	3.66	273	283	220	85
1942	Tallahassee	GFL	41	120	7	23	3	2	0	7	0	9	38	0.192	P	10	59	5	0.932	38	18	14	3.54	285	273	210	146
Rados, Frank		BS																									
1940	Waycross	GFL	<10																								
Radzevich, Edwin "Ed"		BR TR																									
1956	Tifton	GFL	35	67	4	6	0	0	0	3	0	7	20	0.090	P	8	38	4	0.920	35	9	8	3.35	196	182	127	67
Raebum, John		BR																									
1953	Vidalia	GSL	3											0.000													
Raehse, William "Bill"		BL TL																									
1948	LaGrange	GAL	43	160	22	40	6	2	2	26	2	18	20	0.250	1B	335	26	8	0.978								
Rafferty, ---																											
1913	Waycross	ESL	22	75	12	13	0	0	0					0.173	OF	38	39	8	0.906								
1915	Brunswick	FLAG	70	234	36	50	8	0	5		0			0.214	OF	152	17	17	0.909								
Ragsdale, Bob																											
1913	Opelika	GAL	87	309	56	73				35				0.236	OF	160	21	5	0.973								
1914	Anniston	GAL	97	354	43	79				26				0.223	M, OF	268	20	8	0.973								
Ragsdale, Joe Leroy "Joe"																											
1941	Albany	GFL	21	54	9	8	0	1	1	6	0	4	21	0.148	P	1	33	2	0.944	21	8	6	4.86	124	140	64	75
Raines, William "Bill"																											
1949	Dublin	GSL	10	12	2	5	1	0	0	5	0	1	2	0.417													
Rainwater, Dewey																											
1928	Cedartown	GAL	5												P					5	3	2	3.35	43	38	20	16
1929	Cedartown	GAL	39	63	4	10	2	0	1		0	1	20	0.159	P	4	52	4	0.933	37	7	12		168	221	52	60
Raisch, Charles		BR TR																									
1955	Moultrie	GFL	7	4		1								0.250	P					7	0	1		<45			
Raisch, Harry		BL TL																									
1948	Americus	GFL	30	51	6	10	1	0	0	8	0	5	20	0.196	P	2	8	4	0.714	21	1	5	9.18	50	65	26	51
Rakestraw, Donald "Don"		BR TR																									
1955	Waycross	GFL	11	9	0	0	0	0	0	0	0	0	3	0.000	P	0	7	1	0.875	11	0	1		<45			
Rambert, Elmer Donald "Pep"		BR TR 6'0" 175 lbs b. 08/01/1916 Cleveland, OH d. 11/16/1974 West Palm Beach, FL																									
1951	Eastman	GSL	103	363	65	125	29	1	4	82	21	44	15	0.344	M, 1B, OF, P	810	35	6	0.993								
Ramburger, ---																											
1906	Albany	GSL													SS												
Ramey, Jerry		BR TR																									
1955	Cordele	GFL	22	39	6	8	2	0	0	3	0	1	9	0.205	P	5	9	4	0.778	19	4	6	5.54	78	106	47	51
Ramirez, Carlos M.		BR TR																									
1957	Waycross	GFL	98	401	73	127	18	2	1	31	10	60	43	0.317	SS	206	302	35	0.936								
Ramont, Richard "Dick"		BR TR																									
1957	Waycross	GFL	5	3		1								0.333	P					4	1	3		<30			

Georgia Class-D Minor League Baseball Encyclopedia

YR	TEAM	LG	G	AB	R	H	2B	3B	HR	RBI	SB	BB	SO	BA	POS	PO	A	E	FA	GP	W	L	ERA	IP	H	SO	BB
Ramont, Terry		BR TR																									
1958	Brunswick	GFL	17	46	7	6	3	0	1	4	0	1	13	0.130	C	65	2	5	0.931								
Rampola, Joe																											
1937	Albany	GFL	51	103	20	25	3	1	5	16	1	21	31	0.243	P	40	50	3	0.968	34	16	11	3.31	234	234	109	100
1938	Albany	GFL	47	131	17	25	4	0	1	18	2	22	41	0.191	P	43	67	12	0.902	28	13	12	3.83	216	239	101	98
1939	Albany	GFL													P									<45			
Ramsey, ---																											
1906	Cordele	GSL													P, OF												
Ramsey, ---																											
1921	Rome	GSL													OF												
Ramsey, ---																											
1929	Anniston	GAL	8												P					8	2	4		48	68	14	13
Ramsey, Donald "Don"																											
1942	Cordele	GFL	114	397	40	100	10	0	0	41	0	27	43	0.252	C	462	55	17	0.968								
Ramsey, Frank E.		BL TL																									
1955	Brunswick	GFL	17	31	6	5	1	0	0	2	0	7	12	0.161	P	4	11	1	0.938	13	7	2	3.08	79	62	57	49
Ramsey, Paul R.		BR TR																									
1951	Cordele	GFL	11	27	1	5	1	0	0	1	0	8	6	0.185	C	45	10	2	0.965								
Ramsey, Silas I.		BR TR																									
1952	Valdosta	GFL	31	65	4	6	0	1	0	2	0	2	28	0.092	P	3	35	5	0.884	31	9	14	2.87	185	169	107	105
1953	Thomasville	GFL	20	53	9	13	0	0	0	4	0	5	18	0.245	P	4	19	4	0.852	20	7	8	3.44	136	121	87	78
Ramsey, William Thrace "Bill" "Tiny"		BR TR 6'0" 175 lbs b. 10/20/1920 Osceola, AR																									
1942	Waycross	GFL	31	134	19	27	5	2	0	6	0	13	25	0.201	OF	60	6	4	0.943								
Rand, Robert E. "Bob"		BR TR																									
1953	Albany	GFL	122	438	83	117	20	8	8	90	14	60	72	0.267	C	707	65	17	0.978								
Randall, George "Elmer"																											
1913	Gadsden	GAL	72	268	54	110					10			0.410	M, OF	110	11	11	0.917								
Randle, Fred L.		BL TR																									
1953	Thomasville(7) - Waycross(14)	GFL	21	25	10	4	1	0	0	2	0	10	13	0.160	P	4	13	1	0.944	19	6	1	4.17	82	70	41	53
Randolph, W. Harry		BL TL																									
1950	Douglas	GSL	50	199	50	74	13	6	3	37	13	39	21	0.372	OF	83	5	5	0.946								
Rapert, Howard		BR TR																									
1952	Hazlehurst-Baxley	GSL	25	46	7	9	1	1	1	5	1	4	16	0.196	P	3	19	0	1.000	24	8	8	5.31	117	126	54	78
Raphael, Mark		BR TR																									
1952	Brunswick	GFL	40	137	19	30	5	1	1	10	5	18	16	0.219	SS, OF	67	42	18	0.858								
Rasch, Marvin																											
1942	Cordele	GFL	124	467	67	122	20	9	7	70	14	47	101	0.261	OF	227	21	22	0.919								
Raulerson, Harry		BL TR																									
1946	Waycross	GFL	6												P					6	1	2	0.00	24	26	18	11
1948	Waycross	GFL	38	84	15	23	4	0	0	14	0	2	22	0.274	P	11	40	2	0.962	33	13	11	4.74	188	234	129	88
1949	Waycross	GFL	43	93	25	33	9	1	3	14	0	7	7	0.355	P	7	29	4	0.900	27	18	3	3.32	198	198	139	70
1950	Waycross	GFL	7												P					7	2	5	5.94	50	52	26	17
1951	Waycross	GFL	56	140	24	46	7	1	2	21	0	22	14	0.329	P	18	87	6	0.946	35	22	10	1.99	290	243	165	89
Rauseo, Michael J. "Mike"		BR TR																									
1948	Baxley	GSL	109	356	46	71	10	7	1	29	9	46	41	0.199	3B	101	219	38	0.894								
1949	Tifton	GSL	146	498	88	128	29	4	6	69	19	103	56	0.257	3B	189	312	44	0.919								
1952	Tifton	GFL	89	292	39	74	18	1	0	43	15	72	20	0.253	SS	207	282	49	0.909								
Rautzhan, William "Bill"		BR TR																									
1946	Cordele	GFL	118	423	55	117	14	2	0	55	4	78	66	0.277	1B	961	63	40	0.962								
Rawlings, Vernon "Vern"		BL TL																									
1947	Cordele	GFL	13	46	4	7	2	0	0	0	0	2	10	0.152	OF	13	0	2	0.867								
Ray, ---																											
1929	Gadsden	GAL	14	53	4	16	3	1	0		0	1	8	0.302	C	60	12	3	0.960								
1929	Anniston	GAL	39	143	21	41	6	4	0		9	11	15	0.287	OF	39	8	8	0.855								
1930	Anniston	GAL	10	31	2	5	0	0	0		0	3	5	0.161	C	35	3	4	0.905								
Ray, George		BR TR																									
1955	Tifton	GFL	2	0										0.000	P					2	0	1	<45				
Ray, Jere		BS TR																									
1962	Thomasville	GFL	29	63	13	17	1	0	0	8	1	7	15	0.270	P	9	32	3	0.932	29	9	6	5.58	142	144	122	124
Ray, Mathew "Matt"		BR TL																									
1957	Thomasville	GFL	17	20	2	2	0	0	0	0	0	2	3	0.100	P	2	22	2	0.923	17	2	3	4.50	62	74	44	32
Ray, T. Stanley "Stan"		BR																									
1946	Valley	GAL	<10																								
1949	Dublin	GSL	22	68	16	13	2	1	0	4	0	15	10	0.191	OF	34	11	5	0.900								
Ray, Thomas "Tom"		BR TR																									
1948	Valley	GAL	10	31	4	6	0	1	0	2	0	5	3	0.194	SS, OF	32	32	8	0.889								
1949	Valley	GAL	85	277	45	66	11	1	0	33	10	53	42	0.238	SS	114	240	50	0.876								
Reach, Clifton "Cliff"		BL TR																									
1948	Alexander City	GAL	31	86	12	14	2	0	0	6	0	15	17	0.163	3B, OF	33	16	12	0.803								
1949	Alexander City	GAL	82	281	40	58	7	8	4	43	13	54	55	0.206	2B, OF	137	56	17	0.919								
1950	Carrollton(55) - Opelika(42)	GAL	97	337	55	68	12	1	13	51	6	63	90	0.202	2B, OF	193	25	20	0.916								
Ready, Charles "Charlie"		BR TR																									
1952	Jesup	GSL	53	105	10	14	3	0	0	6	0	11	27	0.133	OF, P	27	25	6	0.897	36	4	7	5.56	131	138	78	97
1953	Jesup	GSL	36	87	13	19	2	0	0	7	0	6	22	0.218	P	13	42	3	0.948	32	17	7	4.26	224	208	161	126
Ready, Kenneth "Ken"		BR TR																									
1957	Thomasville	GFL	4	3		1								0.333	P					4	1	1	<30				

Georgia Class-D Minor League Baseball Encyclopedia

YR	TEAM	LG	G	AB	R	H	2B	3B	HR	RBI	SB	BB	SO	BA	POS	PO	A	E	FA	GP	W	L	ERA	IP	H	SO	BB
Reagan, Eddie L. "Kid"																											
1906	Cordele	GSL													2B												
1913	Cordele	ESL	102	367	49	87	7	0	0					0.237	M, 2B	230	283	25	0.954								
1914	Cordele	GSL		362	40	84	16	1	0		8			0.232	M												
1915	Griffin	GAL	39	152	18	33	4	0	0					0.217	M, 2B	80	97	11	0.941								
1916	Griffin	GAL	70	243	20	47					6			0.193	M, 2B												
Reagin, William "Bill"		BR TR																									
1953	Dublin(41) - Sandersville(17)	GSL	58	168	26	38	1	0	0	14	1	14	22	0.226	3B, P	38	99	20	0.873	13	3	2	<45				
Reale, John		BR TR																									
1949	Albany	GFL	137	521	77	130	23	0	4	75	8	62	98	0.250	3B	125	270	45	0.898								
Rechichar, Adrian L.		BR TR																									
1954	Brunswick	GFL	126	462	78	126	24	6	1	62	9	43	76	0.273	2B	290	342	45	0.934								
Recipko, William "Bill"		BR TR																									
1953	Hazlehurst-Baxley	GSL	13	21	1	4	1	0	0	3	0	1	5	0.190	P	3	8	0	1.000	10	1	0	<45				
Reckelhoff, Robert "Bob"		BL																									
1953	Sandersville	GSL	8											0.071													
1954	Waycross	GFL	3	12		1								0.083													
Recurt, Luis		BR TR																									
1956	Brunswick	GFL	97	383	58	89	4	3	2	21	9	39	46	0.232	2B	247	212	17	0.964								
Rediger, Glenn		BR TR																									
1955	Vidalia	GSL	103	372	49	110	19	1	8	56	3	48	43	0.296	1B, OF	651	40	22	0.969								
Reed, ---																											
1929	Anniston	GAL	5												P					5	1	1		30	43	8	9
Reed, James "Jim"		BR TR																									
1946	LaGrange(7) - Carrollton(1)	GAL	8												P					8	0	5	0.00	43	57	31	24
Reed, John "Jack"		BL TR																									
1955	Hazlehurst-Baxley	GSL	27	48	7	11	1	0	0	7	0	2	17	0.229	P	3	27	6	0.833	27	11	5	3.33	127	111	78	49
Reed, Robert H. "Bob"		BR TR																									
1947	Opelika(2) - Alex City(14)	GAL	16	45	6	10	2	0	0	2	4	6	10	0.222	OF	18	1	0	1.000								
Reed, Tommy																											
1938	Moultrie	GFL	53	200	29	55	10	3	3	27	3	23	29	0.275	3B, P	29	90	18	0.869	3	1	1	1.93	14	10	13	6
Reeder, Clyde																											
1939	Moultrie	GFL	139	537	54	154	19	5	4	86	1	44	39	0.287	1B	1223	86	33	0.975								
Reehoff, Ronald "Ron"		BR TR																									
1954	Hazlehurst-Baxley	GSL	28	110	23	26	3	0	0	11	4	15	12	0.236	2B	57	64	7	0.945								
Rees, Ernest		BR TR																									
1949	Newnan	GAL	12	42	5	7	1	0	0	2	0	5	8	0.167	OF	21	2	3	0.885								
1950	Valdosta(25) - Waycross(96)	GFL	121	462	65	107	21	5	0	40	15	68	102	0.232	2B, SS	255	278	58	0.902								
Reese, Aaron Durant "Aaron"		BR TR																									
1953	Waycross	GFL	6											0.000	P					0	1		<45				
Reese, Charles																											
1913	Talladega	GAL	73	255	44	96				14				0.376	M, OF	176	47	14	0.941								
Reese, Eddie		BR TR																									
1946	LaGrange	GAL	93	297	45	66	6	3	0	32	3	54	26	0.222	2B	211	200	29	0.934								
Reese, Edward "Eddie"																											
1929	Carrollton	GAL	37	162	14	45	12	0	4		3	3	24	0.278	SS	70	126	12	0.942								
1930	Carrollton	GAL		47		12								0.255	SS												
1930	Huntsville	GAL	98	390	96	132	37	6	13		10	33	35	0.338	2B, 3B, SS	242	283	39	0.931								
Reese, Joseph "Joe"		BL TR																									
1946	Thomasville	GFL	82	308	50	106	12	2	4	45	7	54	21	0.344	2B	206	198	43	0.904								
1948	Eastman	GSL	19	76	15	31	8	0	0	10	5	7	2	0.408	2B	47	48	8	0.922								
Reese, Red																											
1920	Carrollton	GSL		144	21	32	3	1	0		2			0.222	C, 2B												
Reese, Richard Benjamin "Rich"		BL TL 6'3" 200 lbs b. 09/29/1941 Leipsic, OH																									
1962	Thomasville	GFL	73	259	57	85	11	2	3	42	5	48	44	0.328	1B	571	30	7	0.988								
Reeser, Eddie																											
1941	Moultrie	GFL	28	105	13	28	2	4	0	14	0	14	9	0.267	C	151	24	2	0.989								
Reeves, ---																											
1930	Talladega	GAL	3												P					3	0	2	7.11	19	28	3	12
Reeves, Harold		BR TR																									
1948	Cordele	GFL	81	252	24	58	9	2	0	26	6	27	28	0.230	C	492	46	6	0.989								
1950	Jesup	GSL	140	508	71	134	19	2	8	90	6	69	72	0.264	C	737	90	16	0.981								
1953	Vidalia	GSL	4											0.100													
Reeves, Herbert "Herb"		BR TR																									
1950	Rome	GAL	11	21	2	4	1	0	0	0	0	0	4	0.190	P	3	9	3	0.800	10	2	4	5.33	49	48	24	35
1950	Dublin	GSL	17	22	5	4	0	0	1	5	0	1	4	0.182	P	2	15	1	0.944	17	4	4	6.62	53	49	35	44
1951	Waycross	GFL	28	62	5	9	2	1	0	5	0	4	17	0.145	P	6	36	5	0.894	26	13	7	3.79	171	154	86	79
1952	Waycross	GFL	42	100	12	19	2	0	0	5	0	7	20	0.190	P	20	62	5	0.943	32	15	12	2.45	235	187	137	102
1954	Statesboro	GSL	1	0										0.000	P					1	0	1	<45				
Regan, James "Jim"		BL TL																									
1949	Tallahassee	GFL	91	332	38	81	7	2	0	35	5	34	39	0.244	1B	770	39	22	0.974								
Regan, John B.																											
1941	Albany	GFL	8	30	4	4	0	1	0	0	0	9	8	0.133	OF	10	0	0	1.000								
Regan, William "Bill"		BR																									
1947	LaGrange	GAL	11	22	2	4	1	0	0	1	0	1	5	0.182	P					9	3	3	3.32	57	53	56	33

Georgia Class-D Minor League Baseball Encyclopedia

YR	TEAM	LG	G	AB	R	H	2B	3B	HR	RBI	SB	BB	SO	BA	POS	PO	A	E	FA	GP	W	L	ERA	IP	H	SO	BB
Reggio, Jimmy		BL																									
1940	Albany	GFL	<10																								
Register, ---																											
1920	Carrollton	GSL		85	16	31								0.365	1B, OF, P												
1921	LaGrange	GSL													OF												
Reichelt, Charles																											
1937	Albany	GFL	6												P					6	2	4	6.12	50	52	14	30
Reichert, Arnold		BL TL																									
1946	Valdosta	GFL	2												P					2	0	1	0.00	4	9	1	3
Reichert, Paul		BR TR																									
1946	Valdosta	GFL	37	131	16	24	3	0	1	12	3	12	38	0.183	OF	60	5	4	0.942								
Reichert, Stanley "Stan"		BR TR																									
1951	Moultrie	GFL	24	79	9	16	0	0	0	3	0	16	14	0.203	2B	51	70	11	0.917								
1951	Fitzgerald	GSL	22	85	14	19	2	1	0	5	0	11	19	0.224	2B	37	35	3	0.960								
Reid, Harold L.		BR TR																									
1952	Dublin	GSL	15	59	8	17	3	0	0	9	0	7	5	0.288	SS	21	31	8	0.867								
Reid, James "Jim"		BL TR																									
1948	Cordele	GFL	40	144	14	29	4	0	0	11	1	16	27	0.201	SS	57	88	27	0.843								
Reid, Robert "Bob"		BR TR																									
1952	Eastman	GSL	120	386	97	111	24	3	16	89	6	140	41	0.288	M, 1B	1198	58	11	0.991								
1953	Eastman	GSL	113	340	103	101	20	1	16	90	9	165	42	0.297	M, 1B	986	59	16	0.985								
1954	Sandersville	GSL	33	124	33	39	5	1	8	34	1	38	5	0.315	1B	311	18	5	0.985								
Reid, Russell "Russ"		BR TR																									
1948	Newnan	GAL	13	49	5	14	1	0	1	8	1	5	2	0.286	3B	5	9	3	0.824								
Reid, Warren																											
1942	Tallahassee	GFL	16	23	2	2	1	0	0	3	0	4	13	0.087	P	1	11	1	0.923	17	3	6	5.85	80	69	50	71
Reider, David "Dave"		BL TR																									
1955	Dublin(24) - Statesboro(37)	GSL	61	259	48	77	13	3	5	36	12	31	28	0.297	2B	153	152	26	0.921								
Reidy, John "Jack"																											
1914	Rome	GAL	95	393	76	117					31			0.298	M, OF	193	23	1	0.995								
1915	Dothan	FLAG	75	280	69	78	14	1	1		24			0.279	M, OF	142	6	1	0.993								
Reilly, ---																											
1915	Brunswick	FLAG	60	216	37	65	7	1	0		23			0.301	2B	146	130	16	0.945								
Reilly, Edward "Ed"		BL																									
1946	Albany	GFL	<10																								
Reilly, Louis "Lou"		BR TR																									
1954	Waycross	GFL	6	9		1								0.111	P					4	1	0		<45			
Reiman, Ken		BR TL																									
1956	Brunswick	GFL	19	44	3	5	1	0	0	1	0	2	11	0.114	P	5	32	4	0.902	16	3	10	6.94	109	116	68	83
Reime, Robert "Bob"		BR TR																									
1952	Moultrie	GFL	16	15	0	2	0	0	0	0	0	0	6	0.133	P	1	14	6	0.714								
Reimer, John		BL TL																									
1956	Dublin	GSL	13	31	2	6	1	0	0	2	0	4	6	0.194	P					6	2	3					
Reinagle, Edwin "Ed"		BL TL																									
1949	Tallassee	GAL	17	30	4	2	0	0	0	0	0	4	11	0.067	P	1	20	8	0.724	16	3	8	4.73	78	91	38	64
Reinecker (Smith), Walter Joseph "Wally"		BR TR 5'6" 150 lbs b. 04/21/1890 Pittsburgh, PA d. 04/18/1957 Pittsburgh, PA																									
1913	Gadsden	GAL	89	338	54	75					19			0.222	SS	141	257	43	0.902								
1914	Talladega	GAL	54	266	32	43					8			0.162	SS	128	189	50	0.864								
Reis, ---																											
1921	Carrollton	GSL		52	7	9								0.173	P												
Reiser, Harold Patrick "Pete"		BL TL 5'11" 185 lbs b. 03/17/1919 St. Louis, MO d. 10/25/1981 Palm Springs, CA																									
1955	Thomasville	GFL	1	0										0.000	M												
Reiter, James "Jim"		BR TR																									
1948	Albany	GFL	25	61	6	12	1	0	1	5	0	4	11	0.197	C	100	7	2	0.982								
Reliford, Joe Louis Sr.		BR TR 4'11" 68 lbs b. 11/29/39 Fitzgerald, GA																									
1952	Fitzgerald	GSL	1	1	0	0	0	0	0	0	0	0	0	0.000	OF	1	1	0	1.000								
Rellihan, Jerry		BR TR																									
1952	Valdosta	GFL	34	41	2	4	1	1	0	4	0	13	16	0.098	P	7	25	4	0.889	34	10	7	3.81	144	135	88	105
Rendlesham, Jerry		BR TR																									
1950	Moultrie	GFL	95	332	66	81	17	7	10	83	5	61	63	0.244	1B	573	48	24	0.963								
Renko, Harry																											
1941	Albany	GFL	53	155	29	43	7	3	0	16	1	17	29	0.277	P	48	39	10	0.897	22	11	6	4.44	154	165	82	75
Rentz, Irwin "Irv"		BR TR																									
1948	Cordele	GFL	86	270	36	70	12	1	0	33	3	28	36	0.259	C	375	21	10	0.975								
1949	Cordele	GFL	110	375	52	103	12	4	1	46	2	21	36	0.275	C	561	73	30	0.955								
Resavy, George		BR TR																									
1956	Dublin	GSL	12	39	6	10	1	1	0	4	1	4	13	0.256	OF	17	2	1	0.950								
Ressel, Paul		BR																									
1952	Valdosta	GFL	10	21	4	2	1	0	0	1	0	8	8	0.095													
Restaino, Emil		BR TR																									
1949	Thomasville	GFL	80	322	72	125	18	12	8	72	20	45	15	0.388	OF	141	15	10	0.940								
Restic, Joseph "Joe"		BR TR																									
1947	Americus	GFL	20	34	2	3	0	0	0	3	0	2	11	0.088	P	2	18	1	0.952	19	2	8	6.70	86	112	40	42
Rettie, Joe																											
1948	Griffin	GAL	<10																								

Georgia Class-D Minor League Baseball Encyclopedia

YR	TEAM	LG	G	AB	R	H	2B	3B	HR	RBI	SB	BB	SO	BA	POS	PO	A	E	FA	GP	W	L	ERA	IP	H	SO	BB
Retzer, Kenneth Leo "Ken"		BL TR 6'0" 185 lbs b. 04/30/1934 Wood River, IL																									
1954	Tifton	GFL	130	450	54	138	24	1	8	75	7	48	53	0.307	C	817	122	28	0.971								
Reveira, Frank		BR TR																									
1956	Sandersville	GSL	102	352	74	117	22	3	12	91	8	59	23	0.332	C	610	43	13	0.980								
Revels, William "Bill"		BR TR																									
1948	Carrollton	GAL	12	26	1	5	1	0	0	3	0	1	5	0.192	P	4	17	1	0.955	10	4	5	2.81	64	63	50	39
Rey, Emil		BR TR																									
1941	Valdosta	GFL	127	450	58	92	9	5	0	51	6	60	125	0.204	SS	205	420	74	0.894								
1942	Valdosta	GFL	115	407	72	102	15	5	0	55	9	81	95	0.251	SS	333	402	33	0.957								
1946	Valdosta	GFL	123	401	59	72	7	6	2	42	16	66	96	0.180	SS	106	367	63	0.882								
1947	Valdosta	GFL	112	396	68	86	10	4	1	34	3	73	83	0.217	SS	204	340	41	0.930								
1948	Douglas	GSL	118	412	58	99	12	4	0	42	12	71	66	0.240	M, SS	208	378	38	0.939								
1949	Douglas	GSL	142	503	88	119	18	5	0	65	21	77	65	0.237	SS	297	446	39	0.950								
1950	Douglas	GSL	131	482	65	117	14	2	2	69	14	73	90	0.243	SS	260	449	30	0.959								
1951	Douglas	GSL	86	298	43	68	8	3	0	26	5	59	33	0.228	SS	139	312	22	0.953								
1952	Douglas	GSL	124	443	68	110	18	3	2	74	14	107	52	0.248	SS	211	386	36	0.943								
Reynolds, ---																											
1906	Americus	GSL													P, OF												
Reynolds, Jesse Hammond																											
1915	Waycross	FLAG	71	246	32	69	14	0	7		4			0.280	M, C	409	116	8	0.985								
Reynolds, Robert "Bob"		BL TL																									
1954	Valdosta	GFL	3	1		0								0.000	P					3	0	1	<45				
Reynolds, Wade																											
1914	Brunswick	GSL		301	43	83	16	7	3		14			0.276													
1915	Brunswick	FLAG	61	238	42	72	15	1	3		18			0.303	M, OF, C	147	17	4	0.976								
1916	Anniston	GAL	65	222	36	73					6			0.329	M, OF, 1B												
Rhawn, Robert John "Bobby" "Rocky"		BR TR 5'8" 180 lbs b. 02/13/1919 Catawissa, PA d. 06/09/1984 Danville, PA																									
1938	Albany	GFL	81	264	50	65	10	2	2	32	9	17	26	0.246	UT	189	64	9	0.966								
1939	Albany	GFL	95	354	65	100	21	3	0	47	6	36	45	0.282	UT	153	34	17	0.917								
Rhodes, Herbert "Herb"		BR TR																									
1946	Opelika	GAL	<10																								
1948	Tallahassee	GFL	30	102	14	30	5	4	2	25	3	19	24	0.294	OF	36	1	1	0.974								
1949	Tallahassee	GFL	29	109	15	26	4	2	1	12	1	8	27	0.239	OF	37	8	4	0.918								
Rhodes, Hilman		BR TR																									
1951	Eastman	GSL	111	364	57	90	16	2	15	69	14	68	75	0.247	OF, C	398	34	20	0.956								
Rhyne, Kenneth "Ken"		BL TL																									
1946	Moultrie	GFL	123	467	101	142	28	3	22	129	2	100	23	0.304	1B, OF, P	943	44	17	0.983	4	1	0	0.00	15	17	4	2
1947	Moultrie	GFL	138	540	95	164	29	4	24	141	6	82	63	0.304	1B	1134	40	16	0.987								
1948	Moultrie	GFL	140	523	101	152	22	3	27	115	9	95	51	0.291	1B	1118	55	16	0.987								
1949	Moultrie	GFL	55	178	31	53	15	0	3	30	1	46	23	0.298	1B	421	15	10	0.978								
1951	Moultrie	GFL	48	189	26	47	8	1	4	27	0	29	13	0.249	1B	492	21	8	0.985								
Rhyne, Marvel		BR TR																									
1947	Tallassee	GAL	13	30	3	6	0	0	0	2	1	2	2	0.200	1B	201	9	1	0.995								
Rice, ---																											
1913	Newnan	GAL	61	210	28	68					6			0.324	1B	176	44	10	0.957								
Rice, Harry Francis "Harry"		BL TR 5'9" 185 lbs b. 11/22/1901 Ware Station, IL d. 01/01/1971 Portland, OR																									
1939	Cordele	GFL	45	81	8	25	4	0	1	15	0	6	1	0.309	UT, P	18	30	3	0.941	20	4	5	4.81	88	116	20	17
Rice, Robert Turnbull "Bob"		BR TR 5'10" 170 lbs b. 05/28/1899 Philadelphia, PA d. 02/20/1986 Elizabethtown, PA																									
1935	Albany	GFL	86	243	38	72	17	0	1		7	41	10	0.296	M, IF	73	125	10	0.952								
1936	Albany	GFL	93	336	51	109	27	4	4	65	15			0.324	M, 3B	95	163	13	0.952								
1937	Albany	GFL	104	333	41	86	19	1	2	45	6	39	7	0.258	M, 3B	109	160	15	0.947								
Rice, Rollie		BL TR																									
1952	Albany	GFL	134	519	88	117	12	8	0	45	24	97	77	0.225	OF	263	19	19	0.937								
1956	Albany	GFL	31	103	27	22	5	1	0	11	5	33	18	0.214	OF	54	3	4	0.934								
Rice, Ronald "Ron"		BR TR																									
1954	Vidalia	GSL	18	70	13	20	4	0	0	4	2	9	22	0.286	2B	36	44	7	0.920								
Rich, ---																											
1920	Lindale	GSL		64	11	21								0.328	OF												
1921	Lindale	GSL		116	18	43								0.371	OF												
Rich, Benjamin "Benny"		BR TR																									
1953	Dublin	GSL	19	33	2	5	1	1	0	3	0	3	9	0.152	P	2	6	2	0.800	13	1	6	6.52	58	63	38	67
1954	Dublin	GSL	6	12		1								0.083	P					6	2	0	<45				
1956	Brunswick	GFL	36	92	12	15	1	0	1	11	0	7	28	0.163	P	17	51	10	0.872	34	19	9	2.64	256	208	257	154
Richards, ---																											
1906	Cordele	GSL													3B												
Richards, J.A.																											
1913	Talladega	GAL	33	115	6	35				1				0.304	C	189	33	5	0.978								
1915	Rome	GAL	51	164	19	40	8	0	0					0.244	C	306	67	7	0.982								
Richards, J.W. "Babe"																											
1921	Carrollton	GSL		166	23	60								0.361	OF, P												
Richardson, ---																											
1906	Americus	GSL													P, OF												
Richardson, Clarence		BR TR																									
1950	Eastman	GSL	34	85	9	18	2	0	0	11	0	10	9	0.212	P	9	29	4	0.905	22	13	6	3.13	178	161	130	75
Richardson, Gordon Clark "Gordie"		BR TL 6'0" 185 lbs b. 06/19/1938 Colquitt, GA																									
1957	Albany	GFL	3	4		2								0.500	P					3	0	1	<30				
1958	Albany	GFL	22	42	7	9	1	0	0	3	0	4	11	0.214	P	2	17	3	0.864	21	13	4	2.93	120	111	93	58

Georgia Class-D Minor League Baseball Encyclopedia

YR	TEAM	LG	G	AB	R	H	2B	3B	HR	RBI	SB	BB	SO	BA	POS	PO	A	E	FA	GP	W	L	ERA	IP	H	SO	BB
Richardson, Hugh																											
1949	Tifton	GSL	13	46	12	15	1	0	0	8	0	12	7	0.326	SS	24	36	3	0.952								
Richardson, Lewis H. "Lew"		BR TR																									
1953	Cordele	GFL	77	209	35	54	12	0	6	32	3	40	29	0.258	M, C, P	247	45	15	0.951		0	0	<45				
Richardson, Martin "Marty"		BR TR																									
1962	Thomasville	GFL	114	416	91	116	14	10	7	65	35	66	51	0.279	2B	252	277	29	0.948								
Richardson, Thomas W. "Tom"		BL TL																									
1956	Brunswick	GFL	8	7		0								0.000	P					8	0	3	<45				
Richbourg, Lance Clayton "Lance"		BL TR 5'10" 160 lbs b. 12/18/1897 DeFuniak Springs, FL d. 09/10/1975 Crestview, FL																									
1941	Tallahassee	GFL													M												
Richter, Philip "Phil"		BR TR																									
1953	Vidalia	GSL	2											0.333	P						1	1	<45				
Rickard, ---																											
1915	Griffin	GAL	51	193	24	49	5	2	0					0.254	OF	97	13	2	0.982								
Ricketson, Donald L. "Don"		BR TR																									
1948	Vidalia-Lyons	GSL	14	47	4	10	2	0	1	5	1	3	6	0.213													
1949	Vidalia-Lyons	GSL	146	549	96	156	23	4	26	133	13	79	78	0.284	OF	289	68	34	0.913								
1951	Eastman	GSL	18	64	11	12	4	0	1	8	2	12	3	0.188	OF	21	0	1	0.955								
1953	Vidalia	GSL	25	96	8	27	7	1	1	16	0	9	12	0.281	C	92	4	5	0.950								
Ricks, Lloyd																											
1921	LaGrange	GSL		99	16	30								0.303	1B												
Riddle, Charles L. "Chase"		BR TR																									
1956	Albany	GFL	137	464	115	164	39	3	24	142	35	100	49	0.353	M, 1B, 3B, C, OF, P	531	99	17	0.974	6	0	0	<45				
1957	Albany	GFL	135	485	107	156	27	6	19	89	32	99	53	0.322	M, 1B, C, P	1018	75	16	0.986	5	1	1	<30				
Riddle, James "Jim"		BR TR																									
1947	Opelika	GAL	126	467	93	134	20	7	3	51	13	71	75	0.287	OF	249	16	8	0.971								
1950	Opelika	GAL	82	271	54	79	16	3	0	37	4	56	22	0.292	OF	135	6	5	0.966								
Ridenour, Roy		BR TR																									
1949	Carrollton	GAL	14	38	5	5	1	0	0	4	0	9	12	0.132	SS	29	41	6	0.921								
Ridgeway, Charles R. "Charlie"		BS TR																									
1948	Fitzgerald	GSL	120	477	106	141	13	1	0	40	80	93	44	0.296	2B	354	313	36	0.949								
1949	Fitzgerald	GSL	48	201	42	53	3	5	0	27	36	24	15	0.264	SS	118	129	14	0.946								
1950	Fitzgerald	GSL	140	569	129	183	34	7	5	81	63	104	33	0.322	2B	401	372	50	0.939								
1951	Dublin(54) - Fitzgerald(39)	GSL	93	359	81	113	16	3	0	26	26	81	10	0.315	M, 2B, 3B	173	206	22	0.945								
1952	Fitzgerald	GSL	120	479	108	173	23	5	1	74	52	110	21	0.361	M, 2B	408	348	35	0.956								
1953	Fitzgerald	GSL	136	508	105	140	13	0	0	44	39	119	34	0.276	M, 2B, P	380	318	38	0.948		0	0	<45				
Ridings, Joel "Jack"																											
1937	Tallahassee	GFL	123	497	82	122	15	7	2	40	29	72	51	0.245	3B	110	224	44	0.884								
1938	Tallahassee	GFL	112	472	77	142	21	5	0	49	31	49	28	0.301	2B	246	256	39	0.928								
Ridley, ---																											
1917	Rome-Lindale	GAL	7	14	0	0	0	0	0	0				0.000	P	4	17	1	0.955	6	3	3		51	36	26	15
Riepple, William J. "Jim"		BL TR																									
1953	Thomasville	GFL	24	99	9	18	4	0	0	7	3	11	29	0.182	3B	23	45	11	0.861								
Riesgo, Arnold		BR TR																									
1952	Hazlehurst-Baxley	GSL	86	248	39	74	18	4	5	49	1	68	23	0.298	M, OF, C	310	26	8	0.977								
1953	Hazlehurst-Baxley	GSL	90	297	59	91	22	2	8	80	1	77	23	0.306	M, 2B, C	362	57	8	0.981								
1954	Hazlehurst-Baxley	GSL	63	193	22	53	11	0	0	37	2	33	22	0.275	M, C, P	446	30	7	0.986	1	0	0	<45				
Rigdon, William "Bill"		BR TR																									
1950	Opelika	GAL	59	213	38	72	13	3	5	53	6	28	13	0.338	SS	114	173	24	0.923								
1951	Opelika	GAL	14	49	10	15	2	0	1	6	1	7	2	0.306													
Riggins, ---																											
1915	Waycross	FLAG	74	286	27	64	14	0	1		8			0.224	3B	104	119	31	0.878								
Riggs, ---																											
1915	Rome	GAL	18	59	4	13	0	0	1					0.220	OF	17	2	1	0.950								
Riggs, Arthur																											
1914	Selma	GAL													M												
Riggs, Lawrence "Larry"		BR TR																									
1956	Hazlehurst-Baxley	GSL	3	0										0.000	P					3	0	0					
Rikard, Denver		BL TR																									
1948	Tallassee	GAL	90	343	57	107	21	6	9	59	6	37	45	0.312	OF	135	16	11	0.932								
1949	Tallassee	GAL	121	448	72	130	21	7	17	93	5	53	53	0.290	OF	219	33	5	0.981								
1951	Albany	GFL	125	459	98	150	29	10	13	96	9	92	28	0.327	OF	194	22	10	0.956								
1952	Albany	GFL	138	527	87	160	30	10	7	111	4	78	26	0.304	OF	199	21	10	0.957								
1954	Waycross	GFL	131	471	65	138	40	4	2	73	6	68	37	0.293	OF	194	23	11	0.952								
Rikard, Robert "Bob"		BR TR																									
1955	Albany	GFL	114	387	70	106	14	11	14	76	9	65	70	0.274	OF, C	324	13	17	0.952								
Riles, Stewart		BR TR																									
1950	Moultrie	GFL	58	150	11	28	4	0	0	15	0	15	42	0.187	C	65	25	9	0.909								
1950	Tifton	GSL	25	68	8	12	0	0	0	5	0	7	11	0.176	C	71	7	6	0.929								
Riley, ---		BR TR																									
1949	Tallahassee	GFL	55												3B	64	83	24	0.860								
Riley, B.																											
1914	Americus	GSL		163	31	47	8	2	2		5			0.288													
Riley, Leonard																											
1942	Americus	GFL	28	107	22	28	5	2	3	11	2	11	25	0.262	SS	38	57	21	0.819								

Georgia Class-D Minor League Baseball Encyclopedia

YR	TEAM	LG	G	AB	R	H	2B	3B	HR	RBI	SB	BB	SO	BA	POS	PO	A	E	FA	GP	W	L	ERA	IP	H	SO	BB
Riley, Pat H.		BL TR																									
1938	Albany	GFL	120	488	128	156	17	7	8	75	28	80	25	0.320	OF	217	11	14	0.942								
1939	Albany	GFL	90	345	69	111	30	9	3	53	21	37	21	0.322	OF	142	2	11	0.929								
1940	Valdosta	GFL	92	369	83	113	20	5	6	55	10	53	30	0.306	OF	181	7	8	0.959								
1941	Americus	GFL	134	501	126	161	32	6	11	95	25	84	30	0.321	OF	274	2	16	0.945								
Riley, Robert "Bob"		BR TR																									
1947	Americus	GFL	60	242	71	77	11	1	0	15	23	53	21	0.318	SS	127	178	38	0.889								
Rinaldi, Charles		BL TR																									
1949	Alexander City	GAL	22	40	3	6	0	1	0	3	0	0	15	0.150	P	5	12	1	0.944	22	7	7	4.00	99	103	20	64
Rinker, Robert John "Bob"		BR TR 6'0" 190 lbs b. 04/21/1921 Audenried, PA																									
1949	Griffin	GAL	112	411	68	117	23	4	8	80	16	44	35	0.285	C	217	84	36	0.893								
Riolo, Joseph "Joe"		BR TR																									
1946	Thomasville	GFL	17	59	7	16	3	0	0	12	0	0	6	0.271	3B	9	10	3	0.864								
Rios, Felix		BR TR																									
1940	Cordele	GFL	38	150	27	55	9	7	1	33	4	19	12	0.367	OF, IF	50	31	6	0.931								
Ris, Harry																											
1939	Cordele	GFL													M												
Rist, Ray		BL TR																									
1939	Moultrie	GFL	139	531	76	157	26	11	3	90	9	67	62	0.296	OF	248	12	8	0.970								
1940	Moultrie	GFL	23	74	19	25	3	2	1	14	0	13	8	0.338	OF	48	2	2	0.962								
Ritchie, Edward "Ed"		BR TR																									
1955	Thomasville	GFL	20	16	2	4	1	0	0	1	0	3	4	0.250	P	6	9	2	0.882	19	4	5	2.14	63	61	36	29
Ritter, Arthur "Art"		BR TR																									
1962	Moultrie	GFL	14	22	1	3	0	0	0	2	0	0	10	0.136	P	5	11	0	1.000	14	1	5	4.50	60	59	60	32
Rivera, Florencio		BR TR																									
1951	Dublin	GSL	26	44	6	5	1	0	0	3	1	6	6	0.114	P	3	16	3	0.864	26	7	7	4.81	118	129	71	89
Rivera, Luis		BL TL																									
1950	Fitzgerald	GSL	34	39	5	4	0	1	0	2	0	12	14	0.103	P	3	13	3	0.842	34	3	6	5.63	115	126	59	70
Rivero, Federico "Freddy"		BR TR																									
1963	Moultrie	GFL	10	0	0	0	0	0	0	0	0	0	0	0.000	P	0	1	0	1.000	10	0	0	6.55	11	16	16	2
Rivers, Joseph W. "Joe"		BR TR																									
1952	Waycross	GFL	44	141	17	22	5	0	1	15	0	24	25	0.156	SS	63	118	29	0.862								
Rixey, Benjamin "Ben"		BR TR																									
1947	Tallahassee	GFL	38	128	23	30	6	2	3	30	1	28	40	0.234	OF	34	3	9	0.804								
Rizzetta, Anthony		BL TL																									
1947	Tallassee(8) - Alex City(2)	GAL	10	43	6	8	0	0	1	7	2	3	14	0.186	OF	28	0	1	0.966								
Roberts, ---																											
1913	Talladega	GAL	45	184	18	28				4				0.152	P	60	69	25	0.838								
Roberts, Arthur "Art"		BR																									
1954	Vidalia	GSL	7	13		1								0.077													
Roberts, C.J. "Red"																											
1917	LaGrange	GAL	11	25	2	3	2	0	0		1			0.120	OF, P	8	5	0	1.000	4	0	3		22	21	12	6
1920	Griffin	GSL													OF												
Roberts, Charles Emory "Red"		BR TR 6'0" 170 lbs b. 08/08/1918 Carrollton, GA d. 12/02/1998 Atlanta, GA																									
1946	Carrollton	GAL	67	227	57	70	13	3	3	37	16	43	16	0.308	3B, SS	69	131	20	0.909								
1947	Carrollton	GAL	97	351	75	135	24	5	11	72	10	53	21	0.385	M, SS	169	297	27	0.945								
1948	Carrollton	GAL	86	300	66	101	17	2	4	64	10	71	15	0.337	M, 3B, SS	109	191	21	0.935								
1949	Alexander City	GAL	107	338	70	107	18	6	5	61	19	84	11	0.317	M, SS	174	296	29	0.942								
1950	Alexander City	GAL	43	117	25	34	4	1	1	19	2	29	5	0.291	M, SS	54	65	5	0.960								
Roberts, Glenn		BR																									
1950	Eastman	GSL	12	38	7	11	0	0	0	8	0	6	9	0.289													
Roberts, Howard																											
1936	Albany	GFL	17	66	13	14	4	0	1	15	0			0.212	OF	20	3	3	0.885								
Roberts, James "Jim"		BR																									
1946	Albany	GFL	<10																								
Roberts, John		BR TR																									
1956	Waycross	GFL	3	3		0								0.000	P					3	0	0		<45			
Roberts, Kelvin K.		BL TR																									
1954	Tifton	GFL	140	522	85	173	36	4	5	92	12	87	20	0.331	1B, OF	407	28	19	0.958								
Roberts, Marvin "Marv"		BR TR																									
1948	Fitzgerald	GSL	10	35	5	7	1	0	0	3	0	8	6	0.200	SS	11	21	5	0.865								
Roberts, Ray		BR TR																									
1940	Moultrie	GFL	23	84	14	22	2	4	0	17	1	10	27	0.262	3B	15	47	10	0.861								
1949	Cordele	GFL	55	197	35	50	10	3	2	26	3	22	44	0.254	OF	87	6	10	0.903								
Roberts, Robert "Bob"		BR TR																									
1953	Fitzgerald	GFL	4											0.000	P						1	0		<45			
1956	Moultrie	GFL	36	38	4	4	0	0	0	2	0	9	17	0.105	P	6	43	5	0.907	36	7	11	4.01	139	131	97	83
Roberts, Thomas L. "Tom"		BR TR																									
1952	Thomasville	GFL	31	34	5	1	0	0	0	0	0	3	18	0.029	P	6	34	1	0.976	29	6	6	3.38	125	126	59	74
1953	Valdosta(5) - Tifton(31)	GFL	36	71	7	8	1	1	0	2	0	7	28	0.113	P	7	43	4	0.926	36	15	10	3.32	195	211	80	100
Roberts, Wayne		BR TL																									
1962	Moultrie	GFL	8	0	0	0	0	0	0	0	0	0	1	0.000	P					7	0	3	11.77	13	18	14	13
Robertson, ---																											
1916	Griffin	GAL	31	78	4	14				0				0.179	P												
1917	Griffin	GAL	7	20	2	4	0	0	0	0				0.200	OF, P	3	10	0	1.000	5	1	4		42	43	23	5
1920	Carrollton	GSL	<10												P, OF												

Georgia Class-D Minor League Baseball Encyclopedia

YR	TEAM	LG	G	AB	R	H	2B	3B	HR	RBI	SB	BB	SO	BA	POS	PO	A	E	FA	GP	W	L	ERA	IP	H	SO	BB
Robertson, Everett																											
1938	Moultrie	GFL	51	168	13	40	5	1	0	13	1	12	15	0.238	C	294	39	10	0.971								
Robertson, Preston		BR TR																									
1947	Tallassee	GAL	12	33	2	4	1	0	0	1	0	1	9	0.121	P	8	22	3	0.909	12	6	6	3.60	90	82	48	34
Robertson, Samuel D. "Sam"																											
1949	Douglas	GSL	136	509	51	137	17	3	0	61	6	46	36	0.269	1B	1271	88	15	0.989								
Robertson, William T. "Bill"		BR TR																									
1955	Brunswick	GFL	137	485	94	145	19	8	17	88	11	88	112	0.299	3B	132	225	48	0.881								
1956	Dublin	GSL	30	103	27	33	7	2	5	21	1	16	25	0.320	OF	20	2	3	0.880								
Robinett, Kenneth "Ken"		BL TL																									
1952	Thomasville	GFL	138	500	94	176	29	3	0	54	1	119	45	0.352	1B	1262	49	27	0.980								
Robinette, James L. "Jimmie"		BL TR																									
1953	Fitzgerald	GFL	28	99	17	21	1	2	0	7	1	14	18	0.212	OF	71	3	4	0.949								
1954	Douglas	GSL	83	339	75	102	14	3	17	91	4	42	53	0.301	OF	122	5	9	0.934								
Robinson, ---																											
1913	LaGrange	GAL	51	183	17	41				6				0.224	OF, P	87	9	3	0.970	3	1	2					
1913	Newnan	GAL	65	321	56	89				25				0.277	OF, P	135	30	13	0.927	6	4	2					
1914	Talladega	GAL	35	133	20	37				6				0.278	OF	53	19	8	0.900								
Robinson, ---																											
1914	Cordele	GSL		52	5	15	1	2	1		2			0.288													
Robinson, ---																											
1929	Cedartown	GAL	7												P					7	1	4		28	29	11	16
Robinson, Ben F.		BR TR																									
1953	Albany	GFL	7											0.200													
1953	Hazlehurst-Baxley	GSL	40	144	26	38	9	1	5	33	1	17	40	0.264	OF	90	2	7	0.929								
Robinson, C. Wilbur																											
1936	Tallahassee	GFL	10	27	3	4	1	0	0	3	0			0.148	P					10	5	3	2.65	78		37	28
1937	Tallahassee	GFL	47	102	10	23	1	0	1	10	3	19	16	0.225	P	14	67	3	0.964	37	17	14	3.12	265	272	133	86
Robinson, Donald E. "Don"		BR TR																									
1952	Tifton	GFL	57	143	14	37	8	2	1	22	1	10	27	0.259	OF, P	36	39	5	0.938	20	5	9	4.33	129	128	52	116
1953	Tifton	GFL	93	314	58	80	11	0	3	49	8	59	51	0.255	OF, P	163	10	7	0.961		3	0	<45				
1954	Tifton	GFL	15	30	3	8	1	0	0	4	0	4	5	0.267	P					2	0	0	<45				
1955	Tifton	GFL	125	424	53	126	19	4	9	65	10	34	65	0.297	1B, OF, P	324	29	19	0.949	18	3	3	3.92	62	72	31	33
1956	Tifton	GFL	9	19		6								0.316	P					2	0	0	<45				
Robinson, Everett																											
1958	Waycross	GFL													M												
Robinson, Harold B.																											
1942	Dothan - Cordele	GFL	10	11	0	1	0	0	0	0	0	1	3	0.091	P	3	4	0	1.000	15	2	5	7.60	58	74	14	37
Robinson, James E. "Jim"		BR TR																									
1955	Tifton	GFL	9	18		4								0.222	P					7	2	1	<45				
Robinson, Orem		BR TR																									
1946	Valdosta	GFL	19	36	3	7	0	0	0	3	0	4	12	0.194	P	3	23	2	0.929	19	8	6	4.36	99	99	82	57
1947	Valdosta	GFL	29	64	6	16	2	0	0	5	0	7	16	0.250	P	9	36	3	0.938	26	10	10	2.66	179	158	108	74
Robinson, Sammie		BR TR																									
1963	Moultrie	GFL	37	81	9	8	2	0	0	6	4	9	36	0.099	OF	53	5	7	0.892								
Robinson, Thomas "Tom"		BR TR																									
1942	Waycross	GFL	117	428	55	128	21	4	0	50	11	34	35	0.299	OF	224	113	46	0.880								
1946	Valley	GAL	84	276	33	77	16	2	1	30	1	20	23	0.279	OF	111	5	8	0.935								
Robinson, William Edward "Eddie"		BL TR 6'2" 210 lbs b. 12/15/1920 Paris, TX																									
1939	Valdosta	GFL	136	518	58	129	22	7	7	88	10	26	53	0.249	1B	1227	121	19	0.986								
1940	Valdosta	GFL	137	569	90	184	20	21	8	105	11	39	38	0.323	1B	1239	124	21	0.985								
Robinson, William Henry Jr. "Bill"		BR TR 6'3" 205 lbs b. 06/26/1943 McKeesport, PA																									
1962	Dublin	GFL	62	207	46	63	9	4	8	37	7	33	42	0.304	OF, P	71	1	5	0.935	1	0	0	15.00	3	5	0	1
1963	Waycross	GFL	113	418	69	132	18	10	10	62	29	37	71	0.316	OF	225	10	8	0.967								
Robison, Ronald "Ron"		BR TR																									
1955	Valdosta	GFL	30	107	11	24	2	0	0	17	0	14	6	0.224	SS	56	77	16	0.893								
Robison, Roy		BR																									
1946	Carrollton	GAL	<10																								
Robison, Vince		BR TR																									
1951	Opelika	GAL	12	52	6	12	1	1	0	6	1	3	10	0.231	OF	20	2	3	0.880								
Rochelli, Louis Joseph "Lou"		BR TR 6'1" 175 lbs b. 01/11/1919 Staunton, IL d. 10/23/1992 Victoria, TX																									
1939	Valdosta	GFL	134	534	93	148	21	6	2	61	18	29	66	0.277	2B	334	415	39	0.951								
1948	Valdosta	GFL	131	500	89	148	28	6	6	105	20	82	53	0.296	M, SS	265	399	58	0.920								
Rodd, Donald "Don"		BR TR																									
1948	Baxley	GSL	27	66	7	10	1	1	0	6	0	7	13	0.152	P	6	29	6	0.854	27	17	6	3.30	191	182	139	84
Roddenberry, Warren																											
1958	Albany	GFL	44	78	17	26	8	3	0	20	0	12	15	0.333	P	8	22	4	0.882	26	11	7	3.69	161	156	90	120
Rodgers, ---																											
1917	Talladega	GAL	1	3	0	1	0	0	0		0			0.333	OF	1	0	0	1.000								
Rodriguez, Angel		BR TR																									
1955	Cordele	GFL	20	45	4	7	1	1	0	2	0	4	10	0.156	C	88	7	3	0.969								
Rodriguez, Charles H.		BR TR																									
1950	Hazlehurst-Baxley	GSL	58	223	23	54	8	1	0	32	2	32	25	0.242	2B	137	152	21	0.932								
1951	Alexander City	GAL	67	245	42	67	3	4	1	22	5	44	28	0.273	2B	177	185	24	0.938								
1952	Statesboro	GSL	13	51	7	12	3	0	0	8	0	9	2	0.235	2B	46	46	5	0.948								

Georgia Class-D Minor League Baseball Encyclopedia

YR	TEAM	LG	G	AB	R	H	2B	3B	HR	RBI	SB	BB	SO	BA	POS	PO	A	E	FA	GP	W	L	ERA	IP	H	SO	BB
Rodriguez, Newton		BR TR																									
1962	Dublin	GFL	11	13	4	4	2	0	0	1	0	3	3	0.308	P	1	9	3	0.769	11	1	2	3.69	39	40	27	20
Roe, ---																											
1942	Albany	GFL	13												P					13	0	2	9.00	39	52	21	37
Roe, H.J.																											
1928	Talladega	GAL	14	33	1	8	2	0	0	0	1	11	0.242		P	15	24	0	1.000	13	3	8	5.72	85	118	34	32
Roede, Lou																											
1941	Thomasville	GFL	130	483	86	137	25	14	10	81	10	94	110	0.284	OF	391	24	10	0.976								
Roedel, Robert "Bob"		BR TR																									
1948	Carrollton	GAL	12	42	4	4	1	0	0	2	0	2	6	0.095	C	54	11	1	0.985								
Roesler, Kenneth "Ken"		BL TR																									
1958	Waycross	GFL	54	182	33	49	10	1	1	11	3	35	18	0.269	OF, P	90	4	5	0.949	1	0	0	<30				
Rogers, Ernest		BR TR																									
1951	Valley	GAL	36	63	7	9	1	0	0	4	0	4	18	0.143	P	1	20	3	0.875	31	11	7	4.30	159	186	57	58
1952	Douglas	GSL	24	47	6	6	2	0	0	4	0	13	13	0.128	P	17	20	2	0.949	20	10	6	3.20	132	130	52	57
1953	Douglas	GSL	5											0.000	P					2	2		<45				
Rogers, Francis		BR TR																									
1951	Waycross	GFL	23	78	9	17	1	1	1	10	0	8	23	0.218	OF	23	3	7	0.788								
Rogers, James "Jim"		BR TR																									
1940	Americus	GFL	39	146	20	39	5	2	4	20	6	16	44	0.267	OF	61	4	5	0.929								
Rogers, Louis "Lou"																											
1941	Thomasville	GFL	16	36	1	8	1	0	0	4	0	1	7	0.222	P	9	8	3	0.850	13	3	3	3.00	81	91	32	32
Rogers, Lynn R.		BR TR																									
1953	Thomasville	GFL	9											0.143	P					2	1		<45				
Rogers, Marion		BR TR																									
1950	Valley	GAL	35	48	6	9	2	0	0	1	0	4	14	0.188	P	4	19	6	0.793	30	7	10	5.71	126	153	41	79
Rogers, Walter "Walt"		BS TR																									
1946	Valdosta	GFL	123	490	82	154	21	13	5	61	18	44	51	0.314	3B	154	252	39	0.912								
Rogers, William T. "Bill"																											
1941	Americus	GFL	8	14	1	1	0	0	0	1	0	1	2	0.071	M, P	1	12	0	1.000	7	1	2	6.50	36	51	11	18
Rohe, George Anthony "George"		BR TR 5'9" 165 lbs b. 09/15/1875 Cincinnati, OH d. 06/10/1957 Cincinnati, OH																									
1913	Newnan	GAL	42	154	28	67					15			0.435	3B	57	88	9	0.942								
Rohrbaugh, Glenn		BR TR																									
1948	Douglas	GSL	35	104	6	26	2	0	0	13	3	14	12	0.250	OF, C	113	14	8	0.941								
Rohs, Norman Edwin "Norm"		BR TR																									
1953	Albany	GFL	103	358	42	89	11	3	1	66	1	36	40	0.249	OF, C	171	20	7	0.965								
Roig, Anton Ambrose "Tony"		BR TR 6'1" 180 lbs b. 12/23/1927 New Orleans, LA																									
1949	Dublin	GSL	14	43	4	11	0	0	1	5	2	3	11	0.256	OF	20	0	3	0.870								
1950	Rome	GAL	119	483	85	158	34	4	15	104	21	27	60	0.327	2B, 3B, SS, OF	211	164	47	0.889								
Rolf, ---																											
1906	Americus	GSL													2B												
Rolfs, Frank		BL TL																									
1948	Griffin	GAL	106	401	67	118	8	13	4	63	8	52	72	0.294	1B	800	45	25	0.971								
Rollo, Charles		BR TR																									
1946	Opelika	GAL	13	54	7	13	2	0	0	5	1	1	3	0.241	2B	31	23	3	0.947								
Roman, Carl		BR TR																									
1948	Carrollton	GAL	23	55	0	12	3	0	0	5	2	5	10	0.218	OF	36	5	1	0.976								
Rombach, Robert "Bob"		BR TR																									
1962	Moultrie	GFL	64	206	41	44	3	0	6	25	3	38	67	0.214	OF	80	2	13	0.863								
1963	Moultrie	GFL	97	280	38	49	8	0	1	25	13	53	85	0.175	3B, OF	96	50	19	0.885								
Romello, Americo "Mike"		BR TR 5'4" 160 lbs b. 09/04/1921 Philadelphia, PA																									
1942	Cordele	GFL	14	57	10	15	3	0	0	5	1	6	8	0.263	SS	23	40	15	0.808								
1946	Americus	GFL	114	423	99	116	13	6	2	57	19	70	39	0.274	SS	242	293	43	0.926								
Romeo, John		BR TR																									
1953	Statesboro - Gadsden	GSL	10	16	1	1	1	0	0	0	0	2	10	0.063	P					0	0		<45				
Romeo, Michael "Mike"		BL TL																									
1962	Brunswick	GFL	28	20	0	1	0	0	0	0	0	1	8	0.050	P	4	15	2	0.905	27	2	5	4.85	65	54	58	44
1963	Brunswick	GFL	24	30	2	5	1	0	0	0	0	1	5	0.167	P	3	21	2	0.923	24	5	7	3.88	95	88	78	44
Rommel, John		BR TR																									
1952	Jesup	GSL	45	107	18	19	5	0	0	11	0	13	36	0.178	OF, P	23	39	2	0.969	27	9	5	4.60	129	152	39	54
Rooks, Gerald		BR TR																									
1956	Fitzgerald	GFL	10	21	1	2	0	1	0	1	0	1	9	0.095	P					9	2	4	<45				
Roop, Harvey Joshua Jr. "Harvey" "Babe"		BL TR 6'2" 215 lbs b. 01/22/1928 Concordville, PA																									
1949	Americus	GFL	137	561	79	152	27	6	17	107	4	16	118	0.271	OF, P	173	36	23	0.901	19	11	6	4.11	116	120	66	48
Rosa, Charles		BR																									
1954	Albany	GFL	1	1		0								0.000													
Rose, Hubert		BL TR																									
1950	Moultrie	GFL	124	469	145	159	18	3	0	47	20	140	40	0.339	2B	296	385	33	0.954								
Rose, Robert R. "Bob"		BR TR																									
1948	Eastman	GSL	31	57	5	7	1	1	0	3	0	7	17	0.123	P	4	19	2	0.920	31	16	8	3.55	165	161	67	84
Rose, Russell "Russ"		BR TR																									
1946	Valdosta	GFL	111	412	58	104	15	3	0	49	13	47	73	0.252	2B	313	267	40	0.935								
Rose, Wallace		BL TL																									
1962	Dublin	GFL	8	6	1	0	0	0	0	0	0	3	4	0.000	P					8	0	2	5.19	26	30	12	15

Georgia Class-D Minor League Baseball Encyclopedia

YR	TEAM	LG	G	AB	R	H	2B	3B	HR	RBI	SB	BB	SO	BA	POS	PO	A	E	FA	GP	W	L	ERA	IP	H	SO	BB
Rosett, Jack																											
1936	Cordele	GFL	41	157	19	41	7	2	1	15	5			0.261	OF	55	3	5	0.921								
Rospond, Walter "Walt"																											
1936	Tallahassee	GFL	121	478	106	116	27	13	6	44	30			0.243	SS	258	388	75	0.896								
Ross, Jerome		BR TR																									
1948	Alexander City	GAL	24	77	8	19	4	1	1	13	0	9	16	0.247	3B	23	42	12	0.844								
Ross, Kent		BR TR																									
1963	Thomasville	GFL	15	38	3	8	1	0	0	1	1	5	14	0.211	OF	10	1	0	1.000								
Ross, Ronald "Ron"		BR TR																									
1958	Waycross	GFL	5	8		2								0.250	P					5	0	4		<30			
Rossi, Michael "Mike"		BR TR																									
1949	Vidalia-Lyons	GSL	54	175	21	49	9	0	1	20	0	8	26	0.280	M, P, OF	32	74	8	0.930	47	25	13	2.80	325	140	126	70
1951	Jesup	GSL	63	151	26	39	9	0	1	19	3	29	17	0.258	OF, P	28	35	3	0.955	31	12	9	3.81	182	183	57	54
Rossi, Ronald "Ron"		BR TR																									
1957	Thomasville	GFL	138	517	104	166	22	10	4	91	11	89	36	0.321	OF	273	7	9	0.969								
Roth, Jac E.		BR TR																									
1948	LaGrange	GAL	43	186	27	51	6	4	0	28	7	15	16	0.274	2B	116	102	20	0.916								
1950	Valley	GAL	95	361	80	104	13	5	1	39	34	61	25	0.288	2B	240	229	25	0.949								
1951	Valley	GAL	16	46	15	14	1	3	0	6	5	8	4	0.304	2B	27	29	1	0.982								
Roth, Richard "Dick"		BR TR																									
1954	Douglas	GSL	1	0										0.000	P					1	0	0		<45			
Roth, V.																											
1913	Thomasville	ESL	57	159	23	45	10	0	4					0.283	P, OF	41	62	9	0.920	26	18	8					
1914	Thomasville	GSL		116	24	35	4	3	1		0			0.302													
Rothgeb, John		BL TL																									
1956	Brunswick	GFL	3	1		0								0.000	P					3	0	0		<45			
Rothrock, John Huston "Jack"		BS TR 5'11" 165 lbs b. 03/14/1905 Long Beach, CA d. 02/02/1980 San Bernardino, CA																									
1948	Tallahassee	GFL													M												
Rotondi, Louis "Lou"		BR TR																									
1951	Tifton	GFL	93	362	87	106	26	3	3	42	25	71	39	0.293	3B, SS, OF	122	78	24	0.893								
Rouse, John		BL TR																									
1958	Thomasville	GFL	24	81	14	24	4	1	1	12	0	11	18	0.296	1B	149	12	13	0.925								
Rouse, William "Bill"		BL TR																									
1962	Moultrie	GFL	27	72	7	15	3	0	1	9	0	14	31	0.208	1B, P	123	8	11	0.923	1	0	1	11.25	4	6	3	4
Rovai, Rudy		BL TL																									
1953	Statesboro	GSL	25	56	4	10	2	1	0	8	0	5	14	0.179	P	4	23	0	1.000	20	6	6	4.88	120	127	78	85
Rowe, ---		BR																									
1946	Valley	GAL	<10																								
Rowe, Bob																											
1928	Carrollton - Gadsden	GAL	68	250	27	79	10	4	6		0	15	18	0.316	OF	121	3	5	0.961								
Rowe, Edgar		BR TR																									
1950	Albany	GFL	19	70	23	13	1	1	0	16	12	12	12	0.186	3B	12	33	7	0.865								
Rowe, John																											
1937	Americus	GFL	56	223	30	57	8	1	0	24	2	27	29	0.256	OF	138	3	4	0.972								
1938	Americus	GFL	126	548	115	173	34	9	4	54	40	53	35	0.316	OF	332	14	32	0.915								
Rowe, Joseph "Joe"		BL TR																									
1962	Dublin	GFL	28	70	19	19	3	0	1	10	1	14	17	0.271	OF	5	2	0	1.000								
Rowell, Carvell William "Bama"		BL TR 5'11" 185 lbs b. 01/13/1916 Citronelle, AL d. 08/16/1993 Citronelle, AL																									
1937	Cordele	GFL	101	361	47	87	9	5	4	58	12	25	38	0.241	2B	220	187	38	0.915								
Rowzee, Robert "Bob"		BL TL																									
1952	Waycross	GFL	10	6	0	0	0	0	0	0	0	2	3	0.000													
1954	Waycross	GFL	9	4		0								0.000	P					6	0	3		<45			
Roxie, ---																											
1913	Gadsden	GAL	59	223	23	57					10			0.256	3B	63	106	20	0.894								
Royal, Julian																											
1949	Douglas	GSL	13	14	0	0	0	0	0	1	0	2	3	0.000	P	1	12	0	1.000								
Royce, Gordon		BR TL																									
1954	Thomasville	GFL	12	16	2	2	0	0	0	1	0	1	4	0.125	P	4	15	3	0.864	12	4	1	3.29	52	53	15	19
Royer, Charles		BR TR																									
1952	Hazlehurst-Baxley	GSL	32	83	5	20	0	0	0	5	0	2	9	0.241	P	7	42	3	0.942	28	14	7	3.78	188	161	129	20
Ruark, E. Parnell		BR TR																									
1949	Sparta	GSL	125	505	104	171	38	17	10	10	5	5	90	0.339	SS	64	226	23	0.927								
1950	Dublin	GSL	113	446	100	146	27	1	39	127	8	61	63	0.327	M, OF	190	7	6	0.970								
1951	Dublin	GSL	126	490	130	161	29	3	32	140	14	79	10	0.329	M, OF	205	16	17	0.929								
1952	Tifton	GFL	95	342	66	98	21	0	19	66	6	55	33	0.287	M, OF	185	16	4	0.980								
1953	Sandersville(79) - Dublin(16)	GSL	95	347	72	129	31	7	10	84	8	64	30	0.372	M, OF, P	169	10	16	0.918		0	1		<45			
1954	Vidalia(55) - Sandersville(21)	GSL	76	284	56	84	11	1	15	59	1	46	32	0.296	OF	133	8	6	0.959								
Ruark, James B. "Jim"		BR TR																									
1948	Sparta	GSL	119	402	57	118	27	7	3	66	3	49	68	0.294	C	806	62	25	0.972								
1949	Sparta	GSL	118	443	68	134	22	6	12	101	0	73	61	0.302	M, C	630	56	17	0.976								
1951	Fitzgerald(62) - Jesup(32)	GSL	94	355	60	107	17	2	12	82	1	41	47	0.301	M, OF, C	206	46	25	0.910								
1952	Jesup	GSL	36	143	25	34	9	1	5	19	0	12	22	0.238	C	159	19	6	0.967								
1953	Dublin	GSL	41	156	23	38	8	2	0	4	25	0	24	0.244	C	228	27	8	0.970								
Ruck, Martin		BR TR																									
1963	Moultrie	GFL	16	11	2	0	0	0	0	0	0	1	11	0.000	P	2	3	1	0.833	12	2	1	4.67	27	27	18	10

Georgia Class-D Minor League Baseball Encyclopedia

YR	TEAM	LG	G	AB	R	H	2B	3B	HR	RBI	SB	BB	SO	BA	POS	PO	A	E	FA	GP	W	L	ERA	IP	H	SO	BB
Rucker, ---		BR																									
1946	LaGrange	GAL	<10																								
Rucker, Robert W. "Bob"		BR TR																									
1951	Rome	GAL	114	471	102	156	28	3	13	100	16	45	26	0.331	3B, OF	179	126	25	0.924								
Rucker, William "Bill"		BR TR																									
1940	Waycross	GFL	17	54	7	14	2	3	1	13	1	4	12	0.259	OF	36	4	3	0.930								
1949	Carrollton	GAL	120	427	56	119	10	1	9	2	75	41	49	0.279	M, 1B, OF	323	8	12	0.965								
1950	Alexander City	GAL	105	371	73	99	23	3	11	64	6	62	51	0.267	3B, OF	150	141	33	0.898								
Ruddle, Ed																											
1937	Tallahassee	GFL													P					1	3		22	28	4	14	
Rudolph, Frederick Donald "Don"		BL TL 5'11" 195 lbs b. 08/16/1931 Baltimore, MD d. 09/12/1968 Granada Hills, CA																									
1950	Jesup	GSL	44	89	8	18	6	0	1	6	0	8	17	0.202	P	14	62	1	0.987	37	13	10	3.13	213	192	92	108
1951	Jesup	GSL	57	138	21	27	8	0	0	23	1	21	35	0.196	P	12	69	6	0.931	45	28	8	2.91	285	245	148	139
Rudolph, Thomas "Tom"		BR TR																									
1963	Thomasville	GFL	19	33	1	2	0	0	0	1	0	3	22	0.061	P	5	25	2	0.938	19	6	8	2.31	109	90	81	48
Rufer, Rudolf Joseph "Rudy"		BR TR 6'0" 165 lbs b. 10/28/1926 Ridgewood, NY																									
1956	Thomasville	GFL	38	131	24	37	5	3	0	15	14	8	15	0.282	M, OF	28	1	0	1.000								
1957	Thomasville	GFL	83	337	75	121	19	5	3	44	37	30	21	0.359	M, OF, P	116	7	7	0.946	10	0	0	<30				
1958	Thomasville	GFL													M												
Ruggerio, Patrick "Pat"		BL																									
1956	Fitzgerald	GFL	4	10		1								0.100													
Ruggles, Raymond		BR TR																									
1956	Hazlehurst-Baxley	GSL	51	190	18	36	4	0	0	10	2	13	48	0.189	SS	78	157	37	0.864								
Rullo, Joseph Vincent "Joe"		BR TR 5'11" 168 lbs b. 06/16/1916 New York, NY d. 10/28/1969 Philadelphia, PA																									
1953	Cordele	GFL	40	117	16	35	8	0	0	22	5	16	8	0.299	M, C, P	18	8	0	1.000		0	0	<45				
Rumfield, Lyn																											
1939	Americus	GFL	30	109	20	40	12	3	0	15	2	19	13	0.367	OF	81	6	2	0.978								
Ruminski, Frank																											
1942	Valdosta	GFL	8	20	6	6	1	2	0	3	0	3	3	0.300	P	1	14	0	1.000	9	6	0	1.42	57	14	36	18
Rummans, Elmer		BR TR																									
1940	Valdosta	GFL	44	107	10	25	2	0	0	8	1	7	40	0.234	P					37	18	10	2.19	263	239	220	76
Runyan, Richard "Dick"		BR TR																									
1955	Dublin	GSL	7	9		1								0.111	P					7	1	3					
Rushing, ---																											
1915	Dothan	FLAG	<10																								
Russell, ---																											
1916	Anniston	GAL	16	38	4	6					0			0.158	P												
1917	Tri-Cities	GAL	3	8	1	0	0	0	0		0			0.000	P	2	20	0	1.000	3	1	2		27	21	11	15
Russell, David "Dave"		BL TR																									
1954	Thomasville	GFL	81	237	44	66	7	2	2	37	5	68	41	0.278	OF	115	9	4	0.969								
1955	Thomasville	GFL	47	116	20	25	2	0	0	10	3	27	20	0.216	3B, OF	47	22	10	0.873								
Russell, Edward G. "Ed"		BL TL																									
1953	Vidalia	GSL	68	277	53	81	14	2	5	32	9	35	40	0.292	1B, OF	462	35	21	0.959								
Russell, Kenneth "Ken"		BR TR																									
1957	Albany	GFL	1	1		0								0.000	P					1	0	0	<30				
Russell, Neil "Bing"		BR TR 6'2" b. 1928 NH																									
1948	Carrollton	GAL	78	263	57	67	11	4	4	38	5	44	64	0.255	OF	121	0	6	0.953								
1949	Carrollton	GAL	11	33	2	6	0	0	0	2	0	4	7	0.182	OF	15	1	0	1.000								
Russell, Richard E. "Dick"		BL TR																									
1950	LaGrange	GAL	21	70	10	15	3	1	1	8	0	9	22	0.214	OF	27	0	2	0.931								
Russo, Anthony		BR TR																									
1956	Hazlehurst-Baxley	GSL	10	14	3	3	0	0	0	0	0	2	8	0.214	P	2	6	0	1.000	10	2	3	4.50	44	44	36	38
Russo, Manuel																											
1936	Thomasville	GFL	24	86	15	20	3	3	1	5	5			0.233	3B	17	39	8	0.875								
1941	Tallahassee	GFL	48	186	30	48	13	2	0	26	4	23	15	0.258	3B	62	100	14	0.920								
Rustin, Theodore "Ted"		BR TR																									
1954	Douglas	GSL	34	89	14	19	3	0	0	7	0	11	21	0.213	P	15	43	8	0.879	33	20	8	4.04	243	262	159	86
Rutledge, Robert "Bob"		BR TR																									
1940	Cordele	GFL	74	255	30	63	12	2	0	21	2	30	51	0.247	2B	193	231	43	0.908								
Rutter, Harry		BR TR																									
1955	Waycross	GFL	27	95	20	17	3	2	1	10	0	21	31	0.179	OF	43	2	3	0.938								
Ryan, Dean R.		BS TL																									
1958	Valdosta	GFL	14	21	3	3	1	0	0	2	0	1	4	0.143	P	0	11	0	1.000	14	4	2	4.64	64	62	29	56
Ryan, Fred D.		BR TR																									
1950	Albany	GFL	138	498	92	125	29	8	8	90	12	84	98	0.251	SS	284	398	45	0.938								
1951	Tifton	GFL	36	115	27	29	6	0	2	13	5	34	30	0.252	SS	75	108	13	0.934								
Ryan, James "Jim"		BR																									
1947	Tallassee	GAL	20	67	9	16	2	0	0	3	1	12	17	0.239													
Ryan, Richard B. "Dick"																											
1949	Hazlehurst-Baxley	GSL	34	114	13	26	5	1	0	19	0	8	21	0.228	P	9	35	3	0.936	33	20	11	3.32	252	121	157	96
Ryan, Robert "Bob"		BR TR																									
1940	Moultrie	GFL	11	41	6	10	2	0	0	6	1	3	5	0.244	SS	18	30	6	0.889								
1941	Moultrie	GFL	123	501	71	120	11	1	0	43	1	44	43	0.240	2B	254	335	44	0.930								

Georgia Class-D Minor League Baseball Encyclopedia

YR	TEAM	LG	G	AB	R	H	2B	3B	HR	RBI	SB	BB	SO	BA	POS	PO	A	E	FA	GP	W	L	ERA	IP	H	SO	BB
Ryan, Thomas "Tom"		BR TR																									
1958	Dublin	GFL	46	185	52	56	10	2	10	36	4	38	69	0.303	2B, 3B	131	121	13	0.951								
Ryckman, William "Bill"		BR TR																									
1954	Valdosta	GFL	47	179	24	46	6	1	1	21	8	11	11	0.257	SS	85	116	26	0.885								
1956	Valdosta	GFL	123	500	86	150	20	3	4	59	10	41	51	0.300	SS	208	340	41	0.930								
Ryder, John		BL TL																									
1951	Fitzgerald	GSL	34	110	14	27	5	0	0	11	6	30	11	0.245	OF	79	4	2	0.976								
Ryder, Paul																											
1935	Tallahassee	GFL	110	327	29	77	14	2	0		5	16	50	0.235	IF	152	233	46	0.893								
Sabine, Frank W, "Frank" "Butch"		BR TR 6'1" 185 lbs b. 08/22/1924 Heilwood, PA																									
1947	Americus	GFL	41	84	5	9	1	0	0	3	0	5	29	0.107	P	6	28	1	0.971	31	9	9	3.66	155	154	103	64
Sacchetti, Charles		BR																									
1954	Vidalia	GSL	8	22		2								0.091													
Sadowski, Robert Frank "Bob"		BL TR 6'0" 175 lbs b. 01/15/1937 St. Louis, MO																									
1955	Hazlehurst-Baxley	GSL	106	369	66	95	13	4	7	49	13	59	64	0.257	1B, 3B, SS, P	500	93	41	0.935	1	0	0					
Saffer, Leslie "Les"		BR TR																									
1950	Newnan	GAL	20	41	3	6	4	0	0	3	0	5	11	0.146	P	5	26	0	1.000	19	6	5	5.69	106	124	67	69
Sager, Donald "Don"		BR TR																									
1955	Sandersville	GSL	46	22	3	2	0	0	0	1	0	1	12	0.091	P	5	11	2	0.889	46	3	5	2.84	76	75	43	29
1956	Sandersville	GSL	38	17	1	3	0	0	0	4	0	2	9	0.176	P	3	13	3	0.842	38	7	3	2.55	74	60	49	23
Sala, Frederick "Fred"		BL TL																									
1950	Jesup(7) - Douglas(13)	GSL	20	62	6	8	4	0	0	4	0	10	20	0.129	OF	28	1	6	0.829								
Salas, Bienvenido		BR TR																									
1953	Thomasville	GFL	35	116	25	27	3	1	0	6	1	20	18	0.233	2B, SS	66	84	9	0.943								
Salazar, Enrique		BR TR																									
1954	Thomasville(33) - Albany(74)	GFL	107	348	54	77	11	2	2	45	8	69	78	0.221	SS	181	266	40	0.918								
Salcido, Carlos		BR TR																									
1955	Albany(6) - Tifton(7)	GFL	13	39	3	6	3	0	1	5	2	5	11	0.154	OF	22	2	2	0.923								
Salerno, Louis "Lou"		BL TL																									
1951	Griffin	GAL	103	386	104	102	18	10	9	61	5	110	79	0.264	OF	181	12	21	0.902								
Salerno, Pasquale J.		BR TR																									
1952	Valdosta	GFL	99	353	52	71	10	2	0	86	9	52	49	0.201	OF	153	18	15	0.919								
1955	Thomasville	GFL	94	372	69	114	5	5	7	57	16	33	49	0.306	OF	189	6	8	0.961								
Sallis, Ed		BR TR																									
1951	Brunswick	GFL	51	162	17	31	4	0	1	18	1	25	12	0.191	C	232	44	8	0.972								
Salmonson, Lee		BR TR																									
1955	Douglas	GSL	26	48	6	9	2	0	1	7	0	4	14	0.188	P	6	31	0	1.000	24	8	6	4.01	119	124	49	50
Salter, Desmond		GFL																									
1942	Tallahassee	GFL	64	262	36	72	11	5	2	45	5	26	30	0.275	3B	103	67	21	0.890								
1949	Douglas - Eastman	GSL	28	87	19	26	9	2	2	17	4	21	9	0.299	OF	32	4	5	0.878								
Salter, Fred		BL																									
1955	Tifton	GFL	13	20	3	6	0	0	0	1	0	4	5	0.300													
Salzman, Cy		BR TR																									
1940	Moultrie	GFL	51	194	22	40	2	0	0	10	1	15	38	0.206	SS	90	179	31	0.897								
Samaklis, Charles																											
1941	Valdosta	GFL	36	97	13	19	2	0	0	8	0	6	23	0.196	P	9	56	8	0.890	32	20	6	2.15	226	188	139	82
Sammons, ---																											
1949	Hazlehurst-Baxley	GSL	9												P					9	3	3	6.43	49	45	14	20
Sample, ---																											
1915	Valdosta	FLAG	<10																								
Sampson, Mark		BR TR																									
1956	Tifton	GFL	3	1		0								0.000	P					3	0	1	<45				
Samson, Charles		BR TL																									
1946	Valdosta	GFL	41	145	18	44	6	3	0	16	4	12	12	0.303	OF	76	3	3	0.963								
Samuel, Manuel		BR TR																									
1962	Dublin	GFL	119	461	100	124	11	2	1	48	13	92	75	0.269	SS	178	245	35	0.924								
Sanchez, Jerry		BR																									
1953	Statesboro	GSL	1												0.000													
Sanchez, P. Armando Jr.		BR TR																									
1951	Alex City(26) - Valley(3)	GAL	29	96	9	25	5	1	0	8	0	9	18	0.260	C	107	17	9	0.932								
1951	Valdosta	GFL	10	30	2	3	1	0	0	4	0	1	8	0.100													
1951	Douglas	GSL	27	78	7	22	3	0	0	8	2	8	7	0.282	OF, C	65	10	7	0.915								
Sanders, ---																											
1917	Anniston	GAL	3	4	0	0	0	0	0	0				0.000	P	0	1	1	0.500	3	0	1		11	14	4	2
Sanders, ---																											
1928	Anniston	GAL	92	374	64	109	17	4	1		17	24	15	0.291	2B	238	306	23	0.959								
Sanders, Alfred "Al"		BR																									
1950	Jesup	GSL	11	33	4	6	0	0	0	6	0	8	12	0.182													
Sanders, Alvin "Al"		BR TL																									
1954	Albany	GFL	15	26	4	2	0	0	0	4	1	6	16	0.077	P	8	18	2	0.929	15	7	4	3.79	95	104	51	39
Sanders, C. Henry		BR TR																									
1953	Sandersville	GSL	33	98	13	24	7	1	0	8	0	18	15	0.245	3B	19	71	9	0.909								

Georgia Class-D Minor League Baseball Encyclopedia

YR	TEAM	LG	G	AB	R	H	2B	3B	HR	RBI	SB	BB	SO	BA	POS	PO	A	E	FA	GP	W	L	ERA	IP	H	SO	BB
Sanders, Lewis "Lou"		BR TR																									
1946	Albany	GFL	83	302	68	65	7	6	0	27	23	90	46	0.215	OF	165	7	15	0.920								
1948	Griffin	GAL	16	48	11	18	2	0	0	9	2	16	6	0.375	OF	11	2	0	1.000								
1949	Griffin	GAL	110	409	91	106	16	5	2	25	9	76	42	0.259	M, SS, OF	188	34	12	0.949								
1951	Griffin	GAL	60	236	64	65	16	3	0	27	19	56	20	0.275	OF	103	5	3	0.973								
Sanders, Robert E. "Bob"		BR TR																									
1952	Cordele	GFL	35	76	7	14	2	0	0	11	0	6	15	0.184	P	4	38	6	0.875	34	13	11	3.63	211	194	114	127
Sanders, Warren Williams "War"		BR TL 5'10" 160 lbs b. 08/02/1877 Maynardville, TN d. 08/03/1962 Chattanooga, TN																									
1914	Newnan	GAL	88	345	39	66					9			0.191	M, OF	139	9	4	0.974								
Sanford, ---																											
1929	Lindale	GAL	62	239	45	76	10	2	1		16	29	14	0.318	2B	167	202	21	0.946								
Sanford, Allen																											
1914	Anniston	GAL	33	110	11	22					2			0.200													
1915	Talladega	GAL	26	76	5	16	2	2	0					0.211	P	7	50	1	0.983	18	9	8					
1916	Talladega	GAL	47	128	9	22				0				0.172	OF, P												
Sanford, George Jackson "Jack"		BR TL																									
1946	Americus	GFL	38	79	20	20	8	0	0	12	2	11	10	0.253	M, 1B, P					1	0	1	0.00	6	11	1	4
1947	Americus	GFL	14	47	8	19	5	0	0	18	0	7	3	0.404	M												
Sanford, John Stanley "Jack"		BR TR 6'0" 190 lbs b. 05/18/1929 Wellesley Hills, MA d. 03/07/2000																									
1949	Americus	GFL	35	84	12	26	6	1	1	15	1	3	15	0.310	P	6	26	10	0.762	30	15	9	4.39	207	192	143	135
Sangalli, Frank		BR TR																									
1954	Fitzgerald	GFL	95	333	72	77	9	6	1	30	9	93	40	0.231	2B	243	252	28	0.946								
Sanson, Richard "Dick"		BR TR																									
1954	Waycross	GFL	2	2	0									0.000	P					2	0	0	<45				
Sansosti, Frank																											
1935	Thomasville	GFL	17	34	5	6	0	0	0		0	5	9	0.176	P					17	6	3		93	100	52	31
1936	Thomasville	GFL	11	16	1	3	0	0	0	1	1			0.188	P					11	3	4	5.69	49		9	28
1937	Thomasville	GFL	54	124	14	21	1	0	5	20	0	10	27	0.169	P	18	60	7	0.918	40	21	10	2.81	263	224	114	105
Santmire, Glenn		BR TR																									
1962	Dublin	GFL	9	9	1	3	1	0	0	1	0	1	6	0.333	P					9	1	0	6.12	25	25	31	24
Santoli, Carmen		BR TR																									
1956	Tifton	GFL	53	167	21	36	5	0	0	16	7	34	54	0.216	OF	69	9	11	0.876								
Santomauro, Joe																											
1949	Vidalia-Lyons	GSL	6												M, P					6	2	3	2.59	59	21	11	26
Saporito, John		BR TR																									
1953	Sandersville - Vidalia	GSL	5											0.000	P						0	1	<45				
Sappenfield, Colon																											
1929	Carrollton	GAL	54	229	40	74	5	4	4		2	8	20	0.323	SS	89	150	23	0.912								
1930	Anniston	GAL	85	340	52	111	22	6	7		8	13	31	0.326	SS	159	276	44	0.908								
Sappenfield, Roger		BR TR																									
1951	Waycross	GFL	16	34	4	5	1	0	0	3	0	2	11	0.147	P	8	21	3	0.906	16	7	6	2.21	102	70	143	65
Sardoff, Marty		BR TR																									
1953	Cordele	GFL	16	21	2	2	1	0	0	3	0	0	7	0.095	P	1	6	2	0.778		1	2	<45				
Sargent, ---																											
1921	Cedartown	GSL													2B												
1921	LaGrange	GSL													2B												
Sarmer, Joseph "Joe"		BR TR																									
1956	Waycross	GFL	7	8	0									0.000	P					7	1	0	<45				
1956	Dublin	GSL	11	22	0	2	1	0	0	0	0	3	9	0.091	P	2	13	2	0.882	10	0	5	6.60	60	67	28	37
Sarmiento, Antonio		BR TR																									
1951	Dublin	GSL	30	69	8	9	2	0	0	2	2	6	16	0.130	P	6	36	6	0.875	27	10	6	4.08	161	185	58	59
1952	Tifton	GFL	28	70	5	10	3	0	0	4	1	4	19	0.143	P	4	37	2	0.953	26	16	3	1.26	185	132	89	42
1952	Dublin	GSL	17	28	3	6	2	0	1	5	0	5	8	0.214	P	5	12	1	0.944	16	5	6	7.00	72	102	33	28
1953	Albany(15) - Tifton(13)	GFL	28	73	11	17	4	0	2	11	2	4	28	0.233	P	9	40	5	0.907	25	12	7	2.63	164	145	91	73
1954	Tifton	GFL	38	88	12	14	1	0	0	5	0	3	24	0.159	P	8	44	2	0.963	35	15	13	3.66	224	197	117	90
1955	Tifton	GFL	24	45	5	6	2	0	0	3	2	1	13	0.133	P	3	25	4	0.875	20	5	12	3.65	116	126	60	41
1955	Statesboro	GSL	4	12	2									0.167	P					3	0	2					
Sarno, Anthony		BR TR																									
1953	Douglas	GSL	35	121	26	31	5	1	1	14	1	23	9	0.256	3B	43	86	14	0.902								
Sarros, Jim		BR TR																									
1946	Cordele	GFL	77	263	30	53	6	3	0	18	2	51	65	0.202	2B, 3B	188	178	29	0.927								
Sarver, Daniel "Dan"		BR TR																									
1956	Sandersville	GSL	118	394	95	99	14	1	12	63	22	102	89	0.251	3B, OF	223	64	18	0.941								
Sasek, Richard "Dick"		BL TR																									
1957	Thomasville	GFL	102	341	53	88	21	3	3	53	7	68	69	0.258	OF	142	18	5	0.970								
Sassano, Robert "Bob"		BR TR																									
1951	Douglas	GSL	14	45	2	8	2	0	0	2	0	4	10	0.178	OF	23	3	4	0.867								
Sasse, ---																											
1941	Thomasville	GFL	3												P					3	0	1	5.73	11	17	1	3
Satkowiak, Phillip B. "Phil"		BL TL 6'0" 190 lbs b. 08/30/1930 Flint, MI																									
1950	Americus	GFL	62	219	42	59	10	3	5	50	2	45	48	0.269	1B	434	27	22	0.954								
Satterfield, Arnold		BR TR																									
1951	Opelika	GAL	27	80	5	19	1	1	0	12	0	15	8	0.238	C	93	12	4	0.963								
Satterfield, Cicero		BR TR																									
1946	Valley(9) - LaGrange(26)	GAL	35	103	8	19	0	1	0	12	1	9	20	0.184	C	124	10	5	0.964								

Georgia Class-D Minor League Baseball Encyclopedia

YR	TEAM	LG	G	AB	R	H	2B	3B	HR	RBI	SB	BB	SO	BA	POS	PO	A	E	FA	GP	W	L	ERA	IP	H	SO	BB
Satterfield, Ralph		BR TR																									
1942	Cordele	GFL	27	115	10	26	3	3	0	10	0	2	22	0.226	SS	40	74	17	0.870								
1946	Newnan	GAL	101	402	54	118	22	8	4	58	2	17	38	0.294	1B	900	34	16	0.983								
Satterfield, Ray "Ben"		GFL																									
1942	Cordele	GFL	29	71	2	12	1	0	0	4	0	5	12	0.169	P	45	40	10	0.895	22	5	9	3.96	134	155	57	63
Sauerbrun, Kip		BL TL																									
1935	Tallahassee	GFL	36	93	14	19	2	0	0		0	10	7	0.204	P					34	20	7		209	198	126	76
1940	Thomasville	GFL	22	62	4	13	1	0	0	4	0	6	10	0.210	P, IF					20	12	5	3.32	157	164	81	40
1941	Thomasville - Moultrie	GFL	20	45	3	8	2	0	0	5	0	2	5	0.178	M, P	2	15	0	1.000	20	8	5	1.40	116	93	68	24
1942	Moultrie	GFL	23	64	7	13	0	0	0	6	0	4	5	0.203	P	8	42	2	0.962	25	13	5	1.83	172	175	84	31
Savage, Clifford "Cliff"		BL TL																									
1950	Americus	GFL	37	80	11	17	3	2	0	6	0	5	12	0.213	P	11	57	3	0.958	36	9	11	2.97	227	164	195	140
Savage, John		BR TR																									
1946	Waycross	GFL	25	45	4	10	1	0	0	8	0	4	17	0.222	P	1	25	2	0.929	25	4	7		129	131	78	61
Savage, William "Bill"		BR TR																									
1948	Griffin	GAL	112	455	81	127	9	9	1	39	36	47	63	0.279	OF	228	8	11	0.955								
Savant, Joe																											
1938	Tallahassee	GFL	112	453	75	135	20	6	2	51	11	48	33	0.298	SS	232	384	53	0.921								
Savarese, Alfred "Al"		BR TR																									
1950	Val(2) - Rom(20) - AC(46)	GAL	68	205	37	33	2	0	0	7	7	59	48	0.161	SS	98	185	29	0.907								
Saverine, Charles "Chuck"		BR TR																									
1950	Americus	GFL	122	439	74	113	27	5	9	76	10	85	105	0.257	C	435	94	22	0.960								
Sawyer, ---																											
1906	Americus	GSL													P												
Sawyer, Roger		BL TL																									
1952	Brunswick	GFL	14	32	4	3	1	0	0	1	0	4	10	0.094	P	0	17	1	0.944	12	5	6	2.43	259	242	121	101
Saye, Charles		BR TR																									
1956	Thomson	GSL	53	194	25	58	10	1	0	36	2	25	23	0.299	3B, OF	57	54	9	0.925								
Sayle, Robert "Bob"		BR TR																									
1953	Cordele	GFL	33	47	6	9	0	0	0	3	0	9	7	0.191	P	9	32	2	0.953	32	4	14	6.72	138	173	61	100
Sbashnig, Peter "Pete"		BL TR																									
1950	Valdosta	GFL	12	23	5	4	2	0	0	3	0	8	4	0.174													
1951	Fitzgerald	GSL	88	290	41	71	13	0	2	32	7	54	56	0.245	1B, P	623	36	20	0.971	13	1	5	9.16	57	81	35	78
Scala, Robert "Bob"		BR TR																									
1952	Moultrie	GFL	32	111	11	25	4	0	1	13	2	14	15	0.225	3B	36	50	11	0.887								
1952	Vidalia(13) - Dublin(9)	GSL	22	85	17	15	2	0	1	9	2	18	18	0.176	3B	19	51	12	0.854								
Scalici, Anthony		BR TR																									
1954	Hazlehurst-Baxley	GSL	74	226	20	48	7	2	0	16	3	27	49	0.212	OF, C	307	26	16	0.954								
Scalisi, Robert "Bob"		BR TR																									
1949	Fitzgerald	GSL	31	78	9	15	4	1	0	5	0	6	22	0.192	P	5	30	4	0.897	39	7	12	5.13	193	129	117	87
1950	Fitzgerald	GSL	35	103	7	19	0	3	0	11	1	5	24	0.184	P	6	30	2	0.947	35	19	14	3.74	274	273	236	119
Scannelli, Frank		BR TR																									
1955	Thomasville	GFL	74	244	29	56	7	1	1	26	1	28	32	0.230	C	448	53	8	0.984								
Scariato, Anthony		BL TL																									
1956	Valdosta	GFL	37	125	23	30	6	0	4	20	0	30	13	0.240	OF	57	4	2	0.968								
Scarth, James "Jim"		BR																									
1953	Brunswick	GFL	13	45	7	8	1	0	0	5	3	9	20	0.178													
Scercy, John		BR TR																									
1956	Moultrie	GFL	85	262	43	46	6	2	3	27	4	67	103	0.176	3B	88	138	26	0.897								
1956	Douglas	GSL	21	68	17	18	3	0	3	13	1	16	22	0.265													
Schaeffer, Bernard		BR TR																									
1946	Thomasville	GFL	27	34	4	8	0	0	0	2	0	3	12	0.235	P	5	21	3	0.897	27	1	9	6.03	100	106	40	106
Schaffer, Robert A. "Bob"		BL TR																									
1954	Albany	GFL	42	80	4	18	3	0	0	12	0	8	13	0.225	P	6	19	5	0.833	32	9	12	3.10	212	194	159	65
Schaive, John Edward "Johnny"		BR TR 5'8" 175 lbs b. 02/25/1934 Springfield, IL																									
1952	Thomasville	GFL	22	79	5	15	2	0	1	7	0	0	12	0.190	2B	47	43	6	0.938								
Schall, Eugene "Gene"		BR TR																									
1954	Americus-Cordele	GFL	23	39	3	5	2	1	0	5	0	1	13	0.128	P	1	11	1	0.923	21	4	7	4.27	97	90	68	71
Schamburg, Theodore "Ted"		BL TR																									
1956	Fitzgerald	GFL	64	210	21	63	10	0	1	23	0	26	31	0.300	3B, P	39	104	16	0.899	9	2	4	<45				
Schammel, George		BL TL																									
1955	Dublin	GSL	18	36	5	9	1	0	0	0	0	1	11	0.250	P					7	0	3					
Scheel, Rolf		BR TR																									
1953	Valdosta	GFL	33	49	7	8	0	0	0	0	0	3	15	0.163	P	6	23	3	0.906	33	5	8	5.47	130	125	89	119
Scheffing, Robert Boden "Bob"		BR TR 6'2" 189 lbs b. 08/11/1913 Overland, MO d. 10/26/1985 Phoenix, AZ																									
1936	Albany	GFL	99	368	77	116	25	7	8	72	11			0.315	C	336	57	18	0.956								
Scheidt, Ray		BR TR																									
1952	Moultrie	GFL	47	78	6	10	1	0	0	5	0	7	37	0.128	P	14	49	4	0.940	40	11	21	3.21	224	222	140	113
Scheidts, Edward "Ed"		BR TR																									
1947	Albany	GFL	24	37	2	8	1	0	0	2	0	4	8	0.216	P	3	26	4	0.879	20	5	8	3.60	115	120	61	56
Schellhouse, Fred																											
1941	Tallahassee	GFL	26	96	4	19	1	0	0	8	1	8	25	0.198	2B	45	51	10	0.906								
Schepner, Joseph Maurice "Joe"		BR TR 5'10" 160 lbs b. 08/10/1895 Aliquippa, PA d. 07/25/1959 Mobile, AL																									
1928	Gadsden	GAL	40	126	14	36	8	0	0		5	12	3	0.286	M, 1B	306	19	4	0.988								

Georgia Class-D Minor League Baseball Encyclopedia

YR	TEAM	LG	G	AB	R	H	2B	3B	HR	RBI	SB	BB	SO	BA	POS	PO	A	E	FA	GP	W	L	ERA	IP	H	SO	BB
Scherer, Leon																											
1935	Tallahassee	GFL	14	41	5	10	1	0	0		0	2	4	0.244	P					14	9	1		108	99	57	36
Schiavo, William "Bill"		BR TR																									
1950	Cordele	GFL	23	41	5	7	0	0	0	3	0	6	9	0.171	P	5	23	6	0.824	19	6	6	3.60	105	95	43	72
Schieffer, John		BR TR																									
1955	Albany	GFL	32	71	9	10	0	0	0	5	2	6	31	0.141	P	9	30	5	0.886	32	16	8	3.14	212	206	102	69
Schindler, Alfred "Al"		BR TR																									
1950	Americus	GFL	125	435	74	88	6	6	1	47	5	95	69	0.202	2B	315	389	35	0.953								
Schivone, Ralph		BR																									
1946	Tallassee	GAL	<10																								
Schlett, Robert "Bob"		BL TR																									
1955	Waycross	GFL	6	5	0									0.000	P					6	0	3		<45			
Schmidhausler, Vernon "Vern"		BR																									
1946	Albany	GFL	13	25	1	3	1	0	0	3	0	3	12	0.120													
Schmidt, ---																											
1920	Rome	GSL		304	50	98	14	2	4		7			0.322													
1921	Rome	GSL		60	17	19								0.317	SS												
Schmidt, Donald "Don"		BR TR																									
1940	Cordele	GFL	10	35	7	10	0	0	0	0	0	8	12	0.286	SS	20	25	7	0.865								
Schmidt, Frederick Albert "Freddy"		BR TR 6'1" 185 lbs b. 02/09/1916 Hartford, CT																									
1939	Albany	GFL	31	69	6	19	2	0	0	8	0	2	11	0.275	P	4	27	0	1.000	22	14	5	1.81	164	139	108	57
Schmidt, Haven L.		BL TR																									
1954	Douglas	GSL	83	264	48	80	15	4	7	52	3	18	59	0.303	OF, C	347	24	14	0.964								
1955	Douglas	GSL	104	380	80	95	21	9	19	76	11	64	105	0.250	C	565	52	30	0.954								
Schmidt, Kermit		BR TR																									
1948	Fitzgerald	GSL	34	77	5	13	1	1	0	4	0	4	7	0.169	P	2	30	2	0.941	25	11	7	1.78	147	102	129	65
1949	Fitzgerald	GSL	58	200	31	59	9	3	0	28	0	26	25	0.295	P, IF	83	101	9	0.953	35	13	9	4.17	207	137	132	81
1950	Fitzgerald	GSL	43	102	17	22	4	3	0	9	0	12	9	0.216	P	19	43	6	0.912	30	18	8	3.43	236	196	197	135
1951	Douglas	GSL	63	186	22	47	3	1	0	18	4	19	12	0.253	3B, OF, P	29	55	8	0.913	21	10	6	3.36	126	114	69	79
Schmidt, Robert Aloysius "Joe"		BR TR 5'10" 190 lbs b. 06/09/1918 Belleville, IL																									
1949	Newnan	GAL	123	455	102	140	21	4	17	108	13	93	21	0.308	M, 2B	326	304	17	0.974								
1950	Newnan	GAL	113	409	100	130	31	3	13	100	20	71	13	0.318	M, 2B	305	284	23	0.962								
Schmitt, Fred D.		BL TR																									
1950	Griffin	GAL	119	413	79	127	25	10	7	70	9	92	69	0.308	OF	212	9	13	0.944								
Schmitz, John		BR TR																									
1958	Waycross	GFL	43	163	13	33	2	1	0	12	1	17	29	0.202	SS	62	109	20	0.895								
Schneider, Edwin A. "Ed"		BR TR																									
1953	Fitzgerald	GFL	24	43	6	15	3	1	0	5	4	8	10	0.349	P	9	21	1	0.968	14	6	6	2.96	85	73	41	33
Schnell, Fred		BL TL																									
1952	Thomasville	GFL	17	29	5	3	0	0	0	0	0	10	10	0.103	P	3	34	2	0.949	17	4	8	3.31	98	90	39	76
Schoendienst, Albert Fred "Red"		BS TR 6'0" 170 lbs b. 02/02/1923 Germantown, IL																									
1942	Albany	GFL	68	264	41	71	7	5	1	28	0	22	15	0.269	2B, SS	155	209	27	0.931								
Schoendienst, Elmer		BR TR																									
1946	Albany	GFL	99	371	54	76	17	2	0	29	13	58	96	0.205	SS	173	307	54	0.899								
1947	Albany	GFL	133	497	76	126	26	5	0	67	14	49	63	0.254	3B, SS	144	263	27	0.938								
Schroeder, A.L.																											
1920	Cedartown	GSL													P												
1921	LaGrange	GSL													P												
Schroeder, Alfred C. "Al"		BR TR																									
1948	Valdosta	GFL	23	71	8	16	2	1	1	7	0	10	12	0.225	OF	22	1	2	0.920								
Schrom, Samuel "Sam"		BR																									
1953	Dublin	GSL	2											0.000													
Schubele, Bruce		BR TR																									
1951	Rome	GAL	46	158	31	36	3	0	0	9	2	36	42	0.228	SS	61	82	14	0.911								
Schuck, Charles		BR TR																									
1952	Moultrie	GFL	71	211	19	42	6	0	0	16	1	53	35	0.199	C	262	33	6	0.980								
1952	Douglas	GSL	36	108	20	28	4	0	2	18	1	35	14	0.259	C	215	19	5	0.979								
Schuessler, Zach		BR TL																									
1946	Opelika	GAL	8												M, P					8	0	5	0.00	38	59	23	12
1947	Opelika	GAL	11	25	3	7	0	0	0	5	0	1	2	0.280	P	6	14	5	0.800	11	7	3	4.05	80	99	45	22
Schuler, Ronald "Ron"		BR																									
1962	Thomasville	GFL	8	19	1	5	0	0	0	3	0	5	6	0.263													
Schulte (Schultehenrich), Leonard Bemard "Len"		BR TR 5'10" 160 lbs b. 12/05/1916 St. Charles, MO d. 05/06/1986 Orlando, FL																									
1936	Albany	GFL	29	90	15	24	0	2	1	25	2			0.267	C	86	20	1	0.991								
1937	Albany	GFL	32	131	21	33	4	0	2	15	1	9	5	0.252	OF	79	39	9	0.929								
Schulte, J.																											
1921	Carrollton	GSL		108	12	24								0.222	OF												
Schulte, Robert "Bob"		BR TR																									
1952	Cordele	GFL	20	45	8	7	1	0	0	4	2	8	7	0.156	C	46	5	1	0.981								
Schultis, Peter "Pete"		BL TR																									
1954	Hazlehurst-Baxley	GSL	5	5		2								0.400	P					5	0	2		<45			
Schultz, ---																											
1914	Talladega	GAL	12												P	6	25	7	0.816	12							
Schultz, Glen		BR TR																									
1953	Vidalia	GSL	31	33	3	3	0	0	0	0	1	12	15	0.091	P	4	10	3	0.824	27	3	5	5.14	91	97	30	75

Georgia Class-D Minor League Baseball Encyclopedia

YR	TEAM	LG	G	AB	R	H	2B	3B	HR	RBI	SB	BB	SO	BA	POS	PO	A	E	FA	GP	W	L	ERA	IP	H	SO	BB
Schultz, Harold F. "Hal"		BL TR																									
1939	Tallahassee	GFL	29	109	15	35	6	2	0	13	9	12	4	0.321	SS	57	80	12	0.919								
1940	Tallahassee	GFL	136	599	92	190	16	6	1	57	20	42	20	0.317	M, SS	276	441	55	0.929								
Schultz, Herbert "Herb"		BR TR																									
1951	Griffin	GAL	99	369	62	94	18	3	3	50	4	52	61	0.255	3B, OF	98	105	33	0.860								
Schultz, Jack		BR TR																									
1953	Vidalia	GSL	1											0.667	P					0	0	0	<45				
Schultz, Joseph Charles Jr. "Joe"		BL TR 5'11" 184 lbs b. 08/29/1918 Chicago, IL d. 01/10/1996 St. Louis, MO																									
1936	Albany	GFL								1		25		0.367	C												
1937	Albany	GFL	20	68	18	12	2	3	1	13	0	14	3	0.176	C	86	6	4	0.958								
Schultz, Kenneth "Ken"		BR TR																									
1962	Thomasville	GFL	96	337	79	98	6	0	0	49	11	74	13	0.291	3B	96	160	28	0.901								
Schultz, Otto		BR TR																									
1950	Opelika	GAL	18	62	9	12	2	1	0	6	1	7	8	0.194	OF	11	1	0	1.000								
Schultz, Richard "Dick"		BR TR																									
1953	Valdosta	GFL	17	37	6	10	0	0	0	7	0	4	12	0.270	P	2	18	5	0.800	17	4	3	5.60	82	95	58	75
1954	Americus-Cordele	GFL	20	54	4	14	3	0	0	5	0	6	15	0.259	P	6	26	2	0.941	17	8	7	3.41	124	115	63	57
Schultz, Stanley "Stan"		BL TL																									
1958	Thomasville	GFL	20	76	12	18	3	0	0	3	0	11	6	0.237	OF	30	1	1	0.969								
Schulze, Ed																											
1913	Newnan	GAL													M												
Schuman, ---																											
1914	Brunswick - Waycross	GSL		306	26	97	6	1	0		8			0.317													
Schurrer, Roland		BR TR																									
1954	Sandersville	GSL	15	20	0	1	1	0	0	0	0	0	13	0.050	P	2	9	2	0.846	15	4	4	6.71	51	64	11	21
Schuyler, ---																											
1913	Brunswick	ESL	98	372	45	103	19	3	4					0.277	OF	156	28	2	0.989								
1914	Brunswick	GSL		296	36	91	15	5	4		18			0.307													
Schwab, Robert "Bob"		BR TR																									
1947	Tallassee	GAL	11	45	12	9	1	0	0	2	0	4	4	0.200	OF	20	3	0	1.000								
Schwartz, ---																											
1921	LaGrange	GSL													P												
Schwartz, B.																											
1914	Valdosta	GSL		239	23	58	4	3	2		4			0.243													
1915	Valdosta	FLAG	30	100	12	24	2	2	0		6			0.240	1B	306	12	5	0.985								
Schwartz, F.																											
1913	Valdosta	ESL	71	258	24	53	4	0	1					0.205	SS	141	183	23	0.934								
1915	Valdosta	FLAG	65	334	27	62	4	0	1		9			0.186	2B, SS	132	94	8	0.966								
Schwartz, William Charles "Bill" "Blab"		BR TR 6'2" 185 lbs b. 04/22/1884 Cleveland, OH d. 08/29/1961 Nashville, TN																									
1913	Opelika	GAL	88	312	30	80				11				0.256	1B	631	33	14	0.979								
1914	Opelika	GAL	92	332	38	87				11				0.262	1B	202	55	28	0.902								
1921	Cedartown	GSL													M, 1B												
Schypinski, Gerald Albert "Jerry"		BL TR 5'10" 170 lbs b. 09/16/1931 Detroit, MI																									
1952	Cordele	GFL	125	485	69	144	13	5	0	56	10	51	23	0.297	SS	231	369	45	0.930								
Scobbins, ---		BR																									
1946	LaGrange	GAL	<10																								
Scollard, John Stanley "John"		BR TR																									
1952	Moultrie	GFL	65	232	13	49	11	1	0	15	1	22	24	0.211	1B, OF	287	18	8	0.974								
Scotese, Robert "Bob"		BR TR																									
1951	Cordele	GFL	56	155	37	27	2	0	0	13	14	34	40	0.174	OF	95	3	7	0.933								
Scott, Frank		BL TL																									
1958	Albany	GFL	15	15	2	0	0	0	0	0	0	0	6	0.000	P	0	6	0	1.000	14	3	1	6.08	40	31	31	59
Scott, George		BR TR																									
1956	Thomasville	GFL	47	135	13	32	4	1	1	14	0	17	24	0.237	3B	32	61	16	0.853								
1957	Thomasville	GFL	114	437	52	141	14	8	2	85	3	40	47	0.323	SS	219	339	27	0.954								
Scott, J. Robert "Bob"		BR TR																									
1955	Sandersville	GSL	27	102	8	19	0	0	1	10	1	5	19	0.186	OF	50	2	5	0.912								
Scott, James D. "Jim"		BR TR																									
1946	Opelika	GAL	34	53	7	19	1	0	0	7	0	3	4	0.358	P	6	30	2	0.947	24	6	8	5.72	96	113	54	45
Scott, LeGrant Edward Sr. "LeGrant"		BL TL 5'8" 170 lbs b. 07/25/1910 Cleveland, OH d. 11/12/1993 Birmingham, AL																									
1946	Waycross	GFL	88	250	58	92	20	1	8	63	6	68	7	0.368	M, OF, P	98	10	10	0.915	4	1	0	0.00	6	5	7	6
1947	Waycross	GFL	76	220	52	79	17	1	3	54	4	55	6	0.359	M, OF	89	7	4	0.960								
1948	Americus	GFL	50	113	17	37	5	4	2	31	3	18	4	0.327	M, OF	48	4	0	1.000								
Scott, Richard Lewis "Dick"		BR TL 6'2" 185 lbs b. 03/15/1933 Portsmouth, NH																									
1956	Thomasville	GFL	36	82	7	14	1	1	0	8	0	8	23	0.171	P	4	31	1	0.972	32	15	13	2.13	216	137	251	110
Scott, Siebert		BS TR																									
1957	Thomasville	GFL	66	86	9	14	1	0	1	9	0	6	25	0.163	P	11	30	0	1.000	58	20	9	3.29	205	177	144	92
Scott, Trammel																											
1906	Cordele	GSL													M, 1B												
Scott, Victor John "Vic"		BR TR																									
1951	Valley	GAL	13	33	2	10	0	0	1	6	0	4	10	0.303	P	0	9	3	0.750	11	5	2	5.30	73	102	27	42
Scott, William J. "Bill"		BR TR																									
1947	Cordele	GFL	21	77	11	14	2	1	1	12	2	12	18	0.182	OF	37	3	2	0.952								

Georgia Class-D Minor League Baseball Encyclopedia

YR	TEAM	LG	G	AB	R	H	2B	3B	HR	RBI	SB	BB	SO	BA	POS	PO	A	E	FA	GP	W	L	ERA	IP	H	SO	BB
Scranton, David "Dave"		BR TR																									
1955	Waycross	GFL	43	97	10	18	2	1	0	4	0	4	36	0.186	P	5	49	5	0.915	42	20	10	2.34	258	202	206	91
1956	Waycross	GFL	35	81	6	15	2	0	0	10	1	10	18	0.185	P	10	40	7	0.877	35	19	12	2.91	247	211	202	86
1957	Waycross	GFL	33	71	6	14	4	0	0	4	0	4	14	0.197	P	8	31	3	0.929	30	10	8	2.90	180	172	74	114
Screen, James "Jim"		BR TR																									
1948	Spa(2) - Vid-Lyo(5) - Fit(9)	GSL	16	29	2	4	0	0	0	0	1	2	12	0.138	P	1	24	5	0.833	16	4	6	4.40	86	84	18	40
Scriptjack, Ray		BR TR																									
1953	Vidalia	GSL	5											0.167	P						0	0	<45				
Scroggs, John		BR TR																									
1954	Waycross	GFL	46	98	9	20	1	0	1	10	0	11	16	0.204	P	10	33	6	0.878	33	15	10	3.37	227	215	138	75
1955	Waycross	GFL	30	63	7	9	0	0	0	2	0	16	12	0.143	P	8	27	0	1.000	25	11	8	2.90	155	166	96	39
1956	Waycross	GFL	49	55	9	12	0	1	0	10	1	6	14	0.218	P	8	21	1	0.967	43	9	5	2.79	116	96	92	32
Seagrave, DeMont		BR TR																									
1956	Moultrie(5) - Fitzgerald(5)	GFL	10	22	3	4	0	1	0	3	0	2	8	0.182	P					9	3	4	4.19	58	61	37	18
Seagraves, ---																											
1930	Cedartown	GAL	8												P					8	3	4	6.16	57	84	20	21
Seal, William A. Jr. "Bill"		BR TR																									
1949	Carrollton	GAL	85	293	68	100	22	2	23	97	15	75	17	0.341	M, 3B, SS	165	185	25	0.933								
1950	Dublin	GSL	38	131	32	47	10	3	4	32	3	33	9	0.359	M, 2B	108	120	6	0.974								
Seaman, Albert "Al"		BS TR																									
1950	Newnan	GAL	25	27	4	5	0	0	0	0	0	6	11	0.185	P	1	7	3	0.727	23	2	5	6.93	74	87	39	61
Seaman, Robert "Bob"		BR																									
1953	Sandersville	GSL	5											0.059													
Seaone, Manuel		BR																									
1953	Eastman	GSL	9											0.345													
Seat, Clayton		BR TR																									
1940	Thomasville	GFL	37	93	6	12	1	1	0	7	0	5	37	0.129	P					32	12	9	4.03	221	253	87	104
Secoli, Frank		BR TR																									
1949	Tallahassee	GFL	10	11	0	1	0	0	0	0	0	2	6	0.091	P	1	5	0	1.000								
Sedlack, Robert "Bob"		BR TR																									
1954	Vidalia	GSL	4	6		1								0.167	P					4	0	1	<45				
1955	Thomasville	GFL	32	80	6	14	1	0	0	5	0	0	18	0.175	P	14	39	7	0.883	31	17	7	1.53	229	161	220	81
Seecs, Henry		BR TR																									
1956	Tifton	GFL	5	4		1								0.250	P					5	1	0	<45				
Seegmiller, Craig "Garth"		BR TR																									
1962	Brunswick	GFL	91	314	51	74	11	0	13	56	3	34	77	0.236	3B	64	118	29	0.863								
Seeman, John		BL TL																									
1956	Thomson	GSL	5	2		1								0.500	P					5	0	1					
Seghi, Philip "Phil"		BR TR																									
1947	Tallahassee	GFL	83	312	36	86	10	4	4	64	5	24	29	0.276	M, 3B	70	150	19	0.921								
Seidel, Raymond "Ray"		BR TR																									
1947	Waycross	GFL	48	94	15	22	5	1	0	13	0	6	5	0.234	P	5	31	4	0.900	42	13	9	3.42	187	200	97	69
1948	Waycross	GFL	55	124	12	31	5	0	0	17	0	6	8	0.250	P	17	47	14	0.821	45	23	7	3.54	282	303	164	102
Seiferlein, Donald "Don"		BR TR																									
1957	Valdosta	GFL	6	8		0								0.000	P					5	0	0	<30				
Seigfried, ---																											
1913	Brunswick	ESL	93	332	43	79	18	1	0					0.238	OF	287	78	26	0.934								
1914	Brunswick	GSL		392	76	110	8	2	7		36			0.281													
Seigler, William "Bill"		BR TR																									
1946	Carrollton	GAL	26	41	4	9	2	0	0	5	0	5	2	0.220	P	7	14	2	0.913	23	4	4	5.34	91	102	46	31
Seiler, Dan																											
1942	Tallahassee	GFL	113	389	50	88	12	9	0	38	2	76	77	0.226	2B	240	264	25	0.953								
Selbee, William "Bill"		BR TR																									
1947	Albany	GFL	12	37	7	5	1	1	0	4	2	10	13	0.135	OF	13	2	2	0.882								
Sellars, A.D.		BR TR																									
1951	Americus	GFL	26	36	1	2	1	0	0	0	0	3	10	0.056	P	1	14	3	0.833	24	2	11	5.93	85	106	22	37
Sellergren, Willard																											
1942	Americus	GFL	26	87	9	17	3	1	1	8	3	8	20	0.195	2B	63	51	18	0.864								
Selley, ---																											
1928	Cedartown	GAL	18	45	4	8	0	0	2		0	0	5	0.178	P	5	26	1	0.969	13	4	4	4.33	79	98	39	20
Sells, Albert																											
1915	Thomasville	FLAG	3												P					3	1	1		23	23	7	7
1920	Cedartown	GSL																									
1921	Cedartown	GSL													P													
1921	LaGrange	GSL													P													
Selph, ---																											
1914	Gadsden	GAL	87	312	24	81				6				0.260	3B	90	179	33	0.891								
1915	Americus-Gainesville	FLAG	71	244	19	59	7	1	1	1				0.242	3B, SS	168	108	27	0.911								
1916	Talladega	GAL	23	87	5	16				1				0.184													
Selph, Charles		BR TR																									
1958	Waycross	GFL	46	162	24	34	3	1	0	10	0	30	22	0.210	2B, 3B	55	107	5	0.970								
Sembera, Carroll William "Carroll"		BR TR 6'0" 155 lbs b. 07/26/1941 Shiner, TX																									
1962	Moultrie	GFL	18	36	7	13	0	1	0	6	0	1	8	0.361	P	6	12	1	0.947	17	6	6	3.49	85	73	109	47
Semler, Marion																											
1939	Thomasville	GFL													P								<45				

Georgia Class-D Minor League Baseball Encyclopedia

YR	TEAM	LG	G	AB	R	H	2B	3B	HR	RBI	SB	BB	SO	BA	POS	PO	A	E	FA	GP	W	L	ERA	IP	H	SO	BB
Semonik, Michael "Mike"		BR TR																									
1958	Dublin	GFL	82	301	40	62	9	1	0	25	2	56	42	0.206	2B	173	200	13	0.966								
Sengstock, Wayne		BR TR																									
1950	Hazlehurst-Baxley	GSL	74	148	19	33	2	1	1	9	1	10	21	0.223	OF, P	21	47	4	0.944	42	13	11	4.78	196	227	97	95
1951	Hazlehurst-Baxley	GSL	68	234	24	66	8	3	2	32	10	19	17	0.282	SS, OF, P	99	147	27	0.901								
Senkowitz, John		BR																									
1954	Tifton	GFL	3	4		0								0.000													
Senn, Yancy Jr.																											
1929	Gadsden	GAL	101	363	50	111	15	5	5		15	50	19	0.306	1B	1124	48	21	0.982								
Serafini, Irvin "Irv"		BR TR																									
1955	Brunswick	GFL	21	23	2	2	0	0	0	1	0	2	11	0.087	P	3	15	3	0.857	20	3	5	5.26	77	84	69	60
1956	Dublin	GSL	10	18	3	5	1	0	1	4	0	1	5	0.278	P	3	12	2	0.882	10	2	4	6.89	47	45	42	50
Serbin, Clifford "Cliff"		BR TR																									
1952	Statesboro	GSL	10	11	1	1	0	0	0	0	0	1	3	0.091	P	3	2	1	0.833								
Sermania, Vincent "Vince"		BR TR																									
1952	Cordele	GFL	10	16	0	0	0	0	0	0	0	1	11	0.000	P	1	12	1	0.929	10	1	7	6.07	46	48	19	44
1952	Fitzgerald	GSL	14	19	2	1	1	0	0	4	0	2	5	0.053	P	2	8	0	1.000	13	3	4	7.10	52	62	24	47
Serners, Joe "Yorkey"		BR TR																									
1940	Moultrie	GFL	80	251	21	51	6	0	0	21	1	39	54	0.203	C	325	36	22	0.943								
1941	Moultrie	GFL	8	23	0	4	0	0	0	0	0	1	7	0.174	C	41	1	2	0.955								
Server, Wallace		BR TR																									
1954	Waycross	GFL	28	106	16	26	5	2	0	14	6	10	15	0.245	SS	19	31	10	0.833								
Sessions, E.E. "Pete"																											
1921	Griffin	GSL		9	2	3								0.333													
1921	Carrollton	GSL	<10												3B												
Settles, Wolf		BR TR																									
1940	Tallahassee	GFL	47	119	10	27	4	0	1	16	1	12	33	0.227	P					42	17	14	3.72	281	265	135	137
Severson, Donald "Don"		BR TR																									
1958	Waycross	GFL	102	364	47	112	16	0	3	49	0	55	27	0.308	C	629	63	13	0.982								
Sevier, John		BR																									
1954	Vidalia	GSL	3	6		0								0.000													
Sewell, ---																											
1915	Newnan	GAL	<6												P					<6							
Sewell, Guy B.																											
1935	Panama City	GFL	20	55	2	8	2	0	0		0	2	11	0.145	P					26	7	9		158	161	68	59
1936	Cordele	GFL	32	55	8	15	0	3	1	9	0			0.273	P					32	8	10	5.43	131		42	59
Sewell, Joseph Jr. "Joe"		BR																									
1956	Fitzgerald	GFL	3	4		0								0.000	P					3	0	2					
Sewell, William "Bill"		BR TR																									
1949	Griffin	GAL	26	101	19	39	10	2	3	24	0	9	13	0.386	OF	41	4	3	0.938								
Seymour, George		BR TR																									
1940	Americus	GFL	10	17	2	2	0	0	0	1	0	1	4	0.118	P									<35			
Seymour, Tex R.		BL TL																									
1950	Albany	GFL	115	405	68	110	27	2	10	75	7	41	85	0.272	OF	131	5	16	0.895								
Sezna, Thomas "Tom"		BR TL																									
1947	Tallahassee	GFL	130	503	91	127	14	12	1	57	30	72	55	0.252	OF	214	13	13	0.946								
1948	Tallahassee	GFL	128	500	107	150	17	12	2	71	29	84	45	0.300	OF	232	18	24	0.912								
Shaddix, Willard H.		BL TL																									
1949	Dublin	GSL	11	17	0	5	0	0	0	2	0	5	3	0.294	P					11	1	3	6.35	51	43	39	34
1950	Jesup	GSL	13	29	2	5	2	0	0	4	0	1	8	0.172	P	4	15	3	0.864	10	4	3	4.09	55	52	34	42
Shaffer, Donald "Don"		BR TR																									
1951	Valdosta	GFL	31	61	12	17	3	1	0	5	0	6	12	0.279	P	6	30	6	0.857	29	12	6	2.77	169	146	95	122
1952	Valdosta	GFL	43	98	12	24	6	1	0	17	1	17	18	0.245	P	14	85	5	0.952								
Shaffer, Frank		BR TR																									
1956	Dublin	GSL	2	0										0.000	P					2	0	0					
Shalata, William "Bill"		BL TR																									
1955	Hazlehurst-Baxley	GSL	104	427	74	126	16	12	3	44	13	20	71	0.295	OF, P	240	5	6	0.976	2	0	0					
1956	Hazlehurst-Baxley	GSL	65	250	25	57	12	1	0	25	9	15	35	0.228	OF	127	11	13	0.914								
Shank, Douglas "Doug"																											
1941	Moultrie	GFL	13	17	0	2	0	0	0	0	0	1	5	0.118	P	1	0	1	0.500	12	2	4	7.66	47	63	30	38
Shanle, Delbert "Del"																											
1949	Douglas	GSL	21	54	5	4	1	0	0	5	0	10	19	0.074	C	68	5	3	0.961								
Shannon, ---																											
1915	Griffin	GAL	16	51	2	10	2	0	1					0.196	C	104	17	3	0.976								
Shannon, Jack																											
1941	Cordele	GFL	22	21	2	2	0	0	0	1	1	1	9	0.095	P	4	15	1	0.950	22	2	4	3.84	75	64	51	50
Shannon, Thomas Michael "Mike" "Moonman"		BR TR 6'3" 195 lbs b. 07/05/1939 St. Louis, MO																									
1958	Albany	GFL	62	245	50	79	15	3	6	54	8	25	41	0.322	OF	142	8	9	0.943								
Shannon, Walter Charles Jr. "Wally"		BL TR 6'0" 178 lbs b. 01/23/1933 Cleveland, OH d. 02/08/1992 Creve Coeur, MO																									
1952	Albany	GFL	124	497	66	154	26	4	1	49	17	48	53	0.310	1B	1117	46	25	0.979								
Shapiro, Albert "Al"		BR TR																									
1946	Tallahassee	GFL	9												P					9	2	4	4.15	52	52	24	30
Shapiro, Robert I. "Bob"		BR TR																									
1952	Valdosta(31) - Moultrie(2)	GFL	33	114	30	21	3	0	0	15	7	37	24	0.184	2B	60	72	11	0.923								

Georgia Class-D Minor League Baseball Encyclopedia

YR	TEAM	LG	G	AB	R	H	2B	3B	HR	RBI	SB	BB	SO	BA	POS	PO	A	E	FA	GP	W	L	ERA	IP	H	SO	BB
Sharlinsky, L.																											
1939	Moultrie	GFL													P									<45			
Sharp, ---																											
1914	Selma	GAL	51	193	11	45					3			0.233	SS	84	138	21	0.914								
Sharp, Hubert N.		BL TL																									
1962	Dublin	GFL	15	13	2	2	0	0	0	0	0	4	8	0.154	P	2	6	1	0.889	15	5	2	5.88	49	48	46	36
1963	Waycross	GFL	21	30	1	6	1	0	0	3	0	4	12	0.200	P	2	15	3	0.850	21	7	4	2.76	101	72	97	39
Sharp, Irving "Irv"		BL TR																									
1955	Douglas	GSL	108	393	76	108	22	2	4	54	13	73	64	0.275	2B, 3B	169	292	35	0.929								
Sharp, William "Bill"		BR TR																									
1946	Valley	GAL	17	55	7	14	3	0	0	3	2	4	11	0.255	OF	19	1	3	0.870								
Sharpe, ---																											
1928	Anniston	GAL	32	92	9	19	2	0	0		2	5	13	0.207	P	20	21	1	0.976	31	18	6	2.56	225	212	90	35
Sharpe, Corwin		BR TR																									
1954	Dublin	GSL	2	2		0								0.000	P					1	0	0	<45				
Sharpless, Seaborne		BL TR																									
1947	Cordele	GFL	109	401	51	102	13	10	0	40	1	47	80	0.254	OF	190	10	21	0.905								
Shartzer, Philip "Phil"		BR TR																									
1954	Fitzgerald	GFL	59	218	26	52	9	0	0	28	3	31	38	0.239	SS	84	153	16	0.937								
Shaw, Bennie A.		BL TR																									
1948	Thomasville	GFL	132	452	72	126	28	9	4	91	7	100	71	0.279	OF	152	12	12	0.932								
Shaw, E.N. "Pop"																											
1920	Carrollton	GSL		111	17	30								0.270	OF												
1921	Cedartown	GSL		127	23	41								0.323	OF												
Shaw, Floyd		BR TR																									
1946	Valley	GAL	16	42	4	7	0	0	0	2	0	0	4	0.167	P	6	20	1	0.963	16	8	5	2.08	108	105	45	20
Shaw, H.L.																											
1916	Rome	GAL	67	264	47	89					25			0.337	OF												
Shaw, James "Jim"		BL TR																									
1948	Fitzgerald	GSL	14	45	6	6	0	0	0	3	0	5	14	0.133	SS	15	25	8	0.833								
Shaw, Stephen "Steve"		BR TR																									
1954	Statesboro	GSL	1	3		0								0.000	P					1	0	1	<45				
Shawkey, James Robert "Bob"		BR TR 5'11" 168 lbs b. 12/04/1890 Sigel, PA d. 12/31/1980 Syracuse, NY																									
1949	Tallahassee	GFL													M												
Shawver, Robert "Bob"		BL TR																									
1952	Hazlehurst-Baxley	GSL	122	450	94	139	19	11	12	91	13	88	76	0.309	SS	216	362	68	0.895								
Shea, David J. "Dave"		BR TR																									
1953	Cordele	GFL	129	473	68	141	30	6	4	78	4	56	65	0.298	1B, OF, P	688	55	18	0.976		0	0	<45				
Shean, ---																											
1914	Talladega	GAL	12												P	8	27	1	0.972	12							
Sheeks, William "Bill"		BR TR																									
1953	Hazlehurst-Baxley	GSL	1											0.000	P						0	1	<45				
Sheffield, Frank		BR TR																									
1947	Cordele	GFL	30	57	5	8	1	0	0	4	0	14	18	0.140	P	5	28	2	0.943	30	6	9	5.76	153	196	77	89
1948	Cordele	GFL	10	14	0	2	0	0	0	1	0	1	6	0.143	P	2	2	0	1.000								
Sheldon, Richard "Dick"		BR TR																									
1957	Valdosta	GFL	41	81	10	16	1	0	0	7	0	4	18	0.198	P	8	28	2	0.947	41	13	11	4.06	226	217	213	83
Sheldon, William S. "Bill"		BL																									
1953	Fitzgerald	GFL	4											0.444													
Shelley, William "Bill"		BL																									
1957	Albany	GFL	10	18	2	4	2	0	0	5	0	4	3	0.222													
Shellnut, Wayne		BR TR																									
1957	Albany	GFL	21	25	3	4	0	0	0	1	0	2	7	0.160	P	12	12	2	0.923	21	3	5	4.26	76	69	36	49
Shelton, James "Jim"		BR TR																									
1955	Dublin	GSL	6	11		4								0.364	P					6	1	2					
Sheppard, ---																											
1913	Anniston	GAL	85	281	24	49					8			0.174	C	537	90	15	0.977								
1914	Opelika	GAL	75	244	23	70					3			0.287	C	142	61	20	0.910								
1915	Thomasville	FLAG	54	214	10	38	5	0	0		1			0.178	C, P	304	58	7	0.981	0							
Sheppard, Kenneth "Ken"		BR TR																									
1956	Valdosta	GFL	38	100	7	18	3	0	1	7	0	2	39	0.180	P	9	38	6	0.887	36	17	13	2.20	262	203	271	126
Sherba, Elmer		BR																									
1953	Jesup	GSL	5											0.190													
Sherman, Edward M. "Ed"		BR TR																									
1950	Vidalia-Lyons	GSL	31	75	9	12	3	1	0	8	0	13	16	0.160	P	5	40	5	0.900	31	11	15	4.72	227	248	74	141
1951	Dub(1) - Fit(7) - Jes(2)	GSL	10	22	7	4	1	0	0	4	0	5	4	0.182	P					8	1	7	7.66	47	68	15	26
Shifflett, Harry H.		BR TR																									
1952	Valdosta	GFL	97	351	53	92	21	4	4	46	7	46	84	0.262	2B, OF	179	130	33	0.904								
Shiffner, Raymond "Ray"		BR TR																									
1953	Cordele	GFL	39	140	15	31	5	0	1	12	7	20	19	0.221	OF	100	3	3	0.972								
Shiles, Harold		BR TR																									
1949	Waycross	GFL	127	447	134	117	24	9	21	85	47	114	93	0.262	3B, SS	225	319	57	0.905								
Shima, Thomas "Tom"		BR TR																									
1958	Brunswick	GFL	19	36	8	6	0	0	1	3	0	9	17	0.167	P	11	20	3	0.912	19	8	4	2.89	109	98	79	39

Georgia Class-D Minor League Baseball Encyclopedia

YR	TEAM	LG	G	AB	R	H	2B	3B	HR	RBI	SB	BB	SO	BA	POS	PO	A	E	FA	GP	W	L	ERA	IP	H	SO	BB
Shimko, Robert "Bob"																											
1951	Cordele	GFL	37	50	7	9	0	0	0	2	0	10	13	0.180	P	7	37	2	0.957	37	2	11	5.10	157	187	67	80
Shinault, Enoch Erskine "Ginger"		BR TR 5'11" 170 lbs b. 09/07/1892 Benton, AR d. 12/29/1930 Denver, CO																									
1915	Anniston	GAL	12	41	3	7	1	0	0					0.171	OF	31	2	3	0.917								
Shinnick, Richard "Dick"		BR TR																									
1955	Brunswick	GFL	11	24	3	2	0	0	0	2	0	6	10	0.083	P					8	6	1	2.32	66	55	52	26
Shipley, Jack																											
1928	Cedartown	GAL	59	233	58	78	12	3	8	21	26	19		0.335	2B	145	184	24	0.932								
1929	Cedartown	GAL	101	400	57	138	12	1	8	29	41	20		0.345	2B	254	348	46	0.929								
1930	Cedartown	GAL	101	404	131	155	27	7	10	21	89	29		0.384	OF	220	16	9	0.963								
Shipley, Joseph Clark "Joe" "Moses"		BR TR 6'4" 210 lbs b. 05/09/1935 Morristown, TN																									
1953	Vidalia	GSL	15	27	1	3	1	0	0	0	0	0	13	0.111	P	3	6	0	1.000	15	1	6	6.04	70	52	54	61
Shires, William "Bill"		BL TR																									
1954	Dublin	GSL	98	381	86	119	16	1	6	49	7	60	28	0.312	OF	116	10	3	0.977								
Shirley, ---																											
1914	Selma	GAL	6	19	0	8				0				0.421	OF	4	3	0	1.000								
Shirley, James "Jim"		BL TL																									
1949	Carrollton	GAL	85	265	35	57	9	2	7	44	5	41	74	0.215	1B	645	28	19	0.973								
1950	Carrollton	GAL	105	369	67	87	13	3	17	71	5	72	80	0.236	1B	672	44	11	0.985								
Shirley, Ralph																											
1949	Hazlehurst-Baxley	GSL	30	42	4	3	0	0	0	1	6	4	29	0.071	P	6	23	5	0.853	34	2	10	6.44	137	121	43	76
Shively, James "Jim"		BL TL																									
1957	Brunswick	GFL	21	24	2	2	1	0	0	1	0	7	13	0.083	P	4	13	3	0.850	20	5	3	2.33	81	63	73	49
Shiver, Floyd L.		BR TR																									
1953	Albany	GFL	26	56	5	9	2	0	0	4	0	4	9	0.161	P	6	36	3	0.933	26	11	7	4.25	142	140	81	76
Shivers, ---		BR																									
1946	Carrollton	GAL	<10																								
Shoemake, Benton		BL TL																									
1949	Valley(67) - Newnan(47)	GAL	114	437	72	117	22	1	1	40	8	53	55	0.268	1B, OF	402	19	17	0.961								
Shoemake, Claude		BL TL																									
1946	Newnan	GAL	124	481	63	152	26	2	14	107	4	21	17	0.316	1B, OF, P	418	17	11	0.975	7	4	2	2.39	49	39	23	15
1947	Newnan	GAL	123	498	81	170	34	6	11	101	7	36	18	0.341	OF	144	19	7	0.959								
1950	Carrollton	GAL	62	234	54	80	6	0	18	68	3	27	6	0.342	OF	60	2	3	0.954								
1951	Rome	GAL	110	458	93	171	37	2	26	135	7	38	6	0.373	1B, OF	265	20	7	0.976								
Sholtzs, ---																											
1941	Valdosta	GFL	3	13	4	3	2	0	0	1	0	2	3	0.231	1B	24	2	3	0.897								
Shosty, Robert "Bob"		BR TR																									
1957	Fitzgerald	GFL	55	196	33	56	13	3	3	35	2	27	35	0.286	OF	100	4	9	0.920								
1958	Thomasville	GFL	91	346	52	97	11	2	7	62	2	30	34	0.280	OF	124	6	12	0.915								
Showers, ---																											
1916	Anniston - Newnan	GAL	70	245	25	50					7			0.204	3B												
Shuck, Larry		BR TR																									
1962	Brunswick	GFL	14	7	0	1	0	0	0	0	0	0	0	0.143	P	1	4	1	0.833	13	2	1	3.24	25	23	23	10
Shultis, Peter "Pete"		BR TL																									
1956	Albany	GFL	7	8		1								0.125	P					6	0	3		<45			
1957	Albany	GFL	30	53	7	13	4	2	0	3	0	6	23	0.245	P	1	17	2	0.900	29	8	8	3.99	142	100	157	154
Shumaker, Robert "Bob"																											
1941	Cordele	GFL	29	95	15	29	5	2	0	20	2	10	18	0.305	3B	36	42	13	0.857								
Shuman, ---																											
1913	Waycross	ESL	82	244	26	58	10	1	1					0.238	C, OF	316	58	16	0.959								
1915	Americus-Gainesville	FLAG	60	211	13	48	6	0	0		5			0.227	OF	60	2	4	0.939								
Shumate, Andrew "Andy"		BR TR																									
1956	Sandersville	GSL	118	420	73	89	19	3	5	44	12	72	133	0.212	2B, SS	267	261	26	0.953								
Shuryn, William "Bill"		BR TR																									
1953	Sandersville	GSL	8											0.250	P						2	3		<45			
Shuster, Harold		BR TR																									
1952	Statesboro	GSL	121	463	84	157	31	0	17	100	10	69	32	0.339	OF	296	13	8	0.975								
Sides, William "Bill"		BL TR																									
1950	Cordele	GFL	103	403	74	95	23	4	6	50	10	69	41	0.236	OF	212	7	14	0.940								
1951	Cordele	GFL	125	453	80	135	25	1	3	59	2	106	20	0.298	OF	222	10	13	0.947								
Sidle, Frank																											
1936	Thomasville	GFL	34	63	8	11	1	0	0	2	3			0.175	M, C	56	16	5	0.935								
Sidwell, ---																											
1930	Talladega	GAL	19	59	6	11	2	1	2		0	4	27	0.186	P	4	41	3	0.938	15	9	4	3.87	121	122	52	56
Siebert, James "Jim"		BR																									
1955	Valdosta	GFL	9	24		3								0.125													
Siebold, John		BR TR																									
1955	Hazlehurst-Baxley	GSL	16	36	11	6	0	0	0	3	2	17	7	0.167	SS	17	22	7	0.848								
Siefert, ---																											
1913	Brunswick	ESL	34	126	11	31	0	0	0					0.246	C	170	14	6	0.968								
Siegfield, ---		BR TR																									
1946	Valley	GAL	1												P					1	0	0	0.00	1			
Siemasz, Nick		BR TR																									
1951	Valdosta	GFL	13	38	10	14	3	0	1	10	3	4	5	0.368	OF	14	1	1	0.938								

Georgia Class-D Minor League Baseball Encyclopedia

YR	TEAM	LG	G	AB	R	H	2B	3B	HR	RBI	SB	BB	SO	BA	POS	PO	A	E	FA	GP	W	L	ERA	IP	H	SO	BB
Sierra, Andrew		BL TL																									
1940	Valdosta	GFL	15	31	1	5	1	0	0	3	0	3	11	0.161	P					14	4	5	3.76	79	87	56	27
Siff, Alan		BR TR																									
1952	Jesup	GSL	11	15	2	2	0	0	0	0	0	2	5	0.133	P	1	3	2	0.667								
1953	Dublin	GSL	13	25	1	4	0	0	1	4	0	0	11	0.160	P	1	13	1	0.933	12	2	4	6.17	54	63	28	33
Sigmon, Jesse																											
1913	Gadsden	GAL	43	132	16	24					5			0.182	P					23	14	9					
1914	Gadsden	GAL	39	137	6	28					1			0.204	P	30	77	15	0.877	39							
1915	Anniston	GAL	29	100	8	19	3	0	1					0.190	P	20	69	6	0.937	20	7	13					
1916	Anniston	GAL	24	61	5	10				0				0.164	P												
1917	Rome-Lindale	GAL	7	18	1	4	0	0	0	0				0.222	OF, P	5	10	0	1.000	5	2	2		29	34	12	12
Sigmon, Joe																											
1938	Americus	GFL	29	76	9	14	3	0	0	8	0	4	22	0.184	P	2	34	5	0.878	26	15	10	3.34	202	202	65	49
Sikes, ---																											
1915	Thomasville	FLAG	36	92	8	20	2	0	2		1			0.217	P	10	44	3	0.947	23	11	9		163	173	105	48
Sikes, E.B. "Don"																											
1920	LaGrange	GSL													OF												
1921	LaGrange	GSL		66	11	23								0.348	OF												
1935	Americus	GFL	31	99	11	32	5	2	0		0	6	9	0.323	M, OF	28	2	1	0.968								
Silbersack, Robert "Bob"		BR TR																									
1956	Thomson	GSL	21	76	9	18	2	0	0	9	2	15	12	0.237	2B	55	44	14	0.876								
Silky, Harold																											
1942	Valdosta	GFL	14	33	4	5	0	0	0	0	0	2	7	0.152	P	4	8	0	1.000	13	6	1	2.82	67	67	30	22
Silva, Gilberto "Gil"		BR TR																									
1954	Americus-Cordele	GFL	6	14		2								0.143	P					6	3	3	1.36	53	34	28	18
Silva, Thomas "Tom"		BR TR																									
1956	Thomson	GSL	35	146	24	32	3	0	0	8	7	9	27	0.219	3B	30	81	18	0.860								
Silver, Charles																											
1936	Americus	GFL	8	13	1	3	2	0	0	1	0			0.231	P					8	1	4	7.41	34		11	29
Silverman, Jerome		BR TR																									
1948	Carrollton	GAL	77	289	47	91	17	1	0	32	3	31	6	0.315	1B	663	29	7	0.990								
1948	Vidalia-Lyons	GSL	34	140	23	41	4	6	0	14	4	8	6	0.293	1B	287	8	4	0.987								
1949	Vidalia-Lyons	GSL	144	605	103	180	20	6	1	104	8	54	25	0.298	1B	1224	79	11	0.992								
1950	Vidalia-Lyons	GSL	23	85	14	28	5	1	0	11	0	6	0	0.329	1B	169	11	3	0.984								
Simcich, John		BR TR																									
1958	Brunswick	GFL	119	436	104	156	25	3	15	104	5	103	64	0.358	3B	134	227	29	0.926								
Simmons, ---		BR TR																									
1954	Valdosta	GFL	4												P					4	0	2	<45				
Simmons, Jack		BR TR																									
1950	Newnan	GAL	47	115	21	27	5	0	1	15	3	27	34	0.235	2B, C	183	33	19	0.919								
Simmons, Paul A.		BR TR																									
1948	Fitzgerald	GSL	113	387	64	109	16	5	3	62	6	70	61	0.282	1B, C	703	46	17	0.978								
1949	Dublin	GSL	99	364	67	118	23	7	9	83	12	52	37	0.324	C	554	40	25	0.960								
Simmons, Richard "Dick"		BL TR																									
1952	Thomasville	GFL	13	40	6	4	1	1	0	4	2	13	14	0.100	OF	29	1	3	0.909								
Simmons, Roy G.		BR TR																									
1951	Waycross	GFL	28	101	8	17	5	0	0	9	0	7	22	0.168	3B	24	57	11	0.880								
Simms, Charles		BL TR																									
1950	Albany	GFL	88	346	58	82	12	2	3	32	13	46	53	0.237	2B, 3B	209	227	45	0.906								
Simon, Dewey																											
1921	Cedartown	GSL		258	57	87								0.337	3B												
Simon, Jerome "Jerry"		BR TR																									
1946	Cordele	GFL	5												P					5	0	0	0.00	9			
1949	Dublin - Tifton	GSL	37	94	14	17	0	0	0	9	0	16	18	0.181	P	14	54	1	0.986	46	17	12	3.43	268	124	162	138
1950	Tifton	GSL	36	61	6	8	1	0	0	3	1	15	24	0.131	P	3	33	1	0.973	36	13	13	3.94	201	202	114	98
Simonec, Reuben		BR TR																									
1946	Thomasville	GFL	11	11	0	0	0	0	0	0	0	2	7	0.000	P	1	2	0	1.000	11	2	4	0.00	36	46	16	31
Simonian, Joseph "Joe"		BR TR																									
1951	Eastman	GSL	65	217	42	54	6	2	1	22	8	47	31	0.249	OF	120	10	8	0.942								
Simpson, Charles J.		BR TR																									
1947	Cordele	GFL	32	75	5	12	3	0	0	5	0	7	11	0.160	P, C	6	28	4	0.895	23	1	13	4.35	122	154	67	77
Simpson, Clifford "Cliff"		BR TR																									
1947	Albany	GFL	108	420	80	115	18	4	0	62	11	70	73	0.274	SS	187	297	75	0.866								
Simpson, Warren		BR TR																									
1956	Thomasville	GFL	12	36	4	7	2	0	0	5	3	9	8	0.194	OF	12	1	3	0.813								
Sims, A. Dewey		BR TR																									
1948	Vidalia-Lyons	GSL	69	243	30	54	8	3	0	21	2	18	48	0.222	OF	129	3	11	0.923								
1950	Opelika	GAL	44	141	14	32	10	0	1	16	7	25	27	0.227	OF	71	4	4	0.949								
Sims, Harold		BR TR																									
1956	Vidalia	GSL	29	38	2	1	0	0	0	2	0	3	24	0.026	P	4	12	2	0.889	29	4	10	5.26	125	109	101	111
Sims, Joe																											
1939	Americus	GFL	33	79	3	12	4	0	0	4	0	4	20	0.152	M, P	6	42	6	0.889	27	11	10	2.79	197	204	96	37
Sinay, Andrew "Andy"																											
1938	Moultrie	GFL	30	88	12	22	3	0	0	12	0	2	3	0.250	P	11	30	2	0.953	17	6	6	4.72	124	138	40	60
Siner, ---																											
1906	Albany	GSL													SS												

Georgia Class-D Minor League Baseball Encyclopedia

YR	TEAM	LG	G	AB	R	H	2B	3B	HR	RBI	SB	BB	SO	BA	POS	PO	A	E	FA	GP	W	L	ERA	IP	H	SO	BB
Singer, George		BL TR																									
1950	Valdosta	GFL	31	91	15	19	3	1	0	10	1	13	15	0.209	C	44	21	11	0.855								
Singer, Hal		BL TL																									
1940	Moultrie	GFL	10	26	2	6	1	2	0	3	0	1	9	0.231	P					8	3	4	4.20	60	63	31	27
1941	Moultrie	GFL	4												P					4	0	2	15.23	13	34	13	11
Singleton, Joseph W. "Joe"		BR TR																									
1948	Moultrie	GFL	70	269	32	64	6	1	2	40	10	18	25	0.238	OF	164	9	8	0.956								
1949	Moultrie	GFL	138	542	72	159	22	4	3	81	20	57	40	0.293	OF	348	16	10	0.973								
Singley, Hulen		BR TR																									
1947	Carrollton	GAL	17	44	2	4	1	0	0	2	0	1	6	0.091	P	2	15	2	0.895	16	9	4	4.45	93	96	41	47
Sinnott, John		BR TR																									
1946	Newnan	GAL	<10																								
1948	Sparta	GSL	59	223	40	60	9	4	2	32	9	29	30	0.269	OF	85	5	3	0.968								
Sinquefield, Edgar Benjamin "Ben"		BR TR																									
1952	Fitzgerald	GSL	48	143	23	39	5	2	4	29	4	14	38	0.273	OF, P	86	13	6	0.943								
1953	Brunswick	GFL	128	439	56	116	20	3	7	81	21	82	100	0.264	OF, P	302	23	19	0.945		0	0	<45				
Sinquefield, Roy		BL TR																									
1947	Opelika	GAL	32	91	7	14	0	1	0	7	1	7	13	0.154	P	4	33	5	0.881	26	15	7	2.94	208	188	155	56
Siragusa, Reano "Noddy"																											
1936	Cordele	GFL	37	72	7	10	0	0	0	3	0			0.139	P					37	14	10	3.45	201		92	89
1937	Cordele	GFL	10												P					10	1	4	5.02	52	72	24	15
Sirota, Alexander "Alex"		BR TR																									
1956	Valdosta	GFL	114	400	53	88	15	2	5	60	3	53	96	0.220	C	866	83	20	0.979								
Sirrine, Ernest		BL TR																									
1951	Griffin	GAL	42	145	24	43	6	0	4	18	1	26	15	0.297	3B, C	75	58	16	0.893								
Sisco, Edmund "Ed"		BR TR																									
1950	Vidalia-Lyons	GSL	16	35	1	1	0	0	0	1	0	2	14	0.029	P	2	16	2	0.900	16	5	9	5.52	101	122	43	49
Sisler, George Jr.		BR TR																									
1940	Albany	GFL	<10												P								<35				
1941	Albany	GFL	14	55	9	13	5	0	0	8	0	7	11	0.236	2B	36	47	5	0.943								
1942	Albany	GFL	11	21	4	8	0	1	0	1	0	3	3	0.381	2B	14	12	2	0.929								
Sisolak, Francis "Fred"		BR TR																									
1952	Brunswick	GFL	128	456	83	100	6	8	5	46	26	86	92	0.219	2B, SS	261	362	49	0.927								
1955	Brunswick	GFL	99	370	81	90	15	4	3	30	10	75	48	0.243	2B, SS	185	274	48	0.905								
1956	Brunswick	GFL	128	462	100	115	26	2	7	36	17	113	56	0.249	2B, 3B, SS, OF	259	232	37	0.930								
Sizemore, Paul		BR TR																									
1956	Douglas	GSL	4	0										0.000	P					4	1	0					
Skaggs, Earl																											
1942	Moultrie	GFL	13	39	2	7	1	0	0	2	0	7	10	0.179	C	43	7	2	0.962								
Skalski, Chester		BR TR																									
1947	Newnan	GAL	99	408	74	120	25	2	3	57	15	22	48	0.294	SS	156	325	31	0.939								
Skelton, ---																											
1915	Valdosta	FLAG				0								0.000	P					0							
Skelton, Robert "Bob"		BR TR																									
1952	Albany	GFL	47	144	12	24	5	4	1	17	1	23	23	0.167	C	191	16	9	0.958								
1953	Albany	GFL	37	122	27	31	4	3	2	12	3	27	21	0.254	3B, C	82	21	5	0.954								
Skidgel, Leon																											
1939	Valdosta	GFL													P								<45				
Skinner, Elisha Harrison "Camp"		BL TR 5'11" 165 lbs b. 06/25/1897 Douglasville, GA d. 08/04/1944 Douglasville, GA																									
1920	Cedartown	GSL		298	37	102								0.342	OF												
Slaboszewski, Vincent "Vince"		BR TR																									
1955	Douglas	GSL	19	43	4	6	1	0	0	4	2	8	18	0.140	OF	5	2	2	0.778								
Slater, ---																											
1914	Talladega	GAL	24	78	8	16				2				0.205	2B	45	53	5	0.951								
1915	Talladega	GAL	10	39	4	8	1	0	0					0.205	2B, OF	104	29	9	0.937								
Slaughter, Franklin "Frank"		BR TR																									
1956	Sandersville	GSL	53	88	21	20	4	2	3	14	1	13	30	0.227	P	12	34	2	0.958	38	11	13	4.19	174	147	131	136
Slezak, Francis		BR TR																									
1955	Thomasville	GFL	43	113	11	18	2	1	0	8	2	8	29	0.159	SS	51	83	19	0.876								
1956	Thomasville	GFL	12	36	3	7	0	0	0	6	0	8	12	0.194													
Slike, Max B.		BR TR																									
1953	Albany	GFL	18	49	6	10	0	0	0	8	0	4	13	0.204	P	2	19	1	0.955	18	7	4	4.02	123	125	94	59
Slivnik, Michael "Mike"		BL																									
1963	Waycross	GFL	14	17	0	2	2	0	0	2	0	0	5	0.118													
Slivocka, Ray		BR TR																									
1951	Brunswick	GFL	20	9	1	1	0	0	0	0	0	5	5	0.111	P	2	14	4	0.800	21	4	3	5.07	55	56	34	40
Sloan, ---																											
1915	Valdosta	FLAG	29	94	6	21	3	0	0		0			0.223	P	6	58	2	0.970	22	12	8		190	137	101	68
Sloan, George		BR TR																									
1947	LaGrange	GAL	29	99	12	29	8	0	0	12	1	14	15	0.293	2B	75	84	17	0.903								
Sloan, Michael "Mike"		BL TL																									
1963	Brunswick	GFL	9	18	3	4	0	0	0	2	0	0	6	0.222	P					8	5	1	1.15	55	42	58	19
Smalley, Charles		BR TL																									
1950	Dublin	GSL	38	94	11	19	0	1	0	9	0	13	18	0.202	P	10	43	3	0.946	38	23	7	2.46	256	189	237	124

Georgia Class-D Minor League Baseball Encyclopedia

YR	TEAM	LG	G	AB	R	H	2B	3B	HR	RBI	SB	BB	SO	BA	POS	PO	A	E	FA	GP	W	L	ERA	IP	H	SO	BB
Smart, Charles		BR TR																									
1947	Tallahassee	GFL	36	120	30	37	7	0	0	23	0	19	14	0.308	3B, SS	28	49	14	0.846								
1948	Fitzgerald	GSL	98	389	55	107	14	7	0	51	22	47	40	0.275	3B	98	187	36	0.888								
Smathers, Fred		BR TR																									
1953	Valdosta	GFL	28	104	14	18	2	0	0	8	0	5	6	0.173	C	136	23	7	0.958								
Smeltzer, Charles		BR TR																									
1946	Opelika	GAL	31	98	16	26	1	1	0	22	0	9	5	0.265	C	95	7	4	0.962								
Smeraglia, Anthony		BL																									
1946	Tallassee	GAL	<10																								
Smilee, Gary		BR																									
1958	Valdosta	GFL	3	3		1								0.333													
Smiley, Charles		BL TL																									
1954	Tifton	GFL	42	139	26	38	12	2	5	24	3	18	33	0.273	1B	335	13	14	0.961								
1956	Vidalia	GSL	119	427	87	125	22	11	9	72	8	81	57	0.293	1B, P	905	50	8	0.992	1	0	0					
Smith, ---																											
1913	Cordele	ESL	36	141	20	35	0	0	0					0.248	SS	69	58	35	0.784								
1915	Brunswick	FLAG	<10																								
Smith, ---																											
1914	Newnan	GAL	92	344	165	85				12				0.247	OF	134	32	10	0.943								
Smith, ---																											
1914	Rome	GAL	50	202	29	72					25			0.356	OF	70	6	3	0.962								
1915	Rome	GAL	41	161	18	42	6	0	0					0.261	OF	77	7	5	0.944								
Smith, ---																											
1917	Tri-Cities	GAL	2	8	1	1	0	0	0		0			0.125	OF	1	0	0	1.000								
Smith, ---																											
1917	Anniston	GAL	7	28	1	6	2	0	0		1			0.214	C, 1B	36	4	4	0.909								
Smith, ---																											
1947	Carrollton	GAL	5												P					5	3	2					
Smith, A.																											
1906	Americus	GSL													1B												
Smith, Andrew E. "Andy"		BR TR																									
1946	Cordele	GFL	67	194	22	45	5	3	1	14	3	27	43	0.232	C	281	56	24	0.934								
1954	Statesboro	GSL	1	4		1								0.250													
Smith, Arnold "Arnie"		BR																									
1956	Thomasville	GFL	31	56	4	13	5	0	0	5	0	7	13	0.232													
Smith, Artis																											
1937	Cordele	GFL		46	3	12				1	5	0		0.261	OF	9	0	0	1.000								
Smith, B.																											
1939	Waycross	GFL													P									<45			
Smith, C.																											
1906	Americus	GSL													2B												
Smith, C.H.																											
1929	Lindale	GAL	94	402	66	113	19	2	4		15	33	21	0.281	SS	198	315	46	0.918								
Smith, Charles		BR TR																									
1956	Fitzgerald	GFL	8	10		0								0.000	P					7	0	1	<45				
Smith, Charles N.		BL TL																									
1955	Valdosta	GFL	50	178	17	41	5	1	0	22	1	19	35	0.230	1B	459	19	8	0.984								
Smith, Dalmas "Del"		BR TR																									
1940	Tallahassee	GFL	133	533	73	133	21	13	6	78	6	46	125	0.250	OF	300	18	11	0.967								
1941	Tallahassee - Thomasville	GFL	131	495	69	128	20	9	6	57	12	41	95	0.259	OF	221	14	13	0.948								
Smith, David "Dave"		BL TL																									
1955	Tifton	GFL	23	72	7	18	2	0	2	10	2	5	7	0.250	OF	36	1	1	0.974								
Smith, Dennis		BR TR																									
1963	Brunswick	GFL	21	26	5	8	1	0	0	3	0	10	7	0.308	C	56	5	2	0.968								
Smith, Ed																											
1942	Tallahassee	GFL	11	21	1	1	0	0	0	3	0	1	8	0.048	P	0	9	1	0.900	10	3	1	4.15	52	44	24	28
Smith, Eugene "Gene"		BR TR																									
1953	Statesboro	GSL	4											0.000	P						0	1	<45				
Smith, Frank J.																											
1951	Moultrie	GFL	29	50	3	9	2	0	0	2	0	3	15	0.180	P	10	19	2	0.935	23	3	12	4.08	117	119	71	61
Smith, Frank Q.		BR TR																									
1953	Waycross	GFL	79	269	28	58	6	0	1	20	1	24	56	0.216	1B	661	37	14	0.980								
Smith, Fred L.		BL TR																									
1955	Albany	GFL	135	521	120	140	15	7	3	40	42	82	84	0.269	OF	347	21	29	0.927								
Smith, Garry L.		BL TL																									
1956	Fitzgerald	GFL	53	186	15	40	10	1	3	22	2	17	58	0.215	1B	421	37	10	0.979								
Smith, George		BR TR																									
1955	Cordele	GFL	19	42	7	5	0	0	0	0	0	1	7	0.119	P	6	19	4	0.862	18	7	7	4.08	119	110	68	56
Smith, George C.		BR TR																									
1956	Thomson	GSL	83	322	74	105	21	8	1	45	11	58	18	0.326	2B, P	182	211	11	0.973	1	0	0					
Smith, George F.		BR TR																									
1950	Albany	GFL	15	11	0	3	0	0	0	1	1	3	3	0.273	OF	11	1	0	1.000								
1951	Albany	GFL	125	489	82	125	26	6	1	52	11	66	63	0.256	3B, OF	173	82	17	0.938								

Georgia Class-D Minor League Baseball Encyclopedia

YR	TEAM	LG	G	AB	R	H	2B	3B	HR	RBI	SB	BB	SO	BA	POS	PO	A	E	FA	GP	W	L	ERA	IP	H	SO	BB
Smith, Gilbert C. "Gil"		BS TR																									
1947	Valdosta	GFL	101	301	39	73	9	5	5	47	8	47	68	0.243	OF, C	233	38	10	0.964								
1948	Valdosta	GFL	24	60	13	16	5	0	1	12	0	15	14	0.267	OF	8	1	1	0.900								
1948	Douglas	GSL	71	228	37	48	7	8	1	28	6	33	39	0.211	C	356	42	14	0.966								
Smith, H.T.		GAL																									
1914	Gadsden	GAL	15	43	2	6				2				0.140	2B	26	26	3	0.945								
1915	LaGrange	GAL	50	188	27	54	14	1	1					0.287	3B	14	18	0	1.000								
1916	LaGrange	GAL	66	220	24	53					16			0.241	1B												
1916	Talladega	GAL	70	259	35	69					13			0.266	3B, OF												
1917	LaGrange	GAL	16	52	7	6	1	0	0	4				0.115	2B, SS	72	23	6	0.941								
1929	Lindale	GAL	96	394	65	134	22	3	1	11	16	21		0.340	3B	168	251	27	0.939								
1930	Lindale	GAL	89	391	74	117	24	6	1	9	13	15		0.299	2B, 3B	186	275	35	0.929								
Smith, Harold E.		BR																									
1958	Albany	GFL	1	2		1								0.500													
Smith, Harold J.		BL TL																									
1947	Americus	GFL	14	16	1	2	0	0	0	0	0	3	8	0.125	P	1	5	4	0.600								
Smith, Harold Raymond "Hal" "Cura"		BR TR 5'11" 189 lbs b. 06/01/1931 Barling, AR																									
1949	Albany	GFL	99	321	50	72	12	2	1	31	7	29	39	0.224	C	542	57	19	0.969								
Smith, Howard		BR TR																									
1940	Albany	GFL	<10												P										<35		
Smith, J.																											
1921	Carrollton	GSL		174	15	36								0.207	C												
1921	Lindale	GSL		250	51	94								0.376	OF												
Smith, J.W.																											
1949	Hazlehurst-Baxley	GSL	13	36	7	1	0	0	0	1	15	21		0.028	OF	23	3	2	0.929								
Smith, Jack Hatfield "Jack"		BR TR 6'0" 185 lbs b. 11/15/1935 Pikeville, KY																									
1955	Thomasville	GFL	2	0										0.000	P					2	0	1	<45				
Smith, James "Jim"		BL TR																									
1946	Valdosta	GFL	34	96	16	25	3	2	0	15	7	21	19	0.260	OF	60	7	7	0.905								
Smith, James D. "Jim"		BL TR																									
1957	Albany	GFL	42	152	20	45	6	2	3	19	3	11	26	0.296	SS	49	98	19	0.886								
Smith, James Earl "Earl"		BR TR																									
1953	Brunswick	GFL	6											0.000	P						1	0	<45				
1953	Douglas	GSL	10	15	7	3	0	0	0	2	0	3	5	0.200	P						2	1	<45				
1955	Statesboro	GSL	3	1		0								0.000	P					3	0	0					
Smith, James Hoyt "Jim"		BR TR																									
1948	Vidalia-Lyons	GSL	118	398	63	82	3	2	0	39	18	76	35	0.206	3B, SS	158	286	61	0.879								
1949	Vidalia-Lyons	GSL	146	588	123	182	27	10	4	81	28	78	34	0.310	3B	205	272	53	0.900								
1950	Vidalia-Lyons	GSL	128	494	81	156	14	7	1	67	18	82	31	0.316	M, 3B	172	287	43	0.914								
1951	Eastman	GSL	115	416	74	108	15	3	1	53	5	68	16	0.260	3B	118	246	39	0.903								
1954	Douglas	GSL	1	1		0								0.000													
Smith, Jesse C.																											
1937	Americus	GFL	19	59	10	13	0	2	1	7	3	14	1	0.220	C	60	10	2	0.972								
Smith, John M.																											
1942	Albany	GFL	42	103	14	22	4	0	0	10	1	17	24	0.214	P	15	17	6	0.842	28	14	8	3.05	186	167	107	99
Smith, Joseph "Joe"		BR TR																									
1947	Tallassee	GAL	45	169	28	56	16	4	1	20	7	15	17	0.331	OF	65	5	4	0.946								
Smith, Julius		BL TR																									
1963	Brunswick	GFL	56	138	21	32	7	0	0	11	9	10	31	0.232	OF	66	3	7	0.908								
Smith, Kenneth B. "Ken"		BL TL																									
1950	Opelika(2) - Valley(21)	GAL	23	71	13	9	2	1	0	3	1	17	19	0.127	1B	133	10	2	0.986								
Smith, Larry		BL TL																									
1955	Statesboro	GSL	6	12		0								0.000	P					6	1	3					
Smith, Leo Jr.		BL TR																									
1957	Valdosta	GFL	82	227	30	65	9	3	2	27	1	32	31	0.286	OF, C	231	11	6	0.976								
Smith, Leroy		BR TL																									
1963	Thomasville	GFL	6	13	0	3	0	0	0	0	0	0	3	0.231	P					5	4	0	1.35	40	19	30	9
Smith, Luther E.		BR TR																									
1946	Valley	GAL	26	58	3	9	0	0	0	3	1	2	6	0.155	P	8	17	2	0.926	14	6	5	4.04	89	78	52	47
Smith, Marion		BR TR																									
1949	Valdosta	GFL	13												P	10	10	1	0.952	13	5	6	5.08	78	96	57	17
Smith, Max E.		BL TL																									
1953	Fitzgerald	GFL	45	151	27	39	6	1	0	16	1	32	30	0.258	OF	69	3	8	0.900								
1953	Sandersville	GSL	20	65	11	14	3	0	0	3	2	11	9	0.215	1B	90	0	1	0.989								
Smith, Michael R. "Mike"		BR TR																									
1952	Fitzgerald	GSL	11	20	1	5	0	0	1	4	1	2	4	0.250	P	0	7	0	1.000	10	3	2	4.59	51	49	35	28
Smith, Morton		BL TL																									
1949	Waycross	GFL	131	550	89	178	28	7	2	114	10	52	32	0.324	1B, OF	679	39	32	0.957								
1953	Waycross	GFL	52	199	26	49	9	2	0	24	3	28	14	0.246	M, 1B, P	368	17	2	0.995		0	3	<45				
Smith, Norman K. "Norm"																											
1937	Cordele	GFL	18	33	1	7	0	0	0	7	0	2	8	0.212	P	3	16	3	0.864	14	9	1	3.00	90	80	76	38
1938	Cordele	GFL	12	29	3	8	1	0	0	3	0	3	6	0.276	P	2	17	0	1.000	11	2	8	3.32	76	79	42	39
1940	Americus	GFL	26	63	6	15	4	0	0	9	0	4	10	0.238	P					23	8	8	3.76	146	152	85	55
1941	Americus	GFL	60	142	11	25	7	0	1	26	1	9	15	0.176	P	26	41	6	0.918	38	14	10	3.25	202	216	151	79
Smith, P.																											
1929	Anniston	GAL	62	249	46	67	17	5	6		26	22	31	0.269	OF	179	25	8	0.962								

Georgia Class-D Minor League Baseball Encyclopedia

YR	TEAM	LG	G	AB	R	H	2B	3B	HR	RBI	SB	BB	SO	BA	POS	PO	A	E	FA	GP	W	L	ERA	IP	H	SO	BB
Smith, Paul		BR TR																									
1955	Waycross	GFL	1	0										0.000	P					1	0	0		<45			
Smith, Paul J.																											
1935	Moultrie	GFL	23	53	3	3	0	0	0		1	3	12	0.057	P					25	10	7		145	137	68	39
1936	Moultrie	GFL	39	100	5	12	0	0	0	4	0			0.120	P					39	13	13	3.42	271		72	79
1937	Moultrie	GFL	48	84	11	13	0	0	0	3	1	9	26	0.155	P	9	60	8	0.896	41	14	12	3.04	228	235	66	74
1938	Cordele	GFL	34	83	7	15	0	2	0	5	0	3	18	0.181	P	7	42	3	0.942	34	12	12	3.57	222	241	87	55
1939	Valdosta	GFL	36	103	6	13	0	0	0	3	1	8	40	0.126	P	11	58	8	0.896	35	21	11	2.35	283	276	146	61
Smith, Paul Leslie "Paul"		BL TL 5'8" 165 lbs b. 03/19/1931 New Castle, PA																									
1950	Tallahassee	GFL	139	615	127	196	24	8	7	76	43	56	38	0.319	OF	305	18	10	0.970								
Smith, Red																											
1920	LaGrange	GSL													M, P, OF												
Smith, Reuben		BR TR																									
1946	LaGrange	GAL	25	58	7	10	1	0	0	4	0	11	7	0.172	P	1	30	4	0.886	15	8	6	3.08	114	113	42	34
Smith, Reuben "Rube"																											
1930	Carrollton	GAL	<10												C												
Smith, Richard Arthur "Dick"		BR TR 6'2" 205 lbs b. 05/17/1939 Lebanon, OR																									
1958	Thomasville	GFL	124	445	73	122	11	18	10	73	28	69	119	0.274	OF, P	217	17	15	0.940	11	0	1		<30			
Smith, Richard Harrison "Dick"		BR TR 5'8" 160 lbs b. 07/21/1927 Blandburg, PA																									
1950	Tallahassee	GFL	100	389	85	132	19	11	5	82	22	72	29	0.339	3B	128	192	42	0.884								
Smith, Richard M. "Dick"		BL TL																									
1958	Brunswick	GFL	2	3		0								0.000	P					2	0	1		<30			
Smith, Robert "Bob"		BS TL																									
1940	Americus	GFL	11	29	1	3	0	0	0	0	0	0	12	0.103	P					12	1	8	4.80	75	75	27	54
Smith, Robert F. "Bob"		BR TL																									
1950	Americus	GFL	20	45	6	8	1	0	0	5	1	13	9	0.178	OF	22	2	2	0.923								
Smith, Robert W. "Bob"		BR TR																									
1950	Moultrie	GFL	17	24	1	3	0	0	0	1	0	6	3	0.125	P	3	11	0	1.000	14	2	2	5.81	48	51	24	45
Smith, Ronald "Ron"		BR TR																									
1962	Moultrie	GFL	41	133	18	28	6	0	2	20	0	16	35	0.211	3B, OF	27	23	13	0.794								
Smith, Sherrod Malone "Sherry"		BR TL 6'1" 170 lbs b. 02/08/1891 Monticello, GA d. 09/12/1949 Reidsville, GA																									
1928	Cedartown	GAL	17	34	5	12	1	0	1		0	2	6	0.353	M, P					7	4	1	1.57	46	40	19	0
1929	Cedartown	GAL	31	60	7	22	2	0	1		0	5	6	0.367	M, P	10	25	2	0.946	10	7	0		76	79	25	7
1930	Cedartown	GAL	31	70	11	23	2	0	2		1	2	6	0.329	M, P	11	45	4	0.933	20	14	2	3.34	132	138	69	21
Smith, Thomas "Tom"		BL TL																									
1954	Brunswick	GFL	7	3		0								0.000	P					7	1	0		<45			
1955	Dublin	GSL	10	16	4	2	0	0	0	0	0	3	7	0.125	P	2	11	2	0.867	10	2	3	6.26	46	44	43	38
Smith, Thomas "Tom"		BL TR																									
1962	Dublin	GFL	73	235	29	57	5	0	3	35	4	40	48	0.243	C	593	37	8	0.987								
Smith, Thomas J. "Tom"		BR TR																									
1946	Thomasville	GFL	31	57	2	8	2	0	0	4	0	2	18	0.140	P	9	23	4	0.889	29	5	10	4.40	131	146	69	73
Smith, Thomas S. "Tom"		BR TR																									
1948	Cordele	GFL	67	211	28	61	10	3	0	31	3	8	15	0.289	OF	83	4	8	0.916								
1949	Cordele	GFL	136	558	82	178	24	10	9	102	7	36	57	0.319	OF	232	20	22	0.920								
Smith, Tommie F.		BL TR																									
1962	Brunswick	GFL	55	165	21	39	6	0	5	17	2	11	30	0.236	C	326	29	7	0.981								
1963	Brunswick	GFL	73	203	22	59	17	0	2	20	0	12	25	0.291	1B, C	380	47	14	0.968								
Smith, Walter "Walt"		BR TR																									
1948	Albany	GFL	17	24	0	2	0	0	0	2	0	0	7	0.083	P	3	11	3	0.824	17	2	5	5.50	72	82	57	34
Smith, William R. "Bill"		BR TR																									
1953	Waycross	GFL	58	212	29	40	9	1	1	14	4	42	33	0.189	OF	132	5	3	0.979								
Smithdeal, Sidney "Sid"		BR TR																									
1956	Fitzgerald	GFL	137	507	51	115	16	8	3	59	10	45	43	0.227	OF	228	12	30	0.889								
Smithley, ---																											
1946	Tallassee	GAL	<10																								
Smoll, John		BR TR																									
1940	Waycross	GFL	<10												P									<35			
Snider, Floyd T. "Smokey"		BL TR																									
1942	Dothan	GFL	20	64	18	16	6	0	0	8	0	17	16	0.250	OF	28	0	3	0.903								
1946	Newnan(17) - Carrollton (21)	GAL	38	122	24	27	8	2	3	16	3	28	24	0.221	OF	55	0	6	0.902								
1947	Carrollton	GAL	124	463	95	142	22	9	21	102	12	90	85	0.307	OF	228	10	15	0.941								
1948	Carrollton	GAL	48	166	34	46	7	2	6	34	3	44	28	0.277	1B, OF	158	3	5	0.970								
1948	Vidalia-Lyons	GSL	83	291	56	64	11	3	2	15	14	66	55	0.220	1B, OF	337	9	8	0.977								
1949	Vidalia-Lyons	GSL	142	490	107	119	24	0	14	101	25	139	86	0.243	OF	294	45	17	0.952								
Snider, Walter "Walt"		BL TL																									
1952	Statesboro	GSL	39	127	19	31	4	0	1	15	1	19	14	0.244	1B, P	212	28	3	0.988	13	5	4	3.36	91	85	46	26
Snodgrass, Walter																											
1906	Albany	GSL													M, OF												
Snyder, Bill																											
1935	Panama City	GFL													M												
Snyder, Harry																											
1935	Panama City	GFL	63	225	50	71	19	0	0		3	18	20	0.316	M, IF	139	148	9	0.970								
Snyder, Paul		BR TR																									
1947	Thomasville	GFL	34	69	8	10	0	0	0	3	1	11	20	0.145	P	5	29	1	0.971	33	12	10	4.34	191	169	188	142
Snyder, Ralph																											
1941	Cordele	GFL	47	129	10	22	4	0	0	16	1	10	33	0.171	C	192	19	9	0.959								

Georgia Class-D Minor League Baseball Encyclopedia

YR	TEAM	LG	G	AB	R	H	2B	3B	HR	RBI	SB	BB	SO	BA	POS	PO	A	E	FA	GP	W	L	ERA	IP	H	SO	BB
Snyder, Richard "Dick"		BR TR																									
1956	Albany	GFL	51	175	24	41	3	3	6	39	7	26	34	0.234	SS	63	135	22	0.900								
Snyder, Ronald "Ron"		BR TR																									
1947	Thomasville	GFL	108	369	51	100	18	4	0	54	3	29	42	0.271	C	495	53	15	0.973								
Sobor, ---																											
1906	Americus	GSL													P												
Socha, George		BR TR																									
1950	Valley	GAL	15	28	4	7	1	0	0	1	0	3	6	0.250	P	3	14	0	1.000	11	5	4	4.00	72	70	52	40
Sockman, Ronald "Ron"		BL TR																									
1957	Fitzgerald	GFL	138	574	81	160	18	5	2	49	22	65	102	0.279	2B, OF	286	73	37	0.907								
Sodupe, Francisco		BL																									
1951	Hazlehurst-Baxley	GSL	14	43	10	11	2	0	0	6	0	6	2	0.256													
Sofia, Michael "Mike"		BR TR																									
1946	Waycross	GFL	54	206	43	38	4	1	0	19	17	48	33	0.184	SS	105	151	27	0.905								
Sohni, ---																											
1906	Cordele	GSL													P												
Soja, Thomas "Tom"		BR																									
1953	Jesup	GSL	7											0.273													
Solberg, Herbert "Herb"		BR TR																									
1954	Albany	GFL	4	6		0								0.000	P					3	2	0	<45				
Solt, James Eugene "Gene"		BR TR																									
1948	Vidalia-Lyons	GSL	121	502	77	143	26	11	6	58	7	27	59	0.285	3B, OF	229	38	16	0.943								
1950	Carrollton	GAL	119	460	106	168	27	1	38	151	6	65	38	0.365	OF, C	433	69	30	0.944								
Sommer, William "Bill"		BR TR																									
1950	Valley(8) - Rome(15)	GAL	23	82	13	22	5	0	0	10	1	17	12	0.268	3B	28	30	8	0.879								
Sorrell, Jesse																											
1929	Gadsden	GAL	95	366	54	90	21	8	2		6	38	45	0.246	3B	104	163	25	0.914								
Sorrells, ---																											
1906	Americus	GSL													3B, 1B												
Sorrentino, John		BR TR																									
1956	Hazlehurst-Baxley	GSL	39	50	1	6	0	0	0	3	0	1	20	0.120	P	12	26	6	0.864	37	5	12	5.01	151	148	102	90
Sosebee, James "Jim"		BL TR																									
1951	Jesup	GSL	110	449	76	156	29	4	7	95	14	44	50	0.347	OF	215	16	10	0.959								
1952	Jesup	GSL	125	535	97	173	40	7	14	101	8	49	49	0.323	1B, OF	586	43	18	0.972								
1953	Jesup	GSL	123	504	118	186	42	9	12	118	6	57	35	0.369	OF	298	24	9	0.973								
1955	Statesboro	GSL	31	102	13	27	1	0	2	18	1	20	12	0.265	M, SS, OF	63	29	4	0.958								
Sosmer, Bernard		BR																									
1958	Waycross	GFL	10	37	2	4	3	0	0	2	1	9	7	0.108													
Souillard, Willard Louis "Lou"		BL TL																									
1956	Waycross	GFL	22	45	3	5	0	0	0	3	0	7	10	0.111	P	1	19	0	1.000	22	9	6	2.20	139	114	75	43
1957	Waycross	GFL	15	25	1	2	0	0	0	0	0	3	5	0.080	P	3	16	0	1.000	16	3	7	3.51	77	98	32	20
Soumma, Eugene "Gene"		BR TR																									
1949	Cordele	GFL	50	95	14	20	2	1	0	7	2	17	24	0.211	P	17	76	9	0.912	46	17	17	3.59	248	262	184	89
Souter, George		BR TR																									
1946	Carrollton	GAL	58	193	43	62	16	4	5	37	13	46	28	0.321	3B, OF, P	63	35	7	0.933	4	1	2	0.00	19	18	12	10
South, ---																											
1917	Tri-Cities	GAL	2	2	0	0	0	0	0		0			0.000	P	0	8	1	0.889	2	0	1		12	4	2	5
Southard, Kenneth "Ken"		BL TR																									
1952	Brunswick	GFL	12	26	3	9	0	0	0	2	0	0	9	0.346	P	4	13	2	0.895	12	2	3	4.70	69	78	33	39
Soward, James E. "Jim"																											
1929	Gadsden	GAL	70	222	32	65	12	0	10		2	10	37	0.293	P	53	57	8	0.932	28	17	6		223	192	100	119
1930	Carrollton	GAL		55		15								0.273	P												
1930	Talladega	GAL	42	130	14	37	7	1	4		0	5	20	0.285	OF, P	44	32	6	0.927	13	3	4	6.21	71	85	27	47
Sowell, Julian																											
1941	Waycross	GFL	21	58	5	10	0	1	0	2	0	7	17	0.172	P	5	34	1	0.975	21	12	6	2.22	158	142	88	59
Sowell, William "Bill"		BR TR																									
1949	Thomasville	GFL	50	197	25	46	6	3	2	16	6	19	54	0.234	OF	79	4	5	0.943								
1950	Griffin	GAL	34	142	40	49	5	5	3	27	10	29	27	0.345	3B	36	59	12	0.888								
1950	Thomasville	GFL	55	161	20	34	3	0	2	14	0	31	44	0.211	OF	57	3	3	0.952								
Sowers, R. Walter "Walt"		BL TR																									
1950	Hazlehurst-Baxley	GSL	75	295	55	114	10	5	0	35	13	32	29	0.386	OF	119	0	11	0.915								
Sowins, Raymond "Ray"		BL TL																									
1947	Moultrie	GFL	103	378	97	106	14	6	16	88	22	90	54	0.280	OF	157	8	11	0.938								
1949	Albany	GFL	110	360	94	102	20	4	15	95	20	133	72	0.283	OF	164	18	8	0.958								
Spain, Hinton E. "Hank"		BL TR																									
1948	Cordele	GFL	121	456	83	141	22	6	2	57	15	62	93	0.309	OF	254	16	18	0.938								
1949	Cordele	GFL	76	305	61	82	9	7	2	34	4	42	53	0.269	OF	150	8	12	0.929								
1950	Cordele	GFL	138	480	79	115	18	5	1	47	16	103	109	0.240	OF	296	27	21	0.939								
Spamer, C. William "Bill"		BR																									
1950	Newnan	GAL	16	49	12	13	4	1	2	11	0	8	11	0.265													
Spampinato, Thomas "Tom"		BR TR																									
1955	Tifton	GFL	13	8	3	1	1	0	0	1	0	1	5	0.125	P	1	3	0	1.000	10	3	0	<45				
1955	Statesboro	GSL	3	6		0								0.000	P					3	0	2					
Sparacino, Frank		BR TR																									
1950	Waycross	GFL	33	137	33	33	8	3	0	8	8	24	30	0.241	SS	55	92	25	0.855								

Georgia Class-D Minor League Baseball Encyclopedia

YR	TEAM	LG	G	AB	R	H	2B	3B	HR	RBI	SB	BB	SO	BA	POS	PO	A	E	FA	GP	W	L	ERA	IP	H	SO	BB
Sparks, Ferrell		BR TR																									
1954	Valdosta	GFL	30	99	10	19	1	0	2	16	1	16	31	0.192	C	184	23	5	0.976								
Sparks, Hugh																											
1941	Tallahassee	GFL	11	20	3	3	0	0	0	0	0	3	9	0.150	P	2	15	3	0.850	11	1	5	4.25	53	70	49	22
Sparks, James "Jimmy"		BR TR																									
1950	Rome	GAL	32	66	9	12	1	0	0	7	0	6	16	0.182	P	8	47	3	0.948	30	10	16	2.83	191	173	126	120
Sparks, Oliverio		BR TR																									
1963	Moultrie	GFL	58	190	24	43	6	2	6	21	5	19	55	0.226	OF	65	3	4	0.944								
Spates, Larcus		BL TR																									
1963	Brunswick	GFL	65	208	41	52	5	1	0	17	19	29	32	0.250	2B	135	112	22	0.918								
Spaugh, ---																											
1913	Waycross	ESL	4												P	1	13	1	0.933								
1915	Americus-Gainesville	FLAG	27	78	8	14	1	1	0		0			0.179	P	8	66	7	0.914	24	5	12		179	205	64	23
Spaziano, Alfred "Al"		BR TR																									
1946	Thomasville	GFL	108	366	63	111	20	2	2	46	8	49	67	0.303	1B, OF, C	518	49	19	0.968								
Spears, Jasper		BR TR																									
1949	Valdosta	GFL	28	109	11	29	4	2	0	12	1	10	26	0.266	2B	42	67	5	0.956								
Spence, Edward "Ed"		BR																									
1957	Brunswick	GFL	13	27	5	8	0	0	2	6	0	5	4	0.296													
Spence, Steve		BR TR																									
1953	Waycross	GFL	1											0.000	P						0	1	<45				
Spencer, ---																											
1906	Americus	GSL													P												
Spencer, David "Dave"		BL TR																									
1947	Alexander City	GAL	18	72	8	22	1	2	0	3	3	2	11	0.306	2B	34	24	10	0.853								
Spencer, Roosevelt		BR TR																									
1963	Brunswick	GFL	48	86	3	14	2	0	2	7	0	4	35	0.163	C	186	16	4	0.981								
Spencer, Willard R. "Bill"		BR TR																									
1946	Carrollton	GAL	1												P					1	0	0	0.00	2			
Spier, Robert "Bob"		BL TL																									
1955	Thomasville	GFL	56	97	20	29	3	3	0	19	0	18	5	0.299	P	8	28	4	0.900	25	15	8	3.05	183	173	132	66
Spiezio, Edward Wayne "Ed"		BR TR 5'11" 180 lbs b. 10/31/1941 Joliet, IL																									
1963	Brunswick	GFL	14	42	8	10	2	0	4	10	1	13	5	0.238	SS	7	17	5	0.828								
Spikes, Oliver C.																											
1936	Moultrie	GFL	37	84	8	14	1	2	1	10	1			0.167	P					37	11	17	4.20	210		162	129
Spilman, Harry		BR TR																									
1952	Eastman	GSL	69	226	23	54	8	0	0	26	0	43	32	0.239	C	289	28	5	0.984								
Spinetti, Sam																											
1936	Cordele	GFL													P									<30			
Spinner, Larry		BL TR																									
1954	Tifton	GFL	136	497	95	142	17	7	19	96	15	56	73	0.286	3B, OF, C	259	191	35	0.928								
Spirida, John																											
1938	Thomasville	GFL	30	118	19	33	7	1	0	22	1	13	21	0.280	OF	74	4	6	0.929								
Spittle, Harry		BL TL																									
1954	Valdosta	GFL	11	22	3	5	0	1	0	3	0	1	3	0.227	P	0	6	2	0.750	12	3	6	6.11	56	64	46	30
Spitzer, Lloyd		BR TR																									
1946	Tallassee(8) - LaGrange(6)	GAL	14	40	5	8	2	0	0	6	0	3	7	0.200	OF	17	1	0	1.000								
Spitznagle, ---																											
1913	Opelika	GAL	88	317	62	69					31			0.218	SS	160	252	42	0.907								
1914	Opelika	GAL	91	354	70	95					18			0.268	SS	190	269	61	0.883								
1915	Dothan	FLAG	70	250	33	61	10	1	0		13			0.244	2B	166	197	29	0.926								
Spivey, William "Bill"																											
1941	Waycross	GFL	13	26	4	4	2	0	0	3	0	7	9	0.154	C	39	6	2	0.957								
Sprayberry, James "Jim"		BL TR																									
1946	Valley(1) - Carrollton(1)	GAL	2												P					2	0	0	0.00	4			
1949	Alexander City	GAL	11	15	5	4	0	0	0	3	0	2	3	0.267	P	1	6	0	1.000	11	2	4	4.30	46	41	10	31
Spruill, James W. "Jack"		BR TR																									
1948	Valley	GAL	124	473	63	116	21	7	0	54	7	57	45	0.245	3B	146	231	32	0.922								
1949	Valley	GAL	126	477	95	153	29	8	4	82	11	50	32	0.321	2B, 3B	180	291	40	0.922								
1950	Cordele	GFL	121	460	92	163	33	5	2	88	10	73	40	0.354	1B	916	75	27	0.973								
Spyhalski, James "Jim"		BR TR																									
1956	Hazlehurst-Baxley	GSL	22	86	15	26	1	4	1	14	0	13	8	0.302	OF	36	1	1	0.974								
1957	Valdosta	GFL	138	502	84	125	18	3	19	80	11	80	89	0.249	OF	255	21	7	0.975								
Squibb, Donald "Don"		BL TR																									
1956	Albany	GFL	3	2		0								0.000	P					3	0	1	<45				
Squillace, John		BR TR																									
1951	Brunswick	GFL	47	141	22	27	2	1	0	14	2	39	12	0.191	2B	85	103	14	0.931								
Sroda, Thaddeus "Ted"		BR																									
1954	Tifton	GFL	6	7		0								0.000													
Stacey, ---																											
1915	Waycross - Brunswick	FLAG	62	203	13	41	5	0	0		6			0.202	OF	89	6	4	0.960								
Stack, Lawrence																											
1937	Tallahassee	GFL	28	106	15	32	2	0	0	13	2	13	19	0.302	SS	43	36	16	0.832								
Stackpole, Cecil		BR TR																									
1950	Hazlehurst-Baxley	GSL	10	35	2	5	0	0	0	1	0	4	20	0.143	OF	15	2	1	0.944								

Georgia Class-D Minor League Baseball Encyclopedia

YR	TEAM	LG	G	AB	R	H	2B	3B	HR	RBI	SB	BB	SO	BA	POS	PO	A	E	FA	GP	W	L	ERA	IP	H	SO	BB
Stalcup, Pete		BR TR																									
1940	Americus	GFL	<10												P									<35			
Staley, Donald "Don"		BR TR																									
1946	Valdosta	GFL	1												P					1	0	0	0.00	1			
Stamey, Harold		BL TR																									
1948	Americus	GFL	132	452	83	147	20	12	3	86	12	67	78	0.325	OF	216	14	16	0.935								
1949	Americus	GFL	134	485	88	151	39	12	11	99	17	76	77	0.311	OF	230	14	17	0.935								
Stamey, John		BL TL																									
1948	Valdosta	GFL	37	66	10	15	1	0	0	7	0	11	16	0.227	P	4	40	2	0.957	24	10	3	2.41	138	109	106	84
Stammen, Orville "Pete"		BL TR																									
1948	Valdosta	GFL	132	465	67	150	21	5	2	77	4	69	48	0.323	C	801	97	24	0.974								
Stamos, Peter "Pete"		BR TR																									
1947	Thomasville	GFL	17	25	0	4	1	0	0	1	0	1	3	0.160	P	4	14	3	0.857	17	8	2	1.83	69	54	28	25
1948	Thomasville	GFL	19	46	6	17	5	1	1	15	0	4	12	0.370	P					9	2	1	4.02	47	57	28	31
1949	Thomasville	GFL	55	141	27	36	11	1	3	21	4	31	44	0.255	2B, OF	73	43	8	0.935								
Stamper, Kenneth "Ken"		BR TR																									
1952	Thomasville(46) - Cordele(15)	GFL	61	200	23	44	4	4	0	20	1	31	57	0.220	1B, 3B	182	69	16	0.940								
1952	Dublin	GSL	43	174	21	46	9	2	0	18	1	21	30	0.264	3B	47	64	17	0.867								
Standard, ---		BR TR																									
1946	LaGrange	GAL	1												P					1	0	1	0.00	3	2	1	2
Standering, Dennis		BL TL																									
1952	Moultrie	GFL	39	122	23	23	4	1	0	12	1	36	23	0.189	1B	322	28	10	0.972								
Stanfield, Ralph																											
1928	Lindale	GAL	64	201	21	52	11	2	5		2	11	31	0.259	OF, P	53	54	11	0.907	26	6	14	4.48	193	245	56	36
1929	Carrollton	GAL	26	60	11	10	1	1	1		1	2	12	0.167	P	7	43	2	0.962	21	8	8		135	155	43	27
1930	Carrollton	GAL		111		36								0.324	P, OF												
1930	Anniston	GAL	38	131	24	41	4	0	3		0	1	16	0.313	OF, P	33	35	5	0.932	13	6	4	5.40	100	124	18	50
Stangel, Robert "Bob"		BL TR																									
1955	Albany	GFL	11	43	4	12	1	2	1	7	3	2	10	0.279	OF	15	0	2	0.882								
Stanley, Bill																											
1920	Griffin	GSL													SS, 3B												
1921	Griffin	GSL		285	47	86								0.302	3B												
Stanley, Kenneth "Ken"		BR TR																									
1949	Thomasville	GFL	36	131	15	36	8	2	2	22	0	6	34	0.275	OF	40	1	3	0.932								
1950	Thomasville	GFL	73	276	41	87	12	7	8	58	4	21	57	0.315	OF	94	14	9	0.923								
Stanley, Robert "Bob"		BR TR																									
1946	Newnan	GAL	103	349	43	96	11	2	0	36	9	28	34	0.275	C, P	537	41	9	0.985	1	0	1	0.00	3	7	1	2
1947	Newnan	GAL	115	421	36	106	15	4	1	62	4	43	37	0.252	C	607	58	14	0.979								
Stanton, Robert E. "Bob"		BR TR																									
1948	Albany	GFL	119	409	68	106	15	5	0	59	5	73	38	0.259	M, 2B	310	329	30	0.955								
Stanziani, Nicholas "Nick"		BR TR																									
1953	Dublin	GSL	56	220	50	66	10	4	11	30	5	34	16	0.300	SS	108	189	24	0.925								
Stapenhorst, Jean																											
1941	Cordele	GFL	25	64	4	12	2	0	0	5	1	7	18	0.188	P	17	32	4	0.925	16	3	9	4.35	91	109	34	46
Stapleton, ---																											
1917	LaGrange	GAL	15	56	6	9	3	0	0		2			0.161	C	109	18	4	0.969								
Stapp, John		BR TR																									
1957	Waycross	GFL	67	226	23	42	7	1	0	24	5	26	47	0.186	2B, SS, OF, P	97	71	23	0.880	2	0	1		<30			
1958	Waycross	GFL	37	135	12	23	2	0	0	15	2	17	25	0.170	2B, SS, P	102	87	11	0.945	1	0	0		<30			
Stark, ---																											
1913	Newnan	GAL	7												P					7	3	4					
Stark, Clint		BL TL																									
1963	Brunswick	GFL	19	31	3	9	0	0	1	3	0	1	8	0.290	P	4	11	1	0.938	13	3	3	2.74	46	28	76	32
Stark, Donald P. "Don"		BL TL																									
1949	Tallahassee	GFL	46	197	27	47	9	4	0	15	1	37	50	0.239	OF	95	5	17	0.855								
Starnes, Kendell		BR TR																									
1949	Dublin	GSL	11	33	3	4	0	0	0	1	0	0	5	0.121	P	1	20	2	0.913	11	8	1	1.47	86	28	63	47
1950	Dublin(11) - Eastman(13)	GSL	24	69	9	10	1	0	0	2	0	2	17	0.145	P	3	36	2	0.951	24	10	6	3.94	162	160	101	107
Starr, A.L.																											
1906	Valdosta	GSL													M												
Starrette, George		BR TR																									
1951	Moultrie	GFL	11	12	4	1	0	0	0	1	0	8	4	0.083	P	3	5	1	0.889								
Stasi, Rocco		BR																									
1955	Douglas	GSL	2	7		0								0.000													
Stasko, Julius		BR TR																									
1946	Tallahassee	GFL	115	449	73	124	16	10	2	65	16	39	61	0.276	2B	298	289	35	0.944								
1947	Tallahassee	GFL	141	580	115	154	16	3	0	50	17	78	47	0.266	2B	427	405	34	0.961								
1948	Tallahassee	GFL	136	544	120	161	26	4	0	76	20	88	26	0.296	2B	444	414	37	0.959								
Stathos, Tony		BL TL																									
1957	Albany	GFL	21	38	12	9	1	0	0	1	1	5	13	0.237	P	2	23	0	1.000	21	9	3	3.42	100	86	69	61
Staub, Raymond E. "Ray"		BL TR																									
1962	Moultrie	GFL	74	238	39	75	8	3	0	26	12	52	48	0.315	OF	109	2	6	0.949								
Steadman, Robert "Bob"		BR TR																									
1949	Opelika	GAL	10	17	2	4	1	0	0	0	0	0	5	0.235													
1951	Opelika	GAL	17	18	0	4	2	0	0	2	0	0	8	0.222	P	2	9	2	0.846	17	3	3	3.75	48	48	14	28

Georgia Class-D Minor League Baseball Encyclopedia

YR	TEAM	LG	G	AB	R	H	2B	3B	HR	RBI	SB	BB	SO	BA	POS	PO	A	E	FA	GP	W	L	ERA	IP	H	SO	BB
Steave, John		BR TR																									
1950	Alexander City	GAL	68	183	14	35	1	1	0	18	1	24	36	0.191	C	324	21	8	0.977								
1951	Cordele	GFL	95	318	27	75	11	2	0	33	3	24	47	0.236	C	360	46	16	0.962								
Steckel, Robert "Bob"		BR TR																									
1949	Valley	GAL	56	193	42	49	4	5	1	19	2	31	35	0.254	2B	163	107	8	0.971								
Steedly, Alvin		BR TR																									
1946	Moultrie	GFL	3												P					3	1	1	0.00	20	17	11	9
1947	Moultrie	GFL	42	81	6	17	2	0	0	5	0	5	15	0.210	P	5	31	6	0.857	42	14	10	3.97	197	192	146	120
Steel, ---		BR TR																									
1946	Carrollton	GAL	1												P					1	0	0	0.00	1			
Steele, P.C. "Jack"																											
1914	Opelika	GAL	86	312	60	100					7			0.321	M, OF	121	16	9	0.938								
1915	Anniston	GAL	55	190	19	47	11	1	3					0.247	M, 1B	536	38	16	0.973								
Steele, Ronald "Ron"		BL TR																									
1953	Albany	GFL	38	57	6	18	2	0	0	7	0	14	20	0.316	OF, P	12	5	6	0.739		2	1	<45				
1956	Albany	GFL	43	115	29	27	8	1	0	25	8	32	33	0.235	OF, P	40	4	6	0.880	5	0	0	<45				
Steely, Stan C.																											
1937	Moultrie	GFL	22	54	4	8	1	0	0	4	0	6	16	0.148	P	10	29	8	0.830	20	6	9	2.94	156	145	76	38
Steen, Robert "Bob"		BL TR																									
1955	Thomasville	GFL	29	91	26	23	1	1	0	8	6	17	16	0.253	2B	62	65	12	0.914								
Stefanik, Raymond "Ray"		BR TR																									
1954	Dublin	GSL	17	28	7	4	2	0	0	4	0	8	13	0.143	P	5	13	0	1.000	17	5	3	5.06	80	73	75	50
Stefano, Nicholas "Nick"		BR TR																									
1948	Americus	GFL	40	132	26	35	4	3	0	14	1	32	26	0.265	2B	68	75	13	0.917								
Steffensen, Richard "Dick"		BR TL																									
1949	Cordele	GFL	22	18	1	2	0	0	0	1	1	5	7	0.111	P	2	14	3	0.842	22	2	3	3.86	63	69	36	30
Stegal, ---																											
1915	Americus-Gainesville	FLAG	<10																								
Steger, David "Dave"		BR TR																									
1947	Valdosta	GFL	85	305	39	89	8	5	1	30	6	40	54	0.292	1B, OF	412	22	21	0.954								
Stein, Edward "Ed"		BR TR																									
1957	Waycross	GFL	10	4	1	1	0	0	0	0	0	1	1	0.250	P	1	3	0	1.000	10	1	1	<30				
Stein, Herbert "Herb"		BR TR																									
1950	Jesup	GSL	127	496	82	151	30	3	6	69	5	41	30	0.304	M, 1B, 2B	999	72	28	0.975								
Steinbach, William "Bill"		BL TR																									
1963	Thomasville	GFL	15	35	3	4	0	0	0	1	0	8	16	0.114	C	92	11	0	1.000								
Steinecke, William Robert "Bill"		BR TR 5'8" 175 lbs b. 02/07/1907 Cincinnati, OH d. 07/20/1986 St. Augustine, FL																									
1953	Jesup	GSL													M												
1962	Dublin	GFL													M												
1963	Waycross	GFL													M												
Steinhour, James "Jim"		BR TL																									
1956	Thomasville	GFL	13	9	0	1	0	0	0	0	0	1	5	0.111	P	0	6	0	1.000	12	1	2	<45				
1957	Thomasville	GFL	30	49	2	5	1	0	0	2	0	6	15	0.102	P	5	19	1	0.960	30	13	6	3.10	151	149	117	71
Stempel, Courtney		BR TR																									
1950	Cordele	GFL	44	78	11	16	4	0	0	5	0	8	26	0.205	P	6	33	4	0.907	32	11	15	4.25	201	179	149	166
Stemper, Robb Paul "Robb"		BR TR																									
1955	Cordele	GFL	26	90	8	19	5	1	0	13	0	11	8	0.211	C	83	18	7	0.935								
Stenger, Richard "Dick"		BL TR																									
1948	Douglas	GSL	16	26	1	0	0	0	0	0	0	5	15	0.000	P	2	10	4	0.750	16	1	7	5.77	78	75	55	54
Stephens, Colonel																											
1906	Americus	GSL													C, 1B												
Stephens, Donald S. "Don"		BL TL																									
1947	Albany	GFL	37	71	8	15	1	0	0	4	0	3	12	0.211	P	13	58	11	0.866	36	12	12	3.44	186	176	114	81
1948	Albany	GFL	42	99	16	27	3	1	0	9	2	5	19	0.273	P	9	68	3	0.963	39	17	14	2.27	254	197	221	110
Stephens, Frank		BR TL																									
1947	Alexander City	GAL	14	11	2	3	0	0	0	1	0	1	1	0.273	P	1	5	1	0.857								
Stephens, T.W.		BR																									
1946	LaGrange	GAL	<10																								
Stephenson, ---																											
1913	Anniston	GAL	48	167	24	50					8			0.299	P, OF	49	82	16	0.891	14	7	7					
1914	Anniston	GAL	47	169	16	49					8			0.290	P	246	54	12	0.962	47							
Stephenson, James L. "Sonny"		BL TL																									
1950	Valdosta	GFL	129	477	108	133	19	6	3	55	18	104	53	0.279	1B, OF	294	19	20	0.940								
1953	Thomasville	GFL	140	484	106	161	29	7	0	96	7	140	49	0.333	1B, OF	1024	54	19	0.983								
Sterkenberg, Larry		BR																									
1963	Thomasville	GFL	23	71	6	13	1	1	1	6	1	4	24	0.183													
Stern, Austin		BL TR																									
1953	Cordele	GFL	26	80	11	19	2	0	0	12	1	21	21	0.238	3B, OF	28	26	8	0.871								
Stern, Jerome																											
1949	Vidalia-Lyons	GSL	16	58	8	13	2	0	0	2	0	1	15	0.224	2B	47	51	11	0.899								
Sterns, Roland		BR TR																									
1955	Brunswick	GFL	2	7		3								0.429	P					2	0	2	<45				
Sterrette, Robert "Bob"		BR																									
1953	Vidalia	GSL	8											0.212													

Georgia Class-D Minor League Baseball Encyclopedia

YR	TEAM	LG	G	AB	R	H	2B	3B	HR	RBI	SB	BB	SO	BA	POS	PO	A	E	FA	GP	W	L	ERA	IP	H	SO	BB
Stevens, ---																											
1942	Dothan	GFL	2												P					2	1	1	0.00	18	13	6	3
Stevens, Jim E.																											
1929	Lindale	GAL	49	135	14	31	6	2	0		2	6	6	0.230	C	150	31	16	0.919								
Stevens, Paul		BR TR																									
1948	Sparta	GSL	83	280	31	63	4	1	1	21	6	24	65	0.225	2B, SS, OF	120	192	14	0.957								
Stevens, Walter "Walt" "Monk"		BL TL																									
1951	Americus	GFL	20	33	9	5	1	0	0	0	1	13	22	0.152	P	1	14	2	0.882	10	2	5	5.80	59	78	25	44
Stevens, William E. "Bill"		BR																									
1950	Opelika	GAL	16	55	6	8	0	0	1	5	2	8	12	0.145													
Stevenson, ---																											
1915	Anniston	GAL	27	105	10	18	2	1	0					0.171													
Stevenson, Frederick "Fred"		BR TR																									
1949	LaGrange	GAL	13	26	2	3	0	0	0	2	0	3	7	0.115	OF	19	1	2	0.909								
Stewart, ---																											
1906	Cordele	GSL													OF													
Stewart, ---																											
1913	Americus	ESL	16	47	2	9	4	0	1					0.191	P	5	14	1	0.950	10	4	6					
1913	Brunswick	ESL	9												P	2	20	0	1.000	8	4	4					
1914	Brunswick	GSL		96	4	12	0	0	0		0			0.125													
1915	Brunswick	FLAG	28	77	4	14	0	0	1		0			0.182	P	6	51	5	0.919	22	8	9		170	138	97	37
1915	Valdosta - Waycross	FLAG	71	254	45	62	11	1	2		38			0.244	2B, 3B, P	155	82	11	0.956	0							
Stewart, Buford		BR TR																									
1941	Moultrie	GFL	56	145	10	36	5	1	2	23	0	4	51	0.248	C	178	23	8	0.962								
1946	Moultrie	GFL	15	50	1	10	2	0	0	1	0	3	13	0.200	OF	8	1	1	0.900								
Stewart, Raymond "Ray"		BR TR																									
1947	Cordele	GFL	14	52	8	16	4	0	0	7	0	6	11	0.308	3B	15	21	10	0.783								
Stewart, Robert H. "Bob"		BL TR																									
1954	Valdosta	GFL	122	440	65	125	22	6	4	54	13	60	40	0.284	1B, 3B	250	132	35	0.916								
Stewart, Rudy		BL																									
1953	Sandersville	GSL	8											0.367													
Stewart, Russell "Russ"		BR TR																									
1939	Valdosta	GFL	72	241	27	59	7	1	0	13	5	22	43	0.245	SS	106	216	28	0.920								
1940	Valdosta	GFL	106	413	40	100	11	3	0	33	5	33	67	0.242	SS	199	320	35	0.937								
Stewart, William E. "Bill"		BL TR																									
1954	Dublin	GSL	10	24	1	6	0	0	0	3	0	0	6	0.250	P	2	6	1	0.889	10	4	1	4.78	49	57	30	17
Stewman, Joseph "Joe"		BR																									
1956	Valdosta	GFL	3	6		1								0.167													
Stickney, Floyd		BR TR																									
1940	Albany	GFL	135	557	92	167	28	15	0	69	7	66	34	0.300	3B	142	279	54	0.886								
Stigman, Richard Lewis "Dick"		BR TL 6'3" 200 lbs b. 01/24/1936 Nimrod, MN																									
1954	Tifton	GFL	12	16	0	0	0	0	0	0	0	2	12	0.000	P	0	10	1	0.909	12	0	6	6.71	55	70	37	31
1956	Vidalia	GSL	33	79	7	13	0	0	0	6	0	5	32	0.165	P	5	31	2	0.947	33	17	9	1.44	213	138	263	97
Stiles, ---																											
1913	Thomasville	ESL	23	65	0	10	0	0	0					0.154	P	4	52	9	0.862	21	8	13					
Still, James "Jim"		BR TR																									
1948	Valley	GAL	58	236	44	62	10	5	6	26	9	29	55	0.263	OF	83	2	6	0.934								
1951	Moultrie	GFL	28	103	19	26	5	1	1	9	0	15	25	0.252	OF	65	4	9	0.885								
Stillings, Gerald		BR TR																									
1956	Waycross	GFL	18	49	1	7	2	0	0	4	0	2	8	0.143	P	11	29	2	0.952	17	9	6	2.25	132	85	77	60
1957	Waycross	GFL	23	54	6	22	1	1	1	7	0	0	10	0.407	P	7	16	3	0.885	19	6	6	3.55	109	94	61	60
Stimson, Carl Remus "Carl"		BS TR 6'5" 190 lbs b. 07/18/1894 Hamburg, IA d. 11/09/1936 Omaha, NE																									
1917	Talladega	GAL	5	11	0	2	1	0	0		0			0.182	P, 3B	1	8	0	1.000	4	0	3		26	23	13	8
Stine, ---																											
1928	Gadsden	GAL	24	87	12	23	5	0	0		2	5	7	0.264	OF	35	2	3	0.925								
Stingley, Richard "Dick"		BR TR																									
1949	Tallahassee	GFL	66	180	15	42	1	0	0	12	1	26	41	0.233	C	279	48	20	0.942								
Stinson, Robert W. "Bob"		BL TR																									
1949	Dublin - Eastman	GSL	61	210	23	65	8	0	1	21	3	23	21	0.310	C	294	31	25	0.929								
1950	Eastman	GSL	114	394	60	119	22	0	1	66	7	49	30	0.302	C	596	73	20	0.971								
1951	Eastman	GSL	42	172	18	52	6	0	0	23	3	13	5	0.302	C	120	13	7	0.950								
Stock, Lloyd		BR TR																									
1948	Griffin	GAL	42	142	20	31	1	2	1	18	1	22	30	0.218	2B, SS	94	105	19	0.913								
Stocker, Ronald "Ron"		BL TL																									
1956	Thomson	GSL	31	51	6	3	1	0	0	2	0	2	13	0.059	P	7	38	3	0.938	28	8	10	3.00	141	124	114	90
1957	Fitzgerald	GFL	32	58	7	9	3	0	0	1	0	1	17	0.155	P	10	30	1	0.976	31	9	10	3.34	159	163	116	73
1958	Dublin	GFL	18	25	8	9	3	0	0	2	0	1	9	0.360	P	4	14	1	0.947	17	5	4	4.05	60	55	42	53
Stocker, Stanley "Stan"		BR TL																									
1948	Valdosta	GFL	41	70	7	10	0	2	0	3	0	11	27	0.143	P	5	31	6	0.857	36	12	12	3.05	195	171	120	113
1950	Valdosta	GFL	19	23	0	2	0	0	0	0	0	0	9	0.087	P	1	16	2	0.895	19	5	4	5.14	63	71	37	47
Stockton, Raymond "Ray"		BL TR																									
1950	Tifton	GSL	13	48	5	9	5	0	0	8	2	5	17	0.188	OF	25	1	0	1.000								
Stokes, James Donald "Don"		BL TR 6'1" 184 lbs b. 07/13/1921 Waverly, TN																									
1942	Dothan	GFL	51	176	21	45	3	0	0	16	3	22	28	0.256	3B	42	70	24	0.824								
Stokes, William "Bill"		BR TR																									
1955	Albany	GFL	1	0										0.000	P					1	0	0	<45				

399

Georgia Class-D Minor League Baseball Encyclopedia

YR	TEAM	LG	G	AB	R	H	2B	3B	HR	RBI	SB	BB	SO	BA	POS	PO	A	E	FA	GP	W	L	ERA	IP	H	SO	BB
Stoll, Maxmillian "Max"		BR TR																									
1962	Thomasville	GFL	33	32	3	6	2	0	0	2	0	4	10	0.188	P	5	22	1	0.964	33	8	7	4.73	97	81	68	78
Stolper, Hubert																											
1939	Tallahassee	GFL	129	462	57	104	15	5	0	47	6	40	70	0.225	C	692	86	13	0.984								
Stolte, William "Bill"		BR TR																									
1951	Griffin	GAL	53	132	16	23	5	1	0	14	0	18	33	0.174	P	12	39	3	0.944	35	14	11	4.30	226	273	115	71
Stone, ---																											
1913	Cordele	ESL	27	102	18	30	0	0	0					0.294	OF	41	6	1	0.979								
Stone, Allan		BR TR																									
1954	Fitzgerald	GFL	30	49	6	12	2	1	0	5	0	7	8	0.245	P	8	33	3	0.932	27	10	7	3.95	130	128	59	67
1955	Moultrie	GFL	11	6	2	2	0	0	0	0	0	0	2	0.333	P	0	7	2	0.778	11	0	2	<45				
Stone, Arthur "Art"		BR																									
1953	Jesup	GSL	19	39	7	5	1	0	1	3	4	4	9	0.128													
Stone, Eddie		BR TR																									
1940	Moultrie	GFL	51	208	25	44	6	0	0	14	4	15	54	0.212	3B	53	111	14	0.921								
Stone, Richard "Dick"		BR TR																									
1956	Fitzgerald	GFL	7	16		5								0.313	P					6	2	2	<45				
Stoner, Robert P. "Bob"																											
1936	Albany	GFL	13	50	6	8	2	0	1	4	0			0.160	OF	27	2	2	0.935								
Stoops, William "Bill"		BR TR																									
1949	Tallahassee	GFL	48	167	17	35	9	1	0	8	2	15	40	0.210	3B, OF	59	35	8	0.922								
1950	Tallahassee	GFL	11	29	4	7	1	0	1	7	1	6	6	0.241													
Stopchuck, Michael "Mike"		BR TR																									
1956	Tifton	GFL	76	263	37	82	16	1	10	43	2	14	53	0.312	C, OF	278	28	7	0.978								
1957	Brunswick	GFL	109	439	83	142	23	10	9	92	12	36	49	0.323	1B	847	60	34	0.964								
1958	Brunswick	GFL	114	446	102	141	22	7	11	105	3	61	41	0.316	1B, C, OF, P	466	41	25	0.953	1	0	0	<30				
Storch, Charles		BR TR																									
1948	Moultrie	GFL	22	26	1	5	1	0	0	3	0	3	11	0.192	P	1	16	2	0.895	22	1	5	3.63	72	76	34	47
1949	Moultrie	GFL	11	9	2	1	1	0	0	1	0	0	4	0.111	P	0	3	0	1.000								
Storey, Gordon																											
1939	Cordele	GFL													P								<45				
Storie, Burl		BR TR																									
1940	Tallahassee	GFL	117	373	54	94	24	3	0	42	2	36	61	0.252	C	522	69	29	0.953								
1941	Tallahassee	GFL	124	455	57	122	21	6	1	59	0	67	51	0.268	C	808	102	39	0.959								
Stotler, Roy		BR TR																									
1956	Brunswick	GFL	80	290	31	62	0	1	4	21	4	40	68	0.214	SS	129	194	53	0.859								
Stouch, John		BR TR																									
1946	Cordele	GFL	50	170	31	33	5	4	0	14	3	28	52	0.194	2B, 3B	93	115	25	0.893								
Stoutenborough, Y.C.																											
1929	Lindale	GAL	30	74	11	17	3	0	1		0	2	10	0.230	P	4	42	4	0.920	30	12	8		180	194	86	46
1930	Lindale	GAL	29	80	12	22	2	0	0		0	1	9	0.275	P	5	44	4	0.925	29	16	5	5.46	173	230	53	35
Stover, Dewey																											
1938	Moultrie	GFL	113	422	83	138	20	7	0	52	37	90	29	0.327	M, OF	187	13	12	0.943								
Stowe, John G.		BL BR																									
1946	LaGrange	GAL	77	277	56	95	11	4	13	68	13	29	12	0.343	OF, P	122	17	7	0.952	5	0	2	0.00	19	29	9	13
1950	Rome	GAL	111	374	56	124	28	0	1	66	6	38	20	0.332	M, 1B, 3B, OF, P	293	40	11	0.968	17	4	0	5.44	48	56	23	32
1951	Rome	GAL	104	450	101	166	39	4	6	27	3	31	30	0.369	1B	846	34	26	0.971								
Stowell, Douglas "Doug"		BR TR																									
1956	Thomson	GSL	18	55	8	9	4	0	1	5	0	11	16	0.164	OF	29	1	3	0.909								
Stoyle, James Donald "Jim"		BL TL																									
1946	Carrollton	GAL	90	336	70	118	22	3	7	83	15	28	28	0.351	1B	947	27	23	0.977								
1947	Newnan	GAL	80	316	42	113	16	6	3	61	12	30	36	0.358	1B	745	23	18	0.977								
1949	Sparta	GSL	121	478	92	191	38	18	18	116	1	57	46	0.400	1B	1004	28	22	0.979								
1950	Griffin	GAL	117	439	104	159	22	5	12	121	0	65	34	0.362	1B	888	39	19	0.980								
1951	Jesup	GSL	107	383	90	116	23	1	14	112	10	86	32	0.303	M, 1B	929	33	12	0.988								
1952	Jesup(67) - Fitzgerald(31)	GSL	98	376	55	122	30	4	13	73	2	44	34	0.324	M, 1B	768	29	11	0.986								
1953	Fitzgerald	GFL	127	478	63	158	46	2	7	99	6	51	70	0.331	1B, P	875	46	17	0.982		0	1	<45				
Strachan, Mearl																											
1939	Cordele	GFL	37	89	8	15	0	0	0	3	0	4	19	0.169	P	18	52	3	0.959	32	13	14	3.00	225	134	112	80
Stratton, George E.																											
1949	Tifton	GSL	50	171	32	43	8	2	1	24	1	43	33	0.251	SS	110	76	31	0.857								
Stratton, Harry																											
1939	Waycross	GFL	72	252	45	74	9	8	0	52	11	53	19	0.294	OF	110	6	4	0.967								
Strauss, Harold		BR TR																									
1946	Cordele	GFL	11	40	9	10	1	0	1	6	1	3	3	0.250	2B	24	27	6	0.895								
Strawser, Croyden		BR TR																									
1953	Valdosta	GFL	69	208	24	46	10	2	2	31	3	32	34	0.221	1B, OF, C	353	17	11	0.971								
Strichek, Edwin "Ed"		BR TR																									
1954	Valdosta	GFL	41	57	9	10	5	3	0	9	0	5	11	0.175	P	6	20	0	1.000	31	7	7	3.61	127	125	103	60
1955	Valdosta	GFL	26	57	5	5	0	1	0	4	0	2	8	0.088	P	11	38	1	0.980	19	12	7	2.01	143	112	83	62
Strickland, Donald M. "Don"		BL TL																									
1950	Thomasville	GFL	81	284	47	84	18	6	5	60	4	60	35	0.296	OF	154	14	14	0.923								
Strickland, Norris		BL TR																									
1947	Cordele	GFL	89	343	61	103	10	5	6	52	7	49	87	0.300	1B, OF	197	15	15	0.934								
1948	Cordele	GFL	133	523	108	185	41	13	4	88	17	74	93	0.354	OF	305	19	20	0.942								
1949	Cordele	GFL	29	106	13	33	6	2	0	18	2	20	17	0.311	OF	44	2	3	0.939								

Georgia Class-D Minor League Baseball Encyclopedia

YR	TEAM	LG	G	AB	R	H	2B	3B	HR	RBI	SB	BB	SO	BA	POS	PO	A	E	FA	GP	W	L	ERA	IP	H	SO	BB
Strickland, Walter "Walt"		BR TR																									
1950	Valdosta	GFL	24	54	4	8	1	1	0	2	0	0	17	0.148	P	5	20	2	0.926	20	9	4	2.71	133	101	86	90
Striffler, Charles		BR TR																									
1948	LaGrange	GAL	37	143	16	37	3	1	0	18	6	18	24	0.259	OF	69	4	5	0.936								
Stringfield, ---																											
1914	Rome	GAL	71	225	39	58					16			0.258	3B	105	151	26	0.908								
Strock, Raymond "Ray"		BR TR																									
1957	Waycross	GFL	19	27	3	6	0	1	0	2	0	1	5	0.222	P	4	7	1	0.917	17	0	4	4.57	61	48	35	55
Stroecker, ---																											
1928	Anniston	GAL	21	85	20	21	4	3	1		1	7	16	0.247	OF	38	2	3	0.930								
1929	Gadsden	GAL	26	85	17	22	4	2	0		3	10	11	0.259	OF	31	10	1	0.976								
Stroeker, Arnold		BR TR																									
1949	Cordele	GFL	43	144	10	28	4	0	0	12	1	8	22	0.194	C	241	24	13	0.953								
Strohmeyer, Fred																											
1941	Americus	GFL	13	26	1	2	0	0	0	1	0	2	12	0.077	P	3	14	1	0.944	12	3	4	5.52	62	72	31	35
Strom, Kenneth "Ken"		BR TR																									
1951	Valdosta	GFL	13	20	10	4	0	1	0	1	0	4	5	0.200	P	5	11	4	0.800	13	7	2	2.87	69	53	53	36
Strosser, Walter "Walt"																											
1941	Moultrie	GFL	110	430	78	122	9	10	9	51	18	81	49	0.284	OF	261	13	8	0.972								
Strott, Arthur "Art"																											
1935	Moultrie	GFL	51	185	41	64	5	12	4		4	20	16	0.346	OF	77	5	1	0.988								
Stroud, Earl		BR TR																									
1953	Cordele	GFL	5											0.000	P						1	1	<45				
Stroud, Luther Earl "Earl"		BR TR																									
1949	Vidalia-Lyons	GSL	10	23	3	5	0	0	0	2	0	1	3	0.217	C	26	3	1	0.967								
1950	Moultrie	GFL	17	51	6	6	0	1	0	1	0	11	16	0.118	C	84	2	7	0.925								
1950	Vidalia-Lyons	GSL	16	53	13	10	0	0	0	9	0	11	15	0.189	C	81	16	4	0.960								
Strozyk, Raymond "Ray"		BR TR																									
1956	Thomson	GSL	104	336	42	69	8	2	1	28	2	52	66	0.205	C	754	83	26	0.970								
1957	Fitzgerald	GFL	84	249	41	66	9	2	0	38	4	43	47	0.265	OF, C	224	26	7	0.973								
Stryker, Ernest		BR																									
1949	Cordele	GFL	10	25	0	5	0	0	0	1	0	4	3	0.200													
Stubing, Lawrence George "Moose"		BL TL 6'3" 220 lbs b. 03/31/1938 Bronx, NY																									
1956	Brunswick	GFL	13	44	7	10	0	0	0	6	0	12	10	0.227	1B	95	5	7	0.935								
Stuckey, Rex		BR TR																									
1949	Valley	GAL	19	53	11	14	1	0	0	4	0	12	9	0.264	C	73	6	4	0.952								
Stuckmeyer, Roland "Rollie"		BL TL																									
1953	Valdosta	GFL	79	265	49	78	13	5	2	47	4	63	14	0.294	M, 1B	686	61	13	0.983								
Sturges, Sylvester L.																											
1939	Americus	GFL	20	72	9	18	5	0	1	12	0	6	14	0.250	OF	27	3	1	0.968								
Stutsman, Edward "Ed"		BL TL																									
1955	Tifton	GFL	50	183	19	45	5	1	2	22	0	20	36	0.246	1B	346	22	7	0.981								
Stutts, Robert "Bob"		BR TR																									
1953	Fitzgerald	GFL	114	414	69	118	14	6	10	76	16	45	57	0.285	OF, C	229	14	26	0.903								
1954	Fitzgerald	GFL	65	235	39	62	8	7	3	22	4	33	50	0.264	OF, C	203	10	14	0.938								
Suarez, Oscar		BR TR																									
1952	Douglas	GSL	15	23	0	6	0	0	0	3	0	2	6	0.261	P	2	16	2	0.900	15	2	7	4.43	65	82	15	27
Suarez, Rafael		BR TR																									
1958	Waycross	GFL	12	30	3	6	0	0	0	1	0	10	6	0.200	C	59	7	1	0.985								
Subbiondo, Joseph "Joe"		BR																									
1950	Newnan	GAL	10	33	4	7	1	0	0	4	0	5	14	0.212													
Suggs, Eugene																											
1920	Cedartown	GSL													2B												
1921	Lindale	GSL		23	5	10								0.435													
Sules, John		BR TR																									
1950	Fitzgerald	GSL	21	66	8	14	1	1	0	6	0	16	11	0.212	1B	110	4	8	0.934								
Sullivan, Daniel "Dan"		BR TR																									
1948	Vidalia-Lyons	GSL	59	200	18	38	2	2	0	13	10	14	30	0.190	2B	158	126	19	0.937								
Sullivan, Eugene "Gene"																											
1938	Moultrie	GFL	56	213	24	67	3	4	1	27	3	18	17	0.315	OF	85	2	4	0.956								
Sullivan, James "Jim"																											
1936	Americus	GFL	21	41	4	9	2	0	0	3	0			0.220	P					21	4	6	4.84	80		29	35
1937	Americus	GFL	22	50	4	14	0	0	1	3	0	2	9	0.280	OF, P	19	4	4	0.852	10	3	2	3.88	51	54	23	20
Sullivan, John L.		BR TR																									
1951	Fitzgerald(14) - Eastman(16)	GSL	30	47	3	2	0	0	0	1	0	6	29	0.043	P	1	11	3	0.800	29	6	13	6.35	119	124	77	153
1952	Fitzgerald	GSL	34	43	2	6	0	0	0	2	1	7	16	0.140	P	5	11	3	0.842	32	7	9	3.54	140	144	43	83
1953	Douglas	GSL	1											0.000	P					0	0		<45				
Sullivan, John Paul "John"		BR TR 5'10" 170 lbs b. 11/02/1920 Chicago, IL																									
1941	Thomasville	GFL	136	567	124	183	21	6	1	56	23	72	65	0.323	SS	261	471	83	0.898								
Sullivan, Joseph "Joe"																											
1935	Thomasville	GFL	55	195	34	45	10	1	4		0	27	45	0.231	IF	480	25	13	0.975								
Sullivan, Joseph W. "Joe"		BR TR																									
1948	Americus	GFL	13	21	1	1	0	0	0	0	0	2	12	0.048	P	1	7	2	0.800	12	2	4	5.08	62	60	34	54
Sullivan, Woodward		BR TR																									
1946	Thomasville	GFL	3												P					3	0	0	0.00	11			

YR	TEAM	LG	G	AB	R	H	2B	3B	HR	RBI	SB	BB	SO	BA	POS	PO	A	E	FA	GP	W	L	ERA	IP	H	SO	BB
Sullivant, Mickey E.		BL TL																									
1962	Brunswick	GFL	14	3	0	0	0	0	0	0	0	0	0	0.000	P	0	5	1	0.833	14	0	1	10.42	19	18	13	16
Summ, Jack																											
1938	Tallahassee	GFL	117	448	68	110	18	5	0	48	18	60	66	0.246	OF	308	15	17	0.950								
1939	Tallahassee	GFL	130	498	92	120	23	5	0	43	34	77	47	0.241	UT	320	73	14	0.966								
Summerhill, Steve		BR TR																									
1940	Valdosta	GFL	113	450	83	138	20	13	3	87	23	46	27	0.307	OF	191	17	4	0.981								
1941	Valdosta	GFL	116	476	84	144	20	13	3	63	14	32	24	0.303	3B	162	130	18	0.942								
1942	Valdosta	GFL	114	471	80	165	33	14	2	95	21	43	19	0.350	OF	421	114	18	0.967								
Summerlin, ---																											
1915	Thomasville	FLAG	4			0								0.000	P					4	1	1		20	22	5	1
Summerlin, Fritz																											
1917	LaGrange	GAL	10	32	2	4	1	0	0		5			0.125	OF	16	3	0	1.000								
1920	Carrollton	GSL	<10												OF												
Summit, ---																											
1920	Lindale	GSL		158	21	48								0.304													
Super, Joseph "Joe"		BL TR																									
1952	Brunswick	GFL	29	38	8	8	0	0	0	1	0	7	8	0.211	P	10	16	3	0.897	18	3	5	5.44	81	99	45	49
1952	Fitzgerald	GSL	17	37	8	5	0	0	0	2	0	7	8	0.135	P	1	10	2	0.846	15	6	5	3.13	95	98	60	29
Suplizio, Samuel "Sam"		BR TR																									
1958	Thomasville	GFL	38	88	14	28	2	0	2	11	1	20	7	0.318	M, OF, P	59	1	0	1.000	2	0	0		<30			
Suratt, Clyde																											
1921	Carrollton	GSL	<10												P												
Suspenski, Victor "Vic"		BR TR																									
1952	Moultrie	GFL	63	193	10	32	6	0	0	14	0	19	15	0.166	C	247	34	10	0.966								
Sutfin, Harry		BR TR																									
1953	Jesup	GSL	4											0.333	P					0	0			<45			
Suto, Raymond "Ray"		BS TL																									
1957	Thomasville	GFL	6	4		0								0.000	P					6	0	1		<30			
Sutter, John																											
1939	Tallahassee	GFL	54	188	14	45	2	2	0	20	1	12	32	0.239	SS	84	123	28	0.881								
Sutter, Richard "Dick"		BR TR																									
1949	Tallahassee	GFL	19	40	0	5	0	0	0	0	1	2	13	0.125	P	0	16	2	0.889	19	3	13	5.32	110	121	71	76
Sutton, James "Jim"		BL TL																									
1948	Tallassee	GAL	18	60	8	17	1	1	3	15	4	3	10	0.283	OF	16	1	5	0.773								
Sutton, Lefty		BL TL																									
1920	Carrollton	GSL		7	1	2								0.286	P												
Svenke, ---																											
1949	Eastman	GSL	22												OF	46	0	2	0.958								
Swails, Alex																											
1936	Cordele	GFL	22	40	1	4	1	0	0	3	0			0.100	P					22	4	9	5.30	112		62	105
Swain, Harold		BR																									
1946	Moultrie	GFL	<10																								
Swain, Kurtis		BR TR																									
1949	Tifton	GSL	118	401	52	96	16	3	0	52	6	50	32	0.239	C	652	63	23	0.969								
1950	Tifton	GSL	123	428	51	109	19	2	0	43	7	53	40	0.255	C	585	69	21	0.969								
1951	Douglas	GSL	125	455	48	127	19	3	2	65	7	57	34	0.279	C	619	46	20	0.971								
1955	Tifton	GFL	12	35	4	8	1	0	0	4	2	2	5	0.229	C	59	11	2	0.972								
Swain, Lloyd		BL TL																									
1949	Vidalia-Lyons	GSL	33	54	7	16	0	0	0	4	0	4	7	0.296	P	12	22	4	0.895	39	5	6	5.86	149	122	64	109
1950	Vidalia-Lyons(12) - Dublin(13)	GSL	25	49	13	15	3	1	0	6	0	12	10	0.306	P	4	12	2	0.889	25	9	5	5.30	129	149	82	77
Swann, P.P. "Ducky"																											
1920	Carrollton	GSL		26	1	0	0	0	0	1				0.000	P												
1921	LaGrange	GSL													OF, P												
Swanson, Dale		BR TR																									
1947	Newnan(2) - Griffin(14)	GAL	16	53	4	11	1	1	0	7	5	6	11	0.208	2B	33	37	7	0.909								
Swanson, Donald R. "Don"		BL TR																									
1952	Brunswick	GFL	65	156	18	46	13	2	0	27	2	18	29	0.295	OF	56	3	4	0.937								
1953	Dublin	GSL	38	142	21	35	6	1	3	21	0	22	15	0.246	OF	57	4	2	0.968								
Swanson, Lester "Les"		BR																									
1948	Tallahassee	GFL	19	36	3	3	1	0	0	0	0	4	6	0.083													
Swanson, Phillip "Phil"		BR TR																									
1954	Tifton	GFL	11	15	2	2	0	0	0	2	0	1	7	0.133	P	1	9	3	0.769	11	3	5	7.28	47	47	34	47
1955	Vidalia	GSL	5	7		1								0.143	P					5	2	1					
Swanson, Ralph		BR TR																									
1947	Newnan(5) - Griffin(14)	GAL	19	71	11	27	4	5	0	7	2	9	8	0.380	SS	39	45	14	0.857								
Sweat, J. LeRoy		BR																									
1951	Douglas(12) - Haz-Bax(4)	GSL	16	50	10	15	2	1	0	7	1	10	8	0.300													
Sweatt, William Howard "Bill"		BR TR																									
1946	LaGrange	GAL	3												P					3	0	0	0.00	6			
1950	Newnan	GAL	20	56	8	17	2	2	0	10	0	1	4	0.304	P	2	19	2	0.913	20	7	10	3.88	146	122	147	103
Sweet, J. Harold		BR TR																									
1953	Vidalia	GSL	23	68	9	16	4	2	0	3	0	4	9	0.235	C	46	4	1	0.980								
Swertfager, Frederick "Fred"		BR TR																									
1957	Valdosta	GFL	7	12		1								0.083	P					7	4	2	2.50	36	24	24	23

Georgia Class-D Minor League Baseball Encyclopedia

YR	TEAM	LG	G	AB	R	H	2B	3B	HR	RBI	SB	BB	SO	BA	POS	PO	A	E	FA	GP	W	L	ERA	IP	H	SO	BB
Swidorski, Donald "Don"		BL TL																									
1952	Jesup	GSL	11	29	3	1	0	0	0	1	0	1	14	0.034	P	4	12	2	0.889	10	1	5	3.57	58	62	35	27
Swift, ---																											
1928	Gadsden - Talladega	GAL	35	90	9	18	4	0	3		0	5	18	0.200	P	7	35	0	1.000	23	9	7	4.77	166	215	57	37
Swift, Fred		BR TR																									
1940	Moultrie	GFL	<10												P					8	0	1	4.50	34	48	19	15
Swigler, Norman "Norm"		BR TR																									
1948	Valley	GAL	27	91	12	18	0	1	0	5	2	29	19	0.198	OF	44	1	4	0.918								
Swindell, David "Dave"																											
1935	Albany	GFL	90	340	54	81	14	5	1	11		27	60	0.238	OF	129	6	7	0.951								
Swindle, James "Jim"		BR TR																									
1946	Valdosta	GFL	36	133	18	27	3	0	0	15	5	5	8	0.203	OF	55	3	4	0.935								
Swingle, Russell "Russ"		BR TR																									
1949	Moultrie	GFL	29	63	8	14	2	0	1	7	0	6	18	0.222	P	8	22	5	0.857	23	7	12	3.60	150	171	81	60
Switzer, Marion		BR																									
1940	Americus	GFL	<10																								
Swoboda, Paul		BL TR																									
1939	Thomasville	GFL	129	504	68	126	21	7	3	57	6	38	37	0.250	1B	1300	95	18	0.987								
1940	Thomasville	GFL	22	77	19	26	1	1	0	7	2	9	1	0.338	1B	164	4	4	0.977								
Swygert, Alan		BR TR																									
1946	Albany	GFL	28	87	14	27	10	0	0	10	0	4	20	0.310	OF	15	7	2	0.917								
1947	Newnan	GAL	15	56	8	15	4	1	0	5	0	1	5	0.268	OF	13	2	2	0.882								
1948	Sparta	GSL	108	428	59	145	29	4	2	88	6	24	38	0.339	1B, OF	620	16	5	0.992								
Symko, Anthony		BR TR																									
1963	Thomasville	GFL	84	272	27	51	2	0	1	16	12	17	51	0.188	3B, OF	86	47	18	0.881								
Szolwinski, Sylvester		BR TR																									
1946	Cordele	GFL	10	9	0	0	0	0	0	0	0	0	4	0.000	P	0	9	1	0.900	10	0	6	0.00	25	29	13	24
Szostak, Henry		BR TR																									
1956	Fitzgerald	GFL	35	81	8	11	1	3	0	8	0	6	31	0.136	P	9	37	6	0.885	32	13	8	3.19	186	217	119	83
Tafaro, Dan A.		BR TR																									
1947	Tallahassee	GFL	16	23	2	6	1	0	0	6	0	3	5	0.261	P	3	17	2	0.909	16	0	4	5.26	65	55	46	67
Taitt, Douglas John "Doug" "Poco"		BL TR 6'0" 176 lbs b. 08/03/1902 Bay City, MI d. 12/12/1970 Portland, OR																									
1947	Alexander City	GAL	52	94	7	20	3	1	0	12	1	16	4	0.213	M, 1B	159	11	14	0.924								
Talas, Eftimeo		BR TR																									
1950	Tallahassee	GFL	33	92	8	13	2	0	0	9	0	7	39	0.141	P	10	57	4	0.944	32	20	5	2.73	247	192	222	148
Taliaferro, Clark "Dick" "Tolly"																											
1928	Carrollton	GAL	70	306	61	120	20	8	9		8	10	33	0.392	SS	141	189	24	0.932								
Taliaferro, Raymond "Ray"		BL TL																									
1954	Valdosta	GFL	13	23	1	1	0	0	0	1	0	2	13	0.043	P	2	8	2	0.833	13	4	4	2.91	68	48	71	45
1956	Hazlehurst-Baxley	GSL	18	26	6	6	1	0	0	3	0	2	5	0.231	P	2	8	0	1.000	13	5	3	3.81	59	51	45	36
Talley, J. Samuel "Sam"		BR TR																									
1950	Rome	GAL	38	134	17	29	7	0	2	17	2	13	16	0.216	2B	65	64	8	0.942								
Tally, Bill		BR																									
1955	Sandersville	GSL	1	1		0								0.000													
Tally, Hoover		BL TL																									
1954	Statesboro	GSL	6	9		1								0.111	P					11	1	3	<45				
Tang, Antonio		BR TR																									
1952	Waycross	GFL	18	53	4	7	0	0	0	1	1	7	7	0.132	SS	23	30	4	0.930								
Tanner, J.D.		BL TL																									
1946	Thomasville	GFL	10	32	6	10	1	0	0	3	2	1	8	0.313	P					1	0	0	0.00	3			
Tanner, William "Bill"		BL TL																									
1947	Americus	GFL	33	122	22	34	3	1	0	14	1	19	24	0.279	OF	38	4	8	0.840								
Tannreuther, Charles		BL TL																									
1955	Douglas	GSL	19	34	3	3	0	0	0			4	24	0.088	P	3	12	2	0.882	19	6	5	5.76	89	92	59	58
Taranto, Anthony Christopher "Anthony"		BR TL																									
1962	Moultrie	GFL	25	11	2	1	1	0	0	1	0	4	9	0.091	P	0	3	2	0.600	25	2	3	7.27	52	61	61	59
1963	Moultrie	GFL	11	11	1	2	0	0	0	2	0	2	5	0.182	P	1	4	2	0.714	11	0	6	5.40	40	37	45	35
Tarkington, Rondle		BR TR																									
1963	Waycross	GFL	16	9	0	0	0	0	0	0	0	0	5	0.000	P	3	2	0	1.000	16	0	3	2.68	37	34	39	23
Tarolli, Louis "Lou"		BL TL																									
1949	Tallahassee	GFL	10	9	0	1	0	0	0	1	0	0	4	0.111	P	1	3	1	0.800								
Tarvin, Arthur "Art"		BR TR																									
1946	Opelika	GAL	2												P					2	0	1	0.00	8	8	3	7
Tarzi, ---																											
1942	Tallahassee	GFL	7	26	0	3	0	0	2		0	2	10	0.115	2B	12	11	1	0.958								
Tasker, John		BL TL																									
1956	Hazlehurst-Baxley	GSL	39	122	26	34	8	6	1	25	4	41	28	0.279	1B	290	23	7	0.978								
1957	Valdosta	GFL	66	224	54	57	6	2	3	34	8	65	41	0.254	1B	523	44	10	0.983								
Tate, J.R.																											
1929	Carrollton	GAL		214	28	53								0.248	2B												
1929	Cedartown	GAL	95	353	46	93	15	8	6		7	27	48	0.263	SS	222	255	48	0.909								
Tattler, Henry																											
1920	Cedartown	GSL													C, OF												
1921	Cedartown	GSL		43	6	13								0.302	C, OF												

403

Georgia Class-D Minor League Baseball Encyclopedia

YR	TEAM	LG	G	AB	R	H	2B	3B	HR	RBI	SB	BB	SO	BA	POS	PO	A	E	FA	GP	W	L	ERA	IP	H	SO	BB
Tauscher, Walter Edward "Walt"		BR TR 6'1" 186 lbs b. 11/22/1901 LaSalle, IL d. 11/27/1992 Winter Park, FL																									
1950	Tallahassee	GFL													M												
Taussig, Donald Franklin "Don"		BR TR 6'0" 180 lbs b. 02/19/1932 New York, NY																									
1950	LaGrange	GAL	<10																								
Taylor, ---																											
1914	Selma - Rome	GAL	75	345	57	83					22			0.241	C	497	120	7	0.989								
1915	Valdosta	FLAG	64	306	14	31	5	0	0		2			0.101	C	297	103	8	0.980								
1917	Rome-Lindale	GAL	9	36	3	7	3	1	0		0			0.194	C	40	8	1	0.980								
Taylor, A.																											
1914	Rome	GAL	24	94	8	20					2			0.213	SS	33	24	4	0.934								
Taylor, D.																											
1939	Cordele	GFL													P									<45			
Taylor, Donald R. "Don"		BR TR																									
1947	Valdosta	GFL	31	109	10	25	6	1	0	14	1	11	30	0.229	OF	61	3	5	0.928								
Taylor, Edwin "Ed"		0																									
1938	Thomasville	GFL	48	179	35	48	11	5	0	23	2	26	26	0.268	SS	110	148	40	0.866								
Taylor, Eugene "Gene"		BR																									
1941	Cordele	GFL	29	59	4	4	0	0	0	1	0	4	25	0.068	P	4	28	6	0.842	26	7	15	4.33	158	174	106	83
1957	Waycross	GFL	6	10		1								0.100													
Taylor, Furman E.		BR TR																									
1942	Valdosta	GFL	13	41	10	14	1	1	0	8	0	7	7	0.341	P	3	16	2	0.905	12	5	6	4.22	96	125	43	33
1946	Moultrie	GFL	66	166	22	45	4	2	0	21	1	23	14	0.271	OF, P	36	44	1	0.988	30	13	6	2.66	176	157	112	63
Taylor, H. Ford		BR TR																									
1953	Douglas	GSL	68	262	56	72	8	0	3	48	8	59	21	0.275	3B, SS	104	160	10	0.964								
Taylor, Harry																											
1938	Tallahassee	GFL													P					0	0		<45				
Taylor, Hugh "Q.P."																											
1942	Dothan	GFL	112	374	58	98	12	8	0	53	4	79	38	0.262	C	616	70	22	0.969								
Taylor, J.W. "Bill"																											
1921	Carrollton	GSL		285	37	77								0.270	3B												
Taylor, James E. "Jim"		BL TL																									
1953	Valdosta	GFL	14	43	5	7	2	1	0	7	0	5	9	0.163	OF	15	3	1	0.947								
Taylor, John N.		BR TR																									
1948	Tallassee	GAL	19	26	3	1	0	0	0	1	0	1	8	0.038	P	4	17	0	1.000	17	4	5	5.09	76	46	49	89
1948	Albany	GFL	10	10	2	3	0	0	0	2	0	1	3	0.300													
1949	Sparta	GSL	<10												P								<45				
Taylor, Jose		BR																									
1962	Brunswick	GFL	3	8	1	0	0	0	0	0	0	1	3	0.000													
Taylor, Robert L. "Bob"		BR TR																									
1949	Moultrie	GFL	14	21	4	1	0	0	0	0	0	6	15	0.048	P	1	14	2	0.882	14	1	10	5.29	85	96	20	39
Taylor, Robert W. "Bob"																											
1939	Thomasville	GFL	14	43	6	11	3	0	0	5	0	2	5	0.256	C	42	9	2	0.962								
Taylor, Royce Raymond "Ray"		BL TR 5'9" 152 lbs b. 01/10/1915 Newark, TX																									
1937	Tallahassee	GFL	90	334	46	85	9	11	2	23	9	43	51	0.254	OF	168	32	13	0.939								
Taylor, Spafford		BR TR																									
1949	Newnan	GAL	89	270	43	60	7	1	0	32	6	55	55	0.222	OF	129	5	9	0.937								
Taylor, William "Bill"		BR TR																									
1936	Cordele	GFL	90	344	62	98	14	6	3	35	4			0.285	C	393	82	15	0.969								
1937	Cordele	GFL	123	481	71	133	15	4	4	73	8	55	21	0.277	C	696	88	17	0.979								
1938	Cordele	GFL	115	462	61	140	19	2	0	54	4	42	17	0.303	C	543	87	24	0.963								
1940	Cordele	GFL	90	358	52	98	18	0	0	38	5	23	13	0.274	M, C	362	50	6	0.986								
Taylor, Zachery																											
1930	Carrollton	GAL	55	193	35	68	14	4	4		4	16	15	0.352	C	211	35	7	0.972								
Teague, John																											
1939	Tallahassee	GFL	69	184	15	38	4	1	0	19	0	14	34	0.207	UT, P	68	46	7	0.942	27	6	13	3.89	155	144	82	103
Teal, Harry		BR TR																									
1946	Waycross	GFL	65	239	27	59	12	3	2	37	2	21	41	0.247	1B	524	32	19	0.967								
Teater, Rollie		BR TR																									
1949	Tallassee	GAL	54	150	18	28	4	0	0	15	2	21	23	0.187	C	198	24	3	0.987								
Tefft, Albert "Al"		BR TR																									
1948	Tallassee	GAL	14	47	4	11	1	0	0	1	0	3	6	0.234	3B	22	14	10	0.783								
Tefft, Charles		BR TR																									
1940	Albany	GFL	75	322	50	92	17	3	0	35	10	21	28	0.286	OF	150	8	9	0.946								
Teichert, Robert "Bob"		BR TL																									
1948	Fitzgerald	GSL	28	57	1	3	1	0	0	1	0	3	23	0.053	P	3	29	6	0.842	28	6	11	3.75	163	147	83	86
1949	Fitzgerald	GSL	16	34	2	9	0	0	0	2	0	1	13	0.265	P	2	20	2	0.917	16	0	8	6.65	88	73	47	59
Telford, Dave		BR TR																									
1946	Tallahassee	GFL	28	70	9	10	0	2	0	8	1	3	30	0.143	P	8	29	3	0.925	28	12	7	3.42	187	186	124	78
Teliszewski, Bernard		BR																									
1957	Thomasville	GFL	9	26		4								0.154													
Telkan, ---																											
1914	Brunswick - Thomasville	GSL		49	9	16	0	2	1		1			0.327													
Tennant, Malcolm "Mal"																											
1939	Americus	GFL	17	47	5	14	2	0	0	9	0	8	4	0.298	C	88	9	5	0.951								

Georgia Class-D Minor League Baseball Encyclopedia

YR	TEAM	LG	G	AB	R	H	2B	3B	HR	RBI	SB	BB	SO	BA	POS	PO	A	E	FA	GP	W	L	ERA	IP	H	SO	BB
Tenney, James "Jim"		BR TR																									
1949	Newnan	GAL	18	27	5	4	0	0	0	0	0	8	2	0.148	P	2	15	2	0.895	18	4	5	3.64	94	87	47	51
1950	Newnan	GAL	27	45	6	6	1	0	0	3	0	8	7	0.133	P	2	17	0	1.000	26	5	10	6.05	125	142	66	78
1951	Dublin(3) - Fitzgerald(22)	GSL	25	55	4	5	0	0	0	3	0	8	13	0.091	P	8	19	2	0.931	23	6	9	4.50	130	158	48	57
Tepedino, Frank A.		BR TR																									
1952	Vidalia	GSL	116	432	97	131	21	5	2	67	13	109	26	0.303	SS	256	369	37	0.944								
1953	Vidalia(34) - Statesboro(85)	GSL	119	435	95	123	22	9	9	86	23	92	26	0.283	3B, SS	195	359	29	0.950								
Terrell, Thurman		BR TR																									
1949	Tifton	GSL	14	33	6	8	1	1	0	2	0	5	4	0.242	P	4	8	0	1.000	18	8	6	4.64	99	67	42	67
1950	Newnan	GAL	20	43	6	7	0	0	0	8	0	6	8	0.163	P	8	11	3	0.864	18	6	5	6.31	87	109	52	70
Terry, Horace		BR																									
1946	Carrollton	GAL	<10																								
Terry, William Harold "Bill"		BL TL 6'1" 200 lbs b. 10/30/1898 Atlanta, GA d. 01/09/1989 Jacksonville, FL																									
1915	Dothan	FLAG	<10												P					0							
1915	Newnan	GAL	8												P	2	11	0	1.000	8	7	1					
1916	Newnan	GAL	33	84	15	20				3				0.238	P												
Terwedow, Donald "Don"		BR TR																									
1952	Valdosta	GFL	39	81	9	21	3	2	0	12	0	8	22	0.259	P	5	36	5	0.891	29	14	12	2.89	199	157	109	142
Tesmer, Warren		BS TR																									
1958	Brunswick	GFL	32	119	30	34	6	1	3	15	1	26	19	0.286	3B, OF	63	30	15	0.861								
Tessier, Lawrence		BR TR																									
1948	Thomasville	GFL	35	63	9	9	4	0	0	0	0	5	24	0.143	P	6	29	5	0.875	28	7	8	4.46	115	117	87	109
Tessin, Elmer		BR TR																									
1950	Moultrie	GFL	35	84	10	19	1	1	0	9	0	13	13	0.226	P	6	46	2	0.963	34	16	8	3.97	231	215	139	94
Texanne, Russell "Russ"		BR TR																									
1940	Cordele	GFL	11	31	3	5	1	0	0	4	0	0	2	0.161	P					10	3	6	4.94	62	73	22	30
Teyema, David "Dave"		BR TR																									
1947	Alexander City	GAL	113	421	64	127	27	9	11	65	10	34	62	0.302	SS, OF	236	143	45	0.894								
Thackston, John		BR TR																									
1955	Tifton	GFL	2	0										0.000	P					2	0	1		<45			
Thaxton, Kent		BR TL																									
1962	Moultrie	GFL	13	15	0	2	0	0	0	3	0	0	6	0.133	P	2	1	2	0.600	11	1	5	6.07	43	45	34	43
1963	Moultrie	GFL	30	52	6	16	1	0	1	8	0	0	8	0.308	P	8	18	2	0.929	24	7	7	3.09	131	119	111	53
Then, Jose (Williams)		BR TR																									
1963	Waycross	GFL	6	2	0	0	0	0	0	0	0	1	1	0.000	P					6	2	2	8.10	10	14	11	1
Thode, Neil E.		BR TR																									
1953	Valdosta	GFL	18	31	1	5	3	0	0	4	0	2	10	0.161	P	7	13	2	0.909	18	3	7	4.55	87	94	51	55
Thoele, Walter "Walt"		BR TR																									
1962	Thomasville	GFL	24	59	16	14	1	0	0	5	4	19	14	0.237	SS	26	29	4	0.932								
1963	Thomasville	GFL	116	373	46	78	10	5	1	33	6	73	112	0.209	SS	168	258	44	0.906								
Thomas, ---																											
1914	Selma	GAL	35	241	12	36				5				0.149	OF	57	3	3	0.952								
Thomas, ---																											
1930	Huntsville	GAL	7												P					7	1	2	6.75	28	40	3	8
Thomas, Clarence W.																											
1936	Moultrie	GFL	45	152	36	36	8	3	4	15	5			0.237	OF	114	6	6	0.952								
Thomas, Dallas Glenn		BL TL																									
1946	Carrollton	GAL	16	63	14	16	2	1	0	9	0	8	11	0.254	OF	31	2	2	0.943								
1947	Carrollton	GAL	107	416	79	118	24	5	11	72	14	53	107	0.284	OF	206	12	18	0.924								
Thomas, Donald D. "Don"		BR TR																									
1954	Hazlehurst-Baxley	GSL	4	1		1								1.000	P					4	0	2		<45			
Thomas, Francis		BR TR																									
1957	Albany	GFL	9	6		2								0.333	P					8	0	2		<30			
Thomas, Frank Joseph "Frank"		BR TR 6'3" 205 lbs b. 06/11/1929 Pittsburgh, PA																									
1948	Tallahassee	GFL	138	596	106	176	39	8	14	132	6	37	87	0.295	OF	247	20	12	0.957								
1949	Tallahassee	GFL	74	285	46	93	19	2	10	63	2	19	39	0.326	OF	162	15	2	0.989								
Thomas, Franklin "Frank"		BR TR																									
1963	Moultrie	GFL	31	60	2	16	2	0	1	10	0	1	20	0.267	P	4	34	3	0.927	24	10	7	2.27	143	130	133	42
Thomas, George		BL TR																									
1942	Americus	GFL	14	44	6	8	2	0	0	4	1	11	11	0.182	OF	24	3	4	0.871								
1954	Albany	GFL	52	179	34	51	6	6	2	25	11	23	44	0.285	OF	50	5	7	0.887								
Thomas, Gordon		BR TR																									
1954	Valdosta	GFL	20	49	3	8	1	0	0	7	1	8	15	0.163	1B	129	4	3	0.978								
Thomas, Jim P.																											
1942	Valdosta	GFL	10	37	7	14	0	2	0	7	0	2	3	0.378	OF	11	3	3	0.824								
Thomas, Parks E.		BL TL																									
1949	Newnan	GAL	26	70	10	19	2	0	0	4	0	5	11	0.271	P	6	35	4	0.911	26	12	8	2.59	167	141	112	84
1950	Newnan	GAL	10	29	1	3	0	0	0	0	0	4	7	0.103	P	2	17	1	0.950	10	5	4	3.51	77	80	53	40
1950	Dublin	GSL	18	48	2	7	1	0	0	5	0	4	10	0.146	P	3	25	3	0.903	18	8	5	3.53	125	99	89	87
Thomas, Robert "Bob"		BR TR																									
1954	Americus-Cordele	GFL	22	64	9	10	2	0	0	7	1	14	22	0.156	3B	14	23	2	0.949								
Thomas, Wilbert		BL TR																									
1950	Douglas	GSL	27	44	7	7	0	0	0	2	0	7	14	0.159	P	6	14	2	0.909	27	9	8	3.81	144	142	60	68
1953	Douglas	GSL	2											0.000	P					0	0		<45				
Thomas, William "Bill"		BR TR																									
1957	Waycross	GFL	67	250	50	69	14	2	6	36	15	56	29	0.276	3B, P	64	143	13	0.941	2	0	0		<30			

Georgia Class-D Minor League Baseball Encyclopedia

YR	TEAM	LG	G	AB	R	H	2B	3B	HR	RBI	SB	BB	SO	BA	POS	PO	A	E	FA	GP	W	L	ERA	IP	H	SO	BB
Thomason, Harold		BL TL																									
1940	Waycross - Valdosta	GFL	11	18	0	5	0	0	0	1	0	0	2	0.278	P					10	2	4	4.41	49	54	15	22
Thomassie, Pershing "Pete"		BL TL																									
1939	Waycross	GFL	135	542	107	171	25	9	1	68	33	42	30	0.315	OF	290	21	15	0.954								
1940	Waycross	GFL	139	570	112	193	31	13	4	91	34	37	21	0.339	OF	361	32	37	0.914								
1949	Waycross	GFL	23	97	17	21	3	0	0	18	3	7	5	0.216	OF	35	3	1	0.974								
Thompson, ---																											
1916	LaGrange	GAL	18	51	5	12					0			0.235	P												
1917	Talladega	GAL	4	10	0	2	0	0	0		0			0.200	P	1	8	0	1.000	4	3	0		27	29	10	6
Thompson, Emery		BR TR																									
1946	Albany	GFL	29	84	16	18	2	0	0	17	2	18	11	0.214	OF, C	72	9	4	0.953								
Thompson, J.B.																											
1949	Sparta - Hazlehurst-Baxley	GSL	10	24	3	2	0	0	0	4	0	2	2	0.083	P	4	11	1	0.938	10	1	4	3.75	48	25	13	16
Thompson, James "Jim"		BL TL																									
1955	Douglas	GSL	3	0										0.000	P					3	0	0					
Thompson, James C. "Jim"		BR TR																									
1949	Carrollton	GAL	19	73	10	16	4	2	2	13	0	5	22	0.219	OF	29	2	1	0.969								
1950	Valley	GAL	104	396	67	113	26	8	3	56	14	43	59	0.285	OF	164	7	11	0.940								
1951	Valley	GAL	115	442	68	120	18	4	4	67	17	45	65	0.271	OF	200	13	9	0.959								
Thompson, Jessie		BR TR																									
1956	Tifton	GFL	34	114	11	24	3	0	0	3	1	8	35	0.211	OF	36	2	1	0.974								
Thompson, John "Jack"		BR TR																									
1946	Opelika	GAL	127	487	81	141	17	9	8	77	12	26	26	0.290	OF, P	305	15	16	0.952	1	0	0	0.00	2			
Thompson, Lafayette Fresco "Fresco"		BR TR 5'8" 150 lbs b. 06/06/1902 Centreville, AL d. 11/20/1968 Fullerton, CA																										
1939	Waycross	GFL	84	304	29	95	17	5	0	52	2	25	33	0.313	1B	662	47	10	0.986								
Thompson, Leo																											
1939	Cordele	GFL	27	103	16	29	4	0	0	12	0	5	7	0.282	C	85	9	6	0.940								
Thompson, Leon C.																											
1941	Waycross	GFL	10	37	2	6	0	0	0	2	0	4	10	0.162	1B	80	8	1	0.989								
Thompson, Leroy		BR TR																									
1950	Americus	GFL	17	34	6	5	0	0	0	0	0	2	15	0.147	P	4	11	2	0.882	17	6	6	5.65	86	110	49	57
Thompson, R.L.																											
1928	Anniston	GAL	68	248	47	79	13	7	5		6	29	35	0.319	OF	127	5	1	0.992								
1929	Cedartown	GAL	79	298	49	93	13	6	9		3	34	23	0.312	OF	154	13	3	0.982								
1930	Talladega	GAL	64	252	58	88	18	3	7		9	37	21	0.349	OF	127	9	2	0.986								
Thompson, Richard "Dick"		BR TR																									
1949	Alexander City	GAL	46	95	15	19	2	0	1	8	0	8	22	0.200	P	8	22	5	0.857	35	14	6	2.72	195	167	134	96
Thompson, Robert "Bob"		BR TR																									
1947	Albany	GFL	62	194	15	36	5	2	0	16	1	12	56	0.186	C	308	50	4	0.989								
Thompson, Robert Herman "Herman"		BL																									
1950	Eastman	GSL	11	39	6	7	1	2	0	6	1	8	3	0.179													
Thompson, William																											
1928	Cedartown	GAL	69	299	54	90	19	2	4		7	27	22	0.301	2B, OF	157	38	7	0.965								
Thompson, William C. "Bill"		BR TR																									
1955	Albany	GFL	121	384	42	101	18	4	6	68	4	64	53	0.263	C	713	48	14	0.982								
Thompson, William Erskine "Erskine"																											
1930	Carrollton - Huntsville	GAL	28	103	7	28	2	0	0		1	3	12	0.272	M, C	99	13	5	0.957								
Thompson, William K. "Bill"		BL TL																									
1953	Fitzgerald	GFL	55	194	39	54	10	3	13	42	5	30	51	0.278	1B, OF, P	159	10	10	0.944		0	2	<45				
1954	Fitzgerald	GFL	139	554	86	164	33	6	16	131	21	63	49	0.296	1B	1105	82	14	0.988								
Thorn, George		BR TR																									
1946	Albany	GFL	2												P					2	0	1	0.00	4	8	1	4
Thorne, Joe																											
1937	Albany	GFL	7												P					7	1	5	5.00	45	41	23	35
Thornell, John "Bob"		BR TR																									
1954	Hazlehurst-Baxley	GSL	36	107	19	22	5	1	2	18	1	17	26	0.206	C	189	10	7	0.966								
Thorpe, ---																											
1930	Talladega	GAL	38	132	19	41	3	2	2		0	19	16	0.311	3B	36	59	7	0.931								
Thorpe, Jack		BS TR																									
1952	Moultrie	GFL	29	99	17	27	4	0	0	10	4	28	25	0.273	2B	46	63	20	0.845								
Thrasher, ---																											
1914	Cordele	GSL		102	22	42	4	3	0		7			0.412													
Thrasher, Clifford "Cliff" "Red"		BR TR																									
1952	Statesboro	GSL	53	196	29	50	6	0	6	35	2	30	24	0.255	C	256	36	6	0.980								
1953	Statesboro	GSL	122	465	64	121	28	4	6	91	10	50	43	0.260	M, C, P	605	70	17	0.975		2	3	<45				
1954	Statesboro	GSL	118	448	66	134	19	4	10	79	9	48	41	0.299	OF, C, P	638	52	22	0.969	9	2	3	5.43	58	71	25	18
Thrasher, George																											
1920	LaGrange	GSL		258	32	78								0.302	OF, 2B												
1921	LaGrange	GSL		262	44	101								0.385	OF												
Thrasher, Ike																											
1920	LaGrange	GSL													3B, OF												
1929	Cedartown	GAL	43	152	25	43	5	0	3		4	14	3	0.283	M												
Thrasher, Lewis "Lew"																											
1935	Tallahassee	GFL	13	36	5	4	1	0	0		0	1	10	0.111	P					14	6	5		94	83	45	21
1936	Tallahassee	GFL	12	28	0	2	0	0	0	0	0			0.071	P					12	6	4	2.96	73		23	33

Georgia Class-D Minor League Baseball Encyclopedia

YR	TEAM	LG	G	AB	R	H	2B	3B	HR	RBI	SB	BB	SO	BA	POS	PO	A	E	FA	GP	W	L	ERA	IP	H	SO	BB
Thrasher, Loren																											
1921	Griffin	GSL		253	37	93								0.368	OF												
Thrift, Snyder "Syd"		BL TL																									
1949	LaGrange	GAL	52	157	28	48	4	0	4	27	0	32	25	0.306	1B, P	293	11	10	0.968	8	4	2	3.67	49	44	34	36
Thurman, Clarence		BR TR																									
1957	Thomasville	GFL	5	2		0								0.000	P					5	0	0	<30				
Tice, ---																											
1930	Talladega	GAL	21	55	4	6	2	0	0		1	1	17	0.109	P	4	25	0	1.000	19	4	9	6.69	121	172	39	38
Tice, Paul																											
1936	Cordele	GFL	31	122	21	38	3	2	0	10	8			0.311	OF	53	1	4	0.931								
1937	Cordele	GFL	120	516	90	148	17	6	1	58	16	39	51	0.287	OF	257	12	17	0.941								
Tideman, ---																											
1906	Valdosta	GSL													OF												
Tidwell, Bruce		BL TL																									
1954	Statesboro	GSL	11	11	1	3	0	0	0	2	0	1	4	0.273	P	0	1	1	0.500								
Tidwell, John "Little John"		BR TR 6'1" 180 lbs b. 08/01/1928 Fairfax, AL																									
1949	Carrollton	GAL	39	136	22	43	7	2	5	32	7	15	15	0.316	OF	61	3	3	0.955								
1950	Dublin	GSL	136	579	122	178	39	6	21	114	13	45	45	0.307	OF	245	18	12	0.956								
1951	Tifton	GFL	98	393	56	126	34	4	6	92	6	39	17	0.321	OF	209	23	11	0.955								
1951	Dublin	GSL	27	115	27	35	7	4	3	17	5	11	6	0.304	OF	43	2	2	0.957								
Tidwell, W. Donovan "Don"		BL TL																									
1954	Statesboro	GSL	28	47	4	8	1	0	0	1	0	1	16	0.170	P	1	14	2	0.882	25	4	8	6.44	109	142	58	69
1955	Waycross		36	53	4	12	0	0	0	1	1	8	14	0.226	P	3	26	2	0.935	35	10	9	3.65	158	159	104	71
Tiefenauer, Bobby Gene "Bobby"		BR TR 6'2" 185 lbs b. 10/10/1929 Desloge, MO																									
1948	Tallassee	GAL													P						3	2	4.40				
1949	Tallassee	GAL	38	85	7	17	2	0	0	6	1	7	18	0.200	P	17	41	4	0.935	28	17	6	2.27	206	161	106	73
Tieken, Virgil		BR TR																									
1954	Waycross		56	186	19	39	3	0	0	19	4	16	24	0.210	3B, C	128	57	17	0.916								
Tiemann, Jerome "Jerry"																											
1942	Americus	GFL	121	431	65	136	24	2	0	77	4	55	5	0.316	M, 1B	1080	69	10	0.991								
Tierce, Joel																											
1936	Moultrie	GFL	107	421	61	116	16	3	4	55	13			0.276	SS	174	318	39	0.927								
1938	Moultrie	GFL	112	439	67	127	16	4	0	45	23	46	45	0.289	3B	237	223	49	0.904								
Tierney, Thomas "Tom"		BR TR																									
1958	Waycross	GFL	63	226	37	59	11	1	3	23	3	38	29	0.261	OF	82	5	2	0.978								
Tillery, Thomas "Tom"		BR																									
1946	Valley	GAL	<10																								
Tilley, Terry		BR																									
1954	Fitzgerald	GFL	9	23		4								0.174													
1955	Moultrie	GFL	9	12		1								0.083													
Tilley, Travis		BL TR																									
1947	LaGrange(22) - Carrollton (6)	GAL	28	90	12	22	3	4	0	7	1	9	10	0.244	OF	40	4	4	0.917								
Timberlake, J. Raymond "Ray"		BR TR																									
1951	Hazlehurst-Baxley	GSL	107	418	47	105	10	2	0	35	16	59	66	0.251	OF	266	10	25	0.917								
1952	Douglas	GSL	74	297	52	80	4	3	0	17	11	40	39	0.269	OF	125	5	9	0.935								
1953	Waycross	GFL	8											0.083													
1953	Douglas	GSL	99	401	79	121	5	5	0	57	17	61	32	0.302	OF	224	8	22	0.913								
Tingle, Thomas T. "Tom"		BL TR																									
1952	Vidalia	GSL	17	49	14	11	2	0	0	6	1	10	5	0.224	SS	21	38	10	0.855								
1955	Vidalia	GSL	110	392	72	119	20	5	5	55	13	79	47	0.304	SS, OF	170	112	36	0.887								
1956	Vidalia	GSL	79	262	56	70	14	7	1	29	10	86	36	0.267	3B, OF	109	53	7	0.959								
Tinsley, Arthur "Art"		BR TR																									
1955	Cordele	GFL	17	42	0	2	0	0	0	2	0	1	20	0.048	P	2	14	2	0.889	17	8	8	3.28	118	122	58	47
1956	Thomson	GSL	7	9		0								0.000	P					7	1	2					
Tippett, Frank		BR TR																									
1954	Sandersville	GSL	13	40	5	6	1	0	0	1	0	1	13	0.150	P	6	13	3	0.864	13	4	6	4.65	93	118	29	38
Tipton, William "Bill"		BR																									
1953	Statesboro	GSL	2											0.000													
Tisdale, ---																											
1914	Anniston	GAL	75	290	37	81					13			0.279	C	221	30	12	0.954								
Tisdale, J. William "Bill"		BR TR																									
1950	Opelika	GAL	14	47	6	5	1	0	0	5	0	9	8	0.106	OF	27	3	1	0.968								
Tison, ---																											
1906	Americus	GSL													OF												
Tittl, Robert "Bob"		BL TL																									
1956	Tifton	GFL	9	13		3								0.231	P					9	3	3	<45				
Titus, Lee		BR TR																									
1953	Dublin	GSL	12	12	0	0	0	0	0	1	0	3	3	0.000	P	3	11	0	1.000		2	3	<45				
Todtenhausen, Arthur "Art"		BR TR																									
1963	Thomasville	GFL	10	20	1	0	0	0	0	0	0	4	15	0.000	P	2	13	0	1.000	10	5	1	3.00	60	56	54	36
Tolbert, ---		BR TR																									
1946	Opelika	GAL	1												P					1	0	0	0.00	1			

Georgia Class-D Minor League Baseball Encyclopedia

YR	TEAM	LG	G	AB	R	H	2B	3B	HR	RBI	SB	BB	SO	BA	POS	PO	A	E	FA	GP	W	L	ERA	IP	H	SO	BB
Tolbert, C.																											
1915	Rome	GAL	59	221	30	64	16	0	3					0.290	OF	82	7	7	0.927								
1916	Rome	GAL	67	256	40	75					9			0.293	OF												
1917	Rome-Lindale	GAL	17	65	17	21	2	2	1		5			0.323	OF	31	3	6	0.850								
1920	Cedartown	GSL		170	40	51								0.300	OF												
Tomasello, Theron																											
1935	Americus	GFL	19	45	5	11	2	1	0		2	4	12	0.244	P					10	3	2		51	64	28	28
Tomasic, George		BR TR																									
1949	Griffin	GAL	32	50	6	10	0	0	0	0	0	8	20	0.200	P	14	25	3	0.929	32	11	12	3.74	159	156	79	89
Tomek (Tometchko), Joseph "Joe"		BR TR																									
1948	Douglas	GSL	76	274	19	56	3	5	2	22	3	23	66	0.204	2B, C	235	123	35	0.911								
Tomkinson, Philip "Phil"		BR TR																									
1947	Valdosta	GFL	78	278	37	96	13	8	1	39	5	16	41	0.345	C	380	61	18	0.961								
Tomlin, Edgar "Ed"		BR																									
1946	Valley	GAL	<10																								
Tomter, Harvey		BL TR																									
1954	Americus-Cordele	GFL	36	78	6	14	2	0	0	4	0	7	33	0.179	P	4	37	4	0.911	34	6	17	5.00	205	197	115	130
Tond, Louis "Lou"		BR TR																									
1949	Tallahassee	GFL	10	24	2	6	0	0	0	2	0	1	7	0.250	P	1	18	0	1.000	11	5	3	3.44	81	83	35	9
Tone, Lawrence																											
1938	Americus	GFL	50	177	24	50	5	8	2	27	1	13	23	0.282	OF	107	5	5	0.957								
Torppey, Kevin		BR TR																									
1963	Moultrie	GFL	8	6	0	0	0	0	0	0	0	0	5	0.000	P					8	3	3	4.26	19	17	19	16
Torres, Don Gilberto (Nunez) "Gil"		BR TR 6'0" 155 lbs b. 08/23/1915 Regla, Cuba d. 01/10/1983 Regla, Cuba																									
1953	Valdosta	GFL	46	142	21	42	8	0	3	26	3	24	9	0.296	M, 1B, 2B, P	125	56	5	0.973	14	4	5	3.15	60	55	29	10
Torres, Edward "Ed"		BS TR																									
1954	Tifton	GFL	23	77	8	18	4	0	0	6	4	14	14	0.234	SS	35	34	10	0.873								
1954	Hazlehurst-Baxley	GSL	24	91	9	24	4	1	1	9	2	15	32	0.264	3B	13	32	8	0.849								
Torres, Felix (Sanchrez) "Felix"		BR TR 5'11" 165 lbs b. 05/01/1932 Ponce, PR																									
1955	Douglas	GSL	108	446	101	127	36	4	17	88	9	49	71	0.285	SS	253	319	54	0.914								
Torres, Gerardo "Guerry"		BR TR																									
1956	Brunswick	GFL	17	39	2	3	1	0	0	0	0	3	13	0.077	P	2	21	1	0.958	14	7	5	1.80	110	78	84	57
Torres, Miguel (Laza)		BR TR																									
1962	Moultrie	GFL	47	163	19	29	4	2	0	18	4	28	24	0.178	SS	46	82	21	0.859								
Torres, Victor M.		BR TR																									
1963	Brunswick	GFL	49	189	31	59	8	1	2	42	3	15	10	0.312	SS	58	135	13	0.937								
Towich, Thomas "Tom"		BR TR																									
1955	Albany	GFL	1	1		0								0.000	P					1	0	0		<45			
Townley, David "Dave"		BR																									
1955	Waycross	GFL	9	19		0								0.000													
Towns, James "Jim"		BL TR																									
1946	LaGrange	GAL	99	380	84	116	14	1	4	45	24	42	15	0.305	SS	164	256	46	0.901								
Townsend, ---																											
1914	Talladega	GAL	10												OF	8	1	1	0.900								
Townsend, Arnold																											
1921	Griffin	GSL		144	39	50								0.347	C												
Townsend, Art																											
1935	Thomasville	GFL	45	152	19	32	4	1	1		4	20	20	0.211													
Townsend, Charles		BR TR																									
1957	Waycross	GFL	6	6		0								0.000	P					6	1	0		<30			
1958	Waycross	GFL	9	13		1								0.077	P					9	2	4	4.21	47	44	37	22
Tracewski, Richard Joseph "Dick"		BR TR 5'11" 167 lbs b. 02/03/1935 Eynon, PA																									
1954	Thomasville	GFL	72	274	36	76	7	4	3	32	3	26	41	0.277	SS	138	191	28	0.922								
Tracy, James L. "Jim"		BR TR																									
1948	Americus	GFL	30	61	6	13	2	0	1	10	6	4	15	0.213	P	9	29	3	0.927	28	6	11	5.64	150	203	60	71
1949	Americus	GFL	36	89	11	14	2	0	0	8	0	6	30	0.157	P	4	46	3	0.943	36	16	11	2.91	238	237	130	83
Tracy, William R. Jr. "Bill"																											
1942	Waycross	GFL	59	175	18	41	9	2	0	24	1	6	21	0.234	C	165	17	9	0.953								
Trainor, Bernard																											
1935	Thomasville	GFL	18	46	2	8	2	0	0		0	3	19	0.174	P					19	7	6		105	114	33	26
1936	Moultrie	GFL	30	60	2	10	1	0	0	4	0			0.167	P					30	8	11	5.34	155		45	52
Trammel, Thomas "Tom"		BR TL																									
1956	Valdosta	GFL	2	2		0								0.000	P					2	0	0		<45			
Trammell, Wesley "Wes"		0																									
1942	Tallahassee	GFL	122	478	61	131	19	4	1	46	3	53	56	0.274	SS	211	287	51	0.907								
Trapasso, Lawrence		BR TR																									
1953	Vidalia	GSL	5											0.250	P						0	1		<45			
Travers, Miles		BR TR																									
1958	Thomasville	GFL	4	9		0								0.000	P					4	0	3		<30			
Travers, Thomas "Tom"		BL TL																									
1947	LaGrange	GAL	12	21	0	2	0	0	0	1	0	1	13	0.095	P	2	23	4	0.862	12	1	7	4.78	64	93	24	33
1948	LaGrange	GAL	16	37	9	5	0	1	0	3	1	5	15	0.135	P	0	10	2	0.833	11	3	3	5.94	50	60	26	26
Treadway, Edgar Raymond "Ray"		BL TR 5'7" 150 lbs b. 10/31/1907 Ragland, AL d. 10/12/1935 Chattanooga, TN																									
1928	Cedartown	GAL	90	373	78	135	22	15	10		12	17	23	0.362	3B, SS	134	252	20	0.951								

Georgia Class-D Minor League Baseball Encyclopedia

YR	TEAM	LG	G	AB	R	H	2B	3B	HR	RBI	SB	BB	SO	BA	POS	PO	A	E	FA	GP	W	L	ERA	IP	H	SO	BB
Treadway, Thadford Leon "Red"		BL TR 5'10" 175 lbs b. 04/28/1920 Athlone, NC d. 05/26/1994 Atlanta, GA																									
1954	Fitzgerald	GFL	117	435	87	158	22	10	0	54	21	70	23	0.363	M, OF, P	292	18	10	0.969	8	0	0		<45			
1956	Fitzgerald	GFL	70	204	41	68	6	4	0	22	4	51	12	0.333	M, 1B, OF, P	464	35	15	0.971	7	0	0		<45			
Trew, James "Jim"		BL TR																									
1950	Moultrie	GFL	111	428	113	144	22	3	3	49	20	88	27	0.336	M, 3B, OF	175	45	8	0.965								
Tribble, ---																											
1906	Waycross	GSL													C, OF												
Trinkle, Kenneth Wayne "Ken"		BR TR 6'1" 175 lbs b. 12/15/1919 Paoli, IN d. 05/10/1976 Paoli, IN																									
1939	Thomasville	GFL	36	72	6	17	0	0	0	3	0	2	22	0.236	P	20	53	1	0.986	33	13	8	2.25	204	183	98	57
Triplett, Herman Coaker "Coaker"		BR TR 5'11" 185 lbs b. 12/18/1911 Boone, NC d. 01/30/1992 Boone, NC																									
1935	Tallahassee	GFL	102	401	74	127	25	11	3		26	37	57	0.317	OF	195	11	18	0.920								
Tripod, Jerry		BR TR																									
1950	Hazlehurst-Baxley	GSL	19	63	6	11	2	0	0	8	0	13	13	0.175	C	106	18	4	0.969								
Tripp, Robert "Bob"		BL TR																									
1948	Americus	GFL	101	422	92	126	26	13	1	53	7	80	53	0.299	1B	907	51	12	0.988								
Trojanowski, Edward "Ed"		BR TR																									
1948	Americus	GFL	96	356	72	94	13	3	2	31	25	80	54	0.264	SS	152	320	37	0.927								
1949	Americus	GFL	137	488	141	129	18	11	4	46	69	150	87	0.264	2B	399	422	25	0.970								
Trossen, Thomas F. "Tom"		BR TR																									
1954	Tifton	GFL	21	24	2	0	0	0	0	1	0	5	16	0.000	P	1	9	5	0.667	20	5	4	4.67	79	55	68	85
Trotter, William P. "Bill"		BR TR																									
1948	LaGrange	GAL	59	222	33	54	6	1	0	32	5	29	14	0.243	2B, 3B	118	140	16	0.942								
Troutman, B.K.																											
1916	Rome - Anniston	GAL	22	77	13	15					7			0.195	OF												
Troxell, Clair		BR TR																									
1951	Albany	GFL	85	253	34	59	9	3	0	37	1	29	36	0.233	C	274	47	8	0.976								
1952	Albany	GFL	105	338	52	71	17	5	1	41	5	66	51	0.210	C	561	96	14	0.979								
Troy, Donald "Don"		BR TR																									
1949	Valdosta	GFL	19	75	10	24	2	2	0	6	4	10	17	0.320	2B	33	49	10	0.891								
Troy, Gordon		BR TR																									
1939	Moultrie	GFL	140	547	64	134	17	8	4	68	13	43	94	0.245	OF	312	18	22	0.938								
1940	Thomasville	GFL	104	343	53	92	11	5	0	45	11	41	53	0.268	OF, IF	204	38	21	0.920								
Troy, Herbert "Herb"		BR TR																									
1962	Moultrie	GFL	62	146	23	39	4	0	2	0		55	41	0.267	C	425	28	8	0.983								
Troy, James "Jim"		BR TR																									
1950	LaGrange	GAL	12	15	3	3	2	0	1	5	1	3	8	0.200													
1951	LaGrange	GAL	99	366	79	102	23	4	5	59	13	65	68	0.279	2B, 3B, OF	144	185	28	0.922								
Truitt, D.E.																											
1929	Cedartown	GAL	20	351	6	14	3	0	1		0	2	11	0.040	P	2	18	2	0.909	15	3	7		89	87	58	64
Tsatsa, Paul		BL TL																									
1957	Fitzgerald	GFL	33	28	2	3	0	1	0	0	0	6	15	0.107	P	1	12	1	0.929	33	6	3	4.10	79	76	53	46
Tschannen, Ronald "Ron"		BR TR																									
1951	Albany	GFL	124	463	78	115	19	9	1	42	14	85	73	0.248	SS	255	432	59	0.921								
Tschudin, B. Fred		BR TR																									
1949	Douglas	GSL	135	520	86	182	24	9	4	105	14	67	19	0.350	C	685	82	20	0.975								
1950	Douglas	GSL	137	516	62	147	24	6	2	95	14	64	26	0.285	M, C	686	19	10	0.986								
1951	Tifton	GFL	122	454	68	136	28	1	0	66	5	58	17	0.300	M, C, P	624	84	15	0.979	19	4	1	2.65	68	77	24	14
Tsitouris, John Philip "John"		BR TR 6'0" 175 lbs b. 05/04/1936 Monroe, NC																									
1954	Valdosta	GFL	4	0										0.000	P					3	0	0	24.00	<45			
1955	Valdosta	GFL	31	56	7	6	2	1	0	3	0	14	22	0.107	P	9	32	9	0.820	31	10	9	3.07	173	167	114	87
Tuck, Gerald		BR																									
1955	Cordele	GFL	2	4		0								0.000													
Tucker, Dwight		BL TL																									
1955	Albany	GFL	3	5		1								0.200	P					3	0	2		<45			
Tucker, Jim S.																											
1941	Americus	GFL	3												P					3	0	2	9.00	8	15	6	11
Tucker, Oliver Dinwiddie "Ollie"		BL TR 5'11" 180 lbs b. 01/27/1902 Radiant, VA d. 07/13/1940 Radiant, VA																									
1921	Cedartown	GSL		333	76	146								0.438	OF												
Tucker, Richard "Dick"		BL																									
1958	Thomasville	GFL	13	24	1	5	1	0	0	4	0	3	14	0.208													
Tucker, Roy		BR TR																									
1952	Fitzgerald	GSL	18	61	9	12	3	0	1	6	0	11	18	0.197	OF	47	3	0	1.000								
Tucker, Thomas "Tom"		BR TR																									
1963	Moultrie	GFL	9	8	0	1	0	0	0	0	0	1	5	0.125	P					9	2	1	1.73	26	19	18	17
Tucker, Wilbur																											
1936	Albany	GFL	15	36	0	10	1	0	0	6	0			0.278	OF	26	5	4	0.886								
Tuggle, William "Bill"		BR TR																									
1952	Statesboro	GSL	39	109	17	26	4	0	0	11	0	27	26	0.239	3B	30	56	12	0.878								
Tuholski, James "Jim"		BR TR																									
1963	Thomasville	GFL	27	44	4	6	0	0	0	1	0	4	15	0.136	P	3	26	3	0.906	27	8	8	2.53	139	125	131	54
Tulner, Charles		BR TR																									
1956	Douglas	GSL	40	123	30	28	7	1	4	14	10	36	40	0.228	1B	285	12	4	0.987								
Turbyfill, Harold		BR TL																									
1956	Sandersville	GSL	2	0										0.000	P					2	0	0					

Georgia Class-D Minor League Baseball Encyclopedia

YR	TEAM	LG	G	AB	R	H	2B	3B	HR	RBI	SB	BB	SO	BA	POS	PO	A	E	FA	GP	W	L	ERA	IP	H	SO	BB
Turek, Donald "Don"		BL TL																									
1954	Thomasville	GFL	4	3		0								0.000	P					4	0	1		<45			
Turk, ---																											
1930	Carrollton	GAL		17		2								0.118	C												
Turner, ---																											
1915	Dothan - Valdosta	FLAG	33	113	10	37	5	0	0	6				0.327	OF, C	128	14	7	0.953								
Turner, ---																											
1930	Anniston	GAL	15	28	2	7	3	0	0	0	0		7	0.250	P	1	23	0	1.000	15	4	6	6.48	75	99	18	21
1930	Carrollton	GAL	<10												P												
Turner, James C. "Jim"		BR TR																									
1951	LaGrange	GAL	27	44	4	7	1	0	0	3	0	6	5	0.159	P	1	17	1	0.947	26	9	4	4.67	135	136	51	57
Turner, James M. "Jim"		BR TR																									
1946	Americus	GFL	106	378	55	105	15	5	2	73	13	27	44	0.278	OF, C	517	65	16	0.973								
Turner, McDonald		BL TL																									
1948	Newnan	GAL	125	526	103	155	18	2	3	59	19	42	40	0.295	OF	186	11	15	0.929								
Turner, Richard "Dick"		BR TR																									
1948	Tallahassee	GFL	20	78	24	20	1	8	2	22	2	27	15	0.256	OF	26	4	3	0.909								
Turner, Robert "Bob"		BR																									
1954	Thomasville	GFL	12	24	0	3	0	0	0	3	0	3	13	0.125													
Turturro, Michael "Mike"		BR TR																									
1949	Tallahassee	GFL	115	371	86	79	11	5	8	40	8	91	111	0.213	2B, SS	205	338	44	0.925								
Turtzo, Paul N.		BL TL																									
1948	Thomasville	GFL	131	513	77	140	31	0	3	74	16	63	82	0.273	OF	243	12	17	0.938								
1952	Thomasville	GFL	33	172	31	45	6	2	9	25	3	19	15	0.262	OF	85	4	3	0.967								
1953	Tifton	GFL	135	473	81	136	23	2	6	84	7	103	23	0.288	OF, P	203	22	10	0.957		0	0		<45			
Tuttle, William "Bill"		BR TR																									
1956	Tifton	GFL	5	2		0								0.000	P					5	0	2		<45			
Twitchell, Beech		BR TR																									
1940	Americus	GFL	45	174	26	39	11	5	1	26	3	25	52	0.224	OF	52	85	3	0.979								
Twitchell, Dan		BR TR																									
1940	Americus	GFL	62	208	28	46	15	1	1	27	1	26	37	0.221	C	277	49	11	0.967								
Tyler, James E. "Jim"		BR TR																									
1950	Dublin(10) - Eastman(9)	GSL	19	52	7	13	1	1	0	7	0	5	7	0.250	P	4	19	3	0.885	19	7	7	4.04	136	137	97	69
1951	Eastman	GSL	22	58	1	8	0	0	0	5	0	6	13	0.138	P	13	43	3	0.949	22	9	9	3.48	163	159	95	58
1952	Eastman	GSL	13	30	2	3	0	0	0	3	0	6	7	0.100	P	5	24	0	1.000	13	6	3	4.77	83	92	40	34
1953	Sandersville	GSL	4											0.375	P					2	1			<45			
Tyndall, Dickie Lee "Dick"		BR TR																									
1954	Brunswick	GFL	17	25	3	7	3	0	0	6	1	0	10	0.280	P					4	0	0		<45			
Tysinger, Everett																											
1941	Cordele	GFL	122	472	62	114	14	3	0	53	11	36	60	0.242	SS	190	369	80	0.875								
Tyson, Cecil Washington "Turkey"		BL TR 6'5" 225 lbs b. 12/06/1914 Elm City, NC																									
1938	Tallahassee	GFL	66	248	47	80	9	2	0	37	2	37	18	0.323	1B	600	31	12	0.981								
1939	Tallahassee	GFL	118	429	73	138	19	14	0	74	12	64	32	0.322	1B	1064	80	23	0.980								
Uhle, Stanley "Stan"		BR TR																									
1940	Thomasville - Americus	GFL	134	522	94	157	32	8	2	75	9	93	67	0.301	OF, IF, P	272	41	26	0.923					<35			
Ulisney, Michael Edward "Mike" "Slugs"		BR TR 5'9" 165 lbs b. 09/28/1917 Greenwald, PA																									
1939	Thomasville	GFL	79	273	30	62	4	1	1	30	2	5	24	0.227	C	302	36	20	0.944								
1940	Thomasville	GFL	135	523	56	143	29	8	3	90	8	22	27	0.273	C	752	88	24	0.972								
1941	Thomasville	GFL	66	251	34	56	7	0	1	32	0	11	14	0.223	C	309	38	11	0.969								
Ullmann, John		BR TR																									
1957	Brunswick	GFL	11	36	5	4	0	0	0	3	0	8	14	0.111	OF	30	5	3	0.921								
Ulrich, Lawrence		BR TR																									
1954	Hazlehurst-Baxley	GSL	14	21	3	6	2	0	1	4	1	1	5	0.286	P	3	5	2	0.800	12	2	4	5.79	56	81	29	20
Umbach, Kendall "Ken"		BL TL																									
1950	LaGrange	GAL	34	100	18	23	7	0	1	11	0	29	26	0.230	1B	266	11	8	0.972								
Umbricht, James "Jim"		BR TR 6'4" 215 lbs b. 09/17/1930 Chicago, IL d. 04/08/1964 Houston, TX																									
1953	Waycross	GFL	54	179	15	44	8	1	0	17	0	10	19	0.246	SS, P	48	93	20	0.876	10	4	3	2.87	69	65	60	41
Umscheid, Donald "Don"		BL TL																									
1949	Carrollton(5) - Griffin(6)	GAL	11	13	0	0	0	0	0	0	0	2	2	0.000	P	4	7	0	1.000								
Umstead, Edwin "Ed"		BL TR																									
1948	Valdosta	GFL	12	37	10	16	4	0	0	10	3	9	3	0.432	OF	14	2	0	1.000								
Underwood, ---																											
1915	Ame-Gains - Brunswick	FLAG	<10																									
Underwood, Horace Glenn "Glenn"		BR TL																									
1947	Waycross	GFL	43	40	2	3	0	0	0	3	0	2	16	0.075	P	2	17	5	0.792	43	5	6	5.94	106	130	55	68
1948	Eastman	GSL	20	34	9	6	1	1	0	4	0	1	11	0.176	P	1	19	2	0.909	17	3	9	4.34	110	108	73	68
Unetich, Frank																											
1935	Albany	GFL	13	25	2	3	1	0	0	0	2		5	0.120	P					10	4	3		54	41	43	28
Upchurch, William "Bill"		BR																									
1953	Albany	GFL	2											0.200													
1953	Tifton	GFL	6											0.190													
Upper, Wray		BL TR																									
1952	Moultrie	GFL	39	141	16	33	2	0	2	12	0	17	8	0.234	3B	39	69	11	0.908								
Upshaw, Charles		BR TR																									
1950	Griffin	GAL	25	40	8	12	3	0	0	5	0	5	7	0.300	P	8	14	4	0.846	20	5	7	4.56	77	90	44	37

Georgia Class-D Minor League Baseball Encyclopedia

YR	TEAM	LG	G	AB	R	H	2B	3B	HR	RBI	SB	BB	SO	BA	POS	PO	A	E	FA	GP	W	L	ERA	IP	H	SO	BB
Upton, Lawrence		BR TR																									
1951	Fitzgerald	GSL	31	106	11	26	0	1	0	7	0	18	25	0.245	2B	48	48	10	0.906								
Urban, Hubert																											
1942	Valdosta	GFL	3												P					3	1	0	4.15	13	14	10	10
Urbanski, William "Bill"		BL TR																									
1955	Dublin	GSL	54	214	29	49	4	1	1	20	3	22	16	0.229	2B	134	132	9	0.967								
Urquhart, ---																											
1930	Anniston	GAL	1												P					1	1	0	0.00	7	7	3	1
Urrizola, P. Michael "Mike"		BR TR																									
1958	Brunswick	GFL	31	57	5	5	1	0	0	6	0	7	27	0.088	P	11	28	5	0.886	31	8	13	4.61	158	137	106	141
Urso, Joseph "Joe"		BR TR																									
1947	Tallassee	GAL	116	474	84	133	16	2	2	43	27	39	33	0.281	2B	344	323	45	0.937								
Usciak, Mathew "Matt"																											
1939	Moultrie	GFL	25	81	18	19	2	0	0	8	3	15	9	0.235	SS	38	70	17	0.864								
Utke, John		BR TR																									
1946	Americus	GFL	84	262	28	59	9	2	0	32	4	20	38	0.225	3B, OF	63	46	13	0.893								
Utley, ---																											
1914	Rome	GAL	92	358	53	103					25			0.288	1B	923	43	32	0.968								
1915	Thomasville	FLAG	71	239	29	57	16	2	1		13			0.238	1B	603	37	12	0.982								
Utley, Ewell		BR TR																									
1950	Griffin	GAL	26	44	5	9	2	0	1	7	0	7	13	0.205	P	1	18	1	0.950	19	7	5	4.93	95	106	51	53
1950	Thomasville	GFL	19	32	7	11	2	1	1	10	0	2	10	0.344	P	2	17	1	0.950	14	4	5	6.85	71	84	61	58
Utley, George		BL TL																									
1953	Waycross	GFL	39	92	5	14	1	0	0	7	0	1	15	0.152	P	12	54	10	0.868	31	11	15	3.78	205	219	94	65
Utter, ---																											
1913	Americus - Valdosta	ESL	27	76	4	10	0	0	0					0.132													
1915	Waycross	FLAG		0										0.000													
Utter, Richard "Dick"		BR TR																									
1950	Thomasville	GFL	35	43	5	6	1	0	0			4	16	0.140	P	1	31	5	0.865	37	3	8	5.46	112	144	70	81
Uzelatz, Max		BR																									
1953	Dublin	GSL	2											0.000														
1954	Valdosta	GFL	6	7		0								0.000														
Vaiden, ---																											
1914	Cordele	GSL		92	3	9	0	0	0		2			0.098													
1915	Waycross	FLAG	24	60	2	11	0	0	0		0			0.183	P	3	49	7	0.881	20	10	8		159	131	82	33
Valdez, ---																											
1929	Anniston	GAL	8												P					8	2	2		36	46	13	8
Valdez, Felipe		BR TR																									
1955	Douglas	GSL	32	110	18	28	6	0	1	9	6	24	32	0.255	2B	51	93	24	0.857								
Valencik, Edward "Ed"		BR TR																									
1946	Valdosta	GFL	11	42	5	9	1	2	0	8	3	7	11	0.214	OF	10	2	2	0.857								
Valesky, Donald "Don"		BL TL																									
1956	Vidalia	GSL	57	206	28	51	7	3	0	16	6	28	68	0.248	OF	101	5	6	0.946								
Valle, Sindo																											
1939	Waycross	GFL	139	505	73	133	18	3	0	53	4	46	36	0.263	SS	307	386	53	0.929								
Van Burkleo, Franklin "Dutch"		BL TL																									
1953	Brunswick	GFL	132	443	106	119	13	4	16	109	6	130	60	0.269	1B	1031	59	16	0.986								
Van Landingham, ---																											
1913	Valdosta	ESL	101	422	72	128	24	3	1					0.303	C, OF	321	71	13	0.968								
1914	Valdosta	GSL		348	40	89	9	3	3		22			0.256													
Van Orsdol, Jack																											
1939	Thomasville	GFL	23	62	8	15	3	0	0	5	0	4	7	0.242	P	12	42	3	0.947	23	10	8	2.36	160	147	84	44
Van, John		BL TL																									
1963	Brunswick	GFL	6	13	1	2	1	0	1	4	0	2	3	0.154	P					6	2	3	2.85	41	28	38	20
Vanasse, Robert J. "Bob"		BL TL																									
1953	Brunswick	GFL	6											0.182	P					1	2		<45				
1953	Dublin	GSL	37	84	12	20	0	2	1	10	0	14	27	0.238	OF, P	27	20	7	0.870	16	2	8	4.67	81	88	61	62
1954	Dublin	GSL	17	31	2	6	0	0	1	5	0	1	11	0.194	P	1	23	0	1.000	12	3	5	6.56	59	73	48	53
Vanatistein, Herbert "Herb"		BR TR																									
1949	Opelika	GAL	15	42	4	8	1	0	1	3	1	1	9	0.190	C	57	4	4	0.938								
Vandegraff, ---																											
1913	LaGrange	GAL	44	152	17	39					8			0.257	OF	57	5	6	0.912								
Vander Meer, John Samuel "Johnny"		BS TL 6'1" 190 lbs b. 11/02/1914 Prospect Park, NJ d. 10/06/1997 Tampa, FL																									
1956	Douglas	GSL	4	4		1								0.250	M, P					0	0						
VanDerBeek, James "Jim"		BL TL																									
1953	Vidalia	GSL	23	33	1	4	0	0	0	2	0	4	12	0.121	P	5	14	2	0.905	21	4	5	4.19	86	91	43	34
1954	Vidalia	GSL	31	60	8	7	0	1	0	4	0	7	26	0.117	P	11	32	0	1.000	31	14	9	2.83	191	166	113	73
1955	Vidalia	GSL	10	18	1	1	0	0	0	1	0	1	9	0.056	P					9	2	3					
Vandergriff, H.L.																											
1921	Griffin	GSL		50	8	16								0.320	C												
Vandergrift, Ed																											
1939	Thomasville	GFL	136	502	87	167	32	6	4	79	21	81	55	0.333	2B	415	433	59	0.935								
Vanderlip, ---																											
1913	Valdosta	ESL	8												P					8	3	5					

411

Georgia Class-D Minor League Baseball Encyclopedia

YR	TEAM	LG	G	AB	R	H	2B	3B	HR	RBI	SB	BB	SO	BA	POS	PO	A	E	FA	GP	W	L	ERA	IP	H	SO	BB
Vandiveer, Rodney "Rod"		BR																									
1955	Brunswick	GFL	2	6		0								0.000													
1955	Dublin	GSL	6	14		4								0.286													
Vanowski, ---		BR																									
1953	Dublin	GSL	1											0.000													
Vardeman, F.C.																											
1920	Cedartown	GSL													P												
1921	Cedartown	GSL													P												
Vargo, Stephen "Steve"																											
1937	Albany	GFL	37	95	11	27	1	0	0	13	2	5	8	0.284	P	14	34	5	0.906	29	16	10	2.18	215	182	106	98
1938	Albany	GFL	39	117	18	27	7	4	0	9	1	8	25	0.231	P	22	30	4	0.929	27	15	7	3.11	194	188	74	87
1939	Cordele	GFL													P									<45				
1949	Hazlehurst-Baxley	GSL	10	36	7	4	0	0	0	3	3	12	12	0.111	SS	23	18	7	0.854								
Varner, Glen Gann "Buck"		BL TR 5'10" 170 lbs b. 08/17/1930 Hixson, TN																									
1948	Carrollton	GAL	66	240	52	70	9	3	9	35	3	44	33	0.292	OF	140	4	5	0.966								
Varner, Paul																											
1942		GFL	75	282	51	101	17	7	0	39	8	34	15	0.358	SS	131	262	44	0.899								
Vasquez, Regino		BR TR																									
1953	Hazlehurst-Baxley	GSL	4											0.000	P						0	1	<45				
Vastano, Pasquale "Pat"		BR TR																									
1951	Tifton	GFL	20	74	11	18	2	0	0	4	1	3	9	0.243	SS	29	66	11	0.896								
1951	Haz-Bax(25) - Fitzgerald(7)	GSL	32	115	16	27	3	0	1	9	4	17	8	0.235	SS	47	68	10	0.920								
1951	Fitzgerald	GSL	<10																								
Vasterling, ---																											
1914	Selma	GAL	69	269	37	82				13				0.305	1B	664	35	15	0.979								
Vaughan, James R. "Jim"																											
1937	Americus	GFL	101	378	44	111	12	12	4	51	10	21	36	0.294	OF	183	12	9	0.956								
Vaughn, ---																											
1913	Valdosta	ESL	10	33	3	6	0	0	0					0.182	P	2	18	3	0.870	9	5	4					
1915	Valdosta	FLAG	<10												P	4	21	1	0.962	8	2	2		49	40	18	12
Vaughn, Bobby		BR																									
1956	Fitzgerald	GFL	9	26		1								0.038													
Vaughn, Donald O. "Don"		BL TL																									
1952	Dublin	GSL	44	89	11	19	3	0	0	10	0	6	24	0.213	P	3	27	3	0.909	32	8	12	4.98	188	186	153	173
1953	Fitzgerald	GFL	32	53	7	7	2	1	1	4	1	22	22	0.132	P	3	24	4	0.871	26	11	9	3.73	157	168	120	92
1954	Vidalia	GSL	17	39	7	8	1	0	0	4	0	6	9	0.205	P	3	10	2	0.867	13	9	1	2.07	87	66	81	28
Vaughn, Leroy		BR TR																									
1955	Albany	GFL	13	22	2	2	1	0	0	3	0	2	6	0.091	P	2	8	2	0.833	13	3	2	3.98	61	71	52	26
Vaughn, R. Eugene "Gene"																											
1942	Americus	GFL	61	191	19	60	5	6	2	31	0	12	27	0.314	P, OF	72	38	3	0.973	23	10	9	2.62	172	169	58	45
Veal, William "Bill"		BR																									
1953	Eastman	GSL	7											0.150													
Veale, Frank																											
1937	Cordele	GFL	22	33	1	4	0	0	0	4	0	4	14	0.121	P	3	14	6	0.739	18	4	7	3.39	101	102	48	49
Veazey, Norman "Norm"		BR TR																									
1948	Newnan	GAL	110	422	77	129	18	3	0	74	4	75	17	0.306	M, OF	184	11	14	0.933								
1949	Tallahassee	GFL	35	102	12	20	2	0	0	10	1	18	5	0.196	M, OF	34	1	1	0.972								
1950	Rome	GAL	16	41	6	15	6	1	0	2	0	3	3	0.366	M, OF	14	0	3	0.824								
Veazie, ---																											
1921	Lindale	GSL		57	9	21								0.368	OF												
1921	Rome	GSL													OF												
Veigel, Allen Francis "Al"		BR TR 6'1" 180 lbs b. 01/30/1917 Dover, OH																									
1937	Moultrie	GFL	10												P					10	3	4	5.23	62	58	21	42
Veinot, Kenneth "Ken"		BL																									
1958	Waycross	GFL	7	22		2								0.091													
Vejsicky, Eugene "Gene"		BR																									
1954	Tifton	GFL	4	11		1								0.091													
Venditto, Alfred "Al"		BR TR																									
1950	Alexander City	GAL	30	113	21	37	4	4	0	18	2	28	13	0.327	3B	65	79	12	0.923								
Verbish, George		BR TR																									
1947	Thomasville	GFL	20	52	10	12	1	0	0	4	0	12	10	0.231	C	63	2	2	0.970								
Vereault, George		BR TL																									
1951	Cordele	GFL	37	71	10	14	3	0	0	7	0	9	17	0.197	P	11	43	4	0.931	36	7	14	3.92	202	249	110	85
Verner, Clifford "Cliff"																											
1928	Talladega	GAL	55	203	40	74	14	13	9		2	16	22	0.365	OF	81	6	4	0.956								
1929	Talladega	GAL	79	310	57	105	17	15	12	22	28	35	0.339		OF	129	10	5	0.965								
1930	Anniston	GAL	101	401	84	137	22	13	13	26	51	41	0.342		OF	199	14	14	0.938								
1930	Talladega	GAL	3												P					3	0	2	7.20	20	29	8	4
Verratt, E.A.																											
1916	Talladega	GAL	24	81	4	10				4				0.123	OF, P												
1917	Talladega	GAL	9	20	1	5	0	0		1				0.250	P	3	13	1	0.941	6	3	1		42	33	21	7
Verstraete, Donald "Don"		BR TR																									
1956	Hazlehurst-Baxley	GSL	4	8		0								0.000	P					3	1	1					
Vesek, Steve																											
1938	Moultrie	GFL	123	477	67	119	23	6	0	69	7	63	54	0.249	SS	244	408	53	0.925								

Georgia Class-D Minor League Baseball Encyclopedia

YR	TEAM	LG	G	AB	R	H	2B	3B	HR	RBI	SB	BB	SO	BA	POS	PO	A	E	FA	GP	W	L	ERA	IP	H	SO	BB
Vest, Charles		BR TR																									
1953	Douglas	GSL	1											0.000	P					0	0		<45				
Vest, Milton M. "Milt"																											
1954	Brunswick	GFL	17	26	6	3	0	0	0	0	0	9	17	0.115	P	4	9	1	0.929	17	4	6	5.67	81	80	53	61
1954	Dublin	GSL	16	44	2	3	1	0	0	1	0	4	26	0.068	P	3	15	0	1.000	15	7	5	3.46	117	125	55	59
Vetter, Robert "Bob"		BR TR																									
1950	Jesup	GSL	13	41	3	4	0	0	0	2	0	3	15	0.098	3B	12	21	1	0.971								
Vickers, Dan																											
1939	Waycross	GFL	62	210	20	48	2	0	0	26	0	7	15	0.229	C	278	41	5	0.985								
Vickers, James J. "Jim"		BR TR																									
1946	Opelika	GAL	35	62	2	11	3	0	0	6	0	4	30	0.177	P	11	46	7	0.891	35	9	15	3.84	204	201	90	84
Victor, Ernie																											
1950	Carrollton	GAL	1												P					1							
Vidal, George		BR TR																									
1948	Vidalia-Lyons	GSL	41	225	23	51	1	0	0	15	1	21	29	0.227	1B, P	407	34	8	0.982	16	1	7	6.39	76	75	37	64
Villa, Antonio		BR TR																									
1946	Valdosta	GFL	46	178	30	41	5	3	0	15	5	22	20	0.230	OF	79	3	2	0.976								
Villamea, Raul		BR TR																									
1951	Alexander City	GAL	41	96	9	21	1	1	0	12	1	6	9	0.219	P	8	25	5	0.868	28	12	12	5.66	170	222	75	55
1951	Dublin	GSL	15	44	8	10	3	0	0	2	0	6	9	0.227	P	11	11	0	1.000	12	8	2	1.95	97	80	47	27
1952	Dublin	GSL	73	188	23	38	5	0	2	14	1	13	38	0.202	OF, P	25	48	7	0.913	36	11	20	4.05	258	288	149	88
Vincent, Al																											
1928	Talladega	GAL	97	406	79	126	17	8	13		4	22	28	0.310	2B, SS	229	175	31	0.929								
Vincent, C.E.																											
1928	Talladega	GAL	69	249	36	67	12	3	0		3	22	36	0.269	SS	182	207	28	0.933								
Vines, ---																											
1917	Griffin	GAL	3	7	0	1	0	0	0		0			0.143	P	0	1	2	0.333	3	2	0		14	15	3	2
Vines, Robert Earl "Bob"		BR TR 6'4" 184 lbs b. 02/25/1897 Waxahachie, TX d. 10/18/1982 Orlando, FL																									
1935	Thomasville	GFL													M												
Vingers, Leonard		BR TR																									
1954	Albany	GFL	65	238	44	60	14	1	3	35	2	17	50	0.252	1B	502	27	15	0.972								
Vingle, Richard "Dick"		BR TR																									
1962	Brunswick	GFL	5	3	0	0	0	0	0	0	0	1	1	0.000	P					5	0	2	7.94	17	17	18	21
1963	Brunswick	GFL	3	1	0	0	0	0	0	0	0	0	0	0.000	P					3	0	1	7.71	7	8	4	8
Vinson, Earl		BR TR																									
1947	Opelika	GAL	125	485	59	145	18	2	0	66	3	36	27	0.299	2B	351	311	38	0.946								
Vinson, Eugene "Gene"		BR TR																									
1952	Douglas	GSL	14	16	0	0	0	0	0	0	0	4	7	0.000	P	4	7	3	0.786								
1953	Waycross	GFL	11	19	6	6	1	0	0	0	0	3	10	0.316	P	2	10	0	1.000		0	4	<45				
1954	Waycross	GFL	3	4		1								0.250	P					2	1	0	<45				
Virgil, Dan		BL																									
1948	LaGrange	GAL	10	37	2	6	0	0	0	1	0	5	18	0.162													
Virgona, Alfred "Al"		BR TR																									
1953	Jesup	GSL	52	111	19	24	5	0	1	12	1	6	16	0.216	OF	41	2	1	0.977								
Virkstis, Robert "Bob"		BL TL																									
1954	Thomasville	GFL	50	70	9	17	2	1	1	8	0	1	12	0.243	P	2	34	2	0.947	45	11	8	2.70	190	187	95	48
1955	Thomasville	GFL	33	47	4	9	0	1	0	9	0	2	6	0.191	P	6	24	4	0.882	28	4	6	3.46	112	140	40	30
Vitale, Harold																											
1938	Tallahassee	GFL	10	31	3	6	1	1	0	4	0	1	3	0.194	C	37	8	1	0.978								
Vitale, Peter "Pete"		BR TR																									
1951	LaGrange	GAL	24	102	17	25	3	4	1	22	2	8	12	0.245	2B	54	56	9	0.924								
Vitali, Joseph "Joe"		BR TR																									
1950	Eastman	GSL	36	122	19	28	5	1	2	24	2	34	20	0.230	OF	52	3	4	0.932								
Vitari, Joseph F. Jr. "Joe"																											
1942	Waycross	GFL	21	83	11	21	0	0	0	5	0	14	8	0.253	SS	33	64	13	0.882								
Viteretto, Peter "Pete"		BL TL																									
1954	Valdosta	GFL	103	372	68	104	15	9	5	59	7	43	57	0.280	OF	155	10	12	0.932								
Vitter, James "Jim"		BR TR																									
1947	Cordele	GFL	44	89	14	21	4	1	0	12	0	3	9	0.236	P	9	70	4	0.952	37	11	16	4.24	206	237	92	78
Vitti, Ralph		BR TR																									
1951	Alexander City	GAL	11	14	8	8	3	0	0	3	2	8	4	0.571	SS	21	34	11	0.833								
Voboril, William "Bill"		BL																									
1957	Waycross	GFL	11	14	0	1	0	0	0	0	0	6	5	0.071													
Vogel, William "Bill"		BR TR																									
1963	Thomasville	GFL	5	11	2	2	0	0	2	4	0	0	6	0.182	P					5	1	2	3.55	33	38	12	13
Vogeltanz, Robert "Bob"		BR TR																									
1947	Albany	GFL	48	84	13	21	4	0	0	8	3	1	17	0.250	P	7	37	4	0.917	32	15	6	3.17	199	176	134	102
Vogt, Pete		BR																									
1955	Valdosta	GFL	16	38	5	11	2	0	0	5	1	7	5	0.289													
Voiselle, William Symmes "Bill" "Ninety-six"		BR TR 6'4" 200 lbs b. 01/29/1919 Greenwood, SC																									
1938	Moultrie	GFL	36	86	9	13	3	0	0	5	0	8	22	0.151	P	6	25	6	0.838	29	8	15	4.52	209	202	135	110
Voitier, Robert "Bob"		BL TR																									
1947	Waycross	GFL	104	398	94	135	24	10	10	89	19	75	55	0.339	OF	195	7	8	0.962								
Volan, Edward "Ed"		BL TR																									
1947	Americus	GFL	21	72	24	21	3	2	2	17	4	16	10	0.292	OF	48	2	1	0.980								

Georgia Class-D Minor League Baseball Encyclopedia

YR	TEAM	LG	G	AB	R	H	2B	3B	HR	RBI	SB	BB	SO	BA	POS	PO	A	E	FA	GP	W	L	ERA	IP	H	SO	BB
Volk, Fred		BL TL																									
1952	Moultrie	GFL	48	99	11	13	1	0	1	8	0	25	26	0.131	1B, P	117	48	3	0.982	25	10	9	2.28	174	147	83	74
Volpe, Joseph "Joe"		BR TR																									
1953	Tifton	GFL	15	19	1	0	0	0	0	0	0	2	16	0.000	P	0	7	1	0.875	15	3	1	6.32	47	59	26	51
Votaw, James "Jim"		BR TR																									
1948	Griffin	GAL	10	11	1	1	0	0	0	0	0	0	6	0.091	P	0	2	0	1.000								
Vroman, Larry		BR TR																									
1956	Waycross	GFL	22	33	5	8	0	0	0	4	0	8	13	0.242	P	7	20	2	0.931	22	8	5	4.66	114	95	88	92
1957	Waycross	GFL	39	63	7	11	2	0	0	8	0	8	28	0.175	P	16	33	3	0.942	36	9	11	4.55	172	198	96	110
Vucelich, Milan																											
1942	Cordele	GFL	61	189	17	46	6	3	0	25	0	12	41	0.243	P	68	28	3	0.970	26	4	10	5.47	130	169	59	81
Vukas, Stephen "Steve"		BR TR																									
1946	Moultrie	GFL	45	107	13	26	4	0	0	16	0	6	31	0.243	P	20	44	1	0.985	32	14	8	2.98	184	173	132	60
1947	Moultrie	GFL	27	58	6	8	0	0	0	1	0	12	14	0.138	P	10	25	3	0.921	18	8	6	3.10	125	108	80	51
Wachtman, David "Dave"		BR TR																									
1950	Valley	GAL	11	15	1	1	0	0	0	1	0	3	6	0.067	P	4	14	1	0.947	11	4	4	5.25	48	38	35	49
Wade, Loren		BR																									
1951	Fitzgerald	GSL	17	29	1	4	1	1	0	1	0	2	11	0.138													
Wadewitz, Oswin		BL TL																									
1949	Carrollton	GAL	11	23	0	2	0	0	0	0	0	0	4	0.087	P	0	9	2	0.818	11	2	7	1.88	67	61	34	44
Wadsworth, Hal																											
1949	Vidalia-Lyons - Fitzgerald	GSL	53	193	14	28	1	2	0	16	2	8	30	0.145	2B	117	100	24	0.900								
Wagner, Allen		BL TR																									
1952	Dublin	GSL	116	441	80	105	12	1	2	29	45	89	68	0.238	2B	364	327	31	0.957								
Wagner, Richard "Dick"		BR TR																									
1949	Newnan	GAL	13	25	2	5	1	0	0	3	0	5	11	0.200	P	3	14	2	0.895	13	5	3	3.60	80	66	49	35
Wagner, Theodore "Ted"		BR																									
1956	Douglas	GSL	6	18		4								0.222													
Wagnon, ---																											
1906	Waycross	GSL													SS, OF												
Wagnon, John																											
1913	Americus - Thomasville	ESL	81	308	60	81	12	1	1					0.263	OF	147	8	1	0.994								
1915	Americus-Gainesville	FLAG	26	109	12	29	3	0	0		3			0.266	M, OF	50	2	1	0.981								
Wagoner, Charles		BL TR																									
1955	Statesboro	GSL	8	7		1								0.143	P					8	1	0					
Wahl, William "Bill"																											
1949	Fitzgerald	GSL	37	146	24	31	8	0	0	27	1	20	29	0.212	SS	61	83	14	0.911								
Wahoo, Charles																											
1913	Waycross	ESL	25	60	6	15	0	0	0					0.250	M, C	85	11	5	0.950								
Waits, Frank																											
1935	Tallahassee	GFL	116	431	97	127	18	12	3		18	53	45	0.295	IF	169	325	30	0.943								
1936	Tallahassee	GFL	113	455	91	14	20	7	1	64	23			0.031	3B	148	330	42	0.919								
Waldrip, ---																											
1928	Lindale	GAL	7												P					7	0	6	6.24	49	72	30	11
Waldron, William W.																											
1913	LaGrange	GAL	91	316	63	90				25				0.285	3B	99	181	28	0.909								
1914	LaGrange	GAL	94	343	59	106				12				0.309	3B	118	115	28	0.893								
1916	LaGrange	GAL	70	244	45	64				15				0.262	SS												
1917	Griffin	GAL	16	63	19	24	11	1	0	12				0.381	2B, SS	27	56	6	0.933								
Waldrop, Berman		BR TR																									
1950	Thomasville	GFL	34	77	2	13	0	0	0	7	0	2	18	0.169	P	8	46	4	0.931	34	10	16	5.13	200	240	103	93
Walenczyk, Robert "Bob"		BL TR																									
1963	Moultrie	GFL	99	330	42	78	21	2	5	53	5	56	64	0.236	1B, 3B, OF	578	35	10	0.984								
Walker, ---																											
1913	Brunswick	ESL	41	149	18	36	0	0	0					0.242	OF, P	47	55	6	0.944	13	3	10					
1913	Valdosta	ESL	9												P	13	9	1	0.957								
1915	Brunswick	FLAG	<10												P					0							
Walker, ---																											
1915	Griffin - Newnan	GAL	58	199	30	58	8	2	2					0.291	OF	28	4	2	0.941								
Walker, Ewart Gladstone "Dixie"		BL TR 6'0" 192 lbs b. 06/01/1887 Brownsville, PA d. 11/14/1965 Leeds, AL																									
1930	Anniston	GAL													M												
Walker, Flem																											
1920	Rome	GSL		32	2	1	0	0	0		0			0.031													
Walker, Fred "Dixie"		BL TR 6'1" 175 lbs b. 09/24/1910 Villa Rica, GA d. 05/17/1982 Birmingham, AL																									
1929	Anniston	GAL	29	111	19	36	5	7	5		1	5	9	0.324	OF	44	3	1	0.979								
Walker, Fred D.		BR TR																									
1958	Albany	GFL	50	60	7	10	4	0	0	3	0	2	20	0.167	P	10	31	9	0.820	40	13	8	5.52	155	166	119	128
Walker, Gary N.		BR TR																									
1958	Dublin	GFL	37	143	30	43	3	0	1	9	2	27	10	0.301	SS	63	110	8	0.956								
Walker, Jack L.		BS TL																									
1947	Tallahassee	GFL	40	64	5	14	0	0	0	10	0	16	21	0.219	P	11	46	5	0.919	40	15	14	4.73	194	228	89	112
Walker, John C.		BL TR																									
1948	Valdosta	GFL	22	88	23	32	2	1	0	11	7	15	11	0.364	OF	28	2	2	0.938								

Georgia Class-D Minor League Baseball Encyclopedia

YR	TEAM	LG	G	AB	R	H	2B	3B	HR	RBI	SB	BB	SO	BA	POS	PO	A	E	FA	GP	W	L	ERA	IP	H	SO	BB
Walker, Lewis G.																											
1928	Talladega	GAL	66	256	22	76	9	3	0	1	11		6	0.297	M, 3B	51	108	9	0.946								
1929	Gadsden	GAL	46	143	10	34	3	2	0	0	3		4	0.238	M, OF	43	20	3	0.955								
1930	Huntsville	GAL	58	239	36	81	11	8	2	4	16		23	0.339	OF	93	7	6	0.943								
Walker, Milton "Milt"		BL TR																									
1950	Valley	GAL	80	288	66	76	11	1	5	34	3	48	48	0.264	1B, 2B, OF	238	29	10	0.964								
1950	Waycross	GFL	31	96	15	19	4	1	1	11	0	10	19	0.198	OF	24	1	7	0.781								
1952	Valdosta	GFL	28	95	14	29	6	0	1	7	0	18	13	0.305	OF	43	3	2	0.958								
Walker, Ronald "Ron"		BR																									
1958	Brunswick	GFL	9	25		3								0.120													
Walker, Tom																											
1928	Anniston	GAL	21	46	8	12	2	1	0	1	5		8	0.261	P	2	21	1	0.958	10	3	4	4.50	72	72	29	37
Walker, Wiley		BR TR																									
1954	Vidalia	GSL	7	9		2								0.222	P					5	0	2	<45				
Walker, William M. "Bill"		BR TR																									
1942	Waycross	GFL	31	73	9	16	0	1	0	6	0	12	27	0.219	P	6	38	2	0.957	30	9	11	2.52	214	231	62	94
1946	Way(4) - Alb(7) - Tal(17)	GFL	28	20	3	1	0	0	0	1	0	4	11	0.050	P	2	8	6	0.625	28	6	3	3.36	83	90	45	43
Wall, ---																											
1930	Lindale	GAL	51	181	47	62	10	3	11		7	17	30	0.343	OF, P	76	12	5	0.946	6	2	1	6.84	25	38	9	10
Wall, Curtis		BR																									
1948	Moultrie	GFL	11	14	1	3	0	1	0	2	0	2	5	0.214													
Wall, Fred		BR TL																									
1963	Brunswick	GFL	7	11	3	2	0	0	0	2	0	3	4	0.182	P					7	4	1	3.89	37	30	32	22
Wallace, Elmer		BR TR																									
1949	Newnan	GAL	42	50	3	3	0	0	0	2	0	8	13	0.060	P	2	28	0	1.000	42	9	2	2.02	147	141	56	65
Wallace, James T. "Jim"		BR TR																									
1949	LaGrange	GAL	10	9	1	1	0	0	0	0	0	2	6	0.111	P	1	8	1	0.900								
Wallace, Michael "Mike"		BR TR																									
1957	Brunswick	GFL	37	45	4	8	3	0	0	2	0	1	15	0.178	P	4	31	4	0.897	36	7	8	4.28	120	123	77	70
Wallace, Virgil Wayne "Wayne"		BR TR																									
1956	Haz-Bax(78) - Dublin(32)	GSL	110	402	53	114	25	5	7	88	9	42	22	0.284	M, 1B, P	927	44	7	0.993	3	0	0					
Wallace, William C. "Bill"		BR TR																									
1950	Cordele	GFL	38	48	5	7	0	2	0	10	0	8	22	0.146	P	5	20	0	1.000	32	6	7	4.21	141	156	69	69
1951	Cordele	GFL	34	71	11	9	2	1	0	8	0	13	32	0.127	P	16	33	2	0.961	34	16	14	4.44	223	258	127	76
Waller, ---																											
1928	Talladega	GAL	19	53	3	11	0	1	1		0	2	7	0.208	P	5	33	3	0.927	14	8	5	3.94	96	106	60	22
Wallin, Carl		BR TR																									
1946	Tallassee(5) - Opelika(7)	GAL	12	11	1	1	0	0	0	0	0	2	2	0.091	P	0	6	0	1.000	12	1	2	0.00	37	39	14	21
Wallin, Clyde "Ray"		BR TR																									
1963	Waycross	GFL	43	135	26	35	8	0	5	18	0	41	35	0.259	1B, OF	95	7	2	0.981								
Wallis, Arnold		BR																									
1946	Opelika	GAL	<10																								
Wallis, Gerald		BR TR																									
1949	LaGrange	GAL	33	73	5	9	2	0	1	9	0	4	25	0.123	P	6	21	6	0.818	33	16	8	2.64	194	149	144	97
1950	LaGrange	GAL	30	49	16	14	1	1	0	5	0	15	11	0.286	C, P	157	35	0	1.000	30	17	4	3.04	157	123	103	82
Walls, Boyd		BR TR																									
1947	LaGrange	GAL	13	44	2	7	0	0	0	4	0	2	5	0.159	C	67	4	2	0.973								
1950	LaGrange	GAL	24	91	12	29	3	0	0	11	0	10	4	0.319													
1951	LaGrange	GAL	92	325	42	80	9	2	0	54	2	29	21	0.246	C	468	40	5	0.990								
Walls, Howard		BR TR																									
1946	LaGrange	GAL	117	401	36	94	12	3	0	49	1	34	43	0.234	C, P	554	65	11	0.983	1	0	0		1			
Walsh, Christian "Chris"		BL TL																									
1952	Moultrie	GFL	93	363	35	80	14	2	6	49	3	30	64	0.220	1B, OF	537	32	20	0.966								
Walsh, Michael "Mike"		BL TR																									
1953	Dublin	GSL	53	200	38	53	6	0	6	27	8	32	32	0.265	2B	150	134	12	0.959								
1954	Waycross	GFL	76	259	33	63	9	2	4	36	3	21	43	0.243	3B	74	105	27	0.869								
Walski, Peter "Pete"		BR TR																									
1957	Valdosta	GFL	11	26	1	4	2	1	0	2	0	3	7	0.154	P					1	0	0	<30				
Walston, Robert "Bob"		BR TR																									
1953	Statesboro	GSL	51	203	40	56	7	3	5	22	11	11	47	0.276	OF	104	9	8	0.934								
Walter, Richard "Dick"		BR TR																									
1957	Valdosta	GFL	28	57	8	12	3	0	0	3	0	1	19	0.211	P	9	32	2	0.953	24	12	6	2.49	159	125	123	71
Walters, George		BR TL																									
1955	Valdosta	GFL	8	21		2								0.095	P					8	3	3	5.29	51	54	42	33
Walters, Jerry		BR TR																									
1955	Sandersville	GSL	25	78	10	15	1	0	0	7	1	17	20	0.192	OF	26	0	4	0.867								
Walters, Jim		BR TR																									
1940	Thomasville	GFL	12	27	2	4	1	0	0	0	0	0	10	0.148	P					12	2	4	7.58	57	80	31	31
Walters, Milton E. "Milt"		BR TR																									
1952	Cordele	GFL	124	437	44	95	9	4	0	41	5	68	64	0.217	OF	287	11	14	0.955								
Walters, Peck																											
1906	Valdosta	GSL													M, C												
Walters, Raymond L. "Ray"		BR TR																									
1947	Americus	GFL	103	356	69	122	22	9	2	67	8	52	33	0.343	OF, C	579	45	13	0.980								

Georgia Class-D Minor League Baseball Encyclopedia

YR	TEAM	LG	G	AB	R	H	2B	3B	HR	RBI	SB	BB	SO	BA	POS	PO	A	E	FA	GP	W	L	ERA	IP	H	SO	BB
Walters, William E. "Billy"		BR TR																									
1953	Waycross	GFL	77	277	33	70	9	4	2	28	1	35	49	0.253	2B, 3B	144	173	21	0.938								
1954	Statesboro	GSL	12	45	3	10	1	0	1	5	0	1	10	0.222	2B	29	27	4	0.933								
Walton, James R. "Jim"		BR TR																									
1962	Moultrie	GFL	34	78	14	23	6	0	3	15	2	11	8	0.295	M, P					9	0	2	5.63	24	30	13	14
1963	Moultrie	GFL													M												
Walton, O.C. "Battleaxe"																											
1921	Carrollton	GSL		139	14	39								0.281	C, OF, 1B												
Walton, Tubby																											
1930	Huntsville	GAL													M												
Wanstrath, William "Bill"																											
1942	Cordele	GFL	70	282	34	76	10	2	1	52	0	32	52	0.270	OF	126	6	11	0.923								
Ward, ---																											
1929	Anniston	GAL	29	74	10	23	2	0	0		2	4	12	0.311	P	8	23	7	0.816	22	5	9		128	148	78	48
Ward, ---		BR																									
1946	LaGrange	GAL	<10																								
Ward, Milton "Milt"		BL TL																									
1947	Tallassee	GAL	77	260	35	69	12	3	5	36	11	33	77	0.265	1B, OF	530	30	6	0.989								
Ward, Robert A. "Bob"		BL TL																									
1952	Vidalia	GSL	30	59	10	8	1	0	0	7	1	10	24	0.136	P	4	25	6	0.829	28	13	7	3.62	164	141	125	126
Ward, Warren		BR TR																									
1946	Thomasville	GFL	5												P					5	0	2	0.00	19	21	8	12
Ward, William "Bill" "Little Poison"																											
1941	Cordele	GFL	54	213	52	60	8	6	5	20	5	25	32	0.282	OF	125	21	4	0.973								
Warden, Charles		BR TR																									
1963	Moultrie	GFL	25	53	1	8	1	0	0	6	0	10	16	0.151	C	151	13	4	0.976								
Ware, Bruce		BL TR																									
1947	LaGrange	GAL	98	369	46	108	11	9	5	49	12	20	57	0.293	OF	231	13	8	0.968								
Ware, Charles		BR TR																									
1953	Tifton	GFL	28	85	13	24	2	0	0	13	0	7	22	0.282	3B	20	36	11	0.836								
1953	Sandersville	GSL	3											0.357													
Ware, Dan		BR																									
1946	LaGrange	GAL	<10																								
Wares, ---																											
1917	LaGrange	GAL	1	4	0	0	0	0	0		0			0.000	2B	2	3	1	0.833								
Wargo, Clarence		BR TR																									
1950	Hazlehurst-Baxley	GSL	33	54	6	6	1	0	1	2	0	4	20	0.111	P	5	22	5	0.844	32	5	10	4.40	139	159	77	75
1951	Hazlehurst-Baxley	GSL	20	36	5	6	2	1	0	2	0	9	8	0.167	P	4	5	0	1.000	14	0	5	6.40	45	62	15	34
Warner, ---																											
1930	Talladega	GAL	2												P					2	0	1	6.75	4	3	0	1
Warner, Henry W.		BR TR																									
1953	Cordele	GFL	49	182	32	38	5	0	1	16	3	43	26	0.209	2B	133	136	11	0.961								
Warren, ---																											
1930	Huntsville	GAL	3												P					3	0	3	7.50	12	25	3	2
Warren, James E. "Jim"		BR TR																									
1949	Sparta	GSL	22	76	9	21	1	0	0	9	0	1	6	0.276	P	9	13	2	0.917	12	7	2	3.00	84	36	45	46
1950	Dublin(21) - Jesup(77)	GSL	98	351	74	115	24	2	21	97	4	19	55	0.328	OF, P	98	31	5	0.963	27	11	5	4.65	147	144	127	89
1952	Jesup	GSL	126	526	104	165	30	2	23	117	9	42	43	0.314	M, OF, P	200	33	19	0.925	23	6	11	5.26	130	135	77	104
1953	Jesup	GSL	94	382	58	115	25	3	13	76	9	22	51	0.301	OF, P	130	11	7	0.953	10	6	1	2.02	49	31	47	32
1954	Statesboro	GSL	99	371	70	123	15	1	30	99	15	25	68	0.332	OF, P	112	38	17	0.898	27	15	7	3.19	178	132	169	66
Warren, Jefferson Edward "Jeff"		BR TR																									
1948	Moultrie	GFL	24	32	5	6	0	0	0	4	0	5	12	0.188	P	1	25	0	1.000	24	7	6	4.41	104	113	69	60
1951	Brunswick	GFL	20	27	1	2	0	0	0	2	0	2	6	0.074	P	1	16	0	1.000	20	4	7	5.02	86	99	33	32
Warren, Leon		BL																									
1954	Vidalia	GSL	2	4		0								0.000													
Warren, Malcolm		BL TR																									
1956	Thomson	GSL	36	71	7	12	1	0	0	4	0	2	30	0.169	P	7	26	4	0.892	31	10	7	2.80	167	139	133	86
Warren, Robert C. "Bob"		BR TR																									
1947	Thomasville	GFL	47	188	27	49	5	7	2	25	0	26	35	0.261	3B	46	95	22	0.865								
Warren, Rudolph "Rudy"		BL TR																									
1954	Sandersville	GSL	90	334	42	94	9	2	8	58	6	37	60	0.281	OF	210	12	31	0.877								
1955	Sandersville	GSL	81	303	60	90	15	8	8	43	13	54	49	0.297	OF	192	12	22	0.903								
1958	Waycross(26) - Brunswick(81)	GFL	107	407	87	127	19	5	9	57	10	73	73	0.312	OF	215	14	23	0.909								
Warshaw, Arthur "Art"		BR TR																									
1953	Statesboro	GSL	2											0.000	P					0	0	1		<45			
Wartelle, John "Johnny"		BL TL																									
1955	Cordele	GFL	30	48	5	4	0	0	0	1	0	1	12	0.083	P	3	21	1	0.960	31	6	9	4.99	137	111	163	137
1958	Dublin	GFL	40	54	7	6	0	0	0	0	0	10	13	0.111	P	10	35	3	0.938	35	10	5	5.70	131	134	90	75
Warwick, ---																											
1914	Waycross	GSL		85	15	14	2	0	0		3			0.165													
Warzyniak, Raymond "Ray"		BR TR																									
1953	Eastman	GSL	120	499	99	183	41	11	15	140	9	56	40	0.367	C	583	45	9	0.986								
Wasconis, George		BR TR																									
1952	Valdosta	GFL	10	9	0	2	0	0	0	0	0	1	4	0.222	P	0	8	2	0.800								
1953	Thomasville	GFL	24	49	5	9	1	0	0	4	0	7	11	0.184	P	2	11	1	0.929	22	14	2	3.46	125	118	63	54

Georgia Class-D Minor League Baseball Encyclopedia

YR	TEAM	LG	G	AB	R	H	2B	3B	HR	RBI	SB	BB	SO	BA	POS	PO	A	E	FA	GP	W	L	ERA	IP	H	SO	BB
Wasem, ---																											
1914	Waycross	GSL		329	49	106	16	1	1		14			0.322													
Washington, ---																											
1928	Anniston	GAL	7												P					7	4	3	4.76	51	57	19	20
1929	Anniston	GAL	23	41	3	11	3	0	0	0	0	6		0.268	P	4	25	4	0.879	20	5	4		95	115	27	27
1930	Cedartown	GAL	10	31	4	11	0	1	1		1	0	1	0.355	P	6	10	1	0.941	8	4	3	7.45	58	84	16	22
Wasiak, Stanley "Stan"		BR TR b. 04/08/1920 Chicago, IL d. 11/20/1992 Mobile, AL																									
1940	Americus	GFL	111	466	79	147	16	5	0	32	10	45	23	0.315	3B	182	216	38	0.913								
1950	Valdosta	GFL	138	523	104	163	21	10	0	91	5	77	18	0.312	M, 2B	363	429	30	0.964								
1951	Valdosta	GFL	107	403	83	129	13	5	1	82	6	61	8	0.320	M, 2B	277	293	16	0.973								
1954	Valdosta	GFL	64	232	33	66	9	0	0	20	2	44	13	0.284	M, 2B, 3B, P	136	179	11	0.966	3	0	0	<45				
1955	Valdosta	GFL	96	340	70	104	15	3	0	31	6	71	27	0.306	M, 2B, P	226	273	20	0.961	1	0	0	<45				
1956	Hazlehurst-Baxley	GSL	28	59	10	17	1	1	0	12	0	16	2	0.288	M, 3B	14	30	6	0.880								
1957	Valdosta	GFL	28	69	11	21	0	1	0	15	1	18	8	0.304	M, P					2	0	0	<30				
Wasil, Andrew		BR TR																									
1957	Waycross	GFL	19	21	2	4	0	0	1	3	0	7	11	0.190	P	0	8	0	1.000	15	2	5	4.24	51	66	33	17
Wassel, William "Bill"		BR TR																									
1949	Griffin(11) - Newnan(9)	GAL	20	60	8	10	1	0	0	6	1	5	14	0.167	OF	23	1	0	1.000								
Wassem, ---																											
1913	Cordele	ESL	83	314	64	96	17	3	4					0.306	OF	115	22	11	0.926								
Waters, Rabun		BR TR																									
1954	Hazlehurst-Baxley	GSL	26	39	4	4	1	0	0	2	0	4	12	0.103	P	9	17	2	0.929	26	5	8	6.73	107	117	56	88
Watkins, Louis "Lou"		BR																									
1953	Vidalia	GSL	3											0.444													
Watkins, Robert																											
1915	Brunswick	FLAG	29	80	7	15	3	0	0		2			0.188	P	2	42	2	0.957	27	7	8		116	117	54	21
1916	Newnan	GAL	27	75	9	15					2			0.200	P					15							
Watson, ---																											
1930	Huntsville	GAL	4												P					4	0	3	7.71	21	41	6	8
Watson, Art		BL TL																									
1955	Tifton	GFL	8	6		0								0.000	P					8	0	1		<45			
Watson, Carl		BL TL																									
1952	Cordele	GFL	55	131	16	34	3	3	0	17	1	7	12	0.260	P	14	37	7	0.879	35	13	12	2.90	211	201	82	93
1953	Cordele	GFL	37	87	4	13	1	0	0	10	2	8	15	0.149	1B, P	67	25	6	0.939	23	3	9	3.87	79	80	36	54
Watson, Edward "Ed"		BL TL																									
1947	LaGrange	GAL	11	20	0	3	0	0	0	0	0	0	9	0.150	P	1	9	1	0.909	10	2	5	4.96	49	59	27	31
1948	LaGrange	GAL	39	66	9	13	2	0	0	7	1	11	23	0.197	P	4	36	7	0.851	39	9	10	3.81	175	194	138	84
Watson, Henry																											
1915	Griffin	GAL	19	53	5	11	3	0	0					0.208	P	2	43	7	0.865	9	7	0					
1916	Griffin	GAL	46	118	13	26					1			0.220	OF, P												
Watson, Jules "Old Folks"																											
1916	Rome	GAL	33	119	11	23					5			0.193	2B, P												
1917	Anniston	GAL	15	61	12	19	4	2	0		3			0.311	2B	40	44	10	0.894								
1920	Carrollton	GSL		224	22	62	5	1	0		6			0.277	2B, OF												
1921	Carrollton	GSL		199	19	39								0.196	M, 2B												
1930	Anniston	GAL	59	225	42	59	8	6	3		2	28	15	0.262	2B	156	193	16	0.956								
Watters, Lark																											
1920	Griffin	GSL																									
Wattigney, Ulysses		BR TR																									
1940	Waycross	GFL	<10												P								<35				
Watts, Donald L. "Don"		BR TL																									
1949	Albany	GFL	33	70	10	20	3	1	0	6	0	5	18	0.286	P	6	37	4	0.915	26	13	7	2.71	163	141	125	65
1951	Albany	GFL	13	18	2	3	0	0	0	1	1	1	4	0.167	P	3	7	1	0.909								
Watts, George		BR																									
1946	Waycross	GFL	<10																								
Watts, Lee		BL TL																									
1950	Valdosta	GFL	29	104	27	26	6	3	0	13	6	22	14	0.250	OF	51	1	3	0.945								
Watts, William "Bill"																											
1941	Tallahassee	GFL	44	175	34	39	8	2	0	13	20	27	29	0.223	SS	78	166	26	0.904								
Watts, William L. "Bill"		BL TL																									
1947	Valdosta	GFL	11	22	1	5	1	0	0	3	0	1	7	0.227	P	1	10	3	0.786	11	2	6	4.42	59	41	47	68
Waugh, Arthur "Art"		BR TR																									
1947	Thomasville	GFL	47	139	15	38	7	1	0	27	1	4	23	0.273	C	172	12	8	0.958								
Waugh, James Elden "Jim"		BR TR 6'3" 185 lbs b. 11/25/1933 Lancaster, OH																									
1951	Brunswick	GFL	18	40	8	4	1	0	0	2	0	6	5	0.100	P	2	44	1	0.979	18	10	8	3.40	119	106	88	60
1955	Brunswick	GFL	3	6		0								0.000	P					3	2	1		<45			
Way, Walter "Walt"		BR TR																									
1954	Albany	GFL	134	481	72	131	24	7	1	81	12	57	87	0.272	1B, 3B, OF, P	343	127	42	0.918	1	0	0	<45				
Wayton, Henry J.																											
1937	Albany	GFL	127	468	79	142	21	6	8	93	19	77	65	0.303	SS	253	370	58	0.915								
Weakley, ---																											
1906	Valdosta	GSL													P												
Weathers, Charles "Charlie"		BL TR																									
1947	Waycross	GFL	43	163	27	30	7	2	2	26	6	26	31	0.184	OF	57	7	7	0.901								
1948	Waycross	GFL	138	550	129	158	23	18	13	117	23	98	97	0.287	OF	283	14	20	0.937								

Georgia Class-D Minor League Baseball Encyclopedia

YR	TEAM	LG	G	AB	R	H	2B	3B	HR	RBI	SB	BB	SO	BA	POS	PO	A	E	FA	GP	W	L	ERA	IP	H	SO	BB
Weaver, ---																											
1906	Columbus	GSL													P												
Weaver, C.B.																											
1921	Rome	GSL																									
Weaver, Earl Sidney "Earl"			b. 08/14/1930																								
1957	Fitzgerald	GFL	112	354	70	102	15	3	6	38	8	100	26	0.288	M, 2B, P	321	289	19	0.970	5	1	0	<30				
1958	Dublin	GFL	37	85	27	25	6	0	4	21	0	33	6	0.294	M, 2B, OF, P	58	41	4	0.961	2	0	0	<30				
Weaver, Fred			BR TR																								
1951	Moultrie	GFL	13	26	7	4	0	0	0	2	1	14	10	0.154													
1951	Fitzgerald	GSL	98	331	60	67	5	0	0	23	3	82	64	0.202	2B, SS	235	265	33	0.938								
1952	Fitzgerald	GSL	120	416	78	115	14	0	1	54	17	63	42	0.276	SS	215	330	59	0.902								
1953	Douglas	GSL	4											0.231													
Weaver, Henry			BR TR																								
1939	Albany	GFL													P								<45				
1940	Albany	GFL	42	100	17	19	3	0	0	7	0	8	32	0.190	P					40	15	13	4.41	251	319	109	70
Weaver, Norman "Norm"			BL TL																								
1957	Waycross	GFL	19	70	3	9	0	0	0	1	0	8	9	0.129	1B	162	7	5	0.971								
Weaver, William "Bill"			BR TR																								
1953	Eastman	GSL	1											0.000	P					0	0		<45				
Webb, ---																											
1916	Rome	GAL	21	69	9	17					9			0.246	1B												
Webb, ---																											
1936	Albany	GFL													P								<30				
Webb, ---			BR																								
1946	LaGrange	GAL	<10																								
Webb, Charles W.			BR TR																								
1950	Waycross	GFL	47	165	26	51	10	0	0	25	5	31	14	0.309	M, 3B	48	62	12	0.902								
1951	Waycross	GFL	123	424	85	120	24	7	2	78	17	110	38	0.283	2B	330	323	25	0.963								
1952	Waycross	GFL	65	235	33	51	14	1	0	21	3	45	29	0.217	2B	151	179	16	0.954								
Webb, Lawrence			BR																								
1946	Newnan	GAL	<10																								
Webb, Leroy																											
1941	Thomasville	GFL	48	121	12	29	2	0	0	15	0	6	24	0.240	P	42	40	8	0.911	34	11	14	4.35	205	214	137	116
Webb, Marion			BL TR																								
1948	LaGrange	GAL	65	225	34	64	10	2	0	28	8	31	44	0.284	3B, SS	78	142	34	0.866								
Webb, Thomas "Tom"			BR TR																								
1958	Valdosta	GFL	65	214	40	46	4	3	0	23	7	74	50	0.215	OF	141	2	4	0.973								
Webb, William Frederick "Bill"			BR TR 6'2" 180 lbs b. 12/12/1913 Atlanta, GA d. 06/01/1994 Austell, GA																								
1947	Carrollton	GAL	31	96	16	39	8	0	2	16	0	6	5	0.406	P	15	44	0	1.000	28	22	5	2.40	229	196	131	38
Webber, Donald "Don"			BR TR																								
1955	Hazlehurst-Baxley	GSL	1	1		1								1.000	P					1	0	0					
Webber, Harry																											
1913	Americus	ESL													M												
Webster, Edwin "Ed"			BR TR																								
1950	LaGrange	GAL	11	12	2	3	1	0	0	0	0	0	4	0.250	P	1	7	0	1.000								
Weddle, Billy			BR TR																								
1956	Moultrie	GFL	133	515	82	122	22	2	14	81	14	48	93	0.237	1B, 3B, OF	256	112	30	0.925								
Weed, Clarence			BR TR																								
1951	Albany	GFL	32	65	9	18	3	0	0	6	0	7	14	0.277	P	4	35	2	0.951	29	11	6	3.75	156	123	78	121
Weeks, Ralph			BL TL																								
1947	Thomasville	GFL	138	530	88	170	22	8	1	92	11	55	37	0.321	1B	1260	45	32	0.976								
Wehman, Richard "Dick"			BR TR																								
1954	Fitzgerald	GFL	121	477	79	136	38	2	9	89	9	46	76	0.285	C	673	67	19	0.975								
Weilbacher, David "Dave"			BR TR																								
1957	Brunswick	GFL	26	66	4	11	2	0	0	9	0	3	28	0.167	P	8	25	7	0.825	23	12	7	2.97	176	167	128	82
Weiler, ---																											
1914	Valdosta - Brunswick	GSL		322	35	67	7	2	0		14			0.208													
1915	Brunswick	FLAG	75	286	34	77	7	2	0		9			0.269	SS	191	181	40	0.903								
Weir, Gary			BR TR																								
1955	Brunswick	GFL	20	51	5	6	2	0	2	6	0	3	26	0.118	OF	20	0	1	0.952								
Weisenberg, Aaron			BR TR																								
1946	Valdosta	GFL	32	51	3	5	0	0	0	5	0	5	24	0.098	P	7	34	4	0.911	31	12	9	2.94	150	134	101	83
Weiss, Dennis			BR																								
1956	Vidalia	GSL	10	26	5	8	1	3	0	7	1	8	4	0.308													
Weiss, Sidney "Sid"																											
1937	Tallahassee	GFL	49	205	32	51	9	4	8	40	1	14	39	0.249	OF	85	1	6	0.935								
Welage, Richard "Dick"			BR TR																								
1955	Douglas	GSL	25	57	4	7	1	0	1	5	0	4	13	0.123	P	6	25	3	0.912	24	11	2	2.36	149	123	78	45
Welch, Eacie			BR TR																								
1951	Alexander City	GAL	77	303	35	62	7	6	0	30	6	25	45	0.205	3B, SS	126	249	33	0.919								
Welch, George			BR TR																								
1950	Cordele	GFL	18	57	4	10	3	0	0	7	0	1	16	0.175	OF	32	1	4	0.892								
Welch, Ronald "Ron"			BR TR																								
1956	Valdosta	GFL	133	501	83	143	21	3	9	82	6	82	54	0.285	2B, SS	318	316	21	0.968								

Georgia Class-D Minor League Baseball Encyclopedia

YR	TEAM	LG	G	AB	R	H	2B	3B	HR	RBI	SB	BB	SO	BA	POS	PO	A	E	FA	GP	W	L	ERA	IP	H	SO	BB
Weldon, Larry		BR TR																									
1940	Moultrie	GFL	45	133	13	31	6	0	0	19	2	5	20	0.233	P, IF					28	12	13	4.34	195	244	62	46
Weldon, William "Bill"		BR TR																									
1949	Dublin	GSL	10	22	1	4	0	0	1	3	0	2	9	0.182	P	1	12	1	0.929	13	2	9	6.14	63	49	28	38
1950	Carrollton	GAL	27	51	7	5	1	0	1	6	0	6	10	0.098	P	5	30	3	0.921	26	8	9	5.33	130	147	69	78
Weller, J. Williams "Jay"		BL TL																									
1958	Valdosta	GFL	9	7		1								0.143	P					9	0	1	<30				
Wellman, Robert Joseph "Bob"		BR TR 6'4" 210 lbs b. 07/15/1925 Norwood, OH d. 12/20/1994 Villa Hills, KY																									
1946	Tallassee	GAL	65	265	37	88	13	6	3	40	4	14	36	0.332	OF	95	9	7	0.937								
1955	Douglas	GSL	107	408	87	130	31	0	21	100	4	54	40	0.319	M, 1B, OF, P	803	40	14	0.984	7	1	1					
1956	Moultrie	GFL	137	475	101	165	37	2	30	124	12	82	43	0.347	M, 1B, P	1000	80	23	0.979	15	2	0	2.70	50	45	28	27
Wells, Jack		BR TR																									
1954	Douglas	GSL	24	67	5	11	2	0	0	1	4	4	11	0.164	P	4	18	2	0.917	19	11	4	2.81	141	140	65	40
1955	Douglas	GSL	35	75	5	11	2	0	0	10	0	9	17	0.147	P	5	39	4	0.917	26	10	7	2.93	175	165	91	38
Wells, James "Jim"		BL TR																									
1963	Waycross	GFL	53	153	21	33	3	0	0	4	5	21	42	0.216	2B, 3B	53	71	8	0.939								
Wells, Leslie "Les"																											
1949	Vidalia-Lyons	GSL	25	72	7	9	0	0	0	3	0	4	25	0.125	P	14	34	4	0.923	29	13	9	4.30	180	103	74	75
Wells, Phil																											
1916	Griffin	GAL	41	142	13	33				7				0.232	M, C												
Wells, Ronald		BR TR																									
1954	Thomasville	GFL	34	70	5	10	3	0	0	2	0	1	21	0.143	P	11	40	9	0.850	32	14	11	3.04	207	189	154	75
Wells, William D. "Bill"		BR TR																									
1954	Thomasville	GFL	6	15		5								0.333	P					6	2	1	<45				
1955	Thomasville	GFL	27	54	5	10	3	0	0	4	0	6	20	0.185	P	6	41	1	0.979	25	6	13	3.39	154	144	95	86
Welp, William "Bill"		BR TR																									
1942	Valdosta	GFL	59	235	44	80	18	6	0	33	15	23	17	0.340	C	321	44	7	0.981								
1946	Valdosta	GFL	111	352	65	109	16	10	0	44	21	47	36	0.310	M, C, P	606	90	21	0.971	2	0	0	0.00	6			
Welsh, Daniel "Dan"		BL TL																									
1956	Thomson	GSL	29	39	5	8	0	0	0	5	0	10	10	0.205	P	1	23	2	0.923	25	8	6	5.00	90	93	71	49
Wenclewicz, Walter "Walt"		BR TR																									
1947	Alexander City	GAL	19	34	1	4	1	0	0	1	0	1	8	0.118	P	5	20	0	1.000	18	3	5	3.26	91	79	38	25
Wendell, Herbert "Herb"		BR TR																									
1950	Moultrie	GFL	22	58	11	13	1	1	1	9	1	17	15	0.224	OF	15	0	3	0.833								
Wenitski, Bernard "Bernie"		BR TR																									
1949	Americus	GFL	136	481	59	103	12	2	0	40	11	43	95	0.214	SS	250	427	81	0.893								
1950	Americus	GFL	114	442	76	114	9	5	1	52	14	72	57	0.258	SS	232	335	53	0.915								
Wenrich, David "Dave"		BR TR																									
1958	Brunswick	GFL	30	103	17	24	2	0	2	10	0	9	13	0.233	C	95	2	4	0.960								
Wenson, Ronald "Ron"		BR TR																									
1954	Valdosta	GFL	123	409	76	101	20	0	6	50	34	62	92	0.247	OF	207	12	13	0.944								
1955	Valdosta	GFL	125	443	69	127	26	3	2	75	47	66	90	0.287	OF	216	13	14	0.942								
Wentworth, Richard "Dick"																											
1942	Cordele	GFL	88	271	25	49	9	2	0	30	0	20	61	0.181	C	206	50	26	0.908								
Werk, Frank																											
1937	Tallahassee	GFL	16	65	5	20	2	2	1	7	1	2	0	0.308	P	20	21	4	0.911	8	3	4	3.38	64	70	29	23
Werking, Glenn		BR TR																									
1962	Thomasville	GFL	30	81	6	19	2	2	1	20	1	15	26	0.235	C	175	13	6	0.969								
Werley, George William "George"		BR TR 6'2" 196 lbs b. 09/08/1938 St. Louis, MO																									
1957	Fitzgerald	GFL	22	19	1	6	0	0	0	0	0	3	8	0.316	P	0	5	2	0.714	21	2	4	7.90	49	55	39	76
1958	Dublin	GFL	49	101	17	23	5	0	0	13	0	14	25	0.228	P	13	29	2	0.955	35	16	10	4.28	208	191	133	83
Werner, ---																											
1913	Americus	ESL	43	128	12	34	6	3	1					0.266	P					21	9	12					
Werner, Daniel Jr. "Dan"		BS TR																									
1955	Cordele	GFL	4	1		0								0.000	P					4	0	1	<45				
Werner, G.H.																											
1913	Gadsden	GAL	88	334	48	101				18				0.302	OF	111	13	10	0.925								
1914	Gadsden	GAL	88	338	43	74				11				0.219	OF	151	56	14	0.937								
1915	Rome	GAL	58	223	31	74	18	0	2					0.332	2B	163	185	16	0.956								
1916	Rome	GAL	35	130	24	27				11				0.208	2B												
Wert, Donald Ralph "Don"		BR TR 5'9" 165 lbs b. 07/29/1938 Strasburg, PA																									
1958	Valdosta	GFL	120	457	88	130	17	11	7	81	6	71	52	0.284	2B, 3B, P	126	247	25	0.937	1	0	0	<30				
Werther, ---																											
1942	Cordele	GFL	6												P					6	1	4	4.50	50	63	15	23
Wesley, ---																											
1930	Huntsville	GAL	62	246	48	75	10	6	1		12	26	47	0.305	OF	128	4	16	0.892								
1930	Carrollton	GAL	<10																									
West, ---																											
1914	Americus	GSL		153	19	39	4	1	0		21			0.255													
West, ---																											
1930	Lindale	GAL	85	353	56	133	17	7	6		8	26	24	0.377	3B	99	107	32	0.866								
West, Ira		BR TR																									
1954	Douglas	GSL	23	91	10	21	2	0	2	12	0	4	23	0.231	3B	23	42	5	0.929								
West, Lewis		BR TR																									
1946	Americus	GFL	16	34	4	6	7	0	0	1	0	3	9	0.176	P	4	21	2	0.926	15	5	4	3.17	88	73	55	73

Georgia Class-D Minor League Baseball Encyclopedia

YR	TEAM	LG	G	AB	R	H	2B	3B	HR	RBI	SB	BB	SO	BA	POS	PO	A	E	FA	GP	W	L	ERA	IP	H	SO	BB
West, Richard Thomas "Dick"		BR TR 6'2" 180 lbs b. 11/24/1915 Louisville, KY d. 03/13/1996 Fort Wayne, IN																									
1935	Americus	GFL	89	324	23	107	28	7	6		12	28	45	0.330	C	316	47	16	0.958								
1936	Americus	GFL	89	309	63	103	15	6	4	56	16			0.333	UT	117	131	40	0.861								
1937	Americus	GFL	103	340	63	111	13	6	6	56	11	35	28	0.326	OF	160	18	10	0.947								
West, Ronnie		BR TR																									
1954	Vidalia	GSL	71	229	45	49	3	2	1	26	6	29	34	0.214	2B, SS, OF	103	93	28	0.875								
West, Stan		BL TR																									
1936	Americus	GFL													P						0	0		<30			
1937	Americus	GFL	29												P					29	12	11	2.92	228	193	95	102
1954	Sandersville	GSL	33	70	8	20	4	1	2	12	0	3	12	0.286	M, P	5	29	2	0.944	17	3	4	4.60	94	108	58	19
West, Tom Caldwell Jr. "Tom"																											
1942	Dothan	GFL	29	83	7	21	3	2	0	16	0	3	29	0.253	P	9	39	3	0.941	27	7	11	4.76	176	187	88	102
West, Weldon Edison "Lefty"		BR TL 6'0" 165 lbs b. 09/03/1915 Gibsonville, NC d. 07/23/1979 Hendersonville, NC																									
1939	Americus	GFL	40	110	11	14	2	0	0	9	0	5	35	0.127	P	17	70	6	0.935	35	18	11	2.91	294	240	245	113
West, William "Bill"		BL TL																									
1963	Waycross	GFL	32	48	5	10	1	1	0	7	0	3	21	0.208	P	9	45	3	0.947	30	9	8	3.00	138	129	116	38
Westbrook, ---																											
1906	Americus	GSL													1B, C, OF												
Westbrook, Edward "Ed"		BL TR																									
1947	Tallassee(21) - Newnan(8)	GAL	29	61	5	12	1	0	0	7	0	3	14	0.197	M, P	8	22	2	0.938	29	9	5	3.14	155	172	104	50
Westbrook, John		BR TL																									
1946	Tallassee(5) - Carrollton(11)	GAL	16	35	1	2	0	0	0	1	0	1	6	0.057	P	4	18	2	0.917	16	6	7	2.51	104	96	67	30
Westbrook, Price		BR																									
1953	Hazlehurst-Baxley	GSL	1											0.333													
Westervelt, ---																											
1906	Columbus	GSL													1B												
Westfall, Elmer		BR TR																									
1948	Baxley	GSL	115	424	59	91	15	4	6	49	7	56	93	0.215	3B, OF	194	33	10	0.958								
Weston, E.H.																											
1914	LaGrange	GAL	27	71	7	13				2				0.183	P	22	34	5	0.918	27							
1915	Valdosta	FLAG	1			0								0.000	P					1	1	0		9	7	5	2
1915	LaGrange	GAL	29	75	3	11	1	0	0					0.147	P	3	37	3	0.930	17	5	8					
1916	Rome	GAL	27	67	6	14				0				0.209	P												
1917	Rome-Lindale	GAL	17	65	3	17	3	0	0	2				0.262	OF, P	30	3	7	0.825	1	0	1		8	14	3	7
Wetherton, Carl		BR TR																									
1950	Thomasville	GFL	35	492	110	116	10	11	0	51	22	110	93	0.236	SS	266	337	71	0.895								
Wexler, James "Jim"		BR TR																									
1956	Thomasville	GFL	33	55	9	10	0	4	0	3	0	2	26	0.182	P	3	17	0	1.000	15	4	8	4.32	102	97	121	86
Whalen, ---																											
1941	Moultrie	GFL	4												P					4	0	1	2.57	21	20	8	16
Whalen, Francis "Frank"		BR TR																									
1946	Americus	GFL	119	444	109	119	21	7	1	57	28	65	74	0.268	OF	216	15	5	0.979								
Whalen, James																											
1906	Americus	GSL													M, OF												
Whaley, Charles		BR TR																									
1952	Statesboro	GSL	9												P					9	6	2	3.10	58	43	33	29
1956	Dublin	GSL	19	25	1	2	1	0	0	3	0	4	19	0.080	P	1	7	2	0.800	19	1	7	5.25	84	84	69	58
Whaley, Randy		BS TR																									
1954	Statesboro	GSL	38	82	6	10	3	0	0	1	0	11	43	0.122	P	4	34	5	0.884	33	11	11	4.22	209	173	173	118
Whaley, Walker		BR TR																									
1949	Dublin	GSL	11	34	4	9	0	0	0	7	0	0	6	0.265	P	0	15	2	0.882	14	3	6	7.00	81	81	41	66
1951	Hazlehurst-Baxley	GSL	18	46	3	13	2	0	1	10	0	1	10	0.283	P	4	27	6	0.838	15	4	6	5.18	92	114	34	55
1952	Statesboro	GSL	16	36	2	9	2	0	0	2	0	0	12	0.250	P	2	10	1	0.923	11	2	5	5.14	63	88	24	39
1953	Dublin	GSL	36	84	10	15	2	0	2	6	0	5	30	0.179	OF, P	17	21	1	0.974	25	4	6	7.08	103	144	42	78
Wheat, B.C.																											
1920	Griffin	GSL													C												
Wheat, Lafe																											
1920	Griffin	GSL													P												
1921	Griffin	GSL													P												
Wheeler, ---																											
1928	Talladega	GAL	70	265	38	61	12	0	2		3	12	16	0.230	1B	687	28	3	0.996								
Wheeler, Buck																											
1921	Griffin	GSL																									
Wheeler, Waverly																											
1939	Valdosta	GFL	131	489	82	133	21	6	1	48	17	55	71	0.272	3B	150	267	38	0.916								
Wherry, Kendall		BR TR																									
1949	Moultrie	GFL	22	64	11	14	4	0	0	11	1	26	24	0.219	OF	26	0	3	0.897								
Whetro, Ronald "Ron"		BR TR																									
1955	Valdosta	GFL	15	44	6	8	1	0	2	7	0	6	4	0.182													
Whiddon, John		BR TR																									
1949	Cordele	GFL	11	10	0	0	0	0	0	1	0	2	10	0.000	P	0	3	1	0.750								
Whitaker, James "Jim"		BR TR																									
1948	Valdosta	GFL	43	103	12	21	3	1	0	12	1	29	28	0.204	OF	44	4	5	0.906								
Whitcomb, Donald "Don"		BR TR																									
1956	Brunswick	GFL	122	459	48	106	15	0	23	81	0	18	140	0.231	C	914	92	31	0.970								

Georgia Class-D Minor League Baseball Encyclopedia

YR	TEAM	LG	G	AB	R	H	2B	3B	HR	RBI	SB	BB	SO	BA	POS	PO	A	E	FA	GP	W	L	ERA	IP	H	SO	BB
White, Adel "Abe"		BR TL 6'0" 185 lbs b. 05/16/1904 Winder, GA d. 10/01/1978 Atlanta, GA																									
1928	Carrollton	GAL	29	82	6	14	1	0	1		1	2	18	0.171	P	11	35	5	0.902	29	13	10	3.36	206	217	141	49
1929	Carrollton	GAL	31	85	7	22	3	0	0		0	1	17	0.259	P	6	34	4	0.909	31	10	11		199	214	101	62
1929	Cedartown	GAL	8												P					8	0	5		30	37	9	13
1930	Carrollton	GAL		8		1								0.125	P												
1930	Lindale	GAL	29	79	6	12	0	2	1		0	1	16	0.152	P	4	27	1	0.969	29	11	11	4.35	182	200	143	52
1947	Griffin	GAL	39	89	6	20	0	0	0	8	0	3	12	0.225	M, P	5	34	1	0.975	35	10	13	3.44	220	244	108	32
1948	Griffin	GAL													M												
1950	Griffin	GAL													M												
White, Albert		BR TR																									
1958	Dublin	GFL	18	58	15	16	1	0	0	2	1	20	6	0.276	2B	11	17	3	0.903								
White, Charles		BL																									
1956	Waycross	GFL	3	10		3								0.300													
White, Curtis		BR TR																									
1950	Carrollton	GAL	16	28	3	6	1	0	0	2	0	2	3	0.214	P	1	5	0	1.000	16	4	5	5.55	60	70	35	45
1951	Valley(2) - Alex City(9)	GAL	11	16	3	4	0	0	0	2	1	1	3	0.250	P					9	1	6	7.83	46	64	20	34
1952	Statesboro	GSL	53	134	14	32	5	1	1	11	1	8	27	0.239	P	8	51	1	0.983	37	16	11	2.63	229	179	154	146
1953	Statesboro	GSL	5											0.250													
1954	Statesboro	GSL	2	5		0								0.000	P					2	1	1	<45				
White, E.R.																											
1928	Lindale	GAL	33	125	7	35	1	1	2		2	9	9	0.280	1B	251	21	12	0.958								
1929	Talledega	GAL	28	101	19	22	1	0	0		1	12	8	0.218	SS	56	85	10	0.934								
White, Edward R. "Ed"		BR TR																									
1951	Valdosta	GFL	33	49	7	1	0	0	0	0	0	9	22	0.020	P	8	29	1	0.974	33	10	8	3.99	158	149	75	134
1952	Valdosta	GFL	19	26	7	4	0	0	0	5	0	9	12	0.154	P	3	18	1	0.955	19	8	4	3.92	101	99	54	84
White, Glennwood "Glen"		BR																									
1956	Thomson	GSL	2	10		2								0.200													
White, H.																											
1929	Lindale	GAL	17	66	8	16	2	1	0		3	5	8	0.242	SS	30	30	8	0.882								
1930	Carrollton	GAL	23	84	12	22	5	0	0		0	14	7	0.262	2B	31	38	3	0.958								
White, Jack		BR TR																									
1953	Statesboro	GSL	6											0.667	P						0	4	<45				
White, John F.		BR TR																									
1947	Valley	GAL	28	103	16	23	3	1	1	11	3	9	23	0.223	OF	33	0	3	0.917								
White, John H.		BR TR																									
1955	Moultrie	GFL	8	16		1								0.063	P					8	1	3	<45				
White, Joyner Clifford "Jo-Jo"		BL TR 5'11" 165 lbs b. 06/01/1909 Red Oak, GA d. 10/09/1986 Tacoma, WA																									
1928	Carrollton	GAL	96	364	92	120	14	8	27		18	42	54	0.330	OF	183	21	7	0.967								
White, Ralph																											
1941	Americus	GFL	21	72	8	10	1	1	0	5	0	7	12	0.139	2B	39	28	7	0.905								
White, Randolph		BR TR																									
1952	Fitzgerald	GSL	23	70	6	12	1	1	0	6	0	4	25	0.171	OF	36	0	3	0.923								
White, Robert II "Bob"		BR TR																									
1956	Valdosta	GFL	22	83	12	24	4	1	3	13	2	5	7	0.289	OF	33	2	3	0.921								
1957	Valdosta	GFL	74	254	31	72	11	0	1	28	0	33	22	0.283	1B	567	24	16	0.974								
White, Robert J. "Bob"		BR TR																									
1955	Cordele	GFL	67	223	16	48	7	1	0	21	1	19	47	0.215	C	392	36	16	0.964								
1958	Dublin	GFL	62	211	27	51	10	1	7	46	0	34	28	0.242	C	427	31	8	0.983								
White, Vernon "Vern"		BR TR																									
1956	Sandersville	GSL	4	3		2								0.667	P					4	0	1					
White, William "Bill"		BL TR																									
1946	LaGrange	GAL	24	83	12	19	1	0	0	6	0	7	9	0.229	3B	24	33	11	0.838								
1953	Douglas	GSL	2											0.500													
Whitecavage, Tony		BR TR																									
1952	Brunswick	GFL	19	61	10	8	1	0	2	5	2	10	22	0.131	3B	17	19	8	0.818								
Whited, Gerald		BR TR																									
1949	Carrollton	GAL	12	40	2	8	1	0	0	5	0	0	15	0.200	1B	77	3	1	0.988								
Whitehead, Donald "Don"		BL TL																									
1950	Tifton	GSL	14	18	3	3	1	0	0		0	6	3	0.167	P	0	20	0	1.000	13	3	4	4.34	58	58	16	28
Whiteside, Bright		BR																									
1946	Newnan	GAL	<10																								
Whitfield, ---																											
1913	Talladega	GAL	39	135	11	25					3			0.185	OF	85	19	8	0.929								
1921	Cedartown	GSL													OF												
Whitfield, James "Jim"																											
1941	Albany	GFL	26	105	10	25	7	1	2	14	0	6	17	0.238	OF	54	4	7	0.892								
Whitley, Shirley																											
1941	Valdosta	GFL	4	15	0	2	0	1	0	0	1	1	5	0.133	OF	2	0	0	1.000								
Whitley, Thomas "Tom"		BR																									
1946	LaGrange	GAL	17	50	2	8	2	0	0	2	4	7	21	0.160													
Whitlow, Robert "Bob"																											
1939	Albany	GFL	34	78	6	18	0	1	0	7	0	7	12	0.231	P	11	32	3	0.935	30	17	10	3.10	209	231	113	40
Whitmire, Glen		BL TR																									
1954	Sandersville	GSL	6	21		3								0.143													
1956	Hazlehurst-Baxley	GSL	31	112	13	16	6	0	0	13	1	17	16	0.143	2B	65	74	10	0.933								

Georgia Class-D Minor League Baseball Encyclopedia

YR	TEAM	LG	G	AB	R	H	2B	3B	HR	RBI	SB	BB	SO	BA	POS	PO	A	E	FA	GP	W	L	ERA	IP	H	SO	BB
Whitmore, Donald "Don"		BR TR																									
1946	Moultrie	GFL	34	69	4	15	2	1	0	5	1	3	13	0.217	P	3	33	2	0.947	31	11	10	4.18	168	184	127	65
1947	Moultrie	GFL	13	29	2	3	1	0	0	2	0	2	7	0.103	P	4	10	2	0.875	12	3	4	3.88	65	66	36	26
Whitney, J.F.																											
1914	Newnan	GAL	23	80	90	14					0			0.175	P	10	42	5	0.912	23							
1915	Newnan	GAL	25	77	6	12	3	0	0					0.156	P	9	54	3	0.955	19	8	7					
Whitney, James "Jim"		BR TR																									
1947	Newnan	GAL	29	80	7	14	0	0	0	5	1	5	12	0.175	C	119	10	6	0.956								
Whitson, Howard		BR TR																									
1954	Douglas	GSL	9	16		6								0.375	P					9	2	1	<45				
Whittaker, Charles R.																											
1936	Moultrie	GFL	23	69	11	20	5	3	0	15	0			0.290	OF	23	0	2	0.920								
Whitten, Norman "Norm"		BR																									
1939	Moultrie	GFL	118	418	47	97	13	3	2	38	4	27	60	0.232	C	608	90	24	0.967								
1946	Valley	GAL	<10																								
Whitworth, Robert "Bob"		BR TR																									
1956	Fitzgerald	GFL	13	2473	31	114	24	0	0	54	1	40	41	0.046	C	712	85	22	0.973								
Whitzer, Michael "Mike"		BR TR																									
1954	Douglas	GSL	1	1		0								0.000	P					1	0	0	<45				
Wiacek, Raymond "Ray"		BR TR																									
1948	Newnan	GAL	92	345	55	100	15	4	4	49	8	29	49	0.290	OF	171	14	6	0.969								
Wick, Gilbert "Gil"		BR TR																									
1950	Hazlehurst-Baxley	GSL	11	24	2	6	1	1	0	0	0	1	4	0.250	P	2	12	1	0.933	11	3	7	5.63	64	75	32	50
Wicker (Whicker), Kemp Caswell "K.C."		BR TL 5'11" 182 lbs b. 08/03/1906 Kernersville, NC d. 06/11/1973 Kernersville, NC																									
1928	Carrollton	GAL		7	1	2								0.286	P												
Wicker, ---																											
1914	Cordele - Thomasville	GSL		299	46	79	18	6	8		8			0.264													
1915	Thomasville	FLAG	70	258	24	60	11	1	2		10			0.233	OF	155	18	6	0.966								
Widmayer, Walter "Walt"		BR																									
1955	Waycross	GFL	1	1		1								1.000	M												
Wiebel, Melvin "Mel"																											
1949	Eastman	GSL	116	424	98	113	21	6	2	27	22	104	64	0.267	OF	236	14	11	0.958								
Wieber, Joseph "Joe"		BR TR																									
1953	Douglas	GSL	2											0.000	P					0	0		<45				
Wiegand, Donald "Don"		BR TR																									
1951	Cordele	GFL	29	86	11	16	0	1	0	5	2	14	17	0.186	2B	51	50	12	0.894								
Wiggins, ---																											
1915	Waycross	FLAG	30	43	5	11	1	0	0		4			0.256	P	5	30	3	0.921	18	7	4		121	95	52	28
Wiggins, LeRoy		BR TR																									
1942	Dothan	GFL	13	25	1	2	0	0	0	0	0	4	12	0.080	P	4	19	2	0.920	13	4	1	4.18	71	69	24	28
1942	Americus	GFL	7												P					7	1	2	6.97	31	56	13	11
1946	Valley	GAL	25	48	5	4	0	1	0	3	0	6	16	0.083	P	4	28	1	0.970	23	11	5	3.77	124	119	64	41
1947	Valley(14) - Griffin(13)	GAL	27	64	11	9	0	1	1	3	2	8	24	0.141	P	5	26	3	0.912	24	8	7	3.74	142	158	65	62
Wiggins, Robert "Bob"		BR TR																									
1947	Valley	GAL	16	32	4	4	0	0	0	1	0	3	10	0.125	P	2	8	1	0.909	10	2	4	5.17	54	58	28	39
Wigle, Robert "Bob"		BL TL																									
1950	Americus	GFL	139	526	128	144	25	17	3	71	7	133	73	0.274	OF	244	15	25	0.912								
Wilcox, Ralph		BR TR																									
1951	Brunswick	GFL	126	488	65	122	21	1	8	56	22	41	45	0.250	3B	137	221	49	0.880								
Wilcox, Ronald "Ron"		BR TR																									
1952	Waycross	GFL	21	51	5	6	3	0	0	1	0	2	14	0.118	1B	83	7	7	0.928								
1952	Douglas	GSL	17	41	5	8	1	0	0	3	0	5	15	0.195	P	8	19	1	0.964	14	6	4	3.89	81	77	44	40
Wilcox, Stanley "Stan"		BL TR																									
1951	Americus	GFL	35	130	19	31	4	6	4	21	0	21	22	0.238	OF	58	2	6	0.909								
Wilder, Percy																											
1913	Cordele	ESL	30	95	10	22	2	0	0					0.232	P	9	61	9	0.886	26	16	10					
Wilder, Ralph		BL TL																									
1948	Cordele	GFL	38	85	18	21	2	2	3	13	0	12	24	0.247	P	8	43	5	0.911	30	13	13	3.46	203	209	152	113
Wiley, Jack																											
1941	Thomasville	GFL	28	67	3	7	0	0	0	1	0	5	25	0.104	P	5	42	6	0.887	28	13	7	3.02	179	184	109	59
Wiley, Joseph																											
1915	Talladega	GAL	<10												P	1	7	2	0.800	7	5	2					
1916	Rome	GAL	25	61	7	13					2			0.213	P					15							
Wilhelm, William H. "Bill"		BR																									
1953	Albany	GFL	1											0.000													
Wilkes, ---																											
1913	Thomasville - Cordele	ESL	50	169	18	36	4	7	1					0.213	OF	125	21	7	0.954								
1914	Thomasville	GSL		212	31	48	14	3	2		22			0.226													
1915	Americus-Gainesville	FLAG	71	222	40	57	10	4	5		24			0.257	3B, OF, C	213	81	24	0.925								
Wilkie, ---																											
1928	Lindale	GAL	30	82	8	16	0	0	0		0	3	16	0.195	P	15	34	2	0.961	20	5	14	5.09	145	186	58	30
Wilkinson, David W. "Dave"		BR TR																									
1952	Dublin	GSL	17	21	2	4	0	0	0	2	0	4	3	0.190	P	0	11	2	0.846	14	1	3	6.88	51	63	30	51
Willard, ---																											
1915	Brunswick	FLAG	46	187	33	58	7	2	2		7			0.310	OF	57	8	7	0.903								

Georgia Class-D Minor League Baseball Encyclopedia

YR	TEAM	LG	G	AB	R	H	2B	3B	HR	RBI	SB	BB	SO	BA	POS	PO	A	E	FA	GP	W	L	ERA	IP	H	SO	BB
Willard, Miles		BR TR																									
1954	Statesboro	GSL	47	181	31	49	6	3	2	18	7	15	24	0.271	SS	86	138	25	0.900								
Willard, Stanley "Stan"		BR TR																									
1948	Americus	GFL	126	533	102	161	21	12	2	68	22	40	64	0.302	2B, SS	336	298	74	0.895								
Willett, Charles R.																											
1906	Valdosta	GSL													M												
Willett, Dennis		BR TR																									
1962	Moultrie	GFL	37	122	16	28	2	0	0	8	6	8	21	0.230	SS	45	76	19	0.864								
1963	Moultrie	GFL	111	445	73	130	12	1	1	21	22	35	58	0.292	SS	160	261	31	0.931								
Willett, Raymond "Ray"		BR TR																									
1946	Thomasville	GFL	126	549	72	136	13	2	1	41	19	40	61	0.248	SS	285	432	75	0.905								
1947	Thomasville	GFL	42	164	24	41	8	0	1	7	4	13	12	0.250	SS	65	133	11	0.947								
1952	Thomasville	GFL	132	557	61	135	17	5	2	62	17	27	47	0.242	SS	356	399	39	0.951								
Willey, Joe																											
1941	Moultrie	GFL	16	48	2	9	0	0	0	4	0	3	12	0.188	P	11	21	1	0.970	13	1	6	3.64	89	113	34	26
Williams, ---																											
1913	Opelika	GAL	38	109	14	29					7			0.266	P	28	27	6	0.902	23	10	13					
1914	LaGrange	GAL	31	88	6	14					0			0.159	P	30	53	3	0.965	31							
1916	LaGrange	GAL	26	71	3	12					2			0.169	P												
Williams, ---																											
1913	Gadsden	GAL	90	367	62	101					40			0.275	1B	861	31	19	0.979								
1914	Gadsden	GAL	55	188	18	33					2			0.176	OF	103	11	7	0.942								
Williams, ---																											
1914	Opelika	GAL	89	314	32	74					8			0.236	C	464	78	10	0.982								
Williams, ---																											
1920	LaGrange	GSL																									
Williams, ---																											
1928	Lindale - Anniston	GAL	22	39	2	7	2	0	0		0	1	5	0.179	P	5	26	1	0.969	22	8	8	4.15	115	119	53	30
Williams, ---		BR																									
1946	Tallahassee	GFL	<10																								
Williams, Benjamin "Ben"		BR TR																									
1951	Fitzgerald	GSL	16	44	6	10	1	0	1	3	0	6	7	0.227	3B	9	22	10	0.756								
Williams, Carl		BR																									
1955	Vidalia	GSL	8	19		2								0.105													
Williams, Charles "Charlie"		BR TR																									
1941	Thomasville - Americus	GFL	26	95	9	19	1	1	0	4	1	7	24	0.200	2B	43	53	12	0.889								
1946	Thomasville	GFL	17	71	8	12	1	0	0	4	2	9	13	0.169	2B	38	47	10	0.895								
Williams, Clifford "Cliff"		BR TR																									
1949	Tallahassee	GFL	12	20	1	4	1	1	0	2	0	1	8	0.200	P	0	10	2	0.833	12	1	1	7.71	49	52	27	43
Williams, Curtis		BR TR																									
1947	LaGrange	GAL	14	17	1	3	0	0	0	0	0	2	4	0.176	P	1	4	0	1.000	14	3	4	9.60	45	61	12	30
Williams, David Carlous "Davey"		BR TR 5'10" 160 lbs b. 11/02/1927 Dallas, TX																									
1947	Waycross	GFL	132	464	147	131	34	10	8	75	28	136	53	0.282	2B	377	374	41	0.948								
Williams, Dick		BR TR																									
1938	Thomasville	GFL	12	43	8	11	1	1	0	5	0	4	8	0.256	OF	15	0	2	0.882								
Williams, Don Q.		BR TR																									
1954	Thomasville	GFL	123	418	65	130	22	12	3	59	15	64	53	0.311	C, P	721	90	15	0.982	1	0	0	<45				
Williams, Ed		BL TL																									
1946	Valley	GAL	18	29	2	5	1	1	0	3	0	2	5	0.172	P	5	26	3	0.912	17	7	5	3.47	96	95	59	44
1947	Valley	GAL	9												P					9	4	3	3.33	46	49	15	16
Williams, Franklin		BR TR																									
1955	Dublin	GSL	54	181	24	43	6	0	4	22	3	15	30	0.238	OF	76	7	5	0.943								
Williams, Fred		BL TR																									
1956	Valdosta	GFL	17	58	14	16	3	1	0	7	1	13	5	0.276	2B	22	24	7	0.868								
Williams, Fred "Papa"		BR TR 6'1" 200 lbs b. 07/17/1913 Meridian, MS d. 11/02/1993 Meridian, MS																									
1951	Waycross	GFL	120	465	64	137	19	4	0	79	16	40	9	0.295	M, 1B	1072	86	16	0.986								
1952	Waycross	GFL	113	399	27	98	18	1	0	53	6	26	12	0.246	M, 1B	974	71	16	0.985								
Williams, Galen		BS TR																									
1955	Albany	GFL	132	498	115	159	28	14	6	79	27	103	39	0.319	2B	270	356	38	0.943								
Williams, James "Jim"		BL TL																									
1955	Moultrie	GFL	19	60	13	17	1	0	0	2	2	15	12	0.283	1B	119	14	4	0.971								
1955	Douglas	GSL	14	43	6	8	0	0	2	7	0	10	11	0.186	1B	98	7	4	0.963								
Williams, James "Jim"		BR TR																									
1955	Hazlehurst-Baxley	GSL	39	121	9	27	7	0	0	13	2	20	17	0.223	C	177	21	5	0.975								
1956	Albany	GFL	127	413	48	104	15	1	0	53	11	80	66	0.252	C	977	80	17	0.984								
Williams, Jerry		BR TR																									
1956	Sandersville	GSL	76	157	23	37	7	0	0	21	1	38	41	0.236	OF, P	39	20	3	0.952	30	10	5	3.79	164	158	109	76
Williams, John		BR TR																									
1953	Jesup	GSL	6											0.000	P						0	3	<45				
1954	Thomasville(29) - Ame-Cor(31)	GFL	60	193	16	40	9	1	0	18	2	25	32	0.207	OF	115	2	11	0.914								
1958	Brunswick	GFL	11	8	1	1	0	0	0	0	0	1	3	0.125	P	0	5	1	0.833	10	2	3	<30				
Williams, Kerr		BR TR																									
1940	Moultrie	GFL	31	92	6	23	3	0	0	6	0	1	20	0.250	P					27	10	13	4.52	205	293	53	54
Williams, Luke A.																											
1920	Carrollton	GSL		42	3	7								0.167	SS												

Georgia Class-D Minor League Baseball Encyclopedia

YR	TEAM	LG	G	AB	R	H	2B	3B	HR	RBI	SB	BB	SO	BA	POS	PO	A	E	FA	GP	W	L	ERA	IP	H	SO	BB
Williams, Lynn																											
1939	Thomasville	GFL	12	33	6	9	0	0	0	2	0	5	9	0.273	C	42	10	6	0.897								
Williams, Marvin "Marv"		BL TL																									
1949	Valdosta	GFL	36	81	11	13	1	0	0	3	0	10	32	0.160	P	5	30	9	0.795	33	15	11	2.41	202	151	226	115
Williams, Norman "Norm"																											
1941	Tallahassee	GFL	10	36	2	3	0	0	0	2	0	2	6	0.083	SS	8	33	7	0.854								
Williams, Paul		BR TR																									
1946	Carrollton	GAL	39	119	15	31	2	1	0	14	5	11	16	0.261	3B	33	53	12	0.878								
1957	Fitzgerald	GFL	1	0										0.000	P					1	0	0	<30				
Williams, Richard A. "Dick"		BL TR																									
1958	Dublin	GFL	23	57	10	9	3	0	0	5	2	19	8	0.158	OF	25	2	2	0.931								
Williams, Robert "Bob"		BL																									
1948	Carrollton	GAL	11	24	2	4	0	0	0	1	0	3	7	0.167													
Williams, Robert "Bob"		BR TR																									
1955	Valdosta	GFL	107	399	46	92	15	4	2	41	8	43	64	0.231	SS	203	335	53	0.910								
1956	Valdosta	GFL	7	23		3								0.130													
1956	Hazlehurst-Baxley	GSL	22	70	7	10	2	1	0	6	1	5	20	0.143	SS, P	24	44	9	0.883	6	4	2					
1957	Valdosta	GFL	24	45	3	7	0	1	0	3	0	3	8	0.156	P	2	21	1	0.958	17	4	7	5.11	88	100	52	63
Williams, Wallace																											
1942	Dothan	GFL	17	44	7	11	0	1	0	9	0	4	8	0.250	P	4	0	1	0.800	14	8	3	3.98	86	88	67	36
Williams, Wiley		BR TR																									
1946	Thomasville	GFL	46	142	11	28	7	1	0	14	0	21	47	0.197	1B	397	21	13	0.970								
Williams, William "Bill"		BL																									
1947	Alexander City	GAL	12	26	2	5	0	0	0	0	0	1	9	0.192													
Williams, William "Bill"		BR TR																									
1957	Brunswick	GFL	20	69	11	13	1	1	0	15	0	12	20	0.188	2B	29	32	4	0.938								
Williamson, ---																											
1930	Anniston	GAL	1												P					1	1	0	0.00	1	1	1	0
Williamson, James C. "Jim"		BL TR																									
1958	Brunswick	GFL	61	242	45	73	8	0	2	33	3	39	20	0.302	2B	132	107	11	0.956								
Williamson, Silas Albert "Al"		BR TR 5'11" 160 lbs b. 02/20/1900 Buckville, AR d. 11/29/1978 Hot Springs, AR																									
1921	LaGrange	GSL													P												
Willingham, Coney		BR																									
1946	Newnan	GAL	<10																								
Willingham, Jack		BR																									
1946	Waycross	GFL	<10																								
Willingham, John		BR TR																									
1956	Haz-Bax - Vidalia	GSL	61	155	12	38	8	1	1	22	3	11	21	0.245	C, P	121	32	5	0.968	11	0	2	4.29	42	47	13	19
Willingham, Ralph		BR TR																									
1946	Thomasville	GFL	15	30	3	7	2	0	0	9	0	1	9	0.233	P	1	14	6	0.714	13	4	5	3.97	68	73	52	28
Willis, Charles R.		BR TR																									
1949	Valdosta	GFL	29	47	6	9	0	0	0	3	0	5	16	0.191	P	3	38	4	0.911	27	3	13	4.35	124	108	77	95
Willis, Clarence E.		BR TR																									
1942	Americus	GFL	48	135	12	26	3	1	0	14	2	12	25	0.193	P	28	43	4	0.947	30	9	9	4.12	190	201	91	101
1948	Valdosta	GFL	14	26	4	8	2	0	0	3	0	5	10	0.308	P	3	15	5	0.783	14	3	5	3.63	67	52	51	59
Willis, James "Jim"		BL TR																									
1956	Tifton	GFL	103	382	67	89	9	3	11	51	14	64	94	0.233	OF	141	9	16	0.904								
Willis, Joel		BR																									
1946	Thomasville	GFL	<10																								
Willis, Robert E. "Bob"		BR TR																									
1953	Douglas	GSL	2											0.333	P						0	1	<45				
Willis, Ronald Earl "Ron"		BR TR 6'2" 195 lbs b. 07/12/1943 Willisville, TN d. 11/21/1977 Memphis, TN																									
1962	Brunswick	GFL	57	179	31	45	8	2	5	19	5	15	55	0.251	OF, P	58	25	9	0.902	20	7	6	4.38	78	71	68	55
Willis, Virgil "Bud"		BL TR																									
1955	Tifton	GFL	102	321	53	80	12	1	4	29	10	39	74	0.249	OF	115	5	17	0.876								
Willoughby, Carl																											
1941	Waycross	GFL	123	492	72	129	21	5	4	61	5	53	112	0.262	1B	1081	46	25	0.978								
Willoughby, John																											
1935	Tallahassee	GFL	33	107	10	35	3	1	0		1	12	6	0.327	C	78	11	3	0.967								
1936	Americus	GFL	84	280	41	87	15	2	7	42	1			0.311	C	340	52	10	0.975								
Wills, William "Bill"		BL TL																									
1950	Hazlehurst-Baxley	GSL	16	63	8	9	4	2	0	7	0	6	25	0.143	OF	26	1	3	0.900								
Wilshere, Carl		BR TR																									
1938	Albany	GFL	33	100	12	25	2	0	0	13	1	7	16	0.250	P	17	44	3	0.953	28	17	6	4.03	212	191	120	129
1939	Albany	GFL	38	104	11	23	1	1	0	21	0	5	23	0.221	P	14	50	8	0.889	29	8	12	3.19	206	211	94	93
1940	Albany	GFL	<10												P								<35				
Wilson, ---																											
1906	Waycross	GSL													P, OF												
Wilson, ---																											
1914	Talladega	GAL	72	252	21	56				7				0.222	2B	109	98	28	0.881								
1915	Anniston	GAL	13	42	2	8	3	0	0					0.190	2B	15	35	5	0.909								
1916	LaGrange	GAL	70	271	45	60				22				0.221	OF												
Wilson, ---																											
1928	Anniston	GAL	25	92	12	19	3	2	0	4	4	18	0.207		OF	61	5	3	0.957								
1930	Huntsville	GAL	28	119	23	40	6	0	4	1	6	12	0.336		2B, 3B	51	43	15	0.862								

Georgia Class-D Minor League Baseball Encyclopedia

YR	TEAM	LG	G	AB	R	H	2B	3B	HR	RBI	SB	BB	SO	BA	POS	PO	A	E	FA	GP	W	L	ERA	IP	H	SO	BB
Wilson, Clyde		BR TR																									
1947	Moultrie	GFL	24	38	4	5	0	0	0	2	0	5	15	0.132	C	60	4	0	1.000								
Wilson, Donald Edmond "Ed"		BR TR																									
1950	Jesup	GSL	82	320	71	115	27	10	2	37	13	62	48	0.359	OF	188	13	15	0.931								
1951	Eastman	GSL	18	75	10	27	3	1	1	8	10	10	9	0.360	OF	48	1	5	0.907								
1954	Americus-Cordele	GFL	5	0										0.000													
Wilson, Francis		BR TR																									
1956	Thomasville	GFL	136	560	63	128	17	3	1	45	21	45	99	0.229	OF	247	18	14	0.950								
Wilson, George D.		BL																									
1946	Americus	GFL	7												P					7	3	2	4.70	46	46	56	37
Wilson, Hugh																											
1941	Tallahassee	GFL	83	302	53	75	8	0	0	22	12	79	59	0.248	2B	233	234	41	0.919								
Wilson, Jack																											
1920	Carrollton	GSL		85	8	18								0.212	OF, 2B, 3B, SS												
Wilson, James "Jim"		BR TR																									
1954	Sandersville	GSL	88	365	66	95	13	4	2	20	7	41	52	0.260	2B, 3B, SS, P	140	202	69	0.832	1	1	0		<45			
Wilson, James M. "Jim"																											
1949	Hazlehurst-Baxley	GSL	116	422	54	79	9	4	0	35	11	62	103	0.187	SS	174	237	53	0.886								
Wilson, Lonnie		BR TR																									
1958	Waycross	GFL	18	41	2	5	1	1	0	2	0	5	12	0.122	C	64	7	4	0.947								
1963	Brunswick	GFL	31	20	3	4	1	0	0	3	0	2	7	0.200	OF, P	2	11	1	0.929	22	3	6	6.00	45	49	41	50
Wilson, Martin		BL TL																									
1946	Waycross	GFL	47	192	24	44	14	2	0	36	0	9	20	0.229	1B	439	15	9	0.981								
Wilson, Nesbit Clarence "Nesby"		BR TR 6'0" 200 lbs b. 10/11/1922 East Spencer, NC																									
1946	Tallassee	GAL	31	125	23	40	11	3	2	17	0	12	11	0.320	OF	70	1	2	0.973								
Wilson, Norman "Norm"		BR TR																									
1946	Waycross	GFL	106	347	51	100	21	1	0	58	15	60	40	0.288	C	643	85	19	0.975								
1952	Cordele	GFL	121	368	47	85	24	0	0	49	2	86	41	0.231	M, C	571	69	14	0.979								
Wilson, Richard "Dick"		BL TL																									
1955	Hazlehurst-Baxley	GSL	4	6		0								0.000	P					4	1	2					
Wilson, Robert "Bob"		BR TR																									
1955	Vidalia	GSL	105	429	87	132	24	11	5	70	34	31	45	0.308	3B	131	160	36	0.890								
Wilson, Walter Wood "Walt"		BL TR 6'4" 190 lbs b. 11/24/1913 Glenn, GA d. 04/17/1994 Bremen, GA																									
1947	LaGrange	GAL	17	44	3	10	1	0	0	2	0	5	12	0.227	P	10	23	1	0.971	17	7	9	4.23	117	135	72	30
Wilson, Ward A.		BR TR																									
1953	Douglas	GSL	12	20	1	3	2	0	0	1	0	5	3	0.150	P	5	10	2	0.882	12	3	3	3.88	58	41	37	57
1954	Valdosta	GFL	10	13	1	4	0	0	0	1	0	2	2	0.308	P					9	2	1		<45			
Wilson, Warren J. "Jack"		BL TR																									
1955	Brunswick	GFL	140	502	125	175	26	8	3	97	21	99	38	0.349	OF	331	12	8	0.977								
Wilson, William C. "Bill"		BR TR																									
1952	Hazlehurst-Baxley	GSL	100	377	40	114	13	2	4	73	5	50	47	0.302	3B	121	181	32	0.904								
Winchell, ---																											
1915	Rome	GAL	<10												P					<6							
Winchester, Joseph "Joe"		BR TR																									
1963	Waycross	GFL	24	34	1	6	0	0	0	1	0	4	16	0.176	C	54	2	0	1.000								
Wingard, Ernest James Sr. "Ernie" "Doc"		BL TL 6'2" 176 lbs b. 10/17/1900 Prattville, AL d. 01/17/1977 Prattville, AL																									
1941	Thomasville	GFL	34	96	13	26	3	0	2	15	0	12	13	0.271	1B	254	9	10	0.963								
Wingard, Ernest Jr. "Ernie"		BL TR																									
1950	LaGrange	GAL	103	386	107	118	12	9	20	87	8	89	51	0.306	2B	260	278	37	0.936								
Winges, ---																											
1913	Valdosta	ESL	43	122	6	14	0	0	0					0.115	P, OF	38	69	10	0.915	24	17	7					
1914	Valdosta	GSL		110	14	25	0	0	0		7			0.227													
1915	Valdosta - Thomasville	FLAG	9												P					9	1	6		65	81	14	33
Wingfield, ---																											
1917	Talladega	GAL	16	59	11	17	0	2	0		7			0.288	1B, 3B, SS	87	24	7	0.941								
Wingo, James "Jim"		BR TR																									
1948	Americus	GFL	31	64	8	13	1	0	0	8	0	9	23	0.203	P	8	38	2	0.958	28	11	11	5.02	174	193	110	137
1949	Americus	GFL	16	23	2	4	1	0	0	1	0	4	8	0.174	P	2	16	1	0.947	16	3	7	6.31	77	88	41	45
Wingo, Kelly																											
1941	Moultrie	GFL	38	178	26	41	11	0	0	11	1	12	22	0.230	3B	34	93	16	0.888								
Winkelspecht, Robert "Bob"		BR TR																									
1950	LaGrange	GAL	132	450	69	108	18	5	12	63	5	66	89	0.240	SS	226	358	38	0.939								
Winn, Breezy																											
1929	Carrollton	GAL		12	0	3								0.250	OF, P												
1930	Huntsville	GAL	11	28	4	8	1	1	0		1	2	3	0.286	P					8	1	3	7.24	46	70	13	20
Winters, Charles		BR TL																									
1951	Alexander City	GAL	10	13	3	2	1	0	0	1	0	4	1	0.154													
1951	Brunswick	GFL	11	16	0	2	0	0	0	1	0	1	4	0.125	P	1	12	1	0.929	11	0	7	7.31	48	69	19	29
Winters, William L. "Bill"		BR TR																									
1950	Griffin	GAL	16	21	1	4	0	0	0	1	0	3	4	0.190	P	1	9	0	1.000								
Wiren, John		BR TR																									
1949	Valdosta	GFL	72	185	30	41	4	2	2	35	1	29	60	0.222	OF, C	190	22	13	0.942								
Wishba, Joseph "Joe"		BR TR																									
1948	Fitzgerald	GSL	16	51	3	3	1	0	0	3	1	10	13	0.059	OF	19	0	2	0.905								

Georgia Class-D Minor League Baseball Encyclopedia

YR	TEAM	LG	G	AB	R	H	2B	3B	HR	RBI	SB	BB	SO	BA	POS	PO	A	E	FA	GP	W	L	ERA	IP	H	SO	BB
Wisniewski, John		BR TR																									
1955	Tifton	GFL	97	370	57	104	15	5	0	35	15	55	46	0.281	SS	154	222	40	0.904								
Wissman, Edward H. "Ed"		BL TL																									
1950	Dublin	GSL	62	201	33	46	8	0	10	31	1	26	21	0.229	M, 1B, P	304	28	6	0.982	17	9	4	3.23	117	124	47	41
Witkowski, John		BL																									
1946	Thomasville	GFL	<10																								
Witz, Thomas "Tom"		BR TR																									
1947	Americus	GFL	12	14	0	1	0	0	0	0	0	6	7	0.071	P	2	11	2	0.867	12	1	2	6.80	49	61	15	38
Witzke, Howard		BR TR																									
1947	Griffin	GAL	25	62	8	15	1	1	0	7	3	5	11	0.242	2B	39	33	5	0.935								
Woddail, Charles																											
1941	Waycross	GFL	138	539	102	174	21	8	7	75	5	60	54	0.323	OF	358	9	16	0.958								
Wodka, Richard "Dick"		BR TR																									
1957	Albany	GFL	14	21	3	6	0	0	0	2	0	3	2	0.286	P	4	15	3	0.864	14	4	2	3.36	59	61	43	35
Wojcik, Frank																											
1935	Albany	GFL	72	271	39	73	15	3	3		6	25	43	0.269	IF	142	173	41	0.885								
Woleen, Raymond		BR TL																									
1946	Thomasville	GFL	120	334	40	70	8	4	0	33	5	39	89	0.210	OF	170	10	11	0.942								
Wolf, Hugh		BR TR																									
1950	Tifton	GSL	23	67	10	10	0	0	0	11	1	3	12	0.149	C	46	4	3	0.943								
Wolf, Lawrence																											
1941	Cordele	GFL	124	463	52	112	20	9	7	70	12	61	69	0.242	OF	256	19	14	0.952								
Wolfe, ---																											
1913	Americus	ESL	22	68	9	17	0	0	0					0.250	P	17	20	3	0.925								
Wolfe, Earl		BR TR																									
1948	Cordele	GFL	19	65	9	13	1	0	0	5	3	11	10	0.200	2B	53	33	11	0.887								
Wolfe, Tom																											
1930	Huntsville	GAL	59	217	56	66	14	5	5		16	43	40	0.304	3B, SS, OF	126	118	31	0.887								
Wolfman, Cedric		BR TR																									
1954	Brunswick	GFL	8	11		2								0.182	P					8	2	2	<45				
1955	Statesboro	GSL	10	33	5	10	3	0	0	8	1	0	11	0.303	P					4	0	4					
Wollitz, Herman		BL TL																									
1947	Tallassee	GAL	14	35	7	9	3	0	0	5	0	4	10	0.257	P	3	17	1	0.952	12	5	3	2.97	91	79	31	47
Womack, Alfred "Al"		BL TL																									
1955	Vidalia	GSL	11	10	1	3	0	0	0	2	0	1	4	0.300	P	0	6	3	0.667	10	2	4	10.93	28	41	25	34
Womack, Charles		BR TR																									
1940	Cordele	GFL	11	38	1	6	2	0	0	2	0	1	15	0.158	OF	11	1	7	0.632								
Wood, ---																											
1914	Gadsden	GAL	48	62	4	11					1			0.177	P	16	20	3	0.923	48							
Wood, ---																											
1914	Brunswick	GSL		114	5	15	0	0	0		0			0.132													
Wood, ---																											
1936	Americus	GFL													P									<30			
Wood, Don		BR																									
1950	Albany	GFL	10	20	0	2	0	0	0	0	0	2	8	0.100													
Wood, Gordon		BR TR																									
1951	Rome	GAL	48	76	9	12	2	0	1	9	0	5	24	0.158	P	7	40	4	0.922	38	6	14	4.87	170	203	78	97
Wood, Norman		BR TR																									
1929	Lindale	GAL	18	45	2	7	2	0	0		0	0	8	0.156	P	16	31	4	0.922	15	5	5		95	105	43	28
1930	Lindale	GAL	24	59	11	14	2	1	1		0	0	11	0.237	P	8	21	4	0.879	19	8	7	4.60	133	160	49	29
Wood, Ronald "Ron"																											
1962	Moultrie	GFL	4	5	2	1	0	0	0	0	0	1	2	0.200	P					4	1	1	6.75	12	20	8	9
Wood, Thomas "Tom"		BL TL																									
1957	Albany	GFL	26	57	7	17	0	0	1	10	0	1	9	0.298	P	3	9	4	0.750	13	1	2	5.29	51	47	27	43
1958	Albany	GFL	64	119	17	29	3	1	0	17	1	11	20	0.244	OF, P	26	22	2	0.960	30	14	4	3.31	147	127	103	97
Wood, W.G.																											
1935	Americus	GFL	34	97	5	16	0	1	1		1	6	7	0.165	P					38	16	11		149	258	97	54
Wood, William "Bill"		BR TR																									
1951	Moultrie	GFL	49	195	27	65	7	4	1	24	1	19	3	0.333	OF	141	7	4	0.974								
Woodall, Richard "Dick"		BR																									
1955	Hazlehurst-Baxley	GSL	3	7		0								0.000													
Woodington, ---																											
1936	Cordele	GFL													P								<30				
Woodring, Richard "Dick"		BR TR																									
1948	Valdosta	GFL	22	149	30	44	8	3	3	27	2	21	34	0.295	OF	63	5	7	0.907								
Woodruff, Ernest		BL TR																									
1949	LaGrange	GAL	17	54	10	13	2	0	0	1	1	12	11	0.241	OF	17	3	2	0.909								
1949	Dublin	GSL	12	47	3	10	1	0	0	4	1	6	6	0.213	OF	16	1	0	1.000								
Woodruff, Ridley		BR																									
1946	LaGrange	GAL	<10																								
Woods, Julian R.		BR TR																									
1949	Eastman	GSL	53	189	35	54	9	1	3	35	2	29	20	0.286	OF	130	7	9	0.938								
1950	Eastman	GSL	137	486	87	133	26	6	7	79	14	100	71	0.274	OF	246	9	16	0.941								
Woods, Ralph		BR TR																									
1962	Thomasville	GFL	75	236	53	68	6	3	5	50	8	46	53	0.288	C	545	47	14	0.977								

Georgia Class-D Minor League Baseball Encyclopedia

YR	TEAM	LG	G	AB	R	H	2B	3B	HR	RBI	SB	BB	SO	BA	POS	PO	A	E	FA	GP	W	L	ERA	IP	H	SO	BB
Wooldridge, Floyd Lewis "Floyd"		BR TR 6'1" 185 lbs b. 08/25/1928 Jerico Springs, MO																									
1950	Albany	GFL	54	94	16	22	5	1	0	16	2	13	17	0.234	P	10	41	2	0.962	31	14	12	3.36	201	181	168	105
Wooley, James E. "Jim"		BL TL																									
1948	Alexander City	GAL	102	341	54	91	11	8	2	44	26	64	72	0.267	OF	192	11	16	0.927								
1949	Alexander City	GAL	106	342	90	98	21	5	1	37	29	83	50	0.287	OF	198	8	6	0.972								
1950	Alexander City	GAL	107	377	81	111	12	11	3	36	29	101	41	0.294	OF	258	19	17	0.942								
1951	Alexander City	GAL	23	82	17	20	1	1	0	10	4	16	8	0.244	OF	56	2	4	0.935								
Woolford, Edward "Ed"		BR TR																									
1954	Albany	GFL	26	84	9	18	3	2	0	10	0	7	9	0.214	2B	63	67	8	0.942								
Woolford, Ralph		BL																									
1948	Tallahassee	GFL	7												P					7	7	0	1.64	55	38	72	22
Wooten, Robert "Bob"		BL TL																									
1940	Cordele	GFL	80	314	33	80	9	2	0	26	2	14	33	0.255	1B	504	29	15	0.973								
Wopinek, George		BR TR																									
1948	Tallahassee	GFL	136	560	118	175	25	12	6	83	7	81	69	0.313	SS	240	463	82	0.896								
Workman, Harry Hall "Hoge"		BR TR 5'11" 170 lbs b. 09/25/1899 Huntington, WV d. 05/20/1972 Ft. Myers, FL																									
1921	LaGrange	GSL													P												
Worrell, Joseph "Joe"		BR TR																									
1958	Albany	GFL	7	8		1								0.125	P					7	1	2		<30			
Worsham, Benjamin E. "Ben"		BR TR																									
1949	Eastman	GSL	18	36	5	7	1	0	0	4	0	4	12	0.194	P	6	25	0	1.000	24	4	7	7.60	103	91	57	24
1951	Eastman	GSL	8												P					8	2	3	4.17	54	53	22	25
Wrenn, Milton E. "Milt"		BR TR																									
1947	Moultrie	GFL	100	345	52	100	15	8	3	56	8	42	51	0.290	C	604	70	12	0.983								
1949	Moultrie	GFL	16	46	6	7	0	0	0	1	2	10	9	0.152	C	60	15	3	0.962								
1951	Tifton(26) - Moultrie(78)	GFL	104	349	52	78	18	4	1	26	14	82	36	0.223	OF, C	326	74	20	0.952								
1952	Moultrie	GFL	33	101	11	24	5	0	0	10	1	11	8	0.238	C	160	17	3	0.983								
Wright, ---																											
1915	Valdosta	FLAG	22	70	5	16	2	0	0		2			0.229	OF	14	1	0	1.000								
Wright, ---																											
1930	Anniston	GAL	86	334	52	81	6	7	1		10	38	36	0.243	3B	102	163	18	0.936								
Wright, ---																											
1930	Lindale	GAL	6												P					6	3	2	11.42	26	37	12	17
Wright, Dixie		BR TR																									
1948	Eastman	GSL	55	136	18	35	12	2	1	24	4	15	16	0.257	C	146	13	8	0.952								
1949	Eastman	GSL	46	162	16	37	5	0	0	20	4	12	26	0.228	C	260	19	5	0.982								
1951	Eastman	GSL	16	45	3	12	1	0	0	6	0	3	2	0.267	C	38	4	5	0.894								
1952	Eastman	GSL	42	144	10	32	10	0	0	15	0	11	11	0.222	C	299	12	12	0.963								
Wright, George P.		BR TR																									
1950	Douglas	GSL	12	21	3	6	1	0	0	2	0	2	8	0.286	P	3	13	2	0.889	12	3	4	4.21	62	66	16	32
Wright, James H. "Jim"		BR TR																									
1950	Dublin	GSL	117	442	99	131	33	2	3	65	10	102	52	0.296	SS	194	261	53	0.896								
1956	Thomasville	GFL	8	14		1								0.071													
1957	Thomasville	GFL	5	3		0								0.000													
Wright, Jerry F.		BR TR																									
1953	Thomasville	GFL	13	17	1	1	0	0	0	0	0	3	7	0.059	P	1	10	1	0.917	13	2	1	3.72	46	49	26	40
1956	Thomasville	GFL	5	8		3								0.375	P					5	1	3		<45			
Wright, Kenneth W. "Ken"		BR TR																									
1953	Vidalia	GSL	27	91	16	20	2	1	0	4	4	12	16	0.220	2B, SS	52	72	10	0.925								
Wright, Owen																											
1936	Americus	GFL	11	16	2	5	0	0	0	3	0			0.313	P					11	3	4	7.40	45		26	23
Wright, Paul A.																											
1942	Moultrie	GFL	41	89	10	16	1	1	0	5	0	7	27	0.180	P	6	63	2	0.972	39	20	8	2.57	235	232	95	56
Wright, Richard "Dick"		BR TR																									
1954	Albany	GFL	1	0										0.000	P					1	0	0		<45			
Wright, Richard A. "Dick"		BL TL																									
1954	Douglas	GSL	11	37	3	8	2	0	0	1	0	1	10	0.216	P					8	3	1	3.75	48	54	26	19
Wright, Roger		BR TR																									
1957	Thomasville	GFL	2	2		0								0.000	M, P					2	0	0		<30			
Wright, Tyre Maurice "Maurice"		BR TR																									
1946	Tallassee	GAL	93	362	70	96	17	4	7	45	17	34	47	0.265	SS	185	269	31	0.936								
1947	Tallassee	GAL	125	482	89	123	22	6	5	57	14	61	54	0.255	SS	240	389	58	0.916								
Wright, William "Bill"																											
1939	Thomasville	GFL	11	29	2	6	0	0	0	0	0	0	3	0.207	SS	7	6	1	0.929								
Wright, William "Bill"		BR TR																									
1954	Valdosta	GFL	11	10	2	3	0	0	0	1	0	4	5	0.300	P	4	6	3	0.769	10	0	5		<45			
Wrobke, Floyd E. "Joe"		BR TR																									
1939	Waycross	GFL	7	14	0	2	0	0	0	0	0	1	5	0.143	P	3	13	2	0.889	7	6	1	2.49	47	40	28	16
1940	Waycross	GFL	14	37	7	7	0	0	0	6	0	5	10	0.189	P					12	6	4	3.14	86	82	44	32
Wroblewski, Erwin R.																											
1942	Albany	GFL	95	353	66	92	18	5	0	47	19	40	65	0.261	2B, SS	136	315	52	0.897								
Wrona, Joseph "Joe"		BR TR																									
1954	Douglas	GSL	10	14	2	2	0	0	0	0	0	2	5	0.143	P	0	6	1	0.857	10	3	2		<45			
Wulf, John Eugene "Gene"		BR TR																									
1942	Albany	GFL	8	18	0	5	0	0	0	3	0	1	9	0.278	P	0	7	0	1.000	9	2	6	4.88	48	53	18	26

Georgia Class-D Minor League Baseball Encyclopedia

YR	TEAM	LG	G	AB	R	H	2B	3B	HR	RBI	SB	BB	SO	BA	POS	PO	A	E	FA	GP	W	L	ERA	IP	H	SO	BB
Wulff, Clayton "Clay"		BR TR																									
1954	Sandersville	GSL	30	108	17	18	4	0	0	9	0	33	34	0.167	SS	41	95	23	0.855								
Wyatt, Billy E.		BR TR																									
1956	Tifton	GFL	66	233	25	45	4	1	1	24	1	29	35	0.193	SS	94	178	22	0.925								
Wyatt, Eugene R. "Gene"		BR TR																									
1952	Hazlehurst-Baxley	GSL	103	434	94	122	19	3	12	48	16	42	70	0.281	OF	211	13	8	0.966								
1953	Hazlehurst-Baxley	GSL	98	384	99	101	15	2	19	68	13	68	76	0.263	OF	243	13	11	0.959								
1954	Hazlehurst-Baxley	GSL	41	149	14	22	5	0	0	14	4	17	51	0.148	OF	77	6	1	0.988								
Wyatt, John W.		BR TR																									
1962	Dublin	GFL	10	13	1	1	1	0	0	1	1	2	5	0.077	P	2	2	2	0.667	10	1	4	4.95	40	43	34	17
Wylie, Mark		BR TR																									
1956	Vidalia	GSL	17	29	4	8	1	0	0	1	0	3	3	0.276	M, P	1	6	1	0.875	13	2	1	2.11	47	35	45	12
Wysocki, Stanley "Stan"		BR TR																									
1939	Cordele	GFL	33	77	6	11	1	0	0	5	0	7	22	0.143	P	6	53	3	0.952	29	9	11	4.17	192	200	78	72
1940	Cordele	GFL	47	113	11	13	1	0	0	5	0	13	41	0.115	P					41	8	19	3.85	250	314	79	68
Yablon, Nathan		BR TR																									
1950	Douglas(34) - Tifton(10)	GSL	44	81	6	13	1	1	0	6	0	4	29	0.160	P	18	63	3	0.964	42	9	12	3.79	209	219	81	101
Yance, James Ray "Jim"		BR TL																									
1951	Albany	GFL	14	16	0	3	0	0	0	2	0	1	3	0.188	P	0	6	0	1.000	14	3	0	5.55	47	33	32	76
Yancek, Frank		BR TR																									
1946	Tallahassee	GFL	30	39	9	5	2	0	0	2	1	15	8	0.128	P	5	33	5	0.884	30	8	9	4.74	131	148	79	61
Yancey, ---																											
1906	Americus	GSL													OF												
Yancey, Charles "Carl"		BR TR																									
1948	Opelika	GAL	20	84	13	16	2	0	0	9	0	11	17	0.190	SS	25	37	8	0.886								
Yanchura, John		BR TR																									
1952	Eastman	GSL	108	409	58	101	18	3	0	27	5	44	57	0.247	SS	171	338	57	0.899								
1953	Eastman	GSL	29	117	37	31	6	1	0	12	3	26	21	0.265	SS	61	88	19	0.887								
Yappel, August		BR TR																									
1957	Valdosta	GFL	2	1		0								0.000	P					2	0	1		<30			
Yarborough, Mack		BR TR																									
1949	Carrollton	GAL	4												SS												
1950	Cordele	GFL	138	539	98	94	12	3	1	39	11	110	131	0.174	SS	254	396	74	0.898								
Yarbrough, Daniel "Dan"		BR TR																									
1955	Moultrie	GFL	6	12		1								0.083	P					1	0	0		<45			
Yarbrough, James "Jim"		BR TR																									
1954	Fitzgerald	GFL	9	20		3								0.150													
1955	Moultrie	GFL	138	505	91	118	30	7	14	85	8	95	97	0.234	OF, C	279	23	5	0.984								
1956	Douglas	GSL	25	92	19	26	5	1	4	15	3	16	18	0.283	OF, P	58	4	2	0.969	3	0	1					
Yates, William Bentley "Bill"		BR TR																									
1953	Douglas	GSL	31	111	13	25	4	1	0	13	1	10	15	0.225	3B	26	36	8	0.886								
Yawn, Sidney "Sid"		BR TR																									
1947	Alexander City	GAL	23	66	9	17	2	0	0	4	1	8	11	0.258	C	93	14	6	0.947								
Yearty, Samuel Joseph "Sam"		BR TR																									
1946	Carrollton	GAL	6												P					6	1	0	0.00	20	26	3	3
1953	Sandersville	GSL	25	50	4	8	0	0	0	2	0	1	11	0.160	P	1	13	2	0.875	19	6	6	4.70	92	104	61	34
Yeates, Douglas "Doug"		BR TR																									
1940	Albany	GFL	24	70	2	5	0	0	0	0	0	3	26	0.071	P					24	8	9	3.34	167	156	83	85
Yebernetsky, George		BR TR																									
1947	Tallahassee	GFL	36	67	8	21	6	1	0	8	0	6	10	0.313	P	6	37	5	0.896	35	13	9	3.69	188	180	108	75
1948	Tallahassee	GFL	34	91	14	25	7	1	0	9	0	15	25	0.275	P	4	64	4	0.944	33	16	13	3.74	236	281	142	82
Yeider, Marshall J.		BR TR																									
1952	Vidalia	GSL	19	42	3	8	2	0	0	6	0	3	24	0.190	P	4	21	2	0.926	16	6	8	5.61	101	105	80	62
Yetsko, Andrew "Andy"		BR TR																									
1955	Sandersville	GSL	44	95	15	25	6	1	3	17	0	11	29	0.263	P	7	36	1	0.977	32	10	11	3.48	189	172	128	77
Yoder, Robert L. "Bob"		BL TR																									
1953	Thomasville	GFL	90	346	64	104	16	6	0	50	6	29	25	0.301	2B	221	200	17	0.961								
Yodhes, John		BR TR																									
1958	Thomasville	GFL	30	133	22	41	5	2	1	21	3	14	21	0.308	OF	28	2	0	1.000								
Yohn, Charles		BL TL																									
1947	Thomasville	GFL	39	69	11	13	1	0	0	5	0	3	17	0.188	P	9	34	4	0.915	39	15	7	2.44	192	178	88	74
Yon, ---																											
1915	Anniston	GAL	<6												P					<6							
Yonchuk, Walter "Walt"		BR TR																									
1940	Moultrie	GFL	134	542	87	148	15	8	0	61	7	41	61	0.273	OF, IF	341	173	45	0.919								
York, Lewis "Lew"		BR TR																									
1946	Carrollton	GAL	121	427	71	129	19	0	19	84	11	37	52	0.302	1B, OF, P	444	12	24	0.950	1	0	0	0.00	1			
York, Preston Rudolph "Rudy"		BR TR 6'1" 209 lbs b. 08/17/1913 Ragland, AL d. 02/05/1970 Rome, GA																									
1949	Griffin	GAL	33	80	13	15	2	0	1	9	0	42	20	0.188	M, 1B	163	20	5	0.973								
Yosipovich, Lou		BR TR																									
1940	Thomasville	GFL	10	10	1	1	0	0	0	0	0	5	4	0.100	OF	7	0	0	1.000								
Yost, ---																											
1921	Cedartown	GSL													SS												

Georgia Class-D Minor League Baseball Encyclopedia

YR	TEAM	LG	G	AB	R	H	2B	3B	HR	RBI	SB	BB	SO	BA	POS	PO	A	E	FA	GP	W	L	ERA	IP	H	SO	BB
Young, ---																											
1913	Anniston	GAL	8												P					8	4	4					
1915	Anniston	GAL	<6												P					<6							
Young, Claude B.		BR TR																									
1950	Vidalia-Lyons	GSL	60	239	38	76	11	1	10	38	3	17	35	0.318	2B, OF	95	45	7	0.952								
1951	Dublin	GSL	72	301	69	115	24	2	15	76	4	25	20	0.382	3B	64	134	20	0.908								
Young, Donald J. "Don"		BL TL																									
1955	Hazlehurst-Baxley	GSL	8	8		3								0.375	P					7	0	1					
1956	Hazlehurst-Baxley	GSL	4	4		1								0.250	P					4	0	2					
Young, Donald Wayne "Don"		BR TR 6'2" 185 lbs b. 10/18/1945 Houston, TX																									
1963	Brunswick	GFL	16	50	9	14	4	0	0	5	1	7	12	0.280	OF	28	0	0	1.000								
Young, Ford		BR TR																									
1957	Thomasville	GFL	25	32	0	6	0	0	0	0	0	0	9	0.188	P	4	24	2	0.933	23	2	10	5.14	91	122	57	41
Young, Harmon		BR TR																									
1953	Jesup	GSL	54	186	38	54	17	3	9	40	3	47	28	0.290	3B	70	100	13	0.929								
Young, Herbert "Herb"		BR TR																									
1948	Waycross	GFL	47	103	20	32	7	0	2	14	0	10	10	0.311	P	7	38	7	0.865	26	13	8	4.39	164	172	136	104
1949	Waycross	GFL	21	42	11	15	1	0	3	9	0	4	6	0.357	P	8	11	1	0.950	11	2	7	7.36	55	60	41	53
1950	Waycross	GFL	29	73	11	18	6	0	1	11	1	11	7	0.247	OF	14	2	2	0.889								
Young, Kenneth "Ken"		BR																									
1963	Thomasville	GFL	3	5	0	2	1	0	0	1	0	0	2	0.400													
Young, Phillip "Phil"		BR TR																									
1957	Brunswick	GFL	42	120	14	23	4	0	1	20	1	19	16	0.192	C	202	24	9	0.962								
Young, Texal "Tex"		BL TL																									
1947	Cordele	GFL	19	36	3	5	0	1	0	6	0	0	11	0.139	P	3	19	5	0.815	15	0	8	3.80	71	71	22	35
1948	Vidalia-Lyons	GSL	33	84	11	19	4	1	0	8	1	4	26	0.226	P	6	43	7	0.875	28	14	11	2.82	185	181	109	64
1949	Vidalia-Lyons - Dublin	GSL	23	63	11	15	3	0	0	11	2	7	9	0.238	P	5	39	6	0.880	24	7	10	6.02	142	120	63	52
Young, Wade		BR TR																									
1956	Dublin	GSL	6	9		0								0.000	P					6	0	1					
Young, William Clyde "Bill"																											
1942	Dothan	GFL	26	83	10	22	3	0	0	7	0	16	14	0.265	OF	37	6	3	0.935								
Young, William J. "Bill"		BR TR																									
1952	Moultrie	GFL	141	487	80	119	21	5	7	54	30	120	37	0.244	3B, OF	238	70	22	0.933								
1953	Vidalia	GSL	5											0.000													
Youngblood, Jack		BR TR																									
1952	Jesup	GSL	11	25	1	3	0	0	0	1	0	1	10	0.120													
1953	Sandersville	GSL	3											0.000	P						0	1		<45			
Yow, Forrest R.		BL TL																									
1950	Tifton(61) - Douglas(34)	GSL	95	384	65	108	22	4	7	53	9	34	62	0.281	OF	125	5	13	0.909								
1951	Douglas	GSL	124	496	80	145	23	3	9	89	8	49	34	0.292	OF	175	8	11	0.943								
1952	Douglas	GSL	77	302	53	79	10	1	7	39	8	37	50	0.262	OF	123	5	10	0.928								
Yudin, Robert "Bob"		BR TR																									
1951	Americus	GFL	14	44	0	2	0	0	0	4	0	4	16	0.045	OF	11	5	2	0.889								
Yurman, Frank		BR TR																									
1956	Vidalia	GSL	22	47	5	10	1	0	0	5	0	5	14	0.213	P	1	19	0	1.000	18	11	5	2.25	116	95	68	48
Zabek, Edward "Ed"		BR TR																									
1947	Thomasville	GFL	118	437	61	102	15	4	0	54	2	39	39	0.233	3B, SS	136	309	51	0.897								
Zachritz, Charles																											
1939	Albany	GFL	52	205	28	54	9	7	3	32	5	21	34	0.263	C	271	37	11	0.966								
Zackery, Rollie		BR TR																									
1962	Brunswick	GFL	40	147	29	40	6	1	6	32	4	27	41	0.272	OF	56	3	3	0.952								
Zaden, Louis "Lou"		BR TR																									
1950	Opelika	GAL	41	156	35	59	7	4	5	26	8	15	15	0.378	OF, C	107	17	4	0.969								
1951	Opelika	GAL	13	50	13	11	3	0	2	7	1	9	8	0.220	OF	16	6	2	0.917								
Zajac, Henry																											
1936	Albany	GFL	11	23	2	5	1	0	0	1	0			0.217	P					11	4	3	3.10	61		21	16
Zander, Ronald "Ron"		BR TR																									
1958	Dublin	GFL	39	123	17	15	3	0	2	17	2	33	35	0.122	OF	64	4	5	0.932								
Zangari, Frank		BR TR																									
1951	Albany	GFL	124	434	60	82	8	0	1	43	17	62	63	0.189	2B	339	376	36	0.952								
1952	Thomasville	GFL	53	165	27	33	4	1	1	16	1	37	15	0.200	2B	89	126	16	0.931								
Zapke, ---																											
1914	Americus	GSL		29	1	4	0	0	0		2			0.138													
Zaski, Regis		BL																									
1954	Brunswick	GFL	14	35	11	11	3	2	0	5	1	3	5	0.314													
Zazzera, Marino "Ben"		BR TR																									
1948	LaGrange	GAL	13	39	7	8	0	1	1	3	1	4	13	0.205	OF	11	0	2	0.846								
Zeccola, Peter "Pete"		BR																									
1948	Tallahassee	GFL	13	13	2	3	1	0	0	1	0	1	9	0.231													
Zeihen, Bernard		BR TR																									
1957	Waycross	GFL	39	30	3	4	1	0	0	2	0	7	13	0.133	P	7	23	1	0.968	38	8	5	4.38	109	97	52	52
1958	Waycross	GFL	23	35	9	4	1	0	0	2	1	3	4	0.114	P	4	11	1	0.938	23	5	6	4.17	95	107	58	45
Zeiser, Harry		BR TR																									
1948	Tallahassee	GFL	139	479	82	105	12	1	0	52	4	110	92	0.219	3B	136	229	35	0.913								
Zeitler, John "Jack"		BR TR																									
1954	Valdosta	GFL	24	73	8	18	2	0	1	9	0	17	6	0.247	SS	36	48	17	0.832								

Georgia Class-D Minor League Baseball Encyclopedia

YR	TEAM	LG	G	AB	R	H	2B	3B	HR	RBI	SB	BB	SO	BA	POS	PO	A	E	FA	GP	W	L	ERA	IP	H	SO	BB
Zeleznock, John		BR TR																									
1958	Albany	GFL	53	198	45	55	10	3	9	50	9	31	33	0.278	OF, P	116	2	4	0.967	3	0	0	<30				
Zelinsky, Matt		BR TR																									
1950	Cordele	GFL	48	169	17	49	8	2	0	29	6	28	15	0.290	3B, OF	84	32	6	0.951								
Zeller, Barton Wallace "Bart"		BR TR 6'1" 185 lbs b. 07/22/1941 Chicago Heights, IL																									
1963	Brunswick	GFL	8	23	4	7	4	0	0	6	1	5	1	0.304													
Zellers, ---																											
1913	Valdosta	ESL	51	149	16	31	2	0	0					0.208	P, OF	26	48	8	0.902	28	15	13					
1914	LaGrange	GAL	52	157	18	35					3			0.223	P	38	35	4	0.948	52							
1915	Rome	GAL	10	24	2	7	3	0	0					0.292	P	4	15	0	1.000	6	3	3					
Zellner, Jerome		BR TL																									
1958	Thomasville	GFL	30	37	8	10	0	0	2	3	0	2	10	0.270	P	3	15	3	0.857	29	1	10	7.96	95	98	70	134
Zera, Angelo		BR TR																									
1948	Baxley	GSL	15	55	5	6	1	1	0	4	0	4	17	0.109	OF	12	0	1	0.923								
Zernial, Gus Edward "Gus" "Ozark Ike"		BR TR 6'2" 210 lbs b. 06/27/1923 Beaumont, TX																									
1942	Waycross	GFL	95	367	54	105	25	4	3	49	0	39	98	0.286	OF	162	5	8	0.954								
Zeski, Donald "Don"		BR TR																									
1950	Valdosta	GFL	26	53	1	7	2	0	0	7	0	8	19	0.132	P	5	23	4	0.875	26	10	8	4.33	158	121	203	157
Zgraggen, Orlando		BR TR																									
1954	Sandersville	GSL	2	0										0.000	P					2	0	1	<45				
Zich, Henry		BR TR																									
1948	Tallassee	GAL	126	504	70	147	29	12	0	78	19	39	30	0.292	1B	1143	60	25	0.980								
Zientara, Benedict Joseph "Benny"		BR TR 5'9" 165 lbs b. 02/14/1918 Chicago, IL d. 04/16/1985 Lake Elsinore, CA																									
1957	Brunswick	GFL	1	2	0									0.000	M, P					1	0	0	<30				
Zimmer, Harold		BR TR																									
1952	Dublin	GSL	118	490	75	135	31	4	7	77	14	25	40	0.276	OF, P	182	18	14	0.935	13	3	2	6.67	54	51	38	50
Zimmerlink, Frank Eugene "Gene"		BL TL																									
1954	Dublin	GSL	43	99	13	21	3	1	0	9	0	4	6	0.212	P	5	37	7	0.857	30	13	12	4.61	205	188	200	122
Zimmerman, George		BR TR																									
1939	Valdosta	GFL	10	27	2	11	0	0	0	2	0	0	1	0.407	C	38	9	0	1.000								
1940	Valdosta	GFL	76	269	38	78	10	2	1	32	5	26	19	0.290	C	446	27	9	0.981								
Zimmerman, Glenn		BL TR																									
1951	Americus	GFL	76	304	78	91	12	3	4	41	27	69	27	0.299	2B	198	227	23	0.949								
Zimmerman, Richard "Dick"		BR TL																									
1954	Thomasville	GFL	3	0										0.000	P					3	0	2	<45				
Zirafi, Antonio		BR TR																									
1949	Americus	GFL	13	22	3	3	0	0	0	1	0	2	11	0.136	P	1	18	4	0.826	13	2	8	4.13	72	63	25	35
Zitek, Donald "Don"		BR TR																									
1955	Moultrie	GFL	32	53	2	12	2	2	0	5	0	7	20	0.226	P	10	8	5	0.783	17	4	7	3.62	92	89	37	44
Zivich, George		BR TR																									
1941	Thomasville	GFL	15	57	7	11	2	0	0	4	4	9	15	0.193	OF	22	3	0	1.000								
Zodda, Victor A. "Vic"		BR TR																									
1946	Valdosta	GFL	76	289	44	72	12	3	0	30	11	35	39	0.249	OF, C	204	39	13	0.949								
Zoeller, Simon Lee		BR TR																									
1942	Americus	GFL	36	132	25	33	6	0	0	9	0	13	35	0.250	2B	82	99	13	0.933								
Zolliecoffer, Heartsell R. "Bob"																											
1949	Douglas	GSL	25	66	7	8	1	0	0	1	0	6	16	0.121	P	9	26	3	0.921	30	13	9	4.29	189	106	99	77
Zuccarini, Robert "Bob"		BR TR																									
1952	Hazlehurst-Baxley	GSL	124	449	87	115	21	0	15	82	15	94	115	0.256	OF	257	12	16	0.944								
1953	Hazlehurst-Baxley	GSL	119	411	131	144	24	5	19	12	22	130	58	0.350	OF	231	13	4	0.984								
1956	Waycross	GFL	81	278	51	71	18	2	8	59	3	74	56	0.255	OF	133	2	8	0.944								
Zwierzynski, Adam		BR TR																									
1947	Americus	GFL	20	66	12	12	0	2	0	6	1	12	13	0.182	OF	22	2	2	0.923								
Zwirko, William "Bill"		BR TR																									
1950	Hazlehurst-Baxley	GSL	79	310	29	58	8	1	3	23	1	38	56	0.187	2B	216	236	25	0.948								

Georgia Class-D Minor League Baseball Encyclopedia

Georgia Class-D League Major Leaguers

This section is covers players and managers of the Georgia-Alabama, Georgia-Florida, or Georgia State League who also spent time in the major leagues as a player or manager. While it was most common for a player to advance from the minors into the majors, it was quite common for players to play in the minors after having been in the majors. These listings include each player's full name, years spent in the Georgia leagues, years spent in the majors, and any honors achieved as a major leaguer.

Georgia Class-D Leaguers Who Played in the Majors

Adams, Ace Townsend "Ace"
(1937 Cordele-GFL, 1952 Fitzgerald-GSL)
1941-1946 New York Giants – NL
   All-Star – 1943

Alexander, David Dale "Dale"
(1940 Thomasville-GFL)
1929-1932 Detroit Tigers – AL
1932-1933 Boston Red Sox – AL

Allen, Frank Leon "Frank"
(1928-1929 Gadsden-GAL, 1930 Talladega-GAL)
1912-1914 Brooklyn Dodgers/Superbas/Robins – NL
1914-1915 Pittsburgh Pirates – NL
1916-17 Boston Braves – NL

Alperman, Charles Augustus "Whitey"
(1913 Waycross-ESL)
1906-1909 Brooklyn Superbas – NL

Antolick, Joseph "Joe"
(1948 Moultrie-GFL)
1944 Philadelphia Phillies – NL

Archer, James William "Jim"
(1951 LaGrange-GAL)
1961-1962 Kansas City Athletics – AL

Arcia, Jose Raimundo (Orta) "Jose"
(1962 Moultrie/Thomasville-GFL)
1968 Chicago Cubs – NL
1969-1970 San Diego Padres – NL

Aspromonte, Robert Thomas "Bob"
(1957 Thomasville-GFL)
1956 Brooklyn Dodgers – NL
1960-1961 Los Angeles Dodgers – NL
1962-1968 Houston Colt .45's/Astros – NL
1969-1970 Atlanta Braves – NL
1971 New York Mets – NL
   NLCS – 1969

Azcue, Jose Joaquin (Lopez), "Joe"
(1956 Moultrie-GFL, 1956 Douglas-GSL)
1960 Cincinnati Reds – NL
1962-1963 Kansas City Athletics – AL
1963-1969 Cleveland Indians – AL
1969 Boston Red Sox – AL
1969-1972 California Angels – AL
   All-Star – 1968

Bailey, James Hopkins "Jim"
(1956 Moultrie-GFL)
1959 Cincinnati Reds – NL

Bakenhaster, David Lee "Dave"
(1963 Brunswick-GFL)
1964 St. Louis Cardinals – NL

Baker, Howard Francis "Howard"
(1914-1915 Talladega-GAL)
1912 Cleveland Naps – AL
1914-1915 Chicago White Sox – AL
1915 New York Giants – NL

Bankston, Wilborn Everett "Everett"
(1914 Cordele-GSL)
1915 Philadelphia Athletics – AL

Barbare, Walter Lawrence "Walter"
(1930 Talladega-GAL)
1914-1916 Cleveland Naps/Indians – AL
1918 Boston Red Sox – AL
1919-1920 Pittsburgh Pirates – NL
1921-1922 Boston Braves – NL

Barber, Stephen David "Steve"
(1958 Dublin-GFL)
1960-1967 Baltimore Orioles – AL
1967-1968 New York Yankees – AL
1969 Seattle Pilots – AL
1970 Chicago Cubs – NL
1970-1972 Atlanta Braves – NL
1972-1973 California Angels – AL
1974 San Francisco Giants – NL
   All-Star – 1963, 1966

Georgia Class-D Minor League Baseball Encyclopedia

Barrett, Francis Joseph "Frank"
(1935-1936 Albany-GFL)
1939 St. Louis Cardinals – NL
1944-1945 Boston Red Sox – AL
1946 Boston Braves – NL
1950 Pittsburgh Pirates – NL

Bartley, Boyd Owen "Boyd"
(1954 Thomasville-GFL)
1943 Brooklyn Dodgers – NL

Basgall, Romanus "Monty"
(1942 Valdosta-GFL)
1948-1949, 1951 Pittsburgh Pirates – NL

Bearden, Henry Eugene "Gene"
(1939 Moultrie-GFL)
1947-1950 Cleveland Indians – AL
1950-1951 Washington Senators – AL
1952 St. Louis Browns – AL
1953 Chicago White Sox – AL
   World Series – 1948

Beazley, John Andrew "Johnny"
(1937 Tallahassee-GFL)
1941-1942, 1946 St. Louis Cardinals – NL
1947-1949 Boston Braves – NL
   World Series – 1942, 1946

Behrman, Henry Bernard "Hank"
(1941 Valdosta-GFL)
1946-1948 Brooklyn Dodgers – NL
1947 Pittsburgh Pirates – NL
1949 New York Giants – NL
   World Series – 1947

Belinsky, Robert "Bo"
(1956 Brunswick-GFL)
1962-1964 Los Angeles Angels – AL
1965-1966 Philadelphia Phillies – NL
1967 Houston Astros – NL
1969 Pittsburgh Pirates – NL
1970 Cincinnati Reds – NL

Bell, Gary "Gary"
(1955 Vidalia-GSL)
1958-1967 Cleveland Indians – AL
1967-1968 Boston Red Sox – AL
1969 Seattle Pilots – AL
1969 Chicago White Sox – AL
   All-Star – 1960, 1966, 1968
   World Series – 1967

Benjamin, Alfred Stanley "Stan"
(1937-1938 Thomasville-GFL)
1939-1942 Philadelphia Phillies – NL
1945 Cleveland Indians – AL

Bessent, Fred Donald "Don"
(1950 LaGrange-GAL)
1955-1957 Brooklyn Dodgers – NL
1958 Los Angeles Dodgers – NL
   World Series – 1955, 1956

Bevil (Bevilacqua), Louis Eugene "Lou"
(1941 Thomasville-GFL)
1942 Washington Senators – AL

Bishop, Charles Tuller "Charlie"
(1946 Albany-GFL)
1952-1954 Philadelphia Athletics – AL
1955 Kansas City Athletics – AL

Blackburn, James Ray "Jim"
(1941-1942 Cordele-GFL)
1948, 1951 Cincinnati Reds – NL

Bloodworth, James Henry "Jimmy"
(1935 Panama City-GFL)
1937, 1939-1941 Washington Senators – AL
1942-1943, 1946 Detroit Tigers – AL
1947 Pittsburgh Pirates – NL
1949-1950 Cincinnati Reds – NL
1950-1951 Philadelphia Phillies – NL
   World Series – 1950

Boone, Isaac Morgan "Ike"
(1920 Cedartown-GSL)
1922 New York Giants – NL
1923-1925 Boston Red Sox – AL
1927 Chicago White Sox – AL
1930-1932 Brooklyn Robins/Dodgers – NL

Boozer, John Morgan "John"
(1958 Brunswick-GFL)
1962-1964, 1966-1969 Philadelphia Phillies – NL

Borom, Edward Jones "Red"
(1935 Tallahassee-GFL)
1944-1945 Detroit Tigers – AL

Bosser, Melvin Edward "Mel"
(1939-1940 Thomasville-GFL, 1946 Carrollton-GAL)
1945 Cincinnati Reds – NL

Bowden, David Timon "Tim"
(1920 Rome-GSL)
1914 St. Louis Browns – AL

Bowers, Stewart Cole "Stew"
(1939-1940 Thomasville-GFL)
1935-1936 Boston Red Sox – AL

Bradshaw, George Thomas "George"
(1947 Valdosta-GFL)
1952 Washington Senators – AL

Brady, James Joseph "Jim"
(1958 Thomasville-GFL)
1956 Detroit Tigers – AL

Bray, Clarence Wilbur "Buster"
(1939 Waycross-GFL)
1941 Boston Braves – NL

Breeden, Danny Richard "Danny"
(1963 Brunswick-GFL)
1969 Cincinnati Reds – NL
1971 Chicago Cubs – NL

Breeden, Harold Noel "Hal"
(1963 Waycross-GFL)
1971 Chicago Cubs – NL
1972-1975 Montreal Expos – NL

Breeding, Marvin Eugene "Marv"
(1955 Cordele-GFL)
1960-1962 Baltimore Orioles – AL
1963 Washington Senators – AL

432

Georgia Class-D Minor League Baseball Encyclopedia

1963 Los Angeles Dodgers – NL

Brewster, Charles Lawrence "Charlie"
(1940-1941, 1948, 1954 Waycross-GFL)
1943 Cincinnati Reds – NL
1943 Philadelphia Blue Jays – NL
1944 Chicago Cubs – NL
1946 Cleveland Indians – AL

Brown, Lloyd Andrew "Lloyd"
(1946 Newnan-GAL, 1955 Cordele-GFL, 1956 Thomson-GSL)
1925 Brooklyn Robins – NL
1928-1932 Washington Senators – AL
1933 St. Louis Browns – AL
1933 Boston Red Sox – AL
1934-1937 Cleveland Indians – AL
1940 Philadelphia Phillies – NL

Brown, Norman Ladelle "Norm"
(1937-1938 Moultrie-GFL)
1943, 1946 Philadelphia Athletics – AL

Bruner, Walter Roy "Roy"
(1937-1938 Thomasville-GFL)
1939-1941 Philadelphia Phillies – NL

Brunsberg, Arlo Adolph "Arlo"
(1962 Thomasville-GFL)
1966 Detroit Tigers – AL

Burright, Larry Allen "Larry"
(1957 Thomasville-GFL)
1962 Los Angeles Dodgers – NL
1963-1964 New York Mets – NL

Burrows, John "John"
(1941 Moultrie-GFL)
1943 Philadelphia Athletics – AL
1943-1944 Chicago Cubs – NL

Butler, Cecil Dean "Cecil"
(1958 Waycross-GFL)
1962, 1964 Milwaukee Braves – NL

Cain, Merritt Patrick "Sugar"
(1930 Carrollton-GAL, 1948 Vidalia-Lyons-GSL)
1932-1935 Philadelphia Athletics – AL
1935-1936 St. Louis Browns – AL
1936-1938 Chicago White Sox – AL

Camp, Howard Lee "Howie"
(1913-1915, 1929 Talladega-GAL, 1928 Anniston-GAL)
1917 New York Yankees – AL

Carey, Max George "Max"
(1955 Cordele-GFL)
1910-1926 Pittsburgh Pirates – NL
1926-1929 Brooklyn Robins – NL
Hall of Fame
World Series – 1925

Carlyle, Roy Edward "Roy"
(1921 Griffin-GSL)
1925 Washington Senators – AL
1925-1926 Boston Red Sox – AL
1926 New York Yankees – AL

Carmel, Leon James "Duke"
(1955-1956 Albany-GFL)
1959-1960, 1963 St. Louis Cardinals – NL
1963 New York Mets – NL
1965 New York Yankees – AL

Carroll, Dorsey Lee "Dixie"
(1928 Talladega-GAL, 1929 Anniston-GAL, 1930 Huntsville-GAL)
1919 Boston Braves – NL

Castiglione, Peter Paul "Pete"
(1941 Moultrie-GFL)
1947-1953 Pittsburgh Pirates – NL
1953-1954 St. Louis Cardinals – NL

Cates, Eli Eldo "Eli"
(1913 Brunswick-ESL, 1916 Rome-GAL)
1908 Washington Senators – AL

Cathey, Hardin Abner "Hardin"
(1940 Thomasville-GFL)
1942 Washington Senators – AL

Ceccarelli, Arthur Edward "Art"
(1949 Valdosta-GFL)
1955-1956 Kansas City Athletics – AL
1957 Baltimore Orioles – AL
1959-1960 Chicago Cubs – NL

Center, Marvin Earl "Pete"
(1937 Americus-GFL)
1942-1943, 1945-1946 Cleveland Indians – AL

Chaplin (Chapman), Bert Edgar "Ed"
(1920 Carrollton-GSL)
1920-1922 Boston Red Sox – AL

Chase, Kendall Fay "Ken"
(1935 Panama City-GFL)
1936-1941 Washington Senators – AL
1942-1943 Boston Red Sox – AL
1943 New York Giants – NL

Cheney, Thomas Edgar "Tom"
(1952-1953 Albany-GFL)
1957, 1959 St. Louis Cardinals – NL
1960-1961 Pittsburgh Pirates – NL
1961-1964, 1966 Washington Senators – AL
World Series – 1960

Christenbury, Lloyd Reid "Lloyd"
(1916 Newnan-GAL, 1916-1917 Anniston-GAL)
1919-1922 Boston Braves – NL

Churn, Clarence Nottingham "Chuck"
(1963 Moultrie-GFL)
1957 Pittsburgh Pirates – NL
1958 Cleveland Indians – AL
1959 Los Angeles Dodgers – NL
World Series – 1959

Clancy, John William "Bud"
(1942 Valdosta-GFL)
1924-1930 Chicago White Sox – AL
1932 Brooklyn Dodgers – NL
1934 Philadelphia Phillies – NL

Clark, Glen Ester "Glen"
(1962 Dublin-GFL)
1967 Atlanta Braves – NL

Clark, Philip James "Phil"
(1951, 1953 Albany-GFL)
1958-1959 St. Louis Cardinals – NL

Clary, Ellis "Ellis"
(1935-1936 Americus-GFL)
1942-1943 Washington Senators – AL
1943-1945 St. Louis Browns – AL
  World Series – 1944

Clemens, Chester Spurgeon "Chet"
(1937 Tallahassee-GFL)
1939, 1944 Boston Bees/Braves – NL

Coble, David Lamar "Dave"
(1936 Moultrie-GFL, 1949-1950 Douglas-GSL, 1950 Tifton-GSL)
1939 Philadelphia Phillies – NL

Cohen, Hyman "Hy"
(1948-1949 LaGrange-GAL)
1955 Chicago Cubs – NL

Colcolugh, Thomas Bernard "Tom"
(1915 Americus-Gainesville-FLAG)
1893-1895 Pittsburgh Pirates – NL
1899 New York Giants – NL

Coles, Charles Edward "Chuck"
(1950 Valdosta-GFL)
1958 Cincinnati Reds – NL

Cook, Raymond Clifford "Cliff"
(1955 Moultrie-GFL, 1955 Douglas-GSL)
1959-1962 Cincinnati Reds – NL
1962-1963 New York Mets – NL

Corbett, Eugene Louis "Gene"
(1952 Albany-GFL)
1936-1938 Philadelphia Phillies – NL

Cosman, James Henry "Jim"
(1963 Brunswick-GFL)
1966-1967 St. Louis Cardinals – NL
1970 Chicago Cubs – NL

Costello, Daniel Francis "Dan"
(1917 Anniston-GAL)
1913 New York Yankees – AL
1914-1916 Pittsburgh Pirates – NL

Cottier, Charles Keith "Chuck"
(1954 Americus-Cordele-GFL)
1959-1960 Milwaukee Braves – NL
1961 Detroit Tigers – AL
1961-1965 Washington Senators – AL
1968-1969 California Angels – AL

Coveney, John Patrick "Jack"
(1913-1914 Waycross-ESL/GSL)
1903 St. Louis Cardinals – NL

Craft, Maurice Montague "Molly"
(1928 Anniston/Lindale-GAL)
1916-1919 Washington Senators – AL

Craig, Roger Lee "Roger"
(1950 Valdosta-GFL)
1955-1957 Brooklyn Dodgers – NL
1958-1961 Los Angeles Dodgers – NL
1962-1963 New York Mets – NL
1964 St. Louis Cardinals – NL
1965 Cincinnati Reds – NL
1966 Philadelphia Phillies – NL
  World Series – 1955, 1956, 1959, 1964

Culberson, Delbert Leon "Leon"
(1951 Rome-GAL)
1943-1947 Boston Red Sox – AL
1948 Washington Senators – AL
  World Series – 1946

Currie, William Cleveland "Bill"
(1950 Waycross-GFL)
1955 Washington Senators – AL

Curtis, Vernon Eugene "Vern"
(1942 Waycross-GFL)
1943-1944, 1946 Washington Senators – AL

Cusick, John Peter "Jack"
(1946 Americus-GFL)
1951 Chicago Cubs – NL
1952 Boston Braves – NL

Dahl, Jay Steven "Jay"
(1963 Moultrie-GFL)
1963 Houston Colt .45's – NL

Daniel, Handley Jacob "Jake"
(1946, 1950 Valley-GAL, 1946-1947 LaGrange-GAL, 1947 Newnan-GAL, 1952-1953 Vidalia-GSL)
1937 Brooklyn Dodgers – NL

Davis, John Wilbur "Bud"
(1914 Opelika/Talladega-GAL, 1916 Newnan-GAL)
1915 Philadelphia Athletics – AL

Davis, Woodrow Wilson "Woody"
(1936 Cordele-GFL, 1939-1940 Valdosta-GFL)
1938 Detroit Tigers – AL

Dean, James Harry "Harry"
(1946 Carrollton-GAL)
1941 Washington Senators – AL

Decatur, Arthur Rue "Art"
(1914-1915 Talladega-GAL)
1922-1925 Brooklyn Robins – NL
1925-1927 Philadelphia Phillies – NL

DeKoning, William Callahan "Bill"
(1939 Americus-GFL)
1945 New York Giants – NL

DeShong, James Brooklyn "Jimmie"
(1951 Cordele-GFL)
1932 Philadelphia Athletics – AL
1934-1935 New York Yankees – AL
1936-1939 Washington Senators – AL

Detweiler, Robert Sterling "Ducky"
(1951 Cordele-GFL)
1942, 1946 Boston Braves – NL

Georgia Class-D Minor League Baseball Encyclopedia

DeViveiros, Bernard John "Bernie"
(1940 Americus-GFL)
1924 Chicago White Sox – AL
1927 Detroit Tigers – AL

Diering, Charles Edward Allen "Chuck"
(1942 Albany-GFL)
1947-1951 St. Louis Cardinals – NL
1952 New York Giants – NL
1954-1956 Baltimore Orioles – AL

Dillard, David Donald "Don"
(1955 Vidalia-GSL)
1959-1962 Cleveland Indians – AL
1963, 1965 Milwaukee Braves – NL

Doll, Arthur James "Art"
(1946 Tallahassee-GFL)
1936, 1938 Boston Bees – NL

Douglas, Charles William "Whammy"
(1954-1955 Brunswick-GFL)
1957 Pittsburgh Pirates – NL

Driscoll, James Bernard "Jim"
(1962 Dublin-GFL)
1970 Oakland Athletics – AL
1972 Texas Rangers – AL

Duckworth, James Raymond "Jim"
(1958 Thomasville-GFL)
1963-1966 Washington Senators – AL
1966 Kansas City Athletics – AL

Duffalo, James Francis "Jim"
(1955 Brunswick-GFL)
1961-1965 San Francisco Giants – NL
1965 Cincinnati Reds – NL

Dusak, Ervin Frank "Erv"
(1939-1940 Albany-GFL)
1948, 1950-1951 St. Louis Cardinals – NL
1951 Pittsburgh Pirates – NL
World Series – 1946

Dustal, Robert Andrew "Bob"
(1956 Valdosta-GFL)
1963 Detroit Tigers – AL

East, Carlton William "Carl"
(1914 Thomasville-GSL, 1930 Carrollton-GAL, 1947 LaGrange-GAL)
1915 St. Louis Browns – AL
1924 Washington Senators – AL

East, Gordon Hugh "Hugh"
(1948 Tallassee-GAL)
1941-1943 New York Giants – NL

Easterling, Paul "Paul"
(1951 Hazlehurst-Baxley-GSL)
1928, 1930 Detroit Tigers – AL
1938 Philadelphia Athletics – AL

Elmore, Verdo Wilson "Verdo"
(1929 Anniston-GAL)
1924 St. Louis Browns – AL

Endicott, William Franklin "Bill"
(1937-1938 Albany-GFL)
1946 St. Louis Cardinals – NL

Etchison, Clarence Hampton "Buck"
(1949 Griffin-GAL)
1943-1944 Boston Braves – NL

Federoff, Alfred "Al"
(1963 Thomasville-GFL)
1951-1952 Detroit Tigers – AL

Feller, Jack Leland "Jack"
(1956 Hazlehurst-Baxley-GSL)
1958 Detroit Tigers – AL

Ferens, Stanley "Stan"
(1940 Albany-GFL)
1942, 1946 St. Louis Browns – AL

Fillingim, Dana "Dana"
(1913-1914 Cordele-ESL/GSL)
1915 Philadelphia Athletics – AL
1918-1923 Boston Braves – NL
1925 Philadelphia Phillies – NL

Finley, Robert Edward "Bob"
(1937 Moultrie-GFL)
1943-1944 Philadelphia Blue Jays – NL

Finney, Louis Klopsche "Lou"
(1928-1929 Talladega-GAL, 1930 Carrollton-GAL, 1946 Opelika/Valley-GAL)
1931, 1933-1939 Philadelphia Athletics – AL
1939-1942, 1944-1945 Boston Red Sox – AL
1945-1946 St. Louis Browns – AL
1947 Philadelphia Phillies – NL
All-Star – 1940

Fisher, Harry Devereux "Harry"
(1947 Tallahassee-GFL)
1951-1952 Pittsburgh Pirates – NL

Fisher, Robert Taylor "Bob"
(1906 Columbus-GSL)
1912-1913 Brooklyn Dodgers/Superbas – NL
1914-1915 Chicago Cubs – NL
1916 Cincinnati Reds – NL
1918-1919 St. Louis Cardinals – NL

Fittery, Paul Clarence "Paul"
(1928-1929 Carrollton-GAL, 1930 Anniston-GAL)
1914 Cincinnati Reds – NL
1917 Philadelphia Phillies – NL

Flair, Albert Dell "Al"
(1937-1938 Moultrie-GFL)
1941 Boston Red Sox – AL

Foss, George Dueward "George"
(1915 Thomasville-FLAG)
1921 Washington Senators – AL

Foss, Larry Curtis "Larry"
(1955 Dublin-GSL)
1961 Pittsburgh Pirates – NL
1962 New York Mets – NL

Foytack, Paul Eugene "Paul"
  (1949 Thomasville-GFL)
1953, 1955-1963 Detroit Tigers – AL
1963-1964 Los Angeles Angels – AL

Freese, Eugene Lewis "Gene"
  (1953 Brunswick-GFL)
1955-1958, 1964-1965 Pittsburgh Pirates – NL
1958 St. Louis Cardinals – NL
1959 Philadelphia Phillies – NL
1960, 1965-1966 Chicago White Sox – AL
1961-1963 Cincinnati Reds – NL
1966 Houston Astros – NL
    World Series – 1961

Fricano, Marion John "Marion"
  (1948 Valdosta-GFL)
1952-1954 Philadelphia Athletics – AL
1955 Kansas City Athletics – AL

Friend, Owen Lacey "Owen"
  (1962 Brunswick-GFL)
1949-1950 St. Louis Browns – AL
1953 Detroit Tigers – AL
1953 Cleveland Indians – AL
1955 Boston Red Sox – AL
1955-1956 Chicago Cubs – NL

Gaddy, John Wilson "John"
  (1939 Albany-GFL)
1938 Brooklyn Dodgers – NL

Gallivan, Philip Joseph "Phil"
  (1930 Carrollton-GAL)
1931 Brooklyn Robins – NL
1932, 1934 Chicago White Sox – AL

Gandy, Robert Brinkley "Bob"
  (1915 Waycross/Brunswick-FLAG)
1916 Philadelphia Phillies – NL

Geary, Eugene Francis Joseph "Huck"
  (1938 Thomasville-GFL)
1942-1946 Pittsburgh Pirates – NL

Geary, Robert Norton "Bob"
  (1914 Americus-GSL)
1918-1919 Philadelphia Athletics – AL
1921 Cincinnati Reds – NL

Gentile, Samuel Christopher "Sam"
  (1937 Moultrie-GFL)
1943 Boston Braves – NL

George, Alex Thomas M. "Alex"
  (1956 Fitzgerald-GFL)
1955 Kansas City Athletics – AL

George, Charles Peter "Greek"
  (1951 Americus-GFL, 1951-1952 Tifton-GFL)
1935-1936 Cleveland Indians – AL
1938 Brooklyn Dodgers – NL
1941 Chicago Cubs – NL
1945 Philadelphia Athletics – AL

Gibson, Samuel Braxton "Sam"
  (1949 Griffin-GAL)
1926-1928 Detroit Tigers – AL
1930 New York Yankees – AL
1932 New York Giants – NL

Gilbert, Drew Edward "Buddy"
  (1954 Douglas-GSL)
1959 Cincinnati Reds – NL

Gillis, Grant "Grant"
  (1936-1938 Moultrie-GFL)
1927-1928 Washington Senators – AL
1929 Boston Red Sox – AL

Gladding, Fred Earl "Fred"
  (1956-1957 Valdosta-GFL)
1961-1967 Detroit Tigers – AL
1968-1973 Houston Astros – NL

Glazner, Charles Franklin "Whitey"
  (1913-1915 Anniston-GAL, 1930 Cedartown-GAL)
1920-1923 Pittsburgh Pirates – NL
1923-1924 Philadelphia Phillies – NL

Glynn, William Vincent "Bill"
  (1946 Americus-GFL)
1949 Philadelphia Phillies – NL
1952-1954 Cleveland Indians – AL
    World Series – 1954

Gooch, John Beverley "Johnny"
  (1916 Talladega-GAL)
1921-1928 Pittsburgh Pirates – NL
1928-1929 Brooklyn Robins – NL
1929-1930 Cincinnati Reds – NL
1933 Boston Red Sox – AL
    World Series – 1925, 1927

Good, Wilbur David Sr. "Will"
  (1942 Tallahassee-GFL)
1905 New York Highlanders – AL
1908-1909 Cleveland Indians – AL
1910-1911 Boston Rustlers/Braves – NL
1911-1915 Chicago Cubs – NL
1916 Philadelphia Phillies – NL
1918 Chicago White Sox – AL

Graham, Wayne Leon "Wayne"
  (1957 Brunswick-GFL)
1963 Philadelphia Phillies – NL
1964 New York Mets – NL

Graham, William Albert "Bill"
  (1957 Valdosta-GFL)
1966 Detroit Tigers – AL
1967 New York Mets – NL

Gray, Milton Marshall "Milt"
  (1935 Thomasville-GFL)
1937 Washington Senators – AL

Gray, Richard Benjamin "Dick"
  (1951 Valdosta-GFL)
1958-1959 Los Angeles Dodgers – NL
1959-1960 St. Louis Cardinals – NL

Green, Fred Allen "Fred"
  (1952 Brunswick-GFL)
1959-1961, 1964 Pittsburgh Pirates – NL
1962 Washington Senators – AL
    World Series – 1960

Georgia Class-D Minor League Baseball Encyclopedia

Gremp, Lewis Edward "Buddy"
(1936-1937 Albany-GFL)
1940-1942 Boston Bees/Braves – NL

Griffin, Ivy Moore "Ivy"
(1936-1937 Cordele-GFL)
1919-1921 Philadelphia Athletics – AL

Grzenda, Joseph Charles "Joe"
(1956 Valdosta-GFL)
1961 Detroit Tigers – AL
1964, 1966 Kansas City Athletics – AL
1967 New York Mets – NL
1969 Minnesota Twins – AL
1970-1971 Washington Senators – AL
1972 St. Louis Cardinals – NL
    ALCS – 1969

Guise, Witt Orison "Lefty"
(1951 Douglas-GSL)
1940 Cincinnati Reds – NL

Haefner, Milton Arnold "Mickey"
(1938 Tallahassee-GFL)
1943-1949 Washington Senators – AL
1949-1950 Chicago White Sox – AL
1950 Boston Braves – NL

Hamric, Odbert Herman "Bert"
(1950 Valdosta-GFL)
1955 Brooklyn Dodgers – NL
1958 Baltimore Orioles – AL

Hamrick, Raymond Bernard "Ray"
(1941 Americus-GFL, 1948 Vidalia-Lyons-GSL)
1943-1944 Philadelphia Blue Jays – NL

Hanson, Harry Francis "Harry"
(1913 Newnan-GAL, 1916-1917 Griffin-GAL)
1913 New York Yankees – AL

Harrell, Raymond James "Ray"
(1950 Fitzgerald-GSL)
1935, 1937-1938 St. Louis Cardinals – NL
1939 Chicago Cubs – NL
1939 Philadelphia Phillies – NL
1940 Pittsburgh Pirates – NL
1945 New York Giants – NL

Harris, William Thomas "Bill"
(1951 Valdosta-GFL)
1957 Brooklyn Dodgers – NL
1959 Los Angeles Dodgers – NL

Hasty, Robert Keller "Bob"
(1921 Carrollton-GSL, 1938 Cordele-GFL)
1919-1924 Philadelphia Athletics – AL

Haydel, John Harold "Hal"
(1962 Dublin-GFL)
1970-1971 Minnesota Twins – AL

Head, Ralph "Ralph"
(1913-1915 LaGrange-GAL)
1923 Philadelphia Phillies – NL

Henley, Gail Curtice "Gail"
(1962 Thomasville-GFL)
1954 Pittsburgh Pirates – NL

Hertweck, Neal Charles "Neal"
(1949 Albany-GFL)
1952 St. Louis Cardinals – NL

Heving, John Aloysius "Johnnie"
(1946 Tallassee-GAL, 1949 Tallahassee-GFL)
1920 St. Louis Browns – AL
1924-1925, 1928-1930 Boston Red Sox – AL
1931-1932 Philadelphia Athletics – AL
    World Series – 1931

Hickey, James Robert "Jim"
(1935 Moultrie-GFL)
1942-1944 Boston Braves – NL

Hickman, James Lucius "Jim"
(1956-1957 Albany-GFL)
1962-1966 New York Mets – NL
1967 Los Angeles Dodgers – NL
1968-1973 Chicago Cubs – NL
1974 St. Louis Cardinals – NL
    All-Star – 1970

High, Andrew Aird "Andy"
(1941 Cordele-GFL)
1922-1925 Brooklyn Robins – NL
1925-1927 Boston Braves – NL
1928-1931 St. Louis Cardinals – NL
1932-1933 Cincinnati Reds – NL
1934 Philadelphia Phillies – NL
    World Series – 1928, 1930, 1931

Hill, Oliver Clinton "John"
(1946-1947 Tallassee-GAL, 1947 Newnan-GAL, 1948 Carrollton-GAL)
1939 Boston Bees – NL

Hitchcock, James Franklin "Jim"
(1946 Opelika-GAL)
1938 Boston Bees – NL

Hoag, Myril Oliver "Myril"
(1950 Valley/Rome-GAL)
1931-1932, 1934-1938 New York Yankees – AL
1939-1941 St. Louis Browns – AL
1941-1942, 1944 Chicago White Sox – AL
1944-1945 Cleveland Indians – AL
    All-Star – 1939
    World Series – 1932, 1937, 1938

Hoak, Donald Albert "Don"
(1947 Valdosta-GFL)
1954-1955 Brooklyn Dodgers – NL
1956 Chicago Cubs – NL
1957-1958 Cincinnati Reds – NL
1959-1962 Pittsburgh Pirates – NL
1963-1964 Philadelphia Phillies – NL
    All-Star – 1957
    World Series – 1955, 1960

Hockette, George Edward "George"
(1928-1929 Gadsden-GAL, 1930 Anniston-GAL)
1934-1935 Boston Red Sox – AL

Hoderlein, Melvin Anthony "Mel"
(1942 Cordele-GFL)
1951 Boston Red Sox – AL
1952-1954 Washington Senators – AL

437

Georgia Class-D Minor League Baseball Encyclopedia

Hodge, Clarence Clemet "Shovel"
(1915 Dothan-FLAG)
1920-1922 Chicago White Sox – AL

Hodkey, Aloysius Joseph "Eli"
(1938 Moultrie-GFL)
1946 Philadelphia Phillies – NL

Hofferth, Stewart Edward "Stew"
(1936 Tallahassee-GFL, 1940 Americus-GFL, 1941-1942 Valdosta-GFL)
1944-1946 Boston Braves – NL

Hoffman, Edward Adolph "Tex"
(1935-1937 Tallahassee-GFL)
1915 Cleveland Indians – AL

Holbrook, James Marbury "Sammy"
(1929 Talladega-GAL)
1935 Washington Senators – AL

Holden, Joseph Francis "Joe"
(1939-1940 Moultrie-GFL, 1946 Cordele-GFL)
1934-1936 Philadelphia Phillies – NL

Holloman, Alva Lee "Bobo"
(1946 Moultrie-GFL)
1953 St. Louis Browns – AL

Howard, Lawrence Rayford "Larry"
(1963 Moultrie-GFL)
1970-1973 Houston Astros – NL
1973 Atlanta Braves – NL

Howell, Homer Elliott "Dixie"
(1938 Thomasville-GFL)
1947 Pittsburgh Pirates – NL
1949-1952 Cincinnati Reds – NL
1953, 1955-1956 Brooklyn Dodgers – NL

Howell, Murray Donald "Red"
(1928 Carrollton-GAL)
1941 Cleveland Indians – AL

Hughson, Cecil Carlton "Tex"
(1937 Moultrie-GFL)
1941-1944, 1946-1949 Boston Red Sox – AL
   All-Star – 1942, 1943, 1944
   World Series – 1946

Humphries, John William "Johnny"
(1948 Douglas-GSL)
1938-1940 Cleveland Indians – AL
1941-1945 Chicago White Sox – AL
1946 Philadelphia Phillies – NL

Hurd, Thomas Carr "Tom"
(1946 Cordele-GFL)
1954-1956 Boston Red Sox – AL

Javier, Manuel Julian (Liranzo) "Julian"
(1956 Brunswick-GFL)
1960-1971 St. Louis Cardinals – NL
1972 Cincinnati Reds – NL
   All-Star – 1963, 1968
   World Series – 1964, 1967, 1968, 1972

Jenkins, Thomas Griffith "Tom"
(1916-1917 Griffin-GAL)
1925-1926 Boston Red Sox – AL
1926 Philadelphia Athletics – AL
1929-1932 St. Louis Browns – AL

Johnson, Robert Wallace "Bob"
(1955 Valdosta-GFL)
1960 Kansas City Athletics – AL
1961-1962 Washington Senators – AL
1963-1967 Baltimore Orioles – AL
1967 New York Mets – NL
1968 Cincinnati Reds – NL
1968 Atlanta Braves – NL
1969 St. Louis Cardinals – NL
1969-1970 Oakland Athletics – NL

Jonnard, Clarence James "Bubber"
(1917 Talladega-GAL)
1920 Chicago White Sox – AL
1922 Pittsburgh Pirates – NL
1926-1927, 1935 Philadelphia Phillies – NL
1929 St. Louis Cardinals – NL

Jonnard, Claude Alfred "Claude"
(1917 Talladega-GAL)
1921-1924 New York Giants – NL
1926 St. Louis Browns – AL
1929 Chicago Cubs – NL
   World Series – 1923, 1924

Jordan, Adolf Otto "Dutch"
(1913, 1915 Valdosta-ESL/FLAG, 1914 Brunswick-GSL)
1903-1904 Brooklyn Superbas – NL

Jumonville, George Benedict "George"
(1939-1938 Cordele-GFL, 1939 Thomasville-GFL)
1940-1941 Philadelphia Phillies – NL

Karpel, Herbert "Herb"
(1938 Thomasville-GFL)
1946 New York Yankees – AL

Kazak (Tkaczuk), Edward Terrance "Eddie"
(1940 Valdosta-GFL, 1941 Albany-GFL)
1948-1952 St. Louis Cardinals – NL
1952 Cincinnati Reds – NL
   All-Star – 1949

Kell, Everett Lee "Skeeter"
(1949 Moultrie-GFL, 1950 Cordele-GFL)
1952 Philadelphia Athletics – AL

Koski, William John "Bill"
(1955 Brunswick-GFL)
1951 Pittsburgh Pirates – NL

Kracher, Joseph Peter "Joe"
(1936-1938 Thomasville-GFL)
1939 Philadelphia Phillies – NL

Krapp, Eugene Hamlet "Gene"
(1916 Talladega-GAL)
1911-1912 Cleveland Naps – AL
1914-1915 Buffalo Buffeds/Bisons – FL

Krausse, Lewis Bernard Sr. "Lew"
(1947 Americus-GFL)
1931-1932 Philadelphia Athletics – AL

Kreitner, Albert Joseph "Mickey"
(1941 Americus-GFL)
1943-1944 Chicago Cubs – NL

Georgia Class-D Minor League Baseball Encyclopedia

Kress, Charles Steven "Chuck"
(1941 Cordele-GFL)
1947, 1949 Cincinnati Reds – NL
1949-1950 Chicago White Sox – AL
1954 Detroit Tigers – AL
1954 Brooklyn Dodgers – NL

Lacy, Osceola Guy Sr. "Guy"
(1916-1917 Anniston-GAL, 1937 Americus-GFL)
1926 Cleveland Indians – AL

Lafitte, Edward Francis "Ed"
(1914-1916 LaGrange-GAL)
1909, 1911-1912 Detroit Tigers – AL
1914-1915 Brooklyn Tip-Tops – FL
1915 Buffalo Bisons – FL

Land, William Gilbert "Doc"
(1929 Gadsden-GAL, 1931 Lindale-GAL)
1929 Washington Senators – AL

Lary, Frank Strong "Frank"
(1950 Thomasville-GFL)
1954-1964 Detroit Tigers – AL
1964 Milwaukee Braves – NL
1964-1965 New York Mets – NL
1965 Chicago White Sox - AL
   All-Star – 1960, 1961

Lassetter, Donald O'Neal "Don"
(1952 Albany-GFL)
1957 St. Louis Cardinals – NL

Layne, Ivoria Hillis "Hillis"
(1938 Americus-GFL)
1941, 1944-1945 Washington Senators – AL

Lazor, John Paul "Johnny"
(1937 Moultrie-GFL)
1943-1946 Boston Red Sox – AL

Lee, Harold Burnham "Hal"
(1947-1949 Cordele-GFL)
1930 Brooklyn Robins – NL
1931-1933 Philadelphia Phillies – NL
1933-1936 Boston Braves/Bees – NL

Lee, Roy Edwin "Roy"
(1938 Thomasville-GFL)
1945 New York Giants – NL

Lehman, Kenneth Karl "Ken"
(1947 Valdosta-GFL)
1952, 1956-1957 Brooklyn Dodgers – NL
1957-1958 Baltimore Orioles – AL
1961 Philadelphia Phillies – NL
   World Series – 1952

Leon, Isidoro (Becerra) "Izzy"
(1948 Sparta-GSL)
1945 Philadelphia Phillies – NL

Letchas, Charlie "Charlie"
(1935-1937 Thomasville-GFL)
1939, 1944, 1946 Philadelphia Phillies – NL
1941 Wahsington Senators – AL

Levy (Whitner), Edward Clarence "Ed"
(1955 Vidalia-GSL)
1940 Philadelphia Phillies – NL
1942, 1944 New York Yankees – AL

Lindquist, Carl Emil "Carl"
(1941 Valdosta-GFL)
1943-1944 Boston Braves – NL

Lipetri, Michael Angelo "Angelo"
(1950 Americus-GFL)
1956, 1958 Philadelphia Phillies – NL

Lown, Omar Joseph "Turk"
(1942 Valdosta-GFL)
1951-1954, 1956-1958 Chicago Cubs – NL
1958 Cincinnati Reds – NL
1958-1962 Chicago White Sox – AL
   World Series – 1959

Lukon, Edward Paul "Eddie"
(1939 Valdosta-GFL)
1941, 1945-1947 Cincinnati Reds – NL

Lum, Michael Ken-Wai "Mike"
(1963 Waycross-GFL)
1967-1975, 1979-1981 Atlanta Braves – NL
1976-1978 Cincinnati Reds – NL
1981 Chicago Cubs – NL
   NLCS – 1969, 1976

Madison, David Pledger "Dave"
(1954 Sandersville-GSL)
1950 New York Yankees – AL
1952 St. Louis Browns – AL
1952-1953 Detroit Tigers – AL

Manno, Donald D. "Don"
(1950 Waycross-GFL, 1950 Tifton-GSL)
1941-1942 Boston Bees/Braves – NL

Manush, Frank Benjamin "Frank"
(1916 Rome-GAL, 1920 Griffin-GSL)
1908 Philadelphia Athletics – AL

Marion, John Wyeth "Red"
(1936 Americus-GFL)
1935, 1943 Washington Senators – AL

Marnie, Harry Sylvester "Harry"
(1939 Moultrie-GFL)
1940-1942 Philadelphia Phillies – NL

Marolewski, Fred Daniel "Fred"
(1948 Albany-GFL)
1953 St. Louis Cardinals – NL

Marquis, Roger Julian "Roger"
(1956 Thomson-GSL)
1955 Baltimore Orioles – AL

Matchick, John Thomas "Tom"
(1962 Brunswick-GFL)
1967-1969 Detroit Tigers – AL
1970 Boston Red Sox – AL
1970 Kansas City Royals – AL
1971 Milwaukee Brewers – AL
1972 Baltimore Orioles – AL
   World Series – 1968

Georgia Class-D Minor League Baseball Encyclopedia

McAuliffe, Richard John "Dick"
    (1958 Valdosta-GFL)
1960-1973 Detroit Tigers – AL
1974-1975 Boston Red Sox – AL
    All-Star – 1965, 1966, 1967
    ALCS – 1972
    World Series – 1968

McClellan, Harvey McDowell "Harvey"
    (1917 Talladega-GAL)
1919-1924 Chicago White Sox – AL

McColl, Alexander Boyd "Alex"
    (1938 Americus-GFL)
1933-1934 Washington Senators – AL
    World Series – 1933

McCovey, Willie Lee "Willie"
    (1955 Sandersville-GSL)
1959-1973, 1977-1980 San Francisco Giants – NL
1974-1976 San Diego Padres – NL
1976 Oakland Athletics – AL
    Hall of Fame
    All-Star 1963, 1966, 1968, 1969, 1970, 1971
    NLCS – 1971
    World Series – 1962

McDevitt, Daniel Eugene "Danny"
    (1951 LaGrange-GAL)
1957 Brooklyn Dodgers – NL
1958-1960 Los Angeles Dodgers – NL
1961 New York Yankees – AL
1961 Minnesota Twins – AL
1962 Kansas City Athletics – AL

McGhee, William Mac "Bill"
    (1929-1930 Carrollton-GAL, 1930 Anniston-GAL, 1951 Fitzgerald-GSL, 1954 Hazlehurst-Baxley-GSL)
1944-1945 Philadelphia Athletics – AL

McGowan, Tullis Earl "Mickey"
    1941 Waycross-GFL)
1948 New York Giants – NL

McMillan, Norman Alexis "Norm"
    (1914-1915 Valdosta-GSL/FLAG)
1922 New York Yankees – AL
1923 Boston Red Sox – AL
1924 St. Louis Browns – AL
1928-1929 Chicago Cubs – NL
    World Series – 1922, 1929

McQuaig, Gerald Joseph "Jerry"
    (1935 Americus-GFL, 1936 Moultrie-GFL)
1934 Philadelphia Athletics – AL

Melton, Clifford George "Cliff"
    (1954 Americus-Cordele-GFL)
1937-1944 New York Giants – NL
    All-Star – 1942
    World Series – 1937

Melton, Reuben Franklin "Rube"
    (1937 Albany-GFL)
1941-1942 Philadelphia Phillies – NL
1943-1944, 1946-1947 Brooklyn Dodgers – NL

Mertz, James Verlin "Jim"
    (1939 Waycross-GFL)
1943 Washington Senators – AL

Metheny, Arthur Beauregard "Bud"
    (1948 Baxley-GSL)
1943-1946 New York Yankees – AL
    World Series – 1943

Miller, Rodney Carter "Rod"
    (1958 Thomasville-GFL)
1957 Brooklyn Dodgers – NL

Milosevich, Michael "Mike"
    (1949 Baxley-GSL, 1951 Americus-GFL)
1944-1945 New York Yankees – AL

Minner, Paul Edison "Paul"
    (1941 Thomasville-GFL)
1946, 1948-1949 Brooklyn Dodgers – NL
1950-1956 Chicago Cubs – NL
    World Series – 1949

Mizell, Wilmer David "Vinegar Bend"
    (1949 Albany-GFL)
1952-1953, 1956-1960 St. Louis Cardinals – NL
1960-1962 Pittsburgh Pirates – NL
1962 New York Mets – NL
    All-Star – 1959
    World Series – 1960

Moore, Jackie Spencer "Jackie"
    (1958 Valdosta-GFL)
1965 Detroit Tigers – AL

Morrell, Willard Blackmer "Bill"
    (1939-1940 Valdosta-GFL, 1941 Cordele-GFL)
1926 Washington Senators – AL
1930-1931 New York Giants – NL

Moss, John Lester "Les"
    (1942 Americus-GFL)
1946-1951, 1952-1953 St. Louis Browns – AL
1951 Boston Red Sox – AL
1954-1955 Baltimore Orioles – AL
1955-1958 Chicago White Sox – AL

Mott, Elisha Matthew "Bitsy"
    (1939-1940 Americus-GFL, 1941 Cordele-GFL)
1945 Philadelphia Phillies – NL

Moulder, Glen Hubert "Glen"
    (1940 Americus-GFL)
1946 Brooklyn Dodgers – NL
1947 St. Louis Browns – AL
1948 Chicago White Sox – AL

Murchison, Thomas Malcolm "Tim"
    (1938 Tallahassee-GFL)
1917 St. Louis Cardinals – NL
1920 Cleveland Indians – AL

Murphy, Edward Joseph "Ed"
    (1938 Albany-GFL, 1948-1950 Americus-GFL)
1942 Philadelphia Phillies – NL

Murray, Robert Hayes "Bob"
    (1935 Moultrie-GFL)
1923 Washington Senators – AL

Murrell, Ivan Augustus (Peters) "Ivan"
    (1963 Moultrie-GFL)
1963-1964, 1967-1968 Houston Colt .45's/Astros – NL
1969-1973 San Diego Padres – NL
1974 Atlanta Braves – NL

Georgia Class-D Minor League Baseball Encyclopedia

Nabors, Herman John "Jack"
  (1915 Talladega/Newnan-GAL)
1915-1917 Philadelphia Athletics – AL

Narron, Samuel "Sammy"
  (1935 Albany-GFL)
1935, 1942-1943 St. Louis Cardinals – NL
  World Series – 1943

Navarro, Julio (Ventura) "Julio"
  (1955 Sandersville-GFL)
1962-1964 Los Angeles Angels – AL
1964-1966 Detroit Tigers – AL
1970 Atlanta Braves – NL

Negray, Ronald Alvin "Ron"
  (1949 Valdosta-GFL)
1952 Brooklyn Dodgers – NL
1955-1956 Philadelphia Phillies – NL
1958 Los Angeles Dodgers – NL

Newsome, Lamar Ashby "Skeeter"
  (1930 Talladega-GAL)
1935-1939 Philadelphia Athletics – AL
1941-1945 Boston Red Sox – AL
1946-1947 Philadelphia Phillies – NL

Nicholson, David Lawrence "Dave"
  (1958 Dublin-GFL)
1960, 1962 Baltimore Orioles – AL
1963-1965 Chicago White Sox – AL
1966 Houston Astros – NL
1967 Atlanta Braves – NL

Oertel, Charles Frank "Chuck"
  (1950 Baxley-GSL)
1958 Baltimore Orioles – AL

Oliver, Eugene George "Gene"
  (1956 Albany-GFL)
1959, 1961-1963 St. Louis Cardinals – NL
1963-1965 Milwaukee Braves – NL
1966-1967 Atlanta Braves – NL
1967 Philadelphia Phillies – NL
1968 Boston Red Sox – AL
1968-1969 Chicago Cubs – NL

O'Neil, George Michael "Mickey"
  (1951-1952 Brunswick-GFL)
1919-1925 Boston Braves – NL
1926 Brooklyn Robins – NL
1927 Washington Senators – AL
1927 New York Giants – NL

O'Neil, John Francis "John"
  (1939 Tallahassee-GFL)
1946 Philadelphia Phillies – NL

O'Rourke, James Francis "Frank"
  (1942 Cordele-GFL)
1912 Boston Braves – NL
1917-1918 Brooklyn Robins – NL
1920-1921 Washington Senators – AL
1922 Boston Red Sox – AL
1924-1926 Detroit Tigers – AL
1927-1931 St. Louis Browns – AL

Osborne, Ernest Preston "Tiny"
  (1920-1921 Griffin-GSL)
1922-1924 Chicago Cubs – NL
1924-1925 Brooklyn Robins – NL

Ostendorf, Frederick K. "Fred"
  (1915 Thomasville-FLAG, 1915 Griffin-GAL)
1914 Indianapolis Hoosiers – FL

Overmire, Frank W. "Stubby"
  (1958 Valdosta-GFL)
1943-1949 Detroit Tigers – AL
1950-1951, 1952 St. Louis Browns – AL
1951 New York Yankees – AL
  World Series – 1945

Owen, Marvin James "Marv"
  (1954 Valdosta-GFL)
1931, 1933-1937 Detroit Tigers – AL
1938-1939 Chicago White Sox – AL
1940 Boston Red Sox – AL
  World Series – 1934, 1935

Palmquist, Edwin Lee "Ed"
  (1956 Thomasville-GFL)
1960-1961 Los Angeles Dodgers – NL
1961 Minnesota Twins – AL

Parker, Douglas Woolley "Dixie"
  (1936-1937 Americus-GFL)
1923 Philadelphia Phillies – NL

Parsons, Edward Dixon "Dixie"
  (1946 Waycross/Moultrie-GFL)
1939, 1942-1943 Detroit Tigers – AL

Paschal, Benjamin Edwin "Ben"
  (1915 Dothan-FLAG)
1915 Cleveland Indians – AL
1920 Boston Red Sox – AL
1924-1929 New York Yankees – AL
  World Series – 1926, 1928

Payne, George Washington "George"
  (1914 Brunswick-GSL)
1920 Chicago White Sox – AL

Penson, Paul Eugene "Paul"
  (1956 Tifton-GFL)
1954 Philadelphia Phillies – NL

Pepper, Donald Hoyte "Don"
  (1962-1963 Thomasville-GFL)
1966 Detroit Tigers – AL

Perryman, Emmett Key "Parson"
  (1928 Lindale-GAL)
1915 St. Louis Browns – AL

Peterman, William David "Bill"
  (1949 Moultrie-GFL, 1950 Cordele-GFL)
1942 Philadelphia Phillies – NL

Peterson, Harding William "Hardy"
  (1950 Tallahassee-GFL)
1955, 1957-1959 Pittsburgh Pirates – NL

Pezold, Lorenz Johannes "Larry"
  (1913 Gadsden-GAL)
1914 Cleveland Naps – AL

Pfister, George Edward "George"
(1956 Thomasville-GFL)
1941 Brooklyn Dodgers – NL

Pfund, Le Roy Herbert "Lee"
(1941 Albany-GFL)
1945 Brooklyn Dodgers – NL

Phebus, Raymond William "Bill"
(1949 Dublin-GSL)
1936-1938 Washington Senators – AL

Phillips, John Melvin "Bubba"
(1949 Thomasville-GFL)
1955, 1963-1964 Detroit Tigers – AL
1956-1959 Chicago White Sox – AL
1960-1962 Cleveland Indians – AL
   World Series – 1959

Phillips, William Taylor "Taylor"
(1951-1952 Waycross-GFL)
1956-1957 Milwaukee Braves – NL
1958-1959 Chicago Cubs – NL
1959-1960 Philadelphia Phillies – NL
1963 Chicago White Sox – AL

Pierro, William Leonard "Bill"
(1947 Tallahassee-GFL)
1950 Pittsburgh Pirates – NL

Pignatano, Joseph Benjamin "Joe"
(1950 Valdosta-GFL)
1957 Brooklyn Dodgers – NL
1958-1960 Los Angeles Dodgers – NL
1961 Kansas City Athletics – AL
1962 San Francisco Giants – NL
1962 New York Mets – NL
   World Series – 1959

Podgajny, John Sigmund "Johnny"
(1939 Moultrie-GFL)
1940-1943 Philadelphia Phillies/Blue Jays – NL
1943 Pittsburgh Pirates – NL
1946 Cleveland Indians – AL

Polivka, Kenneth Lyle "Ken"
(1955 Moultrie-GFL)
1947 Cincinnati Reds – NL

Poole, James Robert "Jim"
(1946-1947, 1951 Moultrie-GFL)
1925-1927 Philadelphia Athletics – AL

Powers, John Calvin "John"
(1949 Valley-GAL)
1955-1958 Pittsburgh Pirates – NL
1959 Cincinnati Reds – NL
1960 Baltimore Orioles – AL
1960 Cleveland Indians – AL

Pratt, Francis Bruce "Frank"
(1917 Anniston-GAL, 1920 Carrollton-GSL)
1921 Chicago White Sox – AL

Quick, James Harold "Hal"
(1936-1938 Americus-GFL)
1939 Washington Senators – AL

Rackley, Marvin Eugene "Marv"
(1941 Valdosta-GFL)
1947-1949 Brooklyn Dodgers – NL
1949 Pittsburgh Pirates – NL
1950 Cincinnati Reds – NL
   World Series – 1949

Rambert, Elmer Donald "Pep"
(1951 Eastman-GSL)
1939-1940 Pittsburgh Pirates – NL

Ramsey, William Thrace "Bill"
(1942 Waycross-GFL)
1945 Boston Braves – NL

Reese, Richard Benjamin "Rich"
(1962 Thomasville-GFL)
1964-1972, 1973 Minnesota Twins – AL
1973 Detroit Tigers – AL
   ALCS – 1969, 1970

Reinecke (Smith), Walter Joseph "Wally"
(1913 Gadsden-GAL, 1914 Talladega-GAL)
1915 Baltimore Terrapins – FL

Reiser, Harold Patrick "Pete"
(1955 Thomasville-GFL)
1940-1942, 1946-1948 Brooklyn Dodgers – NL
1949-1950 Boston Braves – NL
1951 Pittsburgh Pirates – NL
1952 Cleveland Indians – AL
   All-Star – 1941, 1942, 1946
   World Series – 1941, 1947

Retzer, Kenneth Leo "Ken"
(1954 Tifton-GFL)
1961-1964 Washington Senators – AL

Rhawn, Robert John "Bobby"
(1938-1939 Albany-GFL)
1947-1949 New York Giants – NL
1949 Chicago White Sox – AL
1949 Pittsburgh Pirates – NL

Rice, Harry Francis "Harry"
(1939 Cordele-GFL)
1923-1927 St. Louis Browns – AL
1928-1930 Detroit Tigers – AL
1930 New York Yankees – AL
1931 Washington Senators – AL
1933 Cincinnati Reds - NL

Rice, Robert Turnbull "Bob"
(1935-1937 Albany-GFL)
1926 Philadelphia Phillies – NL

Richardson, Gordon Clark "Gordie"
(1957-1958 Albany-GFL)
1964 St. Louis Cardinals – NL
1965-1966 New York Mets – NL
   World Series – 1964

Richbourg, Lance Clayton "Lance"
(1941 Tallahassee-GFL)
1921 Philadelphia Phillies – NL
1924 Washington Senators – AL
1927-1931 Boston Braves – NL
1932 Chicago Cubs – NL

Georgia Class-D Minor League Baseball Encyclopedia

Rinker, Robert John "Bob"
(1949 Griffin-GAL)
1950 Philadelphia Athletics – AL

Roberts, Charles Emory "Red"
(1946-1948 Carrollton-GAL, 1949-1950 Alexander City-GAL)
1943 Washington Senators – AL

Robinson, William Edward "Eddie"
(1939-1940 Valdosta-GFL)
1942, 1946-1948, 1957 Cleveland Indians – AL
1949-1950 Washington Senators – AL
1950-1952 Chicago White Sox – AL
1953 Philadelphia Athletics – AL
1954-1956 New York Yankees – AL
1956 Kansas City Athletics – AL
1957 Detroit Tigers – AL
1957 Baltimore Orioles - Al
    All-Star – 1949, 1951, 1952, 1953
    World Series – 1948, 1955

Robinson, William Henry Jr. "Bill"
(1962 Dublin-GFL, 1963 Waycross-GFL)
1966 Atlanta Braves – NL
1967-1969 New York Yankees – AL
1972-1974, 1982-1983 Philadelphia Phillies – NL
1975-1982 Pittsburgh Pirates – NL
    NLCS – 1975, 1979
    World Series – 1979

Rochelli, Louis Joseph "Lou"
(1939, 1948 Valdosta-GFL)
1944 Brooklyn Dodgers – NL

Rohe, George Anthony "George"
(1913 Newnan-GAL)
1901 Baltimore Orioles – AL
1905-1907 Chicago White Sox – AL
    World Series – 1906

Roig, Anton Ambrose "Tony"
(1949 Dublin-GSL, 1950 Rome-GAL)
1953, 1955-1956 Washington Senators – AL

Rothrock, John Huston "Jack"
(1948 Tallahassee-GFL)
1925-1932 Boston Red Sox – AL
1932 Chicago White Sox – AL
1934-1935 St. Louis Cardinals – NL
1937 Philadelphia Athletics – AL
    World Series – 1934

Rowell, Carvel William "Bama"
(1937 Cordele-GFL)
1939-1941, 1946-1947 Boston Bees/Braves – NL
1948 Philadelphia Phillies – NL

Rudolph, Frederick Donald "Don"
(1950-1951 Jesup-GSL)
1957-1959 Chicago White Sox – AL
1959 Cincinnati Reds – NL
1962 Cleveland Indians – AL
1962-1964 Washington Senators – AL

Rufer, Rudolph Joseph "Rudy"
(1956-1958 Thomasville-GFL)
1949-1950 New York Giants – NL

Rullo, Joseph Vincent "Joe"
(1953 Cordele-GFL)
1943-1944 Philadelphia Athletics – AL

Sadowski, Robert Frank "Bob"
(1955 Hazlehurst-Baxley-GSL)
1960 St. Louis Cardinals – NL
1961 Philadelphia Phillies – NL
1962 Chicago White Sox – AL
1963 Los Angeles Angels – AL

Sanders, Warren William "War"
(1914 Newnan-GAL)
1903-1904 St. Louis Cardinals – NL

Sanford, John Stanley "Jack"
(1949 Americus-GFL)
1956-1958 Philadelphia Phillies – NL
1959-1965 San Francisco Giants – NL
1965-1967 California Angels – AL
1967 Kansas City Athletics – AL
    All-Star – 1957
    World Series – 1962

Schaive, John Edward "Johnny"
(1952 Thomasville-GFL)
1958-1960, 1962-1963 Washington Senators – AL

Scheffing, Robert Boden "Bob"
(1936 Albany-GFL)
1941-1942, 1946-1950 Chicago Cubs – NL
1950-1951 Cincinnati Reds – NL
1951 St. Louis Cardinals – NL

Schepner, Joseph Maurice "Joe"
(1928 Gadsden-GAL)
1919 St. Louis Browns – AL

Schmidt, Frederick Albert "Freddy"
(1939 Albany-GFL)
1944, 1946-1947 St. Louis Cardinals – NL
1947 Philadelphia Phillies – NL
1947 Chicago Cubs – NL
    World Series – 1944

Schoendienst, Albert Fred "Red"
(1942 Albany-GFL)
1945-1956, 1961-1963 St. Louis Cardinals – NL
1956-1957 New York Giants – NL
1957-1960 Milwaukee Braves – NL
    Hall of Fame
    All-Star – 1946, 1948, 1949, 1950, 1951, 1952, 1953, 1954, 1955, 1957
    World Series – 1946, 1957, 1958

Schulte (Schultehenrich), Leonard Bernard "Len"
(1936-1937 Albany-GFL)
1944-1946 St. Louis Browns – AL

Schultz, Joseph Charles Jr. "Joe"
(1936-1937 Albany-GFL)
1939-1941 Pittsburgh Pirates – NL
1943-1948 St. Louis Browns – AL

Schwartz, William Charles "Bill"
(1913-1914 Opelika-GAL, 1921 Cedartown-GSL)
1904 Cleveland Naps – AL

Georgia Class-D Minor League Baseball Encyclopedia

Schypinski, Gerald Albert "Jerry"
(1952 Cordele-GFL)
1955 Kansas City Athletics – AL

Scott, LeGrant Edward "LeGrant"
(1946-1947 Waycross-GFL, 1948 Americus-GFL)
1939 Philadelphia Phillies – NL

Scott, Richard Lewis "Dick"
(1956 Thomasville-GFL)
1963 Los Angeles Dodgers – NL
1964 Chicago Cubs – NL

Sembera, Carroll William "Carroll"
(1962 Moultrie-GFL)
1965-1967 Houston Astros – NL
1969-1970 Montreal Expos – NL

Shannon, Thomas Michael "Mike"
(1958 Albany-GFL)
1962-1970 St. Louis Cardinals – NL
   World Series – 1964, 1967, 1968

Shannon, Walter Charles "Wally"
(1952 Albany-GFL)
1959-1960 St. Louis Cardinals – NL

Shawkey, James Robert "Bob"
(1949 Tallahassee-GFL)
1913-1915 Philadelphia Athletics – AL
1915-1927 New York Yankees – AL
   World Series – 1914, 1921, 1922, 1923, 1926

Shinault, Enoch Erskine "Ginger"
(1915 Anniston-GAL)
1921-1922 Cleveland Indians – AL

Shipley, Joseph Clark "Joe"
(1953 Vidalia-GSL)
1958-1960 San Francisco Giants – NL
1963 Chicago White Sox – AL

Skinner, Elisha Harrison "Camp"
(1920 Cedartown-GSL)
1922 New York Yankees – AL
1923 Boston Red Sox – AL

Smith, Harold Raymond "Hal"
(1949 Albany-GFL)
1956-1961 St. Louis Cardinals – NL
1965 Pittsburgh Pirates – NL
   All-Star – 1957, 1959

Smith, Jack Hatfield "Jack"
(1955 Thomasville-GFL)
1962-1963 Los Angeles Dodgers – NL
1964 Milwaukee Braves – NL

Smith, Paul Leslie "Paul"
(1950 Tallahassee-GFL)
1953, 1957-1958 Pittsburgh Pirates – NL
1958 Chicago Cubs – NL

Smith, Richard Arthur "Dick"
(1958 Thomasville-GFL)
1963-1964 New York Mets – NL
1965 Los Angeles Dodgers – NL

Smith, Richard Harrison "Dick"
(1950 Tallahassee-GFL)
1951-1955 Pittsburgh Pirates – NL

Smith, Sherrod Malone "Sherry"
(1928-1930 Cedartown-GAL)
1911-1912 Pittsburgh Pirates – NL
1915-1917, 1919-1922 Brooklyn Robins – NL
1922-1927 Cleveland Indians – AL
   World Series – 1916, 1920

Spiezio, Edward Wayne "Ed"
(1963 Brunswick-GFL)
1964-1968 St. Louis Cardinals – NL
1969-1972 San Diego Padres – NL
1972 Chicago White Sox – AL
   World Series – 1967, 1968

Steinecke, William Robert "Bill"
(1953 Jesup-GSL, 1962 Dublin-GFL, 1963 Waycross-GFL)
1931 Pittsburgh Pirates – NL

Stigman, Richard Lewis "Dick"
(1954 Tifton-GFL, 1956 Vidalia-GSL)
1960-1961 Cleveland Indians – AL
1962-1965 Minnesota Twins – AL
1966 Boston Red Sox – AL
   All-Star – 1960

Stimson, Carl Remus "Carl"
(1917 Talladega-GAL)
1923 Boston Red Sox – AL

Stubing, Lawrence George "Moose"
(1956 Brunswick-GFL)
1967 California Angels – AL

Sullivan, John Paul "John"
(1941 Thomasville-GFL)
1942-1944, 1947-1948 Washington Senators – AL
1949 St. Louis Browns – AL

Taitt, Douglas John "Doug"
(1947 Alexander City-GAL)
1928-1929 Boston Red Sox – AL
1929 Chicago White Sox – AL
1931-1932 Philadelphia Phillies – NL

Tauscher, Walter Edward "Walt"
(1950 Tallahassee-GFL)
1928 Pittsburgh Pirates – NL
1931 Washington Senators – AL

Taussig, Donald Franklin "Don"
(1950 LaGrange-GAL)
1958 San Francisco Giants – NL
1961 St. Louis Cardinals – NL
1962 Houston Colt .45's – NL

Terry, William Harold "Bill"
(1915 Dothan-FLAG, 1915-1916 Newnan-GAL)
1923-1936 New York Giants – NL
   Hall of Fame
   All-Star – 1933, 1934, 1935
   World Series – 1924, 1933, 1936

Thomas, Frank Joseph "Frank"
(1948-1949 Tallahassee-GFL)
1951-1958 Pittsburgh Pirates – NL
1959 Cincinnati Reds – NL
1960-1961, 1966 Chicago Cubs – NL

Georgia Class-D Minor League Baseball Encyclopedia

1961, 1965 Milwaukee Braves – NL
1962-1964 New York Mets – NL
1964-1965 Philadelphia Phillies – NL
1965 Houston Astros – NL
    All-Star – 1954, 1955, 1958

Thompson, Lafayette Fresco "Fresco"
    (1939 Waycross-GFL)
1925 Pittsburgh Pirates – NL
1926 New York Giants – NL
1927-1930 Philadelphia Phillies – NL
1931-1932 Brooklyn Robins/Dodgers – NL
1934 New York Giants – NL

Tiefenauer, Bobby Gene "Bobby"
    (1948-1948 Tallassee-GAL)
1952, 1955, 1961 St. Louis Cardinals – NL
1960, 1965, 1967 Cleveland Indians – AL
1962 Houston Colt .45's – NL
1963-1965 Milwaukee Braves – NL
1965 New York Yankees – AL
1968 Chicago Cubs – NL

Torres, Don Gilberto (Nunez) "Gil"
    (1953 Valdosta-GFL)
1940, 1946 Washington Senators – AL

Torres, Felix (Sanchez) "Felix"
    (1955 Douglas-GSL)
1962-1964 Los Angeles Angels – AL

Tracewski, Richard Joseph "Dick"
    (1954 Thomasville-GFL)
1962-1965 Los Angeles Dodgers – NL
1966-1969 Detroit Tigers – AL
    World Series – 1963, 1965, 1968

Treadway, Edgar Raymond "Ray"
    (1928 Cedartown-GAL)
1930 Washington Senators – AL

Treadway, Thadford Leon "Red"
    (1954, 1956 Fitzgerald-GFL)
1944-1945 New York Giants – NL

Trinkle, Kenneth Wayne "Ken"
    (1939 Thomasville-GFL)
1943, 1946-1948 New York Giants – NL
1949 Philadelphia Phillies – NL

Triplett, Herman Coaker "Coaker"
    (1935 Tallahassee-GFL)
1938 Chicago Cubs – NL
1941-1943 St. Louis Cardinals – NL
1943-1945 Philadelphia Blue Jays/Phillies – NL

Tsitouris, John Philip "John"
    (1954-1955 Valdosta-GFL)
1957 Detroit Tigers – AL
1958-1960 Kansas City Athletics – AL
1962-1968 Cincinnati Reds – NL

Tucker, Oliver Dinwiddie "Ollie"
    (1921 Cedartown-GSL)
1927 Washington Senators – AL
1928 Cleveland Indians – AL

Tyson, Cecil Washington "Turkey"
    (1938-1939 Tallahassee-GFL)
1944 Philadelphia Blue Jays – NL

Ulisney, Michael Edward "Mike"
    (1939-1941 Thomasville-GFL)
1945 Boston Braves – NL

Umbricht, James "Jim"
    (1953 Waycross-GFL)
1959-1961 Pittsburgh Pirates – NL
1962-1963 Houston Colt .45's – NL

Vander Meer, John Samuel "Johnny"
    (1956 Douglas-GSL)
1937-1943, 1946-1949 Cincinnati Reds – NL
1950 Chicago Cubs – NL
1951 Cleveland Indians – AL
    All-Star – 1938, 1939, 1942, 1943
    World Series – 1940

Varner, Glen Gann "Buck"
    (1948 Carrollton-GAL)
1952 Washington Senators – AL

Veigel, Allen Francis "Al"
    (1937 Moultrie-GFL)
1939 Boston Bees – NL

Vines, Robert Earl "Bob"
    (1935 Thomasville-GFL)
1924 St. Louis Cardinals – NL
1925 Philadelphia Phillies – NL

Voiselle, William Symmes "Bill"
    (1938 Moultrie-GFL)
1942-1947 New York Giants – NL
1947-1949 Boston Braves – NL
1950 Chicago Cubs – NL
    All-Star – 1944
    World Series – 1948

Walker, Ewart Gladstone "Dixie"
    (1930 Anniston-GAL)
1909-1912 Washington Senators – AL

Walker, Fred "Dixie"
    (1929 Anniston-GAL)
1931, 1933-1936 New York Yankees – AL
1936-1937 Chicago White Sox – AL
1938-1939 Detroit Tigers – AL
1939-1947 Brooklyn Dodgers – NL
1948-1949 Pittsburgh Pirates – NL
    All-Star – 1943, 1944, 1945, 1946, 1947
    World Series – 1941, 1947

Waugh, James Elden "Jim"
    (1951, 1955 Brunswick-GFL)
1952-1953 Pittsburgh Pirates – NL

Webb, William Frederick "Bill"
    (1947 Carrollton-GAL)
1943 Philadelphia Blue Jays – NL

Wellman, Robert Joseph "Bob"
    (1946 Tallassee-GAL, 1955 Douglas-GSL, 1956 Moultrie-GFL)
1948, 1950 Philadelphia Athletics – AL

Werley, George William "George"
(1957 Fitzgerald-GFL, 1958 Dublin-GFL)
1956 Baltimore Orioles – AL

Wert, Donald Ralph "Don"
(1958 Valdosta-GFL)
1963-1970 Detroit Tigers – AL
1971 Washington Senators – AL
   All-Star – 1968
   World Series – 1968

West, Richard Thomas "Dick"
(1935-1937 Americus-GFL)
1938-1943 Cincinnati Reds – NL

West, Weldon Edison "Lefty"
(1939 Americus-GFL)
1944-1945 St. Louis Browns – AL

White, Adel "Abe"
(1928-1930 Carrollton-GAL, 1929 Cedartown-GAL, 1930 Lindale-GAL, 1947-1948, 1950 Griffin-GAL)
1937 St. Louis Cardinals – NL

White, Joyner Clifford "Jo-Jo"
(1928 Carrollton-GAL)
1932-1938 Detroit Tigers – AL
1943-1944 Philadelphia Athletics – AL
1944 Cincinnati Reds – NL
   World Series – 1934, 1935

Wicker, Kemp Caswell "Kemp"
(1928 Carrollton-GAL)
1936-1938 New York Yankees – AL
1941 Brooklyn Dodgers – NL
   World Series – 1937

Williams, David Carlous "Davey"
(1947 Waycross-GFL)
1949, 1951-1955 New York Giants – NL
   All-Star – 1953
   World Series – 1951, 1954

Williams, Fred "Papa"
(1951-1952 Waycross-GFL)
1945 Cleveland Indians – AL

Williamson, Silas Albert "Al"
(1921 LaGrange-GSL)
1928 Chicago White Sox – AL

Willis, Ronald Earl "Ron"
(1962 Brunswick-GFL)
1966-1969 St. Louis Cardinals – NL
1969 Houston Astros – NL
1970 San Diego Padres – NL
   World Series – 1967, 1968

Wilson, Walter Wood "Walt"
(1947 LaGrange-GAL)
1945 Detroit Tigers – AL

Wingard, Ernest James "Ernie"
(1941 Thomasville-GFL)
1924-1927 St. Louis Browns – AL

Wooldridge, Floyd Lewis "Floyd"
(1950 Albany-GFL)
1955 St. Louis Cardinals – NL

Workman, Harry Hall "Hoge"
(1921 LaGrange-GSL)
1924 Boston Red Sox – AL

York, Preston Rudolph "Rudy"
(1949 Griffin-GAL)
1934, 1937-1945 Detroit Tigers – AL
1946-1947 Boston Red Sox – AL
1947 Chicago White Sox – AL
1948 Philadelphia Athletics – AL
   All-Star – 1938, 1941, 1942, 1943, 1944, 1946, 1947
   World Series – 1940, 1945, 1946

Young, Donald Wayne "Don"
(1963 Brunswick-GFL)
1965, 1969 Chicago Cubs – NL

Zeller, Barton Wallace "Bart"
(1963 Brunswick-GFL)
1970 St. Louis Cardinals – NL

Zernial, Gus Edward "Gus"
(1942 Waycross-GFL)
1949-1951 Chicago White Sox – AL
1951-1954 Philadelphia Athletics – AL
1955-1957 Kansas City Athletics – AL
1958-1959 Detroit Tigers – AL
   All-Star – 1953

Zientara, Benedict Joseph "Benny"
(1957 Brunswick-GFL)
1941, 1946-1948 Cincinnati Reds – NL

Georgia Class-D Leaguers Who Managed in the Majors

Adair, Marion Danne "Bill"
(1956 Valdosta-GFL)
1970 Chicago White Sox - AL

Carey, Max George "Max"
(1955 Cordele-GFL)
1932-1933 Brooklyn Dodgers – NL
   Hall of Fame

Cottier, Charles Keith "Chuck"
(1954 Americus-Cordele-GFL)
1984-1986 Seattle Mariners – AL

Craig, Roger Lee "Roger"
(1950 Valdosta-GFL)
1978-1979 San Diego Padres – NL
1985-1992 San Francisco Giants – NL
   NLCS – 1989
   World Series – 1989

Keane, Johnny
(1938-1939 Albany-GFL)
1961-1964 St. Louis Cardinals – NL
1965-1966 New York Yankees – AL
   World Series – 1964

Lucchesi, Frank
(1952 Thomasville-GFL)
1970-1972 Philadelphia Phillies – NL
1975-1977 Texas Rangers – NL
1987 Chicago Cubs – NL

Moore, Jackie Spencer "Jackie"
(1958 Valdosta-GFL)
1984-1986 Oakland Athletics – AL

Moss, John Lester "Les"
(1942 Americus-GFL)
1968 Chicago White Sox – AL
1979 Detroit Tigers – AL

Scheffing, Robert Boden "Bob"
(1936 Albany-GFL)
1957-1959 Chicago Cubs – NL
1961-1963 Detroit Tigers – AL

Schoendienst, Albert Fred "Red"
(1942 Albany-GFL)
1965-1976, 1980, 1990 St. Louis Cardinals – NL
   World Series – 1967, 1968

Schultz, Joseph Charles Jr. "Joe"
(1936-1937 Albany-GFL)
1969 Seattle Pilots – AL
1973 Detroit Tigers – AL

Shawkey, James Robert "Bob"
(1949 Tallahassee-GFL)
1930 New York Yankees – AL

Stubing, Lawrence George "Moose"
(1956 Brunswick-GFL)
1988 California Angels – AL

Terry, William Harold "Bill"
(1915 Dothan-FLAG, 1915-1916 Newnan-GAL)
1932-1941 New York Giants – NL
   World Series – 1933, 1936, 1937

Tracewski, Richard Joseph "Dick"
(1954 Thomasville-GFL)
1979 Detroit Tigers – AL

Weaver, Earl Sidney "Earl"
(1957 Fitzgerald-GFL, 1958 Dublin-GFL)
1968-1982, 1985-1986 Baltimore Orioles – AL
   ALCS – 1969, 1970, 1971, 1973, 1974, 1979
   World Series – 1969, 1970, 1971, 1979

White, Joyner Clifford "Jo-Jo"
(1928 Carrollton-GAL)
1960 Cleveland Indians – AL

York, Preston Rudolph "Rudy"
(1949 Griffin-GAL)
1959 Boston Red Sox – AL

Georgia Minor League Baseball Reunion

In August 2001, the first reunion of the Georgia-Florida League was held in Moultrie, Georgia. Organized chiefly by Clint Chafin, son of Bobbie Chafin who pitched for Griffin of the Georgia-Alabama League in 1949, along with the Museum of Colquitt County History and the Moultrie-Colquitt County Chamber of Commerce, the historical first reunion drew over thirty former players as well as many fans of the former leagues. Among the players and fans in attendance were some from the Georgia-Alabama League and the Georgia State League. When plans were made for the second annual event, it was decided that players, umpires, batboys, scorekeepers, and anybody who had any connection with any of the three Georgia Class-D leagues, Georgia-Florida, Georgia-Alabama, or Georgia State, would be invited to attend. The second event, also held in Moultrie and also organized by Clint, drew and even bigger crowd than the first.

Plans for the next reunion, which will be the third annual, are finalized for August 1-2, 2003 in Moultrie with golf, stories, a dinner banquet, and much more. The event has expanded yet again to included alumni from neighboring state Alabama and the Alabama-Florida and Alabama State Leagues. Players from these leagues got reunited in 1999 and 2000, but no event has been held since for the Alabama players. As many of the Georgia players also played in the Alabama Class-D circuits, and vice-versa, it was only fitting to hold a joint event for both states this year.

Players who attended the 2002 Georgia Minor League Baseball Reunion:

Dizzy Adams	Otto Kossuth
Blas Arroyo	Joey Laudermilk
Danny Bass	Ken Markham
Billy Bledsoe	Bobby McGee
Wilbur Caldwell	Deane Mink
Joe Chambers	Floyd Moser
Sonny Clements	Chester Ploszaj
Neal Cobb	Thomas Proctor
Jack Crouch	Harry Raulerson
Les Crouch	Rollie Rice
Jack Daughtry	Arthur Schmidt
Mayes Dobbins	Logan Sharpless
Paul Eames	Hal Smith (batboy)
Floyd Faust	Hank Spain
Phil Gilbert	Hillory Stanton
Edsel Griffin	Sonny Stevenson
Jim Harp	Norris Strickland
George Harrington	Walter Strickland
Edd Hartness	Jim Tenney
Arnold Heft	Elmer Tessin
Bob Hegwood	Jim Tyler
Chet Kanavage	Milt Wrenn
Steve Kebler	Tex Young
Bill Kivett	Bob Zuccarini

For information on the 2003 reunion or any future events, please contact Clint Chafin or the Museum of Colquitt County History at the following addresses:

Clint Chafin
4789 Tallokas Road
Moultrie, Georgia 31788

Museum of Colquitt County History
P.O. Box 86
Moultrie, Georgia 31776

Georgia Class-D Minor League Baseball Encyclopedia

Index

Name	Page(s) name appears on						
Aaron, Mack	138	146	155	166			
Aaron, W.M.	11	20	21	212			
Aase, Kermit	51	55	212				
Abadie, Ben	108	212					
Abbott, ---	11	212					
Abell, ---	31	212					
Abercrombie, ---	19	212					
Abrams, Norm	150	153	212				
Abreu, Joe	81	83	212				
Ackerman, Bob	197	212					
Acree, John	112	212					
Acton, Jim	90	92	93	212			
Adair, Bill	181	183	212	447			
Adair, Hubert	152	212					
Adair, Tommy	54	58	76	94	212		
Adam, Dick	167	177	212				
Adamcewicz, Erwin	94	106	212				
Adams, Ace	46	47	49	146	207	208	212	431
Adams, Bob	81	90	91	92	101	103	104	105
	115	118	129	130	131	204	205	212
Adams, Carl	121	212					
Adams, Ellie	146						
Adams, Henry	55	212					
Adams, Jerome	151	166	212	448			
Adams, John	152	212					
Adams, Ken	146	150	212				
Adams, Marvin	34	37	212				
Adams, Phil	96	212					
Adams, Tom	96	212					
Adcock, Bob	102	104	105	108	137	138	212
Addison, George	58	212					
Addison, John	95	213					
Adelhelm, Bill	121	122	213				
Adkinson, Bill	80	213					
Adz, Johnny	54	213					
Agnew, ---	14	213					
Aguilar, Bob	197	198	213				
Ainsworth, Harold	172	213					
Aizupura, Nicomedes	197	198	199	201	202	213	
Akers, Oza	40	41	42	213			
Akins, Jack	172	213					
Albanese, Joe	51	213					
Alberts, Henry	134	142	213				
Albertson, Jerry	125	213					
Albritton, Ervin	117	213					
Albritton, Gene	55	213					
Albury, Charles R.	119						
Alden, Frank	162	213					
Aldridge, R.C. "Bob"	150						
Aleshire, Jim	189	213					
Alexander, ---	11	12	16	24	25	213	
Alexander, Bill	31	32	34	35	37	39	80	81
	213						
Alexander, Bob	201	213					
Alexander, Byron	62						
Alexander, E.D.	4	213					
Alexander, Grant	180	213					
Alexander, Moose	59	60	61	206	213	431	
Alexander, Ted	77	213					
Alexander, Tom	177	213					
Alexson, Andy	108	109	213				
Alford, ---	16	213					
Allegrucci, Don	166	213					
Allen, ---	5	9	11	22	213		
Allen, Bill	122	123	152	153	156	162	214
Allen, Earl	41	44	45	46	213		
Allen, Ed	193	214					
Allen, Frank	31	33	34	38	214	431	
Allen, Harry	27	29	115	128	214		
Allen, Jim	155	214					
Allen, Joel	124	214					
Allen, Johnny	71	81	90	129	130	214	
Allen, L.	55	214					
Alleruzo, Larry	44	214					
Allison, E.B.	19	21	214				
Allison, Jim	184	186	189	214			
Allman, Frank	160	214					
Almeida, Dan	186	187	214				
Almon, ---	31	214					
Alomar, Rafael	175	177	178	214			
Alonso, John	102	124	214				
Alperman, Whitey	7	214	431				
Alrick, Ed	112	113	214				
Altomare, John	146	214					
Altomer, Lou	156	162	214				
Alvares, Ramon	112	214					
Alvarez, Alberto	175	184	187	214			
Alvarez, Demetro	192	214					
Alvarez, Luis	129	214					
Alvarez, Ultus	151	152	153	207	214		
Alves, Joe	150	214					
Amadee, Joe	38	39	214				
Amaral, Dan	44	45	46	47	48	214	
Amazon, H.W.	11	12	19	21	214		
Ambrose, Dick	155	166	214				
Amburgey, Conley	180	184	215				
Ammon, Walt	40	42	45	46	215		
Ammons, Bud	31	32	33	34	215		
Ammons, Dewey	151	215					
Amoroso, Dante	77	215					
Anders, Howard	197	215					
Anderson, ---	7	14	15	16	24	25	38	71
	215						
Anderson, Bill	112	114	185	187	189	215	
Anderson, Carl	147	215					
Anderson, Charles	137						
Anderson, Dick	81	197	198	199	215		
Anderson, Frank	41	44	45	46	215		
Anderson, Gerald M.	93						
Anderson, Harrison	87	215					
Anderson, Jack	64	215					
Anderson, Jim	189	215					
Anderson, Ken	201	215					
Anderson, Lewis A.	93						
Anderson, Lewis E.	84						
Anderson, Marion	34						
	40	215					
Anderson, Martin	82	215					
Anderson, O.B.	77	86	95				
Anderson, Roger	171	215					
Anderson, T.P.	125	215					
Anderson, Victor	19	21	22	215			
Anderson, W.T.	47	50	54	58	66	75	84	93
	106	119	132	140	149	159	169	179
	188	192						
Anderson, Walt	112	215					
Anderton, Sherman	180	215					
Andres, Bob	95	108	215				
Andrews, Charles H.	78	87	96	122			

Georgia Class-D Minor League Baseball Encyclopedia

Name							Name						
Andrews, Chris	172	215					Avery, ---	31	217				
Androsko, Steve	201	215					Avery, Ken	198	199	217			
Androvich, Joe	145	215					Avinger, Frank	146	218				
Angeli, Joe	77	79	215				Aycock, J.B.	176	185				
Angelone, John	142	143	151	153	161	216	Ayers, H.L.	128					
Anile, Joe	149	216					Ayers, Lonzo	81	218				
Anjeski, Elmer	77	86	87	88	216		Ayers, W.F.	54	218				
Annino, Alfio	40	43	216				Aylmer, Bob	180	218				
Annunziato, Al	47	50	216				Azcue, Joe	180	184	218	431		
Annunzio, Joe	44	216					Azzarello, Frank	117	218				
Ansley, ---	16	216					Babcock, Harry	156	218				
Anthon, Fred	200	216					Babcock, Owen	180	218				
Anthony, ---	4	216					Babich, Dick	180	182	218			
Anthony, George	151	216					Bach, Phil	149	218				
Anthony, Stan	117	216					Bacha, Bill	85	218				
Antley, ---	14	17	18	216			Bachars, Medar	152	157	218			
Antolick, Joe	95	216	431				Bachelor, Harry	28	218				
Antonangeli, Don	201	216					Bacque, Gene	190	218				
Apicella, Jim	200	216					Badia, Armenio	162	218				
Appleby, Ellis	67	216					Badour, Bob	151	157	218			
Appling, Horace	44	216					Baggens, ---	13	14	218			
Arbogast, Ford	166	216					Baglivi, Bill	48	49	218			
Archaumbault, Charles	151	216					Bagnall, A.E.	63					
Archer, Dick	155	216					Bagwell, E.	5					
Archer, Jim	129	216	431				Bagwell, E.S.	9	218				
Archipoli, Andy	58	64	216				Bagwell, Jim	121	218				
Arcia, Jose	197	198	216	431			Bahnson, Dick	145	218				
Arcoleo, Frank	98	100	216				Bailey, ---	24	31	77	218		
Ard, Tom	117	216					Bailey, D.M.	103					
Ardis, ---	27	216					Bailey, Don	72	82	83	117	129	218
Arduini, Sal	95	216					Bailey, Freddie	181	218				
Arellanes, Bill	171	181	216				Bailey, George	91	92	93	204	218	
Arent, George	161	165	168	175	177	178 216	Bailey, Jim	180	218	431			
Arlitt, Buzz	63	64	65	216			Bailey, John	201	218				
Armstrong, Carl	62	64	216				Bailey, Paul	58	218				
Arnall, Hamilton C.	81	90					Baines, Alfred	31	32	218			
Arnitz, Pete	192	216					Bakay, John	62	67	69	218		
Arnold, Mel	54	58	216				Bakenhaster, Dave	200	218	431			
Arnone, Bob	200	217					Baker, ---	16	17	219			
Arroyo, Blas	90	116	217	448			Baker, Allen	117	219				
Arterburn, Harry	133	217					Baker, Earl	125	163	219			
Arwood, Dr. W.C.	171	180					Baker, Floyd	163	164	219			
Asbill, Joe	141	217					Baker, George	50	54	219			
Ash, George	132	217					Baker, Howard	12	20	219	431		
Ashcraft, Bill	125	217					Baker, Jake	34	36	38	39	219	
Ashton, Andrew	151	217					Baker, Jerry	150	156	166	219		
Ashworth, Johnny	67	217					Baker, Oscar	16	219				
Asinof, Eliot	59	217					Baker, Ray	112	219				
Askew, ---	9	11	16	217			Baker, Roy	111	124	127	209	219	
Asmer, John	76	79	85	107	207	217	Baker, Royal	95	219				
Aspromonte, Bob	189	217	431				Baker, Winford	142	219				
Astin, Bob	72	81	217				Baktis, Simon	132	219				
Atchison, John	77	217					Bakunas, Al	76	219				
Atchley, Loy	31	217					Balais, Alex	81	219				
Atkinson, Don	54	57	58	62	93	217	Balczac, Ed	189	219				
Attaway, Bob	94	97	217				Baldwin, Jack	181	219				
Attride, ---	16	217					Baldwin, Lamar	124	134	137	219		
Atwater, Charlie	55	60	61	64	217		Baldwin, Robert	165	219				
Atzert, George	95	107	217				Balen, John	75	219				
Aucoin, Al	152	217					Bales, ---	13	17	22	27	219	
Augugliaro, Frank	119	132					Bales, Jack	108	219				
August, Joe	77	217					Ball, Bob	63	219				
Augustoni, Bill	162	164	217				Ball, Jim	82	83	91	92	93 103 104 105 219	
Aurelio, Ed	82	98	217										
Austin, Alvin	96	108	122	217			Ball, John	72	155	158	219		
Austin, Bob	67	217					Balla, John	141	219				
Austin, Forrest	67	217					Ballard, Frank	201	219				
Austin, Robert C.	50						Ballard, Larry	197	219				
Austin, William A.	119						Ballentine, Curtis	68	219				
Avera, Jim	58	217					Ballou, Don	55	220				
Averette, ---	5	217					Balogh, Steve	145	220				
Averette, Dave	44	217					Ban, Dick	132	135	140	220		

Georgia Class-D Minor League Baseball Encyclopedia

Name							
Banas, George	112	220					
Bancroft, Charles	190	194	195	220			
Bandini, Phil	112	220					
Bandoch, Ed	86	95	107	220			
Banks, Gerald	160	161	220				
Bankston, Everett	209	220	431				
Bankston, Will	13	14					
Bannister, ---	9	11	220				
Banta, Sterling	59	220					
Banville, ---	24	220					
Baolto, Vito C.	75						
Barath, Dave	130	220					
Barbare, P.	38	220					
Barbare, Walt	38	220	431				
Barbella, Vic	96	220					
Barber, ---	5	17	18	29	30	220	
Barber, Steve	193	220	431				
Barbero, Frank	48	220					
Barberra, Clem	150	220					
Barbier, John	141	143	144	161	220		
Barbieri, Fernando	134	220					
Barclay, Robert	11	220					
Barfield, Frank	190	220					
Bargas, John	86	220					
Barger, John	90	92	93	206	220		
Barker, George	121	220					
Barker, Norb	115	220					
Barker, Tommy	198	201	220				
Barkley, ---	71	220					
Barlam, Barnett	77	220					
Barlow, M.H.	142	151					
Barna, Dick	185	221					
Barna, Mike	162	220					
Barnard, ---	16	221					
Barnes, ---	5	29	38	221			
Barnes, Bill	76	86	95	98	112	113	114	126
	208	209	221				
Barnes, Bob	126	221					
Barnes, Duge	58	221					
Barnes, Irv	40	221					
Barnes, Luther	98	221					
Barnett, ---	7	14	221				
Barnett, Byron	147	150	155	221			
Barnett, John	59	64	65	208	221		
Barnett, Lowell	59	61	221				
Barnhart, ---	29	221					
Barnhart, Bob	55	221					
Barnhart, Lowell	189	221					
Baron, Vic	192	221					
Barone, Anthony	125	155	221				
Barone, Frank	145	221					
Barone, Les	180	221					
Barrett, Frank	40	43	432				
Barrett, Garland	155	166	221				
Barrett, Mike	201	221					
Barrett, Red	221						
Barron, Norm	185	187	221				
Barron, W.M.	98	112	125				
Barrow, Ray	85	221					
Barry, Berry	221						
Barry, Gene	67	221					
Barry, Jeremiah	48						
Barry, Willie	173	221					
Bartell, ---	16	17	221				
Barth, Al	189	190	221				
Barth, Jerry	172	221					
Bartholomew, ---	67	222					
Bartholomew, Jack	102	150	156	222			
Bartley, Boyd	161	222	432				
Bartley, Don	141	222					
Bartolozzi, Ralph	86	88	222				
Barton, Cecil	160	170	222				
Bartula, Matthew	73	222					
Barty, Warren	197	198	199	222			
Basgall, Monty	68	69	207	222	432		
Baskin, Al	86	112	126	222			
Bass, Danny	120	222	448				
Bass, Les	190	191	222				
Bassett, Grady	34	38	39	222			
Bassetti, Gil	185	187	209	210	222		
Bassignani, Al	112	222					
Bastion, Marv	115	137	165	222			
Batchko, Joe	76	77	222				
Bateman, Ed	150	222					
Bates, ---	29	222					
Battistelli, Angelo	102	116	222				
Battle, Don	161	222					
Battson, Cecil	8	9	10	11	222		
Batty, Bill	160	163	222				
Batty, Tom	126	222					
Bauer, Ed	77	157	222				
Bauman, Walt	145	146	148	222			
Baumgardner, ---	11	222					
Bavasi, E.J.	58	64					
Bavoso, Tom	184	222					
Bayno, Joe	171	222					
Bays, Dick	172	174	222				
Bazner, Henry	41	42	222				
Beach, D.E.	86	95	108	121			
Beach, Ed	101	104	105	222			
Beagle, H.E.	35	223					
Beaird, Dick	103	125	134	223			
Beal, Bill	157	223					
Beall, ---	24	223					
Beall, B.A.	99	112					
Beaman, George	185	223					
Bean, Roger	189	223					
Beane, Bill	175	179	223				
Beane, Ed	67	223					
Bearden, Billy	142	152	167	223			
Bearden, Gene	54	223	432				
Bearden, Jack	111	116	118	119	129	130	131	145
	146	150	204	223			
Beasley, ---	9	10	71	223			
Beasley, E.B	189						
Beasley, John	116	117	223				
Beatty, Arlin	170	223					
Beaty, Frank	111	223					
Beauchamp, Walt	113	116	126	137	223		
Beaugez, Ray	166	223					
Beavers, Jim	82	83	91	146	147	148	167	168
	208	209	223				
Beazley, Johnny	48	223	432				
Beck, ---	27	31	32	223			
Beck, Bill	180	223					
Beck, Dale	129	223					
Beck, Dick	172	181	223				
Beck, Junius F.	93						
Beck, Ted	94	96	223				
Bedingfield, J.R.	27	223					
Bednar, Dave	189	191	193	194	195	223	
Beecher, Bob	137	138	223				
Beheler, Ernest	165	223					
Behrends, Al	59	224					
Behrens, Ed	120	122	224				
Behrman, Hank	64	65	224	432			
Beiler, Carl	161	171	224				
Belaj, Allen	186	224					
Belakovy, Rudy	98	100	101	209	224		
Belcher, Neil	77	224					
Belinsky, Bo	180	224	432				
Belknap, Lyle	54	224					
Bell, Charlie	27	28	224				
Bell, Gary	177	224	432				

Name							
Bell, Gilbert F.	108						
Bell, Jefferson	75	85	96	224			
Bell, John	129	224					
Bell, Russ	176	224					
Belladella, Bob	163	167	224				
Bellamy, Perry	163	224					
Bender, Chief	106	109	120	123	132	135	160	170
	179	188	224				
Benedict, ---	24	224					
Benedict, Cletus	160	224					
Benedict, Hoyt	120	224					
Benezue, ---	73	224					
Benish, Bob	121	224					
Benjamin, Stan	48	49	51	52	53	224	432
Bennett, ---	24	25	224				
Bennett, Charles	71	141	147	224			
Bennett, Craig	77	224					
Bennett, Frank	55	60	61	224			
Bennett, Gerald	177	224					
Benson, Gene	68	224					
Benson, John	157	224					
Benswanger, W.E.	77						
Beran, Lee	133	135	175	224			
Beredino, Joe	170	224					
Berenbrok, Paul W.	89						
Berg, Ed	91	103	105	225			
Bergdoll, Charles	190	225					
Bergen, Robert L.	108						
Berger, Fred	170	173	225				
Berger, Jack	160	170					
Bergesch, L.W.	85	94					
Bergey, Francis	193	225					
Bergey, Jim	181	225					
Bergstraesser, Bill	194	225					
Beringhele, Basil	68	225					
Berman, Buddy	77	102	115	116	225		
Bernat, Walt	63	225					
Bernebrok, Paul W.	80						
Bernhardt, Virgil	180	225					
Bernier, Bill	132	225					
Bernstein, ---	6	225					
Bernsten, Ray	185	225					
Berry, George	40	42	43	225			
Berry, John	41	51	225				
Berry, Larry	55	60	63	225			
Berry, Sam	138	225					
Bertha, Elmer	90	225					
Bertrand, Art	170	225					
Bertschy, Bob	193	225					
Berzonski, John	147	157	225				
Bess, Bob	98	99	225				
Bess, Krim	40	42	43	45	46	50	52	53
	54	208	225				
Bessent, Don	115	116	118	119	205	225	432
Betancourt, Roberto	126	132	134	135	136	208	225
Betcher, George	133	225					
Betcher, Ralph	140	141	225				
Bethea, George	134	225					
Bethman, Carl	54	56	57	206	207	225	
Betsch, Dick	186	225					
Bettin, Bob	155	171	225				
Bettineschi, Frank	147	157	226				
Bettison, ---	37	226					
Bettleyon, Bob	133	226					
Betts, ---	16	226					
Betz, Bob	91	226					
Bevell, Pat	60	226					
Beverly, Charles	108	226					
Beverly, Jack	95	226					
Bevil, Lou	64	65	226	432			
Beyrer, Harold	54	226					
Bianchi, Frank	102	226					
Bianchini, Ray	185	226					
Biassetti, Gil	176	226					
Biel, ---	17	226					
Bieser, Fred	71	226					
Biggerstaff, Jack	111	226					
Biggs, MacDuff	190	226					
Billingsley, ---	9	226					
Billingsley, Donald G.	98						
Billingsley, Ray	194	226					
Bindschadler, Ben	172	226					
Birchfield, Gilbert	62	65	226				
Bird, Bob	189	193	195	226			
Bird, Jim	125	226					
Bisesi, John	149	153	166	226			
Bishop, Charlie	75	226	432				
Bishop, Danny	189	226					
Bishop, Pat	94	226					
Bitting, Earl	7	13	226				
Bivins, E.A.	185						
Black, ---	12	29	226				
Black, Bobby	201	202	226				
Black, Gene	128	130	131	226			
Black, Loyd	62	226					
Black, Ralph	125	226					
Black, Wayne	41	42	226				
Blackburn, H.C.	156						
Blackburn, H.F.	166						
Blackburn, Jim	63	67	211	227	432		
Blackburn, Leo	185						
Blackburn, Tom	82	104	227				
Blackman, Don	86	227					
Blackmon, Grover	78	227					
Blackstock, Hal	44	45	73	81	82	83	84	227
Blackwell, ---	9	11	16	227			
Blackwell, Bill	103	227					
Blackwell, Dan	63	227					
Blackwell, Ken	150	227					
Blackwell, Tom	76	81	90	227			
Blackwell, Verne	54	56	227				
Blair, J.R.	43	47	50	75	76	85	106	119
	132	140	160				
Blansit, ---	16	227					
Blanton, ---	5	227					
Blanton, Hugh	124	137	227				
Blasco, Pete	55	227					
Blaylock, Rodney H.	76						
Blaze, Frank	73	227					
Bledsoe, Billy	108	109	121	123	151	227	448
Bledsoe, Charles	134	136	142	154	157	165	168	227
Bleidistel, Wally	43	227					
Blevins, Jesse	67	227					
Blewster, Dave	55	59	227				
Block, Al	43	44	48	51			
Bloodworth, Charles	108	122	227				
Bloodworth, Jimmy	41	227	432				
Bloom, Don	167	172	227				
Blue, Earl	124						
Blume, Jim	154	156	227				
Bly, John	201	202	203	227			
Boatman, Jim	80	227					
Boatwright, John	107	227					
Bobo, Bill	58	227					
Bobowski, Ed	90	102	103	105	115	116	118	119
	228						
Bodan, Joe	68	228					
Boddy, Bob	124	125	228				
Bodnar, Elmer	106	228					
Boehme, Ken	145	228					
Bogardus, Earl	141	228					
Bogart, Gene	63	228					
Boger, Jim	194	228					
Boggan, George	106	228					

Georgia Class-D Minor League Baseball Encyclopedia

Name								Name						
Boggs, Pat	156	228						Bowen, Harold	67	230				
Boggus, A.A.	99							Bowen, Howard	126	230				
Boggus, T.D.	188							Bowen, J.C.	91					
Bohn, Lloyd	160	228						Bowen, Jack	190	191	230			
Bohonko, John	54	228						Bowen, Rex	40	41	42	43	46	230
Bojorquez, Federico	170	228						Bowers, Stew	55	59	230	432		
Bolam, Bob	133	228						Bowie, Don	170	230				
Bolch, Bill	125	167	228					Bowland, Art	68	69	230			
Bolding, Billy	194	228						Bowman, Clyde	200	230				
Bolin, Joe	193	228						Box, ---	146	230				
Bolin, Pete	149	228						Boxer, Seymour	126	156	158	230		
Boling, Edward	35	38	228					Boyce, George	141	230				
Bollman, Bill	107	109	207	228				Boyce, Ken	151	157	230			
Bolster, Harvey	63	228						Boyd, J.S.	9	20	22	23	230	
Bolt, ---	29	228						Boyd, Smith	4	230				
Bonaparte, Bob	133	135	228					Boyd, Warner	170	230				
Bonavia, Anthony	193	228						Boyer, Bob	188	192	194	195	207	230
Bonczek, Lonegan	192	228						Boyer, Ken	147	230				
Bonds, Ken	106	228						Boyer, Lew	170	230				
Bone, ---	9	228						Boyer, Milt	72	91	230			
Bone, Bill	170	228						Boykin, Gayle	151	231				
Boner, Billy	179	188	228					Boykin, Roma	19	231				
Bonet, Hector	151	228						Boykin, W.J.	8	10				
Bongard, Eddie	59	228						Bozeman, Jim	77	231				
Bonifay, Albert	27	228						Bozich, John	193	231				
Bonifay, R.B. "Bob"	86	151	162	172				Bozzuto, Bert	81	90	102	105	231	
Bonnett, Luther	120	228						Brackens, Samuel J.	140	149				
Bonowitz, Joe	43	45	228					Brackett, Raymond F.	144	149				
Booker, Bill	197	229						Bradberry, Buck	161	165	231			
Booker, John	89	117	229					Braddock, Ron	200	231				
Boone, Ike	27	28	208	229	432			Bradley, Bob	45	231				
Boone, Ron	193	229						Bradley, Don	166	168	176	178	210	231
Boos, Wendell	80	83	229					Bradley, Eugene	20	29	30	231		
Boote, ---	11	229						Bradshaw, George	86	231	432			
Booth, Bill	189	193	229					Bradshaw, Herbert	55	60	78	87	96	108 134
Booth, Jim	112	229						Bradshaw, Hugh	107	116	231			
Booth, Wayne	77	229						Brady, ---	67	231				
Booz, Walter M.	30							Brady, Jim	193	231	432			
Boozer, John	192	229	432					Brady, Ken	63	231				
Boozer, Wes	54	229						Brady, Pat	57					
Bope, George	16	18	21	24	229			Braganca, Joe	103	116	132	231		
Borden, Wallie	60	64	229					Braica, Joseph T.	124	136				
Borders, Aubrey	71	72	229					Brakefield, William	17	231				
Borom, Red	41	229	432					Bramblett, Laura P.	176	185				
Borrett, Curtis	173	229						Brancato, Fred	181	189	231			
Bosarge, Vince	73	74	82	205	229			Brancato, Jim	77	231				
Bosch, Ortelio	152	229						Brand, Clarence	75	231				
Bossard, Belasco	165	167	168	169	229			Brande, Ralph	54	231				
Bosse, Lou	170	229						Brandenburg, Charles	160	231				
Bosser, Mel	55	59	61	71	207	208	229 432	Brandon, Goat	27	28	231			
Bossie, Ron	180	229						Brandt, Fred	161	231				
Bostwick, ---	11	19	229					Brannan, Charles	77	86	231			
Bostwick, Bill	189	229						Brannen, ---	9	231				
Boswell, Brant	31	32	229					Brannon, ---	38	231				
Boswell, John	156	229						Brannon, Shaw	67	231				
Bothell, Hilliery E.	119							Branon, Mike	197	231				
Botkin, Del	197	229						Braun, Ken	77	79	231			
Bottoms, Woodrow	72	73	74	81	82	99	100 104	Braun, Leon	151	156	157	231		
	112	117	204	229				Brawner, Ralph	82	231				
Bottone, Lou	55	229						Bray, ---	11	12	232			
Bottorff, Tom	103	111	229					Bray, Buster	55	232	432			
Bourell, Roy	40	43	230					Bray, Herman E.	146	157	167	176		
Bourgeois, Joe	149	153	230					Brayer, Dennis	200	232				
Bova, Tom	171	177	230					Braze, ---	17	232				
Bowden, ---	6	13	16	17	230			Braziel, Dennis	172	232				
Bowden, Ray	86	230						Brazier, ---	6	7	16	19	232	
Bowden, Russ	172	230						Breadon, S.	75	85				
Bowden, Tim	27	28	230	432				Breaux, Cliff	121	232				
Bowdoin, Lawrence	19	21	22	24	27	230		Breeden, Danny	200	232	432			
Bowen, ---	5	230						Breeden, Hal	201	202	203	232	432	
Bowen, Charlie	103							Breeden, Jack	189	191	193	232		
Bowen, Grady	6	7	8	11	13	22	230	Breeding, Marv	170	173	174	232	432	

Georgia Class-D Minor League Baseball Encyclopedia

Name									Name							
Breedlove, Ernest	193	232								129	131	204	205	234		
Breidt, Bob	156	232							Brown, Bobby	161	234					
Brelich, Mike	59	232							Brown, Christine	62						
Bremer, Walt	87	96	108	122	134	142	143	144	Brown, Clem	176						
	206	232							Brown, Don	132	135	179	188	234		
Brennan, Don	137	138	145	208	232				Brown, Gene	106	234					
Brennan, Wilbert	107	232							Brown, Gimpy	72	74	170	186	234	433	
Brenner, ---	5	232							Brown, Hubert	72	74	234				
Brenner, Herbert	27	29	232						Brown, J.R.	72	103	116				
Breschini, Wes	119	121	123	208	232				Brown, Jerome	201	234					
Brewer, ---	17	232							Brown, John	157	234					
Brewer, George	124	232							Brown, Keith	180	234					
Brewer, Henry	29	232							Brown, Lamar	142	154	234				
Brewer, Orbie	86	232							Brown, Levi	197	234					
Brewer, W.A.	165	175	184						Brown, Lou	179	188	190	191	234		
Brewster, Bill	63	232							Brown, Martin	47	234					
Brewster, Charlie	60	61	64	65	96	97	163	207	Brown, Newton	170	173	234				
	232	433							Brown, Norm	47	49	51	52	234	433	
Brewton, Byron	194	232							Brown, Roger	121	234					
Brick, Jerome	162	232							Brown, Xenophon	59	234					
Bricker, Cy	85	232							Browning, Doug	157	235					
Brickner, Walt	59	61	63	64	232				Browning, Ted	72	73	74	81	83	84	204	205
Bridenbaker, Ray	110									235						
Bridges, Barney	197	232							Brownslow, ---	11	235					
Bridges, Don	190	233							Bruce, Buster	45	46	47	49	235		
Bridges, Floyd	146	233							Bruenjes, Allen	179	185	235				
Bridges, Frank	132	133	233						Brumbaugh, John	149	155	161	180	235		
Bridges, Geneva	166	233							Brummitt, Larry E.	192	196	200				
Bridges, Harold	71	73	233						Bruner, Bruce	29	32	235				
Bridges, J.W.	76	85	94	107	150	160	170		Bruner, C.L.	19						
Bridges, Joe	58								Bruner, Roy	48	51	52	53	235	433	
Briggs, Clyde	167	233							Brunner, Sheldon	45	235					
Briggs, Harold	81	233							Bruno, Bob	99	197	235				
Briggs, Walter O. Jr.	162	172	181	190					Bruns, Don	193	235					
Brightwell, Bill	77	233							Brunsberg, Arlo	198	235	433				
Brill, Jim	172								Brunson, Marion	91	235					
Brill, Stan	107	109	233						Bryant, Bill	55	235					
Briner, Dan	190	191	233						Bryant, Chic	44	235					
Brinkley, Lawrence	186	233							Bryant, Harold	86	95	98	125	235		
Brinkman, Frank	90	233							Bryant, Ira	166	235					
Brinson, ---	27	233							Bryant, Irwin	117	235					
Brinson, Luther	134	142	233						Bryant, Jim	68	69	117	235			
Brinson, W.W.	124	137	145	165	175				Brydon, Bob	64	235					
Brio, Carl	181	233							Bryson, Hoyle	51	52	55	56	235		
Briscoe, Bertram	157	233							Bryson, Joe	72	235					
Brisson, Virgil	141	233							Brzowsky, Emil	60	235					
Britchet, Jackson	67	69	233						Bubeck, Bob	126	235					
Brittian, ---	19	233							Bucco, Dick	106	235					
Britz, Greg	193	233							Bucek, John	72	235					
Brock, ---	24	233							Bucha, Anthony	94	235					
Brock, Ed	58	233							Buchanan, ---	5	235					
Brock, J.L.	117								Buck, Joe	72	235					
Brock, Paul	71	74	80	81	83	84	89	98	Buckles, Jim	141	143	235				
	99	100	101	112	114	150	205	206	Buddhu, Charles	45	236					
	209	210	233						Buell, Sam	165	168	176	208	236		
Brockell, Charlie	161	163	164	170	233				Buesse, Carl	5	236					
Brockelman, Bernard	62	65	207	233					Buesse, F.	5	236					
Brodsky, Sheldon	171	233							Buffington, Jack	63	236					
Brodzinski, Jim	81	82	83	89	233				Buffington, Rex	64	236					
Brogden, Otis	72	233							Buheller, Clarence	155	161	163	164	206	236	
Brooks, Floyd	76	78	233						Buhl, Larry	189	193	236				
Brooks, R.	11	19	233						Buie, ---	16	236					
Brooks, Warren	63	68	69	76	79	81	86	234	Bukowski, John	197	200	236				
Brophy, Jim	86	234							Bullard, Henry	171	236					
Brosnan, Pat	120	162	234						Bullock, Bruce	180	183	236				
Broukal, Bill	107	109	207	234					Bumstead, Dan	150	165	175	236			
Brouthers, Walt	6	7	13	14	15	234			Bunce, Jack	160	164	170	236			
Brown, ---	19	63	77	138	234				Bunch, Jake	44	236					
Brown, Al	107	117	234						Bundrick, Clinton	72	236					
Brown, Arles	85	234							Bundy, ---	6	236					
Brown, Ben	41	42	45	46	234				Bunt, Walter	133	140	149	160	170	179	
Brown, Bill	89	92	102	104	105	107	115	118	Burbank, ---	34	236					

Georgia Class-D Minor League Baseball Encyclopedia

Name									
Burch, H.H.	145								
Burcham, Tom	141	151	152	153	236				
Burchfield, Boyd	55	236							
Burchfield, Ken	197	198	236						
Burden, ---	5	236							
Burford, Lamar	151	153	236						
Burford, Larry	160	236							
Burford, Red	34	236							
Burg, Jerold	166	167	236						
Burgamy, Ralph	111	113	125	127	145	236			
Burger, Bob	201	202	236						
Burgess, ---	20	22	24	27	236				
Burgess, Jay	125	236							
Burgess, O.K.	55	60	64						
Burgess, Ted	172	236							
Burk, Ron	103	237							
Burke, ---	11	17	237						
Burke, Don	189	237							
Burke, Joe	90	237							
Burkey, Melvin	94	237							
Burkhardt, John	86	237							
Burkholder, John	63	237							
Burkwitt, Irwin	76	78	237						
Burleson, Art	20	237							
Burlick, Bill	54	237							
Burnell, Bob	189	237							
Burnett, Ed	72	237							
Burnett, Gerald	146	237							
Burnett, L.W.	43	237							
Burnett, Ray	85	88	208	237					
Burnette, Etheridge	82	237							
Burnette, Tom	167	237							
Burnham, Al	189	193	237						
Burns, ---	17	237							
Burns, Bill	99	112	237						
Burns, Bob	43	237							
Burns, Jim	58	59	61	62	63	65	68	69	
	70	147	148	157	158	197	201	202	
	203	208	209	237					
Burns, Matthew A.	134	151	161	171	181	189	193		
Burnstein, Leonard	102	237							
Burpo, Howard	64	237							
Burress, ---	13	237							
Burright, Possum	189	190	191	237	433				
Burroughs, Gene	194	195	208	237					
Burrows, John	63	237	433						
Burruss, ---	16	18	237						
Burt, Dick	121	237							
Burt, Tommy	55	59	61	64	238				
Burtner, Hugh	184	238							
Burtner, Lou	47	238							
Burton, ---	31	238							
Burton, Jim	146	238							
Burton, Leonard	63	238							
Busa, Al	95	97	107	238					
Busch, August Jr.	149	160	170	179	188	192			
Busch, George	116	117	118	238					
Bush, Carl	72	238							
Bush, Herb	176	238							
Bush, Ray	151	238							
Bussan, Don	141	238							
Bustle, Bill	116	118	119	205	238				
Butchko, Steve	133	238							
Butkus, Carl	68	238							
Butler, C.L.	35	238							
Butler, Cecil	194	195	196	238	433				
Butler, J.L.	171	180							
Buttice, Lou	145	155	238						
Butts, ---	31	238							
Butts, Bobby	176	238							
Butts, Gene	126	238							
Byrd, Charles	200	238							
Byrd, Walt	116	238							
Byrne, John	96	97	208	238					
Cabaniss, Gerald	107	238							
Cabera, ---	16	238							
Cacciola, Jim	116	238							
Cade, Dane	197	238							
Cagle, Lamar	77	238							
Cahall, G.L.	71	103							
Cahall, George	80	81	89	101	115	116	128	129	
Cahill, Norm	77	238							
Cahoon, Jim	182	238							
Cailor, Howard	186	238							
Cain, Charles	137	238							
Cain, George	71	90	238						
Cain, Merritt "Sugar"	37	39	70	99	101	239	433		
Calabrese, Joe	125	239							
Caldara, ---	37	239							
Calder, ---	4	239							
Caldwell, ---	17	24	25	34	239				
Caldwell, Bob	177	239							
Caldwell, Calvin	137	239							
Caldwell, Jim	161	239							
Caldwell, Maurice	155	239							
Caldwell, Wilbur	99	111	125	127	128	137	138	139	
	145	147	155	158	166	167	175	178	
	184	185	209	210	239	448			
Cali, Bill	176	239							
Calkins, Dick	102	239							
Callahan, James	80	89	102	115	129				
Callahan, Mike	157	239							
Callaway, Bill	85	94	239						
Callaway, Charles	161	239							
Callen, Jim	102	239							
Calloway, Don	150	239							
Calobrisi, Frank	147	151	153	239					
Calvetti, Lou	170	239							
Camberari, Rocco	176	239							
Camp, Howie	9	12	20	21	22	31	35	239	
	433								
Camp, Loy	71	74	81	239					
Campbell, Ben	90	239							
Campbell, Bob	172	240							
Campbell, Cliff	77	133	239						
Campbell, Doug	151	153	239						
Campbell, Earl	86	239							
Campbell, Fred	90	91	92	93	129	130	131	204	
	205	240							
Campbell, George	198	201	240						
Campbell, James A.	121	194	198	201					
Campbell, Joe	129	130	131	240					
Campbell, Lem	44	47	240						
Campbell, Nolan	193	240							
Campbell, Paul	90	240							
Campo, Ray	82	240							
Cann, Bill	95	240							
Canning, Bill	201	240							
Cannon, Bill	44	240							
Cannon, Bob	125	138	139	240					
Cannon, Harry	40	240							
Cannon, Shorty	29	240							
Canteley, Maxie	54	58	240						
Cantler, Don	95	240							
Cantley, John	9	10	11	16	240				
Canuso, Joe	161	163	170	173	174	240			
Capone, Bob	150	153	161	163	240				
Cappel, Lou	59	240							
Capps, Bill	180	240							
Capullo, Bob	189	193	240						
Caputo, Lou	170	173	176	240					
Caradori, Jim	186	240							
Carangelo, Ferdinand	172	240							
Carel, Paul	58	240							

Georgia Class-D Minor League Baseball Encyclopedia

Name						
Carey, Elwood	95	97	240			
Carey, Scoops	170	240	433	447		
Carlesi, Vince	142	240				
Carlin, Jim	51	240				
Carlson, Bob	67	133	150	171	241	
Carlson, Les	75	240				
Carlson, Ray	67	240				
Carlyle, Roy	29	241	433			
Carmel, Duke	170	179	241	433		
Carmichael, ---	29	241				
Carmichael, Bryce	98	100	112	114	209	241
Carmichael, Dan	176	241				
Carmichael, Ed	55	80	82	241		
Carmo, Bob	193	241				
Carn, Irv	147	151	157	241		
Caro, Jack	134	135	136	241		
Carolan, Joe	141	143	160	241		
Carpenter, Bill	170	189	241			
Carpenter, John	72	241				
Carpenter, Max	154	172	241			
Carr, Bill	107	241				
Carr, T.C.	176					
Carrasquel, Manuel	186	241				
Carre, L.H	36	37				
Carre, L.M.	36					
Carrico, Edgar	189	241				
Carroll, ---	32	34				
Carroll, Bill	90	241				
Carroll, Dixie	38	241	433			
Carroll, Gerald	197	241				
Carroll, Ray	179	188	241			
Carson, Ray	185	241				
Carter, ---	11	24	29	241		
Carter, Arlen	155	165	241			
Carter, Bob	151	242				
Carter, Emil	71	134	142	143	241	
Carter, Homer	31	37	38	39	241	
Carter, Larry	68	69	242			
Carter, Leon	116	118	119	204	242	
Carter, Mack	51	52	54	242		
Carter, Russ	27	242				
Carter, Steve	80	82	242			
Cartier, Dale	162	172	242			
Cartwright, Don	160	242				
Cartwright, H.L.	181					
Cartwright, James	31	32	242			
Caruso, Enrico	117					
Carver, Jim	193					
Casanega, Dave	162	242				
Casanova, Rudy	197	242				
Case, S.E.	31	32	242			
Casey, Charles	73	104	242			
Cash, ---	31	242				
Cash, Al	142	152	242			
Cash, Jack	130	131	145	242		
Cash, Paul	54	58	61	242		
Cash, Sewell	154	242				
Cashion, ---	24	25	242			
Cassell, Carl	160	176	242			
Cassidy, ---	5	242				
Cassidy, John	189	242				
Castaing, ---	24	242				
Castalado, Jerry	156	242				
Castaneda, Jim	160	242				
Castelgrande, Vito	77	242				
Castelli, Anthony	161	242				
Castiglione, Pete	63	66	242	433		
Castille, Earl	172	242				
Castillo, Celido	41	242				
Castillo, Sergio	146	242				
Caswell, Marv	172	181	243			
Catalano, Pete	124	137	145	146	243	
Cataldo, Tom	129	243				
Catchings, Ben	89	93	243			
Catchpole, Jim	77	243				
Cater, Jim	96	108	142	151	153	243
Cates, Eli	6	8	22	243	433	
Cathey, Abner	59	61	243	433		
Cathey, Bob	107	243				
Cathey, John	137	154	243			
Cato, Roy	145	152	243			
Catterton, Frank	129	131	243			
Caudle, Jim	145	155	157	158	159	171	208	209
	243							
Causion, Bill	165	167	168	243		
Cavallaro, Fred	133	150	154	243		
Cavaness, Jim	67	243				
Cawley, Gaynor	198	199	201	243		
Cearley, Wilbur	54	243				
Ceccarelli, Art	106	108	109	110	208	243	433
Cecil, Ed	200	243				
Celardo, Ed	142	151	243			
Celiberti, Frank	137	243				
Celli, Alfred	140	149				
Celozzi, Joe	156	243				
Center, Pete	47	243	433			
Centi, Dave	190	243				
Ceran, ---	133	243				
Ceravolo, Joe	99	243				
Cercek, Ed	120	243				
Cernich, Joe	201	243				
Chadner, Dick	161	243				
Chadwick, ---	38	244				
Chadwick, Reed	145	146	172	244		
Chaffer, Rudie	85					
Chafin, Bobbie	102	244				
Chafin, Cotton	111	113	151	152	162	208	209	244
Chafin, Mark	172	244				
Chaillot, Emil	155	244				
Chalker, A.G.	22	244				
Chambers, ---	9	11	16	17	18	29	244
Chambers, Bob	141	244				
Chambers, Inman	68	78	244			
Chambers, Jim	200	244				
Chambers, Joe	73	74	82	83	84	91	92	93
	111	129	204	205	244	448		
Champlain, ---	7	8	14	244		
Chance, Jesse	180	244				
Chance, Wendell	167	244				
Chancey, C.M.	6	7	29	208	244	
Chandler, Bill	185	244				
Chandler, Billy	141	144	151	244		
Chandler, Dave	81	244				
Chandler, Jack	73					
Chandler, Norm	142	143	244			
Chandler, Ray	117	244				
Chaplin, Ed	27	28	244	433		
Chaplin, Mel	140	143	244			
Chapman, ---	14	17	244			
Chapman, Herb	104	244				
Chappell, Marv	80	89	102	105	115	116	118	119
	129	131	205	206	244			
Chaptman, Devon	90	93	244			
Charette, Don	156	245				
Charette, Roger	167	245				
Charles, Jim	103	105	245			
Charmolue, Jules	51	245				
Chase, Ken	41	42	245	433		
Chastant, ---	19	20	24	245		
Chatham, Happy	17	27	245			
Chechile, Bill	102	103	104	116	118	245
Cheney, ---	7	22	245			
Cheney, Tom	140	149	245	433		
Cherek, LeRoy	194	245				

Name							Name						
Chergey, Paul	133	154	245				Clement, Ed	60	247				
Chernetsky, Anthony	76	245					Clements, Anthony	176	247				
Cherry, Dick	78	87	245				Clements, Frank	145	148	155	158	209	247
Chestnut, H.C.	29	245					Clements, Mason	117	138	139	247		
Chetaitis, Stan	64	245					Clements, Ralph	103	105	247			
Chew, Ray	63	245					Cleveland, ---	37	38	39	102	205	247
Chiado, Bob	51	245					Click, Jim	67	247				
Chierichella, Carmine	189	245					Clifford, Ernest	141	143	247			
Childers, Jimmy	151	156	245				Clift, Frank	184	247				
Childs, Delton	91	92	93	106	204	205	245	Clifton, Henry	124	145	155	158	247
Childs, Dick	108	109	122	123	207	245	Clifton, John	152	154	163	248		
Childs, Frank	71	72	81	83	245		Clifton, Ralph	189	248				
Chilton, Warren	111	245					Cline, John	186	248				
Chipman, A.B.	27	245					Cline, Leonard	133	248				
Chitty, H.B.	137	145	154	165	175	184	Cloer, Burlon	179	248				
Chitwood, Ed	80	83	205	245			Cloninger, Al	58	248				
Chitwood, Ken	34	37	39	245			Clonts, Ray	44	248				
Chivari, Louis	132						Cloude, Bill	134	248				
Chlebek, Stan	161	245					Cluley, Mike	107	248				
Cholakian, Ed	141	245					Coapland, Bernis	77	248				
Chredar, Steve	85	86	245				Coates, Dick	78	248				
Christakis, George	63	245					Coats, Glenn	76	248				
Christenbury, Low	21	22	24	25	246	433	Cobb, Jim	152	248				
Christiansen, ---	34	246					Cobb, Joe	162	248				
Christie, Frank	112	126	134	146	246		Cobb, Neal	94	248	448			
Christie, Jake	54	246					Cobb, William O.	89	102				
Christie, John	180	183	246				Cobiella, Ricardo	116	248				
Christino, Mike	201	246					Coble, Dave	44	111	124	126	248	434
Christoff, Ernie	190	246					Coccetti, Al	68	69	248			
Christopher, Leo	125	246					Cochran, Bill	133	248				
Christy, Jim	189	246					Cochran, Gene	180	248				
Chulick, Bill	76	246					Cochran, George	160					
Chumbris, Nick	142	246					Cochran, John	20	21	248			
Churlilla, Ed	175	246					Cockrell, Gene	176	248				
Churn, Chuck	201	246	433				Cockroft, Dolly	170					
Ciani, Nick	103	246					Cockroft, Joe	177	248				
Ciatto, Rosario	162	172	246				Coffey, ---	17	248				
Cibrowski, Marion	58	64	65	66	246		Coffey, Herman	172	248				
Cibulski, Floyd	147	148	246				Cohen, Arnold	40	248				
Ciccimarro, John	67	246					Cohen, Henry S.	59					
Ciccone, Nick	76	246					Cohen, Hy	90	103	105	205	248	434
Ciccone, Remo	58	246					Cohen, M.A.	99	112				
Cichon, Frank	90	92	93	102	105	246	Cohick, Harry	58	61	62	248		
Cielesz, Walt	54	56	59	246			Cohn, David	63					
Cierniak, Don	163	167	246				Coho, Russ	160	248				
Cimmino, Vince	166	246					Coker, E.R.	35	37	248			
Cincotta, Joe	185	246					Coker, Jack	87	88				
Clair, Tom	76	246					Coker, Jim	85	89	102	248		
Clancey, ---	7	246					Colangelo, Stan	157	248				
Clancy, Bill	171	181	246				Colcolough, Tom	16	249	434			
Clancy, Bud	68	246	433				Cole, ---	9	249				
Clapham, Brad	142	144	151	246			Cole, Dr. Ray	99	112				
Clapp, Charles	19	20	22	246			Cole, F.G. "Jack"	117	130				
Clarich, Jim	107	247					Cole, Harold	117	249				
Clark, ---	9	10	17	21	247		Cole, Jack	130	249				
Clark, Bob	179	184	185	247			Cole, Joe	47	249				
Clark, Dr. T.H.	111						Cole, Ken	82	249				
Clark, Glen	197	198	199	207	247	434	Cole, Mrs. F.G.	117	130				
Clark, Langdon	14	247					Cole, Sam	40	41	42	43	45	47	249
Clark, Lou	133	247					Coleman, Bill	171	249				
Clark, Phil	132	135	136	149	247	434	Coleman, Malcolm	113	126	137	138	249	
Clark, R.H.	31	32	34	37	39	247	Coleman, Sid	41	42	45	249		
Clark, Ray	91	92	104	116	118	204	205	247	Coles, Chuck	121	122	123	249	434
Clark, Roy	111	247					Colflesh, Jack	106	141	249			
Clark, Walt	48	51	247				Colgan, Bill	59	64	77	87	249	
Clark, William	7	8	247				Colgan, Dick	189	193	249			
Clarke, Bill	145	247					Colina, Eddie	63	249				
Clary, Ellis	40	42	43	247	434		Coller, Jon	197	249				
Claset, John	150	153	161	164	247		Colley, Owen	73	249				
Clawson, Charles	77	247					Collier, ---	4	38	249			
Claypool, Jim	126	137	139	247			Collins, Bill	51	67	138	147	155	249
Clemens, Chet	48	247	434				Collins, Bob	108	116	121	249		

Georgia Class-D Minor League Baseball Encyclopedia

Name								
Collins, Charlie	41	91	115	119	249			
Collins, Howard	193	195	249					
Collins, Jack	99	100	112	114	124	126	127	137
	166	249						
Collins, Jim	154	249						
Collins, John F.	58							
Collins, Lee	80	81	82	249				
Collins, Steve	120	249						
Collum, Ambrose	72	250						
Colombatto, Pete	86	250						
Colon, Joe	185	250						
Colone, Dick	172	250						
Colson, Rod	104	250						
Colter, ---	71	250						
Columbano, Aldo	116	117	250					
Colvard, Herman	197	201	250					
Colvin, Jack	150	156	250					
Combs, ---	19	250						
Combs, M.E.	84							
Combs, Ralph	155	165	250					
Comegys, Clarence	133	250						
Comegys, Howard	150	250						
Comiskey, Bob	91	103	105	250				
Commisso, Dom	141	250						
Comolli, Vic	94	106	110	250				
Comotti, Al	75							
Comotti, Elmo	77	79	250					
Company, Ron	162	250						
Condit, ---	71	72	250					
Condu, Phil	171	173	174	250				
Conhenney, Jim	102	250						
Coniff, E.P.	4	5	250					
Conley, ---	16	250						
Conn, Bob	154	250						
Connell, Guy	55	59	75	84	151	159	162	169
	172	179	181	188	190	192		
Connell, Nina	55	60						
Connell, Truman	99	100	112	250				
Connell, Wes	192	250						
Conner, Jim	125	250						
Conner, John	94	250						
Connor, ---	71	250						
Connor, Charles	182							
Conovan, Mike	91	92	250					
Conquy, Gene	181	250						
Conrad, Bob	172	250						
Conrad, George	185	250						
Conte, Michael	129	250						
Conti, Lou	162	251						
Contini, Bobby	55	60	251					
Contratto, George	193	251						
Conway, Alvin	186	187	251					
Cook, ---	29	146	251					
Cook, Bill	99	101	251					
Cook, Bob	96	251						
Cook, Claude	144	125						
Cook, Cliff	171	175	177	178	251	434		
Cook, Don	134	135	251					
Cook, Dwight	179	251						
Cook, Eason	72	82						
Cook, George	99	112	114	137	139	170	209	210
	251							
Cook, Hugh	117	251						
Cook, John	150	166	197	251				
Cook, Ron	77	251						
Cooke, Jay	181	182	183	251				
Coombs, ---	29	251						
Coombs, Woody	41	251						
Cooper, ---	9	16	251					
Cooper, Bill	94	97	130	150	166	251		
Cooper, Bob	156	251						
Cooper, Carl	103	104	105	116	118	119	129	130
	251							
Cooper, Frank	126	142	151	152	251			
Cooper, Stewart	85	251						
Cop, Milan	155	158	159	166	251			
Copeland, Cliff	186	251						
Copeland, Elmer	71	81	83	84	205	206	251	
Copeland, Harvey J.	71	89	102	115				
Copeland, Jim	146	252						
Coppola, Herb	78	252						
Corbett, ---	16	17	252					
Corbett, Gene	140	252	434					
Corbett, Tom	45	48	49	206	207	252		
Corder, Bob	141	157	252					
Cordero, Manuel	137	252						
Corley, Art	82	83	252					
Corley, Earl	116	252						
Corley, Furman	63	252						
Corley, Harold	94	252						
Corley, Ken	76	78	252					
Corley, Ray	167	252						
Corley, Stan	181	252						
Cornacchia, Arthur J.	80							
Cornelius, Rusty	27	29	30	252				
Cornett, Homer	156	252						
Cornwell, John	162	252						
Corrales, Reggie	116	252						
Correllas, Dick	180	252						
Corso, Gene	133	252						
Corthell, Dick	161	252						
Cosby, ---	31	252						
Cosman, Jim	200	202	252	434				
Coss, Royden	91	93	252					
Costa, Frank	34	35	38	39	205	252		
Costa, Tony	34	35	252					
Costello, Dan	24	25	107	121	252	434		
Costello, Tom	133	252						
Cothran, Bob	163	252						
Cotney, Vern	146	252						
Cottengim, Charles	112	252						
Cotter, Jim	160	252						
Cottier, Chuck	160	163	252	434	447			
Cottle, R.L.	91							
Coulling, Stan	63	68	116	253				
Coultas, Gary	181	253						
Courser, Ron	200	253						
Courtney, Bill	120	123	253					
Courtney, James	103	253						
Coveney, Jack	7	14	253	434				
Cowan, E.	11	12	253					
Cowan, Frank	180	185	253					
Cowan, Jim	133	253						
Cowan, W. W.	11	253						
Cowart, Ike	43							
Cowart, William W.	102							
Cowen, Gerald	186	253						
Cox, ---	14	253						
Cox, Frank	140	143	253					
Cox, George	185	253						
Cox, Jim	41	48	253					
Cox, Max	71	253						
Coy, Hugh	188	191	253					
Cozart, Paul	161	253						
Cozens, John	138	253						
Craddock, ---	27	253						
Craft, Molly	31	253	434					
Crago, Bill	99	100	112	113	125	127	128	208
	253							
Craig, Myron	121	253						
Craig, Roger	121	123	253	434	447			
Craig, Royal	160	253						
Craig, Steve	95	253						
Crain, Paul	81	82	83	84	205	206	253	

Georgia Class-D Minor League Baseball Encyclopedia

Name								Name							
Crandall, Johnny	59	253						Cunningham, Ed	133	255					
Cranston, ---	5	253						Cunningham, Larry	125	126	255				
Craven, Bob	126	138	139	253				Cuoco, Al	121	256					
Craven, Jess	9	11	19	27	28	253		Cuomo, Mario	141	256					
Craven, Jim	177	181	253					Curl, Kedy	160	179	189	191	256		
Craven, Tommy	27	254						Curley, Jim	68	256					
Cravey, Nadine	160	179	188	192				Currie, Bill	122	123	256	434			
Crawford, Jim	146	148	171	254				Currie, Frank	34	256					
Crawford, Wayne	117	254						Curry, ---	38	256					
Crawley, ---	5	254						Curtis, Ira	95	97	256				
Creager, Bill	55	56	254					Curtis, Leonard M.	50						
Creamer, Brice	90	254						Curtis, Turk	68	256	434				
Creel, Jim	117	129	254					Cusick, Jack	76	256	434				
Creel, Scobie	117	254						Cusick, Joe	58	62	67	256			
Creel, Wiley	37							Cutcliff, Tom	107	256					
Creighton, Joe	145	254						Cutter, Ron	193	256					
Cressman, Bob	198	254						Cyrus, Dave	85	88	94	97	106	109	110 256
Crews, ---	5	254						Czjka, Edward P.	75						
Crisler, Joe	41	44	254					Dabbs, Chester	73	94	113	256			
Crisp, Ransom	161	254						Dacey, Red	6	8	256				
Croge, Sam	193	195	254					Dacus, Joe	130	131	152	154	256		
Cromartie, Bill	95	254						Dahl, Jay	200	201	202	256	434		
Cromartie, Henry	107	112	254					Daidone, Joe	165	171	256				
Crone, Bob	180	254						Dairon, Wayne	197	256					
Cronic, George	138	254						Dal Porto, Angelo	155	158	166	176	256		
Cronic, Guin	78	79	87	254				Dale, Paul	181	256					
Cronin, Frank	64	68	254					Daley, ---	7	256					
Cronin, Jim	86	254						Daley, Gil	113	126	127	132	135	136	256
Crook, Don	171	254						Dalton, Elroy	94	256					
Crosby, Ralph	176	254						Daly, Hugh	120	133	150	256			
Crosley, Umpire	4	254						Damaska, Bill	200	256					
Cross, Don	47	51	52	157	254			Dan, Virgil	90	256					
Cross, Jim	181	182	183	190	191	254		Dance, John	75	85	256				
Crosslin, ---	38	254						Dandurand, Tom	182	257					
Crotty, John	193	254						Daniel, Bob	172	257					
Crouch, ---	24	254						Daniel, Doug	125	138	146	156	257		
Crouch, Les	85	94	97	154	157	165	168 169	Daniel, Jake	71	73	74	81	83	117	118 147
	171	254	448						157	204	205	257	434		
Crow, Lee	12	20	255					Daniel, Stewart	126	257					
Crow, Paul	73	255						Daniels, Dick	146	172	173	257			
Crowder, ---	5	73	255					Danielson, Dan	64	257					
Crowder, H.F.	34	37	255					Danish, Chris	81	257					
Crowe, Charles	173	255						Danna, Charles	82	84	91	93	257		
Crowe, Hoyt	31	33	34	255				Danna, Jesse	80	82	83	84	91	92	93 104
Crowl, Ernest	117	255							205	257					
Crowley, ---	5	255						Danowski, Bill	155	257					
Crowley, J.M.	43							D'Antonio, Joe	56	257					
Crowley, Walt	107	109	110	255				Darby, William T.	99						
Crowley, William	184							Darden, Bill	96	257					
Crowson, Marv	71	255						Darden, L.H.	101						
Crucitti, Tony	85	255						Dardes, Nick	112	257					
Crum, McPherson	137	255						Darr, Don	133	257					
Crumley, John	134	255						Daugherty, Mike	72	257					
Crumly, Ivan	77	78	79	255				Daugherty, Norm	41	257					
Crutchfield, Gene	155	255						Dauten, Fred	180	257					
Cruthers, Hal	54	255						Davenport, ---	5	6	7	8	14	29	37 37
Cruz, Jose Ramon	201	255							257						
Cruze, Bob	93	95	97	255				Davenport, Nevil	100	104	111	257			
Cudemo, Mike	116	124	130	255				Davids, Roland	68	257					
Cudillo, Joe	48	255						Davidson, Bob	141	257					
Culberson, Leon	130	255	434					Davis, ---	14	71	257				
Culbreth, Bud	180	255						Davis, Al	176	257					
Cullinan, Craig F.	197							Davis, Alton	151	257					
Culp, ---	29	255						Davis, Alvin	90	103	116				
Culpepper, Bill	80	89	113	129	255			Davis, Art	76	257					
Culpepper, J.E.	27	255						Davis, Bill	99	181	185	259			
Culpepper, J.T.	46							Davis, Bubba	180	258					
Cummings, ---	5	255						Davis, Bud	11	12	22	258	434		
Cummings, Polly	54	56	57	255				Davis, Carl	34	37	38	156	258		
Cummings, Vince	194	255						Davis, Clarence	73	258					
Cumpson, Bill	126	255						Davis, Don	200	258					
Cundiff, Bill	197	199	255					Davis, Ed	40	41	42	207	258		

Georgia Class-D Minor League Baseball Encyclopedia

Name								
Davis, Ernest	200	258						
Davis, Fred	80	89	258					
Davis, Gene	149	152	258					
Davis, Hargrove	64	258						
Davis, Hazen	162	258						
Davis, Homer	50	54						
Davis, Howard	50	125	150	258				
Davis, J.B.	201	258						
Davis, Jack	163	173	258					
Davis, Jim	72	103	258					
Davis, Joe	145	175	184	258				
Davis, Lisle	62	258						
Davis, Max	80	83	89	259				
Davis, Ned	172	258						
Davis, R.C.	71							
Davis, Ralph	80	258						
Davis, Ray	128							
Davis, Spencer	85	258						
Davis, Spike	93							
Davis, Sterling	141	258						
Davis, T.K.	91							
Davis, Thurman	137	138	139	146	161	258		
Davis, Tom	176	258						
Davis, Van	124	127	137	138	139	145	147	148
	154	157	158	165	168	169	184	208
	209							
Davis, Vic	176	178	200	258				
Davis, W.C.	31	33	34	38	259			
Davis, Walter	166	259						
Davis, Wayne	133	134	170	173	174	259		
Davis, Wendell	111	121	133	134	135	259		
Davis, Woody	43	44	45	46	55	60	207	259
	434							
Dawkins, Bob	116	259						
Dawson, Ron	157	259						
Day, ---	6	7	8	14	72	259		
Day, Don	133	141	143	144	259			
Day, Dwight	121	259						
Day, Kenneth	62							
de la Cruz, Ramon	201	259						
de la Torre, Albert	197	259						
Deal, ---	38	259						
Deal, Bill	161	167	171	173	259			
Deal, Marv	141	150	259					
Deal, Nip	71	259						
Deal, Silas	55	259						
Deal, Wally	55	56	60	61	208	259		
Dealing, Ephram	167	259						
Dean, Charles	71	259						
Dean, Harry	71	259	434					
Dean, Ray	163	259						
Dean, Ted	108	259						
DeArman, H.P	31	32	34	35	37	260		
DeArmond, Hollis	86	260						
Deary, Bernard D.	140	149						
DeBosky, Edward	29	260						
DeBruler, Ernest	189	260						
Decatur, Arthur R.	12	20	21	80	89	101	115	128
	260	434						
Deck, Ed	170	260						
Decker, Bob	165	260						
DeCosta, ---	4	5	260					
Dedon, ---	13	14	260					
Deeds, Ray	177	178	260					
Deering, Verne	162	177	260					
Deery, Jim	173	182	260					
DeFalco, Fred	181	260						
DeFeo, Bob	102	103	107	117	260			
DeFoor, Max	185	260						
DeFore, Ed	132	138	151	155	260			
DeGourscey, Joe	116	260						
DeGraaf, Bill	188	191	260					
DeGregorio, Syl	51	260						
Deibler, Mason	91	94	102	103	260			
DeIeso, Vinny	142	260						
Deitch, Elliott	120	126	260					
Deitch, Mike	107	260						
DeJesus, Bill	176	260						
DeJohn, John	60	260						
DeKoning, Bill	54	260	434					
Del Isola, Sal	95	260						
Del Monico, Gerald	186	260						
Del Papa, Frank	76	78	260					
Del Piano, Mike	121	133	260					
DeLeonardis, Ralph	140	149						
Delforge, Ralph	197	201						
Delich, Bill	121	260						
Delida, Bob	176	261						
Delo, Lawrence	107	261						
DeLuca, Ed	176	177	261					
DeLuca, Tom	188	261						
DeLucia, Pasquale	96	261						
DeMatteis, John	117	261						
DeMatteis, Sal	117	261						
Dembek, Joe	134	163	261					
Dembinski, Dan	103	261						
Dembinsky, Charles	197	261						
Demchuk, Bill	68	261						
Demma, Sam	63	64	129	261				
Demont, Paul	107	120	122	141	143	144	170	174
	261							
Dempsey, Frank	112	261						
Dendinger, Dick	81	90	261					
Dendy, Bob	112	121	261					
Deneau, Belmont	151	261						
Denison, Jack	142	143	144	261				
Dennany, Bob	82	91	93	261				
Dennis, C.T.	72	261						
Dennis, Harold	170	261						
Dennis, Jack	116	261						
Denny, Fred	75	261						
Denny, Horace	72	186	261					
Denton, Malcolm	38	261						
DePillo, George	81	261						
Deporto, Jesse	107	261						
Depperschmidt, Gene	108	109	110	207	261			
DeRieux, Bob	121	123	261					
Dernback, Al	50	52	54	56	58	261		
Derry, Stan	166	261						
DeShong, Jimmie	133	261	434					
Desmuke, Harry	75	262						
DeSousa, John	160	262						
DeSouza, Freddie	116	118	204	262				
DeSpirito, Joe	150	262						
D'Esposito, Dan	182	262						
DeStafano, Lou	154	161	262					
DeStefano, Mike	162	262						
Detmers, Larry	171	262						
Detweiler, Ducky	133	134	206	262	434			
Deutch, Morris	47	262						
Devaney, Bob	90	92	205	262				
DeVany, Art	180	262						
Deveney, Jim	161	262						
Devine, Mike	201	262						
DeViveiros, Bernie	58	262	435					
Devlin, Conrad	171	262						
DeWeese, Mal	41	44	45	262				
Dews, Bobby	48	262						
Dexter, Dave	188	262						
Deyo, ---	5	262						
Dezik, John	48	262						
Diahl, Les	189	262						
Diamond, Paul	175	262						
DiBello, Don	129	262						

Georgia Class-D Minor League Baseball Encyclopedia

Name								
Dick, T.S.	38							
Dickerman, Ed	103	126	134	135	142	143	262	
Dickerson, ---	16	17	71	262				
Dickerson, Jerry	192	195	262					
Dickinson, John	72	262						
Dickson, ---	38	262						
Dickson, Ed	103	262						
Dickson, Robin	41	262						
DiCola, Charles	112	262						
Didier, Mel	108	262						
Diehl, Leonard	116	262						
Diering, Chuck	67	69	263	435				
Dietrich, Bill	166	263						
Dietz, Bill	63	65	263					
Dietz, Emmett	180	263						
Diez, Alfredo	166	168	263					
Diffly, Peter	91	263						
DiFranco, Sam	112	125	263					
DiGirolomo, Al	134	263						
DiGirolomo, Rocco	130	263						
Dillard, ---	5	263						
Dillard, Don	177	263	435					
Dillard, Rudy	126	263						
Dillon, Charles	133	263						
Dillon, J.T.R.	27	29	263					
DiLullo, Ralph	108	263						
DiMare, Dom	157	263						
DiMartino, Joe	75	263						
DiMasi, Joe	81	263						
Dimitriadis, Jim	86	263						
DiMott, Don	161	263						
Dinan, Paul	176	177	263					
DiNecci, Al	133	263						
Dingler, George	120	263						
Dingus, Bill	192	195	263					
Dinkelacker, Tim	161	164	263					
DiRoberto, John	151	155	263					
Dispenziere, Carmen	59	63	263					
Dittmer, Charles	155	263						
Dittus, George	67							
Dixon, ---	37	263						
Dixon, Bill	151	153	263					
Dixon, Percy	59	263						
Dixon, Stokely	58	62	68	263				
Doane, Carl	78	87	263					
Dobberstein, Charles	177	180	264					
Dobbins, Howard	34	264						
Dobbins, Mayes	125	129	130	147	157	167	264	448
Dobbins, Ralph	98	113	126	264				
Dobbs, Gil	58	264						
Dobbs, O.R.	55	60						
Dobek, John	156	264						
Dobernic, John	41	42	44	264				
Dobias, John	150	152	264					
Dobner, Charles	47	264						
Dobzanski, Bob	175	178	264					
Dodgin, Jim	111	134	135	141	142	264		
Dodson, ---	32	264						
Dodson, Dick	122	126	264					
Dodson, Sam	167	180	264					
Doehler, Charles	156	264						
Doerflinger, Gene	80	89	90	92	93	205	206	264
Doherty, ---	14	264						
Doherty, Peter	128							
Doke, Ted	160	264						
Doke, Tom	167	264						
Dolan, Lonnie	156	177	264					
Dolhrman, Paul	51	264						
Doligale, John	172	173	264					
Doll, Art	77	264	435					
Dollard, Bob	62	264						
Domalik, Joe	170	264						
Dominy, Clint	193	264						
Dommer, Chuck	76	79	264					
Donahue, Matt	31	264						
Donaldson, Earl	9	10	11	12	16	19	21	22
	24	25	27	30	31	32	38	265
Donaldson, George	120	265						
Donaldson, Jack	9	11	20	21	265			
Donaldson, R.F. Jr.	146	157	167	176				
Donatucci, John	194	265						
Donnelly, Bob	150	265						
Donofry, Don	150	265						
Donovan, Tom	189	265						
Dorin, Henry	63	265						
Dorman, Alfred	146	156	167					
Dorough, John	76	265						
Dorsey, Norris	182	265						
Dorsky, Mike	89	91	117	265				
Dorwin, Rod	95	108	113	265				
Dotlich, Joe	44	45	265					
Dotson, Gene	107	120	265					
Dotterer, Tom	161	163	265					
Doty, Theodore R. "Ted"	150							
Dougan, John	99	265						
Dougan, Stan	99	265						
Douglas, Dan	180	185	265					
Douglas, David	68	265						
Douglas, Ken	170	265						
Douglas, Leroy	162	265						
Douglas, Whammy	160	161	164	170	207	208	265	435
Dove, Pat	51	55	57	59	61	64	76	77
	133	265						
Dow, Bill	186	265						
Dowdy, ---	24	25	265					
Dowling, Edward	98							
Downs, Wilburn	73	265						
Doyle, ---	12	266						
Doyle, Walter Jr.	98							
Dozier, ---	16	266						
Dragotto, Ralph	117	266						
Drake, Enid	186	266						
Drake, Jay	120	266						
Drake, John	194	266						
Drane, Don	180	266						
Drapcho, Al	180	266						
Draper, Dick	161	167	266					
Draper, Lovell	12	266						
Dravecky, Andrew	77	86	95	266				
Dreisbach, Ed	179	266						
Drew, Dick	146	266						
Drewiske, Roger	177	178	266					
Drews, Roy	129	131	266					
Driggers, Bobby	157	167	168	169	177	178	185	208
	209	266						
Driscoll, ---	27	30	266					
Driscoll, Jim	197	266	435					
Driskell, Roy	80	266						
Drostie, Carroll	161	171	266					
Drotar, Joe	170	266						
Druga, Tom	126	127	209	266				
Drummond, Calvin T.	144	154						
Duay, Ted	41	266						
Dubbs, Clayton	106	266						
Duberstein, Ed	41	42	44	45	266			
Duby, Bob	149	266						
Duckworth, Jim	193	266	435					
Duda, John	67	75	266					
Dudas, Al	62	266						
Dudley, ---	4	5	266					
Dudley, John	150	266						
Dudley, Martin	7	14	24	267				
Duenas, Jose	167	168	267					
Duff, ---	32	267						

Name								
Duff, Art	62	65	267					
Duffalo, Jim	170	174	267	435				
Duffy, Joe	186	267						
Dugan, ---	27	267						
Dugan, Joe	179	267						
Dugger, Charles	120	267						
Duke, Bill	167	267						
Duke, Willie	91	267						
Dukovich, ---	68	267						
Dulancy, C.A.	68	267						
Dulick, Pete	54	267						
Dull, Bob	77	267						
Dumas, ---	29	267						
Dumas, Otto	31	267						
Duncan, Bob	190	267						
Duncan, Charles	91	267						
Duncan, Dick	141	267						
Duncan, Frank	62	267						
Duncan, Fred	180	267						
Duncan, Higgins	124	127	210	267				
Duncan, Jim	172	267						
Duncan, John	73	137	138	267				
Duncan, Lindon	176	177	178	267				
Duncan, Troy	71	267						
Dundee, Pat	146	267						
Dunham, ---	16	267						
Dunlap, Bob	156	267						
Dunlap, Don	175	267						
Dunlevy, Harry	59	267						
Dunn, Don	171	267						
Dunn, Ed	68	90	126	267				
Dunn, J.C.	170	173	207	267				
Dunning, Guy	16	17	268					
Dupon, Bart	182	183	268					
Duran, Julio	184	186	187	268				
Durant, Don	166	268						
Duren, Jim	194	268						
Durham, J.C.	27	268						
Durheim, Harry	48	268						
Durkin, Jim	116	119	268					
Durley, George	7	268						
Dusak, Erv	54	56	58	60	61	268	435	
Dusmuke, Herman L.	112							
Dustal, Bob	182	183	268	435				
Dutton, Charles	160	268						
Dutton, Dean	189	190	268					
Duval, ---	29	268						
Duval, Joe	163	268						
Duzyk, Bob	170	173	268					
Dvorak, Ray	58	268						
Dworaczyk, Anthony	180	185	268					
Dwyer, Bill	78	79	87	88	268			
Dwyer, John	176	268						
Dye, Ben	133	268						
Dye, Cliff	186	268						
Dye, Francis	98							
Dye, Hoyle	72	268						
Dyer, Leroy	194	195	268					
Dyer, Penhallow	193	268						
Dyer, Vaughn	157	158	159	177	268			
Dykes, Charlie	76	79	268					
Dykstra, Leonard	189	191						
Dyser, Bill	90	93	268					
Dziedzic, Walt	134	268						
Eames, Paul	120	132	141	143	144	162	163	172
	268	448						
Earl, Les	121	268						
Earley, Jerry	140	268						
Early, ---	32	269						
Earp, Whitfield	30	269						
East, Carl	14	37	38	70	81	99	204	269
	435							
East, Hugh	91	269	435					
Easterling, Gene	137	139	269					
Easterling, Paul	138	269	435					
Eastman, Robert B.	142	151						
Eaton, Dick	108	109	269					
Eaton, Gerald	172	269						
Eaton, Joe	63	65	269					
Ebel, Wally	44	45	48	269				
Ebetino, John	102	116	269					
Ebker, Bob	192	269						
Eckenroth, Bill	58	269						
Eckenroth, Leroy	68	269						
Ecklund, Bill	98	269						
Eckman, Ned	166	168	269					
Edelstein, Jacob	142	143	269					
Edenfield, O.E.	134	152						
Edge, Harvey	91	104	269					
Edge, Roy	77	269						
Edgley, Joe	173	269						
Edmondson, Lee	71	91	269					
Edmondson, W.C.	11	20	269					
Edwards, Bob	82	83	84	91	92	93	204	205
	269							
Edwards, Don	160	166	176	269				
Edwards, Elmer	76	269						
Edwards, Hoyt	90	269						
Edwards, Mac	40	43	269					
Edwards, Ray	82	91	93	102	269			
Ehlers, Arthur	95	107	120	133	141			
Ehnninger, Bob	171	269						
Eidson, Lewis	81	83	269					
Eilbacher, Leo	160	269						
Eilstrop, ---	85	270						
Eiselstein, Bill	201	202	270					
Elder, Gene	161	270						
Eldred, Henry	4	270						
Elenchin, John	76	270						
Elias, Jack	176	177	178	270				
Elkins, Bobby	151	270						
Ellington, ---	27	270						
Ellington, Paul	73	270						
Elliott, Art	149	157	158	160	166	270		
Elliott, Buck	59	270						
Elliott, E.M.	70							
Ellis, ---	13	14	24	25	29	270		
Ellis, George	117	270						
Ellis, Gerhart	90	270						
Ellis, Jerry	201	270						
Ellis, Ralph	59	60	61	206	270			
Ellis, Roy	134	142	173	270				
Ellison, Lee	80	270						
Ello, Jim	81	89	90	102	105	270		
Elmore, Verdo	33	34	35	270	435			
Elmstrom, Carl	201	202	203	208	270			
Elrod, ---	7	16	270					
Elston, Dick	40	42	270					
Embler, Jack	60	270						
Embry, Harry	44	270						
Embry, Joel	91	270						
Emmert, Dick	201	202	270					
Endicott, Bill	47	50	51	52	53	270	435	
Engel, Al	167	168	173	270				
Engel, Ray	173	182	183	270				
England, Jim	151	271						
Engle, Bob	95	271						
Englehart, Bill	172	174	271					
Engler, John	186	271						
English, Edgar	64	271						
Ennis, ---	27	271						
Ennis, Emory	185	271						
Enos, Bill	125	127	209	271				
Enquist, Ernest	156	271						

Georgia Class-D Minor League Baseball Encyclopedia

Name								Name							
Ensley, Jim	142	144	271					Farris, Jimmy	173	176	273				
Epps, George	85	271						Fasanaro, Dick	166	273					
Erickson, Dale	200	271						Fasano, Benny	112	133	135	273			
Erickson, Marlin	171	181	271					Fatui, Charles	41	273					
Ermisch, Howard	81	271						Faucette, Lew	72	273					
Ery, Ed	9	10	11	17	18	271		Fauci, Tom	172	273					
Eskridge, Jim	78	271						Faulk, Leon	156	273					
Esposito, Anthony	126	127	271					Faust, Floyd	150	152	160	161	163	164	206	207
Esser, Bill	47	271							273	448					
Estep, Virgil	162	271						Feaster, ---	44	273					
Estroff, H.B.	167	177	186					Feathers, Beattie	44	45	206	273			
Estroff, William "Bill"	113	126	144	154	165			Fedak, Gene	171	174	175	273			
Etchison, Buck	102	271	435					Federico, Don	179	273					
Eubanks, ---	6	8	13	271				Federoff, Whitey	201	273	435				
Euliss, Walt	67	78	271					Federow, Emil	90	273					
Eure, Carlton	63	271						Feeley, ---	34	273					
Eury, Glenn	133	135	136	207	271			Fehrenbach, Floyd	171	173	273				
Eustice, Willis	91	93	271					Feie, Bill	67	69	273				
Evans, Al H.	161							Feinberg, H.S.	44	48	51	59	64		
Evans, Dean	43	51	52	53	56	271		Feinberg, Joseph	64						
Evans, Frank	106	271						Feinstien, Joe	103	105	273				
Evans, Jim	151	153	271					Felaz, John	133	273					
Evans, Millard	72	74	271					Feldman, Nathan	129	273					
Evans, Robert	67	68	271					Feldstein, Alan	197	274					
Evans, Willard	99	112	271					Feller, Jack	185	274	435				
Everett, ---	5	271						Fenrick, Roger	180	274					
Evernham, George	133	271						Fenster, Aaron	151	274					
Evins, John	90	272						Fenton, ---	7	274					
Ewaniak, John	85	87	88	272				Fenz, Joseph	110						
Ewer, Seaborn	63	272						Feola, Charles	157	274					
Ewin, Dick	193	194	196	272				Ferens, Stan	58	61	208	274	435		
Exline, Bob	194	272						Ferguson, ---	24	73	274				
Ezzell, Bob	34	35	37	39	272			Ferguson, Art	120	274					
Fabbio, Anthony	150	272						Ferguson, Jim	160	274					
Faberlle, Hector	142	143	145	147	209	272		Ferko, Bob	138	274					
Fabrizio, Anthony	150	153	207	272				Fernandez, Cecil	41	45	274				
Fackler, Earl	141	143	170	173	174	272		Fernandez, Jose	156	274					
Factor, Leonard	59	272						Fernandez, Luis	113	114	126	209	210	274	
Faehr, Al	138	272						Fernandez, Marcelo	113	126	127	210	274		
Fahan, Ed	62	272						Fernandez, Mike	116	274					
Fain, Stan	77	272						Fernandez, Rafael	96	274					
Fair, Paul	67	272						Ferra, Joe	77	103	274				
Faircloth, ---	7	272						Ferrand, Ray	201	202	203	274			
Fairley, Florian	77	272						Ferrara, Bernard	171	274					
Falcigno, Harry	115	129	137	138	272			Ferrara, Tony	167	274					
Falcione, Andrew	155	156	272					Ferrell, Beverly	41	42	43	45	46	274	
Falcone, Nick	150	175	272					Ferrell, Richard B.	198	201					
Falconi, Frank	44	272						Ferrerra, Lee	193	274					
Fall, Ralph	113	126	127	137	138	139	209	272	Fesperman, George	55	60	64				
Fallon, Dick	181	272						Fetner, Charles	116	274					
Falls, Tim	166	272						Fetter, Ken	94	274					
Falter, Tom	142	272						Field, Gary	193	274					
Fandozzi, Mike	188	190	191	206	272			Fields, Conrad	24	25	274				
Fann, Ernest	197	272						Fields, Howard	171	177	274				
Fanning, Rip	34	38	272					Fields, Tom	180	274					
Fantasia, Sal	146	272						Fields, Walt	77	274					
Fappiano, Gene	130	131	272					Figueroa, Angel	185	274					
Fappiano, Silvio J.	115							Figueroa, Rodolfo	193	274					
Farington, Gerald	198	272						Fillingim, Dana	6	13	274	435			
Farland, Jim	189	193	272					Filo, Ed	58	60	275				
Farless, Sam	150	161	164	273				Finch, ---	156	275					
Farmer, ---	11	273						Finch, Robert L. Jr.	47						
Farmer, Dave	180	273						Fincher, Bill	189	191	275				
Farmer, Dennis	162	163	167	172	273			Fincher, Bob	71	275					
Farnsworth, Fred	181	273						Fingers, M.	54	275					
Farr, Red	71	273						Fink, Jim	77	86	275				
Farrar, Bill	89	273						Finley, Bob	47	275	435				
Farrar, Charles	56	60	61	64	78	99	112	113	Finley, Doug	98	113	275				
	206	207	273					Finn, Francis	200	275					
Farrar, Jim	177	273						Finney, Bob	73	275					
Farrar, Roger	190	273						Finney, Jack	103						
Farrell, Dick	200	273						Finney, Lou	32	34	37	38	72	73	204	275

Georgia Class-D Minor League Baseball Encyclopedia

Name								
	435							
Fiore, Pat	119	132						
Fiori, Ben	107	275						
Firek, Jan	197	275						
Fish, Hamilton	29	275						
Fisher, ---	37	275						
Fisher, Bob	5	275	435					
Fisher, George	96	108	109	207	275			
Fisher, Harry	86	88	275	435				
Fisher, Robert L.	75							
Fisher, Ron	91	93	275					
Fisher, Stan	166	275						
Fisher, Vern	151	153	275					
Fisher, W.A.	51	275						
Fittery, Paul	30	31	33	34	35	36	37	39
	205	275	435					
Fitzgerald, ---	16	275						
Fitzgerald, John	107	109	275					
Fitzgerald, Lou	67	275						
Flaherty, Chris	103	275						
Flair, Al	47	49	51	52	275	435		
Flair, Elmer	68	275						
Flammia, Rocco Thomas	75							
Flanagan, Bill	141	275						
Flanagan, Jerome	185	275						
Flanigan, Cheri Jim	149	275						
Fleisch, Don	102	149	160	166	276			
Fleischer, Herb	155	276						
Fleming, Doug	150	165	168	276				
Flemming, Wheeler	82	83	91	92	103	104	117	118
	129	205	276					
Fleshman, Elvin	172	182	183	276				
Fletcher, George A.	76	85	94	106				
Fletcher, George F.	120							
Fletcher, Thomas E.	63							
Flohr, ---	27	276						
Flood, Joe	201	276						
Flora, Bill	41	42	45	276				
Flores, Paul	37	102	103	104	105	205	276	
Flowers, ---	24	25	276					
Flowers, B.	11	276						
Flowers, Bob	171	276						
Flowers, Burnice	71	276						
Flowers, H.	11	276						
Flowers, John	197	276						
Floyd, Bob	179	180	276					
Floyd, Buck	31	276						
Floyd, Charles	186	276						
Floyd, Tim	46							
Floyd, Wiley	188							
Flynn, Bob	185	276						
Flynn, Don	20	21	22	23	24	25	276	
Flynn, Tom	180	276						
Foell, George	129	276						
Fogg, Bill	94	97	276					
Fogleman, Oliver	171	276						
Folds, E.V.	115							
Foley, Walt	47	276						
Folk, Dick	171	175	276					
Folson, ---	73	276						
Foltmer, Harold	122	276						
Foote, Ambrose	163	276						
Forbes, John	107	276						
Ford, A.W. "Andy"	31	34	37	70	71	81		
Ford, Bob	151	156	157	158	161	167	277	
Ford, Don	81	82	122	182	276	277		
Ford, John	172	181						
Ford, Leonard	47	277						
Ford, Lonnie	120	277						
Foreman, Dick	193	277						
Foreman, Don	106	277						
Forrest, C.C.	57	62						
Forrest, Dick	171	186	277					
Forrest, Henry	172	277						
Forrest, Jim	60	277						
Forrester, Frank	81	102	277					
Forsythe, Ron	181	277						
Fort, Hollis	40	43						
Fortner, ---	29	30	277					
Fortuna, Walter	64	277						
Foss, Deeby	16	277	435					
Foss, Larry	176	178	277	435				
Foster, ---	5	71	277					
Foster, Dick	129	277						
Foster, Duell	145	152	277					
Foster, R.A.	27	277						
Foster, Ralph	111	277						
Foster, Shelby	166	277						
Foster, Tom	185	277						
Fountain, Harvey	138	277						
Fountain, Ron	142	277						
Fouts, Paul	85	277						
Fowler, ---	34	277						
Fowler, Bob	172	277						
Fowler, Cecil	63	277						
Fowler, Lincoln	113	277						
Fowler, Ted	162	277						
Fowler, Wheeler	138	277						
Fox, Jim	30	278						
Foytack, Paul	108	109	278	436				
Fracaro, Dave	194	278						
Frady, Bill	157	278						
Frady, Herb	117	278						
Fragela, Alberto	142	278						
Fraker, Dick	67	71	278					
Frakes, Ben	31	33	205	278				
Fraley, Carroll	160	278						
Francek, Mike	200	278						
Francis, Charles	176	278						
Francis, Ed	94	278						
Francoline, Jim	51	132	133	135	278			
Francone, Nick	185	278						
Frank, Morris	94	106	109	110	207	208	278	
Franklin, Hal	193	278						
Franks, ---	6	7	278					
Franks, Paul	162	278						
Franson, Carl	90	92	103	104	116	118	133	135
	204	278						
Frantell, Don	106	108	278					
Franz, Bill	94	278						
Frazee, ---	38	278						
Frazier, Andy	108	278						
Frazier, Bill	133	278						
Frazier, Clarence	186	189	278					
Frazier, Dan	130	278						
Frazier, John	91	278						
Frazier, Lance	73	82	104	278				
Frazier, Lee	171	278						
Frazier, Ralph	73	82	278					
Frederick, Bill	72	278						
Fredericks, Harry	120	278						
Freedman, Benny	34	35	279					
Freeland, John	85	279						
Freeman, Harold	54	279						
Freeman, Jim	134	156	279					
Freese, Gene	150	153	279	436				
Fregin, Arnold	161	180	279					
Freis, Clayton	54	56	57	279				
French, A.J.	50	54						
Frentz, ---	9	10	279					
Freund, Norm	47	279						
Frew, Bill	86	279						
Frey, ---	38	279						
Frey, Larry	63	279						

Georgia Class-D Minor League Baseball Encyclopedia

Name							
Friar, Del	44	279					
Fricano, Marion	96	97	279	436			
Friedman, Stan	99	112	279				
Friend, Owen	196	197	279	436			
Frioni, Alfonso	194	279					
Frisinger, Jack	85	88	208	279			
Frost, Bob	54	279					
Froug, Mel	107	279					
Fry, Bob	180	279					
Fryman, Howard	149	279					
Fucci, Dom	129	279					
Fullen, Tom	197	199	279				
Fuller, ---	37	279					
Fuller, A.L.	81						
Fuller, Bertram	27	279					
Fullington, ---	102	279					
Fulton, Bob	103	105	121	122	279		
Fultz, George	96	97	279				
Fulwiler, Harold	63	279					
Funderburk, Dr. A.G.	133	141					
Funk, Ernie	95	97	279				
Fuqua, Roger	31	34	35	37	39	279	
Futcher, John	99	108	279				
Gabriel, Earl	179	280					
Gaddy, John	54	280	436				
Gaffney, George	186	280					
Gagnon, Russ	99	111	114	280			
Gaidzis, John	150	280					
Gaillard, Mel	64	280					
Gaillard, Ted	116	280					
Gaines, R.H.	29	280					
Gaines, Sam	126	280					
Gaisford, Jerry	151	280					
Gaisser, Roy	64	280					
Galasso, Lou	94	280					
Galen, Joe	141	280					
Galey, Bob	84	87	88	108	280		
Galinkin, Norm	96	280					
Gall, Bill	107	280					
Gallagher, ---	13	29	280				
Gallagher, Charles	32	33	59	280			
Gallart, Armando	72	280					
Gallegos, N.F.	44	280					
Gallivan, Phil	37	280					
	436	201	280				
Galloway, Oliver	91	104	125	137	185	280	
Gallucci, Frank	138	280					
Galoffin, Jose	99	100	280				
Ganakas, Michael R.	124	132	140				
Gandy, Bob	16	17	280	436			
Ganong, ---	19	280					
Ganss, Bob	68	280					
Ganzer, Bob	185	280					
Garcia, David	149	280					
Garcia, Jesus	145	156	166	280			
Garcia, Jose	124	280					
Garcia, Manuel	165	171	281				
Garcia, Sergio	171	281					
Gardecki, Stan	59	281					
Gardner, ---	17	18	281				
Gardner, Joel	111	281					
Garmon, Ray	156	166	176	281			
Garner, ---	31	281					
Garner, Bill	95	107	121	281			
Garner, Bob	71	281					
Garner, E.O.	41						
Garner, Homer	103	281					
Garone, Mike	90	281					
Garrecht, Bob	108	281					
Garrett, ---	78	281					
Garrett, Charles	201	281					
Garrett, Tige	12	20	21	22	27	31	281
Garrison, ---	12	281					
Garrison, Bill	180	281					
Garrison, John W.	112						
Garrison, Lyle	75	76	79	281			
Garton, Ed	150	281					
Garvey, ---	29	281					
Garwood, Charlie	58						
Gary, Lou	149	281					
Gaskins, Henry	176	281					
Gassoway, Paul	59	64	206	281			
Gast, Mike	67	281					
Gaston, Bob	163	281					
Gaston, Dave	13	14	15	281			
Gaston, W.S.	70						
Gates, ---	134	281					
Gatza, Paul	194	281					
Gault, Pat	34	36	37	281			
Gautreaux, Joe	68	78	281				
Gavaghan, Tom	95	281					
Gay, Bill	161	282					
Gay, Carlus	193						
Gay, J. Hoyt	73	82	91	104	117		
Gearhart, Earl	161	164	282				
Geary, Bob	13	282	436				
Geary, Henry	134	135	156	282			
Geary, Huck	51	282	436				
Geehring, Don	94	282					
Geels, Bob	186	282					
Geesing, John	189	191	282				
Gehringer, Paul	125	127	128	155	210	282	
Geis, Harry	94	107	109	207	282		
Geminiani, Dick	198	199	201	282			
Gemme, Bernie	189	282					
Gendreau, Ron	133	135					
Genevrino, Mike	120	133	134	135	147	154	282
Gentile, Sam	47	48	282	436			
Gentle, ---	20	282					
Gentry, Dick	162	282					
Gentry, Ed	31	34	37	39	282		
George, Alex	180	282	436				
George, Greek	133	134	142	143	282	436	
George, John D.	155						
George, Johnny	67	111	155	282			
George, Joseph	81	90	102	116	129		
George, Louis	81	90	102	116	129		
George, Milt	72	282					
Gerace, John	133	282					
Gerard, Ray	177	282					
Gergely, Bill	134	142	282				
German, Preston	75	282					
Gershberg, Howard	171	185	282				
Geter, Eldridge	201	203	282				
Ghant, Roland	167	282					
Ghelfi, Dick	155	158	166	282			
Giambelluca, Charles	201	282					
Gianelli, Ray	180	283					
Giaquinto, Frank	121	123	283				
Giavedoni, Nilo	132	283					
Gibbons, Bill	142	172	283				
Gibbs, Powell D.	140						
Gibson, ---	24	29	283				
Gibson, Charlie	63	68	69	283			
Gibson, G.H.	147	157	167	177	186		
Gibson, Hammond	165	283					
Gibson, Sam	102	283	436				
Gibson, William	134	142	151	161	171	181	189	193
Giglio, Joe	38	82	283				
Gilbert, Art	73	74	283				
Gilbert, Buddy	165	167	168	169	208	283	436
Gilbert, Clarence	112	283					
Gilbert, Fred	98	110					
Gilbert, Glenn	170	283					

Georgia Class-D Minor League Baseball Encyclopedia

Name							
Gilbert, Harry	150	283					
Gilbert, Herb	170	185	283				
Gilbert, Jack	98	100	101	125	126	283	
Gilbert, Lewis	27	283					
Gilbert, Phil	138	144	146	148	167	168	169	177
	178	209	210	283	448		
Gilchrist, Jim	182	283					
Gilder, R.T.	184						
Giles, G.W.	145						
Gill, Audis	72	283					
Gill, Bill	108	109	283				
Gillespie, ---	6	283					
Gillespie, Frank	111	283					
Gillet, Al	86	283					
Gilliam, Earl	152	180	283				
Gilliland, ---	24	283					
Gilliland, G.E.	86						
Gillis, Grant	44	47	51	283	436		
Gilmore, Bob	197	283					
Gilmore, Don	75	79	283				
Gilmore, John	91	283					
Gilmore, Russ	151	284					
Gilson, John	71	284					
Gilstrap, John	59	85	284				
Ginn, Stark	22	284					
Giombetti, Eddie	90	284					
Giordano, Al	134	136	142	284			
Gisclair, Clyde	161	284					
Givens, Bill	41	284					
Gladding, Fred	182	190	191	284	436		
Gladich, Frank	121	150	284				
Glamp, Francis	141	284					
Glaser, Bob	181	284					
Glass, ---	9	10	31	33	37	284	
Glass, Dick	75	284					
Glaudi, Benjamin	167	284					
Glaze, Claude	82	89	91	284			
Glaze, Hugh	81	284					
Glazner, Whitey	9	11	19	21	37	284	436
Glenn, ---	185	284					
Glover, Charles	134	284					
Glover, Jim	59	201	202	203			
Glover, Omer	89	90	146	284			
Glynn, Bill	76	78	79	207	284	436	
Godbold, Gus	95	96	97	284			
Godwin, Bill	72	82	129	131	284		
Goeken, Don	130	284					
Goen, ---	16	284					
Goetz, Art	54	58	284				
Goff, Jim	55	103	116	284	285		
Goffney, Carlton	110						
Goggans, Bryant	99	285					
Goggans, G.E. "Cheese"	31	32	34	37	39	73	82	91
	104	117	130	285			
Gohl, Vince	95	285					
Goicoechea, Leo	81	83	285				
Goines, Jim	175	285					
Goins, Preston	155	285					
Goldasich, Paul	51	285					
Golden, ---	20	285					
Goldfield, Alan	197	201	285				
Goldsmith, Ralph	58	285					
Golembiewski, Marion	85	88	121	285			
Gondolfi, Art	22	23	24	285			
Gonet, Bill	151	285					
Gongola, Pete	177	178	285				
Gonzales, Oscar	160	285					
Gonzalez, Cotayo	116	285					
Gonzalez, Tom	190	285					
Gooch, Johnny	22	285	436				
Good, Bill	99	100	101	112	285		
Good, Will	68	285	436				
Goode, ---	37	285					
Goode, Noah	94	285					
Goodlett, Vince	201	285					
Goodrich, ---	5	285					
Goodwin, Fred	129	285					
Goodwin, Gervin	77	285					
Goodwin, Gil	62	285					
Goodwin, Hoyt	130	285					
Goodwin, Troy	112	285					
Goody, Sam	140	143	176	178	285		
Goosetree, Ed	24	25	285				
Gordey, Alex	146	285					
Gordon, ---	13	286					
Gordon, Bob	147	286					
Gordon, Early	182	286					
Gordon, Jerry	155	286					
Gordon, Melvin	64	65	66	286			
Gore, Jack	145	286					
Gormish, Mike	95	286					
Gorton, Ron	185	187	286				
Gottesman, Bert	96	286					
Gottlieb, Martin	125						
Gould, ---	27	286					
Gould, Pete	106	108	286				
Gounaris, Alex	101	103	286				
Gowan, Reid	86	286					
Grabert, Herman	149	152	286				
Grace, John	194						
Graddick, John	94	286					
Grady, Bruce	194	286					
Graf, Phil	193	286					
Graffeo, John	76	286					
Graham, Alvin	47						
Graham, Bernard	161	286					
Graham, Bill	190	286					
Graham, Homer	185	286					
Graham, Joe	181	286					
Graham, Lonnie	180	286					
Graham, Tom	67	69	137	286			
Graham, Wayne	189	191	286	436			
Grammer, Jack	176	286					
Granger, George	38	39	205	286			
Granger, Gerald	125	286					
Grant, Charlie	63	67	286				
Grant, Cy	40	286					
Grant, Gabby	130	156	286				
Grant, Melvin	181	286					
Grasso, Joe	111	114	209	210	286		
Graves, ---	12	287					
Graves, Millard	55	287					
Gravino, Frank	67	69	287				
Gravino, Joe	151	287					
Gray, ---	6	31	32	33	35	38	287
Gray, Dick	134	135	136	287	436		
Gray, Milt	41	42	287	436			
Gray, Ron	161	164	180	287			
Grayston, Eddie	40	42	44	45	46	47	48	49
	287						
Greco, Al	111	287					
Greek, Bill	43	287					
Green, ---	29	64	71	73	287		
Green, Billy	165	168	169	171	174	175	210	287
Green, Bob	77	184	287				
Green, Claude	133	287					
Green, Curtis	180	188					
Green, Curtis E.	150	161					
Green, Fred	140	141	143	144	208	287	436
Green, H.T.	90	102	116				
Green, Harold	167	168	177	209	287		
Green, Jim	162	172	201	202	203	287	
Green, Lee	197	287					
Green, Paul	102	287					

Georgia Class-D Minor League Baseball Encyclopedia

Name									Name							
Green, Ray	38	142	171	287					Gulledge, W.F.	72	82					
Greenamoyer, Bill	108	287							Gulliver, Clark	71	289					
Greenan, Bill	162	287							Gulvas, Joe	151	289					
Greene, ---	35	287							Gums, Marv	186	289					
Greene, Joe	162	164	208	287					Gunn, Dick	179	188	289				
Greene, Ray	31	32	287						Gunnells, Luther	71	73	74	82	83	89	91	92
Greener, Andrew	134	288								93	128	204	205	290		
Greer, Elwyn	58	288							Gunning, Ed	171	184	186	187	290		
Greer, F.L.	98								Gunter, Carl	173	290					
Gregg, Fred	85	87	88	94	96	288			Gunter, Ray	157	290					
Gregg, Jim	111	288							Gupton, Harry	145	290					
Gregory, Bob	91	288							Gurdy, ---	71	290					
Gremp, Buddy	43	47	288	437					Gurri, Anibal	142	147	157	290			
Grice, John	86	87	288						Gusak, Tony	54	58	290				
Grieger, Russ	48	51	288						Gussin, Joe	189	290					
Grier, Harold	198	199	288						Gustavson, Carl	91	290					
Griffin, ---	9	10	13	288					Guth, Gene	67	69	290				
Griffin, Alva	150	288							Guthrie, ---	19	20	290				
Griffin, Ed	81	90	288	448					Guthrie, Bill	197	200	202	290			
Griffin, H.	5	288							Guymon, Darrell	192	290					
Griffin, Hal	6	7	8	20	21	22	24	25	Guyton, ---	71	290					
	288								Guza, Mike	171	290					
Griffin, Ivy	44	47	49	288	437				Haber, Nate	111	126	129	166	290		
Griffin, T.	5	288							Hadden, A. Oswald	155	165	175	184	193		
Griffin, Wes	181	288							Haddican, Harold	77	78	79	290			
Griffin, William	98								Haden, Stan	51	290					
Griffith, Dick	142	288							Hader, George	43	290					
Griffith, Johnny	145								Hadley, Harry	58	290					
Griffith, Ralph	34	35	36	37	288				Haefner, Mickey	51	52	53	290	437		
Griffith, W.D.	44	63	76						Hafey, Will	60	290					
Griffy, Jim	129	172	288						Hafner, Ron	193	290					
Grigg, Bill	111	288							Hagan, ---	146	290					
Griggs, Bill	71	104	125	127	137	288			Hagar, Carl	166	290					
Grilliot, Bill	129	288							Hageman, John	185	290					
Grimes, ---	31	32	288						Hagen, Dick	194	197	199	290			
Grimes, Dave	72	288							Hager, Fred	29	290					
Grimes, Glenn	44	288							Hagle, Don	94	290					
Grimes, Jim	197								Hahn, ---	38	290					
Grimes, Marion	56	288							Hahn, Earl	47	290					
Grimes, Mike	64								Hahn, Lou	141	291					
Grimsley, Weldon	141	288							Haines, William S. Jr.	144						
Grinnells, Harold	129	288							Hair, Bill	67	69	291				
Grish, Steve	67	69	289						Halden, Joe	54	291					
Grissom, Herb	182	289							Hale, Don	90	291					
Grizzell, Bob	129	289							Hall, ---	5	6	8	13	24	28	43	209
Groat, Clarence	68	69	289							291						
Grobar, Jim	161	289							Hall, Alex	44	47	51				
Grogel, Don	120	289							Hall, Bob	81	90	134	142	291		
Gronsky, Steve	141	143	289						Hall, Carl	73	291					
Groome, J.L.	19	20	289						Hall, Floyd	73	291					
Gross, ---	13	28	289						Hall, G.H.	16	18	291				
Gross, Don	85	96	97	108	289				Hall, H.V.	126	134					
Gross, J.F.	30	289							Hall, Jack	141	291					
Gross, Jerrold	141	289							Hall, Jesse	76	91	291				
Gross, Lloyd	54	56	57	207	208	289			Hall, Morris	161	171	291				
Gross, Stephan G.	132								Hall, R.B.	112	126					
Grote, Harold	108	110	289						Hall, R.H.	134						
Grover, Oscar	6								Hallford, Lew	126	127	128	138	139	209	291
Groves, ---	73	289							Hallman, George	145	291					
Gruber, Bob	95	289							Halperin, Philip	150	161					
Grupposo, Vince	78	289							Halsall, Walt	111	291					
Grzenda, Joe	182	183	289	437					Halter, Dick	162	291					
Guenst, Charles	155	176	289						Halverson, Don	180	291					
Guerriero, ---	67	289							Ham, ---	5	291					
Guess, ---	16	17	18	289					Hamende, Joe	200	203	291				
Guettler, Ken	81	83	84	204	289				Hamey, H. Roy	86	95	107	121			
Guido, Ed	90	289							Hamilton, ---	5	291					
Guinn, Jim	44	45	47	50	52	289			Hamilton, Bill	137	291					
Guinty, Charles	94	289							Hamilton, E.D.	162						
Guise, Lefty	137	139	210	289	437				Hamilton, George	117	291					
Guitterez, W.	9	11	22	289					Hamilton, Leon	58	189	291				
Gula, Pete	99	100	112	113	114	289			Hamlin, Bill	133	291					

467

Georgia Class-D Minor League Baseball Encyclopedia

Name									Name							
Hamlin, Nat	138	146	155	166	291				Harrell, Ray	125	128	293	437			
Hamm, Francis	76	291							Harrelson, Cleveland	115	293					
Hammack, Shurley	81	103	291						Harrelson, John	81	293					
Hammel, Wayne	98	291							Harrigan, W.L.	5	293					
Hammen, Floyd	151	160	163	292					Harrington, Fred	189	190	294				
Hammett, Miles	90	292							Harrington, Hayes	40	41	294				
Hammock, Bill	73	292							Harrington, Lou	166	294					
Hammon, Silas	163	292							Harrington, Walter	54	294					
Hammond, J.H.	38	39	204	292					Harris, ---	72	294					
Hammond, Murray S.	129								Harris, Bill	98	125	134	135	136	138	294	437
Hammons, Herb	91	292							Harris, Bob	117	180	294				
Hamner, R.L.	31	292							Harris, C.	34	38	294				
Hamons, Bull	147	150	157	292					Harris, C.E.	44						
Hampshire, Larry	151	152	153	292					Harris, C.W.	4						
Hamric, Bert	121	122	207	292	437				Harris, Darrell	166	294					
Hamrick, Charles	81	292							Harris, Dick	200	201	294				
Hamrick, Connie	198	292							Harris, Jack	35	294					
Hamrick, Ray	62	65	100	207	292	437			Harris, Joe	31	34	294				
Hamrick, Roy	81	113	292						Harris, Mercer	85	294					
Hancock, Leroy	177	292							Harris, Oliver	155	294					
Hand, Dave	193	292							Harris, Raymond	150	161	188				
Hand, Dewey	37	41	292						Harris, Reese	59	294					
Handel, Henry	107	121	292						Harrison, ---	34	294					
Haney, Clay	157	292							Harrison, Bill	104	294					
Haney, Joe	162	292							Harrison, Charles	129	131	205	294			
Haniak, Frank	192	292							Harrison, Dennie	55	56	60	294			
Hanke, Gus C.	62								Harrison, L.H.	151	294					
Hanley, Joseph T.	140	149							Harrison, Michael R.	161						
Hanna, ---	22	292							Harrison, Randy	160	294					
Hanna, John	67	292							Harrison, Robert L.	112	126	138				
Hanna, Perry	157	292							Harrod, Jerrel	142	294					
Hanna, Vic	160	170	172	174	292				Harrow, Herb	156	294					
Hannegan, Robert E.	94								Hart, ---	5	294					
Hannon, Chick	9	292							Hart, Clarence	38	294					
Hansen, Henry	64	292							Hart, Dick	197	198	294				
Hanson, C.W.	30	292							Hart, Gary	201	294					
Hanson, Harry	9	22	24	292	437				Hart, Norm	102	294					
Hanson, J.W.	115	117	292						Hartbarger, Jim	170	294					
Harbison, Douglas	22	292							Harter, E.J.	99						
Hardage, ---	9	292							Hartlein, Bill	82	294					
Hardegree, Bill	75	96	99	102	111	112	293		Hartley, Don	99	112	166	294			
Harden, Jim	98	99	100	101	111	114	125	127	Hartley, G.B.	186						
	137	139	209	293					Hartley, Jim	138	139	295				
Hardin, Henry	58	293							Hartley, Lee	294						
Hardin, Hugh	201	203	293						Hartley, Travis	51	52	55	57	60	61	295
Hardish, Dick	141	293							Hartman, Dick	102	115	295				
Hardison, Jim	176	178	293						Hartman, Earl	75	79	81	83	99	100	113	209
Hardwick, George	34	37	293							295						
Hardwick, Jim	186	293							Hartman, Elmer	171	295					
Hare, Bernard	108	293							Hartman, John	198	201	295				
Hargis, ---	38	293							Hartner, ---	6	8	14	295			
Hargis, Jim	102	103	293						Hartness, Edd	50	52	54	56	57	111	113	114
Hargrett, R.L.	162									124	125	126	127	128	151	152	162
Hargrove, J.Z.	99	136								163	208	209	295	448		
Hargrove, Woody	44	47	49	51	52	64	293		Hartz, John	64	295					
Harjo, Fesser	63	293							Harvey, ---	16	295					
Harkness, Jean	48	293							Harvey, Gene	126	295					
Harms, Carl	67	293							Harvey, Joe	156	295					
Harms, Lionel	163	293							Harwood, ---	5	295					
Harms, Roger	186	293							Harwood, Don	87	96	295				
Harp, Jim	111	114	125	127	137	139	146	148	Haschak, Bill	76	295					
	155	158	159	209	210	293	448		Hash, Frank	186						
Harper, ---	5	293							Haslett, J.E.	50						
Harper, Bill	71	293							Hassler, Percy	86	95	97	207	295		
Harper, Cartha	180	293							Hasty, Bob	29	51	295	437			
Harper, Charles	120	293							Hatcher, Bill	176	295					
Harper, Dean	142	293							Hatcher, Jerry	121	295					
Harper, Luther	138	293							Hatcher, Louis	165	175	184				
Harper, O.L.	146								Hatcher, Marv	121	133	136	172	295		
Harrell, Ben	72	74	81	293					Hatfield, Jim	189	193	194	195	295		
Harrell, Joe	80								Hathaway, R.H.	29	295					
Harrell, Lanier	126								Hathcock, Marlin	73	74	91	204	295		

Georgia Class-D Minor League Baseball Encyclopedia

Name									Name							
Hatter, Curtis	50								Henderson, Bill	125	126	127	160	161	166	209	298
Haury, John	180	295							Henderson, Bob	95	97	298					
Hausfeld, Walt	98	295							Henderson, Chuck	68	69	297					
Haverly, Karl	170	179	295						Henderson, Dave	177	186	298					
Hawkins, ---	5	295							Henderson, Hap	27	298						
Hawkins, Cy	28	29	32	296					Hendricks, O.R.	176							
Hawkins, E.J.	29	295							Henegar, Russ	104	298						
Hawkins, G.B.	6	7	9	10	11	16	18	19	Henkel, Ernest	155	165	298					
	21	27	296						Henkel, Howard	86	95	96	97	206	298		
Hawkins, Jack	7	296							Henley, Gail	198	298	437					
Hawley, Rondell	106	296							Henley, Howard	106	298						
Hay, Bob	126	138	139	146	296				Henne, Bob	141	298						
Hay, Derl	94	296							Henrichs, Russ	194	298						
Hay, Howard	157	296							Henrichsen, Gerald	171	298						
Haydel, Hal	197	296	437						Henrickson, Ed	99	100	112	298				
Hayden, Jim	161	170	174	185	296				Henriquez, Julio	171	298						
Hayden, John	103	296							Henry, ---	5	9	298					
Hayes, Bruce	11	296							Henry, Wilbur	40	298						
Hayes, Ed	133	296							Hensley, Paul	161	298						
Hayes, Frank	72	296							Herald, Ray	133	298						
Hayes, Tom	161	172	296						Herbert, Bentley	142	298						
Haygood, Charles	198	199	296						Herbert, Don	108	298						
Haynes, Bill	67	296							Herbik, John	86	88	95	134	207	298		
Haynes, Hoover	104	296							Herbison, Jim	85	88	298					
Haynes, Willard	89	117	296						Herdt, Don	103	105	298					
Hays, Harold	133	149							Hering, Fred	107	121						
Hayward, Jim	150								Hernandez, John	64	298						
Hayworth, George	197	296							Hernandez, Sam	157	158	159	192	194	195	207	298
Head, Ralph	9	11	20	21	296	437			Herndon, Hardin	27	29	30	298				
Headen, Ray	55	296							Herndon, Roy	54	298						
Heagerty, L.E.	51	296							Herold, Joe	14	298						
Healy, Dick	194	296							Herrell, Don	68	298						
Healy, Francis	85	88	296						Herrera, Ray	155	159	298					
Hearn, Barnie	45	48	296						Herrin, Cecil	172							
Hearn, Douglas	72								Herring, ---	7	298						
Hearn, George	145	296							Herring, Art	181	299						
Hearn, Joshua	142	151	296						Herring, Bill	73	299						
Heath, Harold	171	296							Herring, Bob	170	176	299					
Heath, Norm	116	297							Herring, Earl	115	122	299					
Heathcock, Ennis	141	297							Herringdine, Cecil	126	137	146	156	158	299		
Heaton, Ralph	147	148	155	157	297				Herrington, George	134	299						
Heavener, Reggie	189	297							Herron, James A.	140	149	160	170	180			
Heavner, Jim	126	297							Hersimaki, Fred	95	299						
Hebert, Walter	80	297							Hertweck, Neal	106	109	110	207	299	437		
Heck, ---	16	77	297						Herzog, Tom	190	299						
Heckman, Ernie	171	297							Hession, Bill	133	299						
Hedin, Al	163	172	297						Hessler, Bill	5	299						
Heffline, Bob	76	297							Hester, Jim	200	299						
Heffren, Ron	163	297							Heughens, Ron	145	157	299					
Heflin, Phil	133	134	135	297					Heving, Johnnie	72	73	107	299	437			
Heft, Arnold	51	297	448						Hewitt, Phil	193	299						
Hegedorn, Gary	107	297							Heyer, Dick	130	299						
Heidlebach, ---	34	35	297						Hickey, Jim	41	299	437					
Heidt, ---	6	297							Hickman, Jim	179	188	190	191	207	299	437	
Heins, Bob	132	140	297						Hicks, Dick	166	299						
Heinz, Charles	51	297							Hicks, Elroy	82	299						
Heinz, Martin	161	171	297						Hicks, Henry J.	151							
Heinze, Norm	197	297							Hicks, R.E.	29	299						
Heisig, Bill	90	92	205	297					Hicks, Robah	141	299						
Heisler, Allen	157	297							Hiedel, Dale	189	299						
Heisler, Phil	189	191	297						Higby, Lynn	185	299						
Heistand, Charles	141	297							Higgenbottom, Dizzy	161	299						
Hejnosz, John	171	297							Higginbotham, ---	37	39	204	299				
Helbig, Anthony	133	297							Higginbotham, Milt	162	172	299					
Heller, Harry	58	297							Higginbotham, Morris	73	299						
Heller, Ron	162	297							High, Andy	63	299	437					
Helmick, Julius	175	297							Hightower, Gene	121	299						
Helms, Larry	184	297							Hiland, Jimmie	166	168	169	210	299			
Helsel, John T.	180								Hill, ---	16	17	37	299	300			
Helvey, Bob	41	297							Hill, Bob	63	65	68	69	78	85	88	300
Hemings, Fay	146	297							Hill, Don	192	300						
Hemmerle, Dick	162	164	297						Hill, George	129	300						

Georgia Class-D Minor League Baseball Encyclopedia

Name								Name							
Hill, Jere	179	192	300					Holderfield, Harold	161	302					
Hill, Jim	71	74	81	84	90	300		Holiday, ---	7	302					
Hill, John	73	74	81	82	89	90	300	437	Holland, Fred	47	302					
Hill, Larry	176	300						Holland, Sid	11	20	302				
Hill, Marion	100	101	300					Hollenkamp, Dick	142	151	302				
Hill, Van	150	161	164	171	173	300		Holley, Jim	165	302					
Hilliard, E.E.	175	184						Holliday, ---	24	302					
Hilliard, Grady	122	123	300					Holliday, Hugh	86	87	302				
Hilliard, Mrs. Ruth	184							Hollingsworth, ---	24	25	302				
Hilyer, Ken	149	152	153	300				Hollingsworth, Charles	140	302					
Hines, ---	5	142	300					Hollis, Grady	157	302					
Hines, Jack	157	167	300					Holloman, Bobo	76	79	302	438			
Hinges, ---	24	300						Holloran, ---	34	38	39	302			
Hink, Bill	59	62	64	300				Holloway, A.T.	72						
Hinkle, George	197	300						Holloway, Jim	47	302					
Hinkle, Jack	94	106	300					Holly, Joe	166	302					
Hinkle, Leon	103	300						Holmes, Ducky	9	302					
Hinrichs, Donald	176	300						Holmes, Harry P.	84	93					
Hinrichs, Wayne	63	300						Holmes, Jeptha	146	302					
Hinson, Bill	167	168	169	300				Holmes, Jim	71	302					
Hinton, Dick	172	300						Holmquist, Doug	197	302					
Hinton, Terry	180	300						Holsomback, Squirt	32	34	37	302			
Hinton, Wilton	186							Holt, ---	16	19	303				
Hire, Ashford	171	300						Holt, Bill	126	303					
Hirst, Art	181	300						Holt, Doug	55	303					
Hisey, Ralph	59	61	111	114	210	300		Holt, Raymond	76						
Hitchcock, Jim	72	300	437					Holtz, Red	27	303					
Hite, Bob	166	300						Holyfield, Harold	197	200	303				
Hitson, John	72	74	300					Hominsky, Ivan	111	124	303				
Hitt, Jack	72	301						Hondzinski, Fred	150	303					
Hoag, Myril	117	118	301	437				Honkus, Stan	161	166	176	185	303		
Hoak, Don	86	87	301	437				Hood, Milt	111	112	166	303			
Hoard, ---	19	301						Hooks, Dave	116	303					
Hoard, Dan	125	137	138	139	146	147	208	301	Hopey, Anthony	189	303					
Hobbs, ---	116	301						Hopke, Fred	181	182	183	303			
Hobbs, Tigner	126	301						Hopkins, Bill	125	127	209	303			
Hocevar, Joe	59	301						Hopkins, Bob	152	303					
Hoch, ---	9	301						Hopkins, Joe	173	303					
Hock, Bob	165	301						Hopper, ---	9	303					
Hockette, Lefty	31	33	34	37	39	205	301	437	Horine, Lawrence	150	303					
Hoderlein, Mel	67	69	301	437				Horn, Vern	54	56	57	303			
Hodge, ---	12	13	16	18	22	301		Horne, Armine	155	303					
Hodge, Clarence	75	301						Horne, Tom	151	160	303				
Hodge, Shovel	16	301	438					Hornsberg, Art	73	303					
Hodges, Jim	177	301						Hornsby, Jay	184	303					
Hodgin, W.H.	30	301						Hornsby, Leonard	73	303					
Hodkey, Eli	51	301	438					Horowitz, Ed	181	303					
Hodnett, Ralph	117							Horton, Marv	56	60	61	64	303		
Hodo, D.W.	89	102						Horton, Ralph	167	303					
Hoellman, ---	38	301						Horton, Roger	96	99	303				
Hoenes, Ron	176	180	301					Hoskiewicz, ---	44	303					
Hofferth, Stew	44	58	64	65	66	68	69	301 438	Hoskins, Gerald	162	303					
								Hotard, Leo	162	303					
Hoffman, Bob	75	79	134	135	136	173	301	302	Hottell, Ed	181	303					
Hoffman, Charles	170	301						Houck, Fred	59	303					
Hoffman, Eddie	54	56	58	61	62	64	207	301	Hovell, Bob	102	115	118	304			
Hoffman, Fred	182	188	190	301				Howard, Alton	147	155	157	304			
Hoffman, Karl	51	301						Howard, Bobby	125	127	209	304			
Hoffman, Myron	108	121	301					Howard, Crawford	76	85	87	88	94	96	304
Hoffman, Tex	41	44	48	301	438			Howard, Larry	201	304	438				
Hofheinz, Roy	201							Howard, Tom	162	171	304				
Hoflac, Joe	71	302						Howe, Bob	130	131					
Hoflack, Dan	76	81	302					Howe, F.E.	134	304					
Hogarth, Art	141	143	302					Howe, Theodore Max	154						
Holbrook, Jim	197	199	302					Howell, Bryan	68	69	142	304			
Holbrook, Sammy	35	302	438					Howell, C.L.	102						
Holcomb, E.	38	302						Howell, Dixie	51	67	304	438			
Holcomb, Hot	37	302						Howell, F.M.	155						
Holcomb, Lou	189	191	193	302				Howell, Francis	155	304					
Holden, Joe	54	59	76	302	438			Howell, Jim	85	111	304				
Holdener, Lou	186	302						Howell, L.C.	89						
Holder, Charles	86	88	302					Howell, Lloyd	9	10	11	12	19	31	32	304

470

Georgia Class-D Minor League Baseball Encyclopedia

Name							
Howell, Pete	107	304					
Howell, Red	31	32	204	304	438		
Howerton, Carlson	192	193	304				
Howig, Donald	77	304					
Howser, Tom	180	304					
Howton, Frank	103	105	304				
Howton, George	44	304					
Hoyal, Craig	156	163	166	176	304		
Hoyle, Alex	120	123	304				
Hoyle, W.E. Jr.	99						
Hoyle, W.E. Sr.	99	112					
Hubbard, Carl	71	304					
Hubbard, Charles	107	304					
Hubbard, Herman	62	304					
Huber, Ray	55	304					
Hubert, Stan	185	304					
Hudson, ---	5	304					
Hudson, Bill	55	91	102	103	104	105	116	125
	204	305					
Hudson, Frank	47	304					
Hudson, Phil	82	103	117	129			
Huelfer, Dennis	141	150	305				
Huesman, Jack	80	89	92	101	102	104	105	205
	305						
Huey, O.D.	44	305					
Huffaker, Dorcie E.	180						
Huffaker, Wayne	47	49	305				
Huffman, Bill	185	186	187	305			
Huffman, Bob	80	305					
Huggins, Miller	31	34	305				
Hughes, ---	27	305					
Hughes, Charles	198	201	305				
Hughes, George	117	119	130	131	204	305	
Hughes, Harry	60	61	207	305			
Hughes, Jim	129	131	142	147	151	171	305
Hughes, Norm	151	155	167	193	305		
Hughson, Tex	47	49	305	438			
Huinker, Art	188	305					
Huisking, Charles	41	305					
Hulet, Fred	121	305					
Hull, Tommy	176	178	305				
Hulme, George	80						
Hulsey, DeLane	176	305					
Hultzapple, Ken	197	305					
Humberson, Roxie	71	305					
Humbert, Jimmy	171	305					
Humbracht, Hal	72	305					
Humphress, John Y.	77						
Humphries, ---	6	30	305				
Humphries, Johnny	98	305	438				
Humphries, Roy	37	40	306				
Hungate, Lew	185	187	306				
Hunnicutt, ---	35	306					
Hunnicutt, Oliver	71	81	90	103	116	129	
Hunnicutt, Warner	155	306					
Hunt, Adrian	185	306					
Hunt, Bob	181	182	306				
Hunt, Ray	72	306					
Hunter, ---	31	306					
Hunter, Bob	29	30	306				
Hunter, H.C.	27	306					
Hunter, Mike	200	202	306				
Hurd, Tom	76	79	207	306	438		
Hurley, ---	7	14	71	306			
Hurley, Don	179	185	306				
Hurst, ---	37	306					
Hurst, John	121	306					
Hurst, Leon	170	306					
Hurvitz, Bob	181	306					
Hushebeck, John	120	123	207	306			
Husich, John	150	161	169	171	174	306	
Hutcherson, Billy	63	67	306				
Hutchins, ---	11	20	306				
Hutchins, Barry	154	177	178	306			
Hutchins, Bob	102	116	117	118	130	306	
Hutchinson, Gordon	193	306					
Hutchinson, Jim	98	306					
Hutchison, ---	16	306					
Huthmaker, Fred	146	155	158	159	306		
Hutson, Cecil	156	158	306				
Hyatt, Marion	129						
Hydringer, ---	31	33	306				
Icenhour, Luther	166	177	307				
Icenhour, Phil	86	307					
Ingalls, Jack	96	97	108	307			
Ingram, Clarence	140	188	191	307			
Ingram, Ed	103						
Ingram, Jimmy	27	307					
Ingram, Pete	201	307					
Ippolito, Rocco	95	96	97	206	307		
Irby, Leroy	177	307					
Irons, Ed	117	118	307				
Irvin, Jim	91	307					
Isaacs, Cecil	180	307					
Isaacson, Herb	162	307					
Isbell, Maurice	44	46	307				
Isert, Fred	48	49	307				
Isert, Lou	58	59	307				
Israel, Bill	71	307					
Itkin, Al	126	127	133	307			
Ivester, Neal	112	307					
Ivey, Bill	149	307					
Ivey, Bob	51	111	307				
Ivey, Doug	47	59	307				
Ivy, Harold	121	122	207	307			
Izzo, John	77	307					
Jack, Dick	150	307					
Jackimchuk, Nick	62	307					
Jackson, Bill	170	171	173	181	183	308	
Jackson, Charles	11	20	307				
Jackson, Claude	72	91	92	103	105	117	118	129
	205	307					
Jackson, Earl	68	308					
Jackson, Frank	102	307					
Jackson, Gene	60	307					
Jackson, Harold	156	307					
Jackson, John	165	175	307				
Jackson, Lendon	189	308					
Jacob, Vince	133	308					
Jacobs, George	59	308					
Jacobs, Ottis	104	134	135	136	308		
Jacobs, Will	133	308					
Jacobsen, Ed	133	308					
Jacobus, Steve	197	198	199	200	308		
Jacoby, Brooks	193	308					
Jacquin, Don	181	308					
Jacquot, Jim	85	308					
Jaeckel, Roy	54	58	59	63	67	308	
Jakosh, Lou	185	308					
Jakowczyk, Wally	120	308					
Jakubov, John	111	308					
Jakubowski, Al	180	308					
James, Fob	31	32	34	73	82	91	104	117
	130	308					
James, R.E.	30	308					
Jameson, Don	67	308					
Jamison, Tom	138	308					
Janci, Fred	59	308					
Janelle, Ray	132	308					
Janeway, Gary	185	308					
Jarman, C.F.	44						
Jarvinen, Vern	176	308					
Jarvis, Bob	91	103	116	117	308		
Javier, Julian	180	308	438				

Georgia Class-D Minor League Baseball Encyclopedia

Name							
Jay, Paul	108	109	110	308			
Jay, W.T.	40	43	59				
Jeakle, Ed	116	308					
Jeanes, John	189	308					
Jeffcoat, William	77	308					
Jefferson, Ernest	62	65	308				
Jefts, Virgil	90	102	138	309			
Jemison, Richard	15	21	23				
Jenkins, Alvin	136	138	139	208	309		
Jenkins, Bob	121	309					
Jenkins, Ernest L.	130						
Jenkins, Gary	197	309					
Jenkins, Lee	96	108	109	207	309		
Jenkins, Reynolds	194	309					
Jenkins, Tom	22	24	25	309	438		
Jensen, Dick	201	309					
Jernigan, R.W. Jr.	180	188					
Jesmer, W.H.	28	29	309				
Jessee, Frank	185	309					
Jeter, Cleo	71	72	82	309			
Jezek, Ed	151	153	171	309			
Jezek, Nick	185	309					
Jimenez, Felipe	147	309					
Jiminez, Dan	134	138	157	166	167	309	
Jiminez, Dario	124	127	128	209	210	309	
Jinske, Wayne	201	202	309				
Jobe, Lew	76	79	85	309			
Joergen, Jim	141	309					
Johannsen, ---	21	27	309				
Johengen, George	116	118	119	309			
Johns, Jim	129	309					
Johnsen, Tor	41	309					
Johnson, ---	27	68	309				
Johnson, Albert	117						
Johnson, Bill	145	311					
Johnson, Bob	64	172	310	438			
Johnson, Charles	108	109	309				
Johnson, Clyde	154	309					
Johnson, Don	197	200	309				
Johnson, Doug	77	78	79	207	309		
Johnson, Earl	27	155	160	163	309		
Johnson, Eli	63	310					
Johnson, Elijah	197	199	310				
Johnson, Emmitt	63	310					
Johnson, Eric	181	310					
Johnson, Erin O.	122						
Johnson, Erin W.	134	142	194	196	200		
Johnson, Ernest	170	176	310				
Johnson, Frank	111	124	137	144	145		
Johnson, George	78	89	104	310			
Johnson, Harold	100	101	310				
Johnson, Harry	142	143	144	151	153	167	310
Johnson, Howie	108	310					
Johnson, Ivy	151	182	310				
Johnson, Jerry	193	310					
Johnson, Jim	51	141	182	185	310		
Johnson, Joe	71	73	310				
Johnson, John	70	72	74	310			
Johnson, Larry	177	310					
Johnson, Lee	43	45	47	48	49	134	137	172
	310						
Johnson, Lorne	194	310					
Johnson, Marion	51	54	67	310			
Johnson, Marshall	193	310					
Johnson, Myra	166	310					
Johnson, Norm	58	310					
Johnson, Oscar	107	109	310				
Johnson, Owen	201	310					
Johnson, Red	62	65	67	69	311		
Johnson, Roy	129	310					
Johnson, Rudolph	125	137	138	310			
Johnson, Sid	156	166	311				
Johnson, Thomas P. Jr.	75						
Johnson, Tom	162	311					
Johnson, Walt	192	311					
Johnson, Wilbur	162	311					
Johnston, Bob	122	151	193	311			
Johnston, Jerry	184	187	311				
Johnston, Jim	125	137	139	145	311		
Johnston, Wiley	51						
Jones, ---	7	14	108	311			
Jones, Barry	82	311					
Jones, Bill	72	73	74	81	84	134	142	143
	205	312					
Jones, Billy Joe	150	311					
Jones, Casey	102	116	137	139	312		
Jones, Charles	75	189	311				
Jones, D.	27	311					
Jones, Dick	96	108	109	110	312		
Jones, E.L.	137	145	155				
Jones, Ellis	182	311					
Jones, Fred	171	311					
Jones, H. Phil	76	85	94	106	120		
Jones, Harry	156	311					
Jones, Harvey	166						
Jones, Isom	24	311					
Jones, Jack	157	162	311				
Jones, Jerry	145	148	152	172	209	311	
Jones, Jim	72	311					
Jones, Lawrence	121	311					
Jones, Lew	163	311					
Jones, Lou	116	117	311				
Jones, Mike	197	200	311				
Jones, Murray	72	311					
Jones, R.E.	22	312					
Jones, Ray	145	147	312				
Jones, Ron	162	312					
Jones, Roscoe	47	312					
Jones, Roser	81	312					
Jones, Rudy	87	311					
Jones, Stan	125	312					
Jones, Tom	82	117	312				
Jones, Vern	85	312					
Jones, Ward	72	312					
Jonietz, Ben	193	312					
Jonnard, Bubber	24	312	438				
Jonnard, Claude	24	312	438				
Joratz, Bob	47	48	50	51	53	312	
Jorda, ---	9	312					
Jordan, ---	16	312					
Jordan, Albert	176	312					
Jordan, Dutch	7	8	13	17	18	312	438
Jordan, Joe	176	177	312				
Jordan, Kirby	59	312					
Jordan, Louis	11	312					
Jordan, N.M.	166	176	185				
Jordan, N.M. Jr.	166						
Jordan, Nance	48	312					
Jordan, Ray	180	312					
Jorgenson, Merlin	141	312					
Joseph, Bill	193	312					
Josephs, Al	150	312					
Joyce, Arnold	90	117	312				
Joyner, ---	34	313					
Joyner, Julian	104	120	123	140	143	144	149	153
	160	170	313				
Judy, George	86	88	95	313			
Julian, Al	103	104	117	129	205	313	
Julian, Bob	103	104	117	118	129	131	313
Julian, Charles	193	196	313				
Jumonville, George	44	47	49	51	55	56	313	438
Jungman, Lawrence	177	313					
Jurkovic, Bill	51	313					
Jusino, Ramon	200	313					

Georgia Class-D Minor League Baseball Encyclopedia

Name	Pages
Justiss, Red	34 35 36 37 313
Justus, Dave	182 190 191 313
Kabat, John	197 313
Kabbes, Ron	188 313
Kahle, Huber	194 313
Kahn, Lou	47 313
Kalena, ---	16 313
Kallaher, Bill	80 82 83 89 91 92 93 205 206 313
Kallas, Harry	133 160 172 173 313
Kalmes, Bill	193 195 313
Kalmon, I.J.	13
Kamenski, Bernard	155 158 313
Kanavage, Chet	98 112 113 138 208 313 448
Kane, ---	28 30 313
Kane, Henry	90 91 92 93 313
Kane, Ken	197 313
Kane, Murray	77 87 313
Karczewski, Gerald	170 173 313
Kardos, Jim	172 314
Karpel, Herb	51 314 438
Karpinec, Everett	99 100 314
Karpoe, John	54 314
Kash, Les	99 101 314
Katalinic, John	103 314
Kates, ---	7 314
Katkaveck, Mickey	75 85 96 97 108 314
Kaye, Charles	107 314
Kazak, Eddie	60 61 62 64 65 66 206 314 438
Keane, Johnny	50 52 54 314 447
Kearns, John	40 42 314
Kebler, Steve	186 194 314 448
Keen, Elmer	134 314
Keen, L.P.	193
Keggereis, Bill	149 153 160 166 314
Keister, Harry	160 314
Kelecava, Clem	116 129 131 205 314
Keleher, Oscar	156 314
Kell, Skeeter	107 120 122 123 314 438
Keller, Bob	47 48 314
Keller, Charles	166 314
Keller, Earl R.	80
Keller, Ed	151 156 314
Keller, George	89 91 314
Keller, Gerald	170 179 314
Keller, Harold	186 314
Keller, Ken	121 314
Kelley, ---	14 24 314
Kelley, Bill	200 314
Kelley, Jim	184 314
Kelly, Art	85 87 314
Kelly, Dick	81 83 205 315
Kelly, Fred	180 315
Kelly, George	34 35 37 38 39 154 204 314
Kelly, Harold	34 36 37 315
Kelly, Howard	54 315
Kelly, Jack	64 65 68 69 315
Kelly, Jesse	121 315
Kelly, Joe	47 315
Kelly, Ken	150 315
Kelly, Mason	116 315
Kelly, O.F.	82 91
Kelly, Oliver	64 65 315
Kelsch, Rudy	190 315
Kelton, Wiley	27 29 31 315
Kemmerer, Nathaniel	102 105 116 117 315
Kemp, Roy	150 153 154 315
Kendall, George	134 135 136 315
Kendall, Ralph	50
Kendig, Lawrence	166 170 179 183 315
Kenmore, ---	72 315
Kennedy, ---	24 315
Kennedy, Joe	113 315
Kennedy, L.L.	172
Kennedy, Ray	86 95
Kennedy, Ray L.	108 121
Kennedy, Webb	82
Kenny, Ken	44 315
Kenny, Sherman	156 315
Kenseith, Keith	176 315
Kent, B.B.	40 43
Kent, Otis	72 73 315
Keough, John	64 315
Kerby, Cliff	129
Kerce, Bob	94 315
Kern, Dan	197 198 315
Kernica, Leo	180 315
Kerr, Bill	126 315
Kerr, Jim	51 52 315
Kerr, Tom	76 85 315
Kerrigan, Robert J.	144
Kettle, Jerry	181 315
Keuch, Warren	171 177 315
Key, H.L.	59
Keyes, Warren S.	134
Kidd, Don	166 316
Kienle, Fred	58 316
Kiesman, Bob	193 316
Kiker, B.	5 316
Kildoo, Don	150 153 316
Kilgore, Bill	71 91 92 103 105 205 316
Killian, C.L.	58 316
Killingsworth, ---	11 316
Kimball, ---	11 316
Kimber, Ray	121 316
Kimbrell, Casey	51 55 56 57 59 60 206 316
Kimbrell, Wilbur	67 316
Kimbrough, Charles	194 195 316
Kinard, Buster	86 316
Kinard, Jim	141 316
Kindl, Bill	177 316
King, ---	9 10 11 19 20 34 316
King, B.W. Jr.	154
King, Bill	166 316
King, Claude	81 316
King, Herman	185 316
King, Jack	189
King, Ken	157 316
King, Rowland	186 316
Kingery, ---	17 316
Kingery, Herbert E.	146
Kingery, R. Herbert	156 167 176
Kingsmore, Doug	171 316
Kinnamon, Bill	107 316
Kinnamon, George	140 141 165 166 167 175 176 316
Kinnas, Christ	76 138 316
Kinney, Bill	77 316
Kinsel, Bill	40 316
Kipp, ---	5 14 316
Kirby, Bob	156 316
Kirby, Howard	48 317
Kirby, Jim	67 150 317
Kirincic, Don	166 317
Kirk, Walt	96 108 317
Kirke, M.M.	19 20 21 22 317
Kirkland, Bill	81 317
Kirkland, Dan	68 317
Kirksey, Bill	68 317
Kirksey, Calvin	59 63 65 68 69 70 71 73 207 208 317
Kirksey, George	201
Kirkwood, David C.	75
Kirschner, George	71 317

Name								Name						
Kiser, Bob	185	317						Kosak, Carl	189	319				
Kiser, Ron	170	317						Kosar, Joe	48	319				
Kish, Alex	50	54	317					Koski, Bill	170	319	438			
Kishner, Joseph	182	317						Koski, Bob	166	180	319			
Kissell, George	200	317						Kosmicki, Michael	185					
Kite, Bert	6	13	317					Koss, Ed	125	319				
Kittrell, Ed	102	103	317					Kossuth, Otto	121	319	448			
Kitts, Claude	29	317						Kostner, Dick	145	152	154	158	319	
Kivett, Bill	76	317	448					Koszenski, Stan	162	319				
Klaus, Dick	141	143	317					Kott, Charles	141	143	207	319		
Kleine, George	62	65	317					Koury, Gabriel	98					
Klemme, Stan	141	317						Kovach, Paul	171	319				
Kliewer, Phil	190	191	317					Kovacic, Frank	185	319				
Klimash, Walt	108	317						Kovak, Walter	110					
Klimkowski, Frank	193	317						Koval, George	59	319				
Klingert, John	134	317						Koval, William	110					
Klobe, Ray	106	109	317					Kovaleski, John	141	156	319			
Kloss, Walt	133	146	155	158	317			Kovaluk, Ted	112	319				
Klump, ---	14	317						Kowalczyk, Dick	186	319				
Knabe, Dick	95	108	317					Kowalski, Ed	163	320				
Knapp, Roy	67	69	317					Kozimer, Harry	107	320				
Knappe, John	77	318						Kozubal, Alex	116	320				
Knezevich, Ed	185	318						Kracher, Joe	45	48	51	52	53	320	438
Knight, ---	11	20	318					Kramer, Bob	90	320				
Knight, Harold	129	318						Krane, Henry	115					
Knighton, N.E.	99							Kranitzky, Chuck	94	320				
Knoblauch, Ray	94	318						Krankie, ---	29	320				
Knodel, Len	150	154	318					Krapp, Gene	22	320	438			
Knoke, John	90	318						Kratzer, Duane	43	45	47	320		
Knoll, Dave	194	318						Kraus, Jim	95	320				
Knoll, Frank	67	318						Krause, Bill	180	320				
Knopp, Mel	90	318						Krauss, Bernard	111	114	320			
Knowles, Charles	31	32	34	35	37	204	318	Krausse, Lew	85	320	438			
Knowles, Earl	73	82	318					Kray, Vic	177	320				
Knowles, Lowe	117	118	318					Kreamcheck, Ed	72	320				
Knox, ---	12	22	318					Krebs, ---	16	320				
Knox, Al	176	318						Kreider, Jesse	87	320				
Knox, Bill	160	164	208	318				Kreitner, Mickey	62	320	438			
Knox, Fred	41	318						Kremer, George	85	320				
Knutson, Dick	180	318						Kreshka, Mike	126	320				
Knutson, Larry	193	318						Kress, Charlie	63	65	320	439		
Knutson, Ron	107	318						Kret, Anthony	120	320				
Koart, Bill	107	318						Kriczky, Mike	150	320				
Koby, Dick	107	318						Krings, Dave	103	116	118	119	320	
Kocak, George	176	318						Krinsky, Robert	68	320				
Koch, Art	64	68	77	87	88	318		Kritsky, Walt	72	320				
Kochis, George	185	318						Krochina, John	103	104	204	320		
Koczwara, Bob	151	153	181	207	318			Krohn, Duane	82	320				
Koellmer, Bill	94	98	111	112	125	318		Krohn, Layton	115	118	119	129	320	
Koenig, Herman	20	22	318					Kroll, Jim	60	62	320			
Koenig, Leon	87	318						Kroll, Wayne	197	199	320			
Koenigsmark, Ted	149	151	318					Kromy, Darwin	171	172	174	320		
Koerner, Ted	201	203	318					Kruppa, Paul	157	320				
Kokinchak, William	80							Kubrick, Ed	144	145				
Kolar, John	185	189	191	319				Kucharski, Jerome	181	183	320			
Kolaska, George	176	319						Kucinski, Mickey	54	321				
Koleff, Nick	162	319						Kuczynski, Ed	190	321				
Kollin, Major	177	319						Kuhlman, William	6	8	13	14	321	
Kolson, Tom	179	188	319					Kuhn, George	111	321				
Koltz, Ted	67	319						Kuk, John	198	321				
Komara, Ray	185	319						Kulesa, John	116	321				
Komisarek, Ed	95	319						Kulig, Al	90	93	321			
Konek, Pete	103	141	319					Kummer, Gerald	193	321				
Konneman, W.H.	27	29	319					Kunigonis, John	55	321				
Kopacz, Ed	157	319						Kuppin, ---	9	321				
Kopec, Don	171	319						Kuras, Walt	102	105	321			
Kopp, Clyde	62	319						Kurt, Lyndon	198	321				
Kopp, John	172	182	190					Kurth, Al	172	321				
Koppenhaver, Bob	106	110	319					Kushner, Joe	182	321				
Kops, Willard	112	319						Kushta, Bill	125	137	138	321		
Koranda, Jim	151	319						Kusmierski, Dick	160	321				
Korcheck, Mike	108	121	123	319				Kuwala, Ed	67	321				

Georgia Class-D Minor League Baseball Encyclopedia

Name						
Kuykendall, Bob	167	321				
Kuykendall, Jim	194	321				
Kwiatkowski, Joe	96	97	206	321		
Kyle, Leon	48	49	321			
LaBar, Luther	166	321				
LaCarter, Ray	113	321				
Lacey, ---	31	34	35	37	321	
Lackey, Bill	170	174	188	192	207	321
LaCount, Gerald W.	84					
Lacy, Guy	21	24	25	47	50	321	439
LaFaive, Dick	176	177	208	321		
LaFaive, Verne	41	321				
LaFitte, Ed	11	12	20	22	321	439
LaFrance, Bill	76	86	87	88	321	
Lagan, John	133	322				
Lageman, Ralph	120	122	123	322		
Lagorio, George	108	322				
Lail, Jack	171	322				
Laird, Red	31	322				
Lakatosh, Dean	166	168	209	210	322	
Lakatosh, Denton	166	322				
Lakeman, Charles	198	322				
Lamar, ---	9	10	11	12	205	322
Lamar, Nick	5	322				
Lamb, ---	73	322				
Lamb, A.F. Jr. "Yank"	142					
Lambert, ---	38	322				
Lamey, Walt	106	322				
Laminack, ---	31	32	35	322		
LaMothe, Dennis	185	322				
LaMotte, ---	5	322				
Lampley, Bill	62	322				
Lancaster, B.A.	33					
Land, Curtis	171	322				
Land, Dick	73	322				
Land, Doc	34	35	38	322	439	
Land, P.S.	91					
Lande, Gil	133	322				
Landers, Ken	156	322				
Landis, Dick	58	322				
Landis, Jack	160	322				
Landon, Gardner	141					
Lane, ---	5	322				
Lane, Clyde	157	158	167	322		
Lane, Dave	157	322				
Lane, Eli	77	322				
Lane, Lefty	30	32	33	35	38	322
Lane, Leon	58	59	322			
Laney, Floyd	102	322				
Laney, Lee	116	322				
Langdon, Joe	34	37	39	104	105	204	322
Lange, Ron	198	199	323			
Langella, Ben	146					
Langemeier, Paul	86	95	102	323		
Langer, Jack	171	323				
Langley, Buddy	150	152	323			
Langley, Jim	71	81	83	115	323	
Langlois, Paul	185	323				
Langston, Howard	162	323				
Langston, Jim	130	323				
Langston, Joe	59	63	65	323		
Lanier, Joe	41	42	323			
Lankford, Jerry	141	323				
Lanoux, Harold	184	186	187	209	323	
Lantrip, Bill	73	74	323			
LaPadula, Nick	130	323				
LaPiana, Peter	58	59	323			
Lapovicy, Frank	99	323				
Large, Don	193	323				
Large, George	134	323				
Larimer, Roger	63					
Larimer, Stan	180	323				

Name							
Larivee, Armand	77	323					
Larned, Harold	162	323					
Lary, Frank	121	323	439				
Lasry, Jack	133	323					
Lassetter, Don	140	323	439				
Lassetter, Roy	27	30	323				
Lassiter, Bob	90	323					
Lassiter, Thomas V.	133	141					
Lastinger, John W.	151						
Lastres, Danilo	134	323					
Latham, Don	179	185	323				
Lathrop, James R.	144						
Laton, Bob	201	202	203	323			
Latsko, George	68	69	323				
Latta, John	73	323					
Laubach, Carl	102	323					
Lauderdale, Tom	161	324					
Laudermilk, Joe	180	324	448				
Laumann, Andrew	76	86	87	88	95	207	324
Lauria, Cosmo	78	324					
Laurie, Lawrence	194	324					
Lavender, ---	5	324					
Lavin, Tom	171	177	324				
Law, Gordon	95	324					
Lawhon, Sid	54	324					
Lawlor, Bob	171	324					
Lawman, Gerald	162	324					
Lawrence, Ralph	181	324					
Lawrence, William	194	324					
Lawson, Elwood	56	57	60	61	207	324	
Lawson, Leroy	103	112	324				
Layne, Hillis	50	52	53	324	439		
Layton, Fred	146	155	156	324			
Lazar, Steve	67	324					
Lazarewicz, Bob	201	324					
Lazaro, Joe	112	324					
Lazicky, Dick	117	130	131	166	324		
Lazor, Johnny	47	48	49	324	439		
Lazzari, Jim	103	324					
Leach, Dick	162	324					
Leach, Russ	54	58	60	61	62	64	65	66
	206	324						
Leachman, Don	167	324					
Leake, Darrell	189	324					
Leaman, ---	19	324					
Leamon, Jim	44	324					
Leaphart, Dr. Alvin	156						
Leary, Bill	76	78	324				
Leatherberry, John	166	168	209	324			
Leatherwood, Gil	55	87	324				
Leber, Dick	189	325					
LeBlanc, Carlton	194	325					
LeBlanc, Rollie	62	65	66	325			
Lechtansky, Ed	141	325					
Ledbetter, Bob	37	39	325				
LeDuc, Carl	201	325					
Lee, Dick	149	325					
Lee, Frank	85	91	325				
Lee, Fred	116	137	325				
Lee, Gene	181	193	325				
Lee, George	56	60	325				
Lee, Hal	85	94	107	325			
Lee, Harold	51	52	325				
Lee, Harry Jr.	134						
Lee, Jim	75	325					
Lee, Joe	171	325					
Lee, Norm	157	325					
Lee, Rick	151	325					
Lee, Roy	51	52	325	439			
Lee, Tom	198	325					
Leeper, Mason	78	87	325				
Lefevre, Leroy	121	122	123	325			

Georgia Class-D Minor League Baseball Encyclopedia

Name							
Lefler, Henry	85	325					
Leftridge, Lee	120	325					
Legursky, Carl	173	325					
Lehman, Ken	87	88	325	439			
Lehman, Otto	29	325					
Lehmann, Chauncey	147	325					
Lehner, Collis	129	130	325				
Lehrman, Charles	121	123	325				
Leib, Marv	93	96	97	206	207	325	
Leili, Joe	76	325					
Leininger, ---	6	7	8	325			
Leistritz, Harold	43	325					
Leitz, Al	56	57	60	61	64	65	66	68
	73	326					
Lemish, Gaylord	75	76	79	86	208	326	
Lemons, Carol	151	326					
Lenn, Ed	67	69	326				
Lenn, Wayne	63	326					
Lenoir J.W.	47						
Lentz, Walt	86	326					
Leon, ---	13	14	20	326			
Leon, Sid	99	100	101	209	326	439	
Leonard, ---	13	22	326				
Leonard, Leon	166	326					
Leonard, Richard F.	124	136					
Leshock, Dave	193	326					
Leslie, Paul	125	188	190	191	326		
Lessley, John	34	37	38	326			
Letchas, Charlie	41	42	45	48	49	326	439
Letlow, Lou	117	326					
Leval, Al	180	326					
Leveille, Roland	77	326					
Levin, Ben	46						
Levison, ---	16	326					
Levy, Ed	177	326	439				
Levy, L.A.	167	177	186				
Lewallen, Keith	194	326					
Lewetag, Al	95	326					
Lewis, Bernard	32	35	37	38	39	204	326
Lewis, Bill	90	93	326				
Lewis, Bob	162						
Lewis, Don	125	126	127	128			
Lewis, Dudley D.	5	326					
Lewis, Jim	73	74	82	83	91	92	93	205
	326						
Lewis, Ralph	121	326					
Lewison, Bill	107	326					
L'Hommedieu, F.E.	16	326					
Licata, Vince	156	327					
Lichti, Russell	121	327					
Liddy, George	90	92	93	205	327		
Liddy, Jack	181	327					
Liedtke, Clyde	111	113	117	327			
Lightfoot, Frank	161	186	327				
Liles, Tommy	67	327					
Lillie, Jim	77	327					
Liming, Jim	75	327					
Linderman, Bob	58	327					
Lindermuth, Dick	121	122	123	327			
Lindermuth, Glen	121	122	327				
Lindgren, Lionel	194	195	327				
Lindley, Jack	44	327					
Lindquist, Carl	64	327	439				
Lindsey, Charles	179	185	327				
Lindsey, John	89	92	93	205	206	327	
Lindsley, John	115	118	119	205	327		
Lindstrom, John	55	57	59	61	207	208	327
Lineberger, Don	142	327					
Lines, Don	142	327					
Linnell, Gerald	185	327					
Linneman, Joe	67	327					
LiPetri, Angelo	120	327	439				
Lippold, Greg	44	46	327				
Lipsey, ---	14	327					
Lipstas, Bob	133	180	327				
Liptak, Bill	133	327					
Lisinski, Don	94	327					
Liszewski, Joe	141	327					
Littell, Don	98	327					
Little, ---	29	327					
Little, Elmer	171	327					
Little, Jim	151	327					
Little, Keith	95	97	327				
Little, Walt	71	81	83	90	102	328	
Livingston, ---	27	328					
Livingston, Doug	156	328					
Livingston, F.S.	16	20	21	22	24	25	328
Lloyd, ---	7	328					
Lloyd, Bob	141	328					
Lloyd, L.T.	156						
LoCicero, Dick	190	328					
Lock, Jerry	192	195	328				
Lockamy, John H.	149						
Lockett, Bill	162	328					
Lockhart, Ed	189	328					
Lockman, Charles	59	328					
Lockwood, Howard	171	174	328				
Loehr, Dave	132	328					
Loeser, Dick	94	328					
Loftin, Jackie	180	328					
Lohr, Larry	73	74	81	82	328		
Lokey, George	58	59	328				
Lomas, Wayne	55	328					
Lomberger, John	81	328					
London, Lou	107	121					
Long, Bill	94	328					
Long, Bob	166	328					
Long, Chester	44	328					
Long, Clarence	194	195					
Long, H.L.	11	24	25	26	27	29	34	328
Long, Hoke	40	328					
Long, Howard	78	328					
Long, Jim	58	98	99	155	156	328	
Long, Joel	188	192	328				
Long, Mann	26						
Long, Wallace	121	328					
Longwello, Charles	172	328					
Lonzano, Manuel	137	138	329				
Looney, Bill	140	329					
Looney, Russ	47	60	63	329			
Lopat, Ted	149						
Lopez, ---	34	329					
Lopez, Carlos	102	105	115	116	151	157	158	167
	168	205	329				
Lopez, Chino	171	329					
Lopez, Junior	201	329					
Lopez, Victorino	171	329					
Lord, Donald G.	73	82	91				
Lorenz, Marv	55	329					
Loschke, Bob	162	329					
Loschke, Leo	77	329					
Lott, Edgar	34	37	39	329			
Lott, F.O.	35	36	37	39	329		
Lott, Gerald	98						
Loudermilk, Joe	125	137	329				
Louis, Bob	94	329					
Lourik, Alex	129	329					
Love, ---	138	329					
Love, B.L.	22	329					
Lovelace, ---	4	329					
Lovelady, Willard	90	329					
Loveland, Jim	181	329					
Loveless, Deason	59	329					
Lovell, Charles	141	329					

Georgia Class-D Minor League Baseball Encyclopedia

Name									Name							
Lovell, Hugh	98	329							MacLeod, Don	194	331					
Lovett, ---	9	10	11	329					Macli, Al	77	331					
Lovett, Bill	90	111	125	329					Macrinotis, Lou	67	331					
Lovett, W.E.	111	124	137	145					Madaio, Gene	193	331					
Lovett, W.H.	111	124	137	145	175				Maddick, Russ	197	199	200	331			
Loveys, Bill	99	100	111	114	329				Maddox, Delma	117	118	119	331			
Loving, C. Ray	103								Maderis, Joe	186	331					
Lowe, ---	14	71	329						Madison, Dave	166	331	439				
Lowe, John	111	329							Maelwig, ---	76	331					
Lowe, Lou	59	329							Magee, J.C.	117						
Lowe, Macon	197	330							Maggi, Ernest	126	331					
Lowell, ---	73	330							Maglio, Steve	98	112	125				
Lowery, Cy	51	55	56	59	60	61	63	206	Magnatta, Jim	90	92	205	331			
	330								Maguire, Paul	176	332					
Lowery, D.D.	20	22	28	30	330				Mahaffey, Jim	40	332					
Lowery, Jason	157	167	330						Mahoney, ---	73	332					
Lowery, Les	44	48	49	330					Mahurin, Leman	166	168	176	178	332		
Lowman, Cal	48	330							Maiden, John	121	332					
Lown, Turk	68	69	330	439					Maier, Ed	184	332					
Lowry, ---	31	32	330						Major, Tom	197	332					
Lowry, Fred N.	41	44	48	51	55	59	63	77	Malavase, Allie	193	332					
	86	95	107	121					Malcolm, Lew	71	332					
Lowry, John	182	183	190	330					Maldonado, Ovidio	185	332					
Lowther, ---	16	330							Malesky, William G.	80						
Luberto, Santo	96	97	330						Mallard, John	156	158	167	168	209	332	
Lubieski, Herman	197	201	330						Malone, Frank	67	332					
Lubinski, Dick	171	173	174	330					Maloney, Pat	77	332					
Luby, Jim	76	330							Maloof, Joe	102	332					
Lucabaugh, Charles	160	164	330						Maltby, ---	17	332					
Lucarella, Rinaldo	112	330							Manahan, Gerald	160	332					
Lucchesi, Frank	141	142	143	330	447				Manchester, Dick	6	13	16	19	332		
Luce, Art	82	330							Mancini, Herb	103	105	332				
Luchetta, Frank	122	330							Manes, Jerry	156	332					
Luciano, Mike	160	330							Manfredi, Ralph	134	332					
Luckey, Dick	62	330							Mangieri, Nicholas J.	124	136					
Luckman, Jack	75	330							Manheim, Francis	73	332					
Lucus, ---	28	330							Mankovitch, Frank	193	195	332				
Luddy, Harold	156	330							Mann, C.G.	91						
Lugo, Lou	150	155	330						Mann, E.W. Jr.	125	180					
Lukasiuk, Lou	50	53	54	56	57	330			Mann, Elbert	80	332					
Luker, John	155	330							Mann, Nickey	154						
Lukon, Eddie	55	56	57	330	439				Mann, Tom	77	332					
Lukon, John	60	62	63	65	330				Mann, William	188						
Lukosius, Justin	162	330							Manning, ---	37	51	332				
Lum, Mike	202	331	439						Manning, Bill	95	332					
Luna, C.W.	19	331							Manning, Tommy	62	332					
Lunger, ---	9	331							Manno, Don	122	126	332	439			
Lutes, Bill	86	87	331						Mansfield, Cliff	156	158	332				
Lutes, Jim	72	331							Manson, ---	16	332					
Luttrell, ---	9	10	331						Manush, Frank	22	23	27	332	439		
Lutz, Dave	160	331							Mapes, Carl	138	139	146	166	332		
Lynch, Wayne	94	97	107	109	110	331			Maples, Earl	184	187	333				
Lynn, Fred	77	87	331						Maratowski, Fred	47	333					
Lyons, Bob	96	108	109	206	331				Marbet, Otto	27	333					
Lyons, Don	160	331							Marburger, Bob	186	333					
Lyons, John	156	331							Marcello, Anthony	111	113	333				
Lyons, Pat	103	331							Marhoover, Gary	155	333					
Lyons, Ray	71	331							Maricich, Eli	117	118	130	131	155	157	158	159
Lyons, Tom	121	331								161	190	205	208	209	333	
MacCallum, Nelson	162	331							Marino, Emil	120	333					
MacConnell, Bob	173	331							Marino, Michael J.	84						
MacDonald, Don	145	331							Marion, J.W.	19	20	21	29	333		
MacFarlane, Morley	177	331							Marion, Red	44	46	333	439			
MacIvor, Colin	179	192	331						Markham, Dick	95	112	333				
Mack, Connie	95	107	120	133	141				Markham, Ken	77	86	88	333	448		
Mack, Connie Jr.	107	120							Markland, John	121	333					
Mack, Earle	120	133	141						Markle, Lou	133	333					
Mack, Jerome	87	331							Marks, Max	31	32	33	34	333		
Mack, Roy	107	133	141						Marlow, Walt	94	333					
Mackey, J. Elmer	193								Marnie, Hal	55	333	439				
Mackey, John	63	331							Marockie, Henry	181	333					
Mackie, H.P	10	11	12	20	22	204	331		Marolewski, Fred	94	96	97	206	333	439	

Georgia Class-D Minor League Baseball Encyclopedia

Name									Name							
Maroney, John	180	333							Maurer, Walt	129	335					
Marotta, Dan	126	333							Maust, Tom	197	199	202	335			
Marquez, Humberto	184	187	333						Maxcy, Russ	194	335					
Marquis, Roger	186	333	439						Maxwell, Bob	67	69	70	335			
Marrero, Leonilo	125	333							Maxwell, Elmo	86	335					
Marrochi, Hugo	151	333							Maxwell, Gordon	185	335					
Marrujo, Jimmie	201	333							Maxwell, J.A.	186						
Marsh, Jim E.	51	56	60	333					Maxwell, John	156	177	335				
Marshall, ---	5	20	73	333					May, John	197	335					
Marshall, Dick	116	119	334						May, Ted	166	335					
Marshall, Reavis	111	334							Mayorquinn, Ernesto	134	335					
Marshall, Shorty	71	73	74	81	83	84	90	92	Mays, ---	11	16	335				
	93	116	118	146	204	333			Mays, Everett	145	147	336				
Marsilisi, Mike	141	334							Mazak, Leo	99	111	116	336			
Martellani, Bob	189	334							Maze, John	55	336					
Martin, Amos	37	334							Mazer, Al	51	336					
Martin, Archie	41	44	93	334					Mazzone, ---	76	336					
Martin, Billie	103	117	334						McAdams, Ralph	51	55	336				
Martin, Carl M.	120	133	141						McAfee, Alton	91	92	93	103	104	105	116	205
Martin, Charles	41	334								336						
Martin, Edwin	50	334							McAfee, Bud	197	336					
Martin, Fred	133	334							McAllister, C.B.	146	154	156	167	176		
Martin, Harold	54	334							McAndrew, Bob	102	105	116	118	205	336	
Martin, Jim	99	111	113	124	127	170	208	209	McArthur, Don	107	336					
	334								McAuliffe, ---	29	30	336				
Martin, John	157	334							McAuliffe, Dick	194	195	336	440			
Martin, Kenneth S.	138	146	155	166	176	185			McBride, ---	24	336					
Martin, Lane	160	164	192	334					McBride, Delton	102	336					
Martin, Ray	162								McBride, Harold	64	68	336				
Martin, S.R.	27	29	334						McBride, Tom	91	336					
Martin, Travis	196	197	198	199	207	334			McBryde, Warren	58	77	78				
Martin, W.P.	19	334							McCaffrey, Tom	180	336					
Martinez, Freddie	58	334							McCain, Sam	107	336					
Martini, Fernando	91	334							McCall, Gordon	161	336					
Martini, Paul	122	334							McCallum, Dick	95	121	336				
Martinich, Tony	107	334							McCalman, Jack	125	336					
Martz, ---	31	334							McCann, Cliff	68	336					
Maruschak, Nick	129	131	334						McCarnes, Jim	78	79	336				
Masatto, Frank	157	334							McCarron, Bob	189	336					
Mashburn, Ernest	71	76	85	334					McCarthy, ---	32	336					
Masluk, Paul	98								McCarthy, Dick	76	336					
Mason, George	82	86	334						McCarthy, Frank	186	336					
Mason, J.	32	334							McCarthy, John	146	147	336				
Mason, John	104	334							McCasland, Stan	161	336					
Mason, Max	167	334							McClaskey, Larry	177	178	209	336			
Mason, S.	31	334							McClatchey, Bob	107	336					
Massey, Horace	94	334							McClellan, Harvey	24	25	337	440			
Massey, Terrance	64	334							McClenaghan, Russ	161	170	176	177	194	337	
Masterson, Bill	76	335							McClendon, H.G.	190						
Mastracci, Bob	166	335							McClinton, Gene	155	337					
Matchick, Tom	197	198	199	335	439				McCloskey, Frank	63	337					
Matesich, Joe	150	335							McClure, Jim	44	45	46	207	337		
Mathes, Ed	161	335							McClure, Oscar	55	337					
Mathewson, ---	31	335							McCluskey, Austin	157	337					
Mathey, Bud	104	335							McClusky, Jim	193	337					
Mathieson, Bob	113	335							McClusky, LeRoy	64	337					
Mathis, Joe	181	335							McColl, Red	50	52	53	207	337	440	
Mathis, Willie	68	69	335						McColley, Bill	163	337					
Mathison, Malcolm	163	335							McCollum, ---	32	337					
Matican, Marv	126	335							McCombie, Charles	151	337					
Matt, J.W.	41								McConnell, Ed	72	337					
Matt, Joseph W. Jr.	98	110							McConnell, Mickey	64						
Matthews, Bob	71	74	81	82	83	84	205	206	McCord, Norm	95	337					
	335								McCorkle, Bob	68	337					
Matthews, Harry	20	22	24	29	335				McCormack, ---	4	337					
Matthews, Jim	176	335							McCormack, Tom	157	160					
Matthews, Luther	102	335							McCormick, Dick	85	337					
Matthews, Matty	24	335							McCormick, John	99	101	210	337			
Mauldin, Mason	99	111	112	335					McCorry, ---	63	64	337				
Mauney, John	172	335							McCovey, Willie	176	177	178	337	440		
Maupin, Bill	182	335							McCowan, John F.	125						
Maurer, Ray	129	335							McCoy, ---	14	337					

Georgia Class-D Minor League Baseball Encyclopedia

Name									Name							
McCoy, Bob	167	337								56	59	60	206	339		
McCraney, ---	9	337							McKenzie, William	41	339					
McCraney, Wayne	89	92	102	337					McKeon, Bill	190						
McCrary, Jim	95	150							McKinley, Pete	41	339					
McCravy, Charles	72	82	337						McKinley, Tom	47	339					
McCrone, Tom	141	337							McKinney, ---	31	32	340				
McCue, George	182	190	337						McKinney, Bill	80	340					
McCulley, Melvin	85	337							McKinney, Clarence	126	340					
McCulloch, Bob	103	337							McKinney, Heaford	149	152	153	340			
McCullough, John	85	87	337						McKinnon, Bill	27	340					
McCune, Larry	181	338							McKinstay, John	173	340					
McDaniel, Dan	150	338							McKnight, ---	5	340					
McDaniel, Elmer	198	338							McLaughlin, ---	32	34	340				
McDaniel, Ernest	67	69	338						McLaughlin, Edward	27	29	340				
McDaniel, Joel	194	195	196	338					McLaughlin, Pat	145	340					
McDaniel, Kerry	197	199	338						McLean, Charles	94	96	340				
McDaniels, Don	154	338							McLean, Harvey	155	340					
McDermid, Doug	145	147	338						McLean, John	151	161	340				
McDevitt, Danny	129	338	440						McLemore, Roy	142	143	144	151	340		
McDevitt, Tom	179	182	338						McLendon, ---	7	340					
McDonald, ---	22	34	38	338					McLennan, Don	155	340					
McDonald, Bob	85	99	338						McLeod, George	150	165	340				
McDonald, J.W.	188								McLeod, Jim	90	340					
McDonald, John	150	338							McLeod, Pete	91	340					
McDonald, Russ	160	166	171	338					McLin, ---	11	340					
McDonough, ---	34	338							McMahon, Jim	76	79	340				
McDougald, Julius	126	338							McMahon, Mike	138						
McDuff, ---	24	338							McMannus, ---	7	340					
McDuffie, ---	19	338							McManus, Joe	130	131	340				
McEnroe, Jim	202	338							McMasters, Omer	167	340					
McFadden, John	103	105	205	206	338				McMichael, H.N.	166						
McFadden, Ken	188	338							McMillan, Bob	186	340					
McFarland, ---	14	338							McMillan, Frank	76	340					
McFarland, Bill	82	338							McMillan, Norm	14	17	340	440			
McFarlane, Alex	44	45	48	338					McMullen, Don	189	340					
McFarlin, ---	16	18	338						McMullen, G.	54	340					
McGarity, Les	72	73	100	338					McMullen, Tom	159	161	164	340			
McGarr, Dave	171	338							McMullin, Dale	171	173	340				
McGee, Bob	166	168	209	338	448				McNair, Ralph	47	340					
McGee, Eugene R.	102								McNally, Don	121	123	133	150	161	341	
McGee, Wilson	64	68	72	74	338				McNally, Jim	45	341					
McGhay, Gerald	166	338							McNamara, Charles	112	341					
McGhee, Bill	34	37	39	99	124	125	137	138	McNamee, Bill	200	341					
	139	146	147	148	166	209	339	440	McNease, Harry	112	341					
McGhee, Dick	111	338							McNeely, Bob	166	341					
McGhee, Tom	121	338							McNeil, Bill	182	183	207	341			
McGlade, ---	24	25	339						McNulty, Ed	162	341					
McGovern, Russ	85	149	152	160	163	206	339		McNulty, Jim	87	88	341				
McGowan, Frank	157	339							McNulty, John	87	341					
McGowen, Mickey	64	65	66	339	440				McPartland, Doug	151	156	157	341			
McGrath, John	121	339							McPherson, Roger	147	148	341				
McGrath, M.	4								McPherson, Ron	146	341					
McGrath, Mike	193	339							McPherson, Tom	54	341					
McGravy, Hoyt	142	152	154	339					McQuaig, Jerry	40	44	341	440			
McGraw, Willie	166	339							McQuillen, Jack	67	341					
McGreal, Jimmy	58	339							McRae, Bill	71	72	341				
McGregor, H.H.	142								McRae, Jim	77	341					
McGue, Don	193	339							McShane, Henry	50						
McGuire, Ed	150	339							McSwain, Cliff	38	204	341				
McGuire, Forrest	172	339							McTaggert, Charles	89	92	102	341			
McHale, John J.	162	181	190	194	197	201			McVay, Frosty	51	52	54	59	64	66	68	69
McIntyre, Jim	176	339								341						
McIntyre, Sam	185	187	188	191	339				McVey, David J.	124						
McKay, Dick	107	109	339						McWhorter, Marcus	81	91	92	205	341		
McKay, F.S.	35	38	339						McWhorter, Pierce	87	341					
McKay, Nicholas	75								Meaders, Elden	59	341					
McKay, Roy	154	158	339						Meador, Bob	134	135	341				
McKee, Art	189	193	339						Meadows, Don	190	191	341				
McKenna, Bob	126	339							Meadows, Herman	99	112	114	341			
McKenney, Bill	94	95	339						Meadows, John	130	341					
McKenzie, Bill	44	339							Meads, Charles	117	341					
McKenzie, Sherwood	41	42	45	48	49	51	52	55	Meagher, Bob	150	153	341				

479

Georgia Class-D Minor League Baseball Encyclopedia

Name							Name					
Meder, Dick	165	341					Miller, Bill	166	176	344		
Mediamolle, Frank	58	68	69	342			Miller, Blanton	149	160	170	179	192
Medley, Carl	156	158	342				Miller, Bob	126	201	344		
Medlin, Jim	172	342					Miller, Charles	89	344			
Medlock, ---	7	14	17	342			Miller, Dan	27	344			
Medlock, Frank	72	82	342				Miller, Dean	150	344			
Mee, Joe	172	342					Miller, Dick	134	344			
Meekins, Dennis	166	168	169	176	342		Miller, Don	180	183	208	344	
Meeres, Gordon	122	342					Miller, Ed	165	344			
Mehrens, Wallace	62	342					Miller, Eddie	181	344			
Meier, John	155	342					Miller, Edo	133	140			
Meikleham, Harry P.	28	38					Miller, Frank	41	58	147	344	
Meka, Mark	202	342					Miller, Gerald	160	163	344		
Melanson, Marv	162	164	342				Miller, Gibbs	86	344			
Melbert, Bill	177	342					Miller, Glenn	181	182	183	344	
Mellinger, Jim	91	342					Miller, Harold	63	65	344		
Mello, Ed	201	203	342				Miller, Howard	63	344			
Melton, Cliff	160	342	440				Miller, Joe	177	344			
Melton, Gary	189	342					Miller, Ken	43	45	344		
Melton, Ray	51	56	71	81	342		Miller, Pinkie	54	344			
Melton, Rube	47	342	440				Miller, Ray	67	344			
Melvin, ---	72	342					Miller, Rod	193	195	344	440	
Mena, Ignacio	155	156	342				Miller, Ronald	192	195	344		
Menapace, Ed	147	151	157	342			Miller, Stan	156	158	344		
Mendillo, Anthony	77	342					Milley, Al	186	187	344		
Mendler, Dave	182	342					Mills, ---	7	16	17	344	
Mendoza, Ray	111	342					Mills, Dick	120	141	345		
Menig, Sam	95	342					Mills, Gil	87	344			
Menkel, Ken	181	342					Mills, Harvey	171	174	189	344	
Menna, Frank	167	193	342				Mills, Hop	70				
Merandi, Gene	140	143	207	342			Mills, Joe	197	200	345		
Mercer, ---	5	342					Mills, L.	11	345			
Mercier, Ron	202	342					Milner, Bruce	82	345			
Merget, John	126	127	133	209	343		Milner, Charlie	115	117	345		
Meriwether, Al	162	343					Milner, Holt	27	29	37	67	345
Merlob, Bob	185	343					Milner, Jim	67	69	345		
Merola, Mike	156						Milner, Walt	73				
Merrigan, Walt	181	343					Milo, ---	71	345			
Mertz, Jim	56	343	440				Milosevich, Mike	112	132	133	135	345	440
Messina, Dino	170	185	343				Milster, Jack	125	345			
Metasic, Edward J.	57						Minarck, Bill	82	345			
Metheny, Bud	98	100	343	440			Minch, Charles	186	345			
Methvin, ---	20	22	343				Mincy, Red	111	113	114	345	
Meyer, Bill	171	343					Miner, Dean	182	345			
Meyer, Gary	179	185	343				Minjock, John	150	170	176	185	187	345
Meyer, Russ	197	199	200	343			Mink, Deane	142	151	345	448	
Miali, Jim	201	343					Mink, Joe	99	102	103	345	
Miarka, Stan	150	151	343				Minner, Paul	64	345	440		
Michael, J.E.	117	343					Minor, Howard	71	345			
Michaels, Bill	75	343					Mintz, Dwain	108	345			
Micham, Jerry	184	187	343				Mirande, Anthony	156	345			
Michel, Harold	50	53	54	343			Miscisco, Dan	200	345			
Micheli, Bob	185	343					Miskulin, John	98	100	101	345	
Michelson, Warren	122	343					Mitchell, ---	5	345			
Mickle, ---	24	343					Mitchell, Bill	193	345			
Middiknight, ---	13	16	20	343			Mitchell, Don	192	345			
Middlebrooks, ---	5	343					Mitchell, Ed	55	345			
Midgette, Dennis	193	343					Mitchell, Joe Bob	63	64	65	80	
Miehoff, Sol	54	343					Mitchell, Merv	45	345			
Mihal, Ron	190	343					Mitchell, Orion	106	120			
Mihalik, Mickey	73	89	91	92	93	205	343	Mitchell, Steven	193	345			
Mikesell, Maurice	94	343					Mitskavich, Nestor	94	346			
Mikulski, Stan	145	343					Mittewede, Walter	27	30	346		
Milam, Lawrence	85	343					Mittleman, Dick	40	346			
Milazzo, Basile	43						Mixon, Art	181	182	183	346	
Milcsik, Ray	63	67	343				Mixon, Clark	151	161	346		
Miles, Jerry	186	343					Mize, Mike	77	346			
Miles, R.L.	22	343					Mize, Pope	51	346			
Millard, John	91	92	93	103	104	105	204	205	Mizell, Vinegar Bend	106	109	346	440
	344							Mizerock, John	162	346			
Miller, ---	14	22	24	25	344		Mlynarek, Anthony	90	346			
Miller, Barry	196	197	202	344			Mlynarek, Lawrence	108	346			

Georgia Class-D Minor League Baseball Encyclopedia

Name									Name					
Moate, Marvin E.	99	156							Morgan, Roger	182	183	348		
Mock, ---	156	346							Moriarity, Dean	142	348			
Mock, George	78	346							Moriskiewicz, John	161	163	348		
Moeller, George	108	346							Morlan, Joe	186	348			
Moeller, Rolf	121	123	208	346					Morowski, Gene	201	348			
Moffett, Frank	14	346							Morrell, Bill	55	60	63	348	440
Molck, Larry	142	346							Morris, Al	188	190	191	348	
Molinder, Walt	67	346							Morris, Charles	197	348			
Molokie, Leon	133	346							Morris, Clint	180	348			
Monaco, Frank	91	92	346						Morris, Dave	82				
Monaco, Vince	165	346							Morris, Eddie	54	348			
Monahan, Jim	141	143	346						Morris, J.T.	136				
Monarchi, Gene	90	346							Morris, Milt	166	176	177	178	348
Monarchi, Pete	81	90	100	346					Morris, Ray	72	348			
Monasterio, Eduardo	162	346							Morris, Ted	150	348			
Monfre, John	192								Morris, Teddy	64	348			
Monkarsh, Bill	198	346							Morris, Willard	44	348			
Monroe, M.M.	64	142							Morrisey, Chet	150				
Monroe, M.M. Jr.	172								Morrisey, Gerald J.	119	132			
Monroe, Ray	137	139	346						Morrison, Dean	73	348			
Monson, Ron	182	185	346						Morrison, Harry	11	19	22	24	348
Montalvo, Jose	73	346							Morrison, Jim	108	113	126	127	209 349
Monterio, Dave	172	346							Morrison, Ron	154	349			
Montgomery, Bob	112	346							Morrongiello, Mike	103	104	349		
Montgomery, Walt	120	346							Morrow, ---	30	349			
Moody, Frank	40	346							Morsberger, Charles	186	349			
Moody, Joe	78	79	346						Morse, Whitey	6	7	8	13	14 349
Moon, Eulas	27	346							Morton, ---	19	349			
Moon, H.W.	160								Morton, Bill	192	195	196	200	349
Moore, ---	14	347							Morzenti, Jerome	190	349			
Moore, Bill	160	347							Moseley, ---	16	349			
Moore, Billy Joe	185	347							Mosley, Bob	154	349			
Moore, Bob	200	347							Mosley, C.S.	29	349			
Moore, Charles	121	347							Mosley, Jack	113	126			
Moore, Clem	27	29	347						Moss, Darvin	177	349			
Moore, Duke	172	347							Moss, Jim	181	349			
Moore, Earl	77	347							Moss, Joe	115	117	129	349	
Moore, Ed	67	108	171	347					Moss, Les	67	349	440	447	
Moore, Gayle	173	182	347						Mote, Eldridge	101				
Moore, Gene	120	347							Mote, Galen	189	349			
Moore, H.H.	31	32	347						Mote, John	138	139	349		
Moore, Herb	75	78	79	207	208	347			Motil, Bob	193	349			
Moore, Hugh	46	58	63	67	347				Mott, Bitsy	54	58	61	63	349 440
Moore, J.	31	347							Mottler, Ernest	111	113	349		
Moore, Jack	111	347							Moulder, Glen	58	61	349	440	
Moore, Jackie	194	347	440	447					Moulton, Jack	34	35	38	349	
Moore, James	12	20	347						Mount, Ron	163	349			
Moore, Jewell	72	347							Mounts, Emory	162	172	173	349	
Moore, Jim	137	138	139	194	347				Mowbray, Jim	181	189	349		
Moore, John	157	347							Mozzali, Mo	192	194	195	196	349
Moore, Lamar	163	347							Mueninghoff, Dick	55	56	349		
Moore, Lloyd	132	347							Muhlenbein, Henry	58	349			
Moore, Morris	162	172	347						Muir, Charles	186	349			
Moore, Ray	180	347							Mulkin, ---	31	349			
Moore, Vern	85	347							Mullaney, Tom	189	349			
Moore, Willard	156	166	347						Mullen, John	197				
Moorefield, ---	11	12	347						Mullen, Vincent	77	86	350		
Moorehead, Dick	120	347							Muller, Charles T.	93				
Moran, ---	24	347							Mulligan, ---	17	350			
Moran, Charles	6	347							Mullin, ---	6	8	350		
Moran, Mike	185	348							Mullis, Don	197	350			
Morelli, Jim	102	105	116	118	137	138	139	348	Munch, Bill	86	350			
Moreno, Heliodoro	175	348							Munday, Charles	121	350			
Morgan, Billy	60	64	348						Mundo, Jim	47	350			
Morgan, Cy	48	49	51	52	53	55	57	348	Munford, ---	29	350			
Morgan, Fred	68	348							Munroe, Ken	134	350			
Morgan, George	173	190	348						Muratore, Dick	193	350			
Morgan, Gordon	172	348							Murch, Red	7	14	16	350	
Morgan, Julian	100	113	156	210	348				Murchison, Tim	51	350	440		
Morgan, Lucius	156	158	166	348					Murillo, Jose	180	350			
Morgan, Malvern	73	74	80	82	83	104	105	130	Murphee, Bill	81	350			
	131	204	348						Murphy, ---	7	8	350		

Georgia Class-D Minor League Baseball Encyclopedia

Name							
Murphy, Bill	132	135	350				
Murphy, Bob	130	140	144	350			
Murphy, Dan	129	130	131	147	167	350	
Murphy, Ed	50	52	53	94	106	107	109	120
	350	440					
Murphy, Huey	175	184					
Murphy, Jim	81	350					
Murphy, Lamar	129	350					
Murray, Bill	76	79	351				
Murray, Bob	40	41	351	440			
Murray, Charles	201	202	350				
Murray, Charlie	55	350					
Murray, Don	154	162	177	350			
Murray, Francis	78	350					
Murray, Glenn	41	42	44	45	51	207	350
Murray, Milt	100	113	350				
Murray, Orlene	193	350					
Murray, Ralph	71	350					
Murray, Tom	71	81	351				
Murray, Walt	81	351					
Murrell, Ivan	201	351	440				
Murta, John	181	351					
Muse, Don	90	103	105	351			
Muse, R.E.	81						
Musial, Ed	122	351					
Musillo, John	197	351					
Muskopf, Bob	171	351					
Muskulin, John	77	351					
Musser, Dick	151	157	351				
Musumeci, John	133	351					
Muth, Dick	41	351					
Muti, Nick	73	351					
Myatt, Charles	160	351					
Myatt, Ralph	194	351					
Myers, Bill	157	351					
Myers, Bob	121	351					
Myers, Dick	126	351					
Myers, Don	77	351					
Myers, Jim	68	351					
Myers, John	171	351					
Myers, Ken	186	351					
Mytrysak, John	133	351					
Nabors, Jack	19	20	21	205	351	441	
Nafus, Virgil	63	351					
Nagle, Bob	90	351					
Nagy, Mike	189	351					
Najour, George	72	351					
Nakunas, Steve	55	351					
Nance, ---	16	18	351				
Nance, Hoover	104	351					
Naphole, John	112	351					
Narieka, Joe	63	351					
Narron, Sam	40	41	42	352	441		
Nasworthy, Luther	90	102	352				
Navarro, Henry	108	109	207	352			
Navarro, Ignatius	150	352					
Navarro, Julio	176	352	441				
Naylor, Dick	151	352					
Nazzaro, Carman	90	352					
Nebinger, Dick	193	352					
Neborak, Bill	59	352					
Nedelco, Alex	86	352					
Nee, Dan	44	352					
Needles, ---	9	352					
Neeley, Bob	176	352					
Neeley, Gary	197	352					
Neely, Jess	120	352					
Negray, Ron	108	109	352	441			
Neigefind, Vic	41	352					
Nelms, Charles	185	187	188	352			
Nelson, ---	9	24	352				
Nelson, Bob	63	352					
Nelson, Burel	73	82	83	84	102	352	
Nelson, Charles	137	142	145	352			
Nelson, Dick	99	100	102	352			
Nelson, Don	197	352					
Nelson, F.M.	41						
Nelson, Gene	121	352					
Nelson, Jim	72	82	95	130	352		
Nemeth, Bob	176	352					
Nemeth, Frank	170	352					
Nemier, ---	68	352					
Nesbihal, Ed	163	352					
Nesta, Nick	197	352					
Nester, Jim	190	191	194	353			
Nettles, Hoke	34	353					
Neudecker, Jerome A.	115						
New, Walter	115						
Newcomb, ---	43	353					
Newcomb, Tete	41	44	45	48	50	54	59	353
Newcomer, Jack	197	198	199	353			
Newell, Bob	108	121	122	353			
Newell, Kirk	11	12	20	353			
Newhall, Bob	72	353					
Newkirk, ---	5	9	10	353			
Newlin, Bob	63	353					
Newmarch, Ron	150	155	156	353			
Newsome, Art	73	353					
Newsome, Skeeter	38	39	353	441			
Newton, Cash	20	21	22	353			
Newton, Doc	31	353					
Newton, Leo	200	353					
Newton, Tom	194	353					
Neyen, Bill	162	353					
Nicholas, Alvin	45	48	353				
Nichols, Bruce	201	202	203	353			
Nichols, Charles	175						
Nichols, Fred	80						
Nichols, J.P. Jr.	4	26					
Nichols, Jim	107	171					
Nicholson, Dave	193	353	441				
Nichting, Ray	138	146	147	148	353		
Nickerson, Frank	99	100					
Nickols, Joseph	130						
Nicolai, Mel	76	79	207	353			
Niedowicz, Frank	107						
Niedzowieski, Ron	180	353					
Niemeier, Don	186	353					
Nierpoetter, Billy	103	105	115	117	354		
Niklas, Roger	122	354					
Niles, Harry	194	354					
Nims, Keith	177	354					
Nisewonger, Jim	150	153	170	181	183	194	354
Nitram, ---	27	354					
Nix, George	72	354					
Nix, Henry	75	76	138	354			
Nix, Tom	186	354					
Njirich, Gildo	78	87	354				
Noah, Harold	87	126	354				
Nobles, ---	34	354					
Nobles, Julian	76	77	354				
Noga, George	90	102	105	116	118	119	205	354
Nojunas, Al	95	354					
Nolan, John	198	201					
Nolley, ---	4	354					
Nolly, Rufus	22	23	24	205	354		
Norbert, Ted	194	195	354				
Nordenhold, Henry	184	187	354				
Norman, Jesse	20	21	354				
Norris, Bob	197	354					
Norris, Jim	151	171	354				
Norris, Larry	167	354					
Norris, Ron	197	354					
North, Bob	146	354					

Georgia Class-D Minor League Baseball Encyclopedia

Name								Name					
North, Lamar	99	111	354					Orr, Dick	47	356			
Norton, Harold	151	354						Orr, John	181				
Nossokoff, Arthur	89							Orsatti, Frank	200	356			
Noto, Phil	72	82	103	354				Ortiz, Felix	185	356			
Novak, Walt	200	354						Ortiz, Otoniel	91	356			
Nowak, Ed	43	46	47	64	354			Osborne, Pete	78	79	356		
Nowak, Hank	47	49	50	52	53	355		Osborne, Tiny	27	29	357	441	
Nunley, ---	4	355						Osborne, Wilson	156	357			
Nunn, ---	27	355						Osburn, D.A.	179				
Nunnally, ---	30	355						Osburn, Herman	150	357			
O'Barr, Tom	112	120	130	131	145	148	154	205	Oscher, Bob	41	357		
	355							Osment, ---	5	357			
O'Brentz, Howard	115							Osteen, Bill	80	106	357		
O'Brien, ---	13	14	16	355				Osteen, Frank	80	357			
O'Brien, Bill	95	107	355					Osteen, W.J.	22	357			
O'Brien, Harry J.	94							Ostendorf, Fred	16	19	357	441	
O'Brien, Jim	76	355						Oster, Fred	171	357			
O'Brien, Phil	201	355						Oster, Sandy	163	357			
O'Bryant, Oscar	137	355						Osthoff, Wilbur	111	114	209	357	
O'Callaghan, Tom	122	355						Ostopchuck, Joe	149	153	357		
Oceak, Frank	155	160	161	170	174	180	355	Otey, Dick	166	357			
O'Coine, Marshall	108	355						O'Toole, Dan	67	357			
O'Connell, Joe	155	355						O'Toole, Jim	125	357			
O'Connell, Tom	72	355						Ott, Ron	185	357			
O'Connor, Mike	179	355						Otten, Don	84	87	357		
Odell, Clancy	68	355						Ouchterloney, Don	77	357			
Odom, Charles A.	146	154	155	165	166			Overland, John	95	96	357		
Odom, Harvey D.	119	132						Overmire, Stubby	194	357	441		
Odom, Lilburn	44	45	355					Overstreet, Charles	99	357			
O'Donnell, Harry	41	355						Overton, Dannie	24	357			
O'Donnell, Jim	189	355						Overton, H.A.	12	20	21	28	30	357
O'Donnell, John	90	92	205	355				Owen, Bill	155	156	167	184	357
Odum, Bill	177	355						Owen, Marv	162	357	441		
Oehler, Vic	40	355						Owen, Maurice	104	105	357		
Oertel, Chuck	125	127	209	355	441			Owens, D.L.	41	42	357		
Ogiego, Walt	55	57	355					Owens, Ed	101				
Ogier, T.L.	54	58	355					Owens, William E.	70	89			
Ogle, Fred	48	49	355					Oyler, Dick	45	357			
Ogle, Hugh	34	355						Ozburn, ---	37	39	357		
Oglesby, Alex	121	129	146	355				Pacanowski, Art	134	357			
Oglesby, Hugh	71	355						Pace, Carl	12	357			
O'Higgins, Dennis	45	355						Pacholke, Al	193	357			
Ohr, Cliff	161	356						Padgett, Bill	116	117	129	131	358
O'Kelley, Clyde	72	356						Padgett, Charles	71	72	81	117	126	358
Okey, Kene	67	356						Padgett, Tom	154	358			
O'Kronley, Pete	51	356						Padgett, Travis	55	358			
Olayko, Alex	91	356						Paepke, Jack	149	150	152	358	
Oldershaw, Howard	98	112	114	356				Page, Bill	185	358			
Oldfield, Pat	31	34	37	356				Page, Glen	86	88	358		
Oliver, Ben	77	356						Pagel, Vic	193	358			
Oliver, G.H.	55	59						Paisley, Bill	77	358			
Oliver, Gene	179	356	441					Paison, Bob	76	358			
Oliveri, Fred	112	356						Pakes, Tom	181	358			
Olmstead, Paul	108	356						Palantino, Bob	76	358			
Olmstead, Ted	75	356						Palazzo, Eugene	98				
O'Malley, Dan	125	356						Palko, Bill	197	201	203	358	
O'Mara, Larry	194	195	356					Pallavicini, Vince	198	201	358		
O'Neal, ---	24	25	356					Palmantier, A.B.	28	358			
O'Neal, J.B.	152							Palmer, Bob	176	358			
O'Neal, Tom	157	356						Palmer, Max	122	358			
O'Neil, John	55	181	190	194	356	441		Palmitesso, Fred	185	358			
O'Neil, Mickey	133	140	141	356	441			Palmquist, Ed	181	358	441		
O'Neill, John	160	163	170	356				Palumbo, ---	77	358			
Oneto, Francis	162	356						Palumbo, Bill	96	358			
Oquendo, Noel	112	114	125	127	137	145	148	209	Pancoe, Joe	95	358		
	210	356						Panek, Ed	55	358			
O'Quinn, ---	5	356						Panella, ---	19	358			
Orlandi, Ron	112	125	356					Panella, Joe	201	358			
Orner, Charles	126	356						Pappas, Nick	104	138	358		
O'Rourke, Frank	67	356	441					Pardue, Larry	167	358			
O'Rourke, Tom	155	356						Pare, Al	162				
Orr, Billy	179	356						Pare, John	99	358			

Georgia Class-D Minor League Baseball Encyclopedia

Name								
Parent, Leo	167	358						
Parente, Greg	75	76	79	358				
Parham, Dave	193	358						
Parilla, ---	27	358						
Paris, Lester	197	358						
Park, Ben E.	138							
Park, Loyal	150	359						
Park, Maynard	85	359						
Parker, ---	6	7	13	14	17	18	24	38
	359							
Parker, Charles	111	114	359					
Parker, Dixie	43	44	47	359	441			
Parker, Dudley	51	56	359					
Parker, Lee	37							
Parker, Newton	71	359						
Parker, Ray	134	359						
Parker, Terry	188	359						
Parks, ---	16	17	31	359				
Parks, Jack	73	359						
Parks, James	27	29	30	359				
Parks, John	43	46						
Parks, Woodford	73	359						
Parnell, Gene	124	126	359					
Parnell, M.R.	30	359						
Parquet, Clyde	198	359						
Parri, Carlo	98	359						
Parrish, Allen	172	359						
Parrish, Ron	138	139	156	359				
Parrott, Willie	156	359						
Parsons, Dixie	76	78	359	441				
Parsons, Harold	147	359						
Parsons, Roger	167	359						
Partain, Jim	197	359						
Pasch, Allan	94	359						
Paschal, Ben	16	17	18	359	441			
Pascoe, Ed	189	359						
Passarella, Bob	133	135	359					
Passaro, Roland	188	359						
Passilla, Jim	181	183	359					
Patchell, Stan	161	170	360					
Patchin, Art	56	360						
Pate, Bob	146	360						
Patrick, T.L.	142	151						
Patriss, Bill	157	158	181	360				
Patrow, Eddie	54	360						
Patten, Roger	155	360						
Patterson, ---	24	38	360					
Patterson, Bill	71	81	100	115	116	117	360	
Patterson, Britt	55	67	360					
Patterson, Charles	180	182	360					
Patterson, Derward	80	117	360					
Patterson, Joe	55	56	60	61	360			
Patterson, Ray	186	360						
Patterson, Ted	99	100	110	112	113	114	138	146
	155	156	157	158	208	209	360	
Pattillo, Robert S.	137							
Patton, Henry	34	35	37	360				
Paul, Joseph	152							
Paulick, Frank	76	87	112	360				
Pavelko, Paul	198	199	360					
Pavlick, Pete	176	178	185	186	360			
Pavone, Nick	75	360						
Pavuk, Tom	161	360						
Pawlak, Walt	161	167	360					
Pawlick, John	112	156	360					
Payne, Charles	176	360						
Payne, Dick	161	360						
Payne, George	13	360	441					
Payne, John	160	360						
Payne, Paul	194	360						
Pazienza, Bill	176	360						
Peacock, Arlen	142	361						
Peacock, Cecil	72	361						
Peacock, O.B.	99							
Peacock, T.D.	47	361						
Peake, ---	72	361						
Peale, Anthony	165	361						
Pearce, Ernest	166	361						
Pearson, ---	17	18	361					
Pearson, Ron	193	195	196	361				
Pearson, Tom	99	100	361					
Peddy, ---	16	361						
Peele, Sanford	47	48	361					
Peeler, ---	24	361						
Peeler, Tom	181	361						
Peeples, ---	24	25	26	361				
Pegram, George	77	361						
Pehanick, Al	172	174	361					
Pelat, Frank	44	45	48	49	55	56	59	207
	361							
Pelham, Bill	44	361						
Pellagrini, Al	171	361						
Pellarin, Anthony	166	361						
Pellicier, ---	34	361						
Pelot, Harold	86	361						
Penczak, Joe	120	361						
Pender, Marcus	125	361						
Pender, Wilbert	161	164	171	361				
Pendergraft, Jim	111	361						
Pendley, Jack	166	168	361					
Pennington, Joe	130	131	361					
Pennucci, Pat	198	361						
Pensky, Stan	44	47	58	361				
Penso, John	47	361						
Penson, Paul	181	361	441					
Penton, Henry	106	107	361					
Pepitone, John	78	361						
Pepper, Don	198	201	362	441				
Peppers, Dorsey	60	63	362					
Perada, Orestes	111	114	137	209	362			
Perchak, Charles	121	122	362					
Perdue, Glenn	103	362						
Pereira, Andres	177	362						
Perello, Dave	99	100	112	362				
Perez, Joaquin	182	183	362					
Perez, Simon	197	199	362					
Perez, Tom	133	362						
Perinis, Alex	166	169	170	362				
Perkins, Dave	161	362						
Perlman, Bertram	176	362						
Permeter, Harold	171	362						
Perna, Frank	150	362						
Perry, ---	5	17	362					
Perry, Bob	117	121	362					
Perry, Bush	95	184						
Perry, Charles	188	362						
Perry, Harold	185	362						
Perry, Joe	170	176	180	183	362			
Perry, Ray	179	362						
Perry, Tom	43	46	362					
Perry, Walt	201	362						
Perryman, Parson	32	362	441					
Persons, Earl	33	34	35	204	362			
Persons, Jim	80	362						
Persoskie, Metro	64	362						
Pescitelli, Pasquale	116	362						
Petchulat, George	95	362						
Peterkin, Alfonso	197	199	362					
Peterman, Bill	107	120	363	441				
Peterman, Irv	62	65	207	362				
Peters, Charles	73	363						
Peters, Genie	56	363						
Peters, Gerald	147	148	157	158	167	168	177	209
	363							

Georgia Class-D Minor League Baseball Encyclopedia

Name								Name							
Petersen, Charles	202	363						Pinkston, Ewell	87	365					
Peterson, ---	24							Pinner, Ted	68	365					
Peterson, Hardy	121	363	441					Pinson, Harold	104	205	365				
Peterson, Howard	185	187	363					Pinson, John	117	118	125	365			
Peterson, Jerry	64	363						Pint, Don	166	365					
Peterson, Tom	160	363						Pippin, Fred	146	148	209	210	365		
Peterson, Wright	77	363						Pirela, Julio	184	187	365				
Petraglia, Joe	107	363						Pirkel, Jim	197	365					
Petrella, Joe	45	363						Pittman, ---	17	365					
Petrick, John	155	363						Pittman, Al	71	365					
Petriello, Joe	176	363						Pizzitola, Vince	134	365					
Petrolongo, Joe	108	363						Pizzo, Joe	94	365					
Petrosky, Mike	56	57	363					Place, Paul	73	365					
Petrovich, Ron	161	363						Plaia, Benny	67	69	365				
Petroziello, Carl	68	69	363					Plante, ---	76	365					
Pettis, Tom	85	363						Plaster, Buddy	170	365					
Petty, Fred	155	363						Platt, Ralph	181	189	193	365			
Petty, Gene	122	363						Plaza, Ron	140	143	365				
Petty, Jim	77							Pleau, Andre	189	194	365				
Petty, Tom	179	188						Pliszka, Matt	85	365					
Petty, Vern	67	69	363					Ploszaj, Chester	138	146	148	365	448		
Petty, Virgil	154	156	363					Plushanski, Fred	145	147	157	158	167	168	209	210
Pezold, Larry	9	363	441						365						
Pfander, John	185	363						Pluss, Dave	66	68	69	206	365		
Pfeifer, Cy	145	363						Plyn, Percy	72	95	365				
Pfeifer, Fred	43	363						Podein, George	55	60	63	365			
Pfeifer, Tony	142	363						Podgajny, Johnny	55	365	442				
Pfeiffer, Harry	75	363						Podolski, Dick	150	366					
Pfister, George	161	171	181	193	363	442		Podowski, Phil	160	366					
Pfund, Lee	62	363	442					Poholsky, John	189	366					
Phagan, Fred	193	363						Pohutsky, Chester	161	366					
Phebus, Bill	111	364	442					Poindexter, R.C.	34	366					
Pheister, Paul	90	364						Poitras, Bob	197	366					
Phelan, ---	5	364						Pokorny, Joe	189	193	195	366			
Phelan, Jim	184	187	364					Poland, Bobby	179	366					
Phelps, Ray	176	364						Poland, Eugene	17	20	22	24	366		
Phillips, ---	24	364						Poland, P.	22	366					
Phillips, Bubba	108	109	364	442				Polivka, Ken	171	174	366	442			
Phillips, Dave	67	364						Polk, Roy	181	183	366				
Phillips, Dick	194	195	364					Pollack, Leonard	98	113	114	366			
Phillips, Gene	167	364						Pollard, Gene	102	111	138	366			
Phillips, John	206	207						Pollock, Stan	161	366					
Phillips, Otis	171	364						Polly, Henry	54	366					
Phillips, Randolph	120	123	364					Pompelia, Augie	147	167	366				
Phillips, Ray	77	86	364					Pompelia, Gene	85	366					
Phillips, Sam	150	364						Pomykala, Jim	121	366					
Phillips, Taylor	132	134	135	142	143	144	208	364	Ponce, Catarino	155	366					
	442							Pond, ---	22	24	25	366			
Philpott, Carey	91	118	364					Pontarelli, Lee	189	366					
Pickel, Oliver	55	56	57	364				Ponte, Orville	194	366					
Pickering, Chris	41	364						Poole, ---	4	5	366				
Pickett, ---	24	364						Poole, Benny	161	366					
Pickett, Fred	41	42	364					Poole, Buddy	102	366					
Picklesimer, ---	38	364						Poole, Edward	16	18					
Pidcock, F.R. Jr.	76	86	120					Poole, Eva B.	86						
Piepho, Harry	5	364						Poole, J.R.	86	128					
Pierce, ---	6	7	364					Poole, Jim	76	86	116	133	134	366	442
Pierce, Dick	189							Poole, Phil S.	86						
Pierce, Jerome	150	153	161	364				Poole, Ralph	73	74	366				
Pierce, Pete	56	364						Pope, Ashley	19	20	21	22	367		
Pierotti, Gerald	128							Pope, C.	72	367					
Pierre, Bill	13	14	22	24	38	364		Pope, Jim	152	367					
Pierro, Bill	86	364	442					Popovich, Charles	91	94	367				
Pierson, Argyle	51	55	56	57	364			Poppell, Jack	155	160	163	367			
Piet, Ernie	120	364						Popwell, Julius	150	367					
Pietrewicz, Alex	197	199	364					Porco, Frank	90	367					
Pignatano, Joe	122	364	442					Porreca, Frank	85	88	367				
Pilgrim, Arvie	167	168	173	182	183	207	365	Porter, Bill	47	367					
Pillar, Bill	150	365						Porterfield, Lee	73	367					
Pillow, Clarence	161	365						Portomene, Angelo	145	147	367				
Pine, Ken	58	365						Posey, ---	4	34	367				
Pinion, Willis	146	365						Posey, Walt	73	367					

Georgia Class-D Minor League Baseball Encyclopedia

Name				
Potocnik, Elmer	94	367		
Potts, A.L.	81	90	103	116
Potts, Cliff	51	367		
Poulas, Nick	90	367		
Poulson, Gary	185	367		
Pound, O.C.	99	111	125	
Pounds, J.P.	29	367		
Pounds, Roy	120	123	367	
Poupore, Bernard	194	367		
Powell, ---	30	367		
Powell, Charles O.	59			
Powell, Chester	189	367		
Powell, Cliff	152	367		
Powell, Duane	166	367		
Powell, Franklin	59			
Powell, Hollis	172	182	367	
Powell, Jack	122	367		
Powell, Jim	190	367		
Powell, Joe	142	367		
Powell, John	89	367		
Powell, Kelly	180	367		
Powell, O.T. "Harry"	5	367		
Powell, Quincie	155	367		
Powell, W.J.	48	51		
Powell, W.L.	91			
Powers, ---	9	16	29	367
Powers, Fred	103	368		
Powers, George	171	368		
Powers, John	104	105	368	442
Powers, Ollie	182	368		
Powers, Tom	82	368		
Prados, Bob	99	368		
Prappas, Jim	129	130	368	
Pratt, ---	6	13	16	368
Pratt, Art	146	368		
Pratt, Frank	24	27	368	442
Pratt, George	140	141	368	
Pratt, Tom	71	368		
Pray, Don	172	179	368	
Predovich, Walt	192	368		
Prescott, Andy	176	368		
Prescott, Howard	186	368		
Pressley, Omer	27	368		
Prezina, John	47	368		
Price, ---	16	17	18	368
Price, Charles	147	157	177	185	368
Price, Jake	50	52	368	
Price, Lou	112	368		
Price, Nathan	190	368		
Price, Paul	189	368		
Price, Ron	162	368		
Pride, Jude	67	368		
Priede, Nilo	171	368		
Prince, ---	28	368		
Prince, Bill	44	368		
Prince, Howard	99	100	368	
Prince, Jim	58	368		
Prince, Ralph	171	368		
Pritchett, Doug	71	368		
Probitsky, Burke	176	178	369	
Probst, ---	24	369		
Procopio, Andrew	138	369		
Proctor, ---	27	369		
Proctor, Louis	9	11	369	
Proctor, Tom	160	170	176	369	448
Prozeralik, Nick	185	369		
Pruett, John	91	369		
Pruett, Milton	99	100	369	
Pruitt, ---	37	39	369	
Pruitt, Clyde A.	72	82	91	
Pryor, Shapard	162	369		
Przeworski, Ted	90	93	369	

Name							
Puckett, Vearel	47	49	369				
Puent, Larry	75	369					
Puffer, Gerald	99	118	130	369			
Pugh, Earl	59	369					
Pugh, Gordon	34	38	39	204	369		
Pulcini, John	87	369					
Pulliam, J.C.	27	369					
Punyko, Art	116	369					
Purcell, E.E.	29	369					
Purcell, George	54	369					
Purcey, Walt	51	54	56	58	61	207	208	369
Purdy, John	78	369					
Purnhage, William G.	76						
Puro, Ray	120	369					
Putnam, Basil	71	369					
Puttman, Frank	40	41	42	369			
Pyle, George	173	369					
Quackenbush, Mark	44	369					
Quartuci, Ray	133	369					
Quatro, Leo	175	176	178	369			
Quattrini, Rino	134	135	369				
Quattrone, Joe	121	122	369				
Query, Wray	35	36	38	369			
Quick, Hal	44	47	49	50	52	370	442
Quick, John	72	370					
Quigley, Jim	173	370					
Quilici, Gabe	121	123	370				
Quimby, Chuck	147	148	209	370			
Quinlan, Bud	77	370					
Quinn, Don	146	154	158	159	176	209	370
Quinn, Lew	43	44	47	207	370		
Quinn, Paul	150	370					
Raburn, Charley	20	21	22	24	25	370	
Rac, Russell	106	109	110	207	370		
Rackley, Marv	64	65	370	442			
Rada, Roger	141	370					
Radak, Dudley	110						
Radney, Joe	59	61	63	65	68	69	70	370
Rados, Frank	60	370					
Radzevich, Ed	181	370					
Raeburn, John	157	370					
Raehse, Bill	90	370					
Rafferty, ---	7	16	17	370			
Ragan, H.R.	111	125					
Ragsdale, Bob	9	10	11	370			
Ragsdale, Joe	62	370					
Raines, Bill	111	370					
Rainwater, Dewey	31	34	35	36	370		
Raisch, Charles	171	370					
Raisch, Harry	94	370					
Rakestraw, Don	173	370					
Raley, Frank	172						
Rambert, Pep	137	139	370	442			
Ramburger, ---	4	370					
Ramey, Jerry	171	370					
Ramirez, Carlos	190	370					
Ramont, Dick	190	370					
Ramont, Terry	193	371					
Rampola, Joe	47	49	50	52	54	371	
Ramsey, ---	5	30	34	371			
Ramsey, Bill	68	371	442				
Ramsey, Don	67	371					
Ramsey, Frank	170	174	371				
Ramsey, Paul	133	371					
Ramsey, Silas	142	143	151	371			
Rancher, Dan	91						
Rand, Bob	149	153	371				
Randall, Elmer	9	204	371				
Randle, Fred	151	152	153	371			

Georgia Class-D Minor League Baseball Encyclopedia

Name								
Randolph, Harry	124	126	371					
Rapert, Howard	146	371						
Raphael, Mark	141	371						
Rasch, Marvin	67	69	371					
Raulerson, Harry	78	96	97	108	109	122	134	135
	136	207	208	371	448			
Rauseo, Mike	98	100	113	142	143	371		
Rautzhan, Bill	76	79	371					
Rawlings, Vern	85	371						
Ray, ---	34	37	371					
Ray, George	172	371						
Ray, Jere	198	199	371					
Ray, Macon	128							
Ray, Matt	189	371						
Ray, Stan	73	111	371					
Ray, Tom	91	104	105	371				
Reach, Cliff	89	102	116	117	371			
Ready, Charlie	146	156	158	371				
Ready, Ken	189	371						
Reagan, ---	5							
Reagan, Kid	7	8	13	19	22	372		
Reagin, Bill	155	156	372					
Reale, John	106	372						
Reardon, Joseph F.	94	120						
Reardon, Joseph R.	106							
Reardon, Robert L.	130							
Rechichar, Adrian	161	163	164	372				
Recipko, Bill	155	372						
Reckelhoff, Bob	156	163	372					
Rector, Charles N.	119							
Recurt, Luis	180	372						
Rediger, Glenn	177	178	372					
Reed, ---	34	372						
Reed, Bob	80	82	372					
Reed, Jack	176	372						
Reed, Jim	71	372						
Reed, Tommy	51	372						
Reeder, Clyde	55	56	372					
Reehoff, Ron	166	372						
Rees, Ernest	103	122	372					
Rees, Kenneth J.	91							
Reese, Aaron	152	372						
Reese, Charles	9	372						
Reese, Eddie	34	37	38	39	71	204	372	
Reese, Joe	77	78	99	372				
Reese, Red	27	372						
Reese, Rich	198	199	372	442				
Reeser, Eddie	63	372						
Reeves, ---	38	372						
Reeves, Harold	94	126	157	372				
Reeves, Herb	117	125	134	142	143	167	372	
Reeves, Philip	149							
Reff, Nick R.	144							
Regan, Bill	80	81	372					
Regan, Jim	107	109	372					
Regan, John	62	372						
Reggio, Jimmy	58	373						
Register, ---	27	29	373					
Reichelt, Charles	47	373						
Reichert, Arnold	78	373						
Reichert, Paul	78	373						
Reichert, Stan	134	138	373					
Reid, Bob	145	146	148	155	158	167	209	373
Reid, Harold	145	373						
Reid, Jim	94	373						
Reid, Russ	91	373						
Reid, Warren	68	373						
Reider, Dave	176	177	373					
Reidy, Jack	11	12	16	17	373			
Reilly, ---	16	18	373					
Reilly, Ed	75	373						
Reilly, Lou	163	373						
Reiman, Ken	180	373						
Reime, Bob	141	373						
Reimer, John	185	373						
Reinagle, Ed	104	373						
Reinecke, Wally	9	10	12	373	442			
Reis, ---	29	373						
Reiser, Pete	171	172	373	442				
Reiter, Jim	94	373						
Reliford, Joe	145	146	373					
Rellihan, Jerry	142	373						
Rencher, D.M.	117							
Rendlesham, Jerry	121	373						
Renko, Harry	62	373						
Rentz, Irv	94	107	373					
Resavy, George	185	373						
Ressel, Paul	142	373						
Restaino, Emil	108	109	206	373				
Restic, Joe	85	373						
Rettie, Joe	90	373						
Retzer, Ken	162	163	164	374	442			
Reveira, Frank	186	187	374					
Revels, Bill	89	90	374					
Rey, Emil	64	65	68	69	78	79	87	88
	98	99	100	111	114	124	127	137
	139	145	148	209	374			
Reynolds, ---	5	374						
Reynolds, Bob	85	162	374					
Reynolds, Jesse	17	374						
Reynolds, Wade	13	14	16	17	22	374		
Rhawn, Bobby	50	54	374	442				
Rhodes, Herb	72	95	107	374				
Rhodes, Hilman	137	139	374					
Rhyne, Ken	75	76	78	79	86	87	95	96
	97	107	134	206	207	374		
Rhyne, Marvel	82	374						
Rice, ---	9	374						
Rice, Bob	40	42	43	45	47	49	374	442
Rice, Harry	54	374	442					
Rice, L.H.	72							
Rice, Robert T.	77							
Rice, Rollie	140	143	179	374	448			
Rice, Ron	167	374						
Rich, ---	27	30	374					
Rich, Benny	155	166	180	183	208	374		
Richards, ---	5	374						
Richards, Babe	29	374						
Richards, J.A.	9	20	374					
Richards, Paul	201							
Richardson, ---	5	374						
Richardson, Clarence	124	125	127	128	374			
Richardson, Gordie	188	192	195	374	442			
Richardson, Hugh	113	375						
Richardson, Lew	150	375						
Richardson, Marty	198	199	375					
Richardson, Tom	180	375						
Richbourg, Lance	63	375	442					
Richter, Phil	157	375						
Rickard, ---	19	375						
Ricketson, Don	100	113	114	137	157	375		
Rickey, Branch	58							
Rickey, Branch Jr.	64	77	108	121	133	140	149	160
	170	179						
Ricks, Lloyd	29	375						
Riddle, Chase	179	182	183	188	190	191	206	207
	375							
Riddle, Jim	82	117	375					
Ridenour, Roy	102	375						
Ridgeway, Charlie	98	99	100	112	113	125	126	127
	128	137	138	139	145	146	147	148
	150	153	208	209	375			
Ridings, Jack	48	51	52	375				
Ridley, ---	24	25	375					

Name								Name							
Riepple, Jim	151	375						Robison, Vince	130	377					
Riesgo, Arnold	146	148	155	166	375			Rochelli, Lou	55	56	95	96	97	377	443
Rigdon, Bill	117	119	130	375				Rockett, Grady L. "Pete"	85	94					
Rigell, Al	117	129						Rodd, Don	98	100	101	377			
Riggins, ---	17	18	375					Roddenberry, Warren	192	196	377				
Riggs, ---	20	375						Rodgers, ---	24	377					
Riggs, Arthur	12	375						Rodriguez, Angel	171	377					
Riggs, Larry	185	375						Rodriguez, Charles	125	129	147	377			
Rikard, Bob	170	173	375					Rodriguez, Newton	197	378					
Rikard, Denver	91	104	105	132	135	136	140	143	Roe, ---	67	378				
	144	163	206	375				Roe, H.J.	32	378					
Riles, Stewart	121	126	375					Roede, Lou	64	65	66	378			
Riley, ---	107	375						Roedel, Bob	90	378					
Riley, B.	13	375						Roesler, Ken	194	378					
Riley, Bob	85	376						Roettger, Harold G.	43	77	86	95	133	140	149	160
Riley, Leonard	67	375							170						
Riley, Pat	50	52	54	56	60	63	65	376	Rogers, Bill	62	63	378			
Rinaldi, Charles	102	376						Rogers, Ernest	130	145	154	378			
Rinker, Bob	102	104	376	443				Rogers, Francis	134	378					
Riolo, Joe	77	376						Rogers, Jim	58	378					
Rios, Felix	58	60	376					Rogers, Lou	64	378					
Ris, Harry	54	376						Rogers, Lynn	151	378					
Rist, Ray	55	56	59	376				Rogers, Marion	118	378					
Ritch, Dr. T.G.	126							Rogers, Walt	78	79	378				
Ritchie, Ed	172	376						Rohe, George	9	204	378	443			
Ritter, Art	198	376						Rohrbaugh, Glenn	99	378					
Rivenbark, William D.	55	60	78	87	96	108	134		Rohs, Norm	149	378				
Rivera, Florencio	137	376						Roig, Tony	111	117	118	378	443		
Rivera, Luis	125	376						Rolf, ---	5	378					
Rivero, Freddy	201	376						Rolfe, Robert	95						
Rivers, Joe	142	376						Rolfs, Frank	90	92	378				
Rixey, Ben	86	376						Rollo, Charles	72	378					
Rizzetta, Anthony	80	82	376					Roman, Carl	90	378					
Roberts, ---	9	376						Rombach, Bob	198	201	202	378			
Roberts, Art	167	376						Romello, Mike	67	76	79	378			
Roberts, Bob	150	181	376					Romeo, John	157	378					
Roberts, Charles	101							Romeo, Mike	197	200	378				
Roberts, Glenn	125	376						Rommel, John	146	378					
Roberts, Harry	154	188						Rooks, Gerald	180	378					
Roberts, Howard	43	376						Roop, Harvey	107	109	378				
Roberts, Jim	75	376						Roop, M.C.	115						
Roberts, John	182	376						Rosa, Charles	160	378					
Roberts, Kelvin	162	163	164	376				Rose, Bob	99	100	378				
Roberts, Marv	99	376						Rose, Hubert	121	122	206	378			
Roberts, Ray	59	107	376					Rose, Russ	78	378					
Roberts, Red	24	25	27	71	81	82	84	89	Rose, Wallace	197	378				
	90	91	93	102	115	376	443		Rosett, Jack	44	379				
Roberts, Tom	142	151	376					Rospond, Walt	44	45	46	379			
Roberts, Wayne	198	376						Ross, Jerome	89	379					
Robertson, ---	22	24	25	26	27	376		Ross, Kent	201	379					
Robertson, Bill	170	173	174	185	377			Ross, Ron	194	379					
Robertson, Everett	51	377						Rossi, Mike	110	113	114	138	209	210	379
Robertson, J.L. Jr.	160							Rossi, Ron	189	190	191	379			
Robertson, James	181							Roth, Dick	165						
Robertson, Preston	82	377						Roth, Edward R.	120	132	140				
Robertson, Sam	111	113	209	377				Roth, Edward W.	75	85	106				
Robinett, Ken	142	143	207	377				Roth, Jac	90	118	130	379			
Robinette, Jimmie	150	165	377					Roth, Richard A.	132	140	149				
Robinson, ---	9	12	13	34	377			Roth, V.	7	8	14	379			
Robinson, Ben	149	155	377					Rothgeb, John	180	379					
Robinson, Bill	197	202	203	377	443			Rothrock, Jack	95	379	443				
Robinson, Don	142	151	162	172	181	377		Rotondi, Lou	134	379					
Robinson, Eddie	55	56	60	61	207	377	443	Rouse, Bill	198	379				
Robinson, Everett	194	377						Rouse, John	194	379					
Robinson, Harold	67	68	377					Rovai, Rudy	157	379					
Robinson, Jim	172	377						Rowe, ---	73	379					
Robinson, Orem	78	87	377					Rowe, Bob	31	379					
Robinson, Sammie	201	377						Rowe, Edgar	120	379					
Robinson, Tom	68	73	377					Rowe, Joe	197	379					
Robinson, Wilbur	44	48	49	377				Rowe, John	47	50	52	379			
Robison, Ron	172	377						Rowell, Bama	47	379	443				
Robison, Roy	71	377						Rowzee, Bob	142	163	379				

Georgia Class-D Minor League Baseball Encyclopedia

Name								
Roxie, ---	9	379						
Royal, Ellie	182	190						
Royal, Julian	111	379						
Royce, Gordon	161	379						
Royer, Charles	146	379						
Ruark, Jim	99	100	112	138	146	155	379	
Ruark, Parnell	112	113	124	125	127	128	137	138
	139	142	143	155	156	157	158	167
	208	209	379					
Ruck, Martin	201	379						
Rucker, ---	71	380						
Rucker, Bill	60	102	115	205	380			
Rucker, Bob	130	131	380					
Ruddle, Ed	48	380						
Rudolph Don	126	127	209	210	136	138	139	380
	443							
Rudolph, Tom	201	202	380					
Rufer, Rudy	181	189	190	191	193	194	380	443
Ruggerio, Pat	180	380						
Ruggles, Raymond	185	380						
Rullo, Joe	150	380	443					
Rumfield, Lyn	54	56	380					
Ruminski, Frank	68	380						
Rummans, Elmer	57	60	61	380				
Runyan, Dick	176	380						
Rushing, ---	16	380						
Russell, ---	22	24	25	380				
Russell, Bing	90	102	380					
Russell, Dave	161	172	380					
Russell, Dick	116	380						
Russell, Ed	157	380						
Russell, Ken	188	380						
Russell, Mrs. B.C.	115	129						
Russell, Robert	115	129						
Russo, Anthony	185	380						
Russo, Manuel	45	63	380					
Rustin, Ted	165	168	210	380				
Ruth, Babe	40							
Rutledge, Bob	58	380						
Rutter, Harry	173	380						
Ryan, Bob	59	63	380					
Ryan, Dean	194	380						
Ryan, Dick	112	114	380					
Ryan, Fred	120	122	123	134	380			
Ryan, Jim	82	380						
Ryan, Tom	193	381						
Ryckman, Bill	162	182	183	381				
Ryder, John	138	381						
Ryder, Paul	41	42	381					
Sabine, Frank	85	381						
Sacchetti, Charles	167	381						
Sadowski, Bob	176	178	381	443				
Saffer, Les	117	381						
Sager, Don	176	186	187	381				
Saigh, Fred M. Jr.	94	106	120	132	140			
Sala, Fred	124	126	381					
Salas, Bienvenido	151	381						
Salazar, Enrique	160	161	163	381				
Salcido, Carlos	170	172	381					
Salerno, Lou	129	130	381					
Salerno, Pasquale	142	143	172	381				
Sallis, Ed	133	381						
Salmonson, Lee	175	381						
Salter, Desmond	68	111	381					
Salter, Fred	172	381						
Salzman, Cy	59	381						
Samaklis, Charles	64	65	381					
Sammons, ---	112	381						
Sample, ---	17	381						
Sampson, Mark	181	381						
Samson, Charles	78	381						
Samuel, Manuel	197	198	199	381				
Sanchez, Armando	129	130	134	137	381			
Sanchez, Jerry	157	381						
Sanders, ---	24	31	32	381				
Sanders, Al	126	160	381					
Sanders, Bob	141	382						
Sanders, Henry	156	381						
Sanders, Lou	75	79	90	102	104	129	131	382
Sanders, War	11	382	443					
Sanderson, Joe	117							
Sanderson, R.M.	126	138						
Sanford, ---	34	382						
Sanford, Allen	11	20	21	22	382			
Sanford, Jack	76	79	85	107	109	382	443	
Sangalli, Frank	161	382						
Sanoers, Lester R.	80							
Sanson, Dick	163	382						
Sansosti, Frank	41	45	48	49	382			
Santmire, Glenn	197	382						
Santoli, Carmen	181	382						
Santomauro, Joe	113	382						
Saporito, John	156	157	382					
Sappenfield, Colon	34	37	39	382				
Sappenfield, Roger	134	135	382					
Sappington, Thomas J.	155							
Sardoff, Marty	150	382						
Sargent, ---	29	382						
Sarmer, Joe	182	185	382					
Sarmiento, Antonio	137	140	142	143	144	145	149	151
	159	162	164	172	174	177	207	208
	382							
Sarno, Anthony	154	382						
Sarros, Jim	76	382						
Sarver, Dan	186	187	382					
Sasek, Dick	189	382						
Sassano, Bob	137	382						
Sasse, ---	64	382						
Satkowiak, Phil	120	382						
Satterfield, Arnold	130	382						
Satterfield, Ben	67	383						
Satterfield, Cicero	71	73	382					
Satterfield, Ralph	67	72	74	383				
Sauerbrun, Kip	41	42	59	63	64	68	69	208
	383							
Savage, Bill	89	90	383					
Savage, Cliff	120	123	383					
Savage, John	78	383						
Savant, Joe	51	52	383					
Savarese, Al	115	117	118	383				
Saverine, Chuck	120	383						
Sawyer, ---	5	383						
Sawyer, Roger	141	144	383					
Saye, Charles	186	383						
Sayle, Bob	150	383						
Sbashnig, Pete	122	138	383					
Scala, Bob	141	145	147	383				
Scalici, Anthony	166	383						
Scalisi, Bob	112	125	127	210	383			
Scannelli, Frank	172	383						
Scarborough, C.I.	30	33						
Scariato, Anthony	182	383						
Scarth, Jim	150	383						
Scercy, John	181	184	383					
Schaeffer, Bernard	77	383						
Schaffer, Bob	160	164	383					
Schaffer, Rudie	94	107						
Schaive, Johnny	142	383	443					
Schall, Gene	160	383						
Schamburg, Ted	180	383						
Schammel, George	176	383						
Scheel, Rolf	151	383						
Scheffing, Bob	43	45	46	383	443	447		
Scheidt, Ray	141	143	207	383				

Georgia Class-D Minor League Baseball Encyclopedia

Name							
Scheidts, Ed	85	383					
Schellhouse, Fred	63	383					
Schepner, Joe	31	383	443				
Scherer, Leon	41	42	207	384			
Schiavo, Bill	120	384					
Schieffer, John	170	174	384				
Schindler, Al	120	384					
Schivone, Ralph	73	384					
Schlensker, Albert H.	121						
Schlett, Bob	173	384					
Schmidhausler, Vern	75	384					
Schmidt, ---	28	30	384				
Schmidt, Don	59	384					
Schmidt, Freddy	54	57	384	443			
Schmidt, Haven	165	175	177	178	384		
Schmidt, Joe	103	104	105	116	117	118	119	204	384
Schmidt, Kermit	99	101	112	114	125	127	137	210	384
Schmitt, Fred	116	118	384				
Schmitz, John	194	384					
Schneider, Ed	150	384					
Schnell, Fred	142	384					
Schoendienst, Elmer	75	85	88	384			
Schoendienst, Red	67	384	443	447			
Schroeder, A.L.	27	29	384				
Schroeder, Al	96	384					
Schrom, Sam	155	384					
Schubele, Bruce	130						
Schuck, Charles	141	145	384				
Schuessler, Zach	72	82	83	89	384		
Schuler, Ron	198	384					
Schulte, Bob	141						
Schulte, J.	29	384					
Schulte, Len	43	47	384	443			
Schultis, Pete	166	384					
Schultz, ---	12	384					
Schultz, Dick	151	160					
Schultz, Glen	157	384					
Schultz, Hal	55	59	60	61	206	385	
Schultz, Herb	129	385					
Schultz, Jack	157	385					
Schultz, Joe	43	47	385	443	447		
Schultz, Ken	198	385					
Schultz, Otto	117	385					
Schultz, Stan	194	385					
Schulze, Ed	9	385					
Schuman, ---	13	14	385				
Schurrer, Roland	167	385					
Schuyler, ---	6	8	13				
Schwab, Bob	82	385					
Schwartz, ---	29	385					
Schwartz, B.	14	17	385				
Schwartz, Bill	9	10	11	29	385	443	
Schwartz, F.	7	17	385				
Schypinski, Jerry	141	143	144	385	444		
Scobbins, ---	71	385					
Scollard, John	141	385					
Scotese, Bob	133	385					
Scott, Bill	85	385					
Scott, Bob	176	385					
Scott, Dick	181	183	385	444			
Scott, Frank	192						
Scott, George	181	189	191	385			
Scott, I.J.	82						
Scott, Jim	72	385					
Scott, LeGrant	78	87	88	94	385	444	
Scott, O.E.	63						
Scott, Siebert	189	191	385				
Scott, Trammel	5	385					
Scott, Vic	130	131	385				
Scranton, Dave	173	174	182	183	190	191	386
Screen, Jim	99	100	386				
Scriptjack, Ray	157	386					
Scroggs, John	159	163	164	173	182	386	
Seagrave, DeMont	180	181	386				
Seagraves, ---	37	386					
Seal, Bill	102	104	105	124	125	126	386
Seaman, Al	117	386					
Seaman, Bob	156	386					
Seaone, Manuel	155	386					
Seat, Clayton	59	61	386				
Secoli, Frank	107	386					
Sedlack, Bob	167	172	174	208	386		
Seecs, Henry	181	386					
Seegmiller, Garth	197	198	386				
Seeman, John	186	386					
Seghi, Phil	86	386					
Seidel, Ray	87	96	97	207	208	386	
Seiferlein, Don	190	386					
Seigfried, ---	6	13	14	15	386		
Seigler, Bill	71						
Seiler, Dan	68	386					
Selbee, Bill	85	386					
Sellars, A.D.	133	386					
Sellergren, Willard	67	386					
Selley, ---	31	386					
Sells, Albert	17	27	29	386			
Selph, ---	11	16	22	386			
Selph, Charles	194	386					
Sembera, Carroll	198	386	444				
Semler, Marion	55	386					
Semonik, Mike	193	387					
Sengstock, Wayne	125	138	387				
Senkowitz, John	162	387					
Senn, Yancy	34	35	387				
Senn, Yancy Jr.	205						
Serafini, Irv	170	185	387				
Serbin, Cliff	147	387					
Sermania, Vince	141	146	387				
Serners, Yorkey	59	63	387				
Server, Wallace	163	387					
Sessions, Pete	29	387					
Settles, Wolf	59	61	387				
Severson, Don	194	387					
Sevier, John	167	387					
Sewell, ---	20	387					
Sewell, Bill	102	104					
Sewell, Guy	41	44	387				
Sewell, Joe	180	387					
Seymour, George	58	387					
Seymour, Tex	120	387					
Sezna, Tom	86	87	95	96	387		
Shaddix, Willard	111	126	387				
Shaefer, P.L.	102	115					
Shaffer, Don	132	134	142	144	387		
Shaffer, Frank	185	387					
Shalata, Bill	176	177	185	387			
Shank, Doug	63	387					
Shank, Reed	180						
Shanle, Del	111	387					
Shannon, ---	19	387					
Shannon, Jack	63						
Shannon, Mike	192	194	196	387	444		
Shannon, Wally	140	143	144	387	444		
Shapiro, Al	77	387					
Shapiro, Bob	141	142	387				
Sharlinsky, L.	55	388					
Sharp, ---	12	388					
Sharp, Bill	73	388					
Sharp, Hubert	197	202	388				
Sharp, Irv	175	178	388				
Sharpe, ---	31	33	388				
Sharpe, Corwin	166	388					

Georgia Class-D Minor League Baseball Encyclopedia

Name								
Sharpless, Seaborne	85	388	448					
Shartzer, Phil	161	164	388					
Shaw, Bennie	95	388						
Shaw, Dr. L.O.	162	172						
Shaw, Floyd	73	74	205	388				
Shaw, H.L.	22	23	388					
Shaw, Jim	99	388						
Shaw, Pop	27	29	388					
Shaw, Steve	167	388						
Shawkey, Bob	107	388	444	447				
Shawver, Bob	146	147	148	209	388			
Shea, Dave	150	152	388					
Shean, ---	12	388						
Sheeks, Bill	156	388						
Sheffield, Frank	85	94	388					
Sheldon, Bill	150	388						
Sheldon, Dick	190	191	388					
Shelley, Bill	188	388						
Shellnut, Wayne	188	388						
Shelton, Jim	176	388						
Sheppard, ---	9	10	11	17	388			
Sheppard, Ken	182	183	208	388				
Sherba, Elmer	156	388						
Sherman, Ed	126	127	137	138	209	210	388	
Shifflett, Harry	142	388						
Shiffner, Ray	150	388						
Shiles, Harold	108	109	206	388				
Shima, Tom	193	195	388					
Shimko, Bob	133	389						
Shinault, Ginger	19	389	444					
Shinnick, Dick	170	389						
Shipley, Jack	31	32	34	35	37	38	39	204
	389							
Shipley, Joe	157	389	444					
Shipp, J.H.	44							
Shires, Bill	166	389						
Shirley, ---	12	389						
Shirley, Jim	102	104	116	389				
Shirley, Ralph	112	389						
Shively, Jim	189	389						
Shiver, Floyd	149	389						
Shivers, ---	71	389						
Shoemake, Benton	103	104	389					
Shoemake, Claude	72	73	74	82	83	84	116	130
	131	204	389					
Sholtzs, ---	64	389						
Shosty, Bob	189	194	389					
Showers, ---	22	389						
Shuck, Larry	197	389						
Shultis, Pete	179	188	191	389				
Shumaker, Bob	63	389						
Shuman, ---	7	16	389					
Shumate, Andy	186	187	389					
Shuryn, Bill	156	389						
Shuster, Harold	145	147	389					
Sides, Bill	120	133	389					
Sidle, Frank	44	45	389					
Sidwell, ---	38	39	389					
Siebert, Jim	172	389						
Siebold, John	176	389						
Siefert, ---	6							
Siegfield, ---	73	389						
Siemasz, Nick	134	389						
Sierra, Andrew	60	390						
Siff, Alan	146	155	390					
Sigmon, Jesse	9	10	11	19	21	22	24	25
	390							
Sigmon, Joe	50	390						
Sikes, ---	17	18	390					
Sikes, Don	27	29	40	390				
Silbersack, Bob	186	390						
Silky, Harold	68	69	390					
Silva, Gil	160	390						
Silva, Tom	186	390						
Silver, Charles	44	390						
Silverman, Jerome	90	100	113	114	126	209	390	
Simcich, John	193	194	195	390				
Simmons, ---	162	390						
Simmons, Dick	142	390						
Simmons, Jack	117	390						
Simmons, Paul	99	100	111	390				
Simmons, Roy	134	390						
Simms, Charles	120	390						
Simon, Dewey	29	30	390					
Simon, Jerry	76	111	113	114	126	210	390	
Simonec, Reuben	77	390						
Simonian, Joe	137	390						
Simpson, Charles	85	88	390					
Simpson, Cliff	85	88	390					
Simpson, Warren	181	390						
Sims, Dewey	100	117	390					
Sims, Harold	186	187	390					
Sims, Joe	54	390						
Sinay, Andy	51	390						
Siner, ---	4	390						
Singer, George	122	391						
Singer, Hal	59	63	391					
Singletary, Lee	77							
Singleton, C.W.	86	95						
Singleton, Charles	64							
Singleton, Joe	95	107	391					
Singley, Hulen	81	391						
Sinnott, John	72	99	391					
Sinquefield, Ben	146	150	153	391				
Sinquefield, Roy	82	83	391					
Siragusa, Reano	44	47	391					
Sirocki, Frank S.	89							
Sirota, Alex	182	391						
Sirrine, Ernest	129	391						
Sisco, Ed	126	391						
Sisler, George	58	62	67	391				
Sisolak, Fred	141	143	170	173	180	182	183	391
Sisson, H.M.	86	95	108	121	162	172	181	190
	198	201						
Sizemore, Paul	184	391						
Skaggs, Earl	68	391						
Skalski, Chester	82	391						
Skelton, ---	17	391						
Skelton, Bob	140	149	391					
Skidgel, Leon	55	391						
Skinner, Camp	27	28	391	444				
Slaboszewski, Vince	175	391						
Slack, Eugene	112	126	134					
Slater, ---	12	20	391					
Slaughter, Frank	186	187	391					
Slezak, Francis	172	181	391					
Slike, Max B.	149	391						
Slivnik, Mike	202	391						
Slivocka, Ray	133	391						
Sloan, ---	17	18	391					
Sloan, George	81	391						
Sloan, Mike	200	202	391					
Slocumb, John I. Jr. "Si"	137							
Slocumb, John L. Jr. "Si"	111							
Smalley, Charles	125	127	128	209	210	391		
Smart, Charles	86	99	100	392				
Smathers, Fred	151	392						
Smeltzer, Charles	72	84	392					
Smeraglia, Anthony	73	392						
Smilee, Gary	194	392						
Smiley, Charles	162	186	187	392				
Smith, ---	7	8	11	12	16	20	24	81
	204	392						
Smith, A.	5	392						

Georgia Class-D Minor League Baseball Encyclopedia

Name									Name							
Smith, Andy	76	167	392						Snyder, Harry	41	394					
Smith, Arnie	181	392							Snyder, Paul	86	88	394				
Smith, Artis	47	392							Snyder, Ralph	63	394					
Smith, B.	56	392							Snyder, Richard A.	196						
Smith, Bill	152	394							Snyder, Ron	86	395					
Smith, Bob	58	120	121	394					Sobor, ---	5	395					
Smith, C.	5	392							Socha, George	118	395					
Smith, C.H.	34	35	392						Sockman, Ron	189	190	191	395			
Smith, Charles	172	180	392						Sodupe, Francisco	138	395					
Smith, Dave	172	392							Sofia, Mike	78	395					
Smith, Del	59	63	64	392					Sohni, ---	5	395					
Smith, Dennis	200	392							Soja, Tom	156	395					
Smith, Dick	121	122	123	193	194	195	207	394	Solberg, Herb	160	395					
	444								Solt, Gene	100	115	116	118	119	204	395
Smith, Earl	150	154	177	393					Somers, W. Coite	147						
Smith, Ed	68	392							Sommer, Bill	117	118	395				
Smith, Frank	134	135	152	392					Sorrell, Jesse	34	395					
Smith, Fred	170	173	392						Sorrells, ---	5	395					
Smith, Garry	180	392							Sorrentino, John	185	187	395				
Smith, Gene	157	392							Sosebee, Jim	138	139	146	147	156	157	158	159
Smith, George	120	132	171	186	187	392				177	208	395				
Smith, Gil	87	96	99	393					Sosmer, Bernard	194	395					
Smith, Godfrey	59	63							Souillard, Lou	179	182	183	190	395		
Smith, H.T.	11	20	22	24	35	38	393		Soumma, Gene	107	109	110	395			
Smith, Hal	106	393	444						Souter, George	71	395					
Smith, Harold	85	192	393						South, ---	24	395					
Smith, Howard	58	393							Southard, Ken	141	395					
Smith, J.	29	30	393						Soward, Jim	34	35	36	37	38	395	
Smith, J.W.	112	393							Sowell, Bill	108	116	121	395			
Smith, Jack	172	393	444						Sowell, Julian	64	65	395				
Smith, James W.	47	50							Sowers, Walt	125	126	208	395			
Smith, Jesse	47	393							Sowins, Ray	86	87	106	109	395		
Smith, Jim	78	100	113	114	126	128	137	139	Spain, Hank	94	107	120	395	448		
	165	188	208	209	393				Spain, Thomas	91						
Smith, Joe	82	393							Spamer, Bill	117	395					
Smith, John	67	393							Spampinato, Tom	172	177	395				
Smith, John R.	182	190							Sparacino, Frank	122	395					
Smith, Julius	200	393							Sparks, Ferrell	162	396					
Smith, Ken	117	118	393						Sparks, Hugh	63	396					
Smith, Larry	177	393							Sparks, Jimmy	117	118	119	205	396		
Smith, Leo	190	393							Sparks, Oliverio	201	203	396				
Smith, Leroy	201	393							Spates, Larcus	200	202	396				
Smith, Luther	73	393							Spaugh, ---	7	16	18	396			
Smith, M.M.	111								Spaziano, Al	77	396					
Smith, Marion	108	393							Spears, Jasper	108	396					
Smith, Max	150	156	393						Spence, Ed	189	396					
Smith, Mike	146	393							Spence, Steve	152	396					
Smith, Morton	108	109	152	393					Spencer, ---	5	396					
Smith, Norm	47	51	58	63	207	393			Spencer, Bill	71	396					
Smith, P.	34	35	393						Spencer, Dave	80	396					
Smith, Paul	41	44	45	46	47	49	51	52	Spencer, Roosevelt	200	396					
	53	55	56	57	121	122	123	173	Spier, Bob	169	172	396				
	206	394							Spiezio, Ed	200	396	444				
Smith, Red	27	394							Spikes, Oliver	44	45	46	396			
Smith, Reuben	71	394							Spilman, Harry	146	396					
Smith, Ron	198	394							Spinetti, Sam	44	396					
Smith, Rube	37	394							Spinner, Larry	162	163	396				
Smith, Sherry	31	34	35	37	39	205	394	444	Spirida, John	51	396					
Smith, Tom	77	94	107	109	161	176	197	199	Spittle, Harry	162	396					
	394								Spitzer, Lloyd	71	73	396				
Smith, Tommie	197	200	202	394					Spitznagle, ---	9	10	11	12	16	18	205	396
Smith, Walt	94	394							Spivey, Bill	64	396					
Smith, Wilkins T.	70								Sprayberry, Jim	71	73	102	396			
Smithdeal, Sid	180	182	394						Spruill, Jack	91	104	105	120	122	123	396
Smithley, ---	73	394							Spurlock, E.M.	75						
Smoll, John	60	394							Spyhalski, Jim	185	190	191	396			
Snider, Floyd	68	71	72	81	83	90	100	113	Squibb, Don	179	396					
	394								Squillace, John	133	396					
Snider, Walt	147	394							Sroda, Ted	162	396					
Snodgrass, Walter	4	394							Stacey, ---	16	17	396				
Snyder, Bill	41	394							Stack, Lawrence	48	396					
Snyder, Dick	179	395							Stackpole, Cecil	125	396					

Georgia Class-D Minor League Baseball Encyclopedia

Name							
Stalcup, Pete	58	397					
Staley, Don	78	397					
Stamey, Harold	94	107	109	206	207	397	
Stamey, John	96	97	397				
Stammen, Pete	96	97	397				
Stamos, Pete	86	88	95	108	397		
Stamper, Ken	141	142	145	397			
Standard, ---	71	397					
Standering, Dennis	141	397					
Stanfield, Ralph	32	33	34	37	205	397	
Stangel, Bob	170	397					
Stanley, Bill	27	29	397				
Stanley, Bob	72	82	397				
Stanley, Ken	108	121	397				
Stanton, Bob	94	397					
Stanziani, Nick	155	397					
Stapenhorst, Jean	63	397					
Stapleton, ---	24	25	397				
Stapp, John	190	194	397				
Stark, ---	9	397					
Stark, Clint	200	397					
Stark, Don	108	397					
Starnes, Kendell	111	114	125	397			
Starr, A.L.	5	397					
Starrett, Stan	201						
Starrette, George	134	397					
Stasi, Rocco	175	397					
Stasko, Julius	77	86	87	88	95	97	397
Stathos, Tony	188	191	397				
Staub, Ray	198	199	397				
Steadman, Bob	103	130	397				
Steave, John	115	133	398				
Steckel, Bob	104	398					
Steedly, Alvin	76	86	398				
Steel, ---	71	398					
Steele, Jack	11	12	19	21	398		
Steele, Ron	149	179	398				
Steely, Stan	47	398					
Steen, Bob	172	398					
Stefanik, Ray	166	398					
Stefano, Nick	94	398					
Steffensen, Dick	107	398					
Stegal, ---	16	398					
Steger, Dave	87	398					
Stein, Ed	190	398					
Stein, Herb	126	398					
Steinbach, Bill	201	398					
Steinecke, Bill	156	197	199	201	202	203	398	444
Steinhour, Jim	181	189	398				
Stempel, Courtney	120	123	208	398			
Stemper, Robb	171	398					
Stenger, Dick	99	398					
Stephens, Colonel	5	398					
Stephens, Don	85	93	94	97	398		
Stephens, Frank	80	398					
Stephens, T.W.	71	398					
Stephenson, ---	9	11	398				
Stephenson, Sonny	122	151	152	398			
Sterkenberg, Larry	201	398					
Stern, Austin	150	398					
Stern, Jerome	113	398					
Sterns, Roland	170	398					
Sterrette, Bob	157	398					
Stevens, ---	68	399					
Stevens, Bill	117	399					
Stevens, Jim	35	399					
Stevens, Paul	99	399					
Stevens, Walt	133	399					
Stevenson, ---	19	399					
Stevenson, Fred	103	399					
Stevenson, Mason	57						
Stewart, ---	5	6	13	16	17	18	399

Name							
Stewart, Bill	166	399					
Stewart, Bob	162	164	399				
Stewart, Buford	63	76	399				
Stewart, Joseph C.	192						
Stewart, Ray	85	399					
Stewart, Rudy	156	399					
Stewart, Russ	55	60	399				
Stewman, Joe	182	399					
Stickney, Floyd	58	60	61	399			
Stigman, Dick	162	186	187	209	210	399	444
Stiles, ---	7	8	399				
Stiles, Francis J.	84						
Still, Jim	91	134	399				
Stillings, Gerald	182	190	399				
Stimson, Carl	24	25	399	444			
Stine, ---	31	399					
Stingley, Dick	108	399					
Stinson, Bob	111	125	137	399			
Stock, Lloyd	90	399					
Stocker, Ron	186	187	189	193	399		
Stocker, Stan	96	97	122				
Stockton, Ray	126	399					
Stokes, Bill	170	399					
Stokes, Don	68	399					
Stoll, Max	198	199	400				
Stolper, Hubert	55	400					
Stolte, Bill	129	131	205	400			
Stone, ---	7	400					
Stone, Allan	161	171	400				
Stone, Art	156	400					
Stone, Claude	173						
Stone, Dick	180	400					
Stone, Eddie	59	400					
Stoner, Bob	43	400					
Stoops, Bill	108	121	400				
Stopchuck, Mike	181	189	191	193	194	195	196	400
Stoples, Earl	71						
Storch, Charles	95	107	400				
Storey, Gordon	54	400					
Storie, Burl	59	63	400				
Stotler, Roy	180	183	400				
Stouch, John	76	400					
Stoutenborough, Y.C.	35	36	38	39	400		
Stover, Dewey	51	52	400				
Stover, H.W.	84						
Stover, Harless W.	119						
Stowe, John	72	73	117	118	128	130	131	204	400
Stowell, Doug	186	400					
Stoyle, Jim	71	73	74	82	84	112	113	114
	116	118	119	138	139	146	148	150
	152	204	206	208	209	400		
Strachan, Mearl	54	56	400				
Stratton, George	113	400					
Stratton, Harry	56	400					
Strauss, Harold	76	400					
Strawser, Croyden	152	400					
Streets, Don	62						
Strichek, Ed	162	172	174	400			
Strickland, Don	121	400					
Strickland, Eugene W.	112						
Strickland, Norris	86	94	96	97	107	206	400	448
Strickland, Walt	122	123	401	448			
Striffler, Charles	90	401					
Stringfield, ---	11	401					
Strock, Ray	190	401					
Stroecker, ---	31	34	401				
Stroeker, Arnold	107	401					
Strohmeyer, Fred	63	401					
Strom, Ken	134	135	401				
Strosser, Walt	63	65	401				
Strott, Art	41	42	401				

Georgia Class-D Minor League Baseball Encyclopedia

Name									Name						
Stroud, Earl	113	121	126	150	401				Tafaro, Dan	86	403				
Strozyk, Ray	186	189	401						Taitt, Doug	80	403	444			
Stryker, Ernest	107	401							Talas, Eftimeo	121	123	403			
Stubing, Moose	180	401	444	447					Talbutton, Ben J.	185					
Stuckey, Rex	104	401							Taliaferro, Dick	31	32	204	403		
Stuckey, W.S.	137	145							Taliaferro, Ray	162	185	403			
Stuckmeyer, Rollie	151	152	401						Talley, Sam	117	403				
Stumberg, B.G.	103								Tallis, Cedric	95					
Sturges, Sylvester	54	401							Tally, Bill	176	403				
Stutsman, Ed	172	401							Tally, Hoover	167	403				
Stutts, Bob	150	161	401						Tang, Antonio	142	403				
Suarez, Oscar	145	401							Tanner, Bill	85	403				
Suarez, Rafael	194	401							Tanner, J.D.	77	403				
Subbiondo, Joe	117	401							Tannreuther, Charles	175	403				
Suggs, Eugene	27	30	401						Taranto, Anthony	198	201	403			
Sules, John	125	401							Tarkington, Rondle	202	403				
Sullivan, A.	40	43							Tarolli, Lou	108	403				
Sullivan, Dan	100	401							Tarvin, Art	72	403				
Sullivan, Gene	51	401							Tarzi, ---	68	403				
Sullivan, Jim	44	47	401						Tasker, John	185	190	403			
Sullivan, Joe	41	42	94	401					Tate, J.M.	37					
Sullivan, John	64	65	66	137	138	139	146	154	Tate, J.R.	34	35	403			
	207	210	401	444					Tattler, Henry	27	29	403			
Sullivan, Lakey	89								Tauscher, Walt	121	404	444			
Sullivan, Woodward	77	401							Taussig, Don	116	404	444			
Sullivant, Mickey	197	402							Taylor, ---	11	12	17	24	404	
Summ, Jack	51	55	56	402					Taylor, A.	11	404				
Summerhill, Steve	60	61	64	65	68	69	110	136	Taylor, Bill	29	44	47	49	51	59	404
	402								Taylor, Bob	55	107	404			
Summerlin, ---	17	402							Taylor, D.	54	404				
Summerlin, Fritz	24	27	402						Taylor, Don	87	404				
Summit, ---	27	402							Taylor, Ed	51	404				
Super, Joe	141	146	402						Taylor, Ellis K.	89					
Suplizio, Sam	193	194	402						Taylor, Ford	154	404				
Suratt, Clyde	29	402							Taylor, Furman	68	76	404			
Surprise, Arthur	112								Taylor, Gene	63	65	190	404		
Suspenski, Vic	141	402							Taylor, Harry	51	404				
Sutfin, Harry	156	402							Taylor, Herald	80					
Suto, Ray	189	402							Taylor, Jim	152	404				
Sutter, Dick	108	402							Taylor, John	89	91	94	112	404	
Sutter, John	55	402							Taylor, Jose	197	404				
Sutton, Jim	91	402							Taylor, Q.P.	68	404				
Sutton, Lefty	27	402							Taylor, Ray	48	404				
Svenke, ---	111	402							Taylor, Spafford	103	404				
Swails, Alex	44	46	402						Taylor, W.W.	99	111	125	137	145	155
Swain, Harold	76	402							Taylor, Zachery	37	404				
Swain, Kurtis	113	126	137	172	402				Teague, John	55	57	404			
Swain, Lloyd	113	125	126	402					Teague, S.E.	46	50	53	57	62	
Swann, Ducky	27	29	402						Teal, Harry	78	404				
Swanson, Dale	81	82							Teater, Rollie	104	404				
Swanson, Don	141	155	402						Tefft, Al	91	404				
Swanson, Les	95	402							Tefft, Charles	58	404				
Swanson, Phil	162	177	402						Teichert, Bob	99	101	112	404		
Swanson, Ralph	81	82	402						Telford, Dave	77	404				
Sweat, LeRoy	137	138	402						Telford, John	132					
Sweat, W. Carlton	142	162	173	182					Teliszewski, Bernard	190	404				
Sweatt, Bill	72	115	117	119	402				Telkan, ---	13	14	404			
Sweet, Harold	157	402							Tennant, Mal	54	404				
Swertfager, Fred	190	402							Tenney, Jim	103	117	137	138	405	448
Swidorski, Don	146	403							Tepedino, Frank	147	148	157	158	405	
Swift, ---	31	32	33	403					Terrell, Thurman	113	117	405			
Swift, Fred	59	403							Terres, Francis M.	144	154				
Swigler, Norm	91	403							Terry, Bill	16	19	20	22	405	444	447
Swindell, Dave	40	403							Terry, Everett C.	80	89				
Swindle, Jim	78	403							Terry, Horace	71					
Swingle, Russ	107								Terwedow, Don	140	142	144	405		
Switzer, Marion	58	403							Tesmer, Warren	193	405				
Swoboda, Paul	55	56	59	207	403				Tessier, Lawrence	95	405				
Swygert, Alan	76	82	99	100	403				Tessin, Elmer	121	123	405	448		
Symko, Anthony	201	403							Texanne, Russ	59	405				
Szolwinski, Sylvester	76	403							Teyema, Dave	80	83	405			
Szostak, Henry	179	180	183	403					Thackston, John	172	405				

Georgia Class-D Minor League Baseball Encyclopedia

Thaxton, Kent	198, 201, 203, 405
Then, Jose	202, 405
Thode, Neil	152
Thoele, Walt	198, 201, 202, 405
Thomas, ---	12, 38, 405
Thomas, Bill	190, 405
Thomas, Bob	160, 405
Thomas, Clarence	44, 405
Thomas, Dallas	71, 81, 405
Thomas, Don	166, 405
Thomas, Francis	188, 405
Thomas, Frank	95, 96, 97, 108, 201, 202, 203, 206, 207, 405, 444
Thomas, George	67, 160, 405
Thomas, Gordon	162, 405
Thomas, Jim	68, 405
Thomas, Parks	103, 105, 117, 125, 405
Thomas, Wilbert	124, 154, 405
Thomason, Harold	60, 406
Thomassie, Pete	56, 60, 61, 108, 206, 406
Thompson, ---	22, 24, 25, 406
Thompson, Bill	150, 152, 161, 163, 170, 174, 207, 406
Thompson, Bob	85, 406
Thompson, C.L.	76, 93, 106, 119, 132, 140, 149
Thompson, Dick	102, 406
Thompson, Emery	76, 406
Thompson, Erskine	37, 38, 406
Thompson, Fresco	56, 77, 86, 95, 108, 121, 134, 142, 151, 161, 171, 181, 189, 193, 406, 445
Thompson, Herman	125, 406
Thompson, J.B.	112, 406
Thompson, Jack	72, 74, 406
Thompson, Jessie	181, 406
Thompson, Jim	102, 118, 130, 175, 406
Thompson, Leo	54, 406
Thompson, Leon	64
Thompson, Leroy	120, 406
Thompson, R.L.	31, 34, 38, 406
Thompson, W.W.	176, 185
Thompson, Walter W.	146
Thompson, William	31, 406
Thorn, George	76, 406
Thorne, Joe	47, 406
Thornell, Bob	166, 406
Thorpe, ---	38, 406
Thorpe, Jack	141, 406
Thrasher, ---	13, 14, 208, 406
Thrasher, Cliff	147, 157, 167, 406
Thrasher, George	27, 29, 30, 208, 406
Thrasher, Ike	27, 34, 406
Thrasher, Lew	41, 44, 406
Thrasher, Loren	29, 407
Threlkeld, G.H.	147, 167, 177, 186
Threlkeld, Howard	175, 184
Thrift, Syd	103, 407
Thurman, Clarence	190, 407
Tice, ---	38, 407
Tice, Paul	44, 47, 48, 407
Tideman, ---	5, 407
Tidwell, Bruce	167
Tidwell, Don	167, 173, 407
Tidwell, John	102, 125, 126, 127, 128, 134, 135, 136, 137, 208, 407
Tiefenauer, Bobby	91, 104, 105, 407, 445
Tieken, Virgil	163, 407
Tiemann, Jerry	67, 69, 407
Tierce, Joel	44, 51, 52, 407
Tierney, Tom	194, 407
Tillery, Tom	73, 407
Tilley, Terry	161, 171, 407
Tilley, Travis	81, 407
Timberlake, Ray	138, 145, 152, 154, 407
Tingle, Tom	147, 177, 178, 186, 407
Tingley, Floyd W.	111
Tinsley, Art	171, 186, 407
Tippett, Frank	167, 407
Tipton, Bill	157, 407
Tisdale, ---	11, 407
Tisdale, Bill	117, 407
Tison, ---	5, 407
Tittl, Bob	181, 407
Titus, Lee	155, 407
Todtenhausen, Art	201, 407
Tolbert, ---	72, 407
Tolbert, C.	20, 21, 22, 24, 25, 27, 408
Tomasello, Theron	40, 408
Tomasic, George	102, 408
Tomek, Joe	99, 408
Tomkinson, Phil	87, 88, 408
Tomlin, Ed	73, 408
Tomter, Harvey	160, 164, 408
Tond, Lou	108, 408
Tone, Lawrence	50, 408
Torppey, Kevin	201, 408
Torres, Ed	162, 166, 408
Torres, Felix	175, 177, 178, 408, 445
Torres, Gil	151, 152, 408, 445
Torres, Guerry	180, 183, 208, 408
Torres, Miguel	198, 408
Torres, Victor	200, 202, 408
Towich, Tom	170, 408
Townley, Dave	173, 408
Towns, Jim	72, 74, 408
Townsend, ---	12, 408
Townsend, Arnold	29, 408
Townsend, Art	41, 408
Townsend, Charles	190, 194, 408
Tracewski, Dick	161, 408, 445, 447
Tracy, Bill	68, 408
Tracy, Jim	94, 107, 110, 408
Trainor, Bernard	41, 44, 408
Trammel, Tom	182, 408
Trammell, Wes	68, 69, 408
Trapasso, Lawrence	157, 408
Travers, Miles	194, 408
Travers, Tom	81, 90, 408
Travis, Jess	26, 29
Treadway, Ray	31, 32, 204, 408, 445
Treadway, Red	161, 163, 164, 180, 182, 409, 445
Trew, Jim	120, 121, 409
Tribble, ---	5, 409
Trinkle, Ken	55, 57, 409, 445
Triplett, Coaker	41, 42, 409, 445
Tripod, Jerry	125, 409
Tripp, Bob	94, 96, 97, 409
Trojanowski, Ed	94, 107, 109, 110, 206, 207, 409
Trossen, Tom	162, 409
Trotter, Bill	90, 409
Troutman, B.K.	22, 409
Troxell, Clair	132, 140, 144, 409
Troy, Don	108, 409
Troy, Gordon	55, 59, 409
Troy, Herb	198, 199, 409
Troy, Jim	116, 129, 409
Truhler, Otto	57
Truitt, D.E.	34, 36, 409
Tsatsa, Paul	189, 409
Tschannen, Ron	132, 135, 409
Tschudin, Fred	111, 113, 114, 124, 128, 134, 135, 208, 409
Tsitouris, John	162, 172, 409, 445
Tuck, Gerald	171, 409
Tucker, Dick	194, 409
Tucker, Dwight	170, 409

Name							
Tucker, Jim	63	409					
Tucker, Ollie	28	29	30	208	409	445	
Tucker, Roy	146	409					
Tucker, Tom	201	409					
Tucker, Wilbur	43	409					
Tuggle, Bill	147	409					
Tuholski, Jim	201	202	203	409			
Tulner, Charles	184	409					
Turbyfill, Harold	186	409					
Turek, Don	161	410					
Turk, ---	37	410					
Turner, ---	16	17	37	410			
Turner, Bob	161	410					
Turner, Dick	95	410					
Turner, Herman	103						
Turner, Jim	76	129	410				
Turner, McDonald	91	92	410				
Turner, Mrs. Luther S.	104						
Turturro, Mike	108	410					
Turtzo, Paul	95	142	143	151	410		
Tuttle, Bill	181	410					
Twitchell, Beech	58	410					
Twitchell, Dan	58	410					
Tyler, Jim	125	137	146	156	410	448	
Tyndall, Dick	161	410					
Tysinger, Everett	63	65	207	410			
Tyson, J.W. Jr.	62						
Tyson, Turkey	51	55	56	57	410	445	
Uhle, Stan	58	59	60	410			
Ulisney, Mike	55	59	64	410	445		
Ullmann, John	189	410					
Ulrich, Lawrence	166	410					
Umbach, Ken	116	410					
Umbricht, Jim	152	410	445				
Umscheid, Don	102	410					
Umstead, Ed	96	410					
Underwood, ---	16	410					
Underwood, Glenn	87	99	410				
Unetich, Frank	40	410					
Upchurch, Bill	149	151	410				
Upper, Wray	141	410					
Upshaw, Charles	116	410					
Upton, Earl V.	132						
Upton, Lawrence	138	411					
Urban, Hubert	68	411					
Urbanski, Bill	176	411					
Urquhart, ---	37	411					
Urrizola, Mike	193	195	411				
Urso, Joe	82	83	411				
Usciak, Matt	55	411					
Utke, John	76	411					
Utley, ---	11	12	17	18	411		
Utley, Ewell	116	121	411				
Utley, George	152	153	411				
Utter, ---	6	7	17	411			
Utter, Dick	121	411					
Uzelatz, Max	155	162	411				
Vaiden, ---	14	17	411				
Valdez, ---	34	411					
Valdez, Felipe	175	411					
Valencik, Ed	78	411					
Valesky, Don	186	411					
Valle, Sindo	56	411					
Van Burkleo, Dutch	150	152	153	411			
Van Gilder, William	140						
Van Landingham, ---	7	8	14	15	411		
Van Orsdol, Jack	55	411					
Van, John	200	411					
Vanak, Joseph T.	154						
Vanasse, Bob	150	155	166	411			
Vanatistein, Herb	103	411					
Vandegraff, ---	9	411					
Vander Meer, Johnny	184	411	445				
VanDerBeek, Jim	157	167	168	177	411		
Vandergriff, H.L.	29	411					
Vandergrift, Ed	55	56	57	411			
Vanderlip, ---	7	411					
Vandiveer, Rod	170	176	412				
Vandiver, C.W.	76	86	95	107	120	133	171	189
	197						
Vandiver, H.S.	157						
Vanowski, ---	155	412					
Varble, Charles V.	57	62					
Vardeman, F.C.	27	29	412				
Vargo, Steve	47	49	50	52	54	112	412
Varnedoe, Heeth	77	86	95	108	121	141	151	161
	171	181	189	193	198	201	
Varner, Buck	90	412	445				
Varner, Paul	67	68	412				
Vasquez, Regino	156	412					
Vastano, Pat	134	138	412				
Vasterling, ---	12	412					
Vaughan, Jim	47	48	412				
Vaughn, ---	7	17	412				
Vaughn, Bobby	180	412					
Vaughn, C.C.	6						
Vaughn, Don	145	148	150	167	168	169	209	210
	412						
Vaughn, Gene	67	412					
Vaughn, Leroy	170	412					
Veal, Bill	155	412					
Veale, Frank	47	412					
Veazey, Norm	90	91	107	108	117	412	
Veazie, ---	30	412					
Veigel, Al	47	412	445				
Veinot, Ken	194	412					
Vejsicky, Gene	162	412					
Venditto, Al	115	412					
Venzon, Anthony	124						
Verbish, George	86	412					
Vereault, George	133	135	412				
Vereen, W.C.	120						
Vereen, W.C. Jr.	76						
Verner, Cliff	32	35	37	38	39	204	412
Verratt, E.A.	22	24	25	26	412		
Verstraete, Don	185	412					
Vesek, Steve	51	52	412				
Vest, Charles	154	413					
Vest, Milt	161	166	413				
Vetter, Bob	126	413					
Vick, Clayton D.	70						
Vickers, Dan	56	413					
Vickers, Jim	72	74	205	413			
Vickers, R.G.	43	46	93				
Victor, Ernie	116	413					
Vidal, George	100	413					
Villa, Antonio	78	413					
Villamea, Raul	129	131	137	139	145	148	209	210
	413						
Vincent, Al	32	413					
Vincent, C.E.	32	413					
Vines, ---	24	413					
Vines, Bob	41	413	445				
Vingers, Leonard	160	413					
Vingle, Dick	197	200	413				
Vinson, Earl	82	413					
Vinson, Gene	145	152	163	413			
Virgil, Dan	90	413					
Virgona, Al	156	413					
Virkstis, Bob	161	172	413				
Vitale, Harold	51	413					
Vitale, Pete	129	413					
Vitali, Joe	125	413					
Vitari, Joe	68	413					

Georgia Class-D Minor League Baseball Encyclopedia

Viteretto, Pete	162 163 413
Vitter, Jim	86 88 413
Vitti, Ralph	129 413
Voboril, Bill	190 413
Vocial, Robert W.	75 84
Vogel, Bill	201 413
Vogeltanz, Bob	85 413
Vogt, Pete	172 413
Voight, Fred W.	108 122
Voiselle, Bill	51 52 413 445
Voitier, Bob	87 413
Volan, Ed	85 413
Volk, Fred	141 414
Volpe, Joe	151 414
Votaw, Jim	90 414
Vroman, Larry	182 190 191 414
Vucelich, Milan	67 414
Vukas, Steve	76 86 414
Wachtman, Dave	118 414
Wade, Loren	138 414
Wadewitz, Oswin	102 414
Wadsworth, Hal	112 113 414
Wagner, Allen	145 147 414
Wagner, Dick	103 414
Wagner, Richard	86
Wagner, Ted	184 414
Wagnon, ---	5 414
Wagnon, John	6 7 16 414
Wagoner, Charles	177 414
Wahl, Bill	112 414
Wahoo, Charles	7 414
Wainer, D.S.	108 121 134 142
Waits, Frank	41 42 44 45 46 414
Waldrip, ---	32 414
Waldron, William	9 11 12 22 23 24 25 414
Waldrop, Berman	121 123 414
Walenczyk, Bob	201 202 414
Walker, ---	6 7 16 19 20 414
Walker, A.D.	44 46 50 53 57 62
Walker, B.M. "Buck"	134 142 152
Walker, Bill	68 76 77 78 415
Walker, Christine	50 53 57
Walker, Dixie	34 37 414 445
Walker, Flem	28 414
Walker, Fred	192 195 414
Walker, Gary	193 414
Walker, Jack	86 88 414
Walker, John	96 414
Walker, Lewis	32 34 38 415
Walker, Milt	118 122 142 415
Walker, Ron	193 415
Walker, Tom	31 415
Walker, Wiley	167 415
Wall, ---	38 415
Wall, Curtis	95 415
Wall, Fred	200 415
Wallace, Bill	120 133 135 136 415
Wallace, Elmer	103 105 205 415
Wallace, Jim	103 415
Wallace, Mike	189 415
Wallace, Wayne	184 185 187 415
Waller, ---	32 415
Waller, L.L.	99 113 126
Wallin, Carl	72 73 415
Wallin, Ray	202 415
Wallis, Arnold	72 415
Wallis, Gerald	103 105 116 118 415
Walls, Boyd	81 116 129 415
Walls, Howard	72 415
Walmsley, L.E. "Chick"	106 120
Walsh, Chris	141 415
Walsh, Dick	171 181 189
Walsh, Mike	155 163 415
Walsh, William H.	110
Walsingham, William Jr.	58 94 106 120 132 140 149 160 170
Walski, Pete	190 415
Walston, Bob	157 415
Walter, Dick	190 191 415
Walters, Billy	152 167 416
Walters, George	172 415
Walters, Jerry	176
Walters, Jim	59
Walters, Milt	141 415
Walters, Peck	5 415
Walters, Ray	85 87 415
Walton, Battleaxe	29 416
Walton, H.E.	47 51
Walton, Jim	198 201 416
Walton, Tubby	38 416
Wanstrath, Bill	67 416
Ward, ---	34 72 416
Ward, Bill	63 416
Ward, Bob	147 148 416
Ward, Milt	82 416
Ward, W.P.	154
Ward, W.P. Jr.	98 165 175 184
Ward, Warren	77 416
Warden, Charles	201 416
Ware, Bruce	81 416
Ware, Charles	151 156 416
Ware, Dan	72 416
Wares, ---	24 416
Wargo, Clarence	125 138 416
Warner, ---	38 416
Warner, Henry	150 416
Warren, ---	38 416
Warren, Bob	86 416
Warren, Jeff	95 133 416
Warren, Jim	112 114 125 126 127 146 147 148 156 167 168 169 209 416
Warren, Leon	167 416
Warren, Malcolm	186 416
Warren, Rudy	167 176 177 193 194 416
Warshaw, Art	157 416
Wartelle, Johnny	171 174 193 416
Warwick, ---	14 416
Warzyniak, Ray	155 157 158 159 208 209 416
Wasconis, George	142 149 151 153 207 416
Wasem, ---	14 417
Washington, ---	31 34 37 417
Wasiak, Stan	58 121 122 134 136 162 172 185 190 417
Wasil, Andrew	190 417
Wassel, Bill	103 417
Wassem, ---	7 417
Waters, Homer	137
Waters, Rabun	166 417
Watkins, Lou	157 417
Watkins, Robert	16 22 23 417
Watson, ---	38 417
Watson, Art	172 417
Watson, Carl	141 150 417
Watson, Ed	81 90 417
Watson, Henry	19 22 417
Watson, Jules	22 24 25 27 29 37 417
Watters, Lark	27 417
Watters, S.E.	77
Wattigney, Ulysses	60 417
Watts, Bill	63 87 417
Watts, Don	106 132 417
Watts, George	78 417
Watts, Lee	122 417
Waugh, Art	86 417

Name									Name							
Waugh, Jim	133	170	417	445					West, Ira	165	419					
Way, Walt	160	163	417						West, Lefty	54	56	57	208	420	446	
Wayton, Henry	47	48	49	417					West, Lewis	76	419					
Weakley, ---	5	417							West, Ronnie	167	420					
Weathers, Charlie	87	96	207	417					West, Stan	44	47	49	167	420		
Weaver, ---	5	418							West, Tom	68	420					
Weaver, Bill	155	418							Westbrook, ---	5	420					
Weaver, C.B.	30	418							Westbrook, Ed	81	82	420				
Weaver, Earl	189	193	418	447					Westbrook, John	71	73	74	420			
Weaver, Fred	134	138	146	148	154	209	418		Westbrook, Price	156	420					
Weaver, Henry	54	58	61	208	418				Westervelt, ---	5	420					
Weaver, Norm	190	418							Westfall, Elmer	98	100	420				
Webb, ---	22	43	72	418					Westmoreland, T.D.	81	129					
Webb, Bill	81	83	84	205	418	445			Weston, E.H.	11	17	20	22	24	420	
Webb, Charles	122	134	136	142	418				Wetherton, Carl	121	123	420				
Webb, Lawrence	72	418							Wetzel, H.B. "Buzz"	85	94	107				
Webb, Leroy	64	418							Wexler, Jim	181	420					
Webb, Marion	90	418							Whalen, ---	63	420					
Webb, Tom	194	418							Whalen, Frank	76	78	420				
Webber, Don	176	418							Whalen, James	5	420					
Webber, Harry	6	418							Whaley, Charles	147	185	420				
Webster, Ed	116	418							Whaley, Randy	167	168	420				
Weddle, Billy	181	418							Whaley, W.W. Jr.	165						
Weed, Clarence	132	418							Whaley, Walker	111	138	147	155	420		
Weeks, ---	4								Wheat, B.C.	27	420					
Weeks, Ralph	86	87	88	207	418				Wheat, Lafe	27	29	420				
Wehman, Dick	161	163	418						Wheeler, ---	32	420					
Weilbacher, Dave	189	418							Wheeler, Buck	29						
Weiler, ---	13	14	16	17	18	418			Wheeler, Earl	132	140					
Weir, Gary	170	418							Wheeler, Waverly	55	420					
Weisenberg, Aaron	78	418							Wherry, Kendall	107	420					
Weiss, Dennis	186	418							Whetro, Ron	172	420					
Weiss, Sid	48	418							Whiddon, J.H.	64						
Welage, Dick	175	178	209	418					Whiddon, John	107	420					
Welch, Eacie	129	418							Whitaker, C.A.	98	112					
Welch, George	120	418							Whitaker, Jim	96	420					
Welch, Ron	182	183	418						Whitcomb, Don	180	182	183	207	420		
Weldon, Bill	111	116	419						White, Abe	31	33	34	35	36	37	38	39
Weldon, J.C.	162									81	83	90	116	205	421	446
Weldon, Larry	59	419							White, Albert	193	421					
Weller, Jay	194	419							White, Bill	72	154	421				
Wellman, Bob	73	74	175	177	178	179	180	181	White, Bob	156	171	182	190	193	421	
	182	183	206	207	419	445			White, Charles	182	421					
Wells, Bill	161	172	174	419					White, Curtis	116	129	130	145	147	148	157	167
Wells, Jack	165	168	175	419						421						
Wells, James M.	124	136							White, E.R.	32	35	421				
Wells, Jim	202	419							White, Ed	134	135	142	421			
Wells, Les	113	419							White, Glen	186	421					
Wells, Phil	22	419							White, H.	35	37	421				
Wells, Ronald	161	419							White, Jack	157	421					
Wells, William O.	28								White, John	82	171	421				
Welp, Bill	68	77	78	419					White, Jo-Jo	31	32	204	421	446	447	
Welsh, Dan	186	419							White, Ralph	63	421					
Wenclewicz, Walt	80	419							White, Randolph	146	421					
Wendell, Herb	121	419							White, Vern	186	421					
Wenitski, Bernie	107	109	120	207	419				Whitecavage, Tony	141	421					
Wenrich, Dave	193	419							Whited, Gerald	102	421					
Wenson, Ron	162	163	172	173	419				Whitehead, Don	126	421					
Wentworth, Dick	67	419							Whiteside, Bright	72	421					
Werk, Frank	48	419							Whitfield, ---	9	29	421				
Werking, Glenn	198	419							Whitfield, Jim	62	421					
Werley, George	189	193	195	419	446				Whitley, Marvin E.	124	136					
Werner, ---	6	8	419						Whitley, Shirley	64	421					
Werner, Dan	171	419							Whitley, Tom	72	421					
Werner, G.H.	9	11	20	21	22	419			Whitlow, Bob	54	421					
Wert, Don	194	195	419	446					Whitmire, Glen	167	185	421				
Werther, ---	67	419							Whitmore, Don	76	86	422				
Wesley, ---	37	38	419						Whitney, J.F.	11	12	20	21	422		
Wesson, L.A.	40								Whitney, Jim	82	422					
West, ---	13	38	419						Whitson, Howard	165	422					
West, Bill	202	203	420						Whittaker, Charles	44	422					
West, Dick	40	42	44	46	47	48	420	446	Whitten, Norm	55	73	422				

Georgia Class-D Minor League Baseball Encyclopedia

Name									
Whitworth, Bob	180	422							
Whitzer, Mike	165	422							
Wiacek, Ray	91	422							
Wiche, James	192								
Wick, Gil	125	422							
Wicker, ---	14	17	422						
Wicker, K.C.	31	422	446						
Widmayer, Walt	173	422							
Wiebel, Mel	111	422							
Wieber, Joe	154	422							
Wiegand, Don	133	422							
Wiggins, ---	17	18	422						
Wiggins, Bob	82	422							
Wiggins, LeRoy	67	68	69	73	74	81	82	422	
Wiggins, Morton M.	40	43	47	50	54	58	75	85	
	94	106	120	132	140	149	160	170	
	179	188	192						
Wigle, Bob	120	122	422						
Wilcox, Francis	151								
Wilcox, Ralph	133	422							
Wilcox, Ron	142	145	422						
Wilcox, Stan	133	422							
Wilder, Percy	6	7	8	422					
Wilder, Ralph	94	97	422						
Wiley, Jack	64	422							
Wiley, Joseph	20	22	23	422					
Wilhelm, Bill	149	422							
Wilkes, ---	7	14	15	16	17	18	422		
Wilkie, ---	32	33							
Wilkinson, Dave	145	422							
Wilkinson, Marvin A.	170								
Willard, ---	16	17	422						
Willard, Miles	167	423							
Willard, Stan	94	97	423						
Willett, Charles	5	423							
Willett, Dennis	198	201	202	203	423				
Willett, Ray	77	79	86	142	143				
Willey, Joe	63	423							
Williams, ---	9	10	11	22	27	31	32	77	
	423								
Williams, Ben	138	423							
Williams, Bill	80	189	424						
Williams, Bob	90	172	173	182	185	190	424		
Williams, Carl	177	423							
Williams, Charlie	63	64	77	423					
Williams, Cliff	108	423							
Williams, Curtis	81	423							
Williams, Davey	84	87	88	206	423	446			
Williams, Dick	51	193	423	424					
Williams, Don	161	163	164	423					
Williams, Ed	73	80	82	423					
Williams, Eddie Jr.	124								
Williams, Franklin	176								
Williams, Fred	182	423							
Williams, Galen	170	173	174	423					
Williams, Jerry	186	423							
Williams, Jim	171	175	176	179	183	423			
Williams, John	156	160	161	193	423				
Williams, Kerr	59	208	423						
Williams, Luke	27	423							
Williams, Lynn	55	424							
Williams, Marv	108	109	424						
Williams, Norm	63	424							
Williams, Papa	134	135	142	143	144	423	446		
Williams, Paul	71	189	424						
Williams, Wallace	68	424							
Williams, Wiley	77	424							
Williamson, ---	37	424							
Williamson, Al	28	29	424	446					
Williamson, Jim	193	424							
Willingham, Coney	72	424							
Willingham, Jack	78	424							
Willingham, John	185	186	424						
Willingham, Ralph	77	424							
Willis, Bob	154	424							
Willis, Bud	172	424							
Willis, Charles	108	424							
Willis, Clarence	67	96	424						
Willis, Jim	181	424							
Willis, Joel	77	424							
Willis, Ron	197	424	446						
Willoughby, Carl	64	65	424						
Willoughby, John	41	44	424						
Wills, Bill	125	424							
Wilshere, Carl	50	52	54	58	424				
Wilson, ---	5	12	19	22	23	31	38	424	
Wilson, Bill	146	425							
Wilson, Bob	177	178	425						
Wilson, Clyde	86	425							
Wilson, Dick	176	425							
Wilson, Ed	126	127	137	160	425				
Wilson, Francis	181	183	425						
Wilson, George	76	425							
Wilson, Hugh	64	425							
Wilson, Jack	27	170	173	174	425				
Wilson, Jim	112	114	167	168	209	425			
Wilson, Lonnie	194	200	425						
Wilson, Martin	78	425							
Wilson, Nesby	73	425							
Wilson, Norm	78	79	141	425					
Wilson, Walt	81	425	446						
Wilson, Ward	154	162	425						
Winchell, ---	20	425							
Winchester, Joe	202	425							
Wingard, Ernie	64	116	118	425	446				
Winges, ---	7	8	14	17	425				
Wingfield, ---	24	25	425						
Wingo, Jim	94	97	107	425					
Wingo, Kelly	63	425							
Winkelspecht, Bob	116	118	425						
Winn, Breezy	34	38	425						
Winters, Bill	116	425							
Winters, Charles	129	133	425						
Wiren, John	108	425							
Wishba, Joe	99	425							
Wisniewski, John	172	426							
Wissman, Ed	124	125	127	426					
Witkowski, John	77	426							
Witz, Tom	85	426							
Witzke, Howard	81	426							
Woddail, Charles	64	65	426						
Wodka, Dick	188	426							
Wojcik, Frank	40	426							
Woleen, Raymond	77	426							
Wolf, Hugh	126	426							
Wolf, Lawrence	63	426							
Wolfe, ---	6	426							
Wolfe, Earl	94	426							
Wolfe, Tom	38	426							
Wolfman, Cedric	161	177	426						
Wollitz, Herman	82	426							
Womack, Al	177	426							
Womack, Charles	59	426							
Wood, ---	11	13	44	426					
Wood, Bill	134	426							
Wood, Don	120	426							
Wood, Gordon	130	131	426						
Wood, Norman	35	38	426						
Wood, Ron	198	426							
Wood, Tom	188	192	195	426					
Wood, W.G.	40	42	426						
Woodall, C.T.	155								
Woodall, Dick	176	426							
Woodall, H.C.	142	151							

Georgia Class-D Minor League Baseball Encyclopedia

Name						
Woodington, ---	44	426				
Woodring, Dick	96	426				
Woodruff, Ernest	103	111	426			
Woodruff, Ridley	72	426				
Woods, Julian	111	125	426			
Woods, Ralph	198	199	426			
Wooldridge, Floyd	120	427	446			
Wooley, Jim	89	102	104	115	118	129	427
Woolf, Jesse	43					
Woolford, Ed	160	427				
Woolford, Ralph	95	427				
Wooten, Bob	59	427				
Wopinek, George	95	97	207	427		
Workman, Hoge	29	427	446			
Worrell, Joe	192	427				
Worsham, Ben	111	137	427			
Wrenn, Milt	86	107	134	141	427	448
Wright, ---	17	37	38	427		
Wright, Bill	55	162	427			
Wright, Dick	160	165	427			
Wright, Dixie	99	112	137	146	427	
Wright, George	124	427				
Wright, Jerry	151	181	427			
Wright, Jim	125	127	181	190		
Wright, Ken	157	427				
Wright, Maurice	73	82	83	205	427	
Wright, Owen	44	427				
Wright, Paul	68	69	70	427		
Wright, R.B.	47	51				
Wright, Roger	189	190	427			
Wrobke, Joe	56	60	427			
Wroblewski, Erwin	67	69	427			
Wrona, Joe	165	427				
Wulf, Gene	67	427				
Wulff, Clay	167	428				
Wyatt, Billy	181	428				
Wyatt, Gene	146	156	166	428		
Wyatt, John	197	428				
Wylie, Mark	186	428				
Wysocki, Stan	54	59	61	207	208	428
Yablon, Nathan	124	126	428			
Yance, Jim	132	428				
Yancek, Frank	77	428				
Yancey, ---	5	428				
Yancey, Carl	91	428				
Yanchura, John	146	148	155	428		
Yappel, August	190	428				
Yarborough, Mack	102	120	123	428		
Yarbrough, Dan	171	428				
Yarbrough, Jim	161	171	173	184	428	
Yates, Bill	154	428				
Yawn, Sid	80	428				
Yeargan, Percy	115					
Yearty, Sam	71	156	428			
Yeates, Doug	58	428				
Yebernetsky, George	86	95	97	428		
Yeider, Marshall	147	428				
Yetsko, Andy	176	178	428			
Yoder, Bob	151	428				
Yodhes, John	194	428				
Yohn, Charles	86	88	428			
Yon, ---	19	428				
Yonchuk, Walt	59	428				
York, Lew	71	73	74	428		
York, Rudy	102	103	428	446	447	
Yosipovich, Lou	59	428				
Yost, ---	29	428				
Youmans, Dr. C.R.	138	146	155	166		
Young, ---	9	19	429			
Young, Bill	68	141	143	157	429	
Young, Claude	126	137	138	139	429	
Young, Don	176	185	200	429	446	
Young, Ford	190	429				
Young, Harmon	156	429				
Young, Herb	96	108	122	429		
Young, Ken	201	429				
Young, Phil	189	429				
Young, Raymond T.	154					
Young, Tex	86	100	101	111	113	429	448
Young, W.E.	44	59				
Young, Wade	185	429				
Youngblood, Jack	146	156	429			
Yow, Forrest	124	126	137	145	429	
Yudin, Bob	133	429				
Yurman, Frank	186	187	429			
Zabek, Ed	86	429				
Zabel, Leslie V.	89	101				
Zachritz, Charles	54	429				
Zackery, Rollie	197	429				
Zaden, Lou	117	118	130	429		
Zajac, Henry	43	429				
Zander, Ron	193	429				
Zangari, Frank	132	135	142	429		
Zapke, ---	13	429				
Zaski, Regis	161	429				
Zazzera, Ben	90	429				
Zeccola, Pete	95	429				
Zeihen, Bernard	190	194	429			
Zeiser, Harry	95	429				
Zeitler, Jack	162	429				
Zeleznock, John	192	430				
Zelinsky, Matt	120	430				
Zeller, Bart	200	430	446			
Zellers, ---	7	8	11	20	430	
Zellner, Jerome	194	195	430			
Zera, Angelo	98	430				
Zernial, Gus	68	430	446			
Zeski, Don	122	123	430			
Zgraggen, Orlando	167	430				
Zich, Henry	89	91	92	205	430	
Zientara, Benny	189	430	446			
Zimmer, Harold	145	430				
Zimmerlink, Gene	166	168	430			
Zimmerman, Dick	161	430				
Zimmerman, George	55	60	430			
Zimmerman, Glenn	133	135	430			
Zirafi, Antonio	107	430				
Zitek, Don	171					
Zivich, George	64	430				
Zodda, Victor A.	77	78	86	95	108	121	430
Zoeller, Simon Lee	67	430				
Zolliecoffer, Bob	111	430				
Zorn, G.H.	146					
Zorn, W.A.	146					
Zuccarini, Bob	146	156	157	159	182	208	430	448
Zwierzynski, Adam	85	430				
Zwirko, Bill	125	430				

Bibliography

Americus Times-Recorder, Americus, Georgia, April 1906 through July 1906.

Atlanta Journal-Constitution, Atlanta, Georgia, April 1917 through July 1948.

Bell, John. *PICKLE IT! Minor League Baseball of Carrollton, Georgia.* Carrollton, Georgia: Vabella Publishing, 2002.

Bell, John. *Shoeless Summer: The summer of 1923 when Shoeless Joe Jackson played baseball in Americus, Georgia.* Carrollton, Georgia: Vabella Publishing, 2001.

Carrollton County Georgian, Carrollton, Georgia, August 1947 through August 1965.

Carroll County Times, Carrollton, Georgia, June 1914 through September 1947.

Carroll Free Press, Carrollton, Georgia, June 1914 through August 1929.

Dews, Robert P. *The Georgia-Florida League – Extra Innings.* Edison, Georgia: Rebel Books, 1985.

Johnson, Lloyd. *The Minor League Register.* Durham, North Carolina: Baseball America, Inc., 1994.

Johnson, Lloyd and Miles Wolff. *The Encyclopedia of Minor League Baseball.* Durham, North Carolina: Baseball America, Inc., 1997.

Obojski, Robert. *Bush League, A Colorful, Factual Account of Minor League Baseball from 1877 to the Present.* New York: Macmillan, 1975.

Reach Official American League Base Ball Guide 1914. Philadelphia: A.J. Reach Company, 1915.

Reach Official American League Base Ball Guide 1928. Philadelphia: A.J. Reach Company, 1929.

Reach Official American League Base Ball Guide 1929. Philadelphia: A.J. Reach Company, 1930.

Reach Official American League Base Ball Guide 1930. Philadelphia: A.J. Reach Company, 1931.

Reach Official American League Base Ball Guide 1935. Philadelphia: A.J. Reach Company, 1936.

Reach Official American League Base Ball Guide 1936. Philadelphia: A.J. Reach Company, 1937.

Reach Official American League Base Ball Guide 1937. Philadelphia: A.J. Reach Company, 1938.

Reach Official American League Base Ball Guide 1938. Philadelphia: A.J. Reach Company, 1939.

Spalding's Official Base Ball Guide 1913. New York: American Sports Publishing Company, 1914.

Spalding's Official Base Ball Guide 1915. New York: American Sports Publishing Company, 1916.

Spalding's Official Base Ball Guide 1939. New York: American Sports Publishing Company, 1940.

Spalding's Official Base Ball Guide 1940. New York: American Sports Publishing Company, 1941.

Spalding's Official Baseball Guide 1941. New York: American Sports Publishing Company, 1942.

Spalding's Official Baseball Guide 1942. New York: American Sports Publishing Company, 1943.

Spalding's Official Baseball Guide 1946. New York: American Sports Publishing Company, 1947.

Spalding's Official Baseball Guide 1947. New York: American Sports Publishing Company, 1948.

Spalding's Official Baseball Guide 1948. New York: American Sports Publishing Company, 1949.

Spalding's Official Baseball Guide 1949. New York: American Sports Publishing Company, 1950.

Spalding's Official Baseball Guide 1950. New York: American Sports Publishing Company, 1951.

Spalding's Official Baseball Guide 1951. New York: American Sports Publishing Company, 1952.

Spalding's Official Baseball Guide 1952. New York: American Sports Publishing Company, 1953.

Spalding's Official Baseball Guide 1953. New York: American Sports Publishing Company, 1954.

Spalding's Official Baseball Guide 1954. New York: American Sports Publishing Company, 1955.

Spalding's Official Baseball Guide 1955. New York: American Sports Publishing Company, 1956.

Spalding's Official Baseball Guide 1956. New York: American Sports Publishing Company, 1957.

Spalding's Official Baseball Guide 1957. New York: American Sports Publishing Company, 1958.

Spalding's Official Baseball Guide 1958. New York: American Sports Publishing Company, 1959.

Spalding's Official Baseball Guide 1962. New York: American Sports Publishing Company, 1963.

Spalding's Official Baseball Guide 1963. New York: American Sports Publishing Company, 1964.

The Professional Baseball Player Database, Old-Time Data, Inc.: Shawnee Mission. Version 4.00.

Times-Free Press, Carrollton, Georgia, August 1948 Through August 1965.

www.alabama-florida-league.com, website

www.baseball-reference.com, website.

www.geocities.com/big_bunko/minor.html, website.

Acknowledgments

Special thanks to each of the following:
The Americus Welcome Center
Alf and Marie Bell
Clint Chafin
Steve Densa
Barefoot Bobby Dews
Horton's Books and Gifts
Lloyd Johnson
Paul Steeley

Special thanks to each of the players listed in this book. Without them, there would be nothing but blank pages here.

A very special thanks to my wife, Virginia, and my sons, Jacob and Andrew, for their support and patience during the writing of this book.

Most of all, I thank God for the many blessings He has given me.

About the Author

John Bell was born in Americus, Georgia in 1969 and lived there until 1995. He graduated from Americus High School in 1987 and earned a B.S. in Political Science with a minor in History from Georgia Southwestern State University in Americus in 1993.

John is a member of the Society of American Baseball Research (SABR) and affiliated with the Magnolia Chapter of Atlanta, Georgia of the organization.

In 2001, John published his first book entitled *Shoeless Summer: The summer of 1923 when Shoeless Joe Jackson played baseball in Americus, Georgia*. The book was nominated for SABR's Seymour Medal in 2002. John's second book entitled *PICKLE IT! – Minor League Baseball of Carrollton, Georgia* was published in 2002.

Having lived in Carrollton, Georgia since 1996, John is married to Virginia Bell. They have two sons, Jacob and Andrew.

www.ingramcontent.com/pod-product-compliance
Lightning Source LLC
Chambersburg PA
CBHW080721230426
43665CB00020B/2575